Developing Windows™ Applications with Borland® C++ 3.1

Second Edition

Developing Windows™ Applications with Borland® C++ 3.1

Second Edition

James W. McCord

SAMS
A Division of Prentice Hall Computer Publishing
11711 North College, Carmel, Indiana 46032 USA

SECOND EDITION
FIRST PRINTING—1992

International Standard Book Number: 0-672-30060-5

Library of Congress Catalog Card Number: 91-64302

95 94 93 92 4 3 2 1

Interpretation of the printing code: the rightmost double-digit number is the year of the book's printing; the rightmost single-digit, the number of the book's printing. For example, a printing code of 92-1 shows that the first printing of the book occurred in 1992.

Trademarks

Screen reproductions in this book were created by means of the program Collage Plus from Inner Media, Inc., Hollis, NH.

Composed in ITC Garamond and MCPdigital
Printed in the United States of America

Publisher
Richard K. Swadley

Managing Editor
Neweleen A. Trebnik

Acquisitions Editor
Gregory S. Croy

Development Editor
Stacy Hiquet

Production Editors
Susan Christophersen
Fran Hatton

Editors
Andy Saff
Rich Limacher
Anne Clarke
Gayle Johnson

Editorial Coordinator
Becky Freeman

Editorial Assistant
Rosemarie Graham

Technical Reviewer
Timothy C. Moore

Cover Art
Held & Dietrich Design

Director of Production and Manufacturing
Jeff Valler

Production Manager
Matthew Morrill

Book Designer
Michele Laseau

Production Analyst
Mary Beth Wakefield

Proofreading/Indexing Coordinator
Joelynn Gifford

Graphics Image Specialists
Dennis Sheehan
Jerry Ellis
Sue VanderWalle

Production
Christine Cook
Keith Davenport
Mark Enochs
Tim Groeling
John Kane
Angie Trzepacz
Julie Walker
Kelli Widdifield

Index
Jeanne Clark

Overview

	Preface	xvii
	Introduction	xix
Part I	**Windows Programming with Borland C++**	
1	Introduction to Windows	3
2	Windows Programming Basics	15
3	The Graphics Device Interface (GDI)	31
4	Resources	85
5	The Keyboard and Windows	123
6	The Mouse and Windows	137
7	Windows and Child Windows	147
8	Memory Management and Windows	165
9	The Multiple Document Interface (MDI)	173
10	Dynamic Link Libraries	189
Part II	**Windows Programming with ObjectWindows**	
11	Introduction to ObjectWindows for C++	201
12	Windows Programming Using ObjectWindows	259
Part III	**Reference**	
13	Windows Functions	317
14	Windows Messages	1017
15	Windows Printer Escapes	1163
16	The Resource Workshop	1209
17	ObjectWindows Classes	1229
	Appendixes	
A	Windows Functions Quick Reference Guide	1305
B	Windows Functions by Category	1333
C	Windows Messages Quick Reference Guide	1359
D	The Command-Line Compiler	1381
	Bibliography	1387
	Program Index	1389
	Index	1393

Contents

Part I Windows Programming with Borland C++

1 Introduction to Windows 3

The History of Windows 4
What's New with Windows 3.1 5
Why Windows? 6
  Advantages of Windows to the User 6
  Advantages of Windows to the Programmer 7
The Standard Components of a Window 8
  The Border 9
  The Client Area 9
  The Control Menu 10
  The Horizontal Scroll Bar 10
  The Maximize Button 11
  The Menu Bar 11
  The Minimize Button 11
  The Title Bar 11
  The Vertical Scroll Bar 11
Windows Functions 12
Windows Messages 12
Hungarian Notation 12
Handles 13
The Include File 14

2 Windows Programming Basics 15

Event-Driven Programming 16
The `WinMain` Function 18
The Message Loop 21

Window Procedures 22
Using Projects to Develop Windows Applications 22
The C or C++ Source Code File 24
The Module Definition File 25
The Resource Files 26
A Fundamental Windows Program 26

3 The Graphics Device Interface (GDI) 31

The Device Context 32
The Mapping Mode 33
The Drawing Coordinates 34
GDI Graphics and Points 35
Drawing Lines 39
Pens 46
Drawing Modes 48
Creating Filled Areas 49
Drawing the Borders 50
Filling the Area 53
Text and Fonts 58
Text Drawing Functions 58
Device Context Attributes for Text 67
Using Fonts 68
Text Metrics 73
Aligning Text 75
Scrolling Text Windows 76
Printing 83

4 Resources 85

Using Accelerators 85
Using Bitmaps 90
Using Cursors 96
Using Dialog Boxes 99
Using Icons 106
Using Menus 110
Using Strings 116

5	**The Keyboard and Windows**	**123**
	Keyboard Input	124
	Keyboard Messages	124
	`lParam`	125
	`wParam`	126
	Character Messages	128
	Character Sets	129
	The Caret	129
	The Keyboard Example	130
6	**The Mouse and Windows**	**137**
	Mouse Input	138
	Mouse Messages	139
	The Hit Test Message	139
	Client Area Mouse Messages	140
	Non-Client Area Mouse Messages	141
	The Mouse Example	142
7	**Windows and Child Windows**	**147**
	Creating a Window	147
	Step 1: Defining Window Classes	148
	Step 2: Creating the Window Itself	150
	Child Window Controls	159
	The Child Window Example	161
8	**Memory Management and Windows**	**165**
	The Local and Global Heaps	166
	Segments	170
9	**The Multiple Document Interface (MDI)**	**173**
	MDI Applications	173
	The MDI Message Loop	175
	MDI Messages	176
	Frame and Child Window Functions	177
	The MDI Example	177

10 Dynamic Link Libraries 189

Static Versus Dynamic Linking 189
Import Libraries 190
The DLL Code Structure 191
Creating a DLL 193
Using the DLL from a Windows Application 195

Part II Windows Programming with ObjectWindows

11 Introduction to ObjectWindows for C++ 201

Object-Oriented Programming for C++ 202
Encapsulation 202
Inheritance 204
Polymorphism 207
Object-Oriented Windows Programming with ObjectWindows 209
The ObjectWindows Hierarchy 210
The `Object` Class 211
Application Objects 212
`TApplication` 213
The Application's Main Program 214
Initializing Applications 215
Executing Applications 216
Terminating Applications 216
Interface Objects 217
`TWindowsObject` 217
Window Objects 221
Using Window Objects 222
`TEditWindow` 226
`TFileWindow` 227
`TBWindow` 229
Dialog Objects 229
`TDialog` 229
`TFileDialog` 232
`TInputDialog` 233
`TSearchDialog` 234

Control Objects 235
`TControl` 235
`TButton` 236
`TListBox` 237
`TComboBox` 238
`TCheckBox` 240
`TBCheckBox` 241
`TRadioButton` 242
`TBRadioButton` 242
`TBButton` 243
`TGroupBox` 243
`TBGroupBox` 244
`TStatic` 245
`TEdit` 246
`TBStatic` 248
`TScrollBar` 249
`TBDivider` 251
`TBStaticBmp` 251
MDI Objects 252
`TMDIFrame` 252
`TMDIClient` 254
Scroller Objects 255
`TScroller` 255

12 Windows Programming Using ObjectWindows 259

Windows Application Structure Using ObjectWindows 260
The `WinMain` Function 260
The Message Loop 261
Window Procedures 261
Project Files 262
The Module Definition File 262
Resource Files 263
C++ Source Files 263
Library Files, DLLs, and Import Libraries 264
Using the IDE with ObjectWindows 264

Programming Examples Using ObjectWindows 266
The Basic Window Example 266
The Line Drawing Example 270
The Arc Drawing Example 273
The Filled Figures Example 275
The `TextOut` Example 278
The `TabbedTextOut` Example 281
The Scroller Example 283
The Accelerator Example 286
The Bitmap Example 290
The Cursor Example 293
The Dialog Example 295
The Icon Example 301
The Menu Example 304
The MDI Example 308

Part III Reference

13 Windows Functions 317

14 Windows Messages 1017

15 Windows Printer Escapes 1163

16 The Resource Workshop 1209

Resources 1209
File Types 1211
Projects 1212
The Accelerator Editor 1213
The Dialog Editor 1215
The Dialog Box 1215
The Caption Control 1216
The Tools Palette 1216
The Alignment Palette 1218
The Menu Editor 1219

	The Paint Editor	1220
	The Tools Palette	1221
	The Colors Palette	1223
	The Window Pane	1224
	The String Editor	1226
17	**ObjectWindows Classes**	**1229**
A	**Windows Functions Quick Reference Guide**	**1305**
B	**Windows Functions by Category**	**1333**
	Application Execution Functions	1333
	Atom Functions	1334
	Bitmap Functions	1334
	Caret Functions	1334
	Clipboard Functions	1335
	Clipping Functions	1335
	Color Palette Functions	1336
	Common Dialog Functions	1336
	Communication Functions	1336
	Coordinate Functions	1337
	Cursor Functions	1337
	DDE Functions	1338
	Debugging Functions	1338
	Device Context Functions	1338
	Dialog Box Functions	1339
	Display and Movement Functions	1339
	Drag-Drop Functions	1340
	Drawing Attribute Functions	1340
	Drawing Tool Functions	1340
	Ellipse and Polygon Functions	1341
	Environment Functions	1341
	Error Functions	1341
	File I/O Functions	1342
	Font Functions	1342
	Hardware Functions	1342
	Hook Functions	1343

Icon Functions 1343
Information Functions 1343
Initialization File Functions 1344
Input Functions 1344
Installable Driver Functions 1345
Lempel-Ziv Expansion Functions 1345
Line Output Functions 1345
Mapping Functions 1346
Memory Management Functions 1346
Menu Functions 1347
Message Functions 1347
Metafile Functions 1348
Module Management Functions 1348
Network Functions 1349
OLE Functions 1349
Operating System Interrupt Functions 1350
Optimization Tool Functions 1350
Painting Functions 1351
Printer Control Functions 1352
Property Functions 1352
Rectangle Functions 1352
Region Functions 1353
Registration Functions 1353
Resource Management Functions 1353
Scrolling Functions 1354
Segment Functions 1354
Shell Functions 1354
Stress Functions 1355
String Manipulation Functions 1355
System Functions 1355
Task Functions 1356
Text Functions 1356
Toolhelp Functions 1356
TrueType Functions 1357
Version Functions 1357
Window Creation Functions 1357
Windows Macros/Utility Functions 1358

C	**Windows Messages Quick Reference Guide**	**1359**
D	**The Command-Line Compiler**	**1381**
	Bibliography	**1387**
	Program Index	**1389**
	Index	**1393**

Preface

Borland C++ 3.1 is a powerful tool for the development of C, C++, and Windows applications. Borland C++ 3.1 supports Windows 3.1 functions and capabilities, offers full ANSI C compatibility, provides the features of C++, and includes the Resource Workshop. The Resource Workshop enables you to create and edit resources for Windows applications such as bitmaps, icons, cursors, dialog boxes, strings, menus, and accelerators.

My purpose in writing this book is to provide you, the programmer, with the information that you need to develop Windows applications using Borland C++ 3.1. This book introduces you to the basic programming concepts and principles involved in developing Windows applications.

This book provides three major categories of information that supplement the Borland C++ 3.1 documentation. The first category of information is Windows programming basics. This book introduces you to Windows and to the methods used for Windows application development. The second category of information deals with developing Windows applications using ObjectWindows. The ObjectWindows functions and classes are described in detail and numerous programming examples are provided. The third category of information is reference material for the hundreds of Windows functions, messages, and printer escapes.

The information contained in this book will provide you with the foundation that you need to develop Windows applications using Borland C++ 3.1.

About the Author

James W. McCord is a computer consultant and well-respected author of many computer books. His best-sellers from Prentice Hall Computer Publishing include the *C Programmer's Guide to Graphics*, the *Borland C++ Programmer's Guide to Graphics*, the *Borland C++ Programmer's Reference*, and the *Windows 3.1 Programmer's Reference*.

Acknowledgments

I could not have completed this project without the help of many people. I would like to thank, most of all, my family, Jill, Josh, and Jamie, for their love and support. I would also like to thank the staff at Sams Publishing for all their hard work on putting this book together. It takes a good team to put this much information together and I thank each person involved with this project. Last but not least, I thank T.B.T. for all the great things in my life.

Introduction

This book was developed to accomplish three primary objectives. The first objective is to provide you with a Windows programming foundation for developing Windows applications with Borland C++ 3.1. The second objective is to provide you with reference information and programming examples for using ObjectWindows for Windows application development. The third objective is to provide complete reference material on the Windows functions and messages so that you can continue to build on this Windows programming foundation.

To meet the objectives of this book, the chapters are divided into three sections. Part I, consisting of Chapters 1 to 10, introduces the fundamentals of developing Windows applications using Borland C++. Part II, which includes Chapters 11 and 12, introduces the ObjectWindows features included with Borland C++ 3.1. Part III consists of Chapters 13 to 17 and contains the reference information for each of the Windows functions and messages as well as the Resource Workshop.

The chapters contained in each section are described in the following sections.

Part I—Windows Programming with Borland C++

Chapter 1, "Introduction to Windows," introduces the Windows environment and explains how programming for Windows applications differs from programming for traditional MS-DOS applications. Chapter 2, "Windows Programming Basics," provides the foundation that you will need to develop Windows applications using Borland C++ 3.1. All the basic components of Windows applications—including the `WinMain` function, the message loop, window procedures, and resource files—are explained in this chapter.

Chapter 3, "The Graphics Device Interface (GDI)," covers the capabilities of the Graphics Device Interface. Topics included are lines, brushes, pens, the device context, and text output. Several examples demonstrating the capabilities of the GDI are provided. In Chapter 4, "Resources," you are introduced to accelerator, bitmap, cursor, dialog box, icon, menu, and string resources. An example that creates and uses each type of resource is provided.

The principles of using the keyboard with Windows are addressed in Chapter 5, "The Keyboard and Windows." Topics for this chapter include keyboard messages, character messages, character sets, and the caret. Chapter 6, "The Mouse and Windows," addresses the principles of using the mouse with Windows. The focus of this chapter is Windows mouse messages.

Chapter 7, "Windows and Child Windows," introduces the concepts of windows and child windows inside the Windows environment. This chapter specifically addresses the use of child window controls. Chapter 8, "Memory Management and Windows," addresses Windows' use of local heaps, global heaps, and segments.

The Multiple Document Interface specification is discussed and demonstrated in Chapter 9. Finally, Chapter 10, "Dynamic Link Libraries," presents the concepts and uses of dynamic link libraries. A dynamic link library is created and demonstrated.

Part II—Windows Programming with ObjectWindows

ObjectWindows and the ObjectWindows class hierarchy are discussed in Chapter 11, "Introduction to ObjectWindows for C++." Chapter 12, "Windows Programming Using ObjectWindows," introduces the fundamental concepts behind programming with ObjectWindows and provides numerous programmimg examples of Windows applications using ObjectWindows.

Part III—Reference

Reference material for each of the Windows functions is provided in Chapter 13. The functions are presented alphabetically. Chapter 14 provides reference material for each of the Windows messages, and these are presented alphabetically as well.

Chapter 15, "Windows Printer Escapes," introduces the Windows printer escapes and provides reference information on each escape. Chapter 16 discusses the capabilities and features of the Resource Workshop.

The final chapter, Chapter 17, provides detailed reference information for each of the ObjectWindows classes. You will find descriptions of the data members and member functions of each ObjectWindows class.

Part III also includes Appendixes A through D, which provide a quick reference guide to Windows functions, a list of Windows functions divided by category, a quick reference guide for Windows messages, and a list of the command-line compiler options with their descriptions.

I

Windows Programming with Borland C++

1

Introduction to Windows

Microsoft Windows is a graphical user interface environment for MS-DOS computers. Windows provides a multitasking environment that uses a consistent windowing and menu structure for its applications. Because the windowing and menu structure is consistent between applications, Windows applications are easier for the user to learn and use than are traditional DOS-based programs. The multitasking advantage of Windows enables you to run several applications at a time. This feature performs especially well for those applications that are created for the Windows environment, but Windows provides the capability to run and multitask non-Windows MS-DOS applications as well. The Windows 3.1 environment is shown in Figure 1.1.

This chapter introduces the Windows graphical user interface. You will also find a brief history of the Windows product, a discussion of some new features and the advantages of using Windows, and an overview of the fundamental components of a window.

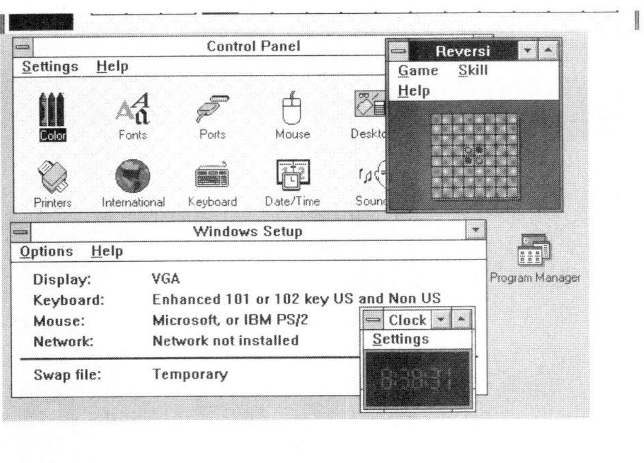

Figure 1.1. *Windows is a multitasking environment.*

Microsoft Windows is "the" graphical user interface environment for MS-DOS machines. Although other graphical user interface environments exist, none can compare with Windows in popularity. Graphical user interfaces use bitmapped displays to convey information. Because the display is not limited to the ASCII character set, as is the case with traditional MS-DOS text-based programs, the image on the display accurately reflects the image produced on an output device such as a printer or plotter. This correlation between the screen image and the output image is called *what-you-see-is-what-you-get* (WYSIWYG) and is one reason graphical user interfaces such as Windows have become so popular. Windows offers the user and the programmer several advantages, which are discussed later in this chapter.

The History of Windows

Microsoft began working on the first version of Windows in 1983, and released version 1.1 of Windows in 1985. This version was designed for a two-floppy 8088 IBM PC system with 256K of RAM. Windows 1.1 automatically tiled the application windows and supported pop-up windows.

In 1987, Microsoft released the next major version of Windows, numbered 2.0. This version contained a new user interface that supported overlapping windows. A major advantage of Windows 2.0 was the improved use of expanded memory. Because Windows 2.0 ran only in real mode, however, the amount of memory that could be addressed was limited to one megabyte.

Microsoft released Windows version 3.0 in 1990. Windows 3.0 added support for owner draw menus, owner draw list boxes, and owner draw buttons, and improved its memory management capabilities. Windows 3.0 quickly became the standard graphical user interface for MS-DOS machines.

In April, 1992, Microsoft released Windows 3.1. Windows 3.1 improved many of the Windows 3.0 features and added new capabilities, including a new File Manager with *file dragging and dropping*, object linking and embedding (OLE), and multimedia extensions.

The new features of Windows 3.1 make the Windows environment more appealing to the user. To take advantage of these features, however, you—the programmer—must understand the new capabilities and the hundreds of functions and messages added to the Windows 3.1 Application Programming Interface (API). In this chapter we take a brief look at some of the new features of Windows 3.1. Part III of this book contains detailed reference information for each of the new Windows 3.1 functions, messages, printer escapes, and data structures.

What's New with Windows 3.1

Windows 3.0 supported three modes of operation: real, standard, and 386 enhanced mode. Windows 3.1 supports only two modes of operation: standard and 386 enhanced mode. Windows 3.1 will run in 386 enhanced mode on 386 (or higher) computers with at least 640K of conventional memory and 1024K of extended memory. Windows 3.1 will run in standard mode on 286 (or higher) computers with at least 640K of conventional memory plus 256K of extended memory. Windows 3.1 runs in standard mode on 386 (or higher) machines with less than 2MB of memory.

Object linking and embedding (OLE) is new for Windows 3.1. With OLE, applications can share data through the embedding or linking of objects. *Object embedding* refers to the capability to insert data such as a sound file or a drawing into another document. Say, for example, that you embedded a bitmapped image into your document and you wanted to edit the bitmap. You would simply select the bitmap from within your word processor, and the bitmap editor that you used to create the embedded bitmap would automatically be started, allowing you to edit the bitmap.

Object linking allows you to share data among applications. For example, you could link a figure into a word processing document, a presentation graphics chart, and a spreadsheet. You could edit the figure from within any of the applications that contain the linked figure. With object linking, only one copy of the linked data exists. Any change to the data, therefore, is reflected in all the documents that are linked to the data. The Windows 3.1 API contains dozens of functions for OLE. These functions are documented in Chapter 13. The OLE functions are easy to find because they all begin with the letters *Ole*.

Another new feature of Windows 3.1 is the support of *file dragging and dropping* in the File Manager. This feature allows the user to easily drag a file to move, print, or copy it. The Windows 3.1 API contains several new functions that you can use to implement this new feature.

Windows 3.1 supports TrueType fonts. TrueType fonts are scalable fonts, meaning that they can be scaled to the exact font size you want. The Windows 3.1 API contains new functions and data structures for the effective implementation of TrueType fonts in your applications.

The multimedia features of Windows 3.1 allow the user to access various multimedia devices and to bring sounds, graphics, animation, and video into the Windows environment. The multimedia features of Windows 3.1 are exciting, but because these new features are part of the multimedia API, they are not documented in this book.

Windows 3.1 offers many new features to the Windows user and many new challenges to the Windows programmer. Borland C++ 3.1 contains features for designing and developing Windows 3.1 applications with either C or C++.

Why Windows?

Windows and its applications offer many advantages over other graphical user interface environments to both the user and the programmer. Users enjoy the benefits of features such as point-and-click capabilities and multitasking. Device-independent graphics and enhanced memory management are helpful for the programmer. The following sections describe some of the advantages of Windows for the user and the programmer.

Advantages of Windows to the User

Users of Windows and Windows applications will appreciate the consistent user interface of this environment. Because most users work with several different software packages, each with its own user interface, the consistency of the user interface's design is very important. Each window in the Windows environment contains the same basic features. Because these basic features are consistent among applications, the user can adapt to new applications more easily.

Windows users also benefit from the use of graphics-based images to represent applications and data. Because Windows is a graphical user interface, graphics images represent physical data structures such as files, applications, windows, and directories. The user can manipulate these physical structures with a mouse by selecting, double-clicking, dragging, and so forth. Double-clicking an icon that represents an application is easier than going to the appropriate directory and typing the name of the file to launch.

What-you-see-is-what-you-get (WYSIWYG) is a major advantage to the user. Most text-based word-processing software packages use the read-only memory, basic input-output system (ROM BIOS) character sets for the screen display. Because the ROM BIOS character sets are not proportional and have no direct correlation to the font used by an application, the text displayed on the screen usually does not correspond to the resulting text output by the printer. With the WYSIWYG feature, however, Windows can treat text as a series of graphics images that are drawn onto the screen as they will appear when printed.

Windows also provides the user with the very important capability of multitasking. Because several applications can run simultaneously, there is no need to save the working file and exit the application to enter another application; the user can simply keep the programs running and switch among applications. Multitasking is enhanced by Windows' memory management capabilities. Windows provides access to all available memory resources, so the user can optimize the system more easily.

Advantages of Windows to the Programmer

Many of the user's advantages in Windows are also utilized by the programmer. The consistent user interface, for example, benefits the programmer because the basic interface design and tools already are established. Because the interface is basically the same for every application, the programmer can spend more time on the application's functionality and less time on the interface design.

The basic design of the graphical user interface is another reason for Windows' popularity. Windows allows the programmer to design graphical representations of physical structures, such as files and directories, and provides convenient features such as pop-up menus and dialog boxes. Windows also supports direct mouse and keyboard input, significantly decreasing application development time.

The programmer will especially appreciate Windows' memory management features. These features enable you to access more memory than you can using traditional MS-DOS applications so that you can make the most of the system memory resources while maintaining flexibility in system design. Chapter 8, "Memory Management and Windows," provides more details on the basic memory management features of Windows.

Windows also provides the capability to develop device-independent graphics. Because well-designed Windows applications do not access the graphics hardware

(the screen and printer) directly, Windows applications operate with any video subsystem or printer that has a Windows device driver. For the programmer, device-independent graphics means that code is not dependent on a certain system configuration. With Windows, there is no need to develop device drivers for all the possible video displays, adapters, and printers for each application.

The Standard Components of a Window

A Windows application uses an application window for input and output to the screen. The Windows application creates the application window and has primary access to the window. The application and Windows, however, share the responsibility of managing the application window. Windows is responsible for managing the size, position, and components of the application window. The application maintains the primary responsibility of managing the client area (working area) of the application window. The application window contains some, and often all, of the following components:

- The window border
- The client area
- The Control menu box
- The Control menu
- The horizontal scroll bar
- The Maximize box
- The menu bar
- The Minimize box
- The title bar
- The vertical scroll bar

The Notepad application window contains each of the components in the previous list. The Notepad application window is shown in Figure 1.2. The following paragraphs describe each component of a typical application window.

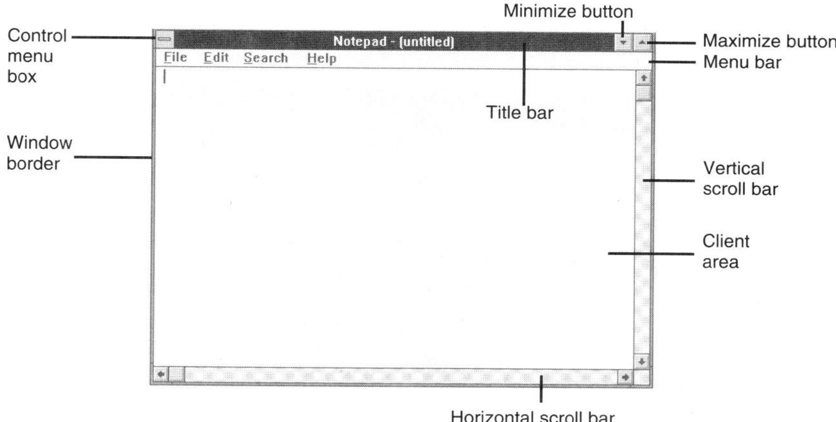

Figure 1.2. *The Notepad window contains the standard window components.*

The Border

The window border surrounds the outside edge of the application window. The window border consists of three basic elements:

- The four corners
- The vertical sides
- The horizontal sides

The four window corners enable you to size the window vertically and horizontally at the same time. The vertical sides of the window border enable you to size the window in the horizontal direction. Finally, you can size the window vertically by using the horizontal sides of the window border.

The Client Area

The client area is the physical part of the window that is not occupied by the menu bar, scroll bars, borders, or other components. The application uses the client area as its workspace. The application maintains the client area, and Windows maintains the position, size, and components of the application window.

The Control Menu

The Control menu box is located in the upper-left corner of the application window. The Control menu box provides access to the Control menu.

Through the menu options of the Control menu, you can restore, move, size, minimize, maximize, and close the application window. The Control menu, also called the *System menu*, provides the primary access to the various components in the application window if you aren't using a mouse. The Control menu for the Notepad application is shown in Figure 1.3.

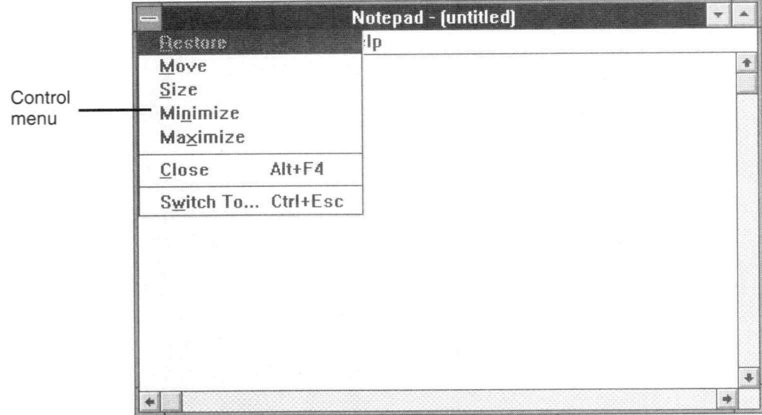

Figure 1.3. *The Control menu for the Notepad application.*

The Horizontal Scroll Bar

With the horizontal scroll bar, you can move through documents and images that are too large for the current size of the client area. The horizontal scroll bar contains three elements. The first element is the left arrow, positioned at the left end of the scroll bar. Clicking this arrow displays a part of the document or image located to the left of the left window border. The second element is the right arrow, positioned at the right end of the scroll bar. Clicking this arrow displays a part of the document or image located to the right of the right window border. The last element, the scroll thumb, indicates the thumb position of the current view area. The solid square in the scroll bar indicates the current view position relative to the far left and far right sides of the document or image.

The Maximize Button

The Maximize button enlarges the application window to fill the screen. After you click the Maximize button, it is replaced with the Restore button. You can click the Restore button to restore the window to its previous size. When the window is restored to its previous size, the Restore button is replaced with the Maximize button.

The Menu Bar

The menu bar lists the menus provided to the user by the application. The File, Edit, and Help menus are common to most applications. As a Windows programmer, however, you can customize the number and type of menus available to the user.

The Minimize Button

The Minimize button shrinks the application window to an icon. When you click the Minimize button, the application is minimized (shrunk to an icon). Double-clicking the minimized window (the icon) restores the window to its previous size.

The Title Bar

The title bar lists the application name and often the active file name for the application window. The title bar of the active window is differentiated by color and/or intensity from the title bar of inactive windows.

The Vertical Scroll Bar

You can use the vertical scroll bar to move through documents and images that are too large for the current size of the client area. The vertical scroll bar contains three components. The first component is the Up arrow, positioned at the top of the scroll bar. Clicking this arrow displays a part of the document or image located above the top window border. The second component is the Down arrow, positioned at the bottom of the scroll bar. Clicking this arrow displays a part of the document or image located below the bottom window border. The last component, the scroll thumb, indicates the thumb position of the current view area. The solid square in the scroll bar indicates the current view position relative to the top and bottom of the document or image.

Windows Functions

The Windows functions are the heart of the Windows application. Most MS-DOS applications written in C or C++ use the functions from the compiler's run-time library to interface with MS-DOS. Functions in the compiler's run-time libraries are oriented specifically for the development of MS-DOS applications running on the 80x86 architecture. When you develop Windows applications, you should use the Windows functions to take advantage of the capabilities of Windows and of its device independence.

There is a wide range of Windows functions. Chapter 13 in Part III provides additional reference information for each of the Windows API functions. You should skim Chapter 13 to get an idea of the almost overwhelming number of Windows functions. Don't be alarmed, however. As happens with most programming libraries, you will soon develop a familiar subset of functions that you will work with frequently.

Windows Messages

Windows applications use Windows messages to communicate with other Windows applications and with the Windows system. Because Windows applications are message, or event, driven, it is important to understand how the Windows messages function. Chapter 14 provides reference information for each of the Windows messages and explains their use. Skim Chapter 14 to get a feel for the number of messages that Windows supports. As with the Windows functions, don't be too alarmed by the sheer number of messages—you will use a small subset of these messages frequently, and you'll soon become familiar with the messages in this subset.

Hungarian Notation

Hungarian notation, a method of creating variable names, is commonly used by Windows programmers. This method was named for the nationality of Microsoft programmer Charles Simonyi and is used extensively by Microsoft for application and operating-system software.

Hungarian notation uses lowercase letters in the prefix of the variable name to indicate the data type of the variable. The remainder of the variable name describes how the variable functions. For example,

```
nCharacterCounter
```

specifies that the variable is an integer (`n`) and represents a character counter (`CharacterCounter`).

The Windows functions and messages listed in Chapters 13 and 14 commonly use the prefixes listed in Table 1.1 in variable and parameter names.

Table 1.1. *Common prefixes for Windows variables.*

Prefix	*Meaning*
`b`	Boolean (nonzero is true, 0 is false)
`c`	Character (one byte value)
`dw`	Long 32-bit unsigned integer
`f`	Bit flags packed into a 16-bit integer
`h`	16-bit handle
`l`	Long 32-bit integer
`lp`	Long 32-bit pointer
`n`	Short 16-bit integer
`p`	Short 16-bit pointer
`pt`	Coordinate pair (x and y) packed into an unsigned 32-bit integer
`rgb`	RGB color value packed into a 32-bit integer
`w`	Short 16-bit unsigned integer

Handles

Handles are fundamental to Windows programming, so it's important that you understand exactly what they are. A *handle* is a unique integer value used by Windows to identify an object in an application such as a window, instance, menu, memory, output device, control, or file. For example, in a module definition file (explained in Chapter 2), menu resources are defined and associated with handles. The first menu item of the first menu in the menu bar of an application, for example,

might be assigned a handle of 100. The second menu item might be assigned a handle of 101. In the application source code, these menu items would be referenced by the handles 100 and 101. The Windows application usually can access only the handle, not the actual data that the handle represents. Windows controls access to the data and, therefore, protects the data in the multitasking environment.

The Include File

Borland C++ provides the windows.h include file so that you can access the various Windows functions and messages from your C or C++ program. windows.h contains the definitions for the Windows constants, variables, data structures, and functions. All Windows applications must include the windows.h file in the source code.

The next chapter introduces you to the basics of programming a Windows application using traditional Windows programming techniques. You will be introduced to the concept of event-driven architectures, and walked through the development of a standard window. The remaining chapters in Part I of this book describe various programming techniques for Windows applications.

2

Windows Programming Basics

Windows programming can be, quite honestly, a major headache to newcomers. Most programmers who are familiar with the traditional, sequential programming methodologies used with C are often not mentally prepared to meet the challenges of Windows programming. Many programmers have the following attitude when approaching Windows programming:

- "A Windows program can't be much different from a C program."
- "I've programmed in C for years, so all I have to do is become familiar with the Windows functions."
- "Windows? C? It's all the same!"

This type of attitude gives Windows programming the unfortunate reputation of being very difficult for programmers.

Learning to program Windows, in itself, is no more difficult than learning the ins and outs of any structured language—you just have to learn the basic code structure and

programming methodologies. For most programmers, the biggest hurdle to learning Windows programming is an unwillingness to discard traditional programming methodologies. If you wholeheartedly adopt the Windows programming methodologies and approach Windows with an open mind, you will quickly adapt to the new programming concepts and methodologies.

This chapter gives you the whirlwind tour of Windows programming. After being introduced to event-driven programming, you'll learn the basic concepts and methodologies for programming Windows applications using Borland C++. The chapter ends by demonstrating these concepts and methodologies with a fundamental Windows program.

Event-Driven Programming

The majority of MS-DOS programs are written using sequential, procedure-driven programming methodologies, which have a distinct beginning, distinct procedures, and a distinct end. The program directly controls the sequence of program events or procedures.

Windows programming methodologies, by contrast, are event driven. Event-driven programs are controlled by the *occurrence* of events, rather than by the *sequence* of them. The following example quickly demonstrates the primary difference between sequential, procedure-driven programs and event-driven programs.

Suppose that you had to write a program that averages the grades of a class which had taken three tests during the semester. You have determined that the procedure for generating the averages is as follows:

1. Enter the names of the students.
2. Enter the grades for test one.
3. Enter the grades for test two.
4. Enter the grades for test three.
5. Calculate and display the averages.

In a sequential, procedure-driven program, the logic flow looks something like that shown in Figure 2.1. The program displays a screen that prompts you for the names of the students. After you enter the names of the students, the next screen prompts you for the grades for test one. Again, another screen prompts you for the grades for test two. After completing the grades for test two, a screen is displayed that enables you to enter grades for test three. After you enter the test three grades, the final screen containing the calculated averages is displayed. This approach is very logical and follows a structured sequence of events. To use the program as intended, however, you must follow the procedure as designed. You can't change a grade in step 3 once you are in step 5, for example.

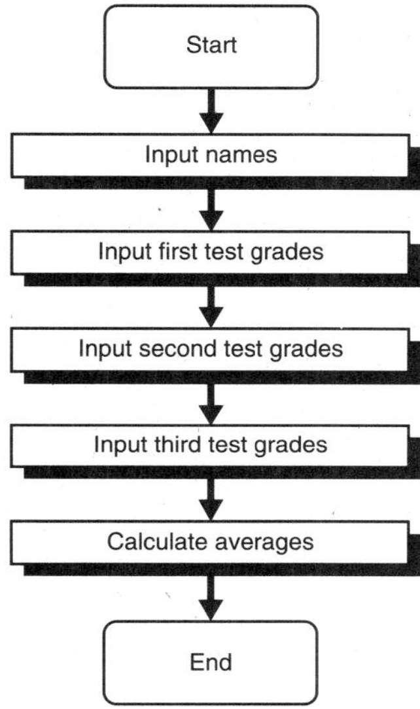

Figure 2.1. *Sequential, procedure-driven methodology.*

Although there are many ways to handle exceptions in sequential, procedure-driven programs such as the one just presented, exceptions also must follow sequential, procedure-driven architectures. Event-driven programs are designed to avoid the limitations of sequential, procedure-driven methodologies by processing events in a nonsequential manner.

Event-driven programming revolves around the generation and processing of messages. A message is information about an event that has occurred. For example, whenever a key or mouse button is pressed, a message is sent. Another message is sent when the key or mouse button is released. Your job as a Windows programmer involves, to a large extent, the sorting and managing of the Windows messages sent to and from the application that you are developing. Because Windows messages are event-driven, messages do not appear in any predefined order.

The previous example of a sequential, procedure-driven application can be easily implemented using event-driven methodologies. Figure 2.2 illustrates the methodology that would be used to implement the application with an event-driven architecture. The full functionality of the sequential, procedure-driven program is still there; however, the user does not have to go through each step, in sequence,

to calculate the grades. The user may skip around the various screens while adding or modifying data at each level. For example, with the event-driven application, you can enter grades for the third test without previously having entered the test scores for tests one and two. With the procedure-driven example, this would not be possible. Event-driven programming methodologies provide many benefits and are very useful for applications that require extensive user interaction.

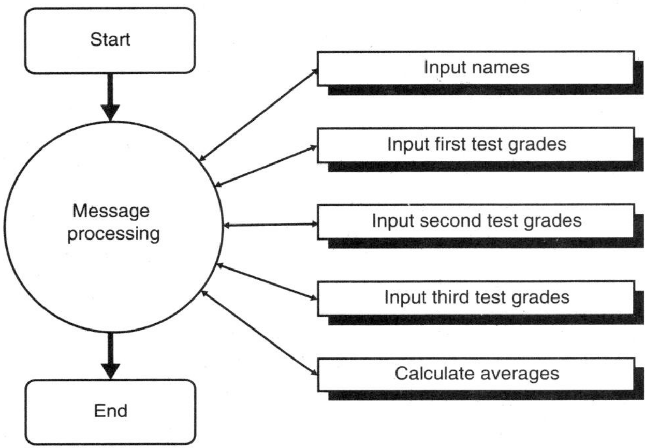

Figure 2.2. *Event-driven program methodology.*

The *WinMain* Function

The `WinMain` function is the entry point for all Windows applications. There are three basic parts to the `WinMain` function: procedure declaration, program initialization, and the message loop. The general form of the `WinMain` function follows.

```
int PASCAL WinMain (HANDLE hInstance, HANDLE hPrevInstance,
                    LPSTR lpszCmdParam, int nCmdShow)

{
HWND hWnd;
MSG Message;
WNDCLASS WndClass;

if (!hPrevInstance)
     {
     WndClass.cbClsExtra = 0;
     WndClass.cbWndExtra = 0;
```

```
          WndClass.hbrBackground = GetStockObject(WHITE_BRUSH);
          WndClass.hCursor = LoadCursor(NULL, IDC_ARROW);
          WndClass.hIcon = LoadIcon (NULL, "END");
          WndClass.hInstance = hInstance;
          WndClass.lpfnWndProc = WndProc;
          WndClass.lpszClassName = "WIN_ONE";
          WndClass.lpszMenuName = NULL;
          WndClass.style = CS_HREDRAW ¦ CS_VREDRAW;

          RegisterClass (&WndClass);
          }

     hWnd = CreateWindow ("WIN_ONE",      /* class name */
               "Fundamental Window",      /* Caption */
               WS_OVERLAPPEDWINDOW,       /* Style */
               CW_USEDEFAULT,             /* x position */
               0,                         /* y position */
               CW_USEDEFAULT,             /* cx - size */
               0,                         /* cy - size */
               NULL,                      /* Parent window */
               NULL,                      /* Menu */
               hInstance,                 /* Program Instance */
               NULL);                     /* Parameters */

     ShowWindow (hWnd, nCmdShow);
     while (GetMessage (&Message, 0, 0, 0))
          {
          TranslateMessage(&Message);
          DispatchMessage(&Message);
          }
     return Message.wParam;
```

The procedure declaration for the `WinMain` function is as follows:

```
int PASCAL WinMain (HANDLE hInstance, HANDLE hPrevInstance,
                    LPSTR lpszCmdLine, int cmdShow);
```

`hInstance` is a handle identifying the program. `hPrevInstance` specifies the program that `hInstance` is related to, if any. Programs are considered related if they share the same module name. `lpszCmdLine` specifies the command-line arguments for the program. `cmdShow` specifies the state of the main window when the window is first opened.

Program initialization is the bulk of the `WinMain` function. In the example later in this chapter (Listing 2.2), the program initialization portion of the `WinMain` function involves the creation of a window. In the process of creating a window, you must define the window class. The first part of the initialization portion of the `WinMain` function defines the various members of a `WndClass` data structure. In this part of the

code, you define the cursor used for the window, the brush used to fill the window background, the name of the window procedure, the window class style, the main menu of the window, and the class name. The program initialization portion of the example presented later in Listing 2.2 is as follows:

```
if (!hPrevInstance)
     {
     WndClass.cbClsExtra = 0;
     WndClass.cbWndExtra = 0;
     WndClass.hbrBackground = GetStockObject(WHITE_BRUSH);
     WndClass.hCursor =  LoadCursor(NULL, IDC_ARROW);
     WndClass.hIcon = LoadIcon (NULL, "END");
     WndClass.hInstance = hInstance;
     WndClass.lpfnWndProc = WndProc;
     WndClass.lpszClassName = "WIN_ONE";
     WndClass.lpszMenuName = NULL;
     WndClass.style = CS_HREDRAW ¦ CS_VREDRAW;

     RegisterClass (&WndClass);
     }

hWnd = CreateWindow ("WIN_ONE",        /* class name */
          "Fundamental Window",        /* Caption */
          WS_OVERLAPPEDWINDOW,         /* Style */
          CW_USEDEFAULT,               /* x position */
          0,                           /* y position */
          CW_USEDEFAULT,               /* cx - size */
          0,                           /* cy - size */
          NULL,                        /* Parent window */
          NULL,                        /* Menu */
          hInstance,                   /* Program Instance */
          NULL);                       /* Parameters */

ShowWindow (hWnd, nCmdShow);
```

The message loop of the `WinMain` function retrieves messages from the application queue and sends each message to the appropriate window function. The message loop from Listing 2.2 follows. More information on the message loop is provided in the following section.

```
while (GetMessage (&Message, 0, 0, 0))
     {
     TranslateMessage(&Message);
     DispatchMessage(&Message);
     }
```

The Message Loop

Windows applications receive input in the form of messages. These messages contain information about the device that generated the input, the current state of the keyboard, the position of the cursor, the state of the mouse, and the system time. Windows monitors all the input devices and places input messages into the system queue. Windows then copies the input messages from the system queue into the appropriate application queue. The application's message loop retrieves the messages from the application queue and sends each message to the appropriate window function. Figure 2.3 diagrams this message-handling process.

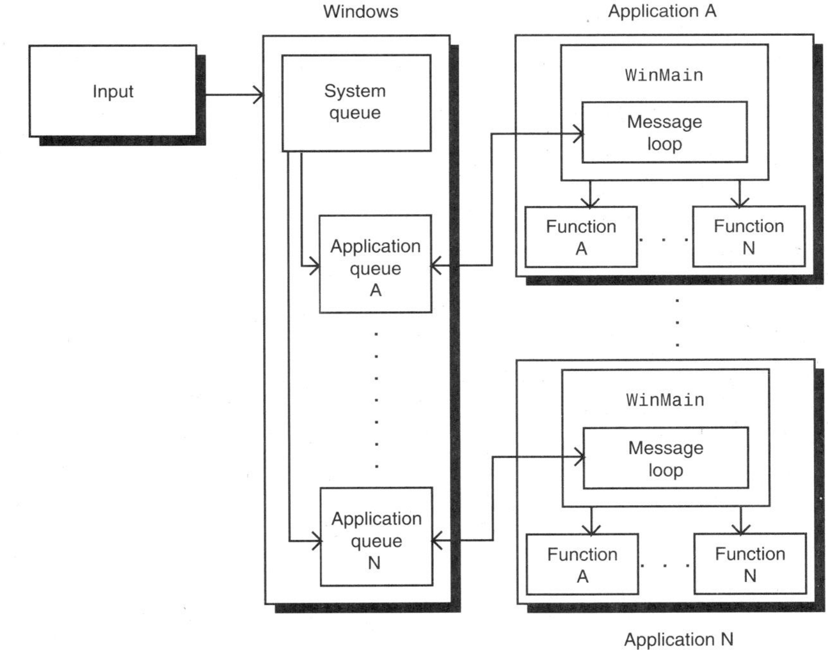

Figure 2.3. *Windows and the message loop.*

The general format for the message loop is as follows:

```
while (GetMessage (&Message, NULL, 0, 0))
     {
     TranslateMessage (&Message);
     DispatchMessage (&Message);
     }
return Message.wParam;
```

In this message loop, `Message` refers to a data structure of type `MSG`. Chapter 13, "Windows Functions," provides information on the `GetMessage`, `TranslateMessage`, and `DispatchMessage` functions used in the message loop.

Window Procedures

Window procedures are functions that receive and process messages. The message loop is responsible for retrieving messages from the application queue and sending the message to the appropriate window procedures. The window procedure determines the action that is taken when a certain message is received.

The window procedure is generally structured using one or more `switch` statements with a `case` for each message. Each `case` reflects the action taken when the corresponding message is received. The following code, which is taken from the example (Listing 2.2) that is presented later in this chapter, represents a simple window procedure:

```
long FAR PASCAL WndProc (HWND hWnd, WORD iMessage, WORD wParam,
                         LONG lParam)
{
switch (iMessage)
     {
     case WM_DESTROY:
          PostQuitMessage(0);
          return 0;
     default:
          return(DefWindowProc(hWnd, iMessage, wParam,
               lParam));
     }
}
```

In this window procedure, only one condition is checked—the receipt of the `WM_DESTROY` message. Although this window procedure is simple, the same structure could be used and expanded for more complex window procedures.

Using Projects to Develop Windows Applications

Several ways to create a Windows application include using the Integrated Development Environment (IDE) and Project Manager, using the command-line compiler, or using a makefile. Whatever method you use, the basic process and the results are the same.

The process for creating a Windows application includes the basic steps shown in Figure 2.4 that follows. C or C++ source files are compiled into object code using the Borland C++ compiler. The resulting object code is linked with definition and library files to form executable code. The resource compiler then binds the resource files with the executable code to create a Windows application.

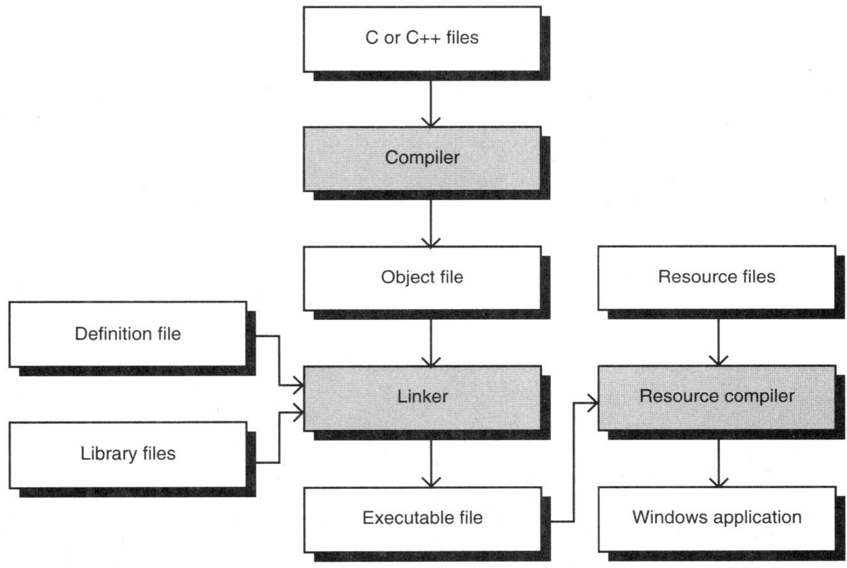

Figure 2.4. *Building a Windows application.*

If you are familiar with previous versions of Borland C++ or have used Turbo C or Turbo C++, using projects to build applications is not a new concept. If you are new to Borland C++, however, or have never developed an application using the Project Manager features of the IDE, you need to understand the use of projects. Now that Borland C++ includes a Windows-based version of the IDE, the IDE project is the most straightforward method for creating Windows applications. For that reason, this book uses the Windows-based IDE and the Project Manager for developing all the examples in this book.

When using the Project Manager and the Windows-based IDE for creating Windows applications, you must follow seven basic steps:

> **Note:** This process is designed for use with Windows-based versions of the IDE. The process used for the DOS-based IDE is similar.

1. Start the IDE by double-clicking the Borland C++ for Windows icon.
2. Create all appropriate C or C++ source files, module definition files, and resource files. More information on these files is included in the following paragraphs.
3. Select `Project ¦ Open`. Type the filename, using a .PRJ extension, in the `Project Name` dialog box. Click the `OK` button, or press Enter to continue.
4. Select `Project ¦ Add item`. Add the appropriate C or C++ source files, module definition files, and resource files. Close the `Project` dialog box when you are done.
5. Select `Options ¦ Application`. The `Set Application Options` dialog box will appear. Select `Windows App` to indicate that you are developing a Windows application.
6. Select `Run ¦ Run`. This selection builds the project into a Windows application and displays your application window if the project compiles successfully.
7. If there are any errors, modify the appropriate file(s) and repeat step 6.

This process is relatively simple and provides you with access to the powerful features of the IDE and Project Manager. Again, this process is used for all the examples in this book. Each example contains a listing of the files used in the application project.

Your windows applications projects generally will contain three types of files: the C or C++ source code file(s), the module definition file, and the resource file(s). Each of these file types is discussed in the following sections.

The C or C++ Source Code File

The source code for the Windows application resides in the C or C++ source code file. As with traditional C or C++ projects, there may be more than one C or C++ file included in a project. The C or C++ source code file contains a combination of

C and/or C++ keywords and functions, Windows functions, Windows messages, and references to include files such as windows.h.

The Module Definition File

The module definition file gives the linker specific information about the application's code and data segments, the size of the application's local heap, and the size of the application's program stack. When using the Borland C++ linker, you don't need to create the module definition file because the linker can determine this information. If you follow the C programming practices described in Part I of this book, however, most of your Windows applications will need the module definition file because its use is customary for developing Windows applications and it enables you to specify settings for the application.

The following lines are included in the module definition file:

```
NAME

DESCRIPTION

EXETYPE

CODE

DATA

HEAPSIZE

STACKSIZE

EXPORTS
```

in which

`NAME` defines a module as an executable.

`DESCRIPTION` adds the specified text to the executable.

`EXETYPE` indicates the type of program the linker should create. `WINDOWS` is used for Windows applications.

`CODE` provides information on the application's code segments. Possible values include `PRELOAD`, `FIXED`, `MOVEABLE`, and `DISCARDABLE`.

`DATA` provides information on the application's data segments. Possible values include `PRELOAD`, `MOVEABLE`, and `MULTIPLE`.

`HEAPSIZE` defines the initial size of the application's local heap.

`STACKSIZE` defines the size of the application's stack.

`EXPORTS` enables you to specify the window and dialog procedures for your application.

Listing 2.1, which appears later in this chapter, is a typical module definition file.

The Resource Files

Most Windows applications use resources such as icons, cursors, bitmaps, and dialog boxes. You can use the Resource Workshop to create these resources. After a resource is created, it is stored in a resource file. Resource files created by the Resource Workshop are source files, and they must be compiled by the Resource Compiler and bound to the executable so that they are available at runtime.

The Resource Compiler compiles the resource source file, binds the compiled file with the compiled .EXE or .DLL module, and generates a Windows-compatible application. When you use the Project Manager to develop Windows applications, the Resource Compiler is invoked automatically.

A Fundamental Windows Program

The example in Listings 2.1 and 2.2 demonstrates a fundamental window. A fundamental window is a window that can be sized, moved, closed, minimized, or maximized. The IDE and the Project Manager were used to create and build the project. The process for creating a Windows application, as described previously in this chapter, was used for this project. The project used to build this example is called WIN_ONE and contains the files WIN_ONE.C and WIN_ONE.DEF. The following project description summarizes the project. A similar summary is used for every example in this book. The window created with this example is shown in Figure 2.5, which follows the listings.

Project Name:	`WIN_ONE`
Files in Project:	`WIN_ONE.C`
	`WIN_ONE.DEF`

Listing 2.1. *The module definition file for the fundamental window example.*

```
NAME            WIN_ONE
DESCRIPTION     'Fundamental Window'
EXETYPE         WINDOWS
CODE            PRELOAD MOVEABLE
DATA            PRELOAD MOVEABLE MULTIPLE
HEAPSIZE        1024
STACKSIZE       5120
EXPORTS         WndProc
```

Listing 2.2. *C source code for the fundamental window example.*

```
#include <windows.h>
#include <stdlib.h>
#include <string.h>

long FAR PASCAL WndProc (HWND hWnd, WORD iMessage,
                WORD wParam, LONG lParam);

int PASCAL WinMain (HANDLE hInstance, HANDLE hPrevInstance,
                    LPSTR lpszCmdParam, int nCmdShow)

{
HWND hWnd;
MSG Message;
WNDCLASS WndClass;

if (!hPrevInstance)
     {
     WndClass.cbClsExtra = 0;
     WndClass.cbWndExtra = 0;
     WndClass.hbrBackground = GetStockObject(WHITE_BRUSH);
     WndClass.hCursor = LoadCursor(NULL, IDC_ARROW);
     WndClass.hIcon = LoadIcon (NULL, "END");
     WndClass.hInstance = hInstance;
     WndClass.lpfnWndProc = WndProc;
     WndClass.lpszClassName = "WIN_ONE";
     WndClass.lpszMenuName = NULL;
     WndClass.style = CS_HREDRAW ¦ CS_VREDRAW;

     RegisterClass (&WndClass);
     }

hWnd = CreateWindow ("WIN_ONE",     /* class name */
          "Fundamental Window",     /* Caption */
```

continues

Listing 2.2. continued

```
          WS_OVERLAPPEDWINDOW,      /* Style */
          CW_USEDEFAULT,            /* x position */
          0,                        /* y position */
          CW_USEDEFAULT,            /* cx - size */
          0,                        /* cy - size */
          NULL,                     /* Parent window */
          NULL,                     /* Menu */
          hInstance,                /* Program Instance */
          NULL);                    /* Parameters */

ShowWindow (hWnd, nCmdShow);
while (GetMessage (&Message, 0, 0, 0))
     {
     TranslateMessage(&Message);
     DispatchMessage(&Message);
     }
return Message.wParam;
}

/***************************************************************/
/*              Window Procedure: WndProc                      */
/***************************************************************/

long FAR PASCAL WndProc (HWND hWnd, WORD iMessage, WORD wParam,
                         LONG lParam)
{
switch (iMessage)
     {
     case WM_DESTROY:
          PostQuitMessage(0);
          return 0;
     default:
          return(DefWindowProc(hWnd, iMessage, wParam,
               lParam));
     }
}
```

As you can see from the size of the listings, a significant number of source code lines are required to generate even a fundamental window. The C source code file contains the WinMain and the WndProc functions. WinMain, which was explained earlier in this chapter, is the entry point for the application. WndProc is the window procedure for the window generated by the application. WndProc is responsible for processing the messages for the resulting window. A typical window procedure, such as in Listing 2.2, contains a switch statement. The actions of the window procedure are triggered by the receipt of certain messages. In Listing 2.2, WndProc monitors and provides actions for only one message, WM_DESTROY; most window procedures, however, define actions for dozens of messages. When WndProc detects the WM_DESTROY message, the PostQuitMessage function is called and the window is terminated. All other messages sent to WndProc are handled by the default window procedure, DefWndProc. When working with window procedures, remember that only Windows calls WndProc; WinMain references WndProc but never calls WndProc directly.

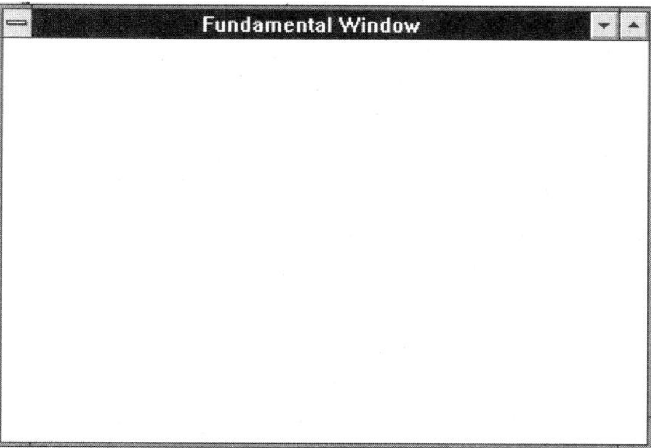

Figure 2.5. *The window created by the fundamental window example.*

This example serves as the baseline for the remainder of the examples in this book. The next chapter introduces the Graphics Device Interface (GDI) and presents numerous examples that build on the basic concepts provided in this chapter.

3

The Graphics Device Interface (GDI)

The Windows Graphics Device Interface (GDI) is designed for device-independent graphics. Because many combinations of output and display devices can be part of a computer system, device-independent graphics enable you to program without being concerned about specific hardware configurations. Many MS-DOS software packages already include more than one executable file to meet different configuration requirements. For example, a software package may contain three executables: one for the Color Graphics Adapter (CGA), one for the Enhanced Graphics Adapter (EGA), and one for the Video Graphics Array (VGA).

Windows applications use the Graphics Device Interface and the Windows device drivers to support device-independent graphics. A device driver converts a general drawing command into the precise actions needed to implement the command on the specified output device. As long as the device driver for the output device is available to Windows, the programmer does not need to be overly concerned with the hardware configuration of the system. This chapter introduces the features and terminology of the Graphics Device Interface.

The Device Context

The *device context* is a set of attributes determining the location and appearance of GDI output for any device. The application cannot access the device context directly, but the application can use the device context's handle *indirectly* to access the device context and its attributes. A device context is created when the program requests the handle for a device context. The created device context contains default values for all its attributes. Table 3.1 lists the default values for each of the device context attributes, any of which can be modified to meet the requirements of the application.

Table 3.1. The device context attributes.

Attribute	Default	Related Function(s)
Background color	White	GetBkColor, SetBkColor
Background mode	OPAQUE	GetBkMode, SetBkMode
Bitmap	None	CreateBitmap, CreateBitmapIndirect, CreateCompatibleBitmap, SelectObject
Brush	WHITE_BRUSH	CreateBrushIndirect, CreateDIBPatternBrush, CreateHatchBrush, CreatePatternBrush, CreateSolidBrush, SelectObject
Brush origin	(0,0)	GetBrushOrg, SetBrushOrg, UnrealizeObject
Clipping region	Display surface	ExcludeClipRect, IntersectClipRect, OffsetClipRgn, SelectClipRgn
Color palette	DEFAULT_PALETTE	CreatePalette, RealizePalette, SelectPalette
Current pen position	(0,0)	GetCurrentPosition, LineTo, MoveTo
Drawing mode	R2_COPYPEN	GetROP2, SetROP2
Font	SYSTEM_FONT	CreateFont, CreateFontIndirect, SelectObject

Attribute	*Default*	*Related Function(s)*
Intercharacter spacing	0	`GetTextCharacterExtra`, `SetTextCharacterExtra`
Mapping mode	`MM_TEXT`	`GetMapMode`, `SetMapMode`
Pen	`BLACK_PEN`	`CreatePen`, `CreatePenIndirect`, `SelectObject`
Polygon filling mode	`ALTERNATE`	`GetPolyFillMode`, `SetPolyFillMode`
Stretching mode	`BLACKONWHITE`	`SetStretchBltMode`
Text color	Black	`GetTextColor`, `SetTextColor`
Viewport extent	(1,1)	`GetViewportExt`, `SetMapMode`, `SetViewportExt`
Viewport origin	(0,0)	`GetViewportOrg`, `OffsetViewportOrg`, `SetViewportOrg`
Window extents	(1,1)	`GetWindowExt`, `SetMapMode`, `SetWindowExt`
Window origin	(0,0)	`GetWindowOrg`, `OffsetWindowOrg`, `SetWindowOrg`

The Mapping Mode

The *mapping mode* affects the appearance of output on the display device and defines the unit of measure used to transform logical units into device units. The mapping mode also defines the orientation of the device's x- and y-axes. The mapping modes defined by Windows are listed in Table 3.2.

Table 3.2. *Windows mapping modes.*

Mapping Mode	*Logical unit*
`MM_ANISOTROPIC`	x and y are arbitrary units where x and y can be scaled independently
`MM_HIENGLISH`	.001 inch

continues

Table 3.2. continued

Mapping Mode	Logical unit
MM_HIMETRIC	.01 mm
MM_ISOTROPIC	x and y are arbitrary units where x and y are scaled uniformly
MM_LOENGLISH	.01 inch
MM_LOMETRIC	.1 mm
MM_TEXT	Pixel
MM_TWIPS	1/1440 inch

The mapping mode that you choose for your application is important. The MM_TEXT mapping mode is most commonly used and is quite sufficient for most purposes. By using the MM_TEXT mode, however, which is based on the pixel, you may get surprising results. For example, a 100-pixel-by-100-pixel image on a VGA screen does not have the same size or appearance as a 100-pixel-by-100-pixel image on a CGA screen. The results, therefore, may not be what you desire. The various mapping modes offer unique advantages and disadvantages, such as direct mapping to pixels, arbitrary scaling, and scaling by inches or millimeters. The requirements of the application indicate the best mapping mode to choose.

The Drawing Coordinates

Windows uses several coordinate systems, which are generally grouped under two classifications: device and logical.

There are three distinct *device* coordinate systems: the *screen* coordinate system, the *whole-window* coordinate system, and the *client area* coordinate system. These device coordinate systems express units of measurement in terms of pixels. Remember that pixels only change relative to video mode; units of measurement change relative to the device context selected as indicated in Table 3.1.

The screen coordinate system uses the entire screen. The upper-left corner of the screen is the origin of the coordinate system. The x-axis increases from left to right; the y-axis increases from top to bottom. Screen coordinates are generally used with functions that move objects relative to a physical location on the screen.

The whole-window coordinate system uses the entire physical size of a window including the window border. The upper-left corner of the window border is the origin of the coordinate system. The x-axis increases from left to right; the y-axis increases from top to bottom. Programmers might use the whole window system when they want to access the entire window to do something unusual like create icons on the window's border—in other words, not very often.

The client area coordinate system is the most commonly used coordinate system. The client area is the working area of the window and excludes the window borders, the Menu bar, and the scroll bars. Because your program generally manipulates only the client area, the client area coordinate system is appropriate for most applications. The upper-left corner of the client area is the origin of the coordinate system. The x-axis increases from left to right; the y-axis increases from top to bottom.

The other grouping of coordinate systems is the *logical* coordinate system. The mapping mode specifies how the logical units specified in GDI functions are converted to device coordinates. Logical units are associated with a window, and device coordinates are associated with a viewport, which usually is the same as the client area. The logical units of a window are expressed in units specified by the mapping mode. Before an object can be drawn, Windows must translate these logical units to one of the device coordinate systems.

GDI Graphics and Points

The GDI is designed for graphic output and contains many functions for displaying graphics such as lines, arcs, and points. The most fundamental element in computer graphics is the point. Therefore, the point is a good subject for beginning this discussion of GDI graphics.

The GDI `SetPixel` function draws a point on the screen, which is the same as illuminating a pixel on the screen because the pixel is the most fundamental screen element. The point example in Listings 3.1 and 3.2 uses the `SetPixel` function to draw a series of alternating blue and red dots in the window's client area.

The point example builds on the fundamental window example from Chapter 2. The only changes made to the `WinMain` function for the point example are the changing of the window caption and the name of the window class. The point example's window procedure, `WndProc`, differs in one major way from the window procedure in the fundamental window example from Chapter 2.

`WndProc` for the point example adds to the capabilities of `WndProc` for the fundamental window example by defining actions for the Windows message `WM_PAINT`. The `WM_PAINT` message is sent to the window procedure when the window first is created and whenever the window is sized. The code that is nested to define the actions for the `WM_PAINT` message is executed whenever the window procedure receives the `WM_PAINT` message. As a result, dots are drawn in the client area of the window with

the SetPixel function when the window is created and each time the window is sized. You can see the effects of responding to the WM_PAINT message by sizing the window created by the code in Listings 3.1 and 3.2. The window resulting from the code in Listings 3.1 and 3.2 is shown in Figure 3.1. Chapter 13 provides additional information on the SetPixel function. Chapter 14 provides additional information on the WM_PAINT message.

> **Note:** This example, as well as the remaining examples in this chapter, uses the MM_ANISOTROPIC mapping mode. The MM_ANISOTROPIC mode allows the x- and y-coordinates to be scaled independently. The SetWindowExt and SetViewportExt functions can be used to specify the units, orientation, and scaling of the axes.

As explained in Chapter 2, the Integrated Development Environment (IDE) and the Project Manager are used in all the examples of this book for code development. The following information describes the files used for the points example project. The project name is WIN_PT. The files that are included in the project are WIN_PT.C and WIN_PT.DEF.

Project Name:	WIN_PT
Files in Project:	WIN_PT.C
	WIN_PT.DEF

Listing 3.1. *The definition file for the point drawing example.*

```
NAME          WIN_PT
DESCRIPTION   'Point Example'
EXETYPE       WINDOWS
CODE          PRELOAD MOVEABLE
DATA          PRELOAD MOVEABLE MULTIPLE
HEAPSIZE      1024
STACKSIZE     5120
EXPORTS       WndProc
```

Listing 3.2. *The C source file for the point drawing example.*

```
#include <windows.h>
#include <stdlib.h>
#include <string.h>
```

```
long FAR PASCAL WndProc (HWND hWnd, WORD iMessage,
                         WORD wParam, LONG lParam);

int PASCAL WinMain (HANDLE hInstance, HANDLE hPrevInstance,
                    LPSTR lpszCmdParam, int nCmdShow)

{
HWND hWnd;
MSG Message;
WNDCLASS WndClass;

if (!hPrevInstance)
     {
     WndClass.cbClsExtra = 0;
     WndClass.cbWndExtra = 0;
     WndClass.hbrBackground = GetStockObject(WHITE_BRUSH);
     WndClass.hCursor =  LoadCursor(NULL, IDC_ARROW);
     WndClass.hIcon = LoadIcon (NULL, "END");
     WndClass.hInstance = hInstance;
     WndClass.lpfnWndProc = WndProc;
     WndClass.lpszClassName = "WIN_PT";
     WndClass.lpszMenuName = NULL;
     WndClass.style = CS_HREDRAW ¦ CS_VREDRAW;

     RegisterClass (&WndClass);
     }

hWnd = CreateWindow ("WIN_PT",            /* class name */
                     "Point Example",     /* Caption */
                     WS_OVERLAPPEDWINDOW,      /* Style */
                     CW_USEDEFAULT,       /* x position */
                     0,                   /* y position */
                     CW_USEDEFAULT,       /* cx - size */
                     0,                   /* cy - size */
                     NULL,                /* Parent window */
                     NULL,                /* Menu */
                     hInstance,           /* Program Instance */
                     NULL);               /* Parameters */

ShowWindow (hWnd, nCmdShow);
while (GetMessage (&Message, 0, 0, 0))
     {
     TranslateMessage(&Message);
     DispatchMessage(&Message);
     }
return Message.wParam;
}
```

continues

Listing 3.2. continued

```
/*****************************************************************/
/*              Window Procedure: WndProc                        */
/*****************************************************************/

long FAR PASCAL WndProc (HWND hWnd, WORD iMessage, WORD wParam,
                         LONG lParam)
{
HDC hDC;
PAINTSTRUCT PtStr;
int x, y;

switch (iMessage)
     {
     case WM_PAINT:

          hDC = BeginPaint(hWnd, &PtStr);
          SetMapMode (hDC, MM_ANISOTROPIC);
          for (x=0; x<640; x=x+10)
               {
               for (y=0; y<480; y=y+10)
                 {
                 SetPixel (hDC,x,y,RGB(255,0,0));
                 SetPixel (hDC,x+5,y,RGB(0,0,255));
                 SetPixel (hDC,x,y+5,RGB(0,0,255));
                 SetPixel (hDC,x+5,y+5,RGB(255,0,0));
                 }
               }
          EndPaint(hWnd,&PtStr);
          return 0;

     case WM_DESTROY:

          PostQuitMessage(0);
          return 0;

     default:

          return(DefWindowProc(hWnd, iMessage, wParam,
                 lParam));
     }
}
```

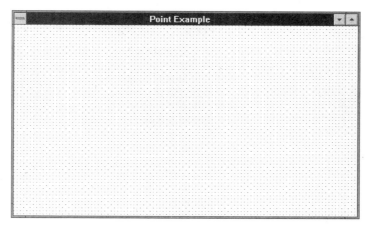

Figure 3.1. *The window created by the point drawing example.*

Drawing Lines

The GDI also provides functions for drawing lines. The `LineTo` and `Polyline` functions are provided to draw straight lines. The `Arc` function is provided to draw elliptical lines. The appearance of the lines drawn by these functions depends on the current pen and the drawing mode. These terms are described later in this chapter. For now, you should focus on how to use these functions.

The `LineTo` function is the most basic line drawing function. The `LineTo` function draws a line from the current pen position to the specified point. The `MoveTo` function often is used to move the pen position before the `LineTo` function is called.

The line drawing example in Listings 3.3 and 3.4 demonstrates the use of the `MoveTo` and `LineTo` functions to draw a series of red, green, and blue lines. This example is structured like the point drawing example presented previously in this chapter. In the line drawing example, however, the `MoveTo` and `LineTo` functions are used to create the lines for the example.

One major difference between the point example and the line drawing example is that the line drawing example defines and uses three colored pens. The `CreatePenIndirect` function is used to create a red, blue, and green logical pen. The `SelectObject` function is used to select one of the created pens before drawing a line. The `MoveTo` function is used to move the current pen position prior to each call to

the LineTo function. When the MoveTo function is called, the pen is moved but no drawing takes place. When the LineTo function is called, a line is drawn using the currently selected pen. Figure 3.2 shows the window created by Listings 3.3 and 3.4.

The description of the project for the line drawing example follows:

Project Name:	WIN_LINE
Files in Project:	WIN_LINE.C
	WIN_LINE.DEF

Listing 3.3. The definition file for the line drawing example.

```
NAME           WIN_LINE
DESCRIPTION    'Line Drawing Example'
EXETYPE        WINDOWS
CODE           PRELOAD MOVEABLE
DATA           PRELOAD MOVEABLE MULTIPLE
HEAPSIZE       1024
STACKSIZE      5120
EXPORTS        WndProc
```

Listing 3.4. The C source file for the line drawing example.

```
#include <windows.h>
#include <stdlib.h>
#include <string.h>

long FAR PASCAL WndProc (HWND hWnd, WORD iMessage,
                         WORD wParam, LONG lParam);

int PASCAL WinMain (HANDLE hInstance, HANDLE hPrevInstance,
                    LPSTR lpszCmdParam, int nCmdShow)

{
HWND hWnd;
MSG Message;
WNDCLASS WndClass;

if (!hPrevInstance)
     {
     WndClass.cbClsExtra = 0;
     WndClass.cbWndExtra = 0;
     WndClass.hbrBackground = GetStockObject(WHITE_BRUSH);
     WndClass.hCursor =  LoadCursor(NULL, IDC_ARROW);
     WndClass.hIcon = LoadIcon (NULL, "END");
```

```
     WndClass.hInstance = hInstance;
     WndClass.lpfnWndProc = WndProc;
     WndClass.lpszClassName = "WIN_LINE";
     WndClass.lpszMenuName = NULL;
     WndClass.style = CS_HREDRAW ¦ CS_VREDRAW;

     RegisterClass (&WndClass);
     }

hWnd = CreateWindow ("WIN_LINE",   /* class name */
                     "Line Drawing Example", /* Caption */
                     WS_OVERLAPPEDWINDOW,    /* Style */
                     CW_USEDEFAULT, /* x position */
                     0,             /* y position */
                     CW_USEDEFAULT, /* cx - size */
                     0,             /* cy - size */
                     NULL,          /* Parent window */
                     NULL,          /* Menu */
                     hInstance,     /* Program Instance */
                     NULL);         /* Parameters */

ShowWindow (hWnd, nCmdShow);
while (GetMessage (&Message, 0, 0, 0))
     {
     TranslateMessage(&Message);
     DispatchMessage(&Message);
     }
return Message.wParam;
}

/****************************************************************/
/*              Window Procedure: WndProc                       */
/****************************************************************/

long FAR PASCAL WndProc (HWND hWnd, WORD iMessage, WORD wParam,
                         LONG lParam)
{
static LOGPEN lpBlue = {PS_SOLID, 1, 1, RGB(0,0,255)},
           lpGreen = {PS_SOLID, 1, 1, RGB(0,255,0)},
           lpRed = {PS_SOLID, 1, 1, RGB(255,0,0)};
HDC hDC;
HPEN hBluePen, hGreenPen, hRedPen;
PAINTSTRUCT PtStr;
short x;

switch (iMessage)
     {
     case WM_PAINT:
```

continues

Listing 3.4. continued

```
            hDC = BeginPaint(hWnd, &PtStr);
            hBluePen = CreatePenIndirect(&lpBlue);
            hGreenPen = CreatePenIndirect(&lpGreen);
            hRedPen = CreatePenIndirect(&lpRed);
            for (x=1; x<640; x=x+2)
                 {
                 SelectObject(hDC,hBluePen);
                 MoveTo(hDC,x,100);
                 LineTo(hDC,x,150);
                 SelectObject(hDC,hGreenPen);
                 MoveTo(hDC,x,150);
                 LineTo(hDC,x,200);
                 SelectObject(hDC,hRedPen);
                 MoveTo(hDC,x,200);
                 LineTo(hDC,x,250);
                 }

            EndPaint(hWnd, &PtStr);
            DeleteObject(hBluePen);
            DeleteObject(hGreenPen);
            DeleteObject(hRedPen);
            return 0;

       case WM_DESTROY:

            PostQuitMessage(0);
            return 0;

       default:

            return(DefWindowProc(hWnd, iMessage, wParam,
                   lParam));
       }
}
```

The `Polyline` function enables you to connect an array of points with lines. The `Polyline` function often is more convenient to use than the `MoveTo` and `LineTo` functions because it enables you to express all the points in an array. The code structure shown in the line drawing example could be used for the `Polyline` function. The only changes to the code that would be necessary are the addition of a defined array containing the points to draw, and a call to the `Polyline` function in place of the `MoveTo` and `LineTo` function calls.

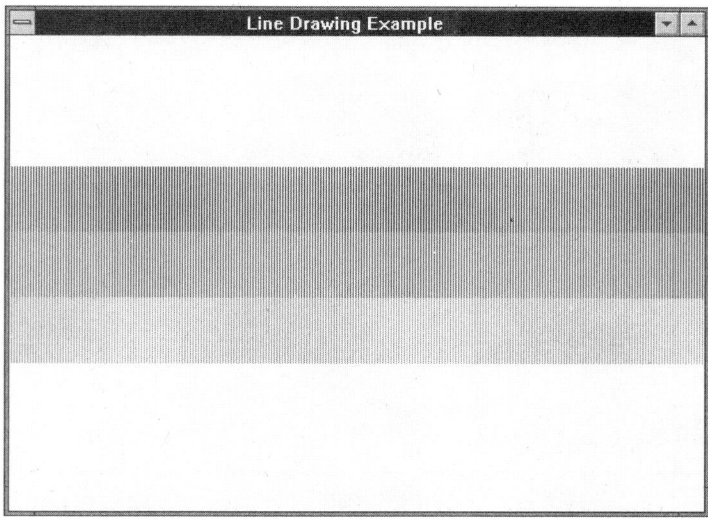

Figure 3.2. *The window created by the line drawing example.*

The `Arc` function draws an elliptical arc. The arc resulting from this function is actually part of an underlying ellipse whose points are calculated but are not actually drawn. The underlying ellipse is specified by the coordinates in the parameters passed to the `Arc` function in X1, Y1, X2, and Y2 (see Chapter 13, "Windows Functions," for information regarding the `Arc` function). These parameters specify the corners of a rectangle that bind the underlying ellipse. The starting point of the ellipse is specified by two other parameters, X3 and Y3. The arc begins at the point where the line—beginning at the center of the underlying ellipse and extending to the point specified in X3 and Y3—intersects the ellipse. The arc is then drawn in a counterclockwise direction until it reaches the point where the line—drawn between the center of the underlying ellipse and the point specified by two additional parameters, X4 and Y4—intersects the ellipse.

The arc drawing example in Listings 3.5 and 3.6 demonstrates the use of the `Arc` function to create an ellipse consisting of four colored line segments. This example is very similar to the previous line drawing example. The listing creates four colored pens by using the `CreatePenIndirect` function, selected with the `SelectObject` function, and uses the pens to draw four different colored arcs that join to form an ellipse. The resulting ellipse contains one red, green, blue, and black elliptical line. Figure 3.3, which follows the listings, shows the window resulting from this example.

The description of the project for the arc drawing example follows:

Project Name:	WIN_ARC
Files in Project:	WIN_ARC.C
	WIN_ARC.DEF

Listing 3.5. *The definition file for the arc drawing example.*

```
NAME            WIN_ARC
DESCRIPTION     'Arc Drawing Example'
EXETYPE         WINDOWS
CODE            PRELOAD MOVEABLE
DATA            PRELOAD MOVEABLE MULTIPLE
HEAPSIZE        1024
STACKSIZE       5120
EXPORTS         WndProc
```

Listing 3.6. *The C source file for the arc drawing example.*

```
#include <windows.h>
#include <stdlib.h>
#include <string.h>

long FAR PASCAL WndProc (HWND hWnd, WORD iMessage,
                         WORD wParam, LONG lParam);

int PASCAL WinMain (HANDLE hInstance, HANDLE hPrevInstance,
                    LPSTR lpszCmdParam, int nCmdShow)

{
HWND hWnd;
MSG Message;
WNDCLASS WndClass;

if (!hPrevInstance)
     {
     WndClass.cbClsExtra = 0;
     WndClass.cbWndExtra = 0;
     WndClass.hbrBackground = GetStockObject(WHITE_BRUSH);
     WndClass.hCursor =  LoadCursor(NULL, IDC_ARROW);
     WndClass.hIcon = LoadIcon (NULL, "END");
     WndClass.hInstance = hInstance;
     WndClass.lpfnWndProc = WndProc;
     WndClass.lpszClassName = "WIN_ARC";
     WndClass.lpszMenuName = NULL;
     WndClass.style = CS_HREDRAW ¦ CS_VREDRAW;
```

```
     RegisterClass (&WndClass);
     }

hWnd = CreateWindow ("WIN_ARC",      /* class name */
          "Arc Drawing Example",     /* Caption */
          WS_OVERLAPPEDWINDOW,       /* Style */
          CW_USEDEFAULT,             /* x position */
          0,                         /* y position */
          CW_USEDEFAULT,             /* cx - size */
          0,                         /* cy - size */
          NULL,                      /* Parent window */
          NULL,                      /* Menu */
          hInstance,                 /* Program Instance */
          NULL);                     /* Parameters */

ShowWindow (hWnd, nCmdShow);
while (GetMessage (&Message, 0, 0, 0))
     {
     TranslateMessage(&Message);
     DispatchMessage(&Message);
     }
return Message.wParam;
}

/*****************************************************************/
/*              Window Procedure: WndProc                        */
/*****************************************************************/

long FAR PASCAL WndProc (HWND hWnd, WORD iMessage, WORD wParam,
                         LONG lParam)
{
static LOGPEN lpBlue = {PS_SOLID, 1, 1, RGB(0,0,255)},
          lpGreen = {PS_SOLID, 1, 1, RGB(0,255,0)},
          lpRed = {PS_SOLID, 1, 1, RGB(255,0,0)},
          lpBlack = {PS_SOLID, 1, 1, RGB(0,0,0)};
HDC hDC;
HPEN hBluePen, hGreenPen, hRedPen, hBlackPen;
PAINTSTRUCT PtStr;

switch (iMessage)
     {
     case WM_PAINT:

          hDC = BeginPaint(hWnd, &PtStr);
          hBluePen = CreatePenIndirect(&lpBlue);
          hGreenPen = CreatePenIndirect(&lpGreen);
          hRedPen = CreatePenIndirect(&lpRed);
          hBlackPen = CreatePenIndirect(&lpBlack);
```

continues

Listing 3.6. continued

```
          SelectObject(hDC,hBluePen);
          Arc(hDC,50,50,200,200,200,50,50,50);

          SelectObject(hDC,hGreenPen);
          Arc(hDC,50,50,200,200,50,50,50,200);

          SelectObject(hDC,hRedPen);
          Arc(hDC,50,50,200,200,50,200,200,200);

          SelectObject(hDC,hBlackPen);
          Arc(hDC,50,50,200,200,200,200,200,50);

          EndPaint(hWnd, &PtStr);
          DeleteObject(hBluePen);
          DeleteObject(hGreenPen);
          DeleteObject(hRedPen);
          DeleteObject(hBlackPen);
          return 0;

     case WM_DESTROY:

          PostQuitMessage(0);
          return 0;

     default:

          return(DefWindowProc(hWnd, iMessage, wParam,
                 lParam));
     }
}
```

Chapter 13, "Windows Functions," provides additional information on the `LineTo`, `MoveTo`, `Arc`, and `Polyline` functions.

Pens

The line drawing functions, as well as some other functions, use the *pen*, which specifies the color, width, and style of the line to be drawn. By default, the pen draws a solid black line that is one pixel wide. You can select predefined pens—called *stock pens*—by using the `GetStockObject` function, or you can create your own pens by using the `CreatePen` or `CreatePenIndirect` functions. Table 3.3 lists the stock pens that you can select with the `GetStockObject` function.

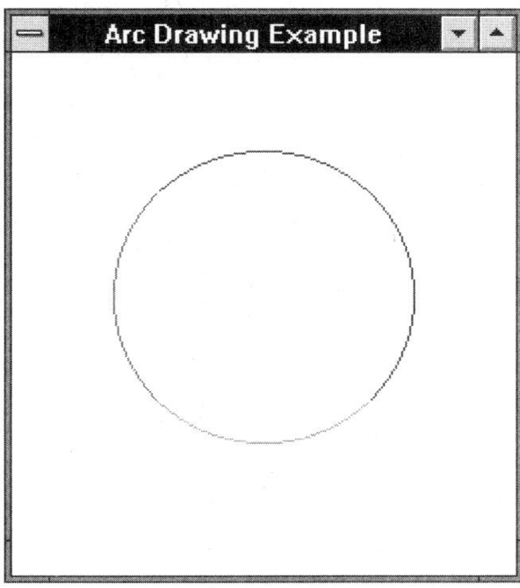

Figure 3.3. *The window created by the arc drawing example.*

Table 3.3. *Stock pens used with the* `GetStockObject` *line drawing function.*

Pen	*Meaning*
`BLACK_PEN`	Black pen
`NULL_PEN`	Null pen (nothing is drawn)
`WHITE_PEN`	White pen

The `CreatePen` and `CreatePenIndirect` functions enable you to create a pen with a specified color, width, and style. You can specify the color of the pen by using the `RGB` macro, which enables you to specify the mix of red, green, and blue intensities for the color (see Chapter 13 for more information on the `RGB` macro). The pen width is specified in logical units. You can select the style of the pen from one of the values listed in Table 3.4 and defined in windows.h.

Table 3.4. Pen styles available using the CreatePen and CreatePenIndirect.

Style	Value
PS_SOLID	0
PS_DASH	1
PS_DOT	2
PS_DASHDOT	3
PS_DASHDOTDOT	4
PS_NULL	5
PS_INSIDEFRAME	6

The previous examples in this chapter used the CreatePenIndirect function to create the pens used for drawing lines. You should review these previous examples to see how pens are created and used. Chapter 13 provides additional information on the GetStockObject, CreatePen, and CreatePenIndirect functions.

Drawing Modes

The *drawing mode* affects the appearance of lines. It defines the way the color of the pen is combined with the color that already exists at the pen location. This combination of the pixel patterns of the pen and destination is called a *binary raster operation*, or ROP2.

The default drawing mode is R2_COPYPEN, which behaves as you might expect a pen to behave. The color of the pen is copied "as is" onto the drawing surface. For most purposes, this mode is sufficient. However, you often can benefit from using other modes to achieve certain effects. For example, you may need to use another mode whenever you require the same pen to draw black on a white background and white on a black background. The various drawing modes, listed in Table 3.5, provide numerous line drawing combinations, such as this one just described.

Table 3.5. Drawing modes.

Mode	Pixel Color
R2_BLACK	Black
R2_COPYPEN	The pen color

Mode	*Pixel Color*
R2_MASKNOTPEN	Combination of the common colors of the display and the inverse of the pen
R2_MASKPEN	Combination of the common colors of the pen and the display
R2_MASKPENNOT	Combination of the common colors of the pen and the inverse of the display color
R2_MERGENOTPEN	Combination of the display color and the inverse of the pen color
R2_MERGEPEN	Combination of the pen and display colors
R2_MERGEPENNOT	Combination of the pen color and inverse of display color
R2_NOP	Not changed
R2_NOT	Inverse of display color
R2_NOTCOPYPEN	Inverse of pen color
R2_NOTMASKPEN	Inverse of R2_MASKPEN
R2_NOTMERGEPEN	Inverse of R2_MERGEPEN
R2_NOTXORPEN	Inverse of R2_XORPEN color
R2_WHITE	White
R2_XORPEN	Combination of the colors in the pen and in the display but not both

The GetROP2 and SetROP2 functions retrieve and set the drawing mode, respectively. Chapter 13, "Windows Functions," provides additional information on these functions.

Creating Filled Areas

Windows creates filled figures by first drawing the border of the figure using the current pen and then filling in the figure with the current brush. The procedures for drawing and filling the figure are explained later in this section. Right now you should focus on the functions used to create filled figures (see Table 3.6). Chapter 13 provides full reference information for each of the functions listed in Table 3.6.

Table 3.6. Functions for drawing filled figures.

Function	*Figure*
`Chord`	Chord
`DrawFocusRect`	Rectangle that indicates focus (which represents the primary selection)
`Ellipse`	Ellipse
`Pie`	Pie
`Polygon`	Polygon
`PolyPolygon`	Series of closed polygons
`Rectangle`	Rectangle
RoundRect	Rounded rectangle

Drawing the Borders

The filled figures example in Listings 3.7 and 3.8 demonstrates the `Pie`, `Ellipse`, `Rectangle`, `Chord`, and `RoundRect` functions. The code structure for this example follows the code structure from the previous examples in this chapter (the line drawing example, arc drawing example, and so on). In this example, a pen and brush are selected using stock objects. The `GetStockObject` function is used to select the `BLACK_PEN` object as the pen and `DKGRAY_BRUSH` object as the brush. The `Pie`, `Ellipse`, `Rectangle`, `Chord`, and `RoundRect` functions are then called to draw the filled figures using the specified pen and brush. Figure 3.4 shows the window resulting from this example.

The description of the project for the filled figure example follows:

Project Name: `WIN_FIGS`
Files in Project: `WIN_FIGS.C`
`WIN_FIGS.DEF`

Listing 3.7. The definition file for the filled figure example.

```
NAME           WIN_FIGS
DESCRIPTION    'Filled Figures Example'
EXETYPE        WINDOWS
CODE           PRELOAD MOVEABLE
DATA           PRELOAD MOVEABLE MULTIPLE
HEAPSIZE       1024
STACKSIZE      5120
EXPORTS        WndProc
```

Listing 3.8. The C source file for the filled figure example.

```
#include <windows.h>
#include <stdlib.h>
#include <string.h>

long FAR PASCAL WndProc (HWND hWnd, WORD iMessage,
                         WORD wParam, LONG lParam);

int PASCAL WinMain (HANDLE hInstance, HANDLE hPrevInstance,
                    LPSTR lpszCmdParam, int nCmdShow)

{
HWND hWnd;
MSG Message;
WNDCLASS WndClass;

if (!hPrevInstance)
     {
     WndClass.cbClsExtra = 0;
     WndClass.cbWndExtra = 0;
     WndClass.hbrBackground = GetStockObject(WHITE_BRUSH);
     WndClass.hCursor =  LoadCursor(NULL, IDC_ARROW);
     WndClass.hIcon = LoadIcon (NULL, "END");
     WndClass.hInstance = hInstance;
     WndClass.lpfnWndProc = WndProc;
     WndClass.lpszClassName = "WIN_FIGS";
     WndClass.lpszMenuName = NULL;
     WndClass.style = CS_HREDRAW ¦ CS_VREDRAW;

     RegisterClass (&WndClass);
     }

hWnd = CreateWindow ("WIN_FIGS",     /* class name */
          "Filled Figures Example", /* Caption */
          WS_OVERLAPPEDWINDOW,      /* Style */
          CW_USEDEFAULT,            /* x position */
          0,                        /* y position */
          CW_USEDEFAULT,            /* cx - size */
          0,                        /* cy - size */
          NULL,                     /* Parent window */
          NULL,                     /* Menu */
          hInstance,                /* Program Instance */
          NULL);                    /* Parameters */

ShowWindow (hWnd, nCmdShow);
while (GetMessage (&Message, 0, 0, 0))
     {
     TranslateMessage(&Message);
```

continues

Listing 3.8. continued

```
     DispatchMessage(&Message);
     }
return Message.wParam;
}

/*****************************************************************/
/*               Window Procedure: WndProc                       */
/*****************************************************************/

long FAR PASCAL WndProc (HWND hWnd, WORD iMessage, WORD wParam,
                         LONG lParam)
{
HDC hDC;
HBRUSH hBrush;
HPEN hPen;
PAINTSTRUCT PtStr;

switch (iMessage)
     {
     case WM_PAINT:

          hDC = BeginPaint (hWnd,&PtStr);

          SetMapMode(hDC, MM_ANISOTROPIC);

          hPen = GetStockObject(BLACK_PEN);
          hBrush = GetStockObject(DKGRAY_BRUSH);
          SelectObject(hDC,hBrush);
          SelectObject(hDC,hPen);

          Rectangle (hDC,50,50,100,100);
          RoundRect (hDC,50,150,100,200,15,15);
          Ellipse (hDC,150,50,200,100);
          Chord (hDC,150,150,200,200,150,150,200,200);
          Pie (hDC,250,50,300,100,250,50,300,50);

          EndPaint(hWnd,&PtStr);
          return 0;

     case WM_DESTROY:

          PostQuitMessage(0);
          return 0;
```

```
        default:

            return(DefWindowProc(hWnd, iMessage, wParam,
                  lParam));
    }
}
```

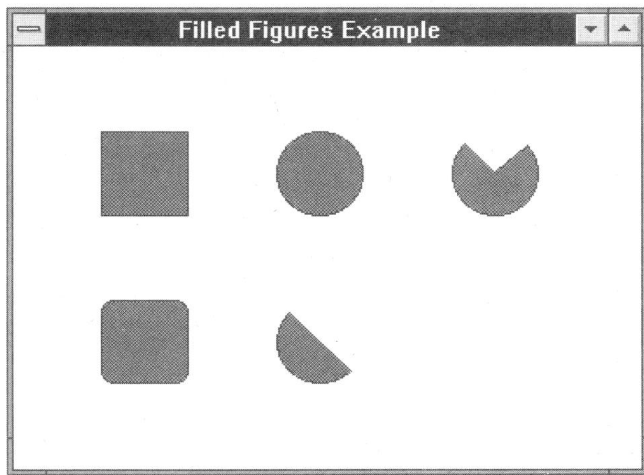

Figure 3.4. *The window created by the filled figure example.*

Filling the Area

The figures created by the functions in Table 3.6 are filled with the current brush. You can choose the brush in two ways:

- Select a predefined stock brush by using the `GetStockObject` function.
- Create a brush by using the `CreateSolidBrush`, `CreateHatchBrush`, `CreatePatternBrush`, or `CreateBrushIndirect` function.

If you select a predefined stock brush by using the `GetStockObject` function, seven brushes are available. Table 3.7 lists these brushes. Listings 3.7 and 3.8 use the `GetStockObject` function to select the dark gray stock brush. These listings also demonstrate the use of the selected stock brush for filling a figure.

Table 3.7. Stock brushes.

Brush	*Meaning*
`BLACK_BRUSH`	Black brush
`DKGRAY_BRUSH`	Dark gray brush
`GRAY_BRUSH`	Gray brush
`HOLLOW_BRUSH`	Hollow brush (which draws borders but does not fill them)
`LTGRAY_BRUSH`	Light gray brush
`NULL_BRUSH`	Null brush
`WHITE_BRUSH`	White brush

You can create your own brush with the `CreateSolidBrush`, `CreateHatchBrush`, `CreatePatternBrush`, or `CreateBrushIndirect` functions. Chapter 13, "Windows Functions," provides reference information on the use of each of these functions. A brush that you create is used just like a stock brush. The fill example in Listings 3.9 and 3.10 demonstrates how to create and select brushes of your own design. The fill example follows the same format as the previous examples in this chapter. The fill example, however, differs from these previous examples because four hatched brushes are created and used. The `CreateHatchBrush` function is used to create four brushes, each consisting of a different fill pattern and fill color. In turn, each brush is selected and a rectangle is drawn using the current pen and filled using the current brush. Like the previous examples, the client area (and the filled figures) is redrawn each time the window is sized. Figure 3.5 shows the window resulting from the listings.

The description of the project for the fill example follows:

Project Name: `WIN_FILL`
Files in Project: `WIN_FILL.C`
`WIN_FILL.DEF`

Listing 3.9. *The definition file for the fill example.*

```
NAME           WIN_FILL
DESCRIPTION    'Fill Example'
EXETYPE        WINDOWS
CODE           PRELOAD MOVEABLE
DATA           PRELOAD MOVEABLE MULTIPLE
HEAPSIZE       1024
STACKSIZE      5120
EXPORTS        WndProc
```

Listing 3.10. The C source file for the fill example.

```
#include <windows.h>
#include <stdlib.h>
#include <string.h>

long FAR PASCAL WndProc (HWND hWnd, WORD iMessage,
                         WORD wParam, LONG lParam);

int PASCAL WinMain (HANDLE hInstance, HANDLE hPrevInstance,
                    LPSTR lpszCmdParam, int nCmdShow)

{
HWND hWnd;
MSG Message;
WNDCLASS WndClass;

if (!hPrevInstance)
     {
     WndClass.cbClsExtra = 0;
     WndClass.cbWndExtra = 0;
     WndClass.hbrBackground = GetStockObject(WHITE_BRUSH);
     WndClass.hCursor =  LoadCursor(NULL, IDC_ARROW);
     WndClass.hIcon = LoadIcon (NULL, "END");
     WndClass.hInstance = hInstance;
     WndClass.lpfnWndProc = WndProc;
     WndClass.lpszClassName = "WIN_FILL";
     WndClass.lpszMenuName = NULL;
     WndClass.style = CS_HREDRAW ¦ CS_VREDRAW;

     RegisterClass (&WndClass);
     }

hWnd = CreateWindow ("WIN_FILL",         /* class name */
          "Fill Example",                /* Caption */
          WS_OVERLAPPEDWINDOW,           /* Style */
          CW_USEDEFAULT,                 /* x position */
          0,                             /* y position */
          CW_USEDEFAULT,                 /* cx - size */
          0,                             /* cy - size */
          NULL,                          /* Parent window */
          NULL,                          /* Menu */
          hInstance,                     /* Program Instance */
          NULL);                         /* Parameters */

ShowWindow (hWnd, nCmdShow);
while (GetMessage (&Message, 0, 0, 0))
     {
     TranslateMessage(&Message);
```

continues

Listing 3.10. continued

```
     DispatchMessage(&Message);
     }
return Message.wParam;
}

/*****************************************************************/
/*              Window Procedure: WndProc                        */
/*****************************************************************/

long FAR PASCAL WndProc (HWND hWnd, WORD iMessage, WORD wParam,
                         LONG lParam)
{

switch (iMessage)
     {
     static HBRUSH hBrush[4];
     static LOGPEN lpBlack = {PS_SOLID,1,1,RGB(0,0,0)};
     HPEN hBlackPen;
     HDC hDC;
     PAINTSTRUCT PtStr;


     case WM_PAINT:

          hBlackPen = CreatePenIndirect(&lpBlack);

          hBrush[0] = CreateHatchBrush(HS_HORIZONTAL,
                   RGB(0,0,0));
          hBrush[1] = CreateHatchBrush(HS_VERTICAL,
                   RGB(255,0,0));
          hBrush[2] = CreateHatchBrush(HS_FDIAGONAL,
                   RGB(0,255,0));
          hBrush[3] = CreateHatchBrush(HS_BDIAGONAL,
                   RGB(0,0,255));

          hDC = BeginPaint(hWnd, &PtStr);

          SelectObject(hDC, hBlackPen);
          SelectObject(hDC, hBrush[0]);
          Rectangle(hDC,10,10,100,200);

          SelectObject(hDC, hBlackPen);
          SelectObject(hDC, hBrush[1]);
          Rectangle(hDC,110,10,200,200);

          SelectObject(hDC, hBlackPen);
          SelectObject(hDC, hBrush[2]);
          Rectangle(hDC,210,10,300,200);
```

```
            SelectObject(hDC, hBlackPen);
            SelectObject(hDC, hBrush[3]);
            Rectangle(hDC,310,10,400,200);

            EndPaint(hWnd, &PtStr);

            DeleteObject(hBlackPen);
            DeleteObject(hBrush[0]);
            DeleteObject(hBrush[1]);
            DeleteObject(hBrush[2]);
            DeleteObject(hBrush[3]);

            return 0;

        case WM_DESTROY:

            PostQuitMessage(0);
            return 0;

        default:

            return(DefWindowProc(hWnd, iMessage, wParam,
                   lParam));
        }
}
```

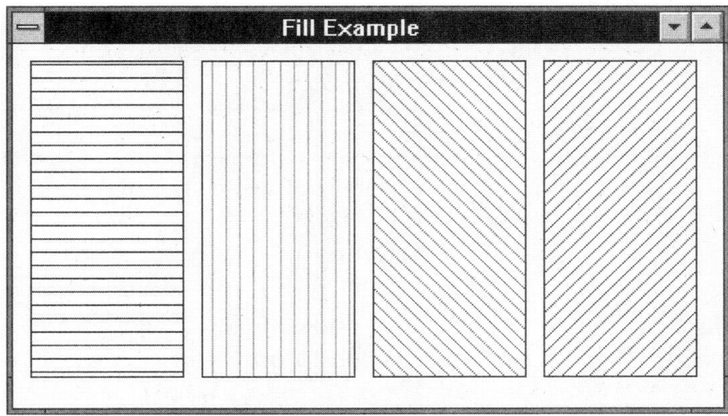

Figure 3.5. *The window created by the fill example.*

The use of brushes is not limited to the filled figures listed in Table 3.6. You can use the `FloodFill`, `FillRect`, and `FillRgn` functions to fill various shapes and types of figures. Chapter 13, "Windows Functions," provides reference information on the `FloodFill`, `FillRect`, and `FillRgn` functions.

Text and Fonts

Windows often uses the Graphics Device Interface for text output. If you have programmed MS-DOS applications, you may think immediately that "graphics" in the Graphics Device Interface and "text" in text output do not mix. MS-DOS applications use two primary modes of operation for the video hardware: graphics and text. *Graphics mode* displays device dependent graphics objects; *text mode* displays text characters. With Windows you don't have this distinction between text and graphics. *Everything* in Windows is, in a sense, treated like a graphics object.

Text characters in Windows are drawn according to a selected font. A *font* contains specific information on the shape and appearance of each character, number, and punctuation mark in a character set. By using defined device-independent font sets, Windows can maintain its device independence while providing the benefits of *what-you-see-is-what-you-get* (WYSIWYG), which means that the text drawn onscreen generally looks the same as it does when drawn by other output devices such as printers or plotters.

Text Drawing Functions

Windows provides several functions for displaying text. These functions are listed in Table 3.8.

Table 3.8. *Text drawing functions.*

Function	*Meaning*
`DrawText`	Draws formatted text in the specified rectangle
`ExtTextOut`	Writes a character string, using the current font, inside a rectangular region
`GrayString`	Writes a string using gray text
`TabbedTextOut`	Writes a character string with expanded tabs
`TextOut`	Writes a character string using the current font

Although all the functions listed in Table 3.8 can be used to display text, `TextOut` and `TabbedTextOut`, both GDI functions, are most commonly used in an application for text output. The `TextOut` example in Listings 3.11 and 3.12 demonstrates how to use the `TextOut` function to display text using the current font.

The `TextOut` example in Listings 3.11 and 3.12 follows the same code structure as the previous examples of this chapter. Therefore, the text displayed by this example is redrawn each time the application window receives a `WM_PAINT` message. In response to the receipt of a `WM_PAINT` message, this example calls the `TextOut` function to display the 30 character strings in the text buffer, `textbuf`. You'll notice that the positional parameters passed to the `TextOut` function, `nXChar` and `nYChar`, are not defined in the `WM_PAINT` code; instead, `nXChar` and `nYChar` are defined in the `WM_CREATE` code. The `WM_CREATE` message is sent when the application window is created. It is often a good idea to define initial values for the application's variables when responding the `WM_CREATE` message. Figure 3.6 shows the window resulting from the `TextOut` example.

The description of the project for the `TextOut` example follows:

Project Name:	`WIN_TXT`
Files in Project:	`WIN_TXT.C`
	`WIN_TXT.DEF`

Listing 3.11. *The definition file for the `TextOut` example.*

```
NAME            WIN_TXT
DESCRIPTION     'TextOut Example'
EXETYPE         WINDOWS
CODE            PRELOAD MOVEABLE
DATA            PRELOAD MOVEABLE MULTIPLE
HEAPSIZE        1024
STACKSIZE       5120
EXPORTS         WndProc
```

Listing 3.12. *The C source file for the `TextOut` example.*

```
#include <windows.h>
#include <stdlib.h>
#include <string.h>

long FAR PASCAL WndProc (HWND hWnd, WORD iMessage,
                         WORD wParam, LONG lParam);

int PASCAL WinMain (HANDLE hInstance, HANDLE hPrevInstance,
                    LPSTR lpszCmdParam, int nCmdShow)

{
HWND hWnd;
MSG Message;
WNDCLASS WndClass;
```

continues

Listing 3.12. continued

```
if (!hPrevInstance)
     {
     WndClass.cbClsExtra = 0;
     WndClass.cbWndExtra = 0;
     WndClass.hbrBackground = GetStockObject(WHITE_BRUSH);
     WndClass.hCursor =  LoadCursor(NULL, IDC_ARROW);
     WndClass.hIcon = LoadIcon (NULL, "END");
     WndClass.hInstance = hInstance;
     WndClass.lpfnWndProc = WndProc;
     WndClass.lpszClassName = "WIN_TXT";
     WndClass.lpszMenuName = NULL;
     WndClass.style = CS_HREDRAW ¦ CS_VREDRAW;

     RegisterClass (&WndClass);
     }

hWnd = CreateWindow ("WIN_TXT",      /* class name */
          "TextOut Example",         /* Caption */
          WS_OVERLAPPEDWINDOW,       /* Style */
          CW_USEDEFAULT,             /* x position */
          0,                         /* y position */
          CW_USEDEFAULT,             /* cx - size */
          0,                         /* cy - size */
          NULL,                      /* Parent window */
          NULL,                      /* Menu */
          hInstance,                 /* Program Instance */
          NULL);                     /* Parameters */

ShowWindow (hWnd, nCmdShow);
while (GetMessage (&Message, 0, 0, 0))
     {
     TranslateMessage(&Message);
     DispatchMessage(&Message);
     }
return Message.wParam;
}

/****************************************************************/
/*              Window Procedure: WndProc                       */
/****************************************************************/

long FAR PASCAL WndProc (HWND hWnd, WORD iMessage, WORD wParam,
                         LONG lParam)
{
static short nXChar, nCaps, nYChar;
HDC hDC;
short x;
```

```
PAINTSTRUCT PtStr;
TEXTMETRIC tm;
short LnCount = 30;
static char *textbuf[] =
     {"One",
     "Two",
     "Three",
     "Four",
     "Five",
     "Six",
     "Seven",
     "Eight",
     "Nine",
     "Ten",
     "Eleven",
     "Twelve",
     "Thirteen",
     "Fourteen",
     "Fifteen",
     "Sixteen",
     "Seventeen",
     "Eighteen",
     "Nineteen",
     "Twenty",
     "Twenty-one",
     "Twenty-two",
     "Twenty-three",
     "Twenty-four",
     "Twenty-five",
     "Twenty-six",
     "Twenty-seven",
     "Twenty-eight",
     "Twenty-nine",
     "Thirty"};

switch (iMessage)
     {

     case WM_CREATE:

          hDC = GetDC(hWnd);

          GetTextMetrics(hDC,&tm);
          nXChar = tm.tmAveCharWidth;
          nYChar = tm.tmHeight + tm.tmExternalLeading;
          nCaps = (tm.tmPitchAndFamily & 1 ?3 : 2) *
               nXChar/2;

          ReleaseDC(hWnd, hDC);
          return 0;
```

continues

Listing 3.12. continued

```
    case WM_PAINT:

         hDC = BeginPaint(hWnd, &PtStr);

         for (x=0; x<LnCount; x=x+1)
              {
              TextOut(hDC,nXChar,nYChar * (1+x),
                textbuf[x],lstrlen(textbuf[x]));
              }

         EndPaint(hWnd, &PtStr);
         return 0;


    case WM_DESTROY:

         PostQuitMessage(0);
         return 0;

    default:

         return(DefWindowProc(hWnd, iMessage, wParam,
                lParam));
    }
}
```

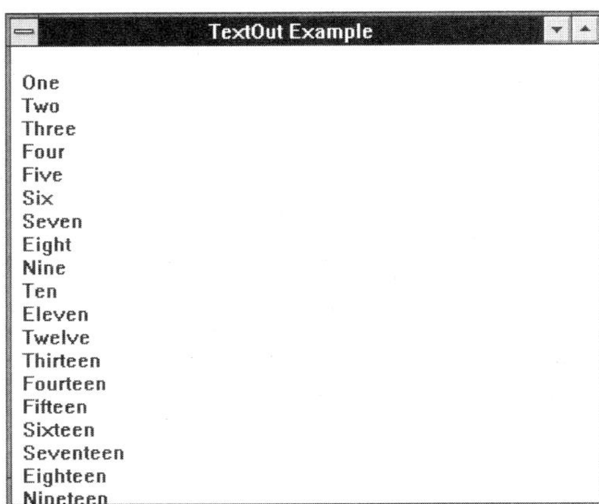

Figure 3.6. *Text output using* `TextOut`.

As Figure 3.6 shows, the example in Listings 3.11 and 3.12 has some limitations. The example displays 30 lines of text; not all these lines, however, can be seen. Because the window has no scroll bar, you cannot view the portion of the text that extends beyond the borders of the window—which is a serious limitation. Therefore, an example that uses both vertical and horizontal scroll bars is presented later in the chapter. For now, however, you need to focus on another method for sending text to a device.

The `TabbedTextOut` example in Listings 3.13 and 3.14 demonstrates how to use the `TabbedTextOut` function for displaying text in the current font and with extended tabs. The `TabbedTextOut` example is almost identical to the `TextOut` example demonstrated previously in this chapter. There are, however, two major differences: the use of the `TabbedTextOut` function and the addition of a tab indicator (`\t`) to the text buffer.

If you compare the code in Listings 3.13 and 3.14 (the `TabbedTextOut` example) to the code in Listings 3.11 and 3.12 (the `TextOut` example), you will notice that the text buffer defined for the `TabbedTextOut` example differs from the text buffer defined for the `TextOut` example. The difference in these text buffers is the addition of tab indicators (`\t`) and a column of additional text to the buffer for the `TabbedTextOut` example. The tab indicator (`\t`) tells the `TabbedTextOut` function to tab over before displaying the text following the indicator. Figure 3.7 shows the window resulting from the `TabbedTextOut` example. Once again, the resulting window has no scroll bars and some of the text sent to the window can't be seen.

The description of the project for the `TabbedTextOut` example follows:

Project Name:	`WIN_TTXT`
Files in Project:	`WIN_TTXT.C`
	`WIN_TTXT.DEF`

Listing 3.13. *The definition file for the* `TabbedTextOut` *example.*

```
NAME            WIN_TTXT
DESCRIPTION     'TabbedTextOut Example'
EXETYPE         WINDOWS
CODE            PRELOAD MOVEABLE
DATA            PRELOAD MOVEABLE MULTIPLE
HEAPSIZE        1024
STACKSIZE       5120
EXPORTS         WndProc
```

Listing 3.14. The C source file for the `TabbedTextOut` example.

```
#include <windows.h>
#include <stdlib.h>
#include <string.h>

long FAR PASCAL WndProc (HWND hWnd, WORD iMessage,
                         WORD wParam, LONG lParam);

int PASCAL WinMain (HANDLE hInstance, HANDLE hPrevInstance,
                    LPSTR lpszCmdParam, int nCmdShow)

{
HWND hWnd;
MSG Message;
WNDCLASS WndClass;

if (!hPrevInstance)
     {
     WndClass.cbClsExtra = 0;
     WndClass.cbWndExtra = 0;
     WndClass.hbrBackground = GetStockObject(WHITE_BRUSH);
     WndClass.hCursor =  LoadCursor(NULL, IDC_ARROW);
     WndClass.hIcon = LoadIcon (NULL, "END");
     WndClass.hInstance = hInstance;
     WndClass.lpfnWndProc = WndProc;
     WndClass.lpszClassName = "WIN_TTXT";
     WndClass.lpszMenuName = NULL;
     WndClass.style = CS_HREDRAW ¦ CS_VREDRAW;

     RegisterClass (&WndClass);
     }

hWnd = CreateWindow ("WIN_TTXT",          /* class name */
          "TabbedTextOut Example",   /* Caption */
          WS_OVERLAPPEDWINDOW,       /* Style */
          CW_USEDEFAULT,             /* x position */
          0,                         /* y position */
          CW_USEDEFAULT,             /* cx - size */
          0,                         /* cy - size */
          NULL,                      /* Parent window */
          NULL,                      /* Menu */
          hInstance,                 /* Program Instance */
          NULL);                     /* Parameters */

ShowWindow (hWnd, nCmdShow);
while (GetMessage (&Message, 0, 0, 0))
     {
     TranslateMessage(&Message);
```

```
     DispatchMessage(&Message);
     }
return Message.wParam;
}

/****************************************************************/
/*              Window Procedure: WndProc                       */
/****************************************************************/

long FAR PASCAL WndProc (HWND hWnd, WORD iMessage, WORD wParam,
                         LONG lParam)
{
int nXText, nYText, nHeight, nTab;
HDC hDC;
short x;
DWORD dwExt;
PAINTSTRUCT PtStr;
short LnCount = 30;
static char *textbuf[] =
     {"One \t1",
     "Two \t2",
     "Three \t3",
     "Four \t4",
     "Five \t5",
     "Six \t6",
     "Seven \t7",
     "Eight \t8",
     "Nine \t9",
     "Ten \t10",
     "Eleven \t11",
     "Twelve \t12",
     "Thirteen \t13",
     "Fourteen \t14",
     "Fifteen \t15",
     "Sixteen \t16",
     "Seventeen \t17",
     "Eighteen \t18",
     "Nineteen \t19",
     "Twenty \t20",
     "Twenty-one \t21",
     "Twenty-two \t22",
     "Twenty-three \t23",
     "Twenty-four \t24",
     "Twenty-five \t25",
     "Twenty-six \t26",
     "Twenty-seven \t27",
     "Twenty-eight \t28",
     "Twenty-nine \t29",
     "Thirty \t30"};
```

continues

Listing 3.14. continued

```
switch (iMessage)
     {

     case WM_PAINT:

          hDC = BeginPaint(hWnd, &PtStr);

          dwExt = GetTextExtent(hDC,"S",1);
          nHeight = HIWORD(dwExt);
          nYText = nHeight;
          nXText = LOWORD(dwExt);
          nTab = 25 * LOWORD(dwExt);
          for (x=0; x<LnCount; x=x+1)
               {
               TabbedTextOut(hDC,nXText,nYText,
                 textbuf[x],lstrlen(textbuf[x]),1,
                 &nTab, nXText);
               nYText = nYText + nHeight;
               }

          EndPaint(hWnd, &PtStr);
          return 0;


     case WM_DESTROY:

          PostQuitMessage(0);
          return 0;

     default:

          return(DefWindowProc(hWnd, iMessage, wParam,
                 lParam));
     }
}
```

The remaining functions in Table 3.8 can generate results similar to those produced by the preceding two examples. Chapter 13, "Windows Functions," provides reference information on each text output function listed in Table 3.8.

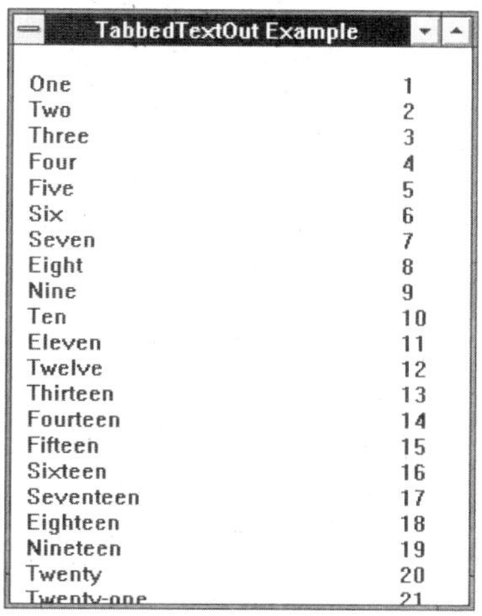

TabbedTextOut Example

One	1
Two	2
Three	3
Four	4
Five	5
Six	6
Seven	7
Eight	8
Nine	9
Ten	10
Eleven	11
Twelve	12
Thirteen	13
Fourteen	14
Fifteen	15
Sixteen	16
Seventeen	17
Eighteen	18
Nineteen	19
Twenty	20
Twenty-one	21

Figure 3.7. *Text output using* `TabbedTextOut`.

Device Context Attributes for Text

As was mentioned previously in this chapter, the device context is a set of attributes that determine the location and appearance of GDI output for a device. The application cannot access the device context directly; the application can, however, use the handle of the device context to indirectly access the device context and its attributes. A device context is created when the program requests the handle for a device context. The created device context contains default values for all its attributes. Table 3.1, shown previously, listed all the device context attributes. Those that affect text are listed in Table 3.9.

Table 3.9. *The device context attributes that affect text.*

Attribute	*Default*	*Related Function(s)*
Background color	White	`GetBkColor`, `SetBkColor`
Background mode	`OPAQUE`	`GetBkMode`, `SetBkMode`
Font	`SYSTEM_FONT`	`CreateFont`, `CreateFontIndirect`, `SelectObject`

continues

Table 3.9. continued

Attribute	*Default*	*Related Function(s)*
Intercharacter spacing	0	`GetTextCharacterExtra`, `SetTextCharacterExtra`
Text color	Black	`GetTextColor`, `SetTextColor`

The *background color* attribute specifies the color that is used to fill the areas around, inside, and between characters. This attribute also is used to fill both the areas between hatches in a hatched brush pattern and the spaces in a styled line pattern. The current background color attribute can be retrieved with the `GetBkColor` function and set with the `SetBkColor` function.

The *background mode* is set to either `OPAQUE` or `TRANSPARENT`. The default setting, `OPAQUE`, turns on the background color. Setting the background mode to `TRANSPARENT` turns off the background color. The `GetBkMode` function retrieves the current background mode. The `SetBkMode` function sets the background mode.

The *font attribute* specifies the current font. A font contains the patterns that specify the shape, size, and appearance of the text characters. Fonts are discussed in more detail in the next section of this chapter.

The *intercharacter spacing* attribute specifies the number of logical units to insert between characters. The `GetTextCharacterExtra` function retrieves the current setting of the intercharacter spacing attribute. The `SetTextCharacterExtra` function sets the intercharacter spacing attribute.

The *text color* attribute specifies the color used to draw the text. This attribute must be a pure color (with no color shades created using hatched or dithered patterns) and is defined using the `SetTextColor` function. The `GetTextColor` function retrieves the current text color.

Using Fonts

A font describes the size, shape, and appearance of the text you display. In other words, the font contains a specific description of each character in a character set. There are two fundamental types of fonts: logical and physical. *Logical* fonts define a character set and are device-independent. *Physical* fonts are designed for a specific device and are, therefore, device-dependent. Logical fonts are more difficult to develop but provide flexibility in use because they are device-independent and often scalable. Physical fonts are easier to develop, but of course, are less flexible because they are device-dependent. Although physical fonts are sometimes scalable, the font resolution is generally poor at larger scales.

You can create logical fonts by using the `CreateFont` or `CreateFontIndirect` functions. The font example in Listings 3.15 and 3.16 demonstrates the use of the `CreateFontIndirect` function to create Times Roman and Helvetica logical fonts.

The font example follows the code structure of the `TabbedTextOut` example. The code to notice in this example is the code written to respond to the `WM_CREATE` and `WM_PAINT` messages. The `WM_CREATE` code, which is executed when the window is created, creates the fonts used for the example with the `CreateFontIndirect` function. The `CreateFontIndirect` function accepts a data structure of type `LOGFONT`, which describes the font to create. The six lines of code that directly precede each `CreateFontIndirect` function call initialize the `LOGFONT` data structure passed to the `CreateFontIndirect` function.

The `WM_PAINT` code selects each font created in the `WM_CREATE` code and displays a line of text. Figure 3.8 shows the window created by the font example. Chapter 13, "Windows Functions," provides reference information on the `CreateFont` and `CreateFontIndirect` functions. Table 3.10 lists the font families and typefaces for the GDI.

The description of the project for the font example follows:

Project Name:	`WIN_FONT`
Files in Project:	`WIN_FONT.C`
	`WIN_FONT.DEF`

Listing 3.15. *The definition file for the font example.*

```
NAME            WIN_FONT
DESCRIPTION     'Font Example'
EXETYPE         WINDOWS
CODE            PRELOAD MOVEABLE
DATA            PRELOAD MOVEABLE MULTIPLE
HEAPSIZE        1024
STACKSIZE       5120
EXPORTS         WndProc
```

Listing 3.16. *The C source file for the font example.*

```
#include <windows.h>
#include <stdlib.h>
#include <string.h>
```

continues

Listing 3.16. continued

```
long FAR PASCAL WndProc (HWND hWnd, WORD iMessage,
                         WORD wParam, LONG lParam);

int PASCAL WinMain (HANDLE hInstance, HANDLE hPrevInstance,
                    LPSTR lpszCmdParam, int nCmdShow)

{
HWND hWnd;
MSG Message;
WNDCLASS WndClass;

if (!hPrevInstance)
     {
     WndClass.cbClsExtra = 0;
     WndClass.cbWndExtra = 0;
     WndClass.hbrBackground = GetStockObject(WHITE_BRUSH);
     WndClass.hCursor =  LoadCursor(NULL, IDC_ARROW);
     WndClass.hIcon = LoadIcon (NULL, "END");
     WndClass.hInstance = hInstance;
     WndClass.lpfnWndProc = WndProc;
     WndClass.lpszClassName = "WIN_FONT";
     WndClass.lpszMenuName = NULL;
     WndClass.style = CS_HREDRAW ¦ CS_VREDRAW;

     RegisterClass (&WndClass);
     }

hWnd = CreateWindow ("WIN_FONT",    /* class name */
          "Font Example",           /* Caption */
          WS_OVERLAPPEDWINDOW,      /* Style */
          CW_USEDEFAULT,            /* x position */
          0,                        /* y position */
          CW_USEDEFAULT,            /* cx - size */
          0,                        /* cy - size */
          NULL,                     /* Parent window */
          NULL,                     /* Menu */
          hInstance,                /* Program Instance */
          NULL);                    /* Parameters */

ShowWindow (hWnd, nCmdShow);
while (GetMessage (&Message, 0, 0, 0))
     {
     TranslateMessage(&Message);
     DispatchMessage(&Message);
     }
return Message.wParam;
}
```

```
/*****************************************************************/
/*              Window Procedure: WndProc                        */
/*****************************************************************/

long FAR PASCAL WndProc (HWND hWnd, WORD iMessage, WORD wParam,
                         LONG lParam)
{
static HANDLE hTmsRmn;
static HANDLE hHelv;
LOGFONT LogFont;
HDC hDC;
PAINTSTRUCT PtStr;

switch (iMessage)
     {

     case WM_CREATE:

          memset(&LogFont,0,sizeof(LOGFONT));
          LogFont.lfHeight = 25;
          LogFont.lfWidth = 15;
          LogFont.lfUnderline = 1;
          LogFont.lfItalic = 1;
          lstrcpy (LogFont.lfFaceName,"Helv");
          hHelv = CreateFontIndirect(&LogFont);

          memset(&LogFont,0,sizeof(LOGFONT));
          LogFont.lfHeight = 25;
          LogFont.lfWidth = 15;
          LogFont.lfUnderline = 1;
          LogFont.lfItalic = 1;
          lstrcpy(LogFont.lfFaceName,"Tms Rmn");
          hTmsRmn = CreateFontIndirect(&LogFont);

          return 0;

     case WM_PAINT:

          hDC = BeginPaint (hWnd, &PtStr);

          SelectObject(hDC, hHelv);
          TextOut(hDC,20,20,
              "Helvetica - Underlined and Italics",34);

          SelectObject(hDC, hTmsRmn);
          TextOut(hDC,20,100,
              "Times Roman - Underlined and Italics",36);

          EndPaint(hWnd,&PtStr);
          return 0;
```

Listing 3.16. continued

```
    case WM_DESTROY:

         DeleteObject(hHelv);
         DeleteObject(hTmsRmn);

         PostQuitMessage(0);
         return 0;

    default:

         return(DefWindowProc(hWnd, iMessage, wParam,
                lParam));
    }
}
```

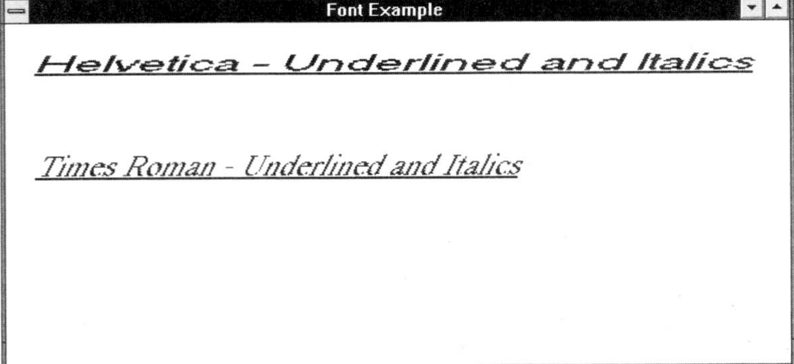

Figure 3.8. *The window created by the font example.*

Table 3.10. *GDI font families and typefaces.*

Font Family	*Font Family Constant*	*Example Typefaces*	*Description*
Dontcare	`FF_DONTCARE`	System	Used when font information is not available or is not important
Decorative	`FF_DECORATIVE`	Symbol	Novelty fonts

Font Family	*Font Family Constant*	*Example Typefaces*	*Description*
Modern	`FF_MODERN`	Courier, Modern, Terminal	Constant stroke width font, may or may not have serifs
Roman	`FF_ROMAN`	Roman, Times Roman	Variable stroke width font with serifs
Script	`FF_SCRIPT`	Script	Resembles handwriting
Swiss	`FF_SWISS`	Helvetica, System	Variable stroke width font without serifs

Text Metrics

The values that describe a font are called the *text metrics* of the font. The `GetTextMetrics` function retrieves a font's text metrics and places them in a data structure of type `TEXTMETRIC`, as follows:

```
typedef struct tagTEXTMETRIC {
     short int tmHeight;
     short int tmAscent;
     short int tmDescent;
     short int tmInternalLeading;
     short int tmExternalLeading;
     short int tmAveCharWidth;
     short int tmMaxCharWidth;
     short int tmWeight
     BYTE tmItalic;
     BYTE tmUnderlined;
     BYTE tmStruckOut;
     BYTE tmFirstChar;
     BYTE tmLastChar;
     BYTE tmDefaultChar;
     BYTE tmBreakChar;
     BYTE tmPitchAndFamily;
     BYTE tmCharSet;
     short int tmOverhang;
     short int tmDigitizedAspectX;
     short int tmDigitizedAspectY;
} TEXTMETRIC;
```

in which

`tmHeight` is the character height

`tmAscent` is the character ascent (units above baseline)

`tmDescent` is the character descent (units below baseline)

`tmInternalLeading` is the amount of space at the top of the character height specified by `tmHeight`

`tmExternalLeading` is the amount of space added between rows

`tmAveCharWidth` is the average character width

`tmMaxCharWidth` is the width of the widest character

`tmWeight` is the font weight

`tmItalic` is nonzero if the font is italic

`tmUnderlined` is nonzero if the font is underlined

`tmStruckOut` is nonzero if the font is struck out

`tmFirstChar` is first character defined for the font

`tmLastChar` is the last character defined for the font

`tmDefaultChar` is the character substituted for characters not in the font

`tmBreakChar` is the character used for word breaks

`tmPitchAndFamily` is the pitch (low-order bit) and family (four high-order bits) of the font

`tmCharSet` is the character set for the font

`tmOverhang` is the extra width added to some synthesized fonts

`tmDigitizedAspectX` is the horizontal aspect of the device the font was designed for

`tmDigitizedAspectY` is the vertical aspect of the device the font was designed for

Most of the fields of the `TEXTMETRIC` data structure are easy to understand. For further explanation, see Figure 3.9, which includes several graphical definitions of a font character cell.

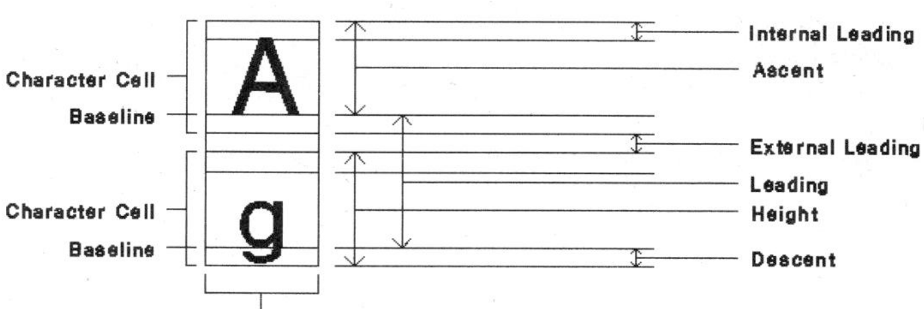

Figure 3.9. *Character cell dimensions.*

Aligning Text

The majority of the text functions listed in Table 3.8 require that the coordinates to a point be passed in the function's argument list. For example, the following line of code from the font example uses the coordinates (20,100) to define the reference point for the text.

```
TextOut(hDC,20,100,"Times Roman - Underlined and Italics",36);
```

The function uses the coordinates of the specified point and the current text alignment to draw the text string. The current text alignment specifies how the string is drawn relative to the passed coordinates. The `SetTextAlign` function sets the current text alignment. (See Chapter 13 for more information on the `SetTextAlign` function.) Table 3.11 lists the horizontal, vertical, and update flags for the `SetTextAlign` function. The default settings for the text alignment flags are `TA_LEFT` (horizontal), `TA_TOP` (vertical), and `TA_NOUPDATECP` (update).

Table 3.11. *Text alignment flags.*

Value	*Meaning*
Horizontal Flags	
`TA_CENTER`	Alignment of y-axis and center of bounding rectangle
`TA_LEFT`	Alignment of y-axis and left side of bounding rectangle
`TA_RIGHT`	Alignment of y-axis and right side of bounding rectangle

continues

Table 3.11. continued

Value	Meaning
Vertical Flags	
TA_BASELINE	Alignment of x-axis and baseline of font within the bounding rectangle
TA_BOTTOM	Alignment of x-axis and bottom of bounding rectangle
TA_TOP	Alignment of x-axis and top of bounding rectangle
Update Flags	
TA_NOUPDATECP	Current position is not updated
TA_UPDATECP	Current position is updated

Note: The default values for these flags are TA_LEFT, TA_TOP, *and* TA_NOUPDATECP.

Scrolling Text Windows

This chapter has presented several examples that displayed text in a window. These examples used a window without scroll bars and, therefore, contained lines of text that could not be viewed. The scrolling text example in Listings 3.17 and 3.18 demonstrates the use of the vertical and horizontal scroll bars for text scrolling.

The first thing to notice about this example is that the window class definition in the WinMain function differs in one major way from the previous examples in this chapter. Because this example requires the use of scroll bars, the WS_VSCROLL and WS_HSCROLL styles are used.

The next thing to be aware of in this example is that the window procedure is quite long and responds to several messages that have not yet been presented: WM_SIZE, WM_HSCROLL, and WM_VSCROLL. Additional messages that are monitored include WM_CREATE and WM_PAINT.

The WM_CREATE code defines initial values for several of the parameters used to track the text positions. The WM_SIZE code defines the scrolling ranges for the vertical and horizontal scroll bars each time the window is sized. The WM_PAINT code draws the text that is to be scrolled.

The most interesting code in the example is the code for the WM_VSCROLL and WM_HSCROLL messages. Both of these message code segments consist of additional switch statements that monitor the scroll bar code that is contained in the wParam parameter of the appropriate message. The nested switch statement determines the direction and amount of scrolling that takes place.

Figure 3.10, which appears following the listings, shows the window resulting from Listings 3.17 and 3.18. Notice that although each character string displayed in the window contains the same number of characters, the right margin of the text is not aligned. This is because the font used to display the text was a proportional font, which means that the width of each character varies. If a fixed font had been used, the right margin of the text would have been aligned.

The description of the project for the scrolling text example follows:

Project Name: `WIN_SCR`
Files in Project: `WIN_SCR.C`
`WIN_SCR.DEF`

Listing 3.17. The definition file for the scrolling text example.

```
NAME            WIN_SCR
DESCRIPTION     'Text Scrolling Example'
EXETYPE         WINDOWS
CODE            PRELOAD MOVEABLE
DATA            PRELOAD MOVEABLE MULTIPLE
HEAPSIZE        1024
STACKSIZE       5120
EXPORTS         WndProc
```

Listing 3.18. The C source file for the scrolling text example.

```
#include <windows.h>
#include <stdlib.h>
#include <string.h>

long FAR PASCAL WndProc (HWND hWnd, WORD iMessage,
                         WORD wParam, LONG lParam);

int PASCAL WinMain (HANDLE hInstance, HANDLE hPrevInstance,
                    LPSTR lpszCmdParam, int nCmdShow)

{
HWND hWnd;
MSG Message;
WNDCLASS WndClass;

if (!hPrevInstance)
     {
     WndClass.cbClsExtra = 0;
     WndClass.cbWndExtra = 0;
     WndClass.hbrBackground = GetStockObject(WHITE_BRUSH);
```

continues

Listing 3.18. continued

```
     WndClass.hCursor =  LoadCursor(NULL, IDC_ARROW);
     WndClass.hIcon = LoadIcon (NULL, "END");
     WndClass.hInstance = hInstance;
     WndClass.lpfnWndProc = WndProc;
     WndClass.lpszClassName = "WIN_SCR";
     WndClass.lpszMenuName = NULL;
     WndClass.style = CS_HREDRAW ¦ CS_VREDRAW;

     RegisterClass (&WndClass);
     }

hWnd = CreateWindow ("WIN_SCR",       /* class name */
          "Text Scrolling Example",   /* Caption */
          WS_OVERLAPPEDWINDOW ¦
          WS_VSCROLL ¦ WS_HSCROLL,    /* Style */
          CW_USEDEFAULT,              /* x position */
          0,                          /* y position */
          CW_USEDEFAULT,              /* cx - size */
          0,                          /* cy - size */
          NULL,                       /* Parent window */
          NULL,                       /* Menu */
          hInstance,                  /* Program Instance */
          NULL);                      /* Parameters */

ShowWindow (hWnd, nCmdShow);
UpdateWindow (hWnd);
while (GetMessage (&Message, 0, 0, 0))
     {
     TranslateMessage(&Message);
     DispatchMessage(&Message);
     }
return Message.wParam;
}

/****************************************************************/
/*               Window Procedure: WndProc                      */
/****************************************************************/

long FAR PASCAL WndProc (HWND hWnd, WORD iMessage, WORD wParam,
                         LONG lParam)
{
static short nXChar, nYChar, nCaps, nXClnt, nYClnt, nMaxWidth,
     nVPos, nVMax, nHPos, nHMax;
HDC hDC;
short x, y, z, nBegin, nEnd, nVInc, nHInc;
PAINTSTRUCT PtStr;
TEXTMETRIC tm;
short LnCount = 30;
```

```
static char *textbuf[] =
       {"One.............................................1",
     "Two.............................................2",
     "Three...........................................3",
     "Four............................................4",
     "Five............................................5",
     "Six.............................................6",
     "Seven...........................................7",
     "Eight...........................................8",
     "Nine............................................9",
     "Ten............................................10",
     "Eleven.........................................11",
     "Twelve.........................................12",
     "Thirteen.......................................13",
     "Fourteen.......................................14",
     "Fifteen........................................15",
     "Sixteen........................................16",
     "Seventeen......................................17",
     "Eighteen.......................................18",
     "Nineteen.......................................19",
     "Twenty.........................................20",
     "Twenty-one.....................................21",
     "Twenty-two.....................................22",
     "Twenty-three...................................23",
     "Twenty-four....................................24",
     "Twenty-five....................................25",
     "Twenty-six.....................................26",
     "Twenty-seven...................................27",
     "Twenty-eight...................................28",
     "Twenty-nine....................................29",
     "Thirty.........................................30"};

switch (iMessage)
     {

     case WM_CREATE:

          hDC = GetDC(hWnd);

          GetTextMetrics(hDC,&tm);
          nXChar = tm.tmAveCharWidth;
          nYChar = tm.tmHeight + tm.tmExternalLeading;
          nCaps = (tm.tmPitchAndFamily & 1 ? 3 : 2) *
               nXChar/2;


          ReleaseDC(hWnd, hDC);
          nMaxWidth = 40 * nXChar + 18 * nCaps;
          return 0;
```

continues

Listing 3.18. continued

```
case WM_SIZE:

     nYClnt = HIWORD(lParam);
     nXClnt = LOWORD(lParam);

     nVMax = max(0,LnCount+2-nYClnt/nYChar);
     nVPos = min(nVPos,nVMax);

     SetScrollRange(hWnd,SB_VERT,0,nVMax,FALSE);
     SetScrollPos(hWnd,SB_VERT,nVPos,TRUE);

     nHMax = max(0,2+(nMaxWidth-nXClnt)/nXChar);
     nHPos = min(nHPos,nHMax);

     SetScrollRange(hWnd,SB_HORZ,0,nHMax,FALSE);
     SetScrollPos(hWnd,SB_HORZ,nHPos,TRUE);
     return 0;

case WM_HSCROLL:

     switch(wParam)
          {
          case SB_LINEUP:
               nHInc = -1;
               break;
          case SB_LINEDOWN:
               nHInc = 1;
               break;
          case SB_PAGEUP:
               nHInc = -8;
               break;
          case SB_PAGEDOWN:
               nHInc = 8;
               break;
          case SB_THUMBPOSITION:
               nHInc = LOWORD(lParam)-nHPos;
               break;
          default:
               nHInc = 0;
          }
     if (nHInc == max(-nHPos,min(nHInc,nHMax-nHPos)))
          {
          nHPos = nHPos + nHInc;
          ScrollWindow(hWnd,-nXChar*nHInc,0,
               NULL,NULL);
          SetScrollPos(hWnd,SB_HORZ,nHPos,TRUE);
```

```
                }
            return 0;

        case WM_VSCROLL:

            switch(wParam)
                {
                case SB_TOP:
                    nVInc = -nVPos;
                    break;
                case SB_BOTTOM:
                    nVInc = nVMax - nVPos;
                    break;
                case SB_LINEUP:
                    nVInc = -1;
                    break;
                case SB_LINEDOWN:
                    nVInc = 1;
                    break;
                case SB_PAGEUP:
                    nVInc = min(-1,-nYClnt/nYChar);
                    break;
                case SB_PAGEDOWN:
                    nVInc = max(1,nYClnt/nYChar);
                    break;
                case SB_THUMBPOSITION:
                    nVInc = LOWORD(lParam)-nVPos;
                    break;
                default:
                    nVInc = 0;
                }
            if (nVInc == max(-nVPos,min(nVInc,nVMax-nVPos)))
                {
                nVPos = nVPos + nVInc;
                ScrollWindow(hWnd,0,-nYChar*nVInc,
                             NULL,NULL);
                SetScrollPos(hWnd,SB_VERT,nVPos,TRUE);
                UpdateWindow(hWnd);
                }
            return 0;

        case WM_PAINT:

            hDC = BeginPaint(hWnd, &PtStr);

            nBegin = max(0,nVPos +
               PtStr.rcPaint.top / nYChar-1);
            nEnd = min(LnCount,nVPos +
               PtStr.rcPaint.bottom / nYChar);
```

continues

Listing 3.18. continued

```
          for (z=nBegin; z<nEnd; z=z+1)
               {
               x = nXChar * (1-nHPos);
               y = nYChar * (1-nVPos+z);

               TextOut(hDC,x,y,textbuf[z],
                  lstrlen(textbuf[z]));
               }

          EndPaint(hWnd, &PtStr);
          return 0;


     case WM_DESTROY:

          PostQuitMessage(0);
          return 0;

     default:

          return(DefWindowProc(hWnd, iMessage, wParam,
                 lParam));
     }
}
```

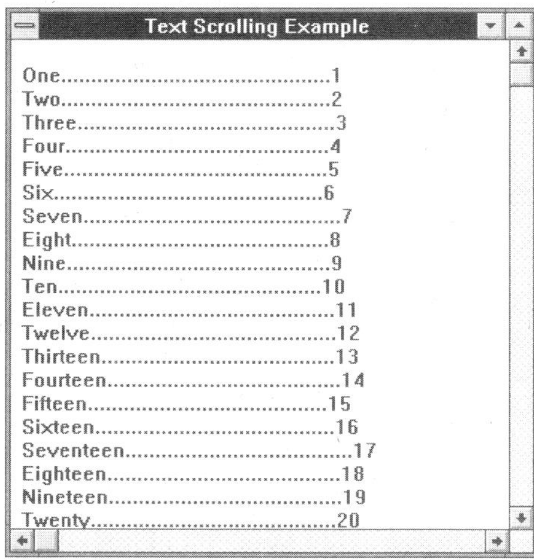

***Figure 3.10.** The window created by the scrolling text example.*

Printing

As I've mentioned before, the GDI is designed to be device-independent. In theory, therefore, the method for printing text on the printer is the same as that for displaying text on the screen. Unfortunately, things are not quite as straightforward as that.

The same GDI functions used to create text and graphics on a screen are used to print text and graphics on a printer. There are fundamental differences, however, in the way both devices operate. For example, not all printers support graphics, and others do not contain enough memory to print a full page of graphics. To account for the differences between printers and the screen, the GDI `Escape` function is provided. An application can use the `Escape` function to access the features of a printer device and to retrieve and modify printer settings. Chapter 13 provides additional information on the `Escape` function. Chapter 15, "Windows Printer Escapes," provides reference information for each of the printer escape subfunctions supported by `Escape`.

Sending output to the printer follows the basic steps outlined in Figure 3.11 that follows. The application calls the `Escape` function which, in turn, is handled by the GDI module. The GDI module calls the `Control` function, which is the printer device driver's equivalent of the `Escape` function and which is also handled by the printer device driver. This driver, with the help of the GDI module, activates the Print Manager.

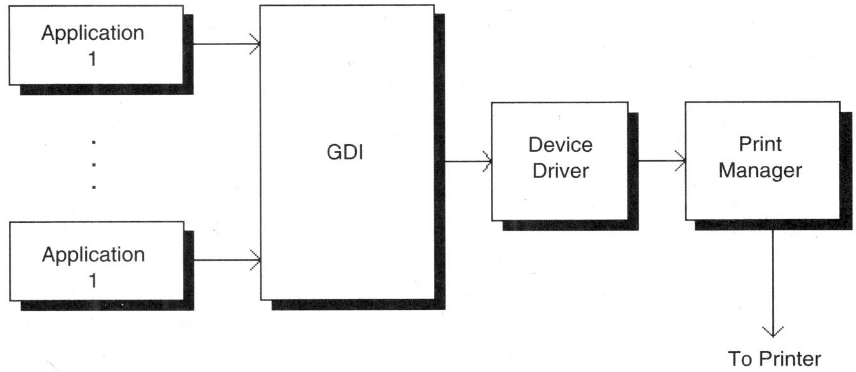

Figure 3.11. *Printer output.*

This chapter has presented the Graphics Device Interface (GDI). The following chapter introduces Windows resources and presents numerous examples that demonstrate the use of menus, bitmaps, accelerators, icons, and more.

4

Resources

Resources are read-only data stored in an application's .EXE file or in a library's .DLL file. Windows uses several different types of resources, including cursors, bitmaps, strings, accelerators, icons, dialog boxes, and menus. You can use the Resource Workshop to create and edit many types of resources used by Windows applications.

This chapter introduces the accelerator, bitmap, cursor, dialog box, icon, menu, and string resources. For each of these types, the resource itself is created—using the Resource Workshop—and incorporated in an example demonstrating the use of that resource.

Using Accelerators

An *accelerator* is a key or key combination used to select a menu item or invoke a command. Using accelerators enables you to access menu items or commands more quickly and conveniently than you can with other methods, such as using pull-down menus.

You can use the Accelerator editor of the Resource Workshop to create accelerator resources.

The accelerator example in Listings 4.1, 4.2, and 4.3 demonstrates the use of accelerators and includes three files: a C source file, a module definition file, and a resource script file. The accelerator table shown in the resource script file (Listing 4.2) was created with the Accelerator editor of the Resource Workshop and saved as an .RC file. Figure 4.1 shows the accelerator resource as it was created with the Accelerator editor.

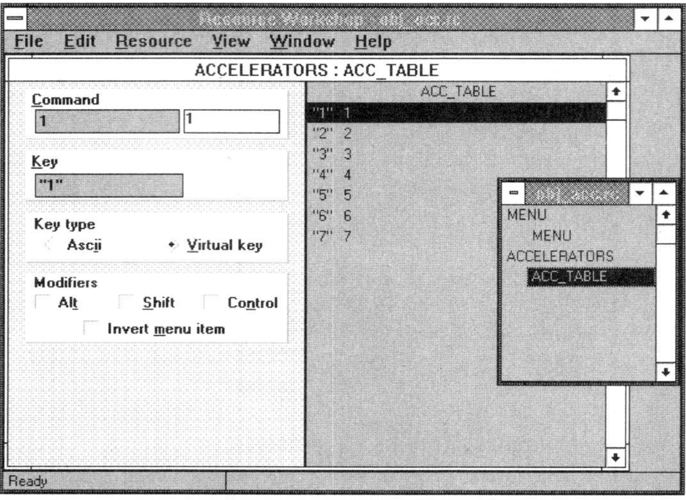

Figure 4.1. *The accelerator resource.*

The accelerators defined for this example are the A, B, C, D, E, F, G, H, and I keys. Whenever you press one of these keys, a message box is displayed that echoes the ID number of the accelerator (see Figure 4.2 following the listings). For this example, the accelerators are not tied to the selection of menu items. Accelerators are generally used, however, as alternatives to selecting items from a menu.

The code structure of this example is similar to code structures already presented in this chapter. The message box that appears when you press an accelerator key is displayed in response to the `WM_COMMAND` message.

The name of this project and the files used to create the accelerator example are as follows:

Project Name:	WIN_ACC
Files in Project:	WIN_ACC.C
	WIN_ACC.DEF
	WIN_ACC.RC

Listing 4.1. *The definition file for the accelerator example.*

```
NAME            WIN_ACC
DESCRIPTION     'Accelerator Example'
EXETYPE         WINDOWS
CODE            PRELOAD MOVEABLE
DATA            PRELOAD MOVEABLE MULTIPLE
HEAPSIZE        1024
STACKSIZE       5120
EXPORTS         WndProc
```

Listing 4.2 *The C source file for the accelerator example.*

```
#include <windows.h>
#include <stdlib.h>
#include <string.h>

long FAR PASCAL WndProc (HWND hWnd, WORD iMessage,
                         WORD wParam, LONG lParam);

int PASCAL WinMain (HANDLE hInstance, HANDLE hPrevInstance,
                    LPSTR lpszCmdParam, int nCmdShow)

{
HWND hWnd;
MSG Message;
WNDCLASS WndClass;
HANDLE hAccel;

if (!hPrevInstance)
     {
     WndClass.cbClsExtra = 0;
     WndClass.cbWndExtra = 0;
     WndClass.hbrBackground = GetStockObject(WHITE_BRUSH);
     WndClass.hCursor =  LoadCursor(NULL, IDC_ARROW);
     WndClass.hIcon = LoadIcon (NULL, "END");
     WndClass.hInstance = hInstance;
     WndClass.lpfnWndProc = WndProc;
     WndClass.lpszClassName = "WIN_ACC";
     WndClass.lpszMenuName = NULL;
     WndClass.style = CS_HREDRAW ¦ CS_VREDRAW;
```

continues

Listing 4.2. continued

```
     RegisterClass (&WndClass);
     }

hWnd = CreateWindow ("WIN_ACC",         /* class name */
          "Accelerator Example",        /* Caption */
          WS_OVERLAPPEDWINDOW,          /* Style */
          CW_USEDEFAULT,                /* x position */
          0,                            /* y position */
          CW_USEDEFAULT,                /* cx - size */
          0,                            /* cy - size */
          NULL,                         /* Parent window */
          NULL,                         /* Menu */
          hInstance,                    /* Program Instance*/
          NULL);                        /* Parameters */

ShowWindow (hWnd, nCmdShow);

hAccel = LoadAccelerators(hInstance,"A_RESOURCE");

while (GetMessage (&Message, 0, 0, 0))
     {
     if (!TranslateAccelerator(hWnd,hAccel,&Message))
          {
          TranslateMessage(&Message);
          DispatchMessage(&Message);
          }
     }
return Message.wParam;
}

/*****************************************************************/
/*               Window Procedure: WndProc                       */
/*****************************************************************/

long FAR PASCAL WndProc (HWND hWnd, WORD iMessage, WORD wParam,
                         LONG lParam)
{
char textout[40];

switch (iMessage)
     {
     case WM_COMMAND:

          wsprintf(textout,"Accelerator ID = %d",wParam);
          MessageBox(hWnd,textout,"Accelerator!",MB_OK);

          return 0;
```

```
    case WM_DESTROY:

         PostQuitMessage(0);
         return 0;

    default:

         return(DefWindowProc(hWnd, iMessage, wParam,
                lParam));
    }
  }
```

Listing 4.3. *The resource file for the accelerator example.*

```
A_RESOURCE ACCELERATORS
BEGIN
"A", 1, VIRTKEY, NOINVERT
"B", 2, VIRTKEY, NOINVERT
"C", 3, VIRTKEY, NOINVERT
"D", 4, VIRTKEY, NOINVERT
"E", 5, VIRTKEY, NOINVERT
"F", 6, VIRTKEY, NOINVERT
"G", 7, VIRTKEY, NOINVERT
"H", 8, VIRTKEY, NOINVERT
"I", 9, VIRTKEY, NOINVERT
END
```

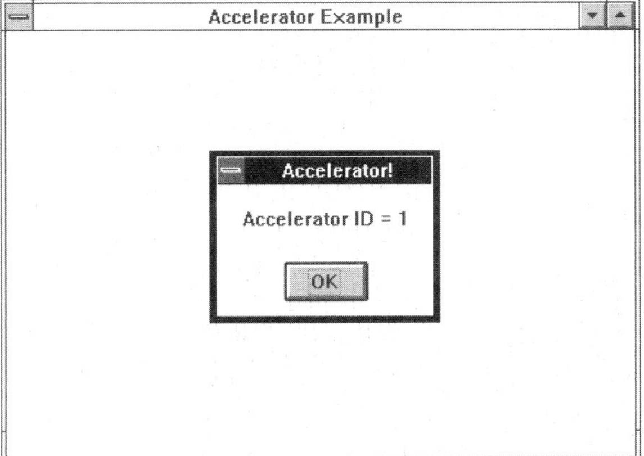

Figure 4.2. *The window created by the accelerator example.*

Using Bitmaps

A *bitmap* is a data series that represents a graphical object. An application uses the bitmap to draw predefined objects quickly onto the screen. The two basic types of bitmaps are the device-dependent bitmap and the device-independent bitmap.

Device-dependent bitmaps are closely tied to a particular output display device, because there is a close correlation between the bits of the bitmaps and the pixels of the output display device. *Device-independent bitmaps*, on the other hand, are not closely tied to a particular display device, because they represent the appearance of the image and not the correlation of the bitmap bits and the pixels of the output device.

You can use preexisting bitmaps or create your own, using the Paint editor of the Resource Workshop (see Chapter 17).

The four bitmap resources used in Listings 4.4, 4.5, and 4.6 were created with the Paint editor of the Resource Workshop. The football and basketball bitmap resources, created with the Paint editor and used for the bitmap example, are shown in Figures 4.3 and 4.4, respectively. The baseball and golf ball bitmap resources used for the bitmap example were created with the Paint editor of the Resource Workshop and are shown in Figures 4.5 and 4.6, respectively.

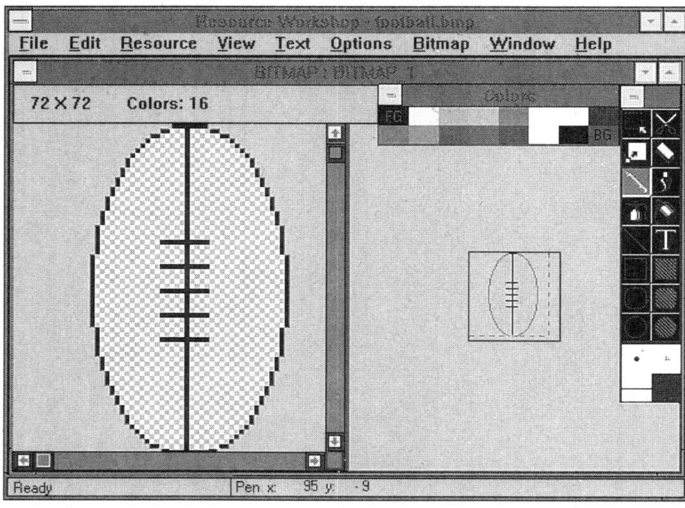

Figure 4.3. *The football bitmap resource.*

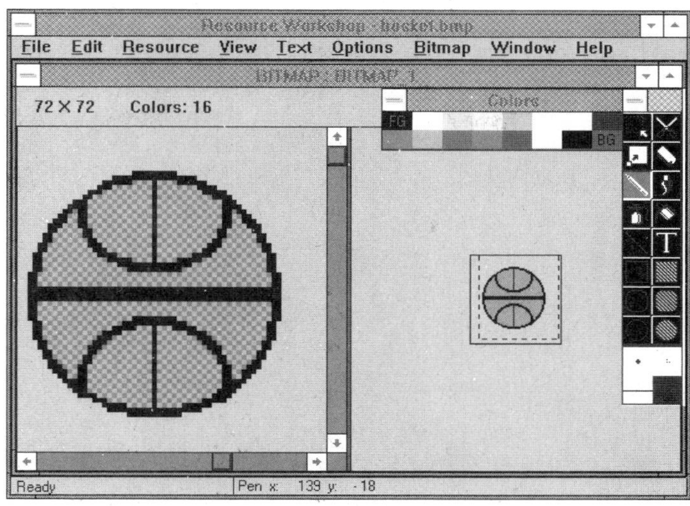

Figure 4.4. *The basketball bitmap resource.*

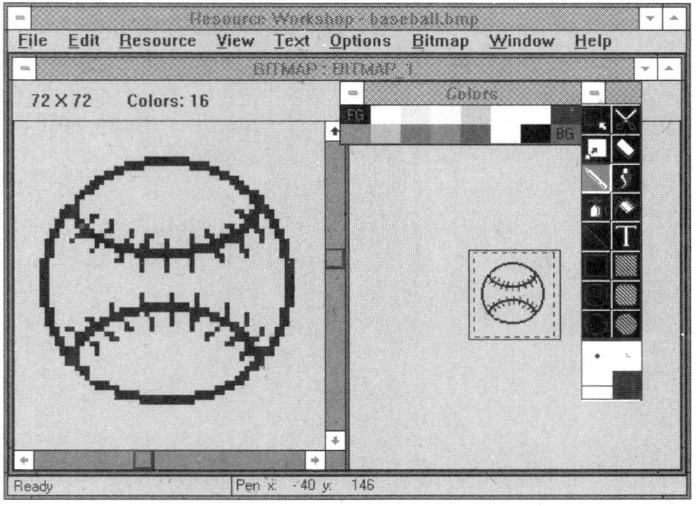

Figure 4.5. *The baseball bitmap resource.*

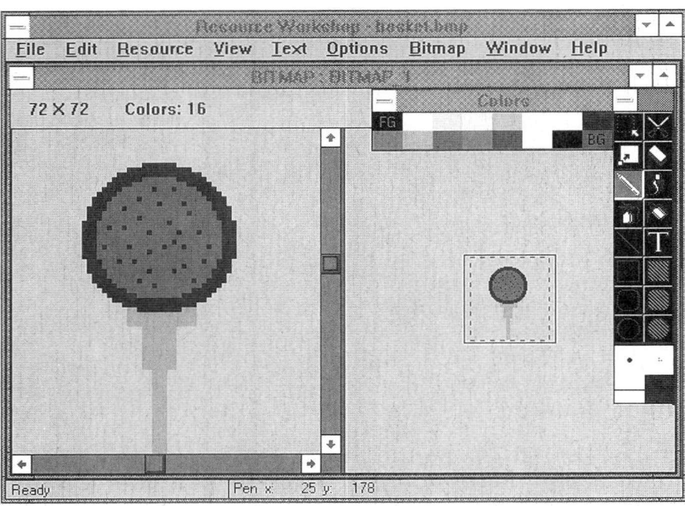

Figure 4.6. *The golf ball bitmap resource.*

The bitmap example contains three files: a module definition file (Listing 4.3), a C source code file (Listing 4.4), and a resource script file (Listing 4.5). The bitmap example loads the four bitmap resources specified in the resource script (.RC) file and displays these bitmaps. Figure 4.7, which follows the listings, shows the window created by the bitmap example. This example demonstrates a straightforward procedure for loading and using bitmap resources.

The bitmaps are loaded in the `WinMain` function using the `LoadBitmap` function. The bitmaps are then drawn on the screen whenever the window procedure receives the `WM_PAINT` message. The `SelectObject` function is used to select the appropriate bitmap. The `BitBlt` function is used to draw the bitmap.

The project name and the files used to create the bitmap example are as follows:

Project Name:	`WIN_BIT`
Files in Project:	`WIN_BIT.C`
	`WIN_BIT.DEF`
	`WIN_BIT.RC`

Listing 4.4. ***The definition file for the bitmap example.***

```
NAME           WIN_BIT
DESCRIPTION    'Bitmap Example'
EXETYPE        WINDOWS
CODE           PRELOAD MOVEABLE
DATA           PRELOAD MOVEABLE MULTIPLE
```

```
HEAPSIZE        1024
STACKSIZE       5120
EXPORTS         WndProc
```

Listing 4.5. *The C source file for the bitmap example.*

```
#include <windows.h>
#include <stdlib.h>
#include <string.h>

static HANDLE hFootball;
static HANDLE hBasketball;
static HANDLE hGolfball;
static HANDLE hBaseball;

long FAR PASCAL WndProc (HWND hWnd, WORD iMessage,
                         WORD wParam, LONG lParam);

int PASCAL WinMain (HANDLE hInstance, HANDLE hPrevInstance,
                    LPSTR lpszCmdParam, int nCmdShow)

{
HWND hWnd;
MSG Message;
WNDCLASS WndClass;

if (!hPrevInstance)
     {
     WndClass.cbClsExtra = 0;
     WndClass.cbWndExtra = 0;
     WndClass.hbrBackground = GetStockObject(WHITE_BRUSH);
     WndClass.hCursor =  LoadCursor(NULL, IDC_ARROW);
     WndClass.hIcon = LoadIcon (NULL, "END");
     WndClass.hInstance = hInstance;
     WndClass.lpfnWndProc = WndProc;
     WndClass.lpszClassName = "WIN_BIT";
     WndClass.lpszMenuName = NULL;
     WndClass.style = CS_HREDRAW ¦ CS_VREDRAW;

     RegisterClass (&WndClass);
     }

hWnd = CreateWindow ("WIN_BIT",      /* class name */
          "Bitmap Example",          /* Caption */
          WS_OVERLAPPEDWINDOW,       /* Style */
          CW_USEDEFAULT,             /* x position */
          0,                         /* y position */
```

continues

Listing 4.5. continued

```
          CW_USEDEFAULT,              /* cx - size */
          0,                          /* cy - size */
          NULL,                       /* Parent window */
          NULL,                       /* Menu */
          hInstance,                  /* Program Instance */
          NULL);                      /* Parameters */

hFootball = LoadBitmap(hInstance,"FOOTBALL");
hBasketball = LoadBitmap(hInstance,"BASKET");
hGolfball = LoadBitmap(hInstance,"GOLFBALL");
hBaseball = LoadBitmap(hInstance,"BASEBALL");

ShowWindow (hWnd, nCmdShow);
UpdateWindow (hWnd);
while (GetMessage (&Message, 0, 0, 0))
     {
     TranslateMessage(&Message);
     DispatchMessage(&Message);
     }
return Message.wParam;
}

/*****************************************************************/
/*              Window Procedure: WndProc                        */
/*****************************************************************/

long FAR PASCAL WndProc (HWND hWnd, WORD iMessage, WORD wParam,
                         LONG lParam)
{
HDC hDC, hMemDC;
short x, y;
PAINTSTRUCT PtStr;

switch (iMessage)
     {

     case WM_PAINT:

          hDC = BeginPaint(hWnd, &PtStr);
          hMemDC = CreateCompatibleDC(hDC);
          for (y=30; y<300; y=y+80)
               {
               SelectObject(hMemDC,hFootball);
               BitBlt(hDC,30,y,72,72,hMemDC,0,0,SRCCOPY);
               SelectObject(hMemDC,hBasketball);
               BitBlt(hDC,130,y,72,72,hMemDC,0,0,SRCCOPY);
               SelectObject(hMemDC,hGolfball);
               BitBlt(hDC,230,y,72,72,hMemDC,0,0,SRCCOPY);
```

```
                SelectObject(hMemDC,hBaseball);
                BitBlt(hDC,330,y,72,72,hMemDC,0,0,SRCCOPY);
                }
            DeleteDC(hMemDC);
            EndPaint(hWnd, &PtStr);
            return 0;

        case WM_DESTROY:

            DeleteObject(hFootball);
            DeleteObject(hBaseball);
            DeleteObject(hBasketball);
            DeleteObject(hGolfball);
            PostQuitMessage(0);
            return 0;

        default:

            return(DefWindowProc(hWnd, iMessage, wParam,
                   lParam));
        }
}
```

Listing 4.6. *The resource file for the bitmap example.*

```
FOOTBALL BITMAP FOOTBALL.BMP
BASKET   BITMAP BASKET.BMP
GOLFBALL BITMAP GOLFBALL.BMP
BASEBALL BITMAP BASEBALL.BMP
```

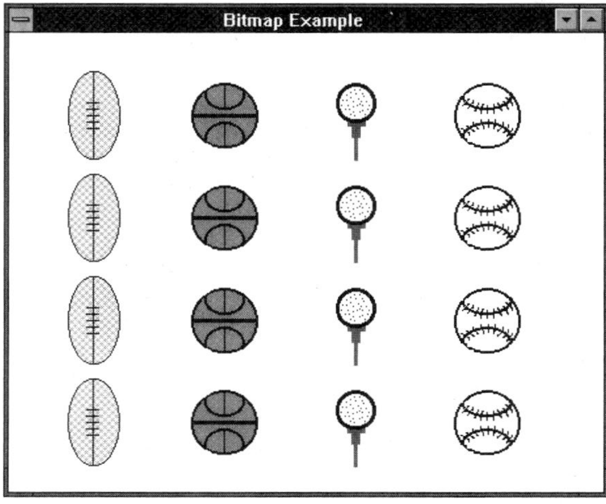

Figure 4.7. *The window created by the bitmap example.*

Using Cursors

A *cursor* is a special 32-by-32-pixel bitmap used to indicate the positions where mouse actions occur. Windows has several predefined cursor types, which are listed in Table 4.1. In addition to using the predefined cursors, you can create your own cursors by using the Paint editor of the Resource Workshop.

Table 4.1. Predefined cursor types.

Constant	*Meaning*
`IDC_ARROW`	Arrow cursor
`IDC_CROSS`	Crosshair cursor
`IDC_IBEAM`	I-beam text cursor
`IDC_ICON`	Empty icon
`IDC_SIZE`	Square with small square in lower-right corner
`IDC_SIZENESW`	Cursor with arrows pointing northeast and southwest
`IDC_SIZENS`	Cursor with arrows pointing north and south
`IDC_SIZENWSE`	Cursor with arrows pointing northwest and southeast
`IDC_SIZEWE`	Cursor with arrows pointing west and east
`IDC_UPARROW`	Vertical arrow cursor
`IDC_WAIT`	Hourglass cursor

The cursor example in Listings 4.7, 4.8, and 4.9 uses a cursor resource created with the Paint editor of the Resource Workshop, saved in .CUR format, and included in the resource script file. Figure 4.8 shows the cursor created with the Paint editor and used in the cursor example.

The cursor example contains three files: the module definition file (Listing 4.7), a C source code file (Listing 4.8), and a resource script file (Listing 4.9). This example loads the cursor resource shown in Figure 4.8 by specifying it as the default cursor for the window class (see the `WndClass.hCursor` line of the `WinMain` function). In this cursor example, the cursor resource is used whenever the current mouse position is within the application window.

The project name and the files used to create the cursor example are as follows:

Project Name:	`WIN_CUR`
Files in Project:	`WIN_CUR.C`
	`WIN_CUR.DEF`
	`WIN_CUR.RC`

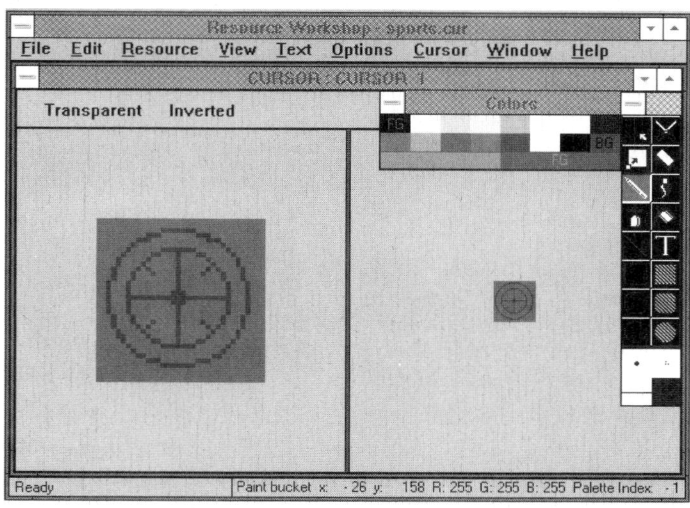

Figure 4.8. *The cursor resource.*

Listing 4.7. *The definition file for the cursor example.*

```
NAME           WIN_CUR
DESCRIPTION    'Cursor Example'
EXETYPE        WINDOWS
CODE           PRELOAD MOVEABLE
DATA           PRELOAD MOVEABLE MULTIPLE
HEAPSIZE       1024
STACKSIZE      5120
EXPORTS        WndProc
```

Listing 4.8. *The C source file for the cursor example.*

```
#include <windows.h>
#include <stdlib.h>
#include <string.h>

long FAR PASCAL WndProc (HWND hWnd, WORD iMessage,
                         WORD wParam, LONG lParam);

int PASCAL WinMain (HANDLE hInstance, HANDLE hPrevInstance,
                    LPSTR lpszCmdParam, int nCmdShow)

{
```

continues

Listing 4.8. continued

```
HWND hWnd;
MSG Message;
WNDCLASS WndClass;

if (!hPrevInstance)
     {
     WndClass.cbClsExtra = 0;
     WndClass.cbWndExtra = 0;
     WndClass.hbrBackground = GetStockObject(WHITE_BRUSH);
     WndClass.hCursor =  LoadCursor(hInstance,"SPORTS");
     WndClass.hIcon = LoadIcon (NULL, "END");
     WndClass.hInstance = hInstance;
     WndClass.lpfnWndProc = WndProc;
     WndClass.lpszClassName = "WIN_CUR";
     WndClass.lpszMenuName = NULL;
     WndClass.style = CS_HREDRAW ¦ CS_VREDRAW;

     RegisterClass (&WndClass);
     }

hWnd = CreateWindow ("WIN_CUR",  /* class name */
          "Cursor Example",       /* Caption */
          WS_OVERLAPPEDWINDOW,    /* Style */
          CW_USEDEFAULT,          /* x position */
          0,                      /* y position */
          CW_USEDEFAULT,          /* cx - size */
          0,                      /* cy - size */
          NULL,                   /* Parent window */
          NULL,                   /* Menu */
          hInstance,              /* Program Instance */
          NULL);                  /* Parameters */

ShowWindow(hWnd,nCmdShow);
UpdateWindow(hWnd);
while (GetMessage (&Message, 0, 0, 0))
     {
     TranslateMessage(&Message);
     DispatchMessage(&Message);
     }
return Message.wParam;
}

/*****************************************************************/
/*               Window Procedure: WndProc                       */
/*****************************************************************/

long FAR PASCAL WndProc (HWND hWnd, WORD iMessage, WORD wParam,
                         LONG lParam)
```

```
{
switch (iMessage)
     {
     case WM_DESTROY:
          PostQuitMessage(0);
          return 0;
     default:
          return(DefWindowProc(hWnd, iMessage, wParam,
                 lParam));
     }
}
```

Listing 4.9. *The resource file for the cursor example.*

```
SPORTS CURSOR SPORTS.CUR
```

Using Dialog Boxes

A *dialog box* is a pop-up window indicating that the application expects some input from, or interaction with, the user. A dialog box enables you to choose from a series of options, each corresponding to a *control* that can consist of such things as radio buttons, checkboxes, input fields, and list boxes.

The examples demonstrated so far in this book have contained two primary elements: the `WinMain` function and the window procedure. Applications that contain a dialog box, however, contain another basic element, the *dialog function*, which is similar to the window procedure except that it processes messages for the dialog box. There are two basic types of dialog boxes: modal and modeless.

A *modal dialog box* disables the parent window and does not let the user return to the parent window until the user makes the appropriate dialog box selections. When a modal dialog box is initiated, the message loop for the dialog box processes messages from the application queue and does not return to the `WinMain` function.

A *modeless dialog box*, in contrast to the modal dialog box, does not disable the parent window. The modeless dialog box receives input from the message loop of the `WinMain` function and does not contain its own message loop. Your use of modal vs. modeless dialog boxes depends on the application and the desired implementation. You can implement the exact same dialog box (as seen by the user) using either modal or modeless.

You can create dialog boxes by using the Dialog editor of the Resource Workshop. This editor contains a variety of tools that you can use to design effective dialog

boxes. The Dialog editor was used to create the dialog box for the dialog box example in Listings 4.10, 4.11, and 4.12. Figure 4.9 shows the dialog box created with the Dialog editor and used in the dialog box example.

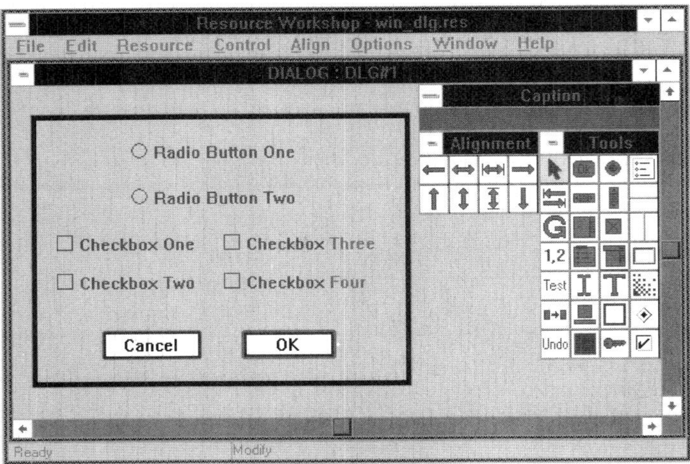

Figure 4.9. *The dialog box resource.*

The dialog box example contains three files: the module definition file (Listing 4.10), a C source code file (Listing 4.11), and a resource script file (Listing 4.12). This example contains a `Help` menu with a `Dialog Box Demo` menu item. (See the "Using Menus" section later in this chapter for more information on creating menus.) When this menu item is selected, the dialog box created with the Dialog editor pops up. You then can select or deselect the controls of that dialog box. Figure 4.10 shows the window and dialog box generated by the dialog box example.

The dialog box format is different from the previously presented examples. The dialog box example contains the usual `WinMain` function and window procedure. However, this example also contains an additional procedure, the dialog procedure, that defines the actions for the dialog buttons. The dialog buttons are referenced in the dialog procedure by the ID defined for each button in the dialog resource.

The project name and the files used to create the dialog box example are as follows:

Project Name:	`WIN_DLG`
Files in Project:	`WIN_DLG.C`
	`WIN_DLG.DEF`
	`WIN_DLG.RC`

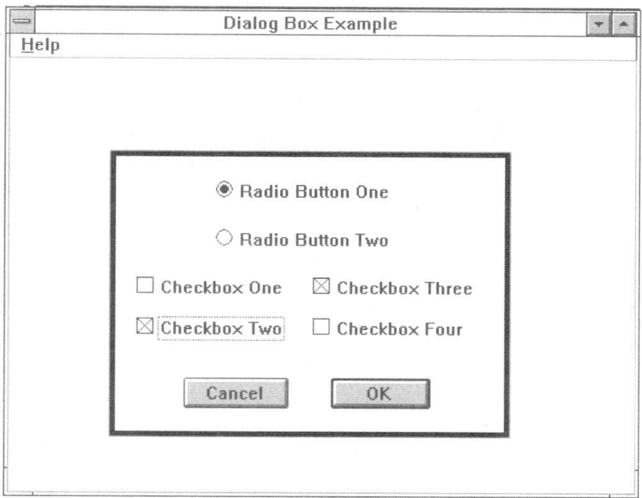

Figure 4.10. *The window and dialog box created by the dialog box example.*

Listing 4.10. *The definition file for the dialog box example.*

```
NAME            WIN_DLG
DESCRIPTION     'Dialog Box Example'
EXETYPE         WINDOWS
CODE            PRELOAD MOVEABLE
DATA            PRELOAD MOVEABLE MULTIPLE
HEAPSIZE        1024
STACKSIZE       5120
EXPORTS         WndProc
                DlgProc
```

Listing 4.11. *The C source file for the dialog box example.*

```
#include <windows.h>
#include <stdlib.h>
#include <string.h>

long FAR PASCAL WndProc (HWND hWnd, WORD iMessage,
                          WORD wParam, LONG lParam);

int PASCAL WinMain (HANDLE hInstance, HANDLE hPrevInstance,
                     LPSTR lpszCmdParam, int nCmdShow)
```

continues

Listing 4.11. continued

```
#define DLG_DEMO 1

{
HWND hWnd;
MSG Message;
WNDCLASS WndClass;

if (!hPrevInstance)
     {
     WndClass.cbClsExtra = 0;
     WndClass.cbWndExtra = 0;
     WndClass.hbrBackground = GetStockObject(WHITE_BRUSH);
     WndClass.hCursor =  LoadCursor(NULL, IDC_ARROW);
     WndClass.hIcon = LoadIcon (NULL, "END");
     WndClass.hInstance = hInstance;
     WndClass.lpfnWndProc = WndProc;
     WndClass.lpszClassName = "WIN_DLG";
     WndClass.lpszMenuName = "DlgMenu";
     WndClass.style = CS_HREDRAW ¦ CS_VREDRAW;

     RegisterClass (&WndClass);
     }

hWnd = CreateWindow ("WIN_DLG",          /* class name */
          "Dialog Box Example",          /* Caption */
          WS_OVERLAPPEDWINDOW,           /* Style */
          CW_USEDEFAULT,                 /* x position */
          0,                             /* y position */
          CW_USEDEFAULT,                 /* cx - size */
          0,                             /* cy - size */
          NULL,                          /* Parent window */
          NULL,                          /* Menu */
          hInstance,                     /* Program Instance */
          NULL);                         /* Parameters */

ShowWindow(hWnd,nCmdShow);
UpdateWindow(hWnd);
while (GetMessage (&Message, 0, 0, 0))
     {
     TranslateMessage(&Message);
     DispatchMessage(&Message);
     }
return Message.wParam;
}

/*****************************************************************/
/*               Dialog Procedure: DlgProc                       */
/*****************************************************************/
```

```
BOOL FAR PASCAL DlgProc(HWND hDlg, WORD iMessage, WORD wParam,
                        LONG lParam)
{
WORD status;

switch(iMessage)
     {
     case WM_INITDIALOG:

          CheckDlgButton(hDlg,101,1);
          return TRUE;

     case WM_COMMAND:

          switch(wParam)
            {
            case 101:
              status = IsDlgButtonChecked(hDlg,101);
              if (status == 0)
                CheckDlgButton(hDlg,101,1);
              else
                CheckDlgButton(hDlg,101,0);
              return TRUE;

            case 102:
               status = IsDlgButtonChecked(hDlg,102);
              if (status == 0)
                CheckDlgButton(hDlg,102,1);
              else
                CheckDlgButton(hDlg,102,0);
              return TRUE;

            case 103:
               status = IsDlgButtonChecked(hDlg,103);
              if (status == 0)
                CheckDlgButton(hDlg,103,1);
              else
                CheckDlgButton(hDlg,103,0);
              return TRUE;

            case 104:
               status = IsDlgButtonChecked(hDlg,104);
              if (status == 0)
                CheckDlgButton(hDlg,104,1);
              else
                CheckDlgButton(hDlg,104,0);
              return TRUE;
```

continues

Listing 4.11. continued

```
            case 105:
               status = IsDlgButtonChecked(hDlg,105);
              if (status == 0)
                CheckDlgButton(hDlg,105,1);
              else
                CheckDlgButton(hDlg,105,0);
              return TRUE;

            case 106:
               status = IsDlgButtonChecked(hDlg,106);
              if (status == 0)
                CheckDlgButton(hDlg,106,1);
              else
                CheckDlgButton(hDlg,106,0);
              return TRUE;

            case 107:
              EndDialog(hDlg,FALSE);
              return TRUE;

            case 108:
              EndDialog(hDlg,TRUE);
              return TRUE;

            }
            break;
     }
return FALSE;
}

/*****************************************************************/
/*              Window Procedure: WndProc                        */
/*****************************************************************/

long FAR PASCAL WndProc (HWND hWnd, WORD iMessage, WORD wParam,
                         LONG lParam)
{
static FARPROC lpfnDlgProc;
static HANDLE hInstance;

switch (iMessage)
     {
     case WM_CREATE:

          hInstance = ((LPCREATESTRUCT)lParam)->hInstance;
          lpfnDlgProc = MakeProcInstance(DlgProc,hInstance);
          return 0;
```

```
     case WM_COMMAND:

          switch(wParam)
           {
           case DLG_DEMO:
                if(DialogBox(hInstance,"DLG#1",hWnd,
                   lpfnDlgProc));
                   InvalidateRect(hWnd,NULL,TRUE);
                return 0;
           }
          break;

     case WM_DESTROY:

          PostQuitMessage(0);
          return 0;

     }

return(DefWindowProc(hWnd,iMessage,wParam,lParam));
}
```

Listing 4.12. *The resource file for the dialog box example.*

```
#include <windows.h>
#define DLG_DEMO 1

DLG#1 DIALOG DISCARDABLE LOADONCALL PURE MOVEABLE 42, 38, 148,
108 STYLE WS_POPUP ¦ WS_DLGFRAME ¦ WS_SYSMENU
  BEGIN
  CONTROL "Radio Button One" 101, "BUTTON", WS_CHILD ¦
     WS_VISIBLE ¦ 0x4L, 38, 6, 74, 14
  CONTROL "Radio Button Two" 102, "BUTTON", WS_CHILD ¦
     WS_VISIBLE ¦ 0x4L, 38, 25, 74, 14
  CONTROL "Checkbox One" 103, "BUTTON", WS_CHILD ¦
     WS_VISIBLE ¦ WS_TABSTOP ¦ 0x2L, 8, 45, 64, 12
  CONTROL "Checkbox Two" 104, "BUTTON", WS_CHILD ¦
     WS_VISIBLE ¦ WS_TABSTOP ¦ 0x2L, 8, 61, 64, 12
  CONTROL "Checkbox Three" 105, "BUTTON", WS_CHILD ¦
     WS_VISIBLE ¦ WS_TABSTOP ¦ 0x2L, 75, 45, 72, 12
  CONTROL "Checkbox Four" 106, "BUTTON", WS_CHILD ¦
     WS_VISIBLE ¦ WS_TABSTOP ¦ 0x2L, 75, 61, 68, 12
  CONTROL "Cancel" 107, "BUTTON", WS_CHILD ¦
     WS_VISIBLE ¦ WS_TABSTOP, 26, 87, 40, 12
  CONTROL "OK" 108, "BUTTON", WS_CHILD ¦
     WS_VISIBLE ¦ WS_TABSTOP ¦ 0x1L, 82, 87, 38, 12
```

continues

Listing 4.12. continued

```
  END

DlgMenu MENU
  {
  POPUP "&Help"
    {
    MENUITEM "&Dialog Demo",  DLG_DEMO
    }
  }
```

Using Icons

An *icon* is a specialized bitmap that represents a minimized application. Double-clicking the icon that represents a minimized application opens that application window.

You can create icons by using the Paint editor of the Resource Workshop. The Paint editor of the Resource Workshop was used to create the icon used for the icon example in Listings 4.13, 4.14, and 4.15. The icon created with the Paint editor and used in the icon example is shown in Figure 4.11.

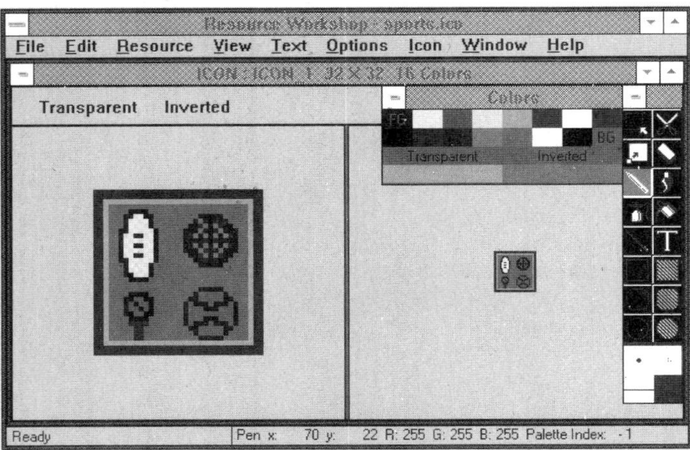

Figure 4.11. *The icon resource.*

The icon example contains three files: the module definition file (Listing 4.13), a C source code file (Listing 4.14), and a resource script file (Listing 4.15). This example is basically the same as the bitmap example demonstrated earlier in this chapter. The only difference is that the icon shown in Figure 4.11 represents the application when the window is minimized. This example loads the icon resource by specifying it as the default icon for the window class. (See the `WndClass.hIcon` line of the `WinMain` function.) Figure 4.12, which appears following the listings, shows the minimized window and icon generated by the icon example.

The project name and the files used to create the icon example are as follows:

Project Name:	`WIN_ICO`
Files in Project:	`WIN_ICO.C`
	`WIN_ICO.DEF`
	`WIN_ICO.RC`

***Listing 4.13.** The definition file for the icon example.*

```
NAME            WIN_ICO
DESCRIPTION     'Icon Example'
EXETYPE         WINDOWS
CODE            PRELOAD MOVEABLE
DATA            PRELOAD MOVEABLE MULTIPLE
HEAPSIZE        1024
STACKSIZE       5120
EXPORTS         WndProc
```

***Listing 4.14.** The C source file for the icon example.*

```
#include <windows.h>
#include <stdlib.h>
#include <string.h>

static HANDLE hFootball;
static HANDLE hBasketball;
static HANDLE hGolfball;
static HANDLE hBaseball;

long FAR PASCAL WndProc (HWND hWnd, WORD iMessage,
                         WORD wParam, LONG lParam);

int PASCAL WinMain (HANDLE hInstance, HANDLE hPrevInstance,
                    LPSTR lpszCmdParam, int nCmdShow)

{
HWND hWnd;
MSG Message;
WNDCLASS WndClass;
```

continues

Listing 4.14. continued

```
if (!hPrevInstance)
     {
     WndClass.cbClsExtra = 0;
     WndClass.cbWndExtra = 0;
     WndClass.hbrBackground = GetStockObject(WHITE_BRUSH);
     WndClass.hCursor =  LoadCursor(NULL, IDC_ARROW);
     WndClass.hIcon = LoadIcon (hInstance, "A_RESOURCE");
     WndClass.hInstance = hInstance;
     WndClass.lpfnWndProc = WndProc;
     WndClass.lpszClassName = "WIN_ICO";
     WndClass.lpszMenuName = NULL;
     WndClass.style = CS_HREDRAW ¦ CS_VREDRAW;

     RegisterClass (&WndClass);
     }

hWnd = CreateWindow ("WIN_ICO",      /* class name */
          "Icon Example",            /* Caption */
          WS_OVERLAPPEDWINDOW,       /* Style */
          CW_USEDEFAULT,             /* x position */
          0,                         /* y position */
          CW_USEDEFAULT,             /* cx - size */
          0,                         /* cy - size */
          NULL,                      /* Parent window */
          NULL,                      /* Menu */
          hInstance,                 /* Program Instance */
          NULL);                     /* Parameters */

hFootball = LoadBitmap(hInstance,"FOOTBALL");
hBasketball = LoadBitmap(hInstance,"BASKET");
hGolfball = LoadBitmap(hInstance,"GOLFBALL");
hBaseball = LoadBitmap(hInstance,"BASEBALL");

ShowWindow (hWnd, nCmdShow);
UpdateWindow (hWnd);
while (GetMessage (&Message, 0, 0, 0))
     {
     TranslateMessage(&Message);
     DispatchMessage(&Message);
     }
return Message.wParam;
}

/*****************************************************************/
/*              Window Procedure: WndProc                        */
/*****************************************************************/
```

```
long FAR PASCAL WndProc (HWND hWnd, WORD iMessage, WORD wParam,
                         LONG lParam)
{
HDC hDC, hMemDC;
short x, y;
PAINTSTRUCT PtStr;

switch (iMessage)
     {

     case WM_PAINT:

          hDC = BeginPaint(hWnd, &PtStr);
          hMemDC = CreateCompatibleDC(hDC);
          for (y=30; y<300; y=y+80)
              {
              SelectObject(hMemDC,hFootball);
              BitBlt(hDC,30,y,72,72,hMemDC,0,0,SRCCOPY);
              SelectObject(hMemDC,hBasketball);
              BitBlt(hDC,130,y,72,72,hMemDC,0,0,SRCCOPY);
              SelectObject(hMemDC,hGolfball);
              BitBlt(hDC,230,y,72,72,hMemDC,0,0,SRCCOPY);
              SelectObject(hMemDC,hBaseball);
              BitBlt(hDC,330,y,72,72,hMemDC,0,0,SRCCOPY);
              }
          DeleteDC(hMemDC);
          EndPaint(hWnd, &PtStr);
          return 0;

     case WM_DESTROY:

          DeleteObject(hFootball);
          DeleteObject(hBaseball);
          DeleteObject(hBasketball);
          DeleteObject(hGolfball);
          PostQuitMessage(0);
          return 0;

     default:

          return(DefWindowProc(hWnd, iMessage, wParam,
                 lParam));
     }
}
```

Listing 4.15. *The resource file for the icon example.*

```
FOOTBALL   BITMAP FOOTBALL.BMP
BASKET     BITMAP BASKET.BMP
GOLFBALL   BITMAP GOLFBALL.BMP
BASEBALL   BITMAP BASEBALL.BMP
A_RESOURCE ICON   SPORTS.ICO
```

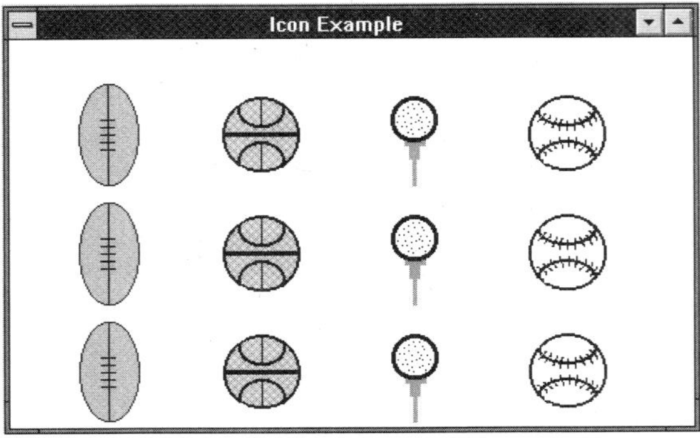

Figure 4.12. *The window created by the icon example.*

Using Menus

A *menu* is a list of application menu items, or commands, that the user can select. A *menu resource* defines the menus that appear on the application's Menu bar. The menu resource also defines the menu items for each of the menus on the Menu bar. Menu items can be represented with either text or bitmaps.

You can create menus by using the Menu editor of the Resource Workshop. The Menu editor contains a variety of tools for designing and creating menus. The Menu editor of the Resource Workshop was used to create the menu used for the menu example in Listings 4.16, 4.17, and 4.18. Figure 4.13 shows the menus created with the Menu editor and used in the menu example.

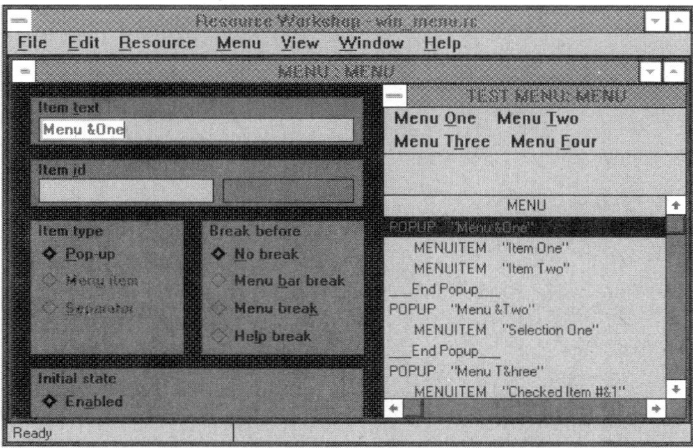

Figure 4.13. *The menu resource.*

The menu example contains three files: the module definition file (Listing 4.16), a C source code file (Listing 4.17), and a resource script file (Listing 4.18). This example contains several menus, each containing at least one menu item. Whenever you select a menu item, a message box appears that echoes the name of the menu item you selected. Figure 4.14 shows the window and message box generated by the menu example.

Adding a menu to your application requires several steps. The first step, of course, is to define the menu resource. As you define the menu resource, you arbitrarily assign unique integer IDs to each of the menu items. Top-level menus are not assigned integer IDs. The menu resource used for the menu example is shown in Figure 4.13.

The second step is to define the created menu resource as the menu for the application. This is accomplished by naming the menu resource as the default menu in the `WndClass.lpszMenuName` line of the window class defined in the `WinMain` function of the application. By declaring the menu in this line of the window class, the menu automatically appears as the application menu. The last step in adding a menu to your application is to define the actions for the menu items.

When you create a menu resource, you are merely defining the menus and menu items. The functionality and actions of the menu items are not defined in the menu resource; they are defined in the window procedure of the application. The action for the menu items is defined in the `WM_COMMAND` code of the window procedure. The `WM_COMMAND` code contains a `switch` statement that contains a `case` for each of the menu item IDs. The code that corresponds to a particular menu item ID defines the actions for that menu item. Although this example merely displays a message box whenever a menu item is selected, you can program a menu item to perform almost any task.

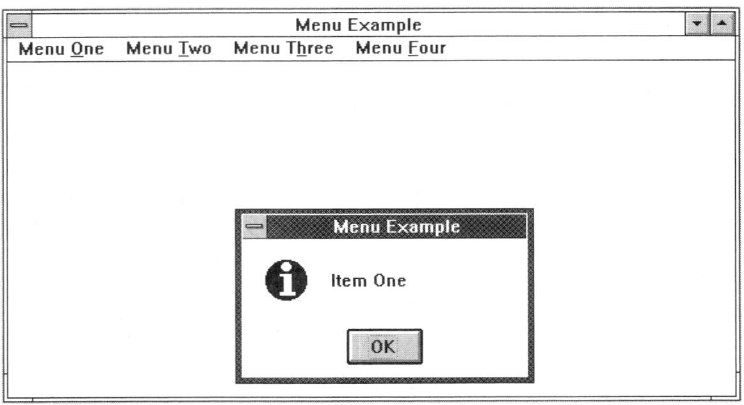

Figure 4.14. *The window created by the menu example.*

The project name and the files used to create the menu example are as follows:

Project Name:	`WIN_MENU`
Files in Project:	`WIN_MENU.C`
	`WIN_MENU.DEF`
	`WIN_MENU.RC`

Listing 4.16. *The definition file for the menu example.*

```
NAME           WIN_MENU
DESCRIPTION    'Menu Example'
EXETYPE        WINDOWS
CODE           PRELOAD MOVEABLE
DATA           PRELOAD MOVEABLE MULTIPLE
HEAPSIZE       1024
STACKSIZE      5120
EXPORTS        WndProc
```

Listing 4.17. *The C source file for the menu example.*

```
#include <windows.h>
#include <stdlib.h>
#include <string.h>

BOOL CheckOne = MF_CHECKED;
BOOL CheckTwo = MF_CHECKED;

long FAR PASCAL WndProc (HWND hWnd, WORD iMessage,
```

```
                          WORD wParam, LONG lParam);

int PASCAL WinMain (HANDLE hInstance, HANDLE hPrevInstance,
                    LPSTR lpszCmdParam, int nCmdShow)

{
HWND hWnd;
MSG Message;
WNDCLASS WndClass;

if (!hPrevInstance)
     {
     WndClass.cbClsExtra = 0;
     WndClass.cbWndExtra = 0;
     WndClass.hbrBackground = GetStockObject(WHITE_BRUSH);
     WndClass.hCursor =  LoadCursor(NULL, IDC_ARROW);
     WndClass.hIcon = LoadIcon (NULL, "END");
     WndClass.hInstance = hInstance;
     WndClass.lpfnWndProc = WndProc;
     WndClass.lpszClassName = "WIN_MENU";
     WndClass.lpszMenuName = "MENU";
     WndClass.style = CS_HREDRAW ¦ CS_VREDRAW;

     RegisterClass (&WndClass);
     }

hWnd = CreateWindow ("WIN_MENU",    /* class name */
          "Menu Example",           /* Caption */
          WS_OVERLAPPEDWINDOW,      /* Style */
          CW_USEDEFAULT,            /* x position */
          0,                        /* y position */
          CW_USEDEFAULT,            /* cx - size */
          0,                        /* cy - size */
          NULL,                     /* Parent window */
          NULL,                     /* Menu */
          hInstance,                /* Program Instance */
          NULL);                    /* Parameters */

ShowWindow(hWnd,nCmdShow);
UpdateWindow(hWnd);
while (GetMessage (&Message, 0, 0, 0))
     {
     TranslateMessage(&Message);
     DispatchMessage(&Message);
     }
return Message.wParam;
```

continues

Listing 4.17. continued

```
}

/*****************************************************************/
/*              Window Procedure: WndProc                        */
/*****************************************************************/

long FAR PASCAL WndProc (HWND hWnd, WORD iMessage, WORD wParam,
                         LONG lParam)
{
HMENU hMenu;

switch (iMessage)
     {
     case WM_COMMAND:
       hMenu = GetMenu(hWnd);

       switch(wParam)
         {
         case 2:
          MessageBox(hWnd,"Item One","Menu Example",
                     MB_ICONINFORMATION¦MB_OK);
          return 0;

         case 3:
          MessageBox(hWnd,"Item Two","Menu Example",
                     MB_ICONINFORMATION¦MB_OK);
          return 0;

         case 5:
          MessageBox(hWnd,"Selection One","Menu Example",
                     MB_ICONINFORMATION¦MB_OK);
          return 0;

         case 7:
          if (CheckOne == MF_CHECKED)
             {
             CheckMenuItem(hMenu,7,MF_BYCOMMAND ¦
                           MF_UNCHECKED);
             CheckOne = MF_UNCHECKED;
             }
             else
             {
             CheckMenuItem(hMenu,7,MF_BYCOMMAND ¦
                           MF_CHECKED);
             CheckOne = MF_CHECKED;
             }
          return 0;
```

```
          case 8:
           if (CheckTwo == MF_CHECKED)
              {
              CheckMenuItem(hMenu,8,MF_BYCOMMAND ¦
                            MF_UNCHECKED);
              CheckTwo = MF_UNCHECKED;
              }
           else
              {
              CheckMenuItem(hMenu,8,MF_BYCOMMAND ¦
                            MF_CHECKED);
              CheckTwo = MF_CHECKED;
              }
           return 0;

          case 10:
           MessageBox(hWnd,"Menu Item One","Menu Example",
                      MB_ICONINFORMATION¦MB_OK);
           return 0;

          case 11:
           MessageBox(hWnd,"Menu Item Two","Menu Example",
                      MB_ICONINFORMATION¦MB_OK);
           return 0;
          }
      break;

      case WM_DESTROY:

        PostQuitMessage(0);
        return 0;

      default:

        return(DefWindowProc(hWnd, iMessage, wParam,
                             lParam));
      }
}
```

Listing 4.18. The resource file for the menu example.

```
MENU  MENU LOADONCALL MOVEABLE PURE DISCARDABLE
BEGIN
  POPUP "Menu &One"
  BEGIN
    MenuItem  "Item One", 2
```

continues

Listing 4.18. continued

```
    MenuItem  "Item Two", 3
  END
  POPUP "Menu &Two"
  BEGIN
    MenuItem  "Selection One", 5
  END
  POPUP "Menu T&hree"
  BEGIN
    MenuItem  "Checked Item #&1", 7, CHECKED
    MenuItem  "Checked Item #&2", 8, CHECKED
  END
  POPUP "Menu &Four"
  BEGIN
    MenuItem  "Menu Item One", 10
    MenuItem  "Menu Item Two", 11
  END
END
```

Using Strings

String resources are text strings that an application can use for menu item names, error messages, dialog box control names, and so forth. String resources are maintained in the resource file of the application. Because the text strings used in an application are all in one location, you can locate and modify the strings easily. Therefore, if you want to display a different string (for example, an error message), you would not need to modify the C source file of the application. You merely modify the line of text in the resource file.

You can create string resources by using the String editor of the Resource Workshop. This editor contains a string table where you can define string resources. The String editor of the Resource Workshop was used to create the strings in the string example in Listings 4.19, 4.20, and 4.21. Figure 4.15 shows the string table created with the String editor and used in the string example.

The string example contains three files: the module definition file (Listing 4.19), a C source code file (Listing 4.20), and a resource script file (Listing 4.21). This example is basically the same as the menu example (a message box appears each time a menu item is selected). The difference is that this example uses references to a string table for the message displayed in the resulting message box. Figure 4.16 shows the window and message box generated by the string example.

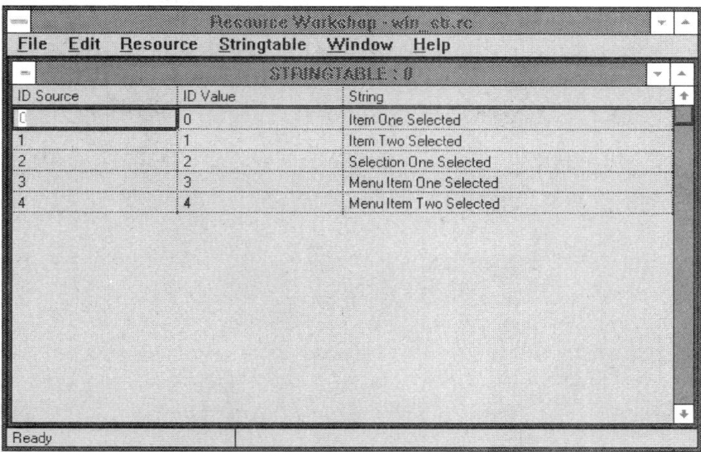

Figure 4.15. *The string resource.*

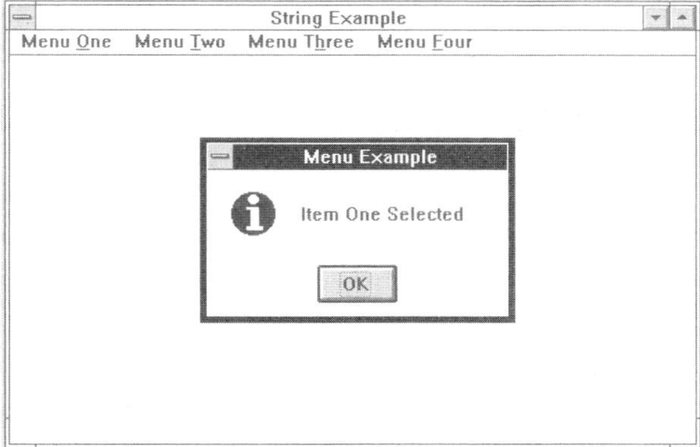

Figure 4.16. *The window created by the string example.*

There are three basic steps for using string tables in an application. The first step is to create the string table. You can create the string table with the String editor or with a simple text editor. The second step is to load the desired string from the string table. This example uses the `LoadString` function to load a string from the string table. The last step is to display the string. In this example, the messages for the message boxes (that are displayed when a menu item is selected) are defined in the string table. The `LoadString` function copies the specified string for the menu item into a buffer, which is then used in the `MessageBox` function to display the specified string.

The following lines show the project name as well as files used to create the string example.

Project Name:	`WIN_STR`
Files in Project:	`WIN_STR.C`
	`WIN_STR.DEF`
	`WIN_STR.RC`

Listing 4.19. *The definition file for the string example.*

```
NAME            WIN_STR
DESCRIPTION     'String Example'
EXETYPE         WINDOWS
CODE            PRELOAD MOVEABLE
DATA            PRELOAD MOVEABLE MULTIPLE
HEAPSIZE        1024
STACKSIZE       5120
EXPORTS         WndProc
```

Listing 4.20. *The C source file for the string example.*

```
#include <windows.h>
#include <stdlib.h>
#include <string.h>

BOOL CheckOne = MF_CHECKED;
BOOL CheckTwo = MF_CHECKED;
HANDLE hIns;

long FAR PASCAL WndProc (HWND hWnd, WORD iMessage,
                         WORD wParam, LONG lParam);

int PASCAL WinMain (HANDLE hInstance, HANDLE hPrevInstance,
                    LPSTR lpszCmdParam, int nCmdShow)

{
HWND hWnd;
MSG Message;
WNDCLASS WndClass;

if (!hPrevInstance)
     {
```

```
     WndClass.cbClsExtra = 0;
     WndClass.cbWndExtra = 0;
     WndClass.hbrBackground = GetStockObject(WHITE_BRUSH);
     WndClass.hCursor =  LoadCursor(NULL, IDC_ARROW);
     WndClass.hIcon = LoadIcon (NULL, "END");
     WndClass.hInstance = hInstance;
     WndClass.lpfnWndProc = WndProc;
     WndClass.lpszClassName = "WIN_STR";
     WndClass.lpszMenuName = "MENU";
     WndClass.style = CS_HREDRAW ¦ CS_VREDRAW;

     RegisterClass (&WndClass);
     }

hIns = hInstance;
hWnd = CreateWindow ("WIN_STR",     /* class name */
          "String Example",         /* Caption */
          WS_OVERLAPPEDWINDOW,      /* Style */
          CW_USEDEFAULT,            /* x position */
          0,                        /* y position */
          CW_USEDEFAULT,            /* cx - size */
          0,                        /* cy - size */
          NULL,                     /* Parent window */
          NULL,                     /* Menu */
          hInstance,                /* Program Instance */
          NULL);                    /* Parameters */

ShowWindow(hWnd,nCmdShow);
UpdateWindow(hWnd);
while (GetMessage (&Message, 0, 0, 0))
     {
     TranslateMessage(&Message);
     DispatchMessage(&Message);
     }
return Message.wParam;
}

/*****************************************************************/
/*              Window Procedure: WndProc                        */
/*****************************************************************/

long FAR PASCAL WndProc (HWND hWnd, WORD iMessage, WORD wParam,
                         LONG lParam)
{
HMENU hMenu;
char buffer[25];

switch (iMessage)
```

continues

Listing 4.20. continued

```
    {
    case WM_COMMAND:
      hMenu = GetMenu(hWnd);

      switch(wParam)
        {
        case 2:
         LoadString(hIns,0,buffer,25);
         MessageBox(hWnd,buffer,"Menu Example",
                    MB_ICONINFORMATION¦MB_OK);
         return 0;

        case 3:
         LoadString(hIns,1,buffer,25);
         MessageBox(hWnd,buffer,"Menu Example",
                    MB_ICONINFORMATION¦MB_OK);
         return 0;

        case 5:
         LoadString(hIns,2,buffer,25);
         MessageBox(hWnd,buffer,"Menu Example",
                    MB_ICONINFORMATION¦MB_OK);
         return 0;

        case 7:
         if (CheckOne == MF_CHECKED)
            {
            CheckMenuItem(hMenu,7,MF_BYCOMMAND ¦
                          MF_UNCHECKED);
            CheckOne = MF_UNCHECKED;
            }
         else
            {
            CheckMenuItem(hMenu,7,MF_BYCOMMAND ¦
                          MF_CHECKED);
            CheckOne = MF_CHECKED;
            }
         return 0;

        case 8:
         if (CheckTwo == MF_CHECKED)
            {
            CheckMenuItem(hMenu,8,MF_BYCOMMAND ¦
                          MF_UNCHECKED);
            CheckTwo = MF_UNCHECKED;
            }
         else
```

```
                {
                CheckMenuItem(hMenu,8,MF_BYCOMMAND ¦
                              MF_CHECKED);
                CheckTwo = MF_CHECKED;
                }
             return 0;

            case 10:
             LoadString(hIns,3,buffer,25);
             MessageBox(hWnd,buffer,"Menu Example",
                        MB_ICONINFORMATION¦MB_OK);
             return 0;

            case 11:
             LoadString(hIns,4,buffer,25);
             MessageBox(hWnd,buffer,"Menu Example",
                        MB_ICONINFORMATION¦MB_OK);
             return 0;
            }
       break;

       case WM_DESTROY:

         PostQuitMessage(0);
         return 0;

       default:

       return(DefWindowProc(hWnd, iMessage, wParam,
             lParam));
       }
}
```

Listing 4.21. *The resource file for the string example.*

```
STRINGTABLE LOADONCALL MOVEABLE PURE DISCARDABLE
BEGIN
  0,  "Item One Selected"
  1,  "Item Two Selected"
  2,  "Selection One Selected"
  3,  "Menu Item One Selected"
  4,  "Menu Item Two Selected"
END

MENU  MENU LOADONCALL MOVEABLE PURE DISCARDABLE
BEGIN
```

continues

Listing 4.21. continued

```
  POPUP "Menu &One"
  BEGIN
    MenuItem  "Item One", 2
    MenuItem  "Item Two", 3
  END
  POPUP "Menu &Two"
  BEGIN
    MenuItem  "Selection One", 5
  END
  POPUP "Menu T&hree"
  BEGIN
    MenuItem  "Checked Item #&1", 7, CHECKED
    MenuItem  "Checked Item #&2", 8, CHECKED
  END
  POPUP "Menu &Four"
  BEGIN
    MenuItem  "Menu Item One", 10
    MenuItem  "Menu Item Two", 11
  END
END
```

This chapter has introduced Windows resources including bitmaps, accelerators, string tables, icons, cursors, and menus. The following chapter provides information on the use of the keyboard as an interface to Windows and your Windows applications.

5

The Keyboard and Windows

The keyboard is a very important input device for Windows applications. Although Windows supports the mouse in its graphical "point-and-click" environment, you do not need to use or even install the mouse to operate Windows successfully. Think of the keyboard, therefore, as the primary input device, although well-designed Windows applications always support both the mouse and the keyboard for input and cursor manipulation.

This chapter introduces the basic concepts and programming principles that you must consider when developing user interfaces that use the keyboard as the primary input device. Chapter 6, "The Mouse and Windows," addresses using the mouse as an input device.

Keyboard Input

A Windows application receives input from the keyboard in the following manner. When you press or release a key, the keyboard device driver passes the appropriate keyboard messages to Windows. The keyboard messages are placed in the system queue and then sent to the message queue of the appropriate application. The application's window procedure then processes the messages. Figure 5.1 shows this procedure.

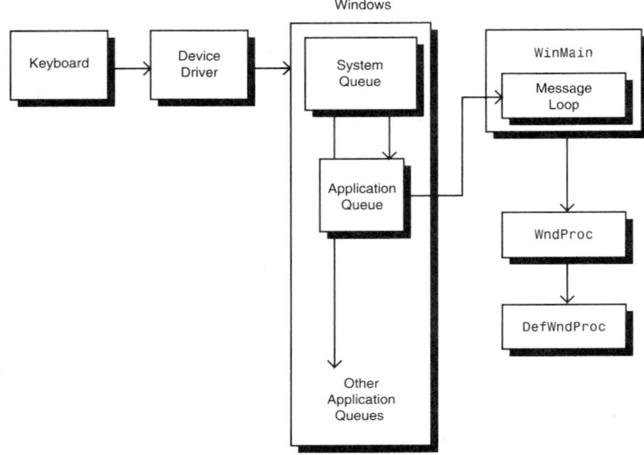

Figure 5.1. *Keyboard input.*

After receiving input from the keyboard, Windows must determine which application should receive the input. Windows solves this problem by sending input messages to the window that has the "input focus," which is either the active window or a "child" of the active window. The window that has the input focus is the targeted recipient of all input messages. The user can distinguish the *active window* in several ways. If the active window has a caption bar, the bar is highlighted. If the active window has a dialog frame, the frame is highlighted. A *child window* that has the input focus usually contains a blinking cursor or caret, and the parent window must be active.

Keyboard Messages

Keyboard input is divided into two categories: keystrokes and characters. Whenever you press or release a key, a *keystroke message* is generated. When a keystroke combination occurs that results in a displayable character, a *character message* is generated—assuming that you are using the traditional message loop that contains the `TranslateMessage` function, as follows:

```
while (GetMessage (&Message, 0, 0, 0))
     {
     TranslateMessage(&Message);
     DispatchMessage(&Message);
     }
return Message.wParam;
```

If you press the A key, for example, two keystroke messages—one for pressing and one for releasing the key—are generated. An additional character message is also sent, however, because the keystroke combination results in a displayable character, the letter *A*. (You learn more about this later in this chapter.)

There are two general types of keystroke messages: system and non-system. Table 5.1 lists these messages. *System messages* correspond only to keystrokes that use the Alt key and invoke options from the application or system menus. *Non-system messages* correspond to virtually all other keystrokes.

Table 5.1. Keystroke messages.

Message	*Type*	*Meaning*
WM_KEYDOWN	Non-system	Non-system key is pressed
WM_KEYUP	Non-system	Non-system key is released
WM_SYSKEYDOWN	System	System key is pressed
WM_SYSKEYUP	System	System key is released

lParam

The keystroke message contains vital information on the keystroke in its two variables, `wParam` and `lParam`. The 32-bit `lParam` variable of the keystroke message is divided into the following six fields:

- Repeat count (bits 0 to 15)
- OEM scan code (bits 16 to 23)
- Extended key flag (bit 24)

- Context code (bit 29)
- Previous key state (bit 30)
- Transition state (bit 31)

> **Note:** Bits 25 to 28 are reserved.

The *repeat count* is the number of keystrokes that the message represents. The repeat count is one, except when the key is held down. The window procedure often is not fast enough to process the key-down messages that result from a key being pressed and held down. When this happens, Windows combines several key-down messages and then increments the repeat count.

The *OEM scan code* is the scan code value sent from the keyboard. Because this field is device-dependent, the value generally is ignored.

The *context code* is set to 1 if the Alt key is pressed. Otherwise, the context code is set to 0.

The *previous key state* helps to determine whether the message is the result of automated typing actions, such as those generated when you hold down a key. The previous key state is 0 if the key was previously up, and 1 if the key was previously down.

The *transition state* indicates whether the key is being pressed or released. The transition state is set to 0 when the key is being pressed down—`WM_KEYDOWN` or `WM_SYSKEYDOWN` key messages. The transition state is set to 1 when the key is being released—`WM_KEYUP` or `WM_SYSKEYUP` key messages.

wParam

The `wParam` parameter of the keystroke message contains the virtual key code that identifies the pressed key. The virtual key code is the device-dependent scan code converted by the Windows system to a device-independent form. Virtual keys are device-independent and are defined in the windows.h include file. Table 5.2 lists the virtual keys and their constants.

Table 5.2. The virtual key codes.

Decimal	*Hex*	*Constant*	*Key*
1	01	VK_LBUTTON	
2	02	VK_RBUTTON	
3	03	VK_CANCEL	Ctrl-break
4	04	VK_MBUTTON	
8	08	VK_BACK	Backspace
9	09	VK_TAB	Tab
12	0C	VK_CLEAR	Numeric keypad 5 with Num Lock off
13	0D	VK_RETURN	Enter
16	10	VK_SHIFT	Shift
17	11	VK_CONTROL	Ctrl
18	12	VK_MENU	Alt
19	13	VK_PAUSE	Pause
20	14	VK_CAPITAL	Caps Lock
27	1B	VK_ESCAPE	Esc
32	20	VK_SPACE	Space bar
33	21	VK_PRIOR	PgUp
34	22	VK_NEXT	PgDn
35	23	VK_END	End
36	24	VK_HOME	Home
37	25	VK_LEFT	Left arrow
38	26	VK_UP	Up arrow
39	27	VK_RIGHT	Right arrow
40	28	VK_DOWN	Down arrow
41	29	VK_SELECT	
42	2A	VK_PRINT	
43	2B	VK_EXECUTE	
44	2C	VK_SNAPSHOT	PrtSc
45	2D	VK_INSERT	Ins
46	2E	VK_DELETE	Del
47	2F	VK_HELP	
48–57	30–39	VK_0 to VK_9	0 to 9 on main keyboard
65–90	41–5A	VK_A to VK_Z	A to Z

continues

Table 5.2. continued

Decimal	Hex	Constant	Key
96–105	60–69	VK_NUMPAD0 to VK_NUMPAD9	Numeric keypad 0 to numeric keypad 9 (Num Lock on)
106	6A	VK_MULTIPLY	* on numeric keypad
107	6B	VK_ADD	+ on numeric keypad
108	6C	VK_SEPARATOR	
109	6D	VK_SUBTRACT	[-] on numeric keypad
110	6E	VK_DECIMAL	. on numeric keypad
111	6F	VK_DIVIDE	/ on numeric keypad
112–123	70–7B	VK_F1 to VK_F12	F1 to F12
124	7C	VK_F13	
125	7D	VK_F14	
126	7E	VK_F15	
127	7F	VK_F16	
144	90	VK_NUMLOCK	Num Lock

Character Messages

The customary message loop of the `WinMain` function contains the `TranslateMessage` function, which translates keystroke messages into character messages. Again, there are two types of character messages: non-system and system. Table 5.3 lists the character messages.

Table 5.3. Character messages.

Message	Type	Meaning
WM_CHAR	Non-system	Non-system character
WM_DEADCHAR	Non-system	Non-system dead character; *dead characters* do not display characters but modify the display of other characters
WM_SYSCHAR	System	System character
WM_SYSDEADCHAR	System	System dead character

The character messages contain the same two variables as the keyboard messages, `wParam` and `lParam`. For the character message, `lParam` is the same as `lParam` for keyboard messages. For the character message, however, `wParam` differs from `wParam` for the keyboard message. For character messages, `wParam` contains the ASCII code for the character.

Character Sets

Windows supports two extended character sets: OEM and ANSI. The *OEM character set* is the IBM character set with which MS-DOS programmers are familiar. However, Windows applications seldom use the OEM character set. Instead, Windows applications most frequently use the *ANSI character set*. Windows provides several functions for the conversion between character sets. Table 5.4 lists these functions and explains their conversions.

Table 5.4. *Conversion functions.*

Function	*Meaning*
`AnsiToOem`	Converts an ANSI string to an OEM character string
`AnsiToOemBuff`	Converts an ANSI string in a buffer to an OEM string
`OemToAnsi`	Converts an OEM character string to an ANSI string
`OemToAnsiBuff`	Converts an OEM character string in a buffer to an ANSI string

The Caret

Windows uses the caret to indicate the current text position. In many environments, the term *cursor* or *text cursor* refers to the current text position. In Windows, however, the term *caret* refers to the current text position and the term *cursor* refers to the current mouse position. The caret is a system resource that is shared among applications, so the Windows environment has only one caret. Only the window that has the input focus can display the caret. The keyboard example in Listings 5.1 and 5.2 demonstrates the use of the caret and the keyboard messages.

The Keyboard Example

The keyboard example in Listings 5.1 and 5.2 demonstrates the use of the caret and keyboard messages for the input and editing of a line of text. This example shows the caret and maintains its position relative to the line of text.

The keyboard example demonstrates how you can create a simple single-line text editor. This example enables you to enter text, and it provides the basic capabilities of an editor. The Left and Right arrow keys enable you to move the caret. The End, Del, and Home keys enable you, respectively, to move the caret to the end of the line, to delete a character at the caret, and to move the caret to the beginning of the line.

The `WinMain` function of this example is similar to what you have already seen in this book. The window procedure, however, contains two significant differences. The window procedure contains the standard switch statement and checks for two keyboard input cases, `WM_CHAR` and `WM_KEYDOWN`. The code for `WM_CHAR` monitors input and checks to make sure that the input is valid. The `WM_KEYDOWN` code updates the caret position and performs the appropriate screen updates for the key that was pressed. Figure 5.2 shows the window created by the keyboard example.

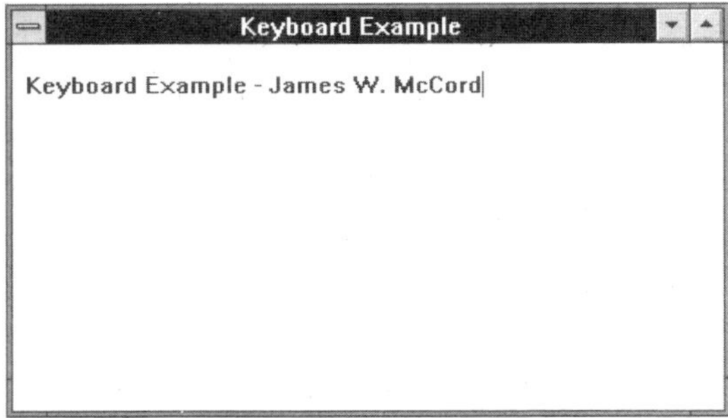

Figure 5.2. *The window created by the keyboard example.*

The project name and the files used to create the keyboard example are as follows:

Project Name:	`WIN_KEY`
Files in Project:	`WIN_KEY.C`
	`WIN_KEY.DEF`

Listing 5.1. ***The definition file for the keyboard example.***

```
NAME            WIN_KEY
DESCRIPTION     'Keyboard Example'
EXETYPE         WINDOWS
```

```
CODE            PRELOAD MOVEABLE
DATA            PRELOAD MOVEABLE MULTIPLE
HEAPSIZE        1024
STACKSIZE       5120
EXPORTS         WndProc
```

Listing 5.2. *The C source file for the keyboard example.*

```
#include <windows.h>
#include <stdlib.h>
#include <string.h>

long FAR PASCAL WndProc (HWND hWnd, WORD iMessage,
                         WORD wParam, LONG lParam);

void NEAR PASCAL CaretPos(HWND hWnd, int nArrayPos,
                          char *cCharBuf, int *xCaret,
                          int *yCaret, int nCharWidth);

int PASCAL WinMain (HANDLE hInstance, HANDLE hPrevInstance,
                    LPSTR lpszCmdParam, int nCmdShow)

{
HWND hWnd;
MSG Message;
WNDCLASS WndClass;

if (!hPrevInstance)
     {
     WndClass.cbClsExtra = 0;
     WndClass.cbWndExtra = 0;
     WndClass.hbrBackground = GetStockObject(WHITE_BRUSH);
     WndClass.hCursor =  LoadCursor(NULL, IDC_ARROW);
     WndClass.hIcon = LoadIcon (NULL, "END");
     WndClass.hInstance = hInstance;
     WndClass.lpfnWndProc = WndProc;
     WndClass.lpszClassName = "WIN_KEY";
     WndClass.lpszMenuName = NULL;
     WndClass.style = CS_HREDRAW ¦ CS_VREDRAW;

     RegisterClass (&WndClass);
     }

hWnd = CreateWindow ("WIN_KEY",      /* class name */
          "Keyboard Example",        /* Caption */
          WS_OVERLAPPEDWINDOW,       /* Style */
          CW_USEDEFAULT,             /* x position */
```

continues

Listing 5.2. continued

```
          0,                         /* y position */
          CW_USEDEFAULT,             /* cx - size */
          0,                         /* cy - size */
          NULL,                      /* Parent window */
          NULL,                      /* Menu */
          hInstance,                 /* Program Instance */
          NULL);                     /* Parameters */

ShowWindow(hWnd,nCmdShow);
while (GetMessage (&Message, 0, 0, 0))
     {
     TranslateMessage(&Message);
     DispatchMessage(&Message);
     }
return Message.wParam;
}

/*****************************************************************/
/*              Window Procedure: WndProc                        */
/*****************************************************************/

long FAR PASCAL WndProc (HWND hWnd, WORD iMessage, WORD wParam,
                         LONG lParam)
{
#define BufSize 40
static unsigned char cCharBuf[BufSize];
static int nNumChar = 0;
static int nArrayPos = 0;
static int nLnHeight;
static int nCharWidth;
static int xCaret, yCaret;
int x;
HDC hDC;
TEXTMETRIC tm;
PAINTSTRUCT PtStr;

switch (iMessage)
     {
     case WM_CHAR:
          {
          if (wParam == VK_BACK)
             {
             if (nArrayPos == 0)
                 MessageBox(hWnd,"Can't Backspace",NULL,
                            MB_OK);
             else
                {
```

```
                nArrayPos = nArrayPos - 1;
                CaretPos(hWnd,nArrayPos,cCharBuf,
                    &xCaret,&yCaret,nCharWidth);
                for (x=nArrayPos; x<nNumChar; x=x+1)
                cCharBuf[x]=cCharBuf[x+1];
                nNumChar= nNumChar - 1;
                InvalidateRect(hWnd,NULL,TRUE);
                }
              break;
              }

        if (wParam <= VK_ESCAPE)
           {
           MessageBox(hWnd,"Try another key",NULL,
                      MB_OK);
           break;
           }

        if (nNumChar >= 40)
           {
           MessageBox(hWnd,"Buffer is full",NULL,
                      MB_OK);
           break;
           }

        for (x=nNumChar;x>nArrayPos;x=x-1)
           cCharBuf[x] = cCharBuf[x-1];
        cCharBuf[nArrayPos] = (unsigned char)wParam;
        nArrayPos = nArrayPos + 1;
        nNumChar = nNumChar + 1;
        CaretPos(hWnd,nArrayPos,cCharBuf,&xCaret,
                 &yCaret,nCharWidth);
        InvalidateRect(hWnd,NULL,TRUE);
        }
        break;


   case WM_CREATE:
        {
        hDC = GetDC(hWnd);
        GetTextMetrics(hDC,&tm);
        nLnHeight = tm.tmHeight + tm.tmExternalLeading;
        nCharWidth = tm.tmAveCharWidth;
        yCaret = nLnHeight;
        ReleaseDC(hWnd,hDC);
        }
        break;
```

continues

Listing 5.2. continued

```
    case WM_SETFOCUS:

         CreateCaret(hWnd,0,0,nLnHeight);
         CaretPos(hWnd,nArrayPos,cCharBuf,&xCaret,
                  &yCaret,nCharWidth);
         ShowCaret(hWnd);
         break;

    case WM_KILLFOCUS:

         DestroyCaret();
         break;

    case WM_KEYDOWN:
         {
         switch(wParam)
           {
           case VK_END:
             nArrayPos = nNumChar;
             CaretPos(hWnd,nArrayPos,cCharBuf,&xCaret,
                      &yCaret,nCharWidth);
             break;;

           case VK_HOME:
             nArrayPos = 0;
             CaretPos(hWnd,nArrayPos,cCharBuf,&xCaret,
              &yCaret,nCharWidth);
             break;

           case VK_DELETE:
             if(nArrayPos == nNumChar)
               MessageBox(hWnd,"End of Buffer",NULL,
                           MB_OK);
             else
               {
               for (x=nArrayPos; x<nNumChar; x=x+1)
               cCharBuf[x] = cCharBuf[x+1];
               nNumChar = nNumChar - 1;
               InvalidateRect(hWnd,NULL,TRUE);
               }
             break;

           case VK_LEFT:
             if (nArrayPos > 0)
               {
               nArrayPos = nArrayPos - 1;
               CaretPos(hWnd,nArrayPos,cCharBuf,&xCaret,
                        &yCaret,nCharWidth);
```

```
                  }
                else
                  MessageBox(hWnd,"Can't move left",NULL,
                             MB_OK);
                break;

              case VK_RIGHT:
                if (nArrayPos < nNumChar)
                 {
                 nArrayPos = nArrayPos + 1;
                 CaretPos(hWnd,nArrayPos,cCharBuf,&xCaret,
                          &yCaret,nCharWidth);
                 }
                else
                 MessageBox(hWnd,"At end of buffer",NULL,
                            MB_OK);
                break;
              }
            }
            break;

      case WM_PAINT:
           {
           hDC = BeginPaint(hWnd,&PtStr);
           TextOut(hDC,nCharWidth,nLnHeight,cCharBuf,
                   nNumChar);
           EndPaint(hWnd,&PtStr);
           }
           break;

      case WM_DESTROY:

           PostQuitMessage(0);
           break;

      default:
           return(DefWindowProc(hWnd,iMessage,wParam,
                  lParam));
      }
return 0;
}

void NEAR PASCAL CaretPos(HWND hWnd, int nArrayPos,
                          char *cCharBuf, int *xCaret,
                          int *yCaret, int nCharWidth)
{
DWORD dWord;
```

continues

Listing 5.2. continued

```
HDC hDC;

hDC = GetDC(hWnd);
dWord = GetTextExtent(hDC,cCharBuf,nArrayPos);
ReleaseDC(hWnd,hDC);
*xCaret = LOWORD(dWord) + nCharWidth;
SetCaretPos(*xCaret,*yCaret);
}
```

This chapter has introduced the keyboard and its use as the interface to Windows and Windows applications. The next chapter presents the use of the mouse as the interface to Windows and your Windows applications.

6

The Mouse and Windows

Many people associate the mouse with Windows. This association is natural because graphical user interfaces such as Windows offer the "point-and-click" advantage. Sometimes the Microsoft Mouse is bundled with the Windows software product. As a Windows programmer you are tempted to assume that the user has a mouse—but don't count on it. As mentioned in Chapter 5, Windows can be installed and operated successfully without a mouse. Therefore, a well-designed Windows program supports the mouse but does not require one.

This chapter introduces the basics of using the mouse as an input device. By combining the information provided in this chapter with the keyboard information in Chapter 5, you can design an effective interface for your Windows application that can be manipulated with either the keyboard or the mouse.

Mouse Input

Most programmers are familiar with the basic operations of the mouse. The cursor, a special bitmap, indicates the current mouse position on the screen. Table 6.1 lists the cursors that Windows has predefined. The mouse cursor moves as the mouse moves and the mouse buttons provide input. The actions resulting from the mouse input depend on the mouse position and the mouse button pressed. Several actions can be taken with the mouse buttons, including clicking, double-clicking, and dragging.

Table 6.1. Predefined cursors.

Constant	*Meaning*
IDC_ARROW	Arrow cursor
IDC_CROSS	Crosshair cursor
IDC_IBEAM	I-beam text cursor
IDC_ICON	Empty icon
IDC_SIZE	Square with small square in lower-right corner
IDC_SIZENESW	Cursor with arrows pointing northeast and southwest
IDC_SIZENS	Cursor with arrows pointing north and south
IDC_SIZENWSE	Cursor with arrows pointing northwest and southeast
IDC_SIZEWE	Cursor with arrows pointing west and east
IDC_UPARROW	Vertical arrow cursor
IDC_WAIT	Hourglass cursor

Clicking refers to pressing and releasing a mouse button. Clicking can be used to select objects and initiate program commands. *Double-clicking* refers to pressing and releasing a mouse button two times in a short time period (1/2 second is the default setting for Windows). Double-clicking activates the default action of the selected item. *Dragging* refers to pressing the mouse button and moving the mouse while the mouse button is still pressed. Dragging often is used for selecting menu items and for moving objects.

Windows receives mouse input through the mouse device driver. The mouse driver, if installed, is loaded when Windows starts (unless the device driver already is loaded) and determines whether a mouse is present. If a mouse is present, the device driver notifies Windows of any mouse event. A window receives a mouse event (in the form of a message) whenever the mouse event occurs within the window. The window receiving the mouse event does not have to be active or have the input focus.

Mouse Messages

The window procedure of a Windows application is notified of a mouse event by a mouse message. There are three general classifications of mouse messages: the hit test message, non-client area messages, and client area messages.

The Hit Test Message

The hit test message is sent before any client or non-client mouse messages. Each time the mouse is moved, the message `WM_NCHITTEST` is sent to the window that contains the cursor to determine the position and region of the mouse (see Chapter 14, "Windows Messages," for more information). The `lParam` parameter of the `WM_NCHITTEST` message contains the x and y screen coordinates of the cursor at the time the message was sent.

The `WM_NCHITTEST` message usually is passed to the `DefWindowProc` function. The return value of the `DefWindowProc` function indicates the area containing the cursor. The `DefWindowProc` function returns one of the hit test values listed in Table 6.2.

Table 6.2. *Hit test codes.*

Hit Test Code	*Meaning*
`HTBOTTOM`	Lower horizontal window border
`HTBOTTOMLEFT`	Lower-left corner of window border
`HTBOTTOMRIGHT`	Lower-right corner of window border
`HTCAPTION`	Caption area
`HTCLIENT`	Client area
`HTERROR`	Screen background or window dividing line; produces a beep on error
`HTGROWBOX`	Size box
`HTHSCROLL`	Horizontal scroll bar
`HTLEFT`	Left window border
`HTMENU`	Menu area
`HTNOWHERE`	Screen background or window dividing line
`HTREDUCE`	Minimize box
`HTRIGHT`	Right window border
`HTSIZE`	Size box

continues

Table 6.2. continued

Hit Test Code	*Meaning*
HTSYSMENU	Control menu box
HTTOP	Upper horizontal window border
HTTOPLEFT	Upper-left corner of window border
HTTOPRIGHT	Upper-right corner of window border
HTTRANSPARENT	Window covered by another window
HTVSCROLL	Vertical scroll bar
HTZOOM	Maximize box

The `WM_NCHITTEST` message generates all other mouse messages. Either a client area or non-client area message is generated, depending on the value that the `DefWindowProc` function returns.

Client Area Mouse Messages

When a mouse event occurs in the client area, a client area mouse message is generated. Table 6.3 lists the client area mouse messages.

Table 6.3. Client area mouse messages.

Message	*Meaning*
WM_LBUTTONDOWN	The left mouse button was pressed in the client area
WM_LBUTTONUP	The left mouse button was released in the client area
WM_LBUTTONDBLCLK	The left mouse button was double-clicked in the client area
WM_MBUTTONDOWN	The middle mouse button was pressed in the client area
WM_MBUTTONUP	The middle mouse button was released in the client area
WM_MBUTTONDBLCLK	The middle mouse button was double-clicked in the client area
WM_MOUSEMOVE	The mouse was moved in the client area
WM_RBUTTONDOWN	The right mouse button was pressed in the client area
WM_RBUTTONUP	The right mouse button was released in the client area
WM_RBUTTONDBLCLK	The right mouse button was double-clicked in the client area

The lParam parameter of each of the client area messages contains the mouse position. The low-order word of lParam contains the x-coordinate of the mouse position; the high-order word of lParam contains the y-coordinate of the mouse position. The coordinates expressed in lParam are relative to the upper-left corner of the window.

The wParam parameter of the client area messages contains a value that indicates the status of the various virtual keys. The wParam parameter can be a combination of the values listed in Table 6.4.

Table 6.4. wParam *values.*

Value	*Meaning*
MK_CONTROL	Ctrl key is down
MK_LBUTTON	Left button is down
MK_MBUTTON	Middle button is down
MK_RBUTTON	Right button is down
MK_SHIFT	Shift key is down

By using the lParam and wParam parameters of the client area mouse messages, you can determine the mouse position and status of the mouse keys.

Non-Client Area Mouse Messages

Whenever a mouse event occurs at a location other than in the client area but still inside the window (such as the menu, caption bar, or scroll bar), a non-client area message is generated. Table 6.5 lists the non-client area mouse messages. Non-client area messages usually are not handled by the application but instead are sent to DefWindowProc.

Table 6.5. *Non-client area mouse messages.*

Message	*Meaning*
WM_LBUTTONDOWN	The left mouse button was pressed in a non-client area
WM_LBUTTONUP	The left mouse button was released in a non-client area
WM_LBUTTONDBLCLK	The left mouse button was double-clicked in a non-client area
WM_MBUTTONDOWN	The middle mouse button was pressed in a non-client area

continues

Table 6.5. continued

Message	*Meaning*
WM_MBUTTONUP	The middle mouse button was released in a non-client area
WM_MBUTTONDBLCLK	The middle mouse button was double-clicked in a non-client area
WM_MOUSEMOVE	The mouse was moved in a non-client area
WM_RBUTTONDOWN	The right mouse button was pressed in a non-client area
WM_RBUTTONUP	The right mouse button was released in a non-client area
WM_RBUTTONDBLCLK	The right mouse button was double-clicked in a non-client area

The `lParam` parameter of the non-client area mouse messages contains the screen coordinates of the mouse position at the time that the message was generated. The low-order word of `lParam` contains the horizontal coordinate of the mouse position; the high-order word of `lParam` contains the vertical coordinate of the mouse position.

The `wParam` parameter of the non-client area mouse messages contains the value determined at the time that the `WM_NCHITTEST` message was generated. This value indicates the non-client area at which the cursor was located when the message was generated. Table 6.3 lists the possible values for `wParam`.

By using the `lParam` and `wParam` parameters of the non-client area mouse messages, you can determine the mouse position and non-client area associated with the message.

The Mouse Example

The mouse example in Listings 6.1 and 6.2 demonstrates one way that you can monitor mouse movements. The example monitors the non-client area message `WM_MOUSEMOVE` and determines whether the mouse is located within the one of nine predefined rectangular regions. Any time the cursor moves within one of the regions, a new cursor is displayed. Ten different cursors can be displayed in this example.

The `WinMain` function follows the same format as the examples previously presented in this book. The window procedure, however, differs from previous examples. The window procedure for the mouse example checks for the `WM_MOUSEMOVE` message. When the `WM_MOUSEMOVE` message is received by the window procedure, the

`WM_MOUSEMOVE` code determines the mouse position. If the mouse position is within any one of nine predefined areas, the cursor is changed using the `LoadCursor` and `SetCursor` functions.

The project name and the files used to create the mouse example are as follows:

Project Name:	`WIN_MOUS`
Files in Project:	`WIN_MOUS.C`
	`WIN_MOUS.DEF`

Listing 6.1. *The definition file for the mouse example.*

```
NAME           WIN_MOUS
DESCRIPTION    'Mouse Example'
EXETYPE        WINDOWS
CODE           PRELOAD MOVEABLE
DATA           PRELOAD MOVEABLE MULTIPLE
HEAPSIZE       1024
STACKSIZE      5120
EXPORTS        WndProc
```

Listing 6.2. *The C source file for the mouse example.*

```
#include <windows.h>
#include <stdlib.h>
#include <string.h>

long FAR PASCAL WndProc (HWND hWnd, WORD iMessage,
                         WORD wParam, LONG lParam);

int PASCAL WinMain (HANDLE hInstance, HANDLE hPrevInstance,
                    LPSTR lpszCmdParam, int nCmdShow)

{
HWND hWnd;
MSG Message;
WNDCLASS WndClass;

if (!hPrevInstance)
     {
     WndClass.cbClsExtra = 0;
     WndClass.cbWndExtra = 0;
     WndClass.hbrBackground = GetStockObject(WHITE_BRUSH);
     WndClass.hCursor = NULL;
     WndClass.hIcon = LoadIcon (NULL, "END");
```

continues

Listing 6.2. continued

```
     WndClass.hInstance = hInstance;
     WndClass.lpfnWndProc = WndProc;
     WndClass.lpszClassName = "WIN_MOUS";
     WndClass.lpszMenuName = NULL;
     WndClass.style = CS_HREDRAW ¦ CS_VREDRAW;

     RegisterClass (&WndClass);
     }

hWnd = CreateWindow ("WIN_MOUS",   /* class name */
          "Mouse Example",         /* Caption */
          WS_OVERLAPPEDWINDOW,     /* Style */
          CW_USEDEFAULT,           /* x position */
          0,                       /* y position */
          CW_USEDEFAULT,           /* cx - size */
          0,                       /* cy - size */
          NULL,                    /* Parent window */
          NULL,                    /* Menu */
          hInstance,               /* Program Instance */
          NULL);                   /* Parameters */

ShowWindow (hWnd, nCmdShow);
UpdateWindow(hWnd);
while (GetMessage (&Message, 0, 0, 0))
     {
     TranslateMessage(&Message);
     DispatchMessage(&Message);
     }
return Message.wParam;
}

/**************************************************************/
/*              Window Procedure: WndProc                     */
/**************************************************************/

long FAR PASCAL WndProc (HWND hWnd, WORD iMessage, WORD wParam,
                         LONG lParam)
{
HDC hDC;
PAINTSTRUCT PtStr;
WORD x, y;
HCURSOR hCursor;

switch (iMessage)
     {

     case WM_MOUSEMOVE:
```

```
x = LOWORD(lParam);
y = HIWORD(lParam);

if (x>=50 && x<=200 && y>=50 && y<=200)
  {

  if (x>=50 && x<=100 && y>=50 && y<=100)
  {
  hCursor = LoadCursor(NULL,IDC_CROSS);
  SetCursor(hCursor);
  }

  if (x>=100 && x<=150 && y>=50 && y<=100)
  {
  hCursor = LoadCursor(NULL,IDC_IBEAM);
  SetCursor(hCursor);
  }

  if (x>=150 && x<=200 && y>=50 && y<=100)
  {
  hCursor = LoadCursor(NULL,IDC_SIZE);
  SetCursor(hCursor);
  }

  if (x>=50 && x<=100 && y>=100 && y<=150)
  {
  hCursor = LoadCursor(NULL,IDC_SIZENESW);
  SetCursor(hCursor);
  }

  if (x>=100 && x<=150 && y>=100 && y<=150)
  {
  hCursor = LoadCursor(NULL,IDC_SIZENS);
  SetCursor(hCursor);
  }

  if (x>=150 && x<=200 && y>=100 && y<=150)
  {
  hCursor = LoadCursor(NULL,IDC_SIZENWSE);
  SetCursor(hCursor);
  }

  if (x>=50 && x<=100 && y>=150 && y<=200)
  {
  hCursor = LoadCursor(NULL,IDC_SIZEWE);
  SetCursor(hCursor);
  }
```

continues

Listing 6.2. continued

```
          if (x>=100 && x<=150 && y>=150 && y<=200)
          {
          hCursor = LoadCursor(NULL,IDC_UPARROW);
          SetCursor(hCursor);
          }

          if (x>=150 && x<=200 && y>=150 && y<=200)
          {
          hCursor = LoadCursor(NULL,IDC_WAIT);
          SetCursor(hCursor);
          }
          }
        else
          {
          hCursor = LoadCursor(NULL,IDC_ARROW);
          SetCursor(hCursor);
          }
        return 0;

     case WM_DESTROY:

          PostQuitMessage(0);
          return 0;

     default:

          return(DefWindowProc(hWnd, iMessage, wParam,
                 lParam));
     }
}
```

This chapter has presented the use of the mouse as an interface to Windows and Windows applications. The next chapter introduces the use of child windows within the client area of a Windows application.

7

Windows and Child Windows

Unlike most previous examples in this book, consisting of only one window, most Windows applications actually consist of several windows. Applications that operate under the multiple document interface (MDI) standard create a unique window for each document in the program. Other applications create multiple windows in the form of edit controls, list boxes, buttons, and so forth.

This chapter focuses on the creation and use of parent and child windows. The following discussion on child windows is limited, though, to the application of child window controls only. Chapter 9 discusses the use of child windows that follow the MDI standard.

Creating a Window

Creating a window consists of two basic steps: creating a window class and creating the window itself.

Step 1: Defining Window Classes

A *window class* provides the information required to create a window, including the name of the window procedure that processes the messages for the window. The examples in this book have registered the window class by using code similar to the following:

```
WNDCLASS WndClass;

if (!hPrevInstance)
     {
     WndClass.cbClsExtra = 0;
     WndClass.cbWndExtra = 0;
     WndClass.hbrBackground = GetStockObject(WHITE_BRUSH);
     WndClass.hCursor =  LoadCursor(NULL, IDC_ARROW);
     WndClass.hIcon = LoadIcon (NULL, "END");
     WndClass.hInstance = hInstance;
     WndClass.lpfnWndProc = WndProc;
     WndClass.lpszClassName = "WIN_ONE";
     WndClass.lpszMenuName = NULL;
     WndClass.style = CS_HREDRAW ¦ CS_VREDRAW;

     RegisterClass (&WndClass);
     }
```

In this block of code, you are defining the fields of a `WNDCLASS` data structure called `WndClass`. To better understand this code, you must examine the `WNDCLASS` data structure that follows:

```
typedef struct tagWNDCLASS {
     WORD style;
     long (FAR PASCAL *lpfnWndProc)();
     int cbClsExtra;
     int cbWndExtra;
     HANDLE hInstance;
     HICON hIcon;
     HCURSOR hCursor;
     HBRUSH hbrBackground;
     LPSTR lpszMenuName;
     LPSTR lpszClassName;
} WNDCLASS;
```

The fields of the `WNDCLASS` structure are the following:

- `style` defines the class style. The `style` field can be any combination (using bitwise OR) of the following values:

Value	*Meaning*
`CS_BYTEALIGNCLIENT`	Aligns a window's client area to the byte boundary in the horizontal direction
`CS_BYTEALIGNWINDOW`	Aligns a window to the byte boundary in the horizontal direction
`CS_CLASSDC`	Gives the window class its own display context
`CS_DBLCLKS`	Sends double-click messages to a window
`CS_GLOBALCLASS`	Indicates that the window class is an application global class
`CS_HREDRAW`	Redraws the window if the horizontal window size is changed
`CS_NOCLOSE`	Disables the close option on the `System` menu
`CS_OWNDC`	Gives each window its own device context
`CS_PARENTDC`	Gives the display context of the parent window to the window class
`CS_SAVEBITS`	Saves the part of the screen image that is covered by a window
`CS_VREDRAW`	Redraws the window if the vertical window size is changed

- `lpfnWndProc` specifies a pointer to the window function.
- `cbClsExtra` indicates the number of bytes to allocate following the window class structure.
- `hInstance` specifies the class module. This field cannot be set to `NULL`.
- `hIcon` specifies the class icon. This field can be set to `NULL` or specify the handle of an icon resource. When `hIcon` is set to `NULL`, its application must draw the icon.
- `hCursor` specifies the class cursor. This field either should identify the handle of a cursor resource or be set to `NULL`. When the field is set to `NULL`, the application must specify the cursor shape.
- `hbrBackground` specifies the class background brush. This field is set to either the handle of a physical brush or to a color value. If the field specifies a color value, 1 must be added; for example, `COLOR_BACKGROUND` + 1. The color values are the following:

`COLOR_ACTIVEBORDER`	`COLOR_HIGHLIGHTTEXT`
`COLOR_ACTIVECAPTION`	`COLOR_INACTIVEBORDER`

COLOR_APPWORKSPACE	COLOR_INACTIVECAPTION
COLOR_BACKGROUND	COLOR_MENU
COLOR_BTNFACE	COLOR_MENUTEXT
COLOR_BTNSHADOW	COLOR_SCROLLBAR
COLOR_BTNTEXT	COLOR_WINDOW
COLOR_CAPTIONTEXT	COLOR_WINDOWFRAME
COLOR_GRAYTEXT	COLOR_WINDOWTEXT
COLOR_HIGHLIGHT	

- `lpszMenuName` contains a pointer to the string that specifies the resource name of the class menu. If this field is set to `NULL`, the windows of the class have no default menu.
- `lpszClassName` contains a pointer to the string that specifies the name of the window class.

As you can see from the number of fields in the `WNDCLASS` structure and from the number of possibilities for each field, the window class is very flexible. When you create a window class, you are, in effect, creating an object class and engaging in a type of object-oriented programming. By creating the window class, you can easily make several windows without redefining the many values contained in the `WNDCLASS` structure for each window.

Step 2: Creating the Window Itself

After the window class is defined, your next step in creating a window is, of course, to create the window itself. You use two Windows functions when creating a window. The first is the `CreateWindow` function, and its syntax is as follows:

```
HWND CreateWindow(lpClassName, lpWindowName, dwStyle, X, Y,
                  nWidth, nHeight, hWndParent, hMenu, hInstance,
                  lpParam)
```

Table 7.1 describes the parameters used in the `CreateWindow` function.

Table 7.1. `CreateWindow` *parameters.*

Parameter	*Type*	*Description*
lpClassname	LPSTR	Pointer to a null-terminated character string that names the window class
lpWindowName	LPSTR	Pointer to a null-terminated character string that represents the window name
dwStyle	DWORD	The style of window to create
X	int	Initial horizontal position of the window's upper-left corner, expressed in screen coordinates
Y	int	Initial vertical position of the window's upper-left corner, expressed in screen coordinates
nWidth	int	Window width in device units
nHeight	int	Window height in device units
hWndParent	HWND	Parent or owner of the window to create
hMenu	HMENU	Menu or child window identifier
hInstance	HANDLE	Instance of module associated with the window
lpParam	LPSTR	Value passed to the window through the CREATESTRUCT data structure referenced by the lParam parameter of the WM_CREATE message

The fundamental window example in Chapter 2 uses the following call to the CreateWindow function to create the basic window. The CreateWindow function usually is followed by the ShowWindow function, which makes the created window visible.

```
hWnd = CreateWindow ("WIN_ONE",       /* class name */
          "Fundamental Window",       /* Caption */
          WS_OVERLAPPEDWINDOW,        /* Style */
          CW_USEDEFAULT,              /* x position */
          0,                          /* y position */
          CW_USEDEFAULT,              /* cx - size */
          0,                          /* cy - size */
          NULL,                       /* Parent window */
          NULL,                       /* Menu */
          hInstance,                  /* Program Instance */
          NULL);                      /* Parameters */
```

The other function used to create a window is the CreateWindowEx function, which is similar to the CreateWindow function except that CreateWindowEx provides several extended style bits. The syntax for the CreateWindowEx function is as follows:

```
HWND CreateWindowEx(dwExStyle, lpClassName, lpWindowName,
                    dwStyle, X, Y, nWidth, nHeight, hWndParent,
                    hMenu, hInstance, lpParam)
```

Table 7.2 describes the additional style bits.

Table 7.2. `CreateWindowEx` ***style bits.***

Parameter	*Type*	*Description*
`dwExStyle`	`DWORD`	Extended style for the window to create. The following values are used for `dwExStyle`: • `WS_EX_DLGMODALFRAME` creates a window with a double border. The window contains a title bar if `WS_CAPTION` is specified in `dwStyle`. • `WS_EX_NOPARENTNOTIFY` creates a child window that will not send the `WM_PARENTNOTIFY` message to the parent window when the child window is created or destroyed.
`lpClassname`	`LPSTR`	Pointer to a null-terminated character string that names the window class
`lpWindowName`	`LPSTR`	Pointer to a null-terminated character string that represents the window name
`dwStyle`	`DWORD`	The style of window to create
`X`	`int`	Initial horizontal position of the window's upper-left corner, expressed in screen coordinates
`Y`	`int`	Initial vertical position of the window's upper-left corner, expressed in screen coordinates
`nWidth`	`int`	Window width in device units
`nHeight`	`int`	Window height in device units
`hWndParent`	`HWND`	Parent or owner of the window to create
`hMenu`	`HMENU`	Menu or child window identifier
`hInstance`	`HANDLE`	Instance of module associated with the window
`lpParam`	`LPSTR`	Value passed to the window through the `CREATESTRUCT` data structure referenced by the `lParam` parameter of the `WM_CREATE` message

With the exception of the `dwExStyle` parameter of the `CreateWindowEx` function, the `CreateWindow` and `CreateWindowEx` functions share the same parameters. Although most of the parameters are fairly self-explanatory, the `lpClassName` and `dwStyle` parameters each have a variety of constants that can be associated with them. The lpClassName parameter specifies the class name. Windows has several predefined public window classes. Table 7.3 lists the values you can use to specify one of the public window classes for the lpClassName parameter.

All the window classes listed in Table 7.3, with the exception of MDICLIENT, correspond to child window controls. In this chapter, a "child window" refers to a child window *control*. Chapter 9 further discusses child windows and the MDI.

Table 7.3. Values for lpClassName.

Value	Meaning
BUTTON	A small rectangular child window representing a two-state button that can be turned on or off
COMBOBOX	A control that contains a selection field and edit control
EDIT	A rectangular child window that accepts user input
LISTBOX	A list of character strings
MDICLIENT	An MDI client window
SCROLLBAR	A rectangle containing a direction arrow at either end and a position indicator
STATIC	A simple text field, box, or rectangle

The dwStyle parameter specifies the style for the created window. Table 7.4 lists the values that you can combine for dwStyle by using bitwise OR.

Table 7.4. Window styles.

Window Styles	
Value	Meaning
DS_LOCALEDIT	Specifies that edit controls in the dialog box will use all memory in the application's data segment
DS_MODALFRAME	Creates a dialog box with a modal dialog box frame
DS_NOIDLEMSG	Suppresses WM_ENTERIDLE messages while the dialog box is displayed
DS_SYSMODAL	Creates a system modal dialog box
WS_BORDER	Creates a window with a border
WS_CAPTION	Creates a window with a Title bar; cannot be used with WS_DLGFRAME

continues

Table 7.4. continued

Window Styles

Value	Meaning
WS_CHILD	Creates a child window; cannot be used with WS_POPUP
WS_CHILDWINDOW	Creates a child window with style WS_CHILD
WS_CLIPCHILDREN	Excludes the area occupied by child windows when drawing within the parent window
WS_CLIPSIBLINGS	Clips child windows relative to each other; for use with WS_CHILD only
WS_DISABLED	Creates a window that is disabled
WS_DLGFRAME	Creates a window with a double border and no title
WS_GROUP	Defines the first control from a group that the user can move from one control to another with the direction keys
WS_HSCROLL	Creates a window with a horizontal scroll bar
WS_ICONIC	Creates an iconic window
WS_MAXIMIZE	Creates a window that is to be maximized
WS_MAXIMIZEBOX	Creates a window with a maximize box
WS_MINIMIZE	Creates a window that is minimum size
WS_MINIMIZEBOX	Creates a window with a minimize box
WS_OVERLAPPEDWINDOW	Creates an overlapped window with styles WS_OVERLAPPED, WS_CAPTION, WS_SYSMENU, WS_THICKFRAME, WS_MINIMIZEBOX, and WS_MAXIMIZEBOX
WS_POPUP	Creates a pop-up window; cannot be used with WS_CHILD
WS_POPUPWINDOW	Creates a pop-up window with styles WS_BORDER, WS_POPUP, and WS_SYSMENU
WS_SYSMENU	Creates a window with a System menu box in the Title bar
WS_TABSTOP	Specifies the controls that a user can move to with the Tab key
WS_THICKFRAME	Creates a window with a thick frame
WS_VISIBLE	Creates a visible overlapped or pop-up window

BUTTON Class Control Styles

Value	Meaning
BS_AUTOCHECK	Creates a small rectangular button that may be checked; button toggles when clicked
BS_AUTORADIOBUTTON	Creates a small circular button that can be checked; when clicked, the checkmarks are removed from the other radio buttons in the group

Value	Meaning
BS_AUTO3STATE	Creates a small rectangular button that changes state when clicked; supports three states: on, off, or grayed
BS_CHECKBOX	Creates a small rectangular button that may be checked
BS_DEFPUSHBUTTON	Designates a button as the default button by its bold border
BS_GROUPBOX	Groups the buttons in the designated rectangle
BS_LEFTTEXT	Forces text to appear on the left side (the right side is the default) for styles BS_CHECKBOX, BS_RADIOBUTTON, and BS_3STATE
BS_OWNERDRAW	Designates an owner draw button; parent is notified when the button is clicked
BS_PUSHBUTTON	Designates a button containing the specified text
BS_RADIOBUTTON	Creates a small circular button that can be checked
BS_3STATE	Creates a small rectangular button that may be checked; supports three states: on, off, and grayed

COMBOBOX Class Control Styles

Value	Meaning
CBS_AUTOHSCROLL	Scrolls the text in the edit control to the right when text reaches the end of the line
CBS_DROPDOWN	Displays the list box only when the icon beside the selection field is selected
CBS_DROPDOWNLIST	Like CBS_DROPDOWN; edit control, however, is replaced by a static text item that displays the current selection from the list box
CBS_HASSTRINGS	Designates that owner-draw combo box contains items that consist of strings
CBS_OEMCONVERT	Converts text from combo box edit control from ANSI to OEM and back to ANSI
CBS_OWNERDRAWFIXED	Designates that the list box owner draws the contents of the list box; contents are all the same height
CBS_OWNERDRAWVARIABLE	Designates that the list box owner draws the contents of the list box; contents are not all the same height
CBS_SIMPLE	Always displays the list box
CBS_SORT	Automatically sorts strings entered in the list box

continues

Table 7.4. continued

EDIT Class Control Styles

Value	*Meaning*
ES_AUTOHSCROLL	Automatically scrolls text to the right 10 spaces when the end of the line is reached
ES_AUTOVSCROLL	Automatically scrolls the text up one page when Enter is pressed on the last line
ES_CENTER	Centers text in a multiline edit control
ES_LEFT	Left justifies text
ES_LOWERCASE	Displays all entered characters as lowercase
ES_MULTILINE	Multiline edit control
ES_NOHIDESEL	Disables the default action of hiding the selection when control loses the input focus and inverting the selection when the control receives the input focus
ES_OEMCONVERT	Converts text in the edit control from ANSI to OEM to ANSI
ES_PASSWORD	Displays asterisk (*) for each character entered into the edit control
ES_RIGHT	Right justifies text in a multiline edit control
ES_UPPERCASE	Displays all entered characters as uppercase

LISTBOX Class Control Styles

Value	*Meaning*
LBS_EXTENDEDSEL	Enables user to select multiple selections from the list box
LBS_HASSTRINGS	Creates an owner-draw list box contains items made up of strings
LBS_MULTICOLUMN	Creates a multicolumn list box with horizontal scroll
LBS_MULTIPLESEL	Toggles the string selection each time a string is clicked or double-clicked; multiple selections can be made
LBS_NOINTEGRALHEIGHT	Creates a list box that has the exact size specified by the application creating the list box
LBS_NOREDRAW	Does not redraw the list box after modification
LBS_NOTIFY	Sends an input message to the parent when a string is clicked or double-clicked
LBS_OWNERDRAWVARIABLE	Enables the list box owner to draw the contents of the list box

Value	*Meaning*
LBS_SORT	Alphabetically sorts strings in the list box
LBS_STANDARD	Alphabetically sorts strings in the list box are sorted alphabetically and sends an input message to the parent window when a string is clicked or double-clicked
LBS_USETABSTOPS	Enables a list box to recognize tab characters when drawing strings
LBS_WANTKEYBOARDINPUT	Sends WM_VKEYTOITEM or WM_CHARTOITEM message to the owner of the list box when a key is pressed while the list box has the input focus

SCROLLBAR Class Control Styles

Value	*Meaning*
SBS_BOTTOMALIGN	Aligns the bottom edge of scroll bar with the bottom edge of the rectangle specified by X, Y, nWidth, and nHeight from the CreateWindow function; used with SBS_HORIZON
SBS_HORZ	Creates a horizontal scroll bar
SBS_LEFTALIGN	Aligns the left edge of scroll bar with the left edge of the rectangle specified by X, Y, nWidth, and nHeight from the CreateWindow function; used with SBS_VERT
SBS_RIGHTALIGN	Aligns the right edge of scroll bar with the right edge of the rectangle specified by X, Y, nWidth, and nHeight from the CreateWindow function; used with SBS_VERT
SBS_SIZEBOX	Specifies a size box
SBS_SIZEBOXBOTTOMRIGHTALIGN	Aligns the lower-right corner of size box with the lower right corner of the rectangle specified by X, Y, nWidth, and nHeight from the CreateWindow function; used with SBS_SIZEBOX
SBS_SIZEBOXTOPLEFTALIGN	Aligns the upper-left corner of size box with the upper-left corner of the rectangle specified by X, Y, nWidth, and nHeight from the CreateWindow function; used with SBS_SIZEBOX
SBS_TOPALIGN	Aligns the top edge of scroll bar with the top edge of the rectangle specified by X, Y, nWidth, and nHeight from the CreateWindow function; used with SBS_HORIZON
SBS_VERT	Creates a vertical scroll bar

Table 7.4. continued

STATIC Class Control Styles

Value	*Meaning*
`SS_BLACKFRAME`	Colors the frame of a box with same color as window frames
`SS_BLACKRECT`	Fills a rectangle with same color as window frames
`SS_CENTER`	Creates a simple rectangle with text centered in rectangle; wraps text to next line if necessary
`SS_GRAYFRAME`	Colors the frame of a box with same color as screen background
`SS_GRAYRECT`	Fills a rectangle the same color as screen background
`SS_ICON`	Displays an icon in the dialog box
`SS_LEFT`	Creates a simple rectangle with text left-justified inside the rectangle; wraps text to next line if necessary
`SS_LEFTNOWORDWRAP`	Creates a simple rectangle with text left-justified inside the rectangle; does not wrap text to the next line
`SS_NOPREFIX`	Without this style, the & character is interpreted as an accelerator prefix character
`SS_RIGHT`	Creates a simple rectangle with text right-justified inside the rectangle; wraps text to the next line if necessary
`SS_SIMPLE`	Creates a simple rectangle with text left-justified; the text cannot be altered
`SS_USERITEM`	Creates a user-defined item
`SS_WHITEFRAME`	Draws the frame of a box in same color as the window background
`SS_WHITERECT`	Fills a rectangle with the same color as the window background

The `CreateWindow` and `CreateWindowEx` functions provide a great deal of flexibility in the specification of a window. The various window and control styles, when combined with the various predefined window classes, provide numerous child window control combinations.

Although the process of creating a window requires only two steps, these steps require much work. To get the most out of your Windows application, it is important that you understand the capabilities provided by Windows for the window creation process. By carefully reviewing the basic concepts of and the features provided by the `WNDCLASS` data structure, the `CreateWindow` function, and the `CreateWindowEx` function, you should be able to create the window that is best for your application.

Child Window Controls

You create child window controls by using the same basic process you used to develop top-level windows. The remainder of this chapter discusses these controls. Do not confuse child window controls, however, with child windows that follow the MDI standard, which are discussed in Chapter 9.

The discussion of the `CreateWindow` and `CreateWindowEx` functions introduced several predefined window classes. The window classes that pertain to child window controls are listed as follows:

- `BUTTON` is a small rectangular child window representing a two-state button that can be turned on or off.
- `COMBOBOX` is a control that contains a selection field and an edit control.
- `EDIT` is a rectangular child window that accepts user input.
- `LISTBOX` is a list of character strings.
- `SCROLLBAR` is a rectangle containing a direction arrow at either end and a position indicator.
- `STATIC` is a simple text field, box, or rectangle.

As the list of predefined classes indicates, child window controls are in the form of buttons, combo boxes, edit boxes, list boxes, scroll bars, and text fields. You can place child window controls inside dialog boxes or on the surfaces of normal, overlapped window client areas.

A child window control communicates with its parent window by sending a `WM_COMMAND` message to the parent. The `WM_COMMAND` message contains three pieces of information. The `wParam` parameter of the message contains the ID of the child window. The low-order word of the `lParam` parameter of the message contains the handle of the child window. The high-order word of the `lParam` parameter of the message contains the notification code. The *notification codes* inform the parent window of the actions that occur within a control.

The following paragraphs briefly describe each of the child window control types. Each description includes a list of the notification codes that apply to that control type.

Button controls—You select a button by clicking on the control. The several button types include push buttons, check boxes, radio buttons, and group boxes. The following notification codes are associated with buttons:

Notification Code	*Meaning*
BN_CLICKED	Specifies that a button has been clicked
BN_DOUBLECLICKED	Specifies that an owner-draw or radio button has been double-clicked

Edit controls—Rectangular child windows that accept input from the user, edit controls are often used to enable the user to type in a filename or keyword. The following notification codes are associated with edit controls:

Notification Code	*Meaning*
EN_CHANGE	Indicates that an action changed the content of the text
EN_ERRSPACE	Specifies that an edit control is out of space
EN_HSCROLL	Specifies that the horizontal scroll bar was clicked and is active
EN_KILLFOCUS	Specifies that the edit control has lost the input focus
EN_MAXTEXT	Specifies that the inserted text exceeds the limits for the edit control
EN_SETFOCUS	Specifies that the edit control has received the input focus
EN_UPDATE	Specifies that the edit control will display altered text
EN_VSCROLL	Specifies that the vertical scroll bar was clicked and is active

List box controls—A list of character strings, the list box control often is used to display a list of options such as files or directories that can be selected. The following notification codes are associated with list box controls:

Notification Code	*Meaning*
LBN_DBLCLK	Specifies that a string was double-clicked
LBN_ERRSPACE	Specifies that there is no more system memory
LBN_KILLFOCUS	Specifies that the list box has lost the input focus
LBN_SELCHANGE	Specifies that the selection was changed
LBN_SETFOCUS	Specifies that the list box has received the input focus

Combo box controls—A combo box contains a selection field and an edit control. The following notification codes are associated with combo boxes:

Notification Code	*Meaning*
CBN_DBLCLK	Sent when a string is double-clicked
CBN_DROPDOWN	Sent to the owner of the combo box when a list box is to be dropped down
CBN_EDITCHANGE	Sent when the text in the edit control is modified
CBN_EDITUPDATE	Specifies that the edit control will display altered text
CBN_ERRSPACE	Sent when there is no more system memory
CBN_KILLFOCUS	Specifies that the combo box no longer has the input focus
CBN_SELCHANGE	Specifies that the selection was modified
CBN_SETFOCUS	Specifies that the combo box received the input focus

Scroll bar controls—Rectangles containing a direction arrow at either end and a position indicator, scroll bars are used to position fields of text or graphics that are too large for the current client area. There are no notification codes associated with scroll bar controls.

Static controls—A simple text field, box, or rectangle, the static control can display messages. There are no notification codes associated with static controls.

The Child Window Example

The child window example in Listings 7.1 and 7.2 demonstrates how you can use child window controls to display three buttons. The first button is a three-state button that automatically cycles between the states when clicked. The second button is a simple push-button. The last button is a check box that is automatically checked or unchecked.

The buttons are created when the WM_CREATE message is received by the window procedure. The three buttons are then created using the CreateWindow function, and the created buttons can be selected by the user. This child window example, however, has not defined any actions for the buttons. To modify this example, you must make the window procedure respond to the WM_COMMAND message.

A child window control communicates with its parent window by sending a WM_COMMAND message to the parent that contains three pieces of information. The wParam parameter of the message contains the ID of the child window. The low-order word of the lParam parameter of the message contains the handle of the child window. The high-order word of the lParam parameter of the message contains the *notification code*, which informs the parent window of the actions that occur

within a control. By evaluating the information sent from the control, the application can be coded to respond accordingly. Figure 7.1 shows the application window and button controls created by this example.

The project name and the files used to create the child window example are as follows:

Project Name:	WIN_CHLD
Files in Project:	WIN_CHLD.C
	WIN_CHLD.DEF

Listing 7.1. *The definition file for the child window example.*

```
NAME            WIN_CHLD
DESCRIPTION     'Child Window Example'
EXETYPE         WINDOWS
CODE            PRELOAD MOVEABLE
DATA            PRELOAD MOVEABLE MULTIPLE
HEAPSIZE        1024
STACKSIZE       5120
EXPORTS         WndProc
```

Listing 7.2. *The C source file for the child window example.*

```
#include <windows.h>
#include <stdlib.h>
#include <string.h>

long FAR PASCAL WndProc (HWND hWnd, WORD iMessage,
                         WORD wParam, LONG lParam);

int PASCAL WinMain (HANDLE hInstance, HANDLE hPrevInstance,
                    LPSTR lpszCmdParam, int nCmdShow)

{
HWND hWnd;
MSG Message;
WNDCLASS WndClass;

if (!hPrevInstance)
     {
     WndClass.cbClsExtra = 0;
     WndClass.cbWndExtra = 0;
     WndClass.hbrBackground = GetStockObject(WHITE_BRUSH);
     WndClass.hCursor =  LoadCursor(NULL, IDC_ARROW);
     WndClass.hIcon = LoadIcon (NULL, "END");
     WndClass.hInstance = hInstance;
```

```
        WndClass.lpfnWndProc = WndProc;
        WndClass.lpszClassName = "WIN_CHLD";
        WndClass.lpszMenuName = NULL;
        WndClass.style = CS_HREDRAW ¦ CS_VREDRAW;

        RegisterClass (&WndClass);
        }

   hWnd = CreateWindow ("WIN_CHLD",      /* class name */
             "Child Window Example",     /* Caption */
             WS_OVERLAPPEDWINDOW,        /* Style */
             CW_USEDEFAULT,              /* x position */
             0,                          /* y position */
             CW_USEDEFAULT,              /* cx - size */
             0,                          /* cy - size */
             NULL,                       /* Parent window */
             NULL,                       /* Menu */
             hInstance,                  /* Program Instance */
             NULL);                      /* Parameters */

   ShowWindow(hWnd,nCmdShow);
   UpdateWindow(hWnd);
   while (GetMessage (&Message, 0, 0, 0))
        {
        TranslateMessage(&Message);
        DispatchMessage(&Message);
        }
   return Message.wParam;
   }

   /*****************************************************************/
   /*               Window Procedure: WndProc                       */
   /*****************************************************************/

   long FAR PASCAL WndProc (HWND hWnd, WORD iMessage, WORD wParam,
                            LONG lParam)
   {
   HDC hDC;
   HWND hWndButton;


   switch (iMessage)
        {
        case WM_CREATE:

             CreateWindow("BUTTON","AUTO3STATE",
               WS_CHILD ¦ WS_VISIBLE ¦ BS_AUTO3STATE,
               100,50,200,50,hWnd,0,
```

continues

Listing 7.2. continued

```
            ((LPCREATESTRUCT)lParam)->hInstance,
            NULL);
          CreateWindow("BUTTON","PUSHBUTTON",
            WS_CHILD ¦ WS_VISIBLE ¦ BS_PUSHBUTTON,
            100,125,200,50,hWnd,0,
            ((LPCREATESTRUCT)lParam)->hInstance,
            NULL);
          CreateWindow("BUTTON","AUTOCHECKBOX",
            WS_CHILD ¦ WS_VISIBLE ¦ BS_AUTOCHECKBOX,
            100,200,200,50,hWnd,0,
            ((LPCREATESTRUCT)lParam)->hInstance,
            NULL);
          return 0;

     case WM_DESTROY:

          PostQuitMessage(0);
          return 0;
     }
return(DefWindowProc(hWnd, iMessage, wParam, lParam));
}
```

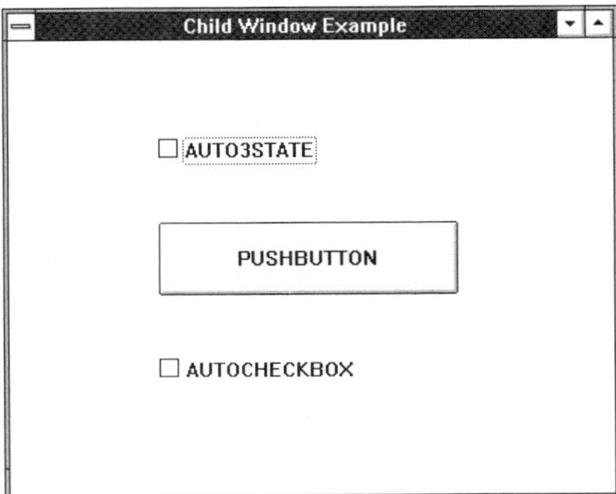

***Figure 7.1.** The window created by the child window example.*

This chapter has introduced you to child window controls and defining window classes. The next chapter discusses Windows' memory management techniques in a multitasking environment.

8

Memory Management and Windows

Windows is a multitasking environment. Because multiple tasks can run at the same time, Windows must carefully manage the system memory so that the memory required by an application is available without affecting the operations of the other tasks. This chapter introduces Windows memory management.

Let's quickly review the way that the Intel 8086 family of microprocessors organizes memory into segments. To begin this review, you also must review the basic operating modes for Windows: real mode, standard mode, and 386 enhanced mode. These terms appear several times during the discussion of memory management and are briefly described as follows:

- Windows *real mode* is designed for machines with less than 1MB of memory. In real mode, Windows can take advantage of expanded memory that follows the Lotus-Intel-Microsoft Expanded Memory Specification 4.0.

- Windows *standard mode* is designed for 80286 machines with at least 1MB of memory or 80386 machines with less than 2MB of memory. Windows standard mode provides the advantages of 80286 protected mode and can address up to 16MB of conventional and extended memory.
- Windows *386 enhanced mode* is designed for 80386 machines with greater than 2MB of memory. The 386 enhanced mode provides the advantages of standard mode while adding the feature of virtual memory and accommodating virtual DOS machines.

Windows 3.0 can operate in real, standard, or 386 enhanced mode. Windows 3.1 does not support real mode—only standard and 386 enhanced mode.

Now that we have reviewed the Windows operating modes, we can begin the discussion of segments and memory addresses.

The microprocessor uses a physical address to read from and write to physical memory. Programmers use the logical address to access physical memory. The logical address consists of two parts. The first part of the logical address is the *segment identifier*. The segment identifier is a 16-bit value that specifies the segment of memory to access. The second part of the logical address is the *offset*. The offset specifies a byte number within the segment. The microprocessor converts the logical address specified by the segment identifier and the offset to a physical address.

In the real mode, the logical address corresponds directly to the physical address. The 20-bit physical address is determined by adding the 16-bit offset and the 16-bit segment address (shifted left four bits) as follows:

Offset	xxxxxxxxxxxxxxxx
Segment	+ xxxxxxxxxxxxxxxx0000
20-bit Physical Address	xxxxxxxxxxxxxxxxxxxx

In the standard mode, the logical address does not correspond to the physical address. Instead, the logical address references the physical address through a descriptor table. The same is true for the 386 enhanced mode. The portion of the logical address referred to as the segment identifier for the real mode is called the *segment selector* for the standard and 386 enhanced modes. The segment selector identifies the segment from an array of segment information records called *segment descriptors*.

The Local and Global Heaps

Windows allocates blocks of memory for an application from either the global or local heap. The *global heap* is memory available to all applications. The *local heap* is memory that is restricted for use by only one application.

The global heap is the memory that Windows controls. The global heap begins at the position at which Windows is loaded into memory and includes the remainder of the available memory. When Windows starts, memory blocks for the code and data are allocated. The memory remaining after the allocation of the memory blocks for the code and data—called *free memory*—can be used by applications. The global heap often is used for allocating large memory blocks; any size of memory block, however, can be allocated.

Blocks of memory are allocated in the global heap according to the following guidelines, which are illustrated in Figure 8.1.

- Fixed segments are allocated from the bottom up.
- Discardable segments are allocated from the bottom down.
- Moveable, nondiscardable data segments are allocated between fixed segments and discardable segments.
- The largest block of free memory usually is located below the discardable segments.

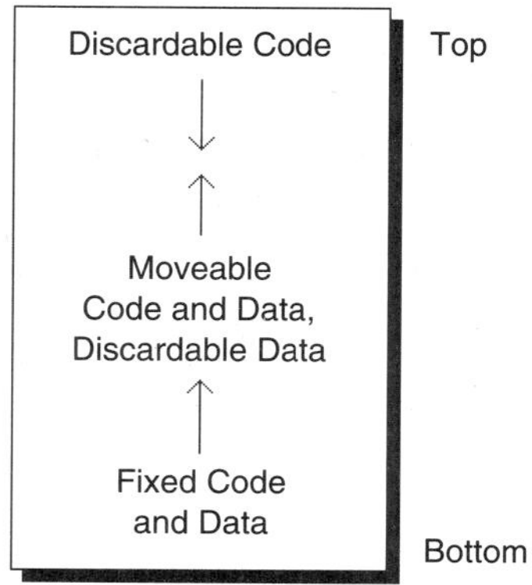

***Figure 8.1.** Global memory.*

Windows provides several functions for managing global memory. Table 8.1 lists these functions. Chapter 13, "Windows Functions," provides additional information for using each of the functions listed in Table 8.1.

Table 8.1. Global memory management functions.

Function	Meaning
GetFreeSpace	Gets the number of bytes available in the global heap
GlobalAlloc	Allocates memory from the global heap
GlobalCompact	Compacts global memory
GlobalDiscard	Discards global memory
GlobalDosAlloc	Allocates global memory
GlobalDosFree	Frees global memory allocated with GlobalDosAlloc
GlobalFix	Keeps a global memory block from being moved in linear memory
GlobalFlags	Gets the flags and lock count of a memory block
GlobalFree	Removes a global block and invalidates the handle
GlobalHandle	Gets the handle of a global memory object
GlobalLock	Gets the pointer for a handle to a global memory block
GlobalLRUNewest	Moves a global memory object to the newest least-recently-used (LRU) position
GlobalLRUOldest	Moves a global memory object to the oldest least-recently-used (LRU) position
GlobalNotify	Installs a notification procedure
GlobalReAlloc	Reallocates a global memory block
GlobalSize	Gets the number of bytes in a global memory block
GlobalUnfix	Unlocks a global memory block
GlobalUnlock	Invalidates the pointer to a global memory block

The local heap contains memory that can be allocated only by the application and is located in the application's data segment. The application's data segment contains three other types of data as shown in Figure 8.2.

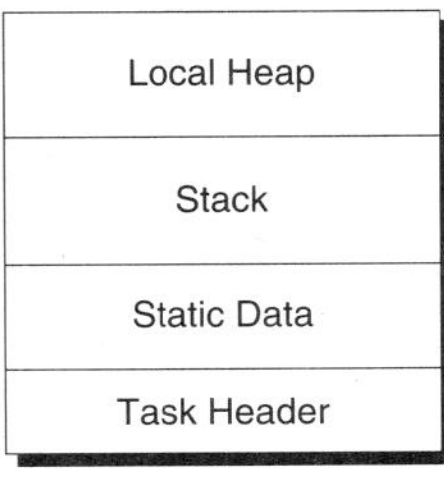

Figure 8.2. The application's data segment.

From top to bottom, as Figure 8.2 shows, the types of data in the application's data segment are the local heap, the stack, the static data, and the task header. The local heap contains all local dynamic data (data allocated using `LocalAlloc`). The stack stores automatic data (variables allocated in the stack when a function is called). Static data refers to all of the variables that are declared to be either `static` or `extern`. The task header contains 16 bytes of information about the application.

The guidelines for allocating memory in the local heap are similar to those used for allocating memory in the global heap. These guidelines (shown in Figure 8.3) are the following:

1. Fixed blocks are located at the bottom of the local heap.
2. Discardable blocks are allocated from the top of the local heap.
3. Nondiscardable, moveable blocks of memory are allocated above the fixed blocks.
4. The largest block of free memory usually is located below the discardable segments.

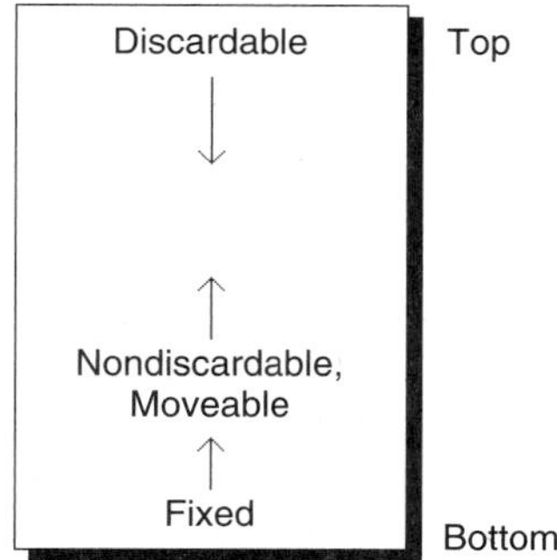

Figure 8.3. *The local heap.*

Windows provides several functions for managing local memory. Table 8.2 lists these functions. Chapter 13 provides additional information for using each of the functions listed in Table 8.2.

Table 8.2. *Local memory management functions.*

Function	Meaning
`LocalAlloc`	Allocates memory from the local heap
`LocalCompact`	Compacts local memory
`LocalDiscard`	Discards local memory when the lock count is zero
`LocalFlags`	Gets the memory type of a local memory block
`LocalFree`	Frees a local memory block when the lock count is zero
`LocalHandle`	Gets the handle of a local memory block
`LocalInit`	Initializes a local heap
`LocalLock`	Locks a local memory block
`LocalReAlloc`	Reallocates a local memory block
`LocalShrink`	Shrinks the local heap
`LocalSize`	Gets the number of bytes in a local memory block
`LocalUnlock`	Unlocks a local memory block

Segments

A block of memory that is associated with a particular segment address is called a *segment*. Segments can vary in size but are limited to 64KB blocks. The memory that Windows controls is divided into segments of varying sizes. Each segment controlled by Windows contains attributes that specify how the segment is to be treated. A segment can be either fixed, moveable, or moveable and discardable.

Fixed segments cannot be moved in memory. Although most segments are moveable, in some cases segments are fixed. When a far pointer references a segment, for example, the segment is fixed. Because fixed segments cannot be moved or discarded, fixed segments quickly use up available memory. You should therefore limit the number of fixed segments.

Moveable segments can be moved in memory. When moveable memory is allocated, a handle that identifies the memory segment is created. Applications use the handle to identify the memory block. Windows uses the handle to locate the memory address of the segment. Windows can relocate moveable segments to make the most efficient use of the memory available on the system.

Moveable segments can be specified as discardable. Windows can remove moveable, discardable segments from memory to make room for memory requests. When the segment is needed, the segment is loaded back into memory from the disk. Code segments are often defined as moveable, discardable segments because code is not changed. When the code must be executed, therefore, it is reloaded into memory. Resources are another example of memory blocks that often are marked as moveable, discardable segments.

Table 8.3 lists several functions that Windows provides for dealing with segments. Chapter 13, "Windows Functions," provides additional information for using each of the functions listed in Table 8.3.

Table 8.3. *Segment functions.*

Function	*Meaning*
`AllocDStoCSAlias`	Returns a code segment selector from the specified data segment selector
`AllocSelector`	Allocates a new selector
`ChangeSelector`	Generates a code or data selector
`DefineHandleTable`	Creates a private handle table in an application's data segment
`FreeSelector`	Frees a selector
`GetCodeInfo`	Gets code segment information
`GlobalFix`	Keeps a global memory block from being moved in linear memory
`GlobalPageLock`	Page locks the memory associated with the specified global selector
`GlobalPageUnlock`	Decreases the page lock count for a block of memory
`GlobalUnfix`	Unlocks a global memory block
`LockSegment`	Locks the specified data segment
`UnlockSegment`	Unlocks the specified data segment

This chapter has introduced the basic memory management techniques for Windows. The following chapter presents the concepts of the Multiple Document Interface (MDI) and demonstrates the techniques for developing an MDI application.

9

The Multiple Document Interface (MDI)

Windows provides the Multiple Document Interface (MDI) specification for applications dealing with documents. The MDI specification standardizes the methods for displaying and manipulating multiple documents from a single application. This chapter introduces the components of an MDI application, the MDI message loop, and the MDI messages.

MDI Applications

MDI applications contain one main window, called the *frame window*, which is similar to most application windows except that the frame window's client area itself contains a child window. This window, called the *client window*, is the background where the other child windows are placed. Each document created by the MDI

application has its own window—a child window—that can be moved, minimized, and maximized. However, this child window is restricted to the area of the client window. Figure 9.1 illustrates the components of an MDI application.

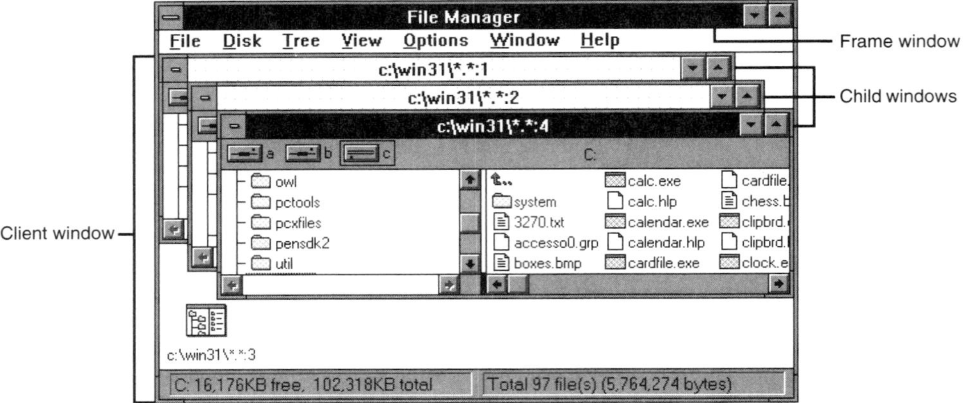

Figure 9.1. *The File Manager, an MDI application.*

The MDI interface is controlled by the passing of messages up and down the hierarchy of windows. The MDI hierarchy begins at the frame window and extends downward to the client window and to its child windows.

The general process for developing an MDI application is about the same as for almost any other Windows application. The differences in the code structure between the traditional Windows application and the MDI application, however, makes the development of the MDI application more difficult.

One noticeable difference between the traditional Windows application and the MDI application occurs during initialization. MDI applications, in general, register at least two window classes. The first window class is for the frame window of the MDI application. The second class—and any other subsequent class—is for the child windows of the MDI application. It is not necessary to register a class for the client window, because Windows has a predefined class for this purpose. When you define the window classes, keep the following in mind:

- The class structure should have an icon, because child windows can be minimized.
- The menu name should be set to `NULL`.
- Additional space should be reserved in the class structure for storing data associated with the window.

The following code is from the MDI example presented later in this chapter. The window class for the frame window is defined first and then registered using the `RegisterClass` function. The window class for the child window follows, and it is also registered using the `RegisterClass` function.

```
if (!hPrevInstance)
     {
     WndClass.cbClsExtra = 0;
     WndClass.cbWndExtra = 0;
     WndClass.hbrBackground = GetStockObject(WHITE_BRUSH);
     WndClass.hCursor =  LoadCursor(NULL, IDC_ARROW);
     WndClass.hIcon = LoadIcon (NULL, IDI_APPLICATION);
     WndClass.hInstance = hInstance;
     WndClass.lpfnWndProc = FrameWndProc;
     WndClass.lpszClassName = "WIN_MDI:FRAME";
     WndClass.lpszMenuName = NULL;
     WndClass.style = CS_HREDRAW ¦ CS_VREDRAW;

     RegisterClass (&WndClass);

     WndClass.cbClsExtra = 0;
     WndClass.cbWndExtra = sizeof(LOCALHANDLE);
     WndClass.hbrBackground = GetStockObject(WHITE_BRUSH);
     WndClass.hCursor =  LoadCursor(NULL, IDC_ARROW);
     WndClass.hIcon = LoadIcon (NULL, IDI_APPLICATION);
     WndClass.hInstance = hInstance;
     WndClass.lpfnWndProc = DocWndProc;
     WndClass.lpszClassName = "WIN_MDI:DOC";
     WndClass.lpszMenuName = NULL;
     WndClass.style = CS_HREDRAW ¦ CS_VREDRAW;

     RegisterClass (&WndClass);
     }
```

The MDI Message Loop

The message loop is another difference between MDI and typical Windows applications. MDI-application message loops use the `TranslateMDISysAccel` function, which is added to the message loop to translate child window accelerators. The reason the MDI message loop differs from the typical Windows application message loop is that system menu accelerators for MDI child windows respond to the Ctrl key rather than the Alt key.

The message loop for an MDI application usually is structured as follows:

```
while (GetMessage (&Message, NULL, 0, 0))
  {
  if (!TranslateMDISysAccel(hWndClient,&Message) &&
      !TranslateAccelerator(hWndFrame,hAccel,&Message))
     {
     TranslateMessage(&Message);
     DispatchMessage(&Message);
     }
  }
```

The MDI example in Listings 9.1, 9.2, and 9.3 presented later in this chapter demonstrates how this message loop is implemented.

MDI Messages

MDI applications control child windows by sending messages to the client window. Windows provides eleven MDI messages to control the child windows of MDI applications. Table 9.1 lists the MDI messages and briefly describes each one. Chapter 14, "Windows Messages," provides additional information for using each of these messages.

Table 9.1. *MDI messages.*

Message	*Meaning*
WM_MDIACTIVATE	Activates a child window
WM_MDICASCADE	Arranges child windows in a cascade fashion
WM_MDICREATE	Creates a child window
WM_MDIDESTROY	Closes a child window
WM_MDIGETACTIVE	Gets the active MDI child window
WM_MDIICONARRANGE	Arranges minimized child windows
WM_MDIMAXIMIZE	Maximizes an MDI child window
WM_MDINEXT	Makes the next child window active
WM_MDIRESTORE	Restores a child window
WM_MDISETMENU	Replaces the menu of the Window pop-up menu, an MDI frame window, or both
WM_MDITILE	Arranges child windows in a tiled format

Frame and Child Window Functions

Typical MDI applications contain at least two window functions. The first window function is for the frame window of the application. The second and every subsequent window function controls the various child window classes specified in `WinMain`.

The frame window procedure of an MDI application is similar to the main window procedure of a typical Windows application. There are some differences, however. The most noticeable difference is that the frame window procedure passes all the messages it does not handle to the `DefFrameProc` function. Typical Windows applications pass all their unhandled messages to the `DefWindowProc` function.

Child window procedures of MDI applications also differ from window procedures of typical Windows applications. The most noticeable difference is that child window procedures in an MDI application pass all messages that they do not handle to the `DefMDIChildProc` function. Typical window procedures pass all their unhandled messages to the `DefWindowProc` function.

The MDI Example

The MDI example presented in Listings 9.1, 9.2, and 9.3 demonstrates how to use the MDI to create a document. Three files are required to create this example. The first file is the *module definition file*. One thing that you should notice about this module definition file (as opposed to other module definition files you have seen in previous examples) is that two window functions are listed after `EXPORTS`: `FrameWndProc` and `DocWndProc`. `FrameWndProc` is the window procedure for the frame window. `DocWndProc` is the window procedure for the document.

The second file is the *C source file*. The overall structure of this example is, for the most part, similar to previous examples demonstrated in the book. Notice some differences, however: first, two window classes are defined; second, one class is defined for the frame window, while another class is defined for the document child window.

The third file in the project is the *resource script file*, which specifies the menus used by the frame and child windows as well as the accelerators for the application.

When this example is executed, the first thing that appears on-screen is the frame window of the application, as shown in Figure 9.2. The menu bar of the frame window contains one menu: `File`, which offers two selections—`New Document` and

`Exit`. Selecting `Exit` from the frame window menu enables you to exit the application. Selecting `New Document` opens a document child window, as shown in Figure 9.3. When the child window is opened, notice that the Menu bar contains the menus and menu options defined for the document child window.

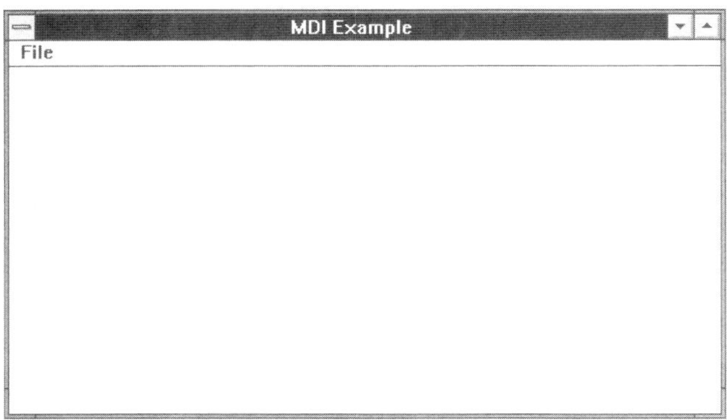

Figure 9.2. *The frame window of the MDI example.*

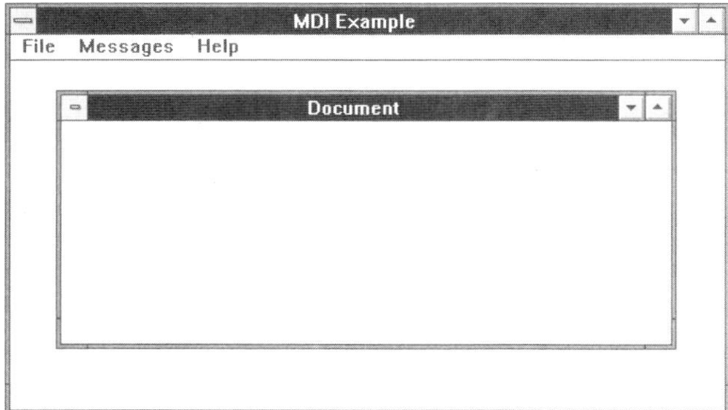

Figure 9.3. *The child window of the MDI example.*

Child windows can be *minimized* or *maximized*. The document child window displayed in Figure 9.3 is shown maximized in Figure 9.4 and minimized in Figure 9.5. There are a few things you should notice when the child window is either minimized or maximized.

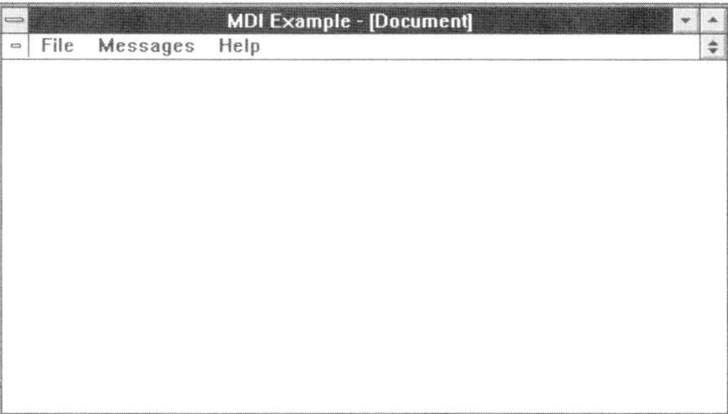

Figure 9.4. *The maximized child window of the MDI example.*

Figure 9.5. *The minimized child window of the MDI example.*

When a child window is minimized, the menu for the child window is still active and the actions resulting from various menu item selections are still active. In Figure 9.5, a message box is displayed that results from selecting the `Message 1` menu item of the `Messages` menu while the document child window is minimized.

When the child window is maximized, a restore button appears in the upper-right corner of the child window (see Figure 9.4). Additionally, a button that enables you to select the system menu for the child window appears below the system menu of the frame window. You may remember, from the discussion of message loops for MDI applications, that the system menu of the child window is selected with the Ctrl key, and the system menu of the frame window is selected with the Alt key. It is important to keep this in mind when using the keyboard to select options from the system menus.

The last thing to notice about the maximized child window is that the name of the child window appears on the caption line of the frame window along with the name of the frame window.

The project name and the files used to create the MDI example are as follows:

Project Name:	`WIN_MDI`
Files in Project:	`WIN_MDI.DEF`
	`WIN_MDI.C`
	`WIN_MDI.RC`

Listing 9.1. *The definition file for the MDI example.*

```
NAME            WIN_MDI
DESCRIPTION     'MDI Example'
EXETYPE         WINDOWS
CODE            PRELOAD MOVEABLE
DATA            PRELOAD MOVEABLE MULTIPLE
HEAPSIZE        1024
STACKSIZE       5120
EXPORTS         FrameWndProc
                DocWndProc
```

Listing 9.2. *The C source file for the MDI example.*

```
#include <windows.h>
#include <stdlib.h>
#include <string.h>

long FAR PASCAL FrameWndProc (HWND hWnd, WORD iMessage,
                              WORD wParam, LONG lParam);

long FAR PASCAL DocWndProc (HWND hWnd, WORD iMessage,
                            WORD wParam, LONG lParam);

HANDLE hInst;
HMENU hMenu, hMenuDoc;
HMENU hMenuWin, hMenuDocWin;
typedef struct
  {
  int x;
  int y;
  }
  DOCDATA;

typedef DOCDATA NEAR *NPDOCDATA;
```

```
int PASCAL WinMain (HANDLE hInstance, HANDLE hPrevInstance,
                    LPSTR lpszCmdParam, int nCmdShow)

{
HWND hWndFrame, hWndClient;
HANDLE hAccel;
MSG Message;
WNDCLASS WndClass;
hInst = hInstance;

if (!hPrevInstance)
     {
     WndClass.cbClsExtra = 0;
     WndClass.cbWndExtra = 0;
     WndClass.hbrBackground = GetStockObject(WHITE_BRUSH);
     WndClass.hCursor =  LoadCursor(NULL, IDC_ARROW);
     WndClass.hIcon = LoadIcon (NULL, IDI_APPLICATION);
     WndClass.hInstance = hInstance;
     WndClass.lpfnWndProc = FrameWndProc;
     WndClass.lpszClassName = "WIN_MDI:FRAME";
     WndClass.lpszMenuName = NULL;
     WndClass.style = CS_HREDRAW ¦ CS_VREDRAW;

     RegisterClass (&WndClass);

     WndClass.cbClsExtra = 0;
     WndClass.cbWndExtra = sizeof(LOCALHANDLE);
     WndClass.hbrBackground = GetStockObject(WHITE_BRUSH);
     WndClass.hCursor =  LoadCursor(NULL, IDC_ARROW);
     WndClass.hIcon = LoadIcon (NULL, IDI_APPLICATION);
     WndClass.hInstance = hInstance;
     WndClass.lpfnWndProc = DocWndProc;
     WndClass.lpszClassName = "WIN_MDI:DOC";
     WndClass.lpszMenuName = NULL;
     WndClass.style = CS_HREDRAW ¦ CS_VREDRAW;

     RegisterClass (&WndClass);
     }

hMenu = LoadMenu(hInst, "MdiMenu");
hMenuDoc = LoadMenu(hInst, "MdiMenuDoc");

hMenuWin = GetSubMenu(hMenu,0);
hMenuDocWin = GetSubMenu(hMenu,1);

hAccel = LoadAccelerators(hInst,"MdiAccel");

hWndFrame = CreateWindow ("WIN_MDI:FRAME", /* class name */
          "MDI Example",          /* Caption */
```

continues

Listing 9.2. continued

```
          WS_OVERLAPPEDWINDOW ¦
          WS_CLIPCHILDREN,        /* Style */
          CW_USEDEFAULT,          /* x position */
          CW_USEDEFAULT,          /* y position */
          CW_USEDEFAULT,          /* cx - size */
          CW_USEDEFAULT,          /* cy - size */
          NULL,                   /* Parent window */
          hMenu,                  /* Menu */
          hInstance,              /* Program Instance */
          NULL);                  /* Parameters */

hWndClient = GetWindow(hWndFrame,GW_CHILD);

ShowWindow (hWndFrame, nCmdShow);
UpdateWindow (hWndFrame);

while (GetMessage (&Message, NULL, 0, 0))
  {
  if (!TranslateMDISysAccel(hWndClient,&Message) &&
      !TranslateAccelerator(hWndFrame,hAccel,&Message))
     {
     TranslateMessage(&Message);
     DispatchMessage(&Message);
     }
  }
return Message.wParam;
}

/****************************************************************/
/*              Window Procedure: FrameWndProc                  */
/****************************************************************/

long FAR PASCAL FrameWndProc (HWND hWnd, WORD iMessage,
                              WORD wParam, LONG lParam)
{
static HWND hWndClient;
HWND hWndChild;
CLIENTCREATESTRUCT clcr;
MDICREATESTRUCT mdi;

switch (iMessage)
     {
     case WM_CREATE:

          clcr.hWindowMenu = hMenuWin;
          clcr.idFirstChild = 100;
```

```
     hWndClient = CreateWindow("MDICLIENT",NULL,
              WS_CHILD¦WS_CLIPCHILDREN¦
              WS_VISIBLE,0,0,0,0,hWnd,1,hInst,
              (LPSTR)&clcr);
     return 0;

case WM_COMMAND:

   switch(wParam)
     {
     case 10:
       mdi.szClass = "WIN_MDI:DOC";
       mdi.szTitle = "Document";
       mdi.hOwner = hInst;
       mdi.x = CW_USEDEFAULT;
       mdi.y = CW_USEDEFAULT;
       mdi.cx = CW_USEDEFAULT;
       mdi.cy = CW_USEDEFAULT;
       mdi.style = 0;
       mdi.lParam = NULL;
       hWndChild = SendMessage(hWndClient,
        WM_MDICREATE,0,
        (LONG)(LPMDICREATESTRUCT)&mdi);
       return 0;

     case 11:
       SendMessage(hWnd,WM_CLOSE,0,0L);
       return 0;

     case 30:
       MessageBox(hWnd,"Help 1","HELP",MB_OK);
       return 0;

     case 31:
       MessageBox(hWnd,"Help 2","HELP",MB_OK);
       return 0;

     case 32:
       MessageBox(hWnd,"Help 3","HELP",MB_OK);
       return 0;

     case 33:
       MessageBox(hWnd,"Help 4","HELP",MB_OK);
       return 0;

     default:
       hWndChild = LOWORD(SendMessage(hWndClient,
                   LM_MDIGETACTIVE,0,0L));
       if(IsWindow(hWndChild))
```

continues

Listing 9.2. continued

```
            SendMessage(hWndChild,WM_COMMAND,wParam,
                        lParam);
            break;
          }
        break;

     case WM_QUERYENDSESSION:

     case WM_CLOSE:

     case WM_DESTROY:
          PostQuitMessage(0);
          return 0;

     }
return DefFrameProc(hWnd,hWndClient,iMessage,wParam,lParam);
}

/***************************************************************/
/*              Window Procedure: DocWndProc                   */
/***************************************************************/

long FAR PASCAL DocWndProc (HWND hWnd, WORD iMessage,
                            WORD wParam, LONG lParam)
{
static HWND hWndClient, hWndFrame;
HDC hDC;
HMENU hMenu;
LOCALHANDLE hDocData;
NPDOCDATA npDocData;

switch(iMessage)
     {
     case WM_CREATE:
          hDocData = LocalAlloc(LMEM_MOVEABLE |
                 LMEM_ZEROINIT,sizeof(DOCDATA));
          npDocData = (NPDOCDATA)LocalLock(hDocData);
          npDocData->x = 10;
          npDocData->y = 10;
          LocalUnlock(hDocData);
          SetWindowWord(hWnd,0,hDocData);
          hWndClient = GetParent(hWnd);
          hWndFrame = GetParent(hWndClient);
          return 0;

     case WM_COMMAND:
       switch(wParam)
```

```
          {
          case 20:
            MessageBox(hWnd,"Message 1","MESSAGE",
                       MB_OK);
            return 0;

          case 21:
            MessageBox(hWnd,"Message 2","MESSAGE",
                       MB_OK);
            return 0;

          case 22:
            MessageBox(hWnd,"Message 3","MESSAGE",
                       MB_OK);
            return 0;

          case 23:
            MessageBox(hWnd,"Message 4","MESSAGE",
                       MB_OK);
            return 0;

          case 25:
            MessageBox(hWnd,"Message 5","MESSAGE",
                       MB_OK);
            return 0;

          default:
            return 0;
          }

     case WM_MDIACTIVATE:
          if(wParam == TRUE)
          SendMessage(hWndClient,WM_MDISETMENU,0,
                      MAKELONG(hMenuDoc,hMenuDocWin));
          if(wParam == FALSE)
          SendMessage(hWndClient,WM_MDISETMENU,0,
                      MAKELONG(hMenu,hMenuWin));
          DrawMenuBar(hWndFrame);
          return 0;

     case WM_QUERYENDSESSION:

     case WM_CLOSE:
          MessageBox(hWnd,"Close Disabled","STOP",
                     MB_ICONSTOP|MB_OK);
          return 0;

     case WM_DESTROY:
```

continues

Listing 9.2. continued

```
          hDocData = GetWindowWord(hWnd,0);
          LocalFree(hDocData);
          return 0;
     }
return DefMDIChildProc(hWnd,iMessage,wParam,lParam);
}
```

Listing 9.3. The resource file for the MDI example.

```
#include <windows.h>
MdiMenu MENU
  {
  POPUP "File"
     {
     MENUITEM "New Document", 10
     MENUITEM "Exit",         11
     }
  }


MdiMenuDoc MENU
  {
  POPUP "File"
     {
     MENUITEM "Exit",         11
     }
  POPUP "Messages",
     {
     MENUITEM "Message 1",    20
     MENUITEM "Message 2",    21
     MENUITEM "Message 3",    22
     MENUITEM "Message 4",    23
     MENUITEM "Message 5",    24
     }
  POPUP "Help",
     {
     MENUITEM "Help 1",       30
     MENUITEM "Help 2",       31
     MENUITEM "Help 3",       32
     MENUITEM "Help 4",       33
     }
  }
```

```
MdiAccel ACCELERATORS
  {
  VK_F1,20,VIRTKEY,SHIFT
  VK_F2,30,VIRTKEY,SHIFT
  }
```

This chapter has presented and demonstrated the concepts of MDI application development. The next chapter introduces dynamic link libraries (DLLs).

10

Dynamic Link Libraries

Dynamic link libraries (DLLs) enable Windows applications to share resources and code. A DLL is actually an executable module that contains functions which can be used by all Windows applications. DLLs are similar to the C run-time libraries that you regularly use when developing C code. DLLs differ from C run-time libraries, however, because DLLs are linked with the application at run time (dynamic linking). C run-time libraries are linked using a linker when the executable is built (static linking). This chapter introduces dynamic link libraries and their use for Windows application development.

Static Versus Dynamic Linking

If you have developed MS-DOS applications using Borland C++, you are familiar with Borland's C run-time library and the many functions that it provides. To use one of the functions provided in the C run-time library, you must include the header file

that contains the function prototype and any constants defined for the function in your C source file. After you include the header file, you then can use the function to develop the application code. When you create the executable, the C source code is compiled into object code using the compiler. The linker then links object code with the run-time library to create the executable code. Using the linker to link the C run-time library is called *static linking*.

Static linking advantageously provides a set of functions that is available to all applications. The application is not required to include the source code for these functions because the linker will copy the appropriate information to the application's executable file during linking.

Although static linking works well for the MS-DOS environments where only one application runs at a time, static linking is not efficient for multitasking environments such as Windows. Because applications share memory resources in a multitasking environment, static linking often results in wasted memory. An example of such waste is two applications using ten of the same functions from a C run-time library. With static linking, the functions are copied into each application during linking. The result is two copies of each of the ten functions in memory—wasted memory. With dynamic linking, applications share resources and functions. This results in the efficient use of memory and system resources.

Import Libraries

An import library has special importance when working with DLLs. The import library helps Windows find code in the DLL. The import library contains the information that connects application modules and DLL modules. An application module is the application's .EXE file and contains the application code. The DLL module is the library module containing the library code, and usually has one of the following extensions: .DLL, .DRV, .FON, or .EXE.

Import libraries are used along with static link libraries to resolve references to external routines. As was mentioned before, when the application references a function from a static link library, the code for the function is copied to the application's executable during linking. However, when the application references a function from a dynamic link library, the linker does not copy the function's code. The linker instead copies information from the import library to indicate the location where the required code can be found during run time.

The DLL Code Structure

When you use Borland C++ for Windows to create a dynamic link library, you follow the same basic steps (outlined in Chapter 2) that you follow to create a Windows application. The main difference, however, is that you select the `Windows DLL` option under `Options | Applications` rather than `Windows App`. The steps to create a Windows DLL are the following:

> **Note:** This process is designed for use with Windows-based versions of the IDE. The process used for the DOS-based IDE is similar.

1. Start the IDE by double-clicking the Borland C++ for Windows icon.
2. Create all appropriate C or C++ source files, module definition files, and resource files. More information on these files is included in the following paragraphs.
3. Select `Project | Open`. Type the filename, using a .PRJ extension, in the `Project Name` dialog box. Click the `OK` button, or press Enter to continue.
4. Select `Project | Add item`. Add the appropriate C or C++ source files, module definition files, and resource files. Close the `Project` dialog box when you are done.
5. Select `Options | Application`. The `Set Application Options` dialog box will appear. Select `Windows DLL` to indicate that you are developing a Windows dynamic link library (DLL).
6. Select `Run | Run`. This selection builds the project into a Windows dynamic link library (DLL).
7. If there are any errors, modify the appropriate file(s) and repeat step 6.

You still can use the Project Manager to develop the DLL. As with Windows applications, the DLL requires two files that you must create: the C source code file and the module definition file.

The C source code file is very different from the C source code files that you have seen so far in this book. The following code outline represents the basic code structure of the C source file for a DLL.

```
#include <windows.h>

int FAR PASCAL LibMain(HANDLE hInstance, WORD wDataSeg,
                       WORD wHeapSize, LPSTR lpszCmdLine)
{
   /*                                 */
   /*     DLL Initialization          */
   /*                                 */

if (cbHeapSize != 0)    /* if MOVEABLE data segment */
   UnlockData(0);

return(1);
}

VOID FAR PASCAL MinRoutine(int iParam1, int iParam2)
{
char cLocalVariable;    /* Local variables on stack */

     /*                                 */
     /*       MinRoutine Code           */
     /*                                 */
}

VOID FAR PASCAL WEP(int iParam)
{
if (nParameter == WEP_SYSTEMEXIT)
   {
   /* System shutdown in progress - respond accordingly */
   return(1);
   }
else
   {if(nParameter == WEP_FREE_DLL)
      {
      /* DLL use count is zero - DLL is free */
      return(1);
      }
    else
      {
      /* ignore undefined value */
      return(1);
      }
   }

}
```

This code structure has three basic components. The first is the `LibMain` function, which is the main entry point for a Windows DLL and is responsible for initializing the DLL. The second component is the `MinRoutine` function, which is simply a representative function in this code structure. The DLL code structure can contain one or more functions; it does not need to have the MinRoutine function. The last component of the code structure is the WEP (Windows Exit Procedure) function. The WEP function, although not necessary, enables the user to define cleanup activities before the DLL is unloaded from memory.

The module definition file is another file that is required for creating DLLs. The module definition file used for DLLs is similar to the module definition files used for Windows applications. It contains the following eight entries:

- LIBRARY specifies that the module is a DLL. The library name follows the LIBRARY keyword.
- DESCRIPTION is a string that describes the DLL.
- EXETYPE WINDOWS is required for Windows applications and DLLs.
- STUB specifies the DOS 2.*x* program that is copied into the body of the library's executable file. When a Windows application is run from DOS instead of Windows, the specified executable stub is executed. If the STUB statement is not used, an executable stub is assigned automatically. Most applications use the WINSTUB.EXE executable file for the executable stub.
- CODE defines the memory attributes of the library's code segments.
- DATA defines the memory attributes of the library's data segment.
- HEAPSIZE defines the initial size of the local heap for the DLL.
- EXPORTS specifies the functions used as entry points from applications or other DLLs.

Creating a DLL

Listings 10.1 and 10.2 demonstrate the creation of a DLL containing two functions: XBox and SlashBox. The XBox function creates a box that has diagonal lines connecting the opposite corners. The SlashBox function creates a box that has one diagonal line connecting the upper-left and lower-right corners. Two files were necessary to create the DLL. Listing 10.1 shows the module definition file. The C source code file, shown in Listing 10.2, contains the functions XBox and SlashBox.

The project name and the files used to create the DLL are as follows:

Project Name:	WIN_DLL
Files in Project:	WIN_DLL.DEF
	WIN_DLL.C

Listing 10.1. The definition file for the DLL.

```
LIBRARY         WIN_DLL
DESCRIPTION     'DLL for DLL Example'
EXETYPE         WINDOWS
CODE            PRELOAD MOVEABLE DISCARDABLE
DATA            PRELOAD MOVEABLE SINGLE
HEAPSIZE        1024
EXPORTS         XBox
                SlashBox
```

Listing 10.2. The C source file for the DLL.

```
#include <windows.h>

int FAR PASCAL LibMain(HANDLE hInstance, WORD wDataSeg,
                       WORD wHeapSize, LPSTR lpszCmdLine)
{
if(wHeapSize != 0)
   UnlockData(0);
return 1;
}

int FAR PASCAL XBox(HDC hDC,int X,int Y)
{
MoveTo(hDC,X,Y);
LineTo(hDC,X+25,Y);
LineTo(hDC,X+25,Y+25);
LineTo(hDC,X,Y+25);
LineTo(hDC,X,Y);
LineTo(hDC,X+25,Y+25);
MoveTo(hDC,X+25,Y);
LineTo(hDC,X,Y+25);
return 1;
}

int FAR PASCAL SlashBox(HDC hDC,int X,int Y)
{
MoveTo(hDC,X,Y);
LineTo(hDC,X+25,Y);
LineTo(hDC,X+25,Y+25);
LineTo(hDC,X,Y+25);
LineTo(hDC,X,Y);
LineTo(hDC,X+25,Y+25);
return 1;
}
```

Using the DLL from a Windows Application

The purpose of a DLL is to provide functions that several Windows applications can use. The `XBox` and `SlashBox` functions of the DLL in Listings 10.1 and 10.2 are used in the DLL example in Listings 10.3 and 10.4. Two files are required for this demonstration. The module definition file of this example (Listing 10.3) looks similar to the module definition files of the previous examples in this book. There is one difference to note, however. The module definition file for this example uses the `IMPORTS` function to specify that the `XBox` and `SlashBox` functions are part of the WIN_DLL dynamic link library and that these functions are necessary for the application.

The C source file in Listing 10.4 is similar to the C source file of the previous examples in this book. The only items of special interest are the function prototypes of the `XBox` and `SlashBox` functions. When the window procedure receives the WM_PAINT message, the `XBox` and `SlashBox` functions are used to draw figures. The DLL example displays nine boxes created with the `XBox` and `SlashBox` functions. Figure 10.1 shows the output of the DLL example.

The project name and the files used to create the DLL example are as follows:

Project Name:	`WIN_DLLE`
Files in Project:	`WIN_DLLE.DEF`
	`WIN_DLLE.C`

Listing 10.3. *The definition file for the DLL example.*

```
NAME            WIN_DLLE
DESCRIPTION     'DLL Example'
EXETYPE         WINDOWS
CODE            PRELOAD MOVEABLE
DATA            PRELOAD MOVEABLE MULTIPLE
HEAPSIZE        1024
STACKSIZE       5120
EXPORTS         WndProc
IMPORTS         WIN_DLL.XBox
                WIN_DLL.SlashBox
```

Listing 10.4. The C source file for the DLL example.

```
#include <windows.h>
#include <stdlib.h>
#include <string.h>

long FAR PASCAL WndProc (HWND hWnd, WORD iMessage,
                         WORD wParam, LONG lParam);

int FAR PASCAL XBox(HDC hDC,int X,int Y);

int FAR PASCAL SlashBox(HDC hDC,int X,int Y);

int PASCAL WinMain (HANDLE hInstance, HANDLE hPrevInstance,
                    LPSTR lpszCmdParam, int nCmdShow)

{
HWND hWnd;
MSG Message;
WNDCLASS WndClass;

if (!hPrevInstance)
     {
     WndClass.cbClsExtra = 0;
     WndClass.cbWndExtra = 0;
     WndClass.hbrBackground = GetStockObject(WHITE_BRUSH);
     WndClass.hCursor =  LoadCursor(NULL, IDC_ARROW);
     WndClass.hIcon = LoadIcon (NULL, IDI_APPLICATION);
     WndClass.hInstance = hInstance;
     WndClass.lpfnWndProc = WndProc;
     WndClass.lpszClassName = "WIN_DLLE";
     WndClass.lpszMenuName = NULL;
     WndClass.style = CS_HREDRAW ¦ CS_VREDRAW;

     RegisterClass (&WndClass);
     }

hWnd = CreateWindow ("WIN_DLLE",  /* class name */
          "DLL Example",          /* Caption */
          WS_OVERLAPPEDWINDOW,    /* Style */
          CW_USEDEFAULT,          /* x position */
          0,                      /* y position */
          CW_USEDEFAULT,          /* cx - size */
          0,                      /* cy - size */
          NULL,                   /* Parent window */
          NULL,                   /* Menu */
          hInstance,              /* Program Instance */
          NULL);                  /* Parameters */
```

```
ShowWindow (hWnd, nCmdShow);
while (GetMessage (&Message, 0, 0, 0))
     {
     TranslateMessage(&Message);
     DispatchMessage(&Message);
     }
return Message.wParam;
}

/*****************************************************************/
/*              Window Procedure: WndProc                        */
/*****************************************************************/

long FAR PASCAL WndProc (HWND hWnd, WORD iMessage, WORD wParam,
                         LONG lParam)
{
HDC hDC;
HPEN hPen;
PAINTSTRUCT PtStr;

switch (iMessage)
     {
     case WM_PAINT:

          hDC = BeginPaint (hWnd,&PtStr);

          SetMapMode(hDC, MM_ANISOTROPIC);

          hPen = GetStockObject(BLACK_PEN);
          SelectObject(hDC,hPen);

          XBox(hDC,50,50);
          SlashBox(hDC,100,50);
          XBox(hDC,150,50);
          SlashBox(hDC,50,100);
          XBox(hDC,100,100);
          SlashBox(hDC,150,100);
          XBox(hDC,50,150);
          SlashBox(hDC,100,150);
          XBox(hDC,150,150);

          EndPaint(hWnd,&PtStr);
          return 0;

     case WM_DESTROY:

          PostQuitMessage(0);
          return 0;
```

continues

Listing 10.4. continued

```
     default:

          return(DefWindowProc(hWnd, iMessage, wParam,
                 lParam));
     }
}
```

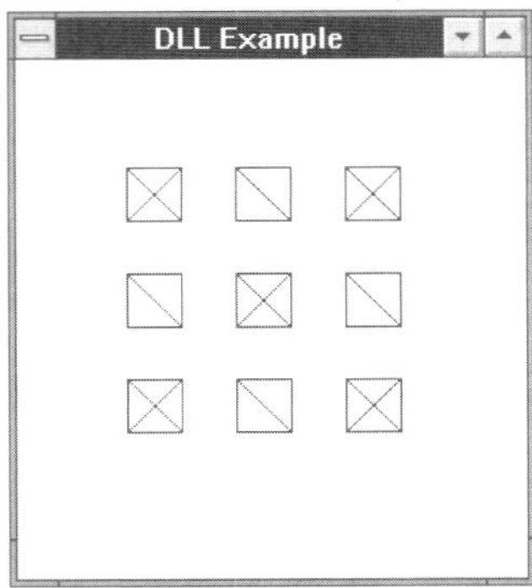

Figure 10.1. *The window created by the DLL example.*

This chapter has introduced the Windows dynamic link library (DLL). The following chapter introduces the ObjectWindows classes.

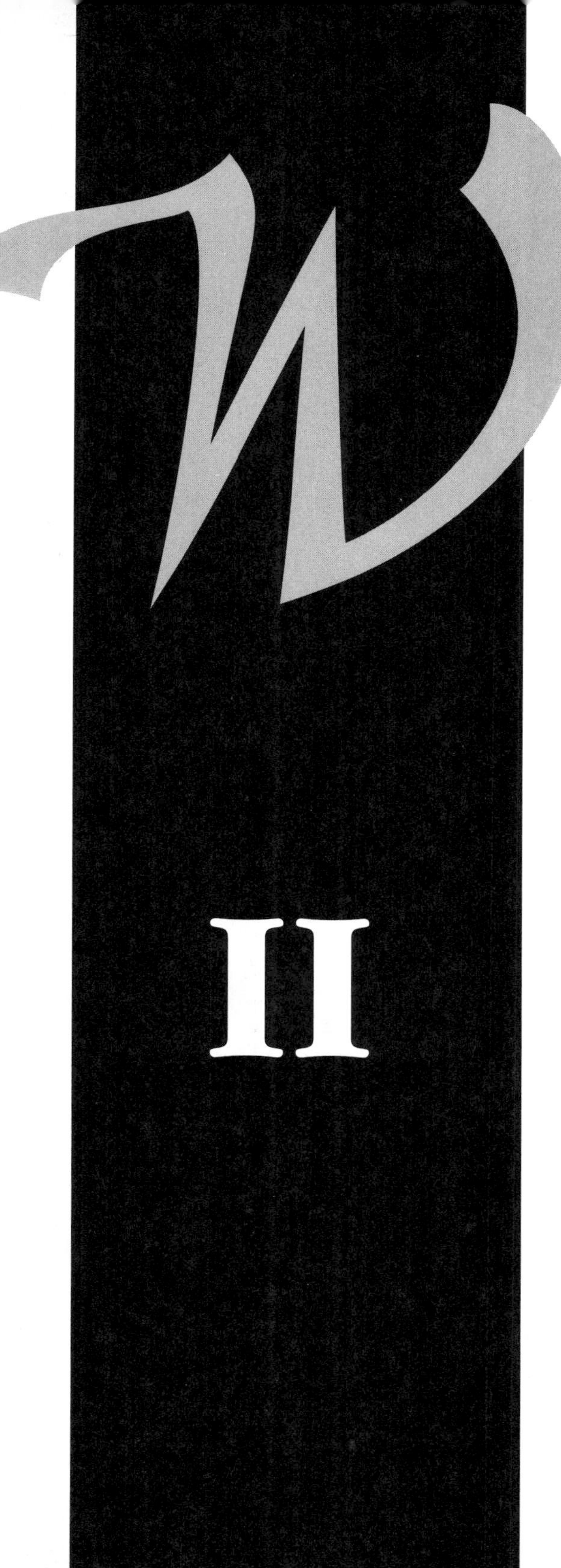

II

Windows Programming with ObjectWindows

11

Introduction to ObjectWindows for C++

Part I of this book introduced traditional Windows programming, whose techniques utilize the C language. Although traditional Windows programs are modular, the resulting code sometimes becomes very long and cumbersome. Part II of the book introduces object-oriented programming techniques and Borland's ObjectWindows for developing Windows applications.

But before you get too far into object-oriented Windows programming using ObjectWindows, you first need to review the basics of object-oriented programming and the C++ language.

Object-Oriented Programming for C++

Object-oriented programming is a relatively new programming methodology. A computer environment is modeled as a collection of objects that interact with each other through messages. Object-oriented programming makes a program more modular and maintainable.

Object-oriented programs, of course, contain objects. Objects contain properties and behaviors. Properties are not directly accessible from outside the object. Instead, the properties are manipulated by the behaviors of the object. The behaviors of the object are invoked when a message is received by the object. This is confusing for newcomers to object-oriented programming, so let's take this one step at a time.

First, we will define an *object*. In the real world, an object has properties and behaviors. For example, a basketball is round and usually orange (its properties) and can be dribbled, passed, or shot (its behaviors). In the programming world, an object also has properties and behaviors. For example, in a graphics application, a circle is described by certain data such as its center, color, radius, and fill pattern (its properties), and can be created, moved, sized, or deleted (its behaviors). Objects in a program can represent the physical entities, such as circles and rectangles, or the more abstract entities, such as stacks and complex data structures.

Object-oriented programming has several characteristics and advantages. First, because objects contain properties and behaviors, objects support modular programming. Modular programming supports ease of development and maintainability of code. The other characteristics and advantages of object-oriented programming involve the properties of encapsulation, inheritance, and polymorphism. The following sections explain these properties.

Encapsulation

Encapsulation is described in the Borland C++ tutorial as combining a data structure with the functions (actions or methods) dedicated to manipulating the data. Encapsulation is achieved by means of a new structuring and data-typing mechanism, the *class*.

To simplify this definition, encapsulation is the practice of using classes to link data and the code used to manipulate the data. In the traditional C programming style, data is usually kept in data structures; functions are then created to manipulate the data. This style is shown as follows:

```
struct data_items
     {
     int a;
     int b;
     int c;
     };

void manipulate_data (int x, int y, int z)
{
data_items.a = data_items.a + x;
data_items.b = data_items.b + y;
data_items.c = data_items.c + z;
}
```

This structure and function then is put into a source file, compiled separately, and treated as a module. The problem with this method is that even though the structure and function are created to be used together, the data can be accessed without using the described function.

The property of encapsulation solves this problem. Encapsulation is provided in C++ by the `struct`, `union`, and `class` keywords. These keywords let you combine data and functions into a class entity. The data items are called data members, whereas the functions are called member functions.

The following is an example of a class:

```
class Circle {
     int x;
     int y;
     int radius;

     int DrawCircle (int a, int b, int rad);
     int DeleteCircle (int a, int b, int rad);
};
```

The data members of the class are `x`, `y`, and `radius`. The member functions of the class are `DrawCircle` and `DeleteCircle`.

By defining the class `Circle`, the properties of the object cannot be directly accessed from outside the object. Only the behaviors of the object, `DrawCircle` and `DeleteCircle`, can manipulate the data. The behaviors of the object can be invoked only by sending a message to the object. By defining an object in this way, the implementation details of the object are not visible to, or accessible by, the outside. This is encapsulation, which leads to modular programming and maintainable, reusable code.

Inheritance

Inheritance is described in the Borland C++ tutorial as building new, derived classes that inherit the data and functions from one or more previously defined base classes, while possibly redefining or adding new data and actions. This creates a hierarchy of classes.

In other words, inheritance is the ability to create a class that has the properties and behaviors of another class. For example, suppose that you start with a class called DOG. This class has several properties, including four legs, a tail, two eyes, two ears, a mouth, and a nose. Under this class you can add classes that provide more specific information.

For our purposes we'll add the `BigDog` class and the `LittleDog` class. The `BigDog` class has the properties of heavy and tall. The `LittleDog` class has the properties of light and short. You could add more classes that provide even more detail. For example, `LongHairBigDog`, `ShortHairBigDog`, `LongHairLittleDog`, and `ShortHairLittleDog` classes could be added. The `LongHairBigDog` and `LongHairLittleDog` classes add the property of long hair. The `ShortHairBigDog` and `ShortHairLittleDog` classes add the property of short hair.

Additional classes could be added which provide even more specifics. We'll add the `IrishSetter` class and the `Chihuahua` class. The `IrishSetter` class adds the property of red hair. The `Chihuahua` class adds the properties of very small and nervous.

The DOG hierarchy is shown in Figure 11.1. By developing a hierarchy, it is possible to classify and inherit properties of objects.

Now let's look at applying this hierarchy. An Irish Setter, for example, has the property of red hair as determined from the derived class `IrishSetter`. Derived classes inherit properties from other classes, called *base classes*. Therefore, the Irish Setter also has the property of the `LongHairBigDog` class, which is long hair. The `LongHairBigDog` class also inherits properties from the `BigDog` class which, in turn, inherits properties from the DOG class. Therefore, you can determine that the Irish Setter has long red hair, is heavy and tall, and has two ears, two eyes, a tail, a mouth, a nose, and four legs. Similarly, you can determine that the Chihuahua is very small and nervous, has short hair, is light and short, and has two ears, two eyes, a tail, a mouth, a nose, and four legs.

Although this is a simple illustration of inheritance, it provides a basic understanding of the power of inheritance. The ability to inherit properties from other classes enables you to generalize data and properties, thus improving programmer efficiency and reducing redundancy in code.

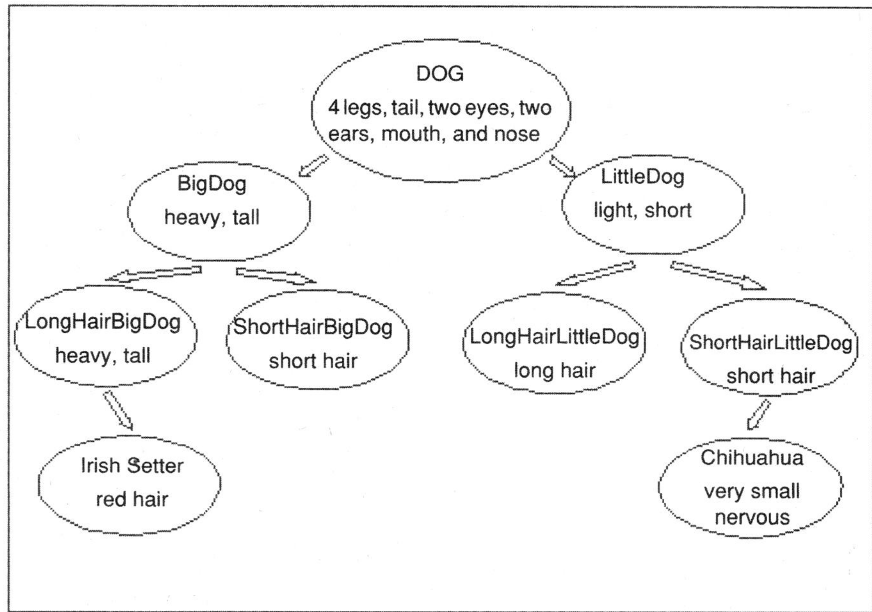

Figure 11.1. *The DOG hierarchy.*

The following example demonstrates the use of the C++ features of inheritance and encapsulation for the implementation of a graphics program:

```
#include <graphics.h>
#include <stdio.h>
#include <stdlib.h>
#include <conio.h>

class Circle {
protected:
   int X;
   int Y;
   int Rad;
public:
   Circle (int InitX, int InitY, int InitRad)
      {X = InitX; Y = InitY; Rad = InitRad;}
};

class SolidCircle : public Circle {
protected:
   int Color;
public:
   SolidCircle (int InitX, int InitY, int InitRad,
```

```
   int InitColor);
};

class ShadedCircle : public Circle {
protected:
   int Color;
public:
   ShadedCircle (int InitX, int InitY, int InitRad,
   int InitColor);
};

SolidCircle::SolidCircle(int InitX, int InitY, int InitRad,
   int InitColor) : Circle (InitX, InitY, InitRad) {
   setfillstyle (SOLID_FILL, InitColor);
   fillellipse (InitX, InitY, InitRad, InitRad);
};

ShadedCircle::ShadedCircle(int InitX, int InitY, int InitRad,
   int InitColor) : Circle (InitX, InitY, InitRad) {
   setfillstyle (HATCH_FILL, InitColor);
   fillellipse (InitX, InitY, InitRad, InitRad);
};


int main()
{
int gdriver = VGA;
int gmode = VGAHI;

int x, y, color, rad, selection;

registerbgidriver(EGAVGA_driver);
registerbgifont(sansserif_font);

initgraph(&gdriver,&gmode,"");

do
{
x = random (639);
y = random (479);
rad = random (51);
color = random (15);
selection = random (2);

if (selection == 0)
     ShadedCircle (x, y, rad + 5, color + 1);
else
     SolidCircle (x, y, rad + 5, color + 1);
```

```
} while (! kbhit());

closegraph();
return 0;
}
```

The program begins by declaring the class `Circle`. The `Circle` class demonstrates the properties of encapsulation through its data `X`, `Y`, and `Rad`. Inheritance is demonstrated by the two derived classes, `ShadedCircle` and `SolidCircle`, of the base class `Circle`.

The program randomly selects the horizontal and vertical coordinates for the center position of a circle. The radius and fill color are then randomly selected. A selection is then made to determine which type of circle will be drawn—either a shaded or solid circle. The shaded or solid circle is then drawn. This continues until a key is pressed.

Polymorphism

Polymorphism is described in the Borland C++ tutorial as giving an action one name or symbol that is shared up and down a class hierarchy, with each class in the hierarchy implementing the action in a way appropriate to itself.

Very simply stated, polymorphism, in C++, is the ability to create several versions of the same function or operator. The Borland C++ Run-Time Library contains several functions that have been "overloaded" to work with various data types. Look at the following function prototypes, for example:

```
int square (int value);
float square (float value);
double square (double square);
```

Each function is designed to accept and return a particular data type: int, float, or double; however, each function is called `square`. In C, you can have only one function with a given name. In C++, on the other hand, function overloading is fully supported as long as the argument lists differ. Therefore, if you call `square` while passing an integer value, the proper function will be called and an integer value will be returned. Similarly, if you call `square` with a float or double value, a float or double value, respectively, will be returned.

The ability to overload functions and operators provides greater flexibility in program design.

The following example demonstrates the overloading of a function:

```
#include <stdio.h>
#include <stdlib.h>
#include <conio.h>
#include <iostream.h>

class squared {
public:
  int squ(int);
  double squ(double);
  long squ(long);
};

int squared::squ(int intval)
{
   int result;

   result = intval * intval;
   return (result);
}

double squared::squ(double dblval)
{
   double result;

   result = dblval * dblval;
   return (result);
}

long squared::squ(long longval)
{
   long result;

   result = longval * longval;
   return (result);
}


int main()
{
squared value;

clrscr();
cout << "The square of 3 is " << value.squ(3) << endl;
cout << "The square of 3.5 is " << value.squ(3.5) << endl;
cout << "The square of 6L is " << value.squ(6L) << endl;

return 0;
}
```

In this example, the class `squared` has three functions called `squ` associated with it. Each function is designed to work with either int, double, or long values. When the function `squ` is called, the value passed as a parameter determines which version of the `squ` function is executed.

Polymorphism is also known either as *late* or *dynamic binding* and is often accomplished using virtual functions.

Now that you have reviewed the basics of object-oriented programming, take a look at Borland's ObjectWindows, an object-oriented library that enables you to take full advantage of object-oriented programming features.

Object-Oriented Windows Programming with ObjectWindows

ObjectWindows is an object-oriented library that incorporates the advantages of object-oriented programming to make programming Windows applications easier for you. With ObjectWindows all major Windows elements, including windows themselves, are treated as objects with defined behaviors, attributes, and data. The three most significant features of ObjectWindows are as follows:

- The encapsulation of window information
- The abstraction of many of the Windows functions
- Automatic message response

The encapsulation of window information is significant in that the behaviors, attributes, and data for the window, dialog box, and control objects (known as *interface objects*) are defined by ObjectWindows. Although ObjectWindows defines the behavior, attributes, and data for interface objects, it is still up to Windows to implement the physical representation of the objects (what you see in the display). The physical representation of the interface objects depends upon Windows structures that are known as *interface elements*.

The interface element's handle is the thread that binds the interface object and the interface element. When the `Create` member function of an interface object is called, the interface element is created and the handle to the element is returned. The `HWindow` data member of the interface object is used to store the handle to the interface element. You must understand the distinction and bond between interface

objects and elements to take full advantage of the features that ObjectWindows offers. Once you understand the basics of ObjectWindows, you can simplify Windows application development by using ObjectWindows' many features.

Another significant feature of ObjectWindows is the abstraction of many Windows functions. Using member functions that abstract a called Windows function makes programming easier for you, because it provides a built-in interface to that function. There are hundreds of Windows functions and, unfortunately, not all of these functions are abstracted. You can call Windows functions directly, however, and many of the parameters you need to call a Windows function are already stored in the data members of the interface objects.

Automatic message response is another significant feature of ObjectWindows. Windows requires its applications to respond to Windows messages that are sent to it. With traditional Windows programming as presented in Part I, a `switch` statement is used to respond to messages. With ObjectWindows, however, Windows messages are handled by object member function calls. A member function can be defined for each message that must be handled. Therefore, when your object receives a message, the appropriate member function is called automatically.

This has been a brief review of the significant features of ObjectWindows. Now let's look at the hierarchy of ObjectWindows classes. Once you review the ObjectWindows hierarchy, you can look more closely at classes that comprise the ObjectWindows library.

The ObjectWindows Hierarchy

ObjectWindows is a library of hierarchical classes that enable you to take advantage of the object-oriented feature of inheritance. The ObjectWindows classes contain data members and member functions that make Windows programming easier. Figure 11.2 illustrates the ObjectWindows hierarchy. The ObjectWindows classes and ObjectWindows member functions are explained in detail in Chapter 17, "ObjectWindows Classes."

The remainder of this chapter provides additional information on the base class `Object` and ObjectWindows application objects, interface objects, window objects, dialog objects, control objects, MDI objects, and `Scroller` objects.

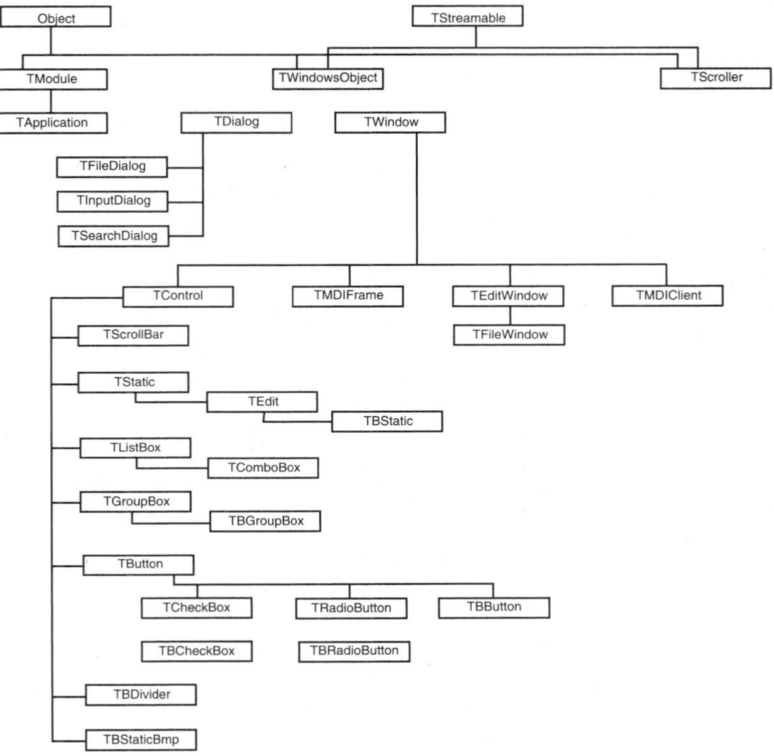

Figure 11.2. *The ObjectWindows hierarchy.*

The *Object* Class

Before you look at application objects, interface objects, window objects, dialog objects, control objects, MDI objects, or `Scroller` objects, you should look at the base class that defines the behaviors, data, and attributes for derived classes. The `Object` class is the base class for all ObjectWindows derived classes. `Object` is an abstract class that defines the behaviors of a derived object and provides the structures for type checking and encapsulation. The `Object` class has the following data members and member functions:

Data Members:

`ZERO` handles problems when the `new` operator cannot allocate space for an object

Member Functions:

Two `Object` constructors

`Object` destructor

`firstThat` finds the first object in the container that meets the specified conditions

`forEach` iterates through each object in the container

`hashValue` returns a hash value

`isA` returns a unique class identifier for the class

`isAssociation` returns zero for the base `Object` class

`isEqual` is a pure virtual function for derived classes

`isSortable` determines whether an object is derived from the class `Sortable`

`lastThat` is identical to `firstThat` for noncontainer objects

`nameOf` enables derived classes to return a class ID string

`new` allocates the specified number of bytes for an object

`printOn` writes the printable representation of the object on a stream

Chapter 17, "ObjectWindows Classes," provides reference information for the data members and member functions of the `Object` class.

Application Objects

Every Windows application developed using ObjectWindows must define an application class derived from `TApplication`. The resulting application object encapsulates the application's behavior, including the creation and display of the main window, the initialization of the first instance of an application, the initialization of every subsequent instance of an application, the processing of messages for the application, and the closing of the application.

For the derived application class, you must define the construction of the main window object and redefine the behaviors for the initialization of instances, the processing of messages, and the closing of the application. Before you go any further into the details of creating and defining the application object, you should quickly review the `TApplication` object.

TApplication

`TApplication` defines the behavior of ObjectWindows applications and provides the structure for them. All ObjectWindows applications derive an application class from `TApplication`. `TApplication` contains the following data members and member functions:

Data Members:

`HAccTable` stores the handle to the current Windows accelerator table

`hPrevInstance` defines the handle of the previous instance of the application

`KBHandlerWnd` points to the active window if the keyboard handler for the window is enabled

`MainWindow` points to the main window of the application

`nCmdShow` specifies whether the application should be displayed as an icon or as an open window

Member Functions:

`TApplication` constructor constructs the `TApplication` object

`~TApplication()` destructor destroys the `TApplication` object

`CanClose` determines whether the application can close

`IdleAction` can be redefined to perform special functions when the application is idle

`InitApplication` makes the initializations required for the first executing instance of the application

`InitInstance` makes the initializations required for all executing instances of the application

`InitMainWindow` constructs a generic `TWindow` class using the application name

`isA` redefines the pure virtual function in class `Object`; this function returns the class ID of `TApplication`

`MessageLoop` manages the message loop of the application

`nameOf` redefines the pure virtual function in class `Object`

`ProcessAccels` processes accelerator messages

`ProcessAppMsg` calls `ProcessDlgMsg`, `ProcessMDIAccels`, and `ProcessAccels` for the processing of modeless dialog messages, MDI accelerator messages, and accelerator messages, respectively

`ProcessDlgMsg` provides message processing of keyboard input for modeless dialog boxes and windows with controls

`ProcessMDIAccels` processes accelerator messages for MDI applications

`Run` initializes the instance and executes the application
`SetKBHandler` enables keyboard handling for the specified window

Chapter 17, "ObjectWindows Classes," provides reference information for the data members and member functions of the `TApplication` class.

The Application's Main Program

All ObjectWindows applications contain a main program that controls the application. For most applications, this main program contains three statements in the format shown in the following code:

```
int PASCAL WinMain(HINSTANCE hInstance, HINSTANCE hPrevInstance,
                   LPSTR lpCmdLine, int nCmdShow)
{
     TAppExample AppExample("Application Example" ,hInstance,
          hPrevInstance, lpCmdLine, nCmdShow);
     AppExample.Run();
     return AppExample.Status;
}
```

The first statement of the main program calls the constructor to construct the application object. When the constructor is called, the data members of the application object are initialized.

The second statement of the main program calls the `Run` member function, which calls `InitApplication` and `InitInstance`. `InitApplication` initializes the first instance of the application. `InitInstance` initializes each instance of the application. After `Run` has called `InitApplication` and `InitInstance`, `InitMainWindow` is called to create a main window. `InitMainWindow` is generally redefined for each application. Lastly, the `Run` member function calls `MessageLoop`. `MessageLoop` receives and processes Windows messages sent to the application.

The third statement of the main program returns the final status of the application. Zero is generally used to represent a normal closing of the application. A nonzero value usually indicates that an error has occurred.

As the three statements indicate, there are three basic steps that occur in the main window:

- The initialization of the application
- The execution of the application
- The termination of the application

The following paragraphs describe each of these steps in more detail.

Initializing Applications

As previously described, the main program generally consists of three statements. Of these three statements, the first two contribute to the initialization of the application. The main window is described in the following paragraphs.

The first statement of the main program called the constructor to the application object. Before you can call the constructor to the application object, however, you must first define an application class derived from `TApplication`. The following code demonstrates how this can be done:

```
class TAppExample : public TApplication
{
public:
     TAppExample(LPSTR AName, HINSTANCE hInstance, HINSTANCE
          hPrevInstance, LPSTR lpCmdLine, int nCmdShow):
          TApplication(AName, hInstance,
          hPrevInstance, lpCmdLine, nCmdShow) {};
     virtual void InitMainWindow();
};
```

In this example you are creating an application class, `TAppExample`, that is derived from `TApplication`. When you create an application object, you must define an `InitMainWindow` member function that constructs and initializes the main window object. Once created, the main window object can be referenced by the `MainWindow` data member. The following code demonstrates how to you can define the `InitMainWindow` member function:

```
void TAppExample::InitMainWindow()
{
     MainWindow = new TAppExampleWindow(NULL, "Main Window");
}
```

The second statement of the main program calls the `Run` member function which, in turn, calls `InitApplication` and `InitInstance`. `InitInstance` then calls `InitMainWindow`.

Therefore, it is obvious that the second statement of the main program plays an important role in application initialization. Because the `Run` member function first calls `InitApplication`, let's look at what happens when you call `InitApplication`.

When the application is executed for the first time (referring to the first time the application has been run since all instances of the application have been terminated), you may want some special initialization of the application to take place. `InitApplication` can be defined to manage the first-time initialization of the application. Subsequent instances of the application do not call `InitApplication`.

The next function that gets called by the `Run` member function is `InitInstance`, which performs initialization for each instance of the application. `InitInstance` also calls `InitMainWindow`. `InitMainWindow` must have been previously defined. The previous paragraphs provide an example of a definition for `InitMainWindow`.

Once all the initializations for the application have been completed, the application is ready to execute.

Executing Applications

The second statement of the main program contributes to the initialization of the application, and it also executes the application. The `Run` member function of the application object calls the `MessageLoop` member function. When the `MessageLoop` function is called, the interactive portion of your application begins. Once the `MessageLoop` function begins processing the messages sent to the application, the application is able to consistently interact with Windows and respond to the messages that are sent to it. The `MessageLoop` function that is inherited by the application works well for most applications and does not need to be modified. If you want special message handling for dialog box, accelerator, or MDI messages, however, you can redefine `MessageLoop`.

`MessageLoop` calls the `ProcessDlgMsg`, `ProcessAccels`, and `ProcessMDIAccels` member functions for the processing of modeless dialog messages, accelerator messages, and MDI accelerator messages, respectively. If your application does not use modeless dialog boxes, accelerators, or MDI accelerators, it may be beneficial for you to redefine `MessageLoop` to eliminate these unnecessary function calls because they require time to execute.

Terminating Applications

The application terminates when the main window is closed. Before the main window can be closed, however, the application must exit `MessageLoop` and agree to terminate. When the user attempts to close an application, the `WM_CLOSE` message is sent to the main window of the application. The `CloseWindow` member function of the main window object is then called. `CloseWindow` calls the `CanClose` member function of the application object to determine whether it is all right to close the application. The application's `CanClose` function returns the result of its call to the `CanClose` function of the main window object. If all agree to close, the application terminates. The third statement of the main program returns the final status of the application.

Interface Objects

Interface objects represent windows, dialog boxes, and controls. As mentioned at the beginning of this chapter, interface objects usually have a corresponding interface element. The interface object provides the functions and data members for initializing, creating, manipulating, and terminating the interface element.

Interface elements are treated as a child window of the parent window. For example, a dialog box is often a child window of the main window. In this case the main window would be the parent window. The dialog box often contains, for example, a list box. The list box contained in the dialog box is considered to be a child window of the dialog box.

Before you go any further into the discussion of interface objects, you should briefly review the class that binds the three basic types of interface objects defined by ObjectWindows, `TWindowsObject`.

TWindowsObject

Derived from `Object`, `TWindowsObject` is an abstract class that defines the behaviors that all interface objects share and maintains a list of child windows. By defining the common behaviors of windows, dialog boxes, and controls and by maintaining a list of child windows, `TWindowsObject` enables interface objects to inherit object behaviors and provides a central location for the maintenance of the child window list. `TWindowsObject` contains the following data members and member functions:

Data Members:

`DefaultProc` holds the address of the default window procedure

`HWindow` specifies the handle of the interface element associated with the interface object

`Parent` points to the interface object that acts as the parent window for the interface object

`Status` can indicate an error in the initialization of an interface object

`Title` points to the caption for the window

`TransferBuffer` points to a buffer used to transfer data

Member Functions:

Two `TWindowsObject` constructors

`TWindowsObject` destructor

`ActivationResponse` either enables or disables keyboard handling when this is being activated and keyboard handling is requested for this

`AfterDispatchHandler` is called by `DispatchAMessage` after responding to a message

`BeforeDispatchHandler` is called by `DispatchAMessage` before invoking a message response

`build` invokes the `TWindowsObject` constructor and constructs an object of type `TWindowsObject` before reading its data members from a stream

`CanClose` determines whether the associated interface element can be closed by calling the `CanClose` member functions of each of the child windows

`ChildWithID` returns the pointer to the child window from the child window list that has the specified ID

`CloseWindow` calls `ShutDownWindow` to close the window

`CMExit` is called when a menu item with an ID of `CM_EXIT` is selected

`Create` is a pure virtual function

`CreateChildren` creates child windows from the child list

`DefChildProc` handles incoming child-ID-based messages by default

`DefCommandProc`, by default, handles command-based messages

`DefNotificationProc` provides the default processing of notification messages and passes these notification messages to the parent as a child-ID-based message

`DefWndProc` handles default message processing

`Destroy` calls an associated interface element

`DisableAutoCreate` disables the autocreate feature

`DisableTransfer` disables the transfer of state data to and from the transfer buffer

`DispatchAMessage` dispatches Windows messages to the appropriate response member function

`DispatchScroll` dispatches messages from scroll bar controls

`DrawItem` is called when a control or menu item needs to be redrawn

`EnableAutoCreate` enables the autocreate feature

`EnableKBHandler` enables windows and modeless dialog boxes to provide a keyboard interface to child controls

`EnableTransfer` enables the transfer of state data to and from the transfer buffer

`FirstThat` calls the specified test function for each child window in `ChildList`

`FirstThat` calls the specified test function for each child window in `ChildList` and takes a member function as a parameter

`ForEach` calls the specified function and passes each child window in `ChildList` as an argument

`ForEach` function is like the previous `ForEach` function except that this function takes a member function as a parameter

`GetApplication` gets the pointer to the `TApplication` object that is associated with `this`

`GetChildPtr` reads a reference to a pointer to a child window from the specified stream

`GetChildren` reads child windows from the specified stream into the child list

`GetClassName` returns the Windows registration class name and must be redefined for derived classes

`GetClient` returns `NULL` for non-MDI interface objects

`GetFirstChild` returns the pointer to the first child window in the child list for the interface object

`GetId` returns zero by default

`GetInstance` returns the instance thunk of the window

`GetLastChild` returns the pointer to the last child window in the child list for the interface object

`GetModule` returns the pointer to the `TModule` that owns the object

`GetSiblingPtr` is used only during a `read` operation to references written by a call to `PutSiblingPtr`

`GetWindowClass` is redefined by derived classes

`hashValue` redefines the pure virtual function in class `Object`

`isA` redefines the pure virtual function in class `Object` and should be redefined to return a unique class ID

`isEqual` redefines the pure virtual function in class `Object`

`IsFlagSet` returns `TRUE` if the bit flag of the `Flags` data member with the specified mask is set

`nameOf` is a pure virtual function

`Next` returns a pointer to the next window in the child window list

`printOn` must be redefined by all objects derived from the base class `Object`

`Previous` returns a pointer to the previous window in the child window list

`PutChildPtr` writes a child window to the specified output stream

`PutChildren` writes child windows in the child list to the specified stream

`PutSiblingPtr` writes the reference to a sibling window to the specified output stream

`read` creates an object instance and calls `GetChildren` to read in the child windows

`Register` registers the Windows registration class of `this`

`RemoveClient` removes the specified client window from the child list

`SetCaption` defines the caption of the interface element as the value specified in `ATitle`

`SetFlags` sets the bit flag of the `Flags` data member with the specified mask according to the value specified in `OnOff`

`SetParent` sets `Parent` to the parent window specified in `NewParent`, removes `this` from the child list of the previous parent, and adds `this` to the child list of the new parent

`SetTransferBuffer` sets `TransferBuffer` to the buffer specified in `ATransferBuffer`

`SetupWindow` attempts to create an associated interface element for each child window in `ChildList` that has the autocreate feature enabled

`Show` displays the interface element as specified in `ShowCmd`

`ShutDownWindow` destroys the associated interface element

`Transfer` transfers data to and from the buffer referenced by `DataPtr`

`TransferData` transfers data between the buffer and the interface object's child windows that have the `WM_TRANSFER` flag set

`WMActivate` enables keyboard handling if requested when a `WM_ACTIVATE` message is detected

`WMClose` calls `CloseWindow` to close the window

`WMCommand` calls the appropriate member functions when command-based, child-ID-based, or notify-based messages are detected

`WMDestroy` handles the `WM_DESTROY` message

`WMDrawItem` dispatches the `WM_DRAWITEM` message for drawable controls

`WMHScroll` calls `DispatchScroll` in response to a `WM_HSCROLL` message

`WMNCDestroy` handles the `WM_NCDESTROY` message

`WMQueryEndSession` calls the appropriate `CanClose` function to determine whether the session can close

`WMVScroll` calls `DispatchScroll` in response to the detection of vertical scroll bar messages

`write` writes `Title`, `Status`, flags, and `CreateOrder` and calls `PutChildren` to write out child windows

Chapter 17, "ObjectWindows Classes," provides reference information for the data members and member functions of the `TWindowsObject` class.

It is important to note that the three primary types of interface objects are derived from `TWindowsObject`: windows, dialog boxes, and controls. Each of these interface types is discussed in more detail later in this chapter.

Window Objects

Window objects are interface objects that are associated with window elements. The basic behaviors of window objects are defined in the `TWindow` class. `TWindow` is derived from `TWindowsObject` and has five classes derived from it: `TMDIFrame`, `TMDIClient`, `TControl`, `TEditWindow`, and `TBWindow`. The following paragraphs briefly explain windows objects and the `TWindow` class.

Using Window Objects

A window object is an interface object and has a corresponding interface element. In order to create a window, you must first define the object and then create the interface element.

ObjectWindows defines a data structure `TWindowAttr` that contains the creation attributes for the window object. The `TWindowAttr` data structure follows:

```
struct_CLASSTYPE TWindowAttr {
     DWORD Style;
     DWORD ExStyle;
     int X, Y, W, H;
     LPSTR Menu;
     int Id;
     LPSTR Param;
     };
```

in which

`Style` is a combination of one or more of the following window style constants:

WS_BORDER	WS_MINIMIZE
WS_CAPTION	WS_MINIMIZEBOX
WS_CHILD	WS_OVERLAPPED
WS_CHILDWINDOW	WS_OVERLAPPEDWINDOW
WS_CLIPCHILDREN	WS_POPUP
WS_CLIPSIBLINGS	WS_POPUPWINDOW
WS_DISABLED	WS_SIZEBOX
WS_DLGFRAME	WS_SYSMENU
WS_GROUP	WS_TABSTOP
WS_HSCROLL	WS_THICKFRAME
WS_ICONIC	WS_VISIBLE
WS_MAXIMIZE	WS_VSCROLL
WS_MAXIMIZEBOX	

`ExStyle` specifies any extended styles. The extended styles follow:

WS_EX_DLGMODALFRAME

WS_EX_NOPARENTNOTIFY

WS_EX_ACCEPTFILES

WS_EX_TOPMOST

WS_EX_TRANSPARENT

in which

X is the x screen coordinate of the upper-left corner of the window

Y is the y screen coordinate of the upper-left corner of the window

W is the width of the window

H is the height of the window

Param contains a value passed to the window when it is created

Menu contains the resource identifier for parent windows

Id holds the child window ID for child windows or the resource identifier for dialog boxes

TWindow

TWindow is an ObjectWindows class that defines the behaviors for the main window and pop-up windows. In general, the main window of an application is an instance of a derived class of TWindow. However, you can create an instance of TWindow. The window defined from the TWindow class is a generic, captioned window that can be minimized, maximized, moved, sized, and closed. The TWindow class contains the following data members and member functions:

Data Members:

Attr references a TWindowAttr structure that specifies the attributes used to create the window including the control ID, menu, text, and style

FocusChildHandle is the child window handle of the child window that had the focus when the window was last activated

Scroller points to the TScroller object used for display scrolling

Member Functions:

Three TWindow constructors

TWindow destructor

ActivationResponse is called by WMActivate and WMMDIActivate to provide a keyboard interface for the window controls

AssignMenu sets Attr.Menu to the specified menu name

`AssignMenu` calls the previous `AssignMenu` function and passes the specifed menu ID

`build` invokes the `TWindow` constructor and constructs an object of type `TWindow` before reading its data members from a stream

`Create` creates an interface element associated with the `TWindow` object

`GetClassName` returns "OWLWindow", the default Windows registration class name for `TWindow`

`GetWindowClass` places the default values for the registration attributes into the window class structure referenced by `AWndClass`

`isA` redefines the pure virtual function in class `Object`

`nameOf` redefines the pure virtual function in class `Object`

`Paint` stores derived types that define `Paint` member functions

`read` uses `TWindowsObject::read` to read the base `TWindowsObject` object

`SetupWindow` initializes the new window

`WMCreate` calls `SetupWindow` when the `WM_CREATE` message is detected

`WMHScroll` handles horizontal scroll bar events

`WMLButtonDown` responds to `WM_LBUTTONDOWN` messages

`WMMDIActivate` sets the parent's (`TMDIFrame`) `ActiveChild` to the window handle specified in the incoming `WM_MDIACTIVATE` message

`WMMove` saves the new window coordinates when a `WM_MOVE` message is detected

`WMPaint` calls `Paint` when a `WM_PAINT` message is detected

`WMSize` calls `SetPageSize` when a window with scrollers has been sized

`WMVScroll` calls `DispatchScroll` when the `WM_VSCROLL` message is detected from a scroll bar control

`write` uses `TWindowsObject::write` to write the base `TWindowsObject` object

Chapter 17, "ObjectWindows Classes," provides reference information for the data members and member functions of the `TWindow` class.

To define the attributes for your window you must first derive a class from `TWindow` and call the constructor of the base class. For example:

```
class TExampleWindow : public TWindow
{
```

```
TExampleWindow(PTWindowsObject AParent, LPSTR ATitle) :
     TWindow(AParent, ATitle) {};
};
```

Once this has been done, you can directly modify the attributes of the window object by defining the `Attr` data member. As an example, you could specify the menu for your window as follows:

```
TExampleWindow::TExampleWindow(PTWindowsObject AParent,
     LPSTR ATitle) : TWindow(AParent, ATitle)
{
AssignMenu("MENUNAME");
}
```

Using Window Elements

Once the window object has been defined, you must create the window element. Fortunately, you do not have to explicitly create the window element because the window element is generally created automatically either when the application is started (main windows) or the `SetupWindow` member function of a parent window is called (child windows). It is, however, a good idea quickly to review the process involved in creating the window element.

The window element is created by calling the `MakeWindow` member function of the application object while passing the window object. `MakeWindow`, in turn, calls `ValidWindow` and `Create`. The `ValidWindow` function determines whether the window object is valid. If valid, `MakeWindow` continues and calls `Create` to create the window element.

Creating Window Classes

Now that you have learned to create the window object and the window element, you may find it necessary to define your own window class that has a specified background, icon, menu, and cursor. In the process of creating the window object, you can define certain attributes, called creation attributes, for each window. Creation attributes include those attributes contained in the `TWindowAttr` data structure. Other attributes, however—including the icon, menu, and background—cannot be defined for each window. Instead, these attributes can be defined only for a window class.

When you decide to modify the attributes (other than creation attributes) of a window, a new window class must be associated with that window. Two member functions of the window must be redefined to accomplish this task of association.

The first member function to redefine is `GetClassName`. The `GetClassName` function returns the name of the window class. For example:

```
LPSTR TCursorWindow::GetClassName()
{
return "CursorWindow";
}
```

The second function to redefine is the `GetWindowClass` function. When you redefine the `GetWindowClass` function, you specify the modified attributes, as in the following example, which redefines the cursor:

```
void TCursorWindow::GetWindowClass(WNDCLASS _FAR & AWndClass)
{
TWindow::GetWindowClass(AWndClass);
AWndClass.hCursor = LoadCursor(0, IDC_CROSS);
}
```

`GetWindowClass` receives a `WNDCLASS` data structure and defines the attributes of the structure relative to what you have specified.

Now that you know how to create window objects, window elements, and window classes, let's look at two classes derived from `TWindow`: `TEditWindow` and `TFileWindow`.

TEditWindow

`TEditWindow` enables you easily to create an edit window that allows the user to enter and modify the text. Edit windows do not, however, enable you to read and write files. The text of the edit window is contained and controlled in a child `TEdit` control that completely fills the client area of the edit window. The `Editor` data member of `TEditWindow` references the instance of `TEdit`. The search and replace capabilities of the edit window are provided by `TEditWindow` and are not a part of `TEdit`.

`TEditWindow` defines a window object that enables the user to enter and edit text. `TEditWindow` is derived from `TWindow` and has one derived class, `TFileWindow`. `TEditWindow` contains the following data members and member functions:

Data Members:

`Editor` points to a multiline edit control that provides text editing for the edit window

`IsReplaceOp` is `TRUE` when the next search will also perform a replace

`SearchStruct` is a transfer buffer used with `TSearchDialog`

Member Functions:

Two `TEditWindow` constructors

`build` invokes the `TEditWindow` constructor and constructs an object of type `TEditWindow` before reading its data members from a stream

`CMEditFind` initiates a text search and displays a search dialog box when a `Find` menu item is selected

`CMEditFindNext` initiates a text search when a `Find Next` menu item is selected

`CMEditReplace` initiates a text search and replace operation and displays a search dialog box when a `Replace` menu item is selected

`DoSearch` offers search functions using the options and features in `SearchStruct`

`read` calls `TWindow::read` to read in the base `TWindow` object

`WMSetFocus` sets the focus to `Editor` edit control when the `WM_SETFOCUS` message is detected

`WMSize` sizes the `Editor` edit control to the `TEditWindow`'s client area when the `WM_SIZE` message is detected

`write` calls `TWindow::write` to write out the base `TWindow` object and then `PutChildPtr` to write out the edit control child window

Chapter 17, "ObjectWindows Classes," provides reference information for the data members and member functions of the `TEditWindow` class.

TFileWindow

`TFileWindow` enables you to easily create a file editing window. Because `TFileWindow` is derived from `TEditWindow`, the file editing window is similar to the edit window. The primary difference between an editing window and a file editing window is that the file editing window enables the user to open a new file, open an existing file, save a file under its current name, and save a file under a new name. The member functions of `TFileWindow` provide these capabilities.

`TFileWindow` defines an editing window that enables the user to read, write, and edit files. `TFileWindow` contains the following data members and member functions:

Data Members:

`FileName` is the name of the file being edited

IsNewFile indicates whether the file being edited is a new file or a previously opened file

Member Functions:

Two TFileWindow constructors

TFileWindow destructor

build invokes the TFileWindow constructor and constructs an object of type TFileWindow before reading its data members from a stream

CanClear determines whether it is all right to clear the text in the editor

CanClose determines whether it is all right to close the file

CMFileNew calls NewFile when a "New" command with a CM_FILENEW ID is detected

CMFileOpen calls Open when an "Open" command with a CM_FILEOPEN ID is detected

CMFileSave calls Save when a "Save" command with a CM_FILESAVE ID is detected

CMFileSaveAs calls SaveAs when a "SaveAs" command with a CM_FILESAVEAS ID is detected

NewFile calls CanClear to determine whether the current text in the editor can be cleared, and if so, opens a new file

Open calls CanClear to determine whether the current text in the editor can be cleared, and if so, displays a file dialog box that enables the user to select a file

Read reads the contents of a file into the editor and sets IsNewFile to FALSE

read calls TEditWindow::read to read in the base TEditWindow object

ReplaceWith replaces the current file in the editor with the specified file

Save saves the current file

SaveAs saves the current file by using a file name retrieved from the user

SetFileName sets the FileName data member and modifies the window caption

SetupWindow establishes the edit window's Editor edit control

Write saves the contents of the editor to the file specified in FileName

write calls TEditWindow::write to write out the base TEditWindow object and then writes out FileName

Chapter 17, "ObjectWindows Classes," provides reference information for the data members and member functions of the `TFileWindow` class.

TBWindow

`TBWindow` enables you to easily create a generic window with a light gray background. `TBWindow` is derived from `TWindow` and has no derived classes. `TBWindow` contains the following data members and member functions:

Data Members:

None

Member Functions:

Two `TBWindow` constructors

`build` creates a `TBWindow` object before its data members are read from a stream

`GetClassName` returns "TBWindow", the default Windows registration class name for `TBWindow`

`GetWindowClass` fills the `WNDCLASS` data structure specified in `AWndClass` with the default registration attributes for `TBWindow`

Chapter 17, "ObjectWindows Classes," provides reference information for the data members and member functions of the `TBWindow` class.

Dialog Objects

Dialog boxes are special purpose child windows that are used as user interfaces for input-related tasks. Dialog boxes are defined in resource files and are referenced in an application by the dialog box ID specified in the resource file. The `TDialog` class is defined by ObjectWindows to create and support dialog boxes.

TDialog

Dialog objects can either be modal or modeless. A modeless dialog box, in effect, is the same as displaying a window. A modal dialog box, on the other hand, disables the parent window and receives all input.

You create modeless dialog boxes by using the `MakeWindow` member function of the application object, as the following example shows:

```
GetModule()->MakeWindow(new TExampleDialog(this,"Dialog"));
```

Modal dialog boxes are created using the `ExecDialog` member function of the application object. For example:

```
GetModule()->ExecDialog(new TExampleDialog(this, "Dialog"));
```

`TDialog` has two members functions, `Ok` and `Cancel`, that are predefined to let you close the dialog box. To use these member functions, the `OK` and `CANCEL` buttons of your dialog box should use the button IDs IDOK and IDCANCEL, respectively. If you want, you can define your own member functions for closing your dialog box.

To manipulate the controls of the dialog box, you must define your own controls and actions. The predefined control classes are not used with dialog boxes. They are for use inside windows other than dialog boxes. The dialog box example in Chapter 12, "Windows Programming Using ObjectWindows," demonstrates one way that you can create a dialog box and define the actions for the controls of the dialog box.

There are three derived classes of `TDialog` that provide special dialog boxes: `TFileDialog`, `TInputDialog`, and `TSearchDialog`. These classes are discussed in the following paragraphs.

`TDialog` is the base class for derived classes that create modal and modeless dialog boxes. `TDialog` is derived from `TWindowsObject` and has three derived classes, `TFileDialog`, `TInputDialog`, and `TSearchDialog`. `TDialog` contains the following data members and member functions:

Data Members:

`Attr` stores the attributes used to create the dialog box

`IsModal` indicates whether the dialog box is modal or modeless

Member Functions:

Three `TDialog` constructors

`TDialog` destructor

`build` invokes the `TDialog` constructor and constructs an object of type `TDialog` before reading its data members from a stream

`Cancel` calls `CloseWindow` using IDCANCEL when the `Cancel` button for the dialog box is selected

`CloseWindow` calls either `TWindowsObject::CloseWindow` when `this` is a modeless dialog box or `CanClose` for a modal dialog box to determine whether the dialog box can be shut; this function returns the specified return value

`CloseWindow` calls either `TWindowsObject::CloseWindow` when `this` is a modeless dialog box or `CloseWindow` for a modal dialog box to determine whether the dialog box can be shut; this function returns `ARetValue`

`Create` creates a modeless dialog box associated with the object

`Destroy` destroys the interface element associated with `TDialog`, and passes a value for a modal dialog box

`Destroy` destroys the interface element associated with `TDialog`, and passes a value for a modeless dialog box

`Execute` executes the modal dialog box associated with `TDialog`

`GetClassName` returns the name of the default Windows class for modal dialog boxes, `OWLDialog`

`GetItemHandle` returns the handle of the dialog control that has the ID specified in `DlgItemID`

`GetWindowClass` fills `AWndClass` (a `WNDCLASS` structure) with the registration attributes for `TDialog`

`isA` redefines the pure virtual function in class `Object`

`nameOf` redefines the pure virtual function in class `Object`; this function returns "TDialog", the class ID string for `TDialog`.

`Ok` calls `CloseWindow` when the `Ok` button of the dialog box is selected, and passes IDOK

`read` calls `TWindowsObject::read` to read in the base `UTWindowsObject` object

`SendDlgItemMsg` sends the control message (`AMsg`) to the dialog box control that has the ID specified in `DlgItemID`

`SetCaption` calls `TWindowsObject::SetCaption` unless `ATitle` is –1

`SetupWindow` calls `SetCaption` and `TWindowsObject::SetupWindow` to set up the dialog box

`ShutDownWindow` calls `TWindowsObject::ShutDownWindow` for modeless dialog boxes or `Destroy` (passing IDCANCEL) for modal dialog boxes to shut down the dialog box

`ShutDownWindow` calls `TWindowsObject::ShutDownWindow` for modeless dialog boxes or `Destroy` (passing `ARetValue`) for modal dialog boxes to shut down the dialog box

WMClose handles the WM_CLOSE message

WMInitDialog calls SetupWindow and is automatically called before the dialog box is displayed

WMQueryEndSession responds when Windows attempts to shut down

write calls TWindowsObject::write to write out the base TWindowsObject object

Chapter 17, "ObjectWindows Classes," provides reference information for the data members and member functions of the TDialog class.

TFileDialog

The file dialog is a special dialog that prompts the user for a file name. The file dialog contains an input line, two list boxes, and two buttons. One list box contains a listing of all the files in the current directory. The other list box specifies the directories visible from the current directory. The two buttons are Ok and Cancel.

The file dialog box constructor requires that the parent window, the resource identifier (SD_FILEOPEN or SD_FILESAVE), and the file name or mask be specified. As the previous line indicates, there are two types of file dialog boxes. The first is the Open dialog box (specified by SD_FILEOPEN). The second is the Save dialog box (specified by SD_FILESAVE).

The following code creates an open file dialog box using "*.*" as the file mask:

```
char NAME[MAXPATH];
_fstrcpy(NAME, "*.*");
GetApplication()->ExecDialog(new TFileDialog(this, SD_FILEOPEN, NAME));
```

The following code creates a save file dialog using DUMMY.DOC as the file mask:

```
char NAME[MAXPATH];
_fstrcpy(NAME, "*.*");
GetApplication()->ExecDialog(new TFileDialog(this, SD_FILESAVE, NAME));
```

TFileDialog defines a dialog box that enables the user to select a file. TFileDialog is derived from TDialog and contains the following data members and member functions:

Data Members:

Extension holds the file name extension

FilePath points to the buffer that returns the file name defined by the user

`FileSpec` contains the current file name

`PathName` contains the current file path

Member Functions:

Two `TFileDialog` constructors

`build` invokes the `TFileDialog` constructor and constructs an object of type `TFileDialog` before reading its data members from a stream

`CanClose` returns `TRUE` when the user entered a valid file name

`HandleDList` responds to messages from the directory list box, calling `UpdateListBoxes` when an entry is double-clicked and `UpdateFileName` otherwise

`HandleFList` responds to messages from the file list box and calls `UpdateFileName` when the list box selection changes

`HandleFName` responds to messages from the edit control and enables the `Ok` button when the edit control contains text

`SelectFileName` selects text from the edit control and sets the focus to the edit control

`SetupWindow` calls `UpDateListBoxes`, `SelectFileName`, and `TWindowsObject::SetupWindow` to set up the dialog box

`UpdateFileName` sets the text of the edit control to `PathName` and selects the text

`UpdateListBoxes` updates the file and directory list boxes

Chapter 17, "ObjectWindows Classes," provides reference information for the data members and member functions of the `TFileDialog` class.

TInputDialog

An input dialog contains a single input line and two buttons. The user can enter a single line of text in the input line. The two buttons in the input dialog are `Ok` and `Cancel`.

The constructor for the input dialog accepts five parameters: the parent window, the dialog caption, the prompt text, the buffer where input is placed, and the size of the input buffer. The following code creates an input dialog with the "Input" caption and the "Enter Text" prompt.

```
PTInputDialog InDlg;
char Txt[79];

strcpy[Txt,""];
InDlg = new TInputDialog(this,"Input","Enter Text", Txt,sizeof(Txt));
```

`TInputDialog` defines a dialog box that enables the user to enter a single line of text. `TInputDialog` is derived from `TDialog` and contains the following data members and member functions:

Data Members:

`Buffer` is a pointer to a buffer that returns the text entered by the user

`BufferSize` stores the size of `Buffer`

`Prompt` points the input dialog box prompt

Member Functions:

Two `TInputDialog` constructor

`build` invokes the `TInputDialog` constructor and constructs an object of type `TInputDialog` before reading its data members from a stream

`read` calls `TDialog::read` to read in the base `TDialog` object

`SetupWindow` calls `TDialog::SetupWindow` to set up the window and limit the number of characters that can be input to `BufferSize` minus 1

`TransferData` transfers input dialog data

`write` calls `TDialog::write` to write out the base `TDialog` object

Chapter 17, "ObjectWindows Classes," provides reference information for the data members and member functions of the `TInputDialog` class.

TSearchDialog

`TSearchDialog` is derived from `TDialog` and provides search-and-replace options for the user. `TSearchDialog` uses a data structure of type `TSearchStruct` to transfer data. Two resource definitions (a search dialog and a replace dialog) are provided in STDWNDS.DLG. `TSearchDialog` contains only the `TSearchDialog` constructor.

Control Objects

Control objects are special windows that serve as user interface elements. Control objects include buttons, scroll bars, list boxes, check boxes, group boxes, edit controls, MDI client controls, and radio buttons. The abstract class `TControl` is the base class for the control objects.

TControl

`TControl` defines member functions for the creation of controls and the processing of messages for derived classes. `TControl` is derived from `TWindow` and has seven derived classes: `TButton`, `TScrollBar`, `TStatic`, `TListBox`, `TGroupBox`, `TBDivider`, and `TBStaticBmp`. `TControl` contains the following data members and member functions:

Data Members:

None

Member Functions:

Three `TControl` constructors

`GetId` returns the window ID, `Attr.Id`

`ODADrawEntire` responds when notified that a drawable control needs to be redrawn

`ODAFocus` responds when notified that the focus has been given to or taken from the drawable control

`ODASelect` responds when notified that the selection state of the drawable control has changed

`WMDrawItem` responds to the `WM_DRAWITEM` message that is sent when the drawable control needs to be redrawn

`WMPaint` calls `DefWndProc` for painting

Chapter 17, "ObjectWindows Classes," provides reference information for the data members and member functions of the `TControl` class. The following paragraphs describe each of the derived classes of `TControl` and explain the various control objects.

TButton

There are two types of button objects. The first is the standard push-button, BS_PUSHBUTTON. The second type of button is the default push-button, BS_DEFPUSHBUTTON. The default push-button is surrounded by a bold border and represents the default action.

The TButton constructor requires the following parameters: the parent window, the control ID, the button text, the location of the button, the size of the button, and a TRUE/FALSE flag indicating whether this button is the default. The following constructs a default button called "Default" (Note: ID_PushButton represents the constant for the button ID):

```
PushButton = new TButton(this, ID_PushButton, "Default", 50,
                         50, 50, 25, TRUE);
```

The TButton class defines push-button interfaces and is derived from TControl. TButton contains the following data members and member functions:

Data Members:

IsDefPB is used for owner-draw buttons and indicates whether the button is the default button

Member Functions:

Three TButton constructors

BMSetStyle determines whether an owner-draw button is the default push button when the button style is set to BS_DEFPUSHBUTTON

build constructs an object of type TButton before reading its member from an input stream

GetClassName returns "BUTTON", the name of TButton's Windows registration class

SetupWindow sends the DM_SETDEFID message to the parent window of an owner-draw button when the button is the default push button

WMGetDlgCode returns default button information for an owner-draw button when the WM_GETDLGCODE message is received

Chapter 17, "ObjectWindows Classes," provides reference information for the data members and member functions of the TButton class.

TListBox

List box controls provide a list of items that the user can select from. The member functions of TListBox can be used to create list boxes, modify the list of the list box, retrieve information about the list, and determine the item that the user has selected.

The TListBox constructor requires the following parameters: the parent window, the control ID, the location of the control, and the size of the control. The TListBox constructor invokes the TControl constructor and adds the LBS_STANDARD style to the default styles for the list box in Attr.Style. Using LBS_STANDARD, the list box alphabetizes the items of the list, notifies the parent of all list box events, is surrounded by a border, and contains a vertical scroll bar. The following code constructs a list box where ID_ListBox is a reference to the constant for the list box ID:

```
ListBox = new TListBox(this, ID_ListBox, 50, 50, 200, 100);
```

The TListBox class defines an interface object that represents a Windows list box. TListBox is used to create and manage list boxes. TListBox is derived from TControl and contains the following data members and member functions. TComboBox is derived from TListBox.

Data Members:

None

Member Functions:

Three TListBox constructors

AddString adds the string specified in AString to the list box

build invokes the TListBox constructor and constructs an object of type TListBox before reading its data members from a stream

ClearList clears all list items

DeleteString deletes the list item at the location specified by Index

FindExactString searches the list box for a string that exactly matches the string specified in AString

FindString searches the list box for a string that begins with the string specified in AString

GetClassName returns "LISTBOX"

GetCount returns the number of list box items when successful

`GetMsgID` returns the Windows list box message ID associated with the specified ObjectWindows message ID

`GetSelCount` returns the number of items currently selected in a list box

`GetSelIndex` returns the position of the currently selected item when successful

`GetSelIndexes` fills the Indexes array with indexes of the selected string

`GetSelString` places the currently selected list item in `AString`

`GetSelStrings` places the currently selected items in `Strings`

`GetString` copies the item at the location specified in `Index` to `AString`

`GetStringLen`, when successful, returns the length of the item at the location specified in `Index`

`InsertString` inserts the string specified in `AString` at the list position specified in `Index`

`SetSelIndex`, when successful, selects the item at the position specified in `Index`

`SetSelIndexes` either selects or deselects the strings at the positions specified in the Indexes array

`SetSelString` selects the list box item that matches `AString`

`SetSelStrings` selects the items in the list box that match the prefixes specified in the `Prefixes` array

`Transfer` uses the buffer pointed to by `DataPtr` to transfer data

Chapter 17, "ObjectWindows Classes," provides reference information for the data members and member functions of the `TListBox` class.

TComboBox

A combo box control is a combination of a list box and an edit control. A combo box control can be any one of three types: simple, drop-down, or drop-down list.

The first type is a simple combo box (`CBS_SIMPLE`). A simple combo box contains an edit control and a list box. The list box of a simple combo box cannot be hidden.

The second type is a drop-down combo box (`CBS_DROPDOWN`). A drop-down combo box is similar to a simple combo box. The difference lies in the list box. With a drop-down combo box, the list area is hidden until the user selects the down-arrow to the right of the list area. The list area is hidden again after the user makes a selection.

The third type is a drop-down list combo box (`CBS_DROPDOWNLIST`). The drop-down list combo box behaves like the drop-down combo box except that the edit control does not accept input directly. Only text from the list items can be displayed in the edit control.

The `TComboBox` constructor requires the following parameters: the parent window, the control ID, the control location, the control size, the combo box type (`CBS_SIMPLE`, `CBS_DROPDOWN`, or `CBS_DROPDOWNLIST`), and the edit control text length. The following code constructs a simple combo box where `ID_ComboBox` represents the constant for the control ID:

```
ComboBox = new TComboBox(this, ID_ComboBox, 50, 50, 100, 150,
                         CBS_SIMPLE, 40);
```

The `TComboBox` class represents a Windows combo box interface. `TComboBox` is derived from `TListBox` and contains the following data members and member functions:

Data Members:

`TextLen` specifies the length of the buffer used for the edit control of the combo box

Member Functions:

Three `TComboBox` constructors

`build` constructs an object of type `TComboBox` before reading its data members from a stream

`Clear` clears the text of the edit control

`GetClassName` returns "COMBOBOX"

`GetEditSel` returns the beginning and ending positions of the currently selected text in the edit control

`GetMsgID` returns the message ID of the Windows combo box message that is associated with the ObjectWindows message ID

`GetText` copies the text of the edit control to the specified string

`GetTextLen` determines the length of the text in the edit control

`HideList` hides the list of a drop-down or drop-down list combo box

`nameOf` redefines the pure virtual function in class `Object`

`read` calls `TWindow::read` to read in the base `TListBox` object

`SetEditSel` selects the characters specified by `StartPos` and `EndPos`

`SetText` selects the first string in the list box that begins with the string specified in `AString`

`SetupWindow` limits the length of the text in the edit control to `TextLen` minus 1 when setting up the combo box

`ShowList` shows the list of a drop-down or drop-down list combo box

`Transfer` moves data to and from a transfer buffer pointed to by uDataPtr

`write` calls `TWindow::write` to write out the base `TListBox` object

Chapter 17, "ObjectWindows Classes," provides reference information for the data members and member functions of the `TComboBox` class.

TCheckBox

A check box control offers the user a selection and represents the state of the selection—either on or off (some check box controls can have a third state—grayed). By default, check boxes are toggled between states when they are selected.

The `TCheckBox` constructor requires the following parameters: the parent window, the control ID, the text associated with the check box, the location of the check box, the size of the check box, and an `AGroup` parameter that helps to group together check and radio boxes. The following code creates the required `AGroup` parameter and a check box:

```
GroupBox = new TGroupBox(this, ID_GroupBox, "Group", 50, 50,
                         100, 100);

CheckBox = new TCheckBox(this, ID_CheckBox, "Box One", 300,
                         200, 50, 50, GroupBox);
```

The `TCheckBox` class represents a Windows check box interface. `TCheckBox` is derived from `TControl` and contains the following data members and member functions. `TRadioButton` is derived from `TCheckBox`.

Data Members:

`Group` is a pointer to the `TGroupBox` control object that groups the check box with other check boxes and radio buttons

Member Functions:

Three `TCheckBox` constructors

`BNClicked` responds to notification messages indicating that the check box was clicked

`build` constructs an object of type `TCheckBox` before reading its data members from an input stream

`Check` places the check box into the checked state by calling `SetCheck`

`GetCheck` determines the check state of the check box

`read` calls `TWindow::read` to read in the base `TWindow` object

`uSetCheck` sets the state of the check box to the state specified in `CheckFlag`—which can be `BF_UNCHECKED` (box is unchecked), `BF_CHECKED` (box is checked), or `BF_GRAYED` (box is grayed)

`Toggle` toggles between the states of the check box

`Transfer` transfers the state of the check box to or from the location pointed to by `DataPtr`

`Uncheck` places the check box in an unchecked state by calling `SetCheck`

`write` calls `TWindow::write` to write the base `TWindow` object

Chapter 17, "ObjectWindows Classes," provides reference information for the data members and member functions of the `TCheckBox` class.

TBCheckBox

`TBCheckBox` creates a BWCC check box control for a parent `TWindow`. `TBCheckBox` is an interface object representing a BWCC check box interface element. `TBCheckBox` is derived from `TCheckBox` and has no derived classes. `TBCheckBox` contains the following data members and member functions:

Data Members:

None

Member Functions:

Three `TBCheckBox` constructors

`build` creates a `TBCheckBox` object before its data members are read from a stream

GetClassName returns "BORCHECK", the name for the `TBCheckBox` Windows registration class

Chapter 17, "ObjectWindows Classes," provides reference information for the data members and member functions of the `TBCheckBox` class.

TRadioButton

A radio button control offers the user a selection and represents the state of the selection—either on or off. By default, radio buttons are toggled between states when they are selected. Radio buttons are usually grouped to provide the user with a choice of mutually exclusive buttons.

The `TRadioButton` constructor requires the following parameters: the parent window, the control ID, the text associated with the radio button, the location of the button, the size of the button, and an `AGroup` parameter that helps to group together check and radio boxes. The following code creates the required `AGroup` parameter and a radio button:

```
GroupBox = new TGroupBox(this, ID_GroupBox, "Group", 50, 50,
                         100, 100);

RadioButton = new TRadioButton(this, ID_RadioButton, "Box One",
                               300, 200, 50, 50, GroupBox);
```

The `TRadioButton` class represents a Windows radio button. A radio button is a two-state button; it can be either checked or unchecked. `TRadioButton` is derived from `TCheckBox` and contains the following data members and member functions:

Data Members:

None

Member Functions:

Three `TRadioButton` constructors

`BNClicked` responds to the `BN_CLICKED` message

`build` invokes the `TRadioButton` constructor and constructs an object of type `TRadioButton` before reading its data members from a stream

Chapter 17, "ObjectWindows Classes," provides reference information for the data members and member functions of the `TRadioButton` class.

TBRadioButton

`TBRadioButton` creates a radio button for a parent `TWindow`. `TBRadioButton` is an interface object that represents a BWCC radio button element. `TBRadioButton` is derived from `TRadioButton` and has no derived classes. `TBRadioButton` contains the following data members and member functions:

Data Members:

None

Member Functions:

Three `TBRadioButton` constructors

`build` creates a `TBRadioButton` object before its data members are read from a stream

`GetClassName` returns "BORRADIO", the name for the `TBRadioButton` Windows registration class

Chapter 17, "ObjectWindows Classes," provides reference information for the data members and member functions of the `TBRadioButton` class.

TBButton

`TBButton` creates a button control for a parent `TWindow`. `TBButton` is an interface object representing a BWCC bitmap push button interface element. `TBButton` is derived from `TButton` and has no derived classes. `TBButton` contains the following data members and member functions:

Data Members:

None

Member Functions:

Three `TBButton` constructors

`build` creates a `TBButton` object before its data members are read from a stream

`GetClassName` returns "BORBTN", the name for the `TBButton` Windows registration class

Chapter 17, "ObjectWindows Classes," provides reference information for the data members and member functions of the `TBButton` class.

TGroupBox

Group box controls simply group a series of controls with a captioned rectangle. The controls within the group box are visually grouped; they are not, however, logically grouped. Logical grouping means that the controls are mutually exclusive. The `WS_GROUP` style for the controls is the only indicator of the logical grouping of controls.

Although group boxes do not logically group controls, they do enable you to define a group response method for the parent window. The group box accepts notification messages from the individual controls and converts the messages to group notification messages.

The `TGroupBox` constructor requires the following parameters: the parent window, the control ID, the text for the group box, the group box location, and the group box size. The following code constructs a group box:

```
GroupBox = new TGroupBox(this, ID_GroupBox, "Options", 50, 50,
                         100, 100);
```

The `TGroupBox` class represents group box elements. `TGroupBox` is derived from `TControl` and contains the following data members and member functions:

Data Members:

`NotifyParent` indicates whether the parent should be notified when one of the group box's selection boxes has changed state

Member Functions:

Three `TGroupBox` constructors

`build` invokes the `TGroupBox` constructor and constructs an object of type `TGroupBox` before reading its data members from a stream

`GetClassName` returns "BUTTON", the name for the `TGroupBox` Windows registration class

`read` calls `TWindow::read` to read in the base `TGroupBox` object

`SelectionChanged` notifies the parent window of a group box that a change has been made in the group box *only* if `NotifyParent` is `TRUE`

`write` calls `TWindow::write` to write out the base `TGroupBox` object

Chapter 17, "ObjectWindows Classes," provides reference information for the data members and member functions of the `TGroupBox` class.

TBGroupBox

`TBGroupBox` creates a group box element. `TBGroupBox` is an interface object representing a gray BWCC group box interface element. `TBGroupBox` is derived from `TBGroupBox` and has no derived classes. `TBGroupBox` contains the following data members and member functions:

Data Members:

None

Member Functions:

Three `TBGroupBox` constructors

`build` creates a `TBGroupBox` object before its data members are read from a stream

`GetClassName` returns "BORSHADE", the name for the `TBGroupBox` Windows registration class

Chapter 17, "ObjectWindows Classes," provides reference information for the data members and member functions of the `TBGroupBox` class.

TStatic

Static controls are graphics or text that can be displayed in the window. Static controls are not selected or modified by the user and do not need unique IDs. Static controls are often used to display "for your information" data.

The `TStatic` constructor requires the following parameters: the parent window, the control ID, the control text, the control location, the control size, and the text length. The following code constructs a static text control. Note: –1 is the ID you should use for static IDs.

```
StaticText = new TStatic(this, -1, "Static Text", 50, 50, 100, 100, 12);
```

The `TStatic` class represents a static text interface element and provides functions for the management of the element. `TStatic` is derived from `TControl` and has one derived class, `TEdit`. TStatic contains the following data members and member functions:

Data Members:

`TextLen` specifies the size of the text buffer for the static control

Member Functions:

Three `TStatic` constructors

`build` invokes the `TStatic` constructor and constructs an object of type `TStatic` before reading its data members from a stream

`Clear` clears the text of the static control

`GetClassName` returns "STATIC", the name for the `TStatic` Windows registration class

`GetText` returns the text of the static control in `ATextString`

`GetTextLen` determines the length of the text in the static control

`nameOf` redefines the pure virtual function in class `Object`

`read` calls `TWindow::read` to read in the base `TWindow` object

`SetText` sets the text of the static control to the string specified in `ATextString`

`Transfer` transfers text to and from the buffer pointed to by `DataPtr`

`write` calls `TWindow::write` to write out the base `TWindow` object

Chapter 17, "ObjectWindows Classes," provides reference information for the data members and member functions of the `TStatic` class.

TEdit

Edit controls enable the user to input text and can be used by a program. Edit controls enable you to cut, copy, and paste using the clipboard and provide many of the features found in text editors.

The `TEdit` constructor requires the following parameters: the parent window, the control ID, the control text, the control location, the control size, the maximum number of characters for the edit control, and a `TRUE/FALSE` flag that indicates whether this is a multiline edit control. By default, edit controls have the following styles: `WS_CHILD`, `WS_VISIBLE`, `WS_TABSTOP`, `ES_LEFT`, `ES_AUTOHSCROLL`, and `WS_BORDER`. Multiline edit controls have the following additional styles: `ES_MULTILINE`, `ES_AUTOVSCROLL`, `WS_HSCROLL`, and `WS_VSCROLL`.

The following code constructs a single-line edit control that can handle up to 80 characters:

```
SingleEdit = new TEdit(this, ID_SingleEdit, "Single Edit", 50,
                       50, 100, 100, 80, FALSE);
```

The following code constructs a multline edit control that can handle up to 300 characters:

```
MultiEdit = new TEdit(this, ID_MultiEdit, "Multi Edit", 50,
                      50, 100, 100, 300, TRUE);
```

The `TEdit` class is the Windows edit control interface and provides the features of a text editor. `TEdit` is derived from `TControl` and contains the following data members and member functions:

Data Members:

None

Member Functions:

Three `TEdit` constructors

`build` invokes the `TEdit` constructor and constructs an object of type `TEdit` before reading its data members from a stream

`CanUndo` indicates whether it is possible to undo the last edit

`ClearModify` resets the edit control change flag

`CMEditClear` calls `Clear` when a menu item with menu ID `CM_EDITCLEAR` is selected

`CMEditCopy` calls `Copy` when a menu item with menu ID `CM_EDITCOPY` is selected

`CMEditCut` calls `Cut` when a menu item with the menu ID `CM_EDITCUT` is selected

`CMEditDelete` calls `DeleteSelection` when a menu item with menu ID `CM_EDITDELETE` is selected

`CMEditPaste` calls `Paste` when a menu item with menu ID `CM_EDITPASTE` is selected

`CMEditUndo` calls `Undo` when a menu item with menu ID `CM_EDITUNDO` is selected

`Copy` copies the selected text to the clipboard

`Cut` deletes the selected text and copies it to the clipboard

`DeleteLine` deletes the line of text specified in `LineNumber`

`DeleteSelection` deletes the selected text

`DeleteSubText` deletes the text between the text positions specified in `StartPos` and `EndPos`

`ENErrSpace` sounds a beep when the edit control cannot allocate more memory

`GetClassName` returns "EDIT"

`GetLine` gets a line of text from the edit control

`GetLineFromPos` gets the line number from a multiline edit control of the line that contains the character position specified in `CharPos`

`GetLineIndex` returns the number of characters prior to the specified line number in a multiline edit control

`GetLineLength` gets the number of characters in a line of text from a multiline edit control

`GetNumLines` gets the number of lines in a multiline edit control

`GetSelection` returns the starting and ending positions of the selected text in `StartPos` and `EndPos`, respectively

`GetSubText` gets the text specified by `StartPos` and `EndPos` and returns the text to `ATextString`

`Insert` inserts the text in `ATextString` into the edit control at the current cursor position

`IsModified` indicates whether the text in the edit control has been modified

`Paste` places the text in the clipboard into the edit control at the current cursor position

`Scroll` scrolls the multiline edit control horizontally or vertically

`Search` searches for the text specified in `AText`

`SetSelection` defines the current text selection

`SetupWindow` defines the limit for the number of characters in the edit control as `TextLen` minus 1

`Undo` performs an "undo" on the last edit

Chapter 17, "ObjectWindows Classes," provides reference information for the data members and member functions of the `TStatic` class.

TBStatic

`TBStatic` creates a static control for a parent `TWindow`. TBStatic is an interface object representing a static text interface element. `TBStatic` is derived from `TStatic` and has no derived classes. `TBStatic` contains the following data members and member functions:

Data Members:

None

Member Functions:

Three `TBStatic` constructors

`build` creates an `TBStatic` object before its data members are read from a stream

`GetClassName` returns "BORSTATIC", the name for the `TBStatic` Windows registration class

Chapter 17, "ObjectWindows Classes," provides reference information for the data members and member functions of the `TBStatic` class.

TScrollBar

Scroll bar controls indicate position relative to a specified range. Scroll bar controls are stand-alone scroll bars and should not be confused with window scroll bars. Scroll bars can be either horizontal or vertical and practically any width and length. `TScrollBar` defines several member functions that enable you to customize and monitor scroll bars.

The `TScrollBar` constructor invokes the `TControl` constructor and adds `SBS_HORIZ` and `SBS_VERT` to the styles for the scroll bar. The parameters required for the `TScrollBar` constructor are as follows: the parent window, the control ID, the control location, the control size, and a `TRUE/FALSE` flag that indicates whether this is a horizontal scroll bar.

The following code constructs a horizontal scroll bar:

```
HorzScroll = new TScrollBar(this, ID_HorzScroll, 50, 50,
                            100, 30, TRUE);
```

The following code constructs a vertical scroll bar:

```
VertScroll = new TScrollBar(this, ID_VertScroll, 50, 50,
                            30, 100, FALSE);
```

The `TScrollBar` class represents and manages stand-alone horizontal and vertical scroll bars. `TScrollBar` is derived from `TControl` and contains the following data members and member functions:

Data Members:

`LineMagnitude` specifies the number of range units that the scroll bar is scrolled when one of the scroll bar arrows is clicked

`PageMagnitude` specifies the number of range units that the scroll bar is scrolled when the scrolling area of the scroll bar is clicked

Member Functions:

Three `TScrollBar` constructors

`build` invokes the `TScrollBar` constructor and constructs an object of type `TScrollBar` before reading its data members from a stream

`DeltaPos` changes the thumb position of the scroll bar by calling `SetPosition`

`GetClassName` returns "SCROLLBAR", the name for the `TScrollBar` Windows registration class

`GetPosition` returns the thumb position of the scroll bar

`GetRange` returns the scroll bar range in `LoVal` and `HiVal`

`read` calls `TWindow::read` to read in the base `TWindow` object

`SBBottom` calls `SetPosition` to move the scroll thumb to the bottom of the scroll bar for vertical scroll bars or to the right for horizontal scroll bars

`SBLineDown` calls `SetPosition` to move the scroll thumb down for vertical scroll bars or right for horizontal scroll bars

`SBLineUp` calls `SetPosition` to move the scroll thumb up for vertical scroll bars or left for horizontal scroll bars

`SBPageDown` calls `SetPosition` to move the scroll thumb down for vertical scroll bars or right for horizontal scroll bars

`SBPageUp` calls `SetPosition` to move the scroll thumb up for vertical scroll bars or left for horizontal scroll bars

`SBThumbPosition` calls `SetPosition` to move the scroll thumb

`SBThumbTrack` calls `SetPosition` to move the scroll thumb to a new position as it is being dragged

`SBTop` calls `SetPosition` to move the scroll thumb to the top for vertical scroll bars or the left for horizontal scroll bars

`SetPosition` moves the thumb position to the position specified in `ThumbPos`

`SetRange` sets to scroll bar range to the values specified in `LoVal` and `HiVal`

`SetupWindow` defines the scroll bar range as 0 to 100

`Transfer` uses the data buffer pointed to by `DataPtr` to transfer scroll bar information

`write` calls `TWindow::write` to write out the base `TWindow` object

Chapter 17, "ObjectWindows Classes," provides reference information for the data members and member functions of the `TScrollBar` class.

TBDivider

`TBDivider` creates either a dip or bump BWCC divider. A dip divider separates areas within a dialog. A bump divider separates areas within a group box. `TBDivider` is an interface object representing a static BWCC divider. `TBDivider` is derived from `TControl` and has no derived classes. `TBDivider` contains the following data members and member functions:

Data Members:

None

Member Functions:

Three `TBDivider` constructors

`build` creates an `TBDivider` object before its data members are read from a stream

`GetClassName` returns "BORSHADE", the name for the `TBDivider` Windows registration class

Chapter 17, "ObjectWindows Classes," provides reference information for the data members and member functions of the `TBDivider` class.

TBStaticBmp

`TBStaticBmp` creates a bitmap control for a parent `TWindow`. `TBStaticBmp` is an interface object representing a static interface element for displaying splash images. `TBStaticBmp` is derived from `TControl` and has no derived classes. `TBStaticBmp` contains the following data members and member functions:

Data Members:

None

Member Functions:

Three `TBStaticBmp` constructors

`build` creates a `TBStaticBmp` object before its data members are read from a stream

`GetClassName` returns "BORBTN", the name for the `TBStaticBmp` Windows registration class

Chapter 17, "ObjectWindows Classes," provides reference information for the data members and member functions of the `TBStaticBmp` class.

MDI Objects

Chapter 9, "The Multiple Document Interface (MDI)," in Part I of this book discussed the multiple document interface standard for Windows. ObjectWindows defines two classes for the creation of MDI applications: `TMDIFrame` and `TMDIClient`. These classes are described in the following paragraphs. The next chapter, Chapter 12, "Windows Programming Using ObjectWindows," provides an example of an MDI application using ObjectWindows.

TMDIFrame

The `TMDIFrame` class represents Multiple Document Interface (MDI) frame windows, the main windows for MDI applications. `TMDIFrame` is derived from `TWindow` and contains the following data members and member functions:

Data Members:

`ActiveChild` is a pointer to the active MDI child window

`ChildMenuPos` stores the top-level menu position for the MDI window

`ClientWnd` is a pointer to the `TMDIFrame` client window

Member Functions:

Four `TMDIFrame` constructors

`TMDIFrame` destructor

`ArrangeIcons` calls the `ArrangeIcons` member function of the client window to arrange the iconized MDI child windows along the bottom of the client window

`build` invokes the `TMDIFrame` constructor and constructs an object of type `TMDIFrame` before reading its data members from a stream

`CascadeChildren` calls the `CascadeChildren` member function of the client window to arrange the MDI child windows that are not iconized in an overlapping style

`CloseChildren` calls the `CanClose` member function of each MDI child window and closes all the child windows if possible

`CMArrangeIcons` calls `ArrangeIcons` when a menu item with a `CM_ARRANGEICONS` ID is selected

`CMCascadeChildren` calls `CascadeChildren` when a menu item with a `CM_CASCADECHILDREN` ID is selected

`CMCloseChildren` calls `CloseChildren` when a menu item with a `CM_CLOSECHILDREN` ID is selected

`CMCreateChild` calls `CreateChild` when a menu item with a `CM_CREATECHILD` ID is selected

`CMTileChildren` calls `TileChildren` when a menu item with a `CM_TILECHILDREN` ID is selected

`CreateChild` creates an MDI child window and returns a pointer to the created child window

`GetClassName` returns "OWLMDIFrame", the name for the `TMDIFrame` Windows registration class

`GetClient` returns the pointer to the client window stored in `ClientWnd`

`GetWindowClass` calls `TWindow::GetWindowClass` and sets `AWndClass.Style` to 0

`InitChild` constructs an instance of `TWindow` as an MDI child window

InitClientWindow constructs the MDI client window as an instance of `TMDIClient`

`read` calls `TWindow::read` to read in the base `TWindow` object

`SetupWindow` calls `InitClientWindow` to construct an MDI client window and creates the interface element

`TileChildren` calls the `TileChildren` member function of the client window to size and arrange the MDI child windows that are not iconized in a non-overlapping style

`WMActivate` responds to the `WM_ACTIVATE` message

`write` calls `TWindow::write` to write out the base `TWindow` object

Chapter 17, "ObjectWindows Classes," provides reference information for the data members and member functions of the `TMDIWindow` class.

The frame window of an MDI application is also the application's main window. The `TMDIFrame` constructor creates the frame window and requires two parameters: the title for the MDI frame window and the handle to an MDI-style menu.

The TMDIFrame constructor calls InitClientWindow to construct the TMDIClient object that serves as the MDI client window. The MDI client window is created by SetupWindow. The TMDIClient class follows.

TMDIClient

The TMDIClient class represents Multiple Document Interface (MDI) client windows and manages the MDI client area and the MDI child windows. TMDIClient is derived from TWindow and contains the following data members and member functions:

Data Members:

ClientAttr stores the attributes of the MDI client window

Member Functions:

Three TMDIClient constructors

TMDIClient destructor

ArrangeIcons aligns MDI child window icons along the bottom of the MDI client window

build invokes the TMDIClient constructor and constructs an object of type TMDIClient before reading its data members from a stream

CascadeChildren adjusts the size of all MDI child windows that are not minimized and arranges them in an overlapping style

GetClassName returns "MDICLIENT", the name for the TMDIClient Windows registration class

read calls TWindow::read to read the base TWindow object

TileChildren adjusts the size of all MDI child windows that are not minimized and arranges them in a non-overlapping, tiled style

WMMDIActivate responds to the WM_MDIACTIVATE message

WMPaint redefines TWindow::WMPaint to call DefWndProc

write calls TWindow::write to write out the base TWindow object

Chapter 17, "ObjectWindows Classes," provides reference information for the data members and member functions of the TMDIClient class.

Scroller Objects

For many applications, you must provide vertical or horizontal scroll bars to view areas that are too large for the current window. The `TScroller` class adds functionality to the scroll bars of a window and can even provide a window with auto-scrolling features. Auto-scrolling refers to the window's capability to scroll when the mouse is dragged from the inside of the window to the outside.

TScroller

The `TScroller` class provides automated scrolling for window displays. `TScroller` is usually associated with scroll bars; however, `TScroller` works with windows without scroll bars. `TScroller` is derived from `TControl` and contains the following data members and member functions.

Data Members:

`AutoMode` indicates whether auto-scrolling is in effect

`AutoOrg` indicates whether the origin of the client area should automatically be offset when preparing the area for painting

`ClassHashValue` contains the hash value of the last constructed instance of `TScroller`

`HasHScrollBar` is `TRUE` when the owner window has a horizontal scroll bar

`HasVScrollBar` is `TRUE` when the owner window has a vertical scroll bar

`InstanceHashValue` contains the hash value of `this`

`TrackMode` indicates whether the display should be scrolled as the scroll thumb is dragged

`Window` points to the owner window

`XLine` specifies the number of horizontal scroll units to move when the scroll arrow is clicked

`XPage` specifies the number of horizontal scroll units to move when the thumb area of the scroll bar is clicked

`XPos` is the horizontal position of the scroller in horizontal scroll units

`XRange` is the maximum number of horizontal scroll units for the window

`XUnit` is the horizontal logical scroll unit used by `TScroller`

YLine is the number of vertical units scrolled when the scroll arrow is clicked

YPage is the number of vertical units scrolled when the thumb area of the scroll bar is clicked

YPos is the current vertical position of the scroller

YRange is the maximum number of vertical scroll units for the window

YUnit is the vertical logical scroll unit used by TScroller

Member Functions:

Two TScroller constructors

TScroller destructor

AutoScroll scrolls the display of the owner window when the mouse is dragged from the inside of the window to the outside

BeginView sets the origin of the owner window's paint display context relative to the current scroller position when AutoOrg is TRUE

build invokes the TScroller constructor and constructs an object of type TScroller before reading its data members from a stream

EndView updates the scroll bar positions to correspond to the position of TScroller

hashValue redefines the pure virtual function in class Object

HScroll calls ScrollTo to handle the specified horizontal scroll event

isA must be redefined by all objects derived from the base class Object

isEqual redefines the pure virtual function in class Object

IsVisibleRect determines whether any part of the specified rectangle is visible in the owner window

nameOf must be redefined by all objects derived from the base class object

printOn must be redefined by all objects derived from the base class object

read reads AutoMode, AutoOrg, HasHScrollBar, HasVScrollBar, TrackMode, XLine, XPage, XPos, XRange, XUnit, YLine, YPage, YPos, YRange, and YUnit

ScrollBy calls ScrollTo to scroll the display the amount specified in Dx and Dy

ScrollTo scrolls the display to the specified position

SetPageSize sets the page width and height to the size of the client area of the owner window

SetRange sets the scroll ranges of TScroller to those specified and calls SetSBarRange to coordinate the ranges of the owner window scroll bars

SetSBarRange sets the range of the scroll bars for the owner window to fit within the range specified for TScroller

SetUnits defines the data members XUnit and YUnit

VScroll calls ScrollTo to handle the specified vertical scroll event

write writes AutoMode, AutoOrg, HasHScrollBar, HasVScrollBar, TrackMode, XLine, XPage, XPos, XRange, XUnit, YLine, YPage, YPos, YRange, and YUnit

XRangeValue converts a horizontal scroll value to a horizontal range value

XScrollValue converts a horizontal range value to a horizontal scroll value

YRangeValue converts a vertical scroll value to a vertical range value

YScrollValue converts a vertical range value to a vertical scroll value

The data members of the TScroller define the characteristics of the scrolling action. Chapter 17, "ObjectWindows Classes," provides reference information for the data members and member functions of the TScroller class.

12

Windows Programming Using ObjectWindows

This chapter introduces you to programming Windows applications using ObjectWindows. Part I of the book already demonstrated many basic Windows programming concepts contained in this chapter. These concepts are reintroduced here in a new light, through the use of object-oriented procedures and ObjectWindows features. This chapter begins with the basic application structure of a Windows program using ObjectWindows and the steps involved in creating the application. Then you learn how to create several Windows applications by using the structures and steps described.

Windows Application Structure Using ObjectWindows

The code structure of a Windows application developed using ObjectWindows differs from the Windows application code structure presented in Part I. ObjectWindows application code uses the features of ObjectWindows classes and takes advantage of object-oriented programming. By using these features and advantages, you usually find that the resulting code is less lengthy and quicker to develop. In addition, you can spend more time on the functionality of the program and less time on the structure, because ObjectWindows has defined the majority of Windows structures that must be defined for each application when you use traditional Windows programming styles.

With a traditional Windows program, there are three fundamental parts to the application: the `WinMain` function, the message loop, and the window procedures. With ObjectWindows applications, these elements are still present; ObjectWindows, however, has already defined objects that enable you to avoid most of the difficulties involved with defining these elements. The following paragraphs review each of these components and describe how each is implemented and handled in ObjectWindows applications.

The *WinMain* Function

As Chapter 11, "Introduction to ObjectWindows Programming for C++" describes, all ObjectWindows applications contain a `WinMain` function that controls the application. For most applications, this main program contains three statements in the format shown in the following code. In general, you do not deviate from this structure.

```
int PASCAL WinMain(HINSTANCE hInstance, HINSTANCE hPrevInstance,
                 LPSTR lpCmdLine, int nCmdShow)
{
     TAppExample AppExample("Application Example", hInstance,
                          hInstance, lpCmdLine, nCmdShow);
     AppExample.Run();
     return AppExample.Status;
}
```

The first statement of the main program calls the constructor that constructs the application object. When the constructor is called, the data members of the application object are initialized. The application object is referenced by the global variable `Application`.

The second statement of the main program calls the Run member function which, in turn, calls InitApplication and InitInstance. InitApplication initializes the first instance of the application. InitInstance initializes each instance of the application. After Run has called InitApplication and InitInstance, InitMainWindow is called to create a main window. InitMainWindow is generally redefined for the application. Last, the Run member function calls MessageLoop, which receives and processes Windows messages sent to the application.

The main program's third statement returns the final status of the application. Zero is generally used to represent a normal closing of the application. A nonzero value usually indicates that an error has occurred.

The Message Loop

In traditional Windows programming styles, the message loop is part of the WinMain function and has the following format:

```
while (GetMessage (&Message, 0, 0, 0))
{
TranslateMessage(&Message);
DispatchMessage(&Message);
}
```

For ObjectWindows applications, the Run member function of the application automatically calls the MessageLoop member function. MessageLoop automatically processes messages and runs until the application is closed. There is no need to define MessageLoop because ObjectWindows has already taken care of it.

Window Procedures

Traditional Windows programming styles use a window procedure to give a window functionality. The window procedure generally consists of at least one switch statement (and often nested switch statements) that handles the various incoming messages. An example of a fundamental window procedure using traditional Windows programming styles is as follows:

```
long FAR PASCAL WndProc (HWND hWnd, WORD iMessage, WORD
                         wParam, LONG lParam)
{
     switch (iMessage)
          {
          case WM_DESTROY:
               PostQuitMessage(0);
               return 0;
```

```
        default:
            return(DefWindowProc(hWnd, iMessage,
                                 wParam, lParam));
        }
}
```

With ObjectWindows, you do not define a window procedure, as previously shown. Instead, you simply define or redefine member functions for the window object. These member functions handle the various messages directed at the window object. Again ObjectWindows has eliminated a lot of the work required to add functionality to window objects. The procedures of defining and redefining window object member functions are demonstrated throughout this chapter.

Project Files

The creation of a Windows application requires several files. The files you most commonly utilize with traditional Windows programming methods include the C source file, the resource file, and the module definition file. The most common way to handle these files during application development is through the Project Manager and the Integrated Development Environment (IDE). The Project Manager and IDE were used extensively in Part I to develop the program examples. A typical Windows project would contain a module definition file (.DEF), a resource file (.RC), and a C source file (.C).

As with Windows applications developed using traditional programming styles, ObjectWindows applications are commonly developed using the Project Manager and the IDE. A typical ObjectWindows project contains a module definition file, a resource file, a C++ source file, and library files. These files are described in more detail in the following sections.

The Module Definition File

The module definition file gives the linker specific information about the application's code and data segments, the size of the application's local heap, and the size of the application's program stack. When you use the Borland C++ linker, it is not really necessary to create the module definition file because the linker is able to determine that information. With traditional Windows programming styles, it is customary, though not necessary, to include the module definition file. With ObjectWindows, however, most projects do not define one but instead use the predefined ObjectWindows definition file OWL.DEF. If you decide to define a module definition file with your ObjectWindows application, this quick description should help you:

```
NAME
DESCRIPTION
EXETYPE
CODE
DATA
HEAPSIZE
STACKSIZE
```

in which

`NAME` defines a module as an executable.

`DESCRIPTION` adds the specified text to the executable.

`EXETYPE` indicates the type of program the linker should create. `WINDOWS` is used for Windows applications.

`CODE` provides information on the application's code segments. possible values include `PRELOAD`, `FIXED`, `MOVEABLE`, and `DISCARDABLE`.

`DATA` provides information on the application's data segments. Possible values include `PRELOAD`, `MOVEABLE`, and `MULTIPLE`.

`HEAPSIZE` defines the initial size of the application's local heap.

`STACKSIZE` defines the size of the application's stack.

Resource Files

Resource files define resources such as menus, dialog boxes, icons, bitmaps, and accelerator tables. Although many things differ between the use of traditional Windows programming styles and the use of ObjectWindows, the resource file is not one of them. You define resource files using the exact same method that you use for applications developed with traditional programming styles for ObjectWindows applications. You can also use the Resource Workshop effectively to generate the resources required for both programming styles.

C++ Source Files

The C++ source file contains the actual code for the application. Because this file is a C++ file, it should contain such items as class definitions and member function definitions. It is in this file that the actual functionality of the application is defined. The examples that appear later in this chapter provide numerous C++ source file listings.

Library Files, DLLs, and Import Libraries

ObjectWindows applications often contain two library files, one for the ObjectWindows library and one for the container class library. The actual library files included in the project depends on the memory model you are using. Table 12.1 lists files that are used for the memory models specified.

Table 12.1. ObjectWindows library files.

Memory Model	ObjectWindows Library	Container Class Library
Small	OWLWS.LIB	TCLASSS.LIB
Medium	OWLWM.LIB	TCLASDBS.LIB
Compact	OWLWC.LIB	TCLASDBL.LIB
Large	OWLWL.LIB	TCLASSL.LIB

Several dynamic link libraries (DLLs) and import libraries are available for use with your ObjectWindows application. Table 12.2 lists these libraries.

Table 12.2. DLLs and import libraries.

Type	DLL	Import Library
ObjectWindows	OWL31.DLL	OWL.LIB
Borland C++	BC30RTL.DLL	CRTLDLL.LIB

If you want your application to use either DLL, you must link the appropriate import library. If your use either of the DLLs, you must use the large memory model and smart callbacks (the `-ml` and `-WS` options).

Using the IDE with ObjectWindows

When the topic of developing Windows applications using Borland C++ was introduced in Part I, there were three different development methods mentioned.

These three methods involved the use of the command-line compiler, the Integrated Development Environment (IDE), and the MAKE utility. Using the IDE and its Program Manager features was selected as the most desirable method for developing Windows applications because this choice offers a more straightforward, procedural approach to development.

The process presented for Windows development in Part I is the same process that you use to develop an ObjectWindows application. Let's review the basic steps to developing an ObjectWindows application:

> **Note:** This process is designed for use with Windows-based versions of the IDE. The process used for the DOS-based IDE is similar.

1. Start the IDE by double-clicking the Borland C++ for Windows icon.
2. Create all appropriate C++ source files, module definition files, and resource files.
3. Select `Project | Open`. Type the filename, using a .PRJ extension, in the `Project Name` dialog box. Click the OK button, or press Enter to continue.
4. Select `Project | Add item`. Add the appropriate C or C++ source files, module definition files, and resource files. Close the `Project` dialog box when you are done.
5. Select `Options | Application`. The `Set Application Options` dialog box will appear. Select `Windows App` to indicate that you are developing a Windows application.
6. Select `Run | Run`. This selection builds the project into a Windows application and displays your application window if the project compiles successfully.
7. If there are any errors, modify the appropriate file(s) and repeat step 6.

This process is rather painless and enables you to take full advantage of the IDE and Project Manager features.

Programming Examples Using ObjectWindows

The remainder of this chapter provides examples on programming with ObjectWindows. Each example contains a full description of the example code and operation.

The Basic Window Example

A good place to begin the examples portion of the chapter is to show a minimal ObjectWindows application. This example displays a window that can respond to events, be resized and moved, manage child windows, and be closed. Note that nothing is displayed inside the client area of the resulting window.

This example, as well as all examples in this chapter, have been created using a project. The project used to build this example is called `OBJ_BAS` and contains the files `OBJ_BAS.CPP` and `OWL.DEF`. The following project description summarizes the project. A similar summary is used for every example in this chapter.

Project Name:	`OBJ_BAS`
Files in Project:	`OBJ_BAS.CPP`
	`OWL.DEF`

Because this example is the fundamental structure used for all the examples in this book, it is important that you understand each component of the code. You should look at each component of the example code individually.

The program begins by including the owl.h header file. Every ObjectWindows program must include this header file.

```
#include <owl.h>
```

The next component of the code, shown as follows, defines a new application class `TBasicDemo`, derived from `TApplication`. An instance of the derived class should be constructed in `WinMain`. `WinMain` appears later in the code. At a minimum, the derived class must redefine the member function `InitMainWindow`. The `InitMainWindow` function is called automatically and constructs the window object that should be the main window of the application.

```
class TBasicDemo : public TApplication
{
public:
    TBasicDemo(LPSTR AName HINSTANCE hInstance, HINSTANCE
```

```
                hPrevInstance, LPSTR lpCmdLine, intCmdShow) :
          TApplication(AName, hInstance, hPrevInstance,
          lpCmdLine, nCmdShow) {};
     virtual void InitMainWindow();
};
```

The following component of code defines the `InitMainWindow` function of the application object `TBasicDemo (TBasicDemo::InitMainWindow)`. The main window object, in this case, is constructed as an instance of `TWindow`. In the remaining examples, however, the main window object should be constructed as an instance of a derived class of `TWindow` or some other ObjectWindows class.

```
void TBasicDemo::InitMainWindow()
{
MainWindow = new TWindow(NULL, "Basic Window
                         Demonstration");
}
```

The last component of code, shown as follows, is the main program of the application. In this section, an instance of the derived class `TBasicDemo` is constructed. All application initializations are made and the message loop is entered. The application exits from the message loop and returns the final status of the application as it closes.

```
int PASCAL WinMain(HINSTANCE hInstance, HINSTANCE
                   hPrevInstance, LPSTR lpCmdLine, int nCmdShow)
{
TBasicDemo BasicDemo("Basic Window", hInstance, hPrevInstance,
                     lpCmdLine, nCmdShow);
BasicDemo.Run();
return(BasicDemo.Status);
}
```

This basic structure is followed throughout the chapter's remaining examples. Listing 12.1 contains the complete code for the basic window example. Figure 12.1 illustrates the output of this example.

Listing 12.1. *The basic window example.*

```
#include <owl.h>

class TBasicDemo : public TApplication
{
public:
     TBasicDemo(LPSTR AName, HINSTANCE hInstance, HINSTANCE
                hPrevInstance, LPSTR lpCmdLine, int nCmdShow) :
```

continues

Listing 12.1. continued

```
        TApplication(AName, hInstance, hPrevInstance,
        lpCmdLine, nCmdShow) {};
     virtual void InitMainWindow();
};


void TBasicDemo::InitMainWindow()
{
MainWindow = new TWindow(NULL, "Basic Window Demonstration");
}

int PASCAL WinMain(HINSTANCE hInstance, HINSTANCE hPrevInstance,
                   LPSTR lpCmdLine, int nCmdShow)
{
TBasicDemo BasicDemo("Basic Window", hInstance, hPrevInstance,
                     lpCmdLine, nCmdShow);
BasicDemo.Run();
return(BasicDemo.Status);
}
```

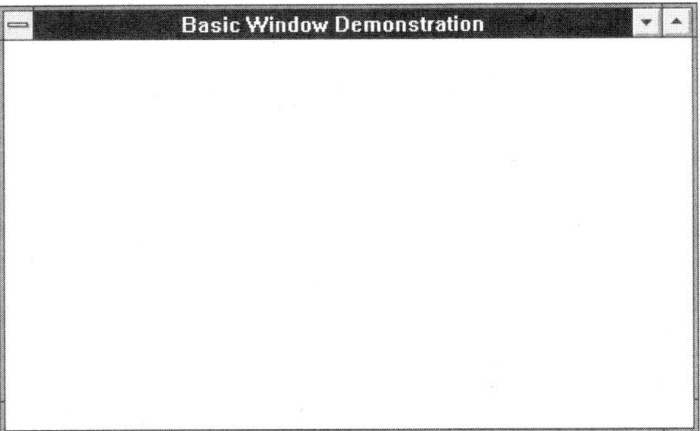

***Figure 12.1.** The output of the basic window example.*

For comparison purposes, the fundamental window example from Part I is included in Listings 12.2 and 12.3. As you can see, ObjectWindows insulates you from the majority of the work required to create a basic window application. The project `WIN_ONE` was used to create this example.

Project Name:	`WIN_ONE`
Files in Project:	`WIN_ONE.C`
	`WIN_ONE.DEF`

Listing 12.2. *The module definition file for the fundamental window example.*

```
NAME            WIN_ONE
DESCRIPTION     'Fundamental Window'
EXETYPE         WINDOWS
CODE            PRELOAD MOVEABLE
DATA            PRELOAD MOVEABLE MULTIPLE
HEAPSIZE        1024
STACKSIZE       5120
```

Listing 12.3. *C source code for the fundamental window example.*

```
#include <windows.h>
#include <stdlib.h>
#include <string.h>

long FAR PASCAL WndProc (HWND hWnd, WORD iMessage,
                         WORD wParam, LONG lParam);

int PASCAL WinMain (HANDLE hInstance, HANDLE hPrevInstance,
                    LPSTR lpszCmdParam, int nCmdShow)

{
HWND hWnd;
MSG Message;
WNDCLASS WndClass;

if (!hPrevInstance)
     {
     WndClass.cbClsExtra = 0;
     WndClass.cbWndExtra = 0;
     WndClass.hbrBackground = GetStockObject(WHITE_BRUSH);
     WndClass.hCursor =  LoadCursor(NULL, IDC_ARROW);
     WndClass.hIcon = LoadIcon (NULL, "END");
     WndClass.hInstance = hInstance;
     WndClass.lpfnWndProc = WndProc;
     WndClass.lpszClassName = "WIN_ONE";
     WndClass.lpszMenuName = NULL;
     WndClass.style = CS_HREDRAW ¦ CS_VREDRAW;

     RegisterClass (&WndClass);
     }

hWnd = CreateWindow ("WIN_ONE",          /* class name */
          "Fundamental Window",          /* Caption */
```

continues

Listing 12.3. continued

```
          WS_OVERLAPPEDWINDOW,          /* Style */
          CW_USEDEFAULT,                /* x position */
          0,                            /* y position */
          CW_USEDEFAULT,                /* cx - size */
          0,                            /* cy - size */
          NULL,                         /* Parent window */
          NULL,                         /* Menu */
          hInstance,                    /* Program Instance */
          NULL);                        /* Parameters */

ShowWindow (hWnd, nCmdShow);
while (GetMessage (&Message, 0, 0, 0))
     {
     TranslateMessage(&Message);
     DispatchMessage(&Message);
     }
return Message.wParam;
}

/*****************************************************************/
/*              Window Procedure: WndProc                        */
/*****************************************************************/

long FAR PASCAL WndProc (HWND hWnd, WORD iMessage, WORD wParam,
                         LONG lParam)
{
switch (iMessage)
          {
     case WM_DESTROY:
          PostQuitMessage(0);
          return 0;
     default:
          return(DefWindowProc(hWnd, iMessage, wParam,
                 lParam));
     }
}
```

The Line Drawing Example

The line drawing example introduces a few concepts beyond the basic window example. In this example, you are using the GDI functions to create pens and draw lines. In addition, you are defining the member function `Paint` to monitor the `WM_PAINT` message. Therefore, when you start the program and every time the window is sized, the specified lines are drawn in the client area. The `OBJ_LINE` project was used to create this example. The code for the C++ source file is provided in Listing 12.4.

Project Name:	`OBJ_LINE`
Files in Project:	`OBJ_LINE.CPP` `OWL.DEF`

Listing 12.4. The line drawing example.

```
#include <owl.h>

class TLineDemo : public TApplication
{
public:
     TLineDemo(LPSTR AName, HINSTANCE hInstance, HINSTANCE
               hPrevInstance, LPSTR lpCmdLine, int nCmdShow) :
        TApplication(AName, hInstance, hPrevInstance,
                     lpCmdLine, nCmdShow) {};
     virtual void InitMainWindow();
};

_CLASSDEF(TLineWindow)

class TLineWindow : public TWindow
{
public:
     TLineWindow(PTWindowsObject AParent, LPSTR ATitle) :
        TWindow(AParent, ATitle) {};
     virtual void Paint(HDC PaintDC, PAINTSTRUCT _FAR &
                        PaintInfo);
};


void TLineWindow::Paint(HDC PaintDC, PAINTSTRUCT _FAR &)
{

     static LOGPEN lpBlue = {PS_SOLID, 1, 1, RGB(0,0,255)},
                   lpRed = {PS_SOLID, 1, 1, RGB(255,0,0)};
     HPEN hBluePen;
     HPEN hRedPen;
     int x1;
     int x2 = 300;

     hBluePen = CreatePenIndirect(&lpBlue);
     hRedPen = CreatePenIndirect(&lpRed);
     for (x1=50; x1<300; x1=x1+5)
       {
       SelectObject(PaintDC, hBluePen);
       MoveTo(PaintDC, x1, 50);
       LineTo(PaintDC, x2, 150);
```

continues

Listing 12.4. continued

```
       SelectObject(PaintDC, hRedPen);
       MoveTo(PaintDC, x2, 50);
       LineTo(PaintDC, x1, 150);
       x2 = x2 - 5;
       }
}


void TLineDemo::InitMainWindow()
{
MainWindow = new TLineWindow(NULL, "Line Drawing Demonstration");
}


int PASCAL WinMain(HINSTANCE hInstance, HINSTANCE hPrevInstance,
                   LPSTR lpCmdLine, int nCmdShow)
{
TLineDemo LineDemo("Line Demo Window", hInstance,
                   hPrevInstance, lpCmdLine, nCmdShow);
LineDemo.Run();
return(LineDemo.Status);
}
```

The program begins much like the basic window example. A derived class of `TApplication`—`TLineDemo`—is defined in the first component of the code. The second component of code, however, differs from the basic window example in that it defines a derived class of `TWindow`—`TLineWindow`. The main window object should be constructed from an instance of the derived class `TLineWindow`. As was already mentioned in the basic window example discussion, the main window object is usually an instance of a derived class of an ObjectWindows class. `TLineWindow` expects the member function `Paint` to be redefined.

The third component of code redefines the `Paint` member function of `TLineWindow` (`TLineWindow::Paint`). This member function defines and creates two pens and uses these pens to draw a series of blue and red lines. Each time the main window receives the `WM_PAINT` message, the `Paint` member function should be called.

The next component constructs the main window object as an instance of `TLineWindow`. The `NULL` parameter indicates that this is to be the main window. The second parameter, "Line Drawing Demonstration", specifies the window title.

The last component is the main program. The main program follows the same principal format as described in the basic window example. The output of this example is shown in Figure 12.2.

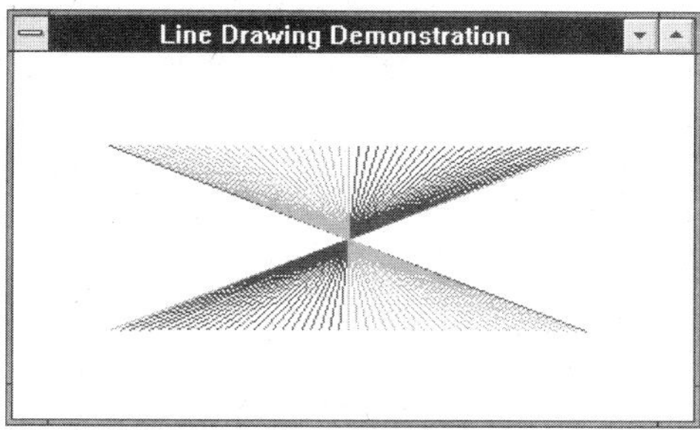

Figure 12.2. *The output of the line drawing example.*

The Arc Drawing Example

The arc drawing example is very similar to the line drawing example. In this example, you are using the GDI functions to create pens and draw arcs. Again, you are redefining the member function `Paint` to monitor the `WM_PAINT` message. The `OBJ_ARC` project was used to create this example. The code for the C++ source file is provided in Listing 12.5.

Project Name:	`OBJ_ARC`
Files in Project:	`OBJ_ARC.CPP`
	`OWL.DEF`

Listing 12.5. *The arc drawing example.*

```
#include <owl.h>

class TArcDemo : public TApplication
{
public:
     TArcDemo(LPSTR AName, HINSTANCE hInstance, HINSTANCE
              hPrevInstance, LPSTR lpCmdLine, int nCmdShow) :
        TApplication(AName, hInstance, hPrevInstance,
                     lpCmdLine, nCmdShow) {};
     virtual void InitMainWindow();
};

_CLASSDEF(TArcWindow)

class TArcWindow : public TWindow
```

continues

Listing 12.5. continued

```
{
public:
     TArcWindow(PTWindowsObject AParent, LPSTR ATitle) :
        TWindow(AParent, ATitle) {};
     virtual void Paint(HDC PaintDC, PAINTSTRUCT _FAR &
                        PaintInfo);
};


void TArcWindow::Paint(HDC PaintDC, PAINTSTRUCT _FAR &)
{

     static LOGPEN lpBlue = {PS_SOLID, 1, 1, RGB(0,0,255)},
                   lpRed = {PS_SOLID, 1, 1, RGB(255,0,0)};
     HPEN hBluePen;
     HPEN hRedPen;
     int x1;
     int y1 = 50;
     int x2 = 350;
     int y2 = 250;

     hBluePen = CreatePenIndirect(&lpBlue);
     hRedPen = CreatePenIndirect(&lpRed);
     for (x1=50; x1<200; x1=x1+5)
       {
       SelectObject(PaintDC, hBluePen);
       Arc(PaintDC, x1, y1, 200, 150, 200, 150, 50, 150);
       SelectObject(PaintDC, hRedPen);
       Arc(PaintDC, 200, 150, x2, y2, 200, 150, 350, 150);
       y1 = y1 + 3;
       x2 = x2 - 5;
       y2 = y2 - 3;
       }
}


void TArcDemo::InitMainWindow()
{
MainWindow = new TArcWindow(NULL, "Arc Demonstration");
}


int PASCAL WinMain(HINSTANCE hInstance, HINSTANCE hPrevInstance,
                   LPSTR lpCmdLine, int nCmdShow)
```

```
{
TArcDemo ArcDemo("Arc Demo Window", hInstance, hPrevInstance,
                lpCmdLine, nCmdShow);
ArcDemo.Run();
return ArcDemo.Status;
}
```

A derived class of `TApplication`—`TArcDemo`—is defined in the first component of the code. The second component of the code defines a derived class of `TWindow`, `TArcWindow`. The main window object is to be constructed from an instance of the derived class `TArcWindow` that expects the member function `Paint` to be redefined.

The third component of code redefines the `Paint` member function of `TArcWindow` (`TArcWindow::Paint`). This member function defines and creates two pens and uses these pens to draw a series of blue and red arcs.

The next component constructs the main window object as an instance of `TArcWindow`. The `NULL` parameter indicates that this is to be the main window. The second parameter, "Arc Demonstration", specifies the window title.

The last component is the main program that follows the same principal format as described in the basic window example. The output of this example is shown in Figure 12.3.

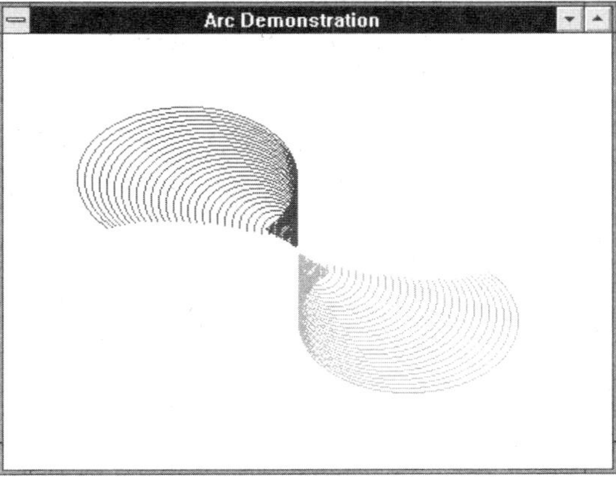

Figure 12.3. *The output of the arc drawing example.*

The Filled Figures Example

The filled figures example is very similar to the previous two examples. In this example, you are using the GDI functions to create brushes and draw several filled figures including a rectangle, a rounded rectangle, a circle, a chorded circle, and a pie-shaped wedge. Again, you are defining the member function `Paint` to monitor the `WM_PAINT` message. The `OBJ_FIG` project was used to create this example. Listing 12.6 shows the code for this C++ source file.

Project Name:	`OBJ_FIG`
Files in Project:	`OBJ_FIG.CPP`
	`OWL.DEF`

Listing 12.6. *The filled figures example.*

```
#include <owl.h>

class TFiguresDemo : public TApplication
{
public:
     TFiguresDemo(LPSTR AName, HINSTANCE hInstance, HINSTANCE
                  hPrevInstance, LPSTR lpCmdLine, int nCmdShow) :
        TApplication(AName, hInstance, hPrevInstance,
                     lpCmdLine, nCmdShow) {};
     virtual void InitMainWindow();
};

_CLASSDEF(TFiguresWindow)

class TFiguresWindow : public TWindow
{
public:
     TFiguresWindow(PTWindowsObject AParent, LPSTR ATitle) :
        TWindow(AParent, ATitle) {};
     virtual void Paint(HDC PaintDC, PAINTSTRUCT _FAR
                        & PaintInfo);
};


void TFiguresWindow::Paint(HDC PaintDC, PAINTSTRUCT _FAR &)
{
     static HBRUSH hBrush[2];
     hBrush[0] = CreateHatchBrush(HS_HORIZONTAL,
                  RGB(0,0,0));
     hBrush[1] = CreateHatchBrush(HS_VERTICAL,
                  RGB(255,0,0));

     SelectObject(PaintDC,hBrush[0]);
     Rectangle (PaintDC,50,50,100,100);
```

```
     SelectObject(PaintDC,hBrush[1]);
     RoundRect (PaintDC,50,150,100,200,15,15);
     Ellipse (PaintDC,150,50,200,100);

     SelectObject(PaintDC,hBrush[0]);
     Chord (PaintDC,150,150,200,200,150,150,200,200);
     Pie (PaintDC,250,50,300,100,250,50,300,50);

}


void TFiguresDemo::InitMainWindow()
{
MainWindow = new TFiguresWindow(NULL, "Figures Demonstration");
}


int PASCAL WinMain(HINSTANCE hInstance, HINSTANCE hPrevInstance,
                   LPSTR lpCmdLine, int nCmdShow)
{
TFiguresDemo FiguresDemo("Figures Demo Window", hInstance,
                         hPrevInstance, lpCmdLine, nCmdShow);
FiguresDemo.Run();
return(FiguresDemo.Status);
}
```

A derived class of `TApplication`—`TFiguresDemo`—is defined in the first component of the code. The second component of the code defines a derived class of `TWindow`: `TFiguresWindow`. `TFiguresWindow` expects the member function `Paint` to be redefined.

The third component of code redefines the `Paint` member function of `TFiguresWindow` (`TFiguresWindow::Paint`). This member function defines and creates two brushes and uses these brushes when drawing the filled figures.

The next component constructs the main window object as an instance of `TFiguresWindow`. The `NULL` parameter indicates that this is to be the main window. The second parameter, "Figures Demonstration", specifies the window title.

The last component is the main program that follows the same principal format as described in the basic window example. The output of this example is shown in Figure 12.4.

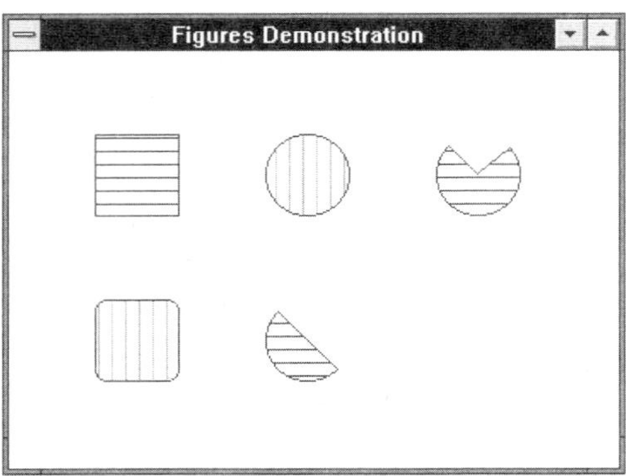

Figure 12.4. *The output of the filled figures example.*

The *TextOut* Example

The `TextOut` example demonstrates how you can generate text in the client area. In this example, you are using the `TextOut` function to display text. This example writes the specified text in response to the `WM_PAINT` message. Therefore, you must redefine the member function `Paint` to draw the text in response to the `WM_PAINT` message. The `OBJ_TXT` project was used to create this example. Listing 12.7 shows the code for this C++ source file.

Project Name:	`OBJ_TXT`
Files in Project:	`OBJ_TXT.CPP`
	`OWL.DEF`

Listing 12.7. *The* `TextOut` *example.*

```
#include <owl.h>

class TTextOutDemo : public TApplication
{
public:
     TTextOutDemo(LPSTR AName, HINSTANCE hInstance, HINSTANCE
                 hPrevInstance, LPSTR lpCmdLine, int nCmdShow) :
        TApplication(AName, hInstance, hPrevInstance,
                    lpCmdLine, nCmdShow) {};
     virtual void InitMainWindow();
};

_CLASSDEF(TTextOutWindow)
```

```
class TTextOutWindow : public TWindow
{
public:
     TTextOutWindow(PTWindowsObject AParent, LPSTR ATitle) :
        TWindow(AParent, ATitle) {};
     virtual void Paint(HDC PaintDC, PAINTSTRUCT _FAR &
        PaintInfo);
};


void TTextOutWindow::Paint(HDC PaintDC, PAINTSTRUCT _FAR &)
{

     int nXText, nYText, nHeight;
     short x;
     DWORD dwExt;
     short LnCount = 15;
     static char *textbuf[] =
          {"One",
          "Two",
          "Three",
          "Four",
          "Five",
          "Six",
          "Seven",
          "Eight",
          "Nine",
          "Ten",
          "Eleven",
          "Twelve",
          "Thirteen",
          "Fourteen",
          "Fifteen"};

          dwExt = GetTextExtent(PaintDC,"S",1);
          nHeight = HIWORD(dwExt);
          nYText = nHeight;
          nXText = LOWORD(dwExt);
          for (x=0; x<LnCount; x=x+1)
               {
               TextOut(PaintDC,nXText,nYText,
                 textbuf[x], lstrlen(textbuf[x]));
               nYText = nYText + nHeight;
               }

}
```

continues

Listing 12.7. continued

```
void TTextOutDemo::InitMainWindow()
{
MainWindow = new TTextOutWindow(NULL, "TextOut Demonstration");
}


int PASCAL WinMain(HINSTANCE hInstance, HINSTANCE hPrevInstance,
                   LPSTR lpCmdLine, int nCmdShow)
{
TTextOutDemo TextOutDemo("TextOut Demo Window", hInstance,
                         hPrevInstance, lpCmdLine, nCmdShow);
TextOutDemo.Run();
return(TextOutDemo.Status);
}
```

A derived class of `TApplication`—`TTextOutDemo`—is defined in the first component of the code. The second component of the code defines a derived class of `TWindow`—`TTextOutWindow`—that expects the member function `Paint` to be redefined.

The third component of code redefines the `Paint` member function of `TTextOutWindow` (`TTextOutWindow::Paint`). This member function defines and displays the 15 specified lines of text. Every time the `WM_PAINT` message is received, the text is redrawn.

The next component constructs the main window object as an instance of `TTextOutWindow`. The `NULL` parameter indicates that this is to be the main window. The second parameter, "`TextOut` Demonstration", specifies the window title.

The last component is the main program that follows the same principal format as described in the basic window example. The output of this example is shown in Figure 12.5.

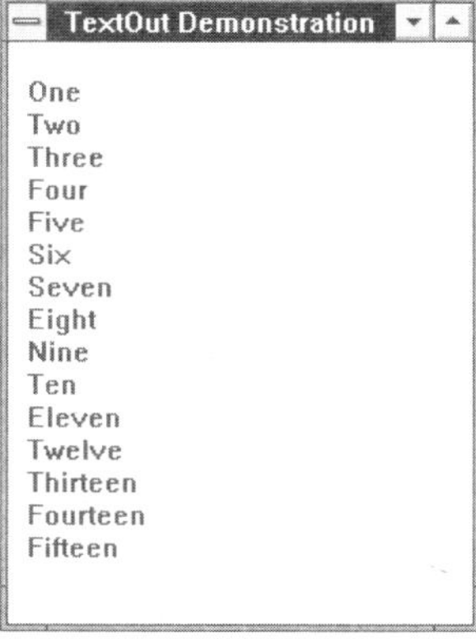

***Figure 12.5.** The output of the `TextOut` example.*

The *TabbedTextOut* Example

The TabbedTextOut example is similar to the TextOut example, except that the TabbedTextOut example demonstrates how you can generate tabbed text in the client area. In this example, you are using the TabbedTextOut function to display text. Again, this example writes the specified text in response to the WM_PAINT message. Therefore, you must redefine the member function Paint to draw text in response to the WM_PAINT message. The OBJ_TTXT project was used to create this example. The code for the C++ source file is provided in Listing 12.8.

Project Name:	OBJ_TTXT
Files in Project:	OBJ_TTXT.CPP
	OWL.DEF

Listing 12.8. *The* TabbedTextOut *example.*

```
#include <owl.h>

class TTTextOutDemo : public TApplication
{
public:
     TTTextOutDemo(LPSTR AName, HINSTANCE hInstance, HINSTANCE
                  hPrevInstance, LPSTR lpCmdLine, int nCmdShow) :
        TApplication(AName, hInstance, hPrevInstance,
                    lpCmdLine, nCmdShow) {};
     virtual void InitMainWindow();
};

_CLASSDEF(TTTextOutWindow)

class TTTextOutWindow : public TWindow
{
public:
     TTTextOutWindow(PTWindowsObject AParent, LPSTR ATitle) :
        TWindow(AParent, ATitle) {};
     virtual void Paint(HDC PaintDC, PAINTSTRUCT _FAR &
                       PaintInfo);
};


void TTTextOutWindow::Paint(HDC PaintDC, PAINTSTRUCT _FAR &)
{

     int nXText, nYText, nHeight, nTab;
     short x;
     DWORD dwExt;
```

continues

Listing 12.8. continued

```
     short LnCount = 13;
     static char *textbuf[] =
          {"Number \tPlayer",
          "______ \t______",
          "One \tJim",
          "Two \tSue",
          "Three \tJohn",
          "Four \tMary",
          "Five \tSally",
          "Six \tGary",
          "Seven \tKenny",
          "Eight \tDonna",
          "Nine \tTony",
          "Ten \tKim",
          "Eleven \tWes"};

          dwExt = GetTextExtent(PaintDC,"S",1);
          nHeight = HIWORD(dwExt);
          nYText = nHeight;
          nXText = LOWORD(dwExt);
          nTab = 25 * LOWORD(dwExt);
          for (x=0; x<LnCount; x=x+1)
               {
               TabbedTextOut(PaintDC,nXText,nYText,
                 textbuf[x],lstrlen(textbuf[x]),1,
                 &nTab,nXText);
               nYText = nYText + nHeight;
               }

}


void TTextOutDemo::InitMainWindow()
{
MainWindow = new TTextOutWindow(NULL, "TabbedTextOut Demonstration");
}


int PASCAL WinMain(HINSTANCE hInstance, HINSTANCE hPrevInstance,
                   LPSTR lpCmdLine, int nCmdShow)
{
TTextOutDemo TTextOutDemo("TTextOut Demo Window",hInstance,
                          hPrevInstance, lpCmdLine, nCmdShow);
TTextOutDemo.Run();
return(TTextOutDemo.Status);
}
```

A derived class of TApplication—TTTextOutDemo—is defined in the first component of the code. The second component of the code defines a derived class of TWindow—TTTextOutWindow—that expects the member function Paint to be redefined.

The third component of code redefines the Paint member function of TTTextOutWindow (TTTextOutWindow::Paint). This member function defines and displays the 15 tabbed lines of text. Every time the WM_PAINT message is received, the text is redrawn.

The next component constructs the main window object as an instance of TTTextOutWindow. The NULL parameter indicates that this is to be the main window. The second parameter, "TabbedTextOut Demonstration", specifies the window title.

The last component is the main program that follows the same principal format as described in the basic window example. The output of this example is shown in Figure 12.6.

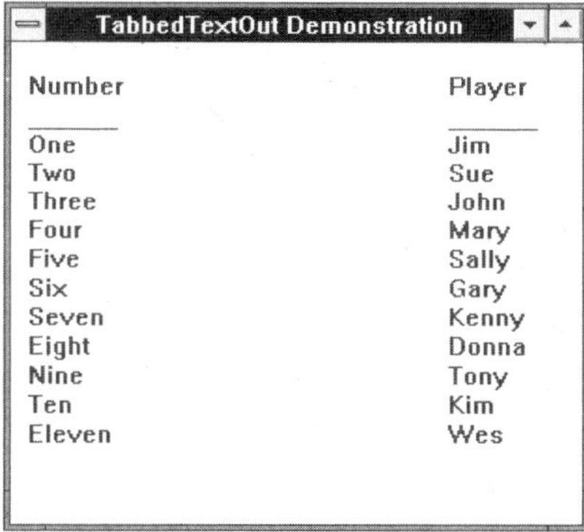

Figure 12.6. *The output of the* `TabbedTextOut` *example.*

The Scroller Example

The scroller example demonstrates the use the scrolling features of TScroller. This example begins by drawing an ellipse that is larger than the current window. The features of TScroller enable you to scroll the image both horizontally and vertically. The OBJ_SCRL project was used to create this example. The code for the C++ source file is provided in Listing 12.9.

Project Name:	OBJ_SCRL
Files in Project:	OBJ_SCRL.CPP
	OWL.DEF

Listing 12.9. The Scroller example.

```
#include <owl.h>

class TScrollerDemo : public TApplication
{
public:
     TScrollerDemo(LPSTR AName, HINSTANCE hInstance, HINSTANCE
                   hPrevInstance, LPSTR lpCmdLine, int nCmdShow) :
        TApplication(AName, hInstance, hPrevInstance,
                     lpCmdLine, nCmdShow) {};
     virtual void InitMainWindow();
};

_CLASSDEF(TScrollerWindow)

class TScrollerWindow : public TWindow
{
public:
     TScrollerWindow(LPSTR ATitle);
     virtual void Paint(HDC PaintDC, PAINTSTRUCT _FAR &
                        PaintInfo);
};


TScrollerWindow::TScrollerWindow(LPSTR ATitle) :
     TWindow(NULL, ATitle)
{
     Attr.Style |= WS_VSCROLL | WS_HSCROLL;
     Scroller = new TScroller(this,5,5,100,100);
}

void TScrollerWindow::Paint(HDC PaintDC, PAINTSTRUCT _FAR &)
{
Ellipse(PaintDC,50,50,500,500);
}


void TScrollerDemo::InitMainWindow()
{
MainWindow = new TScrollerWindow("Scroller Demonstration");
}


int PASCAL WinMain(HINSTANCE hInstance, HINSTANCE hPrevInstance,
                   LPSTR lpCmdLine, int nCmdShow)
{
```

```
TScrollerDemo ScrollerDemo("Scroller Demo Window", hInstance,
                           hPrevInstance, lpCmdLine, nCmdShow);
ScrollerDemo.Run();
return(ScrollerDemo.Status);
}
```

A derived class of `TApplication`—`TScrollerDemo`—is defined in the first component of the code. The second component of the code defines a derived class of `TWindow`—`TScrollerWindow`—that expects the member function `Paint` to be redefined.

The third component of code is unlike any of the components in the previous examples. This component is a constructor for a `TScrollerWindow`, defines the scroll styles, and constructs the `Scroller` object.

The fourth component of code redefines the `Paint` member function of `TScrollerWindow` (`TScrollerWindow::Paint`). This member function generates the oversized ellipse.

The next component constructs the main window object as an instance of `TScrollerWindow`. The second parameter, "`Scroller` Demonstration", specifies the window title.

The last component is the main program that follows the same principal format as described in the basic window example. The output of this example is shown in Figure 12.7.

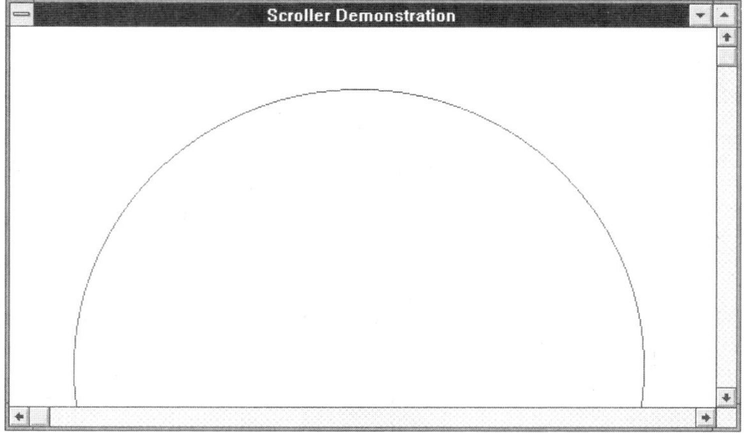

Figure 12.7. *The output of the scroller example.*

The Accelerator Example

The accelerator example demonstrates several new concepts. The first new concept is the use of accelerator and menu resources. Another concept is using and defining the `InitInstance` member function of the application object. Lastly, this example demonstrates the methods for defining actions for menu item and accelerator selection. The `OBJ_ACC` project was used to create this example. Listing 12.10 shows the resource file for this project. The code for the C++ source file is provided in Listing 12.11.

Project Name:	`OBJ_ACC`
Files in Project:	`OBJ_ACC.CPP`
	`OBJ_ACC.RC`
	`OWL.DEF`

Listing 12.10. The resource file for the accelerator example.

```
ACC_TABLE ACCELERATORS
BEGIN
  "1", 1, VIRTKEY, NOINVERT
  "2", 2, VIRTKEY, NOINVERT
  "3", 3, VIRTKEY, NOINVERT
  "4", 4, VIRTKEY, NOINVERT
  "5", 5, VIRTKEY, NOINVERT
  "6", 6, VIRTKEY, NOINVERT
  "7", 7, VIRTKEY, NOINVERT
END

MENU  MENU LOADONCALL MOVEABLE PURE DISCARDABLE
BEGIN
  POPUP "Menu One"
  BEGIN
    MenuItem  "Item One", 1
    MenuItem  "Item Two", 2
  END
  POPUP "Menu Two"
  BEGIN
    MenuItem  "Selection One", 3
  END
  POPUP "Menu Three"
  BEGIN
    MenuItem  "Checked Item #1", 4, CHECKED
    MenuItem  "Checked Item #2", 5, CHECKED
  END
  POPUP "Menu Four"
```

```
  BEGIN
    MenuItem  "Menu Item One", 6
    MenuItem  "Menu Item Two", 7
  END
END
```

Listing 12.11. The C++ source file for the accelerator example.

```
#include <owl.h>

#define CM_ONEONE 1
#define CM_ONETWO 2
#define CM_TWOONE 3
#define CM_THREEONE 4
#define CM_THREETWO 5
#define CM_FOURONE 6
#define CM_FOURTWO 7

class TAcceleratorDemo : public TApplication
{
public:
     TAcceleratorDemo(LPSTR AName, HINSTANCE hInstance,
     HINSTANCE hPrevInstance, LPSTR lpCmdLine, int
     nCmdShow) : TApplication(AName, hInstance,
     hPrevInstance, lpCmdLine, nCmdShow) {};
     virtual void InitMainWindow();
     virtual void InitInstance();
};

_CLASSDEF(TAcceleratorWindow)

class TAcceleratorWindow : public TWindow
{
public:
     TAcceleratorWindow(PTWindowsObject AParent, LPSTR ATitle);
     virtual void CMOneOne(RTMessage Msg) =
          [CM_FIRST + CM_ONEONE];
     virtual void CMOneTwo(RTMessage Msg) =
          [CM_FIRST + CM_ONETWO];
     virtual void CMTwoOne(RTMessage Msg) =
          [CM_FIRST + CM_TWOONE];
     virtual void CMThreeOne(RTMessage Msg) =
          [CM_FIRST + CM_THREEONE];
     virtual void CMThreeTwo(RTMessage Msg) =
          [CM_FIRST + CM_THREETWO];
     virtual void CMFourOne(RTMessage Msg) =
          [CM_FIRST + CM_FOURONE];
```

continues

Listing 12.11. continued

```
     virtual void CMFourTwo(RTMessage Msg) =
          [CM_FIRST + CM_FOURTWO];
};


TAcceleratorWindow::TAcceleratorWindow(PTWindowsObject AParent,
     LPSTR ATitle) : TWindow(AParent, ATitle)
{
AssignMenu("MENU");
};

void TAcceleratorDemo::InitMainWindow()
{
MainWindow = new TAcceleratorWindow(NULL,"Accelerators");
}

void TAcceleratorDemo::InitInstance()
{
TApplication::InitInstance();
HAccTable = LoadAccelerators(hInstance, "ACC_TABLE");
}

void TAcceleratorWindow::CMOneOne(RTMessage)
{
     MessageBox(HWindow,"Menu One - Item One",
       "Accelerator = 1",MB_OK);
}

void TAcceleratorWindow::CMOneTwo(RTMessage)
{
     MessageBox(HWindow,"Menu One - Item Two",
        "Accelerator = 2",MB_OK);
}


void TAcceleratorWindow::CMTwoOne(RTMessage)
{
     MessageBox(HWindow,"Menu Two - Selection One",
        "Accelerator = 3",MB_OK);
}


void TAcceleratorWindow::CMThreeOne(RTMessage)
{
     MessageBox(HWindow,"Menu Three - Checked Item #1",
        "Accelerator = 4",MB_OK);
}
```

```
void TAcceleratorWindow::CMThreeTwo(RTMessage)
{
     MessageBox(HWindow,"Menu Three - Checked Item #2",
        "Accelerator = 5",MB_OK);
}


void TAcceleratorWindow::CMFourOne(RTMessage)
{
     MessageBox(HWindow,"Menu Four - Menu Item One",
        "Accelerator = 6",MB_OK);
}


void TAcceleratorWindow::CMFourTwo(RTMessage)
{
     MessageBox(HWindow,"Menu Four - Menu Item Two",
        "Accelerator = 7",MB_OK);
}


int PASCAL WinMain(HINSTANCE hInstance, HINSTANCE hPrevInstance,
     LPSTR lpCmdLine, int nCmdShow)
{
TAcceleratorDemo AcceleratorDemo("Accelerators Window",
   hInstance, hPrevInstance, lpCmdLine, nCmdShow);
AcceleratorDemo.Run();
return(AcceleratorDemo.Status);
}
```

You should first review the resource file that defines four menus: Menu One, Menu Two, Menu Three, and Menu Four. Menu One contains two items: Item One and Item Two. Menu Two contains one item: Selection One. Menu Three contains two items: Checked Item #1 and Checked Item #2. Menu Four contains two items: Menu Item One and Menu Item Two. Accelerators, keys ranging from 1 to 7, have been defined for each menu item.

Now you should examine the C++ source file. A derived class of `TApplication`—`TAcceleratorDemo`—is defined in the first component of the code. The second component of the code defines a derived class of `TWindow`—`TAcceleratorWindow`—that expects the seven member functions to be defined. Each member function should define the action for a corresponding menu item or accelerator selection.

The third component of code constructs a `TAcceleratorWindow` and loads the specified menu.

The next component constructs the main window object as an instance of `TAcceleratorWindow`. The `NULL` parameter indicates that this is to be the main window. The second parameter, "Accelerators", specifies the window title.

The next component defines the `InitInstance` member function of the application object. This member function initializes each application instance and loads the specified accelerator table.

The seven code components following the definition of the `InitInstance` member function of the application object define the actions to be taken for each of the menu items. The member functions correspond to an appropriate menu item (for example, `CMOneOne` corresponds to Menu One of Item One). The member functions are automatically called in response to the command messages sent when a menu item is selected. Although these member functions only display message boxes, they could easily be redefined to perform more intricate, detailed operations.

The last component is the main program that follows the same principal format as described in the basic window example. The output of this example is shown in Figure 12.8.

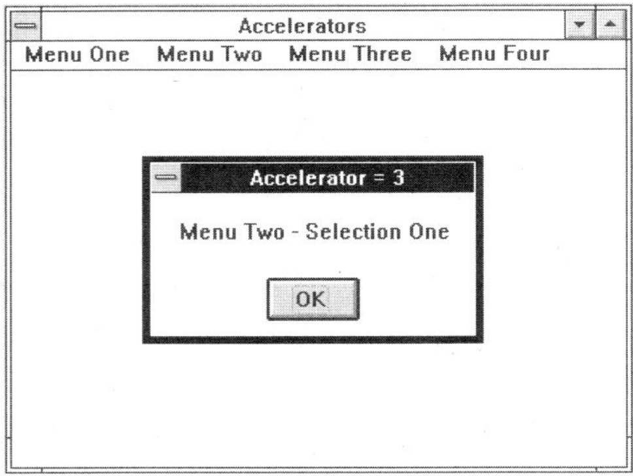

Figure 12.8. *The output of the accelerator example.*

The Bitmap Example

The bitmap example demonstrates the use of bitmap resources by loading and displaying the specified bitmaps. The bitmaps used in this example were created for the bitmap example demonstrated in Chapter 4. With this example, you are once again defining the member function `Paint` to respond to the `WM_PAINT` message. The `OBJ_BIT` project was used to create this example. The code for the resource file is provided in Listing 12.12. The code for the C++ source file is provided in Listing 12.13.

Project Name:	OBJ_BIT
Files in Project:	OBJ_BIT.CPP OBJ_BIT.RC OWL.DEF

Listing 12.12. The resource file for the bitmap example.

```
FOOTBALL BITMAP FOOTBALL.BMP
BASKET   BITMAP BASKET.BMP
GOLFBALL BITMAP GOLFBALL.BMP
BASEBALL BITMAP BASEBALL.BMP
```

Listing 12.13. The C++ source file for the bitmap example.

```
#include <owl.h>
#include <windobj.h>

class TBitmapDemo : public TApplication
{
public:
     TBitmapDemo(LPSTR AName, HINSTANCE hInstance, HINSTANCE
        hPrevInstance, LPSTR lpCmdLine, int nCmdShow) :
        TApplication(AName, hInstance, hPrevInstance,
        lpCmdLine, nCmdShow) {};
     virtual void InitMainWindow();
};

_CLASSDEF(TBitmapWindow)

class TBitmapWindow : public TWindow
{
public:
     HBITMAP hFootball;
     HBITMAP hBasketball;
     HBITMAP hGolfball;
     HBITMAP hBaseball;

     TBitmapWindow(PTWindowsObject AParent, LPSTR ATitle) :
       TWindow(AParent, ATitle) {};
     virtual void Paint(HDC PaintDC, PAINTSTRUCT _FAR &
                        PaintInfo);
};

void TBitmapWindow::Paint(HDC PaintDC, PAINTSTRUCT _FAR &
                          PaintInfo)
```

continues

Listing 12.13. continued

```
{
     HDC hMemDC;

     hMemDC = CreateCompatibleDC(PaintInfo.hdc);
     hFootball = LoadBitmap(GetApplication()->hInstance,
                "FOOTBALL");
     hBasketball = LoadBitmap(GetApplication()->hInstance,
                "BASKET");
     hGolfball = LoadBitmap(GetApplication()->hInstance,
                "GOLFBALL");
     hBaseball = LoadBitmap(GetApplication()->hInstance,
                "BASEBALL");
         SelectObject(hMemDC,hFootball);
         BitBlt(PaintDC,30,50,72,72,hMemDC,0,0,SRCCOPY);
         SelectObject(hMemDC,hBasketball);
         BitBlt(PaintDC,130,100,72,72,hMemDC,0,0,SRCCOPY);
         SelectObject(hMemDC,hGolfball);
         BitBlt(PaintDC,230,150,72,72,hMemDC,0,0,SRCCOPY);

         SelectObject(hMemDC,hBaseball);
         BitBlt(PaintDC,330,200,72,72,hMemDC,0,0,SRCCOPY);
     DeleteDC(hMemDC);
}

void TBitmapDemo::InitMainWindow()
{
MainWindow = new TBitmapWindow(NULL, "Bitmap Demonstration");
}

int PASCAL WinMain(HINSTANCE hInstance, HINSTANCE hPrevInstance,
                   LPSTR lpCmdLine, int nCmdShow)
{
TBitmapDemo BitmapDemo("Bitmap Window", hInstance, hPrevInstance,
                       lpCmdLine, nCmdShow);
BitmapDemo.Run();
return(BitmapDemo.Status);
}
```

The resource file of this project simply defines four bitmaps that were previously created using the Whitewater Resource Toolkit and the Resource Workshop.

In the source file, a derived class of `TApplication`—`TBitmapDemo`—is defined in the first component of the code. The second component of the code defines a derived class of `TWindow`—`TBitmapWindow` that creates the handles for the bitmaps and expects the member function `Paint` to be redefined.

The third component of code redefines the `Paint` member function of `TBitmapWindow` (`TBitmapWindow::Paint`). This member function loads and displays the bitmaps defined in the resource file.

The next component constructs the main window object as an instance of `TBitmapWindow`. The `NULL` parameter indicates that this is to be the main window. The second parameter, "Bitmap Demonstration", specifies the window title.

The last component is the main program that follows the same principal format as described in the basic window example. The output of this example is shown in Figure 12.9.

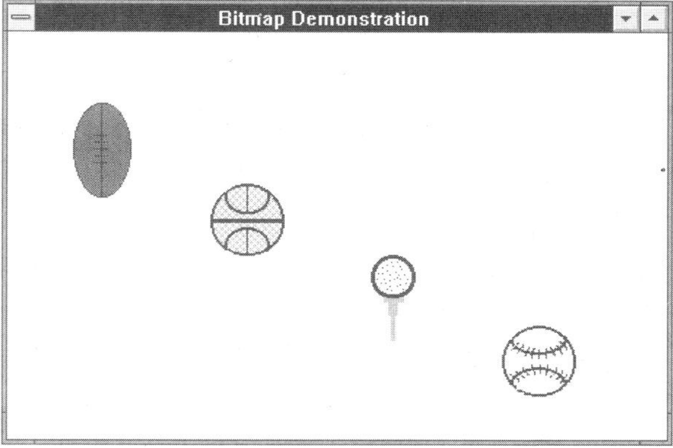

Figure 12.9. *The output of the bitmap example.*

The Cursor Example

This example demonstrates how you can redefine the cursor (that is, modify the predefined cursor or redefine the predefined cursor). Whenever the cursor is located inside the client area of the main window, the cursor is changed to the specified shape. The `OBJ_CUR` project was used to create this example. The code for the C++ source file is provided in Listing 12.14.

Project Name:	`OBJ_CUR`
Files in Project:	`OBJ_CUR.CPP`
	`OWL.DEF`

Listing 12.14. The cursor example.

```
#include <owl.h>

class TCursorDemo : public TApplication
{
public:
     TCursorDemo(LPSTR AName, HINSTANCE hInstance, HINSTANCE
        hPrevInstance, LPSTR lpCmdLine, int nCmdShow) :
        TApplication(AName, hInstance, hPrevInstance,
        lpCmdLine, nCmdShow) {};
     virtual void InitMainWindow();
};

_CLASSDEF(TCursorWindow)

class TCursorWindow : public TWindow
{
public:
     TCursorWindow(PTWindowsObject AParent, LPSTR AName) :
       TWindow (AParent, AName) {};
     virtual void GetWindowClass(WNDCLASS& AWndClass);
};

void TCursorWindow::GetWindowClass(WNDCLASS _FAR & AWndClass)
{
     TWindow::GetWindowClass(AWndClass);
     AWndClass.hCursor = LoadCursor(0, IDC_CROSS);
}


void TCursorDemo::InitMainWindow()
{
MainWindow = new TCursorWindow(NULL, "Cursor Demonstration");
}

int PASCAL WinMain(HINSTANCE hInstance, HINSTANCE hPrevInstance,
                   LPSTR lpCmdLine, int nCmdShow)
{
TCursorDemo CursorDemo("Cursor Window", hInstance,
   hPrevInstance, lpCmdLine, nCmdShow);
CursorDemo.Run();
return(CursorDemo.Status);
}
```

A derived class of `TApplication`—`TCursorDemo`—is defined in the first component of the code. The second component of the code defines a derived class of `TWindow`—`TCursorWindow`—that expects the member function `GetWindowClass` to be redefined.

The third component of code redefines the `GetWindowClass` member function of `TCursorWindow` (`TCursorWindow::GetWindowClass`). This member function loads the specified cursor.

The next component constructs the main window object as an instance of `TCursorWindow`. The `NULL` parameter indicates that this is to be the main window. The second parameter, "Cursor Demonstration", specifies the window title.

The last component is the main program that follows the same principal format as described in the basic window example earlier in this chapter.

The Dialog Example

The dialog example is similar in many respects to the accelerator example: it uses a resource file and demonstrates the methods for defining the actions of dialog controls, such as buttons. The `OBJ_DLG` project was used to create this example. Listing 12.15 shows the resource file for this project. The code for the C++ source file is provided in Listing 12.16.

Project Name:	`OBJ_DLG`
Files in Project:	`OBJ_DLG.CPP`
	`OBJ_DLG.RC`
	`OWL.DEF`

Listing 12.15. *The resource file for the dialog example.*

```
#include <windows.h>
#define DLG_DEMO 1

DLG_1 DIALOG DISCARDABLE LOADONCALL PURE MOVEABLE 42, 38, 148, 108 STYLE
WS_POPUP ¦ WS_DLGFRAME ¦ WS_SYSMENU
  BEGIN
  CONTROL "Radio Button One" 101, "BUTTON", WS_CHILD ¦
     WS_VISIBLE ¦ 0x4L, 38, 6, 74, 14
  CONTROL "Radio Button Two" 102, "BUTTON", WS_CHILD ¦
     WS_VISIBLE ¦ 0x4L, 38, 25, 74, 14
  CONTROL "Checkbox One" 103, "BUTTON", WS_CHILD ¦
     WS_VISIBLE ¦ WS_TABSTOP ¦ 0x2L, 8, 45, 64, 12
  CONTROL "Checkbox Two" 104, "BUTTON", WS_CHILD ¦
     WS_VISIBLE ¦ WS_TABSTOP ¦ 0x2L, 8, 61, 64, 12
  CONTROL "Checkbox Three" 105, "BUTTON", WS_CHILD ¦
     WS_VISIBLE ¦ WS_TABSTOP ¦ 0x2L, 75, 45, 72, 12
  CONTROL "Checkbox Four" 106, "BUTTON", WS_CHILD ¦
     WS_VISIBLE ¦ WS_TABSTOP ¦ 0x2L, 75, 61, 68, 12
  CONTROL "Cancel" 107, "BUTTON", WS_CHILD ¦
     WS_VISIBLE ¦ WS_TABSTOP, 26, 87, 40, 12
```

Listing 12.15. continued

```
  CONTROL "OK" 108, "BUTTON", WS_CHILD |
     WS_VISIBLE | WS_TABSTOP | 0x1L, 82, 87, 38, 12
  END

DlgMenu MENU
  {
  POPUP "&Help"
    {
    MENUITEM "Dialog Demo",  DLG_DEMO
    }
  }
```

Listing 12.16. The C++ source file for the dialog example.

```
#include <owl.h>
#include <dialog.h>

#define CM_DLG 1
#define ID_RADIOONE 101
#define ID_RADIOTWO 102
#define ID_CHECKONE 103
#define ID_CHECKTWO 104
#define ID_CHECKTHREE 105
#define ID_CHECKFOUR 106
#define ID_MYCANCEL 107
#define ID_MYOK 108

class TDlg : public TDialog
{
public:
     TDlg(PTWindowsObject AParent, LPSTR AName)
          : TDialog(AParent, AName) {};
     virtual void RadioOne(RTMessage Msg) =
          [ID_FIRST + ID_RADIOONE];
     virtual void RadioTwo(RTMessage Msg) =
          [ID_FIRST + ID_RADIOTWO];
     virtual void CheckOne(RTMessage Msg) =
          [ID_FIRST + ID_CHECKONE];
     virtual void CheckTwo(RTMessage Msg) =
          [ID_FIRST + ID_CHECKTWO];
     virtual void CheckThree(RTMessage Msg) =
          [ID_FIRST + ID_CHECKTHREE];
     virtual void CheckFour(RTMessage Msg) =
          [ID_FIRST + ID_CHECKFOUR];
     virtual void MyCancel(RTMessage Msg) =
```

```
          [ID_FIRST + ID_MYCANCEL];
     virtual void MyOk(RTMessage Msg) =
          [ID_FIRST + ID_MYOK];

};

_CLASSDEF(TDlgWindow)

class TDlgWindow : public TWindow
{
public:
  TDlgWindow(PTWindowsObject AParent, LPSTR ATitle);
  virtual void CMDlg(RTMessage Msg) =
    [CM_FIRST + CM_DLG];
};


class TDlgApp : public TApplication
{
public:
  TDlgApp(LPSTR AName, HINSTANCE hInstance, HINSTANCE
         hPrevInstance, LPSTR lpCmdLine, int nCmdShow) :
         TApplication(AName, hInstance, hPrevInstance,
         lpCmdLine, nCmdShow) {};
  virtual void InitMainWindow();
};


void TDlg::RadioOne(RTMessage)
{
WORD status;

status = IsDlgButtonChecked(HWindow,101);
if (status == 0)
     CheckDlgButton(HWindow,101,1);
else
     CheckDlgButton(HWindow,101,0);
}


void TDlg::RadioTwo(RTMessage)
{
WORD status;

status = IsDlgButtonChecked(HWindow,102);
if (status == 0)
     CheckDlgButton(HWindow,102,1);
else
```

continues

Listing 12.16. continued

```
     CheckDlgButton(HWindow,102,0);
}


void TDlg::CheckOne(RTMessage)
{
WORD status;

status = IsDlgButtonChecked(HWindow,103);
if (status == 0)
     CheckDlgButton(HWindow,103,1);
else
     CheckDlgButton(HWindow,103,0);
}


void TDlg::CheckTwo(RTMessage)
{
WORD status;

status = IsDlgButtonChecked(HWindow,104);
if (status == 0)
     CheckDlgButton(HWindow,104,1);
else
     CheckDlgButton(HWindow,104,0);
}


void TDlg::CheckThree(RTMessage)
{
WORD status;

status = IsDlgButtonChecked(HWindow,105);
if (status == 0)
     CheckDlgButton(HWindow,105,1);
else
     CheckDlgButton(HWindow,105,0);
}


void TDlg::CheckFour(RTMessage)
{
WORD status;

status = IsDlgButtonChecked(HWindow,106);
if (status == 0)
     CheckDlgButton(HWindow,106,1);
```

```
else
     CheckDlgButton(HWindow,106,0);
}

void TDlg::MyCancel(RTMessage)
{
CloseWindow(0);
}


void TDlg::MyOk(RTMessage)
{
CloseWindow(0);
}


TDlgWindow::TDlgWindow(PTWindowsObject AParent, LPSTR Title)
  : TWindow(AParent, Title)
{
AssignMenu("DlgMenu");
}


void TDlgWindow::CMDlg(RTMessage)
{
GetApplication()->ExecDialog(new TDlg(this, "DLG_1"));
}


void TDlgApp::InitMainWindow()
{
MainWindow = new TDlgWindow(NULL, "Dialogs");
}


int PASCAL WinMain(HINSTANCE hInstance, HINSTANCE hPrevInstance,
                   LPSTR lpCmdLine, int nCmdShow)
{
  TDlgApp DlgApp("Dialogs", hInstance, hPrevInstance,
                 lpCmdLine, nCmdShow);
  DlgApp.Run();
  return (DlgApp.Status);
}
```

You should first review the resource file. The resource file defines one menu with one menu item. The resource file also defines four checkboxes, two radio buttons, an `OK` button, and a `Cancel` button for the dialog box.

Now you should examine the C++ source file. The first component of the code defines a derived class of TDialog—TDlg—that expects eight member functions to be defined, one for each of the elements in the dialog box. Each member function should define the action for the corresponding element.

The second code component defines a derived class of TWindow—TDlgWindow. The CMDlg function is expected to be defined and should launch the dialog box when the one menu item is selected.

A derived class of TApplication—TDlgApp—is defined in the next component of the code.

The next eight code segments define the member functions for TDlg. Each function defines the default action for its corresponding element. For the radio buttons and checkboxes, the state of the button is toggled. For the OK and Cancel buttons, the dialog box is terminated.

The next component of code constructs a TDlgWindow and loads the specified menu. The component following the TDlgWindow constructor defines the action for the CMDlg member function of TDlgWindow. When the appropriate menu item is selected, the dialog box is launched.

The next component constructs the main window object as an instance of TDlgWindow. The NULL parameter indicates that this is to be the main window. The second parameter, "Dialogs", specifies the window title.

The last component is the main program that follows the same principal format as described in the basic window example earlier in this chapter. The output of this example is shown in Figure 12.10.

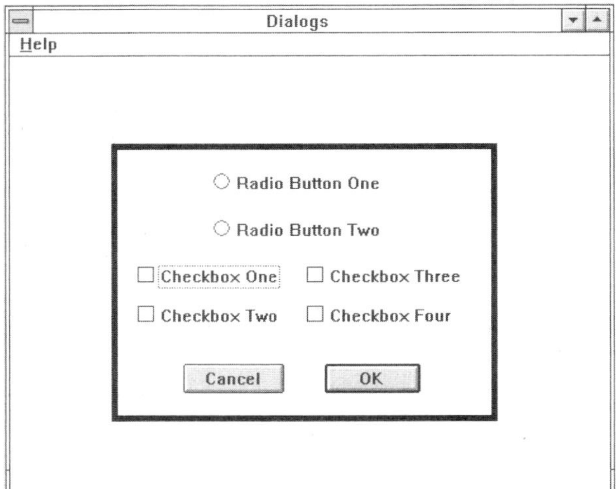

Figure 12.10. *The output of the dialog example.*

The Icon Example

The icon example is almost identical to the bitmap example. The only difference is that the icon example uses an icon created in Listings 4.13, 4.14, and 4.15 to represent the minimized application. The `OBJ_ICON` project was used to create this example. The code for the resource file is provided in Listing 12.17. The code for the C++ source file is provided in Listing 12.18.

Project Name:	`OBJ_ICON`

Files in Project:	`OBJ_ICON.CPP`
	`OBJ_ICON.RC`
	`OWL.DEF`

Listing 12.17. *The resource file for the icon example.*

```
FOOTBALL    BITMAP FOOTBALL.BMP
BASKET      BITMAP BASKET.BMP
GOLFBALL    BITMAP GOLFBALL.BMP
BASEBALL    BITMAP BASEBALL.BMP
SPORTS      ICON   SPORTS.ICO
```

Listing 12.18. *The C++ source file for the icon example.*

```
#include <owl.h>

class TIconDemo : public TApplication
{
public:
     TIconDemo(LPSTR AName, HINSTANCE hInstance, HINSTANCE
        hPrevInstance, LPSTR lpCmdLine, int nCmdShow) :
        TApplication(AName, hInstance, hPrevInstance,
        lpCmdLine, nCmdShow) {};
     virtual void InitMainWindow();
};

_CLASSDEF(TIconWindow)

class TIconWindow : public TWindow
{
public:
     HBITMAP hFootball;
     HBITMAP hBasketball;
     HBITMAP hGolfball;
     HBITMAP hBaseball;
```

continues

Listing 12.18. continued

```
     TIconWindow(PTWindowsObject AParent, LPSTR AName) :
       TWindow (AParent, AName) {};
     virtual void GetWindowClass(WNDCLASS _FAR &
       AWndClass);
     virtual void Paint(HDC PaintDC, PAINTSTRUCT _FAR &
       PaintInfo);
};

void TIconWindow::GetWindowClass(WNDCLASS _FAR & AWndClass)
{
     TWindow::GetWindowClass(AWndClass);
     AWndClass.hIcon =  LoadIcon(GetApplication()->
        hInstance, "SPORTS");
}


void TIconWindow::Paint(HDC PaintDC, PAINTSTRUCT _FAR &
               PaintInfo)
{
     HDC hMemDC;

     hMemDC = CreateCompatibleDC(PaintInfo.hdc);

     hFootball = LoadBitmap(GetApplication()->
          hInstance,"FOOTBALL");
     hBasketball = LoadBitmap(GetApplication()->
          hInstance,"BASKET");
     hGolfball = LoadBitmap(GetApplication()->
          hInstance,"GOLFBALL");
     hBaseball = LoadBitmap(GetApplication()->
          hInstance,"BASEBALL");

     SelectObject(hMemDC,hFootball);
     BitBlt(PaintDC,30,50,72,72,hMemDC,0,0,SRCCOPY);

     SelectObject(hMemDC,hBasketball);
     BitBlt(PaintDC,130,100,72,72,hMemDC,0,0,SRCCOPY);

     SelectObject(hMemDC,hGolfball);
     BitBlt(PaintDC,230,150,72,72,hMemDC,0,0,SRCCOPY);

     SelectObject(hMemDC,hBaseball);
     BitBlt(PaintDC,330,200,72,72,hMemDC,0,0,SRCCOPY);
```

```
     DeleteDC(hMemDC);
}

void TIconDemo::InitMainWindow()
{
MainWindow = new TIconWindow(NULL, "Icon Demonstration");
}

int PASCAL WinMain(HINSTANCE hInstance, HINSTANCE hPrevInstance,
     LPSTR lpCmdLine, int nCmdShow)
{
TIconDemo IconDemo("Icon Window", hInstance, hPrevInstance,
   lpCmdLine, nCmdShow);
IconDemo.Run();
return(IconDemo.Status);
}
```

The resource file of this project simply defines four bitmaps and one icon that were previously created using the Resource Workshop.

In the source file, a derived class of `TApplication`—`TIconDemo`—is defined in the first component of the code. The second component of the code defines a derived class of `TWindow`—`TIconWindow`—that creates handles for the bitmaps and expects the member functions `Paint` and `GetWindowClass` to be redefined.

The third code component redefines the `GetWindowClass` member function of `TIconWindow`. This member function loads the icon used to represent the minimized application.

The next component of code redefines the `Paint` member function of `TIconWindow`. This member function loads and displays the bitmaps defined in the resource file.

The next component constructs the main window object as an instance of `TIconWindow`. The `NULL` parameter indicates that this is to be the main window. The second parameter, "Icon Demonstration", specifies the window title.

The last component is the main program that follows the same principal format as described in the basic window example earlier in this chapter. The output of this example is shown in Figure 12.11.

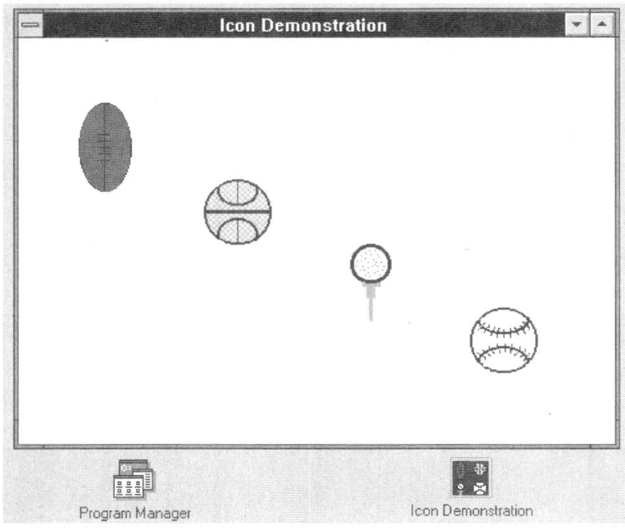

Figure 12.11. *The output of the icon example.*

The Menu Example

The menu example loads a menu resource and defines responses for each of the menu items. Each time a menu item is selected, a message box is displayed. The `OBJ_MENU` project was used to create this example. Listing 12.19 shows the resource file for this project. The code for the C++ source file is provided in Listing 12.20.

Project Name:	`OBJ_MENU`
Files in Project:	`OBJ_MENU.CPP`
	`OBJ_MENU.RC`
	`OWL.DEF`

Listing 12.19. *The resource file for the menu example.*

```
MENU  MENU LOADONCALL MOVEABLE PURE DISCARDABLE
BEGIN
  POPUP "Player One"
  BEGIN
    MenuItem  "Bob", 1
    MenuItem  "Mary", 2
    MenuItem  "John", 3
  END
  POPUP "Player Two"
```

```
  BEGIN
    MenuItem  "Gary", 4
    MenuItem  "Sue", 5
    MenuItem  "Jane", 6
  END
  POPUP "Game"
  BEGIN
    MenuItem  "Checkers", 7
    MenuItem  "Chess", 8
  END
END
```

Listing 12.20. *The C++ source file for the menu example.*

```
#include <owl.h>

#define CM_BOB 1
#define CM_MARY 2
#define CM_JOHN 3
#define CM_GARY 4
#define CM_SUE 5
#define CM_JANE 6
#define CM_CHECKERS 7
#define CM_CHESS 8

class TMenuDemo : public TApplication
{
public:
     TMenuDemo(LPSTR AName, HINSTANCE hInstance, HINSTANCE
        hPrevInstance, LPSTR lpCmdLine, int nCmdShow) :
        TApplication(AName, hInstance, hPrevInstance,
        lpCmdLine, nCmdShow) {};
     virtual void InitMainWindow();
     virtual void InitInstance();
};

_CLASSDEF(TMenuWindow)

class TMenuWindow : public TWindow
{
public:
     TMenuWindow(PTWindowsObject AParent, LPSTR ATitle);
     virtual void CMBob(RTMessage Msg) =
          [CM_FIRST + CM_BOB];
     virtual void CMMary(RTMessage Msg) =
          [CM_FIRST + CM_MARY];
```

continues

Listing 12.20. continued

```
     virtual void CMJohn(RTMessage Msg) =
          [CM_FIRST + CM_JOHN];
     virtual void CMGary(RTMessage Msg) =
          [CM_FIRST + CM_GARY];
     virtual void CMSue(RTMessage Msg) =
          [CM_FIRST + CM_SUE];
     virtual void CMJane(RTMessage Msg) =
          [CM_FIRST + CM_JANE];
     virtual void CMCheckers(RTMessage Msg) =
          [CM_FIRST + CM_CHECKERS];
     virtual void CMChess(RTMessage Msg) =
          [CM_FIRST + CM_CHESS];
};


TMenuWindow::TMenuWindow(PTWindowsObject AParent,
     LPSTR ATitle) : TWindow(AParent, ATitle)
{
AssignMenu("MENU");
};

void TMenuDemo::InitMainWindow()
{
MainWindow = new TMenuWindow(NULL,"Menus");
}

void TMenuDemo::InitInstance()
{
TApplication::InitInstance();
}

void TMenuWindow::CMBob(RTMessage)
{
MessageBox(HWindow, "Bob","Player One",MB_OK);
}

void TMenuWindow::CMMary(RTMessage)
{
MessageBox(HWindow, "Mary","Player One",MB_OK);
}


void TMenuWindow::CMJohn(RTMessage)
{
MessageBox(HWindow, "John","Player One",MB_OK);
}
```

```
void TMenuWindow::CMGary(RTMessage)
{
MessageBox(HWindow, "Gary","Player Two",MB_OK);
}


void TMenuWindow::CMSue(RTMessage)
{
MessageBox(HWindow, "Sue","Player Two",MB_OK);
}


void TMenuWindow::CMJane(RTMessage)
{
MessageBox(HWindow, "Jane","Player Two",MB_OK);
}


void TMenuWindow::CMCheckers(RTMessage)
{
MessageBox(HWindow, "Checkers","Game",MB_OK);
}


void TMenuWindow::CMChess(RTMessage)
{
MessageBox(HWindow, "Chess","Game",MB_OK);
}

int PASCAL WinMain(HINSTANCE hInstance, HINSTANCE hPrevInstance,
                   LPSTR lpCmdLine, int nCmdShow)
{
TMenuDemo MenuDemo("Menu Window", hInstance, hPrevInstance,
                   lpCmdLine, nCmdShow);
MenuDemo.Run();
return(MenuDemo.Status);
}
```

You should quickly review the resource file. The resource file defines three menus: Player One, Player Two, and Game. Player One contains three items: Bob, Mary, and John. Player Two contains three items: Gary, Sue, and Jane. Game contains two items: Checkers and Chess.

Now you should examine the C++ source file. A derived class of `TApplication`—`TMenuDemo`—is defined in the first component of the code. The second component of the code defines a derived class of `TWindow`—`TMenuWindow`—that expects eight member functions to be defined. Each member function should define the action for a corresponding menu item selection.

The third component of code constructs a `TMenuWindow`, loads the specified menu, and sets the state of each menu item.

The next component constructs the main window object as an instance of `TMenuWindow`. The `NULL` parameter indicates that this is to be the main window. The second parameter, "Menus", specifies the window title.

The next component defines the `InitInstance` member function of the application object. This member function actually does nothing; however, it is included to indicate the location where an accelerator table would be loaded if one were defined and required.

The next eight code components define the actions to be taken for each of the menu items. The member functions correspond to an appropriate menu item. The member functions are automatically called in response to the command messages sent when a menu item is selected. Although these member functions only display message boxes, they could easily be redefined to perform more intricate, detailed operations.

The last component is the main program that follows the same principal format as described in the basic window example. The output of this example is shown in Figure 12.12.

Figure 12.12. *The output of the menu example.*

The MDI Example

This example demonstrates a simple MDI application. Child windows can be created, tiled, cascaded, minimized, maximized, arranged, and closed. The `OBJ_MDI` project was used to create this example. Listing 12.21 shows the resource file for this project. The code for the C++ source file is provided in Listing 12.22.

Project Name:	`OBJ_MDI`

Files in Project:	`OBJ_MDI.CPP`
	`OBJ_MDI.RC`
	`OWL.DEF`

Listing 12.21. *The resource file for the MDI example.*

```
#include <windows.h>
#include <owlrc.h>

MENU  MENU
BEGIN
  POPUP "MDI Menu"
  BEGIN
    MENUITEM  "Create Child", CM_CREATECHILD,
    MENUITEM  "Tile", CM_TILECHILDREN,
    MENUITEM  "Cascade", CM_CASCADECHILDREN,
    MENUITEM  "Arrange Icons", CM_ARRANGEICONS,
    MENUITEM  "Close All", CM_CLOSECHILDREN,
  END
END
```

Listing 12.22. *The C++ source file for the MDI example.*

```
#include <owl.h>
#include <mdi.h>

class TMDIDemo : public TApplication
{
public:
     TMDIDemo(LPSTR AName, HINSTANCE hInstance, HINSTANCE
        hPrevInstance, LPSTR lpCmdLine, int nCmdShow) :
        TApplication(AName, hInstance, hPrevInstance,
        lpCmdLine, nCmdShow) {};
     virtual void InitMainWindow();
};

class TMDIDemoFrame : public TMDIFrame
{
WORD ChildNum;

public:
```

continues

Listing 12.22. continued

```
     TMDIDemoFrame(LPSTR ATitle, LPSTR AMenu);
     virtual PTWindowsObject InitChild();
};


void TMDIDemo::InitMainWindow()
{
MainWindow = new TMDIDemoFrame("MDI","MENU");
}


TMDIDemoFrame::TMDIDemoFrame(LPSTR ATitle, LPSTR AMenu)
          : TMDIFrame(ATitle, AMenu) {};


PTWindowsObject TMDIDemoFrame::InitChild()
{
return new TWindow(this, "Child");
}


int PASCAL WinMain(HINSTANCE hInstance, HINSTANCE hPrevInstance,
                   LPSTR lpCmdLine, int nCmdShow)
{
TMDIDemo MDIDemo("MDI Demo Window", hInstance, hPrevInstance,
                 lpCmdLine, nCmdShow);
MDIDemo.Run();
return(MDIDemo.Status);
}
```

The resource file defines the menu for the MDI application. The menu contains five items: Create Child, Tile, Cascade, Arrange Icons, and Close All.

The source file begins by defining a derived class of `TApplication`—`TMDIDemo`. The second code segment of the file defines a derived class of `TMDIFrame`—`TMDIDemoFrame`. The member function `InitChild` is expected to be redefined.

The next component constructs the main window object as an instance of `TMDIDemoFrame` and loads the menu. The next code segment constructs a `TMDIDemoFrame` and defines `ChildNum`. The definition of `TMDIDemoFrame::InitChild` follows. Lastly, the main program is called.

You may have noticed that although a menu was defined, no member functions were defined to handle the actions required of the menu items. ObjectWindows defines several member functions that automatically handle the manipulation of MDI child windows, including creating child windows, tiling child window, arranging icons, and cascading child windows. This saves you a great deal of work! To realize the amount of work that ObjectWindows can save, you should review the MDI example in Part I, Chapter 9.

An MDI application is very flexible and several *screen dumps* (that is, "dumps" of screens or screen shots) of the resulting application have been included. Figure 12.13 illustrates one open window and one minimized window. Figure 12.14 illustrates the result of choosing the Arrange Icons menu item with several minimized child windows. Figure 12.15 illustrates the results of the Tile menu item with four open windows. Figure 12.16 illustrates the results of the Cascade menu item when four windows are open. Figure 12.17 illustrates a maximized MDI child window.

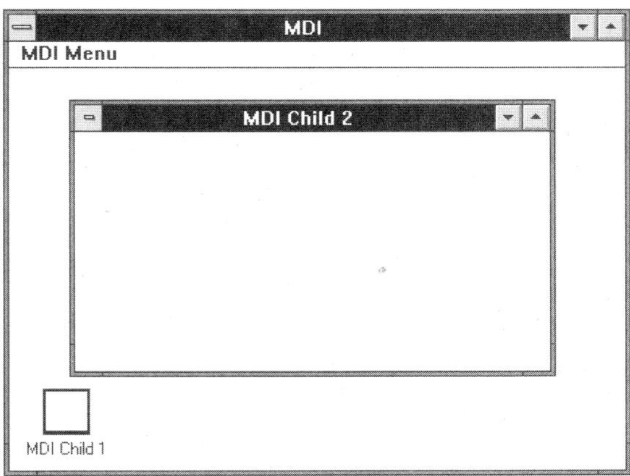

Figure 12.13. *The MDI example.*

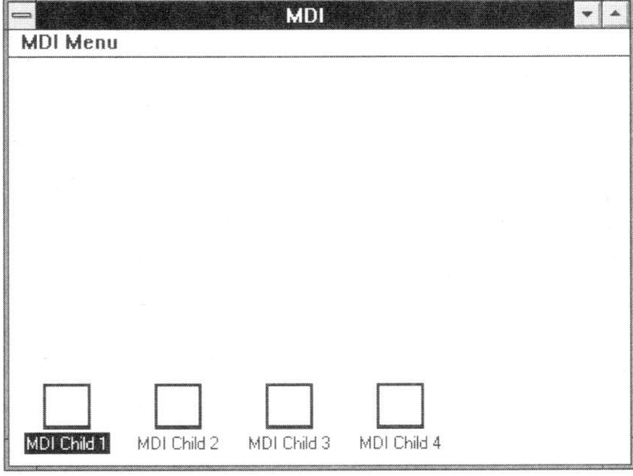

Figure 12.14. *The Arrange Icons option of the MDI example.*

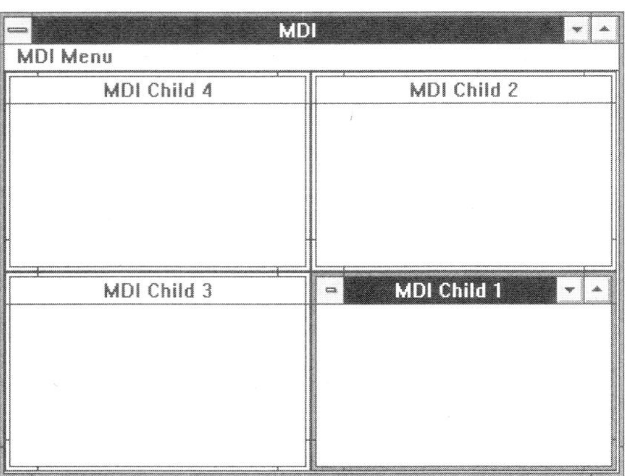

Figure 12.15. *The Tile option of the MDI example.*

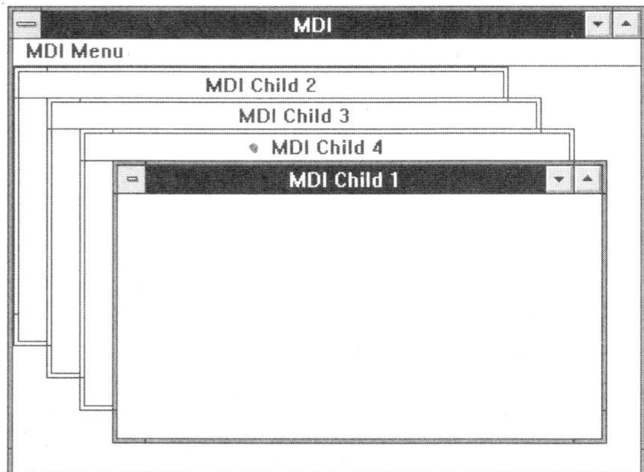

Figure 12.16. *The Cascade option of the MDI example.*

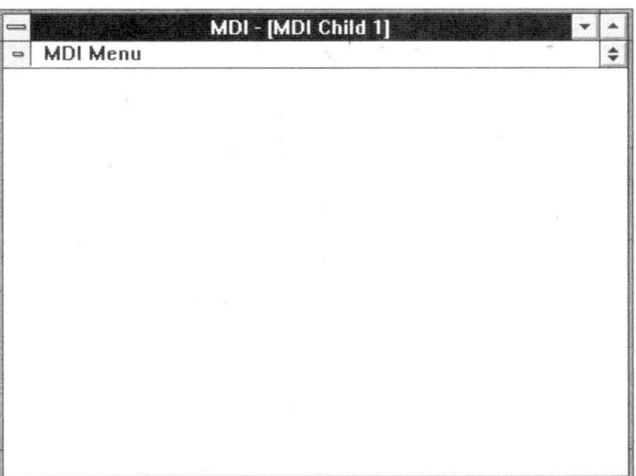

Figure 12.17. *A maximized MDI child window.*

III Reference

13

Windows Functions

This chapter introduces the Windows functions. These functions allow you to take advantage of the Windows user interface, graphics, and memory management capabilities. The functions are listed in alphabetical order and each function is described in the format that follows.

FunctionName

Syntax The syntax for the function is provided.

Parameter	*Type*	*Description*

Each of the function's parameters is described in this section. The parameter, the parameter type, and a brief description of the parameter are provided.

Description A full description of the function is provided in this section. Descriptions of subfunctions appear within a gray screen.

Return Value The function's return value, if any, is described in this section.

Function Category The function's category is provided.

Related Functions This section lists other Windows functions that are similar to or used with the function being described.

This format provides helpful information concerning the purpose and use of the Windows functions.

The remainder of this chapter provides reference information foreach of the Windows functions.

AbortDoc

Syntax `int AbortDoc(hDC)`

Parameter	*Type*	*Description*
hDC	HDC	Device context

Description The `AbortDoc` function replaces the `ABORTDOC` printer escape used for Windows versions 3.0 and earlier. `AbortDoc` ends the current print job. If the print job was sent to the Print Manager, the spool job is erased and nothing is sent to the printer. If the Print Manager was not used, the print job is closed and, if possible, the printer is reset.

Return Value A positive value is returned when successful. A negative value or zero is returned when unsuccessful.

Function Category Printer Control

Related Functions `Escape`, `SetAbortProc`, `StartDoc`

AccessResource

Syntax `int AccessResource(hinst, hrsrc)`

Parameter	*Type*	*Description*
hinst	HINSTANCE	Instance of module whose executable file contains the resource
hrsrc	HRSCR	Resource

Description The AccessResource function reads the resource in hrsrc from the resource file specified in hinst. The function opens the file, moves the file pointer to the beginning of the resource, then reads the resource. The resource file should be closed using the _lclose function.

Return Value The handle to the resource file is returned when successful. –1 is returned when unsuccessful.

Function Category Resource Management

Related Functions FreeResource, LoadResource

AddAtom

Syntax `ATOM AddAtom(lpszName)`

Parameter	*Type*	*Description*
lpszName	LPCSTR	Pointer to the null-terminated string to add to the table

Description The AddAtom function adds the string in lpszName to the atom table. The function returns the atom that identifies the string.

Return Value The atom that identifies the added string is returned when successful. When unsuccessful, zero is returned.

Function Category Atom

Related Functions DeleteAtom, FindAtom, GetAtomName

AddFontResource

Syntax `int AddFontResource(lpszFile)`

Parameter	*Type*	*Description*
`lpszFile`	`LPCSTR`	Specifies either a pointer to a character string that contains the filename of the font resource file, or the handle to a loaded module

Description The `AddFontResource` function adds the font resource from the file specified in `lpszFile` to the font table. Applications that add or remove font resources should send the `WM_FONTCHANGE` message to all top-level windows.

Return Value The number of fonts added to the font table is returned. Zero is returned when unsuccessful.

Function Category Font

Related Functions `CreateFont`, `LoadLibrary`, `RemoveFontResource`

AdjustWindowRect

Syntax `void AdjustWindowRect(lprc, dwStyle, fMenu)`

Parameter	*Type*	*Description*
`lprc`	`RECT FAR*`	Pointer to `RECT` data structure containing coordinates of the client rectangle
`dwStyle`	`DWORD`	Window styles of the window containing the client rectangle
`fMenu`	`BOOL`	Indicates whether the window has a menu

Description The `AdjustWindowRect` function determines the size of the window rectangle based on the specified client rectangle size. The window rectangle can be passed to `CreateWindow` to create a window with the specified client area size. The client rectangle is the smallest rectangle that encloses the client area. The window rectangle is the smallest rectangle that encloses the window. `lprc` points to a data structure or type `RECT` that contains the coordinates of the client rectangle. The `RECT` structure follows.

```
typedef struct tagRECT {
     int left;
     int top;
     int right;
     int bottom;
} RECT;
```

in which

`left` is the x coordinate of the upper-left corner

`top` is the y coordinate of the upper-left corner

`right` is the x coordinate of the lower-right corner

`bottom` is the y coordinate of the lower-right corner.

Return Value There is no return value.

Function Category Window Creation

Related Functions `AdjustWindowRectEx`, `CreateWindow`

AdjustWindowRectEx

Syntax

```
void AdjustWindowRectEx(lprc, dwStyle, fMenu,
                        dwExStyle)
```

Parameter	*Type*	*Description*
`lprc`	`RECT FAR*`	Pointer to `RECT` data structure containing coordinates of the client rectangle
`dwStyle`	`DWORD`	Window styles of the window containing the client rectangle
`fMenu`	`BOOL`	Indicates whether the window has a menu
`dwExStyle`	`DWORD`	Extended style of window being created

Description The `AdjustWindowRectEx` function determines the window rectangle, considering the specified extended style, for the specified client rectangle size. The window rectangle can then be passed to `CreateWindowEx` to create a window with the specified client area size. A client rectangle is the smallest rectangle that encloses the client area. A window rectangle is the smallest rectangle that encloses the window. It is assumed that the menu is a single row menu. `lprc` points to a data structure of type `RECT` that contains the coordinates of the client rectangle. The `RECT` structure follows.

```
typedef struct tagRECT {
     int left;
     int top;
     int right;
     int bottom;
} RECT;
```

in which

`left` is the x coordinate of the upper-left corner

`top` is the y coordinate of the upper-left corner

`right` is the x coordinate of the lower-right corner

`bottom` is the y coordinate of the lower-right corner.

Return Value There is no return value.

Function Category Window Creation

Related Functions `AdjustWindowRect`, `CreateWindowEx`

AllocDiskSpace

Syntax `int AllocDiskSpace(lLeft, wDrive)`

Parameter	*Type*	*Description*
`lLeft`	`LONG`	Number of bytes that should remain free on the disk
`wDrive`	`WORD`	Disk partition on which to create the "stress.eat" file

Description The AllocDiskSpace function creates a file that allocates space on the disk partition specified in wDrive. The created file, "stress.eat," will occupy all free space left on the disk with the exception of the amount specified in lLeft. "stress.eat" will be created in the root directory of the drive specified in wDrive. wDrive is set to one of the following values:

Value	*Meaning*
EDS_WIN	File created on the Windows partition
EDS_CUR	File created on the current partition
EDS_TEMP	File created on partition containing the TEMP directory

Return Value A value greater than zero is returned when successful. Zero is returned when the file could not be created. –1 is returned to indicate that one or more of the parameters of the function is invalid.

Function Category Stress

Related Functions UnAllocDiskSpace

AllocDStoCSAlias

Syntax `UINT AllocDStoCSAlias(uSelector)`

Parameter	*Type*	*Description*
uSelector	UINT	Data segment selector

Description The AllocDStoCSAlias function returns the code segment selector for the data segment selector specified in uSelector. The returned code segment selector can be used to execute code in the data segment. The new selector should not be freed by calling FreeSelector.

Return Value The code segment selector for the specified data segment is returned when successful. Zero is returned when unsuccessful.

Function Category Segment

Related Functions AllocSelector, ChangeSelector, Free Selector

AllocFileHandles

Syntax `int AllocFileHandles(Left)`

Parameter	*Type*	*Description*
`Left`	`int`	Number of file handles to remain free

Description The `AllocFileHandles` function allocates file handles that are available to the current instance of an application. `AllocFileHandles` will allocate up to 50 file handles and will leave the number of file handles specified in `Left` available to the application.

Return Value A value greater than zero indicates that at least one file handle was allocated. Zero indicates that the number of free file handles was less than the number specified in `Left`. A return value of –1 indicates that `Left` was negative.

Function Category Stress

Related Functions `UnAllocFileHandles`

AllocGDIMem

Syntax `BOOL AllocGDIMem(wLeft)`

Parameter	*Type*	*Description*
`wLeft`	`WORD`	Minimum allocation size in bytes

Description The `AllocGDIMem` function allocates all available memory in the GDI heap, leaving only the amount of memory specified in `wLeft` unallocated. All memory previously allocated by a call to `AllocGDIMem` is freed prior to the new allocation of memory.

Return Value A nonzero value is returned when allocation is successful. Zero is returned when unsuccessful.

Function Category Stress

Related Functions `FreeAllGDIMem`

AllocMem

Syntax `BOOL AllocMem(dwLeft)`

Parameter	*Type*	*Description*
dwLeft	DWORD	Minimum allocation size in bytes

Description The `AllocMem` function allocates all available memory except for the number of bytes specified in `dwLeft`. All memory previously allocated by a call to `AllocMem` is freed prior to the new allocation of memory.

Return Value A nonzero value is returned when the allocation is successful. Zero is returned when unsuccessful.

Function Category Stress

Related Functions `FreeAllMem`

AllocResource

Syntax `HGLOBAL AllocResource(hinst, hrsrc, cbResource)`

Parameter	*Type*	*Description*
hinst	HINSTANCE	Instance of module whose executable file contains the resource
hrsrc	HRSRC	Resource
cbResource	DWORD	Allocation override size in bytes

Description The `AllocResource` function allocates memory for the resource specified in `hrsrc`. `cbResource` specifies the number of bytes to allocate for the resource.

Return Value The handle to the allocated global memory block is returned.

Function Category Resource Management

Related Functions `AccessResource`, `FindResource`, `LoadResource`

AllocSelector

Syntax `UINT AllocSelector(uSelector)`

Parameter	*Type*	*Description*
`uSelector`	`UINT`	Selector to copy

Description The `AllocSelector` function allocates a new selector by either copying the selector in `uSelector` when `uSelector` specifies a selector or by creating an uninitialized selector when `uSelector` is zero.

Return Value The selector is returned when successful. Zero is returned when unsuccessful.

Function Category Segment

Related Functions `ChangeSelector, FreeSelector`

AllocUserMem

Syntax `BOOL AllocUserMem(wContig)`

Parameter	*Type*	*Description*
`wContig`	`WORD`	Minimum allocation size in bytes

Description The `AllocUserMem` function allocates all memory in the User heap except for the amount specified in `wContig`. The memory is allocated in sizes at least as large as the value specified in `wContig`. All memory previously allocated by a call to `AllocUserMem` is freed prior to the new allocation of memory.

Return Value A nonzero value is returned when allocation is successful. Zero is returned when unsuccessful.

Function Category Stress

Related Functions `FreeAllUserMem`

AnimatePalette

Syntax `void AnimatePalette(hpal, iStart, cEntries, lppe)`

Parameter	*Type*	*Description*
hpal	HPALETTE	Logical palette
iStart	UINT	First palette entry to animate
cEntries	UINT	Number of entries to animate
lppe	const PALETTEENTRY FAR*	Points to first member of an array of PALETTEENTRY data structures

Description The `AnimatePalette` function replaces palette entries in the logical palette specified in `hpal`. `iStart` and `cEntries` specify the palette entries to replace. `lppe` points to the first member of an array of `PALETTEENTRY` data structures used to replace the specified palette entries. The `PALETTEENTRY` data structure follows.

```
typedef struct
     {
     BYTE peRed;
     BYTE peGreen;
     BYTE peBlue;
     BYTE peFlags;

} PALETTEENTRY;
```

in which

`peRed` is the intensity of red for the palette entry

`peGreen` is the intensity of green for the palette entry

`peBlue` is the intensity of blue for the palette entry

`peFlags` is `NULL` or one of the following values:

Value	Meaning
PC_EXPLICIT	Low-order word of the palette entry contains a hardware palette index
PC_NOCOLLAPSE	Color will be placed in an unused entry in the palette; color will not replace existing entry
PC_RESERVED	Entry is used for palette animation; no color can be matched to this entry

Return Value There is no return value.

Function Category Color Palette

Related Functions `CreatePalette`

AnsiLower

Syntax `char FAR* AnsiLower(lpchString)`

Parameter	Type	Description
lpchString	char FAR*	Pointer to a null-terminated string

Description The `AnsiLower` function converts the characters in the character string pointed to by `lpchString` to lowercase. `lpchString` may also specify a single character. When `lpchString` specifies a single character, the character must be in the low-order byte of the low-order word.

Return Value The pointer to the character string is returned when `lpchString` specifies a character string. When `lpchString` specifies a single character, the low-order byte of the low-order word of the returned 32-bit value contains the converted character.

Function Category String Manipulation

Related Functions `AnsiLowerBuff`, `AnsiUpper`

AnsiLowerBuff

Syntax `UINT AnsiLowerBuff(lpszString, cbString)`

Parameter	*Type*	*Description*
`lpszString`	`LPSTR`	Pointer to a buffer containing the character string
`cbString`	`UINT`	Number of characters in the buffer

Description The `AnsiLowerBuff` function converts the character string in the buffer pointed to by `lpszString` to lowercase. `cbString` specifies the number of characters in the buffer. When `cbString` is set to zero, the length is assumed to be 65,536.

Return Value The length of the converted string is returned.

Function Category String Manipulation

Related Functions `AnsiLower`, `AnsiUpperBuff`

AnsiNext

Syntax `LPSTR AnsiNext(lpchCurrentChar)`

Parameter	*Type*	*Description*
`lpchCurrentChar`	`LPCSTR`	Pointer to a character in a null-terminated string

Description The `AnsiNext` function returns the pointer to the next character in the string after the character pointed to by `lpchCurrentChar`.

Return Value The pointer to the next character is returned.

Function Category String Manipulation

Related Functions `AnsiPrev`

AnsiPrev

Syntax `char FAR* AnsiPrev(lpchStart, lpchCurrentChar)`

Parameter	*Type*	*Description*
`lpchStart`	`const char FAR*`	Pointer to the beginning of the null-terminated string
`lpCurrentChar`	`char FAR*`	Pointer to the current character in the null-terminated string

Description The `AnsiPrev` function returns the pointer to the character from the string that appears just prior to the character specified in `lpchCurrentChar`.

Return Value The pointer to the previous character is returned. If `lpchCurrentChar` and `lpchStart` point to the same character, `lpchStart` is returned.

Function Category String Manipulation

Related Functions `AnsiNext`

AnsiToOem

Syntax `void AnsiToOem(hpszWindows, hpszOem)`

Parameter	*Type*	*Description*
`hpszWindows`	`const char _huge*`	Pointer to null-terminated string containing Windows characters
`hpszOem`	`char _huge*`	Pointer to the string to receive the converted characters

Description The `AnsiToOem` function converts the Windows characters in the string specified in `hpszWindows` to OEM characters and copies the converted characters to the string specified in `hpszOem`. `hpszWindows` and `hpszOem` can point to the same string.

Return Value There is no return value.

Function Category String Manipulation

Related Functions AnsiToOemBuff, OemToAnsi

AnsiToOemBuff

Syntax

```
void AnsiToOemBuff(lpszWindowsStr, lpszOemStr,
                   cbWindowsStr)
```

Parameter	*Type*	*Description*
lpszWindowsStr	LPCSTR	Pointer to a buffer containing Windows characters
lpszOemStr	LPSTR	Pointer to the buffer to receive the converted characters
cbWindowsStr	UINT	Number of characters in lpszWindowsStr

Description The AnsiToOemBuff function converts the Windows characters in the buffer pointed to by lpszWindowsStr into the OEM character set and copies them to the buffer pointed to by lpszOemStr. cbWindowsStr specifies the number of characters in lpszWindowsStr. lpszWindowsStr and lpszOemStr can specify the same buffer.

Return Value There is no return value.

Function Category String Manipulation

Related Functions AnsiToOem, OemToAnsiBuff

AnsiUpper

Syntax

```
LPSTR AnsiUpper(lpszString)
```

Parameter	*Type*	*Description*
lpszString	LPSTR	Pointer to a null-terminated string

Description The `AnsiUpper` function converts the characters in the character string pointed to by `lpszString` to uppercase. `lpszString` may also specify a single character. When `lpszString` specifies a single character, the character must be in the low-order byte of the low-order word.

Return Value The pointer to the character string is returned when `lpszString` specifies a character string. When `lpszString` specifies a single character, the low-order byte of the low-order word of the returned 32-bit value contains the converted character.

Function Category String Manipulation

Related Functions `AnsiLower`, `AnsiUpperBuff`

AnsiUpperBuff

Syntax `UINT AnsiUpperBuff(lpszString, cbString)`

Parameter	*Type*	*Description*
`lpszString`	`LPSTR`	Pointer to a buffer containing the character string
`cbString`	`UINT`	Number of characters in the buffer

Description The `AnsiUpperBuff` function converts the character string in the buffer pointed to by `lpszString` to uppercase. `cbString` specifies the number of characters in the buffer. When `cbString` is set to zero, the length is assumed to be 65,536.

Return Value The length of the converted string is returned.

Function Category `String Manipulation`

Related Functions `AnsiLowerBuff`, `AnsiUpper`

AnyPopup

Syntax `BOOL AnyPopUp()`

Description The AnyPopUp function determines whether any pop-up windows exist on the screen.

Return Value A nonzero value is returned when a pop-up window exists. Zero is returned if no pop-up window exists.

Function Category Information

Related Functions GetLastActivePopup, GetParent, GetWindow

AppendMenu

Syntax

```
BOOL AppendMenu(hmenu, fuFlags, idNewItem,
                lpNewItem)
```

Parameter	*Type*	*Description*
hmenu	HMENU	Menu to modify
fuFlags	UINT	State of new menu item
idNewItem	UINT	Command ID of new menu item; when fuFlags contains MF_POPUP, idNewItem contains the handle of the pop-up menu
lpNewItem	LPCSTR	Content of new menu item; meaning depends on fuFlags settings as follows:
	fuFlags	lpNewItem contains:
	MF_STRING	Long pointer to null-terminated string
	MF_BITMAP	Bitmap handle in the low-order word
	MF_OWNERDRAW	32-bit value supplied by the application

Description The AppendMenu function appends a new menu item to the menu specified in hmenu. The ID of the menu item is specified in idNewItem. lpNewItem specifies the content of the new menu item. fuFlags is a combination of one or more of the following values and provides information on the state of the new menu item:

Value	*Meaning*
MF_BITMAP	A bitmap is used as the menu item; the low-order word of lpNewItem contains the handle of the bitmap
MF_CHECKED	Checkmark is placed beside the menu item
MF_DISABLED	Menu item is disabled
MF_ENABLED	Menu item is enabled
MF_GRAYED	Disables and grays the menu item
MF_MENUBARBREAK	Menu item is placed on new line for static menu bar items; item is placed in a new column for pop-up menus and is divided from the previous column with a vertical line
MF_MENUBREAK	Menu item is placed on a new line for static menu bar items; item is placed in a new column for pop-up menu
MF_OWNERDRAW	Menu item is an owner draw item
MF_POPUP	Menu item has pop-up menu
MF_SEPARATOR	Creates a horizontal line and can be used only for pop-up menus
MF_STRING	Menu item is a character string
MF_UNCHECKED	Menu item is not checked

Return Value A nonzero value is returned when successful. Zero is returned when unsuccessful.

Function Category Menu

Related Functions CreateMenu, InsertMenu

Arc

Syntax

```
BOOL Arc(hdc, nLeftRect, nTopRect, nRightRect, nBottomRect,
         nXStartArc, nYStartArc, nXEndArc, nYEndArc)
```

Parameter	*Type*	*Description*
hdc	HDC	Device context
nLeftRect	int	Logical x coordinate of the upper-left corner of the bounding rectangle

Parameter	Type	Description
nTopRect	int	Logical y coordinate of the upper-left corner of the bounding rectangle
nRightRect	int	Logical x coordinate of the lower-right corner of the bounding rectangle
nBottomRect	int	Logical y coordinate of the lower-right corner of the bounding rectangle
nXStartArc	int	Logical x coordinate of the starting point of the arc
nYStartArc	int	Logical y coordinate of the starting point of the arc
nXEndArc	int	Logical x coordinate of the ending point of the arc
nYEndArc	int	Logical y coordinate of the ending point of the arc

Description The `Arc` function draws an elliptical arc using the current pen. The ellipse from which the arc is derived is defined by the bounding rectangle specified in `(nLeftRect,nTopRect)` and `(nRightRect, nBottomRect)`. The arc begins where the line segment projected from the center of the ellipse to the point specified in `(nXStartArc, nYStartArc)` intersects the ellipse. The arc is then drawn in a counterclockwise direction until it intercepts the line segment projected from the center of the ellipse to the point specified in `(nXEndArc, nYEndArc)`.

Return Value `TRUE` is returned when successful. `FALSE` is returned when unsuccessful.

Function Category Line Output

Related Functions `Chord, Ellipse, LineTo, PolyLine`

ArrangeIconicWindows

Syntax `UINT ArrangeIconicWindows(hWnd)`

Parameter	*Type*	*Description*
hWnd	HWND	Window handle

Description The `ArrangeIconicWindows` function arranges the minimized child windows for the window specified in `hWnd`.

Return Value The height of one row of icons is returned when one or more minimized windows exist. If no minimized windows exist, zero is returned.

Function Category Display and Movement

Related Functions `MoveWindow`, `OpenIcon`

BeginDeferWindowPos

Syntax `HDWP BeginDeferWindowPos(cWindows)`

Parameter	*Type*	*Description*
cWindows	int	Initial number of windows

Description The `BeginDeferWindowPos` function allocates memory for a data structure which will contain the window positions of multiple windows. The amount of memory allocated depends on the number of windows specified in `cWindows`. This function is used with the `DeferWindowPos` and `EndDeferWindowPos` functions. The handle to the data structure is returned.

Return Value The handle for the data structure is returned when successful. `NULL` is returned when unsuccessful.

Function Category Display and Movement

Related Functions `EndDeferWindowPos`

BeginPaint

Syntax `HDC BeginPaint(hwnd, lpps)`

Parameter	Type	Description
hwnd	HWND	Window to repaint
lpps	PAINTSTRUCT FAR*	Pointer to PAINTSTRUCT data structure that is to receive painting information

Description The BeginPaint function gets the window in hwnd ready for painting. lpps points to a data structure of type PAINTSTRUCT that is filled by the function with information about the painting. The application should call BeginPaint only in response to the WM_PAINT message and should have a corresponding EndPaint call. The PAINTSTRUCT structure follows.

```
typedef struct tagPAINTSTRUCT {
     HDC hdc;
     BOOL fErase;
     RECT rcPaint;
     BOOL fRestore;
     BOOL fIncUpdate;
     BYTE rgbReserved[16];
} PAINTSTRUCT;
```

in which

hdc is the display context

fErase is nonzero if the background is to be redrawn, zero if the background will not be redrawn

rcPaint is a data structure containing the upper-left and lower-right corners of the rectangle to paint

fRestore is reserved for use by Windows

fIncUpdate is reserved for use by Windows

rgbReserved[16] is reserved for use by Windows.

Return Value The device context for the window in hwnd is returned.

Function Category Painting

Related Functions EndPaint

BitBlt

Syntax

```
BOOL BitBlt(hdcDest, nXDest, nYDest, nWidth, nHeight,
            hdcSrc, nXSrc, nYSrc, dwRop)
```

Parameter	*Type*	*Description*
hdcDest	HDC	Device context to receive bitmap
nXDest	int	Logical x-coordinate of upper-left corner of destination
nYDest	int	Logical y-coordinate of upper-left corner of destination
nWidth	int	Width of destination rectangle, in logical units
nHeight	int	Height of destination rectangle, in logical units
hdcSrc	HDC	Device context from which bitmap will be copied
nXSrc	int	Logical x-coordinate of upper-left corner of bitmap
nYSrc	int	Logical y-coordinate of upper-left corner of bitmap
dwRop	DWORD	Raster operation to perform

Description The `BitBlt` function copies a bitmap from the source device to the destination device. The source device is specified in `hdcSrc`. The destination device is specified in `hdcDest`. `dwRop` specifies the raster operation to perform. The raster operation specifies how the source and destination will be combined. The following values can be used for `dwRop`:

Value	*Meaning*
BLACKNESS	All output is black
DSTINVERT	Destination bitmap is inverted
MERGECOPY	Uses Boolean AND to combine the pattern and source bitmap
MERGEPAINT	Uses Boolean OR to combine the inverted source bitmap with the destination bitmap
NOTSRCCOPY	Copies the inverted source bitmap to the destination

Value	*Meaning*
NOTSRCERASE	Uses Boolean OR to combine the destination and source, then inverts the combination
PATCOPY	Copies the pattern to the destination bitmap
PATINVERT	Uses Boolean XOR to combine the destination bitmap with the pattern
PATPAINT	Uses Boolean OR to combine the inverted source with the pattern, then uses Boolean OR to combine the result of the previous operation with the destination
SRCAND	Uses Boolean AND to combine the source and destination bitmaps
SRCCOPY	Copies the source bitmap to the destination
SRCERASE	Uses Boolean AND to combine the inverted destination bitmap with the source bitmap
SRCINVERT	Uses Boolean XOR to combine the source and destination bitmaps
SRCPAINT	Uses Boolean OR to combine the source and destination bitmaps
WHITENESS	All output is white

Return Value `TRUE` is returned when the bitmap is drawn. If the bitmap is not drawn, `FALSE` is returned.

Function Category Bitmap

Related Functions `PatBlt`, `StretchBlt`

BringWindowToTop

Syntax `BOOL BringWindowToTop(hWnd)`

Parameter	*Type*	*Description*
hWnd	HWND	Window to be brought to the top

Description The `BringWindowToTop` function brings the pop-up or child window specified in `hWnd` to the top of the windows stack. This function is used to bring windows that are partially covered by other windows to the top.

Return Value A nonzero value is returned when successful. Zero is returned when unsuccessful.

Function Category Display and Movement

Related Functions `ArrangeIconicWindows`, `MoveWindow`, `SetWindowPos`

BuildCommDCB

Syntax `int BuildCommDCB(lpszDef, lpdcb)`

Parameter	*Type*	*Description*
`lpszDef`	`LPCSTR`	Pointer to a null-terminated string that contains the device control information in DOS MODE format
`lpdcb`	`DCB FAR*`	Pointer to a `DCB` data structure receiving the translated string

Description The `BuildCommDCB` function translates the string in `lpszDef` into device control block codes. These codes are then placed into the data structure of type `DCB` pointed to by `lpdcb`. The `DCB` structure follows.

```
typedef struct tagDCB {
     BYTE Id;
     WORD BaudRate;
     BYTE ByteSize;
     BYTE Parity;
     BYTE StopBits;
     WORD RlsTimeout;
     WORD CtsTimeout;
     WORD DsrTimeout;

     WORD fBinary: 1;
     WORD fRtsDisable: 1;
     WORD fParity: 1;
     WORD fOutxCtsFlow: 1;
     WORD fOutxDsrFlow: 1;
     WORD fDummy: 2;
     WORD fDtrDisable: 1;
     WORD fOutX: 1;
     WORD fInX: 1;
```

```
        WORD fPeChar: 1;
        WORD fNull: 1;
        WORD fChEvt: 1;
        WORD fDtrFlow: 1;
        WORD fRtsFlow: 1;
        WORD fDummy2: 1;

        char XonChar;
        char XoffChar;
        WORD XonLim;
        WORD XoffLim;
        char PeChar;
        char EofChar;
        char EvtChar;
        WORD TxDelay;
} DCB;
```

in which

`Id` identifies the communication device

`BaudRate` is the baud rate. The high-order byte should be set to `0xFF`; the low-order byte should then be set to one of the following values:

CBR_110	CBR_2400	CBR_19200
CBR_300	CBR_4800	CBR_38400
CBR_600	CBR_9600	CBR_56000
CBR_1200	CBR_14400	CBR_128000
		CBR_256000

`ByteSize` is the number of bits in a character (4 to 8)

`Parity` is the parity scheme—either EVENPARITY, MARKPARITY, NOPARITY, or ODDPARITY

`StopBits` is the number of stop bits to use—either ONESTOPBIT, ONE5STOPBITS, or TWOSTOPBITS

`RlsTimeout` is the maximum number of milliseconds the device should wait for the receive-line-signal-detect signal

`CtsTimeout` is the maximum number of milliseconds the device should wait for the clear-to-send signal

`DsrTimeout` is the maximum number of milliseconds the device should wait for the data-set-ready signal

`fBinary: 1` specifies binary mode

`fRtsDisable: 1` indicates whether the request-to-send signal is disabled `fParity: 1` indicates whether parity checking is enabled

`fOutxCtsFlow:1` specifies that clear-to-send signal is monitored for output flow control

`fOutxDsrFlow: 1` specifies that data-set-ready signal is monitored for output flow control

`fDummy: 2` is reserved

`fDtrDisable: 1` specifies whether the data-terminal-ready signal is disabled

`fOutX: 1` specifies that XON/XOFF flow control is used during transmission

`fInX: 1` specifies that XON/XOFF flow control is used while receiving

`fPeChar: 1` specifies that characters received with parity errors are to be replaced with the character in the fPeChar field

`fNull: 1` specifies that null characters are discarded

`fChEvt: 1` specifies that reception of the `EvtChar` character is to be flagged

`fDtrFlow: 1` specifies that the data-terminal-ready signal is used for receive flow control

`fRtsFlow: 1` specifies that the ready-to-send signal is used for receive flow control

`fDummy2: 1` is reserved

`XonChar` specifies the value of the XON character

`XoffChar` specifies the value of XOFF character

`XonLim` is the minimum number of characters allowed in the receive queue before the XON character is sent

`XoffLim` specifies the maximum number of characters allowed in the receive queue before the XOFF character is sent

`PeChar` specifies the value of the character used to replace characters received with parity errors

`EofChar` specifies the character used to signal the end of data

`EvtChar` specifies the character used to signal an event

`TxDelay` is not used.

Return Value A zero is returned when successful. –1 is returned when unsuccessful.

Function Category Communication

Related Functions OpenComm, ReadComm, SetCommState

CallMsgFilter

Syntax `BOOL CallMsgFilter(lpMsg, nCode)`

Parameter	*Type*	*Description*
lpMsg	const MSG FAR*	Pointer to MSG data structure containing message
nCode	int	Specifies how message is processed

Description The CallMsgFilter function passes the message pointed to by lpMsg to the current message filter function. The message is stored in a data structure of type MSG, which is shown below. nCode is used by the filter function to determine how to process the message. The SetWindowsHook function is used by the application to specify the filter function.

```
typedef struct tagMSG {
     HWND hwnd;
     WORD message;
     WORD wParam;
     LONG lParam;
     DWORD time;
     POINT pt;
} MSG;
```

in which

hwnd is the window that receives the message

message is the message number

wParam is additional message information

lParam is additional message information

time is the time the message was posted

pt is the screen coordinates of the cursor position when the message was posted.

Return Value Zero is returned when the message requires processing. If no further processing is required, a nonzero value is returned.

Function Category Hook

Related Functions `SetWindowsHook`, `UnhookWindowsHook`

CallNextHookEx

Syntax

```
LRESULT CallNextHookEx(hHook, nCode, wParam,
                       lParam)
```

Parameter	*Type*	*Description*
`hHook`	`HHOOK`	Handle to current hook function
`nCode`	`int`	Hook code to pass to next hook function
`wParam`	`WPARAM`	`wParam` parameter of message being processed by the hook function
`lParam`	`LPARAM`	`lParam` parameter of message being processed by the hook function

Description The `CallNextHookEx` function passes the hook code specified in `nCode` to the next hook function. `hHook` specifies the current hook function.

Return Value The return value depends on the message being processed and the value of `nCode`.

Function Category Window Creation

Related Functions `SetWindowsHookEx`, `UnhookWindowsHookEx`

CallWindowProc

Syntax

```
LRESULT CallWindowProc(wndprcPrev, hwnd, uMsg, wParam,
                       lParam)
```

Parameter	Type	Description
wndprcPrev	WNDPROC	Procedure instance address of the previous window function
hwnd	HWND	Window receiving the message
uMsg	UINT	Message
wParam	WPARAM	Message-dependent information
lParam	LPARAM	Message-dependent information

Description The `CallWindowProc` function is used for window subclassing and passes information to the window procedure specified in `wndprcPrev`. A subclass is created with the `SetWindowLong` function.

Return Value The return value depends on the message that is sent. See the "Windows Messages" reference section for more information on the return values for Windows messages.

Function Category Message

Related Functions `SetWindowLong`

Catch

Syntax `int Catch(lpCatchBuf)`

Parameter	Type	Description
lpCatchBuf	int FAR*	Pointer to the CATCHBUF data structure to receive the execution environment

Description The `Catch` function captures the current execution environment and places it in the data structure of type `CATCHBUF` pointed to by `lpCatchBuf`. The `Throw` function can be used to later restore the execution environment.

Return Value Zero is returned.

Function Category Task

Related Functions `Throw`

ChangeClipboardChain

Syntax `BOOL ChangeClipboardChain(hWnd, hWndNext)`

Parameter	*Type*	*Description*
`hWnd`	`HWND`	Window to be removed from the chain
`hWndNext`	`HWND`	Window that follows `hWnd`

Description The `ChangeClipboardChain` function removes the window specified in `hWnd` from the clipboard chain of viewers. The window specified in `hWndNext` follows the window specified in `hWnd` on the clipboard chain of viewers.

Return Value The `ChangeClipboardChain` function returns a nonzero value when the window in `hWnd` is found and removed. A zero is returned when the window is not found and removed.

Function Category Clipboard

Related Functions `GetClipboardViewer`, `SetClipboardViewer`

ChangeMenu

Description As of Windows 3.0, `ChangeMenu` has been replaced by the following five functions:

`AppendMenu`	Appends a menu item to an existing menu
`DeleteMenu`	Deletes a menu item from an existing menu; the menu item is destroyed
`InsertMenu`	Inserts a menu item into an existing menu
`ModifyMenu`	Modifies a menu item
`RemoveMenu`	Deletes a menu item from an existing menu; the menu item is not destroyed

Function Category Menu

Related Functions AppendMenu, DeleteMenu, InsertMenu, ModifyMenu, RemoveMenu

ChangeSelector

Syntax

```
UINT ChangeSelector(uSourceSelector,
                    uDestSelector)
```

Parameter	*Type*	*Description*
uSourceSelector	UINT	Selector to be converted
uDestSelector	UINT	Selector to receive the converted selector

Description The ChangeSelector function converts a code selector to a data selector or a data selector to a code selector. uSourceSelector specifies the selector that will be converted. uDestSelector specifies the selector that receives the converted selector.

Return Value The resulting selector is returned when successful. Zero is returned when unsuccessful.

Function Category Segment

Related Functions AllocSelector, FreeSelector

CheckDlgButton

Syntax

```
void CheckDlgButton(hwndDlg, idButton, uCheck)
```

Parameter	*Type*	*Description*
hwndDlg	HWND	Dialog box containing the button
idButton	int	Button to modify
uCheck	UINT	Setting for button

Description The CheckDlgButton function alters the setting of a button in the dialog box specified by hwndDlg. The button to modify is specified in idButton. uCheck defines the new setting for the

specified button. When uCheck is a nonzero value, a checkmark is placed next to the button. When uCheck is zero, any checkmark next to the button is removed. For three-state buttons, setting uCheck to 1 will place a checkmark next to the button; setting uCheck to 0 will remove any checkmark next to the button; and setting uCheck to 2 will gray the button. The BM_SETCHECK message is sent to the button by this function.

Return Value There is no return value.

Function Category Dialog Box

Related Functions CheckRadioButton, IsDlgButtonChecked

CheckMenuItem

Syntax `BOOL CheckMenuItem(hmenu, idCheckItem, uCheck)`

Parameter	*Type*	*Description*
hmenu	HMENU	Menu handle
idCheckItem	UINT	Menu item to check
uCheck	UINT	Specifies how to check menu item

Description The CheckMenuItem function puts or removes a checkmark from the menu item in idCheckItem. The menu item in idCheckItem is contained in the pop-up menu specified in hmenu. Top-level menu items cannot be checked with this function. uCheck specifies how to check the menu item. The following flags are used for uCheck. These flags can be combined using the bitwise OR.

Flag	*Meaning*
MF_BYCOMMAND	idCheckItem specifies a menu-item ID; this flag cannot be used with MF_BYPOSITION
MF_BYPOSITION	idCheckItem specifies the menu-item position; this flag cannot be used with MF_BYCOMMAND
MF_CHECKED	Places a checkmark by the item
MF_UNCHECKED	Removes a checkmark by the item

Return Value The previous state of the button, either MF_CHECKED or MF_UNCHECKED, is returned. When the specified menu item is invalid, –1 is returned.

Function Category Menu

Related Functions EnableMenuItem, GetMenuItemCount, GetMenuState

CheckRadioButton

Syntax

```
nIDCheckButtonnIDCheckButton void CheckRadioButton(hwndDlg,
    idFirstButton, idLastButton, idCheckButton)
```

Parameter	*Type*	*Description*
hwndDlg	HWND	Dialog box
idFirstButton	int	First radio button in group
idLastButton	int	Last radio button in group
idCheckButton	int	Radio button to be checked

Description The CheckRadioButton function places a checkmark next to the radio button specified in idCheckButton. Any checkmarks next to the radio buttons in the group of buttons defined by idFirstButton and idLastButton are removed. hwndDlg specifies the dialog box containing the radio buttons. This function sends the BM_SETCHECK message to the radio-button control.

Return Value There is no return value.

Function Category Dialog Box

Related Functions CheckDlgButton, IsDlgButtonChecked

ChildWindowFromPoint

Syntax

```
HWND ChildWindowFromPoint(hwndParent, Pt)
```

Parameter	Type	Description
hwndParent	HWND	Parent window
Pt	POINT	Client coordinates of test point in a POINT data structure

Description The ChildWindowFromPoint function finds the child window containing the point specified in Pt. Pt specifies client coordinates. The parent window is specified in hwndParent.

Return Value The handle for the child window is returned if the specified point lies within a child window. If the point does not lie within a child window, but does lie inside the parent window, the parent window handle is returned. If the point does not lie within the parent window, NULL is returned.

Function Category Coordinate, Information

Related Functions WindowFromPoint

ChooseColor

Syntax `BOOL ChooseColor(lpcc)`

Parameter	Type	Description
lpcc	LPCHOOSECOLOR	Pointer to CHOOSECOLOR data structure containing information to initialize the dialog box

Description The ChooseColor function creates a dialog box that is defined by the system and offers the user a choice of colors. The color choices offered in the dialog box consist of system colors and dithered system colors. lpcc points to a data structure of type CHOOSECOLOR that contains information to initialize the dialog box. When ChooseColor returns, the CHOOSECOLOR data structure contains information about the color selected. The CHOOSECOLOR data structure follows.

```
#include <commdlg.h>
typedef struct
     {
```

```
    DWORD lStructSize;
    HWND hwndOwner;
    HANDLE hInstance;
    DWORD rgbResult;
    LPDWORD lpCustColors;
    DWORD Flags;
    DWORD lCustData;
    WORD(FAR PASCAL *lpfnHook)(HWND, unsigned, WORD, LONG;
    LPSTR lpTemplateName;
} CHOOSECOLOR;
```

in which

`lStructSize` is the length of the structure in bytes

`hwndOwner` is the window that owns the dialog box

`hInstance` specifies the data block containing the dialog template specified in `lpTemplateName`

`rgbResult` contains the initial color selection when the dialog box is created and contains the color selected by the user when the dialog box is closed

`lpCustColors` is a pointer to an array of 16 32-bit values containing the RGB values for custom color boxes in the dialog box

`Flags` is a combination of dialog box initialization flags selected from the following values:

Value	*Meaning*
`CC_ENABLEHOOK`	Enables the hook function in `lpfnHook`
`CC_ENABLETEMPLATE`	Creates a dialog box using the template defined in `hInstance` and `lpTemplateName`
`CC_ENABLETEMPLATEHANDLE`	Indicates that `hInstance` specifies a data block that contains a preloaded dialog template
`CC_FULLOPEN`	Forces the entire dialog box, including the custom colors part, to be visible
`CC_PREVENTFULLOPEN`	Prevents the creation of custom colors

Value	Meaning
CC_RGBINIT	Forces the dialog box to initially select the color in rgbResult
CC_SHOWHELP	Displays the Help push button

lCustData is application-supplied data passed to the hook function in lpfnHook

lpfnHook specifies the hook function that processes the messages for the dialog box

lpTemplateName is a pointer to a null-terminated string naming the dialog box template resource that replaces the standard template.

Return Value TRUE is returned when a color is selected. FALSE is returned when no color is selected or an error occurs.

Function Category Common Dialog

Related Functions ChooseFont

ChooseFont

Syntax `BOOL ChooseFont(lpcf)`

Parameter	Type	Description
lpcf	LPCHOOSEFONT	Pointer to CHOOSEFONT data structure containing information for dialog box initialization

Description The ChooseFont function creates a dialog that is defined by the system and prompts the user to select a font by specifying a facename, point size, color, and style. lpcf points to a data structure of type CHOOSEFONT that contains dialog box initialization data. When ChooseFont returns, the CHOOSEFONT data structure contains information about the font the user selected. The CHOOSEFONT data structure follows.

```
#include <commdlg.h>
typedef struct
     {
     DWORD lStructSize;
     HWND hwndOwner;
     HDC hDC;
     LPLOGFONT lpLogFont;
     int iPointSize;
     DWORD Flags;
     DWORD rgbColors;
     DWORD lCustData;
     WORD(FAR PASCAL*lpfnHook)(HWND, unsigned, WORD, LONG);
     LPSTR lpTemplateName;
     HANDLE hInstance;
     LPSTR lpszStyle;
     WORD nFontType;
     int nSizeMin;
     int nSizeMax;
} CHOOSEFONT;
```

in which

`lStructSize` is the length of the structure in bytes

`hwndOwner` is the window that owns the dialog box

`hDC` specifies the device context for the printer containing the fonts to list

`lpLogFont` points to a `LOGFONT` data structure

`iPointSize` specifies the size of the selected font

`Flags` is a combination of one or more of the following initialization flags:

Value	*Meaning*
CF_APPLY	Enable Apply button
CF_ANSIONLY	Allow only the selection of fonts that use the ANSI character set
CF_BOTH	List available printer and screen fonts
CF_TTONLY	Allow only the selection of TrueType fonts
CF_EFFECTS	Enable color, strikeout, and underline effects
CF_ENABLEHOOK	Enable the hook function in `lpfnHook`

Value	*Meaning*
CF_ENABLETEMPLATE	Indicate that hInstance specifies the data block that contains the template specified by lpTemplateName
CF_ENABLETEMPLATEHANDLE	Indicate that hInstance specifies the data block that contains a preloaded dialog template
CF_FIXEDPITCHONLY	Allow only the selection of fixed pitch fonts
CF_FORCEFONTEXIST	Indicate an error when the user attempts to select a nonexistent font or style
CF_INITTOLOGFONTSTRUCT	Use the LOGFONT structure in lpLogFont to initialize the controls of the dialog box
CF_LIMITSIZE	Allow only the selection of fonts within the size range specified in nSizeMin and nSizeMax
CF_NOFACESEL	Indicate that there is no selection in the Font facename combo box
CF_NOOEMFONTS	Do not allow vector font selections. Same as CF_NOVECTORFONTS.
CF_NOSIMULATIONS	Do not allow GDI font simulations
CF_NOSIZESEL	Indicate that there is no selection in the Size combo box
CF_NOSTYLESEL	Indicate that there is no selection in the Font Style combo box
CF_NOVECTORFONTS	Do not allow vector font selections
CF_PRINTERFONTS	List only fonts supported by the printer associated with the device context in hDC
CF_SCALABLEONLY	Allow only the selection of scalable fonts
CF_SCREENFONTS	List only screen fonts
CF_SHOWHELP	Show the Help push button
CF_TTONLY	Enumerate TrueType fonts only

Value	Meaning
CF_USESTYLE	Indicate lpszStyle points to a buffer containing the style data used for Font Style initialization
CF_WYSIWYG	Allow only the selection of fonts that are available to both the printer and the screen

rgbColors contains an RGB value for the text color when the CF_EFFECTS color is set

lCustData is application-supplied data for the hook function

lpfnHook points to the hook function that processes the dialog box messages

lpTemplateName points to a null-terminated string naming the dialog box template resource that replaces the standard dialog box template

hInstance specifies the data block containing the dialog template specified lpTemplateName

lpszStyle points to a buffer containing style data

nFontType specifies the selected font and is set to one of the following values:

Value	Meaning
BOLD_FONTTYPE	Font is bold
ITALIC_FONTTYPE	Font is italic
REGULAR_FONTTYPE	Font is regular
SIMULATED_FONTTYPE	Font is simulated by GDI
PRINTER_FONTYPE	Font is printer font
SCREEN_FONTTYPE	Font is screen font

nSizeMin is the minimum point size for the font; CF_LIMITSIZE flag must be set

nSizeMax is the maximum point size for the font; CF_LIMITSIZE flag must be set.

Return Value TRUE is returned when successful. FALSE is returned when unsuccessful.

Function Category Common Dialog

Related Functions `ChooseColor`

Chord

Syntax

```
BOOL Chord(hdc, nLeftRect, nTopRect, nRightRect,
           nBottomRect, nXStartLine, nYStartLine,
           nXEndLine, nYEndLine)
```

Parameter	*Type*	*Description*
`hdc`	`HDC`	Device context
`nLeftRect`	`int`	X coordinate of upper-left corner of bounding rectangle
`nTopRect`	`int`	Y coordinate of upper-left corner of bounding rectangle
`nRightRect`	`int`	X coordinate of lower-right corner of bounding rectangle
`nBottomRect`	`int`	Y coordinate of lower-right corner of bounding rectangle
`nXStartLine`	`int`	X coordinate of starting point of line segment
`nYStartLine`	`int`	Y coordinate of starting point of line segment
`nXEndLine`	`int`	X coordinate of ending point of line segment
`nYEndLine`	int	Y coordinate of ending point of line segment

Description The `Chord` function creates a chord. A chord is an ellipse that is cut at the intersections of a line segment. The ellipse is drawn inside the bounding rectangle specified by `(nLeftRect, nTopRect)` and `(nRightRect, nBottomRect)`. The line segment specified by `(nXStartLine, nYStartLine)` and `(nXEndLine, nYEndLine)` intersects the ellipse. The part of the ellipse that is not cut off by the line segment is the chord. The chord is drawn using the selected pen and filled with the selected brush.

Return Value TRUE is returned when successful. FALSE is returned when unsuccessful.

Function Category Ellipse and Polygon

Related Functions Arc, Ellipse

ClassFirst

Syntax BOOL ClassFirst(ceClass)

Parameter	*Type*	*Description*
ceClass	CLASSENTRY FAR*	Pointer to CLASSENTRY data structure that receives class information

Description The ClassFirst function retrieves information about the first class in the Windows class list. ceClass points to the data structure of type CLASSENTRY that stores the retrieved data.

The CLASSENTRY data structure follows.

```
#include <toolhelp.h>
typedef struct tagCLASSENTRY
     {
     DWORD dwSize;
     HANDLE hInst;
     char szClassName[MAX_CLASSNAME + 1];
     WORD wNext;
} CLASSENTRY;
```

in which

dwSize is the size of the CLASSENTRY structure in bytes

hInst is the instance handle

szClassName is the null-terminated string containing the Windows class name

wNext is the next class in the Windows class list.

Return Value TRUE is returned when successful. FALSE is returned when unsuccessful.

Function Category Toolhelp

Related Functions `ClassNext`

ClassNext

Syntax `BOOL ClassNext(ceClass)`

Parameter	*Type*	*Description*
ceClass	CLASSENTRY FAR*	Pointer to a CLASSENTRY data structure that receives class information

Description The `ClassNext` function retrieves information about the next class in the Windows class list. `ceClass` points to the data structure of type `CLASSENTRY` that stores the retrieved data. The `CLASSENTRY` data structure follows.

```
typedef struct tagCLASSENTRY
     {
     DWORD dwSize;
     HANDLE hInst;
     char szClassName[MAX_CLASSNAME + 1];
     WORD wNext;
} CLASSENTRY;
```

in which

`dwSize` is the size of the `CLASSENTRY` structure in bytes

`hInst` is the instance handle

`szClassName` is the null-terminated string containing the Windows class name

`wNext` is the next class in the Windows class list.

Return Value `TRUE` is returned when successful. `FALSE` is returned when unsuccessful.

Function Category Toolhelp

Related Functions `ClassFirst`

ClearCommBreak

Syntax `int ClearCommBreak(idComDev)`

Parameter	Type	Description
idComDev	int	Communication device to restore

Description The `ClearCommBreak` function restores character transmission for the device specified in `idComDev`. The transmission line is placed in a nonbreak state.

Return Value Zero is returned when the function is successful. –1 is returned when unsuccessful.

Function Category Communication

Related Functions `OpenComm`, `SetCommBreak`

ClientToScreen

Syntax `void ClientToScreen(hwnd, lppt)`

Parameter	Type	Description
hwnd	HWND	Window containing client area used for conversion
lppt	POINT FAR*	Pointer to a `POINT` data structure containing the client coordinates to convert

Description The `ClientToScreen` function converts the client coordinates in the data structure of type `POINT`, pointed to by `lppt`, to screen coordinates. The resulting screen coordinates are placed into the `POINT` data structure pointed to by `lppt`. The `POINT` data structure follows.

```
typedef struct tagPOINT {
     int x;
     int y;
} POINT;
```

in which

x specifies the horizontal coordinate of the point

y specifies the vertical coordinate of the point.

Return Value There is no return value.

Function Category Coordinate

Related Functions ScreenToClient

ClipCursor

Syntax `void ClipCursor(lprc)`

Parameter	*Type*	*Description*
lprc	const RECT FAR*	Rectangle coordinates

Description The ClipCursor function restricts the movement of the cursor to the rectangular region defined by lprc. lprc points to a structure of type RECT which holds the screen coordinates of the upper-left and lower-right corners of the rectangular region. The RECT structure is shown as follows. When lprc is set to NULL, the confining rectangular region is defined as the entire screen.

```
typedef struct tagRECT{
     int left;
     int top;
     int right;
     int bottom;
} RECT;
```

in which

left is the x coordinate of the upper-left corner

top is the y coordinate of the upper-left corner

right is the x coordinate of the lower-right corner

bottom is the y coordinate of the lower-right corner.

Return Value There is no return value.

Function Category Cursor

Related Functions `CreateCursor`, `DestroyCursor`, `GetClipCursor`

CloseClipboard

Syntax `BOOL CloseClipboard()`

Description The `CloseClipboard` function closes the clipboard and should be called after a window has finished using the clipboard in order to allow other applications to access and use the clipboard.

Return Value The `CloseClipboard` function returns a nonzero value if the clipboard is closed. A zero is returned if the clipboard is not closed.

Function Category Clipboard

Related Functions `OpenClipboard`

CloseComm

Syntax `int CloseComm(idComDev)`

Parameter	*Type*	*Description*
`idComDev`	`int`	Device to close

Description The `CloseComm` function closes the communication device specified in `idComDev`. All memory allocated for the device queues is freed. The characters in the output queue are transmitted before closing the device.

Return Value Zero is returned when successful. A negative value is returned when unsuccessful.

Function Category Communication

Related Functions `OpenComm`, `ReadComm`, `WriteComm`

CloseDriver

Syntax `LRESULT CloseDriver(hdrvr, lParam1, lParam2)`

Parameter	*Type*	*Description*
`hdrvr`	`HDRVR`	Installable device driver to close. The handle to the driver is obtained by a call to `OpenDriver`.
`lParam1`	`LPARAM`	Driver-specific data
`lParam2`	`LPARAM`	Driver-specific data

Description The `CloseDriver` function closes the installable device driver specified in `hdrvr`.

Return Value A nonzero value is returned when successful. Zero is returned when unsuccessful.

Function Category Installable Driver

Related Functions `OpenDriver`

CloseMetaFile

Syntax `HMETAFILE CloseMetaFile(hdc)`

Parameter	*Type*	*Description*
`hdc`	`HDC`	Metafile device context to close

Description The `CloseMetaFile` function closes the metafile device context specified in `hdc` and creates a metafile handle. The metafile handle can be used to play the metafile.

Return Value The handle for the metafile is returned when successful. `NULL` is returned when unsuccessful.

Function Category Metafile

Related Functions `CreateMetaFile`, `DeleteMetaFile`, `PlayMetaFile`

CloseWindow

Syntax `void CloseWindow(hwnd)`

Parameter	*Type*	*Description*
`hwnd`	`HWND`	Window to minimize

Description The `CloseWindow` function minimizes the window specified in `hwnd`. The function does not work on pop-up or child windows.

Return Value There is no return value.

Function Category Display and Movement

Related Functions `MoveWindow`, `OpenIcon`, `ShowWindow`

CombineRgn

Syntax

```
int CombineRgn(hrgnDest, hrgnSrc1, hrgnSrc2,
               fCombineMode)
```

Parameter	*Type*	*Description*
`hrgnDest`	`HRGN`	Specifies the region to be replaced by the new region
`hrgnSrc1`	`HRGN`	Region to combine
`hrgnSrc2`	`HRGN`	Region to combine
`fCombineMode`	`int`	Method to use to combine the regions

Description The `CombineRgn` function combines the regions specified in `hrgnSrc1` and `hrgnSrc2` to form a new region. `hrgnDest` specifies the new region. `fCombineMode` specifies the method used to combine the regions. One of the following values is used for `fCombineMode`:

Value	*Meaning*
`RGN_AND`	Uses the intersection of the regions
`RGN_COPY`	Creates a copy of `hrgnSrc1`
`RGN_DIFF`	Saves the areas of `hrgnSrc1` that are not part of `hrgnSrc2`

Value	*Meaning*
`RGN_OR`	Creates a union of both regions
`RGN_XOR`	Combines the regions but removes any overlapping areas

Return Value The type of region created by the function is returned. One of the following values is returned:

Value	*Meaning*
`COMPLEXREGION`	New region has overlapping borders
`ERROR`	No region was created
`NULLREGION`	New region is empty
`SIMPLEREGION`	New region has no overlapping borders

Function Category Region

Related Functions `CreateRectRgn`, `PaintRgn`

CommDlgExtendedError

Syntax `DWORD CommDlgExtendedError(VOID)`

Parameter	*Type*	*Description*
None		

Description The `CommDlgExtendedError` function determines whether an error occurred during a `ChooseColor`, `ChooseFont`, `FindText`, `GetFileTitle`, `GetOpenFileName`, `GetSaveFileName`, `PrintDlg`, or `ReplaceText` function call.

Return Value Zero is returned when no error is detected. One of the following values is returned when an error is detected:

Value	*Error*
`CDERR_DIALOGFAILURE`	Dialog box could not be created
`CDERR_FINDRESFAILURE`	Function unable to find the specified resource
`CDERR_INITIALIZATION`	Function failed during initialization

Value	*Error*
CDERR_LOCKRESFAILURE	Function failed to lock the specified resource
CDERR_LOADRESFAILURE	Function failed to load the specified resource
CDERR_LOADSTRFAILURE	Function failed to load the specified string
CDERR_MEMALLOCFAILURE	Function unable to allocate memory for internal data structures
CDERR_MEMLOCKFAILURE	Function unable to lock the memory associated with a handle
CDERR_NOHINSTANCE	Function unable to provide the instance handle needed when the ENABLETEMPLATE flag is set in the Flags member of a common dialog data structure
CDERR_NOHOOK	Function unable to provide the pointer to the hook function needed when the ENABLEHOOK flag is set in the Flags member of a common dialog data structure
CDERR_NOTEMPLATE	Application failed to provide the template needed when the ENABLETEMPLATE flag is set in the Flags member of a common dialog data structure
CDERR_REGISTERMSGFAIL	RegisterWindowMessage function failed when called by common dialog function
CDERR_STRUCTSIZE	The lStructSize member of the common dialog data structure is invalid
CFERR_NOFONTS	No fonts exist
FNERR_BUFFERTOOSMALL	Buffer pointed to by lpstrFile member of structure is too small
FNERR_INVALIDFILENAME	Filename is invalid
FNERR_SUBCLASSFAILURE	Attempt to subclass a list box failed

Value	*Error*
FRERR_BUFFERLENGTHZERO	Member in data structure points to an invalid buffer
PDERR_CREATEICFAILURE	PrintDlg function failed when it attempted to create an information context
PDERR_DNDMMISMATCH	Data in the DEVMODE and DEVNAMES data structures do not define the same printer
PDERR_GETDEVMODEFAIL	Printer device driver failed to initialize a DEVMODE data structure
PDERR_INITFAILURE	PrintDlg function failed during initialization
PDERR_LOADDRVFAILURE	PrintDlg function failed to load the device driver for the printer
PDERR_NODEFAULTPRN	Default printer does not exist
PDERR_NODEVICES	No printer drivers found
PDERR_PARSEFAILURE	Common dialog function failed to parse the strings in the devices section of WIN.INI
PDERR_PRINTERNOTFOUND	Device section of WIN.INI does not contain entry for the requested printer
PDERR_RETDEFFAILURE	PD_RETURNDEFAULT flag was set in the Flags member of the PRINTDLG data structure but either the hDevMode or hDevNames field was nonzero
PDERR_SETUPFAILURE	Common dialog function failed to load required resources

Function Category Common Dialog

Related Functions PrintDlg

CopyCursor

Syntax `HCURSOR CopyCursor(hinst, hcur)`

Parameter	*Type*	*Description*
`hinst`	`HINSTANCE`	Instance of module that will copy the cursor
`hcur`	`HCURSOR`	Cursor to copy

Description The `CopyCursor` function copies the specified cursor. The application should destroy the copied cursor using the `DestroyCursor` function.

Return Value The handle to the copied cursor is returned when successful. `NULL` is returned when unsuccessful.

Related Functions `CopyIcon`, `DestroyCursor`, `GetCursor`, `SetCursor`, `ShowCursor`

CopyIcon

Syntax `HICON CopyIcon(hinst, hicon)`

Parameter	*Type*	*Description*
`hinst`	`HINSTANCE`	Instance of module that will copy the icon
`hicon`	`HICON`	Icon to be copied

Description The `CopyIcon` function copies the specified icon. The application should use `DestroyIcon` to destroy the copied icon.

Return Value The handle to the copied icon is returned when successful. `NULL` is returned when unsuccessful.

Related Functions `CopyCursor`, `DestroyIcon`, `DrawIcon`

CopyLZFile

Syntax `LONG CopyLZFile(hfSource, hfDest)`

Parameter	*Type*	*Description*
`hfSource`	`int`	Source file ID
`hfDest`	`int`	Destination file ID

Description The `CopyLZFile` function copies the source file specified in `hfSource` to the destination file specified in `hfDest`. If the source file is compressed, the resulting destination file is decompressed.

Return Value The number of bytes in the destination file is returned when successful. One of the following values (all less than zero) is returned when an error occurs:

Value	*Meaning*
`LZERROR_BADINHANDLE`	`hfSource` is invalid
`LZERROR_BADOUTHANDLE`	`hfDest` is invalid
`LZERROR_GLOBALALLOC`	Insufficient memory for required buffers
`LZERROR_READ`	File format of source file is invalid
`LZERROR_UNKNOWNALG`	Source file was compressed with an unknown compression algorithm
`LZERROR_WRITE`	Insufficient space in output file

Function Category Lempel-Ziv Encoding

Related Functions `LZCopy`, `LZRead`, `LZStart`

CopyMetaFile

Syntax `HMETAFILE CopyMetaFile(hmfSrc, lpszFile)`

Parameter	*Type*	*Description*
`hmfSrc`	`HMETAFILE`	Source metafile
`lpszFile`	`LPCSTR`	Pointer to a null-terminated string that defines the file to receive the metafile

Description The `CopyMetaFile` function copies the metafile specified in `hmfSrc` to the file specified in `lpszFile`. `lpszFile` can be set to `NULL` to indicate that the source metafile should be copied to a memory metafile.

Return Value The handle for the new metafile is returned when successful. `NULL` is returned when unsuccessful.

Function Category Metafile

Related Functions CreateMetaFile, DeleteMetaFile, PlayMetaFile

CopyRect

Syntax `void CopyRect(lprcDst, lprcSrc)`

Parameter	*Type*	*Description*
lprcDst	RECT FAR*	Pointer to RECT data structure containing coordinates of destination rectangle
lprcSrc	const RECT FAR*	Pointer to RECT data structure containing coordinates of source rectangle

Description The CopyRect function copies the rectangle specified in the data structure of type RECT, pointed to by lprcSrc, to the data structure of type RECT, pointed to by lprcDst. The RECT structure follows.

```
typedef struct tagRECT {
     int left;
     int top;
     int right;
     int bottom;
} RECT;
```

in which

left is the x coordinate of the upper-left corner

top is the y coordinate of the upper-left corner

right is the x coordinate of the lower-right corner

bottom is the y coordinate of the lower-right corner.

Return Value There is no return value.

Function Category Rectangle

Related Functions EqualRect, OffsetRect, SetRect

CountClipboardFormats

Syntax `int CountClipboardFormats()`

Description The `CountClipboardFormats` function gets the number of formats in the clipboard.

Return Value The number of data formats in the clipboard is returned.

Function Category Clipboard

Related Functions `EnumClipboardFormat`, `RegisterClipboardFormat`

CreateBitmap

Syntax
```
HBITMAP CreateBitmap(nWidth, nHeight, cbPlanes,
                     cbBits, lpvBits)
```

Parameter	*Type*	*Description*
nWidth	int	Width of bitmap, in pixels
nHeight	int	Height of bitmap, in pixels
cbPlanes	UINT	Number of color planes in bitmap
cbBits	UINT	Number of color bits per pixel
lpvBits	const void FAR*	Points to an array that contains the bit values for the bitmap

Description The `CreateBitmap` function creates a bitmap with the specified parameters. The resulting bitmap is device dependent. `nWidth` and `nHeight` specifies the size, in pixels, of the bitmap. `cbPlanes` specifies the number of color planes in the bitmap. `cbBits` defines the number of color bits per pixel for the display. `lpvBits` points to an array that contains the bit values for the bitmap. `lpvBits` can be set to `NULL`. When `lpvBits` is `NULL`, the bitmap is uninitialized.

Return Value The handle for the bitmap is returned when successful. `NULL` is returned when unsuccessful.

Function Category Bitmap

Related Functions `CreateBitmapIndirect`

CreateBitmapIndirect

Syntax `HBITMAP CreateBitmapIndirect(lpbm)`

Parameter	*Type*	*Description*
`lpbm`	`BITMAP FAR*`	Pointer to `BITMAP` data structure that contains bitmap information

Description The `CreateBitmapIndirect` function creates a bitmap using the parameters in the data structure of type `BITMAP` that is pointed to by `lpbm`. The `BITMAP` structure follows.

```
typedef struct tagBITMAP {
     int bmType;
     int bmWidth;
     int bmHeight;
     int bmWidthBytes;
     BYTE bmPlanes;
     BYTE bmBitsPixel;
     LPSTR bmBits;
} BITMAP;
```

in which

`bmType` is the bitmap type (zero for logical bitmaps)

`bmWidth` is the bitmap width in pixels

`bmHeight` is the bitmap height in pixels

`bmWidthBytes` is the number of bytes in each raster line

`bmPlanes` is the number of color planes in the bitmap

`bmBitsPixel` points to the number of adjacent color bits in each plane needed to define a pixel

`bmBits` points to the array containing the bit values for the bitmap.

Return Value The handle of the created bitmap is returned when successful. NULL is returned when unsuccessful.

Function Category Bitmap

Related Functions CreateBitmap, CreateCompatibleBitmap

CreateBrushIndirect

Syntax `HBRUSH CreateBrushIndirect(lplb)`

Parameter	*Type*	*Description*
lplb	LOGBRUSH FAR*	Pointer to LOGBRUSH data structure containing information on the brush

Description The CreateBrushIndirect function creates a logical brush. lplb points to the data structure of type LOGBRUSH that contains the style, color, and pattern for the brush. The LOGBRUSH data structure follows.

```
typedef struct tagLOGBRUSH {
     WORD lbStyle;
     COLORREF lbColor;
     short int lbHatch;
} LOGBRUSH;
```

in which

lbStyle is the brush style and is set to one of the following values:

Value	*Meaning*
BS_DIBPATTERN	Pattern brush defined with a device-independent bitmap
BS_HATCHED	Hatched brush
BS_HOLLOW	Hollow brush
BS_PATTERN	Pattern brush defined with a memory bitmap
BS_SOLID	Solid brush

`lbColor` is the color for the brush and is one of the following values:

Value	*Meaning*
DIB_PAL_COLORS	Color table is an array of 16-bit indexes to the logical palette
DIB_RGB_COLORS	Color table contains literal RGB values

`lbHatch` is the hatch style and is interpreted as follows:

If `lbStyle` is BS_DIBPATTERN, `lbHatch` contains the handle to a packed device-independent bitmap.

If `lbStyle` is BS_HATCHED, `lbHatch` contains one of the following values that specify the line orientation of the hatch:

Value	*Meaning*
HS_BDIAGONAL	45-degree upward hatch
HS_CROSS	Crosshatch with vertical/horizontal lines
HS_DIAGCROSS	45-degree crosshatch
HS_FDIAGONAL	45-degree downward hatch
HS_HORIZONTAL	Horizontal hatch
HS_VERTICAL	Vertical hatch

If `lbStyle` is BS_PATTERN, `lbHatch` contains the handle to the bitmap for the pattern.

If `lbStyle` is BS_SOLID or BS_HOLLOW, `lbHatch` is ignored.

Return Value The handle for the created brush is returned when successful. NULL is returned when unsuccessful.

Function Category Drawing Tool

Related Functions `CreatePatternBrush`, `CreateSolidBrush`, `GetStockObject`, `SelectObject`

CreateCaret

Syntax `void CreateCaret(hwnd, hbmp, nWidth, nHeight)`

Parameter	*Type*	*Description*
hwnd	HWND	Window that owns the caret
hbmp	HBITMAP	Bitmap identification for the new caret shape. When Bitmap = NULL, a solid caret is created. When Bitmap = 1, the caret's color is gray.
nWidth	int	Width of the caret in logical units
nHeight	int	Height of the caret in logical units

Description The `CreateCaret` function creates a new shape for the system caret. The caret is owned by the window specified in `hwnd`. `hbmp` defines the new shape of the caret. When `hbmp` is a bitmap handle created with `CreateBitmap`, `CreateDIBitmap`, or `LoadBitmap`, `nWidth` and `nHeight` are determined automatically. For any other value of `hbmp`, `nWidth` and `nHeight` define the number of logical units in the caret's width and height, respectively. By setting `nWidth` and/or `nHeight` to `NULL`, the width and/or height of the caret are automatically set to the dimensions of the window's border.

Return Value There is no return value.

Function Category Caret

Related Functions `DestroyCaret`, `ShowCaret`

CreateCompatibleBitmap

Syntax

```
HBITMAP CreateCompatibleBitmap(hdc, nWidth,
                               nHeight)
```

Parameter	*Type*	*Description*
hdc	HDC	Device context
nWidth	int	Width of bitmap in bits
nHeight	int	Height of bitmap in bits

Description The `CreateCompatibleBitmap` function creates a bitmap that is compatible with the device specified in `hdc`. When `hdc` specifies a device, the bitmap has the number of color planes and bits per pixel defined for the device. When `hdc` specifies a device context, the resulting bitmap has the same format as the current bitmap for the specified device context.

Return Value The handle of the created bitmap is returned when successful. `NULL` is returned when unsuccessful.

Function Category Bitmap

Related Functions `CreateBitmap`, `LoadBitmap`

CreateCompatibleDC

Syntax `HDC CreateCompatibleDC(hdc)`

Parameter	*Type*	*Description*
`hdc`	`HDC`	Device context; can be set to `NULL` to create a memory device context compatible with the system display

Description The `CreateCompatibleDC` function creates a memory device context. The memory device context is compatible with the device specified in `hdc` and represents the display surface in memory.

Return Value The handle for the created memory device context is returned when successful. When unsuccessful, `NULL` is returned.

Function Category Device Context

Related Functions `CreateDC`, `DeleteDC`

CreateCursor

Syntax

```
HCURSOR CreateCursor(hinst, xHotSpot, yHotSpot, nWidth,
                     nHeight, lpvANDplane, lpvXORplane)
```

Parameter	Type	Description
hinst	HINSTANCE	Module creating the cursor
xHotSpot	int	Horizontal position of hotspot
yHotSpot	int	Vertical position of hotspot
nWidth	int	Cursor width in pixels
nHeight	int	Cursor height in pixels
lpvANDplane	const void FAR*	AND mask for the cursor
lpvXORplane	const void FAR*	XOR mask for the cursor

Description The `CreateCursor` function creates the specified cursor. `hinst` specifies the module which is creating the cursor. The cursor hotspot is defined by the horizontal and vertical positions specified in `xHotSpot` and `yHotSpot`, respectively. The size of the cursor is defined in `nWidth` and `nHeight`. `nWidth` defines the cursor width, in pixels. `nHeight` defines the cursor height, in pixels. `lpvANDplane` points to the array which contains the AND mask for the cursor. `lpvXORplane` points to the array which contains the XOR mask for the cursor.

Return Value The handle to the cursor is returned when successful. `NULL` is returned when unsuccessful.

Function Category Cursor

Related Functions `DestroyCursor`, `SetCursor`

CreateDC

Syntax

```
HDC CreateDC(lpszDriver, lpszDevice, lpszOutput,
             lpvInitData)
```

Parameter	Type	Description
lpszDriver	LPCSTR	Pointer to string containing the DOS filename of the device driver
lpszDevice	LPCSTR	Pointer to string containing the name of the device

Parameter	*Type*	*Description*
`lpszOutput`	`LPCSTR`	Pointer to string containing the DOS filename or device name for output
`lpvInitData`	`const void FAR*`	Pointer to a `DEVMODE` data structure containing initialization date for the device driver

Description The `CreateDC` function creates a device context for the device specified by `lpszDriver`, `lpszDevice`, and `lpszOutput`. `lpvInitData` points to a data structure of type `DEVMODE` that contains initialization data for the device driver. The `ExtDevMode` function is used to retrieve this structure and the information for a specified device. The `DEVMODE` structure follows.

```
#include <print.h>
typedef struct _devicemode {
     char dmDeviceName[CCHDEVICENAME];
     WORD dmSpecVersion;
     WORD dmDriverVersion;
     WORD dmSize;
     WORD dmDriverExtra;
     DWORD dmFields;
     short dmOrientation;
     short dmPaperSize;
     short dmPaperLength;
     short dmPaperWidth;
     short dmScale;
     short dmCopies;
     short dmDefaultSource;
     short dmPrintQuality;
     short dmColor;
     short dmDuplex;
     short dmYResolution
     short dmTTOption
} DEVMODE;
```

in which

`dmDeviceName` is the name of the device the driver supports

`dmSpecVersion` is the version number of the initialization date specification (0x30A for Windows 3.1)

`dmDriverVersion` is the printer driver version

`dmSize` is the size in bytes of the `DEVMODE` structure

`dmDriverExtra` is the size of the `dmDriverData` field and the length of the data in the `DEVMODE` structure

`dmFields` is the bitfield that indicates the remaining members in `DEVMODE` that have been initialized. `dmFields` is any combination of the following values:

```
DM_ORIENTATION
DM_PAPERSIZE
DM_PAPERLENGTH
DM_PAPERWIDTH
DM_SCALE
DM_COPIES
DM_DEFAULTSOURCE
DM_PRINTQUALITY
DM_COLOR
DM_DUPLEX
DM_YRESOLUTION
DM_TTOPTION
```

`dmOrientation` is the paper orientation—either `DMORIENT_PORTRAIT` or `DMORIENT_LANDSCAPE`

`dmPaperSize` is the paper size; it is one of the following values:

Value	*Meaning*
DMPAPER_FIRST	DMPAPER_LETTER
DMPAPER_LETTER	8.5 by 11 inch
DMPAPER_LETTERSMALL	Letter small 8.5 by 11 inch
DMPAPER_TABLOID	Tabloid 11 by 17 inch
DMPAPER_LEDGER	Ledger 17 by 11 inch
DMPAPER_LEGAL	8.5 by 14 inch
DMPAPER_STATEMENT	Statement 5.5 by 8.5 inch
DMPAPER_EXECUTIVE	Executive 7.25 by 10 inch
DMPAPER_A3	297 by 420 millimeter
DMPAPER_A4	210 by 297 millimeter
DMPAPER_A4SMALL	Small 210 by 297 millimeter
DMPAPER_A5	148 by 210 millimeter
DMPAPER_B4	250 by 354 millimeter
DMPAPER_B5	182 by 257 millimeter
DMPAPER_FOLIO	Folio 8.5 by 13 inch
DMPAPER_QUARTO	Quarto 215 by 275 millimeter
DMPAPER_10X14	10 by 14 inch

Value	*Meaning*
DMPAPER_11X17	11 by 17 inch
DMPAPER_NOTE	Note 8.5 by 11 inch
DMPAPER_CSHEET	C size sheet
DMPAPER_DSHEET	D size sheet
DMPAPER_ESHEET	E size sheet
DMPAPER_ENV_9	#9 envelope
DMPAPER_ENV_10	#10 envelope
DMPAPER_ENV_11	#11 envelope
DMPAPER_ENV_12	#12 envelope
DMPAPER_ENV_14	#14 envelope
DMPAPER_ENV_DL	DL 110 by 220 millimeter
DMPAPER_ENV_C5	C5 162 by 229 millimeter
DMPAPER_ENV_MONARCH	Monarch 3.875 by 7.5 inch
DMPAPER_LETTER_EXTRA	9\275 by 12 inch
DMPAPER_LEGAL_EXTRA	9\275 by 15 inch
DMPAPER_TABLOID_EXTRA	11.69 by 18 inch
DMPAPER_A4_EXTRA	9.27 by 12.69 inch
DMPAPER_LETTER_TRANSVERSE	11 by 8\275 inch
DMPAPER_A4_TRANSVERSE	297 by 210 millimeter
DMPAPER_LETTER_EXTRA_TRANSVERSE	12 by 9\275 inch
DMPAPER_LAST	Same as DMPAPER_LETTER_ EXTRA_TRANSVERSE
DMPAPER_USER	User defined

`dmPaperLength` is the value to override the paper length in `dmPaperSize` (in tenths of a millimeter)

`dmPaperWidth` is the value to override the paper width in `dmPaperSize` (in tenths of a millimeter)

`dmScale` is the output scale

`dmCopies` is the number of copies to print

`dmDefaultSource` is the default paper bin; it is selected from one of the following values:

```
DMBIN_AUTODMBIN_CASSETTE
DMBIN_ENVELOPE
DMBIN_ENVMANUAL
```

DMBIN_FIRST
DMBIN_LARGECAPACITY
DMBIN_LARGEFMT
DMBIN_LAST
DMBIN_LOWER
DMBIN_MANUAL
DMBIN_MIDDLE
DMBIN_ONLYONE
DMBIN_SMALLFMT
DMBIN_TRACTOR
DMBIN_UPPER

dmPrintQuality is the printer resolution; it is set to one of the following:
DMRES_HIGH
DMRES_MEDIUM
DMRES_LOW
DMRES_DRAFT

dmColor is the color/monochrome switch; it is one of the following:
DMCOLOR_COLOR
DMCOLOR_MONOCHROME

dmDuplex is the indicator for double-sided or duplex printing; it is one of the following:
DMDUP_SIMPLEX
DMDUP_HORIZONTAL
DMDUP_VERTICAL

dmYResolution is the Y-resolution of printer in dots per inch

dmTTOption is the value that indicates how to print TrueType fonts. dmTTOptions is one of the following values:

Value	*Meaning*
DMTT_BITMAP	Print TrueType fonts as graphics
DMTT_DOWNLOAD	Download TrueType fonts
DMTT_SUBDEV	Use device fonts to replace TrueType fonts

Return Value The device context for the specified device is returned when successful. When unsuccessful, NULL is returned.

Function Category Device Context

Related Function `DeleteDC`

CreateDialog

Syntax `HWND CreateDialog(hinst, lpszDlgTemp, hwndOwner, dlgprc)`

Parameter	*Type*	*Description*
`hinst`	`HINSTANCE`	Instance of module that contains the dialog box template
`lpszDlgTemp`	`LPCSTR`	Name of dialog box
`hwndOwner`	`HWND`	Window that owns the dialog box
`dlgprc`	`DLGPROC`	Dialog function

Description The `CreateDialog` function creates a dialog box. `hinst` specifies the instance of the module whose executable file contains the dialog box template. The size, style, and controls for the dialog box are specified in `lpszDlgTemp`. `hwndOwner` specifies the window that owns the dialog box. `dlgprc` points to the dialog function. The dialog function must follow the conventions and formats presented to work properly.

Syntax `BOOL FAR PASCAL DialogProc(hwndDlg, wMsg, wParam, lParam)`

Parameter	*Type*	*Description*
`hwndDlg`	`HWND`	Dialog box receiving message
`wMsg`	`WORD`	Message Number
`wParam`	`WORD`	16 bits of message-dependent information
`lParam`	`DWORD`	32 bits of message-dependent information

Description This function should be used only when the dialog class is used for the dialog box. It should not call the `DefWindowProc`

function to process unwanted messages. The name DialogProc is simply a holder for the real function name. The real name must be exported by using the EXPORTS statement.

Return Value DialogProc should return a nonzero value when the message is successfully handled. Zero should be returned by DialogProc when unable to handle the message. When the WM_INITDIALOG message is sent, zero should be returned if the function calls the SetFocus function. Otherwise, a nonzero value should be returned.

Return Value The handle for the dialog box is returned if the dialog box is created. NULL is returned if the dialog box is not created.

Function Category Dialog Box

Related Functions CreateDialogIndirect, CreateDialogIndirectParam

CreateDialogIndirect

Syntax

```
HWND CreateDialogIndirect(hinst, lpbDlgTemp, hwndOwner,
                          dlgprc)
```

Parameter	*Type*	*Description*
hinst	HINSTANCE	Instance of module that contains the dialog box template
lpbDlgTemp	const BYTE FAR*	Points to structure containing template size, style, control, and so forth
hwndOwner	HWND	Window that owns the dialog box
dlgprc	DLGPROC	Dialog function

Description The CreateDialogIndirect function creates a dialog box. hinst specifies the instance of the module whose executable file contains the dialog-box template. The size, style, and controls for the dialog box are specified in a data structure of type DLGTEMPLATE pointed to by lpbDlgTemp. The DLGTEMPLATE structure is described at the end of this paragraph. hwndOwner specifies the window that owns the dialog box. dlgprc points to the dialog function. The dialog function must follow the conventions and formats in the following paragraphs to work properly.

```
DLGTEMPLATE {
     long dtStyle;
     BYTE dtItemCount;
     int dtX;
     int dtY;
     int dtCX;
     int dtCY;
     char dtMenuName[];
     char dtClassName[];
     char dtCaptionText[];
#ifdef DS_SETFONT_INCLUDED;
     short int dtPointSize;
     char dtTypeFace[];
#endif
     DLGITEM dtDlgItem[];
};
```

in which

`dtStyle` is the dialog box style and can be any combination of the following values:

Value	*Meaning*
`DS_LOCALEDIT`	Text storage for edit controls will be allocated in the application's local data segment
`DS_SYSMODAL`	System-modal dialog box
`DS_MODALFRAME`	Dialog box with modal dialog box border
`DS_ABSALIGN`	`dtX` and `dtY` are relative to screen
`DS_SETFONT`	Use a font other than the system font in the dialog box
`DS_NOIDLEMSG`	The `WM_ENTERIDLE` message will not be sent to the dialog box owner while the box is being displayed

`dtItemCount` is the number of items in the dialog box

`dtX` is the x coordinate of the upper-left corner of the dialog box; it is specified in units of 1/4 the dialog base width unit

`dtY` is the y coordinate of the upper-left corner of the dialog box; it is specified in units of 1/8 the dialog base height unit

`dtCX` is the width of the dialog box; it is specified in units of 1/4 the dialog base width unit

`dtCY` is the height of the dialog box; it is specified in units of 1/8 the dialog base height unit

`dtMenuName` is the name of the menu for the dialog box

`dtClassName` is the name of the class for the dialog box

`dtCaptionText[]` is the caption for the dialog box

`dtPointSize` is the number of points used to draw text in the dialog box (typeface size)

`dtTypeFace` is the name of the typeface used to draw text in the dialog box

`dtDlgItem` is an array of `DLGITEM` structures that define the controls of the dialog box.

Syntax `BOOL FAR PASCAL DialogProc(hwndDlg, wMsg, wParam, lParam)`

Parameter	*Type*	*Description*
`hwndDlg`	`HWND`	Dialog box receiving message
`wMsg`	`WORD`	Message Number
`wParam`	`WORD`	16 bits of message-dependent information
`lParam`	`DWORD`	32 bits of message-dependent information

Description This function should be used only when the dialog class is used for the dialog box. It should not call the `DefWindowProc` function to process unwanted messages. The name `DialogProc` is simply a holder for the real function name. The real name must be exported by using the `EXPORTS` statement.

Return Value `DialogProc` should return a nonzero value when the function successfully handles the message. Zero should be returned when unable to handle the message. When the `WM_INITDIALOG` message is sent, zero should be returned if the function calls the `SetFocus` function. Otherwise, a nonzero value should be returned.

Return Value The handle of the dialog box is returned when successful. When unable to create the dialog box or controls, `NULL` is returned.

Function Category Dialog Box

Related Functions `CreateDialog`, `CreateDialogIndirectParam`, `CreateDialogParam`

CreateDialogIndirectParam

Syntax

```
HWND CreateDialogIndirectParam(hinst,lpbDlgTemp,
                               hwndOwner, dlgprc,
                               lParamInit)
```

Parameter	*Type*	*Description*
hinst	HINSTANCE	Instance of module that contains the dialog box template
lpbDlgTemp	const BYTE FAR*	Points to structure containing template size, style, control, and so forth
hwndOwner	HWND	Window that owns the dialog box
dlgprc	DLGPROC	Dialog function
lParamInit	LPARAM	32-bit value passed to the dialog function when dialog box is created

Description The `CreateDialogIndirectParam` function creates a dialog box. `hinst` specifies the instance of the module whose executable file contains the dialog-box template. The size, style, and controls for the dialog box are specified in a data structure of type `DLGTEMPLATE` pointed to by `lpbDlgTemp`. The `DLGTEMPLATE` structure follows this paragraph. `hwndOwner` specifies the window that owns the dialog box. `dlgprc` points to the dialog function. The dialog function must follow the conventions and formats in the following paragraphs to work properly. `lParamInit` is a 32-bit value passed to the dialog function to initialize dialog box controls.

```
DLGTEMPLATE {
     long dtStyle;
     BYTE dtItemCount;
     int dtX;
     int dtY;
     int dtCX;
     int dtCY;
     char dtMenuName[];
     char dtClassName[];
     char dtCaptionText[];
#ifdef DS_SETFONT_INCLUDED;
     short int dtPointSize;
     char dtTypeFace[];
```

```
#endif
     DLGITEM dtDlgItem[];
};
```

in which

`dtStyle` is the dialog box style and can be any combination of the following values:

Value	*Meaning*
DS_LOCALEDIT	Text storage for edit controls will be allocated in the application's local data segment
DS_SYSMODAL	System-modal dialog box
DS_MODALFRAME	Dialog box with modal dialog box border
DS_ABSALIGN	`dtX` and `dtY` are relative to screen
DS_SETFONT	Use a font other than the system font in the dialog box
DS_NOIDLEMSG	The `WM_ENTERIDLE` message will not be sent to the dialog box owner while the box is being displayed

`dtItemCount` is the number of items in the dialog box

`dtX` is the x coordinate of the upper-left corner of the dialog box; it is specified in units of 1/4 the dialog base width unit

`dtY` is the y coordinate of the upper-left corner of the dialog box; it is specified in units of 1/8 the dialog base height unit

`dtCX` is the width of the dialog box; it is specified in units of 1/4 the dialog base width unit

`dtCY` is the height of the dialog box; it is specified in units of 1/8 the dialog base height unit

`dtMenuName` is the name of the menu for the dialog box

`dtClassName` is the name of the class for the dialog box

`dtCaptionText[]` is the caption for the dialog box

`dtPointSize` is the number of points used to draw text in the dialog box (typeface size)

`dtTypeFace` is the name of the typeface used to draw text in the dialog box

`dtDlgItem` is an array of `DLGITEM` structures that define the controls of the dialog box.

Syntax `BOOL FAR PASCAL DialogProc(hwndDlg, wMsg, wParam, lParam)`

Parameter	*Type*	*Description*
`hwndDlg`	`HWND`	Dialog box receiving message
`wMsg`	`WORD`	Message Number
`wParam`	`WORD`	16 bits of message-dependent information
`lParam`	`DWORD`	32 bits of message-dependent information

Description This function should be used only when the dialog class is used for the dialog box. It should not call the `DefWindowProc` function to process unwanted messages. The name `DialogProc` is simply a holder for the real function name. The real name must be exported by using the `EXPORTS` statement.

Return Value `DialogProc` should return a nonzero value when the function successfully handles the message. Zero should be returned when unable to handle the message. When the `WM_INITDIALOG` message is sent, zero should be returned if the function calls the `SetFocus` function. Otherwise, a nonzero value should be returned.

Return Value The handle of the dialog box is returned when successful. When unable to create the dialog box or controls, `NULL` is returned.

Function Category Dialog Box

Related Functions `CreateDialog`, `CreateDialogIndirect`, `CreateDialogParam`

CreateDialogParam

Syntax

```
HWND CreateDialogParam(hinst, lpszDlgTemp, hwndOwner,
                        dlgprc, lParamInit)
```

Parameter	*Type*	*Description*
`hinst`	`HINSTANCE`	Instance of module that contains the dialog box template
`lpszDlgTemp`	`LPCSTR`	Name of dialog box

Parameter	*Type*	*Description*
`hwndOwner`	`HWND`	Window that owns the dialog box
`dlgprc`	`DLGPROC`	Dialog function
`lParamInit`	`LPARAM`	32-bit value passed to the dialog function

Description The `CreateDialogParam` function creates a dialog box. `hinst` specifies the instance of the module whose executable file contains the dialog box template. The size, style, and controls for the dialog box are specified in `lpszDlgTemp`. `hwndOwner` specifies the window that owns the dialog box. `dlgprc` points to the dialog function. The dialog function must follow the conventions and formats in the following paragraphs to work properly. `lParamInit` is a 32-bit value passed to the dialog function to initialize dialog box controls.

Syntax `BOOL FAR PASCAL DialogProc(hwndDlg, wMsg, wParam, lParam)`

Parameter	*Type*	*Description*
`hwndDlg`	`HWND`	Dialog box receiving message
`wMsg`	`WORD`	Message Number
`wParam`	`WORD`	16 bits of message-dependent information
`lParam`	`DWORD`	32 bits of message-dependent information

Description This function should be used only when the dialog class is used for the dialog box. It should not call the `DefWindowProc` function to process unwanted messages. The name `DialogProc` is simply a holder for the real function name. The real name must be exported using the `EXPORTS` statement.

Return Value `DialogProc` should return a nonzero value when the function successfully handles the message. Zero should be returned when unable to handle the message. When the `WM_INITDIALOG` message is sent, zero should be returned if the function calls the `SetFocus` function. Otherwise, a nonzero value should be returned.

Return Value The handle for the dialog box is returned if the dialog box is created. `NULL` is returned if the dialog box is not created.

Function Category Dialog Box

Related Functions `CreateDialog`, `CreateDialogIndirect`, `CreateDialogIndirectParam`

CreateDIBitmap

Syntax

```
HBITMAP CreateDIBitmap(hdc, lpbmih, dwInit, lpvBits, lpbmi,
                       fnColorUse)
```

Parameter	*Type*	*Description*
`hdc`	`HDC`	Device context
`lpbmih`	`BITMAPINFOHEADER FAR*`	Pointer to `BITMAPINFOHEADER` structure containing size and format information for the bitmap
`dwInit`	`DWORD`	Determines whether bitmap will be initialized
`lpvBits`	`const void FAR*`	Array containing initial bitmap values
`lpbmi`	`BITMAPINFO FAR*`	Pointer to `BITMAPINFO` structure containing dimensions and colors for `lpvBits`
`fnColorUse`	`UNIT`	Set to `DIB_PAL_COLORS` (color table in `lpbmi` contains array of 16-bit indexes for the currently realized logical palette) or `DIB_RGB_COLORS` (color table in `lpbmi` contains RGB values)

Description The CreateDIBitmap function creates a device-specific bitmap from a device-independent bitmap. hdc specifies the device context. lpbmih points to a data structure of type BITMAPINFOHEADER that contains information on the device independent bitmap. The BITMAPINFOHEADER structure follows this paragraph. dwInit determines whether the resulting bitmap will be initialized. When dwInit is set to CBM_INIT, lpvBits and lpbmi are used to initialize the bitmap. lpbmi points to a data structure of type BITMAPINFO. The BITMAPINFO structure is shown after the BITMAPINFOHEADER structure.

```
typedef struct BITMAPINFOHEADER {
     DWORD biSize;
     DWORD biWidth;
     DWORD biHeight;
     WORD biPlanes;
     WORD biBitCount;
     DWORD biCompression;
     DWORD biSizeImage;
     DWORD biXPelsPerMeter;
     DWORD biYPelsPerMeter;
     DWORD biClrUsed;
     DWORD biClrImportant;
} BITMAPINFOHEADER;
```

in which

biSize is the number of bytes required for the structure

biWidth is the width of the bitmap in pixels

biHeight is the height of the bitmap in pixels

biPlanes is the number of planes; must be set to 1

biBitCount is the number of bits per pixel

biCompression is the type of compression and is selected from the following values:

BI_RGB	Bitmap is not compressed
BI_RLE8	Run-length encode format with 8 bits per pixel
BI_RLE4	Run-length encode format with 4 bits per pixel

biSizeImage is the size of the image in bytes

biXPelsPerMeter is the horizontal resolution in pixels per meter for the target device biYPelsPerMeter is the vertical resolution in pixels per meter for the target device

biClrUsed is the number of color indexes in the color table that the bitmap actually uses

biClrImportant is the number of color indexes considered important for the bitmap.

The BITMAPINFO structure is as follows:

```
typedef struct tagBITMAPINFO {
     BITMAPINFOHEADER bmiHeader;
     RGBQUAD bmiColors[1];
} BITMAPINFO;
```

in which

bmiHeader is the BITMAPINFOHEADER structure for the device-independent bitmap

bmiColors is an array of data structures of type RGBQUAD that defines the colors in the bitmap.

Return Value The handle of the created bitmap is returned when successful. NULL is returned when unsuccessful.

Function Category Bitmap

Related Functions CreateBitmap

CreateDIBPatternBrush

Syntax `HBRUSH CreateDIBPatternBrush(hglbDIBPacked, fnColorSpec)`

Parameter	*Type*	*Description*
hglbDIBPacked	HGLOBAL	Global memory object that contains the packed, device-independent bitmap
fnColorSpec	UNIT	Indicates whether the bmiColors[] fields of the BITMAPINFO data structure contains RGB color values or indexes to the logical palette

Description The `CreateDIBPatternBrush` function creates a logical brush using the pattern from a device-independent bitmap. `hglbDIBPacked` specifies the global memory object that contains the packed, device-independent bitmap. The handle for this global object is defined when the `GlobalAlloc` function is called to allocate global memory. The application fills the global memory with a packed, device-independent bitmap that contains a `BITMAPINFO` data structure and array defining the pixels of the bitmap. `fnColorSpec` indicates whether the `bmiColors[]` fields of the `BITMAPINFO` data structure contains RGB color values or indexes to the currently realized logical palette. `fnColorSpec` is set to one of the following values:

Value	*Meaning*
`DIB_PAL_COLORS`	Color table contains 16-bit indexes into the currently realized logical palette
`DIB_RGB_COLORS`	Color table contains literal RGB values

Return Value The handle of the created logical brush is returned when successful. `NULL` is returned when unsuccessful.

Function Category Drawing Tool

Related Functions `CreateBrushIndirect`, `CreatePatternBrush`, `CreateSolidBrush`

CreateDiscardableBitmap

Syntax `HBITMAP CreateDiscardableBitmap(hdc, nWidth, nHeight)`

Parameter	*Type*	*Description*
`hdc`	`HDC`	Device context
`nWidth`	`int`	Width of bitmap in bits
`nHeight`	`int`	Height of bitmap in bits

Description The `CreateDiscardableBitmap` function creates a discardable bitmap. The discardable bitmap is compatible with the device in `hdc`. The number of color planes and bits per pixel for the bitmap are set to the corresponding values for the specified device.

Return Value The handle of the created bitmap is returned when successful. `NULL` is returned when unsuccessful.

Function Category Bitmap

Related Functions `CreateBitmap`, `LoapBitmap`

CreateEllipticRgn

Syntax
```
HRGN CreateEllipticRgn(nLeftRect, nTopRect,
                       nRightRect, nBottomRect)
```

Parameter	*Type*	*Description*
`nLeftRect`	`int`	X coordinate of upper-left corner of the bounding rectangle
`nTopRect`	`int`	Y coordinate of upper-left corner of the bounding rectangle
`nRightRect`	`int`	X coordinate of lower-right corner of the bounding rectangle
`nBottomRect`	`int`	Y coordinate of lower-right corner of the bounding rectangle

Description The `CreateEllipticRgn` function creates an elliptical region within the bounding rectangle specified by `nLeftRect`, `nTopRect`, `nRightRect`, and `nBottomRect`.

Return Value The handle of the new region is returned when successful. `NULL` is returned when unsuccessful.

Function Category Region

Related Functions `CreateEllipticRgnIndirect`

CreateEllipticRgnIndirect

Syntax `HRGN CreateEllipticRgnIndirect(lprc)`

Parameter	*Type*	*Description*
lprc	const RECT FAR*	Pointer to a RECT data structure containing the coordinates of the bounding rectangle

Description The CreateEllipticRgnIndirect function creates an elliptical region within the bounding rectangle specified by the coordinates in the data structure of type RECT pointed to by lprc. The RECT data structure follows.

```
typedef struct tagRECT{
     int left;
     int top;
     int right;
     int bottom;
} RECT;
```

in which

left is the x coordinate of the upper-left corner

top is the y coordinate of the upper-left corner

right is the x coordinate of the lower-right corner

bottom is the y coordinate of the lower-right corner.

Return Value The handle to the new region is returned when successful. NULL is returned when unsuccessful.

Function Category Region

Related Functions CreateEllipticRgn

CreateFont

Syntax

```
HFONT CreateFont(nHeight, nWidth, nEscapement,nOrientation,
                 fnWeight, fbItalic, fbUnderline,
                 fbStrikeout, fbCharSet, fbOutputPrecision,
                 fbClipPrecision, fbQuality,
                 fbPitchandFamily, lpszFace)
```

Parameter	Type	Description
nHeight	int	Desired height of the font in logical units
nWidth	int	Average width of the characters in logical units
nEscapement	int	Angle of each line (using tenths of degrees) of text written in the font with respect to the bottom of the page
nOrientation	int	Angle of each character's baseline (in tenths of degrees) with respect to the bottom of the page
fnWeight	int	Weight of the font. fnWeight is one of the following values:

Constant	Value
FW_DONTCARE	0
FW_THIN	100
FW_EXTRALIGHT	200
FW_ULTRALIGHT	200
FW_LIGHT	300
FW_NORMAL	400
FW_REGULAR	400
FW_MEDIUM	500
FW_SEMIBOLD	600
FW_DEMIBOLD	600
FW_BOLD	700
FW_EXTRABOLD	800
FW_ULTRABOLD	800
FW_BLACK	900
FW_HEAVY	900

Parameter	Type	Description
fbItalic	BYTE	Indicates whether font is italic
fbUnderline	BYTE	Indicates whether font is underlined
fbStrikeout	BYTE	Indicates whether font uses strikeout characters

Parameter	Type	Description
fbCharSet	BYTE	Specifies the character set and is one of the following: ANSI_CHARSET, DEFAULT_CHARSET, OEM_CHARSET, SHIFTJIS_CHARSET, SYMBOL_CHARSET
fbOutputPrecision	BYTE	Specifies output precision and is one of the following: OUT_CHARACTER_PRECIS, OUT_DEVICE_PRECIS, OUT_RASTER_PRECIS, OUT_DEFAULT_PRECIS, OUT_STRING_PRECIS, OUT_STROKE_PRECIS, OUT_TT_PRECIS
fbClipPrecision	BYTE	Specifies the clipping precision nd is one of the following: CLIP_CHARACTER_PRECIS, CLIP_DEFAULT_PRECIS, CLIP_ENCAPSULATE, CLIP_LH_ANGLES CLIP_MASK, CLIP_STROKE_PRECIS, CLIP_TT_ALWAYS
fbQuality	BYTE	Specifies the output quality and is one of the following: DEFAULT_QUALITY, DRAFT_QUALITY, PROOF_QUALITY
fbPitchandFamily	BYTE	Specifies the pitch and family of the font. The two low-order bits define the pitch of the font. The following are used for the pitch: DEFAULT_PITCH, FIXED_PITCH, VARIABLE_PITCH The four high-order bits define the font family. The following are used for the font family: FF_DECORATIVE, FF_DONTCARE, FF_MODERN, FF_ROMAN, FF_SCRIPT, FF_SWISS
lpszFace	LPCSTR	Pointer to a null-terminated character string that contains the typeface name of the font

Description The `CreateFont` function creates a logical font with the characteristics specified in the various arguments.

Return Value The handle for the font is returned when successful. `NULL` is returned when unsuccessful.

Function Category Font

Related Functions `AddFontResource`, `CreateFontIndirect`

CreateFontIndirect

Syntax `HFONT CreateFontIndirect(lplf)`

Parameter	*Type*	*Description*
`lplf`	`const LOGFONT FAR*`	Pointer to `LOGFONT` data structure containing the characteristics of the logical font

Description The `CreateFontIndirect` function creates a logical font using the font characteristics specified in the data structure of type `LOGFONT` pointed to by `lplf`. The `LOGFONT` structure follows.

```
typedef struct tagLOGFONT {
     int lfHeight;
     int lfWidth;
     int lfEscapement;
     int lfOrientation;
     int lfWeight;
     BYTE lfItalic;
     BYTE lfUnderline;
     BYTE lfStrikeOut;
     BYTE lfCharSet;
     BYTE lfOutPrecision;
     BYTE lfClipPrecision;
     BYTE lfQuality;
     BYTE lfPitchAndFamily;
     BYTE lfFaceName[LF_FACESIZE];
} LOGFONT;
```

in which

`lfHeight` is the average height of the font in logical units

`lfWidth` is the average width of the characters in logical units

`lfEscapement` is the angle between the escapement vector and the horizontal axis of the display (expressed in tenths of degrees)

`lfOrientation` is the angle between the baseline of a character and the horizontal axis (expressed in tenths of degrees)

`lfWeight` is the font weight and is selected from the following values:

Constant	*Value*
FW_DONTCARE	0
FW_THIN	100
FW_EXTRALIGHT	200
FW_ULTRALIGHT	200
FW_LIGHT	300
FW_NORMAL	400
FW_REGULAR	400
FW_MEDIUM	500
FW_SEMIBOLD	600
FW_DEMIBOLD	600
FW_BOLD	700
FW_EXTRABOLD	800
FW_ULTRABOLD	800
FW_BLACK	900
FW_HEAVY	900

`lfItalic` indicates whether the font is italic (nonzero for italic)

`lfUnderline` indicates whether the font is underlined (nonzero for underline)

`lfStrikeOut` indicates whether the font is a strikeout font (nonzero for strikeout)

`lfCharSet` is the character set and is one of the following: `ANSI_CHARSET`, `DEFAULT_CHARSET`, `OEM_CHARSET`, `SHIFJIS_CHARSET`, or `SYMBOL_CHARSET` `lfOutPrecision` is the output precision and is one of the following: `OUT_CHARACTER_PRECIS`, `OUT_DEFAULT_PRECIS`, `OUT_DEVICE_PRECIS`, `OUT_RASTER_PRECIS`, `OUT_STRING_PRECIS`, `OUT_STROKE_PRECIS`, `OUT_TT_PRECIS`, or `OUT_TT_ONLY_PRECIS`

`lfClipPrecision` is the clipping precision and is one of the following: `CLIP_CHARACTER_PRECIS`, `CLIP_DEFAULT_PRECIS`, `CLIP_EMBEDDED`, `CLIP_LH_ANGLES`, `CLIP_MASK`, `CLIP_STROKE_PRECIS`, or `CLIP_TT_ALWAYS`

`lfQuality` is the output quality and is one of the following: `DEFAULT_QUALITY`, `DRAFT_QUALITY`, or `PROOF_QUALITY`

`lfPitchAndFamily` is the font pitch and family. The two low-order bits specify the pitch. The following values are used for the pitch: `DEFAULT_PITCH`, `FIXED_PITCH`, `VARIABLE_PITCH`

The four high-order bits specify the font family. The following values are used for the family: `FF_DECORATIVE`, `FF_DONTCARE`, `FF_MODERN`, `FF_ROMAN`, `FF_SCRIPT`, `FF_SWISS`

`lpFaceName` is a null-terminated character string containing the typeface.

Return Value The handle to the logical font is returned when successful. `NULL` is returned when unsuccessful.

Function Category Font

Related Functions `CreateFont`

CreateHatchBrush

Syntax `HBRUSH CreateHatchBrush(fnStyle, clrref)`

Parameter	*Type*	*Description*
`fnStyle`	`int`	Hatch style
`clrref`	`COLORREF`	Foreground color for the brush

Description The `CreateHatchBrush` function creates a logical brush using the hatch style specified in `fnStyle` and the color specified in `clrref`. One of the following values is used for `fnStyle`:

Value	Meaning
HS_BDIAGONAL	45-degree upward hatch
HS_CROSS	Crosshatch with vertical/horizontal lines
HS_DIAGCROSS	45-degree crosshatch
HS_FDIAGONAL	45-degree downward hatch
HS_HORIZONTAL	Horizontal hatch
HS_VERTICAL	Vertical hatch

Return Value The handle for the created logical brush is returned when successful. NULL is returned when unsuccessful.

Function Category Drawing Tool

Related Functions CreatePatternBrush, CreateSolidBrush, SelectObject

CreateIC

Syntax

```
HDC CreateIC(lpszDriver, lpszDevice, lpszOutput,
             lpvInitData)
```

Parameter	Type	Description
lpszDriver	LPCSTR	Pointer to string that contains the DOS filename of the device driver
lpszDevice	LPCSTR	Pointer to string that contains the name of the device
lpszOutput	LPCSTR	Pointer to string that contains the DOS file name or device name for ouput
lpvInitData	const void FAR*	Pointer to initialization data for the device driver. The initialization data is stored in a DEVMODE structure.

Description The CreateIC function creates an information context for the device specified in lpszDriver, lpszDevice, and lpszOutput. lpvInitData points to the initialization data for the device driver.

Return Value The handle for the information context is returned when successful. `NULL` is returned when unsuccessful.

Function Category Device Context

Related Functions `CreateDC`, `DeleteDC`

CreateIcon

Syntax

```
HICON CreateIcon(hinst, nWidth, nHeight, bPlanes,
                 bBitsPixel, lpvANDbits, lpvXORbits)
```

Parameter	*Type*	*Description*
`hinst`	`HINSTANCE`	Instance of module creating the icon
`nWidth`	`int`	Width of icon in pixels
`nHeight`	`int`	Height of icon in pixels
`bPlanes`	`BYTE`	Number of planes in XOR mask of the icon
`bBitsPixel`	`BYTE`	Number of bits per pixel in XOR mask of the icon
`lpvANDbits`	`const void FAR*`	Pointer to an array containing the bits for the AND mask of the icon
`lpvXORbits`	`const void FAR*`	Pointer to an array containing the bits for the XOR mask of the icon

Description The `CreateIcon` function creates an icon using the specified height, width, and patterns.

Return Value The handle to the icon is returned when successful. `NULL` is returned when unsuccessful.

Function Category Painting

Related Functions `DrawIcon`

CreateMenu

Syntax `HMENU CreateMenu()`

Description The `CreateMenu` function creates an empty menu. Menu items are added to the menu using `AppendMenu` or `InsertMenu`.

Return Value The handle of the new menu is returned when successfully created. When unable to create the menu, `NULL` is returned.

Function Category Menu

Related Functions `AppendMenu`, `DeleteMenu`, `DestroyMenu`, `InsertMenu`, `SetMenu`

CreateMetaFile

Syntax `HDC CreateMetaFile(lpszFile)`

Parameter	*Type*	*Description*
`lpszFile`	`LPCSTR`	Pointer to a null-terminated string that defines the name of the metafile

Description The `CreateMetaFile` function creates a metafile device context. `lpszFile` points to the string that defines the name of the metafile. `lpszFile` can be set to `NULL` to create a memory metafile.

Return Value The handle to the metafile device context is returned when successful. `NULL` is returned when unsuccessful.

Function Category Metafile

Related Functions `CloseMetaFile`, `DeleteMetaFile`

CreatePalette

Syntax `HPALETTE CreatePalette(lplgpl)`

Parameter	Type	Description
lplgp lconst	LOGPALETTE FAR*	Pointer to LOGPALETTE structure containing information on the colors in the logical palette

Description The CreatePalette function creates a logical palette using the information in the data structure of type LOGPALETTE pointed to by lplgpl. The LOGPALETTE structure follows.

```
typedef struct tagLOGPALETTE
    {
    WORD palVersion;
    WORD palNumEntries;
    PALETTEENTRY palPalEntry[1];
} LOGPALETTE;
```

in which

palVersion is the Windows version number (0X300 for Windows 3.0 and 3.1)

palNumEntries is the number of entries in the palette

palPalEntry[1] is an array of PALETTEENTRY data structures defining the color and use of each palette entry. The PALETTEENTRY data structure follows.

```
typedef struct
    {
    BYTE peRed;
    BYTE peGreen;
    BYTE peBlue;
    BYTE peFlags;
} PALETTEENTRY;
```

in which

peRed is the intensity of red for the palette entry

peGreen is the intensity of green for the palette entry

peBlue is the intensity of blue for the palette entry

peFlags is NULL or one of the following values:

Value	Meaning
PC_EXPLICIT	Low-order word of the palette entry contains a hardware palette index
PC_NOCOLLAPSE	Color will be placed in an unused entry in the palette; color will not replace existing entry
PC_RESERVED	Entry is used for palette animation; no color can be matched to this entry

Return Value The handle for the logical palette is returned when successful. NULL is returned when unsuccessful.

Function Category Color Palette

Related Functions AnimatePalette, DeleteObject

CreatePatternBrush

Syntax `HBRUSH CreatePatternBrush(hbmp)`

Parameter	Type	Description
hbmp	HBITMAP	Bitmap used for brush pattern

Description The CreatePatternBrush function creates a logical brush that uses the pattern specified in hbmp.

Return Value The handle of the created brush is returned when successful. NULL is returned when unsuccessful.

Function Category Drawing Tool

Related Functions CreateDIBPatternBrush

CreatePen

Syntax `HPEN CreatePen(fnPenStyle, nWidth, clrref)`

Parameter	Type	Description
fnPenStyle	int	Pen style
nWidth	int	Width of pen in logical units
clrref	COLORREF	Color of pen

Description The CreatePen function creates a logical pen. fnPenStyle specifies the style of the pen. nWidth specifies the width, in logical units, of the pen. clrref specifies the pen color. One of the following constants is used for fnPenStyle:

Constant	Meaning
PS_SOLID	Solid pen
PS_DASH	Dashed pen
PS_DOT	Dotted pen
PS_DASHDOT	Dash—dotted pen
PS_DASHDOTDOT	Dash—dot—dotted pen
PS_NULL	Null pen
PS_INSIDEFRAME	Pen that draws line inside the frame of ellipses and rectangles when using the Chord, Ellipse, Pie, Rectangle, and RoundRect functions

Return Value The handle for the created logical pen is returned when successful. NULL is returned when unsuccessful.

Function Category Drawing Tool

Related Functions CreatePenIndirect, SelectObject

CreatePenIndirect

Syntax `HPEN CreatePenIndirect(lplgpn)`

Parameter	Type	Description
lplgpn	LOGPEN FAR*	Pointer to LOGPEN data structure containing information on the logical pen

Description The `CreatePenIndirect` function creates a logical pen using the information in the data structure of type `LOGPEN` pointed to by `lplgpn`. The `LOGPEN` structure follows.

```
typedef struct tagLOGPEN {
     WORD lopnStyle;
     POINT lopnWidth;
     COLORREF lopnColor;
} LOGPEN;
```

in which

`lopnStyle` is the pen style and is chosen from one of the following constants:

Constant	*Value*
PS_SOLID	0
PS_DASH	1
PS_DOT	2
PS_DASHDOT	3
PS_DASHDOTDOT	4
PS_NULL	5
PS_INSIDEFRAME	6

`lopnWidth` is the pen width in logical units

`lopnColor` is the pen color.

Return Value The handle for the created logical pen is returned when successful. `NULL` is returned when unsuccessful.

Function Category Drawing Tool

Related Functions `CreatePen`, `DeleteObject`, `SelectObject`

CreatePolygonRgn

Syntax `HRGN CreatePolygonRgn(lppt, cPoints, fnPolyFillMode)`

Parameter	Type	Description
lppt	const POINT FAR*	Pointer to an array of POINT data structures in which each data structure specifies a point on the polygon
cPoints	int	Number of points in the array
fnPolyFillMode	int	Polygon-filling mode; set to ALTERNATE or WINDING

Description The CreatePolygonRgn function creates a polygonal region using the points specified in lppt. Each point in lppt is specified using a data structure of type POINT. The POINT data structure follows.

```
typedef struct tagPOINT {
    int x;
    int y;
} POINT;
```

in which

x specifies the horizontal coordinate of the point

y specifies the vertical coordinate of the point.

Return Value The handle to the new region is returned when successful. NULL is returned when unsuccessful.

Function Category Region

Related Functions CreatePolyPolygonRgn

CreatePolyPolygonRgn

Syntax

```
HRGN CreatePolyPolygonRgn(lppt, lpnPolyCount, cIntegers,
                          fnPolyFillMode)
```

Parameter	Type	Description
lppt	const POINT FAR*	Pointer to an array of POINT data structures that define the points in the polygons

Parameter	*Type*	*Description*
`lpnPolyCount`	`const int FAR*`	Pointer to an array of integers that define the number of points from `lppt` used for each of the polygons
`cIntegers`	`int`	Total number of integer values in `lpnPolyCount` array
`fnPolyFillMode`	`int`	Polygon-filling mode; either `ALTERNATE` or `WINDING`

Description The `CreatePolyPolygonRgn` function creates a region that is made up of a series of closed, filled polygons. `lppt` is a pointer to an array of `POINT` data structures. These `POINT` data structures contain the individual points for the polygons. The `POINT` data structure follows. The number of points from `lppt` required to create each polygon is contained in the array pointed to by `lpnPolyCount`. The number of polygons to draw is specified in `cIntegers`.

```
typedef struct tagPOINT {
     int x;
     int y;
} POINT;
```

in which

`x` specifies the horizontal coordinate of the point

`y` specifies the vertical coordinate of the point.

Return Value The handle to the new region is returned when successful. `NULL` is returned when unsuccessful.

Function Category Region

Related Functions `CreatePolygonRgn`

CreatePopupMenu

Syntax `HMENU CreatePopupMenu()`

Description The `CreatePopupMenu` function creates an empty pop-up menu. Menu items are added to the menu with `AppendMenu` or `InsertMenu`. The application is responsible for adding the pop-up menu to existing menus.

Return Value The handle of the new pop-up window is returned when successfully created. When unable to create the pop-up window, `NULL` is returned.

Function Category Menu

Related Functions `AppendMenu`, `CreateMenu`, `InsertMenu`, `TrackPopupMenu`

CreateRectRgn

Syntax

```
HRGN CreateRectRgn(nLeftRect, nTopRect, nRightRect,
                    nBottomRect)
```

Parameter	*Type*	*Description*
`nLeftRect`	`int`	X coordinate of upper-left corner of region
`nTopRect`	`int`	Y coordinate of upper-left corner of region
`nRightRect`	`int`	X coordinate of lower-right corner of region
`nBottomRect`	`int`	Y coordinate of lower-right corner of region

Description The `CreateRectRgn` function creates a rectangular region using the coordinates specified in `nLeftRect`, `nTopRect`, `nRightRect`, and `nBottomRect`.

Return Value The handle to the new region is returned when successful. `NULL` is returned when unsuccessful.

Function Category Region

Related Functions `CreateRectRgnIndirect`, `CreateRoundRectRgn`

CreateRectRgnIndirect

Syntax `HRGN CreateRectRgnIndirect(lprc)`

Parameter	*Type*	*Description*
`lprc`	`const RECT FAR*`	Pointer to a `RECT` data structure containing the coordinates of the rectangular region

Description The `CreateRectRgnIndirect` function creates a rectangular region using the coordinates in the data structure of type `RECT` pointed to by `lprc`. The `RECT` data structure follows.

```
typedef struct tagRECT{
     int left;
     int top;
     int right;
     int bottom;
} RECT;
```

in which

`left` is the x coordinate of the upper-left corner

`top` is the y coordinate of the upper-left corner

`right` is the x coordinate of the lower-right corner

`bottom` is the y coordinate of the lower-right corner.

Return Value The handle to the new region is returned when successful. `NULL` is returned when unsuccessful.

Function Category Region

Related Functions `CreateRectRgn`, `CreateRoundRectRgn`

CreateRoundRectRgn

Syntax `HRGN CreateRoundRectRgn(nLeftRect, nTopRect, nRightRect, nBottomRect, nWidthEllipse, nHeightEllipse)`

Parameter	*Type*	*Description*
nLeftRect	int	X coordinate of upper-left corner of rectangular region
nTopRect	int	Y coordinate of upper-left corner of rectangular region
nRightRect	int	X coordinate of lower-right corner of rectangular region
nBottomRect	int	Y coordinate of lower-right corner of rectangular region
nWidthEllipse	int	Width of ellipse used to create the rounded corners
nHeightEllipse	int	Height of ellipse used to create the rounded corners

Description The `CreateRoundRectRgn` function creates a rounded, rectangular region. `(nLeftRect, nTopRect)` specify the coordinates of the upper-left corner of the rectangular region. `(nRightRect:, nBottomRect)` specify the coordinates of the lower-right corner of the rectangular region. `(nWidthEllipse, nHeightEllipse)` specify the shape of the rounded corners of the rounded, rectangular region.

Return Value The handle to the new region is returned when successful. `NULL` is returned when unsuccessful.

Function Category Region

Related Functions `CreateRectRgn`, `CreateRectRgnIndirect`

CreateScalableFontResource

Syntax

```
BOOL CreateScalableFontResource(fHidden, lpszResourceFile,
                                lpszFontFile,
                                lpszCurrentPath)
```

Parameter	*Type*	*Description*
fHidden	UINT	Read-only embedded font flag. Set to zero to indicate that the font has read/write permission. Set to 1 to indicate that the font has read/write permission and should be hidden from other applications.
lpszResourceFile	LPCSTR	Pointer to a null-terminated string that specifies the name of the font resource file
lpszFontFile	LPCSTR	Pointer to a null-terminated string that specifies the name of the scalable font file
lpszCurrentPath	LPCSTR	Pointer to a null-terminated string that specifies the path of the scalable font file

Description The `CreateScalableFontResource` function creates a font resource file and is used by applications that install TrueType fonts. `lpszResourceFile` specifies the name of the resulting font resource file. `lpszFontFile` specifies the name of the scalable font file. `lpszCurrentPath` specifies the path to the scalable font file. The `AddFontResource` function can be used to install the created font.

Return Value `TRUE` is returned when successful. `FALSE` is returned when unsuccessful.

Function Category Font, TrueType

Related Functions `AddFontResource`

CreateSolidBrush

Syntax `HBRUSH CreateSolidBrush(clrref)`

Parameter	*Type*	*Description*
`clrref`	`COLORREF`	Color of brush

Description The `CreateSolidBrush` function creates a logical brush using the solid color specified in `clrref`.

Return Value The handle for the created logical brush is returned when successful. `NULL` is returned when unsuccessful.

Function Category Drawing Tool

Related Functions `CreateBrushIndirect`, `CreateHatchBrush`, `CreatePatternBrush`

CreateWindow

Syntax

```
HWND CreateWindow(lpszClassName, lpszWindowName, dwStyle,
                  X, Y, nWidth, nHeight, hwndParent, hmenu,
                  hinst, lpvParam)
```

Parameter	*Type*	*Description*
`lpszClassName`	`LPCSTR`	Pointer to a null-terminated character string that names the window class
`lpszWindowName`	`LPCSTR`	Pointer to a null-terminated character string that represents the window name
`dwStyle`	`DWORD`	The style of window to create
`X`	`int`	Initial horizontal position of the window's upper-left corner, expressed in screen coordinates. For child windows, X is relative to the client area of the parent window.

Parameter	*Type*	*Description*
Y	int	Initial vertical position of the window's upper-left corner, expressed in screen coordinates. For child windows, Y is relative to the client area of the parent window.
nWidth	int	Window width in device units
nHeight	int	Window height in device units
hwndParent	HWND	Parent or owner of the window to create
hmenu	HMENU	Menu or child window identifier
hinst	HINSTANCE	Instance of module associated with the window
lpvParam	void FAR*	Value passed to the window through the CREATESTRUCT data structure referenced by the lParam parameter of the WM_CREATE message

Description The CreateWindow function creates an overlapped, pop-up, or child window. The CreateWindow sends the WM_CREATE, WM_GETMINMAXINFO, and WM_NCCREATE messages to the specified window. lpszClassName points to a null-terminated string that names the window class. The values that follow can be used for lpszClassName:

Value	*Meaning*
BUTTON	A small rectangular child window representing a two-state button that can be turned on or off
COMBOBOX	A control that contains a selection field and an edit control
EDIT	A rectangular child window that accepts user input
LISTBOX	A list of character strings
MDICLIENT	MDI client window

Value	*Meaning*
SCROLLBAR	A rectangle containing a direction arrow at either end and a position indicator
STATIC	A simple text field, box, or rectangle

`lpszWindowName` points to the string that represents the window name. `dwStyle` specifies the style for the created window. The table that follows shows the values that can be combined, using bitwise OR, for `dwStyle`.

Value	*Meaning*
	Dialog Box
DS_LOCALEDIT	Edit controls in the dialog box will use all memory in the application's data segment
DS_MODALFRAME	Creates a dialog box with a modal dialog box frame
DS_NOIDLEMSG	Suppresses `WM_ENTERIDLE` messages while the dialog box is displayed
DS_SYSMODAL	Creates a system modal dialog box
	Window Styles
WS_BORDER	Creates a window with a border
WS_CAPTION	Creates a window with a title bar; cannot be used with `WS_DLGFRAME`
WS_CHILD	Creates a child window; cannot be used with `WS_POPUP`
WS_CHILDWINDOW	Creates a child window with style `WS_CHILD`
WS_CLIPCHILDREN	Excludes the area occupied by child windows when drawing within the parent window
WS_CLIPSIBLINGS	Clips child windows relative to each other; for use with `WS_CHILD` only
WS_DISABLED	Creates a window that is disabled
WS_DLGFRAME	Creates a window with a double border and no title
WS_GROUP	Defines the first control from a group that the user can move from one control to another with the direction keys

Value	Meaning
WS_HSCROLL	Creates a window with a horizontal scroll bar
WS_ICONIC	Creates an iconic window
WS_MAXIMIZE	Creates a window that is to be maximized
WS_MAXIMIZEBOX	Creates a window with a maximize box
WS_MINIMIZE	Creates a window that is minimum size
WS_MINIMIZEBOX	Creates a window with a minimize box
WS_OVERLAPPED	Creates a window with a border and a caption
WS_OVERLAPPEDWINDOW	Creates an overlapped window with styles WS_OVERLAPPED, WS_CAPTION, WS_SYSMENU, WS_THICKFRAME, WS_MINIMIZEBOX, and WS_MAXIMIZEBOX
WS_POPUP	Creates a pop-up window; cannot be used with WS_CHILD
WS_POPUPWINDOW	Creates a pop-up window with styles WS_BORDER, WS_POPUP, and WS_SYSMENU
WS_SYSMENU	Creates a window with a System menu box in the title bar
WS_TABSTOP	Specifies the controls that a user can move to with the TAB key
WS_THICKFRAME	Creates a window with a thick frame
WS_VISIBLE	Creates a visible overlapped or pop-up window
WS_VSCROLL	Creates a window with a vertical scroll bar
	BUTTON Class Control Styles
BS_AUTOCHECKBOX	Small rectangular button that may be checked; button toggles when clicked
BS_AUTORADIOBUTTON	Small circular button that can be checked; when clicked, the checkmarks are removed from the other radio buttons in the group
BS_AUTO3STATE	Small rectangular button that changes state when clicked; supports three states—on, off,or grayed
BS_CHECKBOX	Small rectangular button that may be checked

Value	Meaning
BS_DEFPUSHBUTTON	Button designated as the default button by its bold border
BS_GROUPBOX	Groups the buttons in the designated rectangle
BS_LEFTTEXT	Forces text to appear on the left side (the right side is the default) for styles BS_CHECKBOX, BS_RADIOBUTTON, and BS_3STATE
BS_OWNERDRAW	Owner draw button; parent is notified when the button is clicked
BS_PUSHBUTTON	Button containing the specified text
BS_RADIOBUTTON	Small circular button that can be checked
BS_3STATE	Small rectangular button that can be checked; supports three states—on, off, and grayed
COMBOBOX Class Control Styles	
CBS_AUTOHSCROLL	Scrolls the text in the edit control to the right when text reaches the end of the line
CBS_DISABLENOSCROLL	Vertical scroll bar of list box disabled when list box does not contain enough items to scroll. Normally, the vertical scroll bar of a list box is hidden when there are not enough items to scroll.
CBS_DROPDOWN	List box is displayed only when the icon beside the selection field is selected
CBS_DROPDOWNLIST	Like CBS_DROPDOWN; edit control, however, is replaced by a static text item that displays the current selection from the list box
CBS_HASSTRINGS	Owner-draw combo box contains items that consist of strings
CBS_NOINTEGRALHEIGHT	Size of combo box is exactly the size specified by the application. Windows normally sizes the combo box.
CBS_OEMCONVERT	Text from combo box edit control is converted from ANSI to OEM and back to ANSI

Value	Meaning
CBS_OWNERDRAWFIXED	List box owner draws the contents of the list box; contents are all the same height
CBS_OWNERDRAWVARIABLE	List box owner draws the contents of the list box; contents are not all the same height
CBS_SIMPLE	List box is always displayed
CBS_SORT	Strings entered in the list box are sorted automatically
EDIT Class Control Styles	
ES_AUTOHSCROLL	Automatically scrolls text to the right 10 spaces when the end of the line is reached
ES_AUTOVSCROLL	Automatically scrolls the text up one page when Enter is pressed on the last line
ES_CENTER	Center text in a multiline edit control
ES_LEFT	Left justifies text
ES_LOWERCASE	Displays all entered characters as lowercase
ES_MULTILINE	Multiline edit control
ES_NOHIDESEL	Disables the default actions of hiding the selection when control loses the input focus and inverting the selection when the control receives the input focus
ES_OEMCONVERT	Converts text in the edit control from ANSI to OEM to ANSI
ES_PASSWORD	Displays * for each character entered into the edit control
ES_READONLY	User cannot enter or edit text on the edit control
ES_RIGHT	Right justifies text in a multiline edit control
ES_UPPERCASE	Displays all entered characters as uppercase
ES_WANTRETURN	Carriage-return is inserted when ENTER key is pressed in a multiline edit control

Value	*Meaning*
	LISTBOX Class Control Styles
LBS_DISABLENOSCROLL	Vertical scroll bar of list box is disabled when list box does not contain enough items to scroll. Normally, the vertical scroll bar is hidden when there are not enough items to scroll.
LBS_EXTENDEDSEL	Allows user to make multiple selections from the list box
LBS_HASSTRINGS	Owner draw list box contains items made up of strings
LBS_MULTICOLUMN	Multicolumn list box with horizontal scroll
LBS_MULTIPLESEL	String selection is toggled each time a string is clicked or double-clicked; multiple selections can be made
LBS_NOINTEGRALHEIGHT	List box has the exact size specified by the application creating the list box
LBS_NOREDRAW	List box is not redrawn after modification
LBS_NOTIFY	Input message is sent to the parent when a string is clicked or double-clicked
LBS_OWNERDRAWFIXED	List box owner draws contents of the list box; all items are same height
LBS_OWNERDRAWVARIABLE	List box owner draws the contents of the list box; items do not have to be the same height
LBS_SORT	Strings in the list box are sorted alphabetically
LBS_STANDARD	Strings in the list box are sorted alphabetically and an input message is sent to the parent window when a string is clicked or double-clicked
LBS_USETABSTOPS	List box recognizes tab characters when drawing strings
LBS_WANTKEYBOARDINPUT	WM_VKEYTOITEM or WM_CHARTOITEM message is sent to the owner of the list box when a key is pressed while the list box has the input focus

Value	Meaning
	SCROLLBAR Class Control Styles
SBS_BOTTOMALIGN	Bottom edge of scroll bar is aligned with the bottom edge of the rectangle specified by X, Y, nWidth, and nHeight from the CreateWindowfunction; used with SBS_HORIZON
SBS_HORZ	Horizontal scroll bar
SBS_LEFTALIGN	Left edge of scroll bar is aligned with the left edge of the rectangle specified by X, Y, nWidth, and nHeight from the CreateWindow function; used with SBS_VERT
SBS_RIGHTALIGN	Right edge of scroll bar is aligned with the right edge of the rectangle specified by X, Y, nWidth, and nHeight from the CreateWindow function; used with SBS_VERT
SBS_SIZEBOX	Specifies a size box
SBS_SIZEBOXBOTTOMRIGHTALIGN	Lower-right corner of size box is aligned with the lower-right corner of the rectangle specified by X, Y, nWidth, and nHeight from the CreateWindow function; used with SBS_SIZEBOX
SBS_SIZEBOXTOPLEFTALIGN	Upper-left corner of size box is aligned with the upper-left corner of the rectangle specified by X, Y, nWidth, and nHeight from the CreateWindow function; used with SBS_SIZEBOX
SBS_TOPALIGN	Top edge of scroll bar is aligned with the top edge of the rectangle specified by X, Y, nWidth, and nHeight from the CreateWindow function; used with SBS_HORIZON
SBS_VERT	Vertical scroll bar
	STATIC Class Control Styles
SS_BLACKFRAME	Box has frame with same color as window frames

Value	*Meaning*
`SS_BLACKRECT`	Rectangle filled with same color as window frames
`SS_CENTER`	Simple rectangle with text centered in rectangle; text is wrapped to next line if necessary
`SS_GRAYFRAME`	Box has frame with the same color as screen background
`SS_GRAYRECT`	Rectangle filled with the same color as screen background
`SS_ICON`	Icon is displayed in the dialog box
`SS_LEFT`	Simple rectangle with text left justified inside the rectangle; text is wrapped to next line if necessary
`SS_LEFTNOWORDWRAP`	Simple rectangle with text left justified inside the rectangle; text is not wrapped to next line
`SS_NOPREFIX`	Without this style, the & character will be interpreted as an accelerator prefix character
`SS_RIGHT`	Simple rectangle with text right justified inside the rectangle; text is wrapped to the next line if necessary
`SS_SIMPLE`	Simple rectangle with text left justified; text cannot be altered
`SS_WHITEFRAME`	Box with frame drawn in the same color as the window background
`SS_WHITERECT`	Rectangle filled with the same color as the window background

Return Value The window handle of the created window is returned when successful. When unable to create the window, `NULL` is returned.

Function Category Window Creation

Related Functions `CreateWindowEx`, `DestroyWindow`

CreateWindowEx

Syntax

```
HWND CreateWindowEx(dwExStyle, lpszClassName,
                    lpszWindowName, dwStyle, X, Y, nWidth,
                    nHeight, hwndParent, hmenu, hinst,
                    lpvCreateParams)
```

Parameter	*Type*	*Description*
`dwExStyle`	`DWORD`	Extended style for the window to create
`lpszClassName`	`LPCSTR`	Pointer to a null-terminated character string that names the window class
`lpszWindowName`	`LPCSTR`	Pointer to a null-terminated character string that represents the window name
`dwStyle`	`DWORD`	The style of window to create
`X`	`int`	Initial horizontal position of the window's upper-left corner, expressed in screen coordinates. For child windows, X is relative to the client area of the parent window.
`Y`	`int`	Initial vertical position of the window's upper-left corner, expressed in screen coordinates. For child windows, Y is relative to the client area of the parent window.
`nWidth`	`int`	Window width in device units
`nHeight`	`int`	Window height in device units
`hwndParent`	`HWND`	Parent or owner of the window to create
`hmenu`	`HMENU`	Menu or child window identifier

Parameter	*Type*	*Description*
`hinst`	`HINSTANCE`	Instance of module associated with the window
`lpvCreateParams`	`void FAR*`	Value passed to the window through the `CREATESTRUCT` data structure referenced by the `lParam` parameter of the `WM_CREATE` message

Description The `CreateWindowEx` function creates an overlapped, pop-up, or child window using the specified extended style. `dwExStyle` specifies the extended style to use. The value for the extended style specified in `dwExStyle` is chosen from the following list:

Value	*Meaning*
`WS_EX_ACCEPTFILES`	Window accepts drag-drop files
`WS_EX_DLGMODALFRAME`	Window with a double border; will contain a title bar if `WS_CAPTION` is specified in dwStyle
`WS_EX_NOPARENTNOTIFY`	A child window with this style will not send the `WM_PARENTNOTIFY` message to the parent window when the child window is created or destroyed
`WS_EX_TOPMOST`	Window is placed on top of all windows and should remain on top even when deactivated

The remainder of the parameters for `CreateWindowEx` are the same as the parameters for `CreateWindow`. See `CreateWindow` in this section for a description of these parameters.

Return Value The handle for the new window is returned. `NULL` is returned when the window cannot be created.

Function Category Window Creation

Related Functions `CreateWindow`, `DestroyWindow`

DdeAbandonTransaction

Syntax

```
BOOL DdeAbandonTransaction(idInst, hConv,
                           idTransaction)
```

Parameter	*Type*	*Description*
idInst	DWORD	Application instance retrieved from previous call to DdeInitialize
hConv	HCONV	Conversation in which transaction was initiated
idTransaction	DWORD	Transaction to terminate; if idTransaction is NULL, all active transactions are abandoned

Description The DdeAbandonTransaction function abandons an asynchronous transaction. idTransaction specifies the transaction to terminate. All resources associated with the transaction are terminated.

Return Value TRUE is returned when successful. FALSE is returned when unsuccessful.

Function Category DDE

Related Functions DdeGetLastError, DdeInitialize

DdeAccessData

Syntax

```
LPBYTE DdeAccessData(hData, lpdwDataLen)
```

Parameter	*Type*	*Description*
hData	HDDEDATA	Global memory object handle to access
lpdwDataLen	LPDWORD	Pointer to value to receive the number of bytes for the global memory object in hData

Description The DdeAccessData function allows the application to read data from the global memory object specified by the handle in hData. When DdeAccessData has finished reading the data, the application should call the DdeUnaccessData function.

Return Value The pointer to the first byte of the global memory object is returned when successful. NULL is returned when unsuccessful.

Function Category DDE

Related Functions DdeGetLastError, DdeUnaccessData

DdeAddData

Syntax

```
HDDEDATA DdeAddData(hData, lpbSrcBuf, cbAddData,
                    offObj)
```

Parameter	*Type*	*Description*
hData	HDDEDATA	Handle of global memory object to receive the additional data
lpbSrcBufLP	BYTE	Pointer to the data buffer to add to the global memory object
cbAddData	DWORD	Number of bytes of data to add to the global memory object
offObj	DWORD	Number of bytes to offset the additional data from the beginning of the global memory object

Description The DdeAddData function adds the data pointed to by pSrcBuf to the global memory object specified by hData. cbAddData specifies the length of the added data. offObj specifies the offset, relative to the beginning of the global memory object, where the data will be added. When the added data overlaps existing data in the global memory object, the new data overwrites the existing data.

Return Value The new handle to the global memory object is returned when successful. Zero is returned when unsuccessful.

Function Category DDE

Related Functions `DdeCreateDataHandle`, `DdeGetLastError`

DdeClientTransaction

Syntax

```
HDDEDATA DdeClientTransaction(lpbData, cbDataLen,
                              hConv, hszItem, wFmt, wType,
                              dwTimeout, lpdwResult)
```

Parameter	*Type*	*Description*
`lpbData`	`LPBYTE`	Pointer to data that will be passed to the server
`cbDataLen`	`DWORD`	Number of bytes of data in `lpbData`. `cbDataLen` is –1 when `lpbData` contains a data handle.
`hConv`	`HCONV`	Specifies the conversation
`hszItem`	`HSZ`	Data item for which data is being exchanged
`wFmt`	`WORD`	Clipboard format for the data
`wType`	`WORD`	Transaction type
`dwTimeout`	`DWORD`	Maximum number of milliseconds that the client should wait for a response from the server during asynchronous transaction
`lpdwResult`	`LPDWORD`	Pointer to variable to receive the result of the transaction; can be `NULL` if there is no need to check the result

Description The `DdeClientTransaction` function initiates a data transaction between the client and server applications. The client application can call this function only after it has initiated a conversation with the server. `lpbData` points to the data passed to the server. `wType` specifies the type of transaction and can be any of the following values:

Value	Meaning
XTYP_ADVSTART	Initiates advise loop. XTYP_ADVSTART can be combined with one or both of the following flags to modify the advise loop type:

Value	Meaning
XTYP_NODATA	Server notifies client of any data change but no data is sent
XTYP_ACKREQ	Server waits for the client to acknowledge receipt of data item before sending next data item
XTYP_ADVSTOP	Ends advise loop
XTYP_EXECUTE	Initiates an execute transaction
XTYP_POKE	Initiates a poke transaction
XTYP_REQUEST	Initiates a request transaction

Return Value The return value is defined as follows for the specified successful conditions. FALSE is returned when unsuccessful.

- Synchronous transactions (client receives and expects data from the server): Data handle of the data is returned.
- Synchronous transactions (client does not expect data from the server): TRUE is returned.
- Asynchronous transactions: TRUE is returned when successful; FALSE is returned when unsuccessful.

Function Category DDE

Related Functions DdeConnect, DdeCreateStringHandle, DdeGetLastError

DdeCmpStringHandles

Syntax `int DdeCmpStringHandles(hsz1, hsz2)`

Parameter	Type	Description
hsz1	HSZ	Handle of first string
hsz2	HSZ	Handle of second string

Description The DdeCmpStringHandles function performs a non-case sensitive comparison of the strings specified in hsz1 and hsz2 and returns the result of the comparison.

Return Value The return value indicates the result of the comparison as follows:

- 1 is returned when hsz1 is 0 or less than hsz2
- 0 is returned when hsz1 and hsz2 are equal
- 1 is returned when hsz2 is 0 or less than hsz1

Function Category DDE

Related Functions DdeAccessData, DDECreateStringHandle, DDEProcStringHandle

DdeConnect

Syntax `HCONV DdeConnect(idInst, hszService, hszTopic, pCC)`

Parameter	*Type*	*Description*
idInst	DWORD	Specifies the application instance obtained through a previous call to DdeInitialize
hszService	HSZ	Specifies the handle of the service name of the server application and is obtained through a previous call to DdeCreateStringHandle
hszTopic	HSZ	Specifies the handle of the string containing the topic name for the conversion to be established and is obtained through a previous call to DdeCreateStringHandle
pCC	PCONVCONTEXT	Pointer to CONVCONTEXT data structure containing conversation context information

Description The DdeConnect function initiates a conversation between the client and server applications. The service and topic names specified in hszService and hszTopic, respectively, defines the conversation. pCC points to a data structure of type CONVCONTEXT that contains conversation context information. The CONVCONTEXT data structure follows.

```
#include <ddeml.h>
typedef struct _CONVCONTEXT
     {
     WORD cb;
     WORD wFlags;
     WORD wCountryID;
     int iCodePage;
     DWORD dwLangID;
     DWORD dwSecurity;
} CONVCONTEXT;
```

in which

cb is the number of bytes in the CONVCONTEXT structure

wFlags specifies conversation context flags; no flags are currently defined

wCountryID is the country code ID for the topic and item name strings

iCodePage is the code page for the topic and item name strings

dwLangID is the language ID for the topic and item name strings

dwSecurity is a private security code defined by the application.

Return Value The conversation handle is returned when successful. NULL is returned when unsuccessful.

Function Category DDE

Related Functions DdeCreateStringHandle, DdeGetLastError

DdeConnectList

Syntax

```
HCONVLIST DdeConnectList(idInst, hszService,
                         hszTopic, hConvList, pCC)
```

Parameter	*Type*	*Description*
idInst	DWORD	Specifies the application instance
hszService	HSZ	Specifies the string that contains the service name of the server application
hszTopic	HSZ	Specifies the string that contains the topic name
hConvList	HCONVLIST	Specifies the conversation list to enumerate
pCC	PCONVCONTEXT	Pointer to a CONVCONTEXT data structure that contains conversation context information

Description The DdeConnectList function initiates conversations with all server applications that support the service and topic names specified in hszService and hszTopic, respectively. This function can also be used to enumerate a list of conversation handles. pCC points to a data structure of type CONVCONTEXT that contains conversation context information. The CONVCONTEXT data structure follows.

```
#include <ddeml.h>
typedef struct _CONVCONTEXT
     {
     WORD cb;
     WORD wFlags;
     WORD wCountryID;
     int iCodePage;
     DWORD dwLangID;
     DWORD dwSecurity;
} CONVCONTEXT;
```

in which

cb is the number of bytes in the CONVCONTEXT structure

wFlags specifies conversation context flags; no flags are currently defined `wCountryID` is the country code ID for the topic and item name strings

`iCodePage` is the code page for the topic and item name strings

`dwLangID` is the language ID for the topic and item name strings

`dwSecurity` is a private security code defined by the application.

Return Value The handle of the new conversation list is returned when successful. `NULL` is returned when unsuccessful.

Function Category DDE

Related Functions `DdeConnect`, `DdeDisconnectList`

DdeCreateDataHandle

Syntax

```
HDDEDATA DdeCreateDataHandle(idInst, lpbSrcBuf,
                             cbInitData, offSrcBuf,
                             hszItem, wFmt, afCmd)
```

Parameter	*Type*	*Description*
`idInst`	`DWORD`	Application instance
`lpbSrcBuf`	`LPBYTE`	Pointer to buffer containing the data to be copied to the global memory object
`cbInitData`	`DWORD`	Number of bytes to allocate for the global memory object
`offSrcBuf`	`DWORD`	Number of bytes of offset for the buffer pointed to by `lpbSrcBuf`
`hszItem`	`HSZ`	String that specifies the data item that corresponds to the global memory object
`wFmt`	`WORD`	Clipboard format of the data
`afCmd`	`WORD`	Creation flag: set to `HDATA_APPOWNED`— Server application that calls `DdeCreateDataHandle` will own the data handle

Description The DdeCreateDataHandle function creates a global memory object. The global memory object is filled with the data in the buffer pointed to by lpbSrcBuf.

Return Value The data handle is returned when successful. NULL is returned when unsuccessful.

Function Category DDE

Related Functions DdeFreeDataHandle, DdeGetLastError

DdeCreateStringHandle

Syntax

```
HSZ DdeCreateStringHandle(idInst, lpszString,
                          idCodePage)
```

Parameter	*Type*	*Description*
idInst	DWORD	Application instance
lpszString	LPSTR	Pointer to buffer containing the string that the handle is to be associated with
idCodePage	int	Code page used to render the string; should be set to CP_WINANSI or the value returned by GetKBCodePage

Description The DdeCreateStringHandle creates a handle to associate with the string specified in lpszString.

Return Value The string handle is returned when successful. NULL is returned when unsuccessful.

Function Category DDE

Related Functions DdeCmpStringHandle, DdeFreeStringHandle, DdeKeepStringHandle

DdeDisconnect

Syntax `BOOL DdeDisconnect(hConv)`

Parameter	*Type*	*Description*
`hConv`	`HCONV`	Conversation to terminate

Description The `DdeDisconnect` function terminates the conversation specified in `hConv`. The specified conversation must have been initiated with `DdeConnect` or `DdeConnectList`.

Return Value `TRUE` is returned when successful. `FALSE` is returned when unsuccessful.

Function Category DDE

Related Functions `DdeConnect`, `DdeConnectList`, `DdeDisconnectList`

DdeDisconnectList

Syntax `BOOL DdeDisconnectList(hConvList)`

Parameter	*Type*	*Description*
`hConvList`	`HCONVLIST`	Conversation list to terminate

Description The `DdeDisconnectList` function terminates the conversations associated with the conversation list specified in `hConvList`. The conversation list specified in `hConvList` must have been created using `DdeConnectList`.

Return Value `TRUE` is returned when successful. `FALSE` is returned when unsuccessful.

Function Category DDE

Related Functions `DdeConnectList`, `DdeDisconnect`

DdeEnableCallback

Syntax `BOOL DdeEnableCallback(idInst, hConv, wCmd)`

Parameter	*Type*	*Description*
`idInstD`	`WORD`	Application instance
`hConv`	`HCONV`	Conversation; can be set to `NULL` to affect all conversations
`wCmd`	`WORD`	Command code

Description The `DdeEnableCallback` function either enables or disables transactions for the conversation specified in `hConv`. When `hConv` is `NULL`, all conversations are affected. `wCmd` specifies the command code and is set to one of the following values:

Value	*Meaning*
`EC_DISABLE`	Disables all blockable transactions for the conversation. Servers can disable the following transactions: `XTYP_ADVSTART`, `XTYP_ADVSTOP`, `XTYP_EXECUTE`, `XTYP_POKE`, `XTYP_REQUEST` Clients can disable the following transactions: `XTYP_ADVDATA`, `XTYP_XACT_COMPLETE`
`EC_ENABLEALL`	Enables all transactions for the conversation
`EC_ENABLEONE`	Enables one transaction for the conversation

Return Value `TRUE` is returned when successful. `FALSE` is returned when unsuccessful.

Function Category DDE

Related Functions `DdeGetLastError`

DdeFreeDataHandle

Syntax `BOOL DdeFreeDataHandle(hData)`

Parameter	Type	Description
hData	HDDEDATA	Handle of global memory object to free

Description The DdeFreeDataHandle function frees the global memory object specified in hData and destroys the data handle. The specified handle must have been created by DdeCreateDataHandle or returned by DdeClientTransaction.

Return Value TRUE is returned when successful. FALSE is returned when unsuccessful.

Function Category DDE

Related Functions DdeCreateDataHandle, DdeGetLastError

DdeFreeStringHandle

Syntax `BOOL DdeFreeStringHandle(idInst, hsz)`

Parameter	Type	Description
idInst	DWORD	Application instance obtained through DdeInitialize function
hsz	HSZ	String handle to free

Description The DdeFreeStringHandle function frees the string handle specified in hsz for the application instance specified in idInst. The specified string handle must have been created by DdeCreateStringHandle.

Return Value TRUE is returned when successful. FALSE is returned when unsuccessful.

Function Category DDE

Related Functions DdeCreateStringHandle, DdeInitialize

DdeGetData

Syntax `DWORD DdeGetData(hData, pDest, cbMax, offSrc)`

Parameter	*Type*	*Description*
hData	HDDEDATA	Handle of global memory object that contains the data to copy
pDest	LPBYTE	Pointer to the buffer to receive the data; if set to NULL, the function returns the number of bytes of data that would be copied
cbMax	DWORD	Maximum number of bytes of data to copy to the buffer
offSrc	DWORD	Offset within the global memory object

Description The DdeGetData function copies the data in the global memory object specified in hData to the buffer specified in pDest. cbMax specifies the maximum number of bytes of data to copy to the buffer. offSrc specifies the global memory offset where copying begins.

Return Value When pDest is not NULL, the lower of the size of the global memory object or the value in cbMax is returned. When pDest is NULL, the size of the global memory object is returned.

Function Category DDE

Related Functions DdeAccessData, DdeGetLastError

DdeGetLastError

Syntax `WORD DdeGetLastError(idInst)`

Parameter	*Type*	*Description*
idInst	DWORD	Application instance identifier obtained from DdeInitialize

Description The `DdeGetLastError` function determines the most recent error for a DDE Management Library function and returns the error value. The error code is reset to `DMLERR_NO_ERROR`. The following table lists the possible return values for each of the listed functions:

Function	*Return Values*
DdeAbandonTransaction	DMLERR_DLL_NOT_INITIALIZED
	DMLERR_INVALIDPARAMETER
	DMLERR_NO_ERROR
	DMLERR_UNFOUND_QUEUE_ID
DdeAccessData	DMLERR_DLL_NOT_INITIALIZED
	DMLERR_INVALIDPARAMETER
	DMLERR_NO_ERROR
DdeAddData	DMLERR_DLL_NOT_INITIALIZED
	DMLERR_INVALIDPARAMETER
	DMLERR_MEMORY_ERROR
	DMLERR_NO_ERROR
DdeClientTransaction	DMLERR_ADVACKTIMEOUT
	DMLERR_BUSY
	DMLERR_DATAACKTIMEOUT
	DMLERR_DLL_NOT_INITIALIZED
	DMLERR_EXECACKTIMEOUT
	DMLERR_INVALIDPARAMETER
	DMLERR_MEMORY_ERROR
	DMLERR_NO_CONV_ESTABLISHED
	DMLERR_NO_ERROR
	DMLERR_NOTPROCESSED
	DMLERR_POKEACKTIMEOUT
	DMLERR_POSTMSG_FAILED
	DMLERR_REENTRANCY
	DMLERR_SERVER_DIED
	DMLERR_UNADVACKTIMEOUT
DdeConnect	DMLERR_DLL_NOT_INITIALIZED
	DMLERR_INVALIDPARAMETER
	DMLERR_NO_CONV_ESTABLISHED
	DMLERR_NO_ERROR

Function	Return Values
DdeConnectList	DMLERR_DLL_NOT_INITIALIZED
	DMLERR_INVALID_PARAMETER
	DMLERR_NO_CONV_ESTABLISHED
	DMLERR_NO_ERROR
	DMLERR_SYS_ERROR
DdeCreateDataHandle	DMLERR_DLL_NOT_INITIALIZED
	DMLERR_INVALIDPARAMETER
	DMLERR_MEMORY_ERROR
	DMLERR_NO_ERROR
DdeCreateStringHandle	DMLERR_INVALIDPARAMETER
	DMLERR_NO_ERROR
	DMLERR_SYS_ERROR
DdeEnableCallback	DMLERR_DLL_NOT_INITIALIZED
	DMLERR_NO_ERROR
	DMLERR_INVALIDPARAMETER
DdeFreeDataHandle	DMLERR_INVALIDPARAMETER
	DMLERR_NO_ERROR
DdeGetData	DMLERR_DLL_NOT_INITIALIZED
	DMLERR_INVALID_HDDEDATA
	DMLERR_INVALIDPARAMETER
	DMLERR_NO_ERROR
DdeNameService	DMLERR_DLL_NOT_INITIALIZED
	DMLERR_DLL_USAGE
	DMLERR_INVALIDPARAMETER
	DMLERR_NO_ERROR
DdePostAdvise	DMLERR_DLL_NOT_INITIALIZED
	DMLERR_DLL_USAGE
	DMLERR_NO_ERROR
DdeQueryConvInfo	DMLERR_DLL_NOT_INITIALIZED
	DMLERR_NO_CONV_ESTABLISHED
	DMLERR_NO_ERROR
	DMLERR_UNFOUND_QUEUE_ID
DdeSetUserHandle	DMLERR_DLL_NOT_INITIALIZED
	DMLERR_INVALIDPARAMETER
	DMLERR_NO_ERROR
	DMLERR_UNFOUND_QUEUE_ID

Function	*Return Values*
DdeUnaccessData	DMLERR_DLL_NOT_INITIALIZED DMLERR_INVALIDPARAMETER DMLERR_NO_ERROR

Return Value The last error code is returned.

Function Category DDE

Related Functions See Description for a list of associated functions.

DdeInitialize

Syntax

```
WORD DdeInitialize(lpidInst, pfnCallback,
                   afCmd, dwRes)
```

Parameter	*Type*	*Description*
lpidInst	LPDWORD	Pointer to application instance identifier
pfnCallback	PFNCALLBACK	Pointer to application-supplied DDE callback function
afCmd	DWORD	Flags specifying initialization instructions
dwRes	DWORD	Reserved; set to OL

Description The `DdeInitialize` function registers the calling application with the DDE Management Library. This function must be called before the application can call other DDE Management Library functions. `lpidInst` points to the application instance identifier. `lpidInst` should be set to OL at initialization. When the function is successful, `lpidInst` points to the application instance identifier. `afCmd` is an array of flags that specifies initialization instructions. `afCmd` can be a combination of any of the following values:

Value	*Meaning*
APPCLASS_MONITOR	Application can monitor DDE activity
APPCLASS_STANDARD	Application is registered as a standard, non-monitoring application
APPCMD_CLIENTONLY	Application cannot be a server for a DDE conversation
APPCMD_FILTERINITS	Application will not receive XTYP_CONNECT and XTYPE_WILDCONNECT transactions until it has created string handles and registered its service name
CBF_FAIL_ALLSVRXACTIONS	Callback function will be prevented from receiving server transactions
CBF_FAIL_ADVISES	Callback function will be prevented from receiving XTYP_ADVSTART and XTYP_ADVSTOP transactions
CBF_FAIL_CONNECTIONS	Callback function will be prevented from receiving XTYP_CONNECT and XTYP_WILDCONNECT transactions
CBF_FAIL_EXECUTES	Callback function will be prevented from receiving XTYP_EXECUTE transactions
CBF_FAIL_POKES	Callback function will be prevented from receiving XTYP_POKE transactions
CBF_FAIL_REQUESTS	Callback function will be prevented from receiving XTYP_REQUEST transactions
CBF_FAIL_SELFCONNECTIONS	Callback function will be prevented from receiving XTYP_CONNECT transactions from the application's own instance
CBF_SKIP_ALLNOTIFICATIONS	Callback function will be prevented from receving any notifications
CBF_SKIP_CONNECT_CONFIRMS	Callback function will be prevented from receiving XTYP_CONNECT_CONFIRM notifications

Value	Meaning
CBF_SKIP_DISCONNECTS	Callback function will be prevented from receiving XTYP_DISCONNECT notifications
CBF_SKIP_REGISTRATIONS	Callback function will be prevented from receiving XTYP_REGISTER notifications
CBF_SKIP_UNREGISTRATIONS	Callback function will be prevented from receiving XTYP_UNREGISTER notifications

Return Value One of the following values is returned:

DMLERR_DLL_USAGE
DMLERR_INVALIDPARAMETER
DMLERR_NO_ERROR
DMLERR_SYS_ERROR

Function Category DDE

Related Functions DdeUninitialize

DdeKeepStringHandle

Syntax `BOOL DdeKeepStringHandle(idInst, hsz)`

Parameter	Type	Description
idInst	DWORD	Application instance identifier obtained from DdeInitialize
hsz	HSZ	String handle

Description The DdeKeepStringHandle function is used by the application to save a string handle that is passed to the application's DDE callback function. Normally, the string handle is destroyed by the callback function. The DdeKeepStringHandle function increments the use count associated with the string handle and, therefore, keeps the string handle from being destroyed.

Return Value TRUE is returned when successful. FALSE is returned when unsuccessful.

Function Category DDE

Related Functions DdeCreateStringHandle, DdeFreeStringHandle

DdeNameService

Syntax `HDDEDATA DdeNameService(idInst, hsz1, hszRes, afCmd)`

Parameter	*Type*	*Description*
idInst	DWORD	Application instance obtained from DdeInitialize
hsz1	HSZ	String specifying the service name
hszRes	HSZ	Reserved; set to NULL
afCmd	WORD	Name service flags

Description The DdeNameService function either registers or unregisters the specified service names and forces the system to send the appropriate XTYP_REGISTER or XTYP_UNREGISTER transactions to DDE Management Library client applications that are running. hsz1 specifies the service name string. afCmd specifies the name service flags and is chosen from the following values:

Value	*Meaning*
DNS_REGISTER	Registers the service name
DNS_UNREGISTER	Unregisters the service name
DNS_FILTERON	Turns initiation filtering on
DNS_FILTEROFF	Turns initiation filtering off

Return Value TRUE is returned when successful. FALSE is returned when unsuccessful.

Function Category DDE

Related Functions DdeConnect, DdeInitialize

DdePostAdvise

Syntax `BOOL DdePostAdvise(idInst, hszTopic, hszItem)`

Parameter	*Type*	*Description*
idInst	DWORD	Application instance obtained from DdeInitialize
hszTopic	HSZ	String containing the topic name
hszItem	HSZ	String containing the item name

Description The DdePostAdvise function forces the system to send an XTYP_ADVREQ transaction to the callback function of the server application for each client application with an active advise loop for the specified topic (hszTopic) and item (hszItem).

Return Value TRUE is returned when successful. FALSE is returned when unsuccessful.

Function Category DDE

Related Functions DdeInitialize

DdeQueryConvInfo

Syntax

```
WORD DdeQueryConvInfo(hConv, idTransaction,
                                 pConvInfo)
```

Parameter	*Type*	*Description*
hConv	HCONV	Conversation
idTransaction	DWORD	Transaction - Obtained from DdeClientTransaction for asynchronous transactions; set to QID_SYNC for synchronous transactions
pConvInfo	PCONVINFO	Pointer to CONVINFO data structure that receives transaction and conversation information

Description The DdeQueryConvInfo function retrieves information on the specified transaction and conversation. hConv specifies the conversation. idTransaction specifies the transaction. pConvInfo points to a data structure of type CONVINFO that receives the transaction and conversation information. The CONVINFO data structure follows.

```
#include <ddeml.h>
typedef struct _CONVINFO
     {
     DWORD cb;
     DWORD hUser;
     HCONV hConvPartner;
     HSZ hszSvcPartner;
     HSZ hszServiceReq;
     HSZ hszTopic;
     HSZ hszItem;
     WORD wFmt;
     WORD wType;
     WORD wStatus;
     WORD wConvst;
     WORD wLastError;
     HCONVLIST hConvList;
     CONVCONTEXT ConvCtxt;
} CONVINFO;
```

in which

cb is the size of the structure in bytes

hUser is the application-supplied data

hConvPartner is the partner application in the DDE conversation

hszSvcPartner is the service name of the partner application

hszServiceReq is the service name of the service application that was requested for connection

hszTopic is the name of the requested topic

hszItem is the name of the requested item

wFmt is the data format of the exchanged data

wType is the transaction type and is selected from one of the following values:

Value	*Meaning*
XTYP_ADVDATA	Tells client that advice data has arrived from the server
XTYP_ADVREQ	Requests the server to send updated data to the client during an advise loop
XTYP_ADVSTART	Requests the server to start an advise loop with the client
XTYP_ADVSTOP	Tells server that an advise loop is terminating
XTYP_CONNECT	Requests the server to create a conversation with a client
XTYP_CONNECT_CONFIRM	Tells a server that a conversation has been established
XTYP_DISCONNECT	Tells a server that a conversation has been terminated
XTYP_ERROR	Tells a DDEML application that a critical error has occurred
XTYP_EXECUTE	Tells the server to execute the command sent by the client
XTYP_MONITOR	Tells application that is registered as APPCMD_MONITOR that data is being sent
XTYP_POKE	Asks the server to accept unsolicited data from a client
XTYP_REGISTER	Tells DDE applications that a server has registered a service name
XTYP_REQUEST	Asks the server to send data to a client
XTYP_UNREGISTER	Tells DDE applications that a server has unregistered a service name
XTYP_WILDCONNECT	Asks the server to establish multiple conversations with the same client
XTYP_XACT_COMPLETE	Tells client that an asynchronous data transaction has finished
wStatus	Conversation status; wStatus is one of the following values: ST_ADVISE ST_BLOCKED ST_BLOCKNEXT

Value	Meaning
	ST_CLIENT ST_CONNECTED ST_INLIST ST_ISLOCAL ST_ISSELF ST_TERMINATED
wConvst	Conversation state; wConvst is one of the following values: XST_ADVACKRCVD XST_ADVDATAACKRCVD XST_ADVDATASENT XST_CONNECTED XST_DATARCVD XST_EXECACKRCVD XST_EXECSENT XST_INCOMPLETE XST_INIT1 XST_INIT2 XST_NULL XST_POKEACKRCVD XST_POKESENT XST_REQSENT XST_UNADVACKRCVD XST_UNADVSENT
wLastError	Error associated with last transaction
hConvList	Conversation list when the handle of the current conversation is a conversation list. Otherwise, hConvList is NULL.
ConvCtxt	Conversation context

Return Value The number of bytes copied to the CONVINFO data structure is returned when successful. 0 is returned when unsuccessful.

Function Category DDE

Related Functions DdeQueryNextServer

DdeQueryNextServer

Syntax `HCONV DdeQueryNextServer(hConvList, hConvPrev)`

Parameter	*Type*	*Description*
`hConvListH`	`CONVLIST`	Conversation list
`hConvPrev`	`HCONV`	Converation handle; set to `NULL` to get the handle of the first conversation

Description The `DdeQueryNextServer` function returns the handle of the next conversation in the conversation list. `hConvList` specifies the handle of the conversation list. `hConvPrev` specifies the conversation handle returned by a previous call to this function. When an application calls `DdeQueryNextServer` for the first time, `hConvPrev` should be set to `NULL` to get the handle of the first conversation in the conversation list.

Return Value A conversation handle is returned. When there are no more conversation handles remaining in the list, `NULL` is returned.

Function Category DDE

Related Functions `DdeConnectList`, `DdeDisconnectList`

DdeQueryString

Syntax

```
DWORD DdeQueryString(idInst, hsz, lpsz, cchMax,
                     codepage)
```

Parameter	*Type*	*Description*
`idInst`	`DWORD`	Application instance identifier obtained through `DdeInitialize`
`hsz`	`HSZ`	String to copy; must be created with `DdeCreateStringHandle`
`lpsz`	`LPSTR`	Pointer to buffer receiving the string

Parameter	Type	Description
cchMax	DWORD	Length of buffer in lpsz
codepage	int	Code page; either CP_WINANSI or a value returned by GetKBCodePage

Description The DdeQueryString function copies the text identified by the string handle in hsz to the buffer pointed to by lpsz. When lpsz is NULL, the length of the string associated with the string handle is returned.

Return Value The length of the copied text is returned when lpsz is a pointer. When lpsz is NULL, the length of the text associated with the string handle is returned.

Function Category DDE

Related Functions DdeCreateStringHandle, DdeInitialize

DdeReconnect

Syntax `HCONV DdeReconnect(hConv)`

Parameter	Type	Description
hConv	HCONV	Conversation to be reestablished. The client must call DdeConnect to obtain this handle.

Description The DdeReconnect function is used by a client DDEML application to attempt to reestablish a conversation. If the conversation is reestablished, the DDEML will attempt to reestablish preexisting advise loops.

Return Value The handle to the reestablished conversation is returned when successful. NULL is returned when unsuccessful.

Related Functions DdeConnect, DdeDisconnect

DdeSetUserHandle

Syntax `BOOL DdeSetUserHandle(hConv, dwID, hUser)`

Parameter	Type	Description
hConv	HCONV	Conversation handle
dwID	DWORD	Transaction identifier
hUser	DWORD	Value associated with the conversation handle

Description The `DdeSetUserHandle` function associates the 32-bit value specified in `hUser` to the conversation handle (`hConv`) and transaction identifier (`dwID`).

Return Value `TRUE` is returned when successful. `FALSE` is returned when unsuccessful.

Function Category DDE

Related Functions `DdeQueryConvInfo`

DdeUnaccessData

Syntax `BOOL DdeUnaccessData(hData)`

Parameter	Type	Description
hData	HDDEDATA	Global memory object handle

Description The `DdeUnaccessData` function frees the global memory object specified in `hData`.

Return Value `TRUE` is returned when successful. `FALSE` is returned when unsuccessful.

Function Category DDE

Related Functions `DdeAccessData`, `DdeCreateDataHandle`, `DdeFreeDataHandle`

DdeUninitialize

Syntax `BOOL DdeUninitialize(idInst)`

Parameter	*Type*	*Description*
`idInst`	`DWORD`	Application instance identifier obtained through `DdeInitialize`

Description The `DdeUninitialize` function frees the DDE Management Library resources allocated for the calling application.

Return Value `TRUE` is returned when successful. `FALSE` is returned when unsuccessful.

Function Category DDE

Related Functions `DdeInitialize`

DebugBreak

Syntax `void DebugBreak()`

Description The `DebugBreak` function forces a break to the debugger.

Return Value There is no return value.

Function Category Debugging

Related Functions `FatalExit`

DefDlgProc

Syntax `LRESULT DefDlgProc(hwndDLG, uMsg, wParam, lParam)`

Parameter	*Type*	*Description*
`hwndDLG`	`HWND`	Dialog box
`uMsg`	`UINT`	Message number
`wParam`	`WPARAM`	16 bits of message-dependent information

Parameter	Type	Description
lParam	LPARAM	32 bits of message-dependent information

Description The DefDlgProc function processes Windows messages that the dialog box with a private window class, specified in hwndDLG, does not process.

Return Value The return value is dependent on the message sent and the result of the message processing.

Function Category Dialog Box, Window Creation

Related Functions DefWindowProc

DefDriverProc

Syntax

```
LRESULT DefDriverProc(dwDriverIdentifier, hdrvr,
                      uMsg, lParam1,lParam2)
```

Parameter	Type	Description
dwDriverIdentifier	DWORD	Installable device driver ID. This parameter is obtained by a previous call to OpenDriver.
hdrvr	HDRVR	Handle of installable driver
uMsg	UINT	Message to be processed
lParam1	LPARAM	Message-dependent information
lParam2	LPARAM	Message-dependent information

Description The DefDriverProc function processes all messages not processed by the installable device driver.

Return Value A nonzero value is returned when successful. Zero is returned when unsuccessful.

Function Category Installable Driver

Related Functions OpenDriver

DeferWindowPos

Syntax `HDWP DeferWindowPos(hdwp, hwnd, hWndInsertAfter, x, y, cx, cy, fwFlags)`

Parameter	*Type*	*Description*
hdwp	HDWP	Handle of window position data structure; returned by BeginDeferWindowPos function
hwnd	HWND	Update information on this window
hWndInsertAfter	HWND	Window following window in hWndInsertAfter can be set to one of the following values:

Value	*Meaning*
HWND_BOTTOM	Window is placed at the bottom of the Z order
HWND_NOTOPMOST	Window is placed at the top of all non topmost windows
HWND_TOP	Window is placed at the top of the Z order
HWND_TOPMOST	Window is placed on top of all non- topmost windows. The window is the topmost window even when the window is deactivated.

Parameter	*Type*	*Description*
x	int	X coordinate of window's upper-left corner
y	int	Y coordinate of window's upper-left corner
cx	int	Window's new width
cy	int	Window's new height
fwFlags	WORD	16-bit value affecting size and position of window

Description The DeferWindowPos function updates the window position data structure initialized by the BeginDeferWindowPos function and specified in hdwp. The data structure is modified for the window specified in hwnd. hWndInsertAfter identifies how the window in hwnd will be positioned. When hWndInsertAfter identifies a window, and the SWP_NOZORDER flag is not specified in fwFlags, the window in hwnd is positioned following the window in hWndInsertAfter. When hWndInsertAfter is NULL, the window in hWnd is placed at the top of the list. When hWndInsertAfter is 1, the window in hwnd is placed at the bottom of the list.

The x and y arguments define the horizontal and vertical coordinates, respectively, of the upper-left corner of the new window position. The cx and cy parameters define the new width and height of the window, respectively.

fwFlags is a 16-bit value affecting the size and position of the specified window. The following constants can be used with fwFlags:

Constant	*Meaning*
SWP_DRAWFRAME	Window is framed
SWP_HIDEWINDOW	Window is hidden
SWP_NOACTIVATE	Window is not activated
SWP_NOMOVE	Position is not updated
SWP_NOREDRAW	Changes are not redrawn
SWP_NOSIZE	Size is not updated
SWP_NOZORDER	Ordering is not updated
SWP_SHOWWINDOW	Window is displayed

Return Value The handle for the updated window position data structure is returned when successful. NULL is returned when unsuccessful.

Function Category Display and Movement

Related Functions EndDeferWindowPos, SetWindowPos

DefFrameProc

Syntax

```
LRESULT DefFrameProc(hwnd, hwndMDIClient, uMsg,
                     wParam, lParam)
```

Parameter	*Type*	*Description*
hwnd	HWND	MDI frame window
hwndMDIClient	HWND	MDI client window
uMsg	UINT	Message number

Parameter	Type	Description
wParam	WPARAM	Additional message information
lParam	LPARAM	Additional message information

Description The `DefFrameProc` function processes the Windows messages that the window function of a multiple document interface (MDI) frame window cannot process. Windows messages not processed by the window function must be passed to the `DefFrameProc` function.

Return Value The return value depends on the message processed.

Function Category Window Creation

Related Functions `DefMDIChildProc`, `DefWindowProc`

DefHookProc

Syntax `DWORD DefHookProc(nCode, uParam, dwParam, lplphkprc)`

Parameter	Type	Description
nCode	int	Specifies how to process message
uParam	UINT	Word parameter of the message
dwParam	DWORD	Long parameter of message
lplphkprc	HOOKPROC FAR*	Pointer to variable that contains the procedure-instance address of the hook function

Description The `DefHookProc` function calls the next function in the hook function chain. The hook function chain is created by Windows when an application defines more than one hook function using `SetWindowsHook`. (This function is obsolete for Windows 3.1. Use `CallNextHookEx` instead.)

Return Value The `DefHookProc` function returns a value relating to the `nCode` parameter.

Function Category Hook

Related Functions `SetWindowsHook`, `UnhookWindowsHook`

DefineHandleTable

Syntax `BOOL DefineHandleTable(wOffset)`

Parameter	*Type*	*Description*
`wOffset`	`WORD`	Offset from beginning of data segment to beginning of private handle table

Description The `DefineHandleTable` function creates a private handle table in a Windows application's default data segment. This table is used to store the segment addresses of global memory objects. `wOffset` specifies the offset for the table from the beginning of the data segment to the beginning of the private handle table. (This function is obsolete for Windows 3.1.)

Return Value A nonzero value is returned when successful. Zero is returned when unsuccessful.

Function Category Segment

Related Functions `GlobalHandle`, `LocalHandle`

DefMDIChildProc

Syntax `LRESULT DefMDIChildProc(hwnd, umsg, wParam, lParam)`

Parameter	*Type*	*Description*
`hwnd`	`HWND`	MDI child window
`umsg`	`UINT`	Message number
`wParam`	`WPARAM`	Additional message information
`lParam`	`LPARAM`	Additional message information

Description The `DefMDIChildProc` function processes the Windows messages that the window function of a multiple document interface (MDI) child window cannot process. Windows messages not processed by the window function must be passed to `DefMDIChildProc`.

Return Value The return value depends on the message processed.

Function Category Window Creation

Related Functions `DefFrameProc`, `DefWindowProc`

DefWindowProc

Syntax `LRESULT DefWindowProc(hwnd, uMsg, wParam, lParam)`

Parameter	*Type*	*Description*
hwnd	HWND	Window receiving message
uMsg	UINT	Message number
wParam	WPARAM	Additional message information
lParam	LPARAM	Additional message information

Description The `DefWindowProc` function processes the Windows messages that the specified application cannot process. Windows messages not processed by the class window function must be passed to `DefWindowProc`.

Return Value The return value depends on the message processed.

Function Category Window Creation

Related Functions `DefDlgProc`, `DefFrameProc`

DeleteAtom

Syntax `ATOM DeleteAtom(atm)`

Parameter	*Type*	*Description*
`atm`	`ATOM`	Atom and character string to delete

Description The `DeleteAtom` function decreases the reference count for the atom in `atm`. If the reference count for the atom is zero, the string associated with the atom is removed.

Return Value Zero is returned when successful. `atm` is returned when unsuccessful.

Function Category Atom

Related Functions `AddAtom`, `FindAtom`

DeleteDC

Syntax `BOOL DeleteDC(hdc)`

Parameter	*Type*	*Description*
`hdc`	`HDC`	Device context

Description The `DeleteDC` function deletes the device context specified in `hdc`.

Return Value `TRUE` is returned if the device context is deleted. `FALSE` is returned when unsuccessful.

Function Category Device Context

Related Functions `CreateDC`, `ReleaseDC`

DeleteMenu

Syntax `BOOL DeleteMenu(hmenu, idItem, fuFlags)`

Parameter	*Type*	*Description*
hmenu	HMENU	Menu to modify
idItem	UINT	Menu item to delete
fuFlags	UINT	Specifies how to interpret idItem

Description The DeleteMenu function deletes a menu item from the menu specified in hmenu. idItem identifies the menu item to delete. idItem is interpreted according to the flag setting in fuFlags. fuFlags can be set to MF_POSITION or MF_BYCOMMAND. When fuFlags is set to MF_BYPOSITION, idItem identifies the menu item position. When fuFlags is set to MF_BYCOMMAND, idItem specifies the command ID of the menu item. If the menu item in idItem has a pop-up menu associated with it, the pop-up menu is destroyed.

Return Value A nonzero value is returned when the item is successfully deleted. Zero is returned when unable to delete the menu item.

Function Category Menu

Related Functions CreateMenu, DestroyMenu

DeleteMetaFile

Syntax `BOOL DeleteMetaFile(hmf)`

Parameter	*Type*	*Description*
hmf	HMETAFILE	Metafile to delete

Description The DeleteMetaFile function denies access to the metafile specified in hmf. The metafile is not destroyed; however, the handle to the metafile is no longer valid.

Return Value TRUE is returned when successful. FALSE is returned when unsuccessful.

Function Category Metafile

Related Functions `CreateMetaFile`, `PlayMetaFile`

DeleteObject

Syntax `BOOL DeleteObject(hgdiobj)`

Parameter	*Type*	*Description*
`hgdiobj`	`HGDIOBJ`	Handle for a logical pen, brush, font, bitmap, region, palette, or icon

Description The `DeleteObject` function deletes the object specified in `hgdiobj`. All system storage associated with the specified object is freed.

Return Value `TRUE` is returned when the object is successfully deleted. `FALSE` is returned when unsuccessful.

Function Category Drawing Tool

Related Functions `GetObject`, `SelectObject`

DestroyCaret

Syntax `void DestroyCaret()`

Description The `DestroyCaret` function is used to destroy the current caret shape. In the process of destroying the caret, the caret is freed from the window that owns it and is cleared from the screen. The caret is destroyed only if a window in the current task owns the caret.

Return Value There is no return value.

Function Category Caret

Related Functions `CreateCaret`, `HideCaret`, `ShowCaret`

DestroyCursor

Syntax `BOOL DestroyCursor(hcur)`

Parameter	*Type*	*Description*
hcur	HCURSOR	Cursor to be destroyed

Description The `DestroyCursor` function destoys the cursor specified in `hcur`. `hcur` should identify only cursors created by the `CreateCursor` function. You should not use `DestroyCursor` to destroy cursors not created with the `CreateCursor` or `LoadCursor` function.

Return Value A nonzero value is returned when successful. Zero is returned when unsuccessful.

Function Category Cursor

Related Functions `CreateCursor`, `SetCursor`

DestroyIcon

Syntax `BOOL DestroyIcon(hicon)`

Parameter	*Type*	*Description*
hicon	HICON	Icon to destroy

Description The `DestroyIcon` function destroys the icon specified by `hicon`. The specified icon must have been created using `CreateIcon` or `LoadIcon`.

Return Value A nonzero value is returned when successful. Zero is returned when unsuccessful.

Function Category Icon

Related Functions `CreateIcon`, `DrawIcon`

DestroyMenu

Syntax `BOOL DestroyMenu(hmenu)`

Parameter	*Type*	*Description*
hmenu	HMENU	Menu to destroy

Description The `DestroyMenu` function destroys the menu specified in `hmenu`.

Return Value A nonzero value is returned if the menu was destroyed. Zero is returned if the menu was not destroyed.

Function Category Menu

Related Functions `CreateMenu`, `DeleteMenu`, `SetMenu`

DestroyWindow

Syntax `BOOL DestroyWindow(hwnd)`

Parameter	*Type*	*Description*
hwnd	HWND	Window to destroy

Description The `DestroyWindow` function destroys the window specified in `hwnd`. The window menu is destroyed, the application queue is flushed, outstanding timers are removed, and the `WM_DESTROY` and `WM_NCDESTROY` messages are sent to the window. If a parent window is specified, the child windows of the parent window are also destroyed.

Return Value A nonzero value is returned if the window was destroyed. Zero is returned if the window was not destroyed.

Function Category Window Creation

Related Functions `CreateWindow`

DeviceCapabilities

Syntax

```
DWORD DeviceCapabilities(lpszDevice, lpszPort,
                         fwCapability, lpszOutput, lpdm)
```

Parameter	*Type*	*Description*
`lpszDevice`	`LPSTR`	Pointer to a null-terminated string containing the name of the printer device
`lpszPort`	`LPSTR`	Pointer to a null-terminated string containing the name of the port where the device is connected
`fwCapability`	`WORD`	Capabilities to query
`lpszOutput`	`LPSTR`	Pointer to an array of bytes
`lpdm`	`LPDEVMODE`	Pointer to a `DEVMODE` data structure

Description The `DeviceCapabilities` function gets the capabilities of the printer device driver for the device specified in `lpszDevice`. `fwCapability` specifies the capabilities to query and is set to one of the following values:

Value	*Meaning*
`DC_BINNAMES`	Copies a structure identical to that returned by the `ENUMPAPERBINS` escape
`DC_BINS`	Gets a list of the available bins; the list of bins is copied into the array pointed to by `lpszOutput`
`DC_COPIES`	Gets the maximum number of copies that the device can generate
`DC_DRIVER`	Gets the version of the printer driver
`DC_DUPLEX`	Returns 1 if the printer supports duplex printing; 0 if duplex printing is not supported
`DC_ENUMRESOLUTIONS`	Returns a list of available resolutions
`DC_EXTRA`	Gets the number of bytes required for the device-specific part of the `DEVMODE` data structure for the printer driver
`DC_FIELDS`	Gets the `dmFields` field of the `DEVMODE` data structure for the printer driver

Value	*Meaning*
DC_FILEDEPENDENCIES	Returns a list of files that must be loaded when a driver is installed
DC_MAXEXTENT	Returns the POINT data structure that contains the maximum paper size specified by the dmPaperLength and dmPaperWidth fields of the DEVMODE data structure for the printer driver
DC_MINEXTENT	Returns the POINT data structure that contains the minimum paper size specified by the dmPaperLength and dmPaperWidth fields of the DEVMODE data structure for the printer driver
DC_ORIENTATION	Determines the number of degrees that portrait orientation is rotated. 0, 90, or 270 is returned.
DC_PAPERNAMES	Determines the list of supported paper names. The list is copied to lpszOutput as an array of paper names in the form of char[cPaperNames, 64].
DC_PAPERS	Places a list of supported paper sizes in lpszOutput
DC_PAPERSIZE	Places the dimensions of supported paper sizes (in tenths of a millimeter) into lpszOutput; the dimensions are stored in POINT data structures
DC_SIZE	Gets the dmSize field of the DEVMODE data structure
DC_TRUETYPE	Determines the print driver's ability to use TrueType fonts. One or more of the following flags can be returned. lpszOutput should be NULL.

Value	*Meaning*
DCTT_BITMAP	TrueType fonts printed as graphics
DCTT_DOWNLOAD	TrueType fonts can be down-loaded
DCTT_SUBDEV	Device fonts substituted for TrueType fonts
DC_VERSION	Gets the specification version to which the printer driver conforms

The DEVMODE structure is used extensively with this function. The DEVMODE structure follows.

```
#include <print.h>
typedef struct _devicemode {
     char dmDeviceName[CCHDEVICENAME];
     WORD dmSpecVersion;
     WORD dmDriverVersion;
     WORD dmSize;
     WORD dmDriverExtra;
     DWORD dmFields;
     short dmOrientation;
     short dmPaperSize;
     short dmPaperLength;
     short dmPaperWidth;
     short dmScale;
     short dmCopies;
     short dmDefaultSource;
     short dmPrintQuality;
     short dmColor;
     short dmDuplex;
     short dmYResolution;
     short dmTTOption;
} DEVMODE;
```

in which

dmDeviceName is the name of the device the driver supports

dmSpecVersion is the version number of the initialization date specification (0x30A for Windows 3.1)

dmDriverVersion is the printer driver version

dmSize is the size in bytes of the DEVMODE structure

dmDriverExtra is the size of the dmDriverData field

dmFields is the bitfield that indicates the initialized members of the DEVMODE structure. dmFields is a combination of the following values:

DM_ORIENTATION	DM_PRINTQUALITY
DM_PAPERSIZE	DM_COLOR
DM_PAPERLENGTH	DM_DUPLEX
DM_SCALE	DM_YRESOLUTION
DM_COPIES	DM_TTOPTION
DM_DEFAULTSOURCE	

dmOrientation is the paper orientation—either DMORIENT_PORTRAIT or DMORIENT_LANDSCAPE `dmPaperSize` is the paper size and is one of the following values:

Value	*Meaning*
DMPAPER_FIRST	Same as DMPAPER_LETTER
DMPAPER_LETTER	8.5 by 11 inch
DMPAPER_LETTERSMALL	Letter Small 8.5 by 11 inch
DMPAPER_TABLOID	Tabloid 11 by 17 inch
DMPAPER_LEDGER	Ledger 17 by 11 inch
DMPAPER_LEGAL	8.5 by 14 inch
DMPAPER_STATEMENT	Statement 5.5 by 8.5 inch
DMPAPER_EXECUTIVE	Executive 7.25 by 10.5 inch
DMPAPER_A3	A3 297 by 420 millimeter
DMPAPER_A4	A4 210 by 297 millimeter
DMPAPER_A4SMALL	A4 small 210 by 297 millimeter
DMPAPER_A5	A5 148 by 210 millimeter
DMPAPER_B4	B4 250 by 354
DMPAPER_B5	B5 182 by 257 millimeter
DMPAPER_FOLIO	Folio 8.5 by 13 inch
DMPAPER_QUARTO	Quarto 215 by 275 millimeter
DMPAPER_10X14	10 by 14 inch
DMPAPER_11X17	11 by 17 inch
DMPAPER_NOTE	Note 8.5 by 11 inch
DMPAPER_CSHEET	17 by 22 inch
DMPAPER_DSHEET	22 by 34 inch
DMPAPER_ESHEET	34 by 44 inch
DMPAPER_ENV_9	#9 envelope
DMPAPER_ENV_10	#10 envelope
DMPAPER_ENV_11	#11 envelope
DMPAPER_ENV_12	#12 envelope
DMPAPER_ENV_14	#14 envelope
DMPAPER_ENV_DL	Envelope DL 110 by 20 millimeter
DMPAPER_ENV_C5	Envelope C5 162 by 229 millimeter
DMPAPER_ENV_MONARCH	Envelope Monarch 3.875 by 7.5 inch
DMPAPER_LETTER_EXTRA	Letter Extra 9.275 by 12 inch
DMPAPER_LEGAL_EXTRA	Legal Extra 9.275 by 15 inch
DMPAPER_TABLOID_EXTRA	Tabloid Extra 11.68 by 18 inch

Value	Meaning
DMPAPER_A4_EXTRA	A4 Extra 9.27 by 12.69 inch
DMPAPER_A4_TRANSVERSE	Transverse 297 by 210 millimeter
DMPAPER_LETTER_EXTRA_TRANSVERSE	Letter Extra Transverse 12 by 9.275 inch
DMPAPER_USER	User defined

dmPaperLength overrides the paper length in dmPaperSize and is measured in tenths of millimeters

dmPaperWidth overrides the paper width in dmPaperSize and is measured in tenths of millimeters

dmScale scales the output by a factor of dmScale/100

dmCopies is the number of copies to print

dmDefaultSource is the default paper bin and is selected from one of the following values:

DMBIN_AUTO
DMBIN_CASSETTE
DMBIN_ENVELOPE
DMBIN_ENVMANUAL
DMBIN_FIRST
DMBIN_LARGECAPACITY
DMBIN_LARGEFMT
DMBIN_LAST
DMBIN_LOWER
DMBIN_MANUAL
DMBIN_MIDDLE
DMBIN_ONLYONE
DMBIN_SMALLFMT
DMBIN_TRACTOR
DMBIN_UPPER

dmPrintQuality defines the printer resolution and can be set to one of the following: DMRES_HIGH, DMRES_MEDIUM, DMRES_LOW, or DMRES_DRAFT. If set to a positive value, dmPrintQuality specifies the number of dots per inch.

dmColor switches between color and monochrome and is one of the following: DMCOLOR_COLOR or DMCOLOR_MONOCHROME

dmDuplex indicates double-sided or duplex printing and is one of the following: DMDUP_SIMPLEX, DMDUP_HORIZONTAL, or DMDUP_VERTICAL

dmYResolution is the y resolution in dots per inch

dmTTOption specifies how TrueType fonts should be printed and is one of the following values:

Value	Meaning
DMTT_BITMAP	Print TrueType as graphics
DMTT_DOWNLOAD	Download TrueType fonts
DMTT_SUBDEV	Substitute device fonts for TrueType fonts

Return Value The return value depends on the setting of `fwCapability`. –1 is returned when the function is unsuccessful.

Function Category Printer Control

Related Functions `DeviceMode`, `Escape`, `LoadLibrary`

DeviceMode

Syntax `void DeviceMode(hwnd, hModule, lpszDevice, lpszOutput)`

Parameter	Type	Description
hwnd	HWND	Window to own dialog box
hModule	HANDLE	Specifies the printer-driver module
lpszDevice	LPSTR	Pointer to a null-terminated string containing the device name
lpszOutput	LPSTR	Pointer to a null-terminated string containing the DOS file name or device name used for output

Description The `DeviceMode` function prompts the user to select a printing mode for the device specified in `lpszDevice`. The selected mode is copied to the environment block associated with the device. This function is part of the printer's device driver. The printer device driver must be loaded using `LoadLibrary`. The address of the function is retrieved using `GetProcAddress`.

Return Value There is no return value.

Function Category Printer Control

Related Functions `DeviceCapabilities`, `ExtDeviceMode`, `LoadLibrary`

DialogBox

Syntax `int DialogBox(hinst, lpszDlgTemp, hwndOwner, dlgprc)`

Parameter	*Type*	*Description*
hinst	HINSTANCE	Instance of module that contains the dialog box template
lpszDlgTemp	LPCSTR	Name of dialog box template
hwndOwner	HWND	Window that owns the dialog box
dlgprc	DLGPROC	Dialog function

Description The `DialogBox` function creates a modal dialog box. `hinst` specifies the instance of the module whose executable file contains the dialog box template. `lpszDlgTemp` is a pointer to a null-terminated string that specifies the dialog box template. `hwndOwner` specifies dialog box's owner. `dlgprc` points to a callback function that processes the messages sent to the dialog box. `DialogProc` must follow the conventions and formats described after this paragraph to operate properly. When `DialogProc` has finished its processing, the dialog box is terminated with a call to the `EndDialog` function.

Syntax `BOOL FAR PASCAL DialogProc(hwndDlg, wMsg, wParam, lParam).`

Parameter	*Type*	*Description*
hDlg	HWND	Dialog box receiving message
wMsg	WORD	Message Number
wParam	WORD	16 bits of message-dependent information
lParam	DWORD	32 bits of message-dependent information

Description This function should be used only when the dialog class is used for the dialog box. It should not call the `DefWindowProc` function to process unwanted messages. The name `DialogProc` is simply a placeholder for the real function name. The real name must be exported using the `EXPORTS` statement.

Return Value `DialogProc` should return a nonzero value when the function successfully handles the message. Zero should be returned when unable to handle the message.

Return Value The `result` parameter of the `EndDialog` function is returned when the dialog box is created. –1 is returned when unable to create the dialog box.

Function Category Dialog Box

Related Functions `DialogBoxIndirect`, `DialogBoxIndirectParam`, `DialogBoxParam`

DialogBoxIndirect

Syntax
```
int DialogBoxIndirect(hinst, hglbDlgTemp, hwndOwner,
                      dlgprc)
```

Parameter	*Type*	*Description*
`hinst`	`HINSTANCE`	Instance of module that creates the dialog box
`hglbDlgTemp`	`HGLOBAL`	Points to structure containing template size, style, control, and so forth
`hwndOwner`	`HWND`	Window that owns the dialog box
`dlgprc`	`DLGPROC`	Dialog function

Description The `DialogBoxIndirect` function creates a modal dialog box. `hinst` specifies the instance of the module whose executable file contains the dialog-box template. The size, style, and controls for the dialog box are specified in a data structure of type `DLGTEMPLATE` pointed to by `hglbDlgTemp`. The `DLGTEMPLATE` structure is described at the end of this paragraph. `hwndOwner` specifies the window that owns the dialog box. `dlgprc` points to the dialog function. The dialog function must follow the conventions and formats presented after the `DLGTEMPLATE` structure to work properly. Once `DialogProc` has finished its processing, the dialog box is terminated with a call to the `EndDialog` function.

```
DLGTEMPLATE {
     long dtStyle;
     BYTE dtItemCount;
     int dtX;
     int dtY;
     int dtCX;
     int dtCY;
     char dtMenuName[];
     char dtClassName[];
     char dtCaptionText[];
#ifdef DS_SETFONT_INCLUDED;
     short int dtPointSize;
     char dtTypeFace[];
#endif
     DLGITEM dtDlgItem[];
};
```

in which

`dtStyle` is the dialog box style and can be any combination of the following values:

Value	*Meaning*
DS_LOCALEDIT	Text storage for edit controls will be allocated in the application's local data segment
DS_SYSMODAL	System-modal dialog box
DS_MODALFRAME	Dialog box with modal dialog box border
DS_ABSALIGN	`dtX` and `dtY` are relative to screen
DS_SETFONT	Use a font other than the system font in the dialog box
DS_NOIDLEMSG	The `WM_ENTERIDLE` message will not be sent to the dialog box owner while the box is being displayed

`dtItemCount` is the number of items in the dialog box

`dtX` is the x coordinate of the upper-left corner of the dialog box; it is specified in units of 1/4 the dialog base width unit

`dtY` is the y coordinate of the upper-left corner of the dialog box; it is specified in units of 1/8 the dialog base height unit

`dtCX` is the width of the dialog box; it is specified in units of 1/4 the dialog base width unit

`dtCY` is the height of the dialog box; it is specified in units of 1/8 the dialog base height unit `dtMenuName` is the name of the menu for the dialog box

`dtClassName` is the name of the class for the dialog box

`dtCaptionText[]` is the caption for the dialog box

`dtPointSize` is the number of points used to draw text in the dialog box (typeface size)

`dtTypeFace` is the name of the typeface used to draw text in the dialog box

`dtDlgItem` is an array of `DLGITEM` structures that define the controls of the dialog box.

Syntax `BOOL FAR PASCAL DialogProc (hwndDlg, wMsg, wParam, lParam)`

Parameter	*Type*	*Description*
`hwndDlg`	`HWND`	Dialog box receiving message
`wMsg`	`WORD`	Message number
`wParam`	`WORD`	16 bits of message-dependent information
`lParam`	`DWORD`	32 bits of message-dependent information

Description This function should be used only when the dialog class is used for the dialog box. It should not call the `DefWindowProc` function to process unwanted messages. The name `DialogProc` is simply a placeholder for the real function name. The real name must be exported using the `EXPORTS` statement.

Return Value `DialogProc` should return a nonzero value when the function successfully handles the message. Zero should be returned when unable to handle the message.

Return Value The `result` parameter of the call to the `EndDialog` function is returned when the dialog box is successfully created. When unable to create the dialog box, –1 is returned.

Function Category Dialog Box

Related Functions `DialogBox`, `DialogBoxIndirectParam`, `DialogBoxParam`

DialogBoxIndirectParam

Syntax

```
int DialogBoxIndirectParam(hinst, hglbDlgTemp,  hwndOwner,
                           dlgprc, lParamInit)
```

Parameter	*Type*	*Description*
`hinst`	`HINSTANCE`	Instance of module that creates the dialog box
`hglbDlgTemp`	`HGLOBAL`	Points to structure containing template size, style, control, and so forth
`hwndOwner`	`HWND`	Window that owns the dialog box
`dlgprc`	`DLGPROC`	Dialog function
`lParamInit`	`LPARAM`	32-bit value passed to the dialog function

Description The `DialogBoxIndirectParam` function creates a modal dialog box. `hinst` specifies the instance of the module whose executable file contains the dialog-box template. The size, style, and controls for the dialog box are specified in a data structure of type `DLGTEMPLATE` pointed to by `hglbDlgTemp`. The `DLGTEMPLATE` structure is presented at the end of this paragraph. `WndParent` specifies the window that owns the dialog box. `dlgprc` points to the dialog function. The dialog function must follow the conventions and formats described after the `DLGTEMPLATE` structure to work properly. Once `DialogProc` has finished its processing, the dialog box is terminated with a call to the `EndDialog` function.

Before the dialog box is displayed, the `WM_INITDIALOG` message is sent to the dialog function.

```
DLGTEMPLATE {
     long dtStyle;
     BYTE dtItemCount;
     int dtX;
     int dtY;
     int dtCX;
     int dtCY;
     char dtMenuName[];
     char dtClassName[];
     char dtCaptionText[];
#ifdef DS_SETFONT_INCLUDED;
     short int dtPointSize;
     char dtTypeFace[];
```

```
#endif
    DLGITEM dtDlgItem[];
};
```

in which

`dtStyle` is the dialog box style and can be any combination of the following values:

Value	*Meaning*
DS_LOCALEDIT	Text storage for edit controls will be allocated in the application's local data segment
DS_SYSMODAL	System-modal dialog box
DS_MODALFRAME	Dialog box with modal dialog box border
DS_ABSALIGN	dtX and dtY are relative to screen
DS_SETFONT	Use a font other than the system font in the dialog box
DS_NOIDLEMSG	The WM_ENTERIDLE message will not be sent to the dialog box owner while the box is being displayed

`dtItemCount` is the number of items in the dialog box

`dtX` is the x coordinate of the upper-left corner of the dialog box; it is specified in units of 1/4 the dialog base width unit

`dtY` is the y coordinate of the upper-left corner of the dialog box; it is specified in units of 1/8 the dialog base height unit

`dtCX` is the width of the dialog box; it is specified in units of 1/4 the dialog base width unit

`dtCY` is the height of the dialog box; it is specified in units of 1/8 the dialog base height unit

`dtMenuName` is the name of the menu for the dialog box

`dtClassName` is the name of the class for the dialog box

`dtCaptionText[]` is the caption for the dialog box

`dtPointSize` is the number of points used to draw text in the dialog box (typeface size)

`dtTypeFace` is the name of the typeface used to draw text in the dialog box

`dtDlgItem` is an array of `DLGITEM` structures that define the controls of the dialog box.

Syntax `BOOL FAR PASCAL DialogProc (hwndDlg, wMsg, wParam, lParam)`

Parameter	*Type*	*Description*
`hwndDlg`	`HWND`	Dialog box receiving message
`wMsg`	`WORD`	Message Number
`wParam`	`WORD`	16 bits of message-dependent information
`lParam`	`DWORD`	32 bits of message-dependent information

Description This function should be used only when the dialog class is used for the dialog box. It should not call the `DefWindowProc` function to process unwanted messages. The name `DialogFunc` is simply a placeholder for the real function name. The real name must be exported by using the `EXPORTS` statement.

Return Value `DialogProc` should return a nonzero value when the function successfully handles the message. Zero should be returned when unable to handle the message. When the `WM_INITDIALOG` message is sent, zero should be returned if the function calls the `SetFocus` function. Otherwise, a nonzero value should be returned.

Return Value The `result` parameter of the call to the `EndDialog` function is returned when successful. When unable to create the dialog box, 1 is returned.

Function Category Dialog Box

Related Functions `DialogBox`, `DialogBoxIndirect`, `DialogBoxParam`

DialogBoxParam

Syntax `int DialogBoxParam(hinst, lpszDlgTemp, hwndOwner, dlgprc, lParamInit)`

Parameter	*Type*	*Description*
`hinst`	`HINSTANCE`	Instance of module that contains the dialog box template

Parameter	*Type*	*Description*
`lpszDlgTemp`	`LPCSTR`	Name of dialog box
`hwndOwner`	`HWND`	Window that owns the dialog box
`dlgprc`	`DLGPROC`	Dialog function
`lParamInit`	`LPARAM`	32-bit value passed to the dialog function

Description The `DialogBoxParam` function creates a modal dialog box. `hinst` specifies the instance of the module whose executable file contains the dialog-box template. The size, style, and controls for the dialog box are specified in `lpszDlgTemp`. `hwndOwner` specifies the window that owns the dialog box. `dlgprc` points to the dialog function. The dialog function must follow the conventions and formats presented after this paragraph to work properly. `lParamInit` is a 32-bit value passed to the dialog function to initialize dialog box controls.

Syntax `BOOL FAR PASCAL DialogProc(hDlg, wMsg, wParam, lParam)`

Parameter	*Type*	*Description*
`hDlg`	`HWND`	Dialog box receiving message
`wMsg`	`WORD`	Message Number
`wParam`	`WORD`	16 bits of message-dependent information
`lParam`	`DWORD`	32 bits of message-dependent information

Description This function should be used only when the dialog class is used for the dialog box. It should not call the `DefWindowProc` function to process unwanted messages. The name `DialogFunc` is simply a placeholder for the real function name. The real name must be exported using the `EXPORTS` statement.

Return Value `DialogProc` should return a nonzero value when the function successfully handles the message. Zero should be returned when unable to handle the message. When the `WM_INITDIALOG` message is sent, zero should be returned if the function calls the `SetFocus` function. Otherwise, a nonzero value should be returned.

Return Value The `result` parameter of the call to the `EndDialog` function is returned when successful. When unable to create the dialog box, –1 is returned.

Function Category Dialog Box

Related Functions `DialogBox`, `DialogBoxIndirectParam`

DirectedYield

Syntax `void DirectedYield(htask)`

Parameter	*Type*	*Description*
`htask`	`HTASK`	Task to execute

Description The `DirectedYield` function stops the current task and executes the task specified in `htask`.

Return Value There is no return value.

Function Category Debugging

Related Functions `TaskFirst`, `TaskNext`, `TaskSwitch`

DispatchMessage

Syntax `LONG DispatchMessage(lpmsg)`

Parameter	*Type*	*Description*
`lpmsg`	`const MSG FAR*`	Pointer to `MSG` data structure containing message information from the Windows application queue

Description The `DispatchMessage` function sends the message pointed to by `lpmsg` to the window function of the specified window. `lpmsg` points to a data structure of type `MSG` that contains message information from the Windows application queue. The `MSG` structure follows.

```
typedef struct tagMSG {
     HWND hwnd;
     WORD message;
     WORD wParam;
     LONG lParam;
     DWORD time;
     POINT pt;
} MSG;
```

in which

`hwnd` is the window receiving the message

`message` is the message number

`wParam` is additional message information

`lParam` is additional message information

`time` is the time the message was posted

`pt` is the cursor position in screen coordinates.

Return Value The value returned from the window function is returned.

Function Category Message

Related Functions `GetMessage`, `PostMessage`, `SendMessage`

DlgDirList

Syntax

```
int DlgDirList(hwndDlg, lpszPath, idListBox,
               idStaticPath, uFileType)
```

Parameter	*Type*	*Description*
hwndDlg	HWND	Dialog box containing list box
lpszPath	LPSTR	Pathname string
idListBox	int	Identifier for list box control
idStaticPath	int	Identifier for displaying the current drive and directory
uFileType	UINT	DOS file attributes

Description The `DlgDirList` function fills a list box control with a file or directory listing. `hwndDlg` identifies the dialog box which contains

the list box. idListBox specifies the list box control to fill. lpszPath is a null-terminated character string specifying the pathname. The format for lpszPath follows.

```
drive:\directory\directory\...\filename
```

Wildcards can be used in the pathname. The list box is filled with the names of all the files matching the pathname in lpszPath. idStaticPath specifies the identifier of the static text control used for displaying the current drive and directory. uFileType specifies the DOS attributes of files to be displayed. The DOS attributes for the uFileType parameter are as follows:

Value	*Meaning*
DDL_READWRITE	Read/Write data files without other attributes
DDL_READONLY	Read-only
DDL_HIDDEN	Hidden files
DDL_SYSTEM	System files
DDL_DIRECTORY	Subdirectories
DDL_ARCHIVE	Archives
DDL_POSTMSGS	LB_DIR flag; if set, messages generated by DlgDirList are sent directly to the application queue. If not set, messages are sent to the dialog box procedure.
DDL_DRIVES	Drives
DDL_EXCLUSIVE	Exclusive bit

In the directory list, subdirectories are enclosed in square brackets ([]); drives are marked as (-a), in which a is the drive name.

The LB_RESETCONTENT and LB_DIR messages are sent to the list box.

Return Value If the list box was successfully created, a nonzero value is returned. When a valid search path is not specified, zero is returned.

Function Category Dialog Box

Related Functions DlgDirListComboBox, DlgDirSelect

DlgDirListComboBox

Syntax

```
int DlgDirListComboBox(hwndDlg, lpszPath, idComboBox,
                       idStaticPath, uFileType)
```

Parameter	*Type*	*Description*
`hwndDlg`	`HWND`	Dialog box containing combo box
`lpszPath`	`LPSTR`	Pathname string
`idComboBox`	`int`	Identifier for combo box control
`idStaticPath`	`int`	Identifier for displaying the current drive and directory
`uFileType`	`UINT`	DOS file attributes

Description The `DlgDirListComboBox` function fills a list box of a combo box control with a file or directory listing. `hwndDlg` identifies the dialog box which contains the list box. `idComboBox` specifies the list box of the combo box to fill. `lpszPath` is a null-terminated character string specifying the pathname. The format for `lpszPath` follows.

```
drive:\directory\directory\...\filename
```

Wildcards can be used in the pathname. The list box is filled with the names of all the files matching the pathname in `lpszPath`. `idStaticPath` specifies the identifier of the static text control used for displaying the current drive and directory. `uFileType` specifies the DOS attributes of files to be displayed. The DOS attributes for the `uFileType` parameter are as follows:

Value	*Meaning*
`DDL_READWRITE`	Read/Write data files without other attributes
`DDL_READONLY`	Read-only
`DDL_HIDDEN`	Hidden files
`DDL_SYSTEM`	System files
`DDL_DIRECTORY`	Subdirectories
`DDL_ARCHIVE`	Archives
`DDL_POSTMSGS`	`LB_DIR` flag; if set, messages generated by `DlgDirList` are sent directly to the application queue. If not set, messages are sent to the dialog box procedure.

Value	*Meaning*
`DDL_DRIVES`	Drives
`DDL_EXCLUSIVE`	Exclusive bit

In the directory list, subdirectories are enclosed in square brackets ([]); drives are marked as (-a-), where a is the drive name.

The `CB_RESETCONTENT` and `CB_DIR` messages are sent to the list box.

Return Value A nonzero value is returned if the listing is generated. Zero is returned when a valid search path was not specified.

Function Category Dialog Box

Related Functions `DlgDirList`, `DlgDirSelectComboBox`

DlgDirSelect

Syntax `BOOL DlgDirSelect(hwndDlg, lpszPath, idListBox)`

Parameter	*Type*	*Description*
`hwndDlg`	`HWND`	Dialog box containing the list box
`lpszPath`	`LPSTR`	Buffer to receive pathname
`idListBox`	`int`	ID of list box control

Description The `DlgDirSelect` function gets the current selection from the list box. `hwndDlg` specifies the dialog box which contains the list box. The `DlgDirSelect` function assumes that the list box, specified by `idListBox`, has been filled. The selection from the list box is copied into the buffer pointed to by `lpszPath`. The `DlgDirSelect` function assumes that the selection is either a drive name, a directory name, or a file name.

The `LB_GETCURSEL` and `LB_GETTEXT` messages are sent to the list box.

Return Value The status of the current selection is returned. The return value is nonzero when a directory name is selected. Zero is returned for all other selections.

Function Category Dialog Box

Related Functions `DlgDirList`, `DlgDirSelectComboBox`

DlgDirSelectComboBox

Syntax `BOOL DlgDirSelectComboBox(hwndDlg, lpszPath, idComboBox)`

Parameter	*Type*	*Description*
`hwndDlg`	`HWND`	Dialog box containing combo box
`lpszPath`	`LPSTR`	Buffer to receive pathname
`idComboBox`	`int`	ID of combo box control

Description The `DlgDirSelectComboBox` function gets the current selection from a list box in the combo box specified by `idComboBox`. `hwndDlg` specifies the dialog box that contains the combo box. `lpszPath` holds the retrieved list box selection. `DlgDirSelectComboBox` assumes that the list box has been filled and that the selection is a drive name, a directory name, or a file name.

The `CB_GETCURSEL` and `CB_GETLBTEXT` messages are sent to the combo box.

Return Value A nonzero value is returned when the current selection is a directory name. Zero is returned for all other selections.

Function Category Dialog Box

Related Functions `DlgDirListComboBox`, `DlgDirSelect`, `DlgDirSelectComboBoxEx`, `DlgDirSelectEx`

DOS3Call

Syntax `extrn DOS3Call :far`

Description The `DOS3Call` function issues a DOS function-request 21H. This function can be called only from an assembly-language routine and is not defined in a Windows include file. All appropriate registers must be set before calling the `DOS3Call` function.

Return Value The registers of the DOS function are returned.

Function Category Operating System Interrupt

Related Functions `NetBIOSCall`

DPtoLP

Syntax `BOOL DPtoLP(hdc, lppt, cPoints)`

Parameter	*Type*	*Description*
`hdc`	`HDC`	Device context
`lppt`	`POINT FAR*`	Points to an array of points defined using the `POINT` data structure
`cPoints`	`int`	Number of points in `lppt`

Description The `DPtoLP` function converts each point defined in the array pointed to by `lppt` from device points to logical points. Each point in the array specified by `lppt` is defined with a data structure of type `POINT`. The `POINT` data structure follows.

```
typedef struct tagPOINT {
     int x;
     int y;
} POINT;
```

in which

`x` specifies the horizontal coordinate of the point

`y` specifies the vertical coordinate of the point.

Return Value `TRUE` is returned if all the points are converted. `FALSE` is returned when unsuccessful.

Function Category Coordinate

Related Functions `LPtoDP`

DragAcceptFiles

Syntax `VOID DragAcceptFiles(hwnd, fAccept)`

Parameter	*Type*	*Description*
`hwnd`	`HWND`	Window that is registering file acceptance or file acceptance cancellation
`fAccept`	`BOOL`	Accept flag

Description The `DragAccept` function defines whether the window in `hwnd` will accept dropped files. `fAccept` is set to `TRUE` to indicate the window will accept dropped files. `fAccept` is set to `FALSE` to indicate that the window will not accept dropped files.

Return Value There is no return value.

Function Category Drag-Drop

Related Functions `DragFinish`

DragFinish

Syntax `VOID DragFinish(hDrop)`

Parameter	*Type*	*Description*
`hDrop`	`HANDLE`	Handle to the internal data structure that describes the dropped files

Description The `DragFinish` function frees the memory that was allocated for the transfer of dropped files.

Return Value There is no return value.

Function Category Drag-Drop

Related Functions `DragAcceptFiles`

DragQueryFile

Syntax `WORD DragQueryFile(hDrop, iFile, lpszFile, cb)`

Parameter	*Type*	*Description*
hDrop	HANDLE	Handle to the internal data structure that defines the dropped files
iFile	WORD	Index of the file to query; if the specified index is valid, the filename for the file index is copied to the buffer pointed to by lpszFile
lpszFile	LPSTR	Pointer to the string where the filename for the file index will be copied
cb	WORD	Number of bytes in lpszFile

Description The `DragQueryFile` function retrieves the name of the dropped file for the specified file index in `iFile`. When `iFile` is set to –1, the number of dropped files is returned.

Return Value When `iFile` specifies a file index, the number of bytes copied to `lpszFile` is returned. When `iFile` is –1, the number of dropped files is returned. If `iFile` is set from 0 to the number of dropped files and `lpszFile` is set to `NULL`, then the return value is the buffer size needed to hold that particular file name.

Function Category Drag-Drop

Related Functions `DragQueryPoint`

DragQueryPoint

Syntax `BOOL DragQueryPoint(hDrop, lppt)`

Parameter	*Type*	*Description*
hDrop	HANDLE	Handle to the internal data structure that defines the dropped file

Parameter	Type	Description
lppt	LPPOINT	Pointer to a POINT data structure that defines the mouse position when the file was dropped

Description The DragQueryPoint function determines the position of the mouse when a file is dropped. lppt points to a data structure of type POINT that stores the mouse coordinates. The POINT data structure follows.

```
typedef struct tagPOINT {
     int x;
     int y;
} POINT;
```

in which

x specifies the horizontal coordinate of the point

y specifies the vertical coordinate of the point.

Return Value TRUE is returned when the file is dropped within the client area of the window. FALSE is returned when the file is dropped outside the client area.

Function Category Drag-Drop

Related Functions DragQueryFile

DrawFocusRect

Syntax `void DrawFocusRect(hdc, lprc)`

Parameter	Type	Description
hdc	HDC	Device context
lprc	const RECT FAR*	Pointer to RECT data structure containing coordinates of rectangle to draw

Description The DrawFocusRect function creates a rectangle in the style that indicates focus. hdc specifies the device context. lprc points to a data structure of type RECT that contains the coordinates of the rectangle to draw. The RECT structure follows. DrawFocusRect uses XOR to draw the rectangle. Therefore, calling this function twice with the same parameters will remove it from the screen.

```
typedef struct tagRECT {
     int left;
     int top;
     int right;
     int bottom;
} RECT;
```

in which

left is the x coordinate of the upper-left corner

top is the y coordinate of the upper-left corner

right is the x coordinate of the lower-right corner

bottom is the y coordinate of the lower-right corner.

Return Value There is no return value.

Function Category Painting, Ellipse and Polygon

Related Functions FrameRect

DrawIcon

Syntax `BOOL DrawIcon(hdc, X, Y, hicon)`

Parameter	*Type*	*Description*
hdc	HDC	Device context
X	int	Logical horizontal coordinate of upper-left corner of icon
Y	int	Logical vertical coordinate of upper-left corner of icon
hicon	HICON	Icon to draw

Description The DrawIcon message draws the icon in hicon at the location specified in X and Y. hdc specifies the device context. The icon specified in hicon must have been loaded with the LoadIcon function.

Return Value A nonzero value is returned when successful. Zero is returned when unsuccessful.

Function Category Painting, Icon

Related Functions `CreateIcon`, `DeleteIcon`, `LoadIcon`

DrawMenuBar

Syntax `void DrawMenuBar(hwnd)`

Parameter	*Type*	*Description*
`hwnd`	`HWND`	Window containing menu to redraw

Description The `DrawMenuBar` function redraws the menu bar associated with the window specified in `hwnd`.

Return Value There is no return value.

Function Category Menu

Related Functions `CreateMenu`, `InsertMenu`

DrawText

Syntax `int DrawText(hdc, lpsz, cb, lprc, fuFormat)`

Parameter	*Type*	*Description*
`hdc`	`HDC`	Device context
`lpsz`	`LPCSTR`	String to draw
`cb`	`int`	Number of bytes in the string; can be set to –1 to indicate that `lpsz` is a long pointer to a null-terminated string and the character count is to be determined automatically

Parameter	Type	Description
lprc	RECT FAR*	Pointer to RECT data structure containing the logical coordinate of the rectangle where the text will be drawn
fuFormat	UINT	Combination of text formats

Description The DrawText function draws the text in lpsz inside the rectangle specified in lprc. lprc points to a structure of type RECT that contains the logical coordinates of the rectangle where the text will be drawn. The RECT structure is shown after the table that follows. The device context in hdc specifies the font, text color, and background color used to draw the text. fuFormat specifies the type of text formatting. fuFormat can be almost any combination (using bitwise OR) of the following values:

Value	Meaning
DT_BOTTOM	Bottom justifies text; used with DT_SINGLELINE
DT_CALCRECT	Determines the width and height of the rectangle
DT_CENTER	Centers text horizontally
DT_EXPANDTABS	Expands the size of tab characters (default is 8)
DT_EXTERNALLEADING	Includes font external leading in line height
DT_LEFT	Left justifies text
DT_NOCLIP	Draws text without clipping
DT_NOPREFIX	Does not allow the processing of prefix characters
DT_RIGHT	Right justifies text
DT_SINGLELINE	Single line only
DT_TABSTOP	Sets the number of characters in the tab stop to the value in the high-order byte of fuFormat
DT_TOP	Top justifies text
DT_VCENTER	Centers text vertically
DT_WORDBREAK	Allows lines to automatically be broken between words

The RECT structure follows.

```
typedef struct tagRECT {
     int left;
     int top;
     int right;
     int bottom;
} RECT;
```

in which

left is the x coordinate of the upper-left corner

top is the y coordinate of the upper-left corner

right is the x coordinate of the lower-right corner

bottom is the y coordinate of the lower-right corner.

Return Value The height of the text is returned.

Function Category Text

Related Functions ExtTextOut, TabbedTextOut, TextOut

Ellipse

Syntax `BOOL Ellipse(hdc, nLeftRect, nTopRect, nRightRect, nBottomRect)`

Parameter	*Type*	*Description*
hdc	HDC	Device context
nLeftRect	int	X coordinate of upper-left corner of bounding rectangle
nTopRect	int	Y coordinate of upper-left corner of bounding rectangle
nRightRect	int	X coordinate of lower-right corner of bounding rectangle
nBottomRect	int	Y coordinate of lower-right corner of bounding rect-angle

Description The `Ellipse` function draws an ellipse inside the rectangle specified by (`nLeftRect`, `nTopRect`) and (`nRightRect`, `nBottomRect`). The current pen is used to draw the ellipse. The current brush is used to fill the ellipse.

Return Value `TRUE` is returned when the ellipse is successfully drawn. `FALSE` is returned when unsuccessful.

Function Category Ellipse and Polygon

Related Functions `Arc`, `Chord`, `Polygon`

EmptyClipboard

Syntax `BOOL EmptyClipboard()`

Description The `EmptyClipboard` function empties the clipboard. All data handles in the clipboard are freed. Ownership of the clipboard is assigned to the window which opened the clipboard. The clipboard must be open when calling this function.

Return Value The `EmptyClipboard` function returns a nonzero value if the clipboard is successfully emptied. A zero is returned when unable to empty the clipboard.

Function Category Clipboard

Related Functions `CloseClipboard`, `OpenClipboard`

EnableCommNotification

Syntax

```
BOOL EnableCommNotification(idComDev, hwnd,
                            cbWriteNotify, cbOutQueue)
```

Parameter	*Type*	*Description*
`idComDev`	`int`	Communication device posting notification messages. This value is returned by `OpenComm`.

Parameter	*Type*	*Description*
`hwnd`	`HWND`	Window that is to be affected by the call; if `hwnd` is `NULL`, the current window will not receive `WM_COMMNOTIFY` messages
`cbWriteNotify`	`int`	Number of bytes the COM driver must write to the input queue of the application before a notification message can be sent
`cbOutQueue`	`int`	Minimum number of bytes in the output queue

Description The `EnableCommNotification` function either enables or disables the posting of the `WM_COMMNOTIFY` message to the window specified in `hwnd`. Applications that use this function must define the constant `USECOMM` before including windows.h.

Return Value `TRUE` is returned when successful. `FALSE` is returned when unsuccessful.

Function Category Communication

Related Functions None

EnableHardwareInput

Syntax `BOOL EnableHardwareInput(fEnableInput)`

Parameter	*Type*	*Description*
`fEnableInput`	`BOOL`	Specifies whether function should save or discard input

Description The `EnableHardwareInput` function enables or disables input from the mouse and keyboard. `fEnableInput` specifies whether input should be saved or discarded. If `fEnableInput` is `TRUE`, input is saved. If `fEnableInput` is `FALSE`, input is discarded.

Return Value A nonzero value is returned if input was enabled prior to the call to `EnableHardwareInput`. Zero is returned if the input was disabled prior to the call to `EnableHardwareInput`.

Function Category Hardware

Related Functions GetInputState

EnableMenuItem

Syntax `BOOL EnableMenuItem(hmenu, idEnableItem, uEnable)`

Parameter	*Type*	*Description*
hmenu	HMENU	Menu handle
idEnableItem	UINT	Menu item to check
uEnable	UINT	Specifies menu item setting

Description The EnableMenuItem function either enables, disables, or grays the menu item specified in idEnableItem. The menu item is contained in the menu specified in hmenu. uEnable specifies the setting for the menu item. The settings for uEnable are listed as follows. These settings can be used in combination by using bitwise OR.

Value	*Meaning*
MF_BYCOMMAND	idEnableItem specifies a menu item ID. This value should not be used with MF_BYPOSITION.
MF_BYPOSITION	idEnableItem specifies the menu item position. This value should not be used with MF_BYCOMMAND.
MF_DISABLED	Disables the menu item. This value should not be used with MF_ENABLED or MF_GRAYED.
MF_ENABLED	Enables the menu item. This value should not be used with MF_DISABLED or MF_GRAYED.
MF_GRAYED	Grays the menu item. This value should not be used with MF_DISABLED or MF_ENABLED.

Return Value The previous state of the menu item is returned when successful. Zero indicates that the item was disabled. 1 indicates that the item was enabled. When unsuccessful, –1 is returned.

Function Category Menu

Related Functions `CheckMenuItem`, `HiliteMenuItem`

EnableScrollBar

Syntax `BOOL EnableScrollBar(hwnd, fnSBFlags, fuArrowFlags)`

Parameter	*Type*	*Description*
`hwnd`	`HWND`	Window or scroll bar control
`fnSBFlags`	`int`	Scroll bar type
`fuArrowFlags`	`UINT`	Scroll bar arrow flags

Description The `EnableScrollBar` function specifies whether the arrows of a scroll bar are enabled or disabled. `fnSBFlags` specifies the scroll bar type and is set to one of the following values:

Value	*Meaning*
`SB_BOTH`	Both vertical and horizontal scroll bars are affected; `hwnd` specifies a window handle
`SB_CTL`	`hwnd` specifies a scroll bar control handle
`SB_HORZ`	Only the horizontal scroll bar is affected; `hwnd` specifies a window handle
`SB_VERT`	Only the vertical scroll bar is affected; `hwnd` specifies a window handle

`fuArrowFlags` specifies which scroll bar arrows are to be enabled or disabled. `fuArrowFlags` is set to one of the following values:

Value	*Meaning*
`ESB_DISABLE_BOTH`	Disables both scroll bar arrows
`ESB_DISABLE_LTUP`	Disables the left arrow of a horizontal scroll bar or the up arrow of a vertical scroll bar
`ESB_DISABLE_RTDN`	Disables the right arrow of a horizontal scroll bar or the down arrow of a vertical scroll bar
`ESB_ENABLE_BOTH`	Enables both scroll bar arrows

Return Value A nonzero value is returned when successful. Zero is returned when unsuccessful.

Function Category Scrolling

Related Functions `ShowScrollBar`

EnableWindow

Syntax `BOOL EnableWindow(hwnd, fEnable)`

Parameter	*Type*	*Description*
`hwnd`	`HWND`	Window handle
`fEnable`	`BOOL`	Specifies whether to enable or disable the window

Description The `EnableWindow` function enables, or disables, all mouse and keyboard input to the window specified in `hwnd`. `fEnable` specifies whether input is enabled or disabled. If `fEnable` is `TRUE`, input is enabled. If `fEnable` is `FALSE`, input is disabled.

Return Value The return value is nonzero if the window was previously disabled. Zero indicates that the window was previously enabled or there was an error.

Function Category Input

Related Functions `IsWindowEnabled`, `SetActiveWindow`

EndDeferWindowPos

Syntax `BOOL EndDeferWindowPos(hdwp)`

Parameter	*Type*	*Description*
`hdwp`	`HDWP`	Handle for window position data structure; the handle is returned by the `BeginDeferWindowPos` or `DeferWindowPos` functions

Description The `EndDeferWindowPos` function updates the size and position of the windows that have window position data in the window position data structure specified by `hdwp`. All updates occur in one screen-refresh cycle.

Return Value A nonzero value is returned when successful. Zero is returned when unsuccessful.

Function Category Display and Movement

Related Functions `BeginDeferWindowPos`

EndDialog

Syntax `void EndDialog(hwndDlg, nResult)`

Parameter	*Type*	*Description*
`hwndDlg`	`HWND`	Dialog box to destroy
`nResult`	`int`	Value to be returned from dialog box

Description The `EndDialog` function removes a modal dialog box created with the `DialogBox` function. `hwndDlg` specifies the modal dialog box to destroy. The results of the `EndDialog` function are returned to the `DialogBox` function that created the dialog box. When the `EndDialog` function is called, an internal flag is set to indicate that the dialog box should be removed. When the dialog function ends, the dialog box is removed.

Return Value There is no return value.

Function Category Dialog Box

Related Functions `CreateDialog`, `DialogBox`

EndDoc

Syntax `int EndDoc(hdc)`

Parameter	*Type*	*Description*
hdc	HDC	Device context

Description The `EndDoc` function ends a print job. The `ENDDOC` printer escape used with Windows 3.0 is replaced by this function.

Return Value A positive value or zero is returned when successful. A negative value is returned when unsuccessful.

Function Category Printer Control

Related Functions `AbortDoc`, `StartDoc`

EndPage

Syntax `int EndPage(hdc)`

Parameter	*Type*	*Description*
hdc	HDC	Device context

Description The `EndPage` function tells the device that the application has finished writing to the page. This function replaces the `NEWFRAME` printer escape used for Windows 3.0.

Return Value A positive value or zero is returned when successful. One of the following values is returned when an error occurs:

Value	*Meaning*
SP_ERROR	General error
SP_APPABORT	Application's abort function returned zero
SP_USERABORT	User terminated the job
SP_OUTOFDISK	Insufficient disk space for spooling
SP_OUTOFMEMORY	Insufficient memory for spooling

Function Category Printer Control

Related Functions `Escape`, `StartPage`

EndPaint

Syntax `void EndPaint(hwnd, lpps)`

Parameter	*Type*	*Description*
`hwnd`	`HWND`	Window to be repainted
`lpps`	`const PAINTSTRUCT FAR*`	Pointer to `PAINTSTRUCT` data structure that contains the paint information from the `BeginPaint` function

Description The `EndPaint` function ends the painting of the window specified in `hwnd`. `lpps` points to the data structure of type `PAINTSTRUCT` that contains the paint information from the `BeginPaint` function. The `PAINTSTRUCT` structure follows.

```
typedef struct tagPAINTSTRUCT {
     HDC hdc;
     BOOL fErase;
     RECT rcPaint;
     BOOL fRestore;
     BOOL fIncUpdate;
     BYTE rgbReserved[16];
} PAINTSTRUCT;
```

in which

`hdc` is the display context

`fErase` is nonzero if the background is to be redrawn, zero if the background will not be redrawn

`rcPaint` is a data structure containing the upper-left and lower-right corners of the rectangle to paint

`fRestore` is reserved for use by Windows

`fIncUpdate` is reserved for use by Windows

`rgbReserved[16]` is reserved for use by Windows.

Return Value There is no return value.

Function Category Painting

Related Functions `BeginPaint`

EnumChildWindows

Syntax `BOOL EnumChildWindows(hwndParent, wndenmprc, lParam)`

Parameter	*Type*	*Description*
hwndParent	HWND	Parent window
wndenmprc	WNDENUMPROC	Procedure instance address of callback function
lParam	LPARAM	Value to pass to callback function

Description The `EnumChildWindows` function enumerates the child windows for the parent window specified in `hwndParent`. The handle of each child window is passed to the callback function that is pointed to by `wndenmprc`. The value in `wndenmprc` is created using `MakeProcInstance`. The callback function is structured as follows. `EnumChildProc` is a placeholder for the actual function name, which must be exported by using `EXPORTS` in the application's module definition file.

```
BOOL FAR PASCAL EnumChildProc(hwnd, lParam)
```

`HWND hwnd;`	Window handle
`DWORD lParam;`	Parameter in `lParam` from `EnumChildWindows`

The callback function should return `TRUE` when enumeration is to continue. To stop enumeration, `FALSE` should be returned.

Return Value A nonzero value is returned when all child windows have been enumerated. Zero is returned when unsuccessful.

Function Category Information

Related Functions `EnumTaskWindows`

EnumClipboardFormats

Syntax `UINT EnumClipboardFormats(uFormat)`

Parameter	*Type*	*Description*
`uFormat`	`UINT`	Known available format

Description The `EnumClipboardFormats` function enumerates the available formats which belong to the clipboard. `uFormat` specifies a format known to be available. The function then returns the next format available in the format list. The first format of the format list can be retrieved when `uFormat` is zero. The clipboard must be open for you to use this function.

Return Value When `uFormat` is zero, the `EnumClipboardFormats` function returns the first format in the clipboard format list. The next available format is returned when `uFormat` specifies a known format. Zero is returned when `wFormat` specifies the last available format or the clipboard is not open.

Function Category Clipboard

Related Functions `GetClipboardFormatName`, `IsClipboardFormatAvailable`

EnumFontFamilies

Syntax

```
int EnumFontFamilies(hdc, lpszFamily, fntenmprc,
                     lpszData)
```

Parameter	*Type*	*Description*
`hdc`	`HDC`	Device context
`lpszFamily`	`LPCSTR`	Pointer to null-terminated string that specifies the family name of the fonts. If set to `NULL`, one font from each family is randomly selected and enumerated.
`fntenmprc`	`FONTENUMPROC`	Procedure-instance address of the application defined callback function
`lpszData`	`LPARAM`	Pointer to data supplied by the application

Description The `EnumFontFamilies` function enumerates the fonts in the font family specified in `lpszFamily`. `fntenmprc` contains the procedure-instance address of the application defined callback function that processes the font information.

Return Value The last value returned by the callback function is returned.

Function Category Font

Related Functions `EnumFonts`

EnumFonts

Syntax `int EnumFonts(hdc, lpszFace, fntenmprc, lpszData)`

Parameter	*Type*	*Description*
hdc	HDC	Device context
lpszFace	LPCSTR	Pointer to a null-terminated character string containing the typeface name of the fonts
fntenmprc	FONTENUMPROC	Procedure instance address of the callback function
lpszData	LPARAM	Pointer to application-supplied data

Description The `EnumFonts` function enumerates the available fonts for the device specified in `hdc`. `lpszFace` contains the typeface name of the font. Information is retrieved for each font that has the specified typeface name. This retrieved information is passed to the callback function specified in `fntenmprc`. The address specified in `fntenmprc` is created using the `MakeProcInstance` function. The callback function uses the following convention and returns an integer value.

```
int FAR PASCAL EnumFontsProc(lplf, lpntm, FontType, lpData)
LPLOGFONT lplf;
LPNEWTEXTMETRIC lpntm;
short FontType;
LPSTR lpData;
```

in which

`lplf` is the pointer to a `LOGFONT` data structure that contains information on the logical attributes of the font

`lpntm` is the pointer to a `NEWTEXTMETRIC` data structure containing the physical attributes of the font when the font is a TrueType font. Otherwise, this parameter points to a `TEXTMETRIC` structure.

`FontType` is the font type: `DEVICE_FONTTYPE`, `RASTER_FONTTYPE`, `TRUETYPE_FONTTYPE`

`lpData` is the pointer to the data passed by `EnumFonts`.

Return Value The last value returned by the callback function is returned by the `EnumFonts` function.

Function Category Font

Related Functions `EnumFontFamilies`

EnumMetaFile

Syntax `BOOL EnumMetaFile(hdc, hlocMF, mfenmprc, lParam)`

Parameter	*Type*	*Description*
`hdc`	`HDC`	Device context
`hlocMF`	`HLOCAL`	Metafile
`mfenmprc`	`MFENUMPROC`	Procedure instance callback function
`lParam`	`LPARAM`	Pointer to data passed to the callback function

Description The `EnumMetaFile` function enumerates the Graphics Device Interface calls within the metafile specified by `hlocMF`. Each Graphics Device Interface call is passed to the application-supplied callback function pointed to by `mfenmprc`. The callback function uses the following convention and returns an integer value (nonzero to continue enumeration, zero to stop).

```
int FAR PASCAL EnumMetaFileProc(hdc, lpht, lpmr, cObj,
                                lParamData)
HDC hdc;
LPHANDLETABLE lpht;
```

```
LPMETARECORD lpmr;
int cObj;
BYTE FAR * lParamData;
```

in which

`hdc` is the device context containing the metafile

`lpht` is the table of handles associated with objects in the metafile

`lpmr` points to a metafile record contained in the metafile

`cObj` is number of objects with handles in the handle table

`lParamData` points to the data supplied by the application.

Return Value `TRUE` is returned when the callback function enumerates the GDI calls in the metafile. Otherwise, `FALSE` is returned.

Function Category Metafile

Related Functions `CreateMetaFile`, `DeleteMetaFile`

EnumObjects

Syntax `int EnumObjects(hdc, fnObjectType, goenmprc, lpData)`

Parameter	*Type*	*Description*
hdc	HDC	Device context
fnObjectType	int	Object type—either OBJ_BRUSH or OBJ_PEN
goenmprc	GOBJENUMPROC	Procedure instance address of the application-supplied callback function
lpData	LPARAM	Pointer to data passed to the callback function

Description The `EnumObjects` function enumerates the pens and brushes available for the device context specified in `hdc`. `fnObjectType` specifies the object type, either `OBJ_BRUSH` or `OBJ_PEN`. `goenmprc` specifies the procedure instance address of the application-supplied callback function. The address for `goenmprc` is created with the `MakeProcInstance` function. The callback function is called for each object and uses the following convention. The callback function returns a nonzero value to continue enumeration. Zero is returned to stop enumeration.

```
int FAR PASCAL EnumObjectsProc(lpLogObject, lpData)
LPSTR lpLogObject;
LPSTR lpData;
```

in which

`lpLogObject` is the pointer to a `LOGPEN` or `LOGBRUSH` data structure containing information on the object

`lpData` is the data passed to the `EnumObjects` function.

Return Value The return value of `EnumObjects` is the value returned by the callback function.

Function Category Drawing Tool

Related Functions `CreateMetaFile`, `DeleteMetaFile` `DeleteObject`, `GetObject`

EnumProps

Syntax `int EnumProps(hwnd, prpenmprc)`

Parameter	*Type*	*Description*
`hwnd`	`HWND`	Window containing property list to enumerate
`prpenmprc`	`PROPENUMPROC`	Procedure instance address of the callback function

Description The `EnumProps` function enumerates the entries in the property list of the window specified in `hwnd`. The callback function specified by `prpenmprc` is used to enumerate the entries. The callback function should not yield control to other tasks or attempt to add properties.

The format of the callback function for fixed data segments is as follows:

```
int FAR PASCAL EnumPropFixedProc(hwnd, lpsz, hData)
HWND hwnd;
LPSTR lpsz;

HANDLE hData;
```

in which

hwnd specifies the window that contains the property list

lpsz points to the null-terminated string associated with the data handle when the property was set

hData is the data handle.

The format for the callback function for moveable data segments is as follows:

```
int FAR PASCAL EnumPropMovableProc(hwnd, wDummy, psz,
                                   hData)
HWND hwnd;
WORD wDummy;
PSTR psz;
HANDLE hData;
```

in which

hwnd specifies the window that contains the property list

wDummy is a dummy parameter

psz points to the null-terminated string associated with the data handle when the property was set

hData is the data handle

EnumPropFixedProc and EnumPropMovableProc are placeholders for the application-supplied function name. The function name must be exported using EXPORTS.

Return Value The last value returned by the callback function is returned. –1 is returned if the function did not find a property to enumerate.

Function Category Property

Related Functions GetProp, RemoveProp, SetProp

EnumTaskWindows

Syntax `BOOL EnumTaskWindows(htask, wndenmprc, lParam)`

Parameter	*Type*	*Description*
`htask`	`HTASK`	Task handle
`wndenmprc`	`WNDENUMPROC`	Procedure instance address forcallback function
`lParam`	`LPARAM`	Value to pass to callback function

Description The `EnumTaskWindows` function enumerates the windows associated with the task specified in `htask`. The value used for `htask` is returned by the `GetCurrentTask` function. `wndenmprc` points to the callback function. The callback function is structured as follows. `EnumTaskWndProc` is a placeholder for the actual function name, which must be exported by using `EXPORTS` in the application's module definition file.

```
BOOL FAR PASCAL EnumTaskWndProc(hwnd, lParam)
```

`HWND hwnd;`	Window associated with current task
`DWORDlParam;`	Parameter in `lParam` from `EnumTaskWindows`

The callback function should return `TRUE` to continue enumeration. It should return `FALSE` to stop enumeration.

Return Value A nonzero value is returned when all windows associated with the task are enumerated. Zero is returned when unsuccessful.

Function Category Information

Related Functions `EnumChildWindows`

EnumWindows

Syntax `BOOL EnumWindows(wndenmprc, lParam)`

Parameter	*Type*	*Description*
`wndenmprc`	`WNDENUMPROC`	Procedure instance address of callback function
`lParam`	`LPARAM`	Value passed to callback function

Description The `EnumWindows` function enumerates the parent windows on the screen. The handle of each function is passed to the callback function pointed to by `wndenmprc`. The callback function is structured as follows. `EnumWindowsProc` is a placeholder for the actual function name, which must be exported by using `EXPORTS` in the application's module definition file.

```
BOOL FAR PASCAL EnumWindowsProc(hwnd, lParam)
```

`HWND hwnd;`	Window handle
`DWORD lParem;`	Parameter in `lParam` from `EnumWindows`

The callback function should return `TRUE` to continue enumeration. It should return `FALSE` to stop enumeration.

Return Value A nonzero value is returned when window enumeration has been completed. Zero is returned when unsuccessful.

Function Category Information

Related Functions `EnumChildWindows`, `EnumTaskWindows`

EqualRect

Syntax `BOOL EqualRect(lprc1, lprc2)`

Parameter	*Type*	*Description*
`lprc1`	`const RECT FAR*`	Pointer to `RECT` data structure containing coordinates of first rectangle
`lprc2`	`const RECT FAR*`	Pointer to `RECT` data structure containing coordinates of second rectangle

Description The `EqualRect` function compares the two rectangles specified in `lprc1` and `lprc2`. `lprc1` and `lprc2` point to data structures of type `RECT` that contain the coordinates of the two rectangles to compare. The `RECT` structure follows. If the two rectangles are equal, a nonzero value is returned.

```
typedef struct tagRECT {
     int left;
     int top;
     int right;
     int bottom;
} RECT;
```

in which

`left` is the x coordinate of the upper-left corner

`top` is the y coordinate of the upper-left corner

`right` is the x coordinate of the lower-right corner

`bottom` is the y coordinate of the lower-right corner.

Return Value A nonzero value is returned when the rectangles are the same. Zero is returned when they are not the same.

Function Category Rectangle

Related Functions `CopyRect`, `FillRect`

EqualRgn

Syntax `BOOL EqualRgn(hrgnSrc1, hrgnSrc2)`

Parameter	*Type*	*Description*
`hrgnSrc1`	`HRGN`	First region
`hrgnSrc2`	`HRGN`	Second region

Description The `EqualRgn` function determines whether the regions specified in `hrgnSrc1` and `hrgnSrc2` are identical.

Return Value `TRUE` is returned when the regions are identical. `FALSE` is returned when the regions are not identical.

Function Category Region

Related Functions `CombineRgn`, `PaintRgn`

Escape

Syntax `int Escape(hdc, nEscape, cbInput, lpszInData, lpvOutData)`

Parameter	*Type*	*Description*
hdc	HDC	Device context
nEscape	int	Escape function
cbInput	int	Number of bytes of data pointed to by lpszInData
lpszInData	LPCSTR	Pointer to the input data structure required for the escape
lpvOutData	void FAR*	Points to the data structure that is to receive output from the escape

Description The Escape function provides access to the facilities of the specified device that cannot be accessed through the Graphics Device Interface. nEscape specifies the escape function to generate. The escape functions are documented in the "Windows Escape Function" reference section presented later in this book.

Return Value A positive value is returned when successful. Zero is returned if the escape was not implemented. A negative value is returned on error. Some of the possible error values are SP_ERROR, SP_OUTOFDISK, SP_OUTOFMEMORY, and SP_USERABORT.

Function Category Printer Control

Related Functions StartDoc, EndDoc

EscapeCommFunction

Syntax `LONG EscapeCommFunction(idComDev, nFunction)`

Parameter	*Type*	*Description*
idComDev	int	Communication device
nFunction	int	Function code of the extended function

Description The `EscapeCommFunction` instructs the communication device in `idComDev` to perform the extended function in `nFunction`. `nFunction` is set to one of the following values:

Value	*Meaning*
CLRDTR	Clears the data-terminal-ready (DTR) signal
CLRRTS	Clears the request-to-send (RTS) signal
GETMAXCOM	Returns the maximum COM port ID supported by the system
GETMAXLPT	Returns the maximum LPT port ID supported by the system
RESETDEV	Resets the device
SETDTR	Sends the data-terminal-ready (DTR) signal
SETRTS	Sends the request-to-send (RTS) signal
SETXOFF	Forces transmission to respond as though an XOFF character had been received
SETXON	Forces transmission to respond as though an XON character had been received

Return Value Zero is returned when successful. A negative value is returned when unsuccessful.

Function Category Communication

Related Functions `OpenComm`, `ReadComm`, `WriteComm`

ExcludeClipRect

Syntax

```
int ExcludeClipRect(hdc, nLeftRect, nTopRect, nRightRect,
                    nBottomRect)
```

Parameter	*Type*	*Description*
hdc	HDC	Device context
nLeftRect	int	Logical x coordinate of upper-left corner of rectangle
nTopRect	int	Logical y coordinate of upper-left corner of rectangle

Parameter	Type	Description
nRightRect	int	Logical x coordinate of lower-right corner of rectangle
nBottomRect	int	Logical y coordinate of lower-right corner of rectangle

Description The `ExcludeClipRect` function excludes the rectangle defined by (`nLeftRect, nTopRect`) and (`nRightRect, nBottomRect`) from the current clipping region.

Return Value One of the following values is returned to describe the resulting clipping region:

Value	Meaning
COMPLEXREGION	Region has overlapping borders
ERROR	No region was created
NULLREGION	Region is empty
SIMPLEREGION	Region has no overlapping borders

Function Category Clipping

Related Functions `GetClipBox`, `IntersectClipRect`

ExcludeUpdateRgn

Syntax `int ExcludeUpdateRgn(hdc, hwnd)`

Parameter	Type	Description
hdc	HDC	Device context associated with clipping region
hwnd	HWND	Window to update

Description The `ExcludeUpdateRgn` function does not allow drawing inside an updated region in the window from a clipping region. `hwnd` specifies the window to update.

Return Value One of the following values is returned to indicate the type of region resulting from the function call:

Value	*Meaning*
COMPLEXREGION	Region has overlapping borders
ERROR	Unable to create a region
NULLREGION	Region is empty
SIMPLEREGION	Region has no overlapping borders

Function Category Painting

Related Functions GetUpdateRgn, ValidateRgn

ExitWindows

Syntax `BOOL ExitWindows(dwReturnCode, uReserved)`

Parameter	*Type*	*Description*
dwReturnCode	DWORD	Return or restart code; either EW_REBOOTSYSTEM or EW_RESTARTWINDOWS
uReserved	UINT	Reserved; set to zero

Description The ExitWindows function attempts to shut down Windows. The WM_QUERYENDSESSION message is sent to all applications. If all applications ok the termination request, the WM_ENDSESSION is sent to all applications before exiting and control is returned to DOS.

Return Value Zero is returned if any one of the applications does not ok the termination request. If all applications ok the termination request, the function does not return.

Function Category Task

Related Functions GetCurrentTask

ExtDeviceMode

Syntax `int ExtDeviceMode(hwnd, hDriver, lpdmOutput, lpszDevice, lpszPort, lpdmInput, lpszProfile, fwMode)`

Parameter	*Type*	*Description*
hwnd	HWND	Window handle
hDriver	HANDLE	Device driver module
lpdmOutput	LPDEVMODE	Pointer to a DEVMODE data structure where the driver writes initialization information from lpdmInput
lpszDevice	LPSTR	Pointer to a null-terminated string containing the device name
lpszPort	LPSTR	Pointer to a null-terminated string containing the name of the port where the device is connected
lpdmInput	LPDEVMODE	Pointer to a DEVMODE data structure supplying initialization data to the printer driver
lpszProfile	LPSTR	Pointer to a null-terminated string containing the name of the file holding initialization data
fwMode	WORD	Mask of the values that specify the operations of the function; set to one or more of the following values:

Value	*Meaning*
DM_IN_BUFFER	Input value; current printer settings are merged with the data in the DEVMODE structure specified in lpdmInput
DM_IN_PROMPT	Input value; Print Setup dialog box is displayed

Value	Meaning
DM_OUT_BUFFER	Output value; Print settings are copied to the DEVMODE structure specified by lpdmOutput
DM_OUT_DEFAULT	Output value; the current printer environment and WIN.INI are updated

Description The ExtDeviceMode function does one of the following:

1. Retrieves device initialization information for the printer driver.
2. Modifies device initialization information for the printer driver.
3. Displays a driver-supplied dialog box used for configuring the printer driver.

This function is actually part of the printer's device driver. The driver must be loaded and the address of the function must be retrieved using GetProcAddress before this function can be used.

Return Value When fwMode is zero, the size of the DEVMODE structure containing the driver initialization data is returned. When the initialization dialog box is displayed, IDOK or IDCANCEL is returned to indicate the button selected. When the function is successful and the dialog box is not displayed, IDOK is returned. A value less than zero is returned when unsuccessful.

Function Category Printer Control

Related Functions DeviceMode, GetModuleHandle

ExtFloodFill

Syntax

```
BOOL ExtFloodFill(hdc, nXStart, nYStart, clrref,
                  fuFillType)
```

Parameter	Type	Description
hdc	HDC	Device context
nXStart	int	Logical x coordinate of fill point

Parameter	Type	Description
nYStart	int	Logical y coordinate of fill point
clrref	COLORREF	Color of boundary or area to fill
fuFillType	UINT	Type of fill to perform

Description The `ExtFloodFill` function fills the specified area of the display using the current brush. `nXStart` and `nYStart` specify the points where the filling will begin. `clrref` specifies the color of the boundary or the color of the area to fill, depending on the setting of `fuFillType`. `fuFillType` is set to one of the following values:

Value	Meaning
FLOODFILLBORDER	`clrref` specifies the color of a boundary; everything within the boundary is filled
FLOODFILLSURFACE	`clrref` specifies the color of an area; everthing in the area that is the specified color is filled

Return Value `TRUE` is returned when successful. `FALSE` is returned when unsuccessful.

Function Category Bitmap

Related Functions `FloodFill`

ExtractIcon

Syntax `HICON ExtractIcon(hInst, lpszExeName, iIcon)`

Parameter	Type	Description
hInst	HANDLE	Application instance
lpszExeName	LPSTR	Pointer to string that specifies the file name

Parameter	Type	Description
iIcon	WORD	Icon index; set to zero to get the handle of the first icon in the file; set to –1 to get the number of icons in the file

Description The `ExtractIcon` function retrieves the handle of an icon from the executable file, dynamic-link library, or icon file specified in `hInst`.

Return Value The handle of an icon is returned when successful. 1 is returned when the specified file is invalid or is not the right type. `NULL` is returned when no icons were found in the file.

Function Category Shell

Related Functions `FindExecutable`, `ShellExecute`

ExtTextOut

Syntax

```
BOOL ExtTextOut(hdc, nXStart, nYStart, fuOptions, lprc,
                lpszString, cbString, lpDx)
```

Parameter	Type	Description
hdc	HDC	Device context
nXStart	int	Logical x coordinate of the character cell for the first character in the string
nYStart	int	Logical y coordinate of the character cell for the first character in the string
fuOptions	UINT	Specifies the rectangle type; can be both/either `ETO_CLIPPED` (text clipped at rectangle's border) and/or `ETO_OPAQUE` (rectangle is filled with the background color)

Parameter	*Type*	*Description*
`lprc`	`const RECT FAR*`	Pointer to a `RECT` data structure containing the coordinates that define the rectangle
`lpszString`	`LPCSTR`	Pointer to the character string
`cbString`	`UINT`	Number of characters in the string
`lpDx`	`int FAR*`	Pointer to an array of values specifying the distance between character cells

Description The `ExtTextOut` function displays the character string specified in `lpszString`, using the current font, inside the rectangle specified by `lprc`. `fuOptions` specifies the rectangle type. `nXStart`, `nYStart`, and `lpDx` provide information used to display the text string.

Return Value `TRUE` is returned when the string is successfully drawn. `FALSE` is returned when unsuccessful.

Function Category Text

Related Functions `DrawText`, `TabbedTextOut`, `TextOut`

FatalAppExit

Syntax `void FatalAppExit(fuAction, lpszMessageText)`

Parameter	*Type*	*Description*
`fuAction`	`UINT`	Must be set to 0
`lpszMessageText`	`LPCSTR`	Pointer to the string to display in the message box

Description The `FatalAppExit` function displays the message in the string pointed to by `lpszMessageText` inside a message box. When the message box is closed, the application is terminated.

Return Value There is no return value.

Function Category Debugging

Related Functions DebugBreak, FatalExit

FatalExit

Syntax `void FatalExit(nErrCode)`

Parameter	*Type*	*Description*
nErrCode	int	Error code to display

Description The FatalExit function is used only for debugging. The current state of Windows is displayed by the function including the error code in nErrCode and a symbolic stack trace.

Return Value There is no return value.

Function Category Debugging

Related Functions DebugBreak, FatalAppExit

FillRect

Syntax `int FillRect(hdc, lprc, hbr)`

Parameter	*Type*	*Description*
hdc	HDC	Device context
lprc	const RECT FAR*	Pointer to RECT data structure containing logical coordinates of rectangle to fill
hbr	HBRUSH	Brush used to fill rectangle

Description The FillRect function fills the rectangle specified in lprc using the brush specified in hbr. The left and top borders of the rectangle are filled; the right and bottom borders are not filled. lprc points to a data structure of type RECT that contains the logical coordinates of the rectangle to fill. The RECT structure follows. hbr specifies the brush used to fill the rectangle. The specified brush should have been previously created with the CreateHatchBrush, CreatePatternBrush, or CreateSolidBrush function. hdc specifies the device context.

```
typedef struct tagRECT {
     int left;
     int top;
     int right;
     int bottom;
} RECT;
```

in which

`left` is the x coordinate of the upper-left corner

`top` is the y coordinate of the upper-left corner

`right` is the x coordinate of the lower-right corner

`bottom` is the y coordinate of the lower-right corner.

Return Value The return value has no significance and is not used.

Function Category Rectangle

Related Functions `CopyRect`, `EqualRect`, `OffsetRect`

FillRgn

Syntax `BOOL FillRgn(hdc, hrgn, hbr)`

Parameter	*Type*	*Description*
`hdc`	`HDC`	Device context
`hrgn`	`HRGN`	Region to fill
`hbr`	`HBRUSH`	Brush to use for filling the region

Description The `FillRgn` function fills the region in `hrgn` using the brush specified in `hbr`. The coordinates for the region in `hrgn` are device coordinates.

Return Value `TRUE` is returned when successful. `FALSE` is returned when unsuccessful.

Function Category Region

Related Functions `CombineRgn`, `FrameRgn`, `PaintRgn`

FindAtom

Syntax `ATOM FindAtom(lpszString)`

Parameter	*Type*	*Description*
`lpszString`	`LPCSTR`	Pointer to the null-terminated string for which to search

Description The `FindAtom` function searches an atom table for the string in `lpszString`. The atom associated with the string is returned when the string is found.

Return Value The atom associated with the string is returned when the string is found. Zero is returned if the string is not found.

Function Category Atom

Related Functions `AddAtom`, `DeleteAtom`

FindExecutable

Syntax `HANDLE FindExecutable(lpszFile, lpszDir, lpszResult)`

Parameter	*Type*	*Description*
`lpszFile`	`LPSTR`	Pointer to the string specifying the filename
`lpszDir`	`LPSTR`	Pointer to the string specifying the default directory
`lpszResult`	`LPSTR`	Pointer to the string to receive the filename

Description The `FindExecutable` function retrieves the filename of the specified file and returns its handle. `lpszResult` receives the retrieved filename.

Return Value The instance handle of the specified executable file is returned when successful. A return value of less than or equal to 32 indicates an error.

Function Category Shell

Related Functions ExtractIcon, ShellExecute

FindResource

Syntax `HRSRC FindResource(hinst, lpszName, lpszType)`

Parameter	*Type*	*Description*
hinst	HINSTANCE	Instance of module whose executable file contains the resource
lpszName	LPCSTR	Pointer to a null-terminated string containing the name of the resource
lpszType	LPCSTR	Pointer to a null-terminated string containing the resource type

Description The FindResource function finds the resource specified by lpszName and lpszType in the resource file specified by hinst. lpszName specifies the name of the resource. lpszType specifies the resource type. The following values are used for lpszType:

Value	*Meaning*
RT_ACCELERATOR	Accelerator table
RT_BITMAP	Bitmap resource
RT_CURSOR	Cursor resource
RT_DIALOG	Dialog box
RT_FONT	Font resource
RT_FONTDIR	Font directory resource
RT_ICON	Icon resource
RT_MENU	Menu resource
RT_RCDATA	User-defined resource
RT_STRING	String resource

Return Value The handle of the specified resource is returned when successful. NULL is returned when unsuccessful.

Function Category Resource Management

Related Functions `AccessResource`, `AllocResource`

FindText

Syntax `HWND FindText(lpfr)`

Parameter	Type	Description
lpfr	LPFINDREPLACE	Pointer to FINDREPLACE data structure containing information used to initialize the dialog box

Description The `FindText` function creates a modeless dialog box defined by the system that allows the user to perform text searches. The actual search operation must be defined by the application. `lpfr` points to a data structure of type `FINDREPLACE` that contains information for initializing the dialog box. The `FINDREPLACE` data structure follows.

```
#include <commdlg.h>
typedef struct
     {
     DWORD lStructSize;
     HWND hwndOwner;
     HANDLE hInstance;
     DWORD Flags;
     LPSTR lpstrFindWhat;
     LPSTR lpstrReplaceWith;
     WORD wFindWhatLen;
     WORD wReplaceWithLen;
     DWORD lCustData;
     WORD (FAR PASCAL *lpfnHook)(HWND, unsigned, WORD,
                                 LONG);
     LPSTR lpTemplateName;
     } FINDREPLACE;
```

in which

`lStructSize` is the size of the structure in bytes

`hwndOwner` is the window that owns the dialog box

`hInstance` specifies the data block that contains the template referenced by `lpTemplateName`

`Flags` is a combination of the following flags:

Value	Meaning
FR_DIALOGTERM	Dialog box is terminating
FR_DOWN	Search is conducted down the document when set
FR_ENABLEHOOK	Enables the hook function in lpfnHook
FR_ENABLETEMPLATE	Enables the use of the template in hInstance and lpTemplateName
FR_ENABLETEMPLATEHANDLE	hInstance specifies a data block containing a pre-loaded dialog template
FR_FINDNEXT	Search for next occurrence of specified text
FR_HIDEMATCHCASE	Match Case check box is hidden and disabled
FR_HIDEWHOLEWORD	Whole Word check box is hidden and disabled
FR_HIDEUPDOWN	Up and Down radio buttons are hidden
FR_MATCHCASE	Search is case-sensitive
FR_NOMATCHCASE	Search is not case-sensitive
FR_NOUPDOWN	Radio direction buttons disabled
FR_NOWHOLEWORD	Whole word checkbox disabled
FR_REPLACE	Replace current text occurrence
FR_REPLACEALL	Replace all text occurrences
FR_SHOWHELP	Help push button shown
FR_WHOLEWORD	Whole word check box shown

lpstrFindWhat is the text string used for the search

lpstrReplaceWith is the text string used to replace the specified text

wFindWhatLen is the length of the lpstrFindWhat string

wReplaceWithLen is the length of the buffer that lpstrReplaceWith points to

lCustData is the application-supplied data passed to the hook function `lpfnHook` points to the hook function that processes the dialog box messages

`lpTemplateName` is a pointer to the string that contains the name of the dialog box template resource used in place of the standard template.

Return Value The handle of the dialog box is returned when successful. When unsuccessful, `NULL` is returned.

Function Category Common Dialog

Related Functions `ReplaceText`

FindWindow

Syntax `HWND FindWindow(lpszClassName, lpszWindowName)`

Parameter	*Type*	*Description*
`lpszClassName`	`LPCSTR`	Window class name
`lpszWindowName`	`LPCSTR`	Window name

Description The `FindWindow` function returns the window handle of the window matching the specified window class name and window name. The window class name is specified in `lpszClassName`. The window name is specified in `lpszWindowName`.

Return Value If a window matching the specifications is found, the window handle is returned. If no matching window is found, `NULL` is returned.

Function Category Information

Related Functions `GetTopWindow`, `GetWindow`

FlashWindow

Syntax `BOOL FlashWindow(hwnd, fInvert)`

Parameter	*Type*	*Description*
hwnd	HWND	Window to flash
fInvert	BOOL	Specifies whether to flash window or return it to its original state

Description The FlashWindow function flashes the window specified in hwnd. By flashing the window, an inactive caption bar becomes active, and an active caption bar becomes inactive. fInvert specifies whether the window should be flashed or returned to its original state. When fInvert is TRUE, the window is flashed. When fInvert is FALSE, the window is returned to its original state.

Return Value A nonzero value is returned when the window was active before calling FlashWindow. Zero is returned when the window was inactive before calling FlashWindow.

Function Category Error

Related Functions MessageBeep, MessageBox

FloodFill

Syntax `BOOL FloodFill(hdc, nXStart, nYStart, clrref)`

Parameter	*Type*	*Description*
hdc	HDC	Device context
nXStart	int	Logical x coordinate of fill point
nYStart	int	Logical y coordinate of fill point
clrref	COLORREF	Color of boundary

Description The FloodFill function fills the specified area of the display using the current brush. nXStart and nYStart specify the points where the filling will begin. clrref specifies the color of the boundary surrounding the area to fill.

Return Value TRUE is returned when successful. When unsuccessful, FALSE is returned.

Function Category Bitmap

Related Functions ExtFloodFill

FlushComm

Syntax `int FlushComm(idComDev, fuQueue)`

Parameter	*Type*	*Description*
idComDev	int	Communication device
fuQueue	int	Queue to flush

Description The FlushComm function flushes the queue in fuQueue of the communication device in idComDev. fuQueue is set to zero to flush the transmission queue. fuQueue is set to 1 to flush the receive queue.

Return Value Zero is returned when successful. A negative value is returned when unsuccessful.

Function Category Communication

Related Functions CloseComm, OpenComm, ReadComm, WriteComm

FrameRect

Syntax `int FrameRect(hdc, lprc, hbr)`

Parameter	*Type*	*Description*
hdc	HDC	Device context
lprc	const RECT FAR*	Pointer to RECT data structure containing the logical coordinates of the rectangle
hbr	HBRUSH	Brush used to frame the rectangle

Description The FrameRect function draws a border around the rectangle specified in lprc. lprc points to a data structure of type RECT containing the logical coordinates of the rectangle. The RECT structure follows. hbr specifies the brush used to draw the border. The specified brush should have been previously created with the CreateHatchbrush, CreatePatternBrush, or CreateSolidBrush function. The border is one logical unit wide and one logical unit high.

```
typedef struct tagRECT {
     int left;
     int top;
     int right;
     int bottom;
} RECT;
```

in which

left is the x coordinate of the upper-left corner

top is the y coordinate of the upper-left corner

right is the x coordinate of the lower-right corner

bottom is the y coordinate of the lower-right corner.

Return Value The return value has no significance and should not be used.

Function Category Painting

Related Functions DrawFocusRect, ValidateRect

FrameRgn

Syntax BOOL FrameRgn(hdc, hrgn, hbr, nWidth, nHeight)

Parameter	*Type*	*Description*
hdc	HDC	Device context
hrgn	HRGN	Specifies the region to frame
hbr	HBRUSH	Brush to use to draw the border
nWidth	int	Width of border in vertical brush strokes (logical units)

Parameter	*Type*	*Description*
`nHeight`	`int`	Height of border in horizontal brush strokes (logical units)

Description The `FrameRgn` function frames the region in `hrgn` with a border. The border is drawn using the brush specified in `hbr`. `nWidth` and `nHeight` specify the width and height of the border, respectively.

Return Value `TRUE` is returned when successful. `FALSE` is returned when unsuccessful.

Function Category Region

Related Functions `FillRgn`, `PaintRgn`

FreeAllGDIMem

Syntax `void FreeAllGDIMem(void)`

Parameter	*Type*	*Description*
None		

Description The `FreeAllGDIMem` function frees all memory allocated by a previous call to the `AllocGDIMem` function.

Return Value There is no return value.

Function Category Stress

Related Functions `AllocGDIMem`, `FreeAllMem`

FreeAllMem

Syntax `void FreeAllMem(void)`

Parameter	*Type*	*Description*
None		

Description The `FreeAllMem` function frees all memory allocated by a previous call to the `AllocMem` function.

Return Value There is no return value.

Function Category Stress

Related Functions `AllocMemm`, `FreeAllGDIMem`, `FreeAllUserMem`

FreeAllUserMem

Syntax `void FreeAllUserMem(void)`

Parameter	*Type*	*Description*
None		

Description The `FreeAllUserMem` function frees all memory previously allocated with the `AllocUserMem` function.

Return Value There is no return value.

Function Category Stress

Related Functions `AllocUserMem`, `FreeAllMem`

FreeLibrary

Syntax `void FreeLibrary(hinst)`

Parameter	*Type*	*Description*
`hinst`	`HINSTANCE`	Loaded library module

Description The `FreeLibrary` function frees the memory associated with the loaded library module in `hinst` when the reference count of the module is zero. Each time the `FreeLibrary` function is called, the reference count for the specified module is decremented.

Return Value There is no return value.

Function Category Module Management

Related Functions `LoadLibrary`

FreeModule

Syntax `BOOL FreeModule(hinst)`

Parameter	*Type*	*Description*
`hinst`	`HINSTANCE`	Loaded module

Description The `FreeModule` function frees the memory associated with the loaded module in `hinst` when the reference count of the module is zero. Each time the `FreeModule` function is called, the reference count for the specified module is decremented.

Return Value Zero is returned if the module's memory is freed. A nonzero value is returned if the memory is not freed.

Function Category Module Management

Related Functions `GetModuleFileName`, `GetModuleHandle`, `GetModuleUsage`, `LoadModule`

FreeProcInstance

Syntax `void FreeProcInstance(lpProc)`

Parameter	*Type*	*Description*
`lpProc`	`FARPROC`	Procedure instance address of the function to free

Description The `FreeProcInstance` function frees the function specified by the procedure instance address in `lpProc`. The address in `lpProc` must have been created with the `MakeProcInstance` function.

Return Value There is no return value.

Function Category Module Management

Related Functions `MakeProcInstance`

FreeResource

Syntax `BOOL FreeResource(hglbResource)`

Parameter	*Type*	*Description*
`hglbResource`	`HGLOBAL`	Data associated with the resource

Description The `FreeResource` function removes the resource in `hglbResource` from memory and frees all associated memory if the reference count for the resource is zero.

Return Value `TRUE` is returned when successful. `FALSE` is returned when unsuccessful.

Function Category Resource Management

Related Functions `AccessResource`, `AllocResource`, `LoadResource`

FreeSelector

Syntax `UINT FreeSelector(uSelector)`

Parameter	*Type*	*Description*
`uSelector`	`UINT`	Selector to free

Description The `FreeSelector` function frees the selector specified by `uSelector`.

Return Value `NULL` is returned when successful. `uSelector` is returned when unsuccessful.

Function Category Segment

Related Functions `AllocSelector`, `ChangeSelector`

GetActiveWindow

Syntax `HWND GetActiveWindow()`

Description The `GetActiveWindow` function returns the handle of the active window. The active window either has the current input focus or has been made the active window by `SetActiveWindow`.

Return Value The handle of the active window is returned. `NULL` is returned if no window is currently active.

Function Category Input

Related Functions `SetActiveWindow`

GetAspectRatioFilter

Syntax `DWORD GetAspectRatioFilter(hdc)`

Parameter	*Type*	*Description*
`hdc`	`HDC`	Device context

Description The `GetAspectRatioFilter` function gets the setting for the current aspect ratio filter for the device specified in `hdc`.

Return Value The high-order word of the return value contains the y coordinate of the aspect ratio used by the aspect ratio filter. The low-order word of the return value contains the x coordinate.

Function Category Font

Related Functions `GetAspectRatioFilterEx`

GetAspectRatioFilterEx

Syntax `BOOL GetAspectRatioFilterEx(hdc, lpAspectRatio)`

Parameter	*Type*	*Description*
`hdc`	`HDC`	Device context that contains the aspect ratio
`lpAspectRatio`	`SIZE FAR*`	Pointer to `SIZE` data structure that will store the retrieved aspect ratio filter

Description The `GetAspectRatioFilterEx` function copies the current aspect ratio filter settings to the data structure pointed to by `lpAspectRatio`. These settings are used to create, select, and display fonts. The `SetMapperFlags` function defines the aspect ratio.

Return Value `TRUE` is returned when successful. `FALSE` is returned when unsuccessful.

Function Category Font

Related Functions `SetMapperFlags`

GetAsyncKeyState

Syntax `int GetAsyncKeyState(vKey)`

Parameter	*Type*	*Description*
`vKey`	`int`	Virtual key code value

Description The `GetAsyncKeyState` function gets the state of the key specified in `vKey`. The return value indicates the state.

Return Value When the most significant bit of the returned value is set, the key is currently pressed down. When the least significant bit of the returned value is set, the key has been pressed since the last call to `GetAsyncKeyState`.

Function Category Hardware

Related Functions `GetKeyState`

GetAtomHandle

Syntax `HLOCAL GetAtomHandle(atm)`

Parameter	*Type*	*Description*
`atm`	`ATOM`	Unsigned integer that identifies the atom

Description The `GetAtomHandle` function gets the handle of the string associated with the atom in `atm`.

Return Value The identifier for the string associated with the atom is returned.

Function Category Atom

Related Functions `AddAtom`, `FindAtom`, `GetAtomName`

GetAtomName

Syntax `UINT GetAtomName(atm, lpszBuffer, cbBuffer)`

Parameter	*Type*	*Description*
`atm`	`ATOM`	Character string to retrieve
`lpszBuffer`	`LPSTR`	Pointer to the buffer to receive the string
`cbBuffer`	`int`	Maximum number of bytes in the buffer

Description The `GetAtomName` function puts a copy of the string associated with `atm` in `lpszBuffer`. `cbBuffer` specifies the maximum number of bytes in the buffer.

Return Value The number of bytes copied to the buffer is returned.

Function Category Atom

Related Functions `AddAtom`, `FindAtom`, `GetAtomHandle`

GetBitmapBits

Syntax `LONG GetBitmapBits(hbm, cbBuffer, lpvBits)`

Parameter	*Type*	*Description*
`hbm`	`HBITMAP`	Bitmap handle
`cbBuffer`	`LONG`	Number of bytes to copy
`lpvBits`	`void FAR*`	Pointer to buffer to receive the bitmap

Description The `GetBitmapBits` function places the bits from the bitmap specified in `hbm` into the buffer pointed to by `lpvBits`. `cbBuffer` specifies the number of bytes to copy. The `GetObject` function can be used to determine the value for `cbBuffer`.

Return Value The number of bytes in the bitmap is returned when successful. When unsuccessful, zero is returned.

Function Category Bitmap

Related Functions `SetBitmapBits`

GetBitmapDimension

Syntax `DWORD GetBitmapDimension(hbm)`

Parameter	*Type*	*Description*
`hbm`	`HBITMAP`	Bitmap handle

Description The `GetBitmapDimension` function gets the dimensions of the bitmap specified in `hbm`.

Return Value The high-order word of the return value contains the height, in tenths of millimeters, of the bitmap. The low-order word of the return value contains the width, in tenths of millimeters, of the bitmap. Zero is returned when unsuccessful.

Function Category Bitmap

Related Functions `SetBitmapDimension`

GetBitmapDimensionEx

Syntax `BOOL GetBitmapDimensionEx(hBitmap, lpDimension)`

Parameter	*Type*	*Description*
`hBitmap`	`HBITMAP`	Bitmap
`lpDimension`	`SIZE FAR*`	Pointer to `SIZE` data structure where the retrieved bitmap dimensions are copied

Description The `GetBitmapDimensionEx` function copies the dimensions of the bitmap specified in `hBitmap` to the data structure pointed to by `lpDimension`. The specified bitmap must have been set by the `SetBitmapDimensionEx` function.

Return Value `TRUE` is returned when successful. `FALSE` is returned when unsuccessful.

Function Category Bitmap

Related Functions `SetBitmapDimensionEx`

GetBkColor

Syntax `COLORREF GetBkColor(hdc)`

Parameter	*Type*	*Description*
`hdc`	`HDC`	Device context

Description The `GetBkColor` function gets the background color for the device context specified in `hdc`.

Return Value The RGB color value of the background color is returned.

Function Category Drawing Attribute

Related Functions `GetBkMode`, `SetBkColor`

GetBkMode

Syntax `int GetBkMode(hdc)`

Parameter	*Type*	*Description*
`hdc`	`HDC`	Device context

Description The `GetBkMode` function gets the background mode for the device context specified in `hdc`.

Return Value The background mode, either `OPAQUE`, `TRANSPARENT`, or `TRANSPARENT1`, is returned.

Function Category Drawing Attribute

Related Functions `GetBkColor`, `SetBkMode`

GetBoundsRect

Syntax `UINT GetBoundsRect(hdc, lprcBounds, flags)`

Parameter	*Type*	*Description*
hdc	HDC	Device context
lprcBounds	RECT FAR*	Pointer to buffer to receive the current bounding rectangle (logical coordinates returned)
flags	UINT	Type of return information. `flags` is set to one of the following values:

Value	*Meaning*
DCB_RESET	Clear bounding rectangle after return
DCB_WINDOWMGR	Retrieve the Windows bounding rectangle, not the application's bounding rectangle

Description The `GetBoundsRect` function returns the bounding rectangle for the device context specified in `hdc`. `flags` specifies the type of data to return.

Return Value The current state of the bounding rectangle is returned. Any combination of the following values may be returned:

Value	*Meaning*
DCB_ACCUMULATE	Bounding rectangle accumulation is occurring
DCB_RESET	Bounding rectangle is empty
DCB_SET	Bounding rectangle is not empty
DCB_ENABLE	Accumulation is enabled
DCB_DISABLE	Accumulation is disabled

Function Category Rectangle

Related Functions `SetBoundsRect`

GetBrushOrg

Syntax `DWORD GetBrushOrg(hdc)`

Parameter	*Type*	*Description*
`hdc`	`HDC`	Device context

Description The `GetBrushOrg` function gets the brush origin for the device context specified in `hdc`.

Return Value The low-order word of the return value contains the x coordinate of the brush origin, in device units. The high-order word of the return value contains the y coordinate of the brush origin, in device units.

Function Category Drawing Tool

Related Functions `SetBrushOrg`

GetBValue

Syntax `BYTE GetBValue(rgbColor)`

Parameter	*Type*	*Description*
`rgbColor`	`DWORD`	RGB color field

Description The `GetBValue` macro gets the blue value from the RGB color value specified in `rgbColor`.

Return Value The blue value from the RGB color field is returned.

Function Category Windows Macros

Related Functions `GetGValue`, `GetRValue`

GetCapture

Syntax `HWND GetCapture()`

Description The `GetCapture` function returns the handle of the window that has the mouse capture. The retrieved handle identifies the window that receives the mouse input.

Return Value The handle of the window that has the mouse capture is returned. If no window has the mouse capture, `NULL` is returned.

Function Category Input

Related Functions `SetCapture`

GetCaretBlinkTime

Syntax `UINT GetCaretBlinkTime()`

Description The `GetCaretBlinkTime` function gets the blink rate of the caret measured in milliseconds.

Return Value The blink rate, measured in milliseconds, is returned.

Function Category Caret

Related Functions `SetCaretBlinkTime`

GetCaretPos

Syntax `void GetCaretPos(lppt)`

Parameter	*Type*	*Description*
`lppt`	`POINT FAR*`	Pointer to the structure which stores the retrieved screen coordinates

Description The `GetCaretPos` function retrieves the screen coordinates of the current caret position. `lppt` points to the structure of type `POINT` which holds the retrieved coordinates. The `POINT` structure follows.

```
typedef struct tagPOINT {
     int x;
     int y;
} POINT;
```

in which

`x` specifies the horizontal coordinate of the caret position

`y` specifies the vertical coordinate of the caret position.

Return Value There is no return value.

Function Category Caret

Related Functions `SetCaretPos`

GetCharABCWidths

Syntax `BOOL GetCharABCWidths(hdc, uFirstChar, uLastChar, lpabc)`

Parameter	*Type*	*Description*
hdc	HDC	Device context
uFirstChar	UINT	First character in character range
uLastChar	UINT	Last character in character range
lpabc	LPABC	Pointer to ABC data structure to receive the character widths

Description The `GetCharABCWidths` function retrieves the character widths of the characters for the current font in the range from `uFirstChar` to `uLastChar`. `lpabc` points to a data structure of type `ABC` that receives the character widths. The `ABC` data structure follows.

```
typedef struct _ABC
     {
     short abcA;
     short abcB;
     short abcC;
     } ABC;
```

in which

`abcA` is the "A" spacing, the distance to add to the current position before drawing the character glyph

`abcB` is the "B" spacing, the width of the drawn portion of the character glyph

`abcC` is the "C" spacing, the distance to add to the current position to provide white space to the right of the character glyph.

Return Value A nonzero value is returned when successful. Zero is returned when unsuccessful.

Function Category Font, TrueType

Related Functions `GetCharWidth`

GetCharWidth

Syntax `BOOL GetCharWidth(hdc, uFirstChar, uLastChar, lpnWidths)`

Parameter	*Type*	*Description*
`hdc`	`HDC`	Device context
`uFirstChar`	`UINT`	First character
`uLastChar`	`UINT`	Last character
`lpnWidths`	`int FAR*`	Pointer to the buffer to receive the widths of the characters

Description The `GetCharWidth` function determines the width of each of the characters from the group of consecutive characters specified by `uFirstChar` and `uLastChar`. The widths of each of the characters are stored in the buffer pointed to by `lpnWidths`.

Return Value A nonzero value is returned when successful. Zero is returned when unsuccessful.

Function Category Font

Related Functions `GetCharABCWidths`

GetClassInfo

Syntax `BOOL GetClassInfo(hinst, lpszClassName, lpWndClass)`

Parameter	*Type*	*Description*
`hinst`	`HINSTANCE`	Instance of the application that created the class
`lpszClassName`	`LPCSTR`	Name of class
`lpWndClass`	`WNDCLASS FAR*`	Pointer to `WNDCLASS` structure where class information will be copied

Description The `GetClassInfo` function gets information about the class specified by `lpszClassName`. `hinst` specifies the instance of the application that created the class. The class information is copied into the data structure of type `WNDCLASS` pointed to by `lpWndClass`.

Return Value A nonzero value is returned if a matching class is found and successfully copied into the structure. Zero is returned if a matching class is not found.

Function Category Window Creation

Related Functions `GetClassLong`, `GetClassName`, `GetClassWord`

GetClassLong

Syntax `LPARAM GetClassLong(hwnd, offset)`

Parameter	*Type*	*Description*
`hwnd`	`HWND`	Window handle
`offset`	`int`	Byte offset of value to retrieve

Description The `GetClassLong` function gets the long value specified in `offset` from the `WNDCLASS` structure for the window in `hwnd`. `offset` specifies the byte offset of the value to retrieve. `offset` can be set to `GCL_WNDPROC` to retrieve a long pointer to the window function or `GCL_MENUNAME` to retrieve a long pointer to the menu-name string.

Return Value The specified long value in the extra class memory is returned when successful. Zero is returned when unsuccessful.

Function Category Window Creation

Related Functions `GetClassInfo`, `GetClassName`, `GetClassWord`

GetClassName

Syntax `int GetClassName(hwnd, lpszClassName, cchClassName)`

Parameter	*Type*	*Description*
`hwnd`	`HWND`	Window handle
`lpszClassName`	`LPSTR`	Buffer to receive class name
`cchClassName`	`int`	Maximum number of bytes to store in `lpszClassName`

Description The `GetClassName` function gets the class name of the window specified in `hwnd`. `lpszClassName` points to the buffer that stores the class name. `cchClassName` specifies the maximum number of bytes copied to `lpszClassName`.

Return Value The number of characters copied to `lpszClassName` is returned when successful. Zero is returned when unsuccessful.

Function Category Window Creation

Related Functions `GetClassInfo`, `GetClassLong`, `GetClassWord`

GetClassWord

Syntax `WPARAM GetClassWord(hwnd, offset)`

Parameter	*Type*	*Description*
`hwnd`	`HWND`	Window handle
`offset`	`int`	Byte offset of value to be retrieved

Description The GetClassWord function gets the word identified by offset from the WNDCLASS structure for the window in hwnd. offset specifies the byte offset of the value to be retrieved. offset can also be set to any of the following values:

Value	*Meaning*
GCW_CBCLSEXTRA	Get number of bytes of additional class information if available
GCW_CBWNDEXTRA	Get number of bytes of additional window information if available
GCW_HBRBACKGROUND	Get the handle for the background brush
GCW_HCURSOR	Get the handle for the cursor
GCW_HICON	Get the handle for the icon
GCW_HMODULE	Get the handle for the module
GCW_STYLE	Get the window-class style bits

Return Value The value in the window's reserved memory is returned when successful. Zero is returned when unsuccessful.

Function Category Window Creation

Related Functions GetClassInfo, GetClassLong, GetClassName

GetClientRect

Syntax `void GetClientRect(hwnd, lprc)`

Parameter	*Type*	*Description*
hwnd	HWND	Window associated with client area
lprc	RECT FAR*	Pointer to RECT data structure where the coordinates of the client area are placed

Description The GetClientRect function places the client coordinates of a client area into the data structure of type RECT pointed to by lprc. The RECT structure follows. The window that contains the client area is specified in hwnd. Client coordinates are defined in relation to the upper left corner of the client area.

```
typedef struct tagRECT {
     int left;
     int top;
     int right;
     int bottom;
} RECT;
```

in which

`left` is the x coordinate of the upper-left corner

`top` is the y coordinate of the upper-left corner

`right` is the x coordinate of the lower-right corner

`bottom` is the y coordinate of the lower-right corner.

Return Value There is no return value.

Function Category Display and Movement

Related Functions `GetWindowRect`

GetClipboardData

Syntax `HANDLE GetClipboardData(uFormat)`

Parameter	*Type*	*Description*
`uFormat`	`UINT`	Data format

Description The `GetClipboardData` function gets clipboard data in the format specified in `uFormat`. The formats available for the clipboard can be determined with the `EnumClipboardFormats` function. For text, two formats are supported: `CF_TEXT`, the default, and `CF_OEMTEXT`, which is used for non-Windows applications.

Return Value The indentifier for the block which contains the clipboard data is returned when successful. `NULL` is returned on error.

Function Category Clipboard

Related Functions `SetClipboardData`

GetClipboardFormatName

Syntax `int GetClipboardFormatName(uFormat,lpszFormatName,cbMax)`

Parameter	*Type*	*Description*
`uFormat`	`UINT`	Format type to retrieve
`lpszFormatName`	`LPSTR`	Pointer to format name
`cbMax`	`int`	Maximum number of bytes for the format name

Description The `GetClipboardFormatName` function gets the name of the format specified in `uFormat`. `lpszFormatName` points to the buffer where the format name will be stored. `cbMax` specifies the maximum length of the buffer.

Return Value The number of bytes copied to the buffer is returned when successful. A zero indicates that the requested format is invalid.

Function Category Clipboard

Related Functions `EnumClipboardFormats`, `RegisterClipboardFormat`

GetClipboardOwner

Syntax `HWND GetClipboardOwner()`

Description The `GetClipboardOwner` function gets the handle of the clipboard's current owner.

Return Value The `GetClipboardOwner` function returns the identifier for the window which currently owns the clipboard. If no window owns the clipboard, `NULL` is returned.

Function Category Clipboard

Related Functions `CloseClipboard`, `OpenClipboard`

GetClipboardViewer

Syntax `HWND GetClipboardViewer()`

Description The `GetClipboardViewer` function retrieves the handle of the first window in the clipboard viewer chain.

Return Value The `GetClipboardViewer` function returns the retrieved window handle. If no viewer is in the clipboard viewer chain, `NULL` is returned.

Function Category Clipboard

Related Functions `SetClipboardViewer`

GetClipBox

Syntax `int GetClipBox(hdc, lprc)`

Parameter	*Type*	*Description*
hdc	HDC	Device context
lprc	RECT FAR*	Points to RECT data structure that receives the dimensions of the rectangle

Description The `GetClipBox` function gets the dimensions of the smallest rectangle that completely encloses the clipping region. The dimensions are placed into the data structure of type `RECT` pointed to by `lprc`. The `RECT` data structure follows.

```
typedef struct tagRECT{
     int left;
     int top;
     int right;
     int bottom;
} RECT;
```

in which

`left` is the x coordinate of the upper-left corner

`top` is the y coordinate of the upper-left corner

`right` is the x coordinate of the lower-right corner

`bottom` is the y coordinate of the lower-right corner.

Return Value One of the following values is returned to describe the clipping region:

Value	*Meaning*
COMPLEXREGION	Region has overlapping borders
ERROR	Device context is invalid
NULLREGION	Region is empty
SIMPLEREGION	Region has no overlapping borders

Function Category Clipping

Related Functions `SelectClipRgn`

GetClipCursor

Syntax `void GetClipCursor(lprc)`

Parameter	*Type*	*Description*
lprc	RECT FAR*	Pointer to RECT data structure that receives the coordinates of the clip rectangle

Description The `GetClipCursor` function gets the coordinates of the cursor clipping rectangle defined by `ClipCursor`. The coordinates are placed in a data structure of type `RECT` pointed to by `lprc`. The `RECT` data structure follows.

```
typedef struct tagRECT{
     int left;
     int top;
     int right;
     int bottom;
} RECT;
```

in which

`left` is the x coordinate of the upper-left corner

`top` is the y coordinate of the upper-left corner

`right` is the x coordinate of the lower-right corner

`bottom` is the y coordinate of the lower-right corner.

Return Value There is no return value.

Function Category Cursor

Related Functions ClipCursor

GetCodeHandle

Syntax `HGLOBAL GetCodeHandle(lpProc)`

Parameter	*Type*	*Description*
lpProc	FARPROC	Procedure instance address

Description The GetCodeHandle function returns the handle of the code segment that contains the function with the procedure instance address in lpProc.

Return Value The handle of the code segment that contains the specified function is returned when successful. NULL is returned when unsuccessful.

Function Category Module Management

Related Functions GetModuleHandle

GetCodeInfo

Syntax `void GetCodeInfo(lpProc, lpSegInfo)`

Parameter	*Type*	*Description*
lpProc	FARPROC	Function address
lpSegInfo	SEGINFO FAR*	Pointer to SEGINFO structure to be filled with code segment information

Description The GetCodeInfo function gets the pointer to an array of values that contain code segment information for the code segment containing the function specified in lpProc. lpSegInfo is a pointer to a SEGINFO structure that is filled with code segment information.

Return Value There is no return value.

Function Category Segment

Related Functions `GetModuleHandle`

GetCommError

Syntax `int GetCommError(idComDev, lpStat)`

Parameter	*Type*	*Description*
`idComDev`	`int`	Communication device
`lpStat`	`COMSTAT FAR*`	Pointer to `COMSTAT` data structure to receive the device status

Description The `GetCommError` function clears the communication port in `idComDev` when the port is locked by Windows as a result of a communications error. The status of the communication device is placed in the data structure of type `COMSTAT` pointed to by `lpStat`. The `COMSTAT` structure follows. When `lpStat` is set to `NULL`, the error code is returned by the function.

```
typedef struct tagCOMSTAT {
     WORD fCtsHold: 1;
     WORD fDsrHold: 1;
     WORD fRlsdHold: 1;
     WORD fXoffHold: 1;
     WORD fXoffSent: 1;
     WORD fEof: 1;
     WORD fTxim: 1;
     WORD cbInQue;
     WORD cbOutQue;
} COMSTAT;
```

in which

`fCtsHold: 1` indicates whether transmission is waiting for the clear-to-send (CTS) signal to be sent

`fDsrHold: 1` indicates whether transmission is waiting for the data-set-ready (DSR) signal to be sent

`fRlsdHold: 1` indicates whether transmission is waiting for the receive-line-signal-detect (RLSD) signal to be sent

`fXoffHold: 1` indicates whether transmission is waiting as a result of the `XoffChar` character being received

`fXoffSent: 1` indicates whether transmission is waiting as a result of the `XoffChar` character being transmitted

`fEof: 1` indicates whether the `EofChar` character has been received

`fTxim: 1` indicates whether a character is waiting to be transmitted

`cbInQue` indicates the number of characters in the receive queue

`cbOutQue` indicates the number of characters in the transmit queue.

Return Value The return value is a combination of one or more error codes returned by the most recent communications function. The possible error codes are as follows:

Value	*Meaning*
`CE_BREAK`	Break condition detected
`CE_CTSTO`	Clear-to-send timeout
`CE_DNS`	Parallel device not selected
`CE_DSRTO`	Data-set-ready timeout
`CE_FRAME`	Framing error detected
`CE_IOE`	I/O error with parallel device
`CE_MODE`	Mode not supported or `idComDev` is invalid
`CE_OOP`	Out-of-paper signal from parallel device
`CE_OVERRUN`	Character lost
`CE_PTO`	Timeout while attempting communication with the parallel port
`CE_RLSDTO`	Receive-line-signal-detect (RLSD) timeout
`CE_RXOVER`	Receive queue overflow
`CE_RXPARITY`	Parity error detected
`CE_TXFULL`	Transmit queue is full

Function Category Communication

Related Functions `GetCommState`

GetCommEventMask

Syntax `UINT GetCommEventMask(idComDev, fnEvtClear)`

Parameter	*Type*	*Description*
`idComDev`	`int`	Communication device
`fnEvtClear`	`int`	Events to enable

Description The `GetCommEventMask` function gets the current event mask for the communication device in `idComDev`. The mask is cleared after the event mask is retrieved. `fnEvtClear` specifies the events to enable. The event values used for `fnEvtClear` are as follows:

Value	*Meaning*
`EV_BREAK`	Sets when a break is detected on input
`EV_CTS`	Sets when the clear-to-send signal changes state
`EV_DSR`	Sets when the data-set-ready signal changes state
`EV_ERR`	Sets when a line status error occurs
`EV_PERR`	Sets when a printer error is detected on a parallel device
`EV_RING`	Sets when a ring indicator is detected
`EV_RSLD`	Sets when the receive-line-signal-detect signal changes state
`EV_RXCHAR`	Sets when a character is received and placed in the receive queue
`EV_RXFLAG`	Sets when the event character is received and placed in the receive queue
`EV_TXEMPTY`	Sets when the last character in the transmit queue is sent

Return Value The current event mask value is returned.

Function Category Communication

Related Functions `GetCommError`, `GetCommState`, `SetCommEventMask`

GetCommState

Syntax `int GetCommState(idComDev, lpdcb)`

Parameter	*Type*	*Description*
idComDev	int	Communication device
lpdcb	DCB FAR*	Pointer to the DCB data structure to receive the device control block

Description The GetCommState function gets the device control block for the communication device in idComDev and places it in the data structure of type DCB pointed to by lpdcb. The DCB data structure follows.

```
typedef struct tagDCB {
    BYTE Id;
    WORD BaudRate;
    BYTE ByteSize;
    BYTE Parity;
    BYTE StopBits;
    WORD RlsTimeout;
    WORD CtsTimeout;
    WORD DsrTimeout;
    WORD fBinary: 1;
    WORD fRtsDisable: 1;
    WORD fParity: 1;
    WORD fOutxCtsFlow: 1;
    WORD fOutxDsrFlow: 1;
    WORD fDummy: 2;
    WORD fDtrDisable: 1;
    WORD fOutX: 1;
    WORD fInX: 1;
    WORD fPeChar: 1;
    WORD fNull: 1;
    WORD fChEvt: 1;
    WORD fDtrflow: 1;
    WORD fRtsflow: 1;
    WORD fDummy2: 1;
    char XonChar;
    char XoffChar;
    WORD XonLim;
    WORD XoffLim;
    char PeChar;
    char EofChar;
    char EvtChar;
    WORD TxDelay;
} DCB;
```

in which

`Id` is the communication device and is set by the device driver

`BaudRate` is the baud rate. When the high-order byte is 0xFF, the low-order byte is one of the following baud-rate index values:

CBR_110	
CBR_300	CBR_14400
CBR_600	CBR_19200
CBR_1200	CBR_38400
CBR_2400	CBR_56000
CBR_4800	CBR_128000
CBR_9600	CBR_256000

When the high-order byte is not 0xFF, `BaudRate`specifies the actual baud rate

`ByteSize` is the number of bits in a character (4 to 8)

`Parity` is the parity scheme—can be `EVENPARITY`, `MARKPARITY`, `NOPARITY`, or `ODDPARITY`

`StopBits` is the number of stop bits to use—can be `ONESTOPBIT`, `ONE5STOPBITS`, or `TWOSTOPBITS`

`RlsTimeout` is the maximum number of milliseconds the device should wait for the receive-line-signal-detect (RLSD) signal

`CtsTimeout` is the maximum number of milliseconds the device should wait for the clear-to-send (CTS) signal

`DsrTimeout` is the maximum number of milliseconds the device should wait for the data-set-ready (DSR) signal

`fBinary` is the binary mode indicator

`fRtsDisable` indicates whether the request-to-send signal is disabled

`fParity` indicates whether the parity checking is enabled

`fOutxCtsFlow` indicates that clear-to-send signal is monitored for output flow control

`fOutxDsrFlow` indicates that data-set-ready signal is monitored for output flow control

`fDummy` is reserved

`fDtrDisable` indicates whether the data-terminal-ready signal is disabled `fOutX` indicates that the XON/XOFF flow control is used during transmission

`fInX` indicates that the XON/XOFF flow control is used while receiving

`fPeChar` indicates that characters received with parity errors are to be replaced with the character in the `fPeChar` field

`fNull` indicates that null characters are discarded

`fChEvt` indicates that reception of the `EvtChar` character is to be flagged as an event

`fDtrflow` indicates that the data-terminal-ready signal is used for receive flow control

`fRtsflow` indicates that the ready-to-send signal is used for receive flow control

`fDummy2` is reserved

`XonChar` is the value of the XON character

`XoffChar` is the value of XOFF character

`XonLim` is the minimum number of characters allowed in the receive queue before the XON character is sent

`XoffLim` is the maximum number of characters allowed in the receive queue before the XOFF character is sent

`PeChar` is the value of the character used to replace characters received with parity errors

`EofChar` is the character used to signal the end of data

`EvtChar` is the character used to signal an event

`TxDelay` is not used.

Return Value Zero is returned when successful. A negative value is returned when unsuccessful.

Function Category Communication

Related Functions `GetCommError`

GetCurrentPDB

Syntax `UINT GetCurrentPDB()`

Description The `GetCurrentPDB` function gets the selector address for the DOS Program Data Base (PDB). The PDB is frequently called the Program Segment Prefix (PSP).

Return Value The selector address of the PDB is returned.

Function Category Task

Related Functions `GetCurrentTask`

GetCurrentPosition

Syntax `DWORD GetCurrentPosition(hdc)`

Parameter	*Type*	*Description*
`hdc`	`HDC`	Device context

Description The `GetCurrentPosition` function gets the logical coordinates of the current position.

Return Value The low-order word of the return value contains the x coordinate of the current position. The high-order word of the return value contains the y coordinate of the current position.

Function Category Coordinate

Related Functions `LineTo`, `MoveTo`

GetCurrentPositionEx

Syntax `BOOL GetCurrentPositionEx(hdc, lppt)`

Parameter	*Type*	*Description*
`hdc`	`HDC`	Device context
`lppt`	`POINT FAR*`	Pointer to `POINT` data structure that receives the current position

Description The `GetCurrentPositionEx` function copies the current position to the data structure pointed to by `lppt`. The current position is specified in logical coordinates.

Return Value `TRUE` is returned when successful. `FALSE` is returned when unsuccessful.

Function Category Coordinate

Related Functions `GetCurrentPosition`

GetCurrentTask

Syntax `HTASK GetCurrentTask()`

Description The `GetCurrentTask` function gets the handle of the current task.

Return Value The handle to the current task is returned when successful. `NULL` is returned when unsuccessful.

Function Category Task

Related Functions `GetNumTasks`

GetCurrentTime

Syntax `DWORD GetCurrentTime()`

Description The `GetCurrentTime` function gets the number of milliseconds elapsed since Windows was started. The retrieved time is called Windows time.

Return Value Windows time, the number of milliseconds since Windows was started, is returned.

Function Category Input

Related Functions `GetTickCount`, `KillTimer`, `SetTimer`

GetCursor

Syntax `HCURSOR GetCursor(void)`

Description The `GetCursor` function gets the handle to the current cursor.

Return Value The retrieved handle is returned when successful. `NULL` is returned when unsuccessful.

Function Categroy Cursor

Related Functions `GetCursorPos`

GetCursorPos

Syntax `void GetCursorPos(lppt)`

Parameter	*Type*	*Description*
`lppt`	`POINT FAR*`	Structure to store cursor coordinates

Description The `GetCursorPos` function retrieves the screen coordinates of the current cursor position. These screen coordinates are then placed in a structure of type `POINT` which is pointed to by `lppt`. The `POINT` structure follows.

```
typedef struct tagPOINT {
     int x;
     int y;
} POINT;
```

in which

`x` is the x screen coordinate of the cursor

`y` is the y screen coordinate of the cursor.

Return Value There is no return value.

Function Category Cursor

Related Functions `SetCursorPos`

GetDC

Syntax `HDC GetDC(hwnd)`

Parameter	*Type*	*Description*
hwnd	HWND	Window handle

Description The `GetDC` function gets the display context for the client area of the window specified in `hwnd`.

Return Value The identifier for the display context is returned when successful. `NULL` is returned when unsuccessful.

Function Category Device Context

Related Functions `CreateDC`, `DeleteDC`

GetDCEx

Syntax `HDC GetDCEx(hwnd, hrgnClip, fdwOptions)`

Parameter	*Type*	*Description*
hwnd	HWND	Windows where drawing is to take place
hrgnClip	HRGN	Clip region; this region can be combined with the visible region of the client window
fdwOptions	DWORD	Device context options. `fdwOptions` is a combination of some of the following values:

Value	*Meaning*
DCX_CACHE	Device context from cache is returned
DCX_CLIPCHILDREN	Visible regions of all child windows are excluded
DCX_CLIPSIBLINGS	Visible regions of all sibling windows are excluded

Value	*Meaning*
DCX_DEFAULTCLIP	Default device context is returned
DCX_EXCLUDERGN	Region in hrgnClip is excluded
DCX_EXCLUDEUPDATE	Update region of window is excluded
DCX_INTERSECTRGN	Region in hrgnClip is intersected with the visible region of the returned device context
DCX_INTERSECTUPDATE	Update region of device context is intersected with the returned device context
DCX_LOCKWINDOWUPDATE	Drawing allowed even if LockWindowUpdate has been called
DCX_NORECOMPUTE	NULL is returned if no match is found in the cache
DCX_NORESETATTRS	Device context attributes are not reset to their default values when the device context is released
DCX_PARENTCLIP	Visible region of the parent window is used
DCX_USESTYLE	Device context type is based on the class styles in the window class
DCX_VALIDATE	When used with DCX_INTERSECTUPDATE, the device context is validated
DCX_WINDOW	The returned device context corresponds to the window rectangle—not the client rectangle

Description The GetDCEx function gets the handle of the device context for the window specified in hwnd. This function provides more direct control over the device context than the GetDC function.

Return Value The device context for the specified window is returned when successful. NULL is returned when unsuccessful.

Function Category Device Context and Painting

Related Category GetDC, ReleaseDC

GetDCOrg

Syntax `DWORD GetDCOrg(hdc)`

Parameter	*Type*	*Description*
hdc	HDC	Device context

Description The GetDCOrg function gets the final translation origin for the device context specified in hdc. The final translation origin is the offset used by Windows to translate device coordinates into client coordinates and is relative to the physical origin of the screen.

Return Value The x coordinate of the final translation origin, in device coordinates, is specified in the low-order word of the return value. The y coordinate of the final translation origin, in device coordinates, is specified in the high-order word of the return value.

Function Category Device Context

Related Functions CreateDC, GetDC, ReleaseDC

GetDesktopWindow

Syntax `HWND GetDesktopWindow()`

Description The GetDesktopWindow function returns the window handle of the Windows desktop window.

Return Value The handle to the Windows desktop window is returned.

Function Category Information

Related Functions GetNextWindow, GetTopWindow

GetDeviceCaps

Syntax `int GetDeviceCaps(hdc, iCapability)`

Parameter	*Type*	*Description*
hdc	HDC	Device context
iCapability	int	Value to return

Description The GetDeviceCaps function gets information on the display device specified in hdc. iCapability specifies the type of information to retrieve. iCapability is set to one of the following values:

Value	*Meaning*
DRIVERVERSION	Version number
TECHNOLOGY	Device technology; is one of the following:
	DT_PLOTTER — vector plotter
	DT_RASDISPLAY — raster display
	DT_RASPRINTER — raster printer
	DT_RASCAMERA — raster camera
	DT_CHARSTREAM — character stream
	DT_METAFILE — metafile
	DT_DISPFILE — display file
HORZSIZE	Width of display in millimeters
VERTSIZE	Height of display in millimeters
HORZRES	Width of display in pixels
VERTRES	Height of display in pixels
LOGPIXELSX	Pixels per logical inch along the display width
LOGPIXELSY	Pixels per logical inch along the display height
BITSPIXEL	Color bits for each pixel
PLANES	Number of color planes
NUMBRUSHES	Number of device-specific brushes
NUMPENS	Number of device-specific pens
NUMMARKERS	Number of device-specific markers
NUMFONTS	Number of device-specific fonts
NUMCOLORS	Number of entries in device color table
ASPECTX	Width of pixel for line drawing
ASPECTY	Height of pixel for line drawing

Value	*Meaning*
ASPECTXY	Diagonal width of pixel for line drawing
PDEVICESIZE	Size of PDEVICE internal data structure
CLIPCAPS	Clipping capabilities; set to one of the following:

Value	*Meaning*
CP_NONE	Output is not clipped
CP_RECTANGLE	Output is clipped to rectangles
CP_REGION	Output is clipped to regions

Value	*Meaning*
SIZEPALETTE	Number of entries in system palette
NUMRESERVED	Number of reserved entries in system palette
COLORRES	Color resolution in bits per pixel
RASTERCAPS	Raster capabilities, described as follows: RC_BANDING — requires banding support RC_BIGFONT — supports fonts larger than 64K RC_BITBLT — can transfer bitmaps RC_BITMAP64 — supports bitmaps larger than 64K RC_DEVBITS — supports device bitmaps RC_DI_BITMAP — supports SetDIBits and GetDIBits RC_DIBTODEV — supports SetDIBitsToDevice RC_FLOODFILL — can floodfill RC_GDI20_OUTPUT — supports Windows 2.0 RC_GDI20_STATE — device context includes a state block RC_NONE — does not support raster operations RC_OP_DX_OUTPUT — supports dev opaque and DX array RC_PALETTE — palette-based device RC_SAVEBITMAP — saves bitmaps locally RC_SCALING — supports scaling RC_STRETCHBLT — supports StretchBlt RC_STRETCHDIB — supports StretchDIBits

Value	*Meaning*
CURVECAPS	Curve capabilities bitmask; bits are as follows: CC_NONE — no curves CC_CIRCLES — does circles CC_PIE — does pie wedges CC_CHORD — does chord arcs CC_ELLIPSES — does ellipses CC_WIDE — does wide borders CC_STYLED — does styled borders CC_WIDESTYLED — does wide, styled borders CC_INTERIORS — does interiors CC_ROUNDRECT — supports rectangles with rounded corners
LINECAPS	Line capabilities bitmask; bits are as follows: LC_NONE — no lines LC_POLYLINE — does polyline LC_MARKERS — does markers LC_POLYMARKER — does polymarkers LC_WIDE — does wide lines LC_STYLED — does styled lines LC_WIDESTYLED — does wide, styled lines LC_INTERIORS — does interiors
POLYGONALCAPS	Polygonal capabilities bitmask; bits are as follows: PC_NONE — no polygons PC_POLYGON — does alternate fill polygon PC_RECTANGLE — does rectangle PC_WINDPOLYGON — does winding number fill polygon PC_SCANLINE — does scan line PC_WIDE — does wide borders PC_STYLED — does styled borders PC_WIDESTYLED — does wide, styled borders PC_INTERIORS — does interiors

Value	Meaning
TEXTCAPS	Text capabilities bitmask; bits are as follows: TC_OP_CHARACTER — does character output precision TC_OP_STROKE — does stroke output precision TC_CP_STROKE — does stroke clip precision TC_CR_90 — does 90-degree character rotation TC_CR_ANY — does any character rotation TC_SF_X_YINDEP — does independent scaling TC_SA_DOUBLE — does doubled character for scaling TC_SA_INTEGER — does integer multiples for scaling TC_SA_CONTIN — does any multiples for scaling TC_EA_DOUBLE — does double-weight characters TC_IA_ABLE — does italicizing TC_UA_ABLE — does underlining TC_SO_ABLE — does strikeouts TC_RA_ABLE — does raster fonts TC_VA_ABLE — does vector fonts TC_RESERVED — reserved; set to zero

Return Value The value of the specified item is returned.

Function Category Environment

Related Functions `GetDC`

GetDialogBaseUnits

Syntax `DWORD GetDialogBaseUnits()`

Description The `GetDialogBaseUnits` function gets the dialog base units that are used by Windows when a dialog box is created. These units are useful for determining the average character width of the system font. The returned dialog base units must be scaled to represent actual dialog units. The horizontal dialog unit is 1/4 the horizontal value returned by `GetDialogBaseUnits`. The vertical dialog unit is 1/8 the vertical value returned by `GetDialogBaseUnits`.

Return Value The value representing the dialog base units is returned. The high-order word contains the height (in pixels) of the current dialog base height unit. The low-order word contains the width (in pixels) of the current dialog base width unit.

Function Category Dialog Box

Related Functions `GetDlgItem`

GetDIBits

Syntax

```
int GetDIBits(hdc, hbmp, nStartScan, cScanLines, lpBits,
              lpBitsInfo, fuColorUse)
```

Parameter	*Type*	*Description*
`hdc`	`HDC`	Device context
`hbmp`	`HBITMAP`	Bitmap handle
`nStartScan`	`UINT`	First scan line of destination bitmap
`cScanLines`	`UINT`	Number of lines to copy
`lpBits`	`void FAR*`	Pointer to buffer to receive the bits for the bitmap in device-independent format
`lpBitsInfo`	`BITMAPINFO FAR*`	Pointer to a `BITMAPINFO` structure containing information for the device-independent bitmap
`fuColorUse`	`UINT`	Set to `DIB_PAL_COLORS` (color table in `lpBitsInfo` contains array of 16-bit indexes for the currently realized logical palette) or `DIB_RGB_COLORS` (color table in `lpBitsInfo` contains RGB values)

Description The `GetDIBits` function retrieves the bits of a bitmap. The bits are then placed into the buffer pointed to by `lpBits` in device-independent format. `hDC` specifies the device context. `hbmp` specifies the bitmap. lpBitsInfo points to a data structure of type BITMAPINFO. The BITMAPINFO structure follows.

```
typedef struct tagBITMAPINFO {
  BITMAPINFOHEADER bmiHeader;
  RGBQUAD bmiColors[1];
} BITMAPINFO;
```

in which

bmiHeader is the BITMAPINFOHEADER structure for the device-independent bitmap

bmiColors is an array of data structures of type RGBQUAD that defines the colors in the bitmap.

The BITMAPINFOHEADER structure follows.

```
typedef struct tagBITMAPINFOHEADER {
  DWORD biSize;
  DWORD biWidth;
  DWORD biHeight;
  WORD biPlanes;
  WORD biBitCount;
  DWORD biCompression;
  DWORD biSizeImage;
  DWORD biXPelsPerMeter;
  DWORD biYPelsPerMeter;
  DWORD biClrUsed;
  DWORD biClrImportant;
} BITMAPINFOHEADER;
```

in which

biSize is the number of bytes required for the structure

biWidth is the width of the bitmap in pixels

biHeight is the height of the bitmap in pixels

biPlanes is the number of planes; must be set to 1

biBitCount is the number of bits per pixel (1, 4, 8, or 24)

biCompression is the type of compression and is selected from the following values:

BI_RGB	Bitmap is not compressed
BI_RLE8	Run-length encode format with 8 bits per pixel

`BI_RLE4` Run-length encode format with 4 bits per pixel

`biSizeImage` is the size of the image in bytes

`biXPelsPerMeter` is the horizontal resolution in pixels per meter for the target device

`biYPelsPerMeter` is the vertical resolution in pixels per meter for the target device

`biClrUsed` is the number of color indexes in the color table the bitmap actually uses

`biClrImportant` is the number of color indexes considered important for the bitmap.

Return Value The number of scan lines copied from the bitmap is returned when successful. Zero is returned if unsuccessful.

Function Category Bitmap

Related Functions `SetDIBits`, `SetDIBitsToDevice`

GetDlgCtrlID

Syntax `int GetDlgCtrlID(hwnd)`

Parameter	*Type*	*Description*
`hwnd`	`HWND`	Child window handle

Description The `GetDlgCtrlID` function returns the child window ID for the child window specified in `hwnd`. This function should not be used when `hwnd` specifies a top-level window because top-level windows have no ID.

Return Value The ID value is returned when successful. When unsuccessful, `NULL` is returned.

Function Category Dialog Box

Related Functions `GetDlgItem`, `SetDlgItemInt`

GetDlgItem

Syntax `HWND GetDlgItem(hwndDlg, idControl)`

Parameter	*Type*	*Description*
`hwndDlg`	`HWND`	Dialog box containing the control
`idControl`	`int`	ID of item to be retrieved

Description The `GetDlgItem` function gets the handle of the control specified by the integer ID in `idControl`. The dialog box containing the control is specified in `hwndDlg`. This function is not limited to dialog boxes. It can be used with any parent-child window pair.

Return Value The handle for the specified control is returned when successful. If no control with the specified ID exists, `NULL` is returned.

Function Category Dialog Box

Related Functions `GetDlgItemInt`, `GetDlgItemText`, `SetDlgItemInt`, `SetDlgItemText`

GetDlgItemInt

Syntax

```
UINT GetDlgItemInt(hwndDlg, idControl,
                   lpfTranslated, fSigned)
```

Parameter	*Type*	*Description*
`hwndDlg`	`HWND`	Dialog box
`idControl`	`int`	Dialog box item to be converted
`lpfTranslated`	`BOOL FAR*`	Boolean variable to receive translated flag
`fSigned`	`BOOL`	Specifies whether value is signed

Description The `GetDlgItemInt` function converts the text of the dialog box item specified in `idControl` to an integer value. `idControl` is contained in the dialog box specified by `hwndDlg`. `fSigned` indicates whether the item is signed. When `fSigned` is a nonzero value, the retrieved text of the specified item is checked for a minus sign. The retrieved text is converted in the following manner. Whitespaces at the beginning of the text are stripped and decimal digits are converted. Conversion stops when a nonnumeric character is found or the end of the string is reached. `lpfTranslated` is set to a nonzero value when no conversion errors occur. It is set to zero when a conversion error occurs. The `WM_GETTEXT` message is sent to the control by `GetDlgItemInt`.

Return Value The converted value of the text for the dialog box item is returned. Use `lpfTranslated` for error detection.

Function Category Dialog Box

Related Functions `GetDlgItem`, `GetDlgItemText`, `SetDlgItemInt`

GetDlgItemText

Syntax `int GetDlgItemText(hwndDlg, idControl, lpsz, cbMax)`

Parameter	*Type*	*Description*
`hwndDlg`	`HWND`	Dialog box containing the control
`idControl`	`int`	Item from which to retrieve text
`lpsz`	`LPSTR`	Buffer to receive text
`cbMax`	`int`	Length of string to be copied

Description The `GetDlgItemText` function gets the text associated with the control item specified in `idControl`. `idControl` is contained in the dialog box specified in `hwndDlg`. The retrieved text is placed in the text buffer pointed to by `lpsz`. The length of the string, in bytes, copied into `lpsz` is limited by the value specified in `cbMax`. The `WM_GETTEXT` message is sent to the control item in `idControl`.

Return Value The number of characters copied into `lpsz` is returned when successful. Zero is returned if no text is copied into `lpsz`.

Function Category Dialog Box

Related Functions `GetDlgItem`, `GetDlgItemInt`, `SetDlgItemText`

GetDOSEnvironment

Syntax `LPSTR GetDOSEnvironment()`

Description The `GetDOSEnvironment` function returns the pointer to the environment string for the current task.

Return Value The far pointer to the environment string of the current task is returned.

Function Category Task

Related Functions `GetCurrentTask`

GetDoubleClickTime

Syntax `WORD GetDoubleClickTime()`

Description The `GetDoubleClickTime` gets the double-click time, measured in milliseconds. The double-click time is a specified maximum number of milliseconds between the first click of a button and the second click of the same button.

Return Value The double-click time, in milliseconds, is returned.

Function Category Input

Related Functions `SetDoubleClickTime`

GetDriverInfo

Syntax `BOOL GetDriverInfo(hdrvr, lpdis)`

Parameter	*Type*	*Description*
`hdrvr`	`HDRVR`	Installable device driver. Get this parameter with the `OpenDriver` function.
`lpdis`	`DRIVERINFOSTRUCT FAR*`	Pointer to `DRIVERINFOSTRUCT` data structure where driver information is copied

Description The `GetDriverInfo` function copies information about the installable device driver specified in `hdrvr`. The information is copied to the data structure pointed to by `lpdis`.

Return Value A nonzero value is returned when successful. Zero is returned when unsuccessful.

Function Category Installable Driver

Related Functions `GetDriverModuleHandle`, `OpenDriver`

GetDriverModuleHandle

Syntax `HINSTANCE GetDriverModuleHandle(hdrvr)`

Parameter	*Type*	*Description*
`hdrvr`	`HDRVR`	Installable device driver. Get this parameter with the `OpenDriver` function.

Description The `GetDriverModuleHandle` function gets the instance handle of the module that contains the installable device driver specified in `hdrvr`.

Return Value The retrieved instance handle is returned when successful. `NULL` is returned when unsuccessful.

Function Category Installable Driver

Related Functions `OpenDriver`

GetDriveType

Syntax `UINT GetDriveType(DriveNumber)`

Parameter	*Type*	*Description*
`DriveNumber`	`int`	Drive number

Description The `GetDriveType` function determines the drive type for the drive number specified in `DriveNumber`: fixed, remote, or removable. DriveNumber is 0 for Drive A, 1 of Drive B, and so forth.

Return Value The type of drive is returned. The drive type values that are returned are as follows:

Value	*Meaning*
0	Cannot determine drive type
DRIVE_FIXED	Disk cannot be removed from the drive
DRIVE_REMOTE	Drive is a remote drive
DRIVE_REMOVABLE	Disk can be removed from the drive

Function Category File I/O

Related Functions GetSystemDirectory, GetTempDrive

GetEnvironment

Syntax `int GetEnvironment(lpszPort, lpvEnviron, cbMaxCopy)`

Parameter	*Type*	*Description*
lpszPort	LPCSTR	Pointer to the string that contains the name of the port
lpvEnviron	void FAR*	Pointer to buffer to receive environment information. The buffer is in the form of a DEVMODE structure.
cbMaxCopy	UINT	Maximum number of bytes to copy to the buffer

Description The GetEnvironment function places the environment associated with the device attached to the system port in lpszPort in the buffer pointed to by lpvEnviron. cbMaxCopy specifies the maximum number of bytes to copy to the buffer.

Return Value The number of bytes copied to lpvEnviron is returned. When lpvEnviron is NULL, the size of the buffer required to store the environment is returned. Zero is returned when unsuccessful.

Function Category Environment

Related Functions `SetEnvironment`

GetExpandedName

Syntax `int GetExpandedName(lpszSource, lpszBuffer)`

Parameter	*Type*	*Description*
`lpszSource`	`LPSTR`	Pointer to string that contains the name of the compressed file
`lpszBuffer`	`LPSTR`	Pointer to buffer that receives the name of the compressed file

Description The `GetExpandedName` function gets the original name of a compressed file. This function works only when the file was compressed using the `COMPRESS.EXE` utility with the `/r` option.

Return Value `TRUE` is returned when successful. A value less than zero is returned when unsuccessful.

Function Category Lempel-Ziv Expansion

Related Functions `LZOpenFile`, `LZRead`

GetFileResource

Syntax

```
BOOL GetFileResource(lpszFileName, lpszResType,
                     lpszResID, dwFileOffset, dwResLen,
                     lpszData)
```

Parameter	*Type*	*Description*
`lpszFileName`	`LPSTR`	Pointer to buffer containing the filename holding the resource
`lpszResType`	`LPSTR`	Pointer to buffer containing the name of the resource type
`lpszResID`	`LPSTR`	Pointer to buffer containing the ID of the resource

Parameter	Type	Description
dwFileOffset	DWORD	Pointer to the offset of the resource within the file
dwResLen	DWORD	Number of bytes in the resource
lpszData	LPSTR	Pointer to buffer to receive a copy of the resource

Description The `GetFileResource` function copies the specified resource to a buffer. The parameters of the function define the location of the resource and the buffer where the resource will be copied.

Return Value `TRUE` is returned when successful. `FALSE` is returned when unsuccessful.

Function Category Version

Related Functions `GetFileResourceSize`

GetFileResourceSize

Syntax

```
DWORD GetFileResourceSize(lpszFileName, lpszResType,
                          lpszResID, lpdwFileOffset)
```

Parameter	Type	Description
lpszFileName	LPSTR	Pointer to buffer containing the filename of file holding the resource
lpszResType	LPSTR	Pointer to buffer containing the resource type
lpszResID	LPSTR	Pointer to buffer containing the name of the resource ID
lpdwFileOffset	DWORD FAR*	Pointer to the offset of the resource within the file

Description The `GetFileResourceSize` function returns the size of the specified resource.

Return Value The number of bytes in the resource is returned when successful. `NULL` is returned when unsuccessful.

Function Category Version

Related Functions `GetFileResource`

GetFileTitle

Syntax `short GetFileTitle(lpszFile, lpszTitle, wBufSize)`

Parameter	*Type*	*Description*
`lpszFile`	`LPSTR`	Pointer to DOS filename
`lpszTitle`	`LPSTR`	Pointer to buffer where filename will be copied
`wBufSize`	`WORD`	Length of buffer pointed to by `lpszTitle`

Description The `GetFileTitle` function copies the title of the file specified in `lpszFile` to the buffer pointed to by `lpszTitle`.

Return Value Zero is returned when successful. If the specified buffer size is too small, a positive value that indicates the required buffer size is returned. A negative return value indicates an error.

Function Category Common Dialog

Related Functions `GetOpenFileName`, `GetSaveFileName`

GetFileVersionInfo

Syntax
```
BOOL GetFileVersionInfo(lpszFileName, dwHandle, dwLen,
                        lpszData)
```

Parameter	*Type*	*Description*
`lpszFileName`	`LPSTR`	Pointer to buffer containing the filename
`dwHandle`	`DWORD`	File version information obtained with `GetFileVersionInfoSize`

Parameter	Type	Description
dwLen	DWORD	Size of buffer pointed to by lpszData; obtained from GetFileVersionInfoSize
lpszData	LPSTR	Pointer to buffer containing file version information

Description The GetFileVersionInfo function copies version information about the file specified in lpszFileName into the buffer pointed to by lpszData. GetFileVersionInfoSize is used to get the required values for dwHandle and dwLen.

Return Value TRUE is returned when successful. FALSE is returned when unsuccessful.

Function Category Version

Related Functions GetFileVersionInfoSize

GetFileVersionInfoSize

Syntax

```
DWORD GetFileVersionInfoSize(lpszFileName,
                             lpdwHandle)
```

Parameter	Type	Description
lpszFileName	LPSTR	Pointer to buffer containing the filename
lpdwHandle	DWORD FAR*	Address of DWORD value where the file version information is copied; this information is used by GetFileVersionInfo

Description The GetFileVersionInfoSize function determines the size of the buffer required to hold the version information. This function obtains a handle for the file version information. The handle is used by the GetFileVersionInfo function.

Return Value The number of bytes required for the buffer that holds the version information is returned when successful. NULL is returned when unsuccessful.

Function Category Version

Related Functions `GetFileVersionInfo`

GetFocus

Syntax `HWND GetFocus()`

Description The `GetFocus` function gets the handle of the window that has the input focus.

Return Value The handle of the window that has the input focus is returned when successful. When unsuccessful, `NULL` is returned.

Function Category Input

Related Functions `GetCapture`, `SetCapture`, `SetFocus`

GetFontData

Syntax
```
DWORD GetFontData(hdc, dwTable, dwOffset,
                  lpvBuffer, cbData)
```

Parameter	*Type*	*Description*
`hdc`	`HDC`	Device context
`dwTable`	`DWORD`	Name of metric table
`dwOffset`	`DWORD`	Offset of table where data retrieval will begin
`lpvBuffer`	`void FAR*`	Pointer to buffer to receive font metric data
`cbData`	`DWORD`	Length of data to retrieve

Description The `GetFontData` function gets font metric data and copies the information into the buffer pointed to by `lpvBuffer`. `dwTable` specifies the name of the metric table to return and is one of the following values:

Value	Meaning
cmap	Character-to-glyph mapping
cvt	Control value table
FOCA	Reserved
fpgm	Font program
glyf	Glyph data
hdmx	Horizontal device metrics
head	Font header
hhea	Horizontal header
hmtx	Horizontal metrics
kern	Kerning
loca	Index to location
maxp	Maximum profile
name	Naming table
OS/2	Metrics for OS/2 and Windows
post	Postscript information
prep	CVT program
WIN	Reserved

Return Value The number of bytes copied to the buffer in `lpvBuffer` is returned when successful. –1 is returned when unsuccessful.

Function Category Font, TrueType

Related Functions `GetOutlineTextMetrics`

GetFreeSpace

Syntax `DWORD GetFreeSpace(fuFlags)`

Parameter	Type	Description
fuFlags	UINT	This parameter is ignored in Windows 3.1.

Description The `GetFreeSpace` function determines the number of bytes of available memory by scanning the global heap.

Return Value The number of available bytes of memory is returned.

Function Category Memory Management

Related Functions `GlobalCompact`, `GlobalDOSFree`, `GlobalFree`, `LocalFree`

GetFreeSystemResources

Syntax `UINT GetFreeSystemResources(fuSysResource)`

Parameter	*Type*	*Description*
`fuSysResource`	`UINT`	Type of resource to evaluate; `fuSysResource` is one of the following values:

Value	*Meaning*
0	Get percentage of free system resource space
1	Get percentage of free GDI resource space
2	Get percentage of free `USER` resource space

Description The `GetFreeSystemResources` function returns the free system resource space specified in `fuSysResource`.

Return Value The appropriate percentage is returned.

Function Category Memory Management

Related Functions `GetFreeSpace`

GetGlyphOutline

Syntax
```
DWORD GetGlyphOutline(hdc, uChar, fuFormat,
                      lpgm, cbBuffer, lpBuffer,lpmat2)
```

Parameter	*Type*	*Description*
`hdc`	`HDC`	Device context
`uChar`	`UINT`	Character for evaluation
`fuFormat`	`UINT`	Curve data format

Parameter	Type	Description
lpgm	LPGLYPHMETRICS	Pointer to GLYPHMETRICS data structure that describes the character cell placement
cbBuffer	DWORD	Size of buffer where information is copied. If set to zero, the required size of the buffer is returned.
lpBuffer	void FAR*	Pointer to buffer where data is copied. If cbBuffer is NULL, the required size of the buffer is returned.
lpmat2	LPMAT2	Pointer to MAT2 data structure that specifies the character transformation matrix

Description The GetGlyphOutline function gets the outline curve data points in the current font for the character specified in uChar. The GLYPHMETRICS data structure pointed to by lpgm follows.

```
typedef struct _GLYPHMETRICS
   {
   WORD gmBlackBoxX;
   WORD gmBlackBoxY;
   POINT gmptGlyphOrigin;
   short gmCellIncX;
   short gmCellIncY;
} GLYPHMETRICS;
```

in which

gmBlackBoxX is the width of the smallest possible rectangle that encloses the glyph

gmBlackBoxY is the height of the smallest possible rectangle that encloses the glyph

gmptGlyphOrigin specifies the coordinates of the upper-left corner of the smallest rectangle that encloses the glyph

gmCellIncX is the horizontal distance from the origin of the current character cell to the origin of the next character cell

gmCellIncY is the vertical distance from the origin of the current character cell to the origin of the next character cell.

`fuFormat` specifies the format of the return data. `fuFormat` is one of the following values:

Value	*Meaning*
`GGO_BITMAP`	Return the glyph bitmap
`GGO_NATIVE`	Return curve data in the rasterizer's native format and use the font's design units

Return Value The return value depends on the setting of `cbBuffer` and `lppt`.

Function Category Font, TrueType

Related Functions `GetOutlineTextMetrics`

GetGValue

Syntax `BYTE GetGValue(rgb)`

Parameter	*Type*	*Description*
`rgb`	`DWORD`	`RGB color field`

Description The `GetGValue` macro gets the green value from the RGB color value specified in `rgb`.

Return Value The green value from the RGB color field is returned.

Function Category Windows Macros

Related Functions `GetBValue`, `GetRValue`

GetInputState

Syntax `BOOL GetInputState()`

Description The `GetInputState` function determines whether there is an input event that needs processing. This function checks mouse, keyboard, and timer events. Mouse events are generated every time the mouse is moved or a mouse button is pressed. Keyboard events are generated whenever a key is pressed. Timer events are generated at specified time intervals. These events are stored in the system queue.

Return Value A nonzero value is returned if there is an input event that needs processing. Zero is returned if there is no input event detected.

Function Category Hardware

Related Functions `EnableHardwareInput`, `GetKeyboardState`

GetInstanceData

Syntax `int GetInstanceData(hinst, npbData, cbData)`

Parameter	*Type*	*Description*
`hinst`	`HINSTANCE`	Previous instance
`npbData`	`BYTE*`	Pointer to a buffer in the current instance
`cbData`	`int`	Number of bytes to copy

Description The `GetInstanceData` function copies data from the previous instance specified in `hinst` to the data area of the current instance specified in `npbData`. `cbData` specifies the number of bytes to copy.

Return Value The number of bytes copied is returned when successful. `NULL` is returned when unsuccessful.

Function Category Module Management

Related Functions `FreeProcInstance`, `MakeProcInstance`

GetKBCodePage

Syntax `int GetKBCodePage()`

Description The `GetKBCodePage` function determines which OEM/ANSI tables are loaded by Windows. The return value indicates the code page that is currently loaded.

Return Value One of the following values is returned to indicate which code page is currently loaded:

Return Value	Meaning
437	USA (default)—there is no OEMANSI.BIN in Windows directory
850	International—OEMANSI.BIN = XLAT850.BIN
860	Portugal—OEMANSI.BIN = XLAT860.BIN
861	Iceland—OEMANSI.BIN = XLAT861.BIN
863	French Canadian—OEMANSI.BIN = XLAT863.BIN
865	Norway/Denmark—OEMANSI.BIN = XLAT865.BIN

Function Category Hardware

Related Functions `GetKeyboardState`, `GetKeyState`

GetKeyboardState

Syntax `void GetKeyboardState(lpbKeyState)`

Parameter	Type	Description
lpbKeyState	BYTE FAR*	Buffer of virtual key codes

Description The `GetKeyboardState` function determines the status of the 256 virtual keyboard keys and places this status into the buffer pointed to by `lpbKeyState`. This buffer contains 256 bytes, one byte for each of the virtual keyboard keys. The key status for each key can be determined by examining the appropriate byte. If the high bit of the byte is set to 1, the key is down. If the high bit of the byte is set to 0, the key is up. If the low bit is set to 1, the key was pressed an odd number of times since startup. The low bit is 0 if the key was pressed an even number of times since startup.

Return Value There is no return value.

Function Category Hardware

Related Functions `GetKeyState`, `SetKeyboardState`

GetKeyboardType

Syntax `int GetKeyboardType(fnKeybInfo)`

Parameter	*Type*	*Description*
`fnKeybInfo`	`int`	Specifies whether a type or subtype of the keyboard is returned

Description The `GetKeyboardType` function gets the system keyboard type. `fnKeybInfo` specifies whether a type or subtype of the keyboard is returned by the function. The following values are used for `fnKeybInfo`:

Value	*Meaning*
0	The keyboard type is returned
1	The keyboard subtype is returned
2	The number of function keys on the keyboard is returned

Return Value A value corresponding to `fnKeybInfo` is returned when successful. If a subtype is returned, the value is OEM-dependent. If a type is returned, the type is one of the following values. Zero is returned when unsuccessful.

Value	*Meaning*
1	IBM PC/XT or compatible keyboard (83 keys)
2	Olivetti "ICO" keyboard (102 keys)
3	IBM AT or compatible keyboard (84 keys)
4	IBM enhanced or similar keyboard (101 or 102 keys)
5	Nokia 1050 or similar keyboard
6	Nokia 9140 or similar keyboard
7	Japanese keyboard

Function Category Hardware

Related Functions `GetKeyboardState`

GetKeyNameText

Syntax `int GetKeyNameText(lParam, lpszBuffer, cbMaxKey)`

Parameter	*Type*	*Description*
`lParam`	`LONG`	Keyboard message being processed
`lpszBuffer`	`LPSTR`	Pointer to buffer to receive key name
`cbMaxKey`	`int`	Maximum length of name

Description The `GetKeyNameText` function gets the name of a key. `lParam` is a 32-bit parameter for the keyboard message being processed by the function. `lpszBuffer` points to the buffer which will store the name of the key. `cbMaxKey` specifies the maximum length of the string, in bytes, and does not count the `NULL` terminator for the string.

Return Value The number of bytes copied to `lpszBuffer` is returned when successful. Zero is returned when unsuccessful.

Function Category Hardware

Related Functions `GetKeyState`

GetKeyState

Syntax `int GetKeyState(vkey)`

Parameter	*Type*	*Description*
`vkey`	`int`	Virtual key

Description The `GetKeyState` function gets the state of the key specified in `vkey`. `vkey` specifies the ASCII or virtual key code of the virtual key. The return value indicates the state of the key.

Return Value The high-order bit of the return value indicates whether the key is down or up. When the high-order bit is 1, the key is down. When the high-order bit is 0, the key is up. If the low-order bit is 1, the key has been pressed an odd number of times since the system was started. If the low-order bit is 0, the key has been pressed an even number of times since the system was started.

Function Category Hardware

Related Functions `GetKeyboardState`, `SetKeyboardState`

GetLastActivePopup

Syntax `HWND GetLastActivePopup(hwndOwner)`

Parameter	*Type*	*Description*
`hwndOwner`	`HWND`	Owner window

Description The `GetLastActivePopup` function gets the pop-up window that was most recently active for the window specified in `hwndOwner`.

Return Value The handle of the pop-up window that was most recently active is returned.

Function Category Window Creation

Related Functions `AnyPopup`, `GetActiveWindow`

GetMapMode

Syntax `int GetMapMode(hdc)`

Parameter	*Type*	*Description*
`hdc`	`HDC`	Device context

Description The `GetMapMode` function gets the current mapping mode.

Return Value The mapping mode is returned. The following values represent the mapping modes.

Value	*Meaning*
`MM_ANISOTROPIC`	Logical units are mapped to arbitrary units with arbitrarily scaled axes
`MM_HIENGLISH`	Each logical unit is mapped to .001 inch; positive x is right, positive y is up

Value	*Meaning*
MM_HIMETRIC	Each logical unit is mapped to .01 millimeter; positive x is right, positive y is up
MM_ISOTROPIC	Logical units are mapped to arbitrary units with equally scaled axes
MM_LOENGLISH	Each logical unit is mapped to .01 inch; positive x is right, positive y is up
MM_LOMETRIC	Each logical unit is mapped to .1 millimeter; positive x is right, positive y is up
MM_TEXT	Each logical unit is mapped to one device pixel; positive x is right, positive y is down
MM_TWIPS	Each logical unit is mapped to one twentieth of a printer's point; positive x is right, positive y is up

Function Category Mapping

Related Functions `SetMapMode`

GetMenu

Syntax `HMENU GetMenu(hwnd)`

Parameter	*Type*	*Description*
hwnd	HWND	Window containing menu

Description The `GetMenu` function gets the handle for the menu of the window specified in `hwnd`.

Return Value The handle of the menu is returned. `NULL` is returned when the specified window has no menu.

Function Category Menu

Related Functions `CreateMenu`, `GetSubMenu`, `SetMenu`

GetMenuCheckMarkDimensions

Syntax `DWORD GetMenuCheckMarkDimensions()`

Description The `GetMenuCheckMarkDimensions` function gets the dimensions for the default checkmark bitmap.

Return Value The dimensions of the default checkmark bitmap are returned. The height, in pixels, is defined in the high-order word of the return value. The width, in pixels, is defined in the low-order word of the return value.

Function Category Menu

Related Functions `CheckMenuItem`, `SetMenuItemBitmaps`

GetMenuItemCount

Syntax `int GetMenuItemCount(hmenu)`

Parameter	*Type*	*Description*
hmenu	HMENU	Menu handle

Description The `GetMenuItemCount` function returns the number of items in the top-level or pop-up menu specified in `hmenu`.

Return Value The number of items in the specified menu is returned when successful. When unsuccessful, –1 is returned.

Function Category Menu

Related Functions `GetMenuItemID`

GetMenuItemID

Syntax `UINT GetMenuItemID(hmenu, pos)`

Parameter	*Type*	*Description*
hmenu	HMENU	Pop-up menu containing the menu item
pos	int	Position of menu item

Description The GetMenuItemID function gets the menu-item ID for the menu item located at the position specified in pos. hmenu specifies the menu that contains the menu item.

Return Value The menu item ID is returned when successful. When unsuccessful, –1 is returned. When pos specifies a SEPARATOR menu item, zero is returned.

Function Category Menu

Related Functions GetMenuItemCount

GetMenuState

Syntax `UINT GetMenuState(hmenu, idItem, fuFlags)`

Parameter	*Type*	*Description*
hmenu	HMENU	Menu handle
idItem	UINT	Menu item ID or position
fuFlags	UINT	Flags indicating whether idItem contains an item ID or position

Description The GetMenuState function either gets the status of a menu item or gets the number of items in a pop-up menu. When hmenu specifies a menu with an associated pop-up menu, the number of items in the pop-up menu is retrieved. When hmenu specifies a pop-up menu, the status of the menu item is retrieved. idItem specifies either a menu item ID or menu item position, depending on the flag settings in fuFlags. If fuFlags contains MF_BYPOSITION, idItem contains a menu item position. If fuFlags contains MF_BYCOMMAND, idItem contains the menu item ID.

Return Value If the menu item does not exist, –1 is returned. When idItem specifies a pop-up window, the high order byte of the return value contains the number of items in the pop-up menu; the low order byte contains the menu flags. For all other cases, the return value identifies the status of the menu item. The status is a combination (using the Boolean OR) of the following flags:

Value	Meaning
MF_BITMAP	Bitmap item
MF_CHECKED	A checkmark is placed next to menu item
MF_DISABLED	Disables the menu item
MF_ENABLED	Enables the menu item
MF_GRAYED	Grays and disables the menu item
MF_MENUBARBREAK	Menu item is placed on a new line. For pop-up menus, the item is placed in a new column with a vertical dividing line.
MF_MENUBREAK	Menu item is placed on a new line. For pop-up menus, the item is placed in a new column without a vertical dividing line.
MF_SEPARATOR	Creates a horizontal dividing line
MF_UNCHECKED	No checkmark is placed next to the menu item

Function Category Menu

Related Functions GetMenu, SetMenu

GetMenuString

Syntax `int GetMenuString(hmenu, idItem, lpsz, cbMax, fwFlag)`

Parameter	Type	Description
hmenu	HMENU	Menu handle
idItem	UINT	Menu item ID or position
lpsz	LPSTR	Pointer to buffer to receive label
cbMax	int	Maximum label length
fwFlag	UINT	Specifies whether idItem contains a menu item ID or position

Description The GetMenuString function places the menu item label for the menu item in idItem into the buffer pointed to by lpsz. The menu item is contained in the menu specified in hmenu. cbMax specifies the maximum number of characters to copy to lpsz. idItem contains either a menu item ID or position. When fwFlag contains MF_BYPOSITION, idItem is a menu item position. When fwFlag contains MF_BYCOMMAND, fwFlag contains a menu item ID.

Return Value The number of bytes copied to lpsz is returned (this value does not include the null terminator).

Function Category Menu

Related Functions GetMenu, SetMenu

GetMessage

Syntax `BOOL GetMessage(lpmsg, hwnd, uMsgFilterMin, uMsgFilterMax)`

Parameter	*Type*	*Description*
lpmsg	MSG FAR*	MSG data structure containing message information from the Windows application queue
hwnd	HWND	Window receiving messages to be examined
uMsgFilterMin	UINT	Lowest message value to retrieve
uMsgFilterMax	UINT	Highest message value to retrieve

Description The GetMessage function places a message retrieved from the application queue into the data structure of type MSG pointed to by lpmsg. The MSG data structure follows. All messages retrieved are associated with the window specified in hwnd. uMsgFilterMin and uMsgFilterMax specify the range of message values that can be retrieved. The WM_KEYFIRST and WM_KEYLAST constants can be used for uMsgFilterMin and uMsgFilterMax, respectively, to retrieve all keyboard-related messages. Similarly, WM_MOUSEFIRST and WM_MOUSELAST can be used to retrieve all mouse-related messages.

```
typedef struct tagMSG {
     HWND hwnd;
     WORD message;
     WORD wParam;
     LONG lParam;
     DWORD time;
     POINT pt;
} MSG;
```

in which

`hwnd` is the window receiving the message

`message` is the message number

`wParam` is additional message information

`lParam` is additional message information

`time` is the time the message was posted

`pt` is the cursor position in screen coordinates.

Return Value A nonzero value is returned when the message retrieved is not `WM_QUIT`. A zero is returned when the message retrieved is `WM_QUIT`.

Function Category Message

Related Functions `GetMessageExtraInfo`, `GetMessagePos`, `GetMessageTime`

GetMessageExtraInfo

Syntax `LONG GetMessageExtraInfo(void)`

Parameter	*Type*	*Description*
None		

Description The `GetMessageExtraInfo` function gets extra information on the last message retrieved with `GetMessage`.

Return Value The extra message information is returned.

Function Category Message

Related Functions `GetMessage`

GetMessagePos

Syntax `DWORD GetMessagePos()`

Description The `GetMessagePos` function gets the value representing the screen coordinates of the cursor position where the last message retrieved by `GetMessage` occurred.

Return Value The low-order word of the return value contains the horizontal coordinate of the cursor position. The high-order word of the return value contains the vertical coordinate of the cursor position.

Function Category Message

Related Functions `GetMessage`, `GetMessageTime`

GetMessageTime

Syntax `LONG GetMessageTime()`

Description The `GetMessageTime` function gets the message time, in milliseconds, for the last message retrieved by `GetMessage`.

Return Value The message time is returned. The message time is the number of milliseconds elapsed from the time the system booted to the time the message was placed in the application queue.

Function Category Message

Related Functions `GetMessage`, `GetMessagePos`

GetMetaFile

Syntax `HMETAFILE GetMetaFile(lpszFile)`

Parameter	*Type*	*Description*
`lpszFile`	`LPCSTR`	Pointer to a null-terminated string that contains the DOS filename of the metafile

Description The `GetMetaFile` function creates a handle for the metafile specified in `lpszFile`.

Return Value The handle of the metafile is returned when successful. `NULL` is returned when unsuccessful.

Function Category Metafile

Related Functions CreateMetaFile, GetMetaFileBits, PlayMetaFile

GetMetaFileBits

Syntax `HGLOBAL GetMetaFileBits(hmf)`

Parameter	*Type*	*Description*
hmf	HMETAFILE	Memory metafile

Description The GetMetaFileBits function gets the handle of the global memory block that contains the bits of the metafile specified in hmf.

Return Value The handle to the global memory block is returned when successful. NULL is returned when unsuccessful.

Function Category Metafile

Related Functions CreateMetaFile, GetMetaFile, PlayMetaFile

GetModuleFileName

Syntax `int GetModuleFileName(hinst, lpszFilename, cbFileName)`

Parameter	*Type*	*Description*
hinst	HINSTANCE	Module or instance of module
lpszFilename	LPSTR	Pointer to the buffer to receive the filename
cbFileName	int	Maximum number of bytes to copy

Description The GetModuleFileName function gets the pathname of an executable file. The module or instance of module specified in hinst was loaded from the retrieved executable file. The pathname is copied into the buffer pointed to by lpszFilename. cbFileName specifies the maximum number of bytes to copy to the buffer.

Return Value The length of the string copied to the buffer is returned.

Function Category Module Management

Related Functions `GetModuleHandle`, `GetModuleUsage`

GetModuleHandle

Syntax `HMODULE GetModuleHandle(lpszModuleName)`

Parameter	*Type*	*Description*
`lpszModuleName`	`LPCSTR`	Pointer to a null-terminated string that defines the module

Description The `GetModuleHandle` function gets the handle for the module specified by the string in `lpszModuleName`.

Return Value The handle to the module is returned when successful. `NULL` is returned when unsuccessful.

Function Category Module Management

Related Functions `GetModuleFileName`, `GetModuleUsage`

GetModuleUsage

Syntax `int GetModuleUsage(hinst)`

Parameter	*Type*	*Description*
`hinst`	`HINSTANCE`	Module or instance of module

Description The `GetModuleUsage` function returns the reference count for the module specified in `hinst`.

Return Value The reference count for the module is returned.

Function Category Module Management

Related Functions `FreeModule`, `LoadModule`

GetNearestColor

Syntax `COLORREF GetNearestColor(hdc, clrref)`

Parameter	*Type*	*Description*
hdc	HDC	Device context
clrref	COLORREF	Color to match

Description The `GetNearestColor` function returns the logical color that is the closest match to the logical color specified in `clrref`. The color returned is the closest matching color from those colors that the specified device can represent.

Return Value An RGB value representing the closest color match is returned.

Function Category Color Palette

Related Functions `GetNearestPaletteIndex`, `UpdateColors`

GetNearestPaletteIndex

Syntax `UINT GetNearestPaletteIndex(hpal, clrref)`

Parameter	*Type*	*Description*
hpal	HPALETTE	Logical palette
clrref	DWORD	Color to match

Description The `GetNearestPaletteIndex` function gets the palette entry index from the logical palette in `hpal` that is most like the color value specified in `clrref`.

Return Value The palette entry index is returned.

Function Category Color Palette

Related Functions `GetNearestColor`, `SelectPaletteEntries`

GetNextDlgGroupItem

Syntax `HWND GetNextDlgGroupItem(hwndDlg, hwndCtl, fPrevious)`

Parameter	Type	Description
hwndDlg	HWND	Dialog box being searched
hwndCtl	HWND	Control where search starts
fPrevious	BOOL	Specifies method of search

Description The `GetNextDlgGroupItem` function searches for the next control in the dialog box specified in `hwndDlg`. The next control is searched for in the control group containing the control specified in `hwndCtl`. A control group has one or more controls with `WS_GROUP` style. The search for the next control begins with the control specified in `hwndCtl`. The previous control is returned when `fPrevious` is `TRUE`. The next control is returned when `fPrevious` is `FALSE`.

Return Value The handle of the next or previous control in the control group is returned. The setting of `fPrevious` determines which control is returned.

Function Category Dialog Box

Related Functions `GetDlgItem`, `GetNextDlgTabItem`

GetNextDlgTabItem

Syntax `HWND GetNextDlgTabItem(hwndDlg, hwndCtl, fPrevious)`

Parameter	Type	Description
hwndDlg	HWND	Dialog box to search
hwndCtl	HWND	Control where search begins
fPrevious	BOOL	Specifies method of search

Description The `GetNextDlgTabItem` function gets the next control in the `hwndDlg` dialog box that has the `WS_TABSTOP` style. The search for the next control begins with the control specified in `hwndCtl`. `fPrevious` defines how the search will be conducted. If `fPrevious` is `TRUE`, `GetNextDlgTabItem` searches for the first previous control that has the `WS_TABSTOP` style. If `fPrevious` is `FALSE`, the next control that has the `WS_TABSTOP` style is returned.

Return Value The handle of the previous or next (depending on the setting of `fPrevious`) control that has the `WS_TABSTOP` style is returned.

Function Category Dialog Box

Related Functions `GetDlgItem`, `GetNextDlgGroupItem`

GetNextDriver

Syntax `HDRVR GetNextDriver(hdrvr, fdwFlag)`

Parameter	*Type*	*Description*
`hdrvr`	`HDRVR`	Installable driver handle. Get this parameter with the `OpenDriver` function.
`fdwFlag`	`DWORD`	Search flag. `fdwFlag` is one of the following values:

Value	*Meaning*
`GND_FIRSTINSTANCEONLY`	Return the handle that identifies the first instance of an installable driver
`GND_REVERSE`	Enumerate instances of the driver as it was loaded; return the handle of the next instance with each subsequent call

Description The `GetNextDriver` function enumerates the instances of the installable device driver specified in `hdrvr`.

Return Value The appropriate value, specified by `fdwFlag`, is returned.

Function Category Installable Driver

Related Functions `GetDriverInfo`

GetNextWindow

Syntax `HWND GetNextWindow(hwnd, uFlag)`

Parameter	*Type*	*Description*
`hwnd`	`HWND`	Current window
`uFlag`	`UINT`	Specifies whether to get next or previous window handle

Description The `GetNextWindow` function returns the next, or previous, window in the window manager's list. `hwnd` specifies the current window (can be either top-level or child window). `uFlag` specifies whether the previous, or the next, window handle will be returned. If `uFlag` is `GW_HWNDNEXT`, the next window handle is returned. If `uFlag` is `GW_HWNDPREV`, the previous window handle is returned.

Return Value The handle for the next, or previous, window (depending on the setting of `uFlag`) is returned.

Function Category Information

Related Functions `FindWindow`, `GetDesktopWindow`, `GetTopWindow`, `GetWindow`

GetNumTasks

Syntax `UINT GetNumTasks()`

Description The `GetNumTasks` function determines the number of executing tasks.

Return Value The number of executing tasks is returned.

Function Category Task

Related Functions `GetCurrentTask`

GetObject

Syntax `int GetObject(hgdiobj, cbBuffer, lpvObject)`

Parameter	*Type*	*Description*
`hgdiobj`	`HGDIOBJ`	Logical pen, brush, font, bitmap, or palette
`cbBuffer`	`int`	Number of bytes to copy to buffer
`lpvObject`	`void FAR*`	Pointer to buffer receiving the information

Description The `GetObject` function gets information on the object specified in `hgdiobj`. The object information is placed in the buffer pointed to by `lpvObject`. `cbBuffer` specifies the number of bytes of information that should be placed in `lpvObject`. For a pen, a `LOGPEN` data structure is retrieved. For a brush, a `LOGBRUSH` data structure is retrieved. For a font, a `LOGFONT` data structure is retrieved. For a bitmap, the width, height, and color information from a `BITMAP` data structure is retrieved. For a palette, a two-byte value specifying the number of entries in the palette is returned.

Return Value The number of bytes copied to the buffer is returned when successful. Zero is returned when unsuccessful.

Function Category Drawing Tool

Related Functions `DeleteObject`, `GetStockObject`, `SelectObject`

GetOpenClipboardWindow

Syntax `HWND GetOpenClipboardWindow(VOID)`

Parameter	*Type*	*Description*
None		

Description The `GetOpenClipboardWindow` function returns the handle of the window that has the clipboard opened.

Return Value The handle of the window that has the clipboard opened is returned. If the clipboard is not opened, `NULL` is returned.

Function Category Clipboard

Related Functions `GetClipboardOwner`, `GetClipboardViewer`

GetOpenFileName

Syntax `BOOL GetOpenFileName(lpofn)`

Parameter	*Type*	*Description*
`lpofn`	`LPOPENFILENAME`	Pointer to `OPENFILENAME` structure containing dialog box initialization information

Description The `GetOpenFileName` function creates a system-defined dialog box that provides the user with the ability to enter the file name of the file to open. `lpofn` points to a data structure of type `OPENFILENAME` that contains initialization information for the dialog box. The `OPENFILENAME` data structure follows.

```
#include <commdlg.h>
typedef structure tagOFN     {
     DWORD lStructSize;
     HWND hwndOwner;
     HANDLE hInstance;
     LPSTR lpstrFilter;
     LPSTR lpstrCustomFilter;
     DWORD nMaxCustFilter;
     DWORD nFilterIndex;
     LPSTR lpstrFile;
     DWORD nMaxFile;
     LPSTR lpstrFileTitle;
     DWORD nMaxFileTitle;
     LPSTR lpstrInitialDir;
     LPSTR lpstrTitle;
     DWORD Flags;
     WORD nFileOffset;
     WORD nFileExtension;
     LPSTR lpstrDefExt;
     DWORD lCustData;
     WORD (FAR PASCAL *lpfnHook)(HWND, unsigned,
                                       WORD, LONG);
     LPSTR lpTemplateName;
} OPENFILENAME;
```

in which

`lStructSize` is the number of bytes in the structure

`hwndOwner` is the handle of the window that owns the dialog box

`hInstance` is the data block that contains the dialog box template specified by `lpTemplateName`

`lpstrFilter` is the pointer to a buffer that contains pairs of null-terminated filter strings. The first string in the pair is the filter description; the second is the filter pattern (for example, "*.doc"). The last string in the buffer must contain two `NULL` characters.

`lpstrCustomFilter` is the pointer to a buffer that contains a pair of filter strings defined by the user. The first string in the pair is the filter description; the second is the filter pattern (for example "*.doc"). The last string in the buffer must contain two `NULL` characters.

`nMaxCustFilter` is the number of bytes for the buffer in `lpstrCustomFilter`

`nFilterIndex` is the index into the buffer pointed to by `lpstrFilter`. This index specifies the initial filter description and pattern to use.

`lpstrFile` is the pointer to a buffer containing the file name used to initialize the File Name edit control

`nMaxFile` is the number of bytes for the buffer pointed to by `lpstrFile`

`lpstrFileTitle` is the pointer to the buffer that is to receive the title of the selected file

`nMaxFileTitle` is the maximum string length for the string copied to `lpstrFileTitle`

`lpstrInitialDir` is the pointer to the string that specified the initial directory

`lpstrTitle` is the pointer to a string used for the title of the dialog box

`Flags` is the dialog box creation flags; `Flags` is a combination of the following flags:

Value	Meaning
OFN_ALLOWMULTISELECT	File Name list box allows multiple selections
OFN_CREATEPROMPT	Dialog function should query the user before creating a file
OFN_ENABLEHOOK	Hook function enabled
OFN_ENABLETEMPLATE	Template specified by `hInstance` and `lpTemplateName` is used
OFN_ENABLETEMPLATEHANDLE	hInstance specifies a data block containing the template
OFN_EXTENSIONDIFFERENT	Extension of returned filename is different than extension in `lpstDefExt`
OFN_FILEMUSTEXIST	User can enter only names of existing files
OFN_HIDEREADONLY	Read-only checkbox is hidden
OFN_NOCHANGEDIR	Dialog box sets current directory to directory that was in effect before the initialization of the dialog box
OFN_NOREADONLYRETURN	Returned file will not have read only attribute set
OFN_NOTESTFILECREATE	File will not be created before returning from dialog box
OFN_NOVALIDATE	Invalid characters may be in returned filename
OFN_OVERWRITEPROMPT	Save As dialog box prompts the user if the selected filename already exists
OFN_PATHMUSTEXIST	User can enter only valid path names
OFN_READONLY	Read-only checkbox is checked
OFN_SHAREAWARE	`OpenFile` call failed due to network sharing violation
OFN_SHOWHELP	Help push button is shown

`nFileOffset` is the offset from the beginning of the path to the filename in the string pointed to by `lpstrFile`

`nFileExtension` is the offset from the beginning of the path to the file extension in the string pointed to by `lpstrFile`

`lpstrDefExt` is the pointer to the buffer containing the default extension

lCustData is the application-defined data passed to the hook function in lpfnHook

lpfnHook is the pointer to the hook function that processes the dialog box messages

lpTemplateName is the pointer to a null-terminated string that names the dialog box template resource which is to replace the standard dialog template

Return Value A nonzero value is returned when the user successfully specifies the file to open. Zero is returned when the user closes or cancels the dialog box.

Function Category Common Dialog

Related Functions GetSaveFileName

GetOutlineTextMetrics

Syntax `DWORD GetOutlineTextMetrics(hdc, cbData, lpOTM)`

Parameter	*Type*	*Description*
hdc	HDC	Device context
cbData	UINT	Number of bytes returned by function
lpOTM	LPOUTLINETEXTMETRIC	Pointer to OUTLINETEXTMETRIC data structure containing font metric data

Description The GetOutlineTextMetrics function gets metric data for TrueType fonts. The metric data is copied to the OUTLINETEXTMETRIC data structure pointed to by lpOTM. The OUTLINETEXTMETRIC data structure follows.

```
typedef struct _OUTLINETEXTMETRIC {
     UINT otmSize;
     TEXTMETRIC otmTextMetrics;
     BYTE otmFiller;
     PANOSE otmPanoseNumber;
     UINT otmfsSelection;
     UINT otmfsType;
     UINT otmsCharSlopeRise;
```

```
    UINT otmsCharSlopeRun;
    UINT otmEMSquare;
    UINT otmAscent;
    UINT otmDescent;
    UINT otmLineGap;
    UINT otmCapEmHeight;
    UINT otmXHeight;
    RECT otmrcFontBox;
    UINT otmMacAscent;
    UINT otmMacDescent;
    UINT otmMacLineGap;
    UINT otmusMinimumPPEM;
    POINT otmptSubscriptSize;
    POINT otmptSubscriptOffset;
    POINT otmptSuperscriptSize;
    POINT otmptSuperscriptOffset;
    UINT otmsStrikeoutSize;
    UINT otmsStrikeoutPosition;
    UINT otmsUnderscoreSize;
    UINT otmsUnderscorePosition;
    PSTR otmpFamilyName;
    PSTR otmpFaceName;
    PSTR otmpStyleName;
    PSTR otmpFullName;
} OUTLINETEXTMETRIC;
```

in which

`otmSize` is the size of the structure in bytes

`otmTextMetrics` is the `TEXTMETRIC` data structure that contains additional information

`otmFiller` is the value that causes the structure to be byte aligned

`otmPanoseNumber` is the panose number for this font

`otmfsSelection` is the nature of the font pattern as follows:

Value	*Meaning*
0	Italic
1	Underscore
2	Negative
3	Outline
4	Strikeout
5	Bold

`otmfsType` indicates whether the font is licensed

`otmsCharSlopeRise` is the slope angle rise—1 if vertical

`otmsCharSlopeRun` is the slope angle run—0 if vertical

`otmEMSSquare` is the number of logical units for the em square of the font

`otmAscent` is the maximum ascent of the font

`otmDescent` is the descent below baseline

`otmLineGap` is the typographic line gap

`otmCapEmHeight` is not supported by Windows

`otmXHeight` is not supported by Windows

`otmrcFontBox` is the font bounding box

`otmMacAscent` is the ascent above baseline for Mac

`otmMacDescent` is the descent below baseline for Mac

`otmMacLineGap` is the line information for Mac

`otmusMinimumPPEM` is the minimum size for font in pixels per em square

`otmptSubscriptSize` is the size of subscript

`otmptSubscriptOffset` is the subscript offset

`otmptSuperscriptSize` is the size of superscript

`otmptSuperscriptOffset` is the offset to superscript

`otmsStrikeoutSize` is the strikeout size

`otmsStrikeoutPosition` is the strikeout position

`otmsUnderscoreSize` is the underscore size

`otmsUnderscorePosition` is the underscore position

`otmpFamilyName` is the pointer to family name

`otmpFaceName` is the pointer to face name

`otmpStyleName` is the pointer to style string

`otmpFullName` is the pointer to full name.

Return Value A nonzero value is returned when the function is successful and `lpOTM` points to a data structure. The number of bytes required for the metric data is returned when `lpOTM` is `NULL` and the function is successful. Zero is returned when the function is unsuccessful.

Function Category Font, TrueType

Related Functions `GetGlyphOutline`, `GetTextMetrics`

GetPaletteEntries

Syntax `UINT GetPaletteEntries(hpal, iStart, cEntries, lppe)`

Parameter	*Type*	*Description*
hpal	HPALETTE	Logical palette
iStart	UINT	First entry of the logical palette to retrieve
cEntries	UINT	Number of palette entries to retrieve
lppe	PALETTEENTRY FAR*	Pointer to an array of PALETTEENTRY data structures receiving the palette entries

Description The `GetPaletteEntries` function gets the palette entries specified by `iStart` and `cEntries` from the palette in `hpal` and places them in the array of data structures of type `PALETTEENTRY` pointed to by `lppe`. The `PALETTEENTRY` structure follows.

```
typedef struct
     {
     BYTE peRed;
     BYTE peGreen;
     BYTE peBlue;
     BYTE peFlags;
} PALETTEENTRY;
```

in which

`peRed` is the intensity of red for the palette entry

`peGreen` is the intensity of green for the palette entry

`peBlue` is the intensity of blue for the palette entry

`peFlags` is `NULL` or one of the following values:

Value	Meaning
PC_EXPLICIT	Low-order word of the palette entry contains a hardware palette index
PC_NOCOLLAPSE	Color will be placed in an unused entry in the palette; color will not replace existing entry
PC_RESERVED	Entry is used for palette animation; no color can be matched to this entry

Return Value The number of entries retrieved from the logical palette is returned. Zero indicates an error.

Function Category Color Palette

Related Functions GetSystemPaletteEntries, SetPaletteEntries

GetParent

Syntax `HWND GetParent(hwnd)`

Parameter	Type	Description
hwnd	HWND	Window handle

Description The GetParent function gets the handle for the parent window of the window specified in hwnd.

Return Value The window handle for the parent window is returned if the specified window has a parent. NULL is returned when the specified window has no parent.

Function Category Information

Related Functions FindWindow, SetParent

GetPixel

Syntax `COLORREF GetPixel(hdc, nXPos, nYPos)`

Parameter	Type	Description
`hdc`	`HDC`	Device context
`nXPos`	`int`	Logical x-coordinate of pixel
`nYPos`	`int`	Logical y-coordinate of pixel

Description The `GetPixel` function determines the RGB color value for the pixel located at the position specified by the logical coordinates in (`nXPos`, `nYPos`). The specified point must lie within the clipping region.

Return Value The RGB color value for the specified position is returned when successful. When unsuccessful, –1 is returned.

Function Category Bitmap

Related Functions `SetPixel`

GetPolyFillMode

Syntax `int GetPolyFillMode(hdc)`

Parameter	Type	Description
`hdc`	`HDC`	Device context

Description The `GetPolyFillMode` function gets the mode used to fill polygons.

Return Value The mode used to fill polygons, either `ALTERNATE` (for alternate mode) or `WINDING` (for winding number mode), is returned.

Function Category Drawing Attribute

Related Functions `SetPolyFillMode`

GetPriorityClipboardFormat

Syntax `int GetPriorityClipboardFormat(lpwPriorityList, cEntries)`

Parameter	*Type*	*Description*
`lpwPriorityList`	`WORD FAR*`	Pointer to list of clipboard formats in priority order
`cEntries`	`int`	Number of items in priority list

Description The `GetPriorityClipboardFormat` function retrieves the first entry in the prioritized clipboard format list. `lpwPriorityList` points to the array which contains the list of prioritized clipboard formats. `cEntries` specifies the number of items in the priority list.

Return Value The `GetPriorityClipboardFormat` function returns the clipboard format with the highest priority from the clipboard format list. If no data exists in the clipboard, `NULL` is returned. –1 is returned when data in the clipboard does not match any format in the clipboard format list.

Function Category Clipboard

Related Functions `EnumClipboardFormats`, `IsClipboardFormatAvailable`, `RegisterClipboardFormat`

GetPrivateProfileInt

Syntax

```
UINT GetPrivateProfileInt(lpszSectionName, lpszKeyName,
                          default, lpszFileName)
```

Parameter	*Type*	*Description*
`lpszSectionName`	`LPCSTR`	Pointer to name of the section heading that appears in the initialization file
`lpszKeyName`	`LPCSTR`	Pointer to the key name that appears in the initialization file
`default`	`int`	Default value for the key
`lpszFileName`	`LPCSTR`	Pointer to the string that contains the name of the initialization file

Description The `GetPrivateProfileInt` function gets the value of the key specified in `lpszKeyName` from the initialization file specified in `lpszFileName`. `lpszSectionName` specifies the application heading that the key name appears under.

Return Value A zero is returned if the value associated with the specified key is not an integer. The value of the entry is returned when successful. `default` is returned if the specified key is not found.

Function Category Initialization File

Related Functions `GetPrivateProfileString`, `WritePrivateProfileString`

GetPrivateProfileString

Syntax

```
int GetPrivateProfileString(lpszSectionName, lpszKeyName,
                            lpszDefault, lpszReturnBuffer,
                            cbReturnBuffer,lpszFileName)
```

Parameter	*Type*	*Description*
`lpszSectionName`	`LPCSTR`	Pointer to the string that specifies the section of the initialization file that contains the entry
`lpszKeyName`	`LPCSTR`	Pointer to a key name that appears in the intialization file
`lpszDefault`	`LPCSTR`	Default value for the key
`lpszReturnBuffer`	`LPSTR`	Pointer to the buffer that receives the character string
`cbReturnBuffer`	`int`	Maximum number of characters to copy to the buffer
`lpszFileName`	`LPCSTR`	Pointer to the name of the initialization file

Description The `GetPrivateProfileString` function copies the string associated with the key name in `lpszKeyName` from the initialization file specified in `lpszFileName` into the buffer pointed to by `lpszReturnBuffer`. `cbReturnBuffer` specifies the maximum number of characters to copy to the buffer.

Return Value The number of characters copied to the buffer is returned. The return value does not include the null terminator.

Function Category Initialization File

Related Functions `GetPrivateProfileInt`, `WritePrivateProfileString`

GetProcAddress

Syntax `FARPROC GetProcAddress(hinst, lpszProcName)`

Parameter	*Type*	*Description*
`hinst`	`HINSTANCE`	DLL module that contains the function
`lpszProcName`	`LPCSTR`	Pointer to the function name

Description The `GetProcAddress` function gets the address of the function specified in `lpszProcName`. `hinst` specifies the module that contains the function. If `hinst` is set to `NULL`, it is assumed that the current module contains the function.

Return Value The pointer to the function's entry point is returned when successful. `NULL` is returned when unsuccessful.

Function Category Module Management

Related Functions `FreeProcInstance`, `MakeProcInstance`

GetProfileInt

Syntax `UINT GetProfileInt(lpszSectionName, lpszKeyName, default)`

Parameter	*Type*	*Description*
`lpszSectionName`	`LPCSTR`	Pointer to the string that specifies the section of the initialization file that contains the entry

Parameter	*Type*	*Description*
`lpszKeyName`	`LPCSTR`	Pointer to the key name that appears in the Windows initialization file
`default`	`int`	Default value for the key

Description The `GetProfileInt` function gets the value of the key specified in `lpszKeyName` from the Windows initialization file. `lpszSectionName` specifies the application heading that the key name appears under.

Return Value A zero is returned if the value associated with the specified key is not an integer. The value of the string is returned when successful. `default` is returned if the specified key is not found.

Function Category Initialization File

Related Functions `GetProfileString`, `WriteProfileString`

GetProfileString

Syntax

```
int GetProfileString(lpszSectionName, lpszKeyName,
                     lpszDefault, lpszReturnBuffer,
                     cbReturnBuffer)
```

Parameter	*Type*	*Description*
`lpszSectionName`	`LPCSTR`	Pointer to the string that specifies the section of the initialization file that contains the entry
`lpszKeyName`	`LPCSTR`	Pointer to a key name that appears in the Windows initialization file
`lpszDefault`	`LPCSTR`	Default value for the key
`lpszReturnBuffer`	`LPSTR`	Pointer to the buffer that receives the character string
`cbReturnBuffer`	`int`	Maximum number of characters to copy to the buffer

Description The `GetProfileString` function copies the string associated with the key name in `lpszKeyName` from the Windows initialization file into the buffer pointed to by `lpszReturnBuffer`. `cbReturnBuffer` specifies the maximum number of characters to copy to the buffer.

Return Value The number of characters copied to the buffer is returned. The null terminator is not included in the return value count.

Function Category Initialization File

Related Functions `GetProfileInt`, `WriteProfileString`

GetProp

Syntax `HANDLE GetProp(hwnd, lpsz)`

Parameter	*Type*	*Description*
`hwnd`	`HWND`	Window containing the property list
`lpsz`	`LPCSTR`	Points to null-terminated string or atom identifying a string

Description The `GetProp` function gets a data handle identified by `lpsz` from the property list for the window specified in `hWnd`. `lpsz` points to either a null-terminated string or an atom that identifies a string. When `lpsz` specifies an atom, the atom (16 bits) is placed in the low-order word of `lpsz`; the high-order word of `lpsz` is set to zero.

Return Value The retrieved data handle is returned when successful. When unsuccessful, `NULL` is returned.

Function Category Property

Related Functions `EnumProps`, `RemoveProp`, `SetProp`

GetQueueStatus

Syntax `DWORD GetQueueStatus(fuFlags)`

Parameter	*Type*	*Description*
`fuFlags`	`UINT`	Queue status flags. `fuFlags` is a combination of the following values:

Value	*Meaning*
`QS_KEY`	`WM_CHAR` message in queue
`QS_MOUSE`	`WM_MOUSEMOVE` or `WM_`... button message is in the queue
`QS_MOUSEMOVE`	`WM_MOUSEMOVE` message in queue
`QS_MOUSEBUTTON`	`WM_`... button message in queue
`QS_PAINT`	`WM_PAINT` message in queue
`QS_POSTMSG`	Message (other than those previously described) in queue
`QS_SENDMSG`	Message from another application in queue
`QS_TIMER`	`WM_TIMER` message in queue

Description The `GetQueueStatus` function determines the type of message that is in the queue. `fuFlags` specifies the queue-status flags to retrieve.

Return Value The high-order word of the return value specifies the message types currently in the queue. The low-order word of the return value indicates the message types added to the queue since the last call to `GetQueueStatus`, `GetMessage`, or `PeekMessage`.

Function Category Message

Related Functions `GetInputState`, `GetMessage`, `PeekMessage`

GetRasterizerCaps

Syntax `BOOL GetRasterizerCaps(lpraststat, cb)`

Parameter	*Type*	*Description*
lpraststat	LPRASTERIZER_STATUS	Pointer to RASTERIZER_STATUS data structure that will receive rasterizer information
cb	int	Number of bytes to be copied to data structure

Description The GetRasterizerCaps function retrieves flags that indicate whether TrueType fonts have been installed. lpraststat points to a data structure of type RASTERIZER_STATUS where the rasterizer information will be copied. The RASTERIZER_STATUS data structure follows.

```
typedef struct _RASTERIZER_STATUS {
     short nSize;
     short wFlags;
     short nLanguageID;
     } RASTERIZER_STATUS;
```

in which

nSize is the size of the structure in bytes

wFlags is TT_AVAILABLE and/or TT_ENABLED to indicate whether a TrueType font is installed and whether TrueType is enabled

nLanguageID is the language specified in SETUP.INF.

Return Value TRUE is returned when successful. FALSE is returned when unsuccessful.

Function Category Font, TrueTypes

Related Functions GetOutlineTextMetrics

GetRgnBox

Syntax `int GetRgnBox(hrgn, lprc)`

Parameter	*Type*	*Description*
hrgn	HRGN	Region
lprc	RECT FAR*	Pointer to a RECT data structure that stores the coordinates of the bounding rectangle of the region

Description The GetRgnBox function gets the coordinates of the rectangle that bounds the region specified in hrgn. The coordinates of the bounding rectangle are placed in the data structure of type RECT pointed to by lprc. The RECT data structure follows.

```
typedef struct tagRECT{
     int left;
     int top;
     int right;
     int bottom;
} RECT;
```

in which

left is the x coordinate of the upper-left corner

top is the y coordinate of the upper-left corner

right is the x coordinate of the lower-right corner

bottom is the y coordinate of the lower-right corner.

Return Value The region's type is returned. One of the following values is returned. ERROR is returned when an error occurs.

Value	*Meaning*
COMPLEXREGION	New region has overlapping borders
NULLREGION	New region is empty
SIMPLEREGION	New region has no overlapping borders

Function Category Region

Related Functions CreateRectRgn, FrameRgn, SetRectRgn

GetROP2

Syntax `int GetROP2(hdc)`

Parameter	*Type*	*Description*
hdc	HDC	Device context

Description The `GetROP2` function gets the drawing mode for the device context specified in `hdc`.

Return Value The drawing mode is returned and is one of the following values:

Value	*Meaning*
R2_BLACK	Pixel is black
R2_COPYPEN	Pixel is the pen color
R2_MASKNOTPEN	Pixel is the combination of the common colors of the display and the inverse of the pen
R2_MASKPEN	Pixel is the combination of the common colors of the pen and the display
R2_MASKPENNOT	Pixel is the combination of the common colors of the pen and the inverse of the display color
R2_MERGENOTPEN	Pixel is the combination of the display color and the inverse of the pen color
R2_MERGEPEN	Pixel is the combination of the pen and display colors
R2_MERGEPENNOT	Pixel is the combination of pen color and inverse of display color
R2_NOP	Pixel is not changed
R2_NOT	Pixel is inverse of display color
R2_NOTCOPYPEN	Pixel is inverse of pen color
R2_NOTMASKPEN	Pixel is the inverse of R2_MASKPEN
R2_NOTMERGEPEN	Pixel is the inverse of R2_MERGEPEN
R2_NOTXORPEN	Pixel is the inverse of R2_XORPEN color
R2_WHITE	Pixel is white
R2_XORPEN	Pixel is the combination of the colors in the pen and in the display, but not both

Function Category Drawing Attribute

Related Functions `SetROP2`

GetRValue

Syntax `BYTE GetRValue(rgb)`

Parameter	*Type*	*Description*
rgb	DWORD	RGB color field

Description The `GetRValue` macro gets the red value from the RGB color value specified in `rgb`.

Return Value The red value from the RGB color field is returned.

Function Category Windows Macros

Related Functions `GetBValue`, `GetGValue`

GetSaveFileName

Syntax `BOOL GetSaveFileName(lpofn)`

Parameter	*Type*	*Description*
lpofn	LPOPENFILENAME	Pointer to `OPENFILENAME` data structure containing dialog box initialization information

Description The `GetSaveFileName` function creates a system-defined dialog box that provides the user with the ability to enter the file name of the file to save. `lpofn` points to a data structure of type `OPENFILENAME` that contains initialization information for the dialog box. The `OPENFILENAME` data structure follows.

```
#include <commdlg.h>
typedef structure tagOFN     {
     DWORD lStructSize;
     HWND hwndOwner;
```

```
    HANDLE hInstance;
    LPSTR lpstrFilter;
    LPSTR lpstrCustomFilter;
    DWORD nMaxCustFilter;
    DWORD nFilterIndex;
    LPSTR lpstrFile;
    DWORD nMaxFile;
    LPSTR lpstrFileTitle;
    DWORD nMaxFileTitle;
    LPSTR lpstrInitialDir;
    LPSTR lpstrTitle;
    DWORD Flags;
    WORD nFileOffset;
    WORD nFileExtension;
    LPSTR lpstrDefExt;
    DWORD lCustData;
    WORD (FAR PASCAL *lpfnHook)(HWND, unsigned,
              WORD, LONG);
    LPSTR lpTemplateName;
} OPENFILENAME;
```

in which

`lStructSize` is the number of bytes in the structure

`hwndOwner` is the handle of the window that owns the dialog box

`hInstance` is the data block that contains the dialog box template specified by `lpTemplateName`

`lpstrFilter` is the pointer to a buffer that contains pairs of null-terminated filter strings. The first string in the pair is the filter description; the second is the filter pattern (for example, "*.doc"). The last string in the buffer must contain two `NULL` characters.

`lpstrCustomFilter` is the pointer to a buffer that contains a pair of filter strings defined by the user. The first string in the pair is the filter description; the second is the filter pattern (for example "*.doc"). The last string in the buffer must contain two `NULL` characters.

`nMaxCustFilter` is the number of bytes for the buffer in `lpstrCustomFilter`

`nFilterIndex` is the index into the buffer pointed to by `lpstrFilter`. This index specifies the initial filter description and pattern to use.

`lpstrFile` is the pointer to a buffer containing the file name used to initialize the File Name edit control `nMaxFile` is the number of bytes for the buffer pointed to by `lpstrFile`

`lpstrFileTitle` is the pointer to the buffer that is to receive the title of the selected file

`nMaxFileTitle` is the maximum string length for the string copied to `lpstrFileTitle`

`lpstrInitialDir` is the pointer to the string that specified the initial directory

`lpstrTitle` is the pointer to a string used for the title of the dialog box

`Flags` is the dialog box creation flags; `Flags` is a combination of the following flags:

Value	*Meaning*
OFN_ALLOWMULTISELECT	File Name list box allows multiple selections
OFN_CREATEPROMPT	Dialog function should query the user before creating a file
OFN_ENABLEHOOK	Hook function enabled
OFN_ENABLETEMPLATE	Template specified by `hInstance` and `lpTemplateName` is used
OFN_ENABLETEMPLATEHANDLE	`hInstance` specifies a data block containing the template
OFN_EXTENSIONDIFFERENT	Extension of returned filename is different than extension in `lpstDefExt`
OFN_FILEMUSTEXIST	User can enter only names of existing files
OFN_HIDEREADONLY	Read-only checkbox is hidden
OFN_NOCHANGEDIR	Dialog box sets current directory to directory that was in effect before the initialization of the dialog box
OFN_NOREADONLYRETURN	Returned file will not have read only attribute set
OFN_NOTESTFILECREATE	File will not be created before returning from dialog box
OFN_NOVALIDATE	Invalid characters may be in returned filename

Value	Meaning
OFN_OVERWRITEPROMPT	Save As dialog box prompts the user if the selected filename already exists
OFN_PATHMUSTEXIST	User can enter only valid path names
OFN_READONLY	Read-only checkbox is checked
OFN_SHAREAWARE	OpenFile call failed due to network sharing violation
OFN_SHOWHELP	Help push button is shown

nFileOffset is the offset from the beginning of the path to the filename in the string pointed to by lpstrFile

nFileExtension is the offset from the beginning of the path to the file extension in the string pointed to by lpstrFile

lpstrDefExt is the pointer to the buffer containing the default extension

lCustData is the application-defined data passed to the hook function in lpfnHook

lpfnHook is the pointer to the hook function that processes the dialog box messages

lpTemplateName is the pointer to a null-terminated string that names the dialog box template resource which is to replace the standard dialog template.

Return Value TRUE is returned when the user specifies a filename. FALSE is returned if the user cancels or closes the dialog box.

Function Category Common Dialog

Related Functions GetOpenFileName

GetScrollPos

Syntax `int GetScrollPos(hwnd, fnbar)`

Parameter	Type	Description
hwnd	HWND	Window containing the scroll bars or scroll control
fnbar	int	Scroll bar

Description The `GetScrollPos` function gets the thumb position of the scroll bar for the window specified in `hwnd`. `fnbar` specifies the scroll bar to evaluate. The value for `fnbar` is selected from the following values. The value returned by the `GetScrollPos` function is relative to the current scrolling range.

Value	Meaning
SB_CTL	Gets the position of a scroll bar control; `hwnd` must specify the window handle of a scroll bar control
SB_HORZ	Gets the position of the horizontal scroll bar
SB_VERT	Gets the position of the vertical scroll bar

Return Value The thumb position of the scroll bar is returned when successful. Zero is returned when unsuccessful.

Function Category Scrolling

Related Functions `GetScrollRange`, `SetScrollPos`

GetScrollRange

Syntax `void GetScrollRange(hwnd, fnBar, lpnMinPos, lpnMaxPos)`

Parameter	Type	Description
hwnd	HWND	Window containing the scroll bars or scroll control
fnBar	int	Scroll bar to retrieve
lpnMinPos	int FAR*	Points to the variable to receive the minimum position
lpnMaxPos	int FAR*	Points to the variable to receive the maximum position

Description The `GetScrollRange` function gets the minimum and maximum ranges for the scroll bar specified in `fnBar` and places these values in `lpnMinPos` and `lpnMaxPos`, respectively. `fnBar` specifies the scroll bar to retrieve. The values for `fnBar` are as follows:

Value	*Meaning*
SB_CTL	Gets the position of a scroll bar control; hWnd must specify the window handle of a scroll bar control
SB_HORZ	Gets the position of the horizontal scroll bar
SB_VERT	Gets the position of the vertical scroll bar

Return Value There is no return value.

Function Category Scrolling

Related Functions `GetScrollPos`, `SetScrollRange`

GetSelectorBase

Syntax `DWORD GetSelectorBase(wSelector)`

Parameter	*Type*	*Description*
wSelector	WORD	Selector

Description The `GetSelectorBase` function gets the base address for the selector specified in `wSelector`.

Return Value The base address of the specified selector is returned.

Function Category Memory Management

Related Functions `GetSelectorLimit`, `SetSelectorBase`

GetSelectorLimit

Syntax `DWORD GetSelectorLimit(wSelector)`

Parameter	Type	Description
wSelector	WORD	Selector

Description The GetSelectorLimit function gets the limit for the selector specified in wSelector.

Return Value The limit for the selector is returned.

Function Category Memory Management

Related Functions GetSelectorBase, SetSelectorLimit

GetStockObject

Syntax `HGDIOBJ GetStockObject(fnObject)`

Parameter	Type	Description
fnObject	int	Type of stock object

Description The GetStockObject function gets the handle for the stock pen, brush, or font specified in fnObject. The following values are used for fnObject:

Brushes

Value	Meaning
BLACK_BRUSH	Black brush
DKGRAY_BRUSH	Dark-gray brush
GRAY_BRUSH	Gray brush
HOLLOW_BRUSH	Hollow brush
LTGRAY_BRUSH	Light-gray brush
NULL_BRUSH	Null brush
WHITE_BRUSH	White brush

Pens

Value	Meaning
BLACK_PEN	Black pen
NULL_PEN	Null pen
WHITE_PEN	White pen

Fonts

Value	*Meaning*
`ANSI_FIXED_FONT`	ANSI fixed system font
`ANSI_VAR_FONT`	ANSI variable system font
`DEVICE_DEFAULT_FONT`	Device-dependent font
`OEM_FIXED_FONT`	OEM-dependent font
`SYSTEM_FONT`	System font
`SYSTEM_FIXED_FONT`	Fixed-width system font

Palettes

Value	*Meaning*
`DEFAULT_PALETTE`	Default color palette

Return Value The handle for the object is returned when successful. `NULL` is returned when unsuccessful.

Function Category Drawing Tool

Related Functions `GetObject`, `SelectObject`

GetStretchBltMode

Syntax `int GetStretchBltMode(hdc)`

Parameter	*Type*	*Description*
`hdc`	`HDC`	Device context

Description The `GetStretchBltMode` function gets the bitmap stretching mode for the device context in `hdc`.

Return Value One of the following stretching modes is returned: `STRETCH_ANDSCANS`, `STRETCH_DELETESCANS`, or `STRETCH_ORSCANS`.

Function Category Drawing Attribute

Related Functions `SetStretchBltMode`, `StretchBlt`

GetSubMenu

Syntax `HMENU GetSubMenu(hmenu, nPos)`

Parameter	*Type*	*Description*
hmenu	HMENU	Menu handle
nPos	int	Menu position

Description The GetSubMenu function gets the handle for the pop-up menu specified by the menu position in nPos. hmenu identifies the menu that contains the pop-up menu.

Return Value The menu handle for the pop-up menu is returned. If a pop-up menu does not exist at the specified position, NULL is returned.

Function Category Menu

Related Functions CreateMenu, DeleteMenu, GetMenu, SetMenu, TrackPopupMenu

GetSysColor

Syntax `DWORD GetSysColor(nDspElement)`

Parameter	*Type*	*Description*
nDspElement	int	Display element

Description The GetSysColor function gets the current color for the display element specified in nDspElement. The index values used for nDspElement are as follows:

Value	*Meaning*
COLOR_ACTIVEBORDER	Active window border
COLOR_ACTIVECAPTION	Active window caption
COLOR_APPWORKSPACE	Background color for MDI applications
COLOR_BACKGROUND	Desktop
COLOR_BTNFACE	Face shading for push buttons
COLOR_BTNHIGHLIGHT	Selected button in a control
COLOR_BTNSHADOW	Edge shading for push buttons

Value	Meaning
COLOR_BTNTEXT	Text on push buttons
COLOR_CAPTIONTEXT	Text for caption, size box, scroll bar arrow box
COLOR_GRAYTEXT	Grayed text
COLOR_HIGHLIGHT	Selected items in a control
COLOR_HIGHLIGHTTEXT	Text of selected items in a control
COLOR_INACTIVEBORDER	Inactive window border
COLOR_INACTIVECAPTION	Inactive window caption
COLOR_INACTIVECAPTIONTEXT	Color of text in an inactive caption
COLOR_MENU	Menu background
COLOR_MENUTEXT	Text for menus
COLOR_SCROLLBAR	Scroll bar gray area
COLOR_WINDOW	Window background
COLOR_WINDOWFRAME	Window frame
COLOR_WINDOWTEXT	Text in windows

Return Value The RGB color value naming the color of the element in `nDspElement` is returned.

Function Category System

Related Functions SetSysColors

GetSysModalWindow

Syntax `HWND GetSysModalWindow()`

Description The `GetSysModalWindow` function returns the handle of a system modal window.

Return Value The window handle for the system modal window is returned when a system modal window is found. If no system modal window is found, `NULL` is returned.

Function Category Information

Related Functions `SetSysModalWindow`

GetSystemDebugState

Syntax `LONG GetSystemDebugState(void)`

Parameter	*Type*	*Description*
None		

Description The `GetSystemDebugState` function returns system state information. The returned information can be used by a Windows-based debugger to determine whether to enter hard or soft mode when a breakpoint in encountered.

Return Value One of the following values is returned:

Value	*Meaning*
`SDS_DIALOG`	A dialog box is displayed
`SDS_MENU`	Menu is displayed
`SDS_NOTASKQUEUE`	Application queue does not exist
`SDS_SYSMODAL`	System modal dialog box is displayed
`SDS_TASKISLOCKED`	Current task is locked and no other tasks are allowed to run

Function Category Debugging

Related Functions `DebugBreak`, `OutputDebugString`

GetSystemDir

Syntax `WORD GetSystemDir(lpszWinDir, lpszBuffer, Size)`

Parameter	*Type*	*Description*
`lpszWinDir`	`LPSTR`	Directory where software is being installed
`lpszBuffer`	`LPSTR`	Pointer to buffer to receive the string containing the pathname
`Size`	`int`	Number of bytes in the buffer pointed to by `lpszBuffer`

Description The `GetSystemDir` function gets the pathname of the Windows system subdirectory and copies the pathname to `lpszBuffer`. This function is supported only in the static-link version of the version library. Applications that do not install software should use the `GetSystemDirectory` function to get the Windows directory.

Return Value The length of the string (including the null terminator) copied to `lpszBuffer` is returned when successful. Zero is returned when unsuccessful.

Function Category Version

Related Functions `GetWindowsDir`

GetSystemDirectory

Syntax `UINT GetSystemDirectory(lpszSysPath, cbSysPath)`

Parameter	*Type*	*Description*
`lpszSysPath`	`LPSTR`	Pointer to the buffer to receive the pathname
`cbSysPath`	`UINT`	Maximum number of bytes in buffer

Description The `GetSystemDirectory` function gets the path of the Windows system subdirectory. The retrieved path is placed in the buffer pointed to by `lpszSysPath`. `cbSysPath` specifies the maximum number of bytes in the buffer.

Return Value The length of the string copied to `lpszSysPath` is returned (excluding the null terminator).

Function Category File I/O

Related Functions `GetWindowsDirectory`

GetSystemMenu

Syntax `HMENU GetSystemMenu(hwnd, fRevert)`

Parameter	Type	Description
hwnd	HWND	Window to own System menu
fRevert	BOOL	Specifies whether to copy or modify

Description The GetSystemMenu function provides access to the System menu. By using this function, an application can copy and modify the System menu. When fRevert is set to TRUE, a copy of the system menu that is owned by the window in hwnd is destroyed and the handle of the original system menu is returned. When fRevert is set to FALSE, the handle of the copy of the System menu owned by the window in hwnd is returned.

Return Value The menu handle for the copy of the System menu is returned when fRevert is FALSE. The return value is undefined when fRevert is TRUE.

Function Category Menu

Related Functions GetMenu, GetSubMenu

GetSystemMetrics

Syntax `int GetSystemMetrics(nIndex)`

Parameter	Type	Description
nIndex	int	Specifies the system measurement to retrieve

Description The GetSystemMetrics function gets the size, or metrics, of the specified display element. nIndex specifies the system measurement to retrieve. The following values are used for nIndex. Measurements are expressed in pixels.

Value	Meaning
SM_CXSCREEN	Screen width
SM_CYSCREEN	Screen height
SM_CXFRAME	Width of window frame that can be sized
SM_CYFRAME	Height of window frame that can be sized

Value	Meaning
SM_CXHSCROLL	Width of arrow bitmap on horizontal scroll bar
SM_CYHSCROLL	Height of arrow bitmap on horizontal scroll bar
SM_CXVSCROLL	Width of arrow bitmap on vertical scroll bar
SM_CYVSCROLL	Height of arrow bitmap on vertical scroll bar
SM_CYCAPTION	Height of caption
SM_CXBORDER	Width of window that cannot be sized
SM_CYBORDER	Height of window that cannot be sized
SM_CXDLGFRAME	Width of frame for window with style WS_DLGFRAME
SM_CYDLGFRAME	Height of frame for window with style WS_DLGFRAME
SM_CXHTHUMB	Width of thumb box on horizontal scroll bar
SM_CYVTHUMB	Height of thumb box on vertical scroll bar
SM_CXICON	Width of icon
SM_CYICON	Height of icon
SM_CXCURSOR	Width of cursor
SM_CYCURSOR	Height of cursor
SM_CYMENU	Height of single-line menu bar
SM_CXFULLSCREEN	Width of client area for full-screen window
SM_CYFULLSCREEN	Height of client area for full-screen window
SM_CYKANJIWINDOW	Height of Kanji window
SM_CXMINTRACK	Minimum tracking width of window
SM_CYMINTRACK	Minimum tracking height of window
SM_CXMIN	Minimum width of window
SM_CYMIN	Minimum height of window
SM_CXSIZE	Width of bitmaps in title bar
SM_CYSIZE	Height of bitmaps in title bar
SM_MOUSEPRESENT	Nonzero if mouse hardware is present
SM_DEBUG	Nonzero if Windows debugging version
SM_SWAPBUTTON	Nonzero if left and right mouse buttons are swapped

Value	Meaning
SM_CXDOUBLECLK	Width (in pixels) of the rectangle around the first click of a double click
SM_CYDOUBLECLK	Height (in pixels) of the rectangle around the first click of a double click
SM_CXICONSPACING	Width of rectangle used to position tiled icons
SM_CYICONSPACING	Height of rectangle used to position tiled icons
SM_DBCSENABLED	Nonzero when Windows uses double-byte characters; zero otherwise
SM_MENUDROPALIGNMENT	Zero if left side of pop-up menu is aligned with left side of menu item; nonzero if left side of pop-up menu is aligned with right side of menu item
SM_PENWINDOWS	Handle of Pen Windows DLL when Pen Windows is installed

Return Value The system metric corresponding to `nIndex` is returned.

Function Category System

Related Functions `GetSysColor`

GetSystemPaletteEntries

Syntax `UINT GetSystemPaletteEntries(hdc, iStart, cEntries, lppe)`

Parameter	Type	Description
hdc	HDC	Device context
iStart	UINT	First entry of the system palette to retrieve
cEntries	UINT	Number of system palette entries to retrieve
lppe	PALETTEENTRY FAR*	Pointer to an array of PALETTEENTRY data structures receiving the palette entries

Description The GetSystemPaletteEntries function gets the palette entries specified by iStart and cEntries from the system palette and places them in the array of data structures of type PALETTEENTRY pointed to by lppe. The PALETTEENTRY structure follows.

```
typedef struct
     {
     BYTE peRed;
     BYTE peGreen;
     BYTE peBlue;
     BYTE peFlags;
} PALETTEENTRY;
```

in which

peRed is the intensity of red for the palette entry

peGreen is the intensity of green for the palette entry

peBlue is the intensity of blue for the palette entry

peFlags is NULL or one of the following values:

Value	*Meaning*
PC_EXPLICIT	Low-order word of the palette entry contains a hardware palette index
PC_NOCOLLAPSE	Color will be placed in an unused entry in the palette; color will not replace existing entry
PC_RESERVED	Entry is used for palette animation; no color can be matched to this entry

Return Value The number of palette entries retrieved from the system palette is returned when successful. Zero is returned when unsuccessful.

Function Category Color Palette

Related Functions GetPaletteEntries, SetPaletteEntries

GetSystemPaletteUse

Syntax UINT GetSystemPaletteUse(hdc)

Parameter	Type	Description
hdc	HDC	Device context

Description The `GetSystemPaletteUse` function determines whether an application has access to the full system palette.

Return Value One of the following values is returned to indicate the current use of the system palette:

Value	Meaning
SYSPAL_NOSTATIC	System palette has no static colors—only black and white
SYSPAL_STATIC	System palette has static colors that will not change when the application realizes its logical palette

Function Category Color Palette

Related Functions `GetSystemPaletteEntries`, `SetSystemPaletteUse`

GetTabbedTextExtent

Syntax

```
DWORD GetTabbedTextExtent(hdc, lpszString, cChars, cTabs,
                          lpnTabs)
```

Parameter	Type	Description
hdc	HDC	Device context
lpszString	LPCSTR	Pointer to the text string
cChars	int	Number of characters in `lpszString`
cTabs	int	Number of tab positions in the array specified in `lpnTabs`
lpnTabs	int FAR*	Pointer to an array of integers specifying the tab stop positions in pixels

Description The `GetTabbedTextExtent` function determines the width and height (in logical units) of the text string specified in `lpszString`. The current font is used when calculating the width and height of the string.

Return Value The low-order word of the return value contains the calculated width. The high-order word of the return value contains the calculated height.

Function Category Text

Related Functions `GetTextExtent`, `GetTextExtentEx`

GetTempDrive

Syntax `BYTE GetTempDrive(bDriveLetter)`

Parameter	*Type*	*Description*
`bDriveLetter`	`char`	This parameter is ignored

Description The `GetTempDrive` function gets the best drive to use for temporary file storage. The best drive is considered to be the drive that has the fastest access time.

Return Value The drive letter of a disk is returned.

Function Category File I/O

Related Functions `GetDriveType`, `GetTempFileName`

GetTempFileName

Syntax

```
int GetTempFileName(bDriveLetter,
                    lpszPrefixString,
                    uUnique, lpszTempFileName)
```

Parameter	*Type*	*Description*
`bDriveLetter`	`BYTE`	Drive for temporary file
`lpszPrefixString`	`LPCSTR`	Pointer to the null-terminated string

Parameter	Type	Description
		containing the filename prefix for the temporary file; characters in the string must be from the OEM character set
`uUnique`	`UINT`	Unsigned short integer
`lpszTempFileName`	`LPSTR`	Pointer to the buffer that receives the temporary filename

Description The `GetTempFileName` function creates a temporary filename. `bDriveLetter` specifies the drive letter for the filename. `lpszPrefixString` specifies the prefix of the filename. `uUnique` is an unsigned short integer which is converted to hexadecimal for use in the filename. `lpszTempFileName` stores the resulting filename in the form of

```
drive:\path\prefixuuuu.tmp
```

in which

`drive` is specified in `bDriveLetter`

`path` is the pathname for the temporary file specified in the `TEMP` environment variable

`prefix` is specified in `lpszPrefixString`

`uuuu` is the hexadecimal equivalent to the value in `uUnique`

`tmp` is the file extension.

Return Value A unique numeric value used in the temporary filename is returned.

Function Category File I/O

Related Functions `GetTempDrive`

GetTextAlign

Syntax `UINT GetTextAlign(hdc)`

Parameter	*Type*	*Description*
`hdc`	`HDC`	Device context

Description The `GetTextAlign` function gets the status of the text alignment flags for the device context specified in `hdc`.

Return Value The return value indicates the status of the text alignment flags. The return value is a combination of one or more of the following values:

Value	*Meaning*
`TA_BASELINE`	Alignment of x axis and baseline of font within the bounding rectangle
`TA_BOTTOM`	Alignment of x axis and bottom of bounding rectangle
`TA_CENTER`	Alignment of y axis and center of bounding rectangle
`TA_LEFT`	Alignment of y axis and left side of bounding rectangle
`TA_NOUPDATECP`	Current position is not updated
`TA_RIGHT`	Alignment of y axis and right side of bounding rectangle
`TA_TOP`	Alignment of x axis and top of bounding rectangle
`TA_UPDATECP`	Current position is updated

Function Category Text

Related Functions `GetTextExtent`, `SetTextAlign`

GetTextCharacterExtra

Syntax `int GetTextCharacterExtra(hdc)`

Parameter	*Type*	*Description*
`hdc`	`HDC`	Device context

Description The `GetTextCharacterExtra` function gets the intercharacter spacing used when the GDI writes a line of text to the device context.

Return Value The current intercharacter spacing is returned.

Function Category Text

Related Functions `ExtTextOut`, `SetTextCharacterExtra`

GetTextColor

Syntax `COLORREF GetTextColor(hdc)`

Parameter	*Type*	*Description*
`hdc`	`HDC`	Device context

Description The `GetTextColor` function gets the text color for the device context in `hdc`. The text color is used to draw text with the GDI text output functions.

Return Value The RGB color value which represents the text color is returned.

Function Category Drawing Attribute

Related Functions `GetBkColor`, `SetTextColor`

GetTextExtent

Syntax `DWORD GetTextExtent(hdc, lpszString, cbString)`

Parameter	*Type*	*Description*
`hdc`	`HDC`	Device context
`lpszString`	`LPCSTR`	Pointer to the text string
`cbString`	`int`	Number of characters in the string

Description The `GetTextExtent` function determines the width and height (in logical units) of the string specified in `lpszString`. The current font is used when calculating the width and height of the string.

Return Value The low-order word of the return value contains the width of the string. The high-order word of the return value contains the height of the string.

Function Category Text

Related Functions `GetTextExtentEx`

GetTextExtentEx

Syntax

```
DWORD GetTextExtentEx(hdc, lpszString, cbString,
                      nMaxExtent, lpnFit, lpnDx)
```

Parameter	*Type*	*Description*
`hdc`	`HDC`	Device context
`lpszString`	`LPCSTR`	Pointer to string used to determine extents
`cbString`	`int`	Number of bytes in string specified by `lpszString`
`nMaxExtent`	`int`	Maximum width of formatted string in logical units
`lpnFit`	`int FAR*`	Pointer to integer that indicates the number of characters that will fit in the space specified by `nMaxExtent`
`lpnDx`	`int FAR*`	Pointer to array of integers containing partial string extents

Description The `GetTextExtentEx` function determines the number of characters from the string specified in `lpszString` that will fit in the space specified in `nMaxExtent`. `lpnFit` points to an integer value indicating the number of characters that will fit in the specified space. `lpnDx` points to an array of integers that contains partial string extents. Each extent specifies the distance between the beginning of the string and one of the characters from the string.

Return Value The low-order word of the return value specifies the width of the string in logical units. The high-order word of the return value specifies the height of the string in logical units.

Function Category Text

Related Functions `GetTextExtent`

GetTextExtentPoint

Syntax

```
BOOL GetTextExtentPoint(hdc, lpszString, cbString,
                        lpSize)
```

Parameter	*Type*	*Description*
`hdc`	`HDC`	Device context
`lpszString`	`LPCSTR`	Pointer to text string
`cbString`	`int`	Number of bytes in text string
`lpSize`	`SIZE FAR*`	Pointer to `SIZE` data structure

Description The `GetTextExtentPoint` function determines the extents of the text string specified in `lpszString`. The width and height, in logical units, of the string is copied to the data structure pointed to by `lpSize`. The current font is used when computing the extents.

Return Value `TRUE` is returned when successful. `FALSE` is returned when unsuccessful.

Function Category Text

Related Functions `SetTextCharacterExtra`

GetTextFace

Syntax `int GetTextFace(hdc, cbBuffer, lpszFace)`

Parameter	*Type*	*Description*
`hdc`	`HDC`	Device context
`cbBuffer`	`int`	Size of buffer in bytes
`lpszFace`	`LPSTR`	Pointer to the buffer to receive the typeface name

Description The `GetTextFace` function gets the typeface name of the current font and places the name into the buffer pointed to by `lpszFace`. `cbBuffer` specifies the maximum number of bytes to copy to the buffer.

Return Value The number of bytes copied to the buffer is returned when successful. Zero is returned when unsuccessful.

Function Category Text

Related Functions `GetTextMetrics`

GetTextMetrics

Syntax `BOOL GetTextMetrics(hdc, lptm)`

Parameter	*Type*	*Description*
`hdc`	`HDC`	Device context
`lptm`	`LPTEXTMETRIC`	Pointer to a `TEXTMETRIC` data structure that receives the text metrics

Description The `GetTextMetrics` function retrieves the metrics for the selected font and places these metrics in the data structure of type `TEXTMETRIC` pointed to by `lptm`. The `TEXTMETRIC` structure follows.

```
typedef struct tagTEXTMETRIC {
     short int tmHeight;
     short int tmAscent;
     short int tmDescent;
     short int tmInternalLeading;
     short int tmExternalLeading;
```

```
    short int tmAveCharWidth;
    short int tmMaxCharWidth;
    short int tmWeight;
    BYTE tmItalic;
    BYTE tmUnderlined;
    BYTE tmStruckOut;
    BYTE tmFirstChar;
    BYTE tmLastChar;
    BYTE tmDefaultChar;
    BYTE tmBreakChar;
    BYTE tmPitchAndFamily;
    BYTE tmCharSet;
    short int tmOverhang;
    short int tmDigitizedAspectX;
    short int tmDigitizedAspectY;
} TEXTMETRIC;
```

in which

`tmHeight` is the character height

`tmAscent` is the character ascent (units above baseline)

`tmDescent` is the character descent (units below baseline)

`tmInternalLeading` is the amount of space at the top of the character height specified by `tmHeight`

`tmExternalLeading` is the amount of space added between rows

`tmAveCharWidth` is the average character width

`tmMaxCharWidth` is the width of the widest character

`tmWeight` is the font weight. `tmWeight` is one of the following values:

Constant	*Value*
FW_DONTCARE	0
FW_THIN	100
FW_EXTRALIGHT	200
FW_ULTRALIGHT	200
FW_LIGHT	300
FW_NORMAL	400
FW_REGULAR	400
FW_MEDIUM	500
FW_SEMIBOLD	600

Constant	Value
FW_DEMIBOLD	600
FW_BOLD	700
FW_EXTRABOLD	800
FW_ULTRABOLD	800
FW_BLACK	900
FW_HEAVY	900

`tmItalic` is nonzero if the font is italic

`tmUnderlined` is nonzero if the font is underlined

`tmStruckOut` is nonzero if the font is struck out

`tmFirstChar` is the first character defined for the font

`tmLastChar` is the last character defined for the font

`tmDefaultChar` is the character substituted for characters not in the font

`tmBreakChar` is the character used for word breaks

`tmPitchAndFamily` is the pitch (low-order bits) and family (four high-order bits) of the font. The low-order bits specify the font type. The following font types are available:

Value	Meaning
TMPF_PITCH	Raster font
TMPF_VECTOR	Vector font
TMPF_TT	TrueType font
TMPF_DEVICE	Device font

The four high-order bits specify the font family. The following font families are available:

Value	Meaning
FF_DECORATIVE	Novelty fonts
FF_DONTCARE	Font family is not important
FF_MODERN	Fonts with constant stroke width
FF_ROMAN	Fonts with variable stroke width and with serifs

Value	*Meaning*
FF_SCRIPT	Fonts similar to handwriting
FF_SWISS	Fonts with variable stroke width and without serifs

tmCharSet is the character set for the font. tmCharSet is one of the following:

ANSI_CHARSET
DEFAULT_CHARSET
OEM_CHARSET
SHIFTIS_CHARSET
SYMBOL_CHARSET

tmOverhang is the extra width added to some synthesized fonts

tmDigitizedAspectX is the horizontal aspect of the device the font was designed for

tmDigitizedAspectY is the vertical aspect of the device the font was designed for.

Return Value TRUE is returned when successful. FALSE is returned when unsuccessful.

Function Category Text

Related Functions GetTextFace

GetTickCount

Syntax `DWORD GetTickCount()`

Description The GetTickCount function gets the number of milliseconds elapsed since Windows was started.

Return Value The number of milliseconds elapsed since Windows was started is returned.

Function Category Input, System

Related Functions KillTimer, SetTimer

GetTopWindow

Syntax `HWND GetTopWindow(hwnd)`

Parameter	*Type*	*Description*
`hwnd`	`HWND`	Parent window

Description The `GetTopWindow` function returns the handle of the top-level child window for the parent window specified in `hwnd`.

Return Value The handle of the top-level child window is returned. If the specified parent window has no child windows, `NULL` is returned.

Function Category Information

Related Functions `FindWindow`, `GetNextWindow`, `GetParent`, `GetWindow`

GetUpdateRect

Syntax `BOOL GetUpdateRect(hwnd, lprc, fErase)`

Parameter	*Type*	*Description*
`hwnd`	`HWND`	Window handle
`lprc`	`RECT FAR*`	`RECT` data structure receiving the client coordinates of the rectangle
`fErase`	`BOOL`	Indicates whether update region is to be erased

Description The `GetUpdateRect` function gets the coordinates of the smallest possible rectangle that encloses the update region of the window specified in `hwnd`. `lprc` points to a data structure of type `RECT` that contains the coordinates of the rectangle. The `RECT` structure follows. If the window in `hwnd` was created with style `CS_OWNDC` and a mapping mode other than `MM_TEXT`, logical coordinates are placed in the structure pointed to by `lprc`. Otherwise, client coordinates are placed in the data structure. When `fErase` is set to `TRUE`, the background of the update region is erased.

```
typedef struct tagRECT {
     int left;
     int top;
     int right;
     int bottom;
} RECT;
```

in which

`left` is the x coordinate of the upper-left corner

`top` is the y coordinate of the upper-left corner

`right` is the x coordinate of the lower-right corner

`bottom` is the y coordinate of the lower-right corner.

Return Value A nonzero value is returned if the update region is not empty. Zero is returned if the update region is empty.

Function Category Painting

Related Functions `GetUpdateRgn`

GetUpdateRgn

Syntax `int GetUpdateRgn(hwnd, hrgn, fErase)`

Parameter	*Type*	*Description*
`hwnd`	`HWND`	Window containing region to be updated
`hrgn`	`HRGN`	Update region
`fErase`	`BOOL`	Indicates whether background should be erased and nonclient areas of child windows drawn. When `fErase` is false, no drawing is done.

Description The `GetUpdateRgn` function copies the update region of a window to the region specified by `hrgn`. Coordinates are expressed in client coordinates.

Return Value The type of resulting region, as indicated by one of the following values, is returned:

Value	Meaning
COMPLEXREGION	Region has overlapping borders
ERROR	Region was not created
NULLREGION	Region is empty
SIMPLEREGION	Region has no overlapping borders

Function Category Painting

Related Functions GetUpdateRect

GetVersion

Syntax `DWORD GetVersion()`

Description The `GetVersion` function determines and returns the Windows version number and the DOS version number.

Return Value The low-order byte of the return value specifies the major Windows version number. The high-order byte of the low-order word of the return value specifies the minor Windows version number. The low-order byte of the high-order word specifies the minor DOS version number. The high-order byte of the high-order word specifies the major DOS version number.

Function Category Module Management

Related Functions None

GetViewportExt

Syntax `DWORD GetViewportExt(hdc)`

Parameter	Type	Description
hdc	HDC	Device context

Description The `GetViewportExt` function gets the width (x extent) and height (y extent) of the viewport for the device context specified in `hdc`. The retrieved extents are expressed in device units.

Return Value The low-order word of the return value contains the width (x extent) of the viewport. The high-order word of the return value contains the height (y extent) of the viewport.

Function Category Mapping

Related Functions `ScaleViewportExt`, `SetViewportExt`

GetViewportExtEx

Syntax `BOOL GetViewportExtEx(hdc, lpSize)`

Parameter	*Type*	*Description*
`hdc`	`HDC`	Device context
`lpSize`	`SIZE FAR*`	Pointer to `SIZE` data structure

Description The `GetViewportExtEx` function copies the extents of the viewport for the device context specified in `hdc` to the data structure pointed to by `lpSize`.

Return Value `TRUE` is returned when successful. `FALSE` is returned when unsuccessful.

Function Category Mapping

Related Functions `GetViewportExt`

GetViewportOrg

Syntax `DWORD GetViewportOrg(hdc)`

Parameter	*Type*	*Description*
`hdc`	`HDC`	Device context

Description The `GetViewportOrg` function gets the coordinates of the origin of the viewport for the device context specified in `hdc`. The retrieved coordinates are expressed in device coordinates.

Return Value The low-order word of the return value contains the x coordinate of the viewport origin. The high-order word of the return value contains the y coordinate of the viewport origin.

Function Category Mapping

Related Functions `OffsetViewportOrg`, `SetViewportOrg`

GetViewportOrgEx

Syntax `BOOL GetViewportOrgEx(hdc, lpPoint)`

Parameter	*Type*	*Description*
`hdc`	`HDC`	Device context
`lpPoint`	`POINT FAR*`	Pointer to `POINT` data structure

Description The `GetViewportOrgEx` function copies the device coordinates of the viewport origin for the device context specified in `hdc` to the data structure pointed to by `lpPoint`.

Return Value `TRUE` is returned when successful. `FALSE` is returned when unsuccessful.

Function Category Mapping

Related Functions `GetViewportOrg`

GetWindow

Syntax `HWND GetWindow(hwnd, fuRel)`

Parameter	*Type*	*Description*
`hwnd`	`HWND`	Window handle
`fuRel`	`UINT`	Window relationship

Description The `GetWindow` function returns the handle of the window which has the specified relationship with the window specified in `hwnd`. The window relationship is specified in `fuRel` and is selected from one of the following values:

Value	*Meaning*
GW_CHILD	First child window
GW_HWNDFIRST	First sibling window for a child window, or first top-level window
GW_HWNDLAST	Last sibling window for a child window, or last top-level window
GW_HWNDNEXT	Next window
GW_HWNDPREV	Previous window
GW_OWNER	Window owner

Return Value If an appropriate window is found, its handle is returned. `NULL` is returned if no window is found or an error occurs.

Function Category Information

Related Functions `FindWindow`, `GetDesktopWindow`, `GetTopWindow`

GetWindowDC

Syntax `HDC GetWindowDC(hwnd)`

Parameter	*Type*	*Description*
hwnd	HWND	Window handle

Description The `GetWindowDC` function retrieves the device context for the window specified in `hwnd`. The display context orgin is in the upper-left corner of the window; therefore, painting is allowed anywhere in the window including caption bars, menus, and scroll bars.

Return Value The device context is returned when successful. `NULL` is returned when unsuccessful.

Function Category Painting

Related Functions `GetDC`, `ReleaseDC`

GetWindowExt

Syntax `DWORD GetWindowExt(hdc)`

Parameter	*Type*	*Description*
`hdc`	`HDC`	Device context

Description The `GetWindowExt` function gets the width (x extent) and height (y extent) of the window for the device context specified in `hdc`. The retrieved extents are expressed in logical units.

Return Value The low-order word of the return value contains the width (x extent) of the window. The high-order word of the return value contains the height (y extent) of the window.

Function Category Mapping

Related Functions `ScaleWindowExt`, `SetWindowExt`

GetWindowLong

Syntax `LPARAM GetWindowLong(hwnd, nOffset)`

Parameter	*Type*	*Description*
`hwnd`	`HWND`	Window handle
`nOffset`	`int`	Byte offset of value to retrieve

Description The `GetWindowLong` function gets information about the window identified in `hwnd`. `nOffset` specifies the byte offset of the value to be retrieved. `nOffset` can also be set to one of the following values:

Value	*Meaning*
`GWL_EXSTYLE`	Extended window style
`GWL_STYLE`	Window style
`GWL_WNDPROC`	Long pointer to the window function

Return Value The specified window information is returned.

Function Category Window Creation

Related Functions `GetWindowWord`, `SetWindowLong`

GetWindowOrg

Syntax `DWORD GetWindowOrg(hdc)`

Parameter	*Type*	*Description*
`hdc`	`HDC`	Device context

Description The `GetWindowOrg` function gets the coordinates of the origin of the window for the device context specified in `hdc`. The retrieved coordinates are expressed in logical coordinates.

Return Value The low-order word of the return value contains the x coordinate of the window origin. The high-order word of the return value contains the y coordinate of the window origin.

Function Category Mapping

Related Functions `SetWindowOrg`

GetWindowOrgEx

Syntax `BOOL GetWindowOrgEx(hdc, lpPoint)`

Parameter	*Type*	*Description*
`hdc`	`HDC`	Device context
`lpPoint`	`POINT FAR*`	Pointer to `POINT` data structure

Description The `GetWindowOrgEx` function copies the logical coordinates of the window origin for the device context specified in `hdc` to the data structure pointed to by `lpPoint`.

Return Value `TRUE` is returned when successful. `FALSE` is returned when unsuccessful.

Function Category Mapping

Related Functions `GetWindowOrg`

GetWindowPlacement

Syntax `BOOL GetWindowPlacement(hwnd, lpwndpl)`

Parameter	*Type*	*Description*
hwnd	HWND	Handle of window
lpwndpl	LPWINDOWREPLACEMENT	Pointer to WINDOWPLACEMENT data structure that stores state and position information

Description The `GetWindowPlacement` function gets the show state and position for the window specified in `hwnd`.

Return Value A nonzero value is returned when successful. Zero is returned when unsuccessful.

Function Category Display and Movement

Related Functions `SetWindowPlacement`

GetWindowRect

Syntax `void GetWindowRect(hwnd, lprc)`

Parameter	*Type*	*Description*
hwnd	HWND	Window handle
lprc	RECT FAR*	Pointer to RECT data structure where screen coordinates of the window are placed

Description The `GetWindowRect` function places the screen coordinates of the window specified in `hwnd` into the data structure of type `RECT` pointed to by `lprc`. The `RECT` structure follows. Screen coordinates are expressed relative to the upper-left corner of the screen.

```
typedef struct tagRECT {
     int left;
     int top;
     int right;
     int bottom;
} RECT;
```

in which

`left` is the x coordinate of the upper-left corner

`top` is the y coordinate of the upper-left corner

`right` is the x coordinate of the lower-right corner

`bottom` is the y coordinate of the lower-right corner.

Return Value There is no return value.

Function Category Display and Movement

Related Functions `GetClientRect`

GetWindowsDir

Syntax `WORD GetWindowsDir(lpszAppDir, lpszBuffer, Size)`

Parameter	*Type*	*Description*
`lpszAppDir`	`LPSTR`	Directory where the software is to be installed
`lpszBuffer`	`LPSTR`	Pointer to buffer that will receive the string containing the pathname
`Size`	`int`	Number of bytes in the buffer specified by `lpszBuffer`

Description The `GetWindowsDir` function copies the path to the Windows directory into the buffer pointed to by `lpszBuffer`. This function is supported only by the static-link version of the version library. The `GetWindowsDirectory` function should be used if your application does not install software.

Return Value The length of the string copied (including the null terminator) to `lpszBuffer` is returned when successful. Zero is returned when unsuccessful.

Function Category Version

Related Functions `GetSystemDir`, `GetWindowsDirectory`

GetWindowsDirectory

Syntax `UINT GetWindowsDirectory(lpszSysPath, cbSysPath)`

Parameter	*Type*	*Description*
`lpszSysPath`	`LPSTR`	Pointer to the buffer to receive the string containing the pathname
`cbSysPath`	`UINT`	Maximum number of bytes in the buffer

Description The `GetWindowsDirectory` function gets the pathname for the Windows directory. The pathname is placed in the buffer pointed to by `lpszSysPath`. `cbSysPath` specifies the maximum number of bytes in the buffer.

Return Value The length of the string placed in the buffer (excluding the null terminator) is returned when successful. Zero is returned when unsuccessful.

Function Category File I/O

Related Functions `GetSystemDirectory`

GetWindowTask

Syntax `HTASK GetWindowTask(hwnd)`

Parameter	*Type*	*Description*
`hwnd`	`HWND`	Window handle

Description The `GetWindowTask` function returns the handle of the task associated with the window specified in `hwnd`.

Return Value The handle of the associated task is returned when successful. `NULL` is returned when unsuccessful.

Function Category Information

Related Functions `EnumTaskWindows`, `GetCurrentTask`

GetWindowText

Syntax `int GetWindowText(hwnd, lpsz, cbMax)`

Parameter	*Type*	*Description*
hwnd	HWND	Window or control handle
lpsz	LPSTR	Buffer to store caption
cbMax	int	Maximum number of characters to store

Description The `GetWindowText` function places the caption of the window, or the text of the control, specified in `hwnd` into the buffer pointed to by `lpsz`. `cbMax` specifies the maximum number of characters that will be placed into `lpsz`. The `WM_GETTEXT` message is sent to the specified control or window.

Return Value The length of the copied string (excluding the null terminator) is returned when successful. If the window has no caption, zero is returned.

Function Category Display and Movement

Related Functions `GetWindowTextLength`, `SetWindowText`

GetWindowTextLength

Syntax `int GetWindowTextLength(hwnd)`

Parameter	*Type*	*Description*
hwnd	HWND	Window or control handle

Description The `GetWindowTextLength` function returns the length of the caption for the window, or the length of the text for the control, specified in `hwnd`.

Return Value The length of the caption or text (excluding the null terminator) is returned. Zero is returned if there is no caption or text.

Function Category Display and Movement

Related Functions `GetWindowText`

GetWindowWord

Syntax `WPARAM GetWindowWord(hwnd, nOffset)`

Parameter	*Type*	*Description*
`hwnd`	`HWND`	Window handle
`nOffset`	`int`	Byte offset of value to retrieve

Description The `GetWindowWord` function gets information about the window indentified in `hwnd`. `nOffset` specifies the byte offset of the value to retrieve. `nOffset` can also be set to one of the following values:

Value	*Meaning*
`GWW_HINSTANCE`	Instance handle of module that owns the window
`GWW_HWNDPARENT`	Handle of the parent window
`GWW_ID`	Control ID of the child window

Return Value The retrieved information is returned.

Function Category Window Creation

Related Functions `GetWindowLong`, `SetWindowWord`

GetWinFlags

Syntax `DWORD GetWinFlags()`

Description The GetWinFlags function returns a value representing the memory configuration of the system in which Windows is running.

Return Value A 32-bit value that contains the flags that define the memory configuration is returned. The following values are flags that may be returned:

Value	*Meaning*
WF_80x87	Intel math coprocessor present
WF_CPU286	80286 CPU present
WF_CPU386	80386 CPU present
WF_CPU486	80486 CPU present
WF_ENHANCED	Windows running in 386 enhanced mode
WF_PAGING	Windows running on system with paged memory
WF_PMODE	Windows running in protected mode
WF_STANDARD	Windows running in standard mode
WF_WIN286	Same as WF_STANDARD
WF_WIN386	Same as WF_ENHANCED
WF_WLO	Windows Library for OS/2 is running under OS/2

Note: *Windows is running in real mode when neither* WF_ENHANCED *nor* WF_STANDARD *is set*.

Function Category Memory Management

Related Functions GlobalFlags, LocalFlags

GlobalAddAtom

Syntax ATOM GlobalAddAtom(lpszString)

Parameter	*Type*	*Description*
lpszString	LPCSTR	Pointer to the null-terminated character string to be added to the table

Description The `GlobalAddAtom` function adds the string in `lpszString` to the atom table and returns a global atom that identifies the string. By referencing the global atom, the string is available to all applications.

Return Value The identifier to the global atom is returned when successful. Zero is returned when unsuccessful.

Function Category Atom

Related Functions `GlobalDeleteAtom`, `GlobalFindAtom`, `GlobalGetAtomName`

GlobalAlloc

Syntax `HGLOBAL GlobalAlloc(fuAlloc, cbAlloc)`

Parameter	*Type*	*Description*
`fuAlloc`	`UINT`	Flags to specify how to allocate memory
`cbAlloc`	`DWORD`	Number of bytes to allocate

Description The `GlobalAlloc` function allocates memory from the global heap. `cbAlloc` specifies the number of bytes allocated from the global heap. `fuAlloc` specifies one or more flags that indicate how the memory is to be allocated. The flags used for `fuAlloc` follow. These flags can be combined.

Value	*Meaning*
`GHND`	Combination of `GMEM_MOVEABLE` and `GMEM_ZEROINIT` flags
`GMEM_DDESHARE`	Shared memory is allocated
`GMEM_DISCARDABLE`	Discardable memory is allocated
`GMEM_FIXED`	Fixed memory is allocated
`GMEM_LOWER`	Same as `GMEM_NOT_BANKED`
`GMEM_MOVEABLE`	Moveable memory is allocated
`GMEM_NOCOMPACT`	Compacting or discarding does not occur to meet the memory allocation requirements
`GMEM_NODISCARD`	Discarding does not occur to meet the memory allocation requirements

Value	*Meaning*
GMEM_NOT_BANKED	Non-banked memory allocated
GMEM_NOTIFY	Notification routine is called if the memory object is discarded
GMEM_ZEROINT	Contents of memory are initialized to zero
GMEM_SHARE	Allocates memory that can be shared with other applications
GPTR	Combination of GMEM_FIXED and GMEM_ZEROINIT flags

Return Value The handle to the allocated memory is returned when successful. NULL is returned when unsuccessful.

Function Category Memory Management

Related Functions GlobalDosAlloc, GlobalReAlloc, LocalAlloc

GlobalCompact

Syntax `DWORD GlobalCompact(dwMinFree)`

Parameter	*Type*	*Description*
dwMinFree	DWORD	Number of bytes to free

Description The GlobalCompact function frees the number of bytes specified in dwMinFree by compacting the global heap. If necessary, unlocked discardable blocks are discarded to free the number of bytes requested.

Return Value The number of bytes in the largest block of free global memory is returned when successful. If dwMinFree is set to zero, the number of bytes in the largest free block that can be generated by Windows is returned.

Function Category Memory Management

Related Functions GlobalAlloc, LocalCompact

GlobalDeleteAtom

Syntax `ATOM GlobalDeleteAtom(atm)`

Parameter	*Type*	*Description*
`atm`	`ATOM`	Atom and character string to delete

Description The `GlobalDeleteAtom` function decreases the reference count for the atom in `atm`. If the reference count is zero, the string associated with the atom is removed.

Return Value Zero is returned when successful. `atm` is returned when unsuccessful.

Function Category Atom

Related Functions `DeleteAtom`, `GlobalAddAtom`, `GlobalFindAtom`

GlobalDiscard

Syntax `HGLOBAL GlobalDiscard(hglb)`

Parameter	*Type*	*Description*
`hglb`	`HGLOBAL`	Global memory block to discard

Description The `GlobalDiscard` function discards the global memory block specified in `hglb`. The lock count of the block must be zero. The handle to the memory block remains valid.

Return Value The handle to the block is returned when successful. `NULL` is returned when unsuccessful.

Function Category Memory Management

Related Functions `GlobalReAlloc`, `LocalDiscard`

GlobalDosAlloc

Syntax `DWORD GlobalDosAlloc(cbAlloc)`

Parameter	*Type*	*Description*
`cbAlloc`	`DWORD`	Number of bytes to allocate

Description The `GlobalDosAlloc` function allocates the number of bytes of global memory specified in `cbAlloc` from the first megabyte of linear address space. This memory can be accessed by DOS in real mode.

Return Value The high-order word of the return value contains a paragraph-segment value. This value can be used to access the memory in real mode. The low-order word of the return value contains a selector. This selector can be used to access the memory in protected mode. Zero is returned when the memory could not be allocated.

Function Category Memory Management

Related Functions `GlobalAlloc`, `GlobalDosFree`

GlobalDosFree

Syntax `UINT GlobalDosFree(uSelector)`

Parameter	*Type*	*Description*
`uSelector`	`UINT`	Memory to free

Description The `GlobalDosFree` function frees the block of memory specified in `uSelector`. The block of memory must have been allocated using `GlobalDosAlloc`.

Return Value Zero is returned when successful. `uSelector` is returned when unsuccessful.

Function Category Memory Management

Related Functions `GlobalDosAlloc`, `GlobalFree`

GlobalEntryHandle

Syntax `BOOL GlobalEntryHandle(geGlobal, hItem)`

Parameter	*Type*	*Description*
geGlobal	GLOBALENTRY FAR*	Pointer to GLOBALENTRY data structure that is to receive the global memory block information
hItem	HANDLE	Global memory block

Description The `GlobalEntryHandle` function retrieves information on the global memory object specified in `hItem` and copies the information into the data structure of type `GLOBALENTRY` pointed to by `geGlobal`. The `GLOBALENTRY` data structure follows.

```
#include <toolhelp.h>
typedef struct tagGLOBALENTRY
     {
     DWORD dwSize;
     DWORD dwAddress;
     DWORD dwBlockSize;
     HANDLE hBlock;
     WORD wcLock;
     WORD wcPageLock;
     WORD wFlags;
     BOOL wHeapPresent;
     HANDLE hOwner;
     WORD wType;
     WORD wData;
     DWORD dwNext;
     DWORD dwNextAlt;
} GLOBALENTRY;
```

in which

`dwSize` is the number of bytes in the data structure

`dwAddress` is the address of the global memory object

`dwBlockSize` is the number of bytes in the global memory object

`hBlock` identifies the global memory block

`wcLock` is the lock count

`wcPageLock` is the page lock count

`wFlags` is set to `GF_PDB_OWNER` to indicate that the process data block is the owner of the memory block `wHeapPresent` indicates whether a local heap exists within the global memory block

`hOwner` is the owner of the memory block

`wType` is the memory block type and is chosen from the following values:

Value	*Meaning*
GT_UNKNOWN	Memory type is unknown
GT_DGROUP	Block contains default data segment and stack segment
GT_DATA	Block contains program data
GT_CODE	Block contains program code
GT_TASK	Block contains task database
GT_RESOURCE	Block contains resource type specified in wData
GT_MODULE	Block contains module database
GT_FREE	Block belongs to free memory pool
GT_INTERNAL	Block reserved for internal use
GT_SENTINEL	Block is first or last block on global heap
GT_BURGERMASTER	Block contains table mapping selectors to arena handles

`wData` is zero when `wType` is not `GT_CODE` or `GT_RESOURCE`. It is the code's segment number when `wType` is `GT_CODE`. It is one of the following when `wType` is `GT_RESOURCE`:

Value	*Meaning*
GD_ACCELERATORS	Block contains data from accelerator table
GD_BITMAP	Block contains data from bitmap
GD_CURSOR	Block contains data from group of cursors
GD_CURSORCOMPONENT	Block contains data from single cursor
GD_DIALOG	Block contains data for dialog box controls
GD_ERRTABLE	Block contains data from error table
GD_FONT	Block contains data describing single font
GD_FONTDIR	Block contains data describing group of fonts
GD_ICON	Block contains data describing group of icons
GD_ICONCOMPONENT	Block contains data describing single icon

Value	Meaning
GD_MENU	Block contains menu data for menu items
GD_NAMETABLE	Block contains data from name table
GD_RCDATA	Block contains data from user-defined resource
GD_STRING	Block contains data from the string table
GD_USERDEFINED	Resource is unknown

dwNext is the next memory block in the global heap

dwNextAlt is the next free block when wType is GT_FREE. It is the next block in the least recently used (LRU) list when wType is not GT_FREE and the block is not discardable. It is NULL when wType is not GT_FREE and the block is not discardable.

Return Value TRUE is returned when successful. FALSE is returned when unsuccessful.

Function Category Toolhelp

Related Functions GlobalEntryModule, GlobalFirst, GlobalNext

GlobalEntryModule

Syntax BOOL GlobalEntryModule(geGlobal, hModule, wSeg)

Parameter	Type	Description
geGlobal	GLOBALENTRY FAR*	Pointer to GLOBALENTRY data structure that receives segment information
hModule	HANDLE	Module that owns the specified segment
wSeg	WORD	Module segment to describe

Description The GlobalEntryModule function retrieves information on the segment specified in wSeg from the module specified in hModule. The segment information is copied to the data structure of type GLOBALENTRY pointed to by geGlobal. The GLOBALENTRY data structure follows.

```
#include <toolhelp.h>
typedef struct tagGLOBALENTRY
     {
     DWORD dwSize;
     DWORD dwAddress;
     DWORD dwBlockSize;
     HANDLE hBlock;
     WORD wcLock;
     WORD wcPageLock;
     WORD wFlags;
     BOOL wHeapPresent;
     HANDLE hOwner;
     WORD wType;
     WORD wData;
     DWORD dwNext;
     DWORD dwNextAlt;
} GLOBALENTRY;
```

in which

`dwSize` is the number of bytes in the data structure

`dwAddress` is the address of the global memory object

`dwBlockSize` is the number of bytes in the global memory object

`hBlock` identifies the global memory block

`wcLock` is the lock count

`wcPageLock` is the page lock count

`wFlags` is set to `GF_PDB_OWNER` to indicate that the process data block is the owner of the memory block

`wHeapPresent` indicates whether a local heap exists within the global memory block

`hOwner` is the owner of the memory block

`wType` is the memory block type and is chosen from the following values:

Value	*Meaning*
GT_UNKNOWN	Memory type is unknown
GT_DGROUP	Block contains default data segment and stack segment
GT_DATA	Block contains program data
GT_CODE	Block contains program code

Value	Meaning
GT_TASK	Block contains task database
GT_RESOURCE	Block contains resource type specified in wData
GT_MODULE	Block contains module database
GT_FREE	Block belongs to free memory pool
GT_INTERNAL	Block reserved for internal use
GT_SENTINEL	Block is first or last block on global heap
GT_BURGERMASTER	Block contains table mapping selectors to arena handles

wData is zero when wType is not GT_CODE or GT_RESOURCE. It is the code's segment number when wType is GT_CODE. It is one of the following when wType is GT_RESOURCE:

Value	Meaning
GD_ACCELERATORS	Block contains data from accelerator table
GD_BITMAP	Block contains data from bitmap
GD_CURSOR	Block contains data from group of cursors
GD_CURSORCOMPONENT	Block contains data from single cursor
GD_DIALOG	Block contains data for dialog box controls
GD_ERRTABLE	Block contains data from error table
GD_FONT	Block contains data describing single font
GD_FONTDIR	Block contains data describing group of fonts
GD_ICON	Block contains data describing group of icons
GD_ICONCOMPONENT	Block contains data describing single icon
GD_MENU	Block contains menu data for menu items
GD_NAMETABLE	Block contains data from name table
D_RCDATA	Block contains data from user-defined resource
GD_STRING	Block contains data from the string table
GD_USERDEFINED	Resource is unknown

dwNext is the next memory block in the global heap

dwNextAlt is the next free block when wType is GT_FREE. It is the next block in the least recently used (LRU) list when wType is not

GT_FREE and the block is not discardable. It is NULL when wType is not GT_FREE and the block is not discardable.

Return Value TRUE is returned when successful. FALSE is returned when unsuccessful.

Function Category Toolhelp

Related Functions GlobalEntryHandle

GlobalFindAtom

Syntax `ATOM GlobalFindAtom(lpszString)`

Parameter	*Type*	*Description*
lpszString	LPCSTR	Pointer to the null-terminated character string to search for

Description The GlobalFindAtom function searches for the string in lpszString in the atom table. If the string is found, the global atom associated with the string is returned.

Return Value The global atom associated with the string is returned when the string is found. Zero is returned if the string is not found.

Function Category Atom

Related Functions GlobalAddAtom, GlobalDeleteAtom

GlobalFirst

Syntax `BOOL GlobalFirst(geGlobal, wFlags)`

Parameter	*Type*	*Description*
geGlobal	GLOBALENTRY FAR*	Pointer to GLOBALENTRY data structure to receive global memory block information

Parameter	*Type*	*Description*
wFlags	WORD	Flag to indicate the heap to use; set to one of the following:

Value	*Meaning*
GLOBAL_ALL	Get information on the first block on the complete global heap
GLOBAL_FREE	Get information on the first block on the free list
GLOBAL_LRU	Get information on the first block on the least recently used (LRU) list

Description The `GlobalFirst` function gets information on the first block of the global heap and copies the information into the data structure of type `GLOBALENTRY` pointed to by `geGlobal`. The `GLOBALENTRY` data structure follows.

```
#include <toolhelp.h>
typedef struct tagGLOBALENTRY
     {
     DWORD dwSize;
     DWORD dwAddress;
     DWORD dwBlockSize;
     HANDLE hBlock;
     WORD wcLock;
     WORD wcPageLock;
     WORD wFlags;
     BOOL wHeapPresent;
     HANDLE hOwner;
     WORD wType;
     WORD wData;
     DWORD dwNext;
     DWORD dwNextAlt;
} GLOBALENTRY;
```

in which

`dwSize` is the number of bytes in the data structure

`dwAddress` is the address of the global memory object

`dwBlockSize` is the number of bytes in the global memory object

`hBlock` identifies the global memory block

`wcLock` is the lock count

`wcPageLock` is the page lock count

`wFlags` is set to `GF_PDB_OWNER` to indicate that the process data block is the owner of the memory block

`wHeapPresent` indicates whether a local heap exists within the global memory block

`hOwner` is the owner of the memory block

`wType` is the memory block type and is chosen from the following values:

Value	*Meaning*
`GT_UNKNOWN`	Memory type is unknown
`GT_DGROUP`	Block contains default data segment and stack segment
`GT_DATA`	Block contains program data
`GT_CODE`	Block contains program code
`GT_TASK`	Block contains task database
`GT_RESOURCE`	Block contains resource type specified in `wData`
`GT_MODULE`	Block contains module database
`GT_FREE`	Block belongs to free memory pool
`GT_INTERNAL`	Block reserved for internal use
`GT_SENTINEL`	Block is first or last block on global heap
`GT_BURGERMASTER`	Block contains table mapping selectors to arena handles

`wData` is zero when `wType` is not `GT_CODE` or `GT_RESOURCE`. It is the code's segment number when `wType` is `GT_CODE`. It is one of the following when `wType` is `GT_RESOURCE`:

Value	*Meaning*
`GD_ACCELERATORS`	Block contains data from accelerator table
`GD_BITMAP`	Block contains data from bitmap
`GD_CURSOR`	Block contains data from group of cursors
`GD_CURSORCOMPONENT`	Block contains data from single cursor
`GD_DIALOG`	Block contains data for dialog box controls
`GD_ERRTABLE`	Block contains data from error table
`GD_FONT`	Block contains data describing single font
`GD_FONTDIR`	Block contains data describing group of fonts

Value	*Meaning*
`GD_ICON`	Block contains data describing group of icons
`GD_ICONCOMPONENT`	Block contains data describing single icon
`GD_MENU`	Block contains menu data for menu items
`GD_NAMETABLE`	Block contains data from name table
`GD_RCDATA`	Block contains data from user-defined resource
`GD_STRING`	Block contains data from the string table
`GD_USERDEFINED`	Resource is unknown

`dwNext` is the next memory block in the global heap

`dwNextAlt` is the next free block when `wType` is `GT_FREE`. It is the next block in the least recently used (LRU) list when `wType` is not `GT_FREE` and the block is not discardable. It is `NULL` when `wType` is not `GT_FREE` and the block is not discardable.

Return Value `TRUE` is returned when successful. `FALSE` is returned when unsuccessful.

Function Category Toolhelp

Related Functions `GlobalInfo`, `GlobalNext`

GlobalFix

Syntax `void GlobalFix(hglb)`

Parameter	*Type*	*Description*
`hglb`	`HGLOBAL`	Global memory block handle

Description The `GlobalFix` function locks the global memory block specified by `hglb` into linear memory at its current address. The lock count for the global block is incremented.

Return Value There is no return value.

Function Category Segment

Related Functions `GlobalUnfix`

GlobalFlags

Syntax `UINT GlobalFlags(hglb)`

Parameter	*Type*	*Description*
`hglb`	`HGLOBAL`	Handle to global memory block

Description The `GlobalFlags` function retrieves and returns information about the global memory block in `hglb`.

Return Value The low-order byte of the return value specifies the lock count of the object. The high-order byte of the return value specifies the memory allocation flag. The flag is one of the following values:

Value	*Meaning*
`GMEM_DDESHARE`	Shared block
`GMEM_DISCARDABLE`	Discardable block
`GMEM_DISCARDED`	Discarded block
`GMEM_NOT_BANKED`	Block cannot be banked

Function Category Memory Management

Related Functions `GetWinFlags`, `LocalFlags`

GlobalFree

Syntax `HGLOBAL GlobalFree(hglb)`

Parameter	*Type*	*Description*
`hglb`	`HGLOBAL`	Global block to free

Description The `GlobalFree` function frees the global memory block specified in `hglb`. The handle to the memory block becomes invalid.

Return Value `NULL` is returned when successful. `hglb` is returned when unsuccessful.

Function Category Memory Management

Related Functions `GlobalDosFree`, `LocalFree`

GlobalGetAtomName

Syntax `UINT GlobalGetAtomName(atom, lpszBuffer, cbBuffer)`

Parameter	*Type*	*Description*
`atom`	`ATOM`	Character string to retrieve
`lpszBuffer`	`LPSTR`	Pointer to the buffer that receives the string
`cbBuffer`	`int`	Maximum number of bytes in the string

Description The `GlobalGetAtomName` function puts a copy of the string associated with `atom` into `lpszBuffer`. `cbBuffer` specifies the maximum number of bytes in the string.

Return Value The number of bytes copied to the buffer is returned.

Function Category Atom

Related Functions `GetAtomName`

GlobalHandle

Syntax `DWORD GlobalHandle(uGlobalSel)`

Parameter	*Type*	*Description*
`uGlobalSel`	`UINT`	Selector of the global memory object

Description The `GlobalHandle` function gets the handle of the global memory object specified by the selector in `uGlobalSel`.

Return Value The low-order word of the return value contains the handle of the memory object. The high-order word of the return value contains the selector of the memory object.

Function Category Memory Management

Related Functions `DefineHandleTable`, `LocalHandle`

GlobalHandleToSel

Syntax `WORD GlobalHandleToSel(hMem)`

Parameter	*Type*	*Description*
`hMem`	`HANDLE`	Global memory object

Description The `GlobalHandleToSel` function creates a selector from the handle specified in `hMem`.

Return Value The selector is returned when successful. Zero is returned when unsuccessful.

Function Category Toolhelp

Related Functions `GlobalAlloc`

GlobalInfo

Syntax `BOOL GlobalInfo(giGlobalInfo)`

Parameter	*Type*	*Description*
`giGlobalInfo`	`GLOBALINFO FAR*`	Pointer to `GLOBALINFO` data structure that receives information on the global heap

Description The `GlobalInfo` function copies global heap information into the data structure of type `GLOBALINFO` pointed to by `giGlobalInfo`. The `GLOBALINFO` data structure follows.

```
#include <toolhelp.h>
typedef struct tagGLOBALINFO
     {
     DWORD dwSize;
     WORD wcItems;
```

```
    WORD wcItemsFree;
    WORD wcItemsLRU;
} GLOBALINFO;
```

in which

dwSize is the number of bytes in the data structure

wcItems is the number of items on the global heap

wcItemsFree is the number of free items on the global heap

wsItemsLRU is the number of least recently used (LRU) items on the global heap.

Return Value TRUE is returned when successful. FALSE is returned when unsuccessful.

Function Category Toolhelp

Related Functions GlobalFirst, GlobalNext

GlobalLock

Syntax void FAR* GlobalLock(hglb)

Parameter	*Type*	*Description*
hglb	HGLOBAL	Global memory block to lock

Description The GlobalLock function gets the pointer to the global memory block specified in hglb. The lock count of the memory object is incremented.

Return Value The pointer to the first byte of memory in the memory block is returned when successful. NULL is returned when unsuccessful.

Function Category Memory Management

Related Functions GlobalUnlock, LocalLock

GlobalLRUNewest

Syntax `HGLOBAL GlobalLRUNewest(hglb)`

Parameter	*Type*	*Description*
hglb	HGLOBAL	Global memory object to move

Description The GlobalLRUNewest function moves the global memory object specified in hglb to the newest, least recently used (LRU) position. The block in hglb must be discardable.

Return Value NULL is returned when hglb is invalid.

Function Category Memory Management

Related Functions GlobalLRUOldest

GlobalLRUOldest

Syntax `HGLOBAL GlobalLRUOldest(hglb)`

Parameter	*Type*	*Description*
hglb	HGLOBAL	Global memory object to move

Description The GlobalLRUOldest function moves the global memory object specified in hglb to the oldest, least recently used (LRU) position. The block in hglb must be discardable.

Return Value NULL is returned when hglb is invalid.

Function Category Memory Management

Related Functions GlobalLRUNewest

GlobalNext

Syntax `BOOL GlobalNext(geGlobal, wFlags)`

Parameter	*Type*	*Description*
geGlobal	GLOBALENTRY FAR*	Pointer to GLOBALENTRY data structure that receives information on the global memory block
wFlags	WORD	Flag to indicate the heap to use; set to one of the following:

Value	*Meaning*
GLOBAL_ALL	Get information on the first block on the complete global heap
GLOBAL_FREE	Get information on the first block on the free list
GLOBAL_LRU	Get information on the first block on the least recently used (LRU) list

Description The GlobalNext function gets information on the next block on the global heap and copies the information to the data structure of type GLOBALENTRY pointed to by geGlobal. The GLOBALENTRY data structure follows.

```
#include <toolhelp.h>
typedef struct tagGLOBALENTRY
     {
     DWORD dwSize;
     DWORD dwAddress;
     DWORD dwBlockSize;
     HANDLE hBlock;
     WORD wcLock;
     WORD wcPageLock;
     WORD wFlags;
     BOOL wHeapPresent;
     HANDLE hOwner;
     WORD wType;
     WORD wData;
     DWORD dwNext;
     DWORD dwNextAlt;
} GLOBALENTRY;
```

in which

`dwSize` is the number of bytes in the data structure

`dwAddress` is the address of the global memory object

`dwBlockSize` is the number of bytes in the global memory object

`hBlock` identifies the global memory block

`wcLock` is the lock count

`wcPageLock` is the page lock count

`wFlags` is set to `GF_PDB_OWNER` to indicate that the process data block is the owner of the memory block

`wHeapPresent` indicates whether a local heap exists within the global memory block

`hOwner` is the owner of the memory block

`wType` is the memory block type and is chosen from the following values:

Value	*Meaning*
`GT_UNKNOWN`	Memory type is unknown
`GT_DGROUP`	Block contains default data segment and stack segment
`GT_DATA`	Block contains program data
`GT_CODE`	Block contains program code
`GT_TASK`	Block contains task database
`GT_RESOURCE`	Block contains resource type specified in `wData`
`GT_MODULE`	Block contains module database
`GT_FREE`	Block belongs to free memory pool
`GT_INTERNAL`	Block reserved for internal use
`GT_SENTINEL`	Block is first or last block on global heap
`GT_BURGERMASTER`	Block contains table mapping selectors to arena handles

`wData` is zero when `wType` is not `GT_CODE` or `GT_RESOURCE`. It is the code's segment number when `wType` is `GT_CODE`. It is one of the following when `wType` is `GT_RESOURCE`:

Value	*Meaning*
GD_ACCELERATORS	Block contains data from accelerator table
GD_BITMAP	Block contains data from bitmap
GD_CURSOR	Block contains data from group of cursors
GD_CURSORCOMPONENT	Block contains data from single cursor
GD_DIALOG	Block contains data for dialog box controls
GD_ERRTABLE	Block contains data from error table
GD_FONT	Block contains data describing single font
GD_FONTDIR	Block contains data describing group of fonts
GD_ICON	Block contains data describing group of icons
GD_ICONCOMPONENT	Block contains data describing single icon
GD_MENU	Block contains menu data for menu items
GD_NAMETABLE	Block contains data from name table
GD_RCDATA	Block contains data from user-defined resource
GD_STRING	Block contains data from the string table
GD_USERDEFINED	Resource is unknown

`dwNext` is the next memory block in the global heap

`dwNextAlt` is the next free block when `wType` is `GT_FREE`. It is the next block in the least recently used (LRU) list when `wType` is not `GT_FREE` and the block is not discardable. It is `NULL` when `wType` is not `GT_FREE` and the block is not discardable.

Return Value `TRUE` is returned when successful. `FALSE` is returned when unsuccessful.

Function Category Toolhelp

Related Functions `GlobalFirst`, `GlobalInfo`

GlobalNotify

Syntax `void GlobalNotify(lpNotifyProc)`

Parameter	*Type*	*Description*
`lpNotifyProc`	`GNOTIFYPROC`	Procedure instance address of the current task's notification procedure

Description The `GlobalNotify` function defines the notification procedure for the current task. `lpNotifyProc` contains the procedure instance address of the current task's notification procedure. The notification procedure is called whenever a global memory block that is allocated with the `GMEM_NOTIFY` flag is about to be discarded. The conventions for the notification procedure follow. The notification procedure should return `FALSE` to indicate that Windows should not discard the memory object or `TRUE` to indicate the memory object can be discarded.

```
BOOL FAR PASCAL NotifyProc(hMem)
HANDLE hMem;
```

`in which`

`hMem` is the handle to the global memory block to evaluate.

Return Value There is no return value.

Function Category Memory Management

Related Functions `GlobalAlloc`, `GlobalReAlloc`

GlobalPageLock

Syntax `UINT GlobalPageLock(hglb)`

Parameter	*Type*	*Description*
`hglb`	`HGLOBAL`	Selector to be locked

Description The `GlobalPageLock` function increments the lock count of the memory associated with the selector specified in `hglb`. The memory associated with the specified selector will not be moved and will remain paged-in as long as the lock count for the memory is greater than zero.

Return Value The resulting lock count is returned when successful. Zero is returned when unsuccessful.

Function Category Segment

Related Functions `GlobalPageUnlock`

GlobalPageUnlock

Syntax `UINT GlobalPageUnlock(hglb)`

Parameter	*Type*	*Description*
`hglb`	`HGLOBAL`	Selector to be unlocked

Description The `GlobalPageUnlock` function decrements the page-lock count of the memory associated with `hglb`. When the page-lock count reaches zero, the block of memory associated with the selector can be moved or paged to disk.

Return Value The resulting page-lock count is returned when successful. Zero is returned when unsuccessful.

Function Category Segment

Related Functions `GlobalPageLock`

GlobalReAlloc

Syntax `HGLOBAL GlobalReAlloc(hglb, cbNewSize, fuAlloc)`

Parameter	*Type*	*Description*
`hglb`	`HGLOBAL`	Global memory block to reallocate
`cbNewSize`	`DWORD`	New size for memory block
`fuAlloc`	`UINT`	Combination of new allocation flags

Description The `GlobalReAlloc` function reallocates the global memory block in `hglb`. `cbNewSize` specifies the new size for the memory block. `fuAlloc` is a combination of flags that indicate how the global block should be reallocted. The following values can be combined using bitwise OR for `fuAlloc`:

Value	*Meaning*
`GMEM_DISCARDABLE`	Memory can be discarded
`GMEM_MODIFY`	Memory flags are modified
`GMEM_MOVEABLE`	Memory is moveable
`GMEM_NODISCARD`	Memory is not discarded to meet the allocation requirements
`GMEM_ZEROINT`	If the block size is increased, any additional memory is initialized to zero

Return Value The handle to the reallocated block is returned when successful. `NULL` is returned when unsuccessful.

Function Category Memory Management

Related Functions `GlobalAlloc`, `GlobalDosAlloc`, `GlobalFree`

GlobalSize

Syntax `DWORD GlobalSize(hglb)`

Parameter	*Type*	*Description*
`hglb`	`HGLOBAL`	Handle to global memory block

Description The `GlobalSize` function gets the number of bytes in the global memory block specified in `hglb`.

Return Value The number of bytes in the block is returned when successful. Zero is returned when unsuccessful.

Function Category Memory Management

Related Functions `GlobalAlloc`, `LocalSize`

GlobalUnfix

Syntax `BOOL GlobalUnfix(hglb)`

Parameter	*Type*	*Description*
`hglb`	`HGLOBAL`	Global memory block to unlock

Description The `GlobalUnfix` function decrements the lock count of the global memory block specified in `hglb`. If the resulting lock count is zero, the block can be moved or discarded.

Return Value `FALSE` is returned if the resulting lock count is zero. `TRUE` is returned if the resulting lock count was not zero.

Function Category Segment

Related Functions `GlobalFix`, `GlobalFlags`

GlobalUnlock

Syntax `BOOL GlobalUnlock(hglb)`

Parameter	*Type*	*Description*
`hglb`	`HGLOBAL`	Handle to global memory block to unlock

Description The `GlobalUnlock` function unlocks the global memory block specified in `hglb`. The lock count for the block is decremented.

Return Value Zero is returned if the lock count was decremented to zero. A nonzero value is returned if the lock count was not decremented to zero.

Function Category Memory Management

Related Functions `GlobalLock`, `LocalUnlock`

GrayString

Syntax `BOOL GrayString(hdc, hbr, gsprc, lParamData, cch, x, y, nWidth, nHeight)`

Parameter	Type	Description
hdc	HDC	Device context
hbr	HBRUSH	Brush used for graying
gsprc	GRAYSTRINGPROC	Procedure instance address of function drawing the string — NULL if TextOut is to be used to draw the string
lParamData	LPARAM	Long pointer to data that is sent to the output function
cch	int	Number of characters to output; if set to zero, the length of the string is calculated automatically
x	int	Logical horizontal coordinate of rectangle enclosing the string
y	int	Logical vertical coordinate of rectangle enclosing the string
nWidth	int	Width of enclosing rectangle in logical units; if set to zero, the width is automatically calculated
nHeight	int	Height of enclosing rectangle in logical units; if set to zero, the height is automatically calculated

Description The `GrayString` function draws grayed text at the position specified in `x` and `y`. `gsprc` is the procedure instance address of the application-supplied function used to draw the text. The following format is used for the function that draws the text:

```
BOOL FAR PASCAL GrayStringProc(hdc, lpData, count)
HDC hdc;
DWORD lpData;

int count;
```

in which

`hdc` is a memory device context

`lpData` points to the string to draw

`count` is the number of characters to output.

The function should return `TRUE` when successful and `FALSE` when unsuccessful. `GrayStringProc` is a placeholder for the function name supplied by the application. The function name must be exported using `EXPORTS`.

`gsprc` can also be set to `NULL` to indicate that the `TextOut` function should be used to draw the string.

Return Value A nonzero value is returned when the string is drawn. Zero is returned when unsuccessful or when `GrayStringProc` returns zero.

Function Category Painting

Related Functions `SetTextColor`, `TextOut`

HIBYTE

Syntax `BYTE HIBYTE(nInteger)`

Parameter	*Type*	*Description*
`nInteger`	`int`	Value to convert

Description The `HIBYTE` macro returns the high-order byte of the value specified in `nInteger`.

Return Value The high-order byte is returned.

Function Category Windows Macros

Related Functions `LOBYTE`

HideCaret

Syntax `void HideCaret(hwnd)`

Parameter	*Type*	*Description*
hwnd	HWND	Window that owns the caret

Description The `HideCaret` function removes the caret from the screen. The caret shape is not destroyed. The caret can be displayed on the screen again by using the `ShowCaret` function. `hwnd` specifies the window that owns the caret. When `hwnd` is `NULL`, the caret is hidden only if a window in the current task owns the caret.

Return Value There is no return value.

Function Category Caret

Related Functions `CreateCaret`, `DestroyCaret`, `ShowCaret`

HiliteMenuItem

Syntax `BOOL HiliteMenuItem(hwnd, hmenu, idHiliteItem, fuHilite)`

Parameter	*Type*	*Description*
hwnd	HWND	Window containing the menu
hmenu	HMENU	Top-level menu containing item to highlight
idHiliteItem	UINT	Menu item ID or position
fuHilite	UINT	Specifies whether menu item should be highlighted; also specifies whether `idHiliteItem` contains a menu item ID or position

Description The `HiliteMenuItem` function either highlights or removes the highlighting from a top-level menu item in the menu specified in `hmenu`. The specified menu is contained in the window in `hwnd`. `idHiliteItem` specifies either the menu item ID or the menu item position. `fuHilite` is a combination (using bitwise OR) of the following flags. When `fuHilite` contains `MF_BYPOSITION`, `idHiliteItem` contains a menu item position. When `fuHilite` contains `MF_BYCOMMAND`, `idHiliteItem` contains a menu item ID.

Value	Meaning
MF_BYCOMMAND	idHiliteItem contains a menu item ID
MF_BYPOSITION	idHiliteItem contains a menu item position
MF_HILITE	Highlights the menu item
MF_UNHILITE	Removes the highlight for the menu item

Return Value A nonzero value is returned if the item is highlighted. Zero is returned if the item is not highlighted.

Function Category Menu

Related Functions CheckMenuItem, EnableMenuItem

HIWORD

Syntax `WORD HIWORD(dwInteger)`

Parameter	Type	Description
dwInteger	DWORD	Value to convert

Description The HIWORD macro returns the high-order word of the value specified in dwInteger.

Return Value The high-order word is returned.

Function Category Window Macros

Related Functions LOWORD

InflateRect

Syntax `void InflateRect(lprc, xAmt, yAmt)`

Parameter	Type	Description
lprc	RECT FAR*	Pointer to RECT data structure to modify

Parameter	Type	Description
xAmt	int	Amount to increase or decrease the width of the rectangle
yAmt	int	Amount to increase or decrease the height of the rectangle

Description The InflateRect function changes the size of the rectangle whose coordinates are stored in the data structure of type RECT pointed to by lprc. The RECT structure follows. xAmt indicates the amount that the width of the rectangle will change. yAmt indicates the amount that the height of the rectangle will change. A positive xAmt or yAmt value increases the width and height, respectively. A negative xAmt or yAmt value decreases the width and height, respectively. The coordinates of the rectangle must not exceed 32,767 or be less than –32,768.

```
typedef struct tagRECT {
     int left;
     int top;
     int right;
     int bottom;
} RECT;
```

in which

left is the x coordinate of the upper-left corner

top is the y coordinate of the upper-left corner

right is the x coordinate of the lower-right corner

bottom is the y coordinate of the lower-right corner.

Return Value There is no return value.

Function Category Rectangle

Related Functions FillRect, OffsetRect, UnionRect

InitAtomTable

Syntax `BOOL InitAtomTable(cTableEntries)`

Parameter	*Type*	*Description*
`cTableEntries`	`int`	Number of entries for the atom hash table (should be a prime number)

Description The `InitAtomTable` function initializes an atom hash table. The number of entries in the table is set to the value in `cTableEntries`. The default size of the atom hash table is 37. This function should be called before calling any of the atom management functions.

Return Value A nonzero value is returned when successful. `FALSE` is returned when unsuccessful.

Function Category Atom

Related Functions `AddAtom`, `DeleteAtom`

InSendMessage

Syntax `BOOL InSendMessage()`

Description The `InSendMessage` function determines whether the current window function is processing a message sent from the `SendMessage` function.

Return Value A nonzero value is returned if the message being processed by the current window function is sent by `SendMessage`. Zero is returned if the message being processed by the current window function is not sent by `SendMessage`.

Function Category Message

Related Functions `SendMessage`

InsertMenu

Syntax `BOOL InsertMenu(hmenu, idItem, fuFlags, idNewItem, lpNewItem)`

Parameter	*Type*	*Description*
hmenu	HMENU	Menu to modify
idItem	UINT	Menu item will be inserted prior to this menu item position
fuFlags	UINT	Specifies state of new menu item
idNewItem	UINT	Menu item ID or menu handle
lpNewItem	LPCSTR	Contents of new menu item

Description The InsertMenu function inserts a new menu item into the menu specified in hmenu. The new menu item will be inserted into the position prior to the menu position specified in idItem. When fuFlags contains MF_BYPOSITION, idItem contains a menu item position. When fuFlags contains MF_BYCOMMAND, idItem contains a menu item ID. fuFlags is a combination of values that specifies the state of the new menu item and how idItem is interpreted. idNewItem contains the command ID of the menu item except when fuFlags contains MF_POPUP. When fuFlags contains MF_POPUP, idNewItem contains the menu handle of the pop-up menu. lpNewItem defines the content of the new menu item.

Value	*Meaning*
MF_BITMAP	Uses a bitmap as the item. The handle of the bitmap is in the low-order word of lpNewItem. This flag should not be used with MF_STRING, MF_OWNERDRAW, or MF_SEPARATOR.
MF_BYCOMMAND	idItem contains a menu item command ID. This flag should not be used with MF_BYPOSITION.
MF_BYPOSITION	idItem contains a menu item position. This flag should not be used with MF_BYCOMMAND.
MF_CHECKED	Puts a checkmark next to the item. This flag should not be used with MF_UNCHECKED.

Value	Meaning
MF_DISABLED	Disables, but does not gray, the menu item. This flag should not be used with MF_ENABLED or MF_GRAYED.
MF_ENABLED	Enables the menu item. This flag should not be used with MF_DISABLED or MF_GRAYED.
MF_GRAYED	Disables and grays the menu item. This flag should not be used with MF_DISABLED or MF_ENABLED.
MF_MENUBARBREAK	Puts menu items on a new line. For pop-up menus, puts the new item in a new column and separates the columns with a vertical line. This flag should not be used with MF_MENUBREAK.
MF_MENUBREAK	Puts menu items on a new line. For pop-up menus, puts the new item in a new column but does not separate the columns with a vertical line. This flag should not be used with MF_MENUBARBREAK.
MF_OWNERDRAW	Item is an owner-draw item. This flag should not be used with MF_BITMAP or MF_STRING.
MF_POPUP	Item has a pop-up menu associated with it. idNewItem specifies the handle of the pop-up window.
MF_SEPARATOR	Creates a horizontal line in the menu in a pop-up menu.
MF_STRING	Menu item is a character string. This flag should not be used with MF_BITMAP or MF_OWNERDRAW.
MF_UNCHECKED	No checkmark is placed by the menu item. This flag should not be used with MF_CHECKED.

Return Value A nonzero value is returned when the function is successful. When unsuccessful, zero is returned.

Function Category Menu

Related Functions AppendMenu, CreateMenu, DeleteMenu, SetMenu

InterruptRegister

Syntax `BOOL InterruptRegister(hTask, lpfnIntCallback)`

Parameter	*Type*	*Description*
hTask	HANDLE	Task registering the callback function
lpfnIntCallback	LPFNINTCALLBACK	Pointer to interrupt callback function that handles interrupts

Description The InterruptRegister function defines a callback function to handle system interrupts. lpfnIntCallback points to the callback function. The callback function has the following format:

```
void *LPFNINTCALLBACK(void)
```

Return Value TRUE is returned when successful. FALSE is returned when unsuccessful.

Function Category Toolhelp

Related Functions InterruptUnRegister

InterruptUnRegister

Syntax `BOOL InterruptUnRegister(hTask)`

Parameter	*Type*	*Description*
hTask	HANDLE	Specifies the task; set to NULL to specify the current task

Description The InterruptUnRegister function removes the callback function used to handle system interrupts for the specified task.

Return Value TRUE is returned when successful. FALSE is returned when unsuccessful.

Function Category Toolhelp

Related Functions `InterruptRegister`

IntersectClipRect

Syntax

```
int IntersectClipRect(hdc, nLeftRect, nTopRect, nRightRect,
                      nBottomRect)
```

Parameter	*Type*	*Description*
`hdc`	`HDC`	Device context
`nLeftRect`	`int`	Logical x coordinate of upper-left corner of rectangle
`nTopRects`	`int`	Logical y coordinate of upper-left corner of rectangle
`nRightRect`	`int`	Logical x coordinate of lower-right corner of rectangle
`nBottomRect`	`int`	Logical y coordinate of lower-right corner of rectangle

Description The `IntersectClipRect` function redefines the clipping region as the intersection of the current clipping region and the rectangle defined by `nLeftRect`, `nTopRect`, `nRightRect`, and `nBottomRect`. The intersection is the smallest rectangle that contains the common parts of both rectangles.

Return Value One of the following values is returned to describe the resulting clipping region:

Value	*Meaning*
`COMPLEXREGION`	Region has overlapping borders
`ERROR`	Device context is invalid
`NULLREGION`	Region is empty
`SIMPLEREGION`	Region has no overlapping borders

Function Category Clipping

Related Functions `RectVisible`, `SelectClipRgn`

IntersectRect

Syntax `BOOL IntersectRect(lprcDst, lprcSrc1, lprcSrc2)`

Parameter	*Type*	*Description*
`lprcDst`	`RECT FAR*`	Pointer to `RECT` data structure to receive the intersection
`lprcSrc1`	`const RECT FAR*`	Pointer to `RECT` data structure containing a source rectangle
`lprcSrc2`	`const RECT FAR*`	Pointer to `RECT` data structure containing a source rectangle

Description The `IntersectRect` function determines the intersection of the rectangles from `lprcSrc1` and `lprcSrc2` and places the coordinates of the intersection rectangle in `lprcDst`. `lprcDst`, `lprcSrc1`, and `lprcSrc2` all point to a data structure of type `RECT`. The `RECT` structure follows.

```
typedef struct tagRECT {
     int left;
     int top;
     int right;
     int bottom;
} RECT;
```

in which

`left` is the x coordinate of the upper-left corner

`top` is the y coordinate of the upper-left corner

`right` is the x coordinate of the lower-right corner

`bottom` is the y coordinate of the lower-right corner.

Return Value A nonzero value is returned when the intersection of the two source rectangles is not empty. Zero is returned when the intersection is empty.

Function Category Rectangle

Related Functions `InflateRect`, `UnionRect`

InvalidateRect

Syntax `void InvalidateRect(hwnd, lprc, fErase)`

Parameter	*Type*	*Description*
hwnd	HWND	Window handle
lprc	const RECT FAR*	Pointer to RECT data structure containing the client coordinates of the rectangle to add to the update region; set to NULL when the entire client area is to be added to the update region
fErase	BOOL	Indicates whether the background in the update region will be erased; set to FALSE to leave the background unchanged; set to TRUE to erase the background

Description The InvalidateRect function adds the client area in the rectangle specified in lprc to the update region of the window in hwnd. This marks the specified area for painting when the next WM_PAINT message is sent. lprc points to a data structure of type RECT that contains the client coordinates of the rectangle to add to the update region. The RECT structure follows.

```
typedef struct tagRECT {
     int left;
     int top;
     int right;
     int bottom;
} RECT;
```

in which

left is the x coordinate of the upper-left corner

top is the y coordinate of the upper-left corner

right is the x coordinate of the lower-right corner

bottom is the y coordinate of the lower-right corner.

Return Value There is no return value.

Function Category Painting

Related Functions `ValidateRectangle`

InvalidateRgn

Syntax `void InvalidateRgn(hwnd, hrgn, fErase)`

Parameter	*Type*	*Description*
`hwnd`	`HWND`	Window handle
`hrgn`	`HRGN`	Region to add to update region
`fErase`	`BOOL`	Indicates whether the background of the update region is to be erased; set to `TRUE` to erase the background; set to `FALSE` to leave the background unchanged

Description The `InvalidateRgn` function adds the client area of the region specified in `hrgn` to the update region of the window in `hwnd`. The added region is, therefore, marked for painting when the next `WM_PAINT` message is sent. `fErase` specifies whether the background of the update region is erased. The region specified in `hrgn` must be created with one of the region functions.

Return Value There is no return value.

Function Category Painting

Related Functions `BeginPaint`, `ValidateRgn`

InvertRect

Syntax `void InvertRect(hdc, lprc)`

Parameter	*Type*	*Description*
`hdc`	`HDC`	Device context

Parameter	Type	Description
lprc	const RECT FAR*	Pointer to RECT data structure containing the logical coordinates of the rectangle to invert

Description The InvertRect function inverts the rectangle specified in lprc. lprc points to a data structure of type RECT that contains the logical coordinates of the rectangle to invert. The RECT structure follows. Each pixel in the rectangle is inverted. The actual color of the inverted pixel depends on the colors available for the display.

```
typedef struct tagRECT {
     int left;
     int top;
     int right;
     int bottom;
} RECT;
```

in which

left is the x coordinate of the upper-left corner

top is the y coordinate of the upper-left corner

right is the x coordinate of the lower-right corner

bottom is the y coordinate of the lower-right corner.

Return Value There is no return value.

Function Category Painting, Rectangle

Related Functions InvertRgn

InvertRgn

Syntax `BOOL InvertRgn(hdc, hrgn)`

Parameter	Type	Description
hdc	HDC	Device context
hrgn	HRGN	Region to fill

Description The `InvertRgn` function inverts all the colors inside the region specified by `hrgn`.

Return Value `TRUE` is returned when successful. `FALSE` is returned when unsuccessful.

Function Category Region

Related Functions `InvertRect`

IsCharAlpha

Syntax `BOOL IsCharAlpha(chTest)`

Parameter	*Type*	*Description*
`chTest`	`char`	Character to test

Description The `IsCharAlpha` function determines whether the character specified in `chTest` is an alphabetical character.

Return Value `TRUE` is returned when the character is alphabetical. `FALSE` is returned if the character is not alphabetical.

Function Category String Manipulation

Related Functions `IsCharAlphNumeric`, `IsCharLower`, `IsCharUpper`

IsCharAlphaNumeric

Syntax `BOOL IsCharAlphaNumeric(chTest)`

Parameter	*Type*	*Description*
`chTest`	`char`	Character to test

Description The `IsCharAlphaNumeric` function determines whether the character specified in `chTest` is alphanumeric.

Return Value `TRUE` is returned if the character is alphanumeric. `FALSE` is returned if the character is not alphanumeric.

Function Category String Manipulation

Related Functions IsCharAlpha, IsCharLower, IsCharUpper

IsCharLower

Syntax `BOOL IsCharLower(chTest)`

Parameter	*Type*	*Description*
chTest	char	Character to test

Description The IsCharLower function determines whether the character specified in chTest is a lowercase character.

Return Value TRUE is returned if the character is lowercase. FALSE is returned if the character is uppercase.

Function Category String Manipulation

Related Functions IsCharAlpha, IsCharAlphNumeric, IsCharUpper

IsCharUpper

Syntax `BOOL IsCharUpper(chTest)`

Parameter	*Type*	*Description*
chTest	char	Character to test

Description The IsCharUpper function determines whether the character specified in chTest is an uppercase character.

Return Value TRUE is returned if the character is uppercase. FALSE is returned if the character is lowercase.

Function Category String Manipulation

Related Functions IsCharAlpha, IsCharAlphaNumeric, IsCharLower

IsChild

Syntax `BOOL IsChild(hwndParent, hwndChild)`

Parameter	*Type*	*Description*
`hwndParent`	`HWND`	Window handle
`hwndChild`	`HWND`	Check this window

Description The `IsChild` function determines whether the window in `hwndChild` is a child window, or descendant, of the window specified in `hwndParent`.

Return Value A nonzero value is returned if `hwndChild` is a child window, or descendant, of `hwndParent`. If not, zero is returned.

Function Category Information

Related Functions `IsWindow`, `SetParent`

IsClipboardFormatAvailable

Syntax `BOOL IsClipboardFormatAvailable(uFormat)`

Parameter	*Type*	*Description*
`uFormat`	`UINT`	Clipboard format

Description The `IsClipboardFormatAvailable` function determines whether data of a specified format exists on the clipboard. `uFormat` specifies the clipboard format for which to check.

Return Value A nonzero value is returned when data which matches the specified format exists in the clipboard. Zero is returned when no matching data is found.

Function Category Clipboard

Related Functions `EnumClipboardFormats`, `GetClipboardFormatName`, `GetPriorityClipboardFormat`, `RegisterClipboardFormat`

IsDBCSLeadByte

Syntax `BOOL IsDBCSLeadByte(bTestChar)`

Parameter	*Type*	*Description*
`bTestChar`	`BYTE`	Character to test

Description The `IsDBCSLeadByte` function determines whether the character specified in `bTestChar` is the first byte of double-byte character.

Return Value `TRUE` is returned if the specified character is the first byte of a double-byte character. `FALSE` is returned if the character is not the first byte of a double-byte character.

Function Category Hardware

Related Functions `GetKeyboardType`

IsDialogMessage

Syntax `BOOL IsDialogMessage(hwndDlg, lpmsg)`

Parameter	*Type*	*Description*
`hwndDlg`	`HWND`	Dialog box
`lpmsg`	`const MSG FAR*`	Data structure containing the message

Description The `IsDialogMessage` function determines whether a particular message is intended for a particular modeless dialog box. `hwndDlg` specifies the modeless dialog box. `lpmsg` points to the `MSG` data structure containing the message. The `MSG` data structure follows this paragraph. If the message is determined to be for the dialog box in `hwndDlg`, the message is processed by `IsDialogMessage`. During the processing of this message, `IsDialogMessage` checks for keyboard messages and processes these messages accordingly. This function sends the `WM_GETDLGCODE` message to the dialog function.

```
typedef struct tagMSG {
     HWND hwnd;
     WORD message;
     WORD wParam;
     LONG lParam;
```

```
    DWORD time;
    POINT pt;
} MSG;
```

in which

`hwnd` is the window receiving the message

`message` is the message

`wParam` is any additional information about the message

`lParam` is any additional information about the message

`time` is the time that the message was posted

`pt` is the screen coordinates of the cursor when the message was posted.

Return Value A nonzero value is returned when the message in `lpmsg` is processed. Zero is returned when the message is not processed.

Function Category Dialog Box

Related Functions `SendDlgItemMessage`

IsDlgButtonChecked

Syntax `UINT IsDlgButtonChecked(hdlg, idButton)`

Parameter	*Type*	*Description*
`hdlg`	`HWND`	Dialog box containing button
`idButton`	`int`	Button control

Description The `IsDlgButtonChecked` function determines the state of the dialog button specified in `idButton`. `hdlg` specifies the dialog box that contains the button in `idButton`. `IsDlgButtonChecked` determines whether the button has been checked (a checkmark placed next to it). If the button is a three-state button, `IsDlgButtonChecked` determines whether the button is checked, not checked, or gray. The `BM_GETCHECK` message is sent to the button control.

Return Value A nonzero value is returned when the button is checked. If no checkmark is beside the button, zero is returned. When a three-state button is grayed, 2 is returned. When a three-state button is checked, 1 is returned. As with normal buttons, a three-state button returns 0 if there is no checkmark beside the button. A return value of −1 indicates that `hdlg` is invalid.

Function Category Dialog Box

Related Functions `CheckDlgButton`, `CheckRadioButton`

IsIconic

Syntax `BOOL IsIconic(hwnd)`

Parameter	*Type*	*Description*
`hwnd`	`HWND`	Window handle

Description The `IsIconic` function determines whether the window specified in `hwnd` is minimized.

Return Value A nonzero value is returned when the window in `hwnd` is minimized. Zero is returned when the window is not minimized.

Function Category Display and Movement

Related Functions `ArrangeIconicWindows`, `ClassWindow`, `IsZoomed`

IsMenu

Syntax `BOOL IsMenu(hmenu)`

Parameter	*Type*	*Description*
`hmenu`	`HMENU`	Handle to test

Description The `IsMenu` function determines whether the handle specified in `hmenu` is a handle for a menu.

Return Value A nonzero value is returned when the specified handle is the handle to a menu. Zero is returned when the handle is not a menu handle.

Function Category Menu

Related Functions `CreateMenu`, `DestroyMenu`, `GetMenu`

IsRectEmpty

Syntax `BOOL IsRectEmpty(lprc)`

Parameter	*Type*	*Description*
`lprc`	`const RECT FAR*`	Pointer to `RECT` data structure containing the coordinates of the rectangle

Description The `IsRectEmpty` function determines whether the rectangle specified by the coordinates in the data structure of type `RECT` pointed to by `lprc` is empty. The `RECT` data structure follows.

```
typedef struct tagRECT {
     int left;
     int top;
     int right;
     int bottom;
} RECT;
```

in which

`left` is the x coordinate of the upper-left corner

`top` is the y coordinate of the upper-left corner

`right` is the x coordinate of the lower-right corner

`bottom` is the y coordinate of the lower-right corner.

Return Value A nonzero value is returned when the rectangle is empty. Zero is returned when the rectangle is not empty.

Function Category Rectangle

Related Functions `SetRectEmpty`

IsTask

Syntax `BOOL IsTask(htask)`

Parameter	*Type*	*Description*
`htask`	`HTASK`	Task handle

Description The `IsTask` function determines whether the task handle specified in `htask` is a valid handle.

Return Value `TRUE` is returned when the specified handle is a valid handle. `FALSE` is returned when the specified handle is not a valid handle.

Function Category Task

Related Functions `GetCurrentTask`

IsWindow

Syntax `BOOL IsWindow(hwnd)`

Parameter	*Type*	*Description*
`hwnd`	`HWND`	Window handle

Description The `IsWindow` function determines whether the window specified in `hwnd` is a valid window.

Return Value A nonzero value is returned if the specified window is a valid window. Zero is returned if it is not a valid window.

Function Category Information

Related Functions `IsWindowEnabled`, `IsWindowVisible`

IsWindowEnabled

Syntax `BOOL IsWindowEnabled(hwnd)`

Parameter	Type	Description
hwnd	HWND	Window handle

Description The `IsWindowEnabled` function determines whether mouse and keyboard input is enabled for the window specified in `hwnd`.

Return Value A nonzero value is returned if input is enabled. Zero is returned if input is disabled.

Function Category Input

Related Functions `IsWindow`, `IsWindowVisible`

IsWindowVisible

Syntax `BOOL IsWindowVisible(hwnd)`

Parameter	Type	Description
hwnd	HWND	Window handle

Description The `IsWindowVisible` function determines whether the window specified in `hwnd` has been made visible using the `ShowWindow` function.

Return Value A nonzero value is returned when the window in `hwnd` has been made visible. Zero is returned if the window has not been made visible.

Function Category Display and Movement

Related Functions `MoveWindow`, `ShowWindow`

IsZoomed

Syntax `BOOL IsZoomed(hwnd)`

Parameter	Type	Description
hwnd	HWND	Window handle

Description The `IsZoomed` function determines whether the window specified in `hwnd` has been maximized.

Return Value A nonzero value is returned when the window in `hwnd` has been maximized. A zero is returned when the window has not been maximized.

Function Category Display and Movement

Related Functions `IsIconic`, `IsWindowVisible`

KillTimer

Syntax `BOOL KillTimer(hwnd, idTimer)`

Parameter	*Type*	*Description*
`hwnd`	`HWND`	Window associated with timer
`idTimer`	`UINT`	Timer event

Description The `KillTimer` function terminates the timer event specified by `hwnd` and `idTimer`. `hwnd` specifies the window associated with the timer event. `idTimer` specifies the timer event.

Return Value A nonzero value is returned if the timer event was terminated. Zero is returned if the timer event was not found.

Function Category Input

Related Functions `SetTimer`

_lclose

Syntax `HFILE _lclose(hf)`

Parameter	*Type*	*Description*
`hf`	`HFILE`	DOS file handle of file to close

Description The `_lclose` function closes the file specified in `hf`.

Return Value Zero is returned when successful. HFILE_ERROR is returned when unsuccessful.

Function Category File I/O

Related Functions _lcreat, _lopen, _lread, _lwrite

_lcreat

Syntax `HFILE _lcreat(lpszFileName, fnAttribute)`

Parameter	*Type*	*Description*
lpszFileName	LPCSTR	Pointer to a null-terminated string naming the file to open; string must contain characters from the ANSI character set
fnAttribute	int	Specifies the file attributes

Description The _lcreat function opens a file using the name in lpszFileName. A new file is created and opened if the specified file does not exist. If the file exists, the file is truncated to zero and opened. fnAttribute specifies the attributes for the file. The following values are used with fnAttribute:

Value	*Meaning*
0	Read and write
1	Read-only
2	Hidden
3	System

Return Value The DOS file handle to the created file is returned when successful. HFILE_ERROR is returned when unsuccessful.

Function Category File I/O

Related Functions _lclose, _lopen, _lread, _lwrite

LineDDA

Syntax

```
void LineDDA(nXStart, nYStart, nXEnd, nYEnd, lnddaprc,
             lParamData)
```

Parameter	*Type*	*Description*
nXStart	int	Logical x coordinate of first endpoint of line
nYStart	int	Logical y coordinate of first endpoint of line
nXEnd	int	Logical x coordinate of second endpoint of line
nYEnd	int	Logical y coordinate of second endpoint of line
lnddaprc	LINEDDAPROC	Procedure instance address of callback function
lParamData	LPARAM	Pointer to application-supplied data

Description The LineDDA function calculates the points that make up the line between the specified endpoints (nXStart, nYStart) and (nXEnd, nYEnd). lnddaprc specifies the procedure instance address of the application-supplied callback function. This address is created using the MakeProcInstance function. Each point on the line is passed to the callback function. lParamData is also passed to the callback function. The callback function uses the following convention and returns no value.

```
void FAR PASCAL LineDDAFunc(xPos, yPos, lpData)
int xPos;
int yPos;

LPSTR lpData;
```

in which

xPos is the x coordinate of the point

yPos is the y coordinate of the point

lpData is the application-supplied data.

Return Value There is no return value.

Function Category Line Output

Related Functions LineTo, Polyline

LineTo

Syntax `BOOL LineTo(hdc, nXEnd, nYEnd)`

Parameter	*Type*	*Description*
hdc	HDC	Device context
nXEnd	int	Logical x coordinate of endpoint
nYEnd	int	Logical y coordinate of endpoint

Description The LineTo function draws a line from the current position to the point specified in (nXEnd, nYEnd). The point (nXEnd, nYEnd) is not drawn. The current pen is used to draw the line. The current position is updated to the point specified in (nXEnd, nYEnd) when the line is successfully drawn.

Return Value TRUE is returned when the line is successfully drawn. FALSE is returned when unsuccessful.

Function Category Line Output

Related Functions LineDDA, MoveTo, Polyline

_llseek

Syntax `LONG _llseek(hf, lOffset, nOrigin)`

Parameter	*Type*	*Description*
hf	HFILE	DOS file handle of file
lOffset	LONG	Number of bytes to move pointer
nOrigin	int	Starting position and direction of pointer

Description The _llseek function repositions the pointer in the opened file specified in hf. lOffset specifies the number of bytes to move the pointer relative to the starting point and direction specified in nOrigin. The following values are used for nOrigin:

Value	*Meaning*
0	Moves the file pointer from the beginning of the file
1	Moves the file pointer from the current pointer position
2	Moves the file pointer from the end of the file

Return Value The new offset of the pointer, in bytes, is returned when successful. HFILE_ERROR is returned when unsuccessful.

Function Category File I/O

Related Functions _lopen, _lread, _lwrite

LoadAccelerators

Syntax `HACCEL LoadAccelerators(hinst, lpszTableName)`

Parameter	*Type*	*Description*
hinst	HINSTANCE	Instance of module whose executable file contains the accelerator table
lpszTableName	LPCSTR	Pointer to a null-terminated string containing the name of the table

Description The LoadAccelerators function loads the accelerator table specified in lpszTableName. hinst specifies the module whose executable file contains the accelerator table to load.

Return Value The handle to the loaded accelerator table is returned when successful. NULL is returned when unsuccessful.

Function Category Resource Management

Related Functions AccessResource, FreeResource

LoadBitmap

Syntax `HBITMAP LoadBitmap(hinst, lpszBitmapName)`

Parameter	*Type*	*Description*
hinst	HINSTANCE	Instance of module whose executable file contains the bitmap
lpszBitmapName	LPCSTR	Name of bitmap

Description The `LoadBitmap` function loads the bitmap resource specified in `lpszBitmapName`. The bitmap is loaded from the executable file for the module specified in `hinst`.

Return Value The bitmap handle is returned when successful. `NULL` is returned when unsuccessful.

Function Category Resource Management

Related Functions `AccessResource`, `DeleteObject`, `FreeResource`

LoadCursor

Syntax `HCURSOR LoadCursor(hinst, lpszCursorName)`

Parameter	*Type*	*Description*
hinst	HINSTANCE	Module that contains the cursor
lpszCursorName	LPCSTR	Name of the cursor resource

Description The `LoadCursor` function loads the cursor specified in `lpszCursorName`. `lpszCursorName` points to a null-terminated character string which holds the name of the cursor resource. `hinst` specifies the module which has the executable file containing the cursor resource. The predefined Windows cursors can be accessed with the `LoadCursor` function by setting `hinst` to `NULL` and `CursorName` to one of the following values:

Constant	*Meaning*
IDC_ARROW	Arrow cursor
IDC_CROSS	Crosshair cursor

Constant	Meaning
IDC_IBEAM	I-beam text cursor
IDC_ICON	Empty icon
IDC_SIZE	Square with small square in lower-right corner
IDC_SIZENESW	Cursor with arrows pointing northeast and southwest
IDC_SIZENS	Cursor with arrows pointing north and south
IDC_SIZENWSE	Cursor with arrows pointing northwest and southeast
IDC_SIZEWE	Cursor with arrows pointing west and east
IDC_UPARROW	Vertical arrow cursor
IDC_WAIT	Hourglass cursor

Return Value The handle of the cursor is returned when successful. When unsuccessful, `NULL` is returned.

Note: If `lpszCursorName` specifies a resource type other than a cursor resource, the return value will not be `NULL`; however, the return value will not be valid.

Function Category Resource Management

Related Functions `SetCursor`, `ShowCursor`

LoadIcon

Syntax `HICON LoadIcon(hinst, lpszIcon)`

Parameter	Type	Description
hinst	HINSTANCE	Instance of module whose executable file contains the icon
lpszIcon	LPCSTR	Pointer to a null-terminated string containing the name of the icon

Description The `LoadIcon` function loads the icon specified in `lpszIcon`. `hinst` specifies the module whose executable file contains the specified icon resource. `LoadIcon` can be used to access the following predefined Windows icons:

Value	*Meaning*
`IDI_APPLICATION`	Default application icon
`IDI_ASTERISK`	Asterisk — used in information messages
`IDI_EXCLAMATION`	Exclamation point — used in warning messages
`IDI_HAND`	Hand-shape — used in serious warning messages
`IDI_QUESTION`	Question mark — used in prompts

Return Value The handle to the icon resource is returned when successful. `NULL` is returned when unsuccessful.

Function Category Resource Management

Related Functions `DrawIcon`

LoadLibrary

Syntax `HINSTANCE LoadLibrary(lpszLibFileName)`

Parameter	*Type*	*Description*
`lpzeLibFileName`	`LPCSTR`	Pointer to a null-terminated string that defines the library file

Description The `LoadLibrary` function loads the library module from the library file specified in `lpszLibFileName`. The function also returns the handle of the loaded module instance.

Return Value The handle of the loaded library module instance is returned when successful. When unsuccessful, one of the following error values is returned:

Value	*Meaning*
0	Out of memory
2	File not found
3	Path not found

Value	Meaning
5	Attempt to dynamically link to a task
6	Library requires separate data segments for each task
8	Insufficient memory to start application
10	Incorrect Windows version
11	Invalid .EXE file
12	OS/2 application
13	DOS 4.0 application
14	Unknown .EXE type
15	Attempt in protected mode to load an .EXE created for an earlier version of Windows
16	Attempt to load a second instance of an .EXE containing multiple, writeable data segments
19	File must be expanded before loaded
20	DLL file was invalid
21	Microsoft Windows 32-bit extensions are required to run the application

Function Category Module Management

Related Functions `FreeLibrary`

LoadMenu

Syntax `HMENU LoadMenu(hinst, lpszMenuName)`

Parameter	Type	Description
`hinst`	`HINSTANCE`	Instance of module whose executable file contains the menu
`lpszMenuName`	`LPCSTR`	Pointer to a null-terminated string containing the name of the menu

Description The `LoadMenu` function loads the menu resource specified in `lpszMenuName`. `hinst` specifies the module whose executable file contains the menu resource.

Return Value The handle to the menu resource is returned when successful. `NULL` is returned when unsuccessful.

Function Category Resource Management

Related Functions `DestroyMenu`, `LoadMenuIndirect`, `SetMenu`

LoadMenuIndirect

Syntax `HMENU LoadMenuIndirect(lpmith)`

Parameter	*Type*	*Description*
`lpmith`	`const MENUITEMTEMPLATEHEADER FAR*`	Points to menu template

Description The `LoadMenuIndirect` function loads the menu specified in `lpmith` into memory. `lpmith` points to a menu template which contains a header and one or more `MENUITEMTEMPLATE` structures. The header and `MENUITEMTEMPLATE` structures follow.

```
typedef struct {
     WORD versionNumber;
     WORD offset;
} MENUITEMTEMPLATEHEADER;
```

in which

`versionNumber` is the version number, usually zero

`offset` is the offset, in bytes, where the menu item list begins.

```
typedef struct {
     WORD mtOption;
     WORD mtID;
     LPSTR mtString;
} MENUITEMTEMPLATE;
```

in which

`mtOption` is a combination of one or more of the following options:

Value	*Meaning*
MF_CHECKED	Checkmark next to item
MF_END	Item is last item in menu
MF_GRAYED	Item is grayed and inactive
MF_HELP	Item has vertical separator on its left
MF_MENUBARBREAK	Item is placed in a new column with a vertical separator
MF_MENUBREAK	Item is placed in a new column without a vertical separator
MF_OWNERDRAW	Owner draws menu item
MF_POPUP	Item displays a pop-up menu

`mtID` is the ID code for the menu (not for pop-up menus)

`mtString` points to the name of the menu item.

Return Value The menu handle is returned when successful. `NULL` is returned when unsuccessful.

Function Category Menu

Related Functions `LoadMenu`, `SetMenu`

LoadModule

Syntax `HINSTANCE LoadModule(lpszModuleName, lpvParameterBlock)`

Parameter	*Type*	*Description*
lpszModuleName	LPCSTR	Pointer to null-terminated string containing the filename of the application to execute
lpvParameterBlock	LPVOID	Pointer to a data structure containing four fields (these are described in the following Description)

Description The `LoadModule` function executes the Windows application specified in `lpszModuleName` or creates a new instance for the Windows application. `lpszModuleName` specifies the name of the application to execute. If a directory path is not given in `lpszModuleName`, Windows searches the current directory, the Windows directory, the system directory, the directories of the PATH environment variable, and the directories mapped in a network, in order. `lpvParameterBlock` points to data structure containing four fields. These fields are as follows:

Field	*Type*	*Description*
`SegEnv`	`WORD`	Segment address of the environment where the module will be run (0 for Windows)
`lpszCmdLine`	`LPSTR`	Pointer to a null-terminated character string that contains the command line
`lpwShow`	`LPWORD`	Pointer to a data structure containing two `WORD` values. The first value is set to 2. The second value is set to one of the values used for the `nCmdShow` parameter of the `ShowWindow` function.
`lpwReserved`	`LPWORD`	Set to `NULL`

Return Value The instance of the loaded module is returned when successful. One of the following values is returned when unsuccessful:

Value	*Meaning*
0	Out of memory
2	File not found
3	Path not found
5	Attempt to dynamically link to a task
6	Library requires separate data segments for each task
8	Insufficient memory to start application
10	Incorrect Windows version
11	Invalid .EXE file
12	OS/2 application
13	DOS 4.0 application
14	Unknown .EXE type
15	Attempt in protected mode to load an .EXE created for an earlier version of Windows

Value	*Meaning*
16	Attempt to load a second instance of an .EXE containing multiple, writeable data segments
17	Attempt in large-frame EMS mode to load a second instance of an application that links to certain nonshareable DLLs already in use
19	Attempt to load a compressed .EXE file
20	Invalid DLL file
21	Microsoft Windows 32-bit extensions required for application

Function Category Application Execution

Related Functions `FreeModule`, `WinExec`

LoadResource

Syntax `HGLOBAL LoadResource(hinst, hrsrc)`

Parameter	*Type*	*Description*
`hinst`	`HINSTANCE`	Instance of module whose executable file contains the resource
`hrsrc`	`HRSRC`	Resource handle

Description The `LoadResource` function loads the resource specified in `hrsrc`. `hinst` specifies the instance of the module whose executable file contains the specified resource.

Return Value The handle to the loaded resource is returned when successful. `NULL` is returned when unsuccessful.

Function Category Resource Management

Related Functions `AccessResource`, `FreeResource`, `LockResource`

LoadString

Syntax `int LoadString(hinst, idResource, lpszBuffer, cbBuffer)`

Parameter	*Type*	*Description*
`hinst`	`HINSTANCE`	Instance of module whose executable file contains the string resource
`idResource`	`UINT`	Integer ID of string to load
`lpszBuffer`	`LPSTR`	Pointer to the buffer to receive the string
`cbBuffer`	`int`	Maximum number of characters to copy to buffer

Description The `LoadString` function copies the string resource specified `idResource` into the buffer pointed to by `lpszBuffer`. `cbBuffer` specifies the maximum number of characters to copy to the buffer. `hinst` specifies the instance of the module whose executable file contains the string resource.

Return Value The number of characters copied to the buffer is returned when successful. Zero is returned when unsuccessful.

Function Category Resource Management

Related Functions `AccessResource`, `FreeResource`

LOBYTE

Syntax `BYTE LOBYTE(wVal)`

Parameter	*Type*	*Description*
`wVal`	`WORD`	Value to convert

Description The `LOBYTE` macro returns the low-order byte of the value specified in `wVal`.

Return Value The low-order byte is returned.

Function Category Windows Macros

Related Functions HIBYTE

LocalAlloc

Syntax `HLOCAL LocalAlloc(fuAllocFlags, fuAlloc)`

Parameter	*Type*	*Description*
fuAllocFlags	UINT	Indicates how the memory is to be allocated
fuAlloc	UINT	Number of bytes to allocate

Description The LocalAlloc function allocates memory from the local heap. The number of bytes of memory to allocate is specified in fuAlloc. fuAllocFlags specifies how the memory is to be allocated. fuAllocFlags is the combination (using bitwise OR) of one or more of the following values:

Value	*Meaning*
LHND	Combination of LMEM_MOVEABLE and LMEM_ZEROINIT
LMEM_DISCARDABLE	Discardable memory is allocated
LMEM_FIXED	Fixed memory is allocated
LMEM_MODIFY	The LMEM_DISCARDABLE flag is modified
LMEM_MOVEABLE	Moveable memory is allocated
LMEM_NOCOMPACT	Memory is not compacted or discarded to meet the memory requirements
LMEM_NODISCARD	Memory is not discarded to meet the memory requirements
LMEM_ZEROINT	The contents of the allocated memory are initialized to zero
LPTR	Combination of LMEM_FIXED and LMEM_ZEROINIT
NONZEROLHND	Same as LMEM_MOVEABLE
NONZEROLPTR	Same as LMEM_FIXED

Return Value The handle to the allocated local memory block is returned when successful. NULL is returned when unsuccessful.

Function Category Memory Management

Related Functions `LocalFree`, `LocalReAlloc`

LocalCompact

Syntax `UINT LocalCompact(uMinFree)`

Parameter	*Type*	*Description*
`uMinFree`	`UINT`	Number of bytes to free

Description The `LocalCompact` function frees the number of bytes specified in `uMinFree` by compacting the local heap. If necessary, unlocked discardable blocks are discarded to free the number of bytes requested.

Return Value The number of bytes in the largest block of free local memory is returned. When `uMinFree` is set to zero, the number of bytes in the largest free block that Windows can generate is returned.

Function Category Memory Management

Related Functions `LocalAlloc`, `LocalLock`

LocalDiscard

Syntax `HLOCAL LocalDiscard(hloc)`

Parameter	*Type*	*Description*
`hloc`	`HLOCAL`	Local memory block to discard

Description The `LocalDiscard` function discards the local memory block specified in `hloc` if the lock count for the memory block is zero. The handle to the memory block remains valid.

Return Value `hloc` is returned when successful. `NULL` is returned when unsuccessful.

Function Category Memory Management

Related Functions LocalFree, LocalReAlloc

LocalFirst

Syntax `BOOL LocalFirst(leLocal, hHeap)`

Parameter	*Type*	*Description*
leLocal	LOCALENTRY FAR*	Pointer to LOCALENTRY data structure that receives local memory block information
hHeap	HANDLE	Local heap

Description The LocalFirst function gets information about the first block on the local heap and copies the information to the data structure of type LOCALENTRY that is pointed to by leLocal. The LOCALENTRY data structure follows.

```
#include <toolhelp.h>
typedef struct tagLOCALENTRY
     {
     DWORD dwSize;
     HANDLE hHandle;
     WORD wAddress;
     WORD wSize;
     WORD wFlags;
     WORD wcLock;
     WORD wType;
     HANDLE hHeap;
     WORD wHeapType;
     WORD wNext;
} LOCALENTRY;
```

in which

dwSize is the number of bytes in the data structure

hHandle is the local memory block

wAddress is the address of the local memory block

wSize is the number of bytes in the local memory block

wFlags is one of the following:

Value	*Meaning*
LF_FIXED	Block is fixed
LF_FREE	Block is part of free memory pool
LF_MOVEABLE	Block can be moved to compact memory

`wcLock` is the lock count

`wType` specifies the contents of the memory block and is set to one of the following values:

Value	*Meaning*
LT_FREE	Belongs to free memory pool
LT_GDI_BITMAP	Contains bitmap object header
LT_GDI_BRUSH	Contains brush object
LT_GDI_DC	Contains device context object
LT_GDI_DISABLED_DC	Reserved for Windows use
LT_GDI_FONT	Contains font object header
LT_GDI_MAX	Reserved for Windows use
LT_GDI_METADC	Contains metafile device context object
LT_GDI_METAFILE	Contains metafile object header
LT_GDI_PALETTE	Contains a palette object
LT_GDI_PEN	Contains a pen object
LT_GDI_RGN	Contains a region object
LT_NORMAL	Reserved for Windows use
LT_USER_ATOMS	Contains atom structure
LT_USER_BWL	Reserved for Windows use
LT_USER_CBOX	Contains combo box structure
LT_USER_CHECKPOINT	Reserved for Windows use
LT_USER_CLASS	Contains a class structure
LT_USER_CLIP	Reserved for Windows use
LT_USER_DCE	Reserved for Windows use
LT_USER_ED	Contains edit control structure
LT_USER_HANDLETABLE	Reserved for Windows use
LT_USER_HOOKLIST	Reserved for Windows use
LT_USER_HOTKEYLIST	Reserved for Windows use
LT_USER_LBIV	Contains a listbox structure

Value	Meaning
LT_USER_LOCKINPUTSTATE	Reserved for Windows use
LT_USER_MENU	Contains a menu structure
LT_USER_MISC	Reserved for Windows use
LT_USER_MWP	Reserved for Windows use
LT_USER_OWNERDRAW	Reserved for Windows use
LT_USER_PALETTE	Reserved for Windows use
LT_USER_POPUPMENU	Reserved for Windows use
LT_USER_PROP	Contains a window property structure
LT_USER_SPB	Reserved for Windows use
LT_USER_STRING	Reserved for Windows use
LT_USER_USERSEEUSERDOALLOC	Reserved for Windows use
LT_USER_WND	Contains a window structure

`hHeap` specifies the local memory heap

`wHeapType` is the local heap type and is set to one of the following values:

Value	Meaning
NORMAL_HEAP	Heap is default heap
USER_HEAP	Heap is used by USER module
GDI_HEAP	Heap is used by GDI module

`wNext` is the next entry in the local heap; reserved for use by Windows.

Return Value `TRUE` is returned when successful. `FALSE` is returned when unsuccessful.

Function Category Toolhelp

Related Functions `LocalInfo`, `LocalNext`

LocalFlags

Syntax `UINT LocalFlags(hloc)`

Parameter	Type	Description
hloc	HLOCAL	Local memory block

Description The `LocalFlags` function returns information on the local memory block specified in `hloc`.

Return Value The high-order byte of the return value contains either `LMEM_DISCARDABLE` (block is discardable) or `LMEM_DISCARDED` (block has been discarded). The low-order byte of the return value contains the reference count for the memory block. The `LMEM_LOCKCOUNT` mask can be used to get the lock count value from the return value.

Function Category Memory Management

Related Functions `GlobalFlags`, `LocalAlloc`

LocalFree

Syntax `HLOCAL LocalFree(hloc)`

Parameter	Type	Description
hloc	HLOCAL	Local memory block to free

Description The `LocalFree` function frees the local memory block specified in `hloc`. The handle of the block becomes invalid.

Return Value `NULL` is returned when the function is successful. `hloc` is returned when unsuccessful.

Function Category Memory Management

Related Functions `LocalFlags`, `LocalLock`

LocalHandle

Syntax `HLOCAL LocalHandle(uLocalMemAddr)`

Parameter	*Type*	*Description*
uLocalMemAddr	UINT	Address of local memory object

Description The LocalHandle function gets the handle of the local memory object that has the address specified in uLocalMemAddr.

Return Value The handle to the local memory object is returned when successful. NULL is returned when unsuccessful.

Function Category Memory Management

Related Functions GlobalHandle, LocalAlloc

LocalInfo

Syntax `BOOL LocalInfo(liLocal, hHeap)`

Parameter	*Type*	*Description*
liLocal	LOCALINFO FAR*	Pointer to LOCALINFO data structure that will receive local heap information
hHeap	HANDLE	Local heap

Description The LocalInfo function gets information on the local heap and places this information in the data structure of type LOCALINFO pointed to by liLocal. The LOCALINFO data structure follows.

```
#include <toolhelp.h>
typedef struct tagLOCALINFO
     {
     DWORD dwSize;
     WORD wcItems;
} LOCALINFO;
```

in which

dwSize is the number of bytes in the data structure

`wcItems` is the total number of items on the local heap.

Return Value `TRUE` is returned when successful. `FALSE` is returned when unsuccessful.

Function Category Toolhelp

Related Functions `LocalFirst`, `LocalNext`

LocalInit

Syntax `BOOL LocalInit(uSegment, uStartAddr, uEndAddr)`

Parameter	*Type*	*Description*
`uSegment`	`UINT`	Segment address
`uStartAddr`	`UINT`	Address of the start of the local heap
`uEndAddr`	`UINT`	Address of the end of the local heap

Description The `LocalInit` function initializes a local heap. `uSegment` specifies the segment where the local heap will be initialized. `uStartAddr` specifies the starting address of the local heap. `uEndAddr` specifies the ending adress of the local heap.

Return Value A nonzero value is returned when the heap is successfully initialized. Zero is returned when unsuccessful.

Function Category Memory Management

Related Functions `LocalAlloc`, `LocalFree`

LocalLock

Syntax `void NEAR* LocalLock(hloc)`

Parameter	*Type*	*Description*
`hloc`	`HLOCAL`	Local memory block to lock

Description The `LocalLock` function locks the local memory block in `hloc` at the given address. The reference count of the block is incremented.

Return Value The pointer to the first byte in the local memory block is returned when successful. `NULL` is returned when unsuccessful.

Function Category Memory Management

Related Functions `GlobalLock`, `LocalUnlock`

LocalNext

Syntax `BOOL LocalNext(leLocal)`

Parameter	*Type*	*Description*
`leLocal`	`LOCALENTRY FAR*`	Pointer to `LOCALENTRY` data structure where the local memory block information is copied

Description The `LocalNext` function retrieves information on the next block on the local heap and copies the information to the data structure of type `LOCALENTRY` pointed to by `leLocal`. The `LOCALENTRY` data structure follows.

```
#include <toolhelp.h>
typedef struct tagLOCALENTRY
     {
     DWORD dwSize;
     HANDLE hHandle;
     WORD wAddress;
     WORD wSize;
     WORD wFlags;
     WORD wcLock;
     WORD wType;
     HANDLE hHeap;
     WORD wHeapType;
     WORD wNext;
} LOCALENTRY;
```

in which

`dwSize` is the number of bytes in the data structure

`hHandle` is the local memory block

`wAddress` is the address of the local memory block

`wSize` is the number of bytes in the local memory block

`wFlags` is one of the following:

Value	*Meaning*
`LF_FIXED`	Block is fixed
`LF_FREE`	Block is part of free memory pool
`LF_MOVEABLE`	Block can be moved to compact memory

`wcLock` is the lock count

`wType` specifies the contents of the memory block and is set to one of the following values:

Value	*Meaning*
`LT_FREE`	Belongs to free memory pool
`LT_GDI_BITMAP`	Contains bitmap object header
`LT_GDI_BRUSH`	Contains brush object
`LT_GDI_DC`	Contains device context object
`LT_GDI_DISABLED_DC`	Reserved for Windows use
`LT_GDI_FONT`	Contains font object header
`LT_GDI_MAX`	Reserved for Windows use
`LT_GDI_METADC`	Contains metafile device context object
`LT_GDI_METAFILE`	Contains metafile object header
`LT_GDI_PALETTE`	Contains a palette object
`LT_GDI_PEN`	Contains a pen object
`LT_GDI_RGN`	Contains a region object
`LT_NORMAL`	Reserved for Windows use
`LT_USER_ATOMS`	Contains atom structure
`LT_USER_BWL`	Reserved for Windows use
`LT_USER_CBOX`	Contains combo box structure
`LT_USER_CHECKPOINT`	Reserved for Windows use
`LT_USER_CLASS`	Contains a class structure
`LT_USER_CLIP`	Reserved for Windows use
`LT_USER_DCE`	Reserved for Windows use
`LT_USER_ED`	Contains edit control structure
`LT_USER_HANDLETABLE`	Reserved for Windows use

Value	*Meaning*
LT_USER_HOOKLIST	Reserved for Windows use
LT_USER_HOTKEYLIST	Reserved for Windows use
LT_USER_LBIV	Contains a listbox structure
LT_USER_LOCKINPUTSTATE	Reserved for Windows use
LT_USER_MENU	Contains a menu structure
LT_USER_MISC	Reserved for Windows use
LT_USER_MWP	Reserved for Windows use
LT_USER_OWNERDRAW	Reserved for Windows use
LT_USER_PALETTE	Reserved for Windows use
LT_USER_POPUPMENU	Reserved for Windows use
LT_USER_PROP	Contains a window property structure
LT_USER_SPB	Reserved for Windows use
LT_USER_STRING	Reserved for Windows use
LT_USER_USERSEEUSERDOALLOC	Reserved for Windows use
LT_USER_WND	Contains a window structure

`hHeap` specifies the local memory heap

`wHeapType` is the local heap type and is set to one of the following values:

Value	*Meaning*
NORMAL_HEAP	Heap is default heap
USER_HEAP	Heap is used by USER module
GDI_HEAP	Heap is used by GDI module

`wNext` is the next entry in the local heap; reserved for use by Windows.

Return Value `TRUE` is returned when successful. `FALSE` is returned when unsuccessful.

Function Category Toolhelp

Related Functions `LocalInfo`, `LocalFirst`

LocalReAlloc

Syntax `HLOCAL LocalReAlloc(hloc, fnNewSize, fuFlags)`

Parameter	*Type*	*Description*
`hloc`	`HLOCAL`	Local memory block to reallocate
`fnNewSize`	`UINT`	New size of memory block
`fuFlags`	`UINT`	Indicates how the memory block is to be reallocated

Description The `LocalReAlloc` function modifies the size of the local memory block in `hloc`. `fnNewSize` specifies the new size of the local memory block. `fuFlags` specifies how the memory block is to be reallocated. One or more of the following values is used for `fuFlags`.

Value	*Meaning*
`LMEM_DISCARDABLE`	Memory is discardable
`LMEM_MODIFY`	Memory flags are modified
`LMEM_MOVEABLE`	Memory is moveable
`LMEM_NOCOMPACT`	Memory is not compacted or discarded to meet the memory requirements
`LMEM_ZEROINT`	Any additional memory allocated to the block is initialized to zero

Return Value The handle to the reallocated local memory is returned when successful. `NULL` is returned when unsuccessful.

Function Category Memory Management

Related Functions `LocalAlloc`, `LocalFree`, `LocalLock`

LocalShrink

Syntax `UINT LocalShrink(hloc, cbNewSize)`

Parameter	*Type*	*Description*
`hloc`	`HLOCAL`	Segment that contains the local heap

Parameter	Type	Description
cbNewSize	UINT	Number of bytes in the heap after it has been sized

Description The `LocalShrink` function shrinks the local heap contained in the segment specified in `hloc`. `cbNewSize` specifies the size of the local heap after it has been sized.

Return Value The final size of the heap is returned.

Function Category Memory Management

Related Functions `GlobalSize`, `LocalReAlloc`, `LocalSize`

LocalSize

Syntax `UINT LocalSize(hloc)`

Parameter	Type	Description
hloc	HLOCAL	Local memory block handle

Description The `LocalSize` function gets the number of bytes in the local memory block specified in `hloc`.

Return Value The number of bytes in the local memory block is returned when successful. Zero is returned when unsuccessful.

Function Category Memory Management

Related Functions `LocalCompact`, `LocalFlags`

LocalUnlock

Syntax `BOOL LocalUnlock(hloc)`

Parameter	Type	Description
hloc	HLOCAL	Local memory block to unlock

Description The `LocalUnlock` function decrements the reference count for the local memory block in `hloc` and unlocks the memory block.

Return Value Zero is returned if the block's reference count is decremented to zero. A nonzero value is returned if the resulting reference count is not zero.

Function Category Memory Management

Related Functions `GlobalUnLock`, `LocalLock`

LockData

Syntax `HANDLE LockData(Dummy)`

Parameter	*Type*	*Description*
`Dummy`	`int`	Should be set to zero and is not used

Description The `LockData` macro locks the current data segment in memory.

Return Value The handle to the locked data segment is returned when successful. `NULL` is returned when unsuccessful.

Function Category Memory Management

Related Functions `LockSegment`

LockInput

Syntax `BOOL LockInput(hReserved, hwndInput, fLock)`

Parameter	*Type*	*Description*
`hReserved`	`HANDLE`	Reserved; set to `NULL`
`hwndInput`	`HWND`	Window to retrieve all input; set to `NULL` when `fLock` is `FALSE`
`fLock`	`BOOL`	Flag to indicate whether to lock or unlock input

Description The `LockInput` function either locks or unlocks input. When `fLock` is `TRUE`, all input to all tasks except the current task is locked and the window specified in `hwndInput` is made system modal (receives all input). When `fLock` is `FALSE`, input is unlocked and the system is restored to its normal, unlocked state.

Return Value A nonzero value is returned when successful. Zero is returned when unsuccessful.

Function Category Debugging

Related Functions `DirectedYield`

LockResource

Syntax `void FAR* LockResource(hglb)`

Parameter	*Type*	*Description*
`hglb`	`HGLOBAL`	Resource handle

Description The `LockResource` function locks the resource specified in `hglb` to its absolute memory address and increments the lock count of the resource.

Return Value The pointer to the first byte of the resource is returned when successful. `NULL` is returned when unsuccessful.

Function Category Resource Management

Related Functions `FreeResource`, `UnlockResource`

LockSegment

Syntax `HGLOBAL LockSegment(uSegment)`

Parameter	*Type*	*Description*
`uSegment`	`UINT`	Segment address of segment to lock

Description The `LockSegment` function locks the segment with the segment address specified in `uSegment`. The segment lock count is incremented.

Return Value The handle to the data segment is returned when successful. `NULL` is returned when unsuccessful.

Function Category Memory Management, Segment

Related Functions `UnlockSegment`

_lopen

Syntax `HFILE _lopen(lpszPathName, fnOpenMode)`

Parameter	*Type*	*Description*
`lpszPathName`	`LPCSTR`	Pointer to a null-terminated string containing the name of the file to open; the string must contain characters from the ANSI character set
`fnOpenMode`	`int`	Indicates the accessibility of the file

Description The `_lopen` function opens a file with the name specified in `lpszPathName`. `fnOpenMode` specifies the accessibility of the file. `fnOpenMode` is a combination of one access mode value and one optional share mode value. The access mode and share mode values follow:

Access Mode

Value	*Meaning*
`READ`	Read only
`READ_WRITE`	Read and write
`WRITE`	Write only

Share Mode

Value	*Meaning*
`OF_SHARE_COMPAT`	Open file with compatibility mode
`OF_SHARE_DENY_NONE`	Open file without denying other processes read or write access
`OF_SHARE_DENY_READ`	Open file and deny other processes read access
`OF_SHARE_DENY_WRITE`	Open file and deny other processes write access
`OF_SHARE_EXCLUSIVE`	Open file with exclusive mode and deny other processes read and write access
`OF_WRITE`	Write only

Return Value The DOS file handle is returned when successful. `HFILE_ERROR` is returned when unsuccessful.

Function Category File I/O

Related Functions `_lclose`, `_lread`, `_lwrite`

LOWORD

Syntax `WORD LOWORD(dwVal)`

Parameter	*Type*	*Description*
`dwVal`	`DWORD`	Value to be converted

Description The `LOWORD` macro returns the low-order word of the value specified in `dwVal`.

Return Value The low-order word is returned.

Function Category Windows Macros

Related Functions `HIWORD`

LockWindowUpdate

Syntax `BOOL LockWindowUpdate(hwndLock)`

Parameter	*Type*	*Description*
`hwndLock`	`HWND`	Window. If `hwndLock` is `NULL`, a locked window is enabled.

Description The `LockWindowUpdate` function either enables or disables drawing in the window specified in `hwndLock`. Windows will only allow one window to be locked at any one time.

Return Value A nonzero value is returned when successful. Zero is returned when unsuccessful.

Function Category Painting

Related Functions `UpdateWindow`

LPtoDP

Syntax `BOOL LPtoDP(hdc, lppt, cPoints)`

Parameter	*Type*	*Description*
`hdc`	`HDC`	Device context
`lppt`	`POINT FAR*`	Points to an array of points defined using the `POINT` data structure
`cPoints`	`int`	Number of points in `lppt`

Description The `LPtoDP` function converts each point defined in the array pointed to by `lppt` from logical points to device points. Each point in the array specified by `lppt` is defined with a data structure of type `POINT`. The `POINT` data structure follows.

```
typedef struct tagPOINT {
     int x;
     int y;
} POINT;
```

in which

x specifies the horizontal coordinate of the point

y specifies the vertical coordinate of the point.

Return Value TRUE is returned if all the points are converted. FALSE is returned when unsuccessful.

Function Category Coordinate

Related Functions DPtoLP

_lread

Syntax `UINT _lread(hFile, hpvBuffer, cbBuffer)`

Parameter	*Type*	*Description*
hFile	HFILE	DOS file handle of file to read
hpvBuffer	void _huge*	Pointer to buffer to receive the data read from the file
cbBuffer	UINT	Number of bytes to read from the file

Description The _lread function reads data from the file associated with the file handle in hFile. The data read from the file is placed in the buffer pointed to by hpvBuffer. cbBuffer specifies the number of bytes to read from the file.

Return Value The number of bytes read from the file is returned when successful. HFILE_ERROR is returned when unsuccessful.

Function Category File I/O

Related Functions _lcreat, _lopen, _lwrite

lstrcat

Syntax `LPSTR lstrcat(lpszString1, lpszString2)`

Parameter	Type	Description
lpszString1	LPSTR	Pointer to byte array containing a null-terminated string
lpszString2	LPCSTR	Pointer to null-terminated string to be appended to lpszString1

Description The lstrcat function appends the string specified in lpszString2 to the string specified in lpszString1 and returns the pointer to the resulting string.

Return Value The pointer to the resulting string in lpszString1 is returned.

Function Category String Manipulation

Related Functions lstrcmp, lstrcpy, lstrlen

lstrcmp

Syntax `int lstrcmp(lpszString1, lpszString2)`

Parameter	Type	Description
lpszString1	LPCSTR	Pointer to a null-terminated string
lpszString2	LPCSTR	Pointer to a null-terminated string

Description The lstrcmp function performs a lexicographic comparison of the two strings specified in lpszString1 and lpszString2. The comparison is case sensitive.

Return Value A value that is less than zero is returned when lpszString1 is less than lpszString2. Zero is returned when the strings are identical. A value that is greater than zero is returned when lpszString1 is greater than lpszString2.

Function Category String Manipulation

Related Functions lstrcmpi, lstrcpy

lstrcmpi

Syntax `int lstrcmpi(lpszString1, lpszString2)`

Parameter	*Type*	*Description*
lpszString1	LPCSTR	Pointer to a null-terminated string
lpszString2	LPCSTR	Pointer to a null-terminated string

Description The `lstrcmpi` function performs a lexicographic comparison of the two strings specified in `lpszString1` and `lpszString2`. The comparison is not case sensitive.

Return Value A value that is less than zero is returned when `lpszString1` is less than `lpszString2`. Zero is returned when the strings are identical. A value that is greater than zero is returned when `lpszString1` is greater than `lpszString2`.

Function Category String Manipulation

Related Functions `lstrcmp`, `lstrcpy`

lstrcpy

Syntax `LPSTR lstrcpy(lpszString1, lpszString2)`

Parameter	*Type*	*Description*
lpszString1	LPSTR	Pointer to buffer to receive `lpszString2`
lpszString2	LPCSTR	Pointer to null-terminated string to copy to `lpszString1`

Description The `lstrcpy` function copies the string pointed to by `lpszString2` to the buffer pointed to by `lpszString1`.

Return Value The pointer to `lpszString1` is returned when successful. `NULL` is returned when unsuccessful.

Function Category String Manipulation

Related Functions `lstrcat`, `lpstrcmp`, `lstrlen`

lstrlen

Syntax `int lstrlen(lpszString)`

Parameter	*Type*	*Description*
`lpszString`	`LPCSTR`	Pointer to null-terminated string

Description The `lstrlen` function returns the number of bytes in the string pointed to by `lpszString`. The null character is not included in the returned count.

Return Value The number of bytes in the string is returned.

Function Category String Manipulation

Related Functions `lstrcat`, `lstrcmp`, `lstrcpy`

_lwrite

Syntax `UINT _lwrite(hf, hpvBuffer, cbBuffer)`

Parameter	*Type*	*Description*
`hf`	`HFILE`	DOS file handle of file to write to
`hpvBuffer`	`const void _huge*`	Pointer to the buffer containing the data to write to the file
`cbBuffer`	`UINT`	Number of bytes to write to the file

Description The `_lwrite` function writes the data in the buffer pointed to by `hpvBuffer` to the file specified by the DOS file handle in `hf`. `cbBuffer` specifies the number of bytes to write to the file.

Return Value The number of bytes written to the file is returned when successful. `HFILE_ERROR` is returned when unsuccessful.

Function Category File I/O

Related Functions `_lcreat`, `_lopen`, `_lread`

LZClose

Syntax `VOID LZClose(hFile)`

Parameter	*Type*	*Description*
`hFile`	`int`	Source file identifier

Description The `LZClose` function closes the file specified in `hFile`. The specified file should have been opened using `LZOpenFile` or `OpenFile`.

Return Value There is no return value.

Function Category Lempel-Ziv Expansion

Related Functions `LZOpenFile`

LZCopy

Syntax `LONG LZCopy(hfSource, hfDest)`

Parameter	*Type*	*Description*
`hfSource`	`int`	Source file handle
`hfDest`	`int`	Destination file handle

Description The `LZCopy` function copies the source file specified in `hfSource` to the destination file specified in `hfDest`. If the source file was compressed using the COMPRESS.EXE utility, the destination file is decompressed. If the source file was not compressed, the destination file is an exact copy of the source file.

Return Value When successful, the size of the destination file is returned. When unsuccessful, one of the following error values is returned:

Value	*Meaning*
LZERROR_BADINHANDLE	hfSource is invalid
LZERROR_BADOUTHANDLE	hfDest is invalid
LZERROR_GLOBALLOC	Insufficient memory to create buffers required for function
LZERROR_GLOBLOCK	Internal data structure handle is invalid
LZERROR_READ	File format of source file is invalid
LZERROR_UNKNOWNALG	Source file was compressed with an unknown compression algorithm
LZERROR_WRITE	Insufficient space for output file

Function Category Lempel-Ziv Expansion

Related Functions CopyLZFile, LZClose, LZOpen

LZDone

Syntax `VOID LZDone(void)`

Parameter	*Type*	*Description*
None		

Description The LZDone function frees all buffers allocated by the LZStart function. LZStart and LZDone should be used when copying multiple files with the CopyLZFile function.

Return Value There is no return value.

Function Category Lempel-Ziv Expansion

Related Functions CopyLZFile, LZStart

LZInit

Syntax `int LZInit(hfSource)`

Parameter	*Type*	*Description*
`hfSource`	`int`	Source file handle

Description The `LZInit` function allocates memory and creates internal data structures that are necessary to decompress files.

Return Value When successful, the file handle of the decompressed file is returned. If the file is not compressed, the original file handle is returned. When unsuccessful, one of the following error values is returned:

Value	*Meaning*
`LZERROR_BADINHANDLE`	`hfSource` is invalid
`LZERROR_GLOBALLOC`	Insufficient memory for the required internal data structures
`LZERROR_GLOBLOCK`	Handle for file is invalid
`LZERROR_READ`	File format of source is invalid
`LZERROR_UNKNOWNALG`	File was compressed with an unknown compression algorithm

Function Category Lempel-Ziv Expansion

Related Functions `LZOpenFile`, `LZStart`

LZOpenFile

Syntax `int LZOpenFile(lpFileName, lpReOpenBuf, wStyle)`

Parameter	*Type*	*Description*
`lpFileName`	`LPSTR`	Pointer to string that contains the name of the file to open
`lpReOpenBuf`	`LPOFSTRUCT`	Pointer to `OFSTRUCT` data structure that receives file information

Parameter	*Type*	*Description*
wStyle	WORD	Combination of flags to indicate the required action

Description The LZOpenFile function can be used for several file operations including creating a file, opening a file, reopening a file, and deleting a file. The file operation is performed on the file with the filename specified in lpFileName. wStyle is a combination of one or more of the following flags and specifies the file operation that the function is to perform:

Value	*Meaning*
OF_CANCEL	Cancel button is added to OF_PROMPT dialog box
OF_CREATE	New file is created; any existing file with the same name is truncated to zero
OF_DELETE	File is deleted
OF_EXIST	Opens and closes to file to determine whether it exists
OF_PARSE	OFSTRUCT data structure is filled; no other action is taken
OF_PROMPT	Dialog box is displayed if the specified file does not exist
OF_READ	File opened for reading only
OF_READWRITE	File opened for reading and writing
OF_REOPEN	File opened using re-open information
OF_SHARE_DENY_NONE	File opened without denying read and write access by other processes
OF_SHARE_DENY_READ	File opened; other processes denied read access
OF_SHARE_DENY_WRITE	File opened; other processes denied write access
OF_SHARE_EXCLUSIVE	File opened; other processes denied both read and write access
OF_WRITE	File opened for writing only

lpReOpenBuf points to a data structure of type OFSTRUCT that receives information on a file when it is first opened. Subsequent calls to LZOpenFile can then refer to the open file. The OFSTRUCT data structure follows.

```
typedef struct tagOFSTRUCT {
     BYTE cBytes;
     BYTE fFixedDisk;
     WORD nErrCode;
     BYTE reserved[4];
     BYTE szPathName[128];
} OFSTRUCT;
```

in which

`cBytes` is the number of bytes in the data structure

`fFixedDisk` is nonzero when the file is on a fixed disk

`nErrCode` is the DOS error code returned if the function fails

`reserved[4]` is reserved

`szPathName[128]` is the pathname of the file and consists of OEM characters.

Return Value The handle of the file is returned when successful. When unsuccessful, –1 is returned.

Function Category Lempel-Ziv Expansion

Related Functions `LZClose`, `LZInit`, `LZRead`

LZRead

Syntax `LONG LZRead(hFile, lpBuffer, nCount)`

Parameter	*Type*	*Description*
`hFile`	`int`	Source file handle
`lpBuffer`	`LPSTR`	Pointer to buffer that will receive the read data
`nCount`	`int`	Number of bytes to read

Description The `LZRead` function reads from the file specified in `hFile`. The data read from the file is placed in the buffer pointed to by `lpBuffer`. `nCount` specifies the maximum number of bytes to read from the file.

Return Value The number of bytes read is returned when successful. A negative value representing one of the following error values is returned when unsuccessful.

Value	*Meaning*
LZERROR_BADINHANDLE	Source file handle is invalid
LZERROR_BADVALUE	nCount is negative
LZERROR_GLOBLOCK	Handle for required initialization data is invalid
LZERROR_READ	File format of source is invalid
LZERROR_UNKNOWNALG	File was compressed with an unknown compression algorithm

Function Category Lempel-Ziv Expansion

Related Functions LZClose, LZOpenFile

LZSeek

Syntax `LONG LZSeek(hFile, lOffset, iOrigin)`

Parameter	*Type*	*Description*
hFile	int	Source file handle
lOffset	long	Offset, in bytes, for file pointer
iOrigin	int	Starting position of pointer: 0 to offset from beginning of file 1 to offset from current position 2 to offset from end of file

Description The LZSeek function positions the file pointer. iOrigin and lOffset define the new position of the file pointer for the file specified in hFile.

Return Value The offset from the beginning of the file to the new file pointer position is returned when successful. When unsuccessful, a negative value representing one of the following errors is returned:

Value	*Meaning*
LZERROR_BADINHANDLE	Source file handle is invalid
LZERROR_BADVALUE	One of the arguments is invalid
LZERROR_GLOBLOCK	Handle to initialization data is invalid

Function Category Lempel-Ziv Expansion

Related Functions LZClose, LZOpenFile

LZStart

Syntax `int LZStart(void)`

Parameter	*Type*	*Description*
None		

Description The LZStart function allocates the buffers required to copy multiple files using the CopyLZFile function. The LZDone function should be called to deallocate the allocated buffers when the application has finished copying files.

Return Value TRUE is returned when successful. LZERROR_GLOBALLOC is returned when unsuccessful.

Function Category Lempel-Ziv Expansion

Related Functions CopyLZFile, LZDone

MAKEINTATOM

Syntax `LPSTR MAKEINTATOM(wInteger)`

Parameter	*Type*	*Description*
wInteger	WORD	Value of the atom's character string

Description The MAKEINTATOM function creates an integer atom representing a character string of decimal digits.

Return Value The pointer to the created atom is returned.

Function Category Windows Macros

Related Functions `MAKEINTRESOURCE`

MAKEINTRESOURCE

Syntax `LPSTR MAKEINTRESOURCE(idResource)`

Parameter	*Type*	*Description*
`idResource`	`int`	Value to convert

Description The `MAKEINTRESOURCE` function converts the value specified in `idResource` to a long pointer to a string. The high-order word of the long pointer is set to zero.

Return Value The pointer to the string is returned. `idResource` is in the low word; zero is in the high word.

Function Category Windows Macros

Related Functions `MAKEINTATOM`

MAKELONG

Syntax `DWORD MAKELONG(wLow, wHigh)`

Parameter	*Type*	*Description*
`wLow`	`WORD`	Low-order word
`wHigh`	`WORD`	High-order word

Description The `MAKELONG` function returns an unsigned long integer created from `wLow` and `wHigh`.

Return Value The created unsigned long integer is returned.

Function Category Windows Macros

Related Functions LOWORD, HIWORD

MAKEPOINT

Syntax `POINT MAKEPOINT(lval)`

Parameter	*Type*	*Description*
lval	DWORD	Coordinates of a point

Description The MAKEPOINT macro fills a POINT data structure using the x and y coordinates contained in lval. The POINT data structure follows.

```
typedef struct tagPOINT {
     int x;
     int y;
} POINT;
```

in which

x is the horizontal coordinate of the point

y is the vertical coordinate of the point.

Return Value The return value specifies the POINT data structure.

Function Category Windows Macros

Related Functions MAKELONG

MakeProcInstance

Syntax `FARPROC MakeProcInstance(lpProc, hinst)`

Parameter	*Type*	*Description*
lpProc	FARPROC	Procedure instance address
hinst	HINSTANCE	Instance associated with the data segment

Description The MakeProcInstance function creates a procedure instance address and binds the data segment for the instance in hinst to the function specified in lpProc.

Return Value The address to the prolog code for the function specified in `lpProc` is returned when successful. `NULL` is returned when unsuccessful.

Function Category Module Management

Related Functions `FreeProcInstance`, `GetProcAddress`

MapDialogRect

Syntax `void MapDialogRect(hwndDlg, lprc)`

Parameter	*Type*	*Description*
`hwndDlg`	`HWND`	Dialog box
`lprc`	`RECT FAR*`	Pointer to `RECT` structure containing coordinates to convert

Description The `MapDialogRect` function converts dialog box units to screen units. `lprc` points to the structure, of type `RECT`, which contains the dialog box units to convert. The `RECT` structure follows this paragraph. `hwndDlg` specifies the dialog box for which unit conversion will be accomplished. Dialog box units are based on the average width and height of the system font. The horizontal dialog box unit is 1/4 the dialog base width unit. The vertical dialog box unit is 1/8 the dialog base height unit. The dialog box units pointed to by `lprc` are replaced with the converted screen units.

```
typedef struct tagRECT {
     int left;
     int top;
     int right;
     int bottom;
} RECT;
```

in which

`left` is the x coordinate of the upper-left corner

`top` is the y coordinate of the upper-left corner

`right` is the x coordinate of the lower-right corner

`bottom` is the y coordinate of the lower-right corner.

Return Value There is no return value.

Function Category Dialog Box

Related Functions `DialogBox`, `GetDialogBaseUnits`

MapVirtualKey

Syntax `UINT MapVirtualKey(uKeyCode, fuMapType)`

Parameter	*Type*	*Description*
`uKeyCode`	`UINT`	Virtual key or scan code
`fuMapType`	`UINT`	Type of mapping to perform

Description The `MapVirtualKey` function returns the scan code, virtual key code, or ASCII value for the virtual key code or scan code specified in `uKeyCode`. When `fuMapType` is set to 0, `uKeyCode` must be a virtual key code and the corresponding scan code is returned. When `fuMapType` is 1, `uKeyCode` must be a scan code and the corresponding virtual key code is returned. When `fuMapType` is 2, `uKeyCode` must be a virtual key code and the corresponding unshifted ASCII value is returned.

Return Value The scan code, virtual key code, or ASCII value is returned as specified by `fuMapType` and described above in Description.

Function Category Hardware

Related Functions `VkKeyScan`

MapWindowPoints

Syntax `void MapWindowPoints(hwndFrom, hwndTo, lppt, cPoints)`

Parameter	*Type*	*Description*
`hwndFrom`	`HWND`	Window from which points are converted
`hwndTo`	`HWND`	Window to which points are converted

Parameter	Type	Description
lppt	POINT FAR*	Pointer to POINT data structures that contain the points
cPoints	UINT	Number of POINT data structures in lppt

Description The MapWindowPoints function converts the set of coordinate points from the coordinate space for hwndFrom to the coordinate space for hwndTo.

Return Value There is no return value.

Function Category Coordinate

Related Functions ClientToScreen, ScreenToClient

max

Syntax `int max(value1, value2)`

Parameter	Type	Description
value1	n/a	First value
value2	n/a	Second value

Description The max macro returns the greater of the values in value1 and value2. value1 and value2 can be any ordered type.

Return Value The greater of value1 and value2 is returned.

Function Category Windows Macros

Related Functions min

MemManInfo

Syntax `BOOL MemManInfo(mmiInfo)`

Parameter	*Type*	*Description*
mmiInfo	MEMMANINFO FAR*	Pointer to MEMMANINFO data structure where memory manager information will be placed

Description The MemManInfo function retrieves information on the memory manager and copies the retrieved information into the data structure of type MEMMANINFO pointed to by mmiInfo. The MEMMANINFO data structure follows.

```
#include <toolhelp.h>
typedef struct tagMEMMANINFO
     {
     DWORD dwSize;
     DWORD dwLargestFreeBlock;
     DWORD dwMaxPagesAvailable;
     DWORD dwMaxPagesLockable;
     DWORD dwTotalLinearSpace;
     DWORD dwTotalUnlockedPages;
     DWORD dwFreePages;
     DWORD dwTotalPages;
     DWORD dwFreeLinearSpace;
     DWORD dwSwapFilePages;
     WORD wPageSize;
} MEMMANINFO;
```

in which

`dwSize` is the number of bytes in the data structure

`dwLargestFreeBlock` is the number of bytes in the largest free block of contiguous linear memory

`dwMaxPagesAvailable` is the maximum number of available pages

`dwMaxPagesLockable` is the maximum number of pages that can be allocated and locked

`dwTotalLinearSpace` is the number of pages of total linear address space

`dwTotalUnlockedPages` is the number of unlocked pages

`dwFreePages` is the number of pages not currently being used `dwTotalPages` is the total number of pages that the virtual memory manager controls (free, locked, and unlocked)

`dwFreeLinearSpace` is the number of pages of free memory in the linear address space

`dwSwapFilePages` is the number of pages in the system swap file

`wPageSize` is the number of bytes in a page.

Return Value `TRUE` is returned when successful. `FALSE` is returned when unsuccessful.

Function Category Toolhelp

Related Functions `GlobalInfo`, `LocalInfo`

MemoryRead

Syntax `DWORD MemoryRead(wSel, dwOffset, lpszBuffer, dwcb)`

Parameter	*Type*	*Description*
`wSel`	`WORD`	Handle or selector of global memory segment to read from
`dwOffset`	`DWORD`	Offset in segment where reading is to start
`lpszBuffer`	`LPSTR`	Pointer to buffer where data will be copied
`dwcb`	`DWORD`	Number of bytes to copy

Description The `MemoryRead` function copies data from the global heap segment specified in `wSel` to the buffer pointed to by `lpszBuffer`. `dwOffset` specifies the segment offset where copying will start. `dwcb` specifies the number of bytes to copy to the buffer.

Return Value The number of characters copied to the buffer is returned when successful. When unsuccessful, zero is returned.

Function Category Toolhelp

Related Functions `MemoryWrite`

MemoryWrite

Syntax `DWORD MemoryWrite(wSel, dwOffset, lpszBuffer, dwcb)`

Parameter	*Type*	*Description*
`wSel`	`WORD`	Handle or selector of global memory segment to write to
`dwOffset`	`DWORD`	Offset in segment where writing is to start
`lpszBuffer`	`LPSTR`	Pointer to buffer from which data will be copied
`dwcb`	`DWORD`	Number of bytes to copy

Description The `MemoryWrite` function copies data from the buffer pointed to by `lpszBuffer` to the global heap segment specified in `wSel`. `dwOffset` specifies the offset in the segment where the data will be copied. `dwcb` specifies the number of bytes to copy from the buffer.

Return Value The number of characters copied is returned when successful. Zero is returned when unsuccessful.

Function Category Toolhelp

Related Functions `MemoryRead`

MessageBeep

Syntax `void MessageBeep(uAlert)`

Parameter	*Type*	*Description*
`uAlert`	`UINT`	Alert level

Description The `MessageBeep` function plays a uniform sound. The sound for each specified alert level is defined in the [sounds] section of WIN.INI. `uAlert` specifies the alert level. The values for `uAlert` follow.

Value	*Meaning*
`MB_OK`	Sound identified by `SystemDefault` is played

Value	*Meaning*
MB_ICONASTERISK	Sound identified by SystemAsterisk is played
MB_ICONEXCLAMATION	Sound identified by SystemExclamation is played
MB_ICONHAND	Sound identified by SystemHand is played
MB_ICONQUESTION	Sound identified by SystemQuestion is played
–1	Standard beep is played

Return Value There is no return value.

Function Category Error

Related Functions `MessageBox`

MessageBox

Syntax `int MessageBox(hwndParent, lpszText, lpszTitle, fuStyle)`

Parameter	*Type*	*Description*
hwndParent	HWND	Window that owns the message box
lpszText	LPCSTR	Message to be displayed
lpszTitle	LPCSTR	Caption for dialog box
fuStyle	UINT	Contents of dialog box

Description The `MessageBox` function creates a window containing a message and caption supplied by the application. The window also contains a combination of icons and buttons. `hwndParent` specifies the owner of this message box. `lpszText` points to the string that contains the string to display. `lpszTitle` points to the string that is used for the dialog box caption. `fuStyle` identifies the contents of the dialog box. `fuStyle` is set to any combination of the following constants. Constants can be combined using the bitwise OR operator.

Message Box Type	*Meaning*
MB_ABORTRETRYIGNORE	Message box contains three buttons — abort, retry, and ignore
MB_APPLMODAL	User must respond to message box before being allowed to continue work in the parent window
MB_DEFBUTTON1	Sets the first button to the default
MB_DEFBUTTON2	Sets the second button to the default
MB_DEFBUTTON3	Sets the third button to the default
MB_ICONASTERISK	Displays an icon showing an i inside a circle
MB_ICONEXCLAMATION	Displays the exclamation point icon
MB_ICONHAND	Displays a stop sign icon
MB_ICONINFORMATION	Displays an icon showing an i inside a circle
MB_ICONQUESTION	Displays a question mark icon
MB_ICONSTOP	Displays a stop sign icon
MB_OK	Displays only one button — the OK button
MB_OKCANCEL	Displays two buttons — OK and Cancel
MB_RETRYCANCEL	Displays two buttons — Retry and Cancel
MB_SYSTEMMODAL	Applications are halted until the user responds to the message box
MB_TASKMODAL	User must respond to the message box before continuing work in the parent window
MB_YESNO	Displays two buttons — Yes and No
MB_YESNOCANCEL	Displays three buttons — Yes, No, and Cancel

Return Value Zero is returned if the dialog box was not created. If the dialog box was created, one of the following is returned:

Return Value	*Meaning*
IDABORT	Abort button selected
IDCANCEL	Cancel button selected
IDIGNORE	Ignore button selected
IDNO	No button selected
IDOK	OK button selected

Return Value	*Meaning*
IDRETRY	Retry button selected
IDYES	Yes button selected

Function Category Error

Related Functions MessageBeep

min

Syntax `int min(value1, value2)`

Parameter	*Type*	*Description*
value1	n/a	First value
value2	n/a	Second value

Description The `min` macro returns the lesser of the values in `value1` and `value2`. `value1` and `value2` can be any ordered type.

Return Value The lesser of `value1` and `value2` is returned.

Function Category Windows Macros

Related Functions max

ModifyMenu

Syntax

```
BOOL ModifyMenu(hmenu, idItem, fuFlags, idNewItem,
                lpNewItem)
```

Parameter	*Type*	*Description*
hmenu	HMENU	Menu to be modified
idItem	UINT	Menu item to modify. When `fuFlags` contains `MF_BYPOSITION`, `idItem` specifies the menu item position. When `fuFlags`

Parameter	Type	Description
		contains MF_BYCOMMAND, idItem specifies the command ID of the menu item.
fuFlags	UINT	Determines how idItem is interpreted and is a combination of items
idNewItem	UINT	When fuFlags contains MF_POPUP, idNewItem specifies the menu handle of the pop-up menu. Otherwise, it specifies the command ID of the modified menu item.
lpNewItem	LPCSTR	Determines the contents of the modified menu item. When fuFlags contains MF_STRING, lpNewItem points to a string. When fuFlags contains MF_BITMAP, lpNewItem contains the handle of a bitmap in its low-order word. When fuFlags contains MF_OWNERDRAW, lpNewItem contains a 32-bit value supplied by the application.

Description The ModifyMenu function modifies an item from the menu specified in hmenu. idItem specifies the menu item to modify. fuFlags specifies the state of the specified menu item. fuFlags is a combination of one or more of the values from the list following this paragraph. idNewItem and lpNewItem contain information on the modified menu item.

Value	Meaning
MF_BITMAP	Uses a bitmap as the item. The handle of the bitmap is in the low-order word of lpNewItem. This flag should not be used with MF_STRING, MF_OWNERDRAW, or MF_SEPARATOR.
MF_BYCOMMAND	idItem contains a menu item command ID. This flag should not be used with MF_BYPOSITION

Value	*Meaning*
MF_BYPOSITION	idItem contains a menu item position. This flag should not be used with MF_BYCOMMAND.
MF_CHECKED	Puts a checkmark next to the item. This flag should not be used with MF_UNCHECKED.
MF_DISABLED	Disables, but does not gray, the menu item. This flag should not be used with MF_ENABLED or MF_GRAYED.
MF_ENABLED	Enables the menu item. This flag should not be used with MF_DISABLED or MF_GRAYED.
MF_GRAYED	Disables and grays the menu item. This flag should not be used with MF_DISABLED or MF_ENABLED.
MF_MENUBARBREAK	Puts menu items on a new line. For pop-up menus, puts the new item in a new column and separates the columns with a vertical line. This flag should not be used with MF_MENUBREAK.
MF_MENUBREAK	Puts menu items on a new line. For pop-up menus, puts the new item in a new column but does not separate the columns with a vertical line. This flag should not be used with MF_MENUBARBREAK.
MF_OWNERDRAW	Item is an owner-draw item. This flag should not be used with MF_BITMAP or MF_STRING.
MF_POPUP	Item has a pop-up menu associated with it. idNewItem specifies the handle of the pop-up window.
MF_SEPARATOR	Creates a horizontal line in the menu in a pop-up menu.
MF_STRING	Menu item is a character string. This flag should not be used with MF_BITMAP or MF_OWNERDRAW.
MF_UNCHECKED	No checkmark is placed by the menu item. This flag should not be used with MF_CHECKED.

Return Value A nonzero value is returned when successful. Zero is returned when unsuccessful.

Function Category Menu

Related Functions AppendMenu, CreateMenu, InsertMenu, SetMenu

ModuleFindHandle

Syntax `HANDLE ModuleFindHandle(meModule, hModule)`

Parameter	*Type*	*Description*
meModule	MODULEENTRY FAR*	Pointer to MODULEENTRY data structure where module information is copied
hModule	HANDLE	Module

Description The ModuleFindHandle function retrieves information on the module specified in hModule and copies the retrieved information into the data structure of type MODULEENTRY pointed to by meModule. The MODULEENTRY data structure follows.

```
#include <toolhelp.h>
typedef struct tagMODULEENTRY
     {
     DWORD dwSize;
     char szModule[MAX_MODULE_NAME + 1];
     HANDLE hModule;
     WORD wcUsage;
     char szExePath[MAX_PATH + 1];
     WORD wNext;
} MODULEENTRY;
```

in which

dwSize is the size of the data structure in bytes

szModule is the string that contains the name of the module

hModule is the handle of the module

wcUsage is the reference count of the module

szExePath is the string that specifies the path to the executable file for the module

wNext is the next module in the module list; reserved for use by Windows.

Return Value The handle to the module is returned when successful. NULL is returned when unsuccessful.

Function Category Toolhelp

Related Functions `ModuleFindName`, `ModuleFirst`, `ModuleNext`

ModuleFindName

Syntax `HANDLE ModuleFindName(meModule, lpszName)`

Parameter	*Type*	*Description*
`meModule`	`MODULEENTRY FAR*`	Pointer to `MODULEENTRY` data structure to receive module information
`lpszName`	`LPSTR`	Module name

Description The `ModuleFindName` function retrieves information on the module specified in `lpszName` and copies the retrieved information to the data structure of type `MODULEENTRY` pointed to by `meModule`. The `MODULEENTRY` data structure follows.

```
#include <toolhelp.h>
typedef struct tagMODULEENTRY
     {
     DWORD dwSize;
     char szModule[MAX_MODULE_NAME + 1];
     HANDLE hModule;
     WORD wcUsage;
     char szExePath[MAX_PATH + 1];
     WORD wNext;
} MODULEENTRY;
```

in which

`dwSize` is the size of the data structure in bytes

`szModule` is the string that contains the name of the module

`hModule` is the handle of the module

`wcUsage` is the reference count of the module

`szExePath` is the string that specifies the path to the executable file for the module

`wNext` is the next module in the module list; reserved for use by Windows.

Return Value The handle to the module specified by lpszName is returned when successful. NULL is returned when unsuccessful.

Function Category Toolhelp

Related Functions ModuleFindHandle, ModuleFirst, ModuleNext

ModuleFirst

Syntax BOOL ModuleFirst(meModule)

Parameter	*Type*	*Description*
meModule	MODULEENTRY FAR*	Pointer to MODULEENTRY data structure where module information is copied

Description The ModuleFirst function retrieves information on the first module from the list of loaded modules and copies this retrieved information to the data structure of type MODULEENTRY pointed to by meModule. The MODULEENTRY data structure follows.

```
#include <toolhelp.h>
typedef struct tagMODULEENTRY
     {
     DWORD dwSize;
     char szModule[MAX_MODULE_NAME + 1];
     HANDLE hModule;
     WORD wcUsage;
     char szExePath[MAX_PATH + 1];
     WORD wNext;
} MODULEENTRY;
```

in which

dwSize is the size of the data structure in bytes

szModule is the string that contains the name of the module

hModule is the handle of the module

wcUsage is the reference count of the module

szExePath is the string that specifies the path to the executable for the module wNext is the next module in the module list; reserved for use by Windows.

Return Value TRUE is returned when successful. FALSE is returned when unsuccessful.

Function Category Toolhelp

Related Functions ModuleNext

ModuleNext

Syntax BOOL ModuleNext(meModule)

Parameter	*Type*	*Description*
meModule	MODULEENTRY FAR*	Pointer to MODULEENTRY data structure where module information is copied

Description The ModuleNext function retrieves information on the next module from the list of all loaded modules and places the retrieved information in the data structure of type MODULEENTRY pointed to by meModule. The MODULEENTRY data structure follows.

```
#include <toolhelp.h>
typedef struct tagMODULEENTRY
     {
     DWORD dwSize;
     char szModule[MAX_MODULE_NAME + 1];
     HANDLE hModule;
     WORD wcUsage;
     char szExePath[MAX_PATH + 1];
     WORD wNext;
} MODULEENTRY;
```

in which

dwSize is the size of the data structure in bytes

szModule is the string that contains the name of the module

hModule is the handle of the module

wcUsage is the reference count of the module

szExePath is the string that specifies the path to the executable for the module

wNext is the next module in the module list; reserved for use by Windows.

Return Value TRUE is returned when successful. FALSE is returned when unsuccessful.

Function Category Toolhelp

Related Functions ModuleFirst

MoveTo

Syntax `DWORD MoveTo(hdc, nXPos, nYPos)`

Parameter	*Type*	*Description*
hdc	HDC	Device context
nXPos	int	Logical x coordinate of point to move to
nYPos	int	Logical y coordinate of point to move to

Description The MoveTo function updates the current position to the point specified by (nXPos, nYPos). No drawing takes place as the current position is updated.

Return Value The low-order word of the return value contains the x coordinate of the previous position. The high-order word of the return value contains the y coordinate of the previous position.

Function Category Line Output

Related Functions LineTo

MoveToEx

Syntax `BOOL MoveToEx(hdc, nX, nY, lpPoint)`

Parameter	Type	Description
hdc	HDC	Device context
nX	int	Logical x coordinate of new position
nY	int	Logical y coordinate of new position
lpPoint	POINT FAR*	Pointer to POINT data structure where the previous current position is placed. If NULL, the previous position is not saved.

Description The MoveToEx function moves the current position to the location specified in (nX, nY). If lpPoint is not NULL, the previous current position is stored in the data structure pointed to by lpPoint.

Return Value TRUE is returned when successful. FALSE is returned when unsuccessful.

Function Category Line Output

Related Functions MoveTo

MoveWindow

Syntax

```
BOOL MoveWindow(hwnd, nLeft, nTop, nWidth, nHeight,
                fRepaint)
```

Parameter	Type	Description
hwnd	HWND	Pop-up or child window
nLeft	int	X coordinate of upper-left corner of window
nTop	int	Y coordinate of upper-left corner of window
nWidth	int	New width of window
nHeight	int	New height of window
fRepaint	BOOL	Specifies whether window is to be repainted

Description The `MoveWindow` function sizes the pop-up or child window specified in `hwnd`. `nLeft` and `nTop` specify the horizontal and vertical coordinates, respectively, of the upper-left corner of the specified window. `nLeft` and `nTop` are expressed in screen coordinates for pop-up windows and in client coordinates for child windows. `nWidth` and `nHeight` express the new width and height, respectively, of the window. `fRepaint` specifies whether the window will be repainted after moving. When `fRepaint` is `TRUE`, the window is repainted. The window is not repainted when `fRepaint` is set to `FALSE`. The `WM_SIZE` message is sent to the window in `hwnd`.

Return Value A nonzero value is returned when successful. Zero is returned when unsuccessful.

Function Category Display and Movement

Related Functions `BringWindowToTop`, `SetWindowPos`

MulDiv

Syntax `int MulDiv(nMultiplicand, nMultiplier, nDivisor)`

Parameter	*Type*	*Description*
`nMultiplicand`	`int`	Multiplied by `nMultiplier`
`nMultiplier`	`int`	Multiplied by `nMultiplicand`
`nDivisor`	`int`	Divide the result of `nMultiplicand` multiplied by `nMultiplier` by this number

Description The `MulDiv` function multiplies `nMultiplicand` and `nMultiplier`, divides the result of the multiplication by `nDivisor`, then returns the result of the division rounded to the nearest integer.

Return Value The resulting integer is returned when successful. –32,768 is returned when unsuccessful.

Function Category Utility

Related Functions `max`, `min`

NetBIOSCall

Syntax `extrn NetBIOSCall :far`

Description The `NetBIOSCall` function generates the `NETBIOS` interrupt 5CH. This function can be called only from an assembly-language routine and is not defined as a Windows include file. All appropriate registers must be set before the `NetBIOSCall` function is called.

Return Value There is no return value.

Function Category Operating System Interrupt

Related Functions `DOS3Call`

NotifyRegister

Syntax `BOOL NotifyRegister(hTask, lpfnCallback, wFlags)`

Parameter	*Type*	*Description*
hTask	HANDLE	Task associated with callback function; NULL indicates the current task is to be associated with the callback function
lpfnCallback	LPFNNOTIFYCALLBACK	Pointer to callback function
wFlags	WORD	Notifications the application will receive; set to NF_NORMAL for the application to receive default notifications; can be set to any combination of the following when NF_NORMAL is not specified:

Value	*Meaning*
NF_TASKSWITCH	Application will receive task switch notifications

Value	*Meaning*
NF_RIP	Application will receive RIP notifications
NF_DEBUGSTR	Application will receive debug string notifications

Description The `NotifyRegister` function defines the notification callback function for the task in `hTask`. The `MakeProcInstance` function is used to obtain the procedure instance address of the callback function. The callback function follows.

```
bool *LPFNNOTIFYCALLBACK(wID, dwData)
WORD wID;
DWORD dwData;
```

in which

`wID` is the type of notification and is selected from the following values:

Value	*Meaning*
NFY_UNKNOWN	Unknown notification
NFY_LOADSEG	`dwData` points to `NFYLOADSEG` structure
NFY_LOGERROR	`dwData` points to `NFYLOGERROR` structure
NFY_LOGPARAMERROR	`dwData` points to `NFYLOGPARAMERROR` structure
NFY_FREESEG	Low word of `dwData` is selector of segment to free
NFY_STARTDLL	`dwData` points to `NFYSTARTDLL` structure
NFY_STARTTASK	`dwData` is CS:IP of task's starting address
NFY_EXITTASK	Low byte of `dwData` contains program exit code
NFY_DELMODULE	Low word of `dwData` contains the handle of the module to free
NFY_RIP	`dwData` points to `NFYRIP` structure
NFY_TASKIN	Low word of `dwData` is handle of old task
NFY_TASKOUT	`dwData` is unused; callback function should perform `GetCurrentTask`
NFY_INCHAR	`dwData` is not used; the callback function should return the ASCII value
NFY_OUTSTR	`dwData` points to the string to display

`dwData` contains the data specified by `wID`.

The callback function returns `TRUE` when the callback handles the notification. `FALSE` is returned when the notification is passed to other callback functions.

Return Value `TRUE` is returned when successful. `FALSE` is returned when unsuccessful.

Function Category Toolhelp

Related Functions `InterruptRegister`, `NotifyUnRegister`

NotifyUnRegister

Syntax `BOOL NotifyUnRegister(hTask)`

Parameter	*Type*	*Description*
`hTask`	`HANDLE`	Task — if `NULL`, specifies the current task

Description The `NotifyUnRegister` function uninstalls the notification callback function associated with the task specified in `hTask`.

Return Value `TRUE` is returned when successful. `FALSE` is returned when unsuccessful.

Function Category Toolhelp

Related Functions `NotifyRegister`

OemKeyScan

Syntax `DWORD OemKeyScan(uOemChar)`

Parameter	*Type*	*Description*
`uOemChar`	`UINT`	ASCII value of OEM character

Description The `OemKeyScan` function maps OEM ASCII codes into OEM scan codes and shift states. `uOemChar` specifies the ASCII value of the OEM character to map. The return value of the function contains information on the scan code and shift state of the specified character.

Return Value The low-order word of the return value indicates the scan code of the OEM character. The high order word of the return value contains flags that indicate the shift state as follows:

Bit	*Meaning*
2	Ctrl pressed
1	Shift pressed

–1 is returned in both the high- and low-order words when the specified character is not defined in the OEM character tables.

Function Category Hardware

Related Functions `VkKeyScan`

OemToAnsi

Syntax `VOID OemToAnsi(hpszOemStr, hpszWindowsStr)`

Parameter	*Type*	*Description*
`hpszOemStr`	`const char _huge*`	Pointer to null-terminated string containing OEM characters
`hpszWindowsStr`	`char _huge*`	Pointer to string to receive the converted characters

Description The `OemToAnsi` function converts the OEM characters in the string pointed to by `hpszOemStr` to ANSI characters and copies the converted characters to the string pointed to by `hpszWindowsStr`. `hpszOemStr` and `hpszWindowsStr` can point to the same string.

Return Value There is no return value.

Function Category String Manipulation

Related Functions AnsiToOem, OemToAnsiBuff

OemToAnsiBuff

Syntax `void OemToAnsiBuff(lpszOemStr, lpszWindowsStr, cbOemStr)`

Parameter	*Type*	*Description*
lpszOemStr	LPCSTR	Pointer to buffer containing OEM characters
lpszWindowsStr	LPSTR	Pointer to the buffer to receive the converted characters
cbOemStr	UINT	Number of characters in lpszOemStr

Description The OemToAnsiBuff function converts the characters in the buffer pointed to by lpszOemStr to ANSI characters and copies the converted characters into the buffer pointed to by lpszWindowsStr. cbOemStr specifies the number of characters in the buffer pointed to by lpszOemStr. When cbOemStr is set to zero, the buffer length is assumed to be 65,536.

Return Value There is no return value.

Function Category String Manipulation

Related Functions AnsiToOemBuff, OemToAnsi

OffsetClipRgn

Syntax `int OffsetClipRgn(hdc, nXOffset, nYOffset)`

Parameter	*Type*	*Description*
hdc	HDC	Device context
nXOffset	int	Number of logical units to move horizontally

Parameter	Type	Description
nYOffset	int	Number of logical units to move vertically

Description The `OffsetClipRgn` function moves the clipping region for the device specified in `hdc` by the amounts specified in `nXOffset` and `nYOffset`. Positive values for `nXOffset` and `nYOffset` move the clipping region to the right and down, respectively. Negative values for `nXOffset` and `nYOffset` move the clipping region to the left and up, respectively.

Return Value One of the following values is returned to describe the clipping region:

Value	Meaning
COMPLEXREGION	Region has overlapping borders
ERROR	Device context is invalid
NULLREGION	Region is empty
SIMPLEREGION	Region has no overlapping borders

Function Category Clipping

Related Functions `SelectClipRgn`

OffsetRect

Syntax `void OffsetRect(lprc, x, y)`

Parameter	Type	Description
lprc	RECT FAR*	Pointer to RECT data structure containing coordinates of the rectangle
x	int	Amount to move rectangle horizontally
y	int	Amount to move rectangle vertically

Description The `OffsetRect` function moves the rectangle specified in `lprc` the amount specified in `x` and `y`. `x` specifies the amount to move in the horizontal direction. y specifies the amount to move in the vertical direction. Positive values of x and y move the rectangle right and down, respectively. Negative values of x and y move the rectangle left and up, respectively. The coordinates of the rectangle must not exceed 32,767 or be less than –32,768. lprc points to a data structure of type RECT. The RECT data structure follows.

```
typedef struct tagRECT {
     int left;
     int top;
     int right;
     int bottom;
} RECT;
```

in which

left is the x coordinate of the upper-left corner

top is the y coordinate of the upper-left corner

right is the x coordinate of the lower-right corner

bottom is the y coordinate of the lower-right corner.

Return Value There is no return value.

Function Category Rectangle

Related Functions InflateRect, OffsetRgn

OffsetRgn

Syntax int OffsetRgn(hrgn, nXOffset, nYOffset)

Parameter	*Type*	*Description*
hrgn	HRGN	Region to move
nXOffset	int	Amount to move in the horizontal direction
nYOffset	int	Amount to move in the vertical direction

Description The OffsetRgn function moves the region specified in hrgn the amounts specified in nXOffset and nYOffset.

Return Value The region's type is returned. One of the following values is returned:

Value	*Meaning*
COMPLEXREGION	New region has overlapping borders
ERROR	No region was created
NULLREGION	New region is empty
SIMPLEREGION	New region has no overlapping borders

Function Category Region

Related Functions `OffsetRect`

OffsetViewportOrg

Syntax `DWORD OffsetViewportOrg(hdc, nXOffset, nYOffset)`

Parameter	*Type*	*Description*
hdc	HDC	Device context
nXOffset	int	Offset in horizontal direction
nYOffset	int	Offset in vertical direction

Description The `OffsetViewportOrg` function moves the origin of the viewport the amount specified by `nXOffset` and `nYOffset`. The values in `nXOffset` and `nYOffset` are added to the current viewport origin coordinates resulting in the new viewport origin position. `nXOffset` and `nYOffset` are expressed in device units.

Return Value The low-order word of the return value contains the x coordinate of the previous viewport origin. The high-order word of the return value contains the y coordinate of the previous return value.

Function Category Mapping

Related Functions `GetViewportOrg`, `SetViewportOrg`

OffsetViewportOrgEx

Syntax `BOOL OffsetViewportOrgEx(hdc, nX, nY, lpPoint)`

Parameter	*Type*	*Description*
`hdc`	`HDC`	Device context
`nX`	`int`	Amount to add to x-coordinate (in device units)
`nY`	`int`	Amount to add to y-coordinate (in device units)
`lpPoint`	`POINT FAR*`	Pointer to `POINT` data structure where previous location is placed. If set to `NULL`, the previous location is not stored.

Description The `OffsetViewportOrgEx` function moves the origin of the viewport the amounts specified in `nX` and `nY`. If `lpPoint` is not `NULL`, the previous position of the origin is stored in the data structure pointed to by `lpPoint`.

Return Value `TRUE` is returned when successful. `FALSE` is returned when unsuccessful.

Function Category Mapping

Related Functions `OffsetViewportOrg`

OffsetWindowOrg

Syntax `DWORD OffsetWindowOrg(hdc, nXOffset, nYOffset)`

Parameter	*Type*	*Description*
`hdc`	`HDC`	Device context
`nXOffset`	`int`	Offset in horizontal direction
`nYOffset`	`int`	Offset in vertical direction

Description The `OffsetWindowOrg` function moves the origin for the window of the device context specified in `hdc`. `nXOffset` and `nYOffset` indicate the number of logical units that the origin will be moved. The values in `nXOffset` and `nYOffset` are added to the coordinates of the current window origin, resulting in the new origin.

Return Value The low-order word of the return value specifies the x coordinate of the previous window origin. The high-order word of the return value specifies the y coordinate of the previous window origin.

Function Category Mapping

Related Functions `GetWindowOrg`, `SetWindowOrg`

OffsetWindowOrgEx

Syntax `BOOL OffsetWindowOrgEx(hdc, nX, nY, lpPoint)`

Parameter	*Type*	*Description*
`hdc`	`HDC`	Device context
`nX`	`int`	Amount to add to x-coordinate (in logical units)
`nY`	`int`	Amount to add to y-coordinate (in logical units)
`lpPoint`	`POINT FAR*`	Pointer to `POINT` data structure where previous location is placed. If set to `NULL`, the previous location is not stored.

Description The `OffsetWindowOrgEx` function moves the origin of the window the amount specified by `nX` and `nY`. If `lpPoint` is not `NULL`, the previous position of the origin is stored in the data structure pointed to by `lpPoint`.

Return Value `TRUE` is returned when successful. `FALSE` is returned when unsuccessful.

Function Category Mapping

Related Functions `OffsetWindowOrg`

OleActivate

Syntax

```
OLESTATUS OleActivate(lpObject, iVerb, fShow,
                      fTakeFocus, hwnd, lpBounds)
```

Parameter	*Type*	*Description*
`lpObject`	`LPOLEOBJECT`	Pointer to object to open
`iVerb`	`WORD`	Operation to perform (0 for primary verb, 1 for secondary verb, and so forth)
`fShow`	`BOOL`	`TRUE` to show window; `FALSE` to hide window
`fTakeFocus`	`BOOL`	`TRUE` when server should take focus, `FALSE` otherwise; relevant only when `fShow` is `TRUE`
`hwnd`	`HWND`	Window containing object
`lpBounds`	`LPRECT`	Pointer to `RECT` data structure that contains the coordinates of the rectangle bounding the object

Description The `OleActivate` function opens the specified object.

Return Value `OLE_OK` is returned when successful. `OLE_BUSY`, `OLE_ERROR_OBJECT`, or `OLE_WAIT_FOR_RELEASE` is returned when unsuccessful.

Function Category OLE Object Management

Related Functions `OleQueryOpen`, `OleSetData`

OleBlockServer

Syntax `OLESTATUS OleBlockServer(lhSrvr)`

Parameter	*Type*	*Description*
lhSrvr	LHSERVER	Server

Description The `OleBlockServer` function forces requests to the server to be sent to a queue until the `OleUnblockServer` function is called.

Return Value `OLE_OK` is returned when successful. `OLE_ERROR_HANDLE` is returned when unsuccessful.

Function Category OLE Server

Related Functions `OleUnblockServer`

OleClone

Syntax
```
OLESTATUS OleClone(lpObject, lpClient, lhClientDoc,
                   lpszObjname, lplpObject)
```

Parameter	*Type*	*Description*
lpObject	LPOLEOBJECT	Pointer to object to copy
lpClient	LPOLECLIENT	Pointer to OLECLIENT structure for the new object
lhClientDoc	LHCLIENTDOC	Client document
lpszObjname	LPSTR	Pointer to null-terminate string containing the client's name for the object
lplpObject	LPOLEOBJECT FAR*	Pointer to variable where the long pointer to the new object will be stored

Description The `OleClone` function makes a duplicate of an object; however, the object is not connected to the server.

Return Value `OLE_OK` is returned when successful. `OLE_BUSY`, `OLE_ERROR_OBJECT`, `OLE_ERROR_HANDLE`, or `OLE_WAIT_FOR_RELEASE` is returned when unsuccessful.

Function Category OLE Object Creation

Related Functions `OleEqual`

OleClose

Syntax `OLESTATUS OleClose(lpObject)`

Parameter	*Type*	*Description*
`lpObject`	`LPOLEOBJECT`	Pointer to object to close

Description The `OleClose` function closes the object specified in `lpObject`. Once an object has been closed, the connection with the server application is terminated.

Return Value `OLE_OK` is returned when successful. `OLE_BUSY`, `OLE_ERROR_OBJECT`, or `OLE_WAIT_FOR_RELEASE` is returned when unsuccessful.

Function Category OLE Client

Related Functions `OleActivate`, `OleDelete`

OleCopyFromLink

Syntax

```
OLESTATUS OleCopyFromLink(lpObject, lpszProtocol,
                          lpClient, lhClientDoc,
                          lpszObjname, lplpObject)
```

Parameter	*Type*	*Description*
`lpObject`	`LPOLEOBJECT`	Pointer to linked object to be embedded
`lpszProtocol`	`LPSTR`	Pointer to null-terminated string that specifies the name of the protocol for the new embedded object; set to "StdFileEditing"
`lpClient`	`LPOLECLIENT`	Pointer to `OLECLIENT` data structure for new object

Parameter	Type	Description
lhClientDoc	LHCLIENTDOC	Client document in which document is being created
lpszObjname	LPSTR	Pointer to null-terminated string containing the client's name for the object
lplpObject	LPOLEOBJECT FAR*	Pointer to variable where the long pointer to the new object will be stored

Description The `OleCopyFromLink` function creates an embedded copy of a linked object. It may be necessary to start the server application before creating the embedded copy.

Return Value `OLE_OK` is returned when successful. `OLE_BUSY`, `OLE_ERROR_HANDLE`, `OLE_ERROR_NAME`, `OLE_ERROR_OBJECT`, `OLE_ERROR_PROTOCOL`, or `OLE_WAIT_FOR_RELEASE` is returned when unsuccessful.

Function Category OLE Object Creation

Related Functions `OleObjectConvert`

OleCopyToClipboard

Syntax `OLESTATUS OleCopyToClipboard(lpObject)`

Parameter	Type	Description
lpObject	LPOLEOBJECT	Pointer to object to be copied to the clipboard

Description The `OleCopyToClipboard` function copies the object pointed to by `lpObject` to the clipboard.

Return Value `OLE_OK` is returned when successful. `OLE_ERROR_OBJECT` is returned when unsuccessful.

Function Category OLE Object Management

Related Functions `OLECreateFromClip`

OleCreate

Syntax

```
OLESTATUS OleCreate(lpszProtocol, lpClient, lpszClass,
                    lhClientDoc, lpszObjname, lplpObject,
                    renderopt, cfFormat)
```

Parameter	*Type*	*Description*
lpszProtocol	LPSTR	Points to null-terminated string that specifies the name of the protocol for the embedded object; set to "StdFileEditing"
lpClient	LPOLECLIENT	Pointer to OLECLIENT data structure for the new object
lpszClass	LPSTR	Pointer to null-terminated string that contains the name of the class of the object to create
lhClientDoc	LHCLIENTDOC	Client document where object is to be created
lpszObjname	LPSTR	Pointer to null-terminated string that contains the client's name for the object
lplpObject	LPOLEOBJECT FAR*	Pointer to variable where the long pointer to the new object is stored
renderopt	OLEOPT_RENDER	Client preference for displaying and printing object; set to one of the following:

Value	*Meaning*
olerender_none	Object is not shown or an object handler does the rendering
olerender_draw	OleDraw function is called; library obtains and manages presentation data
olerender_format	OleGetData function gets data in specified format; library obtains and manages data in requested format in cfFormat

Parameter	Type	Description
cfFormat	OLECLIPFORMAT	Clipboard format requested by client when OleGetData is called; only CF_METAFILEPICT, CF_DIB, and CF_BITMAP formats are supported

Description The OleCreate function creates an embedded object of the class specified in lpszClass. The server is opened for initial editing.

Return Value OLE_OK is returned when successful. OLE_ERROR_HANDLE, OLE_ERROR_NAME, OLE_ERROR_PROTOCOL, or OLE_WAIT_FOR_RELEASE is returned when unsuccessful.

Function Category OLE Object Creation

Related Functions OleCreateFromClip, OleDraw, OldGetData

OleCreateFromClip

Syntax

```
OLESTATUS OleCreateFromClip(lpszProtocol, lpClient,
                            lhClientDoc, lpszObjname,
                            lplpObject, renderopt,
                            cfFormat)
```

Parameter	Type	Description
lpszProtocol	LPSTR	Points to null-terminated string that specifies the name of the protocol for the embedded object; set to "StdFileEditing" for the object linking and embedding protocol or "Static" for uneditable pictures
lpClient	LPOLECLIENT	Pointer to OLECLIENT data structure used to locate callback function
lhClientDoc	LHCLIENTDOC	Client document where object is to be created

Parameter	Type	Description
lpszObjname	LPSTR	Pointer to null-terminated string that contains the client's name for the object
lplpObject	LPOLEOBJECT FAR*	Pointer to variable where the long pointer to the new object is stored
renderopt	OLEOPT_RENDER	Client preference for displaying and printing object; set to one of the following:

Value	Meaning
olerender_none	Object is not shown or an object handler does the rendering
olerender_draw	OleDraw function is called; library obtains and manages presentation data
olerender_format	OleGetData function gets data in specified format; library obtains and manages data in requested format in cfFormat

Parameter	Type	Description
cfFormat	OLECLIPFORMAT	Clipboard format requested by client when OleGetData is called; only CF_METAFILEPICT, CF_DIB, and CF_BITMAP formats are supported

Description The OleCreateFromClip function creates an object from the clipboard.

Return Value The OLE_OK function is returned when successful. OLE_ERROR_CLIP, OLE_ERROR_FORMAT, OLE_ERROR_HANDLE, OLE_ERROR_NAME, OLE_ERROR_OPTION, OLE_ERROR_PROTOCOL, or OLE_WAIT_FOR_RELEASE is returned when unsuccessful.

Function Category OLE Object Creation

Related Functions OleCreate, OleDraw, OleGetData, OleQueryCreateFromClip

OleCreateFromFile

Syntax

```
OLESTATUS OleCreateFromFile(lpszProtocol, lpClient,
                            lpszClass, lpszFile,lhClientDoc,
                            lpszObjname, lplpObject,
                            renderopt, cfFormat)
```

Parameter	*Type*	*Description*
lpszProtocol	LPSTR	Points to null-terminated string that specifies the name of the protocol for the embedded object; set to "StdFileEditing"
lpClient	LPOLECLIENT	Pointer to OLECLIENT data structure used to locate the callback function
lpszClass	LPSTR	Pointer to null-terminated string that contains the name of the class of the object to create
lpszFile	LPSTR	Pointer to null-terminated string identifying the name of the file that contains the object
lhClientDoc	LHCLIENTDOC	Client document where object is to be created
lpszObjname	LPSTR	Pointer to null-terminated string that contains the client's name for the object
lplpObject	LPOLEOBJECT FAR*	Pointer to variable where the long pointer to the new object is stored
renderopt	OLEOPT_RENDER	Client preference for displaying and printing object; set to one of the following:

Value	*Meaning*
olerender_none	Object is not shown or an object handler does the rendering
olerender_draw	OleDraw function is called; library obtains and manages presentation data

Value	*Meaning*
olerender_format	OleGetData function gets data in specified format; library obtains and manages data in requested format in cfFormat

Parameter	*Type*	*Description*
cfFormat	OLECLIPFORMAT	Clipboard format requested by client when OleGetData is called; only CF_METAFILEPICT, CF_DIB, and CF_BITMAP formats are supported

Description The OleCreateFromFile function creates an embedded object from the file specified in lpszFile. The server is started to render the Native and presentation data (if the server is not already open). The server is closed if the function started it; otherwise, the server is left open. The user is not shown the object for editing.

Return Value OLE_OK is returned when successful. OLE_ERROR_CLASS, OLE_ERROR_HANDLE, OLE_ERROR_MEMORY, OLE_ERROR_NAME, OLE_ERROR_PROTOCOL, or OLE_WAIT_FOR_RELEASE is returned when unsuccessful.

Function Category OLE Object Creation

Related Functions OleCreate, OleDraw, OleGetData

OleCreateFromTemplate

Syntax

```
OLESTATUS OleCreateFromTemplate(lpszProtocol,
                                lpClient, lpszTemplate,
                                lhClientDoc, lpszObjname,
                                lplpObject, renderopt,
                                cfFormat)
```

Parameter	*Type*	*Description*
lpszProtocol	LPSTR	Points to null-terminated string that specifies the name of the protocol for

Parameter	Type	Description
		the embedded object; set to "StdFileEditing"
lpClient	LPOLECLIENT	Pointer to OLECLIENT data structure for the new object
lpszTemplate	LPSTR	Pointer to null-terminated string that contains the path to the file to use as a template for the new object
lhClientDoc	LHCLIENTDOC	Client document where object is to be created
lpszObjname	LPSTR	Pointer to null-terminated string that contains the client's name for the object
lplpObject	LPOLEOBJECT FAR*	Pointer to variable where the long pointer to the new object is stored
renderopt	OLEOPT_RENDER	Client preference for displaying and printing object; set to one of the following:

Value	Meaning
olerender_none	Object is not shown or an object handler does the rendering
olerender_draw	OleDraw function is called; library obtains and manages presentation data
olerender_format	OleGetData function gets data in specified format; library obtains and manages data in requested format in cfFormat

Parameter	Type	Description
cfFormat	OLECLIPFORMAT	Clipboard format requested by client when OleGetData is called; only CF_METAFILEPICT, CF_DIB, and CF_BITMAP formats are supported

Description The OleCreateFromTemplate function creates an object by using the specified object as a template. The server is opened for initial editing.

Return Value `OLE_OK` is returned when successful. `OLE_ERROR_CLASS`, `OLE_ERROR_HANDLE`, `OLE_ERROR_MEMORY`, `OLE_ERROR_NAME`, `OLE_ERROR_PROTOCOL`, or `OLE_WAIT_FOR_RELEASE` is returned when unsuccessful.

Function Category OLE Object Creation

Related Functions `OleCreate`, `OleDraw`, `OleGetData`

OleCreateInvisible

Syntax

```
OLESTATUS OleCreateInvisible(lpszProtocol, lpClient,
                             lpszClass, lhClientDoc,
                             lpszObjname, lplpObject,
                             renderopt, cfFormat,
                             fActivate)
```

Parameter	*Type*	*Description*
`lpszProtocol`	`LPSTR`	Pointer to the string that specifies the protocol name
`lpClient`	`LPOLECLIENT`	Pointer to `OLECLIENT` data structure initialized by the client
`lpszClass`	`LPSTR`	Pointer to the string that specifies the registered class name of the object
`lhClientDoc`	`LHCLIENTDOC`	Client document
`lpszObjName`	`LPSTR`	Pointer to the string that specifies the client's name for the object
`lplpObject`	`LPOLEOBJECT FAR*`	Pointer to variable where the object long pointer to the object is stored
`renderopt`	`OLEOPT_RENDER`	Client's preference for data presentation. One of the following values is used:

Value	*Meaning*
`olerender_none`	Client library does not obtain presentation data or draw the object

Value	*Meaning*
olerender_draw	Client calls OleDraw; the library manages presentation data
olerender_format	Client calls OleGetData; the library manages data in the requested format specified in cfFormat

Parameter	*Type*	*Description*
cfFormat	OLECLIPFORMAT	Clipboard format. Only used when renderopt is olerender_format.
fActivate	BOOL	TRUE to start server. FALSE if server not started and blank object is created using the specified class and format

Description The OleCreateInvisible function creates an object. The server application is not displayed to the user. This function can either start the server or create a blank object using the specified class and format without starting the server.

Return Value OLE_OK is returned when successful. OLE_ERROR_HANDLE, OLE_ERROR_NAME, or OLE_ERROR_PROTOCOL is returned when unsuccessful.

Function Category OLE Object Creation

Related Functions OleActivate, OleClose

OleCreateLinkFromClip

Syntax

```
OLESTATUS OleCreateLinkFromClip(lpszProtocol,
                                lpClient, lhClientDoc,
                                lpszObjname, lplpObject,
                                renderopt, cfFormat)
```

Parameter	*Type*	*Description*
lpszProtocol	LPSTR	Points to null-terminated string that specifies the name of the protocol for the

Parameter	Type	Description
		embedded object; set to "StdFileEditing"
lpClient	LPOLECLIENT	Pointer to OLECLIENT data structure used to locate the callback function
lhClientDoc	LHCLIENTDOC	Client document where object is to be created
lpszObjname	LPSTR	Pointer to null-terminated string that contains the client's name for the object
lplpObject	LPOLEOBJECT FAR*	Pointer to variable where the long pointer to the new object is stored
renderopt	OLEOPT_RENDER	Client preference for displaying and printing object; set to one of the following:

Value	Meaning
olerender_none	Object is not shown or an object handler does the rendering
olerender_draw	OleDraw function is called; library obtains and manages presentation data
olerender_format	OleGetData function gets data in specified format; library obtains and manages data in requested format in cfFormat

Parameter	Type	Description
cfFormat	OLECLIPFORMAT	Clipboard format requested by client when OleGetData is called; only CF_METAFILEPICT, CF_DIB, and CF_BITMAP formats are supported

Description The OleCreateLinkFromClip function creates a link to an object from the clipboard.

Return Value OLE_OK is returned when successful. OLE_ERROR_CLIP, OLE_ERROR_FORMAT, OLE_ERROR_HANDLE, OLE_ERROR_NAME, OLE_ERROR_PROTOCOL, or OLE_WAIT_FOR_RELEASE is returned when unsuccessful.

Function Category OLE Object Creation

Related Functions `OleCreate`, `OleDraw`, `OleGetData`, `OleQueryLinkFromClip`

OleCreateLinkFromFile

Syntax

```
OLESTATUS OleCreateLinkFromFile(lpszProtocol,lpClient,
                                lpszClass, lpszFile,
                                lpszItem, lhClientDoc,
                                lpszObjname, lplpObject,
                                renderopt, cfFormat)
```

Parameter	*Type*	*Description*
`lpszProtocol`	`LPSTR`	Points to null-terminated string that specifies the name of the protocol for the embedded object; set to "StdFileEditing"
`lpClient`	`LPOLECLIENT`	Pointer to `OLECLIENT` data structure used to locate the callback function
`lpszClass`	`LPSTR`	Pointer to null-terminated string that contains the name of the class of the object to create
`lpszFile`	`LPSTR`	Pointer to null-terminated string that contains the name of the file containing the object
`lpszItem`	`LPSTR`	Pointer to null-terminated string that specifies the part of the document to link to; set to `NULL` to link to the entire document
`lhClientDoc`	`LHCLIENTDOC`	Client document where object is to be created
`lpszObjname`	`LPSTR`	Pointer to null-terminated string that contains the client's name for the object

Parameter	*Type*	*Description*
lplpObject	LPOLEOBJECT FAR*	Pointer to variable where the long pointer to the new object is stored
renderopt	OLEOPT_RENDER	Client preference for displaying and printing object; set to one of the following:

Value	*Meaning*
olerender_none	Object is not shown or an object handler does the rendering
olerender_draw	OleDraw function is called; library obtains and manages presentation data
olerender_format	OleGetData function gets data in specified format; library obtains and manages data in requested format in cfFormat

cfFormat	OLECLIPFORMAT	Clipboard format requested by client when OleGetData is called; only CF_METAFILEPICT, CF_DIB, and CF_BITMAP formats are supported

Description The OleCreateLinkFromFile function creates a linked object from the specified file containing an object. The server is started (if not open) to render the presentation data. The object is not shown to the user for editing.

Return Value OLE_OK is returned when successful. One of the following is returned when unsuccessful: OLE_ERROR_CLASS, OLE_ERROR_HANDLE, OLE_ERROR_MEMORY, OLE_ERROR_NAME, OLE_ERROR_PROTOCOL, or OLE_WAIT_FOR_RELEASE.

Function Category OLE Object Creation

Related Functions OleCreate, OleDraw, OleGetData

OleDelete

Syntax `OLESTATUS OleDelete(lpObject)`

Parameter	*Type*	*Description*
lpObject	LPOLEOBJECT	Pointer to object to delete

Description The `OleDelete` function deletes the object pointed to by `lpObject`. All memory associated with the object is freed.

Return Value `OLE_OK` is returned when successful. `OLE_BUSY`, `OLE_ERROR_OBJECT`, or `OLE_WAIT_FOR_RELEASE` is returned when unsuccessful.

Function Category OLE Object Management

Related Functions `OleCreate`, `OleRelease`

OleDraw

Syntax

```
OLESTATUS OleDraw(lpObject, hdc, lprcBounds,
                  lprcWBounds, hdcFormat)
```

Parameter	*Type*	*Description*
lpObject	LPOLEOBJECT	Pointer to object to draw
hdc	HDC	Device context
lprcBounds	LPRECT	Pointer to RECT data structure that defines the bounding rectangle where the object is drawn; coordinates expressed in logical units
lprcWBounds	LPRECT	Pointer to RECT data structure that defines the bounding rectangle when hdc specifies a metafile; first coordinate pair specifies the window origin, second coordinate point specifies the window extents
hdcFormat	HDC	Device context of the target device

Description The `OleDraw` function draws the object pointed to by `lpObject` in the appropriate bounding rectangle (`lprcBounds` or `lprcWBounds`) in the device context specified in `hdc`. The device context specified in `hdcFormat` may be used by the library to determine information about the target device if the library is required to use an object handler to render the object.

Return Value `OLE_OK` is returned when successful. `OLE_ERROR_ABORT`, `OLE_ERROR_BLANK`, `OLE_ERROR_DRAW`, `OLE_ERROR_MEMORY`, or `OLE_ERROR_OBJECT` is returned when unsuccessful.

Function Category OLE Object Management

Related Functions `OleSetBounds`

OleEnumFormats

Syntax `OLECLIPFORMAT OleEnumFormats(lpObject, cfFormat)`

Parameter	*Type*	*Description*
`lpObject`	`LPOLEOBJECT`	Pointer to object
`cfFormat`	`OLECLIPFORMAT`	Format returned by last call to `OleEnumFormats`; set to zero when this function is called for the first time

Description The `OleEnumFormats` function enumerates the data formats that describe the object pointed to by `lpObject`. When `cfFormat` is `NULL`, the first available format is returned. Otherwise, the function returns the next available format after the format specified in `cfFormat`.

Return Value The format that follows the specified format is returned. If no more formats are available `NULL` is returned.

Function Category OLE Object Management

Related Functions `OleEnumObjects`, `OleGetData`

OleEnumObjects

Syntax `OLESTATUS OleEnumObjects(lhDoc, lplpObject)`

Parameter	*Type*	*Description*
`lhDoc`	`LHCLIENTDOC`	Document that contains the objects to enumerate
`lplpObject`	`LPOLEOBJECT FAR*`	Pointer to object when function returns; should point to `NULL` object for the first call to this function

Description The `OleEnumObject` function enumerates the objects in the document specified in `lhDoc`. When `lplpObject` points to a `NULL` object, the first object in the document is returned. When `lplpObject` points to an object in the document, the document that follows the document specifed in `lplpObject` is returned.

Return Value `OLE_OK` is returned when successful. `OLE_ERROR_HANDLE` or `OLE_ERROR_OBJECT` is returned when unsuccessful.

Function Category OLE Document

Related Functions `OleDelete`, `OleRelease`

OleEqual

Syntax `OLESTATUS OleEqual(lpObject1, lpObject2)`

Parameter	*Type*	*Description*
`lpObject1`	`LPOLEOBJECT`	Pointer to first object
`lpObject2`	`LPOLEOBJECT`	Pointer to second object

Description The `OleEqual` function determines whether the objects specified in `lpObject1` and `lpObject2` are equal. Embedded objects are considered to be equal if they have the same class, item, and native data. Linked objects are considered to be equal if they have the same class, document, and item.

Return Value `OLE_OK` is returned when the objects are equal. `OLE_ERROR_OBJECT` or `OLE_ERROR_NOT_EQUAL` is returned when unsuccessful.

Function Category OLE Object Management

Related Functions `OleClone`

OleExecute

Syntax `OLESTATUS OleExecute(lpObject, hCommands, wReserved)`

Parameter	*Type*	*Description*
`lpObject`	`LPOLEOBJECT`	Pointer to object that specifies the server where DDE execute commands are sent
`hCommands`	`HANDLE`	Memory that contains DDE execute commands
`wReserved`	`WORD`	Reserved; set to zero

Description The `OleExecute` function sends the DDE execute commands specified in `hCommands` to the server for the object specified in `lpObject`. The `OleQueryProtocol` function should be called prior to this function and should specify the "StdExecute" protocol.

Return Value `OLE_OK` is returned when successful. `OLE_BUSY`, `OLE_ERROR_COMMAND`, `OLE_ERROR_MEMORY`, `OLE_ERROR_NOT_OPEN`, `OLE_ERROR_OBJECT`, `OLE_ERROR_PROTOCOL`, `OLE_ERROR_STATIC`, or `OLE_WAIT_FOR_RELEASE` is returned when unsuccessful.

Function Category OLE Client

Related Functions `OleQueryProtocol`

OleGetData

Syntax `OLESTATUS OleGetData(lpObject, cfFormat, phData)`

Parameter	*Type*	*Description*
`lpObject`	`LPOLEOBJECT`	Pointer to object containing the data to retrieve

Parameter	Type	Description
cfFormat	OLECLIPFORMAT	Format for data is returned; should be set to one of the predefined clipboard formats
phData	HANDLE FAR*	Pointer to handle of memory object to contain the data

Description The OleGetData function gets data from the object specified in lpObject using the format specified in cfFormat. phData points to the handle of the memory object that contains the retrieved data when the function returns.

Return Value OLE_OK is returned when successful. OLE_ERROR_BLANK, OLE_ERROR_FORMAT, OLE_ERROR_OBJECT, or OLE_WARN_DELETE_DATA is returned when unsuccessful.

Function Category OLE Object Management

Related Functions OleSetData

OleGetLinkUpdateOptions

Syntax

```
OLESTATUS OleGetLinkUpdateOptions(lpObject,
                                  lpUpdateOpt)
```

Parameter	Type	Description
lpObject	LPOLEOBJECT	Pointer to object
lpUpdateOpt	OLEOPT_UPDATE FAR*	Pointer to variable where the current value of the link update option for the object is stored; the link option is one of the following:

Value	Meaning
oleupdate_always	Update linked object when possible; supports the automatic link update radio button in the Links dialog box

Value	Meaning
oleupdate_onsave	Update linked object when source document is saved by server
oleupdate_oncall	Update linked object on request by client; supports the Manual link update radio button in the Links dialog box

Description The `OleGetLinkUpdateOptions` function gets the link update options for the object specified in `lpObject`.

Return Value `OLE_OK` is returned when successful. `OLE_ERROR_OBJECT` or `OLE_ERROR_STATIC` is returned when unsuccessful.

Function Category OLE Link

Related Functions `OleSetLinkUpdateOptions`

OleIsDCMeta

Syntax `OLESTATUS OleIsDcMeta(hdc)`

Parameter	Type	Description
hdc	HDC	Device context

Description The `OleIsDcMeta` function determines whether the device context specified in `hdc` is a metafile device context.

Return Value A positive value is returned when the specified device context is a metafile device context. `NULL` is returned if `hdc` is not a metafile device context.

Function Category OLE Object Management

Related Functions `OleActivate`, `OleClose`

OleLoadFromStream

Syntax
```
OLESTATUS OleLoadFromStream(lpStream, lpszProtocol,
                            lpClient, lhClientDoc,
                            lpszObjname, lplpObject)
```

Parameter	*Type*	*Description*
lpStream	LPOLESTREAM	Pointer to OLESTREAM data structure initialized by client application
lpszProtocol	LPSTR	Pointer to null-terminated string that specifies the protocol; set to "StdFileEditing" for object linking and embedding or "Static" for uneditable pictures
lpClient	LPOLECLIENT	Pointer to OLECLIENT data structure initialized by client application and is used to locate the callback function
lhClientDoc	LHCLIENTDOC	Client document where object is to be created
lpszObjname	LPSTR	Pointer to null-terminated string that contains the client's name for the object
lplpObject	LPOLEOBJECT FAR*	Pointer to variable where the pointer to the loaded object is stored

Description The OleLoadFromStream function loads an object from a document.

Return Value OLE_OK is returned when successful. OLE_ERROR_HANDLE, OLE_ERROR_NAME, OLE_ERROR_PROTOCOL, OLE_ERROR_STREAM, or OLE_WAIT_FOR_RELEASE is returned when unsuccessful.

Function Category OLE Object Creation

Related Functions OleSaveToStream

OleLockServer

Syntax `OLESTATUS OleLockServer(lpObject, lphServer)`

Parameter	*Type*	*Description*
`lpObject`	`LPOLEOBJECT`	Pointer to object that represents the open server application
`lphServer`	`LHSERVER FAR*`	Pointer to handle of server application when function returns

Description The `OleLockServer` function keeps the open server application in memory and is called by a client application. The `OleUnlockServer` function is called to release the server from memory.

Return Value `OLE_OK` is returned when successful. `OLE_ERROR_OBJECT`, `OLE_ERROR_LAUNCH`, or `OLE_ERROR_COMM` is returned when unsuccessful.

Function Category OLE Client

Related Functions `OleUnlockServer`

OleObjectConvert

Syntax

```
OLESTATUS OleObjectConvert(lpObject, lpszProtocol,
                           lpClient, lhClientDoc,
                           lpszObjname, lplpObject)
```

Parameter	*Type*	*Description*
`lpObject`	`LPOLEOBJECT`	Pointer to object to convert
`lpszProtocol`	`LPSTR`	Pointer to null-terminated string that specifies the protocol; set to “Static” for uneditable pictures
`lpClient`	`LPOLECLIENT`	Pointer to `OLECLIENT` data structure initialized by client application and is used to locate the callback function

Parameter	Type	Description
lhClientDoc	LHCLIENTDOC	Client document where object is to be created
lpszObjname	LPSTR	Pointer to null-terminated string that contains the client's name for the object
lplpObject	LPOLEOBJECT FAR*	Pointer to variable where the pointer to the loaded object is stored

Description The `OleObjectConvert` function creates a new object by converting an existing object. The specified protocol is supported by the new object. The original object is not modified in any way.

Return Value `OLE_OK` is returned when successful. `OLE_BUSY`, `OLE_ERROR_HANDLE`, `OLE_ERROR_NAME`, `OLE_ERROR_OBJECT`, or `OLE_ERROR_STATIC` is returned when unsuccessful.

Function Category OLE Object Creation

Related Functions `OleClone`

OleQueryBounds

Syntax `OLESTATUS OleQueryBounds(lpObject, lpBounds)`

Parameter	Type	Description
lpObject	LPOLEOBJECT	Pointer to object
lpBounds	LPRECT	Pointer to RECT data structure that defines the bounding rectangle for the object; all coordinates are expressed in MM_HIMETRIC units

Description The `OleQueryBounds` function gets the extents of the rectangle that bounds the target device for the object specified in `lpObject`.

Return Value `OLE_OK` is returned when successful. `OLE_ERROR_MEMORY`, `OLE_ERROR_OBJECT`, or `OLE_ERROR_BLANK` is returned when unsuccessful.

Function Category OLE Object Management

Related Functions `OleSetBounds`

OleQueryClientVersion

Syntax `DWORD OleQueryClientVersion(void)`

Parameter	*Type*	*Description*
None		

Description The `OleQueryClientVersion` function returns the version number of the client library.

Return Value The low byte of the low word of the return value contains the major version number of the client library. The high byte of the low word contains the minor version number of the client library. The high word of the return value is reserved.

Function Category OLE Object Management

Related Functions `OleQueryServerVersion`

OleQueryCreateFromClip

Syntax
```
OLESTATUS OleQueryCreateFromClip(lpszProtocol,
                                 renderopt, cfFormat)
```

Parameter	*Type*	*Description*
`lpszProtocol`	`LPSTR`	Points to null-terminated string that specifies the name of the protocol for the embedded object; set to "StdFileEditing" for object linking and embedding or "Static" for uneditable pictures

Parameter	Type	Description
renderopt	OLEOPT_RENDER	Client preference for displaying and printing object; set to one of the following:

Value	Meaning
olerender_none	Object is not shown or an object handler does the rendering
olerender_draw	OleDraw function is called; library obtains and manages presentation data
olerender_format	OleGetData function gets data in specified format; library obtains and manages data in requested format in cfFormat

Parameter	Type	Description
cfFormat	OLECLIPFORMAT	Clipboard format requested by client when OleGetData is called; only CF_METAFILEPICT, CF_DIB, and CF_BITMAP formats are supported

Description The OleQueryCreateFromClip function determines whether the object on the clipboard supports the protocol and rendering options specified in lpszProtocol and renderopt.

Return Value OLE_OK is returned when successful. OLE_ERROR_FORMAT or OLE_ERROR_PROTOCOL is returned when unsuccessful.

Function Category OLE Object Creation

Related Functions OleCreateFromClip, OleDraw

OleQueryLinkFromClip

Syntax

```
OLESTATUS OleQueryLinkFromClip(lpszProtocol,
                               renderopt,  cfFormat)
```

Parameter	*Type*	*Description*
lpszProtocol	LPSTR	Points to null-terminated string that specifies the name of the protocol for the embedded object; set to "StdFileEditing"
renderopt	OLEOPT_RENDER	Client preference for displaying and printing object; set to one of the following:

Value	*Meaning*
olerender_none	Object is not shown or an object handler does the rendering
	olerender_draw OleDraw function is called; library obtains and manages presentation data
olerender_format	OleGetData function gets data in specified format; library obtains and manages data in requested format in cfFormat

Parameter	*Type*	*Description*
cfFormat	OLECLIPFORMAT	Clipboard format requested by client when OleGetData is called; only CF_METAFILEPICT, CF_DIB, and CF_BITMAP formats are supported

Description The OleQueryLinkFromClip function indicates whether the data on the clipboard can be used by the client application to produce a linked object that supports the protocol and rendering options specified in lpszProtocol and renderopt.

Return Value OLE_OK is returned when successful. OLE_ERROR_FORMAT or OLE_ERROR_PROTOCOL is returned when unsuccessful.

Function Category OLE Link

Related Functions OleCreateLinkFromClip, OleDraw

OleQueryName

Syntax `OLESTATUS OleQueryName(lpObject, lpszObject, lpwBuffSize)`

Parameter	*Type*	*Description*
`lpObject`	`LPOLEOBJECT`	Pointer to object
`lpszObject`	`LPSTR`	Pointer to character array that contains a null-terminated string that specifies the name of the object when the function returns
`lpwBuffSize`	`WORD FAR*`	Pointer to variable that contains the number of bytes pointed to by `lpszObject`

Description The `OleQueryName` function copies the name of the object in `lpObject` to the string contained in the array pointed to by `lpszObject`.

Return Value `OLE_OK` is returned when successful. `OLE_ERROR_OBJECT` is returned when unsuccessful.

Function Category OLE Object Management

Related Functions `OleRename`

OleQueryOpen

Syntax `OLESTATUS OleQueryOpen(lpObject)`

Parameter	*Type*	*Description*
`lpObject`	`LPOLEOBJECT`	Pointer to object

Description The `OleQueryOpen` function determines whether the object in `lpObject` is open.

Return Value `OLE_OK` is returned when successful. `OLE_ERROR_OBJECT`, `OLE_ERROR_STATIC`, or `OLE_ERROR_COMM` is returned when unsuccessful.

Function Category OLE Client

Related Functions `OleActivate`

OleQueryOutOfDate

Syntax `OLESTATUS OleQueryOutOfDate(lpObject)`

Parameter	*Type*	*Description*
`lpObject`	`LPOLEOBJECT`	Pointer to object

Description The `OleQueryOutOfData` function determines whether the object specified in `lpObject` is out of date. Linked objects might be out of date if the source document for the link has been updated. An embedded object might be out of date if the object contains links to other objects.

Return Value `OLE_OK` is returned if the object is not out of date. Otherwise, `OLE_ERROR_OUTOFDATE` or `OLE_ERROR_OBJECT` is returned.

Function Category OLE Link

Related Functions `OleUpdate`

OleQueryProtocol

Syntax `LPVOID OleQueryProtocol(lpobj, lpszprotocol)`

Parameter	*Type*	*Description*
`lpobj`	`LPOLEOBJECT`	Pointer to object
`lpszprotocol`	`LPSTR`	Pointer to null-terminated string containing the name of the protocol; set to “StdFileEditing” or “StdExecute”

Description The `OleQueryProtocol` function determines whether the object in `lpobj` supports the protocol to `lpszprotocol`.

Return Value A `VOID` pointer to an `OLEOBJECT` structure is returned when the protocol is supported. `NULL` is returned when the specified protocol is not supported.

Function Category OLE Object Management

Related Functions `OleExecute`

OleQueryReleaseError

Syntax `OLESTATUS OleQueryReleaseError(lpobj)`

Parameter	*Type*	*Description*
`lpobj`	`LPOLEOBJECT`	Pointer to object

Description The `OleQueryReleaseError` function determines the error value for an asynchronous operation on the object specified in `lpobj`. The client application should call this function when it receives the `OLE_RELEASE` notification indicating that an asynchronous operation has been terminated. `OleQueryReleaseError` will indicate whether the operation terminated normally or as a result of an error.

Return Value `OLE_OK` is returned when the asynchronous operation terminated normally. An error value is returned when the operation terminated as the result of an error.

Function Category OLE Client

Related Functions `OleQueryReleaseMethod`, `OleQueryReleaseStatus`

OleQueryReleaseMethod

Syntax `OLE_RELEASE_METHOD OleQueryReleaseMethod(lpobj)`

Parameter	*Type*	*Description*
`lpobj`	`LPOLEOBJECT`	Pointer to object

Description The `OleQueryReleaseMethod` function determines which operation finished for the object specified in `lpobj`. The client application calls this function when it receives the `OLE_RELEASE` notification to determine the operation that was released.

Return Value When successful, the server operation that finished is returned and is one of the following values. When `lpobj` is invalid, `OLE_ERROR_OBJECT` is returned.

Value	*Meaning*
OLE_NONE	No operation active
OLE_DELETE	Object delete
OLE_LNKPASTE	PasteLink
OLE_EMBPASTE	Paste and Update
OLE_SHOW	Show
OLE_RUN	Run
OLE_ACTIVATE	Activate
OLE_UPDATE	Update
OLE_CLOSE	Close
OLE_RECONNECT	Reconnect
OLE_SETUPDATEOPTIONS	Set update options
OLE_SERVERUNLAUNCH	Stopping server
OLE_LOADFROMSTRING	`LoadFromStream`
OLE_SETDATA	`OleSetData`
OLE_REQUESTDATA	`OleRequestData`
OLE_OTHER	Other asynchronous operations
OLE_CREATE	`Create`
OLE_CREATEFROMTEMPLATE	`CreateFromTemplate`
OLE_CREATELINKFROMFILE	`CreateLinkFromFile`
OLE_COPYFROMLNK	`CopyFromLink`
OLE_CREATEFROMFILE	`CreateFromFile`
OLE_CREATEINVISIBLE	`CreateInvisible`

Function Category OLE Client Server

Related Functions `OleQueryReleaseError`, `OleQueryReleaseStatus`

OleQueryReleaseStatus

Syntax `OLESTATUS OleQueryReleaseStatus(lpobj)`

Parameter	*Type*	*Description*
`lpobj`	`LPOLEOBJECT`	Pointer to object

Description The `OleQueryReleaseStatus` function determines whether an operation has finished for the object specified in `lpobj`.

Return Value `OLE_BUSY` is returned if an operation is still in progress. `OLE_OK` is returned if no operation is in progress. `OLE_ERROR_OBJECT` is returned if `lpobj` is invalid.

Function Category OLE Client

Related Functions `OleQueryReleaseError`, `OleQueryReleaseMethod`

OleQueryServerVersion

Syntax `DWORD OleQueryServerVersion(void)`

Parameter	*Type*	*Description*
None		

Description The `OleQueryServerVersion` function returns the version number for the server library.

Return Value The low byte of the low word of the return value contains the major version number. The high byte of the low word of the return value contains the minor version number. The high word is reserved.

Function Category OLE Server

Related Functions `OleQueryClientVersion`

OleQuerySize

Syntax `OLESTATUS OleQuerySize(lpObject, pdwSize)`

Parameter	*Type*	*Description*
`lpObject`	`LPOLEOBJECT`	Pointer to the object
`pdwSize`	`DWORD FAR*`	Pointer to variable where the object size will be stored

Description The `OleQuerySize` function determines the size of the object specified in `lpObject` and copies the size to the variable pointed to by `pdwSize`.

Return Value `OLE_OK` is returned when successful. `OLE_ERROR_BLANK`, `OLE_ERROR_MEMORY`, or `OLE_ERROR_OBJECT` is returned when unsuccessful.

Function Category OLE Object Management

Related Functions `OleQueryType`

OleQueryType

Syntax `OLESTATUS OleQueryType(lpObject, lpType)`

Parameter	*Type*	*Description*
`lpObject`	`LPOLEOBJECT`	Pointer to object
`lpType`	`LPLONG`	Pointer to `LONG` variable that will contain the object type; it will be one of the following values:

Value	*Meaning*
`OT_EMBEDDED`	Embedded object
`OT_LINK`	Linked object
`OT_STATIC`	Static picture

Description The `OleQueryType` function determines the object type for the object specified in `lpObject` (either embedded, linked, or static) and copies the type to the variable pointed to by `lpType`.

Return Value `OLE_OK` is returned when successful. `OLE_ERROR_OBJECT` or `OLE_ERROR_GENERIC` is returned when unsuccessful.

Function Category OLE Object Management

Related Functions `OleEnumFormats`, `OleQuerySize`

OleReconnect

Syntax `OLESTATUS OleReconnect(lpObject)`

Parameter	*Type*	*Description*
`lpObject`	`LPOLEOBJECT`	Pointer to object

Description The `OleReconnect` function reconnects the object specified in `lpObject`. If the object is not open, the function does not open it.

Return Value `OLE_OK` is returned when successful. `OLE_BUSY`, `OLE_ERROR_NOT_LINK`, `OLE_ERROR_OBJECT`, `OLE_ERROR_STATIC`, or `OLE_WAIT_FOR_RELEASE` is returned when unsuccessful.

Function Category OLE Client

Related Functions `OleActivate`, `OleClose`, `OleUpdate`

OleRegisterClientDoc

Syntax

```
OLESTATUS OleRegisterClientDoc(lpszClass, lpszDoc,
                               reserved, lplhDoc)
```

Parameter	*Type*	*Description*
`lpszClass`	`LPSTR`	Pointer to null-terminated string specifying the client document class
`lpszDoc`	`LPSTR`	Pointer to null-terminated string containing the path and name of the client document
`reserved`	`LONG`	Reserved; set to zero
`lplhDoc`	`LHCLIENTDOC FAR*`	Pointer to the returned handle of the client document

Description The `OleRegisterClientDoc` function registers an open client document with the library. The handle to the registered client document is returned in `lplhDoc`.

Return Value `OLE_OK` is returned when successful. `OLE_ERROR_NAME`, `OLE_ERROR_ALREADY_REGISTERED`, or `OLE_ERROR_MEMORY` is returned when unsuccessful.

Function Category OLE Document

Related Functions `OleRevokeClientDoc`

OleRegisterServer

Syntax

```
OLESTATUS OleRegisterServer(lpszClass, lpsrvr,
                            plhserver, hInst, srvruse)
```

Parameter	*Type*	*Description*
`lpszClass`	`LPSTR`	Pointer to null-terminated string that specifies the class name to register
`lpsrvr`	`LPOLESERVER`	Pointer to `OLESERVER` data structure initialized by the server application
`lplhserver`	`LHSERVER FAR*`	Pointer to variable that contains the handle to the server
`hInst`	`LPLONG`	Instance of server application
`srvruse`	`OLE_SERVER_USE`	Value set to `OLE_SERVER_SINGLE` for servers that use a single instance or `OLE_SERVER_MULTI` for servers that use a multiple instance

Description The `OleRegisterServer` function registers the server, class name, and instance with the server library.

Return Value `OLE_OK` is returned when successful. `OLE_ERROR_PROTECT_ONLY`, `OLE_ERROR_CLASS`, or `OLE_ERROR_MEMORY` is returned when unsuccessful.

Function Category OLE Server

Related Functions `OleRevokeServer`

OleRegisterServerDoc

Syntax

```
OLESTATUS OleRegisterServerDoc(lhsrvr, lpszDocName,
                               lpdoc, lplhdoc)
```

Parameter	*Type*	*Description*
lhsrvr	LHSERVER	Server handle obtained from OleRegisterServer
lpszDocName	LPSTR	Pointer to null-terminated string that contains the path and name to the document
lpdoc	LPOLESERVERDOC	Pointer to OLESERVERDOC data structure initialized by the server application
lplhdoc	LHSERVERDOC FAR*	Pointer to the returned document handle

Description The `OleRegisterServerDoc` function registers the specified document with the server library. This function is used by the server application when it creates or opens a document for any other reason besides a request from the library.

Return Value `OLE_OK` is returned when successful. `OLE_ERROR_ADDRESS`, `OLE_ERROR_HANDLE` or `OLE_ERROR_MEMORY` is returned when unsuccessful.

Function Category OLE Document

Related Functions `OleRevokeServerDoc`

OleRelease

Syntax

```
OLESTATUS OleRelease(lpObject)
```

Parameter	*Type*	*Description*
`lpObject`	`LPOLEOBJECT`	Pointer to object to release

Description The `OleRelease` function releases the object specified in `lpObject` from memory and, if open, closes it. The object is not deleted.

Return Value `OLE_OK` is returned when successful. `OLE_BUSY`, `OLE_ERROR_OBJECT`, or `OLE_WAIT_FOR_RELEASE` is returned when unsuccessful.

Function Category OLE Object Management

Related Functions `OleDelete`

OleRename

Syntax `OLESTATUS OleRename(lpObject, lpszNewname)`

Parameter	*Type*	*Description*
`lpObject`	`LPOLEOBJECT`	Pointer to object to rename
`lpszNewname`	`LPSTR`	Pointer to null-terminated string that contains the new name

Description The `OleRename` function renames the object in `lpObject` and notifies the client library of the name change.

Return Value `OLE_OK` is returned when successful. `OLE_ERROR_OBJECT` is returned when unsuccessful.

Function Category OLE Document

Related Functions `OleQueryName`

OleRenameClientDoc

Syntax `OLESTATUS OleRenameClientDoc(lhClientDoc, lpszNewDocname)`

Parameter	*Type*	*Description*
`lhClientDoc`	`LHCLIENTDOC`	Pointer to document to rename

Parameter	Type	Description
lpszNewDocname	LPSTR	Pointer to null-terminated string that contains the new name

Description The `OleRenameClientDoc` function renames the document specified in `lhClientDoc` and informs the client library of the name change.

Return Value `OLE_OK` is returned when successful. `OLE_ERROR_HANDLE` is returned when unsuccessful.

Function Category OLE Document

Related Functions `OleRegisterClientDoc`, `OleRenameServerDoc`

OleRenameServerDoc

Syntax `OLESTATUS OleRenameServerDoc(lhDoc, lpszDocname)`

Parameter	Type	Description
lhDoc	LHSERVERDOC	Document to rename
lpszDocname	LPSTR	Pointer to null-terminated string that contains the new document name

Description The `OleRenameServerDoc` function renames the document specified in `lhDoc` and notifies the server library of the name change.

Return Value `OLE_OK` is returned when successful. `OLE_ERROR_HANDLE` or `OLE_ERROR_MEMORY` is returned when unsuccessful.

Function Category OLE Document

Related Functions `OOleRegisterServerDoc`, `leRenameClientDoc`

OleRequestData

Syntax `OLESTATUS OleRequestData(lpObject, cfFormat)`

Parameter	Type	Description
lpObject	LPOLEOBJECT	Pointer to object associated with the server
cfFormat	OLECLIPFORMAT	Format for data; can be any of the predefined clipboard formats

Description The `OleRequestData` function requests that the library retrieve data from the server in the specified format.

Return Value `OLE_OK` is returned when successful. `OLE_BUSY`, `OLE_ERROR_NOT_OPEN`, `OLE_ERROR_OBJECT`, or `OLE_ERROR_STATIC`, `OLE_WAIT_FOR_RELEASE` is returned when unsuccessful.

Function Category OLE Client

Related Functions `OleGetData`, `OleSetData`

OleRevertClientDoc

Syntax `OLESTATUS OleRevertClientDoc(lhClientDoc)`

Parameter	Type	Description
lhClientDoc	LHCLIENTDOC	Document reverted to saved state

Description The `OleRevertClientDoc` function tells the client library that the document specified in `lhClientDoc` has reverted to previously saved state.

Return Value `OLE_OK` is returned when successful. `OLE_ERROR_HANDLE` is returned when unsuccessful.

Function Category OLE Document

Related Functions `OleRegisterClientDoc`, `OleRevertServerDoc`

OleRevertServerDoc

Syntax `OLESTATUS OleRevertServerDoc(lhDoc)`

Parameter	*Type*	*Description*
lhDoc	LHSERVERDOC	Document reverted to saved state

Description The `OleRevertServerDoc` function notifies the server library that the document specified in `lhDoc` has been reverted to its saved state.

Return Value `OLE_OK` is returned when successful. `OLE_ERROR_HANDLE` is returned when unsuccessful.

Function Category OLE Document

Related Functions `OleRegisterServerDoc`, `OleRevertClientDoc`

OleRevokeClientDoc

Syntax `OLESTATUS OleRevokeClientDoc(lhClientDoc)`

Parameter	*Type*	*Description*
lhClientDoc	LHCLIENTDOC	Client document

Description The `OleRevokeClientDoc` function notifies the client library that the client document specified in `lhClientDoc` is no longer open.

Return Value `OLE_OK` is returned when successful. `OLE_ERROR_HANDLE` or `OLE_ERROR_NOT_EMPTY` is returned when unsuccessful.

Function Category OLE Document

Related Functions `OleRegisterClientDoc`

OleRevokeObject

Syntax `OLESTATUS OleRevokeObject(lpClient)`

Parameter	*Type*	*Description*
`lpClient`	`LPOLECLIENT`	Pointer to `OLECLIENT` data structure associated with object to revoke

Description The `OleRevokeObject` function revokes the object specified in `lpClient`.

Return Value `OLE_OK` is returned when successful. An error value is returned when unsuccessful.

Function Category OLE Server

Related Functions `OleRevokeServer`

OleRevokeServer

Syntax `OLESTATUS OleRevokeServer(lhServer)`

Parameter	*Type*	*Description*
`lhServer`	`LHSERVER`	Server to revoke

Description The `OleRevokeServer` function closes all documents opened by the server for client applications and ends communications with the client applications.

Return Value `OLE_OK` is returned when successsful. `OLE_ERROR_HANDLE` or `OLE_WAIT_FOR_RELEASE` is returned when unsuccessful.

Function Category OLE Server

Related Functions `OleRegisterServer`, `OleRevokeServerDoc`

OleRevokeServerDoc

Syntax `OLESTATUS OleRevokeServerDoc(lhdoc)`

Parameter	*Type*	*Description*
`lhdoc`	`LHSERVERDOC`	Document to revoke

Description The `OleRevokeServerDoc` function revokes the document specified in `lhdoc`. The document is not available after calling this function.

Return Value `OLE_OK` is returned when successful. `OLE_ERROR_HANDLE` or `OLE_WAIT_FOR_RELEASE` is returned when unsuccessful.

Function Category OLE Document

Related Functions `OleRegisterServerDoc`

OleSavedClientDoc

Syntax `OLESTATUS OleSavedClientDoc(lhClientDoc)`

Parameter	*Type*	*Description*
`lhClientDoc`	`LHCLIENTDOC`	Document that has been saved

Description The `OleSavedClientDoc` function notifies the client library that the document specified by `lhClientDoc` has been saved.

Return Value `OLE_OK` is returned when successful. `OLE_ERROR_HANDLE` is returned when unsuccessful.

Function Category OLE Document

Related Functions `OleRegisterClientDoc`, `OleRevokeClientDoc`

OleSavedServerDoc

Syntax `OLESTATUS OleSavedServerDoc(lhDoc)`

Parameter	*Type*	*Description*
lhDoc	lhDoc	Document that has been saved

Description The OleSavedServerDoc function tells the server library that the document specified in lhDoc has been saved.

Return Value OLE_OK is returned when successful. OLE_ERROR_CANT_UPDATE_CLIENT or OLE_ERROR_HANDLE is returned when unsuccessful.

Function Category OLE Document

Related Functions OleRegisterServerDoc, OleRevokeServerDoc

OleSaveToStream

Syntax `OLESTATUS OleSaveToStream(lpObject, lpStream)`

Parameter	*Type*	*Description*
lpObject	LPOLEOBJECT	Pointer to object to save
lpStream	LPOLESTREAM	Pointer to OLESTREAM data structure initialized by the client application

Description The OleSaveToStream function saves the object specified in lpObject to the stream.

Return Value OLE_OK is returned when successful. OLE_ERROR_BLANK, OLE_ERROR_MEMORY, OLE_ERROR_OBJECT, or OLE_ERROR_STREAM is returned when unsuccessful.

Function Category OLE Object Management

Related Functions OleLoadFromStream

OleSetBounds

Syntax `OLESTATUS OleSetBounds(lpObject, lpBounds)`

Parameter	*Type*	*Description*
lpObject	LPOLEOBJECT	Pointer to object
lpBounds	LPRECT	Pointer to RECT data structure that contains the coordinates of the bounding rectangle; coordinates are expressed in MM_HIMETRIC units

Description The OleSetBounds function defines the coordinates of the bounding rectangle on the target device for the object specified in lpObject. This function has no relevance for linked objects.

Return Value OLE_OK is returned when successful. OLE_BUSY, OLE_ERROR_MEMORY, OLE_ERROR_OBJECT, or OLE_WAIT_FOR_RELEASE is returned when unsuccessful.

Function Category OLE Object Management

Related Functions OleDraw, OleQueryBounds

OleSetColorScheme

Syntax `OLESTATUS OleSetColorScheme(lpObject, lpPalette)`

Parameter	*Type*	*Description*
lpObject	LPOLEOBJECT	Pointer to OLEOBJECT data structure that describes the object
lpPalette	LPLOGPALETTE	Pointer to LOGPALETTE data structure that defines the palette

Description The OleSetColorScheme function defines the palette that the client application recommends for the server application to use when editing the specified object. The server does not have to use the specified palette.

Return Value OLE_OK is returned when successful. OLE_BUSY, OLE_ERROR_COMM, OLE_ERROR_MEMORY, OLE_ERROR_OBJECT, OLE_ERROR_PALETTE, OLE_ERROR_STATIC, or OLE_WAIT_FOR_RELEASE is returned when unsuccessful.

Function Category OLE Object Management

Related Functions OleDraw

OleSetData

Syntax `OLESTATUS OleSetData(lpObject, cfFormat, hData)`

Parameter	*Type*	*Description*
lpObject	LPOLEOBJECT	Pointer to object that specifies the server
cfFormat	OLECLIPFORMAT	Data format
hData	HANDLE	Memory object containing the data

Description The OleSetData function sends data to the server associated with the object specified in lpObject in the format specified in cfFormat.

Return Value OLE_OK is returned when successful. OLE_BUSY, OLE_ERROR_BLANK, OLE_ERROR_MEMORY, OLE_ERROR_NOT_OPEN, OLE_ERROR_OBJECT, or OLE_WAIT_FOR_RELEASE is returned when unsuccessful.

Function Category OLE Object Management

Related Functions OleGetData, OleRequestData

OleSetHostNames

Syntax

```
OLESTATUS OleSetHostNames(lpObject, lpszClient,
                          lpszClientObj)
```

Parameter	*Type*	*Description*
lpObject	LPOLEOBJECT	Pointer to object

Parameter	Type	Description
lpszClient	LPSTR	Pointer to null-terminated string that specifies the name of the container application
lpszClientObj	LPSTR	Pointer to null-terminated string that specifies the container's name for the object

Description The OleSetHostNames function defines the name of the container application and the container's name for the object specified in lpObject. lpszClient specifies the name of the container application. lpszClientObj specifies the container's name for the object.

Return Value OLE_OK is returned when successful. OLE_BUSY, OLE_ERROR_MEMORY, OLE_ERROR_OBJECT, or OLE_WAIT_FOR_RELEASE is returned when unsuccessful.

Function OLE Object Management

Related Functions OleSetTargetDevice

OleSetLinkUpdateOptions

Syntax `OLESTATUS OleSetLinkUpdateOptions(lpObject, UpdateOpt)`

Parameter	Type	Description
lpObject	LPOLEOBJECT	Pointer to object
UpdateOpt	OLEOPT_UPDATE	Link update option; set to one of the following values:

Value	Meaning
oleupdate_always	Update linked object whenever possible
oleupdate_onsave	Update linked object when source document is saved
oleupdate_oncall	Update linked object on request from client application

Description The `OleSetLinkUpdateOptions` function defines the link update options for the object-specified `lpObject`.

Return Value `OLE_OK` is returned when successful. `OLE_BUSY`, `OLE_ERROR_OBJECT`, `OLE_ERROR_OPTION`, `OLE_ERROR_STATIC`, or `OLE_WAIT_FOR_RELEASE` is returned when unsuccessful.

Function Category OLE Link

Related Functions `OleGetLinkUpdateOptions`

OleSetTargetDevice

Syntax `OLESTATUS OleSetTargetDevice(lpObject, hotd)`

Parameter	*Type*	*Description*
`lpObject`	`LPOLEOBJECT`	Pointer to object
`hotd`	`HANDLE`	Handle of `OLETARGETDEVICE` structure that defines the target device

Description The `OleSetTargetDevice` function defines the target output device for the object specified in `lpObject`. `hotd` specifies the target device.

Return Value `OLE_OK` is returned when successful. `OLE_BUSY`, `OLE_ERROR_MEMORY`, `OLE_ERROR_OBJECT`, `OLE_ERROR_STATIC`, or `OLE_WAIT_FOR_RELEASE` is returned when unsuccessful.

Function Category OLE Object Management

Related Functions `OleSetHostNames`

OleUnblockServer

Syntax `OLESTATUS OleUnblockServer(lhSrvr, lpfRequest)`

Parameter	*Type*	*Description*
`lhSrvr`	`LHSERVER`	Handle to a server

Parameter	Type	Description
`lpfRequest`	`BOOL FAR*`	Pointer to flag indicates whether there are any further requests in the queue—`TRUE` for more requests, `FALSE` for no more requests. This flag is set when the function returns.

Description The `OleUnblockServer` function processes a request from a queue. The `OleBlockServer` function forces requests to be sent to a queue.

Return Value `OLE_OK` is returned when successful. `OLE_ERROR_HANDLE` or `OLE_ERROR_MEMORY` is returned when unsuccessful.

Function Category OLE Server

Related Functions `OleBlockServer`

OleUnlockServer

Syntax `OLESTATUS OleUnlockServer(hServer)`

Parameter	Type	Description
`hServer`	`LHSERVER`	Server

Description The `OleUnlockServer` function releases the server specified in `hServer` from memory. The server is locked in memory by `OleLockServer`.

Return Value `OLE_OK` is returned when successful. `OLE_ERROR_HANDLE` or `OLE_WAIT_FOR_RELEASE` is returned when unsuccessful.

Function Category OLE Client

Related Functions `OleLockServer`

OleUpdate

Syntax `OLESTATUS OleUpdate(lpObject)`

Parameter	*Type*	*Description*
`lpObject`	`LPOLEOBJECT`	Pointer to object

Description The `OleUpdate` function updates the presentation of the object specified in `lpObject` and makes sure that the object has been updated relative to the objects that it depends upon.

Return Value `OLE_OK` is returned when successful. `OLE_BUSY`, `OLE_ERROR_OBJECT`, `OLE_ERROR_STATIC`, or `OLE_WAIT_FOR_RELEASE` is returned when unsuccessful.

Function Category OLE Link

Related Functions `OleQueryOutOfDate`

OpenClipboard

Syntax `BOOL OpenClipboard(hwnd)`

Parameter	*Type*	*Description*
`hwnd`	`HWND`	Window to access the clipboard

Description The `OpenClipboard` function allows the window specified in `hwnd` to gain access to the contents of the clipboard. No other application can modify the clipboard until the `CloseClipboard` function is called.

Return Value A nonzero value is returned if the clipboard is opened successfully. Zero is returned if the clipboard cannot be opened or is in use by another application.

Function Category Clipboard

Related Functions `CloseClipboard`, `EmptyClipboard`

OpenComm

Syntax `int OpenComm(lpszDevControl, cbInQueue, cbOutQueue)`

Parameter	*Type*	*Description*
`lpszDevControl`	`LPCSTR`	Pointer to a string containing the name of the communication device
`cbInQueue`	`UINT`	Size of the receive queue
`cbOutQueue`	`UINT`	Size of the transmit queue

Description The `OpenComm` function opens the communication device specified in `lpszDevControl` and assigns a handle to the device. The handle can be used in other communication functions to identify the communication device. `lpszDevControl` points to a string containing the name of the communication device. `lpszDevControl` contains LPT1 for parallel port 1, LPT2 for parallel port 2, COM1 for serial port 1, and so forth. `cbInQueue` and `cbOutQueue` specify the size of the receive and transmit queues, respectively. `cbInQueue` and `cbOutQueue` are ignored for LPT devices.

Return Value The return value identifies the communication device. One of the following values is returned on error:

Value	*Meaning*
`IE_BADID`	Invalid ID
`IE_BAUDRATE`	Unsupported baud rate
`IE_BYTESIZE`	Invalid byte size
`IE_DEFAULT`	Error in default parameters
`IE_HARDWARE`	Hardware not present
`IE_MEMORY`	Unable to allocate queues
`IE_NOPEN`	Device not open
`IE_OPEN`	Device already open

Function Category Communication

Related Functions `CloseComm`, `FlushComm`, `ReadComm`, `WriteComm`

OpenDriver

Syntax `HDRVR OpenDriver(lpDriverName, lpSectionName, lParam)`

Parameter	*Type*	*Description*
`lpDriverName`	`LPCSTR`	Pointer to null-terminated string that contains the name of the installable driver
`lpSectionName`	`LPCSTR`	Pointer to null-terminated string that contains the section name of the SYSTEM.INI file
`lParam`	`LPARAM`	Driver-specific data

Description The `OpenDriver` function performs initialization for the installable driver specified in lpDriverName. `lpDriverName` must contain the same driver name as specified in SYSTEM.INI. `lpSectionName` specifies the name of SYSTEM.INI file that contains the driver name. If the driver name is in the `[driver]` section of SYSTEM.INI, `lpSectionName` should be `NULL`.

Return Value The handle to the driver is returned when successful. `NULL` is returned when unsuccessful.

Function Category Installable Driver

Related Functions `CloseDriver`

OpenFile

Syntax `HFILE OpenFile(lpszFileName, lpOpenBuff, fuMode)`

Parameter	*Type*	*Description*
`lpszFileName`	`LPCSTR`	Pointer to a null-terminated string containing the name of the file to open; the string must contain characters from the Windows character set
`lpOpenBuff`	`OFSTRUCT FAR*`	Pointer to a `OFSTRUCT` data structure receiving

Parameter	Type	Description
		information about the file when the file is opened
fuMode	UINT	Action to take

Description The OpenFile function opens, creates, reopens, or deletes the file with the name specified in lpszFileName. lpOpenBuff points to a data structure of type OFSTRUCT that contains information on the file when it is first opened. The OFSTRUCT structure follows. fuMode specifies the action to take. fuMode is a combination, using bitwise OR, of the following values:

Value	Meaning
OF_CANCEL	Add a Cancel button to the OF_PROMPT dialog box
OF_CREATE	Create a new file
OF_DELETE	Delete the file
OF_EXIST	Open, then close, the file
OF_PARSE	Fill the OFSTRUCT data structure
OF_PROMPT	Display a dialog box if the file does not exist
OF_READ	Open for read only
OF_READWRITE	Open for read and write
OF_REOPEN	Open file with information in reopen buffer
OF_SEARCH	Search directories even when path name is specified
OF_SHARE_COMPAT	Open file with compatibility mode
OF_SHARE_DENY_NONE	Open file without denying other processes read and write access
OF_SHARE_DENY_READ	Open file and deny other processes read access
OF_SHARE_DENY_WRITE	Open file and deny other processes write access
OF_SHARE_EXCLUSIVE	Open file and deny other processes read and write access
OF_VERIFY	Verify date and time
OF_WRITE	Write only

```
typedef struct tagOFSTRUCT {
     BYTE cBytes;
     BYTE fFixedDisk;
     WORD nErrCode;
     BYTE reserved[4];
     BYTE szPathName[120];
} OFSTRUCT;
```

in which

`cBytes` is the length of the `OFSTRUCT` structure in bytes

`fFixedDisk` indicates whether the file is on a fixed disk (0 for not on a fixed disk)

`nErrCode` is the DOS error code if `OpenFile` returns –1

`reserved[4]` is reserved

`szPathName` is the pathname of the file.

Return Value The DOS file handle of the function is returned when successful. `HFILE_ERROR` is returned when unsuccessful.

Function Category File I/O

Related Functions `OpenSystemFile`

OpenIcon

Syntax `BOOL OpenIcon(hwnd)`

Parameter	*Type*	*Description*
`hwnd`	`HWND`	Window handle

Description The `OpenIcon` function displays the minimized window specified in `hwnd` in its original size and position.

Return Value When successful, a nonzero value is returned. Zero is returned when unsuccessful.

Function Category Display and Movement

Related Functions `ArrangeIconicWindows`, `CloseWindow`, `IsIconic`

OutputDebugString

Syntax `void OutputDebugString(lpszOutputString)`

Parameter	*Type*	*Description*
`lpszOutputString`	`LPCSTR`	Pointer to a null-terminated string containing the message to display

Description The `OutputDebugString` function displays the message in `lpszOutputString` on the debugging terminal.

Return Value There is no return value.

Function Category Debugging

Related Functions `DebugBreak`, `GetSystemDebugState`

PaintRgn

Syntax `BOOL PaintRgn(hdc, hrgn)`

Parameter	*Type*	*Description*
hdc	HDC	Device context
hrgn	HRGN	Region to paint. Coordinates are expressed in device units.

Description The `PaintRgn` function paints the region specified in `hrgn`. The region is filled using the selected brush.

Return Value `TRUE` is returned when successful. `FALSE` is returned when unsuccessful.

Function Category Region

Related Functions `FillRgn`, `FrameRgn`, `InvertRgn`

PALETTEINDEX

Syntax `COLORREF PALETTEINDEX(nPaletteIndex)`

Parameter	*Type*	*Description*
`nPaletteIndex`	`int`	Palette entry index containing color to use

Description The `PALETTEINDEX` macro returns the palette entry specifier for the logical color palette entry index specified in `nPaletteIndex`. The palette entry specifier contains a 1 in the high-order byte and the palette entry index in the low-order bytes. The palette entry specifier can be passed to functions that require an RGB value instead of passing the RGB value.

Return Value The palette entry specifier is returned.

Function Category Window Macros

Related Functions `PALETTERGB`, `RGB`

PALETTERGB

Syntax `COLORREF PALETTERGB(cRed, cGreen, cBlue)`

Parameter	*Type*	*Description*
`cRed`	`BYTE`	Red intensity
`cGreen`	`BYTE`	Green intensity
`cBlue`	`BYTE`	Blue intensity

Description The `PALETTERGB` macro returns the palette-relative RGB specifier representing the red, green, and blue color intensities specified in `cRed`, `cGreen`, and `cBlue`, respectively. The resulting RGB specifier contains 2 in the high-order byte and the RGB value in the three low-order bytes.

Return Value The palette-relative RGB specifier is returned.

Function Category Windows Macros

Related Functions `PALETTEINDEX`, `RGB`

PatBlt

Syntax

```
BOOL PatBlt(hdc, nLeftRect, nTopRect, nwidth, nheight,
            fdwRop)
```

Parameter	*Type*	*Description*
hdc	HDC	Device context
nLeftRect	int	Logical x coordinate of upper-left corner of rectangle to receive the pattern
nTopRect	int	Logical y coordinate of upper-left corner of retangle to receive the pattern
nwidth	int	Width of receiving rectangle in logical units
nheight	int	Height of receiving rectangle in logical units
fdwRop	DWORD	Raster operation to perform

Description The `PatBlt` function creates a bit pattern on the specified device that matches the specifications in the paremeters. The resulting pattern is the combination of the selected brush and the existing pattern on the device. `fdwRop` specifies the raster operation to perform. The following values can be used for `fdwRop`:

Value	*Meaning*
BLACKNESS	All output is black
DSTINVERT	Inverts the destination bitmap
PATCOPY	Copies the pattern to the destination bitmap
PATINVERT	Uses Boolean OR to combine the destination bitmap and pattern
PATPAINT	Paints the destination bitmap
WHITENESS	All output is white

Return Value `TRUE` is returned if the bitmap is drawn. `FALSE` is returned if the bitmap is not drawn.

Function Category Bitmap

Related Functions `BitBlt`, `StretchBlt`

PeekMessage

Syntax

```
BOOL PeekMessage(lpmsg, hwnd, uFilterFirst, uFilterLast,
                 fuRemove)
```

Parameter	*Type*	*Description*
`lpmsg`	`MSG FAR*`	`MSG` data structure containing message information from the Windows application queue
`hwnd`	`HWND`	Window receiving messages to be examined
`uFilterFirst`	`UINT`	Lowest message value to retrieve
`uFilterLast`	`UINT`	Highest message value to retrieve
`fuRemove`	`UINT`	Combination of `PM_NOREMOVE`, `PM_NOYIELD`, and `PM_REMOVE` flags

Description The `PeekMessage` function places a message retrieved from the application queue into the data structure of type `MSG` pointed to by `lpmsg`. The `MSG` data structure follows. This message differs from `GetMessage` because it does not wait for a message to be placed in the application queue before returning. All messages retrieved are associated with the window specified in `hwnd`. `uFilterFirst` and `uFilterLast` specify the range of message values that can be retrieved. The `WM_KEYFIRST` and `WM_KEYLAST` constants can be used for `uFilterFirst` and `uFilterLast`, respectively, to retrieve all keyboard-related messages. Similarly, `WM_MOUSEFIRST` and `WM_MOUSELAST` can be used to retrieve all mouse-related messages. `fuRemove` is a combination of the following flags:

Value	*Meaning*
PM_NOREMOVE	Messages aren't removed from the queue after being processed by PeekMessage; not used with PM_REMOVE flag
PM_NOYIELD	Keeps the current task from yielding system resources to another task
PM_REMOVE	Messages are removed from the queue after being processed by PeekMessage; not used with PM_NOREMOVE flag

```
typedef struct tagMSG {
     HWND hwnd;
     WORD message;
     WORD wParam;
     LONG lParam;
     DWORD time;
     POINT pt;
} MSG;
```

in which

hwnd is the window receiving the message

message is the message number

wParam is additional message information

lParam is additional message information

time is the time the message was posted

pt is the cursor position in screen coordinates.

Return Value A nonzero value is returned when a message is found. Zero is returned when a message is not found.

Function Category Message

Related Functions GetMessage, PostMessage, ReplyMessage, SendMessage

Pie

Syntax

```
BOOL Pie(hdc, nLeftRect, nTopRect, nRightRect, nBottomRect,
         nxStartArc, nyStartArc, nxEndArc, nyEndArc)
```

Parameter	*Type*	*Description*
hdc	HDC	Device context
nLeftRect	int	X coordinate of upper-left corner of binding rectangle
nTopRect	int	Y coordinate of upper-left corner of binding rectangle
nRightRect	int	X coordinate of lower-right corner of binding rectangle
nBottomRect	int	Y coordinate of lower-right corner of binding rectangle
nxStartArt	int	X coordinate of the starting point for the arc
nyStartArc	int	Y coordinate of the starting point for the arc
nxEndArc	int	X coordinate of the ending point for the arc
nyEndArc	int	Y coordinate of the ending point for the arc

Description The `Pie` function draws a pie-shaped wedge using the current pen and brush. The pie-shaped wedge is specified with four sets of coordinates. The first and second set, (`nLeftRect`, `nTopRect`) and (`nRightRect`, `nBottomRect`), specify the upper-left and lower-right corners, respectively, of the ellipse that is used to create the pie-shaped wedge. The third set of coordinates, (`nxStartArc`, `nyStartArc`), specifies the point used to determine where the arc for the pie-shaped wedge will begin. A line is projected from the center of the ellipse to the point specified in (`nxStartArc`, `nyStartArc`). The arc for the pie-shaped wedge begins where this projected line intercepts the ellipse. (`nxEndArc`, `nyEndArc`) is used in a similar fashion to determine the ending point of the arc. The arc of the pie-shaped wedge begins at the point where the line segment between the center of the ellipse and (`nxStartArc`, `nyStartArc`) intercepts the ellipse. The arc extends in a counter-clockwise direction and ends at the point where the line segment between the center of the ellipse and (`nxEndArc`, `nyEndArc`) intercepts the ellipse.

Return Value `TRUE` is returned if the pie-shaped wedge is successfully drawn. `FALSE` is returned when unsuccessful.

Function Category Ellipse and Polygon

Related Functions Chord, Ellipse

PlayMetaFile

Syntax `BOOL PlayMetaFile(hdc, hmf)`

Parameter	*Type*	*Description*
hdc	HDC	Device context
hmf	HMETAFILE	Metafile

Description The PlayMetaFile function plays the metafile specified in hmf on the device specified in hdc.

Return Value TRUE is returned when successful. FALSE is returned when unsuccessful.

Function Category Metafile

Related Functions PlayMetaFileRecord

PlayMetaFileRecord

Syntax `void PlayMetaFileRecord(hdc, lpht, lpmr, cHandles)`

Parameter	*Type*	*Description*
hdc	HDC	Device context
lpht	HANDLETABLE FAR*	Pointer to the handle table used for metafile playback
lpmr	METARECORD FAR*	Pointer to the metafile to play
cHandles	UINT	Number of handles in the handle table

Description The PlayMetaFileRecord function plays the metafile record specified in lpmr.

Return Value There is no return value.

Function Category Metafile

Related Functions PlayMetaFile

Polygon

Syntax BOOL Polygon(hdc, lppt, cPoints)

Parameter	*Type*	*Description*
hdc	HDC	Device context
lppt	const POINT FAR*	Pointer to an array of POINT data structures; each data structure specifies a point in the polygon
cPoints	int	Number of points in lppt

Description The Polygon function creates an automatically closed polygon consisting of the points specified in lppt. lppt is a pointer to an array of data structures of type POINT. Each POINT data structure specifies a point in the polygon. The POINT structure follows. cPoints specifies the number of points in lppt. The resulting polygon is filled using the polygon-filling mode.

```
typedef struct tagPOINT {
     int x;
     int y;
} POINT;
```

in which

x specifies the horizontal coordinate of the point

y specifies the vertical coordinate of the point.

Return Value TRUE is returned when successful. FALSE is returned when unsuccessful.

Function Category Ellipse and Polygon

Related Functions PolyPolygon, Rectangle, RoundRect

Polyline

Syntax `BOOL Polyline(hdc, lppt, cPoints)`

Parameter	*Type*	*Description*
`hdc`	`HDC`	Device context
`lppt`	`const POINT FAR*`	Pointer to an array of points to be connected by lines; each point is defined using a `POINT` data structure
`cPoints`	`int`	Number of points in `lppt`

Description The `Polyline` function connects the points in the array pointed to by `lppt` with line segments. Each point in the array pointed to by `lppt` is defined using a data structure of type `POINT`. The `POINT` data structure follows. The current pen is used to draw the line segments.

```
typedef struct tagPOINT {
     int x;
     int y;
} POINT;
```

in which

`x` specifies the horizontal coordinate of the point

`y` specifies the vertical coordinate of the point.

Return Value `TRUE` is returned when successful. `FALSE` is returned when unsuccessful.

Function Category Line Output

Related Functions `LineDDA`, `LineTo`, `MoveTo`

PolyPolygon

Syntax `BOOL PolyPolygon(hdc, lppt, lpnPolyCounts, cPolygons)`

Parameter	*Type*	*Description*
hdc	HDC	Device context
lppt	const POINT FAR*	Pointer to an array of POINT data structures; each data structure specifies a point in a polygon
lpnPolyCounts	int FAR*	Pointer to an array of integers; each integer specifies the number of points from lppt required for one polygon
cPolygons	int	Number of integers in lpnPolyCounts

Description The PolyPolygon function draws a series of closed polygons. The number of closed polygons is specified in cPolygons. The points for all of the polygons are contained in the array pointed to by lppt. Each point is specified in a POINT data structure. The POINT data structure follows. lpnPolyCounts points to an array of integers. Each integer represents the number of points from lppt used to create the closed polygon. Each polygon is filled using the current polygon-filling mode and is not closed automatically.

```
typedef struct tagPOINT {
     int x;
     int y;
} POINT;
```

in which

x specifies the horizontal coordinate of the point

y specifies the vertical coordinate of the point.

Return Value TRUE is returned when successful. FALSE is returned when unsuccessful.

Function Category Ellipse and Polygon

Related Functions Polygon, Rectangle, RoundRect

PostAppMessage

Syntax `BOOL PostAppMessage(htask, uMsg, wParam, lParam)`

Parameter	*Type*	*Description*
`htask`	`HTASK`	Task to receive message
`uMsg`	`UINT`	Type of message posted
`wParam`	`WPARAM`	Additional message information
`lParam`	`LPARAM`	Additional message information

Description The `PostAppMessage` function posts a message to the application with the task handle specified in `htask`. The function returns without waiting for the application to process the message.

Return Value A nonzero value is returned if the message is posted. Zero is returned if the message is not posted.

Function Category Message

Related Functions `GetMessage`, `PeekMessage`

PostMessage

Syntax `BOOL PostMessage(hwnd, uMsg, wParam, lParam)`

Parameter	*Type*	*Description*
`hwnd`	`HWND`	Window to receive message
`uMsg`	`UINT`	Type of message posted
`wParam`	`WPARAM`	Additional message information
`lParam`	`LPARAM`	Additional message information

Description The `PostMessage` function places a message in the application queue of the window specified in `hwnd`. The function does not wait for the window to process the message before returning. The `PostMessage` function should never be used to send a message to a control.

Return Value A nonzero value is returned when the message is posted. Zero is returned if the message is not posted.

Function Category Message

Related Functions `PostAppMessage`, `SendMessage`

PostQuitMessage

Syntax `void PostQuitMessage(nExitCode)`

Parameter	*Type*	*Description*
`nExitCode`	`int`	Application exit code

Description The `PostQuitMessage` function posts the `WM_QUIT` message with the application. The function does not wait for the application to process the message before returning. The function is used to inform Windows that the application wants to quit. `nExitCode` specifies the application exit code that is used as the `wParam` parameter for the `WM_QUIT` message.

Return Value There is no return value.

Function Category Message

Related Functions `GetMessage`

PrintDlg

Syntax `BOOL PrintDlg(lppd)`

Parameter	*Type*	*Description*
`lppd`	`LPPRINTDLG`	Pointer to `PRINTDLG` data structure containing dialog box initialization information

Description The `PrintDlg` function displays one of two dialog boxes: a print dialog box or a setup dialog box. The print dialog box prompts the user to select the print job properties. The setup dialog box prompts the user to configure the printer. `lppd` points to a data structure of type `PRINTDLG`. The `PRINTDLG` structure follows.

```
typedef struct tagPD {
     DWORD lStructSize;
     HWND hwndOwner;
     HANDLE hDevMode;
     HANDLE hDevNames;
     HDC hDC;
     DWORD Flags;
     WORD nFromPage;
     WORD nToPage;
     WORD nMinPage;
     WORD nMaxPage;
     WORD nCopies;
     HANDLE hInstance;
     DWORD lCustData;
     int (FAR PASCAL *lpfnPrintHook)(HWND, WORD,
              WORD, LONG);
     int (FAR PASCAL *lpfnSetupHook)(HWND, WORD,
              WORD, LONG);
     LPSTR lpPrintTemplateName;
     LPSTR lpSetupTemplateName;
     HANDLE hPrintTemplate;
     HANDLE hSetupTemplate;
} PRINTDLG;
```

in which

`lStructSize` is the number of bytes in the structure

`hwndOwner` is the window handle of the window that owns the dialog box

`hDevMode` is the movable global memory object that contains a `DEVMODE` data structure. This data structure contains data used to initialize the dialog controls. When `PrintDlg` returns, the structure contains information on the state of the dialog controls.

`hDevNames` is the moveable global memory object that contains a `DEVNAMES` data structure. The strings in this data structure are used to initialize dialog controls. When `PrintDlg` returns, this data structure contains the strings entered by the user.

`hDC` is the device or information context. When `Flags` contains `PD_RETURNDC`, `hDC` is a device context. When `Flags` contains `PD_RETURNIC`, `hDC` is an information context. When `Flags` contains both `PD_RETURNDC` and `PD_RETURNIC`, `hDC` is `PD_RETURNDC`.

`Flags` is a combination of the following dialog box initialization flags:

Value	*Meaning*
`PD_ALLPAGES`	The ALL radio button is selected when the dialog box is created
`PD_COLLATE`	Collate checkbox is checked when dialog box is created
`PD_DISABLEPRINTOFILE`	Print to File check box is disabled
`PD_ENABLEPRINTHOOK`	Hook function specified in `lpfnPrintHook` enabled
`PD_ENABLEPRINTTEMPLATE`	Dialog box created using template specified in `hInstance` and `lpPrintTemplateName`
`PD_ENABLEPRINTTEMPLATEHANDLE`	Dialog box created using preloaded dialog template in `hInstance`
`PD_ENABLESETUPHOOK`	Hook function in `lpfnSetupHook` enabled
`PD_ENABLESETUPTEMPLATE`	Dialog box created using template specified by `hInstance` and `lpSetupTemplateName`
`PD_ENABLESETUPTEMPLATEHANDLE`	Dialog box created using preloaded dialog template in `hInstance`
`PD_HIDEPRINTTOFILE`	Check box is hidden and disabled
`PD_NOPAGENUMS`	Pages radio button and edit control disabled
`PD_NOSELECTION`	Selection radio button disabled
`PD_NOWARNING`	Warning message is not displayed if there is no default printer
`PD_PAGENUMS`	Pages radio button is enabled and set to selected state
`PD_PRINTSETUP`	Print setup dialog box is displayed
`PD_PRINTTOFILE`	Print to File check box is placed in checked state

Value	Meaning
PD_RETURNDC	PrintDlg function returns a device context that matches the user's selections
PD_RETURNDEFAULT	PrintDlg returns DEVMODE and DEVNAME data structures that are initialized for the system default printer
PD_RETURNIC	PrintDlg function returns an information context that matches the user's selections
PD_SELECTION	Selection radio button is enabled and set to selected state
PD_SHOWHELP	Help push button shown
PD_USEDEVMODECOPIES	Copies edit control is disabled for printer drivers that do not support multiple copies

nFromPage is the value for the starting page edit control

nToPage is the value for the ending page edit control

nMinPage is the minimum value for page range in nFromPage and nToPage

nMaxPage is the maximum value for page range in nFromPage and nToPage

nCopies defines the number of copies for the Copies edit control

hInstance is the data block that contains the preloaded dialog box template

lCustData is the application-defined data passed to the hook function in lpfnHook

lpfnPrintHook is the function for print dialog messages

lpfnSetupHook is the function for setup dialog messages

lpPrintTemplateName is the pointer to the null-terminated string that specifies the substitute dialog box template

lpSetupTemplateName is the pointer to the null-terminated string that specifies the dialog box template substituted for the standard dialog template in COMMDLG `hPrintTemplate` is the handle to the global memory object that contains the preloaded dialog template used to replace the default print dialog

`hSetupTemplate` is the handle to the global memory object that contains the preloaded dialog template used to replace the default setup dialog.

Return Value `TRUE` is returned when successful. `FALSE` is returned when unsuccessful.

Function Category Common Dialog

Related Functions `GetOpenFileName`, `GetSaveFileName`

ProfClear

Syntax `void ProfClear()`

Description The `ProfClear` function discards the samples in the sampling buffer. This function is used with the Windows Profiler.

Return Value There is no return value.

Function Category Optimization Tools

Related Functions `ProfFinish`, `ProfFlush`, `ProfStop`

ProfFinish

Syntax `void ProfFinish()`

Description The `ProfFinish` function ends the sampling session and flushes the output buffer to disk. This function is used with the Windows Profiler.

Return Value There is no return value.

Function Category Optimization Tools

Related Functions `ProfClear`, `ProfFlush`, `ProfStop`

ProfFlush

Syntax `void ProfFlush()`

Description The `ProfFlush` function flushes the sampling buffer to disk. This function is used with the Windows Profiler.

Return Value There is no return value.

Function Category Optimization Tools

Related Functions `ProfClear`, `ProfFinish`, `ProfStop`

ProfInsChk

Syntax `ProfInsCheck()`

Description The `ProfInsCheck` function indicates whether the Windows Profiler is installed.

Return Value Zero is returned if the Profiler is not installed. 1 is returned if the Profiler is installed for any mode other than 386 enhanced mode. 2 is returned if the Profiler is installed for 386 enhanced mode.

Function Category Optimization Tools

Related Functions `ProfSetup`, `ProfStart`

ProfSampRate

Syntax `void ProfSampRate(nRate286, nRate386)`

Parameter	*Type*	*Description*
`nRate286`	`int`	Sampling rate if application is not running with Windows in 386 enhanced mode
`nRate386`	`int`	Sampling rate if application is running with Windows in 386 enhanced mode

Description The `ProfSampRate` function specifies the sampling rate for the Windows Profiler. `nRate386` specifies the sampling rate in milliseconds if the application is running with Windows in 386 enhanced mode and ranges from 1 to 1000. `nRate286` specifies the sampling rate if the application is not running with Windows in 386 enhanced mode. One of the following values is used for `nRate286`:

Value	*Meaning*
1	122.070 microseconds
2	244.141 microseconds
3	488.281 microseconds
4	976.562 microseconds
5	1.953125 milliseconds
6	3.90625 milliseconds
7	7.8125 milliseconds
8	15.625 milliseconds
9	31.25 milliseconds
10	62.5 milliseconds
11	125 milliseconds
12	250 milliseconds
13	500 milliseconds

Return Value There is no return value.

Function Category Optimization Tools

Related Functions `ProfSetup`, `ProfStart`

ProfSetup

Syntax `void ProfSetup(nBufferKB, nSamplesKB)`

Parameter	*Type*	*Description*
`nBufferKB`	`int`	Number of kilobytes in output buffer
`nSamplesKB`	`int`	Amount of sampling data to write to disk

Description The `ProfSetup` function defines the size of the output buffer and the amount of sampling data to write to disk. `nBufferKB` specifies the number of kilobytes in the output buffer. `nBufferKB` can range between 1 and 1064 and has the default value of 64. `nSamplesKB` specifies the amount of sampling data to write to the disk. When `nSamplesKB` is zero, the default value, the amount of data written to the disk, is unlimited. The `ProfSetup` function is used with the Window Profiler. Windows must be running in 386 enhanced mode or the function has no effect.

Return Value There is no return value.

Function Category Optimization Tools

Related Functions `ProfStartup`, `ProfStop`

ProfStart

Syntax `void ProfStart()`

Description The `ProfStart` function initiates a sampling session. The `ProfStart` function is used with the Windows Profiler.

Return Value There is no return value.

Function Category Optimization Tools

Related Functions `ProfSetup`, `ProfStop`

ProfStop

Syntax `void ProfStop()`

Description The `ProfStop` function terminates a sampling session. The `ProfStop` function is used with the Windows Profiler.

Return Value There is no return value.

Function Category Optimization Tools

Related Functions `ProfSetup`, `ProfStartup`

PtInRect

Syntax `BOOL PtInRect(lprc, Pt)`

Parameter	*Type*	*Description*
lprc	const RECT FAR*	Pointer to RECT data structure containing the coordinates of the rectangle
Pt	POINT	POINT data structure containing the point to check

Description The PtInRect function determines whether the point in Pt lies within the rectangle in lprc. lprc points to the data structure of type RECT that contains the coordinates for the rectangle. Pt points to the data structure of type POINT that contains the coordinates of the point. The point is considered to be within the rectangle if it lies within the rectangle's borders or on the left or top borders. If the point is on the right or bottom borders, it is not considered to be inside the rectangle. The RECT and POINT data structures follow.

```
typedef struct tagRECT {
     int left;
     int top;
     int right;
     int bottom;
} RECT;
```

in which

left is the x coordinate of the upper-left corner

top is the y coordinate of the upper-left corner

right is the x coordinate of the lower-right corner

bottom is the y coordinate of the lower-right corner.

```
typedef struct tagPOINT {
     int x;
     int y;
} POINT;
```

in which

x is the horizontal coordinate of the point

y is the vertical coordinate of the point.

Return Value A nonzero value is returned if the point lies within the given rectangle. Zero is returned if the point does not lie within the given rectangle.

Function Category Rectangle

Related Functions `IntersectRect`, `PtInRegion`, `UnionRect`

PtInRegion

Syntax `BOOL PtInRegion(hrgn, nXPos, nYPos)`

Parameter	*Type*	*Description*
`hrgn`	`HRGN`	Region
`nXPos`	`int`	Logical x coordinate of point to check
`nYPos`	`int`	Logical y coordinate of point to check

Description The `PtInRegion` function determines whether the point specified by (`nXPos`, `nYPos`) lies within the region specified in `hRgn`.

Return Value `TRUE` is returned if the point lies within the specified region. `FALSE` is returned if the point does not lie within the specified region.

Function Category Region

Related Functions `RectInRegion`

PtVisible

Syntax `BOOL PtVisible(hdc, nXPos, nYPos)`

Parameter	*Type*	*Description*
`hdc`	`HDC`	Device context
`nXPos`	`int`	Logical x coordinate of point

Parameter	Type	Description
nYPos	int	Logical y coordinate of point

Description The PtVisible function determines whether the point specified by (nXPos, nYPos) lies in the clipping region of the device context specified in hdc.

Return Value A nonzero value is returned if the point is within the clipping region. Zero is returned if the point is not within the clipping region.

Function Category Clipping

Related Functions RectVisible

QuerySendMessage

Syntax `BOOL QuerySendMessage(NULL, NULL, NULL, lpMessage)`

Parameter	Type	Description
lpMessage	LPMSG	Pointer to MSG data structure

Description The QuerySendMessage function returns a value that indicates whether the message sent by SendMessage originated within the current task. lpMessage points to the MSG data structure where the message is placed when the message originated within the current task. The MSG data structure follows.

```
typedef struct tagMSG {
     HWND hwnd;
     WORD message;
     WORD wParam;
     LONG lParam;
     DWORD time;
     POINT pt;
} MSG;
```

in which

hwnd is the window receiving the message

message is the message number

`wParam` is additional message information

`lParam` is additional message information

`time` is the time the message was posted

`pt` is the cursor position in screen coordinates.

Return Value Zero is returned when the message originated within the current task. A nonzero value is returned when unsuccessful or the message did not originate from within the current task.

Function Category Debugging

Related Functions `SendMessage`

ReadComm

Syntax `int ReadComm(idComDev, lpvBuf, cbRead)`

Parameter	*Type*	*Description*
`idComDev`	`int`	Communcation device
`lpvBuf`	`void FAR*`	Pointer to buffer to receive characters
`cbRead`	`int`	Number of characters to read

Description The `ReadComm` function reads from the communication device specified in `idComDev`. The characters read are copied into the buffer pointed to by `lpvBuf`. `cbRead` specifies the number of characters to read.

Return Value The number of characters read from the device is returned. For parallel ports, the return value is zero. A negative value indicates an error.

Function Category Communication

Related Functions `OpenComm`, `WriteComm`

RealizePalette

Syntax `UINT RealizePalette(hdc)`

Parameter	*Type*	*Description*
hdc	HDC	Device context

Description The `RealizePalette` function maps entries in the logical palette for the device context specified in `hdc` to the system palette.

Return Value The number of logical palette entries mapped to the system palette is returned.

Function Category Color Palette

Related Functions `CreatePalette`, `SelectPalette`

Rectangle

Syntax
```
BOOL Rectangle(hdc, nLeftRect, nTopRect, nRightRect,
               nBottomRect)
```

Parameter	*Type*	*Description*
hdc	HDC	Device context
nLeftRect	int	X coordinate of upper-left corner of rectangle
nTopRect	int	Y coordinate of upper-left corner of rectangle
nRightRect	int	X coordinate of lower-right corner of rectangle
nBottomRect	int	Y coordinate of lower-right corner of rectangle

Description The `Rectangle` function creates a rectangle using the logical coordinates in (`nLeftRect`, `nTopRect`) and (`nRightRect`, `nBottomRect`). The rectangle's border is drawn with the current pen. The rectangle is filled using the current brush.

Return Value A nonzero value is returned when successful. Zero is returned when unsuccessful.

Function Category Ellipse and Polygon

Related Functions Polygon, RoundRect

RectInRegion

Syntax `BOOL RectInRegion(hrgn, lprc)`

Parameter	*Type*	*Description*
hrgn	HRGN	Region
lprc	const RECT FAR*	Pointer to a data structure of type RECT containing the coordinates of the rectangle to check

Description The RectInRegion function determines whether any part of the rectangle specified in lprc lies within the region specified in hrgn. lprc points to a data structure of type RECT that contains the coordinates of the rectangle. The RECT data structure follows.

```
typedef struct tagRECT{
     int left;
     int top;
     int right;
     int bottom;
} RECT;
```

in which

left is the x coordinate of the upper-left corner

top is the y coordinate of the upper-left corner

right is the x coordinate of the lower-right corner

bottom is the y coordinate of the lower-right corner.

Return Value A nonzero value is returned if any part of the rectangle lies within the region. Zero is returned if no part of the rectangle lies within the region.

Function Category Region

Related Functions `PtInRegion`

RectVisible

Syntax `BOOL RectVisible(hdc, lprc)`

Parameter	*Type*	*Description*
`hdc`	`HDC`	Device context
`lprc`	`const RECT FAR*`	Pointer to `RECT` data structure containing the coordinate of the rectangle

Description The `RectVisible` function determines whether any part of the rectangle specified in the data structure of type `RECT` pointed to by `lprc` lies within the clipping region of the device context specified in `hdc`. The `RECT` data structure follows.

```
typedef struct tagRECT{
     int left;
     int top;
     int right;
     int bottom;
} RECT;
```

in which

`left` is the x coordinate of the upper-left corner

`top` is the y coordinate of the upper-left corner

`right` is the x coordinate of the lower-right corner

`bottom` is the y coordinate of the lower-right corner.

Return Value A nonzero value is returned if any part of the specified rectangle lies within the clipping region. Zero is returned if no part of the specified rectangle lies within the clipping region.

Function Category Clipping

Related Functions `PtVisible`

RedrawWindow

Syntax

```
BOOL RedrawWindow(hwnd, lprcUpdate, hrgnUpdate,
                  fuRedraw)
```

Parameter	*Type*	*Description*
hwnd	HWND	Window to redraw. If set to NULL, the entire screen is updated.
lprcUpdate	const RECT FAR*	Pointer to RECT data structure that contains the coordinates of the update rectangle
hrgnUpdate	HRGN	Update region. If hrgnUpdate and lprcUpdate are both NULL, the client area is added to the update region
fuRedraw	UINT	Combination of redraw flags

Description The RedrawWindow function updates the rectangle or region of the client area specified in lprcUpdate or hrgnUpdate. fuRedraw specifies a combination of the following redraw flags:

Invalidation Flags

Value	*Meaning*
RDW_INTERNALPAINT	WM_PAINT message is posted to the window
RDW_INVALIDATE	The area in lprcUpdate or hrgnUpdate (whichever is not NULL) is invalidated. If both are NULL, the entire window is invalidated
RDW_ERASE	Window receives a WM_ERASEBKGND message when the window is repainted. RDW_ERASE must also be specified for this flag to work.

Validation Flags

Value	*Meaning*
RDW_NOERASE	Pending WM_ERASEBKGND messsages are suppressed
RDW_NOINTERNALPAINT	Pending WM_PAINT messages are suppressed
RDW_VALIDATE	The area in lprcUpdate or hrgnUpdate (whichever is not NULL) is validated. If both are NULL, the entire window is validated.

Enumeration Control Flags

Value	*Meaning*
RDW_ALLCHILDREN	Include child windows when repainting
RDW_NOCHILDREN	Do not include child windows when repainting
RDW_ERASENOW	Window receives WM_ERASEBKGND message before the function returns
RDW_UPDATENOW	Window receives WM_PAINT or WM_PAINTICON message before the function returns

Return Value: A nonzero value is returned when successful. Zero is returned when unsuccessful.

Function: Category Painting

Related: Functions GetUpdateRect, GetUpdateRgn, InvalidateWindow, InvalidateRgn

RegCloseKey

Syntax `LONG RegCloseKey(hkey)`

Parameter	*Type*	*Description*
hkey	HKEY	Key to close

Description The `RegCloseKey` closes the key specified in `hkey`. When a key is closed, all data for the key is written to the system registration database and the key handle is released.

Return Value `ERROR_SUCCESS` is returned when successful. An error value is returned when unsuccessful.

Function Category Registration

Related Functions `RegDeleteKey`, `RegOpenKey`

RegCreateKey

Syntax `LONG RegCreateKey(hkey, lpszSubKey, phkResult)`

Parameter	*Type*	*Description*
`hkey`	`HKEY`	Key handle
`lpszSubKey`	`LPSTR`	Pointer to null terminated string that specifies the subkey to open or create
`phkResult`	`PHKEY`	Pointer to handle of key that is opened or created

Description The `RegCreateKey` function either creates or opens the specified key. The key is created when the specified key does not exist. If the specified key exists, it is opened. The key created or opened is usually a subkey of the key specified in `hkey`.

Return Value `ERROR_SUCCESS` is returned when successful. An error value is returned when unsuccessful.

Function Category Registration

Related Functions `RegOpenKey`, `RegSetValue`

RegDeleteKey

Syntax `LONG RegDeleteKey(hkey, lpszSubKey)`

Parameter	Type	Description
hkey	HKEY	Key handle
lpszSubKey	LPSTR	Pointer to null-terminated string that specifies the subkey to delete

Description The RegDeleteKey function deletes a key. The key that is deleted is specified in lpszSubKey and is usually a subkey of the key specified in hkey. When lpszSubKey is set to NULL, the key in hkey is deleted.

Return Value ERROR_SUCCESS is returned when successful. An error value is returned when unsuccessful.

Function Category Registration

Related Functions RegCloseKey

RegEnumKey

Syntax `LONG RegEnumKey(hkey, iSubkey, lpszBuffer, cbBuffer)`

Parameter	Type	Description
hkey	HKEY	Key handle
iSubkey	DWORD	Index of subkey to retrieve; set to zero for first call to RegEnumKey
lpszBuffer	LPSTR	Pointer to buffer where the name of the subkey will be copied
cbBuffer	DWORD	Number of bytes in buffer pointed to by lpszBuffer

Description The RegEnumKey function enumerates the subkeys for the key specified in hkey. iSubkey should be set to zero on the first call to this function and incremented for each subsequent call. The name of the enumerated subkey is copied to the buffer pointed to by lpszBuffer.

Return Value ERROR_SUCCESS is returned when successful. An error value is returned when unsuccessful.

Function Category Registration

Related Functions `RegQueryValue`

RegisterClass

Syntax `ATOM RegisterClass(lpwc)`

Parameter	*Type*	*Description*
`lpwc`	`const WNDCLASS FAR*`	Points to `WNDCLASS` structure that contains the class attributes

Description The `RegisterClass` function registers a window class. `lpwc` points to a data structure of type `WNDCLASS` that contains the attributes for the window class.

Return Value For Windows 3.0 and earlier: A nonzero value is returned if the class is successfully registered. Zero is returned if the class is not registered. For Windows 3.1: The atom that identifies the class is returned.

Function Category Window Creation

Related Functions `UnregisterClass`

RegisterClipboardFormat

Syntax `UINT RegisterClipboardFormat(lpszFormatName)`

Parameter	*Type*	*Description*
`lpszFormatName`	`LPCSTR`	Name of new format

Description The `RegisterClipboardFormat` function registers a new clipboard format. `lpszFormatName` points to the name of the new format. The name is a null-terminated character string. The new format will be added to the format list for the clipboard.

Return Value Zero is returned if the format cannot be registered. A value in the range of 0xC000 to 0xFFFF which identifies the new format is returned when successful.

Function Category Clipboard

Related Functions `EnumClipboardFormats`, `GetClipboardFormatName`, `GetPriorityClipboardFormat`

RegisterWindowMessage

Syntax `UINT RegisterWindowMessage(lpszString)`

Parameter	*Type*	*Description*
`lpszString`	`LPCSTR`	Pointer to the message string to register

Description The `RegisterWindowMessage` function defines a new, unique window message. `lpszString` specifies the message string to register.

Return Value An unsigned short integer within the range of 0xC000 to 0xFFFF is returned when the message is registered successfully. Zero is returned when unsuccessful.

Function Category Message

Related Functions `PostMessage`, `SendMessage`

RegOpenKey

Syntax `LONG RegOpenKey(hkey, lpszSubKey, phkResult)`

Parameter	*Type*	*Description*
`hkey`	`HKEY`	Key handle
`lpszSubKey`	`LPSTR`	Pointer to null-terminated string that contains the name of the subkey to open
`phkResult`	`PHKEY`	Pointer to handle of key to open

Description The `RegOpenKey` function opens the specified key. The key that is opened is usually a subkey of the key specified in `hkey`. When `hkey` is `NULL`, the key specified in `lpszSubKey` is opened. If the specified key does not exist, the key is not created.

Return Value `ERROR_SUCCESS` is returned when successful. An error value is returned when unsuccessful.

Function Category Registration

Related Functions `RegCreateKey`

RegQueryValue

Syntax `LONG RegQueryValue(hkey, lpszSubKey, lpszValue, pcb)`

Parameter	*Type*	*Description*
`hkey`	`HKEY`	Key handle
`lpszSubKey`	`LPSTR`	Pointer to null-terminated string that contains the name of the subkey
`lpszValue`	`LPSTR`	Pointer to buffer where the text string will be copied
`lpcb`	`LONG FAR*`	Pointer to variable that specifies the number of bytes for the value in `lpszValue`; this variable contains the size of the string copied to `lpszValue` when the function returns

Description The `RegQueryValue` function copies the text string associated with the specified key to the buffer pointed to by `lpszValue`.

Return Value `ERROR_SUCCESS` is returned when successful. An error value is returned when unsuccessful.

Function Category Registration

Related Functions `RegEnumKey`

RegSetValue

Syntax `LONG RegSetValue(hkey, lpszSubKey, fdwType, lpszValue, cb)`

Parameter	*Type*	*Description*
hkey	HKEY	Key handle or HKEY_CLASSES_ROOT
lpszSubKey	LPSTR	Pointer to null-terminated string that contains the name of the subkey
fdwType	DWORD	String type; set to REG_SZ
lpszValue	LPSTR	Pointer to null-terminated string that specifies the text string to associate with the specified key
cb	DWORD	Number of bytes in the string pointed to by lpszValue

Description The `RegSetValue` function associates the text string specified in `lpszValue` with the specified key. A key is created if the specified key does not exist.

Return Value `ERROR_SUCCESS` is returned when successful. An error value is returned when unsuccessful.

Function Category Registration

Related Functions `RegCreateKey`, `RegQueryValue`

ReleaseCapture

Syntax `void ReleaseCapture()`

Description The `ReleaseCapture` function restores normal input processing by releasing the mouse capture.

Return Value There is no return value.

Function Category Input

Related Functions `GetCapture`, `SetCapture`

ReleaseDC

Syntax `int ReleaseDC(hwnd, hdc)`

Parameter	*Type*	*Description*
`hwnd`	`HWND`	Window handle
`hdc`	`HDC`	Device context to release

Description The `ReleaseDC` function releases the device context in `hdc` for the window in `hwnd`. The device context is then free to be used by other applications. Only common and window device contexts are freed.

Return Value Zero is returned when the device context is not released. 1 is returned when the device context is released.

Function Category Device Context, Painting

Related Functions `CreateDC`, `DeleteDC`, `GetDC`, `SaveDC`

RemoveFontResource

Syntax `BOOL RemoveFontResource(lpszFile)`

Parameter	*Type*	*Description*
`lpszFile`	`LPCSTR`	Specifies either a pointer to a character string that contains the filename of the font resource file, or the handle to a loaded module in the low-order word (high-order word must be set to zero)

Description The `RemoveFontResource` function removes the font resource specified by `lpszFile` from the font table.

Return Value A nonzero value is returned when successful. Zero is returned when unsuccessful.

Function Category Font

Related Functions AddFontResource, CreateScalableFontResource

RemoveMenu

Syntax `BOOL RemoveMenu(hmenu, idItem, fuFlags)`

Parameter	*Type*	*Description*
hmenu	HMENU	Menu to modify
idItem	UINT	Menu item to remove
fuFlags	UINT	Specifies meaning of idItem

Description The RemoveMenu function deletes the menu item specified in idItem from the menu specified in hmenu. The menu item specified in idItem must have a pop-up menu associated with it. The handle for the pop-up menu is not destroyed; therefore, it is able to be reused. idItem contains the command ID of the menu item when fuFlags is set to MF_BYCOMMAND. idItem contains the menu item position when fuFlags is set to MF_BYPOSITION. The values used for fuFlags are as follows:

Value	*Meaning*
MF_BYCOMMAND	The command ID of the menu item is contained in idItem
MF_BYPOSITION	The menu item position is contained in idItem

The GetSubMenu function is used to retrieve the handle of the pop-up menu before the RemoveMenu function is called. The DrawMenuBar function should be called after the menu has been changed.

Return Value A nonzero value is returned when successful. When unsuccessful, zero is returned.

Function Category Menu

Related Functions CreateMenu, DeleteMenu, DestroyMenu, GetSubMenu

RemoveProp

Syntax `HANDLE RemoveProp(hwnd, lpsz)`

Parameter	*Type*	*Description*
hwnd	HWND	Window containing property list to modify
lpsz	LPCSTR	Points to null-terminated string or atom identifying the entry to remove

Description The RemoveProp function removes the entry specified in lpsz from the property list of the window specified in hwnd. lpsz points to either a null-terminated string or an atom that identifies a string. When lpsz specifies an atom, the atom (16-bits) is placed in the low-order word of lpsz; the high-order word of lpsz is set to zero.

Return Value The specified string is returned when successful. When unsuccessful, NULL is returned.

Function Category Property

Related Functions EnumProps, GetProp, SetProp

ReplaceText

Syntax `HWND ReplaceText(lpfr)`

Parameter	*Type*	*Description*
lpfr	LPFINDREPLACE	Pointer to FINDREPLACE data structure containing dialog box initialization data

Description The ReplaceText function creates a system-defined modeless dialog box for locating and replacing text. The application is responsible for defining the actions for the dialog box. lpfr points to a data structure of type FINDREPLACE that contains initialization information for the dialog box. The FINDREPLACE data structure follows.

```
#include <commdlg.h>
typedef struct     {
     DWORD lStructSize;
     HWND hwndOwner;
     HANDLE hInstance;
     DWORD Flags;
     LPSTR lpstrFindWhat;
     LPSTR lpstrReplaceWith;
     WORD wFindWhatLen;
     WORD wReplaceWithLen;
     DWORD lCustData;
     BOOL (FAR PASCAL *lpfnHook)(HWND, unsigned,
                                  WORD, LONG);
     LPSTR lpTemplateName;
} FINDREPLACE;
```

in which

`lStructSize` is the size of the structure in bytes

`hwndOwner` is the window that owns the dialog box

`hInstance` is the data block that contains the template referenced by `lpTemplateName`

`Flags` is the dialog box intialization flags. `Flags` is a combination of the following values:

Value	*Meaning*
`FR_DIALOGTERM`	Dialog box is terminating
`FR_DOWN`	Search is conducted down the document when set
`FR_ENABLEHOOK`	Enables the hook function in `lpfnHook`
`FR_ENABLETEMPLATE`	Enables the use of the template in `hInstance` and `lpTemplateName`
`FR_ENABLETEMPLATEHANDLE`	`hInstance` specifies a data block containing a pre-loaded dialog template
`FR_FINDNEXT`	Search for next occurrence of the specified text
`FR_HIDEMATCHCASE`	Match case check box is hidden and disabled
`FR_HIDEWHOLEWORD`	Whole word check box is hidden and disabled

Value	Meaning
FR_HIDEUPDOWN	Up and Down radio buttons are hidden
FR_MATCHCASE	Search is case sensitive
FR_NOMATCHCASE	Search is not case sensitive
FR_NOUPDOWN	Radio direction buttons disabled
FR_NOWHOLEWORD	Whole word checkbox disabled
FR_REPLACE	Replace current text occurrence
FR_REPLACEALL	Replace all text occurrences
FR_SHOWHELP	Help push button shown
FR_WHOLEWORD	Whole word check box is checked

`lpstrFindWhat` is the text string used for the search

`lpstrReplaceWith` is the text string used to replace the specified text

`wFindWhatLen` is the length of the `lpstrFindWhat` string in bytes

`wReplaceWithLen` is the length of the `lpstrReplaceWith` buffer in bytes

`lCustData` is the application-supplied data passed to the hook function

`lpfnHook` is the pointer to the hook function that processes the dialog box messages

`lpTemplateName` is the pointer to the null-terminated string that contains the name of the dialog box template resource used in place of the standard template.

Return Value The handle to the dialog box is returned when successful. `NULL` is returned when unsuccessful.

Function Category Common Dialog

Related Functions `FindText`

ReplyMessage

Syntax `void ReplyMessage(lResult)`

Parameter	Type	Description
lResult	LRESULT	Result of message processing

Description The `ReplyMessage` function replies to a message sent by the `SendMessage` function. Control is not returned to the function that called `SendMessage`.

Return Value There is no return value.

Function Category Message

Related Functions `SendMessage`

ResetDC

Syntax `HDC ResetDC(hdc, lpdm)`

Parameter	Type	Description
hdc	HDC	Device context
lpdm	LPDEVMODE	Pointer to DEVMODE structure that contains information about the new device context

Description The `ResetDC` function uses the information pointed to by `lpdm` to update the device context specified in `hdc`.

Return Value The handle to the device context is returned when successful. `NULL` is returned when unsuccessful.

Function Category Device Context

Related Functions `DeviceCapabilities`, `ExtDeviceMode`

ResizePalette

Syntax `BOOL ResizePalette(hpal, cEntries)`

Parameter	*Type*	*Description*
hpal	HPALETTE	Palette to modify
cEntries	UINT	New number of palette entries

Description The `ResizePalette` function modifies the size of the logical palette specified in `hpal`. `cEntries` specifies the number of palette entries in the resized palette.

Return Value A nonzero value is returned when successful. Zero is returned when unsuccessful.

Function Category Color Palette

Related Functions `CreatePalette`, `SetPaletteEntries`

RestoreDC

Syntax `BOOL RestoreDC(hdc, nSavedDC)`

Parameter	*Type*	*Description*
hdc	HDC	Device context
nSavedDC	int	Device context to restore; if set to –1, the most recently saved device context is restored

Description The `RestoreDC` function restores the device context in `hdc` to the state specified in `nSavedDC`. The state information is saved in the context stack by a previous call to the `SaveDC` function.

Return Value `TRUE` is returned when successful. `FALSE` is returned when unsuccessful.

Function Category Device Context

Related Functions `CreateDC`, `ReleaseDC`, `SaveDC`

RGB

Syntax `COLORREF RGB(cRed, cGreen, cBlue)`

Parameter	*Type*	*Description*
cRed	BYTE	Red intensity
cGreen	BYTE	Green intensity
cBlue	BYTE	Blue intensity

Description The RGB macro selects an RGB color. The intensities specified in cRed, cGreen, and cBlue and the capabilities of the output device are considered before a color is selected.

Return Value The selected RGB color is returned.

Function Category Windows Macros

Related Functions PALETTERGB

RoundRect

Syntax

```
BOOL RoundRect(hdc, nLeftRect, nTopRect, nRightRect,
               nBottomRect, nEllipseWidth, nEllipseHeight)
```

Parameter	*Type*	*Description*
hdc	HDC	Device context
nLeftRect	int	X coordinate of upper-left corner of rectangle
nTopRect	int	Y coordinate of upper-left corner of rectangle
nRightRect	int	X coordinate of lower-right corner of rectangle
nBottomRect	int	Y coordinate of lower-right corner of rectangle
nEllipseWidth	int	Width of ellipse used to draw the rounded corners of the rectangle
nEllipseHeight	int	Height of the ellipse used to draw the rounded corners of the rectangle

Description The `RoundRect` function creates a rounded rectangle. (`nLeftRectX1`, `nTopRect`) and (`nRightRect`, `nBottomRect`) specify the size of the rectangle. `nEllipseWidth` and `nEllipseHeight` describe the shape and size of the rounded corners. The rectangle's border is drawn using the current pen. The rectangle is filled using the current brush.

Return Value A nonzero value is returned when successful. Zero is returned when unsuccessful.

Function Category Ellipse and Polygon

Related Functions `Polygon`, `PolyPolygon`, `Rectangle`

SaveDC

Syntax `int SaveDC(hdc)`

Parameter	*Type*	*Description*
`hdc`	`HDC`	Device context to save

Description The `SaveDC` function saves the state of the device context specified in `hdc`. The state information is copied onto the context stack.

Return Value The saved device context is returned when successful. When unsuccessful, zero is returned.

Function Category Device Context

Related Functions `CreateDC`, `DeleteDC`, `RestoreDC`

ScaleViewportExt

Syntax `DWORD ScaleViewportExt(hdc, nXNum, nXDenom, nYNum, nYDenom)`

Parameter	*Type*	*Description*
`hdc`	`HDC`	Device context
`nXNum`	`int`	Numerator of the amount to scale the width (x extent) of the viewport

Parameter	*Type*	*Description*
nXDenom	int	Denominator of the amount to scale the width (x extent) of the viewport
nYNum	int	Numerator of the amount to scale the height (y extent) of the viewport
nYDenom	int	Denominator of the amount to scale the height (y extent) of the viewport

Description The `ScaleViewportExt` function scales the width (x extent) and height (y extent) of the viewport for the device context specified in `hdc`. The width (x extent) is multiplied by the fraction specified by `nXNum/nXDenom`. The height is multiplied by the fraction specified by `nYNum/nYDenom`.

Return Value The low-order word of the return value specifies the previous width (x extent) of the viewport in device units. The high-order word of the return value specifies the previous height (y extent) of the viewport in device units.

Function Category Mapping

Related Functions `GetViewportExt`, `SetViewportExt`

ScaleViewportExtEx

Syntax

```
BOOL ScaleViewportExtEx(hdc, nXnum, nXdenom, nYnum,
                        nYdenom, lpSize)
```

Parameter	*Type*	*Description*
hdc	HDC	Device context
nXnum	int	Value to multiply the current horizontal extent
nXdenom	int	Value to divide the current horizontal extent
nYnum	int	Value to multiply the current vertical extent

Parameter	Type	Description
nYdenom	int	Value to divide the current vertical extent
lpSize	SIZE FAR*	Pointer to SIZE data structure where the previous viewport extents are stored

Description The ScaleViewportExtEx function changes the current viewport extents using the values in nXnum, nXdenom, nYnum, and nYdenom. These values are used as follows:

```
xNewVE = (xOldVE * nXnum)/nXdenom

yNewVE = (yOldVE * nYnum)/nYdenom
```

The previous viewport extents are stored in a data structure of type SIZE pointed to by lpSize.

Return Value TRUE is returned when successful. FALSE is returned when unsuccessful.

Function Category Mapping

Related Functions ScaleViewportExt, SetViewportExt

ScaleWindowExt

Syntax `DWORD ScaleWindowExt(hdc, nXNum, nXDenom, nYNum, nYDenom)`

Parameter	Type	Description
hdc	HDC	Device context
nXNum	int	Numerator of the amount to scale the width (x extent) of the window
nXDenom	int	Denominator of the amount to scale the width (x extent) of the window
nYNum	int	Numerator of the amount to scale the height (y extent) of the window

Parameter	Type	Description
nYDenom	int	Denominator of the amount to scale the height (y extent) of the window

Description The `ScaleWindowExt` function scales the width (x extent) and height (y extent) of the window for the device context specified in `hdc`. The width (x extent) is multiplied by the fraction specified by `nXNum/nXDenom`. The height is multiplied by the fraction specified by `nYNum/nYDenom`.

Return Value The low-order word of the return value specifies the previous width (x extent) of the window in logical units. The high-order word of the return value specifies the previous height (y extent) of the window in logical units.

Function Category Mapping

Related Functions `GetWindowExt`, `SetWindowExt`

ScaleWindowExtEx

Syntax

```
BOOL ScaleWindowExtEx(hdc, nXnum, nXdenom, nYnum,
                      nYdenom, lpSize)
```

Parameter	Type	Description
hdc	HDC	Device context
nXnum	int	Value to multiply the current horizontal extent
nXdenom	int	Value to divide the current horizontal extent
nYnum	int	Value to multiply the current vertical extent
nYdenom	int	Value to divide the current vertical extent
lpSize	SIZE FAR*	Pointer to `SIZE` data structure where the previous viewport extents are stored

Description The `ScaleWindowExtEx` function changes the current window extents using the values in `nXnum`, `nXdenom`, `nYnum`, and `nYdenom`. These values are used as follows:

```
xNewWE = (xOldWE * nXnum)/nXdenom

yNewWE = (yOldWE * nYnum)/nYdenom
```

The previous window extents are stored in a data structure of type `SIZE` pointed to by `lpSize`.

Return Value `TRUE` is returned when successful. `FALSE` is returned when unsuccessful.

Function Category Mapping

Related Functions `ScaleWindowExt`, `SetWindowExt`

ScreenToClient

Syntax `void ScreenToClient(hwnd, lppt)`

Parameter	*Type*	*Description*
hwnd	HWND	Window containing client area used for conversion
lppt	POINT FAR*	Pointer to a `POINT` data structure containing the screen coordinates to convert

Description The `ScreenToClient` function converts the screen coordinates in the data structure of type `POINT`, pointed to by `lppt`, to client coordinates. The resulting client coordinates are placed into the `POINT` data structure pointed to by `lppt`. The `POINT` data structure follows.

```
typedef struct tagPOINT {
     int x;
     int y;
} POINT;
```

in which

`x` specifies the horizontal coordinate of the point

`y` specifies the vertical coordinate of the point.

Return Value There is no return value.

Function Category Coordinate

Related Functions `ClientToScreen`

ScrollDC

Syntax

```
BOOL ScrollDC(hdc, dx, dy, lprcScroll, lprcClip,
              hrgnUpdate, lprcUpdate)
```

Parameter	*Type*	*Description*
`hdc`	`HDC`	Device context
`dx`	`int`	Number of horizontal scroll units
`dy`	`int`	Number of vertical scroll units
`lprcScroll`	`const RECT FAR*`	Pointer to `RECT` structure that contains the coordinates of the scrolling rectangle
`lprcClip`	`const RECT FAR*`	Pointer to `RECT` structure that contains the coordinates of the clipping region
`hrgnUpdate`	`HRGN`	Region that is uncovered by the scrolling
`lprcUpdate`	`const RECT FAR*`	Pointer to `RECT` structure that contains the coordinates of the rectangle that binds the update region

Description The `ScrollDC` function scrolls a rectangle of bits the amount specified in `dx` and `dy`. `lprcScroll` points to the data structure of type `RECT` that contains the coordinates of the rectangle to scroll. `lprcClip` and `lprcUpdate` both point to data structures of type `RECT`. The `RECT` structure follows.

```
typedef struct tagRECT {
     int left;
     int top;
```

```
    int right;
    int bottom;
} RECT;
```

in which

`left` is the x coordinate of the upper-left corner

`top` is the y coordinate of the upper-left corner

`right` is the x coordinate of the lower-right corner

`bottom` is the y coordinate of the lower-right corner.

Return Value A nonzero value is returned when scrolling occurs. Zero is returned when unsuccessful.

Function Category Scrolling

Related Functions `ScrollWindow`

ScrollWindow

Syntax `void ScrollWindow(hwnd, dx, dy, lprcScroll, lprcClip)`

Parameter	*Type*	*Description*
hwnd	HWND	Window containing client area to scroll
dx	int	Number of device units to scroll horizontally
dy	int	Number of device units to scroll vertically
lprcScroll	const RECT FAR*	Pointer to RECT data structure containing the coordinates of the area to scroll; if set to NULL, the entire client area is scrolled
lprcClip	const RECT FAR*	Pointer to RECT data structure containing the coordinates of the clipping rectangle to scroll; if set to NULL, the entire window is scrolled

Description The `ScrollWindow` function scrolls the window in `hwnd`. The contents of the client area for the window in `hwnd` are moved the number of device units specified in `dx` and `dy`. `dx` describes the amount to scroll in the horizontal direction. `dy` describes the amount to scroll in the vertical direction. Positive values for `dx` and `dy` move the client area right and down, respectively. Negative values for `dx` and `dy` move the client area left and up, respectively. `lprcScroll` and `lprcClip` point to data structures of type `RECT`. The `RECT` data structure follows.

```
typedef struct tagRECT {
     int left;
     int top;
     int right;
     int bottom;
} RECT;
```

in which

`left` is the x coordinate of the upper-left corner

`top` is the y coordinate of the upper-left corner

`right` is the x coordinate of the lower-right corner

`bottom` is the y coordinate of the lower-right corner.

Return Value There is no return value.

Function Category Scrolling

Related Functions `ScrollDC`, `ScrollWindowEx`

ScrollWindowEx

Syntax

```
int ScrollWindowEx(hwnd, dx, dy, lprcScroll,
                   lprcClip, hrgnUpdate, lprcUpdate,
                   fuScroll)
```

Parameter	*Type*	*Description*
`hwnd`	`HWND`	Window to scroll
`dx`	`int`	Number of device units to scroll horizontally (negative value to scroll left; positive value to scroll right)

Parameter	*Type*	*Description*
dy	int	Number of device units to scroll vertically (negative value to scroll up; positive value to scroll down)
lprcScroll	const RECT FAR*	Pointer to a RECT data structure that defines the portion of the client area to scroll. Set to NULL to scroll the entire client area.
lprcClip	const RECT FAR*	Pointer to RECT data structure that defines the clipping rectangle to scroll. Set to NULL to scroll the entire client area. This parameter has precedence over lprcScroll.
hrgnUpdate	HRGN	Region that is modified to hold the region invalidated by scrolling. hrgnUpdate can be NULL.
lprcUpdate	RECT FAR*	Pointer to a RECT data structure where the boundaries of the invalidated rectangle are copied. lprcUpdate can be NULL.
fuScroll	UINT	Scrolling flags. fuScroll is set to one of the following values:

Value	*Meaning*
SW_SCROLLCHILDREN	All children that intersect the rectangle specified in lprcScroll are scrolled the amount specfied in dx and dy.
SW_INVALIDATE	Region specfied in hrgnUpdate is invalidated after scrolling

Value	Meaning
SW_ERASE	If used with SW_INVALIDATE, the WM_ERASEBKGND message is sent to the window and the newly invalidated region is erased

Description The ScrollWindowEx function scrolls the specified contents of the client area of the window. This function behaves like the ScrollWindow function but has enhanced capabilities.

Return Value One of the following values is returned:

Value	Meaning
ERROR	Error in region
NULLREGION	No invalidation produced during scrolling
SIMPLEREGION	Rectangular invalidation produced during scrolling
COMPLEXREGION	Nonrectangular invalidation produced during scrolling

Function Category Scrolling

Related Functions ScrollWindow, UpdateWindow

SelectClipRgn

Syntax `int SelectClipRgn(hdc, hrgn)`

Parameter	Type	Description
hdc	HDC	Device context
hrgn	HRGN	Region to select

Description The SelectClipRgn function sets the region specified in hrgn as the clipping region for the device context specified in hdc.

Return Value One of the following values is returned to describe the clipping region.

Value	*Meaning*
COMPLEXREGION	Region has overlapping borders
ERROR	Device context or region handle is invalid
NULLREGION	Region is empty
SIMPLEREGION	Region has no overlapping borders

Function Category Clipping

Related Functions GetClipBox, OffsetClipRgn

SelectObject

Syntax `HGDIOBJ SelectObject(hdc, hgdiobj)`

Parameter	*Type*	*Description*
hdc	HDC	Device context
hgdiobj	HGDIOBJ	Handle of bitmap, brush, font, pen, or region to select

Description The `SelectObject` function selects the object specified in `hgdiobj` as the current object selected for the device context in `hdc`.

Return Value The handle of the previously selected object is returned when successful. `NULL` is returned when unsuccessful.

Function Category Drawing Tool

Related Functions GetObject, GetStockObject, UnrealizeObject

SelectPalette

Syntax `HPALETTE SelectPalette(hdc, hpal, fPalBack)`

Parameter	*Type*	*Description*
hdc	HDC	Device context
hpal	HPALETTE	Logical palette

Parameter	*Type*	*Description*
`fPalBack`	`BOOL`	Set to a nonzero value if the logical palette is a background palette; set to zero if the logical palette is a foreground palette when the window has the input focus

Description The `SelectPalette` function selects the logical palette in `hpal` for the palette object of the device context in `hdc`. The selected palette is used by the Graphics Device Interface to control colors displayed in the device context.

Return Value The handle for the previous logical palette used by the Graphics Device Interface is returned when successful. When unsuccessful, `NULL` is returned.

Function Category Color Palette

Related Functions `CreatePalette`, `RealizePalette`

SendDlgItemMessage

Syntax

```
LRESULT SendDlgItemMessage(hwndDlg, idDlgItem, uMsg,
                           wParam, lParam)
```

Parameter	*Type*	*Description*
`hwndDlg`	`HWND`	Dialog box containing control
`idDlgItem`	`int`	Item to receive message
`uMsg`	`UINT`	Message value
`wParam`	`WPARAM`	Additional message information
`lParam`	`LPARAM`	Additional message information

Description The `SendDlgItemMessage` function sends a message to a control. The control that receives the message is specified in `idDlgItem`. The specified control is contained in the dialog box specified in

hwndDlg. uMsg contains the message value of the message to send to the control. wParam and lParam contain additional information on the message in uMsg.

Return Value The value returned by SendDlgItemMessage is the value returned by the control's window function. If idDlgItem identifies an invalid control, zero is returned.

Function Category Dialog Box

Related Functions DefDlgProc

SendDriverMessage

Syntax

```
LRESULT SendDriverMessage(hdrvr, wMsg, lParam1,
                          lParam2)
```

Parameter	*Type*	*Description*
hdrvr	HDRVR	Installable driver
wMsg	WORD	Message that the driver must process
lParam1	LPARAM	First message parameter
lParam2	LPARAM	Second message parameter

Description The SendDriverMessage function sends the message specified in wMsg to the installable device driver specified in hdrvr. lParam1 and lParam2 specify the message parameters.

Return Value A nonzero value is returned when successful. Zero is returned when unsuccessful.

Function Category Installable Driver

Related Functions DefDriverProc

SendMessage

Syntax

```
LRESULT SendMessage(hwnd, uMsg, wParam, lParam)
```

Parameter	*Type*	*Description*
hwnd	HWND	Window to receive message
uMsg	UINT	Message to be sent
wParam	WPARAM	Additional message information
lParam	LPARAM	Additional message information

Description The `SendMessage` function sends the message in `uMsg` to the window specified in `hwnd`, and then waits for the message to be processed. The message will not be placed in the destination application's queue.

Return Value The value returned by the window function receiving the message is returned.

Function Category Message

Related Functions `GetMessage`, `InSendMessage`, `PostMessage`

SetAbortProc

Syntax `int SetAbortProc(hdc, abrtprc)`

Parameter	*Type*	*Description*
hdc	HDC	Device context
abrtprc	ABORTPROC	Pointer to abort function

Description The `SetAbortProc` function defines the application-supplied abort function. The abort function allows the user to cancel a print job during spooling. The address specified in `abrtprc` is created using `MakeProcInstance`. The abort function uses the following conventions:

```
FARPROC AbortProc(hdc, error)
HDC hdc;

int error;
```

in which

`hdc` is the device context

`error` indicates whether an error has occurred; zero for no error or `SP_OUTOFDISK` if the Print Manager is out of disk space.

The abort function should return `TRUE` to continue the print job and `FALSE` to cancel the print job.

Return Value A positive value is returned when successful. A negative value is returned when unsuccessful.

Function Category Printer Control

Related Functions `AbortDoc`, `Escape`

SetActiveWindow

Syntax `HWND SetActiveWindow(hwnd)`

Parameter	*Type*	*Description*
`hwnd`	`HWND`	Top-level window to activate

Description The `SetActiveWindow` function designates the top-level window in `hwnd` as the active window.

Return Value The handle of the previously active window is returned.

Function Category Input

Related Functions `GetActiveWindow`

SetBitmapBits

Syntax `LONG SetBitmapBits(hbmp, cBits, lpvBits)`

Parameter	*Type*	*Description*
`hbmp`	`HBITMAP`	Bitmap to set
`cBits`	`DWORD`	Number of bytes in `lpvBits`

Parameter	*Type*	*Description*
lpvBits	const void FAR*	Pointer to array containing the bitmap bits

Description The SetBitmapBits function sets the bits for the bitmap specified in hbmp to the bit values contained in the array pointed to by lpvBits. cBits specifies the number of bits in the array pointed to by lpvBits.

Return Value The number of bytes used to set the bitmap bits is returned when successful. Zero is returned when unsuccessful.

Function Category Bitmap

Related Functions GetBitmapBits

SetBitmapDimension

Syntax `DWORD SetBitmapDimension(hbmp, nWidth, nHeight)`

Parameter	*Type*	*Description*
hbmp	HBITMAP	Bitmap handle
nWidth	int	Width of bitmap in tenths of millimeters
nHeight	int	Height of bitmap in tenths of millimeters

Description The SetBitmapDimension function sets the width and height dimensions for the bitmap in hbmp to the values expressed in nWidth and nHeight, respectively.

Return Value The high-order word of the return value contains the previous height of the bitmap. The low-order word of the return value contains the previous width of the bitmap.

Function Category Bitmap

Related Functions GetBitmapDimension

SetBitmapDimensionEx

Syntax `BOOL SetBitmapDimensionEx(hbm, nX, nY, lpSize)`

Parameter	*Type*	*Description*
`hbm`	`HBITMAP`	Bitmap
`nX`	`int`	Width of bitmap in tenths of millimeters
`nY`	`int`	Height of bitmap in tenths of millimeters
`lpSize`	`SIZE FAR*`	Pointer to `SIZE` data structure where the previous bitmap dimensions are placed. `lpSize` can be `NULL`.

Description The `SetBitmapDimensions` function defines the preferred bitmap size in tenths of millimeter units. These values are not used by the Graphics Device Interface (GDI). `nX` and `nY` specify the bitmap dimensions.

Return Value `TRUE` is returned when successful. `FALSE` is returned when unsuccessful.

Function Category Bitmap

Related Functions `SetBitmapDimension`

SetBkColor

Syntax `COLORREF SetBkColor(hdc, clrref)`

Parameter	*Type*	*Description*
`hdc`	`HDC`	Device context
`clrref`	`COLORREF`	New background color

Description The `SetBkColor` function sets the background color for the device context in `hdc` to the color specified in `clrref` (the nearest physical color to `clrref` is used if the device cannot use the RGB value specified in `clrref`).

Return Value The previous background color is returned as an RGB value when successful. When unsuccessful, 0x80000000 is returned.

Function Category Drawing Attribute

Related Functions `GetBkColor`, `SetBkMode`

SetBkMode

Syntax `int SetBkMode(hdc, fnBkMode)`

Parameter	*Type*	*Description*
`hdc`	`HDC`	Device context
`fnBkMode`	`int`	Background mode

Description The `SetBkMode` function sets the background mode for the device context in `hdc`. The background mode is defined in `fnBkMode`. The following values are used for `fnBkMode`:

Value	*Meaning*
`OPAQUE`	Background is filled with the background color before any drawing takes place
`TRANSPARENT`	Background is not changed before drawing takes place

Return Value The previous background mode, either `OPAQUE` or `TRANSPARENT`, is returned.

Function Category Drawing Attribute

Related Functions `GetBkMode`, `SetBkColor`

SetBoundsRect

Syntax `UINT SetBoundsRect(hdc, lprcBounds, flags)`

Parameter	*Type*	*Description*
`hdc`	`HDC`	Device context

Parameter	Type	Description
lprcBounds	const RECT FAR*	Pointer to rectangle that defines the bounding rectangle. Values are expressed in logical coordinates. lprcBounds can be set to NULL.
flags	UINT	New rectangle to combine with accumulated rect-angle. flags is a combination of the following values:

Value	Meaning
DCB_ACCUMULATE	Adds the rectangle specified by lprcBounds to the bounding rectangle
DCB_DISABLE	Disables bounds accumulation
DCB_ENABLE	Enables bounds accumulation
DCB_RESET	Defines the bounding rectangle as empty
DCB_SET	Defines the bounding rectangle as the rectangle specified in lprcBounds

Description The SetBoundsRect function defines the bounding rectangle for the device context specified in hdc.

Return Value The current state of the bounding rectangle is returned. The return value is a combination of the following values:

Value	Meaning
DCB_ACCUMULATE	Bounds rectangle accumulation occurring
DCB_DISABLE	Bounds accumulation is disabled
DCB_ENABLE	Bounds accumulation is enabled
DCB_RESET	Bounding rectangle is empty
DCB_SET	Bounding rectangle is not empty

Function Category Rectangle

Related Functions `GetBoundsRect`

SetBrushOrg

Syntax `DWORD SetBrushOrg(hdc, nXOrg, nYOrg)`

Parameter	*Type*	*Description*
`hdc`	`HDC`	Device context
`nXOrg`	`int`	X coordinate of new origin, in device units
`nYOrg`	`int`	Y coordinate of new origin, in device units

Description The `SetBrushOrg` function sets the origin of the currently selected brush for the device context in `hdc` to the point specified in `nXOrg` and `nYOrg`. `nXOrg` and `nYOrg` are the horizontal and vertical device coordinates, respectively, for the new origin and must be in the range of 0 to 7.

Return Value The low-order word of the return value contains the x coordinate of the previous origin. The high-order word of the return value contains the y coordinate of the previous origin.

Function Category Drawing Tool

Related Functions `GetBrushOrg`

SetCapture

Syntax `HWND SetCapture(hwnd)`

Parameter	*Type*	*Description*
`hwnd`	`HWND`	Window to receive mouse input

Description The `SetCapture` function sends all subsequent mouse input to the window specified in `hwnd`.

Return Value The handle of the window that previously had the mouse capture is returned. If no window previously had the mouse capture, `NULL` is returned.

Function Category Input

Related Functions `GetCapture`, `ReleaseCapture`

SetCaretBlinkTime

Syntax `void SetCaretBlinkTime(uMSeconds)`

Parameter	*Type*	*Description*
`uMSeconds`	`UINT`	New blink rate measured in milliseconds

Description The `SetCaretBlinkTime` function defines the caret blink rate. The blink rate is set to the number of milliseconds specified in `uMSeconds`.

Return Value There is no return value.

Function Category Caret

Related Functions `GetCaretBlinkTime`

SetCaretPos

Syntax `void SetCaretPos(X, Y)`

Parameter	*Type*	*Description*
`X`	`int`	Horizontal logical coordinate
`Y`	`int`	Vertical logical coordinate

Description The `SetCaretPos` function places the caret at the position specified in `X` and `Y`. `X` and `Y` are expressed in logical coordinates. The caret is moved only if the caret is owned by a window in the current task.

Return Value There is no return value.

Function Category Caret

Related Functions `GetCaretPos`

SetClassLong

Syntax `LPARAM SetClassLong(hwnd, nIndex, lNewLong)`

Parameter	*Type*	*Description*
`hwnd`	`HWND`	Window handle
`nIndex`	`int`	Byte offset of word to change
`lNewLong`	`LPARAM`	New value

Description The `SetClassLong` function sets the value identified by `nIndex` to the value specified in `lNewLong`. `nIndex` specifies the byte offset of the value to change from the `WNDCLASS` data structure. `nIndex` can also be set to the following values:

Value	*Meaning*
`GCL_MENUNAME`	Sets new long pointer to menu name
`GCL_WNDPROC`	Sets new long pointer to window function

Return Value The previous value of the changed long integer is returned when successful. Zero is returned when unsuccessful.

Function Category Window Creation

Related Functions `GetClassLong`, `SetClassWord`

SetClassWord

Syntax `WPARAM SetClassWord(hwnd, nIndex, wNewWord)`

Parameter	*Type*	*Description*
`hwnd`	`HWND`	Window handle

Parameter	*Type*	*Description*
`nIndex`	`int`	Byte offset of word to change
`wNewWord`	`WPARAM`	New value

Description The `SetClassWord` function sets the value identified by `nIndex` to the value specified in `wNewWord`. `nIndex` specifies the byte offset of the word to change from the `WNDCLASS` data structure. `nIndex` can also be set to the following values:

Value	*Meaning*
`GCW_CBCLSEXTRA`	Sets two new bytes of additional window class data
`GCW_CBWNDEXTRA`	Sets two new bytes of additional window call data
`GCW_HBRBACKGROUND`	Sets a new handle to a background brush
`GCW_HCURSOR`	Sets a new handle to a cursor
`GCW_HICON`	Sets a new handle to an icon
`GCW_STYLE`	Sets a new style bit for the window class

Return Value The previous value of the specified word is returned when successful. Zero is returned when unsuccessful.

Function Category Window Creation

Related Functions `GetClassWord`, `SetClassLong`

SetClipboardData

Syntax `HANDLE SetClipboardData(uFormat, hData)`

Parameter	*Type*	*Description*
`uFormat`	`UINT`	Data format
`hData`	`HANDLE`	Location of data

Description The `SetClipboardData` function defines a data handle for the data specified in `hData`. `uFormat` specifies the format of the data. The data formats in the following list can be used for `uFormat`. Format values obtained via the `RegisterClipboardFormat` function can also be used for `uFormat`. Once the `SetClipboardData` function has been called, the specified data becomes the property of the clipboard.

Format	*Meaning*
`CF_BITMAP`	Handle to a bitmap
`CF_DIB`	Block containing a `BITMAPINFO` data structure and the bitmap
`CF_DIF`	Software Art's Data Interchange Format
`CF_DSPBITMAP`	Bitmap format which corresponds to a private format
`CF_DSPMETAFILEPICT`	Metafile format which corresponds to a private format
`CF_DSPTEXT`	Text display format which corresponds to a private format
`CF_METAFILEPICT`	Metafile defined by the `METAFILEPICT` structure
`CF_OEMTEXT`	Text format using the OEM character set
`CF_OWNERDISPLAY`	Owner display format
`CF_PALETTE`	Color palette handle
`CF_PRIVATEFIRST` to `CF_PRIVATELAST`	Used for private formats
`CF_SYLK`	Microsoft Symbolic Link Format
`CF_TEXT`	Text format
`CF_TIFF`	Tag Image File Format

Return Value The data handle is returned when successful. `NULL` is returned when unsuccessful.

Function Category Clipboard

Related Functions `GetClipboardData`

SetClipboardViewer

Syntax `HWND SetClipboardViewer(hwnd)`

Parameter	*Type*	*Description*
`hwnd`	`HWND`	Window to be added to chain

Description The `SetClipboardViewer` function puts the window specified in `hwnd` on the chain of windows notified when the clipboard is modified. The `WM_DRAWCLIPBOARD` message is sent to each window in the chain when the contents of the clipboard are modified.

Return Value The handle for the next window in the chain is returned and should be used to respond to clipboard-viewer chain messages.

Function Category Clipboard

Related Functions `ChangeClipboardChain`, `GetClipboardViewer`

SetCommBreak

Syntax `int SetCommBreak(idComDev)`

Parameter	*Type*	*Description*
`idComDev`	`int`	Communication device

Description The `SetCommBreak` function suspends character transmission for the device in `idComDev`. The device is placed in a break state.

Return Value Zero is returned when successful. A negative value is returned when unsuccessful.

Function Category Communication

Related Functions `ClearCommBreak`

SetCommEventMask

Syntax `WORD FAR* SetCommEventMask(idComDev, fuEvtMask)`

Parameter	*Type*	*Description*
`idComDev`	`int`	Communication device
`fuEvtMask`	`UINT`	Events to enable

Description The `SetCommEventMask` function sets the event mask for the communication device in `idComDev`. `fuEvtMask` specifies the events to enable. The event values used for `fuEvtMask` are as follows:

Value	*Meaning*
`EV_BREAK`	Set when a break is detected on input
`EV_CTS`	Set when the clear-to-send signal changes state
`EV_CTSS`	Set to indicate current status of clear-to-send signal
`EV_DSR`	Set when the data-set-ready signal changes state
`EV_DSRS`	Set to indicate current status of data-set-ready signal
`EV_ERR`	Set when a line status error occurs
`EV_PERR`	Set when a printer error is detected on a parallel device
`EV_RING`	Set when a ring indicator is detected
`EV_RSLD`	Set when the receive-line-signal-detect signal changes state
`EV_RSLDS`	Set to indicate current status of receive-line-signal-detect signal
`EV_RXCHAR`	Set when a character is received and placed in the receive queue
`EV_RXFLAG`	Set when the event character is received and placed in the receive queue
`EV_TXEMPTY`	Set when the last character in the transmit queue is sent

Return Value The pointer to the event mask is returned.

Function Category Communication

Related Functions `GetCommEventMask`

SetCommState

Syntax `int SetCommState(lpdcb)`

Parameter	*Type*	*Description*
`lpdcb`	`const DCB FAR*`	Pointer to a `DCB` data structure containing the settings for the device

Description The `SetCommState` function sets the state of a communication device to the settings specified in the data structure of type `DCB` pointed to by `lpdcb`. The `DCB` data structure follows.

```
typedef struct tagDCB {
     BYTE Id;
     WORD BaudRate;
     BYTE ByteSize;
     BYTE Parity;
     BYTE StopBits;
     WORD RlsTimeout;
     WORD CtsTimeout;
     WORD DsrTimeout;

     WORD fBinary: 1;
     WORD fRtsDisable: 1;
     WORD fParity: 1;
     WORD fOutxCtsFlow: 1;
     WORD fOutxDsrFlow: 1;
     WORD fDummy: 2;
     WORD fDtrDisable: 1;

     WORD fOutX: 1;
     WORD fInX: 1;
     WORD fPeChar: 1;
     WORD fNull: 1;
     WORD fChEvt: 1;
     WORD fDtrflow: 1;
     WORD fRtsflow: 1;
     WORD fDummy2: 1;

     char XonChar;
     char XoffChar;
     WORD XonLim;
     WORD XoffLim;
     char PeChar;
     char EofChar;
     char EvtChar;
     WORD TxDelay;
} DCB;
```

in which

`Id` is the communication device and is set by the device driver

`BaudRate` is the baud rate. When the high-order byte is 0xFF, the low-order byte is one of the following baud-rate index values:

```
CBR_110
CBR_300
CBR_600
CBR_1200
CBR_2400
CBR_4800
CBR_9600
CBR_14400
CBR_19200
CBR_38400
CBR_56000
CBR_128000
CBR_256000
```

When the high-order byte is not 0xFF, `BaudRate` specifies the actual baud rate.

`ByteSize` is the number of bits in a character (4 to 8)

`Parity` is the parity scheme—can be `EVENPARITY`, `MARKPARITY`, `NOPARITY`, or `ODDPARITY`

`StopBits` is the number of stop bits to use—can be `ONESTOPBIT`, `ONE5STOPBITS`, or `TWOSTOPBITS`

`RlsTimeout` is the maximum number of milliseconds the device should wait for the receive-line-signal-detect (RLSD) signal

`CtsTimeout` is the maximum number of milliseconds the device should wait for the clear-to-send (CTS) signal

`DsrTimeout` is the maximum number of milliseconds the device should wait for the data-set-ready (DSR) signal

`fBinary` is the binary mode indicator

`fRtsDisable` indicates whether the request-to-send signal is disabled

`fParity` indicates whether the parity checking is enabled

`fOutxCtsFlow` indicates that clear-to-send signal is monitored for output flow control

`fOutxDsrFlow` indicates that data-set-ready signal is monitored for output flow control

`fDummy` is reserved

`fDtrDisable` indicates whether the data-terminal-ready signal is disabled

`fOutX` indicates that the XON/XOFF flow control is used during transmission

`fInX` indicates that the XON/XOFF flow control is used while receiving

`fPeChar` indicates that characters received with parity errors are to be replaced with the character in the `fPeChar` field

`fNull` indicates that null characters are discarded

`fChEvt` indicates that reception of the `EvtChar` character is to be flagged as an event

`fDtrflow` indicates that the data-terminal-ready signal is used for receive flow control

`fRtsflow` indicates that the ready-to-send signal is used to receive flow control

`fDummy2` is reserved

`XonChar` is the value of the XON character

`XoffChar` is the value of XOFF character

`XonLim` is the minimum number of characters allowed in the receive queue before the XON character is sent

`XoffLim` is the maximum number of characters allowed in the receive queue before the XOFF character is sent

`PeChar` is the value of the character used to replace characters received with parity errors

`EofChar` is the character used to signal the end of data

`EvtChar` is the character used to signal an event

`TxDelay` is not used.

Return Value Zero is returned when successful. A negative value is returned when unsuccessful.

Function Category Communication

Related Category `GetCommState`

SetCursor

Syntax `HCURSOR SetCursor(hcur)`

Parameter	*Type*	*Description*
`hcur`	`HCURSOR`	Cursor resource

Description The `SetCursor` function redefines the shape of the cursor. The cursor is set to the shape specified in `hcur`. `hcur` must identify a resource which has been loaded with the `LoadCursor` function. If `hcur` is `NULL`, the cursor is removed from the screen.

Return Value The handle which identifies the previous cursor shape is returned. The return value is `NULL` if no previous shape exists.

Function Category Cursor

Related Functions `CreateCursor`, `LoadCursor`, `SetCursorPos`

SetCursorPos

Syntax `void SetCursorPos(X, Y)`

Parameter	*Type*	*Description*
`X`	`int`	X screen coordinate of cursor
`Y`	`int`	Y screen coordinate of cursor

Description The `SetCursorPos` function places the cursor at the screen coordinates specified in `X` and `Y`. `X` specifies the horizontal screen coordinate of the cursor; `Y` specifies the vertical screen coordinate of the cursor.

Return Value There is no return value.

Function Category Cursor

Related Functions `GetCursorPos`

SetDIBits

Syntax

```
int SetDIBits(hdc, hBitmap, uStartScan, cScanLines,
              lpvBits, lpbmi, fuColorUse)
```

Parameter	*Type*	*Description*
hdc	HDC	Device context
hBitmap	HANDLE	Bitmap handle
uStartScan	UINT	First scan line in lpvBits buffer
cScanLines	UINT	Number of lines in lpvBits buffer to copy to device
lpvBits	const void FAR*	Pointer to buffer that stores the bitmap bits for the device-independent bitmap
lpbmi	BITMAPINFO FAR*	Pointer to a BITMAPINFO structure containing information for the device-independent bitmap
fuColorUse	UINT	Set to DIB_PAL_COLORS (color table in lpbmi contains array of 16-bit indexes for the currently realized logical palette) or DIB_RGB_COLORS (color table in lpbmi contains RGB values)

Description The SetDIBits function sets the bits of a bitmap. The bits are placed into the buffer pointed to by lpvBits in device-independent format. hdc specifies the device context. hBitmap specifies the bitmap. lpbmi points to a data structure of type BITMAPINFO. The BITMAPINFO structure follows.

```
typedef struct tagBITMAPINFO {
     BITMAPINFOHEADER bmiHeader;
     RGBQUAD bmiColors[1];
} BITMAPINFO;
```

in which

bmiHeader is the BITMAPINFOHEADER structure for the device-independent bitmap

bmiColors is an array of data structures of type RGBQUAD that defines the colors in the bitmap.

The BITMAPINFOHEADER structure follows.

```
typedef struct BITMAPINFOHEADER {
     DWORD biSize;
     DWORD biWidth;
     DWORD biHeight;
     WORD biPlanes;
     WORD biBitCount;
     DWORD biCompression;
     DWORD biSizeImage;
     DWORD biXPelsPerMeter;
     DWORD biYPelsPerMeter;
     DWORD biClrUsed;
     DWORD biClrImportant;
} BITMAPINFOHEADER;
```

in which

biSize is the number of bytes required for the structure

biWidth is the width of the bitmap in pixels

biHeight is the height of the bitmap in pixels

biPlanes is the number of planes; must be set to 1

biBitCount is the number of bits per pixel

biCompression is the type of compression and is selected from the following values:

BI_RGB	Bitmap is not compressed
BI_RLE8	Run-length encode format with 8 bits per pixel
BI_RLE4	Run-length encode format with 4 bits per pixel

biSizeImage is the size of the image in bytes

biXPelsPerMeter is the horizontal resolution in pixels per meter for the target device

biYPelsPerMeter is the vertical resolution in pixels per meter for the target device

biClrUsed is the number of color indexes in the color table that the bitmap actually uses

biClrImportant is the number of color indexes considered important for the bitmap.

Return Value The number of scan lines copied is returned when successful. Zero is returned if unsuccessful.

Function Category Bitmap

Related Functions `GetDIBits`, `SetDIBitsToDevice`

SetDIBitsToDevice

Syntax
```
int SetDIBitsToDevice(hdc, uXDest, uYDest, uWidth, uHeight,
                      uXSrc, uYSrc, uStartScan, cScanLines,
                      lpvBits, lpbmi, fuColorUse)
```

Parameter	*Type*	*Description*
hdc	HDC	Device context
uXDest	UINT	X coordinate of origin for destination rectangle
uYDest	UINT	Y coordinate of origin for destination rectangle
uWidth	UINT	Width of the rectangle in the device-independent bitmap
uHeight	UINT	Height of the rectangle in the device-independent bitmap
uXSrc	UINT	X coordinate of the source in the device-independent bitmap
uYSrc	UINT	Y coordinate of the source in the device-independent bitmap
uStartScan	UINT	First scan line in `lpvBits` buffer
cScanLines	UINT	Number of scan lines in `lpvBits` buffer to copy to device
lpvBits	void FAR*	Pointer to buffer that stores the bitmap bits for the device-independent bitmap
lpbmi	BITMAPINFO FAR*	Pointer to a `BITMAPINFO` structure containing information for the device-independent bitmap

Parameter	*Type*	*Description*
fuColorUse	UINT	Set to DIB_PAL_COLORS (color table in lpbmi contains array of 16-bit indexes for the currently realized logical palette) or DIB_RGB_COLORS (color table in lpbmi contains RGB values)

Description The SetDIBitsToDevice function sets the bits from a device-independent bitmap onto the display surface of the output device specified by hdc. uXDest and uYDest specify the location of the destination rectangle. uWidth, uHeight, uXSrc, and uYSrc define the source rectangle in the device-independent bitmap. lpbmi points to a data structure of type BITMAPINFO. The BITMAPINFO structure follows.

```
typedef struct tagBITMAPINFO {
     BITMAPINFOHEADER bmiHeader;
     RGBQUAD bmiColors[1];
} BITMAPINFO;
```

in which

bmiHeader is the BITMAPINFOHEADER structure for the device-independent bitmap

bmiColors is an array of data structures of type RGBQUAD that defines the colors in the bitmap.

The BITMAPINFOHEADER structure follows.

```
typedef struct BITMAPINFOHEADER {
     DWORD biSize;
     DWORD biWidth;
     DWORD biHeight;
     WORD biPlanes;
     WORD biBitCount;
     DWORD biCompression;
     DWORD biSizeImage;
     DWORD biXPelsPerMeter;
     DWORD biYPelsPerMeter;
     DWORD biClrUsed;
     DWORD biClrImportant;
} BITMAPINFOHEADER;
```

in which

`biSize` is the number of bytes required for the structure

`biWidth` is the width of the bitmap in pixels

`biHeight` is the height of the bitmap in pixels

`biPlanes` is the number of planes; must be set to 1

`biBitCount` is the number of bits per pixel

`biCompression` is the type of compression and is selected from the following values:

`BI_RGB`	Bitmap is not compressed
`BI_RLE8`	Run-length encode format with 8 bits per pixel
`BI_RLE4`	Run-length encode format with 4 bits per pixel

`biSizeImage` is the size of the image in bytes

`biXPelsPerMeter` is the horizontal resolution in pixels per meter for the target device

`biYPelsPerMeter` is the vertical resolution in pixels per meter for the target device

`biClrUsed` is the number of color indexes in the color table that the bitmap actually uses

`biClrImportant` is the number of color indexes considered important for the bitmap.

Return Value The number of scan lines set is returned when successful. Zero is returned if unsuccessful.

Function Category Bitmap

Related Functions `SetDIBits`, `StretchDIBits`

SetDlgItemInt

Syntax `void SetDlgItemInt(hwndDlg, idControl, uValue, fSigned)`

Parameter	*Type*	*Description*
`hwndDlg`	`HWND`	Dialog box containing the control

Parameter	Type	Description
`idControl`	`int`	Control to be altered
`uValue`	`UINT`	Value to set
`fSigned`	`BOOL`	Specifies sign

Description The `SetDlgItemInt` function sets the text of a control to the specified value. The control to alter is specified in `idControl`. `hwndDlg` specifies the dialog box which contains the control. The text of the control is set to the string that represents the integer value specified in `uValue`. The value in `uValue` is converted to a string of decimal digits. `fSigned` specifies whether `uValue` is signed. When `fSigned` is set to a nonzero value, `uValue` is signed. The `WM_SETTEXT` message is sent to the control.

Return Value There is no return value.

Function Category Dialog Box

Related Functions `GetDlgItemInt`, `SetDlgItemText`

SetDlgItemText

Syntax `void SetDlgItemText(hwndDlg, idControl, lpsz)`

Parameter	Type	Description
`hwndDlg`	`HWND`	Dialog box containing the control
`idControl`	`int`	Dialog box control
`lpsz`	`LPCSTR`	Text string for the control

Description The `SetDlgItemText` function sets the text of the control specified in `idControl`. The specified control is contained in the dialog box defined in `hwndDlg`. The text of the control is set to the text string pointed to by `lpsz`. The `WM_SETTEXT` message is sent to the control.

Return Value There is no return value.

Function Category Dialog Box

Related Functions `GetDlgItemText`, `SetDlgItemInt`

SetDoubleClickTime

Syntax `void SetDoubleClickTime(uInterval)`

Parameter	*Type*	*Description*
`uInterval`	`UINT`	Double-click time in milliseconds

Description The `SetDoubleClickTime` function defines the maximum number of milliseconds between two clicks of a button (a double click). `uInterval` specifies the double-click time. If `uInterval` is set to 0, the default double-click time of 500 milliseconds is used.

Return Value There is no return value.

Function Category Input

Related Functions `GetDoubleClickTime`

SetEnvironment

Syntax `int SetEnvironment(lpszPort, lpvEnviron, cbMaxCopy)`

Parameter	*Type*	*Description*
`lpszPort`	`LPCSTR`	Pointer to the string that contains the name of the port
`lpvEnviron`	`const void FAR*`	Pointer to the buffer containing the new environment
`cbMaxCopy`	`UINT`	Number of bytes to copy from the buffer

Description The `SetEnvironment` function sets the environment associated with the device attached to the system port specified in `lpszPort` to the contents of the buffer pointed to by `lpvEnviron`. `cbMaxCopy` specifies the number of bytes to copy from the buffer.

Return Value The number of bytes copied from the buffer to the environment is returned when successful. Zero is returned when unsuccessful. When the environment is deleted and not replaced, 1 is returned.

Function Category Environment

Related Functions `GetEnvironment`

SetErrorMode

Syntax `UINT SetErrorMode(fuErrorMode)`

Parameter	*Type*	*Description*
`fuErrorMode`	`UINT`	Error mode flag

Description The `SetErrorMode` function defines the way that the DOS function 24H is handled. `fuErrorMode` specifies one of the following error mode flags:

Flag	*Meaning*
`SEM__FAILCRITICALERRORS`	Critical-error-handler message is not displayed. The error is returned to the calling application.
`SEM_NOGPFAULTERRORBOX`	General-protection-fault message box is not displayed. Use only with debugging applications that handle GP faults.
`SEM__NOOPENFILEERRORBOX`	Message box is not displayed when a file can be found.

Return Value The previous value of the error mode flag is returned.

Function Category Task

Related Functions `GetDOSEnvironment`

SetFocus

Syntax `HWND SetFocus(hwnd)`

Parameter	*Type*	*Description*
hwnd	HWND	Window to receive keyboard input

Description The SetFocus function sends all keyboard input (the input focus) to the window specified in hwnd. When hwnd is NULL, all keyboard input is ignored. The WM_KILLFOCUS message is sent to the window that previously held the input focus. The WM_SETFOCUS message is sent to the window in hwnd.

Return Value The handle of the window that previously held the input focus is returned. If no window previously held the input focus, NULL is returned.

Function Category Input

Related Functions GetFocus

SetHandleCount

Syntax `UINT SetHandleCount(cHandles)`

Parameter	*Type*	*Description*
cHandles	UINT	Number of file handles for the application; must be 255 or less

Description The SetHandleCount function defines the number of file handles available for the application. cHandles specifies the number of file handles needed by the application. The default number of file handles is 20. cHandles cannot exceed 255.

Return Value The number of file handles available to the application is returned.

Function Category File I/O

Related Functions OpenFile

SetKeyboardState

Syntax `void SetKeyboardState(lpbKeyState)`

Parameter	*Type*	*Description*
`lpbKeyState`	`BYTE FAR*`	Array containing keyboard key states

Description The `SetKeyboardState` function sets the Windows keyboard state table to the values in the 256-byte array pointed to by `lpbKeyState`. The LEDs and BIOS flags for the NUM LOCK, CAPS LOCK, and SCROLL LOCK keys are set according to the corresponding values in the array.

Return Value There is no return value.

Function Category Hardware

Related Functions `GetKeyboardState`

SetMapMode

Syntax `int SetMapMode(hdc, fnMapMode)`

Parameter	*Type*	*Description*
`hdc`	`HDC`	Device context
`fnMapMode`	`int`	Mapping mode

Description The `SetMapMode` function defines the mapping mode for the device context specified in `hdc`. `fnMapMode` specifies the mapping mode to set. The following values are used for the `fnMapMode` function. The mapping mode is used to convert logical coordinates into device coordinates.

Value	*Meaning*
`MM_ANISOTROPIC`	Logical units are mapped to arbitrary units with arbitrarily scaled axes
`MM_HIENGLISH`	Each logical unit is mapped to .001 inch; positive x is right, positive y is up
`MM_HIMETRIC`	Each logical unit is mapped to .01 millimeter; positive x is right, positive y is up

MM_ISOTROPIC	Logical units are mapped to arbitrary units with equally scaled axes
MM_LOENGLISH	Each logical unit is mapped to .01 inch; positive x is right, positive y is up
MM_LOMETRIC	Each logical unit is mapped to .1 millimeter; positive x is right, positive y is up
MM_TEXT	Each logical unit is mapped to one device pixel; positive x is right, positive y is down
MM_TWIPS	Each logical unit is mapped to one twentieth of a printer's point; positive x is right, positive y is up

Return Value The previous mapping mode is returned.

Function Category Mapping

Related Functions GetMapMode

SetMapperFlags

Syntax `DWORD SetMapperFlags(hdc, fdwMatch)`

Parameter	*Type*	*Description*
hdc	HDC	Device context containing the font-mapper flag
fdwMatch	DWORD	When fdwMatch is set to ASPECT_FILTERING, only fonts with x-aspects and y-aspects that match the specified device are selected.

Description The SetMapperFlags function modifies the algorithm used by the font mapper. The algorithm is used to map logical fonts to physical fonts. fdwMatch indicates whether the font mapper will try to match the aspect height and width for the font to the specified device.

Return Value The previous value of the font-mapper flag is returned.

Function Category Font

Related Functions `CreateFont`

SetMenu

Syntax `BOOL SetMenu(hwnd, hmenu)`

Parameter	*Type*	*Description*
`hwnd`	`HWND`	Window containing menu to modify
`hmenu`	`HMENU`	New menu

Description The `SetMenu` function sets the menu for the window specified in `hwnd` to the menu specified in `hmenu`. The window is redrawn when the function is called. If `hmenu` is set to `NULL`, the current menu for the window specified in `hwnd` is removed.

Return Value A nonzero value is returned when the menu is changed. Zero is returned if the menu was not changed.

Function Category Menu

Related Functions `CreateMenu`, `GetMenu`

SetMenuItemBitmaps

Syntax

```
BOOL SetMenuItemBitmaps(hmenu, idItem, fuFlags,
                        hbmUnchecked, hbmChecked)
```

Parameter	*Type*	*Description*
`hmenu`	`HMENU`	Menu to change
`idItem`	`UINT`	Menu item to change
`fuFlags`	`UINT`	Specifies meaning of `idItem`
`hbmUnchecked`	`HBITMAP`	Bitmap to use when a menu item is not checked
`hbmChecked`	`HBITMAP`	Bitmap to use when the menu item is checked

Description The `SetMenuItemBitmaps` function defines the bitmaps associated with the menu item specified in `idItem` from the menu specified

in `hmenu`. The value of `fuFlags` specifies the meaning of the value in `idItem`. The values for `fuFlags` are as follows:

Value	*Meaning*
`MF_BYCOMMAND`	`idItem` contains the control ID of the menu item
`MF_BYPOSITION`	`idItem` contains the position of the menu item

`hbmUnchecked` and `hbmChecked` specify the bitmaps place by the menu item when the item is unchecked and checked, respectively. When either `hbmUnchecked` or `hbmChecked` is `NULL`, nothing is displayed beside the menu item for the corresponding selection. When both are `NULL`, the default checkmark is used when the menu item is checked and nothing is used when the menu item is unchecked.

Return Value A nonzero value is returned when successful. Zero is returned when unsuccessful.

Function Category Menu

Related Functions `CheckMenuItem`, `GetMenuCheckMarkDimensions`, `HiliteMenuItem`

SetMessageQueue

Syntax `BOOL SetMessageQueue(cMsg)`

Parameter	*Type*	*Description*
`cMsg`	`int`	Maximum number of messages that a new queue can hold

Description The `SetMessageQueue` function creates a new message queue that will hold the number of messages specified in `cMsg`. When the new queue is created, the old queue is destroyed. This function must be called from `WinMain` before any windows are created and before any messages are sent.

Return Value A nonzero value is returned if a new queue is created. Zero is returned if the new queue could not be created.

Function Category Message

Related Functions `GetMessage`, `PeekMessage`

SetMetaFileBits

Syntax `HGLOBAL SetMetaFileBits(hmf)`

Parameter	*Type*	*Description*
`hmf`	`HMETAFILE`	Global memory block containing the metafile data

Description The `SetMetaFileBits` function creates a memory metafile using the data in the global memory block specified in `hmf`.

Return Value The handle for the memory metafile is returned when successful. `NULL` is returned when unsuccessful.

Function Category Metafile

Related Functions `GetMetaFileBits`

SetMetaFileBitsBetter

Syntax `HGLOBAL SetMetaFileBitsBetter(hmf)`

Parameter	*Type*	*Description*
`hmf`	`HMETAFILE`	Global memory block that contains the metafile data. Use `GetMetaFileBits` to create this block.

Description The `SetMetaFileBitsBetter` function uses the data specified in `hmf` to create a memory metafile.

Return Value The ID to the memory metafile is returned when successful. `NULL` is returned when unsuccessful.

Function Category Metafile

Related Functions `GetMetaFileBits`, `SetMetaFileBits`

SetPaletteEntries

Syntax `UINT SetPaletteEntries(hpal, iStart, cEntries, lppe)`

Parameter	*Type*	*Description*
`hpal`	`HPALETTE`	Logical palette
`iStart`	`UINT`	First entry of the logical palette to set
`cEntries`	`UINT`	Number of palette entries to set
`lppe`	`const PALETTEENTRY FAR*`	Pointer to an array of `PALETTEENTRY` data structures containing the RGB values and flags

Description The `SetPaletteEntries` function defines the palette entries specified by `sStartIndex` and `cEntries` for the palette in `hpal`, using the array of data structures of type `PALETTEENTRY` pointed to by `lppe`. The `PALETTEENTRY` structure follows.

```
typedef struct
     {
     BYTE peRed;
     BYTE peGreen;
     BYTE peBlue;
     BYTE peFlags;
} PALETTEENTRY;
```

in which

`peRed` is the intensity of red for the palette entry

`peGreen` is the intensity of green for the palette entry

`peBlue` is the intensity of blue for the palette entry

`peFlags` is `NULL` or one of the following values:

Value	*Meaning*
`PC_EXPLICIT`	Low-order word of the palette entry contains a hardware palette index
`PC_NOCOLLAPSE`	Color will be placed in an unused entry in the palette; color will not replace existing entry
`PC_RESERVED`	Entry is used for palette animation; no color can be matched to this entry

Return Value The number of entries defined for the logical palette is returned when successful. Zero is returned when unsuccessful.

Function Category Color Palette

Related Functions `GetPaletteEntries`

SetParent

Syntax `HWND SetParent(hwndChild, hwndNewParent)`

Parameter	*Type*	*Description*
`hwndChild`	`HWND`	Child Window
`hwndNewParent`	`HWND`	New parent window

Description The `SetParent` function sets the parent window of the child window in `hwndChild` to the window in `hwndNewParent`.

Return Value The window handle of the previous parent window for `hwndChild` is returned.

Function Category Information

Related Functions `GetParent`, `IsChild`

SetPixel

Syntax `COLORREF SetPixel(hdc, nXPos, nYPos, clrref)`

Parameter	*Type*	*Description*
`hdc`	`HDC`	Device context
`nXPos`	`int`	Logical x coordinate of point
`nYPos`	`int`	Logical y coordinate of point
`clrref`	`COLORREF`	Color to paint point

Description The `SetPixel` function paints the pixel at the point specified by `nXPos` and `nYPos` the color specified in `clrref`. The specified point must lie within the clipping region.

Return Value The actual RGB color value that the point was painted is returned when successful. This value may differ from the color specified in `clrref`. –1 is returned when unsuccessful.

Function Category Bitmap

Related Functions `GetPixel`

SetPolyFillMode

Syntax `int SetPolyFillMode(hdc, fnMode)`

Parameter	*Type*	*Description*
`hdc`	`HDC`	Device context
`fnMode`	`int`	Filling mode

Description The `SetPolyFillMode` function sets the polygon filling mode for the device context in `hdc`. The polygon filling mode is used by Graphics Device Interface functions that require the computation of interior points using the polygon algorithm. The filling mode is specfied in `fnMode`. The following values are used for `fnMode`:

Value	*Meaning*
`ALTERNATE`	Alternate mode
`WINDING`	Winding number mode

Return Value The previous filling mode, either `ALTERNATE` or `WINDING`, is returned when successful. When unsuccessful, zero is returned.

Function Category Drawing Attribute

Related Functions `GetPolyFillMode`

SetProp

Syntax `BOOL SetProp(hwnd, lpsz, hData)`

Parameter	*Type*	*Description*
`hwnd`	`HWND`	Windows that contains the property list to receive the new entry
`lpsz`	`LPSTR`	Points to null-terminated string or atom identifying the entry to add
`hData`	`HANDLE`	Data handle to be copied to property list

Description The `SetProp` function either adds or modifies the entry specified in `lpsz` in the property list of the window specified in `hwnd`. When an entry matching `lpsz` doesn't exist, an entry containing the string in `lpsz` and the data handle in `hData` is added to the property list. When an entry matching `lpsz` exists, the data handle in `hData` is assigned to the entry. `lpsz` points to either a null-terminated string or an atom that identifies a string. When `lpsz` specifies an atom, the atom (16-bits) is placed in the low-order word of `lpsz`; the high-order word of `lpsz` is set to zero.

Return Value A nonzero value is returned if the data handle and string are added to the property list. Otherwise, zero is returned.

Function Category Property

Related Functions `EnumProps`, `GetProp`, `RemoveProp`

SetRect

Syntax `void SetRect(lprc, nLeft, nTop, nRight, nBottom)`

Parameter	*Type*	*Description*
`lprc`	`RECT FAR*`	Pointer to `RECT` data structure to receive the rectangle coordinates
`nLeft`	`int`	X coordinate of upper-left corner of rectangle

Parameter	Type	Description
nTop	int	Y coordinate of upper-left corner of rectangle
nRight	int	X coordinate of lower-right corner of rectangle
nBottom	int	Y coordinate of lower-right corner of rectangle

Description The `SetRect` function creates a new rectangle. The coordinates specified in (`nLeft`, `nTop`) and (`nRight`, `nBottom`) define the new rectangle. These coordinates are placed in the data structure of type `RECT` pointed to by `lprc`. The `RECT` data structure follows.

```
typedef struct tagRECT {
     int left;
     int top;
     int right;
     int bottom;
} RECT;
```

in which

`left` is the x coordinate of the upper-left corner

`top` is the y coordinate of the upper-left corner

`right` is the x coordinate of the lower-right corner

`bottom` is the y coordinate of the lower-right corner.

Return Value There is no return value.

Function Category Rectangle

Related Functions `SetRectEmpty`

SetRectEmpty

Syntax `void SetRectEmpty(lprc)`

Parameter	Type	Description
lprc	RECT FAR*	RECT data structure that will receive the empty rectangle

Description The `SetRectEmpty` function creates an empty rectangle and stores the coordinates of the rectangle (all zero) in the data structure of type `RECT` pointed to by `lprc`. The `RECT` structure follows.

```
typedef struct tagRECT {
     int left;
     int top;
     int right;
     int bottom;
} RECT;
```

in which

`left` is the x coordinate of the upper-left corner

`top` is the y coordinate of the upper-left corner

`right` is the x coordinate of the lower-right corner

`bottom` is the y coordinate of the lower-right corner.

Return Value There is no return value.

Function Category Rectangle

Related Functions `SetRect`

SetRectRgn

Syntax `void SetRectRgn(hrgn, nLeftRect, nTopRect, nRightRect, nBottomRect)`

Parameter	*Type*	*Description*
`hrgn`	`HRGN`	Region
`nLeftRect`	`int`	X coordinate of upper-left corner of rectangular region
`nTopRect`	`int`	Y coordinate of upper-left corner of rectangular region
`nRightRect`	`int`	X coordinate of lower-right corner of rectangular region
`nBottomRect`	`int`	Y coordinate of lower-right corner of rectangular region

Description The `SetRectRgn` function creates a rectangular region but does not use additional memory for the GDI heap, as the

CreateRectRegion function does. The space allocated to the region specified by hrgn is used by the SetRectRgn function.

Return Value There is no return value.

Function Category Region

Related Functions CreatePolygonRgn, CreateRectRgn

SetResourceHandler

Syntax

```
RSRCHDLRPRC SetResourceHandler(hInstance, lpType,
                               lpLoadFunc)
```

Parameter	*Type*	*Description*
hInstance	HINSTANCE	Instance of module whose executable file contains the resource
lpType	LPCSTR	Pointer to resource type
lpLoadFunc	RSRCHDLRPRC	Procedure instance address of the callback function

Description The SetResourceHandler function installs the callback function specified in lpLoadFunc. The callback function is used to load the resource type specified in lpType. The following conventions are used for the callback function.

```
FARPROC LoadProc(hglbMem, hinst, hrsrcResInfo)
HGLOBAL hglbMem;
HINSTANCE hinst;

HRSRC hrsrcResInfo;
```

in which

hglbMem is a stored resource

hinst is the instance of the module whose executable file contains the resource

hrsrcResInfo is the resource.

Return Value The pointer to the previously installed resource handler is returned. If a resource handler has not been installed, the pointer to the default handler is returned.

Function Category Resource Management

Related Functions `AllocResource`, `LockResource`

SetROP2

Syntax `int SetROP2(hdc, fnDrawMode)`

Parameter	*Type*	*Description*
`hdc`	`HDC`	Device context
`fnDrawMode`	`int`	Drawing mode

Description The `SetROP2` function sets the drawing mode for the device context specified in `hdc`. The drawing mode is specified in `fnDrawMode`. The following values are used for `fnDrawMode`:

Value	*Meaning*
`R2_BLACK`	Pixel is black
`R2_COPYPEN`	Pixel is the pen color
`R2_MASKNOTPEN`	Pixel is the combination of the common colors of the display and the inverse of the pen
`R2_MASKPEN`	Pixel is the combination of the common colors of the pen and the display
`R2_MASKPENNOT`	Pixel is the combination of the common colors of the pen and the inverse of the display color
`R2_MERGENOTPEN`	Pixel is the combination of the display color and the inverse of the pen color
`R2_MERGEPEN`	Pixel is the combination of the pen and display colors
`R2_MERGEPENNOT`	Pixel is the combination of pen color and inverse of display color
`R2_NOP`	Pixel is not changed
`R2_NOT`	Pixel is the inverse of display color
`R2_NOTCOPYPEN`	Pixel is the inverse of pen color
`R2_NOTMASKPEN`	Pixel is the inverse of `R2_MASKPEN`
`R2_NOTMERGEPEN`	Pixel is the inverse of `R2_MERGEPEN`
`R2_NOTXORPEN`	Pixel is the inverse of `R2_XORPEN` color

Value	*Meaning*
R2_WHITE	Pixel is white
R2_XORPEN	Pixel is the combination of the colors in the pen and in the display, but not both

Return Value The previous drawing mode is returned.

Function Category Drawing Attribute

Related Functions GetROP2

SetScrollPos

Syntax `int SetScrollPos(hwnd, fnBar, nPos, fRedraw)`

Parameter	*Type*	*Description*
hwnd	HWND	Window containing scroll bar to set
fnBar	int	Scroll bar to set
nPos	int	New thumb position of scroll bar
fRedraw	BOOL	Set to nonzero if the scroll bar is to be redrawn; zero if it is not to be redrawn

Description The `SetScrollPos` function sets the thumb position of the scroll bar specified in `fnBar` to the position specified in `nPos`. The scroll bar is redrawn if `fRedraw` is set to a nonzero value. `fnBar` is set to one of the following values:

Value	*Meaning*
SB_CTL	Sets the position of a scroll-bar control; hwnd must specify the window handle of a scroll-bar control
SB_HORZ	Sets the position of the horizontal scroll bar
SB_VERT	Sets the position of the vertical scroll bar

Return Value The previous thumb position of the scroll bar is returned when successful. Zero is returned when unsuccessful.

Function Category Scrolling

Related Functions `GetScrollPos`, `SetScrollRange`

SetScrollRange

Syntax `void SetScrollRange(hwnd, fnBar, nMin, nMax, fRedraw)`

Parameter	*Type*	*Description*
`hwnd`	`HWND`	Window containing scroll bar to set
`fnBar`	`int`	Scroll bar to set
`nMin`	`int`	Minimum scrolling position
`nMax`	`int`	Maximum scrolling position
`fRedraw`	`BOOL`	Set to `TRUE` if the scroll bar is to be redrawn; `FALSE` if it is not to be redrawn

Description The `SetScrollRange` function defines the range of the scroll bar specified in `fnBar`. The minimum and maximum positions for the scroll bar are defined by `nMin` and `nMax`, respectively. The scroll bar is redrawn if `fRedraw` is set to a nonzero value. `fnBar` is set to one of the following values:

Value	*Meaning*
`SB_CTL`	Sets the range of a scroll-bar control; `hwnd` must specify the window handle of a scroll-bar control
`SB_HORZ`	Sets the range of the horizontal scroll bar
`SB_VERT`	Sets the range of the vertical scroll bar

Return Value There is no return value.

Function Category Scrolling

Related Functions `GetScrollRange`, `SetScrollPos`

SetSelectorBase

Syntax `WORD SetSelectorBase(wSelector, dwBase)`

Parameter	*Type*	*Description*
`wSelector`	`WORD`	New selector value
`dwBase`	`DWORD`	New base value

Description The `SetSelectorBase` function defines the base and limit of the selector. `wSelector` specifies the new selector value. `dwBase` specifies the new base value.

Return Value The new selector value is returned.

Function Category Memory Management

Related Functions `GetSelectorBase`, `GetSelectorLimit`, `SetSelectorLimit`

SetSelectorLimit

Syntax `WORD SetSelectorLimit(wSelector, dwBase)`

Parameter	*Type*	*Description*
`wSelector`	`WORD`	New selector value
`dwBase`	`DWORD`	Current base value for `wSelector`

Description The `SetSelectorLimit` function defines the limit of the selector. `wSelector` specifies the new selector value. `dwBase` specifies the current base value for the selector.

Return Value The new selector value is returned.

Function Category Memory Management

Related Functions `GetSelectorBase`, `GetSelectorLimit`, `SetSelectorBase`

SetStretchBltMode

Syntax `int SetStretchBltMode(hdc, fnStretchMode)`

Parameter	Type	Description
hdc	HDC	Device context
fnStretchMode	int	Stretching mode

Description The `SetStretchBltMode` function sets the stretching mode for the device context specified in `hdc`. The stretching mode determines the scan lines and columns that are eliminated when a bitmap is contracted. `fnStretchMode` specifies the stretching mode. The following values are used for `fnStretchMode`.

Value	Meaning
STRETCH_ANDSCANS	Black pixels are preserved by using the AND operator on all eliminated and remaining lines
STRETCH_DELETESCANS	All eliminated lines are deleted
STRETCH_ORSCANS	White pixels are preserved by using the OR operator on all eliminated and remaining lines

Return Value The previous stretching mode (one of the following) is returned: `STRETCH_ANDSCANS`, `STRETCH_DELETESCANS`, or `STRETCH_ORSCANS`.

Function Category Drawing Attribute

Related Functions `GetStretchBltMode`, `StretchBlt`

SetSwapAreaSize

Syntax `LONG SetSwapAreaSize(cCodeParagraphs)`

Parameter	Type	Description
cCodeParagraphs	UINT	Number of 16-byte paragraphs requested by the application

Description The `SetSwapAreaSize` function defines the amount of memory available for use by an application for code segments. `cCodeParagraphs` specifies the number of 16-byte paragraphs to be used for code segments. Only one-half the memory available after Windows is loaded can be used. When `cCodeParagraphs` is zero, the current size of code-segment space is returned.

Return Value The low-order word of the return value contains the number of paragraphs that can be used for code segments. The high-order word of the return value specifies the maximum size available.

Function Category Memory Management

Related Functions `GetNumTasks`

SetSysColors

Syntax
```
void SetSysColors(cDspElements, lpnDspElements,
                  lpdwRgbValues)
```

Parameter	*Type*	*Description*
`cDspElements`	`int`	Number of system colors to change
`lpnDspElements`	`const int FAR*`	Array of index values that indicate the display elements to change
`lpdwRgbValues`	`const COLORREF FAR*`	Array of unsigned long integers containing the new RGB values for the display elements

Description The `SetSysColors` function sets the system color for the specified display elements. The number of elements to change is specified in `cDspElements`. `lpnDspElements` points to an array containing the index values for the display elements to change. The following values are used for `lpnDspElements`:

Value	*Meaning*
`COLOR_ACTIVEBORDER`	Active window border
`COLOR_ACTIVECAPTION`	Active window caption
`COLOR_APPWORKSPACE`	Background color for MDI applications
`COLOR_BACKGROUND`	Desktop
`COLOR_BTNFACE`	Face shading for push buttons
`COLOR_BINHIGHLIGHT`	Selected bottom in a control
`COLOR_BTNSHADOW`	Edge shading for push buttons

Value	Meaning
COLOR_BTNTEXT	Text on push buttons
COLOR_CAPTIONTEXT	Text for caption, size box, scroll bar arrow box
COLOR_GRAYTEXT	Grayed text
COLOR_HIGHLIGHT	Selected items in a control
COLOR_HIGHLIGHTTEXT	Text of selected items in a control
COLOR_INACTIVEBORDER	Inactive window border
COLOR_INACTIVECAPTION	Inactive window caption
COLOR_INACTIVECAPTIONTEXT	Text color in an inactive caption
COLOR_MENU	Menu background
COLOR_MENUTEXT	Text for menus
COLOR_SCROLLBAR	Scroll bar gray area
COLOR_WINDOW	Window background
COLOR_WINDOWFRAME	Window frame
COLOR_WINDOWTEXT	Text in windows

Return Value There is no return value.

Function Category System

Related Functions GetSysColor

SetSysModalWindow

Syntax `HWND SetSysModalWindow(hwnd)`

Parameter	Type	Description
hwnd	HWND	Window to be made system modal

Description The SetSysModalWindow function makes the window specified in hwnd a system modal window.

Return Value The handle of the previous system modal window is returned.

Function Category Input

Related Functions `SetActiveWindow`

SetSystemPaletteUse

Syntax `UINT SetSystemPaletteUse(hdc, fuStatic)`

Parameter	*Type*	*Description*
`hdc`	`HDC`	Device context
`fuStatic`	`UINT`	New use of system palette

Description The `SetSystemPaletteUse` function provides an application with full access to the system palette. `hdc` must specify a device context that supports color palettes. `fuStatic` specifies the new use of the system palette and is selected from one of the following values:

Value	*Meaning*
`SYSPAL_NOSTATIC`	System palette has no static colors—only black and white
`SYSPAL_STATIC`	System palette has static colors that will not change when the application realizes its logical palette

Return Value Either `SYSPAL_NOSTATIC` or `SYSPAL_STATIC` (see table under Description for this function) is returned, which represents the previous use of the system palette.

Function Category Color Palette

Related Functions `GetSystemPaletteUse`

SetTextAlign

Syntax `UINT SetTextAlign(hdc, fuAlign)`

Parameter	*Type*	*Description*
`hdc`	`HDC`	Device context
`fuAlign`	`UINT`	Specifies the text alignment

Description The `SetTextAlign` function sets the text alignment flags for the device context specified in `hdc` to the mask of values specified in `fuAlign`. `fuAlign` is a combination of the following values:

Value	*Meaning*
TA_BASELINE	Alignment of x axis and baseline of font within the binding rectangle
TA_BOTTOM	Alignment of x axis and bottom of binding rectangle
TA_CENTER	Alignment of y axis and center of binding rectangle
TA_LEFT	Alignment of y axis and left side of binding rectangle
TA_NOUPDATECP	Current position is not updated
TA_RIGHT	Alignment of y axis and right side of binding rectangle
TA_TOP	Alignment of x axis and top of binding rectangle
TA_UPDATECP	Current position is updated

Return Value The low-order word of the return value specifies the previous horizontal alignment. The high-order word of the return value specifies the previous vertical alignment.

Function Category Text

Related Functions `GetTextAlign`

SetTextCharacterExtra

Syntax `int SetTextCharacterExtra(hdc, nExtraSpace)`

Parameter	*Type*	*Description*
hdc	HDC	Device context
nExtraSpace	int	Extra space added to each character in logical units

Description The `SetTextCharacterExtra` function sets the amount of intercharacter spacing for the device in `hdc` to the amount specified in `nExtraSpace`.

Return Value The previous amount of intercharacter spacing is returned.

Function Category Text

Related Functions `GetTextCharacterExtra`

SetTextColor

Syntax `COLORREF SetTextColor(hdc, clrref)`

Parameter	*Type*	*Description*
`hdc`	`HDC`	Device context
`clrref`	`COLORREF`	Text color

Description The `SetTextColor` function sets the text color for the device context in `hdc` to the text color specified in `clrref`. The text color is set to the closest physical color if the specified device cannot represent the specified color.

Return Value The RGB color value for the previous text color is returned.

Function Category Drawing Attribute

Related Functions `GetTextColor`

SetTextJustification

Syntax `int SetTextJustification(hdc, nExtraSpace, cBreakChars)`

Parameter	*Type*	*Description*
`hdc`	`HDC`	Device context
`nExtraSpace`	`int`	Total extra space in logical units
`cBreakChars`	`int`	Number of break characters in the line

Description The `SetTextJustification` function tells the Graphics Device Interface how to justify a line of text. `nExtraSpace` and `cBreakChars` specify the justification parameters. The `SetTextJustification` function is used with the `GetTextExtent` function. The text width calculated with `GetTextExtent` is needed to determine the `nExtraSpace` value.

Return Value A 1 is returned when successful. Zero is returned when unsuccessful.

Function Category Text

Related Functions `GetTextExtent`, `GetTextMetrics`, `SetTextAlign`

SetTimer

Syntax `UINT SetTimer(hwnd, idTimer, uTimeout, tmprc)`

Parameter	*Type*	*Description*
`hwnd`	`HWND`	Window associated with timer
`idTimer`	`UINT`	Timer event
`uTimeout`	`UINT`	Time elapsed between timer events
`tmprc`	`TIMERPROC`	Procedure instance address of timer function

Description The `SetTimer` function creates a system timer event. `hwnd` specifies the window associated with the timer. `hwnd` is set to `NULL` if no window is associated with the timer. `idTimer` specifies the timer event when `hwnd` is not `NULL`. `uTimeout` defines the number of milliseconds elapsed between timer events. `tmprc` contains the procedure instance address of the function that processes the event. The `WM_TIMER` message is sent to the function specified in `tmprc` when a timer event occurs. When `tmprc` is `NULL`, the `WM_TIMER` message is placed in the application queue. The timer function must follow the format below. `TimerProc` is a placeholder for the function name that is supplied by the application. The function name must be exported using `EXPORTS` in the application's module definition file.

```
WORD FAR PASCAL TimerProc(hwnd, wMsg, TimerID, dwTime)
```

`HWND hwnd;`	Window associated with timer event
`WORD wMsg;`	Specifies `WM_TIMER` message
`int TimerID;`	Timer identification
`DWORD dwTime;`	System time

Return Value The integer identifier for the new timer event is returned. Zero is returned when the timer could not be created.

Function Category Input

Related Functions `KillTimer`

SetViewportExt

Syntax `DWORD SetViewportExt(hdc, nXExtent, nYExtent)`

Parameter	*Type*	*Description*
`hdc`	`HDC`	Device context
`nXExtent`	`int`	Width (x extent) of viewport in device units
`nYExtent`	`int`	Height (y extent) of viewport in device units

Description The `SetViewportExt` function defines the width (x extent) and height (y extent) of the viewport for the device context specified in `hdc`. `nXExtent` and `nYExtent` specify the width (x extent) and height (y extent) of the viewport, respectively. If any of the following mapping modes are set, the call to the `SetViewportExt` function is ignored:

```
MM_HIENGLISH
MM_HIMETRIC
MM_LOENGLISH
MM_LOMETRIC
MM_TEXT
MM_TWIPS
```

Return Value The low-order word of the return value contains the previous width (x extent) of the viewport. The high-order word of the return value contains the previous height (y extent) of the viewport. The return value is zero when the function is unsuccessful.

Function Category Mapping

Related Functions `GetViewportExt`, `ScaleViewportExt`

SetViewportExtEx

Syntax `BOOL SetViewportExtEx(hdc, nX, nY, lpSize)`

Parameter	*Type*	*Description*
hdc	HDC	Device context
nX	int	Horizontal extent of the viewport in device units
nY	int	Vertical extent of the viewport in device units
lpSize	SIZE FAR*	Pointer to SIZE data structure where the previous viewport extents are copied. lpSize can be NULL.

Description The `SetViewportExtEx` function defines the viewport extents for the device context specified in `hdc`. This function is ignored if any of the following mapping modes are in effect:

```
MM_HIENGLISH
MM_HIMETRIC
MM_LOENGLISH
MM_LOMETRIC
MM_TEXT
MM_TWIPS
```

Return Value `TRUE` is returned when successful. `FALSE` is returned when unsuccessful.

Function Category Mapping

Related Functions `SetWindowExtEx`

SetViewportOrg

Syntax `DWORD SetViewportOrg(hdc, nXOrigin, nYOrigin)`

Parameter	*Type*	*Description*
hdc	HDC	Device context
nXOrigin	int	X coordinate of the origin of the viewport in device coordinates
nYOrigin	int	Y coordinate of the origin of the viewport in device coordinates

Description The `SetViewportOrg` function sets the origin of the viewport for the device context specified in `hdc`. `nXOrigin` and `nYOrigin` specify the horizontal and vertical device coordinates of the viewport origin, respectively.

Return Value The low-order word of the return value specifies the x device coordinate of the previous viewport origin. The high-order word of the return value specifies the y device coordinate of the previous viewport origin.

Function Category Mapping

Related Functions `GetViewportOrg`, `OffsetViewportOrg`

SetViewportOrgEx

Syntax `BOOL SetViewportOrgEx(hdc, nX, nY, lpPoint)`

Parameter	*Type*	*Description*
hdc	HDC	Device context
nX	int	Horizontal coordinate of viewport origin
nY	int	Vertical coordinate of viewport origin
lpPoint	POINT FAR*	Pointer to `POINT` data structure where the coordinates of the previous origin are copied

Description The `SetViewportOrgEx` function defines the viewport origin for the device context specified in `hdc`. `nX` and `nY` specify the device coordinates of the viewport origin.

Return Value `TRUE` is returned when successful. `FALSE` is returned when unsuccessful.

Function Category Mapping

Related Functions `SetViewportOrg`, `SetWindowOrgEx`

SetWindowExt

Syntax `DWORD SetWindowExt(hdc, nXExtent, nYExtent)`

Parameter	*Type*	*Description*
hdc	HDC	Device context
nXExtent	int	Width (x extent) of window in logical units
nYExtent	int	Height (y extent) of window in logical units

Description The `SetWindowExt` function defines the width (x extent) and height (y extent) of the window for the device context specified in `hdc`. `nXExtent` and `nYExtent` specify the width (x extent) and height (y extent) of the window, respectively. If any of the following mapping modes are set, the call to the `SetWindowExt` function is ignored:

```
MM_HIENGLISH
MM_HIMETRIC
MM_LOENGLISH
MM_LOMETRIC
MM_TEXT
MM_TWIPS
```

Return Value The low-order word of the return value contains the previous width (x extent) of the window. The high-order word of the return value contains the previous height (y extent) of the window. The return value is zero when the function is unsuccessful.

Function Category Mapping

Related Functions `GetWindowExt`, `ScaleWindowExt`

SetWindowExtEx

Syntax `BOOL SetWindowExtEx(hdc, nX, nY, lpSize)`

Parameter	*Type*	*Description*
hdc	HDC	Device context
nX	int	Horizontal extent of window
nY	int	Vertical extent of window
lpSize	SIZE FAR*	Pointer to SIZE data structure where the previous window extents are copied. lpSize can be set to NULL.

Description The SetWindowExtEx function defines the window extents for the device context specified in hdc. nX and nY define the window extents using logical units. This function is ignored if any of the following mapping modes are in effect:

```
MM_HIENGLISH
MM_HIMETRIC
MM_LOENGLISH
MM_LOMETRIC
MM_TEXT
MM_TWIPS
```

Return Value TRUE is returned when successful. FALSE is returned when unsuccessful.

Function Category Mapping

Related Functions `SetViewportExtEx`, `SetWindowExt`

SetWindowLong

Syntax `LPARAM SetWindowLong(hwnd, nOffset, lParamNew)`

Parameter	Type	Description
hwnd	HWND	Window handle
nOffset	int	Byte offset of attribute to change
lParamNew	LPARAM	New value

Description The `SetWindowLong` function sets the attribute value identified by `nOffset` to the value specified in `lParamNew`. `nOffset` specifies the byte offset of the attribute to change. `nOffset` can also be set to the following values:

Value	Meaning
GWL_EXSTYLE	Sets a new extended window style
GWL_STYLE	Sets a new window style
GWL_WNDPROC	Sets a new long pointer to the window procedure

Return Value The previous value of the specified long integer is returned when successful. Zero is returned when unsuccessful.

Function Category Window Creation

Related Functions `GetWindowLong`, `SetWindowText`, `SetWindowWord`

SetWindowOrg

Syntax `DWORD SetWindowOrg(hdc, nXOrigin, nYOrigin)`

Parameter	Type	Description
hdc	HDC	Device context
nXOrigin	int	X coordinate of the origin of the window in logical coordinates
nYOrigin	int	Y coordinate of the origin of the window in logical coordinates

Description The SetWindowOrg function sets the origin of the window for the device context specified in hdc. nXOrigin and nYOrigin specify the horizontal and vertical logical coordinates of the window origin, respectively.

Return Value The low-order word of the return value specifies the x logical coordinate of the previous window origin. The high-order word of the return value specifies the y logical coordinate of the previous window origin.

Function Category Mapping

Related Functions GetWindowOrg, OffsetWindowOrg

SetWindowOrgEx

Syntax `BOOL SetWindowOrgEx(hdc, nX, nY, lpPoint)`

Parameter	*Type*	*Description*
hdc	HDC	Device context
nX	int	Horizontal coordinate of new window origin
nY	int	Vertical coordinate of new window origin
lpPoint	POINT FAR*	Pointer to POINT data structure where the previous window origin is copied. lpPoint can be set to NULL.

Description The SetWindowOrgEx function defines the window origin of the device context specified in hdc. nX and nY define the logical coordinates of the new window origin.

Return Value TRUE is returned when successful. FALSE is returned when unsuccessful.

Function Category Mapping

Related Functions SetViewportOrgEx, SetWindowOrg

SetWindowPlacement

Syntax `BOOL SetWindowPlacement(hwnd, lpwndpl)`

Parameter	*Type*	*Description*
`hwnd`	`HWND`	Window handle
`lpwndpl`	`LPWINDOWPLACEMENT`	Pointer to `WINDOWPLACEMENT` data structure that contains the new window show state and position

Description The `SetWindowPlacement` data structure defines window placement information. `lpwndpl` points to a data structure of type `WINDOWPLACEMENT` that defines the show state and the normal, minimized, and maximized positions of the window.

Return Value A nonzero value is returned when successful. Zero is returned when unsuccessful.

Function Category Display and Movement

Related Functions `GetWindowPlacement`

SetWindowPos

Syntax

```
void SetWindowPos(hwnd, hwndInsertAfter, x, y, cx, cy,
                  fuFlags)
```

Parameter	*Type*	*Description*
`hwnd`	`HWND`	Window handle
`hwndInsertAfter`	`HWND`	Window in hwnd will be positioned after this window
`x`	`int`	X coordinate of window's upper-left corner
`y`	`int`	Y coordinate of window's upper-left corner
`cx`	`int`	Window's new width

Parameter	*Type*	*Description*
`cy`	`int`	Window's new height
`fuFlags`	`UINT`	16-bit value affecting size and position of window

Description The `SetWindowPos` function alters the size, position, and order of the window specified in `hwnd`. `x` and `y` identify the horizontal and vertical coordinates, respectively, of the upper-left corner of the specified window. `cx` and `cy` specify the new width and height, respectively, of the window. `hwndInsertAfter` specifies a window from the window manager's window list. The window in `hwnd` will be placed after the window in `hwndInsertAfter` when the `SWP_NOZORDER` flag is set and `hwndInsertAfter` contains a valid window handle. `hwndInsertAfter` must be one of the following values if `hwndInsertAfter` does not contain a valid window handle:

Value	*Meaning*
`HWND_BOTTOM`	Window is placed at the bottom of the Z order
`HWND_TOP`	Window is placed at the top of the Z order
`HWND_TOPMOST`	Window is placed above all non-topmost windows
`HWND_NOTOPMOST`	Window is placed above all non-topmost windows but not above topmost windows

`fuFlags` is a 16-bit value affecting the size and position of the specified window. The following constants can be used with `fuFlags`:

Constant	*Meaning*
`SWP_DRAWFRAME`	Window is framed
`SWP_HIDEWINDOW`	Window is hidden
`SWP_NOACTIVATE`	Window is not activated
`SWP_NOMOVE`	Position is not updated
`SWP_NOREDRAW`	Changes are not redrawn
`SWP_NOSIZE`	Size is not updated
`SWP_NOZORDER`	Ordering is not affected
`SWP_SHOWWINDOW`	Window is displayed

Return Value A nonzero value is returned when successful. Zero is returned when unsuccessful.

Function Category Display and Movement

Related Functions `BeginDeferWindowPos`, `DeferWindowPos`, `EndDeferWindowPos`, `MoveWindow`

SetWindowsHook

Syntax `HHOOK SetWindowsHook(idHook, hkPrc)`

Parameter	*Type*	*Description*
`idHook`	`int`	System hook to install
`hkPrc`	`HOOKPROC`	Procedure instance address of the filter function

Description The `SetWindowsHook` function installs the system hook specified in idHook. `hkPrc` is the procedure instance address of the filter function. The filter function handles events before they go to the application's message loop. (This function is obsolete for Windows 3.1. Use `SetWindowsHookEx` instead.) The valid system hooks for `idHook` are as follows:

System Hook	*Meaning*
`WH_CALLWNDPROC`	Window function filter installed
`WH_CBT`	Computer-based training filter installed
`WH_DEBUG`	Debugging filter installed
`WH_GETMESSAGE`	Message filter installed
`WH_HARDWARE`	Hardware-message filter installed
`WH_JOURNALPLAYBACK`	Journaling playback filter installed
`WH_JOURNALRECORD`	Journaling record filter installed
`WH_KEYBOARD`	Keyboard filter installed
`WH_MOUSE`	Mouse-message filter installed
`WH_MSGFILTER`	Message filter installed
`WH_SHELL`	Shell-application filter installed
`WH_SYSMSGFILTER`	System-wide message filter installed

Return Value The pointer to the previous procedure instance address for the previous filter function is returned. `NULL` is returned if there is no previous filter installed. ((FARPROC) 0xFFFFFFFF) is returned when unsuccessful.

Function Category Hook

Related Functions SetWindowHookEx, UnhookWindowsHook

SetWindowsHookEx

Syntax `HHOOK SetWindowsHookEx(idHook, hkprc, hinst, htask)`

Parameter	*Type*	*Description*
idHook	int	Type of hook to install
hkprc	HOOKPROC	Procedure instance address of hook procedure
hinst	HINSTANCE	Instance of module that contains the hook function. If set to NULL, the installed hook function is local to the current process.
htask	HTASK	Task for hook installation. If set to NULL, the hook function can be called by any process or task.

Description The SetWindowsHookEx function is similar to the SetWindowsHook function but offers extended functionality. SetWindowHookEx installs an application-defined hook function. idHook specifies the type of hook to install and is one of the following values:

Value	*Meaning*
WH_CALLWNDPROC	Window function filter installed
WH_CBT	Comptuer-based training filter installed
WH_DEBUG	Debugging filter installed
WH_GETMESSAGE	Message filter installed
WH_HARDWARE	Non-standared hardware message filter installed
WH_JOURNAL_PLAYBACK	Journaling playback filter installed
WH_JOURNAL_RECORD	Journaling record filter installed
WH_KEYBOARD	Keyboard filter installed

Value	*Meaning*
`WH_MOUSE`	Mouse message filter installed
`WH_MSGFILTER`	Message filter installed
`WH_SYSMSGFILTER`	System-wide message filter installed

Return Value The handle to the installed hook is returned when successful. `NULL` is returned when unsuccessful.

Function Category Hook

Related Functions `SetWindowsHook, UnhookWindowsHookEx`

SetWindowText

Syntax `void SetWindowText(hwnd, lpsz)`

Parameter	*Type*	*Description*
`hwnd`	`HWND`	Window or control handle
`lpsz`	`LPCSTR`	New text or caption

Description The `SetWindowText` function sets the caption of the window, or the text for the control, specified in `hwnd`. `lpsz` points to the character string containing the new text or caption.

Return Value There is no return value.

Function Category Display and Movement

Related Functions `GetWindowText, SetWindowPos`

SetWindowWord

Syntax `WPARAM SetWindowWord(hwnd, nOffset, wParamNew)`

Parameter	*Type*	*Description*
`hwnd`	`HWND`	Window handle
`nOffset`	`int`	Byte offset of word to change

Parameter	Type	Description
wParamNew	WPARAM	New value

Description The SetWindowWord function sets the attribute identified by nOffset to the value specified in hwNewWord. nOffset specifies the byte offset of the attribute to change. nOffset can also be set to the following values:

Value	Meaning
GWW_HINSTANCE	Instance handle of the module that owns the window
GWW_ID	Control ID of the child window

Return Value The previous value of the specified word is returned when successful. Zero is returned when unsuccessful.

Function Category Window Creation

Related Functions GetWindowWord, SetWindowLong

ShellExecute

Syntax

```
HANDLE ShellExecute(hwnd, lpszOp, lpszFile,
                    lpszParams, lpszDir,fwShowCmd)
```

Parameter	Type	Description
hwnd	HWND	Parent window
lpszOp	LPSTR	Pointer to null-terminated string that specifies the operation, either "open" or "print"
lpszFile	LPSTR	Pointer to null-terminated string that specifies the file to open
lpszParams	LPSTR	Pointer to null-terminated string that specifies the parameters to pass to the executable file in lpszFile; when lpszFile specifies a document file, lpszParams is NULL

`lpszDir`	`LPSTR`	Pointer to null-terminated string specifying the default directory
`fwShowCmd`	`WORD`	Indicates whether to show the program when it is opened. `fwShowCmd` can be one of the following values:

Value	*Meaning*
`SW_HIDE`	Window is hidden and not active
`SW_MINIMIZE`	Window is minimized and top-level window is activated
`SW_RESTORE`	Identical to `SW_SHOWNORMAL`
`SW_SHOW`	Window is activated and shows in its current size and position
`SW_SHOWMAXIMIZED`	Window is activated and maximized
`SW_SHOWMINIMIZED`	Window is activated and iconic
`SW_SHOWMINNOACTIVE`	Window is iconic but not active
`SW_SHOWNA`	Window is shown in current state but is not activated
`SW_SHOWNOACTIVATE`	Window is shown in its most recent size and position but is not activated
`SW_SHOWNORMAL`	Activates and displays the window using its original size and position

Description The `ShellExecute` either opens or prints the file specified in `lpszFile`. When `lpszFile` specifies a document file, the specified file can be opened or printed. When `lpszFile` specifies an executable file, the file can only be opened.

Return Value The instance handle of the program is returned when successful. One of the following error values is returned when unsuccessful:

Value	*Meaning*
0	System out of memory
2	File not found
3	Path not found
5	Function attempted to dynamically link to task
6	Library requires separate data segments for each task
8	Insufficient memory to start application

Value	Meaning
10	Windows version incorrect
11	.EXE file invalid
12	OS/2 application
13	DOS 4.0 application
14	.EXE type unknown
15	Program attempted to load an .EXE file created for earlier version of Windows in protected mode
16	Program attempted to load a second instance of the .EXE file containing multiple, writeable data segment
19	Program attempted to load a compressed .EXE file
20	Program attempted to load an invalid DLL file
21	Program requires Windows 32-bit extensions

Function Category Shell

Related Functions `FindExecutable`

ShowCaret

Syntax `void ShowCaret(hwnd)`

Parameter	Type	Description
`hwnd`	`HWND`	Window that owns the caret

Description The `ShowCaret` function displays the caret at its current position. The caret is not shown if a shape has not been defined, the caret has been hidden two or more times, or the caret is not owned by the window in `hwnd`. When `hwnd` is `NULL`, a window in the current task must own the caret for the caret to be shown.

Return Value There is no return value.

Function Category Caret

Related Functions `CreateCaret`, `HideCaret`

ShowCursor

Syntax `int ShowCursor(fShow)`

Parameter	*Type*	*Description*
fShow	BOOL	Effect on display count

Description The `ShowCursor` function can either hide or show the cursor. `fShow` determines the action of the `ShowCursor` function. If `fShow` is `TRUE`, the cursor display counter is incremented. If `fShow` is `FALSE`, the cursor display counter is decremented. The cursor display counter is a value maintained internally which determines whether the cursor is shown or hidden. The initial value of the display counter is zero when a mouse is installed and –1 when no mouse is installed. By calling the `ShowCursor` function, the display counter is modified. Whenever the cursor display counter is greater than or equal to zero, the cursor is displayed.

Return Value The value of the cursor display counter is returned.

Function Category Cursor

Related Functions `CreateCursor`, `LoadCursor`, `SetCursor`

ShowOwnedPopups

Syntax `void ShowOwnedPopups(hwnd, fShow)`

Parameter	*Type*	*Description*
hwnd	HWND	Window that owns the pop-up windows
fShow	BOOL	Specifies whether pop-up windows are hidden

Description The `ShowOwnedPopups` function either shows or hides the pop-up windows that are owned by the window specified in `hwnd`. `fShow` determines whether the pop-up windows will be shown or hidden. If `fShow` is `FALSE`, all visible pop-up windows will be hidden. If `fShow` is `TRUE`, all hidden pop-up windows will be shown.

Return Value There is no return value.

Function Category Display and Movement

Related Functions `ShowWindow`

ShowScrollBar

Syntax `void ShowScrollBar(hwnd, fnBar, fShow)`

Parameter	*Type*	*Description*
`hwnd`	`HWND`	Window containing scroll bar or scroll bar control
`fnBar`	`int`	Value indicating meaning of `hwnd` and scroll bar position
`fShow`	`BOOL`	Set to `FALSE` to hide scroll bar; set to `TRUE` to show the scroll bar

Description The `ShowScrollBar` function either hides or shows the scroll bar in `hwnd`. `fShow` specifies whether the scroll bar is to be hidden or shown. `fnBar` specifies the meaning of `hwnd` and the scroll bar position. `fnBar` is set to one of the following values:

Value	*Meaning*
`SB_BOTH`	Hide/show both horizontal and vertical scroll bars; `hwnd` specifies a window containing a scroll bar in its nonclient area
`SB_CTL`	Hide/show the scroll bar control; `hwnd` specifies the scroll bar control
`SB_HORZ`	Hide/show the horizontal scroll bar; `hwnd` specifies a window containing a scroll bar in its nonclient area
`SB_VERT`	Hide/show the vertical scroll bar; `hwnd` specifies a window containg a scroll bar in its nonclient area

Return Value There is no return value.

Function Category Scrolling

Related Functions `SetScrollPos`, `SetScrollRange`

ShowWindow

Syntax `BOOL ShowWindow(hwnd, nCmdShow)`

Parameter	*Type*	*Description*
`hwnd`	`HWND`	Window handle
`nCmdShow`	`int`	Defines how window is shown

Description The `ShowWindow` function either displays or removes the window specified in hwnd. `nCmdShow` specifies the way in which the function behaves. The constants used for `nCmdShow` are as follows:

Constant	*Meaning*
`SW_HIDE`	Hides the window and another window becomes active
`SW_MINIMIZE`	Minimizes the window and the top-level window becomes active
`SW_RESTORE`	Activates and displays the window
`SW_SHOW`	Activates and displays the window in its current size and position
`SW_SHOWMAXIMIZED`	Activates, displays, and maximizes the window
`SW_SHOWMINIMIZED`	Activates and displays the window as minimized
`SW_SHOWMINNOACTIVE`	Displays the window as minimized
`SW_SHOWNA`	Displays the window in its current state
`SW_SHOWNOACTIVE`	Displays the window in its most recent size and position
`SW_SHOWNORMAL`	Activates and displays the window

Return Value A nonzero value is returned if the previous state of the window was visible. Zero is returned if the previous state of the window was hidden.

Function Category Display and Movement

Related Functions `ShowOwnedPopups`

SizeofResource

Syntax `DWORD SizeofResource(hinst, hrsrc)`

Parameter	*Type*	*Description*
`hinst`	`HINSTANCE`	Instance of module whose executable file contains the resource
`hrsrc`	`HRSRC`	Resource handle

Description The `SizeofResource` function returns the number of bytes in the resource specified in `hrsrc`. `hinst` specifies the instance of the module whose executable file contains the specified resource.

Return Value The number of bytes in the resource is returned when successful. Zero is returned when unsuccessful.

Function Category Resource Management

Related Functions `AllocResource`, `FreeResource`

StackTraceCSIPFirst

Syntax
```
BOOL StackTraceCSIPFirst(steStackTrace, wSS,
                         wCS, wIP, wBP)
```

Parameter	*Type*	*Description*
`steStackTrace`	`STACKTRACEENTRY FAR*`	Pointer to `STACKTRACEENTRY` data structure where stack information is copied
`wSS`	`WORD`	Value in stack segment register
`wCS`	`WORD`	Value in code segment register
`wIP`	`WORD`	Value in instruction pointer
`wBP`	`WORD`	Value in base pointer

Description The StackTraceCSIPFirst function retrieves information on the stack frame defined by wSS, wCS, wIP and wBP and copies the information to the data structure of type STACKTRACEENTRY pointed to by steStackTrace. The STACKTRACEENTRY data structure follows.

```
#include <toolhelp.h>
typedef struct tagSTACKTRACEENTRY {
     DWORD dwSize;
     HANDLE hTask;
     WORD wSS;
     WORD wBP;
     WORD wCS;
     WORD wIP;
     HANDLE hModule;
     WORD wSegment;
     WORD wFlags;
} STACKTRACEENTRY;
```

in which

dwSize is the size of the data structure in bytes

hTask is the stack's task handle

wSS is the value in the stack segment register

wBP is the value in the base pointer register

wCS is the value in the code segment register

wBP is the value in the base pointer register

wCS is the value of the instruction pointer register

wIP is the value of the instruction pointer register

hModule is the module that contains the currently executing function

wSegment is the segment number of the current selector

wFlags is the frame type: FRAME_FAR when the CS register contains a valid code segment or FRAME_NEAR when the CS register is NULL.

Return Value A nonzero value is returned when successful. Zero is returned when unsuccessful.

Function Category Toolhelp

Related Functions StackTraceNext, StackTraceFirst

StackTraceFirst

Syntax `BOOL StackTraceFirst(steStackTrace, hTask)`

Parameter	*Type*	*Description*
steStackTrace	STACKTRACEENTRY FAR*	Pointer to STACKTRACEENTRY data structure where stack frame information is copied
hTask	HANDLE	Task

Description The StackTraceFirst function copies information on the first stack frame in the task specified in hTask to the data structure of type STACKTRACEENTRY pointed to by steStackTrace. The STACKTRACEENTRY data structure follows.

```
#include <toolhelp.h>
typedef struct tagSTACKTRACEENTRY {
     DWORD dwSize;
     HANDLE hTask;
     WORD wSS;
     WORD wBP;
     WORD wCS;
     WORD wIP;
     HANDLE hModule;
     WORD wSegment;
     WORD wFlags;
} STACKTRACEENTRY;
```

in which

dwSize is the size of the data structure in bytes

hTask is the stack's task handle

wSS is the value in the stack segment register

wBP is the value in the base pointer register

wCS is the value in the code segment register

wIP is the value of the instruction pointer register

`hModule` is the module that contains the currently executing function

`wSegment` is the segment number of the current selector

`wFlags` is the frame type: `FRAME_FAR` when the CS register contains a valid code segment or `FRAME_NEAR` when the CS register is `NULL`.

Return Value A nonzero value is returned when successful. Zero is returned when unsuccessful.

Function Category Toolhelp

Related Functions `StaceTraceCSIPFirst`, `StackTraceNext`

StackTraceNext

Syntax `BOOL StackTraceNext(steStackTrace)`

Parameter	*Type*	*Description*
`steStackTrace`	`STACKTRACEENTRY FAR*`	Pointer to `STACKTRACEENTRY` data structure where stack frame information is copied

Description The `StackTraceNext` function copies information on the next stack frame in the stack trace to the data structure of type `STACKTRACEENTRY` pointed to by `steStackTrace`. The `STACKTRACEENTRY` data structure follows.

```
#include <toolhelp.h>
typedef struct tagSTACKTRACEENTRY {
     DWORD dwSize;
     HANDLE hTask;
     WORD wSS;
     WORD wBP;
     WORD wCS;
     WORD wIP;
     HANDLE hModule;
     WORD wSegment;
     WORD wFlags;
} STACKTRACEENTRY;
```

in which

`dwSize` is the size of the data structure in bytes

`hTask` is the stack's task handle

`wSS` is the value in the stack segment register

`wBP` is the value in the base pointer register

`wCS` is the value in the code segment register

`wIP` is the value of the instruction pointer register

`hModule` is the module that contains the currently executing function

`wSegment` is the segment number of the current selector

`wFlags` is the frame type: `FRAME_FAR` when the CS register contains a valid code segment or `FRAME_NEAR` when the CS register is `NULL`.

Return Value A nonzero value is returned when successful. Zero is returned when unsuccessful.

Function Category Toolhelp

Related Functions `StackTraceCSIPFirst`, `StackTraceFirst`

StartDoc

Syntax `int StartDoc(hdc, lpdi)`

Parameter	*Type*	*Description*
hdc	HDC	Device context
lpdi	DOCINFO FAR*	Pointer to DOCINFO structure containing the name of the document and output file

Description The `StartDoc` function initiates a print job. Windows 3.1 applications should use this function instead of the `STARTDOC` pointer escape. `lpdi` points to a `DOCINFO` data structure. The `DOCINFO` data structure follows.

```
typedef struct {
     short cbSize;
     LPSTR lpszDocName;
     LPSTR lpszOutput;
} DOCINFO;
```

in which

`cbSize` is the size of the structure in bytes

`lpszDocName` is a pointer to a null-terminated string that specifies the name of the document

`lpszOutput` is a pointer to a null-terminated string that specifies the name of the output file. If set to `NULL`, the output goes to the device for the specified device context.

Return Value A positive value is returned when successful. `SP_ERROR` is returned when unsuccessful.

Function Category Printer Control

Related Functions `EndDoc`, `Escape`

StartPage

Syntax `int StartPage(hdc)`

Parameter	*Type*	*Description*
`hdc`	`HDC`	Device context

Description The `StartPage` function initializes the printer driver for incoming data.

Return Value A positive value is returned when successful. Zero or a negative value is returned when unsuccessful.

Function Category Printer Control

Related Functions `EndPage`, `Escape`

StretchBlt

Syntax

```
BOOL StretchBlt(hdcDest, nXOriginDest, nYOriginDest,
                nWidthDest, nHeightDest, hdcSrc,
                nXOriginSrc, nYOriginSrc, nWidthSrc,
                nHeightSrc, fdwRop)
```

Parameter	*Type*	*Description*
hdcDest	HDC	Device context receiving bitmap
nXOriginDest	int	Logical x coordinate of upper-left corner of destination rectangle
nYOriginDest	int	Logical y coordinate of upper-left corner of destination rectangle
nWidthDest	int	Width of destination rectangle in logical units
nHeightDest	int	Height of destination rectangle in logical units
hdcSrc	HDC	Device context to source bitmap
nXOriginSrc	int	Logical x coordinate of upper-left corner of source rectangle
nYOriginSrc	int	Logical y coordinate of upper-left corner of source rectangle
nWidthSrc	int	Width of source rectangle in logical units
nHeightSrc	int	Height of source rectangle in logical units
fdwRop	DWORD	Raster operation to perform

Description The `StretchBlt` function places the bitmap in the source rectangle into the destination rectangle. The bitmap is stretched or compressed to fit the destination rectangle. `hdcDest`, `nXOriginDest`, `nYOriginDest`, `nWidthDest`, and `nHeightDest` provide information on the destination rectangle and bitmap.

`hdcSrc`, `nXOriginSrc`, `nYOriginSrc`, `nWidthSrc`, and `nHeightSrc` provide information on the source rectangle and bitmap. `fdwRop` specifies the raster operation to perform. The following values are used for `fdwRop`:

Value	*Meaning*
`BLACKNESS`	All output is black
`DSTINVERT`	Destination bitmap is inverted
`MERGECOPY`	Uses Boolean AND to combine the pattern and source bitmap
`MERGEPAINT`	Uses Boolean OR to combine the inverted source bitmap with the destination bitmap
`NOTSRCCOPY`	Copies the inverted source bitmap to the destination
`NOTSRCERASE`	Uses Boolean OR to combine the destination and source, then inverts the combination
`PATCOPY`	Copies the pattern to the destination bitmap
`PATINVERT`	Uses Boolean XOR to combine the destination bitmap with the pattern
`PATPAINT`	Uses Boolean OR to combine the inverted source with the pattern, then uses Boolean OR to combine the result of the previous operation with the destination
`SRCAND`	Uses Boolean AND to combine the source and destination bitmaps
`SRCCOPY`	Copies the source bitmap to the destination
`SRCERASE`	Uses Boolean AND to combine the inverted destination bitmap with the source bitmap
`SRCINVERT`	Uses Boolean XOR to combine the source and destination bitmaps
`SRCPAINT`	Uses Boolean OR to combine the source and destination bitmaps
`WHITENESS`	All output is white

Return Value A nonzero value is returned if the bitmap is drawn. Zero is returned if the bitmap is not drawn.

Function Category Bitmap

Related Functions `BitBlt`, `PatBlt`

StretchDIBits

Syntax

```
int StretchDIBits(hdc, uXOriginDest, uYOriginDest,
                  uWidthDest, uHeightDest, uXOriginSrc,
                  uYOriginSrc, uWidthSrc, uHeightSrc,
                  lpvBits, lpbmi, fuColorUse, fdwRop)
```

Parameter	*Type*	*Description*
`hdc`	`HDC`	Device context receiving bitmap
`uXOriginDest`	`UINT`	Logical x coordinate of upper-left corner of destination rectangle
`uYOriginDest`	`UINT`	Logical y coordinate of upper-left corner of destination rectangle
`nDestWidth`	`UINT`	Width of destination rectangle in logical units
`uHeightDest`	`UINT`	Height of destination rectangle in logical units
`uXOriginSrc`	`UINT`	Logical x coordinate of upper-left corner of source rectangle
`uYOriginSrc`	`UINT`	Logical y coordinate of upper-left corner of source rectangle
`uWidthSrc`	`UINT`	Width of source rectangle in logical units
`uHeightSrc`	`UINT`	Height of source rectangle in logical units
`lpvBits`	`const void FAR*`	Points to array of device-independent bitmap bits
`lpbmi`	`BITMAPINFO FAR*`	Points to `BITMAPINFO` data structure containing information on the device-independent bitmap
`fuColorUse`	`UINT`	Set to `DIB_PAL_COLORS` (color table in `lpbmi` contains array of 16-bit indexes for the currently realized logical palette) or `DIB_RGB_COLORS` (color table in `lpbmi` contains RGB values)

Parameter	*Type*	*Description*
`fdwRop`	`DWORD`	Raster operation to perform

Description The `StretchDIBits` function places the device-independent bitmap in the source rectangle into the specified destination rectangle. The bitmap is stretched or compressed to fit the destination rectangle. `lpvBits`, `lpbmi`, and `fuColorUse` specify the device-independent bitmap. `lpbmi` points to a data structure of type `BITMAPINFO`. The `BITMAPINFO` structure appears after the following table. `uXOriginSrc`, `uYOriginSrc`, `uWidthSrc`, and `uHeightSrc` specify the source rectangle. `uXOriginDest`, `uYOriginDest`, `uWidthDest`, and `uHeightDest` specify the destination rectangle. `fdwRop` specifies the raster operation to perform. The following values are used for `fdwRop`:

Value	*Meaning*
`BLACKNESS`	All output is black
`DSTINVERT`	Destination bitmap is inverted
`MERGECOPY`	Uses Boolean AND to combine the pattern and source bitmap
`MERGEPAINT`	Uses Boolean OR to combine the inverted source bitmap with the destination bitmap
`NOTSRCCOPY`	Copies the inverted source bitmap to the destination
`NOTSRCERASE`	Uses Boolean OR to combine the destination and source, then inverts the combination
`PATCOPY`	Copies the pattern to the destination bitmap
`PATINVERT`	Uses Boolean XOR to combine the destination bitmap with the pattern
`PATPAINT`	Uses Boolean OR to combine the inverted source with the pattern, then uses Boolean OR to combine the result of the previous operation with the destination
`SRCAND`	Uses Boolean AND to combine the source and destination bitmaps
`SRCCOPY`	Copies the source bitmap to the destination
`SRCERASE`	Uses Boolean AND to combine the inverted destination bitmap with the source bitmap
`SRCINVERT`	Uses Boolean XOR to combine the source and destination bitmaps

Value	Meaning
SRCPAINT	Uses Boolean OR to combine the source and destination bitmaps
WHITENESS	All output is white

```
typedef struct tagBITMAPINFO {
     BITMAPINFOHEADER bmiHeader;
     RGBQUAD bmiColors[1];
} BITMAPINFO;
```

in which

`bmiHeader` is the `BITMAPINFOHEADER` structure for the device-independent bitmap

`bmiColors` is an array of data structures of type `RGBQUAD` that defines the colors in the bitmap.

The `BITMAPINFOHEADER` structure follows.

```
typedef struct BITMAPINFOHEADER {
     DWORD biSize;
     DWORD biWidth;
     DWORD biHeight;
     WORD biPlanes;
     WORD biBitCount;
     DWORD biCompression;
     DWORD biSizeImage;
     DWORD biXPelsPerMeter;
     DWORD biYPelsPerMeter;
     DWORD biClrUsed;
     DWORD biClrImportant;
} BITMAPINFOHEADER;
```

in which

`biSize` is the number of bytes required for the structure

`biWidth` is the width of the bitmap in pixels

`biHeight` is the height of the bitmap in pixels

`biPlanes` is the number of planes; must be set to 1

`biBitCount` is the number of bits per pixel

`biCompression` is the type of compression and is selected from the following values:

`BI_RGB`	Bitmap is not compressed
`BI_RLE8`	Run-length encode format with 8 bits per pixel
`BI_RLE4`	Run-length encode format with 4 bits per pixel

`biSizeImage` is the size of the image in bytes

`biXPelsPerMeter` is the horizontal resolution in pixels per meter for the target device

`biYPelsPerMeter` is the vertical resolution in pixels per meter for the target device

`biClrUsed` is the number of color indexes in the color table the bitmap actually uses

`biClrImportant` is the number of color indexes considered important for the bitmap

Return Value The number of scan lines copied is returned.

Function Category Bitmap

Related Functions `GetDIBits`, `SetDIBits`, `SetStretchBltMode`

SwapMouseButton

Syntax `BOOL SwapMouseButton(fSwap)`

Parameter	*Type*	*Description*
`fSwap`	`BOOL`	Specifies whether to reverse or restore mouse button meanings

Description The `SwapMouseButton` function redefines the way that the left and right mouse buttons are interpreted. When `fSwap` is set to `TRUE`, right mouse button messages are generated by the left mouse button; the left mouse button generates right mouse button messages. When `fSwap` is `FALSE`, the mouse buttons are interpreted normally.

Return Value A nonzero value is returned when the mouse buttons have been swapped. Zero is returned when the buttons are set normally.

Function Category Input

Related Functions SetCapture, SetDoubleClickTime

SwitchStackBack

Syntax `void SwitchStackBack()`

Description The SwitchStackBack function returns the stack of the current task to the data segment of the task.

Return Value There is no return value.

Function Category Memory Management

Related Functions SwitchStackTo

SwitchStackTo

Syntax `void SwitchStackTo(uStackSegment, uStackPointer, uStackTop)`

Parameter	*Type*	*Description*
uStackSegment	UINT	Data segment to contain the stack
uStackPointer	UINT	Offset of the beginning of the stack
uStackTop	UINT	Offset of the top of the stack

Description The SwitchStackTo function changes the stack of the current task to the segment in uStackSegment. uStackPointer and uStackTop specify the beginning and top of the stack, respectively.

Return Value There is no return value.

Function Category Memory Management

Related Functions SwitchStackBack

SystemHeapInfo

Syntax `BOOL SystemHeapInfo(shiSysHeap)`

Parameter	*Type*	*Description*
`shiSysHeap`	`SYSHEAPINFO FAR*`	Pointer to `SYSHEAPINFO` data structure where the User and GDI heap information is copied

Description The `SystemHeapInfo` function copies USER.EXE and GDI.EXE heap information to the data structure of type `SYSHEAPINFO` pointed to by `shiSysHeap`.

Return Value A nonzero value is returned when successful. Zero is returned when unsuccessful.

Function Category Toolhelp

Related Functions None

SystemParametersInfo

Syntax

```
BOOL SystemParametersInfo(uAction, uParam, lpvParam,
                          fuWinIni)
```

Parameter	*Type*	*Description*
`uAction`	`UINT`	System-wide parameter to query or set
`uParam`	`UINT`	Value depends on `uAction`
`lpvParam`	`void FAR*`	Value depends on `uAction`
`fuWinIni`	`UINT`	Set to one of the following:

`SPIF_UPDATEINIFILE` to write the new system-wide parameter setting to WIN.INI, or `SPIF_SENDWININICHANGE` to broadcast the `WM_WININICHANGE` message after updating WIN.INI

Description The `SystemParametersInfo` function sets or queries system-wide parameters. `uAction` specifies the parameter to query or set. `uAction` is one of the following values:

Value	Meaning
SPI_GETBEEP	Gets the BOOL value that specifies whether the warning beeper is on or off
SPI_GETBORDER	Gets the multiplier factor used to define the width of a window's sizing border
SPI_GETFASTTASKSWITCH	Determines whether fast task switching is on or off
SPI_GETGRIDGRANULARITY	Gets the granularity value of the desktop sizing grid
SPI_GETICONTITLELOGFONT	Gets logical font information for the current icon-title font
SPI_GETICONTITLEWRAP	Determines whether icon title wrapping is on or off
SPI_GETKEYBOARDDELAY	Gets the keyboard repeat-delay setting
SPI_GETKEYBOARDSPEED	Gets the keyboard repeat-speed setting
SPI_GETMENUDROPALIGNMENT	Gets the pop-up menu alignment
SPI_GETMOUSE	Gets the mouse speed and the mouse threshold values
SPI_GETSCREENSAVEACTIVE	Determines whether screen saving is on or off
SPI_GETSCREENSAVETIMEOUT	Gets the screen-saver timeout values
SPI_ICONHORIZONTALSPACING	Defines the width of the icon cell in pixels
SPI_ICONVERTICALSPACING	Defines the height of the icon cell in pixels
SPI_LANGDRIVER	Loads a new language driver
SPI_SETBEEP	Turns the warning beeper on or off
SPI_SETBORDER	Defines the multiplier factor used to determine the width of the window's sizing border
SPI_SETDESKPATTERN	Defines the current desktop pattern

Value	*Meaning*
SPI_SETDESKWALLPAPER	Defines the filename containing the bitmap used for the desktop wallpaper
SPI_SETDOUBLECLKHEIGHT	Defines the height of the double-click rectangle
SPI_SETDOUBLECLICKTIME	Defines the mouse double-click time
SPI_SETDOUBLECLKWIDTH	Defines the width of the double-click rectangle
SPI_SETFASTTASKSWITCH	Turns fast task switching on or off
SPI_SETGRIDGRANULARITY	Defines the granularity of the desktop sizing grid
SPI_SETICONTITLELOGFONT	Defines the font used for icon titles
SPI_SETICONTITLEWRAP	Turns icon title wrapping on or off
SPI_SETKEYBOARDDELAY	Defines the keyboard repeat-delay setting
SPI_SETKEYBOARDSPEED	Defines the keyboard repeat-speed setting
SPI_SETMENUDROPALIGNMENT	Defines pop-up menu alignment
SPI_SETMOUSE	Defines the mouse speed and threshold values
SPI_SETMOUSEBUTTONSWAP	Swaps or restores the right and left mouse buttons
SPI_SETSCREENSAVEACTIVE	Defines the screen saver state
SPI_SETSCREENSAVETIMEOUT	Defines the screen saver timeout value

The `uParam` and `lpvParam` parameter settings depend on the setting of `uAction`. For a complete description of these parameters, refer to the SDK reference manuals.

Return Value A nonzero value is returned when successful. Zero is returned when unsuccessful.

Function Category System

Related Functions None

TabbedTextOut

Syntax

```
LONG TabbedTextOut(hdc, xPosStart, yPosStart, lpszString,
                   cbString, cTabStops, lpnTabPositions,
                   nTabOrigin)
```

Parameter	*Type*	*Description*
`hdc`	`HDC`	Device context
`xPosStart`	`int`	Logical x coordinate of the starting point for the string
`yPosStart`	`int`	Logical y coordinate of the starting point for the string
`lpszString`	`LPCSTR`	Pointer to the character string
`cbString`	`int`	Number of characters in `lpszString`
`cTabStops`	`int`	Number of tab stop positions in `lpnTabPositions`
`lpnTabPositions`	`int FAR*`	Pointer to an array of integers that specify the tab stop positions in pixels
`nTabOrigin`	`int`	Logical x coordinate of the starting position where tabs are expanded

Description The `TabbedTextOut` function displays the character string specified in `lpszString` using the current font and expanding tabs to columns as specified in `lpnTabPositions`.

Return Value The low-order word of the return value specifies the height of the displayed string in logical units. The high-order word of the return value specifies the width of the displayed string in logical units. Zero is returned when unsuccessful.

Function Category Text

Related Functions `DrawText`, `TextOut`

TaskFindHandle

Syntax `BOOL TaskFindHandle(teTask, hTask)`

Parameter	*Type*	*Description*
teTask	TASKENTRY FAR*	Pointer to TASKENTRY data structure where task information is copied
hTask	HANDLE	Task

Description The `TaskFindHandle` function copies information about the task specified in `hTask` to the data structure of type `TASKENTRY` pointed to by `teTask`. The `TASKENTRY` data structure follows.

```
#include <toolhelp.h>
typedef struct tagTASKENTRY {
     DWORD dwSize;
     HANDLE hTask;
     HANDLE hTaskParent;
     HANDLE hInst;
     HANDLE hModule;
     WORD wSS;
     WORD wSP;
     WORD wStackTop;
     WORD wStackMinimum;
     WORD wStackBottom;
     WORD wcEvents;
     HANDLE hQueue;
     char szModule[MAX_MODULE_NAME + 1];
     WORD wPSPOffset;
     HANDLE hNext;
} TASKENTRY;
```

in which

`dwSize` is the size of the structure in bytes

`hTask` is the stack's task handle

`hTaskParent` is the parent of the task

`hInst` is the instance handle of the task

`hModule` is the module that contains the currently executing function `wSS` is the stack segment

`wSP` is the value of the stack pointer

`wStackTop` is the offset of the top of the stack

`wStackMinimum` is the stack's lowest segment number

`wStackBottom` is the offset to the bottom of the stack

`wcEvents` is the number of pending events

`hQueue` is the task's queue

`szModule` is the name of the module that contains the currently executing function

`wPSPOffset` is the offset of the PSP to the beginning of the executable code segment

`hNext` is the next entry in the task list. This field is reserved for use by Windows.

Return Value A nonzero value should be returned when successful. Zero is returned when unsuccessful.

Function Category Toolhelp

Related Functions `TaskFirst`, `TaskNext`

TaskFirst

Syntax `BOOL TaskFirst(teTask)`

Parameter	*Type*	*Description*
`teTask`	`TASKENTRY FAR*`	Pointer to `TASKENTRY` data structure where task information is copied

Description The `TaskFirst` function copies information about the first task in the task queue to the data structure of type `TASKENTRY` pointed to by `teTask`. The `TASKENTRY` data structure follows.

```
#include <toolhelp.h>
typedef struct tagTASKENTRY {
     DWORD dwSize;
     HANDLE hTask;
     HANDLE hTaskParent;
```

```
    HANDLE hInst;
    HANDLE hModule;
    WORD wSS;
    WORD wSP;
    WORD wStackTop;
    WORD wStackMinimum;
    WORD wStackBottom;
    WORD wcEvents;
    HANDLE hQueue;
    char szModule[MAX_MODULE_NAME + 1];
    WORD wPSPOffset;
    HANDLE hNext;
} TASKENTRY;
```

in which

`dwSize` is the size of the structure in bytes

`hTask` is the stack's task handle

`hTaskParent` is the parent of the task

`hInst` is the instance handle of the task

`hModule` is the module that contains the currently executing function

`wSS` is the stack segment

`wSP` is the value of the stack pointer

`wStackTop` is the offset of the top of the stack

`wStackMinimum` is the stack's lowest segment number

`wStackBottom` is the offset to the bottom of the stack

`wcEvents` is the number of pending events

`hQueue` is the task's queue

`szModule` is the name of the module that contains the currently executing function

`wPSPOffset` is the offset of the PSP to the beginning of the executable code segment

`hNext` is the next entry in the task list. This field is reserved for use by Windows.

Return Value A nonzero value is returned when successful. Zero is returned when unsuccessful.

Function Category Toolhelp

Related Functions TaskFindHandle, TaskNext

TaskGetCSIP

Syntax `DWORD TaskGetCSIP(hTask)`

Parameter	*Type*	*Description*
hTask	HANDLE	Task

Description The TaskGetCSIP function returns the next CS:IP value for the task specified in hTask.

Return Value A DWORD containing the next CS:IP value is returned when successful. Zero is returned when unsuccessful.

Function Category Toolhelp

Related Functions TaskSetCSIP, TaskSwitch

TaskNext

Syntax `BOOL TaskNext(teTask)`

Parameter	*Type*	*Description*
teTask	TASKENTRY FAR*	Pointer to TASKENTRY data structure where task information is copied

Description The TaskNext function copies information about the next task on the task queue to the data structure of type TASKENTRY pointed to by teTask. The TASKENTRY data structure follows.

```
#include <toolhelp.h>
typedef struct tagTASKENTRY {
     DWORD dwSize;
     HANDLE hTask;
     HANDLE hTaskParent;
     HANDLE hInst;
```

```
        HANDLE hModule;
        WORD wSS;
        WORD wSP;
        WORD wStackTop;
        WORD wStackMinimum;
        WORD wStackBottom;
        WORD wcEvents;
        HANDLE hQueue;
        char szModule[MAX_MODULE_NAME + 1];
        WORD wPSPOffset;
        HANDLE hNext;
} TASKENTRY;
```

in which

`dwSize` is the size of the structure in bytes

`hTask` is the stack's task handle

`hTaskParent` is the parent of the task

`hInst` is the instance handle of the task

`hModule` is the module that contains the currently executing function

`wSS` is the stack segment

`wSP` is the value of the stack pointer

`wStackTop` is the offset of the top of the stack

`wStackMinimum` is the stack's lowest segment number

`wStackBottom` is the offset to the bottom of the stack

`wcEvents` is the number of pending events

`hQueue` is the task's queue

`szModule` is the name of the module that contains the currently executing function

`wPSPOffset` is the offset of the PSP to the beginning of the executable code segment

`hNext` is the next entry in the task list. This field is reserved for use by Windows.

Return Value A nonzero value is returned when successful. Zero is returned when unsuccessful.

Function Category Toolhelp

Related Functions TaskFindHandle, TaskFirst

TaskSetCSIP

Syntax `DWORD TaskSetCSIP(hTask, wCS, wIP)`

Parameter	*Type*	*Description*
hTask	HANDLE	Task
wCS	WORD	Value for code segment register
wIP	WORD	Value for instruction pointer register

Description The TaskSetCSIP function defines the code segment and instruction pointer for the task specified in hTask. wCS specifies the code segment register. wIP specifies the instruction pointer register.

Return Value A DWORD value that contains the new CS:IP value is returned when successful. NULL is returned when unsuccessful.

Function Category Toolhelp

Related Functions TaskGetCSIP, TaskSwitch

TaskSwitch

Syntax `BOOL TaskSwitch(hTask, dwNewCSIP)`

Parameter	*Type*	*Description*
hTask	HANDLE	New task
dwNewCSIP	DWORD	Address for task execution

Description The TaskSwitch function switches to the task specified in hTask. dwNewCSIP specifies the address where the task will begin to be executed.

Return Value TRUE is returned when successful. FALSE is returned when unsuccessful.

Function Category Toolhelp

Related Functions `TaskGetCSIP`, `TaskSetCSIP`

TerminateApp

Syntax `void TerminateApp(hTask, wFlags)`

Parameter	*Type*	*Description*
`hTask`	`HANDLE`	Task— set to `NULL` to specify the current task
`wFlags`	`WORD`	Flags that indicate how the task is to be terminated

Description The `TerminateApp` function terminates the application specified in `hTask` and should be used only by debugger applications. `wFlags` indicates how the task should be terminated and is set to one of the following values:

Value	*Meaning*
`UAE_BOX`	Kernel module is called to display the UAE box and end the task
`NO_UAE_BOX`	Kernel module is called to end the task. The UAE box is not displayed.

Return Value There is no return value.

Function Category Toolhelp

Related Functions `InterruptRegister`, `NotifyRegister`

TextOut

Syntax `BOOL TextOut(hdc, nXStart, nYStart, lpszString, cbString)`

Parameter	*Type*	*Description*
`hdc`	`HDC`	Device context
`nXStart`	`int`	Logical x coordinate of text starting point

Parameter	Type	Description
InYStart	int	Logical y coordinate of text starting point
lpszString	LPCSTR	Pointer to the character string to draw
cbString	int	Number of characters in lpszString

Description The TextOut function displays the character string specified in lpszString using the current font. nXStart and nYStart specify the logical coordinates of the starting point for the text.

Return Value A nonzero value is returned when the string is successfully drawn. Zero is returned when unsuccessful.

Function Category Text

Related Functions DrawText, TabbedTextOut

Throw

Syntax `void Throw(lpCatchBuf, nErrorReturn)`

Parameter	Type	Description
lpCatchBuf	const WORD FAR*	Pointer to an array that contains the execution environment
nErrorReturn	int	Value to be returned to Catch

Description The Throw function sets the execution environment to the values stored in the buffer pointed to by lpCatchBuf. nErrorReturn specifies the return value to the Catch function.

Return Value There is no return value.

Function Category Task

Related Functions Catch, Yield

TimerCount

Syntax `BOOL TimerCount(tiTimer)`

Parameter	*Type*	*Description*
tiTimer	TIMERINFO FAR*	Pointer to TIMERINFO data structure where execution times are copied

Description The TimerCount function copies execution time information about the current task and Virtual Machine and copies this information to the data structure of type TIMERINFO pointed to by tiTimer. The TIMERINFO data structure follows.

```
typedef struct tagTIMERINFO
     {
     DWORD dwSize;
     DWORD dwmsSinceStart;
     DWORD dwmsThisVM;
} TIMERINFO;
```

in which

dwSize is the number of bytes in the data structure

dwmsSinceStart is the number of milliseconds the current task has been executing

dwmsThisVM is the number of milliseconds the current Virtual Machine has been executing.

Return Value TRUE is returned when successful. FALSE is returned when unsuccessful.

Function Category Toolhelp

Related Functions GetTickCount

ToAscii

Syntax `int ToAscii(uVirtKey, uScanCode, lpbKeyState, lpdwTransKey, fuState)`

Parameter	*Type*	*Description*
uVirtKey	UINT	Virtual key code
uScanCode	UINT	Scan code of key
lpbKeyState	BYTE FAR*	Pointer to an array of key states
lpdwTransKey	DWORD FAR*	Pointer to 32-bit buffer that receives the translated ANSI character
fuState	UINT	Bit 0 flag's menu display

Description The `ToAscii` function converts the virtual key code specified in `uVirtKey` to the corresponding ANSI character or characters. `uScanCode` and `lpbKeyState` are used in the conversion. The translated character or characters are copied to `lpdwTransKey`.

Return Value A negative number is returned when unsuccessful. The number of characters copied to `lpdwTransKey` is returned when successful. The following values are returned to indicate success:

Value	*Meaning*
0	There is no translation possible
1	One ANSI character copied
2	Two characters copied—usually an accent and dead-key character

Function Category String Manipulation

Related Functions `OemKeyScan`, `VkKeyScan`

TrackPopupMenu

Syntax `BOOL TrackPopupMenu(hmenu, fuFlags, x, y, nReserved, hwnd, lprc)`

Parameter	*Type*	*Description*
hmenu	HMENU	Pop-up menu to display
fuFlags	UINT	Screen position and mouse button flag. The possible screen position flags are the following:

Value	*Meaning*
TPM_CENTERALIGN	Centers the menu horizontally on x
TPM_LEFTALIGN	Menu's left side aligned on x
TPM_RIGHTALIGN	Menu's right side aligned on x.

The possible mouse button flags include:

Value	*Meaning*
TPM_LEFTBUTTON	Menu tracks left mouse button
TPM_RIGHTBUTTON	Menu tracks right mouse button

x	int	Horizontal screen coordinate of upper- left corner of menu
x	int	Vertical screen coordinate of upper-left corner of menu nReserved int. Set to zero; reserved
hwnd	HWND	Window that owns the pop-up menu
lprc	const RECT FAR*	Set to NULL; reserved

Description The TrackPopupMenu function places the pop-up menu specified in hmenu at the position specified in x and y. The menu and its items are automatically tracked by the function. The handle of the pop-up menu is obtained with the CreatePopupMenu or GetSubMenu functions.

Return Value A nonzero value is returned when successful. Zero is returned when unsuccessful.

Function Category Menu

Related Functions CreatePopupMenu, GetSubMenu

TranslateAccelerator

Syntax `int TranslateAccelerator(hwnd, haccl, lpmsg)`

Parameter	*Type*	*Description*
hwnd	HWND	Window containing messages to be translated
haccl	HACCEL	Accelerator table
lpmsg	MSG FAR*	Points to retrieved message

Description The `TranslateAccelerator` function translates keyboard accelerators for use with menus commands. `WM_KEYUP` and `WM_KEYDOWN` messages are translated to `WM_COMMAND` (for all menu item accelerators except System menu accelerators) or `WM_SYSCOMMAND` (for System menu accelerators) messages. The `WM_COMMAND` or `WM_SYSCOMMAND` message is sent to the window, not to the application queue. The `TranslateAccelerator` function does not return until the message is processed. `lpmsg` points to a message retrieved with the `GetMessage` or `PeekMessage` function. The message must contain information about the Windows application queue and be an `MSG` data structure. The `MSG` data structure follows.

```
typedef struct tagMSG {
     HWND hwnd;
     WORD message;
     WORD wParam;
     LONG lParam;
     DWORD time;
     POINT pt;
} MSG;
```

in which

`hwnd` is the window receiving the message

`message` is the message number

`wParam` is additional message information

`lParam` is additional message information

`time` is the time the message was posted

`pt` is the cursor position in screen coordinates.

Return Value A nonzero value is returned when translation is successful. Zero is returned when translation is unsuccessful.

Function Category Message

Related Functions GetMessage, LoadAccelerator, PeekMessage

TranslateMDISysAccel

Syntax `BOOL TranslateMDISysAccel(hwndClient, lpmsg)`

Parameter	*Type*	*Description*
hwndClient	HWND	Parent MDI client window
lpmsg	MSG FAR*	Points to retrieved message

Description The TranslateMDISysAccel function translates keyboard accelerators for multiple document interface (MDI) child window System menu commands. WM_KEYUP and WM_KEYDOWN messages are translated to WM_SYSCOMMAND messages. lpmsg points to a message retrieved with the GetMessage or PeekMessage function. The message must contain information about the Windows application queue and be an MSG data structure. The MSG data structure follows.

```
typedef struct tagMSG {
     HWND hwnd;
     WORD message;
     WORD wParam;
     LONG lParam;
     DWORD time;
     POINT pt;
} MSG;
```

in which

hwnd is the window receiving the message

message is the message number

wParam is additional message information

lParam is additional message information

time is the time the message was posted

pt is the cursor position in screen coordinates.

Return Value A nonzero value is returned if translation was successful. Zero is returned when unsuccessful.

Function Category Message

Related Functions `GetMessage`, `PeekMessage`

TranslateMessage

Syntax `BOOL TranslateMessage(lpmsg)`

Parameter	*Type*	*Description*
`lpmsg`	`const MSG FAR*`	Points to retrieved message

Description The `TranslateMessage` function translates virtual key messages into character messages. `WM_KEYDOWN`, `WM_KEYUP` message combinations are translated to `WM_CHAR` or `WM_DEADCHAR` messages. `WM_SYSKEYDOWN`, `WM_SYSKEYUP` message combinations are translated to `WM_SYSCHAR` or `WM_SYSDEADCHAR` messages. The translated character messages are posted to the application queue. `lpmsg` points to a message retrieved with the `GetMessage` or `PeekMessage` function. The message must contain information about the Windows application queue and be an `MSG` data structure. The `MSG` data structure follows.

```
typedef struct tagMSG {
     HWND hwnd;
     WORD message;
     WORD wParam;
     LONG lParam;
     DWORD time;
     POINT pt;
} MSG;
```

in which

`hwnd` is the window receiving the message

`message` is the message number

`wParam` is additional message information

`lParam` is additional message information

`time` is the time the message was posted

`pt` is the cursor position in screen coordinates.

Return Value A nonzero value is returned when translation is successful. Zero is returned when unsuccessful.

Function Category Message

Related Functions `GetMessage`, `PeekMessage`, `TranslateAccelerator`

TransmitCommChar

Syntax `int TransmitCommChar(idComDev, chTransmit)`

Parameter	*Type*	*Description*
`idComDev`	`int`	Communication device
`chTransmit`	`char`	Character to transmit

Description The `TransmitCommChar` function places the character in `chTransmit` at the head of the transmit queue for the device in `idComDev`.

Return Value Zero is returned when successful. A negative value is returned when unsuccessful.

Function Category Communication

Related Functions `UngetCommChar`

UnAllocDiskSpace

Syntax `void UnAllocDiskSpace(wDrive)`

Parameter	*Type*	*Description*
`wDrive`	`WORD`	Drive containing "stress.eat"

Description The `UnAllocDiskSpace` function deletes the "stress.eat" file created to allocate disk space by the `AllocDiskSpace` function. `wDrive` specifies the disk partition that contains the "stress.eat" file. `wDrive` is set to one of the following values:

Value	*Meaning*
`EDS_WIN`	Windows partition
`EDS_CUR`	Current partition
`EDS_TEMP`	Partition containing the TEMP directory

Return Value There is no return value.

Function Category Stress

Related Functions `AllocDiskSpace`

UnAllocFileHandles

Syntax `void UnAllocFileHandles(void)`

Parameter	*Type*	*Description*
None		

Description The `UnAllocFileHandles` function frees the file handles allocated with the `AllocFileHandles` function.

Return Value There is no return value.

Function Category Stress

Related Functions `AllocFileHandles`

UngetCommChar

Syntax `int UngetCommChar(idComDev, chUnget)`

Parameter	*Type*	*Description*
`idComDev`	`int`	Communication device
`chUnget`	`char`	Character to place in receive queue

Description The `UngetCommChar` function puts the character in `chUnget` at the head of the receive queue for the device in `idComDev`. The character placed in the receive queue will be the next character read from the queue.

Return Value Zero is returned when successful. A negative value is returned when unsuccessful.

Function Category Communication

Related Functions `TransmitCommChar`

UnhookWindowsHook

Syntax `BOOL UnhookWindowsHook(idHook, hkprc)`

Parameter	*Type*	*Description*
`idHook`	`int`	Type of hook function to remove
`hkprc`	`HOOKPROC`	Procedure instance address of hook function

Description The `UnhookWindowsHook` function removes the hook function specified in `hkprc`. The type of hook function to remove is specified in `idHook`. The values used for `idHook` are as follows:

Value	*Meaning*
`WH_CALLWNDPROC`	Window function filter removed
`WH_CBT`	Computer Base Training filter removed
`WH_DEBUG`	Debugging filter removed
`WH_GETMESSAGE`	Message filter removed
`WH_HARDWARE`	Hardware filter removed
`WH_JOURNALPLAYBACK`	Journaling playback filter removed
`WH_JOURNALRECORD`	Journaling record filter removed
`WH_KEYBOARD`	Keyboard filter removed
`WH_MOUSE`	Mouse message filter removed
`WH_MSGFILTER`	Message filter removed

Note: This function is for use with Windows 3.0 and earlier. Use `SetWindowsHookEx` for Windows 3.1.

Return Value A nonzero value is returned when successful. When unsuccessful, zero is returned.

Function Category Hook

Related Functions `DefHookProc`, `SetWindowsHook`

UnhookWindowsHookEx

Syntax `BOOL UnhookWindowsHookEx(hhook)`

Parameter	*Type*	*Description*
`hhook`	`HHOOK`	Hook function to remove. This value is returned by the `SetWindowsHookEx` function.

Description The `UnhookWindowsHookEx` function removes the application-defined hook function specified in `hhook`.

Return Value A nonzero value is returned when successful. Zero is returned when unsuccessful.

Function Category Hook

Related Functions `SetWindowsHookEx`

UnionRect

Syntax `BOOL UnionRect(lprcDst, lprcSrc1, lprcSrc2)`

Parameter	*Type*	*Description*
`lprcDst`	`RECT FAR*`	Pointer to `RECT` data structure that receives the union
`lprcSrc1`	`const RECT FAR*`	Pointer to `RECT` data structure containing a source rectangle

Parameter	*Type*	*Description*
`lprcSrc2`	`const RECT FAR*`	Pointer to `RECT` data structure containing a source rectangle

Description The `UnionRect` function stores the coordinates of the smallest rectangle that contains both of the rectangles in `lprcSrc1` and `lprcSrc2` (the union of `lprcSrc1` and `lprcSrc2`) in `lprcDst`. `lprcDst`, `lprcSrc1`, and `lprcSrc2` all point to a structure of type `RECT` that contains the coordinates of the respective rectangle. The `RECT` structure follows.

```
typedef struct tagRECT {
     int left;
     int top;
     int right;
     int bottom;
} RECT;
```

in which

`left` is the x coordinate of the upper-left corner

`top` is the y coordinate of the upper-left corner

`right` is the x coordinate of the lower-right corner

`bottom` is the y coordinate of the lower-right corner.

Return Value A nonzero value is returned when the union of the rectangles is not empty. If the union is empty, zero is returned.

Function Category Rectangle

Related Functions `IntersectRect`

UnlockData

Syntax `HANDLE UnlockData(dummy)`

Parameter	*Type*	*Description*
`dummy`	`int`	Should be set to zero and not used

Description The `UnlockData` function unlocks the current data segment.

Return Value Zero is returned if the lock count for the segment is decreased to zero. Otherwise, a nonzero value is returned.

Function Category Memory Management

Related Functions `LockData`, `UnlockSegment`

UnlockResource

Syntax `BOOL UnlockResource(hResData)`

Parameter	*Type*	*Description*
`hResData`	`HANDLE`	Global memory block to unlock

Description The `UnlockResource` function unlocks the resource specified in `hResData`. The reference count for the specified resource is decremented.

Return Value `FALSE` is returned when the reference count for the resource is decremented to zero. `TRUE` is returned if the resource is not decremented to zero.

Function Category Resource Management

Related Functions `LockResource`

UnlockSegment

Syntax `void UnlockSegment(uSegment)`

Parameter	*Type*	*Description*
`uSegment`	`UINT`	Segment address of segment to unlock. If set to –1, the current data segment is unlocked.

Description The `UnlockSegment` function unlocks the segment specified by the segment address in `uSegment`. The lock count of the segment is decremented.

Return Value The return value is placed in the CX register. Check this register using assembly language.

Function Category Memory Management, Segment

Related Functions `LockSegment`

UnrealizeObject

Syntax `BOOL UnrealizeObject(hgdiobj)`

Parameter	*Type*	*Description*
`hgdiobj`	`HGDIOBJ`	Object to reset

Description The `UnrealizeObject` function resets the origin of a brush or realizes a palette. When `hgdiobj` specifies a brush, the Graphics Device Interface resets the origin of the brush. When `hgdiobj` specifies a logical palette, the Graphics Device Interface realizes the palette, even if previously realized.

Return Value A nonzero value is returned when successful. Zero is returned when unsuccessful.

Function Category Drawing Tool

Related Functions `RealizePalette`, `SelectObject`

UnregisterClass

Syntax `BOOL UnregisterClass(lpszClassName, hinst)`

Parameter	*Type*	*Description*
`lpszClassName`	`LPCSTR`	String containing the class name
`hinst`	`HINSTANCE`	Instance of module that created the class

Description The `UnregisterClass` function removes the window class, whose name is specified in `lpszClassName`, from the window class table. `hinst` identifies the module that created the class.

Return Value A nonzero value is returned when the window class is successfully removed. Zero is returned when unable to remove the window class.

Function Category Window Creation

Related Functions `RegisterClass`

UpdateColors

Syntax `int UpdateColors(hdc)`

Parameter	*Type*	*Description*
hdc	HDC	Device context

Description The `UpdateColors` function updates the client area of the device context in `hdc`. Colors in the client area are matched to the system palette pixel by pixel.

Return Value The return value has no significance and is not used.

Function Category Color Palette

Related Functions `CreatePalette`, `GetSystemPaletteEntries`

UpdateWindow

Syntax `void UpdateWindow(hwnd)`

Parameter	*Type*	*Description*
hwnd	HWND	Window to update

Description The `UpdateWindow` function updates the client area of the window in `hwnd`. The update is accomplished by sending a `WM_PAINT` message to the window if the update region for the window is not empty. No message is sent if the update region is empty.

Return Value There is no return value.

Function Category Painting

Related Functions `ExcludeUpdateRgn`

ValidateCodeSegments

Syntax `void ValidateCodeSegments()`

Description The `ValidateCodeSegments` function sends debugging information whenever a code segment has been modified by random memory overwrites. This function is for use when operating in real mode or in the debugging version of Windows.

Return Value There is no return value.

Function Category Debugging

Related Functions `ValidateFreeSpaces`

ValidateFreeSpaces

Syntax `LPSTR ValidateFreeSpaces()`

Description The `ValidateFreeSpaces` function checks free segments in memory for valid contents. When an invalid byte is encountered, debugging information is displayed and a fatal exit is initiated. This function is for only the debugging version of Windows.

Return Value There is no return value.

Function Category Debugging

Related Functions `ValidateCodeSegments`

ValidateRect

Syntax `void ValidateRect(hwnd, lprc)`

Parameter	*Type*	*Description*
hwnd	HWND	Window handle
lprc	const RECT FAR*	Pointer to RECT structure containing the client coordinates of the rectangle to remove from the update region

Description The ValidateRect function removes the rectangle specified in lprc from the update region for the window in hwnd. lprc points to the data structure of type RECT that contains the client coordinates of the rectangle to remove from the update region. The RECT structure follows. If lprc is set to NULL, the entire window is validated.

```
typedef struct tagRECT {
     int left;
     int top;
     int right;
     int bottom;
} RECT;
```

in which

left is the x coordinate of the upper-left corner

top is the y coordinate of the upper-left corner

right is the x coordinate of the lower-right corner

bottom is the y coordinate of the lower-right corner.

Return Value There is no return value.

Function Category Painting

Related Functions InvalidateRect, ValidateRgn

ValidateRgn

Syntax `void ValidateRgn(hwnd, hrgn)`

Parameter	Type	Description
hwnd	HWND	Window handle
hrgn	HRGN	Region to be removed from the update region

Description The ValidateRgn function removes the region specified in hrgn from the update region of the window in hwnd. When hrgn is set to NULL, the entire window is validated. Otherwise, hrgn must have been created using one of the region functions.

Return Value There is no return value.

Function Category Painting

Related Functions InvalidateRgn, ValidateRect

VerFindFile

Syntax

```
WORD VerFindFile(wFlags, lpszFileName, lpszWinDir,
                 lpszAppDir, lpszCurDir, lpwCurDirLen,
                 lpszDestDir, lpwDestDirLen)
```

Parameter	Type	Description
wFlags	WORD	Bitmask set to VFFF_ISSHAREDFILE to indicate the source file may be shared by multiple applications
lpszFileName	LPSTR	Pointer to string containing filename of file to install
lpszWindDir	LPSTR	Pointer to string directory that contains Windows; can be retrieved using GetWindowsDir
lpszAppDir	LPSTR	Pointer to string that specifies the directory where the installation routine is installing related files

Parameter	Type	Description
lpszCurDir	LPSTR	Pointer to buffer where path to current version of file is copied
lpwCurDirLen	LPWORD	Pointer to size of buffer specified in szCurDir
lpszDestDir	LPSTR	Pointer to buffer where installation path specified by VerFindFile is copied
lpwDesDirLen	LPWORD	Pointer to size of buffer specified in lpszDestDir

Description The VerFindFile function indicates where a file should be installed. The function looks for other versions of the same file. szCurDir and lpszDestDir are used when calling the VerInstallFile function.

Return Value A bitmask indicating the status of the file is returned. The bitmask may contain one or more of the following values:

Value	Meaning
VFF_CURNEDEST	Current version of file is not at the destination recommended by the function
VFF_FILEINUSE	Windows is using the current version of the file
VFF_BUFFTOOSMALL	At least one buffer was too small

Function Category Version

Related Functions VerInstallFile

VerInstallFile

Syntax

```
DWORD VerInstallFile(wFlags, lpszSrcFileName,
                     lpszDestFileName, lpszSrcDir,
                     lpszDestDir, lpszCurDir, lpszTmpFile,
                     lpwTmpFileLen)
```

Parameter	*Type*	*Description*
`wFlags`	`WORD`	Bitmask which may contain the following: `VIFF_FORCEINSTALL` to install the file regardless of version numbers; `VIFF_DONTDELETEOLD` to install the file without deleting the old file when the old file is not in the destination directory
`lpszSrcFileName`	`LPSTR`	Pointer to string that contains the name of the file to install
`lpszDestFileName`	`LPSTR`	Pointer to string that contains the name of the new file
`lpszSrcDir`	`LPSTR`	Pointer to string that contains the name of the directory that holds the new file
`lpszDestDir`	`LPSTR`	Pointer to string that contains the name of the directory where the file is to be installed
`lpszCurDir`	`LPSTR`	Pointer to string that contains the name of the directory where the pre-existing version of the file can be found
`lpszTmpFile`	`LPSTR`	Pointer to string where the name of the temporary copy of the source file is placed. This parameter should be `NULL` for the first call to `VerInstallFile`.
`lpwTmpFileLen`	`LPWORD`	Pointer to length of buffer in `lpszTmpFile`. This parameter holds the number of bytes returned in `lpszTmpFile` when the function returns.

Description The `VerInstallFile` function installs a file using information retrieved from the `VerFindFile` function. The file is decompressed when necessary and a unique filename is assigned.

Return Value A bitmask that contains one or more of the following values is returned when unsuccessful.

Value	*Meaning*
VIF_TEMPFILE	Temporary copy of new file is in destination directory
VIF_MISMATCH	New file attributes differ from previous file attributes
VIF_SRCOLD	New file is older that previous file
VIF_DIFFLANG	New file has different language or code page values
VIF_DIFFCODEPG	New file requires code page that cannot be displayed using current version of Windows
VIF_DIFFTYPE	New file has different type, subtype, or operating system than previous file
VIF_WRITEPROT	Previous file is write-protected
VIF_FILEINUSE	Previous file is being used by Windows
VIF_OUTOFSPACE	Temporary file cannot be created due to lack of disk space
VIF_ACCESSVIOLATION	Operation failed because of access operation
VIF_SHARINGVIOLATION	Operation failed because of sharing violation
VIF_CANNOTCREATE	Temporary file cannot be created
VIF_CANNOTDELETE	Previous file or destination file cannot be deleted
VIF_CANNOTRENAME	Temporary file cannot be renamed
VIF_OUTOFMEMORY	Operation failed due to lack of memory
VIF_CANNOTREADSRC	Source file cannot be read
VIF_CANNOTREADDST	Destination file cannot be read
VIF_BUFFTOOSMALL	Buffer in `lpszTmpFile` is too small

Function Category Version

Related Functions `VerFindFile`

VerLanguageName

Syntax `WORD VerLanguageName(wLang, lpszLang, wSize)`

Parameter	*Type*	*Description*
`wLang`	`WORD`	Binary Microsoft language ID
`lpszLang`	`WORDLPSTR`	Pointer to buffer where language string is copied
`wSize`	`WORD`	Number of bytes in `wLang` buffer

Description The `VerLanguageName` function copies the text that represents the binary Microsoft language ID specified in `wLang` to the buffer pointed to by `lpszLang`.

Return Value The length of the string that corresponds to `wLang` is returned when successful. Zero is returned when unsuccessful.

Function Category Version

Related Functions `GetFileVersionInfoSize`

VerQueryValue

Syntax

```
BOOL VerQueryValue(lpvBlock, lpszSubBlock,
                   lplpBuffer, lpwLen)
```

Parameter	*Type*	*Description*
`lpvBlock`	`LPVOID`	Pointer to block
`lpszSubBlock`	`LPSTR`	Pointer to buffer containing the path of block in `lpvBlock`
`lplpBuffer`	`VOID FAR* FAR*`	Pointer to buffer where far pointer to file version information value is placed

Parameter	Type	Description
lpwLen	LPWORD	Pointer to buffer where file version information value length is placed

Description The `VerQueryValue` function retrieves version information for the block specified in `lpvBlock`. The `GetFileVersionInfo` function is called prior to this function to get an appropriate value for `lpvBlock`.

Return Value `TRUE` is returned when successful. `FALSE` is returned when unsuccessful.

Function Category Version

Related Functions `GetFileVersionInfo`

VkKeyScan

Syntax `UINT VkKeyScan(uChar)`

Parameter	Type	Description
uChar	char	ANSI character

Description The `VkKeyScan` function returns the virtual key code and shift state for the ANSI character specified in `uChar`.

Return Value The low order byte of the returned value specifies the virtual key code. The high order byte of the returned value specifies the shift states as follows.

Value	Meaning
0	No shift
1	Shifted character
2	Control character
6	Control + ALT character
7	Shift + Control + ALT character
3, 4, 5	Shift key combination

1 is returned in both the low and high order bytes when no key code is found that matches the specified character.

Function Category Hardware

Related Functions MapVirtualKey, OemKeyScan

WaitMessage

Syntax `void WaitMessage()`

Description The `WaitMessage` function suspends the application when the application has no task to perform, yields control to another application, and returns only after a message has been placed in the application queue.

Return Value There is no return value.

Function Category Message

Related Functions GetMessage, PeekMessage, SendMessage

WindowFromPoint

Syntax `HWND WindowFromPoint(pt)`

Parameter	*Type*	*Description*
pt	POINT	POINT data structure containing the specified point

Description The `WindowFromPoint` function determines which window contains the point specified in `pt`. The screen coordinates for the point are stored in a data structure of type `POINT`. The `POINT` structure is shown below.

```
typedef struct tagPOINT {
     int x;
     int y;
} POINT;
```

in which

`x` is the horizontal coordinate of the point

`y` is the vertical coordinate of the point.

Return Value The window handle of the window containing the point is returned. If no window contains the specified point, NULL is returned.

Function Category Coordinate, Information

Related Functions ChildWindowFromPoint

WinExec

Syntax `UINT WinExec(lpszCmdLine, fuCmdShow)`

Parameter	*Type*	*Description*
lpszCmdLine	LPCSTR	Pointer to null-terminated character string containing the command line for application
fuCmdShow	UINT	Indicates how the application window will be shown

Description The WinExec function executes a Windows or non-Windows application. lpszCmdLine specifies the name of the application to execute. If a directory path is not given in lpszCmdLine, Windows searches the current directory, the Windows directory, the system directory, the directories of the PATH environment variable, and the directories mapped in a network, in order. fuCmdShow specifies the state of the application window. The following constants are used for fuCmdShow.

Constant	*Meaning*
SW_HIDE	Hides the window and another window becomes active
SW_MINIMIZE	Minimizes the window and the top level window becomes active
SW_RESTORE	Activates and displays the window
SW_SHOW	Activates and displays the window in its current size and position
SW_SHOWMAXIMIZED	Activates, displays, and maximizes the window

Constant	*Meaning*
SW_SHOWMINIMIZED	Activates and displays the window as minimized
SW_SHOWMINNOACTIVE	Displays the window as minimized
SW_SHOWNA	Displays the window in its current state
SW_SHOWNOACTIVE	Displays the window in its most recent size and position
SW_SHOWNORMAL	Activates and displays the window

Return Value A value greater than 32 is returned when successful. A value less than 32 indicates an error. The following values represent the error values returned by the function.

Value	*Meaning*
0	Out of memory
2	File not found
3	Path not found
5	Attempt to dynamically link to a task
6	Library requires separate data segments for each task
8	Insufficient memory to start application
10	Incorrect Windows version
11	Invalid .EXE file
12	OS/2 application
13	DOS 4.0 application
14	Unknown .EXE type
15	Attempt in protected mode to load an .EXE created for an earlier version of Windows
16	Attempt to load a second instance of an .EXE containing multiple, writeable data segments
19	Attempt to load compressed .EXE file
20	Attempt to load invalid DLL file
21	Application requires Windows 32-bit extensions

Function Category Application Execution

Related Functions `LoadModule`, `WinHelp`

WinHelp

Syntax `BOOL WinHelp(hwnd, lpszHelpFile, fuCommand, dwData)`

Parameter	*Type*	*Description*
hwnd	HWND	Window requesting help
lpszHelpFile	LPCSTR	Pointer to a null-terminated string containing the directory and file name of the help file to display
fuCommand	UINT	Type of help requested
dwData	DWORD	Context or key word of help requested

Description The `WinHelp` function launches the Windows Help application. `hwnd` specifies the window that requests help. `lpszHelpFile` contains the directory and file name of the help file to display. `fuCommand` specifies the type of help requested. The following values are used for `fuCommand`.

Value	*Meaning*
HELP_CONTEXT	Displays help for the context in `dwData`
HELP_CONTENTS	Displays help contents topic as defined in `OPTIONS` section of the Help Project File
HELP_SET_CONTENTS	Displays a Help topic in a pop-up window if `dwData` is 0x0104
HELP_HELPONHELP	Displays help on using the help application
HELP_INDEX	Displays the index of a help file
HELP_KEY	Displays help for the key word in `dwData`
HELP_MULTIKEY	Displays help for a key word in an alternate keyword table
HELP_QUIT	Tells the help application that the help file is not being used
HELP_SETINDEX	Sets the context in `dwData` as the current index for the help file specified by `lpszHelpFile`

Depending on the setting of `fuCommand`, `dwData` specifies the context or key word of the help requested. When `fuCommand` is `HELP_CONTEXT`, `dwData` contains a 32-bit unsigned integer containing a context-identifier number. When `fuCommand` is `HELP_KEY`, `dwData` is a long pointer to a null-terminated string containing the key word identifying the help topic. When `fuCommand` is `HELP_MULTIKEY`, `dwData` is a long pointer to a data structure of type `MULTIKEYHELP`.

Return Value A nonzero value is returned when successful. Zero is returned when unsuccessful.

Function Category Application Execution

Related Functions `LoadModule`, `WinExec`

WNetAddConnection

Syntax

```
UINT WNetAddConnection(lpszNetPath, lpszPassword,
                       lpszLocalName)
```

Parameter	*Type*	*Description*
`lpszNetPath`	`LPSTR`	Pointer to null-terminated string that specifies the shared device or remote server
`lpszPassword`	`LPSTR`	Pointer to null-terminated string that specifies the network password
`lpszLocalName`	`LPSTR`	Pointer to null-terminated string that specifies the local drive or device to redirect

Description The `WNetAddConnection` function redirects the device specified in `lpszLocalName` to the shared device specified in `lpszNetPath`.

Return Value One of the following values is returned:

Value	*Meaning*
`WN_SUCCESS`	Success
`WN_NOT_SUPPORTED`	Function not supported
`WN_OUT_OF_MEMORY`	Out of memory
`WN_NET_ERROR`	Network error
`WN_BAD_POINTER`	Invalid pointer
`WN_BAD_NETNAME`	Invalid network resource name
`WN_BAD_LOCALNAME`	Invalid local device name

Value	*Meaning*
WN_BAD_PASSWORD	Invalid password
WN_ACCESS_DENIED	Security violation
WN_ALREADY_CONNECTED	Local device already connected to remote resource

Function Category Network

Related Functions WNetCancelConnection, WNetGetConnection

WNetCancelConnection

Syntax `UINT WNetCancelConnection(lpszName, fForce)`

Parameter	*Type*	*Description*
lpszName	LPSTR	Pointer to name of redirected local device or a fully-qualified network path
fForce	BOOL	Indicates whether any open files or open print jobs on the device should be closed before the connection is cancelled

Description The WNetCancelConnection function cancels the specified connection.

Return Value One of the following values is returned:

Value	*Meaning*
WN_SUCCESS	Success
WN_NOT_SUPPORTED	Function not supported
WN_OUT_OF_MEMORY	Out of memory
WN_NET_ERROR	Network error
WN_BAD_POINTER	Invalid pointer

Value	*Meaning*
WN_BAD_VALUE	lpszName is an invalid local device or network name
WN_NOT_CONNECTED	lpszName is not a redirected local device or currently accessed network resource
WN_OPEN_FILES	Files are open and fForce is FALSE. The connection was not cancelled.

Function Category Network

Related Functions WNetAddConnection, WNetGetConnection

WNetGetConnection

Syntax

```
UINT WNetGetConnection(lpszLocalName, lpszRemoteName,
                       cbBufferSize)
```

Parameter	*Type*	*Description*
lpszLocalName	LPSTR	Pointer to zero-terminated string that specifies the name of the redirected device
lpszRemoteName	LPSTR	Pointer to buffer that receives the zero-terminated name of the remote network resource
cbBufferSize	WORD FAR*	Pointer to variable that specifies the maximum number of bytes for the buffer specified in lpszRemoteName

Description The WNetGetConnection function gets the name of the network resource associated with the redirected local device specified in lpszLocalName. lpszRemoteName points to the buffer that receives the name of the remote network resource.

Return Value One of the following values is returned:

Value	Meaning
WN_SUCCESS	Success
WN_NOT_SUPPORTED	Function not supported
WN_OUT_OF_MEMORY	Out of memory
WN_NET_ERROR	Network error
WN_BAD_POINTER	Invalid pointer
WN_BAD_VALUE	lpszLocalName is an invalid local device
WN_NOT_CONNECTED	lpszLocalName is not a redirected local device
WN_MORE_DATA	Buffer was too small

Function Category Network

Related Functions WNetAddConnection, WNetCancelConnection

WriteComm

Syntax `int WriteComm(idComDev, lpvBuf, cbWrite)`

Parameter	Type	Description
idComDev	int	Communication device
lpvBuf	const void FAR*	Pointer to buffer containing the characters to write
cbWrite	int	Number of characters to write

Description The WriteComm function writes the characters in the buffer pointed to by lpvBuf to the communication device specified in idComDev. cbWrite specifies the number of characters to write.

Return Value The number of characters written is returned.

Function Category Communication

Related Functions GetCommError, OpenComm, ReadComm

WritePrivateProfileString

Syntax

```
BOOL WritePrivateProfileString(lpszSectionName,
                               lpszKeyName, lpszString,
                               lpszFileName)
```

Parameter	*Type*	*Description*
lpszSectionName	LPCSTR	Pointer to the name of a Windows application appearing in the initialization file
lpszKeyName	LPCSTR	Pointer to a key name that appears in the initialization file
lpszString	LPCSTR	Pointer to the string containing the new key value
lpszFileName	LPCSTR	Pointer to the string containing the name of the initialization file

Description The `WritePrivateProfileString` function writes the string pointed to by `lpszString` to the initialization file specified in `lpszFileName`. The string will be assigned to the key specified in `lpszKeyName`. `lpszSectionName` specifies the application heading that the key name appears under.

Return Value A nonzero value is returned when successful. Zero is returned when unsuccessful.

Function Category Initialization File

Related Functions GetPrivateProfileInt, GetPrivateProfileString

WriteProfileString

Syntax
```
BOOL WriteProfileString(lpszSectionName,lpszKeyName,
                                        lpszString)
```

Parameter	*Type*	*Description*
lpszSectionName	LPCSTR	Pointer to the name of a Windows application appearing in the Windows initialization file
lpszKeyName	LPCSTR	Pointer to a key name that appears in the Windows initialization file
lpszString	LPCSTR	Pointer to the string containing the new key value

Description The `WriteProfileString` function writes the string pointed to by `lpszString` to the Windows initialization file. The string will be assigned to the key specified in `lpszKeyName`. `lpszSectionName` specifies the application heading that the key name appears under.

Return Value A nonzero value is returned when successful. Zero is returned when unsuccessful.

Function Category Initialization File

Related Functions `GetProfileInt`, `GetProfileString`

wsprintf

Syntax
```
int_cdecl wsprintf(lpszOutput, lpszFormat[,argument]...)
```

Parameter	*Type*	*Description*
lpszOutput	LPSTR	Pointer to string to receive the formatted output
lpszFormat	LPSTR	Pointer to format control string
argument	n/a	One or more arguments for the format control string

Description The `wsprintf` function formats a series of characters and stores the formatted values in the buffer pointed to by `lpszOutput`. `lpszFormat` specifies the format control string. The format control string contains format specifiers that control the format of the output. A format specifier follows the format of

```
%[-][#][0][width][.precision]type
```

in which

`-` indicates to pad the output right and left justify

`#` indicates to precede hexadecimal values with 0x or 0X

`0` indicates that the output value should be padded with zeroes to fill the width of the field

`width` specifies the minimum number of characters to output

`.precision` specifies the minimum number of character to output

`type` indicates the output type. `type` is selected from the following:

Value	*Meaning*
s	String argument referenced by a long pointer
c	Single character argument
d,i	Signed decimal integer
ld,li	Long signed decimal integer
u	Unsigned integer argument
lu	Long unsigned integer argument
`x,X`	Unsigned hexadecimal integer
`lx, lX`	Long unsigned hexadecimal integer

`argument` refers to one or more arguments that correspond to the format specifiers in the format control string.

Return Value The number of characters stored in `lpszOutput`, excluding the null terminator, is returned.

Function Category String Manipulation

Related Functions `wvsprintf`

wvsprintf

Syntax `int wvsprintf(lpszOutput, lpszFormat, lpvArglist)`

Parameter	*Type*	*Description*
`lpszOutput`	`LPSTR`	Pointer to a null-terminated string to receive the formatted output
`lpszFormat`	`LPCSTR`	Pointer to null-terminated string containing the format control string
`lpvArglist`	`const void FAR*`	Pointer to an array of arguments for the format control string

Description The `wvsprintf` function formats a series of characters and stores the formatted characters in the buffer pointed to by `lpszOutput`. `lpszFormat` points to the string containing the format control string. The format control string contains format specifiers that control the format of the output. A format specifier follows the format of

```
%[-][#][0][width][.precision]type
```

in which

`-` indicates to pad the output right and left justify

`#` indicates to precede hexadecimal values with 0x or 0X

`0` indicates that the output value should be padded with zeroes to fill the width of the field

`width` specifies the minimum number of characters to output

`.precision` specifies the minimum number of character to output

`type` indicates the output type. `type` is selected from the following:

Value	*Meaning*
s	String argument referenced by a long pointer
c	Single character argument
d,i	Signed decimal integer

Value	Meaning
ld,li	Long signed decimal integer
u	Unsigned integer argument
lu	Long unsigned integer argument
x,X	Unsigned hexadecimal integer
lx, lX	Long unsigned hexadecimal integer

`lpvArglist` points to an array that contains the arguments for the format control string.

Return Value The number of characters stored in `lpszOutput`, excluding the null terminator, is returned.

Function Category String Manipulation

Related Functions `wsprintf`

Yield

Syntax `void Yield()`

Description The `Yield` function halts the current task. Waiting tasks can be started.

Return Value There is no return value.

Function Category Task

Related Functions `PeekMessage`, `TranslateMessage`

14

Windows Messages

This chapter provides reference information on the various Window messages. These messages are used by Windows applications to communicate with the Windows system and other Windows applications.

A message consists of three parts. The first is the message number that is identified by the message name. The second part is a word parameter, referenced as `wParam`. The third part is a long parameter, referenced as `lParam`. In this chapter you will find a description of each of these three parts for every message. Descriptions of the function and the return value are also provided, along with a list of related messages. This information appears in the following format.

MESSAGE_NAME

wParam Description of the word parameter.

lParam Description of the long parameter.

Description Provides information on the message.

Return Value Provides information on the return value.

Related Messages Lists the messages that are related to the described message.

The remainder of this chapter provides the reference material for the window messages.

BM_GETCHECK

wParam Not used.

lParam Not used.

Description The BM_GETCHECK message determines whether a radio button or check box is checked.

Return Value One of the following values is returned when the BS_AUTOCHECKBOX, BS_AUTORADIOBUTTON, BS_AUTO3STATE, BS_CHECKBOX, BS_RADTIOBUTTON, or BS_3STATE style is used:

0	Unchecked
1	Checked
2	Cannot determine state (for three-state buttons)

Buttons using other styles return zero.

Related Messages BM_GETSTATE, BM_SETCHECK

BM_GETSTATE

wParam Not used.

lParam Not used.

Description The BM_GETSTATE message determines the state of a button control.

Return Value The state of the button control is returned. The following masks can be used with the return value to determine state information:

Mask	*Description*
0x0003	Determines the check state of radio buttons and check boxes. Zero indicates that the button is not checked. One indicates that the button is checked. Two indicates that the state cannot be determined.

Mask	*Description*
0x0004	Determines the highlight state of a button. A nonzero value indicates that the button is highlighted.
0x0008	Determines the focus state of a button. A nonzero value indicates that the button has the focus.

Related Messages BM_GETCHECK, BM_SETSTATE

BM_SETCHECK

wParam Defines the state of the button control. wParam is set to one of the following values:

0	Button is not checked
1	Button is checked
2	Button state is indeterminate (three-state buttons only)

lParam Not used.

Description The BM_SETCHECK message specifies the check state for button controls. wParam defines the state of the button control.

Return Value Zero is returned.

Related Messages BM_GETCHECK, BM_GETSTATE, BM_SETSTATE

BM_SETSTATE

wParam Set to a nonzero value to highlight the button. wParam is set to zero to return the button to its normal unhighlighted state.

lParam Not used.

Description The BM_SETSTATE message sets the highlight state of a button control. wParam defines the highlight state of the button control.

Return Value Zero is returned.

Related Messages BM_GETSTATE, BM_SETCHECK

BM_SETSTYLE

wParam Defines the style for a button. The value for wParam is selected from one of the following:

Value	*Meaning*
BS_AUTOCHECKBOX	Box that may be checked. Toggles between states when selected.
BS_AUTORADIOBUTTON	Small circular button that may be checked. When this button is selected, all checkmarks on other buttons in the group are removed.
BS_AUTO3STATE	Box that may be checked, unchecked, or grayed (three states). Button state is toggled when selected.
BS_CHECKBOX	Box that may be checked.
BS_DEFPUSHBUTTON	Button with a bold border. The bold border designates this button as the default button.
BS_GROUPBOX	Rectangle where other buttons are grouped. Text is displayed in upper-left corner.
BS_LEFTTEXT	Used with radio button and check box styles to make text appear on the left side of the radio button or check box. The default is for text to appear on the right side.
BS_OWNERDRAW	Owner draw button. Owner window is told when the button is selected. Owner window is also sent WM_MEASUREITEM and WM_DRAWITEM messages.
BS_PUSHBUTTON	Button containing text. WM_COMMAND message is sent to the parent window when the button is selected.
BS_RADIOBUTTON	Small circular button that may be checked. Often grouped with other radio buttons.
BS_3STATE	Box that may be checked or grayed.

lParam Set to TRUE if the button should be redrawn. Set to FALSE if the button should not be redrawn.

Description The BM_SETSTYLE message modifies the button style. wParam specifies the new button style. lParam indicates whether the buttons are to be redrawn.

Return Value Zero is returned.

Related Messages BM_SETCHECK, BM_SETSTATE

BN_CLICKED

wParam Specifies the control ID.

lParam The low-order word of lParam specifies the handle for the button control. The high-order word of lParam specifies the BN_CLICKED notification code.

Description The BN_CLICKED code is sent through a WM_COMMAND message from a button control to the parent window when the button has been clicked. Disabled buttons do not send a BN_CLICKED notification message.

Related Messages BN_DOUBLECLICKED, WM_COMMAND

BN_DOUBLECLICKED

wParam Specifies the control ID.

lParam The low-order word of lParam contains the handle of the button control. The high-order word of lParam contains the BN_DOUBLECLICKED notification code.

Description The BN_DOUBLECLICKED code is sent through a WM_COMMAND message to the parent window when a button has been double-clicked. The button must have style BS_RADIOBUTTON or BS_OWNERDRAW.

Related Messages BN_CLICKED, WM_COMMAND

CB_ADDSTRING

wParam Not used.

lParam Points to the null-terminated string that will be added to the list box of the combo box.

Description The CB_ADDSTRING message adds the string in lParam to the list box of a combo box. If the list box is a sorted list box (CBS_SORT style), the string will be sorted and placed in the appropriate position. If the list box is not sorted, the string is added to the end of the list.

Return Value The index to the added string is returned. CB_ERR is returned upon the occurrence of an error. CB_ERRSPACE is returned if there is not enough space to store the new string. The WM_COMPAREITEM message is sent to the owner of an owner draw combo box created with the CBS_SORT style but not the CBS_HASSTRINGS style to place the item in the list box.

Related Messages CB_DELETESTRING, CB_INSERTSTRING, WM_COMPAREITEM

CB_DELETESTRING

wParam Specifies the index of the string that is to be deleted from the list box of a combo box.

lParam Not used.

Description The CB_DELETESTRING message deletes the string with the index specified in wParam from the list boxes of combo boxes.

Return Value The number of strings left in the list is returned. CB_ERR is returned when wParam contains an invalid index.

Related Messages CB_ADDSTRING, WM_DELETEITEM

CB_DIR

wParam Specifies the DOS attributes. The DOS attributes which can be used for wParam are as follows:

Value	*Meaning*
0x0000	Read/write; no additional attributes
0x0001	Read only
0x0002	Hidden file
0x0004	System file
0x0010	lParam specifies a subdirectory
0x0020	Archive

Value	*Meaning*
0x4000	Include drives that match the name in `lParam`
0x8000	Exclusive bit

lParam Points to the file specification string.

Description The `CB_DIR` message puts a list of the files from the current directory into the list box. The files that are added to the list must match the DOS attributes specified in `wParam` and the file specification string in `lParam`.

Return Value The index to the last filename added to the list is returned. `CB_ERR` is returned when an error occurs. `CB_ERRSPACE` is returned if there is not enough memory available.

Related Messages `CB_ADDSTRING`, `CB_INSERTSTRING`

CB_FINDSTRING

wParam Specifies the item just prior to the first item to search. When `wParam` is –1, the list box is searched starting from the top.

lParam Points to the null-terminated string containing the prefix text.

Description The `CB_FINDSTRING` message searches the list box of a combo box for the first occurrence of the prefix string specified in `lParam`. The value in `wParam` specifies the index of the item just prior to the item where the search begins. The search begins with the item after the item specified in `wParam` and continues to the end of the list, begins again at the top, and terminates on the item in `wParam` (when no match is found). `lParam` points to the null terminated string that contains the prefix text. The search is case independent.

Return Value The index of the matching item is returned when a match is found. `CB_ERR` is returned when the search is unsuccessful.

Related Messages `CB_SETCURSEL`

CB_GETCOUNT

wParam Not used.

lParam Not used.

Description The CB_GETCOUNT message gets the number of items in a list box of a combo box.

Return Value The number of items in the list box is returned when successful. CB_ERR is returned when unsuccessful.

Related Messages CB_ADDSTRING, CB_INSERTSTRING

CB_GETCURSEL

wParam Not used.

lParam Not used.

Description The CB_GETCURSEL message gets the index of the selected item in a list box of a combo box.

Return Value The index of the selected item is returned. CB_ERR is returned when no item is currently selected.

Related Messages CB_SETCURSEL

CB_GETDROPPEDCONTROLRECT

wParam Not used.

lParam Points to a RECT data structure that receives the coordinates of the dropped-down list box of a combo box.

Description The CB_GETDROPPEDCONTROLRECT message retrieves the screen coordinates of the dropped-down list box of a combo box. lParam points to a data structure of type RECT that stores the coordinates of the dropped-down list box. The RECT data structure follows.

```
typedef struct tagRECT {
     int left;
     int top;
     int right;
     int bottom;
} RECT;
```

in which

left is the horizontal coordinate of the upper-left corner of the rectangular region `top` is the vertical coordinate of the upper-left corner of the rectangular region

`right` is the horizontal coordinate of the lower-right corner of the rectangular region

`bottom` is the vertical coordinate of the lower-right corner of the rectangular region.

Return Value `CB_OKAY` is returned.

Related Messages `CB_GETDROPPEDSTATE`, `CB_SETDROPPEDSTATE`

CB_GETDROPPEDSTATE

wParam Not used.

lParam Not used.

Description The `CB_GETDROPPEDSTATE` message determines whether the list box of a combo box is dropped down and visible.

Return Value A nonzero value is returned when the list box is dropped down and visible. Zero is returned if the list box is not dropped down and visible.

Related Messages `CB_SHOWDROPDOWN`

CB_GETEDITSEL

wParam Not used.

lParam Not used.

Description The `CB_GETEDITSEL` message gets the beginning and ending character positions of the selected text. `CB_GETEDITSEL` is used with the edit control of a combo box.

Return Value The low-order word of the returned value contains the starting position of the selected text. The high-order word of the return value contains the ending position.

Related Messages `CB_SETEDITSEL`

CB_GETEXTENDEDUI

wParam Not used.

lParam Not used.

Description The CB_GETEXTENDEDUI message determines whether a combo box has the default or the extended user interface. The extended user interface adds the following characteristics to the default interface:

- Clicking the static text field displays the list box for combo boxes with CBS_DROPDOWNLIST style.
- Pressing the DOWN arrow displays the list box (F4 disabled).
- Static text field scrolling is disabled when the item list is not visible.

Return Value A nonzero value is returned when the combo box has the extended user interface. Zero is returned when the combo box has the default user interface.

Related Messages CB_SETEXTENDEDUI

CB_GETITEMDATA

wParam Contains the index to an item in a combo box.

lParam Not used.

Description The CB_GETITEMDATA message returns the value associated with the combo box item specified in wParam. The retrieved value is a 32-bit value provided by the application. When the specified item is an owner draw combo box with style CBS_HASSTRINGS, the return value is the lParam parameter of CB_ADDSTRING or CB_INSERTSTRING. Otherwise, the return value is the lParam parameter of the CB_SETITEMDATA message.

Return Value The 32-bit value associated with the item is returned when successful. CB_ERR is returned when an error occurs.

Related Messages CB_SETITEMDATA

CB_GETITEMHEIGHT

wParam Specifies the combo box component to evaluate. When `wParam` is –1, the height of the edit control of the combo box is returned. When the combo box has style `CBS_OWNERDRAWVARIABLE`, `wParam` contains the index of the list item to evaluate.

lParam Not used.

Description The `CB_GETITEMHEIGHT` message determines the height of the combo box component specified in `wParam`.

Return Value The height, in pixels, of the specified combo box component is returned when successful. `CB_ERR` is returned when unsuccessful.

Related Messages `CB_SETITEMHEIGHT`

CB_GETLBTEXT

wParam Contains the index of the string to copy.

lParam Points to the buffer where the string will be stored.

Description The `CB_GETLBTEXT` message places the string from a list box of a combo box into the buffer pointed to by `lParam`. `wParam` specifies the index of the string to copy.

Return Value The number of bytes in the string, excluding the null character, is returned when successful. When unsuccessful, `CB_ERR` is returned.

Related Messages `CB_GETLBTEXTLEN`

CB_GETLBTEXTLEN

wParam Specifies the index of the string to evaluate.

lParam Not used.

Description The `CB_GETLBTEXTLEN` message determines the length of the string specified in `wParam`. The string is contained in the list box of a combo box.

Return Value The number of bytes in the string, not counting the null character, is returned when successful. `CB_ERR` is returned if an invalid index is specified in `wParam`.

Related Messages CB_GETLBTEXT

CB_INSERTSTRING

wParam Specifies the position index where the string will be inserted. If wParam is set to –1, the string is put at the bottom of the list.

lParam lParam points to the null-terminated string to be inserted into the list.

Description The CB_INSERTSTRING message inserts the string pointed to by lParam into the list box of a combo box. wParam specifies the position where the string will be inserted.

Return Value The position index of the inserted string is returned when successful. When an error occurs, CB_ERR is returned. If there is insufficient memory to store the string, CB_ERRSPACE is returned.

Related Messages CB_ADDSTRING, CB_DELETESTRING

CB_LIMITTEXT

wParam Defines the maximum number of bytes that can be entered into the edit control of a combo box. If wParam is set to zero, the default length of 65,535 is used.

lParam Not used.

Description The CB_LIMITTEXT message restricts the number of bytes that a user can enter into the edit control of a combo box to the value specified in wParam.

Return Value 1 is returned when successful. CB_ERR is returned when the combo box has CBS_DROPDOWNLIST style.

Related Messages CB_GETLBTEXTLEN

CB_RESETCONTENT

wParam Not used.

lParam Not used.

Description The CB_RESETCONTENT message removes all the strings from the list box and edit control of a combo box. All memory associated with the removed strings is freed. The WM_DELETEITEM message is sent to the owner of owner draw combo boxes without the CBS_HASSTRINGS style for each item being deleted from the combo box.

Return Value CB_OKAY is returned.

Related Messages WM_DELETEITEM

CB_SELECTSTRING

wParam Specifies the index of the item just prior to the first item to search. The item specified by wParam is the last item to search. If wParam is set to –1, the search begins at the top of the list.

lParam Points to the null-terminated prefix string.

Description The CB_SELECTSTRING message selects the item from the list box of a combo box that matches the string pointed to by lParam. The search begins with the next item after the item specified in wParam. The search continues down the list and begins again at the top if no match is found by the time the bottom of the list is reached. The last item searched is the item specified in wParam. The edit control text of the combo box displays the selected text. The search is not case sensitive.

Return Value The index of the selected item is returned when successful. When unsuccessful, CB_ERR is returned.

Related Messages CB_FINDSTRING

CB_SETCURSEL

wParam Specifies the index of the selected string. When wParam is –1, nothing in the list box is selected and the edit control is cleared.

lParam Not used.

Description The CB_SETCURSEL message selects the string specified in wParam. The combo box edit control text displays the selected string.

Return Value The index of the selected item is returned when successful. When an invalid index is specified, CB_ERR is returned.

Related Messages `CB_FINDSTRING`, `CB_GETCURSEL`

CB_SETEDITSEL

wParam Not used.

lParam Defines the position of the selected text. The beginning position is specified in the low-order word; the ending position is specified in the high-order word. When the beginning position is set to –1, the current selection is "unselected." When the ending position is set to –1, the current selection extends from the starting position to the last character of the edit control.

Description The `CB_SETEDITSEL` message selects a block of text in the edit control of a combo box. The starting position of the block is specified in the low-order word of `lParam`. The ending position of the block is specified in the high-order word of `lParam`. The first character of the edit control is referenced as character zero.

Return Value A nonzero value is returned when successful. When unsuccessful, zero is returned. If the message is sent to a combo box with style `CBS_DROPDOWNLIST`, `CB_ERR` is returned.

Related Messages `CB_GETEDITSEL`

CB_SETEXTENDEDUI

wParam Set to `TRUE` to use the extended user interface; set to `FALSE` to use the default user interface.

lParam Not used.

Description The `CB_SETEXTENDEDUI` message specifies the user interface type, either extended or default, for a combo box that has the `CBS_DROPDOWN` or `CBS_DROPDOWNLIST` style. The extended user interface adds the following characteristics to the default interface:

- Clicking the static text field displays the list box for combo boxes with the CBS_DROPDOWNLIST style.
- Pressing the DOWN arrow displays the list box (F4 disabled).
- Static text field scrolling is disabled when the item list is not visible.

Return Value CB_OKAY is returned when successful. CB_ERR is returned when unsuccessful.

Related Messages CB_GETEXTENDEDUI

CB_SETITEMDATA

wParam Specifies the index to the item in the combo box.

lParam Specifies the value to be associated with the item in the combo box.

Description The CB_SETITEMDATA message defines the 32-bit value associated with the combo box item specified in wParam. The new value to associate with the item is specified in lParam.

Return Value CB_ERR is returned when an error occurs.

Related Messages CB_ADDSTRING, CB_INSERTSTRING

CB_SETITEMHEIGHT

wParam Specifies the component that will be set. When wParam is –1, the height of the edit control or static text is set. When the combo box has the CBS_OWNERDRAWVARIABLE style, wParam contains the index of the list item to set. When wParam is zero, the height of all list items is set.

lParam Specifies the height, in pixels, of the combo box component.

Description The CB_SETITEMHEIGHT message sets the height of the combo box component specified in wParam to the value specified in lParam.

Return Value CB_ERR is returned when unsuccessful.

Related Messages CB_GETITEMHEIGHT

CB_SHOWDROPDOWN

wParam Specifies whether to show or hide the drop-down list box on a combo box. wParam is set to TRUE to show the list box. It is set to FALSE to hide the list box.

lParam Not used.

Description The CB_SHOWDROPDOWN message either shows or hides the drop-down list box of a combo box. wParam specifies whether the list box is shown or hidden. The drop-down list box must be created with the CBS_DROPDOWN or CBS_DROPDOWNLIST style.

Return Value A nonzero value is always returned.

Related Messages CB_GETDROPPEDSTATE, CB_GETDROPPEDCONTROLRECT

CBN_CLOSEUP

wParam Contains the control ID for the combo box control.

lParam The low-order word of lParam contains the handle of the combo box control. The high-order word of lParam contains the CBN_CLOSEUP code.

Description The CBN_CLOSEUP code is sent to the parent window of a combo box when the list box of the combo box is hidden. This code is not used with combo boxes that have the CBS_SIMPLE style.

Related Messages CBN_DROPDOWN, WM_COMMAND

CBN_DBLCLK

wParam Contains the control ID for the combo box control.

lParam The low-order word of lParam contains the handle of the combo box control. The high-order word of lParam contains the CBN_DBLCLK notification code.

Description The CBN_DBLCLK code is sent through a WM_COMMAND message from a control to the parent window when a string in the list box of a combo box has been double-clicked.

Related Messages CBN_SELCHANGE, WM_COMMAND

CBN_DROPDOWN

wParam Specifies the control ID for the combo box control.

lParam The low-order word of lParam contains the handle of the combo box control. The high-order word of lParam contains the CBN_DROPDOWN code.

Description The CBN_DROPDOWN code is sent through a WM_COMMAND message from a control to the parent window when a list box of a combo box is to be dropped down. This code is sent prior to the list box becoming visible.

Related Messages CBN_CLOSEUP, WM_COMMAND

CBN_EDITCHANGE

wParam Specifies the control ID for the combo box control.

lParam The low-order word of lParam contains the handle of the combo box control. The high-order word of lParam contains the CBN_EDITCHANGE code.

Description The CBN_EDITCHANGE code is sent through a WM_COMMAND message from a control to the parent window when the text in an edit control of a combo box may have been modified by the user. This code is sent after Windows updates the display.

Related Messages CBN_EDITUPDATE, WM_COMMAND

CBN_EDITUPDATE

wParam Contains the control ID for the combo box control.

lParam The low-order word of lParam contains the handle of the combo box control. The high-order word of lParam contains the CBN_EDITUPDATE code.

Description The CBN_EDITUPDATE code is sent through a WM_COMMAND message from a control to the parent window when the text for an edit control of a combo box may have been altered by the user. This code is sent before Windows updates the display.

Related Messages CBN_EDITCHANGE, WM_COMMAND

CBN_ERRSPACE

wParam Contains the control ID for the combo box control.

lParam The low-order word of `lParam` contains the handle of the combo box control. The high-order word of `lParam` contains the `CBN_ERRSPACE` code.

Description The `CBN_ERRSPACE` code is sent through a `WM_COMMAND` message from a control to the parent window when the list box of a combo box cannot allocate the memory it needs.

Related Messages `WM_COMMAND`

CBN_KILLFOCUS

wParam Contains the control ID for the combo box control.

lParam The low-order word of `lParam` contains the handle of the combo box control. The high-order word of `lParam` contains the `CBN_KILLFOCUS` code.

Description The `CBN_KILLFOCUS` code is sent through a `WM_COMMAND` message from a control to the parent window when the combo box control loses the input focus.

Related Messages `CBN_SETFOCUS`, `WM_COMMAND`

CBN_SELCHANGE

wParam Contains the control ID of the combo box control.

lParam The low-order word of `lParam` contains the handle of the combo box control. The high-order word of `lParam` contains the `CBN_SELCHANGE` code.

Description The `CBN_SELCHANGE` code is sent through a `WM_COMMAND` message from a control to the parent window when a selection of the list box of a combo box is modified by the user.

Related Messages `CBN_DBLCLK`, `WM_COMMAND`

CBN_SELENDCANCEL

wParam Contains the control ID of the combo box control.

lParam The low-order word of `lParam` contains the handle of the combo box control. The high-order word of `lParam` contains the `CBN_SELENDCANCEL` code.

Description The `CBN_SELENDCANCEL` code is sent whenever the user selects an item, then clicks outside the control to close the combo box control. This code is sent to the `CBN_CLOSEUP` code to indicate that the selection made by the user should be ignored.

Related Messages `CBN_SELENDOK`, `WM_COMMAND`

CBN_SELENDOK

wParam Contains the control ID of the combo box control.

lParam The low-order word of `lParam` contains the handle of the combo box control. The high-order word of `lParam` contains the `CBN_SELENDOK` code.

Description The `CBN_SELENDOK` code is sent whenever the user selects an item, then presses Enter or the Down arrow key. This code is sent prior to the `CBN_CLOSEUP` code to indicate that the selection made by the user is valid.

Related Messages `CBN_SELENDCANCEL`, `WM_COMMAND`

CBN_SETFOCUS

wParam Contains the control ID of the combo box control.

lParam The low-order word of `lParam` contains the handle of the combo box control. The high-order word of `lParam` contains the `CBN_SETFOCUS` code.

Description The `CBN_SETFOCUS` code is sent through a `WM_COMMAND` message from a control to the parent window when the combo box receives the input focus.

Related Messages `WM_COMMAND`

DM_GETDEFID

wParam Not used.

lParam Not used.

Description The DM_GETDEFID message gets the default push button control ID for a dialog box.

Return Value A 32-bit value is returned. The high-order word of the return value contains DC_HASDEFID when the default button exists. The low-order word of the return value contains the ID of the default button when the high-order word contains DC_HASDEFID. Zero is returned when the default push button does not have an ID.

Related Messages DM_SETDEFID

DM_SETDEFID

wParam Specifies the ID of the default push button.

lParam Not used.

Description The DM_SETDEFID message changes the ID of the default push button control for a dialog box.

Return Value A nonzero value is always returned.

Related Messages DM_GETDEFID

DRV_CLOSE

Note: The DRV_CLOSE message is used with installable drivers and the DriverProc function. Therefore, the parameters of the DRV_CLOSE message differ from the parameters of typical Windows messages and notification codes. The DriverProc function is the main function within an installable driver. The DriverProc function is provided by the developer of the driver.

Parameter	Description
dwDriverIdentifier	The unique 32-bit identifier returned by the OpenDriver function
hDriver	Instance of the installable driver to close

lParam1 Driver-specific data.

lParam2 Driver-specific data.

Description The DRV_CLOSE message is sent to an installable driver when the application calls the CloseDriver function. lParam1 and lParam2 are the same values as the lParam1 and lParam2 parameters of the CloseDriver function. When the driver receives this message, the private use-count variable should be decremented. The driver is closed when the use-count variable is zero.

Return Value A nonzero value should be returned by the installable driver when the DriverProc function closed the driver. Zero should be returned when the driver was not closed.

Related Messages DRV_OPEN

DRV_CONFIGURE

> **Note:** The DRV_CONFIGURE message is used with installable drivers and the DriverProc function. Therefore, the parameters of the DRV_CONFIGURE message differ from the parameters of typical Windows messages and notification codes. The DriverProc function is the main function within an installable driver. The DriverProc function is provided by the developer of the driver.

Parameter	Description
dwDriverIdentifier	The unique 32-bit identifier that specifies the installable driver
hDriver	Instance of the installable driver

lParam1 The low-word of lParam1 specifies the handle of the parent window of the configuration dialog box.

lParam2 Pointer to an optional DRVCONFIGINFO data structure.

Description The DRV_CONFIGURE message informs the installable driver that its configuration dialog box should be displayed. The installable driver is expected to provide the dialog template and dialog procedure.

Return Value A nonzero value is returned to indicate that the installable driver processed the message. Zero is returned to indicate that the installable driver did not process the message.

Related Messages DRV_QUERYCONFIGURE

DRV_DISABLE

> **Note:** The DRV_DISABLE message is used with installable drivers and the DriverProc function. Therefore, the parameters of the DRV_DISABLE message differ from the parameters of typical Windows messages and notification codes. The DriverProc function is the main function within an installable driver. The DriverProc function is provided by the developer of the driver.

Parameter	*Description*
dwDriverIdentifier	dwDriverIdentifier is not used
hDriver	Instance of the installable driver

lParam1 Not used.

lParam2 Not used.

Description The DRV_DISABLE message notifies an installable driver that the driver is going to be removed from the system by Windows.

Return Value Zero is returned when the installable driver processes the message.

Related Messages DRV_CLOSE

DRV_ENABLE

> **Note:** The `DRV_ENABLE` message is used with installable drivers and the `DriverProc` function. Therefore, the parameters of the `DRV_ENABLE` message differ from the parameters of typical Windows messages and notification codes. The `DriverProc` function is the main function within an installable driver. The `DriverProc` function is provided by the developer of the driver.

Parameter	*Description*
`dwDriverIdentifier`	`dwDriverIdentifier` is not used
`hDriver`	Instance of the installable driver

lParam1 Not used.

lParam2 Not used.

Description The `DRV_ENABLE` message notifies the installable driver under one of the following conditions:

- The driver is loaded.
- The driver is reloaded.
- Windows is reinstalled after executing a DOS application.

Return Value Zero is returned when the installable driver processes the message.

Related Messages `DRV_OPEN`

DRV_FREE

> **Note:** The DRV_FREE message is used with installable drivers and the DriverProc function. Therefore, the parameters of the DRV_FREE message differ from the parameters of typical Windows messages and notification codes. The DriverProc function is the main function within an installable driver. The DriverProc function is provided by the developer of the driver.

Parameter	Description
`dwDriverIdentifier`	`dwDriverIdentifier` is not used
`hDriver`	Instance of the installable driver

lParam1 Not used.

lParam2 Not used.

Description The `DRV_FREE` message is sent to the installable driver when the driver is going to be discarded by Windows. The `DriverProc` function for the installable driver should free all memory allocated for the driver.

Return Value Zero is returned when the installable driver processes the message.

Related Messages `DRV_CLOSE`, `DRV_DISABLE`

DRV_INSTALL

> **Note:** The `DRV_INSTALL` message is used with installable drivers and the `DriverProc` function. Therefore, the parameters of the `DRV_INSTALL` message differ from the parameters of typical Windows messages and notification codes. The `DriverProc` function is the main function within an installable driver. The `DriverProc` function is provided by the developer of the driver.

Parameter	Description
`dwDriverIdentifier`	Unique 32-bit value that identifies the installable driver
`hDriver`	Instance of the installable driver

lParam1 Not used.

lParam2 Pointer to optional `DRVCONFIGINFO` data structure.

Description The `DRV_INSTALL` message is sent to the installable driver during driver initialization so that the appropriate driver entry for the SYSTEM.INI file can be made.

Return Value A nonzero value should be returned by the installable driver when the message is processed. Zero should be returned when the message was not processed.

Related Messages `DRV_CLOSE`, `DRV_LOAD`

DRV_LOAD

> **Note:** The `DRV_LOAD` message is used with installable drivers and the `DriverProc` function. Therefore, the parameters of the `DRV_LOAD` message differ from the parameters of typical Windows messages and notification codes. The `DriverProc` function is the main function within an installable driver. The `DriverProc` function is provided by the developer of the driver.

Parameter	*Description*
`dwDriverIdentifier`	`dwDriverIdentifier` is not used
`hDriver`	Instance of the installable driver

lParam1 Not used.

lParam2 Not used.

Description The `DRV_LOAD` message notifies the installable driver that the driver has been loaded.

Return Value A nonzero value should be returned by the installable driver when the `DriverProc` function loaded the driver. Zero should be returned when the driver was not loaded.

Related Messages `DRV_DISABLE`, `DRV_INSTALL`

DRV_OPEN

> **Note:** The DRV_OPEN message is used with installable drivers and the DriverProc function. Therefore, the parameters of the DRV_OPEN message differ from the parameters of typical Windows messages and notification codes. The DriverProc function is the main function within an installable driver. The DriverProc function is provided by the developer of the driver.

Parameter	*Description*
`dwDriverIdentifier`	Unique 32-bit identifier for the installable driver
`hDriver`	Instance of the installable driver

lParam1 Pointer to null-terminated string containing the ASCII characters that follow the driver name in SYSTEM.INI.

lParam2 Data specified by the third argument of the `OpenDriver` function.

Description The `DRV_OPEN` message is sent to an installable driver whenever the driver is opened.

Return Value A nonzero value is returned by the installable driver when the message is processed. Zero is returned if the message is not processed.

Related Messages `DRV_CLOSE`, `DRV_DISABLE`

DRV_QUERYCONFIGURE

> **Note:** The DRV_QUERYCONFIGURE message is used with installable drivers and the DriverProc function. Therefore, the parameters of the DRV_QUERYCONFIGURE message differ from the parameters of typical Windows messages and notification codes. The DriverProc function is the main function within an installable driver. The DriverProc function is provided by the developer of the driver.

Parameter	*Description*
dwDriverIdentifier	Unique 32-bit identifier for the installable driver
hDriver	Instance of the installable driver

lParam1 Not used.

lParam2 Not used.

Description The DRV_QUERYCONFIGURE message determines whether an installable driver can be configured by the user.

Return Value A nonzero value should be returned by the installable driver when the driver can be configured by the user. Zero should be returned when the driver cannot be configured by the user.

Related Messages DRV_CONFIGURE

DRV_POWER

> **Note:** The DRV_POWER message is used with installable drivers and the DriverProc function. Therefore, the parameters of the DRV_POWER message differ from the parameters of typical Windows messages and notification codes. The DriverProc function is the main function within an installable driver. The DriverProc function is provided by the developer of the driver.

Parameter	*Description*
dwDriverIdentifier	Unique 32-bit identifier for the installable driver
hDriver	Instance of the installable driver

lParam1 Not used.

lParam2 Not used.

Description The DRV_POWER message is sent to an installable driver whenever the power to the device associated with the driver is going to be turned off or on.

Return Value A nonzero value should be returned by the installable driver when the message is processed. Zero should be returned when the message was not processed.

Related Messages DRV_CONFIGURE

DRV_REMOVE

> **Note:** The DRV_REMOVE message is used with installable drivers and the DriverProc function. Therefore, the parameters of the DRV_REMOVE message differ from the parameters of typical Windows messages and notification codes. The DriverProc function is the main function within an installable driver. The DriverProc function is provided by the developer of the driver.

Parameter	*Description*
dwDriverIdentifier	Unique 32-bit identifier for the installable driver
hDriver	Instance of the installable driver

lParam1 Not used.

lParam2 Not used.

Description The DRV_REMOVE message is sent to an installable driver by the application during driver configuration. This message is the fourth message sent by the application to the installable driver. The driver should remove the appropriate entries from the SYSTEM.INI file when the DRV_REMOVE message is received.

Return Value A nonzero value should be returned by the installable driver when the message is processed. Zero should be returned when the message is not processed.

Related Messages DRV_CLOSE, DRV_INSTALL, DRV_OPEN

DRV_USER

> **Note:** The DRV_USER message is used with installable drivers and the DriverProc function. Therefore, the parameters of the DRV_USER message differ from the parameters of typical Windows messages and notification codes. The DriverProc function is the main function within an installable driver. The DriverProc function is provided by the developer of the driver.

Parameter	*Description*
dwDriverIdentifier	dwDriverIdentifier is driver-dependent
hDriver	hDriver is driver-dependent

lParam1 lParam1 is driver-dependent.

lParam2 lParam2 is driver-dependent.

Description The DRV_USER message is defined by the user and is driver-dependent.

Return Value The return value is driver-dependent.

Related Messages DRV_OPEN

EM_CANUNDO

wParam Not used.

lParam Not used.

Description The EM_CANUNDO message indicates whether an edit control has the ability to respond to an EM_UNDO message (the last edit control operation can be undone).

Return Value A nonzero value is returned when the edit control is able to process the EM_UNDO message. Zero is returned when the edit control is not able to process the EM_UNDO message.

Related Messages EM_UNDO

EM_EMPTYUNDOBUFFER

wParam Not used.

lParam Not used.

Description The `EM_EMPTYUNDOBUFFER` message clears the undo flag of an edit control. When the undo flag is set, the last edit operation can be undone.

Return Value There is no return value.

Related Messages `EM_CANUNDO`, `EM_SETHANDLE`, `EM_UNDO`, `WM_SETTEXT`

EM_FMTLINES

wParam Specifies whether soft linebreak characters should be used with word-wrapped text. When `wParam` is set to `TRUE`, soft linebreak characters are used. When `wParam` is set to `FALSE`, soft linebreak characters are not used.

lParam Not used.

Description The `EM_FMTLINES` message determines whether a multiline edit control will add or remove soft linebreak characters from word-wrapped text. `wParam` specifies how the soft linebreak characters are handled. A soft linebreak is a combination of carriage return\carriage return\linefeed.

Return Value `TRUE` is returned when soft linebreak characters are used. `FALSE` is returned when soft linebreak characters are not used.

Related Messages `EM_GETHANDLE`, `WM_GETTEXT`

EM_GETFIRSTVISIBLELINE

wParam Not used.

lParam Not used.

Description The `EM_GETFIRSTVISIBLELINE` message determines the topmost visible line of the edit control.

Return Value The retrieved zero-based index is returned.

Related Messages `EM_GETLINECOUNT`, `EM_LINEINDEX`

EM_GETHANDLE

wParam Not used.

lParam Not used.

Description The `EM_GETHANDLE` message gets the data handle of the buffer that stores the contents of a multiline edit control. This message is used only with multiline edit controls.

Return Value The retrieved handle is returned when successful. Zero is returned when unsuccessful or when the message is sent to a single-line edit control.

Related Messages `EM_SETHANDLE`

EM_GETLINE

wParam Defines the line number in the edit control. The first line of the control is numbered 0.

lParam Points to the buffer where the line will be placed. The maximum number of bytes to copy to the buffer is defined in the first word of the buffer.

Description The `EM_GETLINE` message gets the line, as specified in `wParam`, from the edit control and places it in the buffer pointed to by `lParam`. The null-terminator is not copied.

Return Value The number of bytes copied to the buffer is returned when successful. Zero is returned when unsuccessful.

Related Messages `EM_GETLINECOUNT`

EM_GETLINECOUNT

wParam Not used.

lParam Not used.

Description The `EM_GETLINECOUNT` message gets the number of text lines in a multiline edit control. This message is not processed by single-line edit controls.

Return Value The number of text lines in the edit control is returned. If the edit control contains no text, 1 is returned.

Related Messages EM_GETLIN E

EM_GETMODIFY

wParam Not used.

lParam Not used.

Description The EM_GETMODIFY message gets the value of the modify flag for an edit control. The modify flag is set whenever text is modified in the control.

Return Value A nonzero value is returned when the contents of the edit control have been modified (modify flag is set). Zero is returned when the contents of the edit control have not been modified (modify flag is not set).

Related Messages EM_SETMODIFY

EM_GETPASSWORDCHAR

wParam Not used.

lParam Not used.

Description The EM_GETPASSWORDCHAR message retrieves the password character that is displayed in an edit control when the user enters text. Edit controls with style ES_PASSWORD display an asterisk (*) by default when the user enters text.

Return Value The character displayed in the edit control is returned.

Related Messages EM_SETPASSWORDCHAR

EM_GETRECT

wParam Not used.

lParam Points to a structure of type RECT that holds the dimensions for the control. The RECT structure follows.

```
typedef struct tagRECT {
     int left;
     int top;
     int right;
     int bottom;
} RECT;
```

in which

`left` is the horizontal coordinate of the upper-left corner of the rectangular region

`top` is the vertical coordinate of the upper-left corner of the rectangular region

`right` is the horizontal coordinate of the lower-right corner of the rectangular region

`bottom` is the vertical coordinate of the lower-right corner of the rectangular region.

Description The `EM_GETRECT` message gets the dimensions of the formatting rectangle for the edit control. The formatting rectangle limits the text of the edit control and does not necessarily correspond to the size of the edit control window.

Return Value There is no meaningful return value.

Related Messages `EM_SETRECT`

EM_GETSEL

wParam Not used.

lParam Not used.

Description The `EM_GETSEL` message gets the starting and ending positions for the currently selected text in the edit control.

Return Value The low-order word of the return value contains the starting position of the selected text. The high-order word of the return value contains the ending position of the selected text (the first non-selected character after the end of the current selection).

Related Messages `EM_SETSEL`

EM_GETWORDBREAKPROC

wParam Not used.

lParam Not used.

Description The `EM_GETWORDBREAKPROC` message retrieves the current word-break function for an edit control. A word-break function first determines whether a line of text will fit into the edit control, and then breaks the line at the appropriate point if necessary.

Return Value The procedure-instance address of the application-defined word-break function is returned.

Related Messages `EM_SETWORDBREAKPROC`

EM_LIMITTEXT

wParam Defines the maximum number of bytes the user can enter. When `wParam` is zero, the maximum number of bytes that can be entered is set to 65,535.

lParam Not used.

Description The `EM_LIMITTEXT` message limits the maximum number of bytes that the user can enter into an edit control to the value specified in `wParam`. Text set by the `WM_SETTEXT` message is not affected by this message.

Return Value There is no return value.

Related Messages `WM_SETTEXT`

EM_LINEFROMCHAR

wParam Specifies the index value of the character when not set to –1. When `wParam` is set to –1, `EM_LINEFROMCHAR` gets the line number containing the first character of the selection.

lParam Not used.

Description The `EM_LINEFROMCHAR` message gets the line number of the line that contains the character at the index value specified in `wParam` (when `wParam` is not –1). When `wParam` is –1, the `EM_LINEFROMCHAR` message gets the line number that contains the first character of the selection. The `EM_LINEFROMCHAR` message is used with multiline edit controls only.

Return Value When `wParam` is –1, the line number that contains the first character of the selection is returned. When `wParam` is not –1, the line number containing the character at the specified index value is returned.

Related Messages `EM_LINEINDEX`

EM_LINEINDEX

wParam Defines the line number used for evaluation. When `wParam` is –1, the line number for the line that contains the caret is used.

lParam Not used.

Description The `EM_LINEINDEX` message determines the number of character positions that precede the line number specified in `wParam`. This message is not processed by single-line edit controls.

Return Value The number of character positions that precede the specified line number (the character index of the line) is returned. –1 is returned when the specified line number is greater than the number of lines in the edit control.

Related Messages `EM_LINEFROMCHAR`

EM_LINELENGTH

wParam Specifies the index of the character in the specified line. When `wParam` is –1, the line that contains the caret is evaluated. For single-line edit controls, `wParam` is ignored.

lParam Not used.

Description The `EM_LINELENGTH` message determines the number of bytes in a line from the text buffer of the edit control. The line number to evaluate is specified in `wParam`.

Return Value For multiline edit controls, the number of bytes in a line from the text buffer of the edit control is returned. For single line edit controls, the length of the text in the edit control is returned.

Related Messages `EM_LINEINDEX`

EM_LINESCROLL

wParam Not used.

lParam The low-order word of `lParam` contains the number of lines to scroll in the vertical direction. The high-order word of `lParam` contains the number of character positions to scroll in the horizontal direction.

Description The `EM_LINESCROLL` message scrolls the contents of the multiline edit control. `lParam` specifies the number of lines to scroll the contents of the edit control in both the vertical and horizontal directions.

Return Value A nonzero value is returned when the message is sent to a multiline edit control. If the message is sent to a single-line edit control, zero is returned.

EM_REPLACESEL

wParam Not used.

lParam Points to the null-terminated string that contains the replacement text.

Description The `EM_REPLACESEL` message replaces the currently selected text from an edit control with the text string pointed to by `lParam`.

Return Value There is no return value.

Related Messages `EM_GETSEL`, `EM_SETSEL`

EM_SETHANDLE

wParam Specifies the handle for the buffer used to store the contents of a multiline edit control. The handle must have been created using `LocalAlloc` with the `LMEM_MOVEABLE` flag.

lParam Not used.

Description The `EM_SETHANDLE` function specifies the text buffer that stores the contents of a multiline edit control. Single-line edit controls do not process this message.

Return Value There is no return value.

Related Messages EM_GETHANDLE, EM_GETMODIFY

EM_SETMODIFY

wParam Defines the setting for the modify flag. TRUE is used to indicate that the text has been modified. FALSE is used to indicate that the text has not been modified.

lParam Not used.

Description The EM_SETMODIFY message sets the value of the modify flag for an edit control to the value in wParam.

Return Value There is no return value.

Related Messages EM_GETMODIFY

EM_SETPASSWORDCHAR

wParam Defines the character that will be displayed whenever the user presses a key during password entry. When wParam is zero, the actual character entered is displayed.

lParam Not used.

Description The EM_SETPASSWORDCHAR message specifies the password character that will be displayed by an edit control. wParam defines the character that will displayed. For edit controls with style ES_PASSWORD, the default character is *. The ES_PASSWORD style is removed from the edit control when EM_SETPASSWORD is sent to the control with wParam set to zero.

Return Value A nonzero value is returned when the message is sent to an edit control.

Related Messages EM_SETREADONLY

EM_SETREADONLY

wParam Specifies the read-only state of an edit control. wParam is set to TRUE to set the read-only state. wParam is set to FALSE to remove the read-only state.

lParam Not used.

Description The `EM_SETREADONLY` message sets the read-only state of an edit control. `wParam` specifies the read-only state. When the read-only state is set, the user cannot modify the edit control text.

Return Value A nonzero value is returned when successful. Zero is returned when unsuccessful.

Related Messages `EM_SETPASSWORDCHAR`

EM_SETRECT

wParam Not used.

lParam Points to the data structure of type `RECT` that contains the rectangle's new dimensions. The `RECT` structure follows.

```
typedef struct tagRECT {
     int left;
     int top;
     int right;
     int bottom;
} RECT;
```

in which

`left` is the horizontal coordinate of the upper-left corner of the rectangular region

`top` is the vertical coordinate of the upper-left corner of the rectangular region

`right` is the horizontal coordinate of the lower-right corner of the rectangular region

`bottom` is the vertical coordinate of the lower-right corner of the rectangular region.

Description The `EM_SETRECT` message sets the formatting rectangle for a control to the dimensions stored in the data structure pointed to by `lParam`. The formatting rectangle limits the text of a multiline edit control. Single-line edit controls do not process this message.

Return Value There is no return value.

Related Messages `EM_GETRECT`, `EM_SETRECTNP`

EM_SETRECTNP

wParam Not used.

lParam Points to the data structure of type `RECT` that contains the rectangle's new dimensions. The `RECT` structure follows.

```
typedef struct tagRECT {
     int left;
     int top;
     int right;
     int bottom;
} RECT;
```

in which

`left` is the horizontal coordinate of the upper-left corner of the rectangular region

`top` is the vertical coordinate of the upper-left corner of the rectangular region

`right` is the horizontal coordinate of the lower-right corner of the rectangular region

`bottom` is the vertical coordinate of the lower-right corner of the rectangular region.

Description The `EM_SETRECTNP` message sets the formatting rectangle for a control to the dimensions stored in the data structure pointed to by `lParam`. The formatting rectangle limits the text of a multiline edit control. This message is similar to the `EM_SETRECT` message, except that the control is not repainted. Single-line edit controls do not process this message.

Return Value There is no return value.

Related Messages `EM_SETRECT`

EM_SETSEL

wParam Not used.

lParam The low-order word of `lParam` contains the starting character position of the text to select. The high-order word of `lParam` contains the ending character position of the text to select. When the low-order word is zero and the high-order word is –1, the entire text is selected. When the low-order word is –1, no selections are made.

Description The EM_SETSEL message selects the characters specified by the values in lParam from the current text of an edit control.

Return Value A nonzero value is returned when the message is sent to an edit control.

Related Messages EM_GETSEL, EM_REPLACESEL

EM_SETTABSTOPS

wParam Defines the number of tab stops in the edit control. When wParam is zero, default tab stops are set (every 32 dialog units). When wParam is 1, lParam specifies the distance between tab stops. When wParam is greater than 1, lParam points to an array of tab stops.

lParam When wParam is greater than one, lParam points to the first member of the array that contains the tab stop positions. When wParam is 1, lParam points to an unsigned integer that specifies the distance between tab stops. Tab stop positions are measured in dialog units.

Description The EM_SETTABSTOPS message positions the tab stops for a multiline edit control. wParam defines the number of tab stops. lParam specifies the distance between tab stops. Single-line edit controls do not process this message.

Return Value A nonzero value is returned when successful. Zero is returned when unsuccessful.

Related Messages EM_SETWORDBREAK

EM_SETWORDBREAKPROC

wParam Not used.

lParam Specifies the procedure instance address for the callback function.

Description The EM_SETWORDBREAKPROC message is sent to inform a multiline edit control that a new word break function has been installed by the application. A word break function determines where a line of text should be broken; the remainder of the text is carried to the next line. lParam specifies the procedure instance address of the callback function. The application-defined word break function is structured as follows:

```
LPSTR FAR PASCAL WordBreakProc(lpszEditText,ichCurrentWord,
                               cchEditText, wActionCode);
```

`LPSTR lpszEditText;`	Address of edit text
`short ichCurrentWord;`	Index of starting point
`short cchEditText;`	Length of edit text
`WORD wActionCode;`	Action. `wActionCode` is one of the following values:

Value	*Meaning*
`WB_LEFT`	Search for beginning of word at left of current position
`WB__RIGHT`	Search for beginning of word at right of current position
`WB_ISDELIMITER`	Check character at current position to determine whether the character is a delimiter

`WordBreakFunc` is a placeholder for the supplied function name. The supplied function name must be exported using `EXPORTS`.

The pointer to the first byte of the next word in the edit control text is returned by `WordBreakProc`. When the current word is the last word of text, the pointer to the first byte that follows the last word is returned.

`WordBreakProc` returns `TRUE` when `wActionCode` is `WB_ISDELIMITER` and the character is a delimiter (`FALSE` is returned if the character is not a delimiter). The index to the beginning of the word in the text buffer is returned otherwise.

Return Value There is no return value.

Related Messages `EM_SETTABSTOPS`

EM_UNDO

wParam Not used.

lParam Not used.

Description The EM_UNDO message performs an "undo" on the last edit operation for the edit control.

Return Value A nonzero value is always returned for single-line edit controls. For multiline edit controls, a nonzero value is returned when successful and zero is returned when unsuccessful.

Related Messages EM_CANUNDO

EN_CHANGE

wParam Specifies the control ID for edit control.

lParam The low-order word of lParam contains the edit control window handle. The high-order word of lParam contains the EN_CHANGE code.

Description The EN_CHANGE code is sent through a WM_COMMAND message to the parent window of an edit control when text may have been altered by the user. This code is sent after Windows updates the display.

Related Messages EN_UPDATE, WM_COMMAND

EN_ERRSPACE

wParam Specifies the control ID of the edit control.

lParam The low-order word of lParam contains the edit control window handle. The high-order word of lParam contains the EN_ERRSPACE code.

Description The EN_ERRSPACE code is sent through a WM_COMMAND message to the parent window of an edit control when the edit control cannot allocate the memory that it needs.

Related Messages WM_COMMAND

EN_HSCROLL

wParam Specifies the control ID of the edit control.

lParam The low-order word of lParam contains the edit control window handle. The high-order word of lParam contains the EN_HSCROLL code.

Description The EN_HSCROLL code is sent through a WM_COMMAND message to the parent window of an edit control when the horizontal scroll bar for the edit control has been clicked. This code is sent before Windows updates the display.

Related Messages EN_VSCROLL, WM_COMMAND

EN_KILLFOCUS

wParam Specifies the control ID of the edit control.

lParam The low-order word of lParam contains the edit control window handle. The high-order word of lParam contains the EN_KILLFOCUS code.

Description The EN_KILLFOCUS code is sent through a WM_COMMAND message to the parent window of an edit control when the edit control has lost the input focus.

Related Messages EN_SETFOCUS, WM_COMMAND

EN_MAXTEXT

wParam Specifies the control ID of the edit control.

lParam The low-order word of lParam contains the edit control window handle. The high-order word of lParam contains the EN_MAXTEXT code.

Description The EN_MAXTEXT code is sent through a WM_COMMAND message to the parent window of an edit control when the current insertion of text exceeds the control's specified limits. This notification is also sent if inserting text into the edit control would either exceed the width of the edit control and the ES_AUTOHSCROLL style is not set, or exceed the height of an edit control and the ES_AUTOVSCROLL is not set.

Related Messages EM_LIMITTEXT, WM_COMMAND

EN_SETFOCUS

wParam Specifies the control ID of the edit control.

lParam The low-order word of lParam contains the edit control window handle. The high-order word of lParam contains the EN_SETFOCUS code.

Description The EN_SETFOCUS code is sent through a WM_COMMAND message to the parent window of an edit control when the edit control receives the input focus.

Related Messages EN_KILLFOCUS, WM_COMMAND

EN_UPDATE

wParam Specifies the control ID of the edit control.

lParam The low-order word of lParam contains the edit control window handle. The high-order word of lParam contains the EN_UPDATE code.

Description The EN_UPDATE code is sent through a WM_COMMAND message to the parent window of an edit control when text has been altered by the user and the edit control of a combo box control will display altered text. This code is sent before Windows updates the display.

Related Messages EN_CHANGE, WM_COMMAND

EN_VSCROLL

wParam Specifies the control ID of the edit control.

lParam The low-order word of lParam contains the edit control window handle. The high-order word of lParam contains the EN_VSCROLL code.

Description The EN_VSCROLL code is sent through a WM_COMMAND message to the parent window of an edit control when the vertical scroll bar for the edit control has been clicked. This code is sent before Windows updates the display.

Related Messages EN_HSCROLL, WM_COMMAND

LB_ADDSTRING

wParam Not used.

lParam Points to the null-terminated text string that should be added.

Description The `LB_ADDSTRING` message adds the string pointed to by `lParam` to a list box. The string is added to the bottom of the list if the list box is not sorted (has style `CBS_SORT`). If the list box is sorted, the string is added at the appropriate position.

Return Value The index to the added string is returned when successful. On error, `LB_ERR` is returned. `LB_ERRSPACE` is returned when there is not enough space to store the string.

Related Messages `LB_DELETESTRING`, `LB_INSERTSTRING`

LB_DELETESTRING

wParam Specifies the index of the string to delete.

lParam Not used.

Description The `LB_DELETESTRING` message removes the list box string specified by the index value in `wParam`.

Return Value The number of strings left in the list is returned when the string is successfully deleted. `LB_ERR` is returned when unsuccessful.

Related Messages `LB_ADDSTRING`, `LB_INSERTSTRING`

LB_DIR

wParam Specifies the DOS attribute value. The DOS attribute values that can be used for `wParam` follow.

Value	*Meaning*
0x0000	Read/write; no additional attributes
0x0001	Read only
0x0002	Hidden file
0x0004	System file
0x0010	Subdirectory

Value	Meaning
0x0020	Archived file
0x4000	All drives included that match name in lParam
0x8000	Exclusive bit

lParam Points to the null-terminated file specification string (wildcards allowed).

Description The LB_DIR message builds a list of files for the list box. The files added to the list must contain the DOS attribute specified in wParam, and match the file specification in lParam.

Return Value The index of the last item added to the list is returned when successful. LB_ERR is returned when an error is generated. LB_ERRSPACE is returned when there is not enough space available to store the list.

Related Messages LB_ADDSTRING, LB_INSERTSTRING

LB_FINDSTRING

wParam Specifies the index of the item just before the first item to search. When wParam is –1, the list box is searched starting from the top.

lParam Points to the null-terminated string containing the prefix text.

Description The LB_FINDSTRING message searches the list box for the first occurrence of the prefix string specified in lParam. The value in wParam specifies the index of the item just prior to the item where the search begins. The search begins with the item after the item specified in wParam and continues to the end of the list, begins again at the top, and terminates on either the found text or the item in wParam. lParam points to the null-terminated string that contains the prefix text.

Return Value The index of the matching item is returned when a match is found. LB_ERR is returned when the search is unsuccessful.

Related Messages LB_ADDSTRING, LB_INSERTSTRING, LB_SELECTSTRING

LB_GETCARETINDEX

wParam Not used.

lParam Not used.

Description The `LB_GETCARETINDEX` message determines the index of the item from a multi-selection list box that has the focus rectangle. The item does not have to be selected.

Return Value For list boxes that allow multiple selections, the index of the item that has the focus rectangle is returned. For single-selection list boxes, the index of the selected item is returned.

Related Messages `LB_SETCARETINDEX`

LB_GETCOUNT

wParam Not used.

lParam Not used.

Description The `LB_GETCOUNT` message determines the number of items in the list box.

Return Value The number of items in the list box is returned when successful. When unsuccessful, `LB_ERR` is returned.

Related Messages `LB_GETSELCOUNT`

LB_GETCURSEL

wParam Not used.

lParam Not used.

Description The `LB_GETCURSEL` message gets the item index of the selected item for a single-selection list box.

Return Value The item index of the selected item is returned. When no item is selected, `LB_ERR` is returned.

Related Messages `LB_GETCARETINDEX`, `LB_SETCURSEL`

LB_GETHORIZONTALEXTENT

wParam Not used.

lParam Not used.

Description The LB_GETHORIZONTALEXTENT message determines the scrollable width, in pixels, of the list box. The list box must have style WS_HSCROLL (horizontal scroll bar).

Return Value The scrollable width of the list box, in pixels, is returned.

Related Messages LB_SETHORIZONTALEXTENT

LB_GETITEMDATA

wParam Specifies the item index for the list box item.

lParam Not used.

Description The LB_GETITEMDATA message gets the 32-bit value, supplied by the application, that is associated with the list box item specified in wParam.

Return Value The retrieved 32-bit value is returned when successful. When unsuccessful, LB_ERR is returned.

Related Messages LB_SETITEMDATA

LB_GETITEMHEIGHT

wParam Specifies the index of the list-box item to evaluate when the list box has style LBS_OWNERDRAWVARIABLE. Otherwise, wParam is zero.

lParam Not used.

Description The LB_GETITEMHEIGHT message determines the height of the specified item from a list box.

Return Value The height, in pixels, of the item is returned when successful. LB_ERR is returned when unsuccessful.

Related Messages LB_SETITEMHEIGHT

LB_GETITEMRECT

wParam Specifies the item index for the list box item.

lParam Points to the data structure of type RECT that stores the client coordinates of the list box item. The RECT structure follows.

```
typedef struct tagRECT {
     int left;
     int top;
     int right;
     int bottom;
} RECT;
```

in which

left is the horizontal coordinate of the upper-left corner of the rectangular region

top is the vertical coordinate of the upper-left corner of the rectangular region

right is the horizontal coordinate of the lower-right corner of the rectangular region

bottom is the vertical coordinate of the lower-right corner of the rectangular region.

Description The LB_GETITEMRECT message gets the dimensions of the rectangle surrounding the list box item specified in wParam. The dimensions of the rectangle are stored in the data structure pointed to by lParam.

Return Value LB_ERR is returned when unsuccessful.

Related Messages LB_GETITEMDATA, LB_GETITEMHEIGHT

LB_GETSEL

wParam Contains the item index.

lParam Not used.

Description The LB_GETSEL message gets the selection state of the item specified in wParam.

Return Value A positive value is returned when the specified item is selected. Zero is returned if the item is not selected. LB_ERR is returned when unsuccessful.

Related Messages LB_SETSEL

LB_GETSELCOUNT

wParam Not used.

lParam Not used.

Description The LB_GETSELCOUNT message gets the number of items selected from a multi-selection list box.

Return Value The number of items selected from the multi-selection list box is returned when successful. LB_ERR is returned when unsuccessful or if the list box is a single-selection list box.

Related Messages LB_GETSELITEMS

LB_GETSELITEMS

wParam Specifies the maximum number of selected items to place in the buffer pointed to by lParam.

lParam Points to the buffer in which the selected item numbers are stored.

Description The LB_GETSELITEMS message places the item numbers of the selected items from a multi-selection list box in the buffer pointed to by lParam. wParam specifies the maximum number of item numbers to place into the buffer.

Return Value The number of items placed in the buffer is returned when successful. LB_ERR is returned when unsuccessful or when the list box is a single-selection list box.

Related Messages LB_GETSEL, LB_SETSEL

LB_GETTEXT

wParam Specifies the index of the string to copy.

lParam Points to the buffer where the string will be placed.

Description The LB_GETTEXT message copies the string identified by the index in wParam into the buffer pointed to by lParam.

Return Value The number of bytes in the string, not counting the null terminator, is returned when successful. LB_ERR is returned when unsuccessful.

Related Messages LB_GETTEXTLEN

LB_GETTEXTLEN

wParam Specifies the index to the string to examine.

lParam Not used.

Description The LB_GETTEXTLEN message determines the length of the list box string specified in wParam.

Return Value The number of bytes in the string, not counting the null terminator, is returned when successful. LB_ERR is returned when unsuccessful.

Related Messages LB_GETTEXT

LB_GETTOPINDEX

wParam Not used.

lParam Not used.

Description The LB_GETTOPINDEX message gets the item index for the first visible item in the list box.

Return Value The index for the first visible item in the list box is returned.

Related Messages LB_SETTOPINDEX

LB_INSERTSTRING

wParam Specifies the index where the string will be inserted into the list box. When wParam is –1, the string is added to the end of the list.

lParam Points to the null-terminated string to insert into the list box.

Description The LB_INSERTSTRING message inserts the string pointed to by lParam into the list box at the position specified in wParam. The LB_INSERTSTRING message will not sort a list box with style LBS_SORT.

Return Value The index of the position where the string was inserted is returned when successful. When an error occurs, LB_ERR is returned. If there is not enough space to store the string, LB_ERRSPACE is returned.

Related Messages LB_ADDSTRING, LB_DELETESTRING

LB_RESETCONTENT

wParam Not used.

lParam Not used.

Description The LB_RESETCONTENT message deletes all items from the list box.

Return Value There is no return value.

Related Messages LB_DELETESTRING

LB_SELECTSTRING

wParam Specifies the index of the item just prior to the first item to search. If wParam is set to –1, the search begins at the top of the list.

lParam Points to the null-terminated prefix string.

Description The LB_SELECTSTRING message selects the item from the list box of a combo box that matches the string pointed to by lParam. The search begins with the next item after the item specified in wParam. The search continues down the list and begins again at the top if no match is found by the time the bottom of the list is reached. The last item searched is the item specified in wParam. The search is not case sensitive.

Return Value The index of the selected item is returned when successful. When unsuccessful, LB_ERR is returned.

Related Messages LB_FINDSTRING

LB_SELITEMRANGE

wParam Specifies the selection setting. When wParam is a nonzero value, the specified items are selected and highlighted. When wParam is zero, the items are not selected and not highlighted (any existing highlights are removed).

lParam The low-order word of lParam contains the item index of the first item. The high-order word of lParam contains the item index of the last item.

Description The LB_SELITEMRANGE sets the selection settings for a range of items in a multi-selection list box. The first item to set is specified in the low-order word of lParam. The high-order word of lParam specifies the last item.

Return Value LB_ERR is returned when unsuccessful.

Related Messages LB_GETSELITEMS

LB_SETCARETINDEX

wParam Specifies the index of the item that is to receive the focus rectangle.

lParam Not used.

Description The LB_SETCARETINDEX message gives the focus rectangle to the item specified in wParam from a multi-selection list box.

Return Value LB_ERR is returned when unsuccessful.

Related Messages LB_GETCARETINDEX

LB_SETCOLUMNWIDTH

wParam Specifies the column width in pixels.

lParam Not used.

Description The LB_SETCOLUMNWIDTH message defines the column width, in pixels, for a multi-column list box with style LBS_MULTICOLUMN. The column width is specified in wParam.

Return Value There is no return value.

Related Messages LB_GETHORIZONTALEXTENT, LB_SETHORIZONTALEXTENT

LB_SETCURSEL

wParam Specifies the index of the string to select. When wParam is –1, nothing is selected.

lParam Not used.

Description The LB_SETCURSEL message selects the string specified in wParam. If the selected string is not visible in the list box, the string is scrolled into view. This message is used with single-selection list boxes.

Return Value LB_ERR is returned when unsuccessful or when wParam is set to –1.

Related Messages LB_GETCURSEL

LB_SETHORIZONTALEXTENT

wParam Specifies the horizontal scroll width in pixels.

lParam Not used.

Description The LB_SETHORIZONTALEXTENT message sets the horizontal scroll width of a list box to the value specified in wParam. The horizontal scroll width is the width that a list box can be scrolled horizontally. The list box must have the style WS_HSCROLL.

Return Value There is no return value.

Related Messages LB_GETHORIZONTALEXTENT

LB_SETITEMDATA

wParam Specifies the item index of the item to which the new data will be attached.

lParam Specifies the value to associate with the item in wParam.

Description The LB_SETITEMDATA message associates the 32-bit value in lParam with the item identified by the index specified in wParam.

Return Value LB_ERR is returned when unsuccessful.

Related Messages LB_GETITEMDATA

LB_SETITEMHEIGHT

wParam Specifies the index of the item when the list box has the LBS_OWNERDRAWVARIABLE style. If the list box does not have the LBS_OWNERDRAWVARIABLE style, wParam should be zero.

lParam Specifies the height, in pixels, of the item.

Description The LB_SETITEMHEIGHT message sets the height of the item specified in wParam to the value specified in lParam when the list box has style LBS_OWNERDRAWVARIABLE. If the list box does not have the LBS_OWNERDRAWVARIABLE style, all items in the list box are set to the specified height.

Return Value LB_ERR is returned when unsuccessful.

Related Messages LB_GETITEMHEIGHT

LB_SETSEL

wParam Specifies the selection setting. When wParam is TRUE, the specified items are selected and highlighted. When wParam is FALSE, the items are not selected and highlighting is removed.

lParam The low-order word of lParam specifies the index of the string to set. When lParam is –1, all items are either selected or unselected, depending upon wParam.

Description The LB_SETSEL message either selects or unselects a string from a multi-selection list box. The string is specified in lParam. wParam specifies whether the string will be selected or unselected. This message is for use with multi-selection list boxes.

Return Value LB_ERR is returned when unsuccessful.

Related Messages LB_GETSEL

LB_SETTABSTOPS

wParam Defines the number of tab stops in the list box.

lParam Points to the first member of the array that contains the tab stop positions. Tab stop positions are measured in dialog units.

Description The LB_SETTABSTOPS message positions the tab stops for a list box. wParam defines the number of tab stops. lParam points to the first member of the array that contains the tab stop positions. The list box must have the style LBS_USETABSTOPS. The relationship between wParam and lParam is as follows:

When wParam is zero and lParam is NULL, the tab stops are set every two dialog units.

When wParam is 1, lParam specifies the distance between tab stops.

When lParam points to more than one value, a tab stop will be set for each value of lParam.

Return Value A nonzero value is returned when successful. Zero is returned when unsuccessful.

Related Messages EM_SETTABSTOPS

LB_SETTOPINDEX

wParam Specifies the index of the list box item.

lParam Not used.

Description The LB_SETTOPINDEX message makes the list box item specified in wParam the first visible item in the list box .

Return Value LB_ERR is returned when unsuccessful.

Related Messages LB_GETTOPINDEX

LBN_DBLCLK

wParam Specifies the control ID of the list box.

lParam The low-order word of lParam contains the list box control handle. The high-order word of lParam contains the LBN_DBLCLK code. The list box control must have the style LBS_NOTIFY.

Description The LBN_DBLCLK code is sent through a WM_COMMAND message to the parent window of the list box control when a string from the list box has been double-clicked.

Related Messages WM_COMMAND

LBN_ERRSPACE

wParam Specifies the control ID of the list box.

lParam The low-order word of lParam contains the list box control handle. The high-order word of lParam contains the LBN_ERRSPACE code.

Description The LBN_ERRSPACE code is sent through a WM_COMMAND message to the parent window of the list box control when the list box control is unable to allocate the memory it needs.

Related Messages WM_COMMAND

LBN_KILLFOCUS

wParam Specifies the control ID of the list box.

lParam The low-order word of lParam contains the list box control handle. The high-order word of lParam contains the LBN_KILLFOCUS code.

Description The LBN_KILLFOCUS code is sent through a WM_COMMAND message to the parent window of a list box control when the list box loses the input focus.

Related Messages LBN_SETFOCUS, WM_COMMAND

LBN_SELCHANGE

wParam Specifies the control ID of the list box.

lParam The low-order word of lParam contains the list box control handle. The high-order word of lParam contains the LBN_SELCHANGE code.

Description The LBN_SELCHANGE code is sent through a WM_COMMAND message to the parent window of a list box control when a selection in the list box has been modified. The list box must have the style LBS_NOTIFY.

Related Messages LBN_DBLCLK, WM_COMMAND

LBN_SETFOCUS

wParam Specifies the control ID of the list box.

lParam The low-order word of lParam contains the list box control handle. The high-order word of lParam contains the LBN_SETFOCUS code.

Description The LBN_SETFOCUS code is sent through a WM_COMMAND message to the parent window of a list box when the list box receives the input focus.

Related Messages LBN_KILLFOCUS, WM_COMMAND

STM_GETICON

wParam Not used.

lParam Not used.

Description The STM_GETICON message retrieves the handle of the icon that is associated with an icon control.

Return Value When successful, the handle of the associated icon is returned. Zero is returned when no icon is associated with the icon control or when an error occurs.

Related Messages STM_SETICON

STM_SETICON

wParam Contains the handle of the icon to be associated with the icon control.

lParam Not used.

Description The STM_SETICON message associates the icon specified in wParam with an icon control.

Return Value The handle of the icon that was previously associated with the icon control is returned when successful. Zero is returned when unsuccessful.

Related Messages STM_GETICON

WM_ACTIVATE

wParam Specifies the state of the window. The following values are used for wParam:

Value	*Meaning*
WA_INACTIVE	Window is being deactivated
WA_ACTIVE	Window is being activated without a mouse click
WA_CLICKACTIVE	Window is being activated with a mouse click

lParam Set as follows:

When the window is minimized, the high-order word of lParam is nonzero. When the window is not minimized, the high-order word of lParam is zero. The low-order word of lParam contains a handle to the window being activated or deactivated.

Description The WM_ACTIVATE message is sent whenever a window is activated or deactivated. The window that is being deactivated receives this message before the window that is being activated.

Return Value Zero should be returned by the application if the message is processed.

Related Messages WM_ACTIVATEAPP, WM_MOUSEACTIVATE, WM_NCACTIVATE

WM_ACTIVATEAPP

wParam A nonzero value when a window is to be activated. wParam is zero when a window is to be deactivated.

lParam When wParam is a nonzero value, the low-order word of lParam specifies the task handle of the application that owns the window to be deactivated. When wParam is zero, the low-order word of lParam specifies the task handle of the application that owns the window to be activated. The high-order word of lParam is not used.

Description The WM_ACTIVATEAPP message is sent to the applications whose windows are being activated and deactivated whenever the window being activated belongs to a different task than the currently active window.

Return Value Zero should be returned by the application if the message is processed.

Related Messages WM_ACTIVATE

WM_ASKCBFORMATNAME

wParam Specifies the maximum number of bytes to copy.

lParam Points to the buffer where the copied format name is to be placed.

Description The WM_ASKCBFORMATNAME message is sent when the following conditions are met:

- The clipboard contains a data handle for the CF_OWNERDISPLAY format.
- The clipboard requests a copy of the format name.

wParam specifies the maximum number of bytes to copy into the buffer pointed to by lParam.

Return Value Zero should be returned by the application if the message is processed.

Related Messages WM_DRAWCLIPBOARD, WM_PAINTCLIPBOARD

WM_CANCELMODE

wParam Not used.

lParam Not used.

Description The `WM_CANCELMODE` message cancels the current system mode. This message is sent whenever a message box is displayed.

Return Value Zero should be returned by the application if the message is processed.

Related Messages None

WM_CHANGECBCHAIN

wParam Contains the window handle that is being removed from the clipboard viewer chain.

lParam The low-order word of `lParam` contains the window handle for the window that follows the window specified in `wParam`.

Description The `WM_CHANGECBCHAIN` message is sent to the first window in the clipboard-viewer chain to indicate that a window is being removed from the chain. Each window that receives this message should send the message to the next window in the clipboard viewer chain using the `SendMessage` function. `wParam` contains the window handle of the window being removed from the chain. The low-order word of `lParam` contains the window handle of the window that follows the window in `wParam`.

Return Value There is no meaningful return value. Zero should be returned by the application if the message is processed.

Related Messages `WM_DESTROYCLIPBOARD`, `WM_DRAWCLIPBOARD`

WM_CHAR

wParam Contains the virtual key code value of the key.

lParam Contains a 32-bit value. This value represents the repeat count, scan code key-transition code, previous key state, and context code as follows:

Bits	*Value*
0-15	The number of times the keystroke is repeated
16-23	Scan code
24	Set to 1 if extended key

Bits	Value
25-26	Not used
27-28	Used only by Windows
29	Context code; set to 1 if ALT key is pressed
30	Previous state; 1 if key is down before message is sent
31	Transition state; 1 if key is being released

Description The WM_CHAR message is sent whenever a WM_KEYUP and WM_KEYDOWN message are translated. wParam and lParam contain information about the key being pressed or released.

Return Value Zero should be returned by the application if the message is processed.

Related Messages WM_KEYDOWN, WM_KEYUP

WM_CHARTOITEM

wParam Contains the value of the pressed key.

lParam The low-order word of lParam contains the window handle of the list box. The high-order word of lParam contains the current caret position.

Description The WM_CHARTOITEM message is sent in response to a WM_CHAR message. A list box with the style LBS_WANTKEYBOARDINPUT sends this message to its owner. This message is received only by owner draw list boxes that do not have the LBS_HASSTRINGS style.

Return Value A –2 is returned when the application needs no further action from the list box. A –1 is returned when the list box should perform the default action. A return value of zero or greater (where the return value represents the index to an item in the list box) is returned when the list box should perform the action for the list box item that corresponds to the returned index number.

Related Messages WM_CHAR, WM_VKEYTOITEM

WM_CHILDACTIVATE

wParam Not used.

lParam Not used.

Description The WM_CHILDACTIVATE message is sent to a child window when the title bar of the window is clicked or the window is sized or moved. For MDI child windows, the message is sent when the title bar is clicked or the window is activated, moved, or sized.

Return Value Zero should be returned by the application if the message is processed.

Related Messages WM_ACTIVATE, WM_NCACTIVATE

WM_CHOOSEFONT_GETLOGFONT

wParam Not used.

lParam Pointer to a LOGFONT data structure where information on the current logical font is stored.

Description The WM_CHOOSEFONT_GETLOGFONT message is sent by an application to the Font dialog box to get information about the current font. The Font dialog box is created by the ChooseFont function. The current LOGFONT data structure contains information about the current font.

Return Value There is no return value.

Related Messages WM_GETFONT

WM_CLEAR

wParam Not used.

lParam Not used.

Description The WM_CLEAR message deletes the current selection in an edit control.

Return Value A nonzero value is returned when the message is sent to an edit control or a combo box.

Related Messages WM_COPY, WM_CUT, WM_PASTE

WM_CLOSE

wParam Not used.

lParam Not used.

Description The WM_CLOSE message is sent whenever a window or application should close.

Return Value Zero should be returned by the application if the message is processed.

Related Messages WM_DESTROY, WM_QUIT

WM_COMMAND

wParam Contains a menu item or control ID.

lParam When wParam contains a control ID, the low-order word of lParam contains the window handle of the control; the high-order word contains the notification code. The high word of the lParam is 1 if the message was from an accelerator. It is zero if the message was sent from a menu.

Description The WM_COMMAND message is sent when a menu item is selected, a control passes a message to its parent window, or an accelerator keystroke is translated.

Return Value Zero should be returned by the application if the message is processed.

Related Messages WM_SYSCOMMAND

WM_COMMNOTIFY

wParam Contains the ID of the communication device.

lParam The low-order word of lParam contains the notification status. The high-order word of lParam contains zero. The following values are used for the low-order word of lParam:

Value	*Meaning*
CN__EVENT	An event has occurred that was enabled in the event word of the communication device
CN_RECEIVE	The number of bytes specified by the cbWriteNotify parameter of the EnableCommNotification function, at a minimum, are in the input queue
CN_TRANSMIT	There are fewer bytes in the output queue than were specified in the cbOutQueue parameter of the EnableCommNotification function

Description The WM_COMMNOTIFY message is sent when a COM port event occurs and indicates the status of the input and output queues of the window.

Return Value Zero should be processed by the application if the message is processed.

Related Messages None

WM_COMPACTING

wParam Specifies the ratio of CPU time Windows spends compacting memory.

lParam Not used.

Description The WM_COMPACTING message is sent to all top-level windows when Windows is spending more than 12.5% of its CPU time compacting memory. This message is usually an indicator that memory is running low and the application should free as much memory as possible.

Return Value Zero should be processed by the application if the message is processed.

Related Messages None

WM_COMPAREITEM

wParam ID of the control that sent the WM_COMPAREITEM message.

lParam Pointer to a structure of type COMPAREITEMSTRUCT that contains the identifiers and data for two items of the combo or list box. The COMPAREITEMSTRUCT structure follows.

```
typedef struct tagCOMPAREITEMSTRUCT {
     WORD CtlType;
     WORD CtlID;
     HWND hwndItem;
     WORD itemID1;
     DWORD itemData1;
     WORD itemID2;
     DWORD itemData2;
} COMPAREITEMSTRUCT;
```

in which

CtlType is ODT_LISTBOX for owner draw list box or ODT_COMBOBOX for owner draw combo box

CtlID is the control ID for the list or combo box

hwndItem is the window handle of the control

itemID1 is the first-item index to compare from the list or combo box

itemData1 is the application-supplied data for the first item to compare

itemID2 is the second-item index to compare from the list or combo box

itemData2 is the application-supplied data for the second item to compare.

Description The WM_COMPAREITEM message determines the position of a new item for a sorted owner draw combo box or list box. This message is often sent several times to determine the position of the new item. This message is sent to the owner of a combo box or list box created with the CBS_SORT or LBS_SORT style.

Return Value The position of one item, relative to the other, is returned as follows:

Value	Meaning
–1	Item 1 before Item 2
0	Items are the same
1	Item 2 before Item 1

Related Messages WM_DELETEITEM

WM_COPY

wParam Not used.

lParam Not used.

Description The WM_COPY message copies the current selection onto the clipboard using the CF_TEXT format.

Return Value TRUE is returned when the message is sent to an edit control or a combo box.

Related Messages WM_CUT, WM_PASTE

WM_CREATE

wParam Not used.

lParam Points to data structure of type CREATESTRUCT that contains the parameters passed to the CreateWindowEx function. The CREATESTRUCT structure follows.

```
typedef struct tagCREATESTRUCT {
     LPSTR lpCreateParams;
     HANDLE hInstance;
     HANDLE hMenu;
     HWND hwndParent;
     int cy;
     int cx;
     int y;
     int x;
     LONG style;
     LPSTR lpszName;
     LPSTR lpszClass;
     DWORD dwExStyle;
} CREATESTRUCT;
```

in which

`lpCreateParams` points to data to create the window

`hInstance` is the module instance handle of the module that owns the new window

`hMenu` is the menu the new window will use

`hwndParent` is the window that owns the created window

`cy` is the height of the created window

`cx` is the width of the created window

`y` is the vertical coordinate of the upper-left corner of the created window

`x` is the horizontal coordinate of the upper-left corner of the created window

`style` is the style for the created window

`lpszName` is the name for the created window

`lpszClass` is the string that specifies the class name of the created window

`dwExStyle` is the extended style for the created window.

Description The `WM_CREATE` message is sent by the `CreateWindow` or `CreateWindowEx` function to allow the window procedure to perform initialization.

Return Value When the application processes this message, it returns zero to create the window and –1 to destroy the window. If the window is not created, the `CreateWindow` or `CreateWindowEx` function will return `NULL`.

Related Messages `WM_NCCREATE`

WM_CTLCOLOR

wParam Specifies the handle for the display context for the child window.

lParam The low-order word of `lParam` contains the handle for the child window. The high-order word of `lParam` specifies the type of control. The high-order word is selected from the following:

Value	*Meaning*
CTLCOLOR_BTN	Button control
CTLCOLOR_DLG	Dialog Box
CTLCOLOR_EDIT	Edit control
CTLCOLOR_LISTBOX	List box control
CTLCOLOR_MSGBOX	Message box
CTLCOLOR_SCROLLBAR	Scroll bar control
CTLCOLOR_STATIC	Static control

Description The WM_CTLCOLOR message is sent to the parent window of the control or message box to be drawn. The parent window is then able to set the background and text colors for the child window.

Return Value Applications that process this message should return a handle to the brush that is used for painting the control background. Otherwise, NULL should be returned.

Related Messages WM_PAINT, WM_PAINTICON

WM_CUT

wParam Not used.

lParam Not used.

Description The WM_CUT messages copies the current selection onto the clipboard in CF_TEXT format. The selection is then deleted from the control window.

Return Value TRUE is returned when the message is sent to an edit control or combo box.

Related Messages WM_COPY, WM_PASTE

WM_DDE_ACK

wParam Specifies the handle of the window that posts the message.

lParam Contains one of the following, depending on the message to which WM_DDE_ACK is responding:

`WM_DDE_INITIATE:`

The low-order word of `lParam` (`aApplication`) contains the name of the replying application. The high-order word of `lParam` (`aTopic`) contains the topic associated with the replying server window.

`WM_DDE_EXECUTE:`

The low-order word of `lParam` (`wStatus`) contains a series of flags that indicate the response status. The high-order word of `lParam` (`hCommands`) contains the handle of the data item that contains the command string.

All other messages:

The low-order word of `lParam` (`wStatus`) contains a series of flags that indicate the status of the response. The high-order word of `lParam` (`aItem`) identifies the item for which the response is sent.

When the low-order word of `lParam` is `wStatus` and contains a series of status flags, the following information is provided in a `DDEACK` data structure:

Bit	*Name*	*Meaning*
15	`fAck`	1 = Request accepted; 0 = request not accepted
14	`fBusy`	1= busy; 0 = not busy
13-8	Reserved	
7-0	`bAppReturnCode`	Application-specific return codes

Description The `WM_DDE_ACK` message tells the application that a `WM_DDE_INITIATE`, `WM_DDE_EXECUTE`, `WM_DDE_DATA`, `WM_DDE_ADVISE`, `WM_DDE_UNADVISE`, `WM_DDE_POKE`, or `WM_DDE_REQUEST` message has been received.

Posting:

The `WM_DDE_ACK` message is posted using the `PostMessage` function when responding to all messages except `WM_DDE_INITIATE`. The `WM_DDE_ACK` message is posted using `SendMessage` in response to `WM_DDE_INITIATE`.

Receiving:

Applications that receive the `WM_DDE_ACK` message should delete all atoms that accompany the message. When `WM_DDE_ACK` is received with an accompanying `hData` object, the `hData` object should be deleted. If a negative WM_DDE_ACK message is received in response to WM_DDE_ADVISE, the hOptions object should be deleted. If a negative WM_DDE_ACK message is received in response to WM_DDE_EXECUTE, the hCommands object should be deleted.

Related Messages WM_DDE_INITIATE, WM_DDE_EXECUTE, WM_DDE_DATA, WM_DDE_ADVISE, WM_DDE_UNADVISE, WM_DDE_POKE, WM_DDE_REQUEST

WM_DDE_ADVISE

wParam Specifies the sending window.

lParam The low-order word of lParam (hOptions) is a handle to a global memory object specifying the method for sending the data. The high-order word of lParam (aItem) is an atom that specifies the requested data item.

Description The WM_DDE_ADVISE message is posted by a client application to request a data item update from the server application. wParam specifies the sending window. lParam specifies the data requested and the means to send the data.

hOptions contains a DDEADVISE data structure as follows:

Word	*Name*	*Meaning*
1	fAckReq	When bit 15 is 1, the server application should send the WM_DDE_DATA message with fAckReq set.
	fDeferUpd	When bit 14 is 1, the server should send the WM_DDE_DATA message with a NULL hData handle.
	Reserved	Bits 13-0 are reserved.
2	cfFormat	Specifies the data type requested by the client application. cfFormat must specify a standard or registered clipboard data format number.

Posting:

The WM_DDE_ADVISE message is posted using the PostMessage function. hOptions is allocated with the GlobalAlloc function

(use the GMEM_DDE_SHARE option). aItem is allocated using the GlobalAddAtom function.

Receiving:

The WM_DDE_ACK message is posted for both positive and negative responses. When the WM_DDE_ACK message is negative, the hOptions object should be deleted.

Related Messages WM_DDE_ACK, WM_DDE_DATA

WM_DDE_DATA

wParam Specifies the window that is posting the message.

lParam The low-order word of lParam (hData) contains the handle identifying the global memory object that contains the data. hData should be set to NULL when the data has changed during a warm link (client sends a WM_DDE_ADVISE message with the fDeferUpd bit set). The high-order word of lParam (aItem) specifies the data item.

Description The WM_DDE_DATA message is posted by the server application and sends a data item value to the client application. The WM_DDE_DATA message can also be used to notify the client that data is available.

hData identifies a global memory object consisting of two words. The first word contains one or more of the following flags:

0x8000	Application receiving WM_DDE_DATA message should send WM_DDE_ACK to acknowledge receipt of data.
0x2000	Application receiving WM_DDE_DATA message should free the memory specified in low-order word of lParam.
0x1000	Data was sent in response to WM_DDE_REQUEST. When this flag is not set, the data was sent in response to a WM_DDE_ADVISE message.

The second word specifies the data format. The data format can be any standard or registered clipboard format. The standard clipboard formats follow:

```
CF_BITMAP
CF_DIB
CF_DIF
CF_METAFILEPICT
CF_OEMTEXT
CF_PALETTE
CF_SYLK
CF_TEXT
CF_TIFF
```

Posting:

The WM_DDE_DATA message is posted using PostMessage. hData is allocated using GlobalAlloc (with the GMEM_DDESHARE option). aItem is allocated using GlobalAddAtom.

Receiving:

When fAckReq is 1, the WM_DDE_ACK message is used to respond positively or negatively. When fAckReq is 0, aItem should be deleted. If hData is specified as NULL, the client application can post the WM_DDE_REQUEST message to request the data. When hData is not NULL, and after the WM_DDE_DATA message has been processed, hData can be deleted unless the fRelease flag is zero or the fRelease flag is 1 while the client application responds with a negative WM_DDE_ACK message.

Related Messages WM_DDE_POKE, WM_DDE_REQUEST

WM_DDE_EXECUTE

wParam Specifies the sending window.

lParam The low-order word of lParam is reserved. The high-order word of lParam (hCommands) identifies a global memory object that contains the commands to be executed.

Description The WM_DDE_EXECUTE message is posted by a client application and sends a command string to the server application. The null-terminated command string contains one or more opcode strings formatted as follows:

```
opcode[[(parameter[[,parameter]]...)]]
```

in which opcode is the application-defined single token, parameter is an application-defined value, and double brackets ([[ ]]) are optional syntax elements.

The server application should post the WM_DDE_ACK message in response to the WM_DDE_EXECUTE message.

Posting:

The WM_DDE_EXECUTE message is posted using the PostMessage function. hCommands is allocated using GlobalAlloc (use the GMEM_DDESHARE option).

Receiving:

The WM_DDE_ACK message is posted using the hCommands object to respond positively or negatively.

Related Messages WM_DDE_ACK

WM_DDE_INITIATE

wParam Specifies the sending window.

lParam The low-order word of lParam (aApplication) contains an atom specifying the name of the application. If aApplication is NULL, conversation with all applications is requested. The high-order word of lParam (aTopic) specifies the topic for conversation. If aTopic is NULL, all topics are available.

Description The WM_DDE_INITIATE message initiates conversations with applications that respond to the application and topic specified in lParam. Clients send this message. All server applications that have names and topics matching those specified in lParam are expected to respond with the WM_DDE_ACK message when receiving the WM_DDE_INITIATE message.

Sending:

The WM_DDE_INITIATE message is sent using the SendMessage function. The message is sent to all windows when the first parameter of SendMessage is –1. aApplication and aTopic are allocated using GlobalAddAtom.

Receiving:

The WM_DDE_ACK message is used to complete the initiation of a conversation. One WM_DDE_ACK message is sent for each topic.

New aApplication and aTopic atoms should be created for the WM_DDE_ACK message.

Related Messages WM_DDE_ACK

WM_DDE_POKE

wParam Specifies the handle of the posting window.

lParam The low-order word of lParam (hData) specifies the handle of the data. The high-order word of lParam (aItem) contains the global atom identifying the data being sent.

Description The WM_DDE_POKE message is sent by the client application to send unexpected data to a server application. The server is expected to acknowledge this message with the WM_DDE_ACK message. WM_DDE_POKE can be sent with either the SendMessage or PostMessage functions. With SendMessage, the sending application will not continue until the server has processed the message. With PostMessage, the sending application continues to execute and the message is placed in the server's message queue.

Related Messages WM_DDE_DATA

WM_DDE_REQUEST

wParam Specifies the sending window.

lParam The low-order word of lParam (cfFormat) contains a standard or registered clipboard format number. The high-order word of lParam (aItem) contains an atom that specifies the requested data item.

Description The WM_DDE_REQUEST message is posted by a client application and requests that the server application provide the value of a data item.

Posting:

The WM_DDE_REQUEST message is posted using the PostMessage function. aItem is allocated using the GlobalAddAtom function.

Receiving:

The server application sends either the WM_DDE_DATA message containing the data or a negative WM_DDE_ACK message.

WM_DDE_TERMINATE

wParam Specifies the sending window.

lParam Not used.

Description The WM_DDE_TERMINATE message terminates a conversation and can be posted by either a client or server application.

Posting:

The WM_DDE_TERMINATE message is posted using the PostMessage function. The sending application should not acknowledge any other messages sent by the receiving application.

Receiving:

The receiving application should respond by posting a WM_DDE_TERMINATE message.

Related Messages WM_DDE_INITIATE

WM_DDE_UNADVISE

wParam Specifies the sending window.

lParam The low-order word of lParam (cfFormat) specifies the clipboard format of the data item specifying the clipboard format. cfFormat can be set to NULL to terminate all conversations for the item. The high-order word of lParam (aItem) specifies the data for which the update request is being retracted. If aItem is NULL, all WM_DDE_ADVISE conversations associated with the client are terminated.

Description The WM_DDE_UNADVISE message is sent by the client application to inform the server application that the specified item or clipboard format should not be updated.

Posting:

The WM_DDE_UNADVISE message is posted using the PostMessage function. aItem is allocated using the GlobalAddAtom function.

Receiving:

The WM_DDE_ACK message is posted to respond either positively or negatively.

Related Messages WM_DDE_ACK, WM_DDE_ADVISE

WM_DEADCHAR

wParam Holds the character value of the dead key.

lParam The value in lParam represents the repeat count, the scan code, the previous key state, and context code. The bits of this value are interpreted as follows:

Bits	*Meaning*
0-15	Repeat count: the number of times the keystroke is repeated
16-23	Scan code
24	1 if dead key is an extended key
25-26	Not used
27-28	Used only by Windows
29	Context code; 1 if ALT key is pressed
30	Previous key state; 1 if key is down before the message is sent
31	Transition state; 1 if key is being released

Description The WM_DEADCHAR message is sent when a WM_KEYUP and a WM_KEYDOWN message are translated. wParam specifies the character value of the dead key. A dead key character value is one that is combined with other character values to form a distinct character.

Return Value Zero should be returned by the application if the message is processed.

Related Messages WM_KEYDOWN, WM_KEYUP

WM_DELETEITEM

wParam ID of control that sent the WM_DELETEITEM message.

lParam Points to a data structure of type DELETEITEMSTRUCT that contains information on the deleted item. The DELETEITEMSTRUCT structure follows.

```
typedef struct tagDELETEITEMSTRUCT
 {
     WORD CtlType;
     WORD CtlID;
     WORD itemID;
     HWND hwndItem;
     DWORD itemData;
 } DELETEITEMSTRUCT;
```

in which

CtlType is ODT_LISTBOX for owner draw list box or ODT_COMBOBOX for owner draw combo box

CtlID is the control ID for the list or combo box

itemID is the item index for the deleted item

hwndItem is the window handle of the control

itemData is the value passed to the control in lParam from LB_INSERTSTRING, LB_ADDSTRING, CB_INSERTSTRING, or CB_ADDSTRING when the item was originally added to the list box.

Description The WM_DELETEITEM message is sent to the owner of an owner draw list or combo box when the list or combo box is destroyed, or an item is removed using LB_DELETESTRING, LB_RESETCONTENT, CB_DELETESTRING, or CB_RESETCONTENT.

Return Value Zero should be returned by the application if the message is processed.

Related Messages CB_DELETESTRING, CB_RESETCONTENT, LB_DELETESTRING, LB_RESETCONTENT

WM_DESTROY

wParam Not used.

lParam Not used.

Description The `WM_DESTROY` message is sent to the window procedure of a window to notify the window that it is being destroyed.

Return Value Zero should be returned by the application if the message is processed.

Related Messages `WM_CLOSE`

WM_DESTROYCLIPBOARD

wParam Not used:

lParam Not used.

Description The `WM_DESTROYCLIPBOARD` message is sent to the owner of the clipboard whenever the contents of the clipboard are emptied by a call to the `EmptyClipboard` function.

Return Value Zero should be returned by the application if the message is processed.

Related Messages `WM_DRAWCLIPBOARD`

WM_DEVMODECHANGE

wParam Not used.

lParam Points to the specified device name in WIN.INI (the Windows initialization file).

Description The `WM_DEVMODECHANGE` message is sent to all top-level windows when device mode settings are modified.

Return Value Zero should be returned by the application if the message is processed.

Related Messages `WM_WININICHANGE`

WM_DRAWCLIPBOARD

wParam Not used.

lParam Not used.

Description The WM_DRAWCLIPBOARD message is sent to the first window of the clipboard viewer chain whenever the contents of the clipboard are modified. Each window that receives this message should pass it to the next window in the clipboard viewer chain using the SendMessage function.

Return Value Zero should be returned by the application if the message is processed.

Related Messages WM_PAINTCLIPBOARD

WM_DRAWITEM

wParam ID of the control that sent the WM_DRAWITEM message. Zero if message is sent by a menu.

lParam Points to a structure of type DRAWITEMSTRUCT which contains information about the item to draw. The DRAWITEMSTRUCT structure follows.

```
typedef struct tagDRAWITEMSTRUCT
 {
     WORD CtlType;
     WORD CtlID;
     WORD itemID;
     WORD itemAction;
     WORD itemState;
     HWND hwndItem;
     HDC hDC;
     RECT rcItem;
     DWORD itemData;
 } DRAWITEMSTRUCT;
```

in which

CtlType is the control type—ODT_BUTTON for owner draw button, ODT_COMBOBOX for owner draw combo box, ODT_LISTBOX for owner draw list box, ODT_MENU for owner draw menu

CtlID is the control ID for the combo box, list box, or button

itemID is the menu item ID (for a menu) or the item index (for a list box or combo box)

itemAction is the drawing action—ODA_DRAWENTIRE when the entire control needs to be redrawn, ODA_FOCUS when the control gets or loses the input focus, ODA_SELECT when the selection status changes

itemState is the state of the item after drawing—ODS_CHECKED when the menu item is to be checked, ODS_DISABLED to disable the item, ODS_FOCUS when the item has the input focus, ODS_GRAYED when the item is grayed, ODS_SELECTED when the item is selected

hwndItem is the window handle of the control

hDC is the device context

rcItem is a rectangle in the device context that defines the boundaries of the control

itemData is the value passed in lParam from CB_ADDSTRING, CB_INSERTSTRING, LB_ADDSTRING, or LB_INSERTSTRING.

Description The WM_DRAWITEM message is sent to an owner draw button, a combo box, a list box, or a menu when the control has visually changed.

Return Value Zero should be returned by the application if the message is processed.

Related Messages WM_COMPAREITEM, WM_DELETEITEM

WM_DROPFILES

wParam Contains a handle to the internal data structure that describes the dropped files.

lParam Not used.

Description The WM_DROPFILES message is sent when the selected files are released over an application window that is registered to receive dropped files. The handle specified in wParam is used by the DragFinish, DragQueryFile, and DragQueryPoint functions to retrieve information on the dropped files.

Return Value Zero should be returned by the application if the message is processed.

Related Messages None

WM_ENABLE

wParam TRUE when the window has been enabled; FALSE when the window has been disabled.

lParam Not used.

Description The WM_ENABLE message is sent whenever a window has been enabled or disabled. wParam specifies whether the window was enabled or disabled.

Return Value Zero should be returned by the application if the message is processed.

Related Messages WM_ACTIVATE

WM_ENDSESSION

wParam TRUE when the session is ending. wParam is FALSE when the session is not ending.

lParam Not used.

Description The WM_ENDSESSION message is sent to an application that returns TRUE in response to the WM_QUERYENDSESSION message. The value in wParam indicates whether the session is actually ending.

Return Value Zero should be returned by the application if the message is processed.

Related Messages WM_QUERYENDSESSION

WM_ENTERIDLE

wParam Indicates whether the message resulted from the displaying of a dialog box or menu. The following values are used for wParam:

Value	*Meaning*
MSGF_DIALOGBOX	Dialog box is being displayed
MSGF_MENU	Menu is being displayed

lParam The low-order word of lParam contains the handle of the dialog box, when wParam is MSGF_DIALOGBOX, or the handle of the window that contains the menu, when wParam is MSGF_MENU. The high-order word of lParam is not used.

Description The WM_ENTERIDLE message is sent to an application's main window procedure when a modal dialog box or menu is going into an idle state.

Return Value Zero should be returned by the application if the message is processed.

Related Messages None

WM_ERASEBKGND

wParam Contains the device context handle.

lParam Not used.

Description The WM_ERASEBKGND message is sent when the background of a window needs repainting. The class background brush specified in the hbrbackground field of the class structure is used to erase the background.

Return Value If the background is successfully erased, TRUE is returned. FALSE is returned when unsuccessful.

Related Messages WM_ICONERASEBKGND, WM_PAINT

WM_FONTCHANGE

wParam Not used.

lParam Not used.

Description The WM_FONTCHANGE message should be sent to all top-level windows whenever a font resource is added or removed by the application.

Return Value Zero should be returned by the application if the message is processed.

Related Messages WM_GETFONT, WM_SETFONT

WM_GETDLGCODE

wParam Not used.

lParam Not used.

Description The WM_GETDLGCODE message is sent to the input procedure for a control. Windows sends this message to an application so that the application can process certain types of input generally handled by Windows.

Return Value The types of input that the application processed are returned. One or more of the following values is returned:

Value	*Meaning*
DLGC_DEFPUSHBUTTON	Default push button
DLGC_HASSETSEL	EM_SETSEL messages
DLGC_PUSHBUTTON	Push button
DLGC_RADIOBUTTON	Radio button
DLGC_WANTALLKEYS	All keys
DLGC_WANTARROWS	Direction keys
DLGC_WANTCHARS	WM_CHAR messages
DLGC_WANTMESSAGE	All keys; message is passed to control
DLGC_WANTTAB	TAB key

Related Messages EM_SETSEL, WM_CHAR, WM_NEXTDLGCTL

WM_GETFONT

wParam Not used.

lParam Not used.

Description The WM_GETFONT message gets the current font used by a control.

Return Value The handle for the retrieved font is returned. NULL is returned if the control uses the system font.

Related Messages WM_FONTCHANGE, WM_SETFONT

WM_GETHOTKEY

wParam Not used.

lParam Not used.

Description The WM_GETHOTKEY function determines the hot key associated with a window.

Return Value The virtual key code of the hot key associated with the window is returned. NULL is returned if no hot key is associated with the window.

Related Messages WM_SETHOTKEY

WM_GETMINMAXINFO

wParam Not used.

lParam Points to a MINMAXINFO data structure as follows:

```
typedef struct tagMINMAXINFO {
     POINT ptReserved;
     POINT ptMaxSize;
     POINT ptMaxPosition;
     POINT ptMinTrackSize;
     POINT ptMaxTrackSize;
} MINMAXIINFO;
```

in which

ptReserved is reserved

ptMaxSize is the maximized width (.x) and height (.y) of window

ptMaxPosition is left (.x) and top (.y) of maximized window

ptMinTrackSize is the minimum tracking width (.x) and height (.y) of window

ptMaxTrackSize is the maximum tracking width (.x) and height (.y) of window.

Description The WM_GETMINMAXINFO message is sent by Windows to a window to retrieve the maximized window size, the minimum and maximum tracking size, and the maximized window position.

Return Value Zero should be returned by the application if the message is processed.

Related Messages WM_GETTEXTLEN, WM_SIZE

WM_GETTEXT

wParam Contains the maximum number of bytes to copy and includes the null terminator.

lParam Points to the buffer where the text will be placed.

Description The WM_GETTEXT message copies text to a buffer. The contents of the edit control are copied for edit controls including combo box edit controls. The button name is copied for buttons. The selected item is copied from list boxes. The window caption is copied for windows.

Return Value The number of bytes copied is returned. CB_ERR is returned if the combo box does not have an edit control.

Related Messages WM_GETTEXTLENGTH, WM_SETTEXT

WM_GETTEXTLENGTH

wParam Not used.

lParam Not used.

Description The WM_GETTEXTLENGTH message determines the length, in bytes and not including the null terminator, for the specified text. The text in the edit control is evaluated for edit controls and combo box edit controls. The selected item is evaluated for list boxes. The button name is evaluated for button controls. The window caption is evaluated for windows.

Return Value A WORD specifying the number of bytes in the text, not including the null terminator, is returned.

Related Messages LB_GETTEXTLEN, WM_GETTEXT

WM_HSCROLL

wParam Specifies the scroll bar code. The scroll bar code is selected from the following values:

Value	*Meaning*
SB_LEFT	Scroll to far left
SB_LINELEFT	Scroll left
SB_LINERIGHT	Scroll right
SB_PAGELEFT	Scroll one page left
SB_PAGERIGHT	Scroll one page right
SB_RIGHT	Scroll to far right
SB_THUMBPOSITION	Scroll to absolute position; low-order word of lParam contains thumb position
SB_THUMBTRACK	Move thumb position to position specified in low-word of lParam

lParam When the WM_HSCROLL message is sent by a scroll bar control, the high-order word of lParam specifies the window handle for the control. The low-order word is used only if wParam contains SB_THUMBPOSITION or SB_THUMBTRACK.

Description The WM_HSCROLL message is sent when the horizontal scroll bar is clicked and active.

Return Value Zero should be returned by the application if the message is processed.

Related Messages WM_HSCROLLCLIPBOARD, WM_VSCROLL

WM_HSCROLLCLIPBOARD

wParam Contains the clipboard application window handle.

lParam The high-order word of lParam contains the thumb position when the low-order word is SB_THUMBPOSITION. The low-order word of lParam contains the scroll bar code. The scroll bar codes are as follows:

Value	Meaning
SB_BOTTOM	Scroll to lower right
SB_ENDSCROLL	End scroll
SB_LINEDOWN	Scroll down one line
SB_LINEUP	Scroll up one line
SB_PAGEDOWN	Scroll down one page
SB_PAGEUP	Scroll up one page
SB_THUMBPOSITION	Scroll to absolute position. When specified, the high-order word of lParam contains the thumb position of the scroll bar code.
SB_TOP	Scroll to upper left

Description The WM_HSCROLLCLIPBOARD message is sent when the following conditions are met:

- The clipboard contains the data handle for the CF_OWNERDISPLAY format.
- A component of the clipboard application's horizontal scroll bar is selected.

wParam contains the clipboard application window handle. lParam contains the scroll bar code.

Return Value Zero should be returned by the application if the message is processed.

Related Messages WM_HSCROLL, WM_VSCROLLCLIPBOARD

WM_ICONERASEBKGND

wParam Contains the device context handle of the icon.

lParam Not used.

Description The WM_ICONERASEBKGND message is sent to a minimized window when the icon's background has to be filled before the icon is painted. A class icon must be registered for a window to receive this message.

Return Value Zero should be returned by the application if the message is processed.

Related Messages WM_ERASEBKGND

WM_INITDIALOG

wParam Specifies the first item from the dialog box that is able to receive the input focus.

lParam Contains the value passed as the parameter `dwInitParam` when the dialog box was created with the `CreateDialogParam`, `DialogBoxIndirectParam`, or `DialogBoxParam` functions. When the dialog box was not created with any of these functions, `lParam` is not used.

Description The `WM_INITDIALOG` message is sent before a dialog box is displayed. This allows the application to initialize the dialog box before it is displayed. If the application returns a nonzero value when responding to this message, the input focus is given to the control item specified in `wParam`. If `FALSE` is returned by the application, the application must set the input focus.

Return Value `TRUE` is returned by the application to set the input focus to the specified item. `FALSE` is returned if the `SetFocus` function is used to set the input focus.

Related Messages WM_GETDLGCODE, WM_NEXTDLGCTL

WM_INITMENU

wParam Holds the menu handle of the menu to initialize.

lParam Not used.

Description The `WM_INITMENU` message is sent before a menu is displayed. The application, therefore, has the opportunity to initialize the menu.

Return Value Zero should be returned by the application if the message is processed.

Related Messages WM_INITMENUPOPUP

WM_INITMENUPOPUP

wParam Specifies the menu handle of the pop-up menu.

lParam The low-order word of `lParam` specifies the index of the pop-up menu in the main menu. The high-order word of `lParam` contains a nonzero value when the pop-up menu is the system menu. The high-order word contains zero when the pop-up menu is not the system menu.

Description The `WM_INITMENUPOPUP` message is sent before a pop-up menu is displayed. This gives the application the opportunity to initialize the menu before it is displayed.

Return Value Zero should be returned by the application if the message is processed.

Related Messages `WM_INITMENU`

WM_KEYDOWN

wParam Specifies the virtual-key code.

lParam Specifies the repeat count, the scan code, the previous key state, and the context code. The bits in `lParam` are interpreted as follows:

Bits	*Meaning*
0-15	Repeat count: the number of times the keystroke is repeated
16-23	Scan code
24	1 if the key is an extended key
25-26	Not used
27-28	Used only by Windows
29	Context code; 1 if ALT key is down
30	Previous key state; 1 if key is down before the message is sent
31	Transition state; 0 for key being pressed, 1 for key being released

Description The WM_KEYDOWN message is sent when a nonsystem key is pressed. Nonsystem keys are keys that are pressed without holding the ALT key down or keys that are pressed while a window has the input focus.

Return Value Zero should be returned by the application if the message is processed.

Related Messages WM_KEYUP, WM_SYSKEYDOWN

WM_KEYUP

wParam Specifies the virtual-key code.

lParam Specifies the repeat count, the scan code, the previous key state, and the context code. The bits in lParam are interpreted as follows:

Bits	*Meaning*
0-15	Repeat count: the number of times the keystroke is repeated
16-23	Scan code
24	1 if the key is an extended key
25-26	Not used
27-28	Used only by Windows
29	Context code; 1 if ALT key is down
30	Previous key state; 1 if key is down before the message is sent
31	Transition state; 1 for key being released

Description The WM_KEYUP message is sent when a nonsystem key is released. Nonsystem keys are keys that are pressed without holding the ALT key down or keys that are pressed while a window has the input focus.

Return Value Zero should be returned by the application if the message is processed.

Related Messages WM_KEYDOWN, WM_SYSKEYUP

WM_KILLFOCUS

wParam Specifies the handle of the window receiving the input focus.

lParam Not used.

Description The `WM_KILLFOCUS` message is sent just before a window loses the input focus.

Return Value Zero should be returned by the application if the message is processed.

Related Messages `WM_SETFOCUS`

WM_LBUTTONDBLCLK

wParam Indicates which virtual keys are down. The following values, in any combination, indicate the virtual keys that are down:

Value	*Meaning*
MK_CONTROL	Control key is down
MK_LBUTTON	Left button is down
MK_MBUTTON	Middle button is down
MK_RBUTTON	Right button is down
MK_SHIFT	Shift key is down

lParam The low-order word of `lParam` contains the horizontal coordinate of the cursor. The high-order word of `lParam` contains the vertical coordinate of the cursor. These coordinates are expressed relative to the upper-left corner of the window.

Description The `WM_LBUTTONDBLCLK` message is sent when the left mouse button is double-clicked.

Return Value Zero should be returned by the application if the message is processed.

Related Messages `WM_LBUTTONDOWN`, `WM_LBUTTONUP`

WM_LBUTTONDOWN

wParam Indicates which virtual keys are down. The following values, in any combination, indicate the virtual keys that are down:

Value	Meaning
MK_CONTROL	Control key is down
MK_MBUTTON	Middle button is down
MK_RBUTTON	Right button is down
MK_SHIFT	Shift key is down

lParam The low-order word of lParam contains the horizontal coordinate of the cursor. The high-order word of lParam contains the vertical coordinate of the cursor. These coordinates are expressed relative to the upper-left corner of the window.

Description The WM_LBUTTONDOWN message is sent when the left mouse button is pressed.

Return Value Zero should be returned by the application if the message is processed.

Related Messages WM_LBUTTONDBLCLK, WM_RBUTTONDOWN

WM_LBUTTONUP

wParam Indicates which virtual keys are down. The following values, in any combination, indicate the virtual keys that are down:

Value	Meaning
MK_CONTROL	Control key is down
MK_MBUTTON	Middle button is down
MK_RBUTTON	Right button is down
MK_SHIFT	Shift key is down

lParam The low-order word of lParam contains the horizontal coordinate of the cursor. The high-order word of lParam contains the vertical coordinate of the cursor. These coordinates are expressed relative to the upper-left corner of the window.

Description The WM_LBUTTONUP message is sent when the left mouse button is released.

Return Value Zero should be returned by the application if the message is processed.

Related Messages WM_LBUTTONDBLCLK, WM_LBUTTONDOWN

WM_MBUTTONDBLCLK

wParam Indicates which virtual keys are down. The following values, in any combination, indicate the virtual keys that are down:

Value	*Meaning*
MK_CONTROL	Control key is down
MK_LBUTTON	Left button is down
MK_MBUTTON	Middle button is down
MK_RBUTTON	Right button is down
MK_SHIFT	Shift key is down

lParam The low-order word of `lParam` contains the horizontal coordinate of the cursor. The high-order word of `lParam` contains the vertical coordinate of the cursor. These coordinates are expressed relative to the upper-left corner of the window.

Description The `WM_MBUTTONDBLCLK` message is sent when the middle mouse button is double-clicked.

Return Value Zero should be returned by the application if the message is processed.

Related Messages `WM_MBUTTONDOWN`, `WM_MBUTTONUP`

WM_MBUTTONDOWN

wParam Indicates which virtual keys are down. The following values, in any combination, indicate the virtual keys that are down:

Value	*Meaning*
MK_CONTROL	Control key is down
MK_LBUTTON	Left button is down
MK_RBUTTON	Right button is down
MK_SHIFT	Shift key is down

lParam The low-order word of `lParam` contains the horizontal coordinate of the cursor. The high-order word of `lParam` contains the vertical coordinate of the cursor. These coordinates are expressed relative to the upper-left corner of the window.

Description The WM_BUTTONDOWN message is sent when the middle mouse button is pressed.

Return Value Zero should be returned by the application if the message is processed.

Related Messages WM_MBUTTONDBLCLK, WM_MBUTTONUP

WM_MBUTTONUP

wParam Indicates which virtual keys are down. The following values, in any combination, indicate the virtual keys that are down:

Value	*Meaning*
MK_CONTROL	Control key is down
MK_LBUTTON	Left button is down
MK_RBUTTON	Right button is down
MK_SHIFT	Shift key is down

lParam The low-order word of lParam contains the horizontal coordinate of the cursor. The high-order word of lParam contains the vertical coordinate of the cursor. These coordinates are expressed relative to the upper-left corner of the window.

Description The WM_MBUTTONUP message is sent when the middle button is released.

Return Value Zero should be returned by the application if the message is processed.

Related Messages WM_MBUTTONDBLCLK, WM_MBUTTONDOWN

WM_MDIACTIVATE

wParam Contains the window handle of the MDI child window to activate when the application sends the message to the client window. When the client window sends the message to a child window, wParam contains TRUE if the child is to be activated or FALSE if the child is to be deactivated.

lParam The high-order byte of `lParam` contains the window handle of the child window being deactivated and the low-order byte of `lParam` contains the window handle of the child window being activated when the message is sent to an MDI child window. `lParam` is zero when the message is sent to the client window.

Description The `WM_MDIACTIVATE` message is sent by an application to a multiple document interface (MDI) client window. When the client window receives the message, the `WM_MDIACTIVATE` message is sent to the child window to be activated and the child window to be deactivated.

Return Value Zero should be returned by the application if the message is processed.

Related Messages `WM_MDIDESTROY`, `WM_MDIGETACTIVE`

WM_MDICASCADE

wParam Contains the cascade flag `MDITILE_SKIPDISABLED`. This flag prevents disabled MDI child windows from being cascaded.

lParam Not used.

Description The `WM_MDICASCADE` message places the child windows of a multiple document interface (MDI) client window in a cascade fashion.

Return Value Zero should be returned by the application if the message is processed.

Related Messages `WM_MDIICONARRAGE`, `WM_MDITILE`

WM_MDICREATE

wParam Not used.

lParam `lParam` points to the data structure of type `MDICREATESTRUCT`. The `MDICREATESTRUCT` structure follows.

```
typedef struct tagMDICREATESTRUCT{
     LPSTR szClass;
     LPSTR szTitle;
     HANDLE hOwner;
     int x;
     int y;
     int cx;
     int cy;
     LONG style;
     LONG lParam;
 } MDICREATESTRUCT;
```

in which

`szClass` is a pointer to the application-defined class of the MDI child window

`szTitle` is a pointer to the title of the MDI child window

`hOwner` is the instance handle of the application

`x` is the position of the left side of the MDI child window

`y` is the position of the top edge of the MDI child window

`cx` is the width of the child window

`cy` is the height of the child window

`style` is chosen from one or more of the following styles:

Style	*Meaning*
WS_MINIMIZE	MDI child window is minimized when it is created
WS_MAXIMIZE	MDI child window is maximized when it is created
WS_HSCROLL	MDI child window contains a horizontal scroll bar when created
WS_VSCROLL	MDI child window contains a vertical scroll bar when created

and

`lParam` is a 32-bit value defined by the application.

Description The WM_MDICREATE message is sent to the multiple document interface (MDI) client window. A child window is then created with the following style bits:

```
WS_CHILD
WS_CLIPSIBLINGS
WS_CLIPCHILDREN
WS_SYSMENU
WS_CAPTION
WS_THICKFRAME
WS_MINIMIZEBOX
WS_MAXIMIZEBOX
```

The child window may also have additional style bits as defined in the MDICREATESTRUCT structure pointed to by lParam.

Return Value The low-order word of the return value contains the handle of the new window. The high-order word contains zero.

Related Messages WM_MDIACTIVATE, WM_MDIDESTROY

WM_MDIDESTROY

wParam Specifies the handle of the child window to close.

lParam Not used.

Description The WM_MDIDESTROY message is sent to a multiple document interface (MDI) client window. The child window specified in wParam is then closed.

Return Value Zero should be returned by the application if the message is processed.

Related Messages WM_MDIACTIVATE, WM_MDICREATE

WM_MDIGETACTIVE

wParam Not used.

lParam Not used.

Description The WM_MDIGETACTIVE message gets the handle for the active multiple document interface (MDI) child window. In addition, the flag which indicates whether the child window is maximized is also retrieved.

Return Value The low-order word of the return value contains the handle of the active child window. The high-order word of the return value contains 1 when the child window is maximized or 0 when the child window is not maximized.

Related Messages WM_MDIACTIVATE

WM_MDIICONARRANGE

wParam Not used.

lParam Not used.

Description The WM_MDIICONARRANGE message arranges the minimized child windows for a multiple document interface (MDI) client window.

Return Value Zero should be returned by the application if the message is processed.

Related Messages WM_MDICASCADE, WM_MDITILE

WM_MDIMAXIMIZE

wParam Specifies the window handle of the child window.

lParam Not used.

Description The WM_MDIMAXIMIZE message is sent to a multiple document interface (MDI) client window and causes the child window specified in wParam to be maximized.

Return Value Zero should be returned by the application if the message is processed.

Related Messages WM_MDIRESTORE

WM_MDINEXT

wParam Not used.

lParam Not used.

Description The `WM_MDINEXT` message is sent to the multiple document interface (MDI) client window. The message activates the MDI child window that is directly behind the active child window (the formerly active window is then pushed behind all other windows).

Return Value Zero should be returned by the application if the message is processed.

Related Messages `WM_MDIACTIVATE`

WM_MDIRESTORE

wParam Specifies the window handle of the child window to restore.

lParam Not used.

Description The `WM_MDIRESTORE` message restores the multiple document interface (MDI) child window specified in `wParam` from a maximized or minimized state.

Return Value Zero should be returned by the application if the message is processed.

Related Messages `WM_MDIMAXIMIZE`

WM_MDISETMENU

wParam Set to `TRUE` to refresh the current menus. Set to `FALSE` to use the menus in `lParam` as new menus.

lParam The low-order word of `lParam` contains the menu handle of the new frame window menu. The high-order word of `lParam` contains the menu handle of the new pop-up menu. The corresponding menu is not changed if either word is set to zero.

Description The `WM_MDISETMENU` message replaces either the menu of the MDI frame window, the Window pop-up menu, or both as specified by the high-order and low-order words in `lParam`.

Return Value The handle of the frame window menu that was replaced is returned.

Related Messages `WM_MDICREATE`

WM_MDITILE

wParam Set to one of the following tiling flags:

Value	*Meaning*
MDITILE_HORIZONTAL	MDI child windows are tiled horizontally (one beside the other)
MDITILE_SKIPDISABLED	Disabled MDI child windows are not tiled
MDITILE_VERTICAL	MDI child windows are tiled vertically (one over the other)

lParam Not used.

Description The WM_MDITILE message arranges the child windows of a multiple document interface (MDI) client area in a tiled format.

Return Value Zero should be returned by the application if the message is processed.

Related Messages WM_MDICASCADE, WM_MDIICONARRANGE

WM_MEASUREITEM

wParam ID of control that sent the WM_MEASUREITEM message.

lParam Points to a data structure of type MEASUREITEMSTRUCT that contains the dimensions of an owner draw control. The MEASUREITEMSTRUCT structure follows.

```
typedef struct tagMEASUREITEMSTRUCT{
     WORD CtlType;
     WORD CtlID;
     WORD itemID;
     WORD itemWidth;
     WORD itemHeight;
     DWORD itemData;
 } MEASUREITEMSTRUCT;
```

in which

CtlType is the control type—ODT_BUTTON for owner draw button, ODT_COMBOBOX for owner draw combo box, ODT_LISTBOX for owner draw list box, ODT_MENU for owner draw menu

`CtlID` is the control ID for a combo box, list box, or button

`itemID` is either a menu ID or a list box item ID

`itemWidth` is the width of a menu item

`itemHeight` is the height of an item in a menu or list box

`itemData` is the value passed to the control in `lParam` from `CB_ADDSTRING`, `CB_INSERTSTRING`, `LB_ADDSTRING`, or `LB_INSERTSTRING`.

Description The `WM_MEASUREITEM` message is sent to the owner of an owner draw button, list box, combo box, or menu item when the control is created. The `MEASUREITEM` data structure is then filled by the owner.

Return Value Zero should be returned by the application if the message is processed.

Related Messages `WM_COMPAREITEM`, `WM_DRAWITEM`

WM_MENUCHAR

wParam Specifies the ASCII character entered.

lParam The low-order word of `lParam` contains `MF_POPUP` if the menu is a pop-up menu or `MF_SYSMENU` if the menu is a System menu. The high-order word of `lParam` contains the handle for the menu.

Description The `WM_MENUCHAR` message is sent to the owner of the menu when a mnemonic character is entered that doesn't match the mnemonic characters defined for the current menu.

Return Value One of the following command codes is returned in the high-order byte of the Return Value

0 – The entered character is discarded and the system speaker is beeped. The low-order word of the return value is ignored.

1 – The current menu should be closed. The low-order word of the return value is ignored.

2 – The low-order word of the return value contains the menu item number for an item.

Related Messages `WM_MENUSELECT`

WM_MENUSELECT

wParam Contains a menu item ID when a menu item is selected. wParam contains the handle to a pop-up menu when the selected item contains a pop-up menu.

lParam The low-order word of lParam contains one or more of the following menu flags. The high-order word of lParam is not used except when the low-order word contains MF_SYSMENU.

Value	*Meaning*
MF_BITMAP	Bitmap item
MF_CHECKED	Checked item
MF_DISABLED	Disabled item
MF_GRAYED	Grayed item
MF_MOUSESELECT	Item selected with a mouse
MF_OWNERDRAW	Owner draw item
MF_POPUP	Contains pop-up menu
MF_SEPARATOR	Menu item separator
MF_SYSMENU	Item is in System menu; the high-order word of lParam specifies the menu associated with the message

Description The WM_MENUSELECT message indicates that a menu item has been selected.

Return Value Zero should be returned by the application if the message is processed.

Related Messages WM_MENUCHAR

WM_MOUSEACTIVATE

wParam Specifies the window handle of the topmost parent window for the activated window.

lParam The low-order word of lParam contains the hit test code. A hit test checks the location of the mouse. The hit test codes used for the low-order word of lParam follow. The high-order word of lParam contains the mouse message number.

Hit Test Code	Meaning
HTBOTTOM	Lower horizontal window border
HTBOTTOMLEFT	Lower-left corner of window border
HTBOTTOMRIGHT	Lower-right corner of window border
HTCAPTION	Caption area
HTCLIENT	Client area
HTERROR	Screen background or window dividing line; produces a beep on error
HTGROWBOX	Size box
HTHSCROLL	Horizontal scroll bar
HTLEFT	Left window border
HTMENU	Menu area
HTNOWHERE	Screen background or window dividing line
HTREDUCE	Minimize box
HTRIGHT	Right window border
HTSIZE	Size box
HTSYSMENU	Control menu box
HTTOP	Upper horizontal window border
HTTOPLEFT	Upper-left corner of window border
HTTOPRIGHT	Upper-right corner of window border
HTTRANSPARENT	Window covered by another window
HTVSCROLL	Vertical scroll bar
HTZOOM	Maximize box

Description The `WM_MOUSEACTIVATE` message is sent when the cursor is moved to an inactive window and a mouse button is pressed. The `DefWindowProc` function should be used by the child window to pass this message to the parent window.

Return Value One of the following values is returned:

Value	Meaning
MA_ACTIVATE	Activate the window
MA_NOACTIVATE	Do not activate the window
MA_ACTIVATEANDEAT	Activate the window and discard mouse event
MA_NOACTIVATEANDEAT	Do not activate the window and discard the mouse event

Related Messages WM_MOUSEMOVE

WM_MOUSEMOVE

wParam Indicates which virtual keys are down. The following values, in any combination, indicate the virtual keys that are down:

Value	*Meaning*
MK_CONTROL	Control key is down
MK_LBUTTON	Left button is down
MK_MBUTTON	Middle button is down
MK_RBUTTON	Right button is down
MK_SHIFT	Shift key is down

lParam The low-order word of lParam contains the horizontal coordinate of the cursor. The high-order word of lParam contains the vertical coordinate of the cursor. These values are expressed in screen coordinates.

Description The WM_MOUSEMOVE message is sent whenever the mouse is moved. The MAKEPOINT macro can be used to convert the value in lParam to a structure of type POINT.

Return Value Zero should be returned by the application if the message is processed.

Related Messages WM_MOUSEACTIVATE

WM_MOVE

wParam Not used.

lParam The low-order word of lParam specifies the horizontal screen coordinate for the new location of the upper-left corner of the client area. The high-order word of lParam specifies the vertical screen coordinate for the new location of the upper-left corner of the client area.

Description The WM_MOVE message is sent when a window has been moved.

Return Value Zero should be returned by the application if the message is processed.

Related Messages WM_SIZE

WM_NCACTIVATE

wParam TRUE when an active caption or icon is to be drawn. wParam is FALSE for inactive captions or icons.

lParam Not used.

Description The WM_NCACTIVATE message is sent to a window when its nonclient area needs updating to reflect an active or inactive state.

Return Value When wParam is FALSE, the application should return TRUE for default processing or FALSE to prevent the icon or caption bar from being deactivated. When wParam is TRUE, the return value should be ignored.

Related Messages WM_NCCREATE

WM_NCCALCSIZE

wParam TRUE if application specifies the valid part of the client area. FALSE otherwise.

lParam Points to the data structure of type NCCALCSIZE_PARAMS that contains the screen coordinates of the window. The NCCALCSIZE_PARAMS structure follows.

```
typedef struct tagNCCALCSIZE_PARAMS {
     RECT rgrc[3]
     WINDOWPOS FAR* lppos;
} NCCALCSIZE_PARAMS;
```

in which

rgrc[3] is an array of rectangles. First contains new window coordinates for a moved or resized window; second contains original coordinates of window; third contains original coordinates of window's client area

lppos is a pointer to the WINDOWPOS data structure.

Description The WM_NCCALCSIZE message is sent to determine the size of window's client area.

Return Value When wParam is FALSE, zero should be returned. When wParam is TRUE, zero or a combination of the following flags can be returned:

WVR_ALIGNTOP
WVR_ALIGNLEFT
WVR_ALIGNBOTTOM
WVR_ALIGNRIGHT
WVR_HREDRAW
WVR_REDRAW
WVR_VALIDRECTS
WVR_VREDRAW

Related Messages WM_NCCREATE

WM_NCCREATE

wParam Not used.

lParam Points to a data structure of type CREATESTRUCT. The CREATESTRUCT follows.

```
typedef struct tagCREATESTRUCT {
     LPSTR lpCreateParams;
     HANDLE hInstance;
     HANDLE hMenu;
     HWND hwndParent;
     int cy;
     int cx;
     int y;
     int x;
     long style;
     LPSTR lpszName;
     LPSTR lpszClass;
     long  dwExStyle;
} CREATESTRUCT;
```

in which

lpCreateParams points to data to create the window

hInstance is the module instance handle of the module that owns the new window

hMenu is the menu the new window will use

hwndParent is the window that owns the created window

`cy` is the height of the created window

`cx` is the width of the created window

`y` is the vertical coordinate of the upper-left corner of the created window

`x` is the horizontal coordinate of the upper-left corner of the created window

`style` is the style for the created window

`lpszName` is the name for the created window

`lpszClass` is the string that specifies the class name of the created window

`dwExStyle` is the extended style for the created window.

Description The `WM_NCCREATE` message is sent before the `WM_CREATE` message when a window is created.

Return Value A nonzero value is returned if the nonclient area is created. Zero is returned when unsuccessful.

Related Messages `WM_CREATE`, `WM_NCDESTROY`

WM_NCDESTROY

wParam Not used.

lParam Not used.

Description The `WM_NCDESTROY` message is sent to a window when the window's nonclient area is being destroyed. This message is sent after the `WM_DESTROY` message.

Return Value Zero should be returned by the application if the message is processed.

Related Messages `WM_NCCREATE`

WM_NCHITTEST

wParam Not used.

lParam The low-order word of `lParam` contains the horizontal screen coordinate of the current cursor position. The high-order word of lParam contains the vertical screen coordinate of the current cursor position. The MAKEPOINT macro can be used to convert lParam to a POINT structure.

Description The WM_NCHITTEST message is sent to the window that contains the cursor whenever the mouse is moved.

Return Value The return value indicates the cursor position and is one of the following values:

Hit Test Code	*Meaning*
HTBORDER	Border of window without sizing border
HTBOTTOM	Lower horizontal window border
HTBOTTOMLEFT	Lower-left corner of window border
HTBOTTOMRIGHT	Lower-right corner of window border
HTCAPTION	Caption area
HTCLIENT	Client area
HTERROR	Screen background or window dividing line; produces a beep on error
HTGROWBOX	Size box
HTHSCROLL	Horizontal scroll bar
HTLEFT	Left window border
HTMAXBUTTON	Maximize button
HTMENU	Menu area
HTMINBUTTON	Minimize button
HTNOWHERE	Screen background or window dividing line
HTREDUCE	Minimize box
HTRIGHT	Right window border
HTSIZE	Size box
HTSYSMENU	Control menu box
HTTOP	Upper horizontal window border
HTTOPLEFT	Upper-left corner of window border
HTTOPRIGHT	Upper-right corner of window border
HTTRANSPARENT	Window covered by another window
HTVSCROLL	Vertical scroll bar
HTZOOM	Maximize box

Related Messages WM_MOUSEMOVE

WM_NCLBUTTONDBLCLK

wParam Contains the hit test code returned by `WM_NCHITTEST`. It can be any of the following values:

Hit Test Code	*Meaning*
HTBORDER	Border of window without sizing bar
HTBOTTOM	Lower horizontal window border
HTBOTTOMLEFT	Lower-left corner of window border
HTBOTTOMRIGHT	Lower-right corner of window border
HTCAPTION	Caption area
HTCLIENT	Client area
HTERROR	Screen background or window dividing line; produces a beep on error
HTGROWBOX	Size box
HTHSCROLL	Horizontal scroll bar
HTLEFT	Left window border
HTMAXBUTTON	Maximize button
HTMENU	Menu area
HTMINBUTTON	Minimize button
HTNOWHERE	Screen background or window dividing line
HTREDUCE	Minimize box
HTRIGHT	Right window border
HTSIZE	Size box
HTSYSMENU	Control menu box
HTTOP	Upper horizontal window border
HTTOPLEFT	Upper-left corner of window border
HTTOPRIGHT	Upper-right corner of window border
HTTRANSPARENT	Window covered by another window
HTVSCROLL	Vertical scroll bar
HTZOOM	Maximize box

lParam Low-order word of `lParam` contains the horizontal screen coordinates of the cursor. High-order word of `lParam` contains the vertical screen coordinates of the cursor.

Description The `WM_NCLBUTTONDBLCLK` message is sent to a window when the left mouse button is double-clicked with the cursor in a non-client area.

Return Value Zero should be returned by the application if the message is processed.

Related Messages WM_NCHITTEST, WM_LBUTTONDOWN, WM_LBUTTONUP

WM_NCLBUTTONDOWN

wParam Contains the hit test code returned by WM_NCHITTEST. It can be any of the following values:

Hit Test Code	*Meaning*
HTBORDER	Border of window without sizing bar
HTBOTTOM	Lower horizontal window border
HTBOTTOMLEFT	Lower-left corner of window border
HTBOTTOMRIGHT	Lower-right corner of window border
HTCAPTION	Caption area
HTCLIENT	Client area
HTERROR	Screen background or window dividing line; produces a beep on error
HTGROWBOX	Size box
HTHSCROLL	Horizontal scroll bar
HTLEFT	Left window border
HTMAXBUTTON	Maximize button
HTMENU	Menu area
HTMINBUTTON	Minimize button
HTNOWHERE	Screen background or window dividing line
HTREDUCE	Minimize box
HTRIGHT	Right window border
HTSIZE	Size box
HTSYSMENU	Control menu box
HTTOP	Upper horizontal window border
HTTOPLEFT	Upper-left corner of window border
HTTOPRIGHT	Upper-right corner of window border
HTTRANSPARENT	Window covered by another window
HTVSCROLL	Vertical scroll bar
HTZOOM	Maximize box

lParam The low-order word of `lParam` contains the horizontal screen coordinates of the cursor. The high-order word of `lParam` contains the vertical screen coordinates of the cursor.

Description The `WM_NCLBUTTONDOWN` message is sent to a window when the left mouse button is pressed with the cursor in a nonclient area.

Return Value Zero should be returned by the application if the message is processed.

Related Messages `WM_NCHITTTEST`, `WM_NCLBUTTONDBLCLK`, `WM_NCLBUTTONUP`

WM_NCLBUTTONUP

wParam Contains the hit test code returned by `WM_NCHITTEST`. It can be any of the following values:

Hit Test Code	*Meaning*
HTBORDER	Border of window without sizing bar
HTBOTTOM	Lower horizontal window border
HTBOTTOMLEFT	Lower-left corner of window border
HTBOTTOMRIGHT	Lower-right corner of window border
HTCAPTION	Caption area
HTCLIENT	Client area
HTERROR	Screen background or window dividing line; produces a beep on error
HTGROWBOX	Size box
HTHSCROLL	Horizontal scroll bar
HTLEFT	Left window border
HTMAXBUTTON	Maximize button
HTMENU	Menu area
HTMINBUTTON	Minimize button
HTNOWHERE	Screen background or window dividing line
HTREDUCE	Minimize box
HTRIGHT	Right window border
HTSIZE	Size box
HTSYSMENU	Control menu box
HTTOP	Upper horizontal window border
HTTOPLEFT	Upper-left corner of window border
HTTOPRIGHT	Upper-right corner of window border

Hit Test Code	Meaning
HTTRANSPARENT	Window covered by another window
HTVSCROLL	Vertical scroll bar
HTZOOM	Maximize box

lParam The low-order word of lParam contains the horizontal screen coordinates of the cursor. The high-order word of lParam contains the vertical screen coordinates of the cursor.

Description The WM_NCLBUTTONUP message is sent to a window when the left mouse button is released with the cursor in a nonclient area.

Return Value Zero should be returned by the application if the message is processed.

Related Messages WM_NCHITTEST, WM_NCLBUTTONDBLCLK, WM_NCLBUTTONDOWN

WM_NCMBUTTONDBLCLK

wParam Contains the hit test code returned by WM_NCHITTEST. It can be any of the following values:

Hit Test Code	Meaning
HTBORDER	Border of window without sizing bar
HTBOTTOM	Lower horizontal window border
HTBOTTOMLEFT	Lower-left corner of window border
HTBOTTOMRIGHT	Lower-right corner of window border
HTCAPTION	Caption area
HTCLIENT	Client area
HTERROR	Screen background or window dividing line; produces a beep on error
HTGROWBOX	Size box
HTHSCROLL	Horizontal scroll bar
HTLEFT	Left window border
HTMAXBUTTON	Maximize button
HTMENU	Menu area
HTMINBUTTON	Minimize button
HTNOWHERE	Screen background or window dividing line
HTREDUCE	Minimize box

Hit Test Code	Meaning
HTRIGHT	Right window border
HTSIZE	Size box
HTSYSMENU	Control menu box
HTTOP	Upper horizontal window border
HTTOPLEFT	Upper-left corner of window border
HTTOPRIGHT	Upper-right corner of window border
HTTRANSPARENT	Window covered by another window
HTVSCROLL	Vertical scroll bar
HTZOOM	Maximize box

lParam The low-order word of `lParam` contains the horizontal screen coordinates of the cursor. The high-order word of `lParam` contains the vertical screen coordinates of the cursor.

Description The `WM_NCMBUTTONDBLCLK` message is sent to a window when the middle mouse button is double-clicked with the cursor in a nonclient area.

Return Value Zero should be returned by the application if the message is processed.

Related Messages `WM_NCHITTEST`, `WM_NCMBUTTONDOWN`, `WM_NCBUTTONUP`

WM_NCMBUTTONDOWN

wParam Contains the hit test code returned by `WM_NCHITTEST`. It can be any of the following values:

Hit Test Code	Meaning
HTBORDER	Border of window without sizing bar
HTBOTTOM	Lower horizontal window border
HTBOTTOMLEFT	Lower-left corner of window border
HTBOTTOMRIGHT	Lower-right corner of window border
HTCAPTION	Caption area
HTCLIENT	Client area
HTERROR	Screen background or window dividing line; produces a beep on error
HTGROWBOX	Size box
HTHSCROLL	Horizontal scroll bar

Hit Test Code	Meaning
HTLEFT	Left window border
HTMAXBUTTON	Maximize button
HTMENU	Menu area
HTMINBUTTON	Minimize button
HTNOWHERE	Screen background or window dividing line
HTREDUCE	Minimize box
HTRIGHT	Right window border
HTSIZE	Size box
HTSYSMENU	Control menu box
HTTOP	Upper horizontal window border
HTTOPLEFT	Upper-left corner of window border
HTTOPRIGHT	Upper-right corner of window border
HTTRANSPARENT	Window covered by another window
HTVSCROLL	Vertical scroll bar
HTZOOM	Maximize box

lParam The low-order word of lParam contains the horizontal screen coordinates of the cursor. The high-order word of lParam contains the vertical screen coordinates of the cursor.

Description The WM_NCMBUTTONDOWN message is sent to a window when the middle mouse button is pressed with the cursor in a nonclient area.

Return Value Zero should be returned by the application if the message is processed.

Related Messages WM_NCHITTEST, WM_NCMBUTTONDBLCLK, WM_NCMBUTTONUP

WM_NCMBUTTONUP

wParam Contains the hit test code returned by WM_NCHITTEST. It can be any of the following values:

Hit Test Code	Meaning
HTBORDER	Border of window without sizing bar
HTBOTTOM	Lower horizontal window border
HTBOTTOMLEFT	Lower-left corner of window border

Hit Test Code	*Meaning*
HTBOTTOMRIGHT	Lower-right corner of window border
HTCAPTION	Caption area
HTCLIENT	Client area
HTERROR	Screen background or window dividing line; produces a beep on error
HTGROWBOX	Size box
HTHSCROLL	Horizontal scroll bar
HTLEFT	Left window border
HTMAXBUTTON	Maximize button
HTMENU	Menu area
HTMINBUTTON	Minimize button
HTNOWHERE	Screen background or window dividing line
HTREDUCE	Minimize box
HTRIGHT	Right window border
HTSIZE	Size box
HTSYSMENU	Control menu box
HTTOP	Upper horizontal window border
HTTOPLEFT	Upper-left corner of window border
HTTOPRIGHT	Upper-right corner of window border
HTTRANSPARENT	Window covered by another window
HTVSCROLL	Vertical scroll bar
HTZOOM	Maximize box

lParam The low-order word of `lParam` contains the horizontal screen coordinates of the cursor. The high-order word of `lParam` contains the vertical screen coordinates of the cursor.

Description The `WM_NCMBUTTONUP` message is sent to a window when the middle mouse button is released with the cursor in a nonclient area.

Return Value Zero should be returned by the application if the message is processed.

Related Messages `WM_NCHITTEST`, `WM_NCMBUTTONDBLCLK`, `WM_NCMBUTTONDOWN`

WM_NCMOUSEMOVE

wParam Contains the hit test code returned by WM_NCHITTEST. It can be any of the following values:

Hit Test Code	*Meaning*
HTBORDER	Border of window without sizing bar
HTBOTTOM	Lower horizontal window border
HTBOTTOMLEFT	Lower-left corner of window border
HTBOTTOMRIGHT	Lower-right corner of window border
HTCAPTION	Caption area
HTCLIENT	Client area
HTERROR	Screen background or window dividing line; produces a beep on error
HTGROWBOX	Size box
HTHSCROLL	Horizontal scroll bar
HTLEFT	Left window border
HTMAXBUTTON	Maximize button
HTMENU	Menu area
HTMINBUTTON	Minimize button
HTNOWHERE	Screen background or window dividing line
HTREDUCE	Minimize box
HTRIGHT	Right window border
HTSIZE	Size box
HTSYSMENU	Control menu box
HTTOP	Upper horizontal window border
HTTOPLEFT	Upper-left corner of window border
HTTOPRIGHT	Upper-right corner of window border
HTTRANSPARENT	Window covered by another window
HTVSCROLL	Vertical scroll bar
HTZOOM	Maximize box

lParam The low-order word of lParam contains the horizontal screen coordinates of the cursor. The high-order word of lParam contains the vertical screen coordinates of the cursor.

Description The WM_NCMOUSEMOVE message is sent to a window when the cursor is moved in a nonclient area.

Return Value Zero should be returned by the application if the message is processed.

Related Messages WM_NCHITTEST

WM_NCPAINT

wParam Not used.

lParam Not used.

Description The WM_NCPAINT message is sent to a window when the window frame needs to be painted. The DefWindowProc function is used to paint the window frame.

Return Value Zero should be returned by the application if the message is processed.

Related Messages WM_ACTIVATE, WM_NCCREATE

WM_NCRBUTTONDBLCLK

wParam Contains the hit test code returned by WM_NCHITTEST. It can be any of the following values:

Hit Test Code	*Meaning*
HTBORDER	Border of window without sizing bar
HTBOTTOM	Lower horizontal window border
HTBOTTOMLEFT	Lower-left corner of window border
HTBOTTOMRIGHT	Lower-right corner of window border
HTCAPTION	Caption area
HTCLIENT	Client area
HTERROR	Screen background or window dividing line; produces a beep on error
HTGROWBOX	Size box
HTHSCROLL	Horizontal scroll bar
HTLEFT	Left window border
HTMAXBUTTON	Maximize button
HTMENU	Menu area
HTMINBUTTON	Minimize button

Hit Test Code	Meaning
HTNOWHERE	Screen background or window dividing line
HTREDUCE	Minimize box
HTRIGHT	Right window border
HTSIZE	Size box
HTSYSMENU	Control menu box
HTTOP	Upper horizontal window border
HTTOPLEFT	Upper-left corner of window border
HTTOPRIGHT	Upper-right corner of window border
HTTRANSPARENT	Window covered by another window
HTVSCROLL	Vertical scroll bar
HTZOOM	Maximize box

lParam The low-order word of `lParam` contains the horizontal screen coordinates of the cursor. The high-order word of `lParam` contains the vertical screen coordinates of the cursor.

Description The `WM_NCRBUTTONDBLCLK` message is sent to a window when the right mouse button is double-clicked with the cursor in a nonclient area.

Return Value Zero should be returned by the application if the message is processed.

Related Messages `WM_NCHITTEST`, `WM_NCRBUTTONDOWN`, `WM_NCRBUTTONUP`

WM_NCRBUTTONDOWN

wParam Contains the hit test code returned by `WM_NCHITTEST`. It can be any of the following values:

Hit Test Code	Meaning
HTBORDER	Border of window without sizing bar
HTBOTTOM	Lower horizontal window border
HTBOTTOMLEFT	Lower-left corner of window border
HTBOTTOMRIGHT	Lower-right corner of window border
HTCAPTION	Caption area
HTCLIENT	Client area
HTERROR	Screen background or window dividing line; produces a beep on error

Hit Test Code	*Meaning*
HTGROWBOX	Size box
HTHSCROLL	Horizontal scroll bar
HTLEFT	Left window border
HTMAXBUTTON	Maximize button
HTMENU	Menu area
HTMINBUTTON	Minimize button
HTNOWHERE	Screen background or window dividing line
HTREDUCE	Minimize box
HTRIGHT	Right window border
HTSIZE	Size box
HTSYSMENU	Control menu box
HTTOP	Upper horizontal window border
HTTOPLEFT	Upper-left corner of window border
HTTOPRIGHT	Upper-right corner of window border
HTTRANSPARENT	Window covered by another window
HTVSCROLL	Vertical scroll bar
HTZOOM	Maximize box

lParam The low-order word of `lParam` contains the horizontal screen coordinates of the cursor. The high-order word of `lParam` contains the vertical screen coordinates of the cursor.

Description The `WM_NCRBUTTONDOWN` message is sent to a window when the right mouse button is pressed with the cursor in a nonclient area.

Return Value Zero should be returned by the application if the message is processed.

Related Messages `WM_NCHITTEST`, `WM_RBUTTONDBLCLK`, `WM_RBUTTONUP`

WM_NCRBUTTONUP

wParam Contains the hit test code returned by `WM_NCHITTEST`. It can be any of the following values:

Hit Test Code	*Meaning*
HTBORDER	Border of window without sizing bar
HTBOTTOM	Lower horizontal window border
HTBOTTOMLEFT	Lower-left corner of window border
HTBOTTOMRIGHT	Lower-right corner of window border
HTCAPTION	Caption area
HTCLIENT	Client area
HTERROR	Screen background or window dividing line; produces a beep on error
HTGROWBOX	Size box
HTHSCROLL	Horizontal scroll bar
HTLEFT	Left window border
HTMAXBUTTON	Maximize button
HTMENU	Menu area
HTMINBUTTON	Minimize button
HTNOWHERE	Screen background or window dividing line
HTREDUCE	Minimize box
HTRIGHT	Right window border
HTSIZE	Size box
HTSYSMENU	Control menu box
HTTOP	Upper horizontal window border
HTTOPLEFT	Upper-left corner of window border
HTTOPRIGHT	Upper-right corner of window border
HTTRANSPARENT	Window covered by another window
HTVSCROLL	Vertical scroll bar
HTZOOM	Maximize box

lParam The low-order word of `lParam` contains the horizontal screen coordinates of the cursor. The high-order word of `lParam` contains the vertical screen coordinates of the cursor.

Description The `WM_NCRBUTTONUP` message is sent to a window when the right mouse button is released with the cursor in a nonclient area.

Return Value Zero should be returned by the application if the message is processed.

Related Messages `WM_NCHITTEST`, `WM_NCRBUTTONDBLCLK`, `WM_NCRBUTTONDOWN`

WM_NEXTDLGCTL

wParam Specifies the control that will receive the control focus.

lParam Determines how to interpret the value in wParam.

Description The WM_NEXTDLGCTL message, which is sent to the window function for a dialog box, gives the control focus to the control specified in wParam. lParam specifies how the value in wParam is interpreted. The following applies to the relationship between lParam and wParam.

lParam is nonzero – wParam contains the handle for the control which will receive the control focus.

lParam is zero – wParam is a flag to indicate whether the previous or next control with the tab-stop style will be given the control focus. When wParam is zero, the next control will be given the control focus. When wParam is nonzero, the previous control will be given the control focus.

Return Value Zero should be returned by the application if the message is processed.

Related Messages WM_GETDLGCODE

WM_PAINT

wParam Not used.

lParam Not used.

Description The WM_PAINT message is sent when a request is made to repaint an application's window.

Return Value Zero should be returned by the application if the message is processed.

Related Messages WM_PAINTCLIPBOARD

WM_PAINTCLIPBOARD

wParam Contains the clipboard application window handle.

lParam The low-order word of lParam points to a data structure of type PAINTSTRUCT. The data structure defines the client area that is to be painted. The PAINTSTRUCT structure follows. The high-order word of lParam is not used.

```
typedef struct tagPAINTSTRUCT {
     HDC hdc;
     BOOL fErase;
     RECT rcPaint;
     BOOL fRestore;
     BOOL fIncUpdate;
     BYTE rgbReserved[16];
} PAINTSTRUCT;
```

in which

`hdc` is the display context used for painting

`fErase` specifies whether the background should be redrawn (nonzero if redrawn, otherwise zero)

`rcPaint` identifies the upper-left and lower-right corners of the rectangle to paint

`fRestore` is reserved for use only by Windows

`fIncUpdate` is reserved for use only by Windows

`rgbReserved[16]` is reserved for use only by Windows.

Description The WM_PAINTCLIPBOARD message is sent to the owner of the clipboard and requests that the clipboard application's client area be repainted. This message is sent only when the following conditions are met:

- The clipboard contains a data handle for the CF_OWNERDISPLAY format.
- The clipboard application's client area needs to be repainted.

Return Value Zero should be returned by the application if the message is processed.

Related Messages WM_DRAWCLIPBOARD, WM_PAINT

WM_PALETTECHANGED

wParam Specifies the handle of the window causing the change to the system palette.

lParam Not used.

Description The WM_PALETTECHANGED message is sent to all windows when the window with the input focus realizes its logical palette. When the window realizes its logical palette, the system palette is changed, and windows that do not have the input focus and that use a color palette should realize their logical palette and update their client area.

Return Value Zero should be returned by the application if the message is processed.

Related Messages WM_QUERYNEWPALETTE

WM_PARENTNOTIFY

wParam Defines the reason the parent window is being notified. The values for wParam follow.

Value	*Meaning*
WM_CREATE	Creating child window
WM_DESTROY	Destroying child window
WM_LBUTTONDOWN	Left button clicked on a child window
WM_MBUTTONDOWN	Middle button clicked on a child window
WM_RBUTTONDOWN	Right button clicked on a child window

lParam lParam contains the child window's window handle (low word) and control ID (high word) only when wParam contains the WM_CREATE and WM_DESTROY messages. For the other values of wParam, lParam contains the x (horizontal) coordinate of the cursor in the low word and the y (vertical) coordinate of the cursor in the high word.

Description The WM_PARENTNOTIFY message is sent to the child window's parent and ancestor windows when the child window is created, destroyed, or clicked.

Return Value Zero should be returned by the application if the message is processed.

Related Messages WM_CREATE, WM_DESTROY

WM_PASTE

wParam Not used.

lParam Not used.

Description The WM_PASTE message pastes the contents of the clipboard (the contents must be in CF_TEXT format) into the control window at the current position of the cursor.

Return Value TRUE is returned when the message is sent to an edit control or combo bar.

Related Messages WM_CUT, WM_COPY

WM_POWER

wParam Specifies the power event notification code. wParam is one of the following:

Value	*Meaning*
PWR_SUSPENDREQUEST	System is about to enter the suspended mode
PWR_SUSPENDRESUME	System resuming operation after entering suspended mode normally
PWR_CRITICALRESUME	System resuming operation after a suspended mode was entered with a PWR_SUSPENDREQUEST notification

lParam Not used.

Description The WM_POWER message indicates that the system is about to enter a suspended mode. The system should conform to the advanced power management (APM) BIOS specification.

Return Value When wParam is PWR_SUSPENDREQUEST, PWR_FAIL or PWR_OK should be returned. When wParam is PWR_SUSPENDRESUME or PWR_CRITICALRESUME, zero should be returned.

Related Messages None

WM_QUERYDRAGICON

wParam Not used.

lParam Not used.

Description The WM_QUERYDRAGICON message is sent to a minimized window that has no icon defined for its class. When this happens, Windows replaces the icon with the default icon.

Return Value The low-order word of the return value contains the handle of the cursor displayed while the icon is moved. NULL is returned when Windows displays the default icon cursor.

Related Messages WM_PAINTICON, WM_QUERYOPEN

WM_QUERYENDSESSION

wParam Not used.

lParam Not used.

Description The WM_QUERYENDSESSION message is sent when the End Session command is chosen. If any of the applications return zero, the session is not ended.

Return Value TRUE is returned when the application is able to shut down. FALSE is returned when the application is unable to shut down.

Related Messages WM_ENDSESSION

WM_QUERYNEWPALETTE

wParam Not used.

lParam Not used.

Description The WM_QUERYNEWPALETTE message is sent to a window before it receives the input focus. When the window receives the input focus, the window should return an indication of whether it was able to realize its logical palette.

Return Value TRUE is returned when the logical palette is realized. FALSE is returned when unable to realize the logical palette.

Related Messages WM_PALETTECHANGED

WM_QUERYOPEN

wParam Not used.

lParam Not used.

Description The WM_QUERYOPEN message is sent to an icon when a request has been made to open the icon into a window.

Return Value FALSE is returned when the application does not allow the icon to be opened. TRUE is returned when the icon can be opened.

Related Messages WM_QUERYDRAGICON

WM_QUEUESYNC

wParam Not used.

lParam Not used.

Description The WM_QUEUESYNC message delimits the messages that Windows CBT sends to an application via the WH_JOURNALPLAYBACK hook. The WM_QUEUESYNC message is the first and last message rendered when the Windows CBT uses the journaling playback hook.

Return Value Zero should be returned by the CBT application if the message is processed.

Related Messages None

WM_QUIT

wParam Specifies the exit code from the call to PostQuitMessage.

lParam Not used.

Description The WM_QUIT message is sent when the PostQuitMessage function is called by the application (indicating a termination request) and causes the GetMessage function to return zero.

Return Value There is no return value.

Related Messages WM_DESTROY, WM_QUERYENDSESSION

WM_RBUTTONDBLCLK

wParam Indicates which virtual keys are down. The following values, in any combination, indicate the virtual keys that are down:

Value	*Meaning*
MK_CONTROL	Control key is down
MK_LBUTTON	Left button is down
MK_MBUTTON	Middle button is down
MK_RBUTTON	Right button is down
MK_SHIFT	Shift key is down

lParam The low-order word of `lParam` contains the horizontal coordinate of the cursor. The high-order word of `lParam` contains the vertical coordinate of the cursor. These coordinates are expressed relative to the upper-left corner of the window.

Description The `WM_RBUTTONDBLCLK` message is sent when the right mouse button is double-clicked.

Return Value Zero should be returned by the application if the message is processed.

Related Messages `WM_RBUTTONDOWN`, `WM_RBUTTONUP`

WM_RBUTTONDOWN

wParam Indicates which virtual keys are down. The following values, in any combination, indicate the virtual keys that are down:

Value	*Meaning*
MK_CONTROL	Control key is down
MK_LBUTTON	Left button is down
MK_MBUTTON	Middle button is down
MK_SHIFT	Shift key is down

lParam The low-order word of `lParam` contains the horizontal coordinate of the cursor. The high-order word of `lParam` contains the vertical coordinate of the cursor. These coordinates are expressed relative to the upper-left corner of the window.

Description The `WM_RBUTTONDOWN` message is sent when the right mouse button is pressed.

Return Value Zero should be returned by the application if the message is processed.

Related Messages `WM_RBUTTONDBLCLK, WM_RBUTTONUP`

WM_RBUTTONUP

wParam Indicates which virtual keys are down. The following values, in any combination, indicate the virtual keys that are down:

Value	*Meaning*
MK_CONTROL	Control key is down
MK_LBUTTON	Left button is down
MK_MBUTTON	Middle button is down
MK_SHIFT	Shift key is down

lParam The low-order word of `lParam` contains the horizontal coordinate of the cursor. The high-order word of `lParam` contains the vertical coordinate of the cursor. These coordinates are expressed relative to the upper-left corner of the window.

Description The `WM_RBUTTONUP` message is sent when the right mouse button is released.

Return Value Zero should be returned by the application if the message is processed.

Related Messages `WM_RBUTTONDBLCLK, WM_RBUTTONDOWN`

WM_RENDERALLFORMATS

wParam Not used.

lParam Not used.

Description The `WM_RENDERALLFORMATS` message is sent to the clipboard owner when the application is being destroyed. This allows the application to render the clipboard data in all available formats by passing the handle of each format to the `SetClipboardData` function.

Return Value Zero should be returned by the application if the message is processed.

Related Messages WM_RENDERFORMAT

WM_RENDERFORMAT

wParam Defines the data format. The data format is selected from any of the following:

Format	*Meaning*
CF_BITMAP	Handle to a bitmap
CF_DIB	Block containing a BITMAPINFO data structure and the bitmap
CF_DIF	Software Art's Data Interchange Format
CF_DSPBITMAP	Bitmap format which corresponds to a private format
CF_DSPMETAFILEPICT	Metafile format which corresponds to a private format
CF_DSPTEXT	Text display format which corresponds to a private format
CF_METAFILEPICT	Metafile defined by the METAFILEPICT structure
CF_OEMTEXT	Text format using the OEM character set
CF_OWNERDISPLAY	Owner display format
CF_PALETTE	Color palette handle
CF_PRIVATEFIRST to CF_PRIVATELAST	Used for private formats
CF_SYLK	Microsoft Symbolic Link Format
CF_TEXT	Text format
CF_TIFF	Tag Image File Format

lParam Not used.

Description The WM_RENDERFORMAT message is sent to the cliboard owner. The clipboard owner should format the data in the clipboard to the format in wParam and pass the handle of the formatted data to the clipboard.

Return Value Zero should be returned by the application if the message is processed.

Related Messages WM_RENDERALLFORMATS

WM_SETCURSOR

wParam Specifies the window handle for the window that contains the cursor.

lParam The low-order word of `lParam` contains the hit test code. A hit test checks the location of the mouse. The hit test codes used for the low-order word of `lParam` follow. The high-order word of `lParam` contains the mouse message number.

Hit Test Code	*Meaning*
HTBORDER	Border of window without sizing bar
HTBOTTOM	Lower horizontal window border
HTBOTTOMLEFT	Lower-left corner of window border
HTBOTTOMRIGHT	Lower-right corner of window border
HTCAPTION	Caption area
HTCLIENT	Client area
HTERROR	Screen background or window dividing line; produces a beep on error
HTGROWBOX	Size box
HTHSCROLL	Horizontal scroll bar
HTLEFT	Left window border
HTMAXBUTTON	Maximize button
HTMENU	Menu area
HTMINBUTTON	Minimize button
HTNOWHERE	Screen background or window dividing line
HTREDUCE	Minimize box
HTRIGHT	Right window border
HTSIZE	Size box
HTSYSMENU	Control menu box
HTTOP	Upper horizontal window border
HTTOPLEFT	Upper-left corner of window border
HTTOPRIGHT	Upper-right corner of window border
HTTRANSPARENT	Window covered by another window
HTVSCROLL	Vertical scroll bar
HTZOOM	Maximize box

Description The WM_SETCURSOR message is sent when the cursor is moved due to mouse movement and the input is not captured.

Return Value Zero should be returned by the application if the message is processed.

Related Messages WM_MOUSEMOVE

WM_SETFOCUS

wParam Specifies the handle of the window that loses the input focus.

lParam Not used.

Description The WM_SETFOCUS message is sent when a window receives the input focus.

Return Value Zero should be returned by the application if the message is processed.

Related Messages None

WM_SETFONT

wParam Specifies the handle of the font to use. If wParam is NULL, the system font will be used.

lParam Specifies whether the control should be redrawn. If lParam is TRUE, the control is redrawn. If lParam is FALSE, the control is not redrawn.

Description The WM_SETFONT message sets the font used by the dialog box control to the font specified in wParam.

Return Value Zero should be returned by the application if the message is processed.

Related Messages WM_GETFONT

WM_SETHOTKEY

wParam Specifies the virtual key code of the hot key to associate with the window. If wParam is NULL, the current hot key associated with the window is removed.

lParam Not used.

Description The WM_SETHOTKEY message associates the hot key specified in wParam with the window. A hot key activates its associated window and cannot be used with a child window.

Return Value One of the following is returned:

2	Another window already has hot key
1	Successful
0	Window is invalid
–1	Hot key is invalid

Related Messages WM_GETHOTKEY

WM_SETREDRAW

wParam Nonzero to set the redraw flag; zero to clear the redraw flag.

lParam Not used.

Description The WM_SETREDRAW message sets or clears the redraw flag and is sent by an application to a window. The redraw flag indicates whether changes made in the window can be redrawn. When the redraw flag is set, the control can be redrawn to reflect changes. When the redraw flag is cleared, the control cannot be redrawn.

Return Value Zero should be returned by the application if the message is processed.

Related Messages None

WM_SETTEXT

wParam Not used.

lParam Points to a null-terminated string containing the window text.

Description The WM_SETTEXT message defines the text for a window. The text of the edit control is set for edit controls and combo box edit controls. The button name is set for buttons. The window caption is set for windows.

Return Value LB_ERRSPACE for a list box or CB_ERRSPACE for a combo box is returned when there is not enough memory for the text. CB_ERR is returned if the combo box receiving the message does not have an edit control.

Related Messages WM_GETTEXT

WM_SHOWWINDOW

wParam TRUE when the window is visible, or shown; FALSE if the window is hidden.

lParam Zero if the message is sent as a result of a call to the ShowWindow function; SW_PARENTCLOSING when the parent window is closing or a pop-up window is being hidden. lParam is SW_PARENTOPENING when the parent window is opening or a pop-up window is shown.

Description The WM_SHOWWINDOW message is sent when a window is being shown or hidden.

Return Value Zero should be returned by the application if the message is processed.

Related Messages WM_ACTIVATE, WM_CREATE

WM_SIZE

wParam Specifies the type of sizing and is selected from the following values:

Value	*Meaning*
SIZE_MAXIMIZED	Window maximized
SIZE_MINIMIZED	Window minimized
SIZE_RESTORED	Window resized
SIZE_MAXHIDE	Message sent to all pop-up windows when another window is maximized
SIZE_MAXSHOW	Message sent to all pop-up windows when another window is restored to its previous size

lParam The low-order word of lParam contains the new width of the client area. The high-order word of lParam contains the new height of the client area.

Description The WM_SIZE message is sent whenever a window is sized.

Return Value Zero should be returned by the application if the message is processed.

Related Messages WM_MOVE, WM_SIZECLIPBOARD

WM_SIZECLIPBOARD

wParam Contains the clipboard application window ID.

lParam The low-order word of lParam contains the reference to the data structure of type RECT that defines the area to paint. The RECT structure follows. The high-order word of lParam is not used.

```
typedef struct tagRECT {
     int left;
     int top;
     int right;
     int bottom;
} RECT;
```

in which

left is the horizontal coordinate of the upper-left corner of the rectangular region

top is the vertical coordinate of the upper-left corner of the rectangular region

right is the horizontal coordinate of the lower-right corner of the rectangular region

bottom is the vertical coordinate of the lower-right corner of the rectangular region.

Description The WM_SIZECLIPBOARD message is sent when the following conditions are met:

- The clipboard contains a data handle for the CF_OWNERDISPLAY format.
- The clipboard application window's size has been modified.

Return Value Zero should be returned by the application if the message is processed.

Related Messages WM_SIZE

WM_SPOOLERSTATUS

wParam Contains SP_JOBSTATUS.

lParam The low-order word of lParam contains the number of jobs left in the Print Manager queue. The high-order word of lParam is not used.

Description The WM_SPOOLERSTATUS message is sent whenever the Print Manager queue is modified by adding or removing a print job.

Return Value Zero should be returned by the application if the message is processed.

Related Messages None

WM_SYSCHAR

wParam Contains the ASCII key code of a System menu key.

lParam Specifies the repeat count, scan code, key transition code, previous key state, and context code. The value of lParam is interpreted as follows:

Bits	*Meaning*
0-15	Repeat count: the number of times the key is repeated
16-23	Scan code
24	1 if extended key
25-26	Not used
27-28	Used by Windows
29	Context code; 1 if ALT key is down
30	Previous key state; 1 if key is down before the message is sent
31	Transition state; 1 if key is being released

Description The WM_SYSCHAR message specifies the virtual-key code of the System-menu key and is sent when WM_SYSKEYUP and WM_SYSKEYDOWN messages are translated.

Return Value Zero should be returned by the application if the message is processed.

Related Messages WM_SYSKEYDOWN, WM_SYSKEYUP

WM_SYSCOLORCHANGE

wParam Not used.

lParam Not used.

Description The WM_SYSCOLORCHANGE message is sent to all top-level windows when the system color setting has been modified. The WM_PAINT message is sent by Windows to all the windows affected by the change.

Return Value Zero should be returned by the application if the message is processed.

Related Messages WM_PAINT

WM_SYSCOMMAND

wParam Specifies the system command. The following values are used for wParam:

Value	*Meaning*
SC_CLOSE	Close window
SC_HOTKEY	Activate window associated with the hot key; low-order word of lParam specifies the window to activate
SC_HSCROLL	Horizontal scroll
SC_KEYMENU	Get menu with key stroke
SC_MAXIMIZE	Maximize window
SC_MINIMIZE	Minimize window
SC_MOUSEMENU	Get menu with key stroke
SC_MOVE	Move window

Value	Meaning
SC_NEXTWINDOW	Go to next window
SC_PREVWINDOW	Go to previous window
SC_RESTORE	Checkpoint
SC_SCREENSAVE	Screen save application
SC_SIZE	Size window
SC_TASKLIST	Task Manager application
SC_VSCROLL	Vertical Scroll

lParam When the mouse is used to choose a System menu command, the low-order word of `lParam` contains the horizontal coordinate of the cursor position; the high-order word of `lParam` contains the vertical coordinate. When the mouse is not used, `lParam` is ignored.

Description The `WM_SYSCOMMAND` message is sent when a System menu command is selected or the minimize or maximize box is selected.

Return Value Zero should be returned by the application if the message is processed.

Related Messages `WM_COMMAND`

WM_SYSDEADCHAR

wParam Specifies the dead key character value.

lParam The low-order word of `lParam` contains the repeat count. The high-order word of `lParam` contains the auto-repeat count.

Description The `WM_SYSDEADCHAR` message specifies the dead key character value and is sent when `WM_SYSKEYUP` and `WM_SYSKEYDOWN` messages are translated.

Return Value Zero should be returned by the application if the message is processed.

Related Messages `WM_SYSKEYDOWN`, `WM_SYSKEYUP`

WM_SYSKEYDOWN

wParam Contains the virtual-key code of the pressed key.

lParam `lParam` specifies the repeat count, scan code, key transition code, previous key state, and context code. The value of `lParam` is interpreted as follows:

Bits	*Meaning*
0-15	Repeat count: the number of times the key is repeated
16-23	Scan code
24	1 if extended key
25-26	Not used
27-28	Used by Windows
29	Context code; 1 if ALT key is down
30	Previous key state; 1 if key is down before the message is sent
31	Transition state; 0 for `WM_KEYDOWN`

Description The `WM_SYSKEYDOWN` message is sent either when an ALT-key sequence is pressed or there is not a window that has the input focus. The message is sent to the active window when no window has the input focus.

Return Value Zero should be returned by the application if the message is processed.

Related Messages `WM_SYSDEADCHAR, WM_SYSKEYUP`

WM_SYSKEYUP

wParam Contains the virtual-key code of the released key.

lParam Specifies the repeat count, scan code, key transition code, previous key state, and context code. The value of `lParam` is interpreted as follows:

Bits	*Meaning*
0-15	Repeat count: the number of times the key is repeated
16-23	Scan code
24	1 if extended key
25-26	Not used
27-28	Used by Windows

Bits	Meaning
29	Context code; 1 if ALT key is down
30	Previous key state; 1 if key is down before the message is sent
31	Transition state; 1 for WM_SYSKEYUP

Description The WM_SYSKEYUP message is sent when an ALT-key sequence is released or when there is not a window that contains the input focus. When no window has the input focus, the WM_SYSKEYUP message is sent to the active window.

Return Value Zero should be returned by the application if the message is processed.

Related Messages WM_SYSDEADCHAR, WM_SYSKEYDOWN

WM_SYSTEMERROR

wParam wParam must be set to 1 to indicate that the error occurred when a task or library was terminating.

lParam Not used.

Description The WM_SYSTEMERROR message indicates that the Windows kernel has detected an error but is unable to display the system error message box.

Return Value Zero should be returned by the application if the message is processed.

Related Messages None

WM_TIMECHANGE

wParam Not used.

lParam Not used.

Description The WM_TIMECHANGE message indicates that the system time has been changed. This message should be sent to all top-level windows by the application that makes the modification.

Return Value Zero should be returned by the application if the message is processed.

Related Messages None

WM_TIMER

wParam Contains the timer ID.

lParam Points to the function specified when the `SetTimer` function was called and the `WM_TIMER` message is sent to this function. When `lParam` is `NULL`, the `WM_TIMER` message is sent to the window function.

Description The `WM_TIMER` message is sent when the time limit for the timer specified in `wParam` has expired.

Return Value Zero should be returned by the application if the message is processed.

Related Messages None

WM_UNDO

wParam Not used.

lParam Not used.

Description The `WM_UNDO` message performs an "undo" on the last operation.

Return Value `TRUE` is returned when successful. `FALSE` is returned when unsuccessful.

Related Messages `WM_CANUNDO`, `WM_COPY`, `WM_CUT`

WM_VKEYTOITEM

wParam Contains the virtual-key code of the pressed key.

lParam The high-order word of `lParam` contains the position of the caret. The low-order word of `lParam` contains the window handle for the list box.

Description The WM_VKEYTOITEM message is sent in response to a WM_KEYDOWN message. A list box with the style LBS_WANTKEYBOARDINPUT sends this message to its owner.

Return Value The return value is –2 when the application needs no further action from the list box. The return value is –1 when the list box should perform the default action for the key stroke. The return value is greater than or equal to zero when the return value represents the index of the list box item that should perform the default action for the key stroke.

Related Messages WM_KEYDOWN

WM_VSCROLL

wParam Contains the scroll bar code. The scroll bar code is selected from the following values:

Value	*Meaning*
SB_BOTTOM	Scroll to bottom
SB_ENDSCROLL	End scroll
SB_LINEDOWN	Scroll down one line
SB_LINEUP	Scroll up one line
SB_PAGEDOWN	Scroll down one page
SB_PAGEUP	Scroll up one page
SB_THUMBPOSITION	Scroll to absolute position. When specified, the low-order word of lParam contains the thumb position of the scroll bar.
SB_THUMBTRACK	Move thumb position to a specified position in lParam
SB_TOP	Scroll to top

lParam The high-order word of lParam contains the control ID when the message is sent by a scroll bar control. The low-order word of lParam is used when wParam contains SB_THUMBPOSITION or SB_THUMBTRACK.

Description The WM_VSCROLL message is sent when the vertical scroll bar is selected and active.

Return Value Zero should be returned by the application if the message is processed.

Related Messages WM_HSCROLL, WM_VSCROLLCLIPBOARD

WM_VSCROLLCLIPBOARD

wParam Specifies the clipboard application window handle.

lParam The low-order word of lParam specifies the scroll bar code. The scroll bar code is selected from the following values:

Value	*Meaning*
SB_BOTTOM	Scroll to lower right
SB_ENDSCROLL	End scroll
SB_LINEDOWN	Scroll down one line
SB_LINEUP	Scroll up one line
SB_PAGEDOWN	Scroll down one page
SB_PAGEUP	Scroll up one page
SB_THUMBPOSITION	Scroll to absolute position. When specified, the high-order word of lParam contains the thumb position of the scroll bar code.
SB_TOP	Scroll to upper left

The high-order word of lParam contains the thumb position only when the scroll bar code is SB_THUMBPOSITION.

Description The WM_VSCROLLCLIPBOARD message is sent when the following conditions are met:

- The clipboard contains the data handle for the CF_OWNERDISPLAY format.
- A component of the clipboard application's vertical scroll bar is selected.

wParam contains the clipboard application window handle.

lParam contains the scroll bar code.

Return Value Zero should be returned by the application if the message is processed.

Related Messages WM_HSCROLLCLIPBOARD, WM_VSCROLL

WM_WINDOWPOSCHANGED

wParam Not used.

lParam Pointer to a WINDOWPOS data structure that contains information about the size and position of the window.

Description The WM_WINDOWPOSCHANGED message notifies a window that its size, position, and/or order has been changed by a call to one of the window management functions. lParam points to the data structure that contains the new size and position of the window.

Return Value Zero should be returned by the application if the message is processed.

Related Messages WM_MOVE, WM_SIZE, WM_WINDOWPOSCHANGING

WM_WINDOWPOSCHANGING

wParam Not used.

lParam Pointer to a WINDOWPOS data structure that contains information about the size and position of the window.

Description The WM_WINDOWPOSCHANGING message notifies a window that its size, position, and/or order is about to be changed by a call to one of the window management functions. lParam points to the data structure that contains the new size and position of the window.

Return Value Zero should be returned by the application if the message is processed.

Related Messages WM_MOVE, WM_SIZE, WM_WINDOWPOSCHANGED

WM_WININICHANGE

wParam Not used.

lParam Points to the string that contains the name of the modified section.

Description The WM_WININICHANGE message indicates that WIN.INI, the Windows initialization file, is modified. The application that modifies WIN.INI should send this message to all top-level windows.

Return Value Zero should be returned by the application if the message is processed.

Related Messages WM_DEVMODECHANGE

15

Windows Printer Escapes

This chapter provides reference information for the Microsoft Windows printer escapes used with the Microsoft Windows function `Escape`. The printer escapes provide more direct control over the output device and enhance the capabilities of the Graphics Device Interface (GDI). All printer escapes are supported by Windows 3.0; not all these escapes, however, are supported by Windows 3.1. The printer escapes are presented in the format that follows.

NAME

Syntax The syntax for the escape. Parameters for the escape are explained.

Description A description of the proper use of the escape.

Return Value A description of the possible values returned by the escape.

REVISED 3.1 This icon indicates changes that have occurred in printer escapes between the release of Windows 3.0 and Windows 3.1.

ABORTDOC

Syntax `short Escape(hDC, ABORTDOC, NULL, NULL, NULL)`

Parameter	*Type*	*Description*
hDC	HDC	Device context

Description The ABORTDOC escape aborts the current job. When the job is terminated, all data sent to the device since the previous ENDDOC escape is erased.

Return Value There is no return value.

REVISED 3.1 For Windows version 3.1, the ABORTDOC escape has been replaced by the AbortDoc function.

BANDINFO

Syntax

```
short Escape(hDC, BANDINFO,
             sizeof(BANDINFOSTRUCT), lpInData,
             lpOutData)
```

Parameter	*Type*	*Description*
hDC	HDC	Device context
lpInData	BANDINFOSTRUCT FAR*	Pointer to a BANDINFOSTRUCT data structure containing information for the driver
lpOutData	BANDINFOSTRUCT FAR*	Pointer to a BANDINFOSTRUCT data structure containing information from the driver

Description The BANDINFO escape retrieves information about devices with banding capabilities. Banding refers to the capability to store a page of output in a metafile that is divided into bands. lpInData points to a data structure of type BANDINFOSTRUCT and contains information that is sent to the device driver from the application. lpOutData points to a data structure of type BANDINFOSTRUCT and stores information about the device. The BANDINFOSTRUCT data structure follows.

```
typedef struct {
     BOOL fGraphicsFlag;
     BOOL fTextFlag;
     RECT GraphicsRect;
} BANDINFOSTRUCT;
```

For `lpInData`, the fields of the `BANDINFOSTRUCT` structure are interpreted as follows:

`fGraphicsFlag` is `TRUE` when the application is sending graphics on the page

`fTextFlag` is `TRUE` when the application is sending text on the page

`GraphicsRect` defines the rectangle that binds the graphics for the page using a `RECT` data structure.

For `lpOutData`, the fields of the `BANDINFOSTRUCT` structure are interpreted as follows:

`fGraphicsFlag` is `TRUE` when the device is expecting graphics on the page

`fTextFlag` is `TRUE` when the device is expecting text on the page

`GraphicsRect` contains no valid data.

Return Value A 1 is returned when successful. A zero is returned when unsuccessful.

This escape is obsolete for Windows 3.1.

BEGIN_PATH

Syntax `short Escape(hDC, BEGIN_PATH, NULL, NULL, NULL)`

Parameter	*Type*	*Description*
`hDC`	`HDC`	Device context

Description The `BEGIN_PATH` escape is used with the `END_PATH` escape to create a path. Paths consist of a series of primitives drawn in succession. Paths can be used to create complex shapes and images on a device. The `END_PATH` escape specifies the path.

Return Value The number of `BEGIN_PATH` escape calls that do not have a corresponding `END_PATH` escape call is returned when successful. Zero is returned when unsuccessful.

CLIP_TO_PATH

Syntax

```
short Escape(hDC, CLIP_TO_PATH, sizeof(int), lpClipMode,
                NULL)
```

Parameter	*Type*	*Description*
hDC	HDC	Device context
lpClipMode	LPINT	Pointer to clipping mode

Description The CLIP_TO_PATH escape specifies a clipping region that is bounded by the open path. lpClipMode specifies the clipping mode and is selected from one of the following values:

Constant	*Value*	*Meaning*
CLIP_SAVE	0	Saves the clipping region
CLIP_RESTORE	1	Restores the clipping region
CLIP_INCLUSIVE	2	Defines an inclusive clipping region. Primitives that extend beyond the borders of the clipping region are clipped.
CLIP_EXCLUSIVE	3	Defines an exclusive clipping region. Primitives that are inside the clipping region are clipped.

The following steps are used to define and implement a clipping region using a path.

1. Use CLIP_TO_PATH to save the current clipping region.
2. Use BEGIN_PATH to begin a path.
3. Draw the primitives bounding the clipping region.
4. Use CLIP_TO_PATH to define the clipping region.
5. Use END_PATH to end the path.
6. Draw the primitives (these will be clipped).
7. Use CLIP_TO_PATH to restore the original clipping region.

Return Value A nonzero value is returned when successful. Zero is returned when unsuccessful.

DEVICEDATA

Syntax `short Escape(hDC, DEVICEDATA, nCount, lpInData, lpOutData)`

Parameter	*Type*	*Description*
hDC	HDC	Device context
nCount	short	Number of bytes that lpInData points to
lpInData	LPSTR	Pointer to data structure of input data
lpOutData	LPSTR	Pointer to data structure of output data

Description The DEVICEDATA escape is used to send data to the printer while bypassing the print-driver code. nCount specifies the number of bytes pointed to by lpInData. lpInData points to a data structure containing the input data. The first word of the data structure contains the number of bytes of input data. This escape is equivalent to the PASSTHROUGH escape.

Return Value The number of bytes sent to the device is returned when successful. A return value of zero or less indicates that the escape was not successful.

With Windows 3.1, the PASSTHROUGH escape should be used rather than the DEVICEDATA escape. The PASSTHROUGH escape will provide the same functionality.

DRAFTMODE

Syntax

```
short Escape(hDC, DRAFTMODE, sizeof(int), lpDraftMode,
             NULL)
```

Parameter	*Type*	*Description*
hDC	HDC	Device context
lpDraftMode	LPINT	Specifies the draft mode

Description The DRAFTMODE escape is used to specify the draft mode of the device. lpDraftMode points to the value that specifies the draft mode. The following values are used for lpDraftMode. The draft mode is off by default.

Value	*Meaning*
0	Draft mode off
1	Draft mode on

Return Value A positive value is returned when successful. A negative value or zero is returned when unsuccessful.

This escape is superceded in Windows 3.1. By setting the `dmPrintQuality` member of the `DEVMODE` structure to `DMRES_DRAFT` when calling the `ResetDC` function, the application can achieve the same results generated with the `DRAFTMODE` escape.

DRAWPATTERNRECT

Syntax

```
short Escape(hDC, DRAWPATTERNRECT,
                sizeof(PRECT_STRUCT), lpInData, NULL)
```

Parameter	*Type*	*Description*
hDC	HDC	Device context
lpInData	PRECT_STRUCT FAR*	Pointer to a PRECT_STRUCT data structure that specifies the rectangle

Description The `DRAWPATTERNRECT` escape is used to draw a rectangle on Hewlett-Packard Laserjet or compatible printers. A patterned, gray-scaled, or filled rectangle can be generated using the Hewlett-Packard Page Control Language. `lpInData` points to a data structure of type `PRECT_STRUCT` that specifies the rectangle to draw. The `PRECT_STRUCT` data structure follows.

```
struct PRECT_STRUCT {
     POINT ptPosition;
     POINT ptSize;
     WORD wStyle;
     WORD wPattern;
} ;
```

in which

`ptPosition` is the upper-left corner of the rectangle

`ptSize` is the lower-right corner of the rectangle

`wStyle` is the type of pattern. The following values are used for `wStyle`:

Value	Meaning
0	Black rule
1	White rule – HP Laserjet IIP only
2	Gray scale
3	HP defined

`wPattern` is the pattern. When `wStyle` is 0, `wPattern` is ignored. When `wStyle` is 2, `wPattern` specifies a percentage of gray for the gray scale. When `wStyle` is 3, `wPattern` is one of six HP defined patterns.

Return Value 1 is returned when successful. Zero is returned when unsuccessful.

ENABLEDUPLEX

Syntax

```
short Escape(hDC, ENABLEDUPLEX, sizeof(WORD), lpInData,
             NULL)
```

Parameter	Type	Description
`hDC`	`HDC`	Device context
`lpInData`	`LPWORD`	Pointer to value that specifies either duplex or simplex printing

Description The `ENABLEDUPLEX` escape is used to select either duplex or simplex printing for devices that are capable of printing on both sides of the paper. `lpInData` points to a value that specifies either duplex or simplex printing. The following values are used for `lpInData`:

Value	Meaning
0	Simplex printing
1	Duplex printing with vertical binding
2	Duplex printing with horizontal binding

Return Value 1 is returned when successful. Zero is returned when unsuccessful.

The `ExtDeviceMode` function can be used to achieve the same results as this escape for Windows 3.1.

ENABLEPAIRKERNING

Syntax

```
short Escape(hDC, ENABLEPAIRKERNING, sizeof(int),
             lpNewKernFlag, lpOldKernFlag)
```

Parameter	*Type*	*Description*
`hDC`	`HDC`	Device context
`lpNewKernFlag`	`LPINT`	Pointer to value specifying whether automatic pair kerning is enabled or disabled (1 and 0, respectively)
`lpOldKernFlag`	`LPINT`	Pointer to value to receive the previous automatic pair kerning setting

Description The `ENABLEPAIRKERNING` escape either enables or disables automatic pair kerning. The device driver automatically modifies the space between characters in text strings according to the font's character pair kerning table when automatic pair kerning is enabled. By default, automatic pair kerning is disabled. `lpNewKernFlag` points to a value that specifies the new setting for automatic pair kerning. The previous automatic pair kerning setting is stored in the value pointed to by `lpOldKernFlag`.

Return Value 1 is returned when successful. Zero is returned when unsuccessful.

ENABLERELATIVEWIDTHS

Syntax

```
short Escape(hDC, ENABLERELATIVEWIDTHS,
             sizeof(int), lpNewWidthFlag,
             lpOldWidthFlag)
```

Parameter	*Type*	*Description*
`hDC`	`HDC`	Device context
`lpNewWidthFlag`	`LPINT`	Pointer to value that indicates whether to enable or disable relative widths (0=disable, 1=enable)
`lpOldWidthFlag`	`LPINT`	Pointer to value to receive the previous relative width setting

Description The ENABLERELATIVEWIDTHS escape is used to either enable or disable relative character widths. The value pointed to by lpNewWidthFlag specifies whether relative character widths are enabled or disabled. When lpNewWidthFlag is 0, relative widths are disabled and the width of each character is the same number of device units. When lpNewWidthFlag is 1, relative widths are enabled and the width of each character is defined by the font's extent table. By default, relative character widths are disabled.

Return Value 1 is returned when successful. Zero is returned when unsuccessful.

ENDDOC

Syntax `short Escape(hDC, ENDDOC, NULL, NULL, NULL)`

Parameter	*Type*	*Description*
hDC	HDC	Device context

Description The ENDDOC escape ends the print job initiated by a STARTDOC escape.

Return Value A positive value is returned when successful. A negative value or zero is returned when unsuccessful.

This escape has been superceded by the EndDoc function for Windows 3.1.

END_PATH

Syntax
```
short Escape(hDC, END_PATH, sizeof(PATH_INFO), lpInData,
             NULL)
```

Parameter	*Type*	*Description*
hDC	HDC	Device context
lpInData	PATH_INFO FAR*	Pointer to a PATH_INFO data structure that specifies the path to create

Description The END_PATH escape ends a path initiated with a BEGIN_PATH escape. Paths consist of a series of primitives drawn in succession. Paths can be used to create complex shapes and

images on a device. A path is defined in the data structure of type `PATH_INFO` pointed to by `lpInData`. The `PATH_INFO` data structure follows.

```
struct PATH_INFO {
     short RenderMode;
     BYTE FillMode;
     BYTE BkMode;
     LOGPEN Pen;
     LOGBRUSH Brush;
     DWORD BkColor;
} ;
```

in which

`RenderMode` specifies how the path is to be created. The following values are used for `RenderMode`:

Constant	*Value*	*Meaning*
NO_DISPLAY	0	Path is not drawn
OPEN	1	Path is open polygon
CLOSED	2	Path is closed polygon

`FillMode` specifies how the path is to be filled. The following values are used for `FillMode`:

Constant	*Value*	*Meaning*
ALTERNATE	1	Fill uses alternate fill algorithm
WINDING	2	Fill uses winding fill algorithm

`BkMode` specifies the background mode used to fill the path. The following values are used for `BkMode`:

Constant	*Meaning*
OPAQUE	Background is filled with the background color before the brush is drawn
TRANSPARENT	Background is not modified

`Pen` specifies the pen used to draw the path

`Brush` specifies the brush used to fill the path

`BkColor` specifies the color used to fill the path.

Return Value The number of BEGIN_PATH escapes without a matching END_PATH escape is returned when successful. –1 is returned when unsuccessful.

ENUMPAPERBINS

Syntax

```
short Escape(hDC, ENUMPAPERBINS, sizeof(int),
             lpNumBins, lpOutData)
```

Parameter	*Type*	*Description*
hDC	HDC	Device context
lpNumBins	LPINT	Pointer to value specifying the number of bins
lpOutData	LPSTR	Pointer to a data structure where paper bin information will be stored

Description The ENUMPAPERBINS escape is used to gather information about the paper bins of the device. The number of paper bins for which to retrieve information is specified in lpNumBins. The information about the paper bins is copied to the data structure pointed to by lpOutData. This data structure contains two arrays. The first array contains the paper bin identification numbers, as follows:

```
short BinList[cBinMax]
```

in which cBinMax is equal to lpNumBins.

The second array is an array of characters as follows:

```
char PaperNames[cBinMax][cchBinName]
```

in which cBinMax is equal to lpNumBins and cchBinName is the length of each string (24).

Return Value 1 is returned when successful. Zero is returned when unsuccessful.

For Windows 3.1, the functionality of this escape is superceded by the functionality of the DeviceCapabilities function.

ENUMPAPERMETRICS

Syntax
```
short Escape(hDC, ENUMPAPERMETRICS, sizeof(int), lpMode,
             lpOutData)
```

Parameter	*Type*	*Description*
hDC	HDC	Device context
lpMode	LPINT	Pointer to value specifying the escape mode
lpOutData	LPRECT	Pointer to array of RECT data structures

Description The ENUMPAPERMETRICS escape works in two ways. When lpMode is set to 0, the ENUMPAPERMETRICS escape returns the number of paper types supported by the device. The returned value is then used to allocate an array of RECT data structures. When lpMode is set to 1, the ENUMPAPERMETRICS escape returns one or more RECT data structures defining the page regions able to receive an image. The array of RECT data structures receiving the page region information is pointed to by lpOutData.

Return Value A positive value is returned when successful. A negative value is returned when unsuccessful. If the escape is not implemented, zero is returned.

For Windows 3.1, the functionality of this escape is superceded by the functionality of the DeviceCapabilities function.

EPSPRINTING

Syntax
```
short Escape(hDC, EPSPRINTING, sizeof(BOOL),
             lpBool, NULL)
```

Parameter	*Type*	*Description*
hDC	HDC	Device context
lpBool	BOOL FAR*	Pointer to value specifying whether to enable or disable downloading (TRUE=enable, FALSE=disable)

Description The EPSPRINTING escape either enables or disables the output of the Windows Postscript header control section. GDI calls cannot be used by applications generating this escape.

Return Value A positive value is returned when successful. A negative value is returned when unsuccessful. If the escape is not implemented, zero is returned.

EXT_DEVICE_CAPS

Syntax

```
short Escape(hDC, EXT_DEVICE_CAPS, sizeof(int),
             lpIndex, lpCaps)
```

Parameter	*Type*	*Description*
`hDC`	`HDC`	Device context
`lpIndex`	`LPINT`	Pointer to value indicating the capability to retrieve
`lpCaps`	`DWORD FAR*`	Pointer to value to receive capability information

Description The `EXT_DEVICE_CAPS` escape determines the capabilities of a device. `lpIndex` points to a value that specifies the capability to examine. The values for `lpIndex` follow. `lpCaps` points to the value where the retrieved capability information is stored.

Constant	*Value*	*Meaning*
`R2_CAPS`	1	The value returned in `lpCaps` indicates which of the 16 binary raster operations are supported by the device driver
`PATTERN_CAPS`	2	The low-order word of `lpCaps` contains the maximum width of a pattern brush bitmap. The high-order word of `lpCaps` contains the maximum height of a pattern brush bitmap
`PATH_CAPS`	3	The logical `OR` operation can be used with the `lpCaps` value to determine whether paths can use alternate or winding interiors or whether the device supports inclusive and exclusive clipping. The following values are used with logical `OR` to determine the capabilities:

Constant	*Value*	*Meaning*
		PATH_ALTERNATE, PATH_WINDING, PATH_INCLUSIVE, PATH_EXCLUSIVE
POLYGON_CAPS	4	The value in lpCaps indicates the maximum number of polygon points that the device supports
PATTERN_COLOR_CAPS	5	The value in lpCaps indicates whether monochrome pattern bitmaps can be converted to color (1 if conversions are supported, 0 if not supported)
R2_TEXT_CAPS	6	The low-order word of lpCaps indicates the raster operations the device supports for text. The high-order word of the lpCaps indicates the type of text for the raster operations. The following values can be used with the logical OR operation to determine the text type: RASTER_TEXT, DEVICE_TEXT, VECTOR_TEXT.
POLYMODE_CAPS	7	Specifies which polygon modes are supported by the device driver.

Return Value A nonzero value is returned when the specified capability is supported. Zero is returned when the specified capability is not supported.

The GetDeviceCaps function is used to achieve the same results as this escape for Windows 3.1.

EXTTEXTOUT

Syntax

```
short Escape(hDC, EXTTEXTOUT, sizeof(EXTTEXT_STRUCT,
             lpInData, NULL)
```

Parameter	*Type*	*Description*
hDC	HDC	Device context
lpInData	EXTTEXT_STRUCT FAR*	Pointer to EXTTEXT_STRUCT data structure

Description The EXTTEXTOUT escape allows the application to call the GDI TextOut function while specifying string characteristics. This function is provided for compatibility with earlier versions of Windows. lpInData points to a data structure of type EXTTEXT_STRUCT. This data structure contains information on the characteristics of the character string. The EXTTEXT_STRUCT data structure follows.

```
typedef struct {
     WORD X;
     WORD Y;
     LPWORD lpText;
     LPWORD lpWidths;
} EXTTEXT_STRUCT;
```

in which

X is the x coordinate of the upper-left corner of the starting point for the string

Y is the y coordinate of the upper-left corner of the starting point for the string

lpText is a pointer to an array of character codes

lpWidths is a pointer to an array of character widths used to print the string.

Return Value 1 is returned when successful. Zero is returned when unsuccessful.

The ExtTextOut function is used with Windows 3.1 to achieve the same results as this escape.

FLUSHOUTPUT

Syntax `short Escape(hDC, FLUSHOUTPUT, NULL, NULL, NULL)`

Parameter	*Type*	*Description*
hDC	HDC	Device context

Description The `FLUSHOUTPUT` escape flushes output from the device buffer.

Return Value A positive value is returned when successful. A negative value is returned when unsuccessful.

GETCOLORTABLE

Syntax
```
short Escape(hDC, GETCOLORTABLE, sizeof(int),
             lpIndex, lpColor)
```

Parameter	*Type*	*Description*
`hDC`	`HDC`	Device context
`lpIndex`	`LPINT`	Pointer to value specifying the color index
`lpColor`	`LPDWORD`	Pointer to value where RGB value is stored

Description The `GETCOLORTABLE` escape copies the RGB value for the color table index specified in `lpIndex` to the value pointed to by `lpColor`.

Return Value A positive value is returned when successful. A negative value or zero is returned when unsuccessful.

GETEXTENDEDTEXTMETRICS

Syntax
```
short Escape(hDC, GETEXTENDEDTEXTMETRICS,
             sizeof(WORD), lpInData, lpOutData)
```

Parameter	*Type*	*Description*
`hDC`	`HDC`	Device context
`lpInData`	`LPWORD`	Pointer to value specifying the number of bytes pointed to by `lpOutData`
`lpOutData`	`EXTTEXTMETRIC FAR*`	Pointer to `EXTTEXTMETRIC` data structure

Description The `GETEXTENDEDTEXTMETRICS` escape retrieves extended text metrics for the selected font. The text metrics are placed in the data structure of type `EXTTEXTMETRIC` pointed to by `lpOutData`. The `EXTTEXTMETRIC` structure follows.

```
struct EXTTEXTMETRIC {
     short etmSize;
     short etmPointSize;
     short etmOrientation;
     short etmMasterHeight;
     short etmMinScale;
     short etmMaxScale;
     short etmMasterUnits;
     short etmCapHeight;
     short etmXHeight;
     short etmLowerCaseAscent;
     short etmLowerCaseDescent;
     short etmSlant;
     short etmSuperScript;
     short etmSubScript;
     short etmSuperScriptSize;
     short etmSubScriptSize;
     short etmUnderlineOffset;
     short etmUnderlineWidth;
     short etmDoubleUpperUnderlineOffset;
     short etmDoubleLowerUnderlineOffset;
     short etmDoubleUpperUnderlineWidth;
     short etmDoubleLowerUnderlineWidth;
     short etmStrikeOutOffset;
     short etmStrikeOutWidth;
     WORD etmKernPairs;
     WORD etmKernTracks;
} ;
```

in which

`etmSize` is the number of bytes in the structure

`etmPointSize` is the point size in twips (twentieths of a point or 1/1440 inches)

`etmOrientation` is the font orientation (0=either, 1=portrait, 2=landscape)

`etmMasterHeight` is the font size in device units

`etmMinScale` is the minimum size for the font

`etmMaxScale` is the maximum size for the font

`etmMasterUnits` is the same as `etmMasterHeight`, except `etmMasterUnits` is expressed in font units

`etmCapHeight` is the height (font units) of uppercase letters

`etmXHeight` is the height (font units) of lowercase letters

`etmLowerCaseAscent` is the number of font units that the ascender of lowercase letters extends above the baseline

`etmLowerCaseDescent` is the number of font units that the descender of lowercase letters extends below the baseline

`etmSlant` is the angle of slant for the font; this angle is measured in tenths of degrees clockwise from the vertical font

`etmSuperScript` is the number of font units used to offset superscript characters from the baseline

`etmSubScript` is the number of font units used to offset subscript characters from the baseline

`etmSuperScriptSize` is the number of font units used for superscript characters

`etmSubScriptSize` is the number of font units used for subscript characters

`etmUnderlineOffset` is the number of font units from the baseline where the top of an underline bar is to be located

`etmUnderlineWidth` is the thickness (font units) of the underline bar

`etmDoubleUpperUnderlineOffset` is the number of font units from the baseline where the top of an upper, double-underline bar is to be located

`etmDoubleLowerUnderlineOffset` is the number of font units from the baseline where the top of a lower, double-underline bar is to be located

`etmDoubleUpperUnderlineWidth` is the thickness (font units) of the upper underline bar

`etmDoubleLowerUnderlineWidth` is the thickness (font units) of the lower underline bar

`etmStrikeOutOffset` is the number of font units from the baseline where the top of the strike-out bar is to be located

`etmStrikeOutWidth` is the thickness (font units) of the strike-out bar

`etmKernPairs` is the number of kerning pairs defined for the font

`etmKernTracks` is the number of kerning tracks defined for the font.

Return Value The number of bytes copied to the data structure is returned when successful. Zero is returned when unsuccessful.

GETEXTENTTABLE

Syntax

```
short Escape(hDC, GETEXTENTTABLE,
             sizeof(CHAR_RANGE_STRUCT), lpInData,
             lpOutData)
```

Parameter	*Type*	*Description*
hDC	HDC	Device context
lpInData	LPSTR	Pointer to CHAR_RANGE_STRUCT data structure defining a range of characters
lpOutData	LPINT	Pointer to array which stores the retrieved character widths

Description The GETEXTENTTABLE escape determines the character width of each character in a specified range of characters. lpInData points to a data structure of type CHAR_RANGE_STRUCT that defines the range of characters. The CHAR_RANGE_STRUCT data structure follows. lpOutData points to an array of integers in which the widths of the specified characters are stored. The size of the array is chLast – chFirst + 1.

```
struct CHAR_RANGE_STRUCT {
     BYTE chFirst;
     BYTE chLast;
} ;
```

in which

chFirst is the character code of the first character in the character range

chLast is the character code of the last character in the character range.

Return Value 1 is returned when successful. Zero is returned when unsuccessful.

GETFACENAME

Syntax
```
short Escape(hDC, GETFACENAME, NULL, NULL,
             lpFaceName)
```

Parameter	*Type*	*Description*
hDC	HDC	Device context
lpFaceName	LPSTR	Pointer to buffer that is to receive the face name

Description The GETFACENAME escape retrieves the face name of the current font and stores it in the buffer pointed to by lpFaceName.

Return Value A positive value is returned when successful. A negative value is returned when unsuccessful. Zero is returned when the escape is not implemented.

GETPAIRKERNTABLE

Syntax
```
short Escape(hDC, GETPAIRKERNTABLE, NULL, NULL,
             lpOutData)
```

Parameter	*Type*	*Description*
hDC	HDC	Device context
lpOutData	KERNPAIR FAR*	Pointer to array of KERNPAIR data structures

Description The GETPAIRKERNTABLE escape retrieves the character pair kerning table for the font and places the table in the array pointed to by lpOutData. lpOutData points to an array of data structures of type KERNPAIR. The KERNPAIR data structure follows.

```
struct KERNPAIR {
     union {
           BYTE each [2];
           WORD both;
           } kpPair;
     short kpKernAmount;
} ;
```

in which

`kpPair.each[0]` is the character code of the first character in the kerning pair

`kpPair.each[1]` is the character code of the second character in the kerning pair

`kpPair.both` contains the first character of the kerning pair in the low-order byte and the second character of the kerning pair in the high-order byte

`kpKernAmount` is the amount of kerning involved when the characters in the kerning pair are placed next to each other.

Return Value The number of data structures copied to the buffer is returned when successful. Zero is returned when unsuccessful.

GETPHYSPAGESIZE

Syntax

```
short Escape(hDC, GETPHYSPAGESIZE, NULL, NULL,
             lpDimensions)
```

Parameter	*Type*	*Description*
hDC	HDC	Device context
lpDimensions	LPPOINT	Pointer to POINT data structure that will store the page size

Description The `GETPHYSPAGESIZE` escape determines the page size and stores the page size in the `POINT` data structure pointed to by `lpDimensions`. The `POINT` data structure follows.

```
typedef struct tagPOINT {
     int x;
     int y;
} POINT;
```

in which

`x` specifies the horizontal page size in device units

`y` specifies the vertical page size in device units.

Return Value A positive value is returned when successful. A negative value or zero is returned when unsuccessful.

GETPRINTINGOFFSET

Syntax

```
short Escape(hDC, GETPRINTINGOFFSET, NULL, NULL,
             lpOffset)
```

Parameter	*Type*	*Description*
hDC	HDC	Device context
lpOffset	LPPOINT	Pointer to POINT data structure that will store the offset

Description The GETPRINTINGOFFSET escape determines the printing offset of the page in device units. The offset is considered to be the upper-left corner of the page where printing begins. The offset is placed in the data structure of type POINT pointed to by lpOffset. The POINT data structure follows.

```
typedef struct tagPOINT {
     int x;
     int y;
} POINT;
```

in which

x specifies the horizontal device coordinate of the offset

y specifies the vertical device coordinate of the offset.

Return Value A positive value is returned when successful. A negative value or zero is returned when unsuccessful.

GETSCALINGFACTOR

Syntax

```
short Escape(hDC, GETSCALINGFACTOR, NULL, NULL,
             lpFactors)
```

Parameter	*Type*	*Description*
hDC	HDC	Device context
lpFactors	LPPOINT	Pointer to POINT data structure that will hold the scaling factor

Description The GETSCALINGFACTOR escape determines the scaling factors for the axes of the device. The scaling factors are copied to the data structure of type POINT pointed to by lpFactors and are exponents of 2 (for example, 3 indicates 2^3 or 8). The POINT data structure follows.

```
typedef struct tagPOINT {
     int x;
     int y;
} POINT;
```

in which

x specifies the horizontal axis scaling factor

y specifies the vertical axis scaling factor.

Return Value A positive value is returned when successful. A negative value or zero is returned when unsuccessful.

GETSETPAPERBINS

Syntax

```
short Escape(hDC, GETSETPAPERBINS, nCount,
             lpInData, lpOutData)
```

Parameter	*Type*	*Description*
hDC	HDC	Device context
nCount	int	Number of bytes pointed to by lpInData
lpInData	BinInfo FAR*	Pointer to BinInfo data structure specifying new bin
lpOutData	BinInfo FAR*	Pointer to BinInfo data structure containing bin information

Description The GETSETPAPERBINS escape determines the number of paper bins for the device and specifies the bin to use. lpInData and lpOutData can either point to a data structure of type BinInfo or be set to NULL. When lpInData is NULL and lpOutData points to a BinInfo data structure, the current bin number and the number of bins is retrieved. When both lpInData and lpOutData point to a BinInfo data structure, lpInData specifies the new bin to use and lpOutData stores the previous bin number. When lpInData points to a BinInfo data structure and lpOutData is NULL, lpInData specifies the new bin number. The BinInfo data structure follows.

```
struct BinInfo{
     int BinNumber;
     int cBins;
     int Reserved;
     int Reserved;
     int Reserved;
     int Reserved;
} ;
```

in which

`BinNumber` is the paper bin number

`cBins` is the number of paper bins available.

Return Value A positive value is returned when successful. Zero or a negative value is returned when unsuccessful.

This escape has been superceded in Windows 3.1. To achieve the same results as this escape, call the `DeviceCapabilities` function to determine the number of paper bins, call the `ExtDeviceMode` function to determine the current bin, and call the `ResetDC` function to set the new current bin.

GETSETPAPERMETRICS

Syntax

```
short Escape(hDC, GETSETPAPERMETRICS, sizeof(RECT),
             lpNewPaper, lpPrevPaper)
```

Parameter	*Type*	*Description*
hDC	HDC	Device context
lpNewPaper	LPRECT	Pointer to RECT data structure specifying the new area
lpPrevPaper	LPRECT	Pointer to RECT data structure where previous area is stored

Description The `GETSETPAPERMETRICS` escape stores the previous paper metrics information and defines the paper type using the specified paper metrics information. `lpNewPaper` points to a data structure of type `RECT` that specifies the usable region of the page. `lpPrevPaper` points to a data structure of type `RECT` that stores the previous usable region.

Return Value A positive value is returned when successful. A negative value is returned when unsuccessful. When the escape is not implemented, zero is returned.

For Windows 3.1, this escape is superceded by the `DeviceCapabilities` and `ExtDeviceMode` functions.

GETSETPAPERORIENT

Syntax

```
short Escape(hDC, GETSETPAPERORIENT, nCount,
                lpInData, NULL)
```

Parameter	*Type*	*Description*
hDC	HDC	Device context
nCount	int	Number of bytes pointed to by lpInData
lpInData	ORIENT FAR*	Pointer to ORIENT data structure defining the paper orientation

Description The `GETSETPAPERORIENT` escape either determines or defines the paper orientation. When `lpInData` is `NULL`, the current paper orientation is returned. When `lpInData` is not `NULL`, `lpInData` points to a data structure of type `ORIENT` that defines the new paper orientation. The `ORIENT` data structure follows.

```
struct ORIENT {
     DWORD Orientation;
     DWORD Reserved;
     DWORD Reserved;
     DWORD Reserved;
     DWORD Reserved;
} ;
```

in which

`Orientation` is either 1 for portrait or 2 for landscape.

Return Value When `lpInData` is `NULL`, the current orientation is returned. If `lpInData` is not `NULL`, the previous orientation is returned. When unsuccessful, –1 is returned.

For Windows 3.1, this function is superceded by the `DeviceCapabilities` and `ExtDeviceMode` functions.

GETSETSCREENPARAMS

Syntax

```
short Escape(hDC, GETSETSCREENPARAMS,
             sizeof(SCREENPARAMS), lpInData,
             lpOutData)
```

Parameter	*Type*	*Description*
hDC	HDC	Device context
lpInData	SCREENPARAMS FAR*	Pointer to SCREENPARAMS data structure that specifies new screen information
lpOutData	SCREENPARAMS FAR*	Pointer to SCREENPARAMS data structure where previous screen information is stored

Description The GETSETSCREENPARAMS escape sets or determines screen information. lpInData and lpOutData will either point to a data structure of type SCREENPARAMS or be set to NULL. The behavior of the escape depends on the settings of lpInData and lpOutData. The SCREENPARAMS data structure follows.

```
struct SCREENPARAMS {
     int angle;
     int frequency;
} ;
```

in which

angle is the angle of the halftone screen in degrees

frequency is the screen frequency.

Return Value A positive value is returned when successful. A negative value is returned when unsuccessful.

GETTECHNOLOGY

Syntax

```
short Escape(hDC, GETTECHNOLOGY, NULL, NULL,
             lpTechnology)
```

Parameter	*Type*	*Description*
hDC	HDC	Device context
lpTechnology	LPSTR	Pointer to buffer where the string that describes the device technology is placed

Description The GETTECHNOLOGY escape determines the printer technology type and copies a string that describes the technology type to the buffer pointed to by lpTechnology.

Return Value 1 is returned when successful. Zero is returned when unsuccessful.

This escape is obsolete for Windows 3.1.

GETTRACKKERNTABLE

Syntax

```
short Escape(hDC, GETTRACKKERNTABLE, NULL, NULL,
                    lpOutData)
```

Parameter	*Type*	*Description*
hDC	HDC	Device context
lpOutData	KERNTRACK FAR*	Pointer to array of KERNTRACK data structures

Description The GETTRACKKERNTABLE escape copies the track kerning table for the current font to the array pointed to by lpOutData. lpOutData points to an array of KERNSTACK data structures. The KERNSTACK data structure follows. The array must contain enough structures to hold all the kerning tracks for the font. The EXTTEXTMETRIC structure returned by the GETEXTENDEDTEXTMETRICS escape can be used to determine the number of kerning tracks for the font.

```
struct KERNTRACK {
     short Degree;
     short MinSize;
     short MinAmount;
     short MaxSize;
     short MaxAmount;
} ;
```

in which

Degree is the amount of track kerning

MinSize is the minimum font size (device units) where linear track kerning applies

MinAmount is the amount of track kerning (logical units) applied to fonts that are less than or equal to the size specified in MinSize

MaxSize is the maximum font size (device units) where linear track kerning applies

MaxAmount is the amount of track kerning (logical units) applied to fonts that are greater than or equal to the size specified in MaxSize.

Return Value The number of data structures copied is returned when successful. Zero is returned when unsuccessful.

GETVECTORBRUSHSIZE

Syntax

```
short Escape(hDC, GETVECTORBRUSHSIZE, sizeof(LOGBRUSH),
             lpInData, lpOutData)
```

Parameter	*Type*	*Description*
hDC	HDC	Device context
lpInData	LOGBRUSH FAR*	Pointer to LOGBRUSH data structure specifying the brush
lpOutData	LPPOINT	Pointer to POINT data structure specifying the width of the pen

Description The GETVECTORBRUSHSIZE escape determines the size of the pen (in device units) used for filling figures. lpInData points to a data structure of type LOGBRUSH that defines the brush. The LOGBRUSH data structure follows. lpOutData points to a data structure of type POINT that specifies the width of the pen. The second word of the POINT data structure contains the pen width in device units.

```
typedef struct tagLOGBRUSH {
     WORD lbStyle;
     DWORD lbColor;
     short int lbHatch;
} LOGBRUSH;
```

in which

`lbStyle` is the brush style and is set to one of the following values:

Value	*Meaning*
BS_DIBPATTERN	Pattern brush defined with a device independent bitmap
BS_HATCHED	Hatched brush
BS_HOLLOW	Hollow brush
BS_INDEXED	Indexed brush
BS_NULL	Null brush
BS_PATTERN	Pattern brush defined with a memory bitmap
BS_SOLID	Solid brush

`lbColor` is the color for the brush and is one of the following values:

Value	*Meaning*
DIB_PAL_COLORS	Color table is an array of 16-bit indexes to the logical palette
DIB_RGB_COLORS	Color table contains literal RGB values

`lbHatch` is the hatch style and is interpreted as follows: If `lbStyle` is `BS_DIBPATTERN`, `lbHatch` contains the handle to a packed, device-independent bitmap. If `lbStyle` is `BS_HATCHED`, `lbHatch` contains one of the following values that specify the line orientation of the hatch:

Value	*Meaning*
HS_BDIAGONAL	45-degree upward hatch
HS_CROSS	Crosshatch with vertical/horizontal lines
HS_DIAGCROSS	45-degree crosshatch
HS_FDIAGONAL	45-degree downward hatch
HS_HORIZONTAL	Horizontal hatch
HS_VERTICAL	Vertical hatch

If `lbStyle` is `BS_PATTERN`, `lbHatch` contains the handle to the bitmap for the pattern. If `lbStyle` is `BS_SOLID` or `BS_HOLLOW`, `lbHatch` is ignored.

Return Value 1 is returned when successful. Zero is returned when unsuccessful.

GETVECTORPENSIZE

Syntax

```
short Escape(hDC, GETVECTORPENSIZE,
             sizeof(LOGPEN), lpInData, lpOutData)
```

Parameter	*Type*	*Description*
hDC	HDC	Device context
lpInData	LOGPEN FAR*	Pointer to LOGPEN data structure specifying the pen
lpOutData	LPPOINT	Pointer to POINT data structure specifying the pen width

Description The GETVECTORPENSIZE escape determines the size of the pen (in device units) used for drawing. lpInData points to a data structure of type LOGPEN that defines the pen. The LOGPEN data structure follows. lpOutData points to a data structure of type POINT that specifies the width of the pen. The second word of the POINT data structure contains the pen width in device units.

```
typedef struct tagLOGPEN {
     WORD lopnStyle;
     POINT lopnWidth;
     DWORD lopnColor;
} LOGPEN;
```

in which

lopnStyle is the pen style and is chosen from one of the following constants:

Constant	*Value*
PS_SOLID	0
PS_DASH	1
PS_DOT	2
PS_DASHDOT	3
PS_DASHDOTDOT	4
PS_NULL	5
PS_INSIDEFRAME	6

lopnWidth is the pen width in logical units

lopnColor is the pen color.

Return Value 1 is returned when successful. Zero is returned when unsuccessful.

MFCOMMENT

Syntax `BOOL Escape(hDC, MFCOMMENT, nCount, lpComment, NULL)`

Parameter	*Type*	*Description*
`hDC`	`HDC`	Device context
`nCount`	`short`	Number of characters pointed to by `lpComment`
`lpComment`	`LPSTR`	Pointer to the string containing the comment to appear in the metafile

Description The `MFCOMMENT` escape adds the comment in the string pointed to by `lpComment` to a metafile. `nCount` specifies the number of characters in the buffer pointed to by `lpComment`.

Return Value A positive value is returned when successful. –1 is returned when unsuccessful.

NEWFRAME

Syntax `short Escape(hDC, NEWFRAME, NULL, NULL, NULL)`

Parameter	*Type*	*Description*
`hDC`	`HDC`	Device context

Description The `NEWFRAME` escape is used to indicate that the application is done writing to the page.

Return Value A positive value is returned when successful. When unsuccessful, one of the following values is returned:

Value	*Meaning*
`SP_APPABORT`	Job terminated due to a return value of zero from the application's abort function
`SP_ERROR`	Error
`SP_OUTOFDISK`	Insufficient disk space for spooling
`SP_OUTOFMEMORY`	Insufficient memory for spooling
`SP_USERABORT`	Job terminated by user through Print Manager

REVISED 3.1 There have been no changes to this escape for Windows 3.1. However, the `StartPage` and `EndPage` functions should be used rather than this escape.

NEXTBAND

Syntax `short Escape(hDC, NEXTBAND, NULL, NULL, lpBandRect)`

Parameter	*Type*	*Description*
hDC	HDC	Device context
lpBandRect	LPRECT	Pointer to RECT data structure to receive next band coordinates

Description The NEXTBAND escape is used to indicate that the application has completed the writing of a band. The device then sends the band to the Print Manager and returns the coordinates of the next band. lpBandRect points to the data structure of type RECT that receives the band coordinates. The RECT data structure follows.

```
typedef struct tagRECT{
     int left;
     int top;
     int right;
     int bottom;
} RECT;
```

in which

left is the x coordinate of the upper-left corner

top is the y coordinate of the upper-left corner

right is the x coordinate of the lower-right corner

bottom is the y coordinate of the lower-right corner.

Return Value A positive value is returned when successful. When unsuccessful, one of the following values is returned:

Value	*Meaning*
SP_APPABORT	Job terminated due to a return value of zero from the application's abort function
SP_ERROR	Error
SP_OUTOFDISK	Insufficient disk space for spooling
SP_OUTOFMEMORY	Insufficient memory for spooling
SP_USERABORT	Job terminated by user through Print Manager

PASSTHROUGH

Syntax `short Escape(hDC, PASSTHROUGH, NULL, lpInData, NULL)`

Parameter	*Type*	*Description*
hDC	HDC	Device context
lpInData	LPSTR	Pointer to data structure of input data

Description The PASSTHROUGH escape is used to send data to the printer while bypassing the print-driver code. lpInData points to a data structure containing the input data. The first word of the data structure contains the number of bytes of input data.

Return Value The number of bytes sent to the device is returned when successful. A return value of zero or less indicates that the escape was not successful.

QUERYESCSUPPORT

Syntax
```
short Escape(hDC, QUERYESCSUPPORT, sizeof(int),
             lpEscNum, NULL)
```

Parameter	*Type*	*Description*
hDC	HDC	Device context
lpEscNum	LPINT	Pointer to value specifying the escape

Description The QUERYESCSUPPORT escape determines whether the device driver implements the escape specified in lpEscNum.

Return Value A nonzero value is returned when the specified escape is implemented. Zero is returned when the specified escape is not implemented. When lpEscNum is DRAWPATTERNRECT, one of the following values is returned:

Value	*Meaning*
0	DRAWPATTERNRECT not implemented
1	DRAWPATTERNRECT implemented for printer other than HP Laserjet IIP (white rules supported)
2	DRAWPATTERNRECT implemented for HP Laserjet IIP

RESTORE_CTM

Syntax `short Escape(hDC, RESTORE_CTM, NULL, NULL, NULL)`

Parameter	*Type*	*Description*
hDC	HDC	Device context

Description The RESTORE_CTM escape restores the transformation matrix to its previous state.

Return Value The number of SAVE_CTM calls without corresponding RESTORE_CTM calls is returned when successful. –1 is returned when unsuccessful.

SAVE_CTM

Syntax `short Escape(hDC, SAVE_CTM, NULL, NULL, NULL)`

Parameter	*Type*	*Description*
hDC	HDC	Device context

Description The SAVE_CTM escape saves the current transformation matrix. The transformation matrix determines how coordinates are translated, rotated, and scaled by the device.

Return Value The number of SAVE_CTM calls without corresponding RESTORE_CTM calls is returned when successful. Zero is returned when unsuccessful.

SETABORTPROC

Syntax `short Escape(hDC, SETABORTPROC, NULL, lpAbortFunc, NULL)`

Parameter	*Type*	*Description*
hDC	HDC	Device context
lpAbortFunc	FARPROC	Pointer to abort function

Description The SETABORTPROC escape defines the abort function for the print job. lpAbortFunc points to the abort function supplied by the application. The abort function has the following conventions:

```
short FAR PASCAL AbortFunc(hPr, code)
HDC hPr;
short code;
```

in which

`hPr` is the device context

`code` indicates whether an error has occurred

The abort function should return a nonzero value to continue the print job and a zero to cancel the print job.

Return Value A positive value is returned when successful. A negative value is returned when unsuccessful.

The `SetAbortProc` function must be used to achieve the same results as this escape for Windows 3.1.

SETALLJUSTVALUES

Syntax

```
short Escape(hDC, SETALLJUSTVALUES, sizeof(EXTTEXTDATA),
             lpInData, NULL)
```

Parameter	*Type*	*Description*
hDC	HDC	Device context
lpInData	EXTTEXTDATA FAR*	Pointer to EXTTEXTDATA data structure defining the justification

Description The `SETALLJUSTVALUES` escape defines the justification values for text. The text justification values are defined in the data structure of type `EXTTEXTDATA` pointed to by `lpInData`. The `EXTTEXTDATA` data structure follows.

```
typedef struct {
     short nSize;
     LPALLJUSTREC lpInData;
     LPFONTINFO lpFont;
     LPTEXTXFORM lpXForm;
     LPDRAWMODE lpDrawMode;
} EXTTEXTDATA;
```

The `EXTTEXTDATA` structure contains the following `JUST_VALUE_STRUCT` data structure:

```
typedef struct {
     short nCharExtra;
     WORD nCharCount;
     short nBreakExtra;
     WORD nBreakCount;
} JUST_VALUE_STRUCT;
```

in which

nCharExtra is the extra space to be allocated between the characters defined in nCharCount (in font units)

nCharCount is the number of characters over which the extra space in nCharExtra is distributed

nBreakExtra is the extra space to be allocated between the characters defined in nBreakCount (in font units)

nBreakCount is the number of characters over which the extra space in nBreakExtra is distributed.

Return Value 1 is returned when successful. Zero is returned when unsuccessful.

SET_ARC_DIRECTION

Syntax

```
short Escape(hDC, SET_ARC_DIRECTION, sizeof(int),
                lpDirection, NULL)
```

Parameter	*Type*	*Description*
hDC	HDC	Device context
lpDirection	LPINT	Pointer to value indicating arc direction

Description The SET_ARC_DIRECTION escape defines the direction, either counterclockwise or clockwise, used by the Windows function Arc when drawing elliptical arcs. lpDirection points to the value that specifies the arc direction. The following values are used for the value pointed to by lpDirection:

Constant	*Value*	*Meaning*
COUNTERCLOCKWISE	0	Arc drawn counterclockwise
CLOCKWISE	1	Arc drawn clockwise

Return Value The previous arc direction is returned.

SET_BACKGROUND_COLOR

Syntax

```
short Escape(hDC, SET_BACKGROUND_COLOR, nCount,
                  lpNewColor, lpOldColor)
```

Parameter	*Type*	*Description*
hDC	HDC	Device context
nCount	int	Number of bytes pointed to by lpNewColor
lpNewColor	LPDWORD	Pointer to new background color
lpOldColor	LPDWORD	Pointer to value that receives the previous background color

Description The SET_BACKGROUND_COLOR escape defines the background color for the device. lpNewColor points to a 32-bit value that specifies the new background color. lpOldColor points to the 32-bit value that receives the previous background color. The background color, by default, is white.

Return Value A nonzero value is returned when successful. Zero is returned when unsuccessful.

SET_BOUNDS

Syntax

```
short Escape(hDC, SET_BOUNDS, sizeof(RECT), lpInData, NULL)
```

Parameter	*Type*	*Description*
hDC	HDC	Device context
lpInData	LPRECT	Pointer to RECT data structure that contains the coordinates of the image

Description The SET_BOUNDS escape defines a rectangle for an image produced by file formats such as Encapsulated Postscript or Hewlett-Packard Graphics Language. lpInData points to a data structure of type RECT that defines the rectangle that binds the image. The RECT data structure follows.

```
typedef struct tagRECT{
     int left;
     int top;
     int right;
     int bottom;
} RECT;
```

in which

`left` is the x coordinate of the upper-left corner

`top` is the y coordinate of the upper-left corner

`right` is the x coordinate of the lower-right corner

`bottom` is the y coordinate of the lower-right corner.

Return Value A nonzero value is returned when successful. Zero is returned when unsuccessful.

SETCOLORTABLE

Syntax

```
short Escape(hDC, SETCOLORTABLE, sizeof(COLORTABLE_STRUCT),
             lpInData, lpColor)
```

Parameter	*Type*	*Description*
hDC	HDC	Device context
lpInData	COLORTABLE_STRUCT FAR*	Pointer to COLORTABLE_STRUCT data structure defining the color table entry
lpColor	LPDWORD	Pointer to value to receive the RGB color value

Description The `SETCOLORTABLE` escape defines an RGB value for the color table. `lpInData` points to a data structure of type `COLORTABLE_STRUCT` that defines the index and RGB value of the color table entry. The `COLORTABLE_STRUCT` data structure follows.

```
struct COLORTABLE_STRUCT {
     WORD Index;
     DWORD rgb;
} ;
```

in which

`Index` is the color table index (0 = first entry)

`rgb` is the RGB color value.

Return Value A positive value is returned when successful. A negative value is returned when unsuccessful.

SETCOPYCOUNT

Syntax

```
short Escape(hDC, SETCOPYCOUNT, sizeof(int),
             lpNumCopies, lpActualCopies)
```

Parameter	*Type*	*Description*
hDC	HDC	Device context
lpNumCopies	LPINT	Pointer to value that indicates the number of uncollated copies to print
lpActualCopies	LPINT	Pointer to value that will store the number of copies to print

Description The SETCOPYCOUNT escape defines the number of uncollated copies of each page that should be printed.

Return Value 1 is returned when successful. Zero is returned when unsuccessful.

Windows 3.1 applications should use the ExtDeviceMode function instead of this escape.

SETKERNTRACK

Syntax

```
short Escape(hDC, SETKERNTRACK, sizeof(int), lpNewTrack,
             lpOldTrack)
```

Parameter	*Type*	*Description*
hDC	HDC	Device context
lpNewTrack	LPINT	Pointer to value specifying the track to use; setting lpNewTrack to zero disables this feature
lpOldTrack	LPINT	Pointer to the value receiving the previous kerning track

Description The SETKERNTRACK escape defines the kerning track used by device drivers that support automatic track kerning. By default, automatic kerning is disabled. lpNewTrack points to the value that specifies the kerning track to be used by the device drivers.

Return Value 1 is returned when successful. Zero is returned when unsuccessful.

SETLINECAP

Syntax

```
short Escape(hDC, SETLINECAP, sizeof(int), lpNewCap,
                lpOldCap)
```

Parameter	*Type*	*Description*
hDC	HDC	Device context
lpNewCap	LPINT	Pointer to value that specifies the end-cap type
lpOldCap	LPINT	Pointer to value that specifies the previous end-cap type

Description The SETLINECAP escape sets the line end-cap, the portion of the line segment that appears on either end of the line segment. lpNewCap points to the value that specifies the new end-cap type. The following values are used for lpNewCap:

Value	*Meaning*
–1	Line segments are drawn with default GDI end-caps
0	Line segments are drawn with squared end points; end points do not extend past the defined line segment
1	Line segments are drawn with rounded end points; the diameter of the rounded portion of the segment is equal to the line width
2	Line segments are drawn with squared end points; end points extend one-half the line width past the defined line segment

Return Value A positive value is returned when successful. A negative value is returned when unsuccessful.

SETLINEJOIN

Syntax
```
short Escape(hDC, SETLINEJOIN, sizeof(int), lpNewJoin,
             lpOldJoin)
```

Parameter	*Type*	*Description*
hDC	HDC	Device context
lpNewJoin	LPINT	Pointer to the value specifying the intersection type
lpOldJoin	LPINT	Pointer to the value that receives the previous intersection type

Description The `SETLINEJOIN` escape defines the intersection type for intersecting line segments. `lpNewJoin` specifies the intersection type. The following values are used for `lpNewJoin`.

Value	*Meaning*
–1	Default GDI intersection
0	Mitered corner (miter join)
1	Rounded corner (round join)
2	Squared end point (bevel join)

Return Value A positive value is returned when successful. A negative value is returned when unsuccessful.

SET_MIRROR_MODE

Syntax
```
short Escape(hdc, SET_MIRROR_MODE, sizeof(WORD),
             lpMirrorMode, (LPSTR) NULL)
```

Parameter	*Type*	*Description*
hdc	HDC	Device context
lpMirrorMode	LPINT	Pointer mirror mode. `lpMirrorMode` is one of the following values:

Value	Meaning
MIRROR_BOTH	Mirroring about horizontal and vertical axes
MIRROR_NONE	Mirroring disabled
MIRROR_HORIZONTAL	Mirroring about horizontal axis
MIRROR_VERTICAL	Mirroring about vertical axis

Description The SET_MIRROR_MODE escape sets the mirror mode to the value specified in lpMirrorMode. To mirror a page, issue the SET_MIRROR_MODE escape before the first primitive to mirror and again after the last primitive to mirror.

Return Value The previous mirror mode is returned.

SETMITERLIMIT

Syntax

```
short Escape(hDC, SETMITERLIMIT, sizeof(int), lpNewMiter,
             lpOldMiter)
```

Parameter	Type	Description
hDC	HDC	Device context
lpNewMiter	LPINT	Pointer to value specifying the new miter limit
lpOldMiter	LPINT	Pointer to value containing the previous miter limit

Description The SETMITERLIMIT escape defines the miter limit for the device. lpNewMiter points to the value that specifies the new miter limit. When the value pointed to by lpNewMiter is –1, the device driver will use the default GDI miter limit. The miter limit is used to define the angle where the device driver will replace a miter join with a bevel join.

Return Value A positive value is returned when successful. A negative value is returned when unsuccessful.

SET_POLY_MODE

Syntax

```
short Escape(hDC, SET_POLY_MODE, sizeof(int), lpMode, NULL)
```

Parameter	Type	Description
hDC	HDC	Device context
lpMode	LPINT	Pointer to value specifying the poly mode

Description The SET_POLY_MODE escape defines the poly mode. The poly mode is used to specify how calls to the Windows functions Polygon and Polyline are handled. lpMode points to the value that specifies the poly mode. The following values are used for the value pointed to by lpMode:

Value	Meaning
PM_POLYLINE	Points define standard polygon or polyline
PM_BEZIER	Points define a 4-point Bezier spline curve; the first and last points are endpoints; the second and third points are control points and are used to specify the shape and direction of the curve
PM_POLYLINESEGMENT	Points define a list of coordinate pairs; these pairs are connected with lines
PM_POLYSCANLINE	Points define a list of coordinate pairs; line segments connect the points. Each line segment must be horizontal or vertical.

Return Value The previous poly mode is returned when successful. A negative value is returned when unsuccessful.

SET_SCREEN_ANGLE

Syntax

```
short Escape(hDC, SET_SCREEN_ANGLE, sizeof(int), lpAngle,
            NULL)
```

Parameter	Type	Description
hDC	HDC	Device context
lpAngle	LPINT	Pointer to value specifying the screen angle

Description The SET_SCREEN_ANGLE escape defines the screen angle. lpAngle points to the value that specifies the screen angle in tenths of a degree (counterclockwise). The screen angle is used by an application for image color separation.

Return Value The previous screen angle is returned.

SET_SPREAD

Syntax `short Escape(hDC, SET_SPREAD, sizeof(int), lpSpread, NULL)`

Parameter	*Type*	*Description*
hDC	HDC	Device context
lpSpread	LPINT	Pointer to value specifying the number of pixels that nonwhite primitives are to be expanded

Description The SET_SPREAD function defines the number of pixels that nonwhite primitives are expanded. lpSpread points to the value that specifies the amount of expansion. Expansion is often desired to correct for flaws during printing. By default, the spread is zero.

Return Value The previous spread value is returned.

STARTDOC

Syntax `short Escape(hDC, STARTDOC, nCount, lpDocName, NULL)`

Parameter	*Type*	*Description*
hDC	HDC	Device context
nCount	short	Number of characters pointed to by lpDocName
lpDocName	LPSTR	Pointer to null-terminated string specifying the document name

Description The STARTDOC escape is used to start a new print job. All NEWFRAME escape calls that are generated after the STARTDOC escape and prior to an ENDDOC escape are spooled under the specified job name. lpDocName points to the string that contains the document name.

Return Value A positive value is returned when successful. –1 is returned when unsuccessful.

REVISED 3.1 The `StartDoc` function replaces this escape for Windows 3.1.

TRANSFORM_CTM

Syntax `short Escape(hDC, TRANSFORM_CTM, 36, lpMatrix, NULL)`

Parameter	*Type*	*Description*
`hDC`	`HDC`	Device context
`lpMatrix`	`LPSTR`	Pointer to array of values defining the new transformation matrix

Description The `TRANSFORM_CTM` escape modifies the current transformation matrix by defining a matrix (pointed to by `lpMatrix`) that will be used with the current transformation matrix to create the new current transformation matrix. The new current transformation matrix is the product of the current transformation matrix and the matrix pointed to by `lpMatrix`.

Return Value A nonzero value is returned when successful. Zero is returned when unsuccessful.

16

The Resource Workshop

The Resource Workshop provides the editors and the Resource Compiler that you need to create your own Windows 3.1 compatible resources. The Resource Workshop includes an Accelerator editor, Dialog editor, Menu editor, Paint editor, String editor, and Text editor. With the Resource Workshop you can edit both binary files and resource scripts. You can create and edit the resources described in the following section using the Resource Workshop.

Resources

Windows applications generally contain numerous graphical elements ranging from dialog boxes to cursors. Under Windows, each of these elements is stored as a resource that can be loaded into the application. Resources are separated from the source code and thus offer several advantages in application development. One advantage is that by separating the resource, you can use a resource definition for several applications. This reduces development time for subsequent applications.

Another advantage is that you can modify a resource without affecting the source code. This enables you to develop resources and source code simultaneously while shortening software modification phases.

It's important to understand that resources do not define interface functionality. Resources are merely the visual representation of program elements. For example, you can define a dialog box resource that contains a series of buttons and that your application can display. The user can select the buttons of the dialog box; however, nothing happens when the buttons are selected unless the application defines the action for each button. The dialog box resource merely defines the location and appearance (the visual representation) of the buttons. The application must define the action of each button in the dialog box (the interface functionality). You can create and edit the following resources with the Resource Workshop:

- *Accelerators* - Keyboard combinations that generate a response by the application. Accelerators are usually tied to menu item selections as alternatives to selecting the menu item with the mouse. Accelerators are created and edited with the Accelerator editor of the Resource Workshop.
- *Bitmaps* - Binary representations of graphical images. Bitmaps frequently used in Windows applications include the scroll bars, the Minimize arrow, and the Maximize arrow. Bitmaps are created and edited with the Paint editor of the Resource Workshop.
- *Cursors* - 32-by-32-pixel bitmaps that indicate the current screen position of the mouse. The most common cursor used by Windows applications is the arrow. Cursors are created and edited with the Paint editor of the Resource Workshop.
- *Dialog boxes* - Windows that contain controls, such as buttons and check boxes, that enable the user to select options. Dialog boxes are created and edited with the Dialog editor of the Resource Workshop.
- *Fonts* - Define the typeface, size, and style of text characters. The Paint editor is used to create and edit font resources.
- *Icons* - Bitmaps that represent minimized windows. Icons are usually either 32 by 32 pixels or 16 by 32 pixels. The Paint editor of the Resource Workshop is used to create and edit icons.
- *Menus* - Provide the user with a hierarchy of choices for using the application. The Menu editor of the Resource Workshop is used to create and edit menu resources.
- *String tables* - Define a table of text strings that the application can display. For example, a string table may contain all the error messages that the application can display. String tables can be created and edited with the String editor of the Resource Workshop.

- *User defined and* `rcdata` *resources* - Consist of data (generally read-only text) that you need to add to your executable file.

File Types

The Resource Workshop enables you to edit and create both binary and text files. The following standard Windows file formats are supported by the Resource Workshop:

File Type	*Description*
.BMP	Contains a bitmap resource in binary format.
.CUR	Contains a cursor resource in binary format.
.DLL	Contains a dynamic link library (DLL). You can use the Resource Workshop to bind resources to DLLs. You can also use the Resource Workshop to decompile a .DLL file and edit the resources contained in that .DLL file.
.EXE	Executable files. You can use the Resource Workshop to bind resources to .EXE files. You can also use the Resource Workshop to decompile an .EXE file and edit the resources contained in that .EXE file.
.FNT	Binary font files that contain the definition of a font.
.FON	Font library files that contain a font directory and one or more font definitions. You cannot create .FON files with the Resource Workshop; you can, however, use the Resource Workshop to edit .FON files.
.ICO	Contains an icon resource in binary format.
.RC	Resource compiler script file that contains the definitions of one of more resources.
.RES	Resource file that contains one or more compiled resources.

The Resource Workshop uses projects to group the various resource types used by an application.

Projects

When you start the Resource Workshop, you will either create a new project or open an existing project. A project file is usually an .RC file that often contains references to other resources. The .RC file can reference other .RC files, .DLG files, .BMP files, .ICO files, .CUR files, .FNT files, header files, include files, and .PAS (Pascal) files.

You are not limited to creating projects based on an .RC file. You can also create a project based on .RES, .CUR, .ICO, .BMP, or .FNT files. Most projects, however, are based on the .RC file because you can combine numerous types of resources into one file.

When a project has been created or an existing project has been opened, the Project window of the Resource Workshop is displayed. The Project window lists the files in the project, the types of resources in each file, and the identifiers associated with the resources (as long as the file is not an .EXE, .DLL, or .RES file). The project window for the Solitaire game of Windows (SOL.EXE) is shown in Figure 16.1.

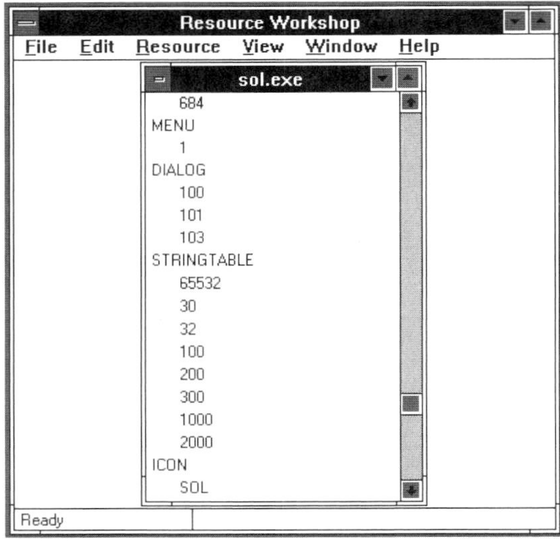

Figure 16.1. *The Project window.*

The View menu of the Resource Workshop lets you define the way that the Project window displays the resource information. The following options are included in the View menu:

- `By type` groups resources according to the resource type.
- `By file` groups resources according to the files that they are in.
- `Show identifiers` shows any identifiers in the project.
- `Show resources` lists the name of each resource in the project.
- `Show items` displays items within each resource.
- `Show unused types` displays all types of resources, even if some might not be included in the project. To use this option, you must check the `By type` option.

You can edit and add resources to the project by using the various editors of the Resource Workshop. The remainder of this chapter introduces the editors of the Resource Workshop.

The Accelerator Editor

The Accelerator editor of the Resource Workshop enables you to create and edit accelerators for your application. Accelerators are key combinations that are often used as a substitute to menu commands to initiate an action in the application. Accelerators are stored in an accelerator table. Each accelerator table entry defines a key combination—an accelerator.

The Accelerator editor is divided into two panes: the outline pane and the dialog box. Figure 16.2 illustrates the Accelerator editor and the Project window. The accelerator table that is loaded into the Accelerator editor in Figure 16.2 is the `PBRUSH` accelerator table from the Windows Paintbrush executable file.

The outline pane of the Accelerator editor (shown on the right side of the editor in Figure 16.2) lists the accelerators, or key combinations, defined in the accelerator table `PBRUSH`. The lines that follow the accelerator table name `PBRUSH` are entries to the accelerator table.

An accelerator table entry has two parts. The first part is the accelerator key. The key can be either a virtual key or an ASCII key. Virtual keys represent keys such as the function and arrow keys. ASCII keys represent the upper- and lowercase letters. You can join both virtual and ASCII keys with any combination of the Ctrl, Alt, or Shift keys. The second part of an accelerator key entry is the integer ID of the command that the accelerator invokes. This integer ID is usually the ID of a menu item.

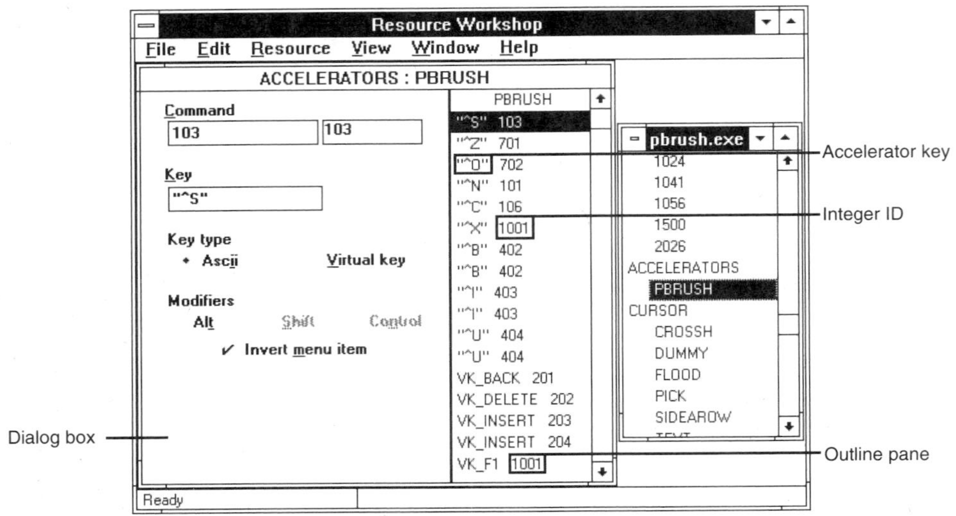

Figure 16.2. *The Accelerator editor.*

The Dialog Box pane of the Accelerator editor (shown on the left side of the editor) reflects the settings of the currently selected accelerator. The selections of the dialog box are the following:

- `Command` is the item ID of the command that is invoked by the accelerator. Either an integer or an identifier can be added.
- `Key` is the accelerator key. Highlight this field and press the appropriate key sequence. The editor will automatically fill this field and select the appropriate key type (the appropriate radio button in the `Key type` field is selected automatically).
- `Key type` is the key type of the accelerator: either ASCII or virtual. This field is automatically selected when you enter the accelerator in the `Key` field.
- `Modifiers` are the check boxes that define the key combination used for the accelerator. The Alt, Shift, and Ctrl boxes, when checked, indicate that the appropriate button is a part of the key combination. The `Invert menu item` box, when checked, causes the associated menu bar command to flash.

When creating or editing an accelerator table, you should start the Menu editor so that you can easily see the menu items and IDs that you need to accurately define the accelerators in the table.

The Dialog Editor

The Dialog editor of the Resource Workshop enables you to graphically create dialog boxes. A dialog box is generally a pop-up window that provides the user with a number of choices. Dialog boxes contain controls such as radio buttons and check boxes that enable the user to specify settings and other types of information.

Figure 16.3 shows the Dialog editor. In this figure, the Options dialog box of the Windows Solitaire game is opened for editing. There are four basic parts to the Dialog Editor: the dialog box, the Caption control, the Tools palette, and the Alignment palette. The sections that follow describe these parts.

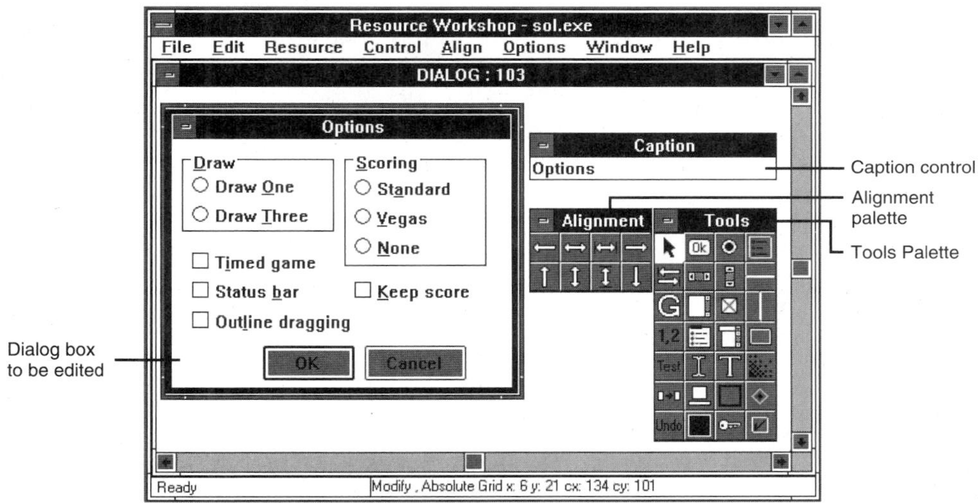

Figure 16.3. *The Dialog editor.*

The Dialog Box

The actual dialog box that you are creating or editing is displayed on the left side of the Dialog editor. The dialog box can be moved, sized, and edited. You can use the features of the Tools palette, the Caption control, and the Alignment palette to edit or create controls in the dialog box. In Figure 16.3, the Options dialog box of the Solitaire game is opened and appears on the left side of the dialog box.

The Caption Control

The Caption control enables you to add a caption to your dialog box. To add text to the control, and thus to your dialog box caption, select the field with the mouse and type in the appropriate text. In Figure 16.3, the dialog box caption is `Options`. The Caption control contains, appropriately, the text `Options`.

The Tools Palette

The Tools palette of the Dialog editor enables you to add buttons, scroll bars, list boxes, edit controls, static controls, and combo boxes to the dialog box. In Figure 16.3, the Tools palette is shown on the right side of the Dialog editor. The following tools are provided in the Tools palette:

The *Pick Rectangle* tool returns the cursor to the standard arrow shape and lets you select controls in the dialog box.

The *Tab Set* tool enables you to modify a tab stop.

The *Set Groups* tool changes the cursor to a G icon and enables you to group controls.

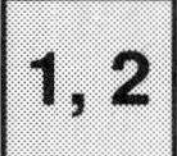

The *Set Order* tool changes the cursor to a Set Order icon and enables to you change the order of the controls.

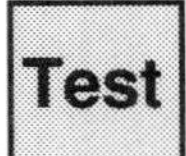

The *Test Dialog* tool enables you to test your dialog box.

The *Duplicate* tool enables you to duplicate controls.

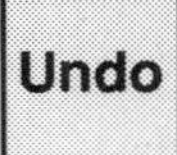

The *Undo* tool performs an "undo" on the last edit to the dialog box.

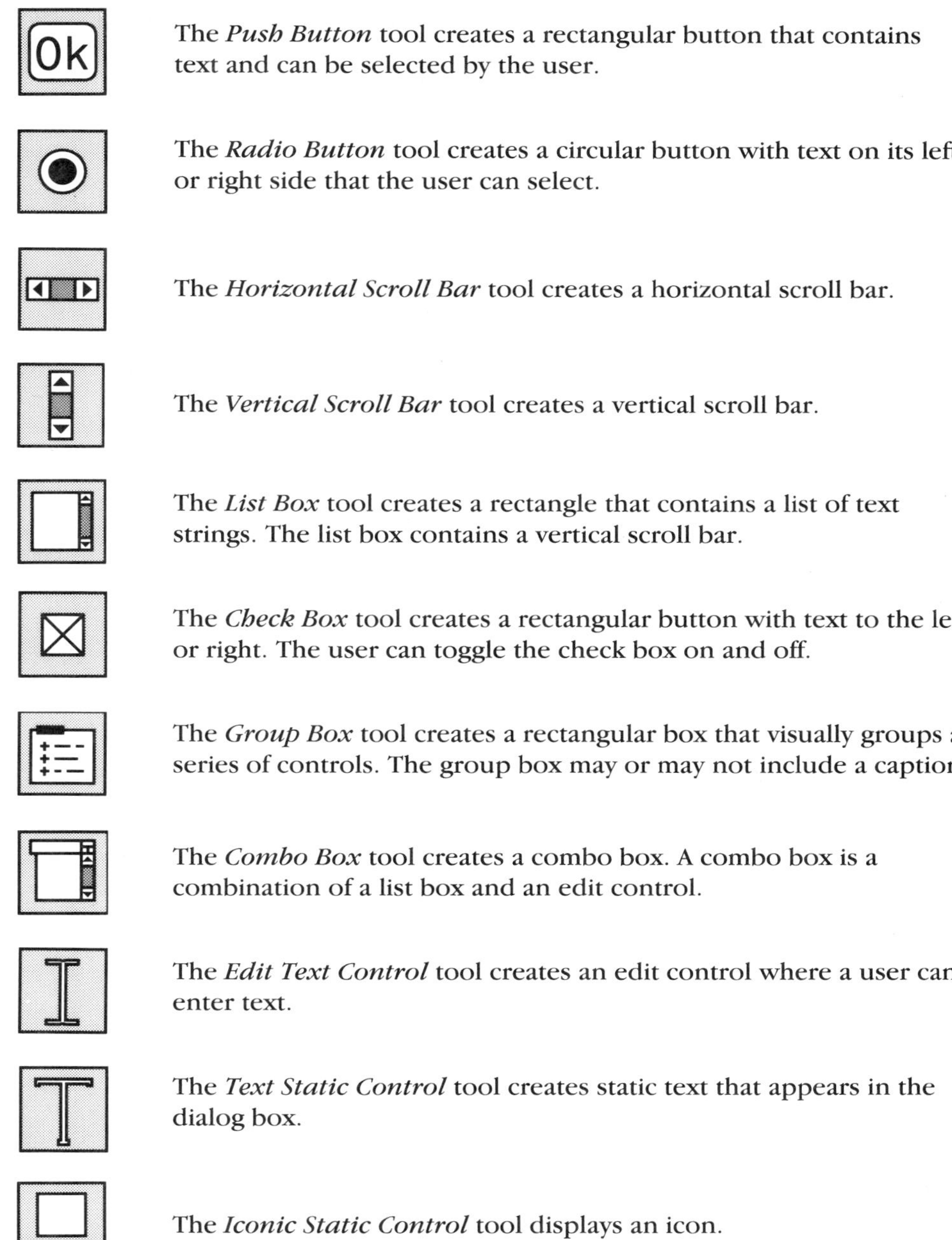

The *Push Button* tool creates a rectangular button that contains text and can be selected by the user.

The *Radio Button* tool creates a circular button with text on its left or right side that the user can select.

The *Horizontal Scroll Bar* tool creates a horizontal scroll bar.

The *Vertical Scroll Bar* tool creates a vertical scroll bar.

The *List Box* tool creates a rectangle that contains a list of text strings. The list box contains a vertical scroll bar.

The *Check Box* tool creates a rectangular button with text to the left or right. The user can toggle the check box on and off.

The *Group Box* tool creates a rectangular box that visually groups a series of controls. The group box may or may not include a caption.

The *Combo Box* tool creates a combo box. A combo box is a combination of a list box and an edit control.

The *Edit Text Control* tool creates an edit control where a user can enter text.

The *Text Static Control* tool creates static text that appears in the dialog box.

The *Iconic Static Control* tool displays an icon.

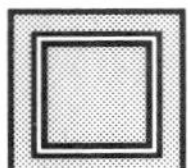

The *White Frame Static Control* tool creates a rectangular, empty frame that is the color of the current background and therefore is invisible.

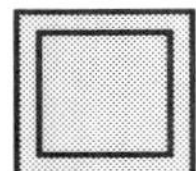

The *Black Rectangle* tool displays a static control icon—a black rectangle.

The *Custom Control* tool creates a control that doesn't match predefined Windows types and has a customized window class.

The Alignment Palette

The Alignment palette enables you to align the controls in the dialog box. In Figure 16.3, the Alignment palette appears between the Tools palette and the dialog box. The Alignment palette includes the following tools:

This tool moves the controls horizontally and aligns them along the left side of the sizing frame.

This tool moves the controls horizontally and centers the controls in the sizing frame.

This tool moves the sizing frame and the controls horizontally and centers them in the dialog box.

This tool moves controls horizontally and aligns the controls along the right side of the sizing frame.

This tool moves the controls vertically and aligns them at the top of the sizing frame.

This tool moves the controls vertically and centers the controls in the sizing frame.

This tool moves the controls vertically and aligns the controls at the bottom of the sizing frame.

This tool moves the sizing frame and the controls vertically and centers them in the dialog box.

The Dialog editor is very flexible and enables you to quickly create dialog boxes.

The Menu Editor

A menu provides the user with a hierarchical choice of options for controlling the application. The Resource Workshop's Menu editor (shown in Figure 16.4) enables you to create and test menus. In Figure 16.4, one of the menus from the Windows Solitaire game has been opened for editing.

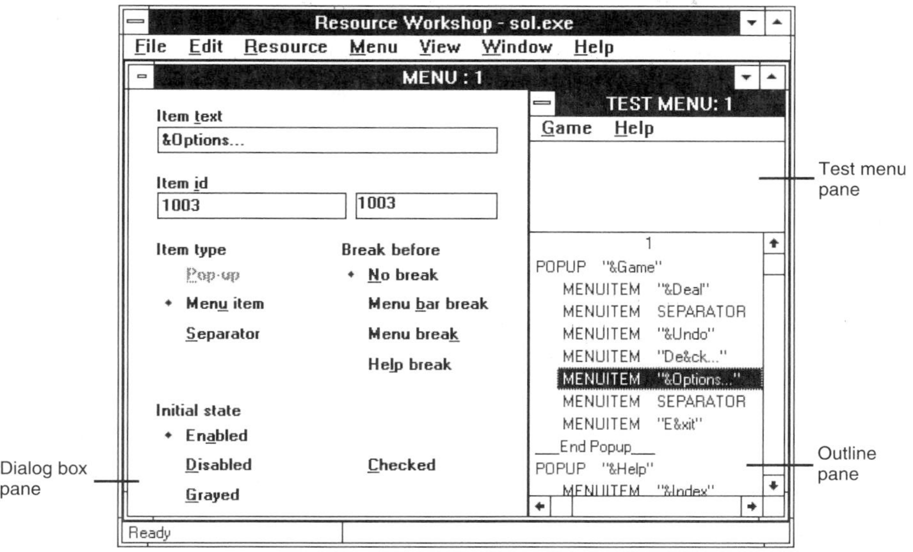

Figure 16.4. The Menu editor.

The Menu editor contains three panes: the outline pane, the test menu pane, and the dialog box pane.

The outline pane is shown in the lower-right corner of the Menu editor in Figure 16.4. The outline pane contains the pseudocode of the menu. You can select lines from this pane to edit. In addition, any lines added to the menu are reflected in this pane.

The test menu pane displays your menu and enables you to test it. In Figure 16.4, the test menu pane is shown in the upper-right corner of the Menu editor.

The dialog box pane enables you to create and edit menu items and pop-up menus. In Figure 16.4, the dialog box pane is shown on the left side of the Menu editor. The selections of the dialog pane are as follows:

- `Item text` is the name of the menu or pop-up command.
- `Item id` is the menu item ID. Pop-up commands and separators have no ID.
- `Item type` is the type of item being created or edited: either pop-up, menu item, or separator.
- `Break before` is the format of the menu commands: either `No break` (no break before command), `Menu bar break` (new line or new column, and you will use vertical line separator), `Menu break` (new line or new column), or `Help break` (move menu item to far right of Menu bar).

The Menu editor is easy to use and enables you to quickly develop and test menu resources.

The Paint Editor

The Paint editor of the Resource Workshop is used to create and edit bitmap, cursor, font, and icon resources. The Paint editor, shown in Figure 16.5, contains three fundamental parts: the Tools palette, the Colors Palette, and the window pane.

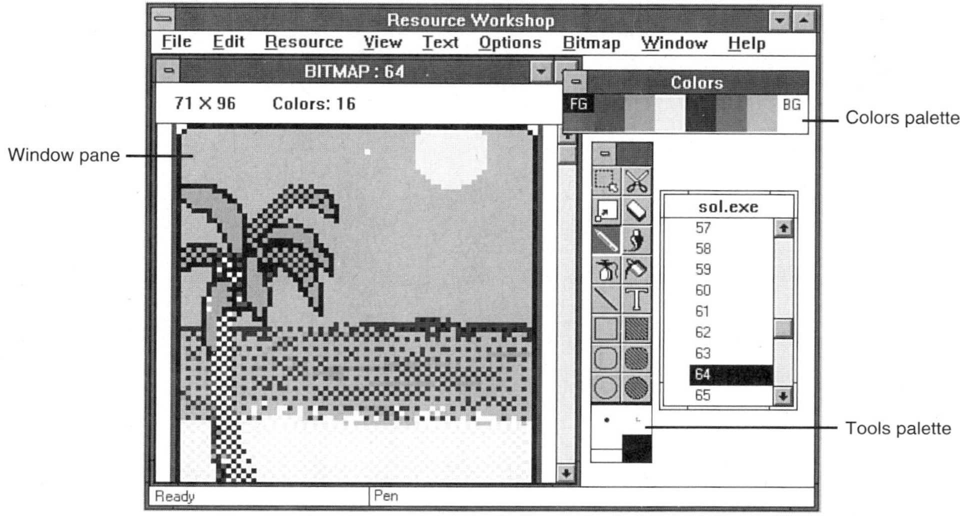

Figure 16.5. *Bitmaps and the Paint editor.*

The Tools Palette

The Tools palette provides a series of tools that enable you to create and edit the resource. The tools of the Tools palette are similar to the painting tools of most paintbrush programs, including Windows Paintbrush. The following tools are included in the Tools palette:

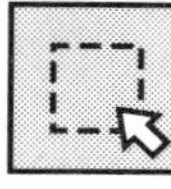

The *Pick Rectangle* tool enables you to select a rectangular area of the screen for moving, copying, or deleting.

[The *Scissors* tool enables you to select a region of the screen for moving, copying, or deleting. The region does not have to be rectangular.

The *Zoom* tool enables you to zoom the image in or out by multiples of 400% (1600% maximum, 100% minimum).

The *Eraser* tool fills a small rectangular area with the current background.

The *Pen* tool draws freehand lines and shapes using either the current background color (press the right mouse button) or the current foreground color (press the left mouse button).

The *Paintbrush* tool paints free-form patterns using the current foreground color (press the left mouse button) or the current background color (press the right mouse button). The paintbrush uses the current brush shape and pattern.

The *Airbrush* tool paints free-form patterns like Paintbrush; however, Airbrush works more like a spray paint can—the faster you move the cursor, the thinner the painted pattern.

The *Paint Can* tool fills an area with the current color. Only a single color is filled.

The *Line* tool draws a straight line using the current foreground color (press the left mouse button) or the current background color (press the right mouse button). The line is drawn using the current line width and style.

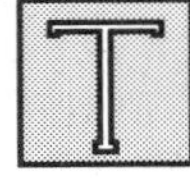

The *Text* tool enables you to add text to the image. The text is drawn using the current font and text alignment.

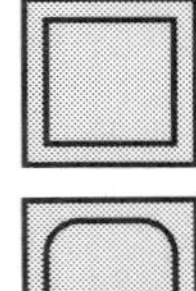

The *Empty Frames* tools enable you to create empty rectangles, rounded boxes, or ellipses. The foreground color (press the left mouse button) or the background color (press the right mouse button) is used to draw the frames. The current line style is used when the image is drawn.

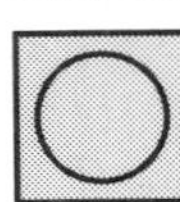

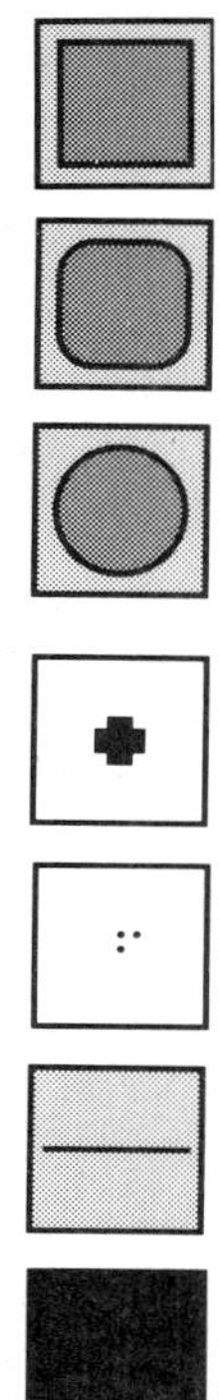

The *Filled-in Frames* tools enable you to create filled rectangles, rounded boxes, or ellipses. The foreground color (press the left mouse button) or the background color (press the right mouse button) is used to draw the figures. The current line style and fill pattern is used when the image is drawn.

The *Style Selections* tools indicate the paintbrush shape, the airbrush shape, the line style, and the patterns used by the other drawing tools.

The Colors Palette

The Colors palette, shown in Figure 16.6, enables you to select the color that you want to use for drawing. The Colors palette generally works in the same way for all the resources that can be edited by the Paint editor. With the Colors palette, you can select the foreground and background colors and the inverted and transparent areas:

- The *foreground (FG) color* is the color typically used to draw figures such as rectangles and ellipses.
- The *background (BG) color* is the color that appears to be underneath the figure.
- The *Inverted area* is the color of the area behind the inverted area and shows through the icon or cursor.
- The *Transparent area* (icons and cursors only) is the color of the area behind the transparent area that shows through the icon or cursor.

The Window Pane

The window pane is where the actual creating and editing of the figure takes place. The window pane can be split into two sections, as shown in Figure 16.6, or it can be one pane, as shown in Figure 16.5. The window pane can be zoomed in and out to make editing the figure easier.

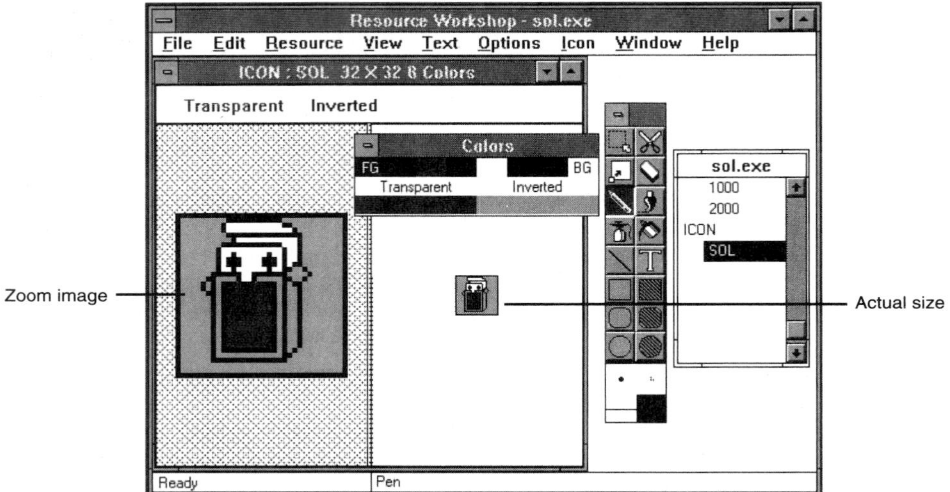

Figure 16.6. *Icons and the Paint editor.*

It was stated previously that the Paint editor is used to create and edit bitmaps, among other things. Figure 16.5 shows a bitmap being edited with the Paint editor. The bitmap that is being edited is one of the bitmaps used for the Windows Solitaire game.

The Paint editor can also be used to create and edit icons, as shown in Figure 16.6. In Figure 16.6, the icon used for the Windows Solitaire game has been opened and is ready for editing.

Another task performed by the Paint editor is creating and editing cursor resources. In Figure 16.7, the Paint editor is being used to edit the paintbrush cursor of the Windows Paintbrush program.

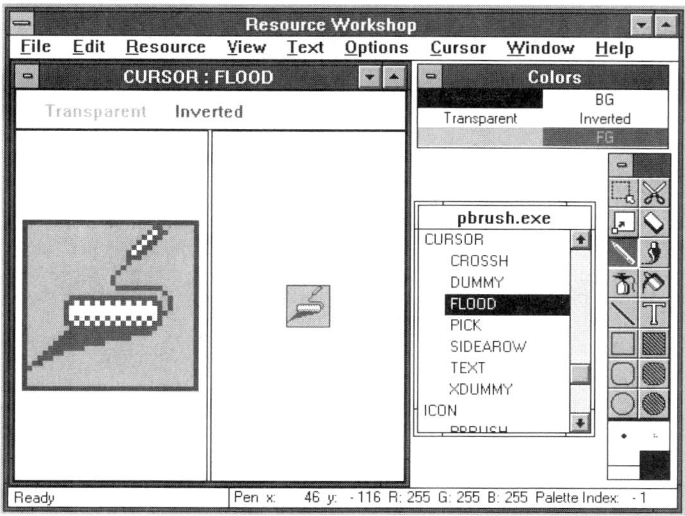

Figure 16.7. *Cursors and the Paint editor.*

In addition to creating and editing icons, cursors, and bitmaps, you can use the Paint editor to create and edit font resources. Figure 16.8 shows the Paint editor being used to create a symbol for a font.

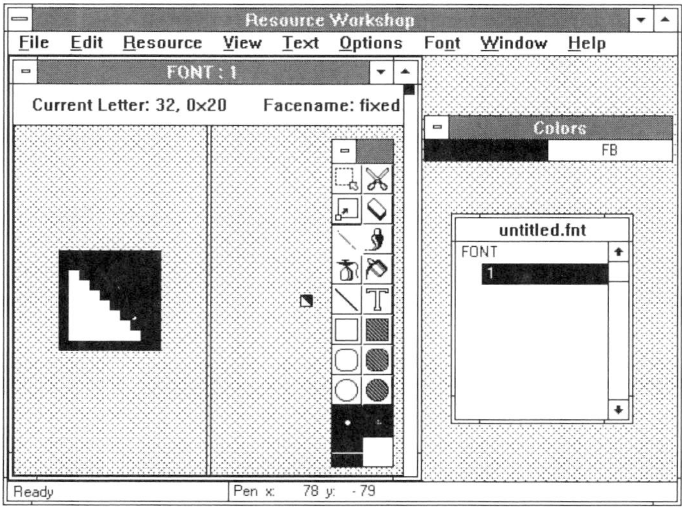

Figure 16.8. *Fonts and the Paint editor.*

The String Editor

The String editor of the Resource Workshop enables you to create and edit string tables. A string table holds a list of text strings that the application can display.

As Figure 16.9 shows, the String editor contains three columns: the `ID Source` column, the `ID Value` column, and the `String` column.

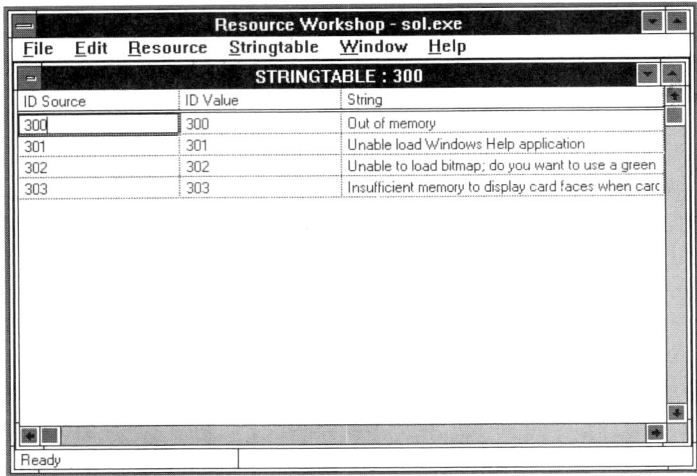

Figure 16.9. *The String editor.*

The ID Source column contains an integer for the string. In this column, you can assign an identifier for the string, such as `sth_FileNew`. If no identifier is specified, however, the integer ID of the string, as specified in the ID Value column, will appear in the ID Source column. In Figure 16.9, notice that the ID Source column and the ID Value column contain the same value. In this instance, no identifier has been assigned for the string.

The ID Value column always contains the integer ID for the string. If the ID Source column contains an identifier rather than the integer ID for the string, both the ID and the identifier can be used in the application to reference the string.

The String column contains the string that the application can display. The string in the String column can be referenced in the application by either the value in the ID Source column or the value in the ID Value column.

Although you can create string tables with a standard text editor, the String editor of the Resource Workshop provides an quick, easy, and efficient way to create string tables.

17

ObjectWindows Classes

This chapter introduces the ObjectWindows classes. The ObjectWindows classes follow:

```
Object              TCheckBox           TMDIClient
TApplication        TComboBox           TMDIFrame
TBButton            TControl            TModule
TBCheckBox          TDialog             TRadioButton
TBDivider           TEdit               TScrollBar
TBGroupBox          TEditWindow         TScroller
TBRadioButton       TFileDialog         TStatic
TBStatic            TFileWindow         TStreamable
TBStaticBmp         TGroupBox           TWindow
TButton             TInputDialog        TWindowsObject
TBWindow            TListBox
```

As described previously in Part II of this book, the ObjectWindows library consists of a hierarchy of classes. Figure 11.2 in Chapter 11, "Introduction to ObjectWindows for C++," shows this hierarchy of ObjectWindows classes.

The descriptions for each class include the class header file, a description of the class, the data members, the constructors and the destructor, and the member functions. Each class is described in the following format:

Class Name:

This heading lists the name of the class.

Class Header File:

This section lists the class header file.

Description:

This section provides a brief description of the class.

Data Member(s):

This section lists the data members for the class and provides the syntax and a description of each data member. The member access for the data member follows the description and is enclosed in brackets. The format for the presentation of data member information is as follows:

`Data Member Name` `Data Member Syntax`

Data Member Description [Member Access]

Constructor(s):

This section lists the constructors for the class. The member access for the constructor follows the description and is enclosed in brackets. The format for the presentation of constructor information is as follows:

`Constructor Syntax` Constructor Description [Member Access]

Destructor:

This section provides the syntax and a description of the destructor. The member access for the destructor follows the description and is enclosed in brackets. The format for the presentation of destructor information is as follows:

`Destructor Syntax` Destructor Description [Member Access]

Additional Member Function(s):

This section lists the member functions of the class, excluding constructors and destructors. The format provides the function name, syntax, and a description of the function. The member access for the member function follows the description and is enclosed in brackets. The format for the presentation of additional member function information is as follows:

`Function Name` `Function Syntax`

Function Description [Member Access]

It is important to remember that properties of classes are inherited from base classes. The descriptions in this chapter list only the functions and data members that are new or modified for the class. Therefore, when you review a class, keep in mind the properties of its base classes.

Class Name: Object

Class Header File:

object.h

Description:

The `Object` class is the base class for all ObjectWindows-derived classes. `Object` provides type checking and encapsulation.

Data Member(s):

`ZERO` `Static PObject ZERO;`

`ZERO` is a pointer to an error object used by a private class.

Constructor(s):

`Object();` Constructs an instance of `Object` [Public]

`Object(RCObject);` Copies data on to another instance [Public]

Destructor:

`virtual ~Object();` Destroys an instance [Public]

Additional Member Function(s):

`firstThat`

```
virtual RCObject firstThat(condFuncType,
        Pvoid) const;
```

The `firstThat` function calls the specified test function for an object. This function returns the object when the specified test is successful. A return value of `NOOBJECT` indicates that the test is unsuccessful. [Public]

`forEach`

```
virtual void forEach(iterFuncType,
        Pvoid);
```

The `forEach` function calls the specified iterator for an object. This function iterates through each object in the container. [Public]

```
hashValue                virtual hashValueType hashValue()
                              const = 0;
```

The `hashValue` function is a pure virtual function for derived classes. The function returns a hash value. [Public]

```
isA                      virtual classType isA() const = 0;
```

The `isA` function is a pure virtual function for derived classes. The function returns a unique class ID for the class. [Public]

```
isAssociation            virtual int isAssociation() const;
```

The `isAssociation` function determines whether or not an object is derived from the class `Association`. [Public]

```
isEqual                  virtual int isEqual(RCObject) const = 0;
```

The `isEqual` function is a pure virtual function for derived classes. [Public]

```
isSortable               virtual int isSortable() const;
```

The `isSortable` function determines whether or not an object is derived from the class `Sortable`. [Public]

```
lastThat                 virtual RCObject lastThat(condFuncType,
                              Pvoid) const;
```

The `lastThat` function is identical to `firstThat` for noncontainer objects. [Public]

```
nameOf                   virtual Pchar nameOf() const = 0;
```

The `nameOf` function is a pure virtual function enabling derived classes to return a class ID string. [Public]

```
new                      Pvoid operator new(size_t);
```

The `new` function allocates the specified number of bytes for an object. ZERO is returned when the function cannot allocate the required space. [Public]

```
printOn                  virtual void printOn(Rostream) const=0;
```

The `printOn` function is a pure virtual function for derived classes. This function writes the printable representation of the object on a stream. [Public]

Class Name: TApplication

Class Header File:

applicat.h

Description:

The `TApplication` class provides the structure of, and defines the behavior for, ObjectWindows applications. All ObjectWindows applications contain a derived class of `TApplication`.

Data Member(s):

`HAccTable` `HANDLE HAccTable;`

`HAccTable` stores the handle to the current Windows accelerator table. [Public]

`hPrevInstance` `HANDLE hPrevInstance;`

`hPrevInstance` defines the handle of the previous instance of the application; `hPrevInstance` is 0 when there is no previous instance. [Public]

`KBHandlerWnd` `PTWindowsObject KBHandlerWnd;`

`KBHandlerWnd` points to the active window if the keyboard handler for the window is enabled. [Public]

`MainWindow` `PTWindowsObject MainWindow;`

`MainWindow` points to the main window of the application. [Public]

`nCmdShow` `int nCmdShow;`

`nCmdShow` specifies whether the application should be displayed as an icon or as an open window. [Public]

Constructor(s):

`TApplication(LPSTR AName,`
`HANDLE AnInstance,`
`HANDLE APrevInstance,`
`LPSTR ACmdLine,`
`int ACmdShow);`
	Constructs the `TApplication` object [Public]

Destructor:

`~TApplication();`	Destroys the `TApplication` object [Public]

Additional Member Function(s):

```
CanClose                 virtual BOOL CanClose();
```

The `CanClose` function determines whether the application can close. The function calls the `CanClose` member function of the main window and returns the value returned by that `CanClose` member function. `TRUE` is returned when the application can close. [Public]

```
IdleAction               virtual void IdleAction();
```

The `IdleAction` function is invoked when the application is idle. This function can be redefined to perform special functions when the application is idle. [Protected]

```
InitApplication          virtual void InitApplication();
```

The `InitApplication` function makes the initializations required for the first executing instance of the application. `InitApplication` can be redefined by derived classes for custom initializations. [Protected]

```
InitInstance             virtual void InitInstance();
```

The `InitInstance` function makes the initializations required for all executing instances of the application. [Protected]

```
InitMainWindow           virtual void InitMainWindow();
```

The `InitMainWindow` function constructs a generic `TWindow` object using the application name; `InitMainWindow` can be redefined to construct a main window object of a derived class. [Protected]

```
isA                      virtual classType isA() const;
```

The `isA` function redefines the pure virtual function in class `Object`. This function returns the class ID of `TApplication`. [Public]

```
MessageLoop              virtual void MessageLoop();
```

The `MessageLoop` function manages the message loop of the application. [Protected]

```
nameOf                   virtual Pchar nameOf() const;
```

The `nameOf` function redefines the pure virtual function in class `Object`. This function returns "`TApplication`," the class ID string [Public]

```
ProcessAccels            virtual BOOL ProcessAccels(LPMSG
                              PMessage);
```

The `ProcessAccels` function processes accelerator messages. [Protected]

```
ProcessAppMsg            virtual BOOL ProcessAppMsg(LPMSG
                              PMessage);
```

The `ProcessAppMsg` function calls `ProcessDlgMsg`, `ProcessMDIAccels`, and `ProcessAccels` for the processing of modeless dialog messages, MDI accelerator messages, and accelerator messages, respectively. This function returns `TRUE` when any modeless dialog message, MDI accelerator message, or accelerator message is encountered. [Protected]

`ProcessDlgMsg` `virtual BOOL ProcessDlgMsg(LPMSG PMessage);`

The `ProcessDlgMsg` function provides message processing of keyboard input for modeless dialog boxes and windows with controls. [Protected]

`ProcessMDIAccels` `virtual BOOL ProcessMDIAccels(LPMSG PMessage);`

The `ProcessMDIAccels` function processes accelerator messages for MDI applications. [Protected]

`Run` `virtual void Run();`

The `Run` function initializes the instance and executes the application. `InitApplication` is called if no other instances of the application are running. `MessageLoop` is called to begin the execution of the application if initialization is successful. [Public]

`SetKBHandler` `void SetKBHandler(PTWindowsObject AWindowsObject);`

The `SetKBHandler` function enables keyboard handling for the specified window. [Public]

Class Name: TBButton

Class Header File:

bbutton.h

Description:

The `TBButton` class represents a BWCC bitmap push button interface. `TBButton` creates a push button control for a parent `TWindow`. `TBButton` can also be used for communications between the application and the button controls of a `TDialog`.

Data Member(s):

None.

Constructor(s):

`TBButton(PTWindowsObject AParent, int AnId, LPSTR AText, int X, int Y, int W, int H, BOOL IsDefault, PTModule AModule = NULL);`	Constructs a button object with the specified parent window, control ID, associated text, position, width, and height [Public]
`TBButton(PTWindowsObject AParent, int ResourceId, PTModule AModule = NULL);`	Constructs a `TBButton` object to be associated with a button control[Public]
`TBButton(StreamableInit);`	`TBButton` stream constructor [Protected]

Destructor:

None.

Additional Member Function(s):

`build` `static PTStreamable build();`

The `build` function constructs an object of type `TBButton` before reading its data members from an input stream. [Protected]

`GetClassName` `virtual LPSTR GetClassName();`

The `GetClassName` function returns "BORBTN", the name of `TBButton`'s Windows registration class. [Protected]

Class Name: TBCheckBox

Class Header File:

bchkbox.h

Description:

The `TBCheckBox` class represents a BWCC check box interface element. `TBCheckBox` creates a BWCC check box control for a parent `TWindow`. `TBCheckBox` can also be used for communications between an application and the check box controls of a `TDialog`.

Data Member(s):

None.

Constructor(s):

`TBCheckBox(PTWindowsObject AParent, int AnId, LPSTR ATitle, int X, int Y, int W, int H, PTGroupBox AGroup, PTModule ATModule = NULL);`	Constructs a check box object with the specified parent window, control ID, associated text, position, width, and height [Public]
`TBCheckBox(PTWindowsObject AParent, int ResourceId, PTGroupBox AGroup, PTModule ATModule = NULL);`	Constructs a `TBCheckBox` object to be associated with a check box control [Public]
`TBCheckBox(StreamableInit);`	`TBCheckBox` stream constructor [Protected]

Destructor:

None.

Additional Member Function(s):

`build` `static PTStreamable build();`

The `build` function constructs an object of type `TBCheckBox` before reading its data members from an input stream. [Public]

`GetClassName` `virtual LPSTR GetClassName();`

The `GetClassName` function returns "BORCHECK", the name of `TBCheckBox`'s Windows registration class. [Protected]

Class Name: TBDivider

Class Header File:

bdivider.h

Description:

The `TBDivider` class represents a static BWCC divider interface element. `TBDivider` creates a static BWCC divider. Divider can either be dips or bumps. Dip dividers separate areas within a dialog. Bump dividers separate areas within a group box.

Data Member(s):

None.

Constructor(s):

`TBDivider(PTWindowsObject AParent, int AnId, LPSTR AText, int X, int Y, int W, int H, BOOL IsVertical, BOOL IsBump, PTModule AModule = NULL);`	Constructs static divider with the specified parent window, control ID, associated text, position, width, and height [Public]
`TBDivider(PTWindowsObject AParent, int ResourceId, PTModule AModule = NULL);`	Constructs a `TBDivider` object to be associated with a static divider [Public]
`TBDivider(StreamableInit);`	`TBDivider` stream constructor [Protected]

Destructor:

None.

Additional Member Function(s):

`build` `static PTStreamable build();`

The `build` function constructs an object of type `TBDivider` before reading its data members from an input stream. [Protected]

`GetClassName` `virtual LPSTR GetClassName();`

The `GetClassName` function returns "BORSHADE", the name of `TBDivider`'s Windows registration class. [Protected]

Class Name: TBGroupBox

Class Header File:

bgrpbox.h

Description:

The `TBGroupBox` class represents a BWCC group box interface element. `TBGroupBox` creates a gray BWCC group box element. Group boxes physically group other interface elements such as check boxes and radio buttons.

Data Member(s):

None.

Constructor(s):

`TBGroupBox(PTWindowsObject AParent, int AnId, LPSTR AText, int X, int Y, int W, int H, PTModule AModule = NULL);`	Constructs a group box object with the specified parent window, control ID, associated text, position, width, and height [Public]
`TBGroupBox(PTWindowsObject AParent, int ResourceId, PTModule ATModule = NULL);`	Constructs a `TBGroupBox` object to be associated with a group box [Public]
`TBGroupBox(StreamableInit);`	`TBGroupBox` stream constructor [Protected]

Destructor:

None.

Additional Member Function(s):

`build` `static PTStreamable build();`

The `build` function constructs an object of type `TBGroupBox` before reading its data members from an input stream. [Public]

`GetClassName` `virtual LPSTR GetClassName();`

The `GetClassName` function returns "BORSHADE", the name of `TBGroupBox`'s Windows registration class. [Protected]

Class Name: TBRadioButton

Class Header File:

bradio.h

Description:

The `TBRadioButton` class represents a BWCC radio button interface element. `TBRadioButton` creates a BWCC radio button control for a parent `TWindow`. `TBRadioButton` can also be used for communications between an application and the radio button controls of a `TDialog`.

Data Member(s):

None.

Constructor(s):

`TBRadioButton(PTWindowsObject AParent, int AnId, LPSTR ATitle, int X, int Y, int W, int H, PTGroupBox AGroup, PTModule AModule = NULL);`	Constructs a radio button object with the specified parent window, control ID, associated text, position, width, and height [Public]
`TBRadioButton(PTWindowsObject AParent, int ResourceId, PTGroupBox AGroup, PTModule ATModule = NULL);`	Constructs a `TBRadioButton` object to be associated with a radio button control [Public]
`TBRadioButton (StreamableInit);`	`TBRadioButton` stream constructor [Protected]

Destructor:

None.

Additional Member Function(s):

`build` `static PTStreamable build();`

The `build` function constructs an object of type `TBRadioButton` before reading its data members from an input stream. [Public]

`GetClassName` `virtual LPSTR GetClassName();`

The `GetClassName` function returns "BORRADIO", the name of `TBRadioButton`'s Windows registration class. [Protected]

Class Name: TBStatic

Class Header File:

bstatic.h

Description:

The `TBStatic` class represents a static text interface element. `TBStatic` creates a static text control for a parent `TWindow`. `TBStatic` can also be used to modify the text of static controls of a `TDialog`.

Data Member(s):

None.

Constructor(s):

`TBStatic(PTWindowsObject AParent, int AnId, LPSTR ATitle, int X, int Y, int W, int H, WORD ATextLen, PTModule AModule = NULL);`	Constructs a static control object with the specified parent window, control ID, associated text, position, width, and height [Public]
`TBStatic(PTWindowsObject AParent, int ResourceId, WORD ATextLen, PTModule AModule = NULL);`	Constructs a `TBStatic` object to be associated with a static text control [Public]
`TBStatic(StreamableInit)`	`TBStatic` stream constructor [Protected]

Destructor:

None.

Additional Member Function(s):

`build` `static PTStreamable build();`

The `build` function constructs an object of type `TBStatic` before reading its data members from an input stream. [Public]

`GetClassName` `virtual LPSTR GetClassName();`

The `GetClassName` function returns "BORSTATIC", the name of `TBStatic`'s Windows registration class. [Protected]

Class Name: TBStaticBmp

Class Header File:

bstatbmp.h

Description:

The `TBStaticBmp` class represents a static text interface element used to display splash images. `TBStaticBmp` creates a bitmap control for a parent `TWindow`. `TBStaticBmp` can also be used to modify the text of bitmap controls of a `TDialog`.

Data Member(s):

None.

Constructor(s):

`TBStaticBmp(PTWindowsObject AParent, int AnId, LPSTR ATitle, int X, int Y, int W, int H, PTModule AModule = NULL);`	Constructs a bitmap control object with the specified parent window, control ID, associated text, position, width, and height [Public]
`TBStaticBmp(PTWindowsObject AParent, int ResourceId, PTModule AModule = NULL);`	Constructs a `TBStaticBmp` object to be associated with a static text control [Public]
`TBStaticBmp(StreamableInit)`	`TBStaticBmp` stream constructor [Protected]

Destructor:

None.

Additional Member Function(s):

`build` `static PTStreamable build();`

The `build` function constructs an object of type `TBStaticBmp` before reading its data members from an input stream. [Public]

`GetClassName` `virtual LPSTR GetClassName();`

The `GetClassName` function returns "BORBTN", the name of `TBStaticBmp`'s Windows registration class. [Protected]

Class Name: TButton

Class Header File:

button.h

Description:

The `TButton` class represents a Windows push button interface. There are two primary types of push buttons:

- Default buttons. The default button has a heavy, thick border. This button performs the default action of a window. Each window can have only one default button.
- Regular buttons. Regular buttons (buttons that are not the default button) appear with a thin border and can be programmed to perform various actions.

Data Member(s):

`IsDefPB`	`BOOL IsDefPB;`

`IsDefPB` indicates whether an owner-draw button is the default push button.

Constructor(s):

`TButton(PTWindowsObject AParent, int AnId, LPSTR AText, int X, int Y, int W, int H, BOOL IsDefault, PTModule AModule = NULL);`	Constructs a button object with the specified parent window, control ID, associated text, position, width, and height [Public]
`TButton(PTWindowsObject AParent, int ResourceId, PTModule AModule = NULL);`	Constructs a `TButton` object to be associated with a button control of `TDialog` [Public]
`TButton(StreamableInit);`	`TButton` stream constructor [Protected]

Destructor:

None.

Additional Member Function(s):

`BMSetStyle`
```
virtual void BMSetStyle(RTMessage Msg) =
    [WM_FIRST + BM_SETSTYLE];
```

The `BMSetStyle` function determines whether an owner-draw push button is the default push button.

`build`
```
static PTStreamable build();
```

The `build` function constructs an object of type `TButton` before reading its data members from an input stream. [Public]

`GetClassName`
```
virtual LPSTR GetClassName();
```

The `GetClassName` function returns "BUTTON", the name of `TButton`'s Windows registration class. [Protected]

`SetupWindow`
```
virtual void SetupWindow();
```

The `SetupWindow` function sends the `DM_SETDEFID` message to the parent window of the button when the button is the default push button and is an owner-draw button.

`WMGetDlgCode`
```
virtual void WMGetDlgCode(RTMessage Msg)
  =[WM_FIRST + WM_GETDLGCODE];
```

The WMGetDlgCode function responds to the WM_GETDLGCODE message. If the button is an owner-draw button, the function returns information that indicates whether the button is the default button.

Class Name: TBWindow

Class Header File:

bwindow.h

Description:

The TBWindow class creates a window with a light gray background.

Data Member(s):

None.

Constructor(s):

`TBWindow(PTWindowsObject AParent, LPSTR ATitle, PTModule AModule = NULL);`	Constructs a generic window [Public]
`TBWindow(StreamableInit)`	TBWindow stream constructor [Protected]

Destructor:

None.

Additional Member Function(s):

`build`	`static PTStreamable build();`

The build function constructs an object of type TBWindow before reading its data members from an input stream. [Public]

`GetClassName`	`virtual LPSTR GetClassName();`

The GetClassName function returns "TBWindow", the name of TBWindow's Windows registration class. [Protected]

`GetWindowClass`	`virtual void GetWindowClass(WNDCLASS &AWndClass);`

The GetWindowClass function fills the WNDCLASS structure specified in AWndClass with the default registration attributes for a TBWindow.

Class Name: TCheckBox

Class Header File:

checkbox.h

Description:

The `TCheckBox` class represents a Windows check box interface. There are two primary types of check boxes:

- Two-state boxes, which are either checked or unchecked
- Three-state boxes, which are checked, grayed, or unchecked

Data Member(s):

`Group`	`PTGroupBox Group;`

`Group` is a pointer to the `TGroupBox` control object that groups the check box with other check boxes and radio buttons. `Group` is `NULL` if the check box is not grouped. [Public]

Constructor(s):

`TCheckBox(PTWindowsObject AParent, int AnId, LPSTR ATitle, int X, int Y, int W, int H, PTGroupBox AGroup, PTModule ATModule = NULL);`	Constructs a check box object using the specified parent window, control ID, associated text, position, width, height, and group box [Public]
`TCheckBox(PTWindowsObject AParent, int ResourceId, PTGroupBox AGroup, PTModule ATModule = NULL);`	Constructs a `TCheckBox` object associated with a check box control of `TDialog` [Public]
`TCheckBox (StreamableInit)`	`TCheckBox` stream constructor [Protected]

Destructor:

None.

Additional Member Function(s):

`BNClicked`	`virtual void BNClicked(RTMessage Msg) = [NF_FIRST + BN_CLICKED];`

The `BNClicked` function responds to notification messages indicating that the check box was clicked. When the check box is a part of a group, `TGroupBox` is notified of the change in the check box state. [Protected]

`build` `static PTStreamable build();`

The `build` function constructs an object of type `TCheckBox` before reading its data members from an input stream. [Public]

`Check` `void Check();`

The `Check` function places the check box into the checked state by calling `SetCheck`. [Public]

`GetCheck` `WORD GetCheck();`

The `GetCheck` function determines the check state of the check box. This function returns `BF_UNCHECKED` if the check box is unchecked, `BF_CHECKED` if the check box is checked, or `BF_GRAYED` if the check box is grayed. [Public]

`read` `virtual Pvoid (Ripstream is);`

The `read` function calls `TWindow::read` to read in the base `TWindow` object. [Protected]

`SetCheck` `void SetCheck(WORD CheckFlag);`

The `SetCheck` function sets the state of the check box to the state specified in `CheckFlag`—which can be `BF_UNCHECKED` (box is unchecked), `BF_CHECKED` (box is checked), or `BF_GRAYED` (box is grayed). [Public]

`Toggle` `void Toggle();`

The `Toggle` function toggles between the states of the check box. [Public]

`Transfer`
```
virtual WORD Transfer(Pvoid DataPtr,
     WORD TransferFlag);
```

The `Transfer` function transfers the state of the check box to or from the location pointed to by `DataPtr`. `TransferFlag` specifies whether data is transferred to or from the check box:

- When `TransferFlag` is `TF_GETDATA`, `Transfer` transfers the state of the check box to the memory location pointed to by `DataPtr`
- When `TransferFlag` is `TF_SETDATA`, `Transfer` sets the state of the check box to the state specified in the location pointed to by `DataPtr`
- When `TransferFlag` is `TF_SIZEDATA`, `Transfer` returns the size of the transfer data [Public]

`Uncheck` `void Uncheck();`

The `Uncheck` function places the check box in an unchecked state by calling `SetCheck`. [Public]

`write` `virtual void write (Ropstream os);`

The `write` function calls `TWindow::write` to write the base `TWindow` object. [Protected]

Class Name: TComboBox

Class Header File:

combobox.h

Description:

The `TComboBox` class represents a Windows combo box interface. There are three primary types of combo boxes:

- Simple. `CBS_SIMPLE` specifies a simple combo box.
- Drop-down. `CBS_DROPDOWN` specifies a drop-down combo box.
- Drop-down list. `CBS_DROPDOWNLIST` specifies a drop-down list combo box.

Data Member(s):

`TextLen` `WORD TextLen;`

`TextLen` specifies the length of the buffer used for the edit control of the combo box. The maximum length of the buffer is `TextLen` minus one. [Public]

Constructor(s):

`TComboBox(PTWindowsObject AParent, int AnId, int X, int Y, int W, int H, DWORD AStyle, WORD ATextLen, PTModule ATModule = NULL);`	Constructs a combo box object with the given parent window, control ID, position, width, height, style, and text length [Public]
`TComboBox(PTWindowsObject AParent, int ResourceId, WORD ATextLen, PTModule ATModule = NULL);`	Constructs a `TComboBox` object to be associated with a combo box control of `TDialog` [Public]
`TComboBox (StreamableInit);`	`TComboBox` stream constructor [Protected]

Destructor:

None.

Additional Member Function(s):

```
build                    static PTStreamable build();
```

The `build` function constructs an object of type `TComboBox` before reading its data members from a stream. [Public]

```
Clear                    void Clear();
```

The `Clear` function clears the text in the edit control. [Public]

```
GetClassName             virtual LPSTR GetClassName();
```

The `GetClassName` function returns "COMBOBOX", the `TComboBox` Windows registration class. [Protected]

```
GetEditSel               int GetEditSel(Rint StartPos,
                                        Rint EndPos);
```

The `GetEditSel` function returns the starting and ending positions of the text currently selected in the edit control. [Public]

```
GetMsgID                 virtual WORD GetMsgID(WORD AnId);
```

The `GetMsgID` function returns the message ID of the Windows combo box message that is associated with the ObjectWindows message ID. [Protected]

```
GetText                  int GetText(LPSTR AString,
                                 int MaxChars);
```

The `GetText` function copies the text of the edit control to the string specified in `AString`. The maximum number of characters copied is specified in `MaxChars`. The number of characters copied to the string is returned. [Public]

```
GetTextLen               int GetTextLen();
```

The `GetTextLen` function returns the length of the text in the edit control. [Public]

```
HideList                 void HideList();
```

The `HideList` function hides the list of a drop-down or drop-down list combo box. [Public]

```
nameOf                   virtual Pchar nameOf()const;
```

The `nameOf` function redefines the pure virtual function in class `Object`. This function returns "TComboBox", the class ID string for `TComboBox`. [Public]

```
read                     virtual Pvoid read(Ripstream is);
```

The `read` function calls `TListBox::read` to read in the base `TListBox` object. [Protected]

```
SetEditSel              int SetEditSel(int StartPos,
                                       int EndPos);
```

The `SetEditSel` function selects the text in the edit control specified by the positions in `StartPos` and `EndPos`. [Public]

```
SetText                 void SetText(LPSTR AString);
```

The `SetText` function finds the first string in a list box that starts with the characters specified in `AString` and selects the matching string. If no matching string is found, the text of the edit control is filled with the specified string and the specified string is selected. [Public]

```
SetupWindow             virtual void SetupWindow();
```

The `SetupWindow` function limits the length of the text in the edit control to `TextLen` minus 1 when setting up the combo box. [Protected]

```
ShowList                void ShowList();
```

The `ShowList` function shows the list of a drop-down or drop-down list combo box. [Public]

```
Transfer                virtual WORD Transfer(Pvoid DataPtr,
                             WORD TransferFlag);
```

The `Transfer` function moves data to and from a transfer buffer pointed to by `DataPtr`. The transfer buffer should point to a `PTComboBoxData` object.

The `TransferFlag` parameter of the `Transfer` function can be set to `TF_SETDATA`, `TF_GETDATA`, or `TF_SIZEDATA` as follows:

- Set `TransferFlag` to `TF_SETDATA` to fill the list of the combo box from the data in the transfer buffer
- Set `TransferFlag` to `TF_GETDATA` to copy the current list selection to the transfer buffer
- Set `TransferFlag` to `TF_SIZEDATA` to return the size of the transfer data; no data is transferred in this case. [Public]

```
write                   virtual void write(Rostream os);
```

The `write` function calls `TWindow::write` to write out the base `TListBox` object. [Protected]

Class Name: TControl

Class Header File:

control.h

Description:

The `TControl` class is an abstract class that is an ancestor to the derived control classes. This class defines functions to create controls and process messages for the derived control classes.

Data Member(s):

None.

Constructor(s):

`TControl(PTWindowsObject AParent, int AnId, LPSTR ATitle, int X, int Y, int W, int H, PTModule ATModule = NULL);`	Constructs a control object using the specified parent window, control ID,associated text, position, width, and height [Public]
`TControl(PTWindowsObject AParent, int ResourceId, PTModule ATModule = NULL);`	Constructs a control object to be associated with a control of `TDialog` [Public]
`TControl (StreamableInit);`	`TControl` stream constructor [Protected]

Destructor:

None.

Additional Member Function(s):

```
GetId                    virtual int GetId();
```

The `GetId` function returns the window ID, `Attr.Id`. [Public]

```
ODADrawEntire            virtual void ODADrawEntire
                              (DRAWITEMSTRUCT _FAR & DrawInfo);
```

The `ODADrawEntire` function responds when notified that a drawable control needs to be redrawn. [Protected]

```
ODAFocus                 virtual void ODAFocus
                              (DRAWITEMSTRUCT _FAR & DrawInfo);
```

The ODAFocus function responds when notified that the focus has been given to or taken from the drawable control. [Protected]

```
ODASelect                  virtual void ODASelect
                                (DRAWITEMSTRUCT _FAR & DrawInfo);
```

The ODASelect function responds when notified that the selection state of the drawable control has changed. [Protected]

```
WMDrawItem                 virtual void WMDrawItem(RTMessage Msg) =
                                [WM_FIRST + WM_DRAWITEM];
```

The WMDrawItem function responds to the WM_DRAWITEM message that is sent when the drawable control needs to be redrawn. [Public]

```
WMPaint                    virtual void WMPaint(RTMessage Msg) =
                                [WM_FIRST + WM_PAINT];
```

The WMPaint function calls DefWndProc for painting. [Public]

Class Name: TDialog

Class Header File:

dialog.h

Description:

The TDialog class is the base class for modal and modeless dialog interface elements. For each dialog box there exists a resource definition that describes its controls. The resource definition identifier must be provided to the TDialog constructor. The member functions of this class handle communications between the dialog box and its controls.

Data Member(s):

```
Attr                       TDialogAttr Attr;
```

Attr stores the attributes used to create the dialog box. [Public]

```
IsModal                    BOOL IsModal;
```

IsModal indicates whether the dialog box is modal or modeless. TRUE indicates that the dialog box is modal. FALSE indicates that the dialog box is modeless. [Public]

Constructor(s):

`TDialog(PTWindowsObject AParent, LPSTR AName, PTModule AModule = NULL)`	Invokes `TWindowsObject's` constructor [Public]
`TDialog(PTWindowsObject AParent, int ResourceId, PTModule AModule = NULL);`	Invokes a `TWindowsObject` constructor and calls `DisableAutoCreate` [Public]
`TDialog(StreamableInit);`	`TDialog` stream constructor [Protected]

Destructor:

`virtual ~TDialog();`	Frees the memory allocated to `TDialog` [Public]

Additional Member Function(s):

`build` `static PTStreamable build();`

The `build` function invokes the `TDialog` constructor and constructs an object of type `TDialog` before reading its data members from a stream. [Public]

`Cancel`

```
virtual void Cancel(RTMessage Msg) =
     [ID_FIRST + IDCANCEL];
```

The `Cancel` function calls `CloseWindow` using IDCANCEL when the `Cancel` button for the dialog box is selected. [Protected]

`CloseWindow` `virtual void CloseWindow(int ARetValue);`

The `CloseWindow` function calls `TWindowsObject::CloseWindow` when `this` is a modeless dialog box or `CanClose` for a modal dialog box to determine whether the dialog box can be shut. If `CanClose` is called and returns `TRUE`, the function calls `TransferData` and then `ShutDownWindow` and passes `ARetValue`. [Public]

`CloseWindow` `virtual void CloseWindow();`

The `CloseWindow` function calls `TWindowsObject::CloseWindow` when `this` is a modeless dialog box or `CloseWindow` for a modal dialog box to determine whether the dialog box can be shut. IDCANCEL is passed as the integer `ARetValue`. [Public]

`Create` `virtual BOOL Create();`

The `Create` function creates a modeless dialog box associated with the object. This function returns `TRUE` when successful or `FALSE` when unsuccessful. [Public]

`Destroy` `virtual void Destroy(int ARetValue);`

The Destroy function destroys the interface element associated with TDialog. TWindowsObject::Destroy is called for modeless dialog boxes. [Public]

```
Destroy                 virtual void Destroy();
```

The Destroy function destroys the interface element associated with TDialog. TWindowsObject::Destroy is called for modeless dialog boxes. Destroy is called, with IDCANCEL passed as ARetValue, for modal dialog boxes. [Public]

```
Execute                 virtual int Execute();
```

The Execute function executes the modal dialog box associated with TDialog. The function should not return until the dialog box is closed. [Public]

```
GetClassName            virtual LPSTR GetClassName();
```

The GetClassName function returns the name of the default Windows class for modal dialog boxes. The function returns "OWLDialog" for modeless dialog boxes. [Protected]

```
GetItemHandle           HWND GetItemHandle(int DlgItemID);
```

The GetItemHandle function returns the handle of the dialog control that has the ID specified in DlgItemID. [Public]

```
GetWindowClass          virtual void GetWindowClass(WNDCLASS
                             FAR & AWndClass);
```

The GetWindowClass function fills AWndClass (a WNDCLASS structure) with the registration attributes for TDialog. This function can be redefined to change the default registration attributes. [Protected]

```
isA                     virtual classType isA() const;
```

The isA function redefines the pure virtual function in class Object. This function returns the class ID of TDialog. [Public]

```
nameOf                  virtual Pchar nameOf()const;
```

The nameOf function redefines the pure virtual function in class Object. This function returns "TDialog", the class ID string for TDialog. [Public]

```
Ok                      virtual void Ok(RTMessage Msg) =
                             [ID_FIRST + IDOK];
```

The Ok function calls CloseWindow when the Ok button of the dialog box is selected, and passes IDOK. [Protected]

```
read                    virtual Pvoid read(Ripstream is);
```

The read function calls TWindowsObject::read to read in the base TWindowsObject object. [Protected]

SendDlgItemMsg

```
DWORD SendDlgItemMsg(int DlgItemID,
     WORD AMsg, WORD WParam, DWORD
     LParam);
```

The SendDlgItemMsg function sends the control message (AMsg) to the dialog box control that has the ID specified in DlgItemID. WParam and LParam are message parameters. SendDlgItemMsg returns the value returned by the control when successful. A return value of zero indicates that the specified ID is invalid. [Public]

SetCaption

```
void SetCaption(LPSTR ATitle);
```

The SetCaption function calls TWindowsObject::SetCaption unless ATitle is –1. [Public]

SetupWindow

```
virtual void SetupWindow();
```

The SetupWindow function calls SetCaption and TWindowsObject::SetupWindow to set up the dialog box. [Protected]

ShutDownWindow

```
virtual void ShutDownWindow();
```

The ShutDownWindow function calls TWindowsObject::ShutDownWindow for modeless dialog boxes or Destroy (passing IDCANCEL) for modal dialog boxes to shut down the dialog box. [Public]

ShutDownWindow

```
virtual void ShutDownWindow(int ARetValue);
```

The ShutDownWindow function calls TWindowsObject::ShutDownWindow for modeless dialog boxes or Destroy (passing ARetValue) for modal dialog boxes to shut down the dialog box. [Public]

WMClose

```
virtual void WMClose(RTMessage Msg) =
     [WM_FIRST + WM_CLOSE];
```

The WMClose function handles the WM_CLOSE message. [Protected]

WMInitDialog

```
virtual void WMInitDialog(RTMessage
     Msg) = [WM_FIRST + WM_INITDIALOG];
```

The WMInitDialog function calls SetupWindow and is automatically called before the dialog box is displayed. [Protected]

WMQueryEndSession

```
virtual void WMQueryEndSession(RTMessage
     Msg) = [WM_FIRST +
     WM_QUERYENDSESSION];
```

The WMQueryEndSession function responds when Windows attempts to shut down. [Protected] `write` — `virtual void write(Ropstream os);`

The `write` function calls `TWindowsObject::write` to write out the base `TWindowsObject` object. [Protected]

Class Name: TEdit

Class Header File:

edit.h

Description:

The `TEdit` class is the Windows edit control interface and provides the features of a text editor. There are two basic types of edit controls:

- Single-line edit controls. These controls contain only one line.
- Multiline edit controls. These contain more than one line of text and may contain vertical scroll bars.

Data Member(s):

None.

Constructor(s):

`TEdit(PTWindowsObject AParent, int AnId, LPSTR AText, int X, int Y, int W, int H, WORD ATextLen, BOOL Multiline, PTModule AModule = NULL);`	Constructs an edit control object with the specified parent window, text, position, width, height, and buffer length [Public]
`TEdit(PTWindowsObject AParent, int ResourceId, WORD ATextLen, PTModule AModule = NULL);`	Invokes `TStatic`'s constructor [Public]
`TEdit(StreamableInit);`	`TEdit` stream constructor [Protected]

Destructor:

None.

Additional Member Function(s):

`build` — `static PTStreamable build();`

The `build` function invokes the `TEdit` constructor and constructs an object of type `TEdit` before reading its data members from a stream. [Public]

```
CanUndo                    BOOL CanUndo();
```

The `CanUndo` function indicates whether it is possible to undo the last edit. This function returns `TRUE` when it is possible to undo the last edit. [Public]

```
ClearModify                void ClearModify();
```

The `ClearModify` function resets the edit control change flag. [Public]

```
CMEditClear                virtual void CMEditClear(RTMessage
                                Msg) = [CM_FIRST + CM_EDITCLEAR];
```

The `CMEditClear` function calls `Clear` when a menu item with menu ID `CM_EDITCLEAR` is selected. [Protected]

```
CMEditCopy                 virtual void CMEditCopy(RTMessage
                                Msg) = [CM_FIRST + CM_EDITCOPY];
```

The `CMEditCopy` function calls `Copy` when a menu item with menu ID `CM_EDITCOPY` is selected. [Protected]

```
CMEditCut                  virtual void CMEditCut(RTMessage Msg) =
                                [CM_FIRST + CM_EDITCUT];
```

The `CMEditCut` function calls `Cut` when a menu item with the menu ID `CM_EDITCUT` is selected. [Protected]

```
CMEditDelete               virtual void CMEditDelete(RTMessage Msg)
                                = [CM_FIRST + CM_EDITDELETE];
```

The `CMEditDelete` function calls `DeleteSelection` when a menu item with menu ID `CM_EDITDELETE` is selected. [Protected]

```
CMEditPaste                virtual void CMEditPaste(RTMessage Msg)
                                = [CM_FIRST + CM_EDITPASTE];
```

The `CMEditPaste` function calls `Paste` when a menu item with menu ID `CM_EDITPASTE` is selected. [Protected]

```
CMEditUndo                 virtual void CMEditUndo(RTMessage Msg)
                                = [CM_FIRST + CM_EDITUNDO];
```

The `CMEditUndo` function calls `Undo` when a menu item with menu ID `CM_EDITUNDO` is selected. [Protected]

```
Copy                       void Copy();
```

The `Copy` function copies the selected text to the clipboard. [Public]

```
Cut                      void Cut();
```

The `Cut` function deletes the selected text and copies it to the clipboard. [Public]

```
DeleteLine               BOOL DeleteLine(int LineNumber);
```

The `DeleteLine` function deletes the line of text specified in `LineNumber`. This function returns `TRUE` when successful. [Public]

```
DeleteSelection          BOOL DeleteSelection();
```

The `DeleteSelection` function deletes the selected text. This function returns `TRUE` when successful. A return value of `FALSE` indicates that no text was selected. [Public]

```
DeleteSubText            BOOL DeleteSubText(int StartPos, int
                              EndPos);
```

The `DeleteSubText` function deletes the text between the text positions specified in `StartPos` and `EndPos`. This function returns `TRUE` when successful. [Public]

```
ENErrSpace               virtual void ENErrSpace(RTMessage Msg)
                              = [NF_FIRST + EN_ERRSPACE];
```

The `ENErrSpace` function sounds a beep when the edit control cannot allocate more memory. [Protected]

```
GetClassName             virtual LPSTR GetClassName();
```

The `GetClassName` function returns "EDIT", the `TEdit` Windows registration class. [Protected]

```
GetLine                  BOOL GetLine(LPSTR ATextString, int
                              StrSize, int LineNumber);
```

The `GetLine` function gets a line of text from the edit control. `LineNumber` specifies the line number to retrieve. `ATextString` specifies the location where the line of text is copied. `StrSize` specifies the number of characters to retrieve. [Public]

```
GetLineFromPos           int GetLineFromPos(int CharPos);
```

The `GetLineFromPos` function gets the line number from a multiline edit control of the line that contains the character position specified in `CharPos`. [Public]

```
GetLineIndex             int GetLineIndex(int LineNumber);
```

The `GetLineIndex` function returns the number of characters prior to the specified line number in a multiline edit control. [Public]

```
GetLineLength            int GetLineLength(int LineNumber);
```

The `GetLineLength` function gets the number of characters in a line of text from a multiline edit control. `LineNumber` specifies the line number. [Public]

```
GetNumLines              int GetNumLines();
```

The `GetNumLines` function gets the number of lines in a multiline edit control. [Public]

```
GetSelection             void GetSelection(Rint StartPos,
                              Rint EndPos);
```

The `GetSelection` function returns the starting and ending positions of the selected text in `StartPos` and `EndPos`, respectively. [Public]

```
GetSubText               void GetSubText(LPSTR ATextString,
                              int StartPos, int EndPos);
```

The `GetSubText` function gets the text specified by `StartPos` and `EndPos` and returns the text to `ATextString`. [Public]

```
Insert                   void Insert(LPSTR ATextString);
```

The `Insert` function inserts the text in `ATextString` into the edit control at the current cursor position. [Public]

```
IsModified                BOOL IsModified();
```

The `IsModified` function indicates whether the text in the edit control has been modified. This function returns `TRUE` when the text has been modified. [Public]

```
Paste                     void Paste();
```

The `Paste` function places the text in the clipboard into the edit control at the current cursor position. [Public]

```
Scroll                    void Scroll(int HorizontalUnit,
                              int VerticalUnit);
```

The `Scroll` function scrolls the multiline edit control horizontally or vertically. `HorizontalUnit` specifies the number of characters to scroll horizontally. `VerticalUnit` specifies the number of characters to scroll vertically. Positive values scroll right and down; negative values scroll left and up. [Public]

```
Search                    int Search(int StartPos, LPSTR AText,
                              BOOL CaseSensitive);
```

The `Search` function searches for the text specified in `AText`. `StartPos` specifies the starting point for the search. `CaseSensitive` indicates whether the text search is case-sensitive. [Public]

```
SetSelection            BOOL SetSelection(int StartPos,
                             int EndPos);
```

The `SetSelection` function defines the current text selection. `StartPos` specifies the first character in the selected text. `EndPos` marks the location immediately after the last character in the selected text. [Public]

```
SetupWindow             virtual void SetupWindow();
```

The `SetupWindow` function defines the limit for the number of characters in the edit control as `TextLen` minus 1. [Protected]

```
Undo                    void Undo();
```

The `Undo` function performs an "undo" on the last edit. [Public]

Class Name: TEditWindow

Class Header File:

editwnd.h

Description:

The `TEditWindow` class defines an object for text editing. `TEditWindow` is derived from `TWindow`.

Data Member(s):

```
Editor                  PTEdit Editor;
```

`Editor` points to a multiline edit control that provides text editing for the edit window. [Public]

```
IsReplaceOp             BOOL IsReplaceOp;
```

`IsReplaceOp` is `TRUE` when the next search will also perform a replace. [Public]

```
SearchStruct            TSearchStruct SearchStruct;
```

`SearchStruct` is a transfer buffer used with `TSearchDialog`. [Public]

Constructor(s):

`TEditWindow (PTWindowsObject AParent, LPSTR ATitle, PTModule AModule = NULL);`	Initializes Editor and SearchStruct [Public]
`TEditWindow (StreamableInit);`	`TEditWindow` stream constructor [Protected]

Destructor:

None.

Additional Member Function(s):

```
build                    static PTStreamable build();
```

The `build` function invokes the `TEditWindow` constructor and constructs an object of type `TEditWindow` before reading its data members from a stream. [Public]

```
CMEditFind               virtual void CMEditFind(RTMessage Msg)
                              = [CM_FIRST + CM_EDITFIND];
```

The `CMEditFind` function initiates a text search and displays a search dialog box when a `Find` menu item is selected. After the user has made selections to the dialog box, `SearchStruct` is updated to reflect the user's selections, `IsReplaceOp` is set to `FALSE`, and `DoSearch` is called. [Protected]

```
CMEditFindNext           virtual void CMEditFindNext(RTMessage
                              Msg) = [CM_FIRST + CM_EDITFINDNEXT];
```

The `CMEditFindNext` function initiates a text search when a `Find Next` menu item is selected. No dialog box is displayed since it is assumed that `SearchStruct` contains the proper settings. `DoSearch` is called by `CMEditFindNext`. [Protected]

```
CMEditReplace            virtual void CMEditReplace(RTMessage
                              MSG) = [CM_FIRST + CM_EDITREPLACE];
```

The `CMEditReplace` function initiates a text search and replace operation and displays a search dialog box when a `Replace` menu item is selected. After the user has made selections to the dialog box, `SearchStruct` is updated to reflect the user's selections, `IsReplaceOp` is set to `TRUE`, and `DoSearch` is called. [Protected]

```
DoSearch                 void DoSearch();
```

The `DoSearch` function offers search functions using the options and features in `SearchStruct`. [Public]

```
read                     virtual Pvoid read(Ripstream is);
```

The `read` function calls `TWindow::read` to read in the base `TWindow` object. [Protected]

```
WMSetFocus               virtual void WMSetFocus(RTMessage Msg)
                            = [WM_FIRST + WM_SETFOCUS];
```

The `WMSetFocus` function sets the focus to Editor edit control when the `WM_SETFOCUS` message is detected. [Protected]

```
WMSize                    virtual void WMSize(RTMessage Msg) =
                               [WM_FIRST + WM_SIZE];
```

The `WMSize` function sizes the Editor edit control to the `TEditWindow`'s client area when the `WM_SIZE` message is detected. [Protected]

```
write                     virtual void  write(Ropstream os);
```

The `write` function calls `TWindow::write` to write out the base `TWindow` object and then `PutChildPtr` to write out the edit control child window. [Protected]

Class Name: TFileDialog

Class Header File:

filedial.h

Description:

The `TFileDialog` class creates a dialog box that enables the user to select a file for opening or saving. An open and save dialog box resource are provided in the FILEDIAL.DLG dialog box resource.

Data Member(s):

```
Extension                 char Extension[MAXTEXT];
```

`Extension` holds the file name extension. [Public]

```
FilePath                  LPSTR FilePath;
```

`FilePath` points to the buffer that returns the file name defined by the user. [Public]

```
FileSpec                  char FileSpec[FILESPEC];
```

`FileSpec` contains the current file name. [Public]

```
PathName                  char PathName[MAXPATH];
```

`PathName` contains the current file path. [Public]

Constructor(s):

`TFileDialog (PTWindowsObject AParent, int ResourceId, LPSTR AFilePath, PTModule AModule = NULL);`	Invokes the `TDialog` constructor [Public]

`TFileDialog(StreamableInit);`	`TFileDialog` stream constructor [Protected]

Destructor:

None.

Additional Member Function(s):

`build`	`static PTStreamable build();`

The `build` function invokes the `TFileDialog` constructor and constructs an object of type `TFileDialog` before reading its data members from a stream. [Public]

`CanClose`	`virtual BOOL CanClose();`

The `CanClose` function returns `TRUE` when the user entered a valid file name. A return value of `FALSE` indicates that the user did not enter a valid file name. [Public]

```
HandleDList          virtual void HandleDList(RTMessage Msg)
                          = [ID_FIRST + ID_DLIST];
```

The `HandleDList` function responds to messages from the directory list box. This function call `UpdateListBoxes` when an entry is double clicked. Otherwise, `UpdateFileName` is called. [Protected]

```
HandleFList          virtual void HandleFList(RTMessage Msg)
                          = [ID_FIRST + ID_FLIST];
```

The `HandleFList` function responds to messages from the file list box and calls `UpdateFileName` when the list box selection changes. [Protected]

```
HandleFName          virtual void HandleFName(RTMessage Msg)
                          = [ID_FIRST + ID_FNAME];
```

The `HandleFName` function responds to messages from the edit control and enables the `OK` button when the edit control contains text. [Protected]

`SelectFileName`	`void SelectFileName();`

The `SelectFileName` function selects text from the edit control and sets the focus to the edit control. [Public]

`SetupWindow`	`virtual void SetupWindow();`

The `SetupWindow` function calls `TDialog::SetupWindow` to set up the dialog box. [Protected]

`UpdateFileName`	`void UpdateFileName();`

The `UpdateFileName` function sets the text of the edit control to `PathName` and selects the text. [Public]

`UpdateListBoxes` `BOOL UpdateListBoxes();`

The `UpdateListBoxes` function updates the file and directory list boxes. `TRUE` is returned when updating is successful. [Public]

Class Name: TFileWindow

Class Header File:

filewnd.h

Description:

The `TFileWindow` class is derived from `TEditWindow` and provides the capability to open, read, write, and save files.

Data Member(s):

`FileName` `LPSTR FileName;`

`FileName` is the name of the file being edited. [Public]

`IsNewFile` `BOOL IsNewFile;`

`IsNewFile` indicates whether the file being edited is a new file or a previously opened file. `TRUE` indicates a new file. `FALSE` indicates a previously opened file. [Public]

Constructor(s):

`TFileWindow (PTWindowsObject AParent, LPSTR ATitle, LPSTR AFileName, PTModule AModule = NULL);`	Invokes the `TEditWindow` constructor [Public]
`TFileWindow (StreamableInit);`	`TFileWindow` stream constructor [Protected]

Destructor:

`virtual ~TFileWindow();`	Frees memory associated with `TFileWindow` [Public]

Additional Member Function(s):

`build` `static PTStreamable build();`

The `build` function invokes the `TFileWindow` constructor and constructs an object of type `TFileWindow` before reading its data members from a stream. [Public]

CanClear virtual BOOL CanClear();

The CanClear function determines whether it is all right to clear the text in the editor. This function returns TRUE if the text has not been modified. A return value of FALSE indicates that the text has been modified. [Public]

CanClose virtual BOOL CanClose();

The CanClose function determines whether it is all right to close the file. This function calls CanClear and returns the value returned by CanClear. [Public]

CMFileNew
```
virtual void CMFileNew(RTMessage Msg)
     = [CM_FIRST + CM_FILENEW];
```

The CMFileNew function calls NewFile when a "FILE New" command with a CM_FILENEW ID is detected. [Protected]

CMFileOpen
```
virtual void CMFileOpen(RTMessage Msg)
     = [CM_FIRST + CM_FILEOPEN];
```

The CMFileOpen function calls Open when an "FILE Open" command with a CM_FILEOPEN ID is detected. [Protected]

CMFileSave
```
virtual void CMFileSave(TMessage& Msg)
     = [CM_FIRST + CM_FILESAVE];
```

The CMFileSave function calls Save when a "FILE Save" command with a CM_FILESAVE ID is detected. [Protected]

CMFileSaveAs
```
virtual void CMFileSaveAs(RTMessage Msg)
     = [CM_FIRST + CM_FILESAVEAS];
```

The CMFileSaveAs function calls SaveAs when a "FILE SaveAs" command with a CM_FILESAVEAS ID is detected. [Protected]

NewFile void NewFile();

The NewFile function calls CanClear to determine whether the current text in the editor can be cleared. If the existing text can be cleared, a new file is opened. [Public]

Open void Open();

The Open function calls CanClear to determine whether the current text in the editor can be cleared. If the existing text can be cleared, Open displays a file dialog box that enables the user to select a file. Once a file has been selected, Open calls ReplaceWith and passes the selected file name. [Public]

Read BOOL Read();

The `Read` function reads the contents of a file into the editor and sets `IsNewFile` to `FALSE`. [Public]

`read` `virtual Pvoid read(Ripstream is);`

The `read` function calls `TEditWindow::read` to read in the base `TEditWindow` object. [Protected]

`ReplaceWith` `void ReplaceWith(LPSTR AFileName);`

The `ReplaceWith` function replaces the current file in the editor with the specified file. `ReplaceWith` calls `SetFileName` and `Read`. [Public]

`Save` `BOOL Save();`

The `Save` function saves the current file. When `IsNewFile` is `TRUE`, `Save` calls `SaveAs`. When `IsNewFile` is `FALSE`, `Save` calls `Write`. `Save` returns the result of the call to the appropriate function. [Public]

`SaveAs` `BOOL SaveAs();`

The `SaveAs` function saves the current file by using a file name retrieved from the user. A "Save" file dialog is displayed to prompt for the file name. Once a file name has been established, `SaveAs` calls `SetFileName` and `Write`. `SaveAs` returns `TRUE` when the file is successfully saved. [Public]

`SetFileName` `void SetFileName(LPSTR AFileName);`

The `SetFileName` function sets the `FileName` data member and modifies the window caption. [Public]

`SetupWindow` `virtual void SetupWindow();`

The `SetupWindow` function establishes the edit window's `Editor` edit control. [Protected]

`Write` `BOOL Write();`

The `Write` function saves the contents of the editor to the file specified in `FileName`. `TRUE` is returned when the file is successfully saved. [Public]

`write` `virtual void write(Ropstream os);`

The `write` function calls `TEditWindow::write` to write out the base `TEditWindow` object then writes out `FileName`. [Protected]

Class Name: TGroupBox

Class Header File:

groupbox.h

Description:

The `TGroupBox` class is an interface object representing group box elements. Group boxes are used to group a series of check boxes and radio buttons that usually represent user options and application settings.

Data Member(s):

`NotifyParent`	`BOOL NotifyParent;`

`NotifyParent` indicates whether the parent should be notified when one of the group box's selection boxes has changed state. [Public]

Constructor(s):

`TGroupBox(PTWindowsObject AParent, int AnId, LPSTR AText, int X, int Y, int W, int H, PTModule AModule = NULL);`	Constructs a group box object using the specified parent window, control ID, text, position, width, and height [Public]
`TGroupBox(PTWindowsObject AParent, int ResourceId, PTModule AModule = NULL);`	Constructs a `TGroupBox` object to be associated with `TDialog` group box control [Public]
`TGroupBox (StreamableInit);`	`TGroupBox` stream constructor [Protected]

Destructor:

None.

Additional Member Function(s):

`build`	`static PTStreamable build();`

The `build` function invokes the `TGroupBox` constructor and constructs an object of type `TGroupBox` before reading its data members from a stream. [Public]

`GetClassName`	`virtual LPSTR GetClassName();`

The `GetClassName` function returns "BUTTON", the `TGroupBox` Windows registration class. [Protected]

`read`	`virtual Pvoid read(Ripstream is);`

The `read` function calls `TWindow::read` to read in the base `TGroupBox` object. [Protected]

`SelectionChanged`	`virtual void SelectionChanged(int ControlId);`

The `SelectionChanged` function notifies the parent window of a group box that a change has been made in the group box *only* if `NotifyParent` is `TRUE`. [Public]

`write`	`virtual void write(Ropstream os);`

The `write` function calls `TWindow::write` to write out the base `TGroupBox` object. [Protected]

Class Name: TInputDialog

Class Header File:

inputdia.h

Description:

The `TInputDialog` class defines a dialog box that enables the user to input a single text item.

Data Member(s):

`Buffer`	`LPSTR Buffer;`

`Buffer` is a pointer to a buffer that returns the text entered by the user. [Public]

`BufferSize`	`WORD BufferSize;`

`BufferSize` stores the size of `Buffer`. [Public]

`Prompt`	`LPSTR Prompt;`

`Prompt` points the input dialog box prompt. [Public]

Constructor(s):

`TInputDialog (PTWindowsObject AParent, LPSTR ATitle, LPSTR APrompt, LPSTR ABuffer, WORD ABufferSize, PTModule AModule = NULL);`	Invokes the `TDialog` constructor [Public]
`TInputDialog(StreamableInit);`	`TInputDialog` stream constructor. [Protected]

Destructor:

None.

Additional Member Function(s):

`build` `static PTStreamable build();`

The `build` function invokes the `TInputDialog` constructor and constructs an object of type `TInputDialog` before reading its data members from a stream. [Public]

`read` `virtual Pvoid read(Ripstream is);`

The `read` function calls `TDialog::read` to read in the base `TDialog` object. [Protected]

`SetupWindow` `virtual void SetupWindow();`

The `SetupWindow` function calls `TDialog::SetupWindow` to set up the window and limit the number of characters that can be input to `BufferSize` minus 1. [Protected]

`TransferData` `void TransferData(WORD Direction);`

The `TransferData` function transfers input dialog data. `Direction` can be set to `TF_SETDATA` or `TF_GETDATA`. When `Direction` is `TF_SETDATA`, the text for the controls is set to the text in `Prompt` and `Buffer`. When `Direction` is set to `TF_GETDATA`, the current text in the editor is copied to `Buffer`. [Public]

`write` `virtual void write(Ropstream os);`

The `write` function calls `TDialog::write` to write out the base `TDialog` object. [Protected]

Class Name: TListBox

Class Header File:

listbox.h

Description:

The `TListBox` class is an interface object that represents a Windows list box. `TListBox` creates and manages list boxes.

Data Member(s):

None.

Constructor(s):

`TListBox(PTWindowsObject AParent, int AnId, int X, int Y, int W, int H, PTModule AModule = NULL);`	Constructs a list box object using the specified parent window, control ID, position, width, and height [Public]

`TListBox(PTWindowsObject AParent, int ResourceId, PTModule AModule = NULL);`	Constructs a `TListBox` object to be associated with a `TDialog` list box [Public]
`TListBox (StreamableInit);`	`TListBox` stream constructor [Protected]

Destructor:

None.

Additional Member Function(s):

`AddString` `int AddString(LPSTR AString);`

The `AddString` function adds the string specified in `AString` to the list box. This function returns the string's position in the list box when successful. A negative return value indicates that the function cannot add the string to the list box. [Public]

`build` `static PTStreamable build();`

The `build` function invokes the `TListBox` constructor and constructs an object of type `TListBox` before reading its data members from a stream. [Public]

`ClearList` `void ClearList();`

The `ClearList` function clears all list items. [Public]

`DeleteString` `int DeleteString(int Index);`

The `DeleteString` function deletes the list item at the location specified by `Index`. When successful, this function returns the number of list items remaining. A negative return value indicates that the function cannot delete the list item. [Public]

`FindExactString` `int FindExactString(LPSTR AString, int SearchIndex);`

The `FindExactString` function searches the list box for a string that exactly matches the string specified in `AString`. The search begins at the index specified in `SearchIndex`. The index of the matching string is returned. [Public]

`FindString` `int FindString(LPSTR AString, int SearchIndex);`

The `FindString` function searches the list box for a string that begins with the string specified in `AString`. The search begins at the index specified in `SearchIndex`. The index of the matching string is returned. [Public]

`GetClassName` `virtual LPSTR GetClassName();`

The `GetClassName` function returns "LISTBOX", the `TListBox` Windows registration class. [Protected]

```
GetCount                    int GetCount();
```

When successful, the GetCount function returns the number of list box items. A negative return value indicates that the function is unsuccessful. [Public]

```
GetMsgID                    virtual WORD GetMsgID(WORD AMsg);
```

The GetMsgID function returns the Windows list box message ID associated with the specified ObjectWindows message ID. [Protected]

```
GetSelCount                 int GetSelCount();
```

The GetSelCount function returns the number of items that are currently selected in a list box. [Public]

```
GetSelIndex                 int GetSelIndex();
```

When successful, the GetSelIndex function returns the position of the currently selected item. A negative return value indicates that the function is unsuccessful. [Public]

```
GetSelIndexes               int GetSelIndexes(Pint Indexes,
                                 int MaxCount);
```

The GetSelIndexes function copies the indexes of the selected strings in the list box to the array specified in Indexes. MaxCount specifies the maximum number of indexes to copy. The number of item indexes copied to the array is returned. [Public]

```
GetSelString                int GetSelString(LPSTR AString, int
                                 MaxChars);
```

The GetSelString function places the currently selected list item in AString. MaxChars specifies the maximum number of characters to copy. When successful, this function returns the length of the copied string. A negative return value indicates that the function is unsuccessful. [Public]

```
GetSelStrings               int GetSelStrings(LPSTR *Strings, int
                                MaxCount, int MaxChars);
```

The GetSelStrings function copies the currently selected items in the list box to the Strings array. MaxCount specifies the maximum number of items to copy to Strings. MaxChars specifies the maximum number of characters in a string to copy to Strings. Strings entries should be able to store MaxChars characters plus a null terminator. [Public]

```
GetString                   int GetString(LPSTR AString, int Index);
```

The GetString function copies the item at the location specified in Index to AString. When successful, this function returns the length of the copied string. A negative return value indicates that the function is unsuccessful. [Public]

```
GetStringLen            int GetStringLen(int Index);
```

When successful, the `GetStringLen` function returns the length of the item at the location specified in `Index`. A negative return value indicates that the function is unsuccessful. [Public]

```
InsertString            int InsertString(LPSTR AString, int
                             Index);
```

The `InsertString` function inserts the string specified in `AString` at the list position specified in `Index`. When successful, this function returns the string's list position. A negative return value indicates that the function is unsuccessful. [Public]

```
SetSelIndex             int SetSelIndex(int Index);
```

When successful, the `SetSelIndex` function selects the item at the position specified in `Index`. This function returns a negative value when unsuccessful. `Index` can be set to –1 to clear all selections. [Public]

```
SetSelIndexes           int SelSelIndexes(Pint Indexes, int
                             NumSelections, BOOL ShouldSet);
```

The `SetSelIndexes` function either selects or deselects the strings associated with the indexes specified in `Indexes`. `NumSelections` specifies the number of indexes in `Indexes` to use. `ShouldSet` specifies whether to select to deselect the strings. If `ShouldSet` is `TRUE`, the strings are selected. If `ShouldString` is `FALSE`, the strings are deselected. [Public]

```
SetSelString            int SetSelString(LPSTR AString, int
                             AIndex);
```

The `SetSelString` function selects the list box item that matches `AString`. The search for a match begins at the position specified by `AIndex`. When successful, this function returns the position of the matching item. A negative return value indicates that the function is unsuccessful. [Public]

```
SetSelStrings           int SetSelStrings(LPSTR *Prefixes, int
                             NumSelections, BOOL ShouldSet);
```

The `SetSelStrings` function selects or deselects the strings in the list box that match the prefix strings specified in the `Prefixes` array. `ShouldSet` indicates whether the strings should be selected or deselected. If `ShouldSet` is `TRUE`, matching strings are selected. If `ShouldSet` is `FALSE`, matching strings are deselected. [Public]

```
Transfer                virtual WORD Transfer(Pvoid DataPtr,
                             WORD TransferFlag);
```

The Transfer function uses the buffer pointed to by DataPtr to transfer data. The transfer buffer contains a pointer to a PTListBoxData object.

The TransferFlag parameter of the Transfer function can be set to TF_SETDATA, TF_GETDATA, or TF_SIZEDATA as follows:

- Set TransferFlag to TF_SETDATA to fill the list and select one or more items using the data in the buffer.
- Set TransferFlag to TF_GETDATA to fill the buffer using the current list and selection(s) from the list box.
- Set TransferFlag to TF_SIZEDATA to return the size of PTListBoxData. No data is transferred in this case. [Public]

Class Name: TMDIClient

Class Header File:

mdi.h

Description:

The TMDIClient class represents Multiple Document Interface (MDI) client windows and manages the MDI client area and the MDI child windows.

Data Member(s):

`ClientAttr`	`LPCLIENTCREATESTRUCT ClientAttr;`

ClientAttr stores the attributes of the MDI client window. [Public]

Constructor(s):

`TMDIClient(PTMDIFrame AParent, PTModule AModule = NULL);`	Constructs an MDI client window object [Public]
`TMDIClient(PTMDIFrame AParent, HWND AnHWindow, PTModule AModule = NULL);`	Constructs an MDI client object to be associated with the MDI client window. [Public]
`TMDIClient (StreamableInit);`	TMDIClient stream constructor [Protected]

Destructor:

`~TMDIClient();`	Frees the ClientAttr structure [Public]

Additional Member Function(s):

`ArrangeIcons` `virtual void ArrangeIcons();`

The `ArrangeIcons` function aligns MDI child window icons along the bottom of the MDI client window. [Public]

`build` `static PTStreamable build();`

The `build` function invokes the `TMDIClient` constructor and constructs an object of type `TMDIClient` before reading its data members from a stream. [Public]

`CascadeChildren` `virtual void CascadeChildren();`

The `CascadeChildren` function adjusts the size of all MDI child windows that are not minimized and arranges them in an overlapping style. [Public]

`GetClassName` `virtual LPSTR GetClassName();`

The `GetClassName` function returns "MDICLIENT", the `TMDIClient` Windows registration class name. [Protected]

`read` `virtual Pvoid read(Ripstream is);`

The `read` function calls `TWindows::read` to read the base `TWindows` object. [Protected]

`TileChildren` `virtual void TileChildren();`

The `TileChildren` function adjusts the size of all MDI child windows that are not minimized and arranges them in a non-overlapping, tiled style. [Public]

`WMMDIActivate`
```
virtual void WMMDIActivate(RTMessage)
= [WM_FIRST + WM_MDIACTIVATE];
```

The `WMMDIActivate` function responds to the `WM_MDIACTIVATE` message. [Protected]

`WMPaint`
```
virtual void WMPaint(RTMessage Msg)
= [WM_FIRST + WM_PAINT];
```

The `WMPaint` function redefines `TWindow::WMPaint` to call `DefWndProc`. [Protected]

`write` `virtual void write (Ropstream os);`

The `write` function calls `TWindow::write` to write out the base `TWindow` object. [Protected]

Class Name: TMDIFrame

Class Header File:

mdi.h

Description:

The TMDIFrame class represents Multiple Document Interface (MDI) frame windows, the main windows for MDI applications. TMDIFrame can automatically create and manipulate MDI child windows.

Data Member(s):

ActiveChild PTWindow ActiveChild;

ActiveChild points to the active MDI child window of a TMDIFrame. [Public]

ChildMenuPos int ChildMenuPos;

ChildMenuPos stores the top-level menu position for the MDI submenu. [Public]

ClientWnd PTMDIClient ClientWnd;

ClientWnd is a pointer to the TMDIFrame client window. [Public]

Constructor(s):

TMDIFrame(LPSTR ATitle, int MenuId, PTModule AModule = NULL);	Constructs an MDI frame window object using the specified caption and menu [Public]
TMDIFrame(LPSTR ATitle, LPSTR MenuName, PTModule AModule = NULL);	Constructs an MDI window object using the specified options and integer resource identifier [Public]
TMDIFrame(HWND AnHWindow, HWND ClientWnd);	Constructs an MDI window object associated with the specified handle. [Public]
TMDIFrame (StreamableInit);	TMDIFrame stream constructor [Protected]

Destructor:

virtual ~TMDIFrame();	Deletes the MDI client window object [Public]

Additional Member Function(s):

ArrangeIcons virtual void ArrangeIcons();

The ArrangeIcons function calls the ArrangeIcons member function of the client window to arrange the iconized MDI child windows along the bottom of the client window. [Public]

build static PTStreamable build();

The `build` function invokes the `TMDIFrame` constructor and constructs an object of type `TMDIFrame` before reading its data members from a stream. [Public]

```
CascadeChildren          virtual void CascadeChildren();
```

The `CascadeChildren` function calls the `CascadeChildren` member function of the client window to arrange the MDI child windows that are not iconized in an overlapping style. [Public]

```
CloseChildren            virtual BOOL CloseChildren();
```

The `CloseChildren` function calls the `CanClose` member function of each MDI child window and closes all the child windows if possible. [Public]

```
CMArrangeIcons           virtual void CMArrangeIcons(RTMessage
                              Msg) = [CM_FIRST +
                              CM_ARRANGEICONS];
```

The `CMArrangeIcons` function calls `ArrangeIcons` when a menu item with a `CM_ARRANGEICONS` ID is selected. [Protected]

```
CMCascadeChildren        virtual void CMCascadeChildren(RTMessage
                              Msg) = [CM_FIRST +
                              CM_CASCADECHILDREN];
```

The `CMCascadeChildren` function calls `CascadeChildren` when a menu item with a `CM_CASCADECHILDREN` ID is selected. [Protected]

```
CMCloseChildren          virtual void CMCloseChildren(RTMessage
                              Msg) = [CM_FIRST +
                              CM_CLOSECHILDREN];
```

The `CMCloseChildren` function calls `CloseChildren` when a menu item with a `CM_CLOSECHILDREN` ID is selected. [Protected]

```
CMCreateChild            virtual void CMCreateChild(RTMessage
                              Msg) = [CM_FIRST + CM_CREATECHILD];
```

The `CMCreateChild` function calls `CreateChild` when a menu item with a `CM_CREATECHILD` ID is selected. [Protected]

```
CMTileChildren           virtual void CMTileChildren(RTMessage
                              Msg) = [CM_FIRST +
                              CM_TILECHILDREN];
```

The `CMTileChildren` function calls `TileChildren` when a menu item with a `CM_TILECHILDREN` ID is selected. [Protected]

```
CreateChild              virtual PTWindowsObject CreateChild();
```

The `CreateChild` function creates a MDI child window and returns a pointer to the created child window. [Public]

```
GetClassName              virtual LPSTR GetClassName();
```

The `GetClassName` function returns "OWLMDIFrame". [Protected]

```
GetClient                 virtual PTMDIClient GetClient();
```

The `GetClient` function returns the pointer to the client window stored in `ClientWnd`. [Public]

```
GetWindowClass            virtual void GetWindowClass(WNDCLASS _FAR &
                                AWndClass);
```

The `GetWindowClass` function calls `TWindow::GetWindowClass` and sets `AWndClass.Style` to 0. [Protected]

```
InitChild                 virtual PTWindowsObject InitChild();
```

The `InitChild` function constructs an instance of `TWindow` as an MDI child window. This function returns the pointer to the instance. You can redefine this member function in the derived window class to construct an instance of a derived MDI child class. [Public]

```
InitClientWindow          virtual void InitClientWindow();
```

The `InitClientWindow` function constructs the MDI client window as an instance of `TMDIClient`. The pointer to the client window is stored in `ClientWnd`. [Public]

```
read                      virtual Pvoid read (Ripstream is);
```

The `read` function calls `TWindow::read` to read in the base `TWindow` object. [Protected]

```
SetupWindow               virtual void SetupWindow();
```

The `SetupWindow` function calls `InitClientWindow` to construct an MDI client window and creates the interface element. [Protected]

```
TileChildren              virtual void TileChildren();
```

The `TileChildren` function calls the `TileChildren` member function of the client window to size and arrange the MDI child windows that are not iconized in a non-overlapping style. [Public]

```
WMActivate                virtual void WMActivate(RTMessage Msg) =
                               [WM_FIRST + WM_ACTIVATE];
```

The `WMActivate` function responds to the `WM_ACTIVATE` message. [Protected]

```
write                     virtual void write(Ropstream os);
```

The `write` function calls `TWindow::write` to write out the base `TWindow` object. [Protected]

Class Name: TModule

Class Header File:

module.h

Description:

The `TModule` class defines behaviors shared by library and application modules. Instances of `TModule` act as stand-ins for library (DLL) modules.

Data Member(s):

`hInstance` `HANDLE hInstance;`

`hInstance` stores the handle of the currently executing instance of the application. [Public]

`lpCmdLine` `LPSTR lpCmdLine;`

`lpCmdLine` points to the command line string. [Public]

`Name` `LPSTR Name;`

`Name` is the application name or DLL module name. [Public]

`Status` `int Status;`

`Status` indicates whether an error has been generated that could keep the application from creating the main window or entering the message loop. [Public]

Constructor(s):

`TModule(LPSTR AName,`
`HANDLE AnInstance,`
`LPSTR ACmdLine);`
	Initializes the data members for the object [Public]

Destructor:

`virtual ~TModule();`	Destroys a `TModule` object [Public]

Additional Member Function(s):

`Error` `virtual void Error(int ErrorCode);`

The `Error` function processes the error specified in `ErrorCode`. `ErrorCode` can be defined by the application or can be one of the following ObjectWindows errors:

```
EM_INVALIDWINDOW
EM_OUTOFMEMORY
EM_INVALIDCLIENT
EM_INVALIDCHILD
EM_INVALIDMAINWINDOW
EM_INVALIDMODULE
```

The `Error` function displays a message box that lists the error code and asks the user to proceed. Depending on the input from the user, the program may continue or be terminated. [Public]

```
ExecDialog              virtual int ExecDialog(PTWindowsObject
                             ADialog);
```

The `ExecDialog` function determines whether the specified dialog object is valid and, if so, executes the dialog object. This function returns IDCANCEL when the specified dialog object is not valid. [Public]

```
GetClientHandle         HWND GetClientHandle(HWND AnHWindow);
```

The `GetClientHandle` function returns the handle of the MDI client window for the specified window. This function returns zero when the window has no MDI client window. [Public]

```
GetParentObject         virtual PTWindowsObject
                        GetParentObject(HWND ParentHandle);
```

The `GetParentObject` function is called in a DLL to get a pointer to a parent window object. [Public]

```
hashValue               virtual hashValueType hashValue() const;
```

The `hashValue` function must be redefined by all objects derived from the base class `Object`. This function returns the hash value of `TModule`, `hInstance`. [Public]

```
isA                     virtual classType isA() const;
```

The `isA` function must be redefined by all objects derived from the base class object. This function returns the object ID of `TModule`, `moduleClass`. [Public]

```
isEqual                 virtual int isEqual(RCObject module)
                             const;
```

The `isEqual` function redefines the pure virtual function in class `Object`. [Public]

```
LowMemory               BOOL LowMemory();
```

The `LowMemory` function returns `TRUE` when the safety pool has been used up. [Public]

```
MakeWindow              virtual PTWindowsObject MakeWindow
                             (PTWindowsObject AWindowsObject);
```

The `MakeWindow` function creates a window or modeless dialog element and associates it with the specified object as long as the specified object is valid. A return value of NULL indicates that the function is unsuccessful. [Public]

```
nameOf                  virtual Pchar nameOf() const;
```

The `nameOf` function redefines the pure virtual function in class `Object`. This function returns the class ID string of `TModule`, "TModule." [Public]

```
printOn                  virtual void printOn(Rostream
                              outputStream) const;
```

The `printOn` function redefines the pure virtual function in class `Object`. The hexadecimal value of the instance handle for the module is printed on the specified stream. [Public]

```
RestoreMemory            void RestoreMemory();
```

The `RestoreMemory` function allocates a safety pool. [Public]

```
ValidWindow              virtual PTWindowsObject ValidWindow
                              (PWindowsObject AWindowsObject);
```

The `ValidWindow` function determines whether the specified object is valid. This function returns the pointer to the object when the object is valid. The object is deleted and `NULL` is returned when the object is not valid. [Public]

Class Name: TRadioButton

Class Header File:

radiobut.h

Description:

The `TRadioButton` class is derived from `TCheckBox` and represents a Windows radio button. A radio button is a two-state button; it can either be checked or unchecked. `TRadioButton` creates and manages radio buttons.

Data Member(s):

None.

Constructor(s):

`TRadioButton (PTWindowsObject AParent, int AnId, LPSTR ATitle, int X, int Y, int W, int H, PTGroupBox AGroup, PTModule AModule = NULL);`	Constructs a radio button object using the specified parent, control ID, text, position, width, height, and group [Public]

`TRadioButton (PTWindowsObject AParent, int ResourceId, PTGroupBox AGroup, PTModule AModule = NULL);`	Constructs a `TRadioButton` object [Public]
`TRadioButton (StreamableInit);`	`TRadioButton` stream constructor [Protected]

Destructor:

None.

Additional Member Function(s):

```
BNClicked               virtual void BNClicked(RTMessage Msg)
                           = [NF_FIRST + BN_CLICKED];
```

The `BNClicked` function responds to the `BN_CLICKED` message. [Protected]

```
build                   static PTStreamable build();
```

The `build` function invokes the `TRadioButton` constructor and constructs an object of type `TRadioButton` before reading its data members from a stream. [Public]

Class Name: TScrollBar

Class Header File:

scrollba.h

Description:

The `TScrollBar` class represents and manages stand-alone horizontal and vertical scroll bars. Do not use `TScrollBar` objects with windows that contain the `WS_HSCROLL` or `WS_VSCROLL` style attributes.

Data Member(s):

```
LineMagnitude           int LineMagnitude;
```

`LineMagnitude` specifies the number of range units that the scroll bar is scrolled when one of the scroll bar arrows is clicked. By default, `LineMagnitude` is 1 and the scroll range is 0 to 100. [Public]

```
PageMagnitude           int PageMagnitude;
```

`PageMagnitude` specifies the number of range units that the scroll bar is scrolled when the scrolling area of the scroll bar is clicked. By default, `PageMagnitude` is 10 and the scroll range is 0 to 100. [Public]

Constructor(s):

`TScrollBar (PTWindowsObject AParent, int AnId, int X, int Y, int W, int H, BOOL IsHScrollBar, PTModule AModule = NULL);`	Constructs a scroll bar object using the specified parent, control ID, position, width, and height; set `IsHScrollBar` to `TRUE` to add `SBS_HORZ` to the styles in `Attr.Style` or `FALSE` to add `SBS_VERT` to the styles in `Attr.Style` [Public]
`TScrollBar (PTWindowsObject AParent int ResourceId, PTModule AModule = NULL);`	Constructs a `TScrollBar` object [Public]
`TScrollBar (StreamableInit);`	`TScrollBar` stream constructor [Protected]

Destructor:

None.

Additional Member Function(s):

`build` `static PTStreamable build();`

The `build` function invokes the `TScrollBar` constructor and constructs an object of type `TScrollBar` before reading its data members from a stream. [Public]

`DeltaPos` `int DeltaPos(int Delta);`

The `DeltaPos` function changes the thumb position of the scroll bar by calling `SetPosition`. `Delta` specifies the amount to move the thumb position (negative for left or up, positive for right or down). `DeltaPos` returns the new thumb position. [Public]

`GetClassName` `virtual LPSTR GetClassName();`

The `GetClassName` function returns "SCROLLBAR", the `TScrollBar` Windows registration class name. [Protected]

`GetPosition` `int GetPosition();`

The `GetPosition` function returns the thumb position of the scroll bar. [Public]

`GetRange` `void GetRange(Rint LoVal, Rint HiVal);`

The `GetRange` function returns the scroll bar range in `LoVal` and `HiVal`. [Public]

`read` `virtual Pvoid read (Ripstream is);`

The `read` function calls `TWindow::read` to read in the base `TWindow` object. [Protected]

`SBBottom`

```
virtual void SBBottom(RTMessage Msg) =
     [NF_FIRST + SB_BOTTOM];
```

The `SBBottom` function calls `SetPosition` to move the scroll thumb to the bottom of the scroll bar for vertical scroll bars or to the right for horizontal scroll bars. [Protected]

`SBLineDown`

```
virtual void SBLineDown(RTMessage Msg) =
     [NF_FIRST + SB_LINEDOWN];
```

The `SBLineDown` function calls `SetPosition` to move the scroll thumb down for vertical scroll bars or right for horizontal scroll bars. `LineMagnitude` defines the number of range units the thumb is moved. [Protected]

`SBLineUp`

```
virtual void SBLineUp(RTMessage Msg) =
     [NF_FIRST + SB_LINEUP];
```

The `SBLineUp` function calls `SetPosition` to move the scroll thumb up for vertical scroll bars or left for horizontal scroll bars. `LineMagnitude` defines the number of range units the thumb is moved. [Protected]

`SBPageDown`

```
virtual void SBPageDown(RTMessage Msg) =
     [NF_FIRST + SB_PAGEDOWN];
```

The `SBPageDown` function calls `SetPosition` to move the scroll thumb down for vertical scroll bars or right for horizontal scroll bars. `PageMagnitude` defines the number of range units the thumb is moved. [Protected]

`SBPageUp`

```
virtual void SBPageUp(RTMessage Msg) =
     [NF_FIRST + SB_PAGEUP];
```

The `SBPageUp` function calls `SetPosition` to move the scroll thumb up for vertical scroll bars or left for horizontal scroll bars. `PageMagnitude` defines the number of range units the thumb is moved. [Protected]

`SBThumbPosition`

```
virtual void SBThumbPosition(RTMessage
     Msg) = [NF_FIRST +
     SB_THUMBPOSITION];
```

The `SBThumbPosition` function calls `SetPosition` to move the scroll thumb. [Protected]

```
SBThumbTrack              virtual void SBThumbTrack(RTMessage
                               Msg) = [NF_FIRST + SB_THUMBTRACK];
```

The `SBThumbTrack` function calls `SetPosition` to move the scroll thumb to a new position as it is being dragged. [Protected]

```
SBTop                     virtual void SBTop(RTMessage Msg) =
                               [NF_FIRST + SB_TOP];
```

The `SBTop` function calls `SetPosition` to move the scroll thumb to the top for vertical scroll bars or the left for horizontal scroll bars. [Protected]

```
SetPosition               void SetPosition(int ThumbPos);
```

The `SetPosition` function moves the thumb position to the position specified in `ThumbPos`. The thumb position will not be moved outside the range of the scroll bar. [Public]

```
SetRange                  void SetRange(int LoVal, int HiVal);
```

The `SetRange` function sets to scroll bar range to the values specified in `LoVal` and `HiVal`. [Public]

```
SetupWindow               virtual void SetupWindow();
```

The `SetupWindow` function defines the scroll bar range as 0 to 100. [Protected]

```
Transfer                  virtual WORD Transfer(Pvoid DataPtr,
                               WORD TransferFlag);
```

The `Transfer` function uses the data buffer pointed to by `DataPtr` to transfer scroll bar information. `DataPtr` should point to a `TScrollBarData` structure, as follows:

```
struct TScrollBarData {
     int LowValue;
     int HighValue;
     int Position;
};
```

[Public]

```
write                     virtual void write(Ropstream os);
```

The `write` function calls `TWindow::write` to write out the base `TWindow` object. [Protected]

Class Name: TScroller

Class Header File:

scroller.h

Description:

The `TScroller` class provides automated scrolling for window displays. `TScroller` is usually associated with scroll bars; however, `TScroller` works with windows without scroll bars. Windows without scroll bars are automatically scrolled when the mouse is dragged from inside the client area to outside the client area.

Data Member(s):

`AutoMode` `BOOL AutoMode;`

`AutoMode` indicates whether auto-scrolling is in effect. `TRUE` indicates auto-scrolling is in effect. `FALSE` indicates auto-scrolling is not in effect. By default, `AutoMode` is `TRUE`. [Public]

`AutoOrg` `BOOL AutoOrg;`

`AutoOrg` indicates whether the origin of the client area should automatically be offset when preparing the area for painting. `TRUE` indicates automatic offset. [Public]

`ClassHashValue` `static hashValueType ClassHashValue;`

`ClassHashValue` contains the hash value of the last constructed instance of `TScroller`. [Protected]

`HasHScrollBar` `BOOL HasHScrollBar;`

The `HasHScrollBar` function is `TRUE` when the owner window has a horizontal scroll bar. [Public]

`HasVScrollBar` `BOOL HasVScrollBar;`

The `HasVScrollBar` function is `TRUE` when the owner window has a vertical scroll bar. [Public]

`InstanceHashValue` `hashValueType InstanceHashValue;`

`InstanceHashValue` contains the hash value of `this`. [Protected]

`TrackMode` `BOOL TrackMode;`

The `TrackMode` function indicates whether the display should be scrolled as the scroll thumb is dragged. `TRUE`, the default, indicates that the display should be scrolled as the thumb is dragged. `FALSE` indicates that the display should not be scrolled as the thumb is dragged. [Public]

`Window` `PTWindow Window;`

`Window` points to the owner window.

`XLine` `int XLine;`

`XLine` specifies the number of horizontal scroll units to move when the scroll arrow is clicked. The default value for `XLine` is 1. [Public]

`XPage` `int XPage;`

`XPage` specifies the number of horizontal scroll units to move when the thumb area of the scroll bar is clicked. The default value for `XPage` is equal to the current window width. [Public]

`XPos` `long XPos;`

`XPos` is the horizontal position of the scroller in horizontal scroll units. [Public]

`XRange` `long XRange;`

`XRange` is the maximum number of horizontal scroll units for the window. [Public]

`XUnit` `int XUnit;`

`XUnit` is the horizontal logical scroll unit used by `TScroller`. `XUnit` is expressed in device units. [Public]

`YLine` `int YLine;`

`YLine` is the number of vertical units scrolled when the scroll arrow is clicked. The default is 1. [Public]

`YPage` `int YPage;`

`YPage` is the number of vertical units scrolled when the thumb area of the scroll bar is clicked. `YPage` is set to the number of vertical units in the window. [Public]

`YPos` `long YPos;`

`YPos` is the current vertical position of the scroller. [Public]

`YRange` `long YRange;`

`YRange` is the maximum number of vertical scroll units for the window. [Public]

`YUnit` `int YUnit;`

`YUnit` is the vertical logical scroll unit used by `TScroller`. `YUnit` is expressed in device units. [Public]

Constructor(s):

`TScroller(PTWindow TheWindow, int TheXUnit, int TheYUnit, long TheXRange, long TheYRange);`	Constructs a `TScroller` object using the specified owner window, `x` unit, `y` unit, `x` range, and `y` range [Public]

`TScroller (StreamableInit);`	`TScroller` stream constructor [Protected]

Destructor:

`~TScroller();`	Destroys a `TScroller` object [Public]

Additional Member Function(s):

`AutoScroll` `virtual void AutoScroll();`

The `AutoScroll` function scrolls the display of the owner window when the mouse is dragged from the inside of the window to the outside. [Public]

`BeginView`
```
virtual void BeginView(HDC PaintDC,
     PAINTSTRUCT _FAR & PaintInfo);
```

The `BeginView` function sets the origin of the owner window's paint display context relative to the current scroller position when `AutoOrg` is `TRUE`. [Public]

`build` `static PTStreamable build();`

The `build` function invokes the `TScroller` constructor and constructs an object of type `TScroller` before reading its data members from a stream. [Public]

`EndView` `virtual void EndView();`

The `EndView` function updates the scroll bar positions to correspond to the position of `TScroller`. [Public]

`hashValue`
```
virtual hashValueType hashValue()
     const;
```

The `hashValue` function redefines the pure virtual function in class `Object`. This function returns the unique ID of a `TScroller` instance. [Public]

`HScroll`
```
virtual void HScroll(WORD ScrollEvent,
     int ThumbPos);
```

The `HScroll` function calls `ScrollTo` or `ScrollBy` to handle the specified horizontal scroll event. `ThumbPos` specifies the current thumb position. [Public]

`isA` `virtual classType isA() const;`

The `isA` function must be redefined by all objects derived from the base class `Object`. This function returns the class ID of `TScroller`. [Public]

`isEqual`
```
virtual int isEqual(RCObject
     testobj) const;
```

The `isEqual` function redefines the pure virtual function in class `Object`. This function returns `TRUE` when `this` points to `testobj`. [Public]

```
IsVisibleRect             BOOL IsVisibleRect(long X, long Y, int
                               XExt, int YExt);
```

The `IsVisibleRect` function determines whether any part of the specified rectangle is visible in the owner window. This function returns `TRUE` if any part of the rectangle is visible. [Public]

```
nameOf                    virtual Pchar nameOf() const;
```

The `nameOf` function must be redefined by all objects derived from the base class object. This function returns "TScroller", the class ID string. [Public]

```
printOn                   virtual void printOn(Rostream
                               outputStream) const;
```

The `printOn` function must be redefined by all objects derived from the base class `Object`. [Public]

```
read                      virtual Pvoid read(Ripstream is);
```

The `read` function reads `AutoMode`, `AutoOrg`, `HasHScrollBar`, `HasVScrollBar`, `TrackMode`, `XLine`, `XPage`, `XPos`, `XRange`, `XUnit`, `YLine`, `YPage`, `YPos`, `YRange`, and `YUnit`. [Protected]

```
ScrollBy                  void ScrollBy(long Dx, long Dy);
```

The `ScrollBy` function calls `ScrollTo` to scroll the display the amount specified in `Dx` and `Dy`. [Public]

```
ScrollTo                  virtual void ScrollTo(long X, long Y);
```

The `ScrollTo` function scrolls the display to the specified position. [Public]

```
SetPageSize               virtual void SetPageSize();
```

The `SetPageSize` function sets the page width and height to the size of the client area of the owner window. [Public]

```
SetRange                  void SetRange(long TheXRange, long
                               TheYRange);
```

The `SetRange` function sets the scroll ranges of `TScroller` to those specified and calls `SetSBarRange` to coordinate the ranges of the owner window scroll bars. [Public]

```
SetSBarRange              virtual void SetSBarRange();
```

The `SetSBarRange` function sets the range of the scroll bars for the owner window to fit within the range specified for `TScroller`. [Public]

`SetUnits` `void SetUnits(int TheXUnit, int TheYUnit);`

The `SetUnits` function defines the data members `XUnit` and `YUnit`. [Public]

`VScroll` `virtual void VScroll(WORD ScrollEvent, int ThumbPos);`

The `VScroll` function calls `ScrollTo` or `ScrollBy` to handle the specified vertical scroll event. `ThumbPos` specifies the current thumb position. [Public]

`write` `virtual void write(Ropstream os);`

The `write` function writes `AutoMode`, `AutoOrg`, `HasHScrollBar`, `HasVScrollBar`, `TrackMode`, `XLine`, `XPage`, `XPos`, `XRange`, `XUnit`, `YLine`, `YPage`, `YPos`, `YRange`, and `YUnit`. [Protected]

`XRangeValue` `long XRangeValue(int AScrollUnit);`

The `XRangeValue` function converts a horizontal scroll value to a horizontal range value. [Public]

`XScrollValue` `int XScrollValue(long ARangeUnit);`

The `XScrollValue` function converts a horizontal range value to a horizontal scroll value. [Public]

`YRangeValue` `long YRangeValue(int AScrollUnit);`

The `YRangeValue` function converts a vertical scroll value to a vertical range value. [Public]

`YScrollValue` `int YScrollValue(long ARangeUnit);`

The `YScrollValue` function converts a vertical range value to a vertical scroll value. [Public]

Class Name: TStatic

Class Header File:

static.h

Description:

The `TStatic` class represents a static text interface element and provides functions for the management of the element.

Data Member(s):

`TextLen` `WORD TextLen;`

`TextLen` specifies the size of the text buffer for the static control. [Public]

Constructor(s):

`TStatic(PTWindowsObject AParent, int AnId, LPSTR ATitle, int X, int Y, int W, int H, WORD ATextLen, PTModule AModule = NULL);`	Constructs a static control object using the specified parent window, control ID, text, position, width, height, and text length [Public]
`TStatic(PTWindowsObject AParent, int ResourceId, WORD ATextLen, PTModule AModule = NULL);`	Constructs a `TStatic` object to be associated with `TDialog` [Public]
`TStatic (StreamableInit);`	`TStatic` stream constructor [Protected]

Destructor:

None.

Additional Member Function(s):

`build` `static PTStreamable build();`

The `build` function invokes the `TStatic` constructor and constructs an object of type `TStatic` before reading its data members from a stream. [Public]

`Clear` `void Clear();`

The `Clear` function clears the text of the static control. [Public]

`GetClassName` `virtual LPSTR GetClassName();`

The `GetClassName` function returns "STATIC". [Protected]

`GetText` `int GetText(LPSTR ATextString, int MaxChars);`

The `GetText` function returns the text of the static control in `ATextString`. `MaxChars` specifies the size of `ATextString`. [Public]

`GetTextLen` `int GetTextLen();`

The `GetTextLen` function returns the length of the text in the static control. [Public]

`nameOf` `virtual Pchar nameOf() const;`

The `nameOf` function redefines the pure virtual function in class `Object`. This function returns "TStatic", the class ID string. [Public]

`read` `virtual Pvoid read(Ripstream is);`

The `read` function calls `TWindow::read` to read in the base `TWindow` object. [Protected]

```
SetText                  void SetText(LPSTR ATextString);
```

The `SetText` function sets the text of the static control to the string specified in `ATextString`. [Public]

```
Transfer                 virtual WORD Transfer(Pvoid DataPtr,
                              WORD TransferFlag);
```

The `Transfer` function transfers text to and from the buffer pointed to by `DataPtr`. The `TransferFlag` parameter of the `Transfer` function can be set to `TF_SETDATA`, `TF_GETDATA`, or `TF_SIZEDATA` as follows:

- Set `TransferFlag` to `TF_SETDATA` to copy the text from the buffer to the static control.
- Set `TransferFlag` to `TF_GETDATA` to copy the text of the static control to the transfer buffer.
- When `TransferFlag` is set to `TF_SIZEDATA`, this function returns `TextLen`. [Public]

```
write                    virtual void write(Ropstream os);
```

The `write` function calls `TWindow::write` to write out the base `TWindow` object. [Protected]

Class Name: TStreamable

Class Header File:

objstrm.h

Description:

`TStreamable` is an abstract class. Classes (known as streamable classes) can inherit from `TStreamable`; however, no object can be instantiated from this class. Objects of streamable classes can read from and write to streams. Classes that inherit from `TStreamable` must redefine the pure virtual member functions described in following sections.

Data Member(s):

None.

Constructor(s):

None.

Destructor:

None.

Additional Member Function(s):

`read` `virtual Pvoid read(Ripstream) = 0;`

The `read` function is a pure virtual function that must be redefined by all derived classes. The `read` function permits the application to read from the specified input stream. [Protected]

`streamableName` `virtual const Pchar streamableName() const = 0;`

The `streamableName` function is a pure virtual function that must be redefined by all derived classes. The name of the streamable class of the object is returned. [Private]

`write` `virtual void write(Ropstream) = 0;`

The `write` function is a pure virtual function that must be redeclared by all derived classes. The `write` function permits the application to write to the specified output stream. [Protected]

Class Name: TWindow

Class Header File:

window.h

Description:

The `TWindow` class is derived from `TWindowsObject` and offers the fundamental features for a window. `TWindow` objects are basic windows and can be used as application main windows or pop-up windows.

Data Member(s):

`Attr` `TWindowAttr Attr;`

`Attr` references a `TWindowAttr` structure that specifies the attributes used to create the window including the control ID, menu, text, and style. [Public]

`FocusChildHandle` `HANDLE FocusChildHandle;`

`FocusChildHandle` is the child window handle of the child window that had the focus when the window was last activated. [Public]

`Scroller` `PTScroller Scroller;`

`Scroller` points to the `TScroller` object used for display scrolling. [Public]

Constructor(s):

`TWindow(PTWindowsObject AParent, LPSTR ATitle, PTModule AModule = NULL);`	Constructs a window object using the specified parent window and text [Public]
`TWindow(HWND AnHWindow);`	Constructor for a `TWindow` that is to be used in a DLL as an alias for a non-`ObjectWindows` window [Public]
`TWindow(StreamableInit);`	`TWindow` stream constructor [Protected]

Destructor:

`virtual ~TWindow();`	Frees `Attr.Menu` and deletes `Scroller` [Public]

Additional Member Function(s):

`ActivationResponse` `virtual void ActivationResponse(WORD Activated, BOOL IsIconified);`

The `ActivationResponse` function provides a keyboard interface for window controls and is called by `WMActivate` and `WMMDIActivate`. [Public]

`AssignMenu` `virtual BOOL AssignMenu(LPSTR MenuName);`

The `AssignMenu` function sets `Attr.Menu` to the specified menu name. [Public]

`AssignMenu` `virtual BOOL AssignMenu(int MenuId);`

The `AssignMenu` function passes the specified menu ID to the previous `AssignMenu` function. The other `AssignMenu` function assigns the corresonding menu to the window. [Public]

`build` `static PTStreamable build();`

The `build` function invokes the `TWindow` constructor and constructs an object of type `TWindow` before reading its data members from a stream. [Public]

`Create` `virtual BOOL Create();`

The `Create` function creates an interface element associated with the `TWindow` object. `Create` returns `TRUE` when successful. When unsuccessful, this function calls `Error` and returns `FALSE`. [Public]

`GetClassName` `virtual LPSTR GetClassName();`

The `GetClassName` function returns “OWLWindow”, the default Windows registration class name for `TWindow`. [Protected]

```
GetWindowClass          virtual void GetWindowClass(WndClass _FAR &
                             AWndClass);
```

The `GetWindowClass` function places the default values for the registration attributes into the window class structure referenced by `AWndClass`. [Protected]

```
isA                     virtual classType isA() const;
```

The `isA` function redefines the pure virtual function in class `Object`. This function returns the class ID of `TWindow`. [Public]

```
nameOf                  virtual Pchar nameOf() const;
```

The `nameOf` function redefines the pure virtual function in class `Object`. This function returns "TWindow," the class ID string of `TWindow`. [Public]

```
Paint                   virtual void Paint(HDC PaintDC,
                             PAINTSTRUCT _FAR & PaintInfo);
```

The `Paint` function stores derived types that define `Paint` member functions. `Paint` is called automatically when a `WM_PAINT` message is detected. [Protected]

```
read                    virtual Pvoid read(Pipstream is);
```

The `read` function uses `TWindowsObject::read` to read the base `TWindowsObject` object. [Protected]

```
SetupWindow             virtual void SetupWindow();
```

The `SetupWindow` function initializes the new window by calling `TWindowsObject::SetupWindow`. [Protected]

```
WMCreate                virtual void WMCreate(RTMessage Msg) =
                             [WM_FIRST + WM_CREATE];
```

The `WMCreate` function calls `SetupWindow` when the `WM_CREATE` message is detected. [Protected]

```
WMHScroll               virtual void WMHScroll(RTMessage Msg) =
                             [WM_FIRST + WM_HSCROLL];
```

The `WMHScroll` function handles horizontal scroll bar events. [Protected]

```
WMLButtonDown           virtual void WMLButtonDown(RTMessage
                             Msg) = [WM_FIRST + WM_LBUTTONDOWN];
```

The `WMLButtonDown` function responds to `WM_LBUTTONDOWN` messages. [Protected]

```
WMDIActivate            virtual void WMDIActivate (RTMessage
                             Msg) = [WM_FIRST + WM_MDIACTIVATE];
```

The `WMMDIActivate` function responds to the `WM_MDIACTIVATE` message and calls `DefWndProc`. This function sets the parent's `ActiveChild` parameter to the window handle specified in the message. [Protected]

```
WMMove                  virtual void WMMove(RTMessage Msg) =
                             [WM_FIRST + WM_MOVE];
```

The `WMMove` function saves the new window coordinates in the `X` and `Y` members of `Attr` when a `WM_MOVE` message is detected. [Protected]

```
WMPaint                 virtual void WMPaint(RTMessage Msg) =
                             [WM_FIRST + WM_PAINT];
```

The `WMPaint` function calls `Paint` when a `WM_PAINT` message is detected. [Protected]

```
WMSize                  virtual void WMSize(RTMessage Msg) =
                             [WM_FIRST + WM_SIZE];
```

The `WMSize` function calls `SetPageSize` when a window with scrollers has been sized. [Protected]

```
WMVScroll               virtual void WMVScroll(RTMessage Msg) =
                             [WM_FIRST + WM_VSCROLL];
```

The `WMVScroll` function calls `DispatchScroll` when the `WM_VSCROLL` message is detected from a scroll bar control. [Protected]

```
write                   virtual void write(Ropstream os);
```

The `write` function uses `TWindowsObject::write` to write the base `TWindowsObject` object. [Protected]

Class Name: TWindowsObject

Class Header File:

windobj.h

Description:

The `TWindowsObject` class is an abstract class and defines behaviors for ObjectWindows interface objects including windows, dialogs, and controls. The member functions of this class create window objects, handle message processing, and destroy window objects.

Data Member(s):

```
DefaultProc             FARPROC DefaultProc;
```

`DefaultProc` holds the address of the default window procedure. [Protected]

`HWindow`	`HWND HWindow;`

`HWindow` specifies the handle of the interface element associated with the interface object. [Public]

`Parent`	`PTWindowsObject Parent;`

`Parent` points to the interface object that acts as the parent window for the interface object. [Public]

`Status`	`int Status;`

`Status` can indicate an error in the initialization of an interface object. [Public]

`Title`	`LPSTR Title;`

`Title` points to the caption for the window. [Public]

`TransferBuffer`	`Pvoid TransferBuffer;`

`TransferBuffer` points to a buffer used to transfer data. [Protected]

Constructor(s):

`TWindowsObject (PTWindowsObject AParent, PTModule AModule = NULL);`	Sets the Parent data member to the the value specified in `AParent` [Public]
`TWindowsObject (StreamableInit);`	`TWindowsObject` stream constructor [Protected]

Destructor:

`virtual ~TWindowsObject();`	Calls `Destroy` to destroy the interface element [Public]

Additional Member Function(s):

`ActivationResponse`	`virtual void ActivationResponse(WORD Activated, BOOL IsIconified);`

The `ActivationResponse` function enables keyboard handling if `this` is being activated and keyboard handling has been requested for `this`. [Public]

`AfterDispatchHandler`	`virtual void AfterDispatchHandler();`

The `AfterDispatchHandler` message is called by `DispatchAMessage` after responding to a message. This function should be redefined to perform postprocessing for incoming messages. [Public]

`BeforeDispatchHandler` `virtual void BeforeDispatchHandler();`

The `BeforeDispatchHandler` function is called by `DispatchAMessage` before invoking a message response. This function should be redefined to process incoming messages. [Public]

`build` `static PTStreamable build();`

The `build` function invokes the `TWindowsObject` constructor and constructs an object of type `TWindowsObject` before reading its data members from a stream. [Public]

`CanClose` `virtual BOOL CanClose();`

The `CanClose` function determines whether the associated interface element can be closed by calling the `CanClose` member functions of each of the child windows. This function returns `TRUE` when the window can be closed or `FALSE` if any of the `CanClose` member functions of the child windows returned `FALSE`. [Public]

`ChildWithId` `PTWindowsObject ChildWithId(int Id);`

The `ChildWithID` function returns the pointer to the child window from child window list that has the specified ID. A `NULL` return value indicates that no child window has the ID specified. [Public]

`CloseWindow` `void CloseWindow();`

The `CloseWindow` function calls `ShutDownWindow` to close the window. [Public]

```
CMExit                  virtual void CMExit
                            (RTMessage Msg) = [CM_FIRST +
                            CM_EXIT];
```

The `CMExit` function is called when a menu item with an ID of `CM_EXIT` is selected. When `this` is the main window, `CloseWindow` is called. [Protected]

`Create` `virtual BOOL Create() = 0;`

The `Create` function is a pure virtual function. `Create` should be redefined in derived types to create the associated interface element. [Public]

`CreateChildren` `BOOL CreateChildren();`

The `CreateChildren` function creates child windows from the child list. The child windows must contain the `WB_AUTOCREATE` mask. [Public]

```
DefChildProc            virtual void DefChildProc(RTMessage
                            Msg);
```

By default, the `DefChildProc` function handles incoming child-ID-based messages. [Protected]

```
DefCommandProc          virtual void DefCommandProc(RTMessage
                             Msg);
```

The `DefCommandProc` function, by default, handles command-based messages. [Protected]

```
DefNotificationProc     virtual void DefNotificationProc
                             (RTMessage Msg);
```

The `DefNotificationProc` function provides the default processing of notification messages and passes these notification messages to the parent as a child-ID-based message. [Protected]

```
DefWndProc              virtual void DefWndProc(RTMessage Msg);
```

The `DefWndProc` function handles default message processing. [Public]

```
Destroy                 virtual void Destroy();
```

The `Destroy` function destroys an associated interface element. [Public]

```
DisableAutoCreate       void DisableAutoCreate();
```

The `DisableAutoCreate` function disables the autocreate feature. The autocreate feature allows the interface object to be created and displayed as a child window. [Public]

```
DisableTransfer         void DisableTransfer();
```

The `DisableTransfer` function disables the transfer of state data to and from the transfer buffer. [Public]

```
DispatchAMessage        virtual void DispatchAMessage(WORD AMsg,
                             RTMessage AMessage, void
                             (TWindowsObject::*)(RTMessage));
```

The `DispatchAMessage` function dispatches Windows messages to the appropriate response member function. [Public]

```
DispatchScroll          void DispatchScroll(RTMessage Msg);
```

The `DispatchScroll` function dispatches messages from scroll bar controls. [Protected]

```
DrawItem                virtual void DrawItem(DRAWITEMSTRUCT _FAR &
                             DrawInfo);
```

The `DrawItem` function is called when a control or menu item needs to be redrawn. [Public]

```
EnableAutoCreate        void EnableAutoCreate();
```

The EnableAutoCreate function enables the autocreate feature. The autocreate feature allows the interface object to be created and displayed as a child window. [Public]

```
EnableKBHandler          void EnableKBHandler();
```

The EnableKBHandler function enables windows and modeless dialog boxes to provide a keyboard interface to child controls. [Public]

```
EnableTransfer           void EnableTransfer();
```

The EnableTransfer function enables the transfer of state data to and from the transfer buffer. [Public]

```
FirstThat                PTWindowsObject FirstThat(TCondFunc
                              Test, Pvoid PParamList);
```

The FirstThat function calls the specified test function for each child window in the child list. When TRUE is returned by the test function, testing stops and FirstThat returns the child window object that was successfully tested. Otherwise, testing continues until the child list is exhausted, then the function returns NULL. [Public]

```
FirstThat                TWindowsObject FirstThat(TCondMemFunc Test,
                              Pvoid PParamList);
```

The FirstThat function calls the specified test function for each child window in the child list. When TRUE is returned by the test function, testing stops and FirstThat returns the child window object that was successfully tested. Otherwise, this function returns a value of NULL and testing continues. [Public]

```
ForEach                  void ForEach(TActionFunc Action, Pvoid
                              PParamList);
```

The ForEach function calls the specified function and passes each child window in the child list as an argument. [Public]

```
ForEach                  void ForEach(TActionMemFunc Action, Pvoid
                              PParamList);
```

This ForEach function is like the previous ForEach function with the exception that this function takes a member function as a parameter. [Public]

```
GetApplication           PTApplication GetApplication();
```

The GetApplication function gets the pointer to the TApplication object that is associated with this. [Public]

```
GetChildPtr              void GetChildPtr(Ripstream is,
                              RPTWindowsObject P);
```

The GetChildPtr function reads a reference to a pointer to a child window from the specified stream. [Protected]

```
GetChildren             void GetChildren(Ripstream is);
```

The GetChildren function reads child windows from the specified stream into the child list. [Public]

```
GetClassName            virtual LPSTR GetClassName() = 0;
```

The GetClassName function returns the Windows registration class name and must be redefined for derived classes. [Protected]

```
GetClient               virtual PTMDIClient GetClient();
```

The GetClient function returns NULL for non-MDI interface objects. TMDIFrame redefines this function to return a pointer to the MDI client window. [Public]

```
GetFirstChild           PTWindowsObject GetFirstChild();
```

The GetFirstChild function returns the pointer to the first child window in the child list for the interface object. [Public]

```
GetId                   virtual int GetId();
```

The GetId function returns 0 by default. TControl redefines this function to return the control ID of the class. [Public]

```
GetInstance             FARPROC GetInstance();
```

The GetInstance function returns the instance thunk of the window. [Public]

```
GetLastChild            PTWindowsObject GetLastChild();
```

The GetLastChild function returns the pointer to the last child window in the child list for the interface object. [Public]

```
GetModule               PTModule GetModule();
```

The GetModule function returns the pointer to the TModule that owns the object. [Public]

```
GetSiblingPtr           void GetSiblingPtr(Ripstream is,
                             RPTWindowsObject P);
```

The GetSiblingPtr function is used only during a read operation to references written by a call to PutSiblingPtr. [Protected]

```
GetWindowClass          virtual void GetWindowClass(WNDCLASS _FAR &
                             AWndClass);
```

The GetWindowClass function fills the specified Windows registration class with attributes. [Protected]

`hashValue` `virtual hashValueType hashValue() const;`

The `hashValue` function must be redefined by all objects derived from the base class object. This function returns the hash value of `TWindowsObject`, `HWindow`. [Public]

`isA` `virtual classType isA() const = 0;`

The `isA` function redefines the pure virtual function in class `Object` and should be redefined to return a unique class ID. [Public]

`isEqual` `virtual int isEqual(RCObject testwin) const;`

The `isEqual` function redefines the pure virtual function in class `Object`. This function returns `TRUE` when `this` points to `testwin`. [Public]

`IsFlagSet` `BOOL IsFlagSet(WORD Mask);`

The `IsFlagSet` function returns `TRUE` if the bit flag of the specified mask is set. Otherwise, this function returns `FALSE`. [Public]

`nameOf` `virtual Pchar nameOf() const = 0;`

The `nameOf` function is a pure virtual function. This function should be redefined by derived classes to return a class ID string. [Public]

`Next` `PTWindowsObject Next();`

The `Next` function returns a pointer to the next window in the child window list. [Public]

`printOn` `virtual void printOn(Rostream outputStream) const;`

The `printOn` function redefines the pure virtual function in class `Object`. [Public]

`Previous` `PTWindowsObject Previous();`

The `Previous` function returns a pointer to the previous window in the child window list. [Public]

`PutChildPtr` `void PutChildPtr(Ropstream os, PTWindowsObject P);`

The `PutChildPtr` function writes a child window to the specified output stream and should only be used during a `write` operation to write pointers that `GetChildPtr` can read. [Protected]

`PutChildren` `void PutChildren(Ropstream os);`

The `PutChildren` writes child windows to the specified stream. [Public]

PutSiblingPtr `void PutSiblingPtr(Ropstream os, PTWindowsObject P);`

The PutSiblingPtr function writes the reference to a sibling window to the specified output stream and should only by used during a write operation to write a pointer that GetSiblingPtr can read. [Protected]

read `virtual Pvoid read(Ripstream is);`

The read function creates an object instance and calls GetChildren to read in the child windows. The child list, HWindow, Parent, and TransferBuffer are set to 0. Title, Status, flags, and CreateOrder are read in. [Protected]

Register `virtual BOOL Register();`

The Register function registers the Windows registration class of this. This function returns TRUE if the class is successfully registered. [Public]

RemoveClient `void RemoveClient();`

The RemoveClient function removes the specified client window from the child list. [Protected]

SetCaption `void SetCaption(LPSTR ATitle);`

The SetCaption function defines the caption of the interface element as the value specified in ATitle. [Public]

SetFlags `void SetFlags(WORD Mask, BOOL OnOff);`

The SetFlags function sets the bit flag of the Flags data member with the specified mask according to the value specified in OnOff. [Public]

SetParent `virtual void SetParent(PTWindowsObject NewParent);`

The SetParent function sets Parent to the parent window specified in NewParent, removes this from the child list of the previous parent, and adds this to the child list of the new parent. [Public]

SetTransferBuffer `void SetTransferBuffer (Pvoid ATransferBuffer);`

The SetTransferBuffer function sets TransferBuffer to the buffer specified in ATransferBuffer. [Public]

SetupWindow `virtual void SetupWindow();`

The SetupWindow function attempts to create an associated interface element for each child window in the child list that has the autocreate feature enabled. [Protected]

Show `void Show(int ShowCmd);`

The Show function displays the interface element as specified in ShowCmd. ShowCmd can be any of the following values:

Value	Meaning
SW_HIDE	Hidden
SW_SHOW	Shown using window's current size and position
SW_SHOWMAXIMIZED	Shown maximized and active
SW_SHOWMINIMIZED	Shown minimized and active
SW_SHOWNORMAL	Shown restored and active [Public]

```
ShutDownWindow          virtual void ShutdownWindow();
```

The `ShutDownWindow` function destroys the associated interface element. [Public]

```
Transfer                virtual WORD Transfer(Pvoid DataPtr,
                             WORD TransferFlag);
```

The `Transfer` function transfers data to and from the buffer referenced by `DataPtr`. `TransferFlag` specifies how the buffer is used:

- When `TransferFlag` is set to `TF_GETDATA`, information is copied to the buffer.
- When `TransferFlag` is set to `TF_SETDATA`, information is retrieved from the buffer.
- When `TransferFlag` is set to `TF_SIZEDATA`, the size of the transfer data is returned. [Public]

```
TransferData            virtual void TransferData(WORD
                             Direction);
```

The `TransferData` function transfers data between the buffer and the interface object's child windows that have the `WM_TRANSFER` flag set. `TranferData` calls `Transfer` for each child window and uses `Direction` to specify how data is transferred. `Direction` can be set to `TF_SETDATA`, `TF_GETDATA`, or `TF_SIZEDATA`:

- When `Direction` is set to `TF_SETDATA`, the list is filled and item(s) selected using the data in the buffer.
- When `Direction` is set to `TF_GETDATA`, the buffer is filled using the current list and selection(s) from the list box.
- When `Direction` is set to `TF_SIZEDATA`, the size of the transfer data is returned and no data is transferred. [Public]

```
WMActivate              virtual void WMActivate(RTMessage Msg)
                             = [WM_FIRST + WM_ACTIVATE];
```

The `WMActivate` function enables keyboard handling if requested when a `WM_ACTIVATE` message is detected. [Protected]

```
WMClose                  virtual void WMClose(RTMessage Msg) =
                              [WM_FIRST + WM_CLOSE];
```

The `WMClose` function calls `CloseWindow` to close the window. [Protected]

```
WMCommand                virtual void WMCommand(RTMessage Msg)
                              = [WM_FIRST + WM_COMMAND];
```

The `WMCommand` function calls the appropriate member functions when command-based, child-ID-based, or notify-based messages are detected. [Protected]

```
WMDestroy                virtual void WMDestroy(RTMessage Msg)
                              = [WM_FIRST + WM_DESTROY];
```

The `WMDestroy` function handles the `WM_DESTROY` message. [Protected]

```
WMDrawItem               virtual void WMDrawItem(RTMessage Msg)
                              = [WM_FIRST + WM_DRAWITEM];
```

The `WMDrawItem` function dispatches the `WM_DRAWITEM` message for drawable controls. [Protected]

```
WMHScroll                virtual void WMHScroll(RTMessage Msg)
                              = [WM_FIRST + WM_HSCROLL];
```

The `WMHScroll` function calls `DispatchScroll` in response to a `WM_HSCROLL` message. [Protected]

```
WMNCDestroy              virtual void WMNCDestroy(RTMessage Msg)
                              = [WM_FIRST + WM_NCDESTROY];
```

The `WMNCDestroy` function handles the `WM_NCDESTROY` message. [Protected]

```
WMQueryEndSession        virtual void WMQueryEndSession(RTMessage Msg)
                            = [WM_FIRST + WM_QUERYENDSESSION];
```

The `WMQueryEndSession` function calls the appropriate `CanClose` function to determine whether the session can close. [Protected]

```
WMVScroll                virtual void WMVScroll(RTMessage Msg)
                              = [WM_FIRST + WM_VSCROLL];
```

The `WMVScroll` function calls `DispatchScroll` in response to the detection of vertical scroll bar messages. [Protected]

```
write                    virtual void write(Ropstream os);
```

The `write` function writes `Title`, `Status`, flags, and `CreateOrder` and calls `PutChildren` to write out child windows. [Protected]

1

A

Windows Functions Quick Reference Guide

This appendix serves as a quick reference guide to the Windows functions. The "Meaning" column contains a brief description of the function.

Function	*Meaning*
AbortDoc	Terminates a print job
AccessResource	Opens a resource
AddAtom	Creates an atom for a character string
AddFontResource	Adds a font resource to the system font table
AdjustWindowRect	Determines the window size for the specified client area
AdjustWindowRectEx	Determines the window size with extended style for the specified client area
AllocDiskSpace	Creates a file that allocates space on a disk partition
AllocDStoCSAlias	Returns a code segment selector from the specified data segment selector

Function	*Meaning*
`AllocFileHandles`	Allocates up to 256 file handles
`AllocGDIMem`	Allocates all available memory in the GDI heap
`AllocMem`	Allocates all memory
`AllocResource`	Allocates memory for a resource
`AllocSelector`	Allocates a new selector
`AllocUserMem`	Allocates all available memory in the User heap
`AnimatePalette`	Replaces entries in a logical palette
`AnsiLower`	Converts a string to lowercase
`AnsiLowerBuff`	Converts a buffered string to lowercase
`AnsiNext`	Gets the long pointer to the next character in a string
`AnsiPrev`	Gets the long pointer to the previous character in a string
`AnsiToOem`	Converts an ANSI string to an OEM string
`AnsiToOemBuff`	Converts an ANSI string in a buffer to an OEM string
`AnsiUpper`	Converts a string to uppercase
`AnsiUpperBuff`	Converts a string in a buffer to uppercase
`AnyPopup`	Determines whether a pop-up window exists
`AppendMenu`	Appends a menu item to the menu
`Arc`	Draws an arc
`ArrangeIconicWindows`	Arranges minimized child windows
`BeginDeferWindowPos`	Allocates memory for `DeferWindowPos`
`BeginPaint`	Prepares a window for painting
`BitBlt`	Copies a bitmap from a source to the specified device
`BringWindowToTop`	Brings a window to the top of the stack
`BuildCommDCB`	Loads a device control block with control codes
`CallMsgFilter`	Passes a message to the current filter function
`CallNextHookEx`	Passes hook information down the hook chain
`CallWindowProc`	Sends message information to the specified function
`Catch`	Places the execution environment in a buffer
`ChangeClipboardChain`	Removes a window from the clipboard viewer chain

`ChangeMenu`	This function has been replaced with the following five functions:
	`AppendMenu`
	`DeleteMenu`
	`InsertMenu`

Function	Meaning
	ModifyMenu
	RemoveMenu
ChangeSelector	Generates a code or data selector
CheckDlgButton	Modifies the state of a button
CheckMenuItem	Either puts or removes a checkmark beside a pop-up menu item
CheckRadioButton	Puts a check beside a button while removing the check from all other buttons in a group
ChildWindowFromPoint	Finds the child window that contains a specified point
ChooseColor	Creates a color-selection dialog box
ChooseFont	Creates a font-selection dialog box
Chord	Draws a chord
ClassFirst	Gets information about the first class in the class list
ClassNext	Gets information about the next class in the class list
ClearCommBreak	Clears the communication break state of a communication device
ClientToScreen	Converts client coordinates to screen coordinates
ClipCursor	Confines the cursor to a rectangular region
CloseClipboard	Closes the clipboard
CloseComm	Closes a communication device
CloseDriver	Closes an installable driver
CloseMetafile	Closes a metafile and creates a metafile handle
CloseWindow	Hides or minimizes a window
CombineRgn	Creates a new region by combining two regions
CommDlgExtendedError	Retrieves error data
CopyCursor	Copies a cursor
CopyIcon	Copies an icon
CopyLZFile	Copies a file and expands it if compressed
CopyMetaFile	Copies a metafile to a file
CopyRect	Copies a rectangle
CountClipboardFormats	Gets the number of formats the clipboard can render
CreateBitmap	Creates a bitmap
CreateBitmapIndirect	Creates a bitmap using the data from a BITMAP structure
CreateBrushIndirect	Creates a logical brush
CreateCaret	Creates a caret

Function	*Meaning*
`CreateCompatibleBitmap`	Creates a bitmap compatible with the specified device
`CreateCompatibleDC`	Creates a memory device context
`CreateCursor`	Creates a cursor from two bit masks
`CreateDC`	Creates a device context
`CreateDialog`	Creates a modeless dialog box
`CreateDialogIndirect`	Creates a modeless dialog box from a template
`CreateDialogIndirectParam`	Creates a modeless dialog box from a template and passes initialization data
`CreateDialogParam`	Creates a modeless dialog box and passes initialization data
`CreateDIBitmap`	Creates a device-specific memory bitmap
`CreateDIBPatternBrush`	Creates a logical brush using a device-independent bitmap
`CreateDiscardableBitmap`	Creates a bitmap that is discardable and compatible with the specified device
`CreateEllipticRgn`	Creates an elliptical region
`CreateEllipticRgnIndirect`	Creates an elliptical region using a `RECT` data structure
`CreateFont`	Creates a logical font
`CreateFontIndirect`	Creates a logical font using information from a `LOGFONT` data structure
`CreateHatchBrush`	Creates a logical brush with a hatched pattern
`CreateIC`	Creates an information context
`CreateIcon`	Creates an icon
`CreateMenu`	Creates an empty menu
`CreateMetaFile`	Creates a metafile
`CreatePalette`	Creates a logical palette
`CreatePatternBrush`	Creates a logical brush with a specified pattern
`CreatePen`	Creates a logical pen
`CreatePenIndirect`	Creates a logical pen using a `LOGPEN` data structure
`CreatePolygonRgn`	Creates a polygonal region
`CreatePolyPolygonRgn`	Creates a polygonal region made up of a series of closed, filled polygons
`CreatePopupMenu`	Creates an empty pop-up menu
`CreateRectRgn`	Creates a rectangular region
`CreateRectRgnIndirect`	Creates a rectangular region using a `RECT` data structure

Function	*Meaning*
`CreateRoundRectRgn`	Creates a rounded rectangular region
`CreateScalableFontResource`	Creates a resource file with font information
`CreateSolidBrush`	Creates a logical brush using a solid color
`CreateWindow`	Creates a window
`CreateWindowEx`	Creates a window with extended style
`DdeAbandonTransaction`	Abandons an asynchronous transaction
`DdeAccessData`	Accesses a DDE global memory object
`DdeAddData`	Adds data to a DDE global memory object
`DdeCallback`	Processes DDEML transactions
`DdeClientTransaction`	Begins a DDE data transaction
`DdeCmpStringHandles`	Compares two DDE string handles
`DdeConnect`	Establishes a conversation with a server
`DdeConnectList`	Establishes multiple DDE conversations
`DdeCreateDataHandle`	Creates a DDE data handle
`DdeCreateStringHandle`	Creates a DDE string handle
`DdeDisconnect`	Terminates a DDE conversation
`DdeDisconnectList`	Destroys a DDE conversation list
`DdeEnableCallback`	Enables or disables a DDE conversation
`DdeFreeDataHandle`	Frees a global memory object
`DdeFreeStringHandle`	Frees a DDE string handle
`DdeGetData`	Copies data from a memory object to a buffer
`DdeGetLastError`	Returns an error code set by a DDEML function
`DdeInitialize`	Registers an application with the DDEML
`DdeKeepStringHandle`	Increments the use count for a string handle
`DdeNameService`	Registers or unregisters a server application
`DdePostAdvise`	Prompts server to send advise data to a client
`DdeQueryConvInfo`	Gets information about a DDE conversation
`DdeQueryNextServer`	Gets the next handle in a conversation list
`DdeQueryString`	Copies the string handle text to a buffer
`DdeReconnect`	Reestablishes a DDE conversation
`DdeSetUserHandle`	Associates a user-defined handle with a transaction
`DdeUnaccessData`	Frees a DDE global memory object
`DdeUninitialize`	Frees DDEML resources for an application
`DebugBreak`	Forces a break to the debugger
`DefDlgProc`	Processes messages that a dialog box with a private window class cannot process

Function	*Meaning*
`DefDriverProc`	Calls the default installable driver procedure
`DeferWindowPos`	Stores window position information for `EndDeferWindowPos`
`DefFrameProc`	Provides default processing for MDI frame window messages
`DefHookProc`	Calls the next function in the filter function chain
`DefMDIChildProc`	Provides default processing for MDI child window messages
`DefWindowProc`	Provides default processing for window messages
`DeleteAtom`	Deletes an atom when the reference count is zero
`DeleteDC`	Deletes a device context
`DeleteMenu`	Deletes a menu item
`DeleteMetaFile`	Deletes a metafile
`DeleteObject`	Deletes a pen, brush, font, bitmap, or region
`DestroyCaret`	Destroys a caret
`DestroyCursor`	Destroys a cursor
`DestroyIcon`	Destroys an icon
`DestroyMenu`	Destroys a menu
`DestroyWindow`	Destroys a window
`DeviceCapabilities`	Gets the printer device driver capabilities
`DeviceMode`	Sets the printing modes
`DialogBox`	Creates a modal dialog box
`DialogBoxIndirect`	Creates a modal dialog box from a template
`DialogBoxIndirectParam`	Creates a modal dialog box from a template and passes initialization data
`DialogBoxParam`	Creates a modal dialog box and passes initialization data
`DirectedYield`	Forces execution to continue at a specified task
`DispatchMessage`	Sends a message to the window function of the specified window
`DlgDirList`	Fills the list box with filenames that match the specified path
`DlgDirListComboBox`	Fills a combo box with filenames that match the specified path
`DlgDirSelect`	Copies the current selection of a list box to a string
`DlgDirSelectComboBox`	Copies the current selection of a combo box to a string

Function	*Meaning*
DlgDirSelectComboBoxEx	Enhanced version of DlgDirSelectCombo
DlgDirSelectEx	Enhanced version of DlgDirSelect
DOS3Call	Generates a DOS 21H interrupt
DPtoLP	Converts device points to logical points
DragAcceptFiles	Indicates whether a window accepts dropped files
DragFinish	Releases memory allocated for dropped files
DragQueryFile	Gets the filename for a dropped file
DragQueryPoint	Gets the mouse position where the file was dropped
DrawFocusRect	Draws a rectangle that indicates focus
DrawIcon	Draws an icon
DrawMenuBar	Redraws the menu bar
DrawText	Draws the specified string
DriverProc	Processes messages for an installable driver
Ellipse	Draws an ellipse
EmptyClipboard	Empties the clipboard
EnableCommNotification	Either enables or disables the posting of WM_COMMNOTIFY
EnableHardwareInput	Either enables or disables keyboard and mouse input
EnableMenuItem	Sets the state of a menu item
EnableScrollBar	Either enables or disables scroll-bar arrows
EnableWindow	Either enables or disables mouse and keyboard input for the application
EndDeferWindowPos	Used with DeferWindowPos to move or size one or more windows
EndDialog	Terminates a modal dialog box
EndDoc	Ends a print job
EndPage	Ends a page
EndPaint	Ends window repainting
EnumChildWindows	Enumerates the child windows that belong to the specified parent window
EnumClipboardFormats	Enumerates all the clipboard formats available
EnumFontFamilies	Gets fonts from the specified family
EnumFonts	Enumerates the available fonts
EnumMetaFile	Enumerates the GDI calls within the metafile
EnumObjects	Enumerates all pens and brushes
EnumProps	Enumerates the window's properties

Function	*Meaning*
`EnumTaskWindows`	Enumerates the windows associated with the specified task
`EnumWindows`	Enumerates the windows currently displayed
`EqualRect`	Determines whether two rectangles are equal
`EqualRgn`	Determines whether two regions are the same
`Escape`	Allows an application to access a device that is not available through the GDI
`EscapeCommFunction`	Specifies that the device is to carry out an extended function
`ExcludeClipRect`	Excludes the specified rectangle from the clipping region
`ExcludeUpdateRgn`	Prevents drawing in invalid window areas
`ExitWindows`	Starts the Windows shutdown procedure
`ExtDeviceMode`	Provides access to driver configurations and device initialization information
`ExtFloodFill`	Fills the specified display surface
`ExtTextOut`	Writes a character string inside a rectangular region using the specified font
`ExtractIcon`	Gets the handle of an icon from an executable file
`FatalAppExit`	Displays a message box and terminates the application
`FatalExit`	Displays the current state of Windows and prompts the user for information to proceed
`FillRect`	Fills a rectangle
`FillRgn`	Fills a region
`FindAtom`	Finds the atom associated with a character string
`FindExecutable`	Gets the name and handle of a program for a file
`FindResource`	Gets the location of a resource
`FindText`	Creates a find-text dialog box
`FindWindow`	Gets the window handle for the specified class and caption
`FlashWindow`	Flashes a window
`FloodFill`	Fills the display area surrounded by the specified border
`FlushComm`	Flushes the characters from a communication device
`FrameRect`	Draws a border on the specified rectangle
`FrameRgn`	Draws a border around a region
`FreeAllGDIMem`	Frees memory allocated by `AllocGDIMem`

Function	*Meaning*
FreeAllMem	Frees memory allocated by AllocMem
FreeAllUserMem	Frees memory allocated by AllocUserMem
FreeLibrary	Decreases the reference count of a library
FreeModule	Decreases the reference count of a module
FreeProcInstance	Removes a function instance entry to an address
FreeResource	Removes a resource from memory
FreeSelector	Frees a selector
GetActiveWindow	Gets the handle of the active window
GetAspectRatioFilter	Gets the setting for the aspect-ratio filter
GetAspectRatioFilterEx	Enhanced version of GetAspectRatioFilter
GetAsyncKeyState	Gets interrupt-level information on the key state
GetAtomHandle	Gets the handle of the string that corresponds to an atom
GetAtomName	Gets the character string associated with an atom
GetBitmapBits	Gets the bitmap bits for the specified bitmap
GetBitmapDimension	Gets the dimensions for the specified bitmap
GetBitmapDimensionEx	Enhanced version of GetBitmapDimension
GetBkColor	Gets the background color
GetBkMode	Gets the background mode
GetBoundsRect	Gets the accumulated bounding rectangle
GetBrushOrg	Gets the current brush origin
GetBValue	Gets the blue value from an RGB color value
GetCapture	Gets the handle of the window that has the mouse capture
GetCaretBlinkTime	Gets the caret blink time
GetCaretPos	Gets the caret position
GetCharABCWidths	Gets the widths of consecutive characters
GetCharWidth	Gets the width of a character
GetClassInfo	Gets information on the specified class
GetClassLong	Gets a long integer from a WNDCLASS structure
GetClassName	Gets a class name
GetClassWord	Gets a word from a WNDCLASS structure
GetClientRect	Gets the coordinates of a window's client area
GetClipboardData	Gets data from the clipboard
GetClipboardFormatName	Gets the format for the clipboard
GetClipboardOwner	Gets the window handle associated with the clipboard owner

Function	*Meaning*
`GetClipboardViewer`	Gets the handle of the first window in the clipboard viewer chain
`GetClipBox`	Gets the dimensions of the bounding rectangle for the clipping region
`GetClipCursor`	Gets the coordinates of the rectangle that confines the cursor
`GetCodeHandle`	Finds the code segment that contains the specified function
`GetCodeInfo`	Gets code segment information
`GetCommError`	Gets the communication status
`GetCommEventMask`	Gets and clears an event mask
`GetCommState`	Loads a buffer with a device control block
`GetCurrentPDB`	Gets the DOS Program Data Base (PDB), also called the Program Segment Prefix (PSP)
`GetCurrentPosition`	Gets the logical coordinates of the current position
`GetCurrentPositionEx`	Enhanced version of `GetCurrentPosition`
`GetCurrentTask`	Gets the handle of the current task
`GetCurrentTime`	Gets the Windows time
`GetCursor`	Gets the current cursor handle
`GetCursorPos`	Gets the screen coordinates of the cursor position
`GetDC`	Gets the display context for a client area
`GetDCEx`	Enhanced version of `GetDC`
`GetDCOrg`	Gets the translation origin for a device context
`GetDesktopWindow`	Gets the window handle of the Windows desktop window
`GetDeviceCaps`	Gets information on a display device
`GetDialogBaseUnits`	Gets the base dialog units
`GetDIBits`	Gets the bits for a device-independent bitmap
`GetDlgCtrlID`	Gets the ID value of a control window
`GetDlgItem`	Gets the handle of an item from the specified dialog box
`GetDlgItemInt`	Converts the item's control text to an integer
`GetDlgItemText`	Copies an item's control text to a string
`GetDOSEnvironment`	Gets the environment string for the current task
`GetDoubleClickTime`	Gets the mouse double-click time
`GetDriverInfo`	Gets information about an installable driver
`GetDriverModuleHandle`	Gets the handle of an installable driver instance

Function	*Meaning*
GetDriveType	Determines the drive type: fixed, removable, or remote
GetEnvironment	Places environment information in a buffer
GetExpandedName	Gets the original filename of a compressed file
GetFileResource	Copies a resource to a buffer
GetFileResourceSize	Gets the size of a resource
GetFileTitle	Gets a filename
GetFileVersionInfo	Gets file version information
GetFileVersionInfoSize	Gets the size of the file version information
GetFocus	Gets the handle of the window that has the input focus
GetFontData	Gets font metric data
GetFreeFileHandles	Returns the number of file handles available
GetFreeSpace	Determines the number of available bytes in the global heap
GetFreeSystemResources	Gets the percentage of free system space
GetGlyphOutline	Gets data for curves of an outline character
GetGValue	Gets the green value from an RGB color value
GetInputState	Determines whether there is any mouse or keyboard input
GetInstanceData	Moves the data from the offset in an instance to the offset in another instance
GetKBCodePage	Gets the current code page
GetKeyboardState	Gets the state of the keyboard keys
GetKeyboardType	Gets the system keyboard type
GetKeyNameText	Gets the string that contains the name of a key
GetKeyState	Gets the state of a virtual key
GetLastActivePopup	Gets the most recently active pop-up window
GetMapMode	Gets the current mapping mode
GetMenu	Gets the menu handle for a window
GetMenuCheckMarkDimensions	Gets the dimensions of the default menu checkmark bitmap
GetMenuItemCount	Gets the number of items in a menu
GetMenuItemID	Gets the ID for a menu item
GetMenuState	Gets the status for a menu item
GetMenuString	Copies a menu label to a string
GetMessage	Gets a message

Function	*Meaning*
`GetMessageExtraInfo`	Gets information about a hardware message
`GetMessagePos`	Gets the position of the mouse when the message was retrieved
`GetMessageTime`	Gets the time when the message was retrieved
`GetMetaFile`	Creates a handle for a metafile
`GetMetaFileBits`	Retrieves and stores the bits of a metafile
`GetModuleFileName`	Gets the file name of a module
`GetModuleHandle`	Gets the handle of a module
`GetModuleUsage`	Gets the reference count of a module
`GetNearestColor`	Gets the closest logical color to the specified color
`GetNearestPaletteIndex`	Gets the index of a logical palette that is the closest match to the specified RGB value
`GetNextDlgGroupItem`	Gets the handle for the next item in the group
`GetNextDlgTabItem`	Gets the handle of the next or previous item
`GetNextDriver`	Enumerates the installable driver instances
`GetNextWindow`	Gets the handle for the next or previous window
`GetNumTasks`	Gets the number of executing tasks
`GetObject`	Gets the bytes of data that define an object
`GetOpenClipboardWindow`	Gets the handle of the window that opened the clipboard
`GetOpenFileName`	Creates an open-filename dialog box
`GetOutlineTextMetrics`	Gets metrics for TrueType fonts
`GetPaletteEntries`	Gets entries from a logical palette
`GetParent`	Gets the window handle for the parent window of the specified window
`GetPixel`	Gets the RGB value for a pixel
`GetPolyFillMode`	Gets the mode for filling polygons
`GetPriorityClipboardFormat`	Gets data in the first format from a prioritized format list
`GetPrivateProfileInt`	Gets an integer value in a section from a private initialization file
`GetPrivateProfileString`	Gets a string in a section from a private initialization file
`GetProcAddress`	Gets the address of a function in a module
`GetProfileInt`	Gets an integer value in a section from WIN.INI
`GetProfileString`	Gets a string in a section from WIN.INI
`GetProp`	Gets the handle for the specified string

Function	*Meaning*
GetQueueStatus	Gets the queued message type
GetRasterizerCaps	Gets the status of TrueType fonts on the system
GetRgnBox	Gets the coordinates of the rectangle bounding the region
GetROP2	Gets the drawing mode
GetRValue	Gets the red value from an RGB color value
GetSaveFileName	Creates a save-filename dialog box
GetScrollPos	Gets the thumb position of a scroll bar
GetScrollRange	Gets the position range for a scroll bar
GetSelectorBase	Gets the base of a selector
GetSelectorLimit	Gets the limit of a selector
GetStockObject	Gets the handle to a predefined stock pen, brush, font, or color palette
GetStretchBltMode	Gets the stretching mode
GetSubMenu	Gets the menu handle for a pop-up menu
GetSysColor	Gets the system color
GetSysModalWindow	Gets the handle of a system modal window
GetSystemDebugState	Gets system state information
GetSystemDir	Gets the Windows system subdirectory
GetSystemDirectory	Gets the pathname for the subdirectory for the Windows system
GetSystemMenu	Provides access to the System menu
GetSystemMetrics	Gets system metrics information
GetSystemPaletteEntries	Gets palette entries from the system palette
GetSystemPaletteUse	Determines whether an application has access to the full system palette
GetTabbedTextExtent	Determines the width and height of a line of text that contains tab characters
GetTempDrive	Gets the drive letter for the best drive to use for temporary file storage
GetTempFileName	Creates a temporary filename
GetTextAlign	Gets a mask of text alignment flags
GetTextCharacterExtra	Gets the current intercharacter spacing
GetTextColor	Gets the text color
GetTextExtent	Gets the width and height of text
GetTextExtentEx	Gets an array of substring lengths
GetTextExtentPoint	Gets the dimensions of a string

Function	*Meaning*
`GetTextFace`	Copies the font name to a buffer
`GetTextMetrics`	Copies the metrics for a font to a buffer
`GetThresholdEvent`	Gets a long pointer to a threshold flag
`GetThresholdStatus`	Gets the threshold event status for each voice
`GetTickCount`	Gets the number of timer ticks that have occurred since the system was booted
`GetTimerResolution`	Gets the timer resolution
`GetTopWindow`	Gets the handle to the top-level child window
`GetUpdateRect`	Gets the dimensions of the rectangle around the update region
`GetUpdateRgn`	Copies the update region of a window
`GetVersion`	Gets the Windows version number
`GetViewportExt`	Gets the viewport extents for a device context
`GetViewportExtEx`	Enhanced version of `GetViewportExt`
`GetViewportOrg`	Gets the viewport origin for a device context
`GetViewportOrgEx`	Enhanced version of `GetViewportOrgEx`
`GetWindow`	Gets a window handle from the window manager's list
`GetWindowDC`	Gets the display context for a window
`GetWindowExt`	Gets the window extents for a device context
`GetWindowLong`	Gets a long integer descriptor for the window
`GetWindowOrg`	Gets the window origin for a device context
`GetWindowOrgEx`	Enhanced version of `GetWindowOrg`
`GetWindowPlacement`	Gets the window show state and the minimized and maximized window positions
`GetWindowRect`	Gets the coordinates of a window
`GetWindowsDir`	Gets the Windows directory
`GetWindowsDirectory`	Gets the pathname for the Windows directory
`GetWindowTask`	Gets a task handle for the task associated with the window
`GetWindowText`	Copies the window caption to a buffer
`GetWindowTextLength`	Gets the number of characters in the window caption or text
`GetWindowWord`	Gets a word descriptor for the window
`GetWinFlags`	Gets information on the system memory configuration
`GlobalAddAtom`	Creates a global atom for a character string

Function	*Meaning*
`GlobalAlloc`	Allocates memory from the global heap
`GlobalCompact`	Compacts global memory
`GlobalDeleteAtom`	Deletes a global atom when the reference count is zero
`GlobalDiscard`	Discards global memory
`GlobalDosAlloc`	Allocates global memory
`GlobalDosFree`	Frees global memory allocated with `GlobalDosAlloc`
`GlobalEntryHandle`	Gets information about a global memory block
`GlobalEntryModule`	Gets information about a specific memory block
`GlobalFindAtom`	Gets the global atom associated with a character string
`GlobalFirst`	Gets information about the first global memory block
`GlobalFix`	Keeps a global memory block from being moved in linear memory
`GlobalFlags`	Gets the flags and lock count of a memory block
`GlobalFree`	Removes a global block and invalidates the handle
`GlobalGetAtomName`	Gets the character string associated with a global atom
`GlobalHandle`	Gets the handle of a global memory object
`GlobalHandleToSel`	Converts a global handle to a selector
`GlobalInfo`	Gets information about the global heap
`GlobalLock`	Gets the pointer for a handle to a global memory block
`GlobalLRUNewest`	Moves a global memory object to the newest least-recently-used (LRU) position
`GlobalLRUOldest`	Moves a global memory object to the oldest least-recently-used (LRU) position
`GlobalNext`	Gets information about the next global memory block
`GlobalNotify`	Installs a notification procedure
`GlobalPageLock`	Page-locks the memory associated with the specified global selector
`GlobalPageUnlock`	Decreases the page lock count for a block of memory
`GlobalReAlloc`	Reallocates a global memory block
`GlobalSize`	Gets the number of bytes in a global memory block
`GlobalUnfix`	Unlocks a global memory block
`GlobalUnlock`	Invalidates the pointer to a global memory block
`GlobalUnWire`	Decreases the lock count and unlocks the memory block when the count is zero

Function	*Meaning*
`GlobalWire`	Moves an object to low memory and increases the lock count
`GrayString`	Writes a string in gray text
`HIBYTE`	Gets the high-order byte of an integer
`HideCaret`	Removes the caret from a window
`HiliteMenuItem`	Either highlights or removes the highlight from a top-level menu item
`HIWORD`	Gets the high-order word of a long integer
`InflateRect`	Sizes the specified rectangle
`InitAtomTable`	Initializes an atom hash table
`InSendMessage`	Determines whether the current window function is processing a message
`InsertMenu`	Inserts a menu item into a menu
`InterruptRegister`	Installs a function to handle system interrupts
`InterruptUnRegister`	Removes the function installed by `InterruptRegister`
`IntersectClipRect`	Creates a new clipping region from the intersection of the clipping region and a rectangle
`IntersectRect`	Determines the intersection of two rectangles
`InvalidateRect`	Defines a rectangle for repainting
`InvalidateRgn`	Defines a region for repainting
`InvertRect`	Inverts the bits of the specified rectangle
`InvertRgn`	Inverts the colors in the region
`IsCharAlpha`	Determines whether a character is alphabetical
`IsCharAlphaNumeric`	Determines whether a character is alphnumeric
`IsCharLower`	Determines whether a character is lowercase
`IsCharUpper`	Determines whether a character is uppercase
`IsChild`	Determines whether a window is a descendant of the specified window
`IsClipboardFormatAvailable`	Determines whether data is available in the specified format
`IsDBCSLeadByte`	Determines whether a character is a DBCS lead byte
`IsDialogMessage`	Determines whether a message is sent to the specified dialog box
`IsDlgButtonChecked`	Determines whether a button is checked
`IsIconic`	Determines whether a window is minimized
`IsMenu`	Determines whether a menu handle is valid

Function	*Meaning*
`IsRectEmpty`	Determines whether a rectangle is empty
`IsTask`	Determines whether a task handle is valid
`IsWindow`	Determines whether a window is valid
`IsWindowEnabled`	Determines whether mouse and keyboard input is enabled for the specified window
`IsWindowVisible`	Determines whether a window is visible
`IsZoomed`	Determines whether a window is maximized
`KillTimer`	Kills the specified timer event
`_lclose`	Closes a file
`_lcreat`	Creates a new file or opens an existing file
`LineDDA`	Calculates each point on a line
`LineTo`	Draws a line
`_llseek`	Sets the pointer to a file
`LoadAccelerators`	Loads an accelerator table
`LoadBitmap`	Loads the specified bitmap
`LoadCursor`	Loads a cursor resource
`LoadIcon`	Loads an icon resource
`LoadLibrary`	Loads a library module
`LoadMenu`	Loads a menu resource
`LoadMenuIndirect`	Loads a menu resource using a template
`LoadModule`	Executes a Windows application and uses a DOS Function 4BH, Code 00H, parameter block
`LoadResource`	Loads a resource
`LoadString`	Loads a string resource
`LOBYTE`	Gets the low-order byte of an integer
`LocalAlloc`	Allocates memory from the local heap
`LocalCompact`	Compacts local memory
`LocalDiscard`	Discards local memory when the lock count is zero
`LocalFirst`	Gets information about the first local memory block
`LocalFlags`	Gets the memory type of a local memory block
`LocalFree`	Frees a local memory block when the lock count is zero
`LocalHandle`	Gets the handle of a local memory block
`LocalInfo`	Copies local heap information to a data structure
`LocalInit`	Initializes a local heap
`LocalLock`	Locks a local memory block
`LocalNext`	Gets information about the next local memory block

Function	*Meaning*
LocalReAlloc	Reallocates a local memory block
LocalShrink	Shrinks the local heap
LocalSize	Gets the number of bytes in a local memory block
LocalUnlock	Unlocks a local memory block
LockData	Locks the current data segment
LockResource	Gets the absolute memory address of a resource
LockSegment	Locks the specified data segment
_lopen	Opens an existing file
LOWORD	Gets the low-order word of a long integer
LPtoDP	Converts logical points to device points
_lread	Reads from a file
lstrcat	Concatenates two strings
lstrcmp	Compares two strings and is case sensitive
lstrcmpi	Compares two strings and is not case sensitive
lstrcpy	Copies one string to another
lstrlen	Gets the length of a string
_lwrite	Writes to a file
LZClose	Closes a file
LZCopy	Copies a file and expands it if it was compressed
LZDone	Frees the buffers allocated by LZStart
LZInit	Initializes the data structure required for file decompression
LZOpenFile	Opens both compressed and uncompressed files
LZRead	Reads from a compressed file
LZSeek	Moves the file pointer
LZStart	Allocates the buffers required for the CopyLZFile function
MAKEINTATOM	Casts an integer for use as a function argument
MAKEINTRESOURCE	Converts an integer value to a long pointer to a string
MAKELONG	Creates an unsigned long integer
MAKEPOINT	Converts a long value that specifies the coordinates of a point into a POINT data structure
MakeProcInstance	Gets a function instance address
MapDialogRect	Converts dialog box coordinates to client coordinates
MapVirtualKey	Gets the scan code, virtual key code, or ASCII value for the specified virtual key code or scan code
max	Determines the greater of two values

Function	*Meaning*
`MapWindowPoints`	Converts points to a different coordinate system
`MemManInfo`	Gets information about the memory manager
`MemoryRead`	Reads memory from a global heap object
`MemoryWrite`	Writes memory to a global heap object
`MessageBeep`	Sends a beep out the system speaker
`MessageBox`	Creates a window containing the specified caption and text
`min`	Determines the lesser of two values
`ModifyMenu`	Modifies a menu item
`ModuleFindHandle`	Gets information about a module
`ModuleFindName`	Gets specific information about the specified module
`ModuleFirst`	Gets information about the first module
`ModuleNext`	Gets information about the next module
`MoveTo`	Moves the current position to the specified point
`MoveToEx`	Enhanced version of `MoveTo`
`MoveWindow`	Changes the size and position of a window
`MulDiv`	Multiplies two values and divides the result by a third value
`NetBIOSCall`	Generates a NETBIOS 5CH interrupt
`NotifyRegister`	Installs a notification callback function
`NotifyUnRegister`	Removes a notification callback function
`OemKeyScan`	Maps OEM ASCII codes 0 to 0x0FF into the OEM scan codes and shift states
`OemToAnsi`	Converts an OEM string to an ANSI string
`OemToAnsiBuff`	Converts an OEM string in a buffer to an ANSI string
`OffsetClipRgn`	Moves the clipping region
`OffsetRect`	Moves a rectangle
`OffsetRgn`	Moves the region
`OffsetViewportOrg`	Moves the viewport origin
`OffsetViewportOrgEx`	Enhanced version of `OffsetViewportOrg`
`OffsetWindowOrg`	Moves the window origin
`OffsetWindowOrgEx`	Enhanced version of `OffsetWindowOrg`
`OleActivate`	Activates an object
`OleBlockServer`	Queues requests for the server
`OleClone`	Copies an object
`OleClose`	Closes the specified object

Function	*Meaning*
`OleCopyFromLink`	Makes a local embedded copy of a linked object
`OleCopyToClipboard`	Puts an object on the clipboard
`OleCreate`	Creates an object of the specified class
`OleCreateFromClip`	Creates an object from the clipboard
`OleCreateFromFile`	Creates an object from a file
`OleCreateFromTemplate`	Creates an object from a template
`OleCreateInvisible`	Creates an object but does not display it
`OleCreateLinkFromClip`	Creates a link to an object from the clipboard
`OleCreateLinkFromFile`	Creates a link to an object in a file
`OleDelete`	Deletes an object
`OleDraw`	Draws an object
`OleEnumFormats`	Enumerates data formats for an object
`OleEnumObjects`	Enumerates objects in a document
`OleEqual`	Compares two objects
`OleExecute`	Sends DDE execute commands to a server
`OleGetData`	Gets data for an object in a specified format
`OleGetLinkUpdateOptions`	Gets update options for an object
`OleLoadFromStream`	Loads an object from a document
`OleLockServer`	Keeps the server in memory
`OleObjectConvert`	Creates a new object using the specified protocol
`OleQueryBounds`	Gets the bounding rectangle for an object
`OleQueryClientVersion`	Gets the client library version
`OleQueryCreateFromClip`	Gets create data for a clipboard object
`OleQueryLinkFromClip`	Gets link data for a clipboard object
`OleQueryName`	Gets the name of the object
`OleQueryOpen`	Determines whether an object is open
`OleQueryOutOfDate`	Determines whether an object is out of date
`OleQueryProtocol`	Determines whether a protocol is supported
`OleQueryReleaseError`	Determines the status of a released operation
`OleQueryReleaseMethod`	Determines the operation that was released
`OleQueryReleaseStatus`	Determines whether an operation is released
`OleQueryServerVersion`	Gets the server library version
`OleQuerySize`	Gets the size of the object
`OleQueryType`	Gets the object type
`OleReconnect`	Reconnects to an open, linked object
`OleRegisterClientDoc`	Registers a document with a library

Function	*Meaning*
`OleRegisterServer`	Registers a server
`OleRegisterServerDoc`	Registers a document with a server library
`OleRelease`	Releases an object from memory
`OleRename`	Tells the library that an object has been renamed
`OleRenameClientDoc`	Tells the library that a document has changed
`OleRenameServerDoc`	Tells the library that a document has changed
`OleRequestData`	Gets data from a server
`OleRevertClientDoc`	Tells the library that a document has reverted to its saved state
`OleRevertServerDoc`	Tells the library that a document has reset to its saved state
`OleRevokeClientDoc`	Tells the library that a document is not open
`OleRevokeObject`	Revokes access to a document
`OleRevokeServer`	Revokes a server
`OleRevokeServerDoc`	Revokes the specified document
`OleSavedClientDoc`	Tells the library that a client document has been saved
`OleSavedServerDoc`	Tells the library that a server document has been saved
`OleSaveToStream`	Saves an object to the stream
`OleSetBounds`	Defines the bounding rectangle for an object
`OleSetColorScheme`	Defines the client's recommended colors for the object
`OleSetData`	Sends data to the server
`OleSetHostNames`	Sets the container name and the container's object name
`OleSetLinkUpdateOptions`	Sets update options for an object
`OleSetTargetDevice`	Sets the target device for an object
`OleUnblockServer`	Processes requests from the queue
`OleUnlockServer`	Releases a server locked with the `OleLockServer` function
`OleUpdate`	Updates an object
`OpenClipboard`	Opens the clipboard
`OpenComm`	Opens a communication device
`OpenDriver`	Opens an installable device driver
`OpenFile`	Creates, opens, or deletes a file
`OpenIcon`	Opens a minimized window

Function	*Meaning*
`OutputDebugString`	Sends a debugging message
`PaintRgn`	Fills the region using the specified brush pattern
`PALETTEINDEX`	Converts an integer to a `COLORREF` value
`PALETTERGB`	Converts the red, green, and blue values into a palette-relative `COLORREF` value
`PatBlt`	Creates a bit pattern
`PeekMessage`	Checks the application queue
`Pie`	Draws a pie
`PlayMetaFile`	Plays the contents of a metafile
`PlayMetaFileRecord`	Plays a metafile record
`Polygon`	Draws a polygon
`Polyline`	Draws a series of line segments
`PolyPolygon`	Draws a series of closed polygons
`PostAppMessage`	Sends a message to the application
`PostMessage`	Puts a message in the application queue
`PostQuitMessage`	Sends `WM_QUIT` to the application
`PrintDlg`	Creates a print-text dialog box
`ProfClear`	Discards the contents of the Profiler sampling buffer
`ProfFinish`	Stops Profiler sampling and flushes the buffer to disk
`ProfFlush`	Flushes the sampling buffer for the Profiler to disk
`ProfInsChk`	Determines whether Profiler is installed
`ProfSampRate`	Sets the Profiler sampling rate
`ProfSetup`	Sets the Profiler sampling buffer and recording rate
`ProfStart`	Begins Profiler sampling
`ProfStop`	Ends Profiler sampling
`PtlnRect`	Determines whether the specified point is within the rectangle
`PtlnRegion`	Determines whether a point is in the region
`PtVisible`	Determines whether the point lies in the region
`QuerySendMessage`	Determines whether the message originated within the task
`ReadComm`	Reads from a communication device
`RealizePalette`	Maps entries from a logical palette to the system palette
`Rectangle`	Draws a rectangle
`RectInRegion`	Determines whether any part of the rectangle is in the region

Function	Meaning
RectVisible	Determines whether part of the specified rectangle lies within the clipping region
RedrawWindow	Updates the client rectangle or region
RegCloseKey	Closes a key
RegCreateKey	Creates a key
RegDeleteKey	Deletes a key
RegEnumKey	Enumerates subkeys of specified key
RegisterClass	Registers the window class
RegisterClipboardFormat	Registers a new clipboard format
RegisterWindowMessage	Defines a new, unique message
RegOpenKey	Opens a key
RegQueryValue	Gets the text string with a specified key
RegSetValue	Associates a text string with a specified key
ReleaseCapture	Releases the mouse capture
ReleaseDC	Releases the display context
RemoveFontResource	Removes a font resource from the font table
RemoveMenu	Removes an item from a menu
RemoveProp	Removes the specified string from the property list
ReplaceText	Creates a replace-text dialog box
ReplyMessage	Replies to a message
ResetDC	Updates a device context
ResizePalette	Changes the size of the color palette
RestoreDC	Restores a device context
RGB	Converts the red, green, and blue values into an explicit COLORREF value
RoundRect	Draws a rounded rectangle
SaveDC	Saves the state of a device context
ScaleViewportExt	Alters the viewport extents
ScaleViewportExtEx	Enhanced version of ScaleViewportExt
ScaleWindowExt	Alters the window extents
ScaleWindowExtEx	Enhanced version of ScaleWindowExt
ScreenToClient	Converts screen coordinates to client coordinates
ScrollDC	Scrolls a rectangle vertically and horizontally
ScrollWindow	Moves the contents of the client area
ScrollWindowEx	Enhanced version of ScrollWindow
SelectClipRgn	Selects a clipping region

Function	*Meaning*
`SelectObject`	Selects an object
`SelectPalette`	Selects a logical palette
`SendDlgItemMessage`	Sends a message to a dialog box
`SendDriverMessage`	Sends a message to an installable driver
`SendMessage`	Sends a message
`SetAbortProc`	Sets the abort function for a print job
`SetActiveWindow`	Makes a window the active window
`SetBitmapBits`	Sets the bits for a bitmap
`SetBitmapDimension`	Defines the dimensions of a bitmap
`SetBitmapDimensionEx`	Enhanced version of `SetBitmapDimension`
`SetBkColor`	Sets the background color
`SetBkMode`	Sets the background mode
`SetBoundsRect`	Sets bounding-rectangle accumulation
`SetBrushOrg`	Sets the origin for the selected brushes
`SetCapture`	Gives the mouse capture to the specified window
`SetCaretBlinkTime`	Sets the caret blink time
`SetCaretPos`	Moves the caret to the specified position
`SetClassLong`	Replaces a long integer in a `WNDCLASS` structure
`SetClassWord`	Replaces a word in a `WNDCLASS` structure
`SetClipboardData`	Copies a handle for data
`SetClipboardViewer`	Adds a handle to the clipboard viewer chain
`SetCommBreak`	Sets the break state for a communication device
`SetCommEventMask`	Gets and sets an event mask
`SetCommState`	Sets the state of the communication device to the state in the device control block
`SetCursor`	Sets the shape of the cursor
`SetCursorPos`	Moves the cursor to the specified position
`SetDIBits`	Sets the bits for a device-independent bitmap
`SetDIBitsToDevice`	Sets bits on a device directly from a device-independent bitmap
`SetDlgItemInt`	Sets the caption or text for an item to a string representing an integer
`SetDlgItemText`	Sets the caption or text for an item to a string
`SetDoubleClickTime`	Sets the mouse double-click time
`SetEnvironment`	Sets the environment associated with a device attached to a system port

Function	*Meaning*
SetErrorMode	Specifies whether Windows or the application handles DOS 24H errors
SetFocus	Gives the input focus to the specified window
SetHandleCount	Sets the number of file handles available for a task
SetKeyboardState	Sets the state of keyboard keys
SetMapMode	Sets the mapping mode
SetMapperFlags	Modifies the algorithm used by the font mapper
SetMenu	Defines a new menu for the window
SetMenuItemBitmaps	Defines bitmaps for a menu item
SetMessageQueue	Creates a new message queue
SetMetaFileBits	Creates a memory metafile
SetMetaFileBitsBetter	Enhanced version of SetMetaFileBits
SetPaletteEntries	Sets the palette entries for a logical palette
SetParent	Sets the parent window for a child window
SetPixel	Defines the RGB value for a pixel
SetPolyFillMode	Sets the mode for filling polygons
SetProp	Adds an entry to the property list
SetRect	Creates a new rectangle
SetRectEmpty	Creates an empty rectangle
SetRectRgn	Creates a rectangular region
SetResourceHandler	Defines a function to load resources
SetROP2	Sets the drawing mode
SetScrollPos	Sets the thumb position of the scroll bar
SetScrollRange	Sets the position range for a scroll bar
SetSelectorBase	Sets the base of a selector
SetSelectorLimit	Sets the limit of a selector
SetStretchBltMode	Sets the stretching mode
SetSwapAreaSize	Sets the amount of memory reserved for code segments of an application
SetSysColors	Modifies system colors
SetSysModalWindow	Defines the specified window as a system modal window
SetSystemPaletteUse	Gives the application access to the full system palette
SetTextAlign	Positions text on the display or device
SetTextCharacterExtra	Sets intercharacter spacing
SetTextColor	Sets the text color
SetTextJustification	Sets the text line justification

Function	*Meaning*
`SetTimer`	Creates a system timer event
`SetViewportExt`	Sets the viewport extents for a device context
`SetViewportExtEx`	Enhanced version of `SetViewportExt`
`SetViewportOrg`	Sets the viewport origin for a device context
`SetViewportOrgEx`	Enhanced version of `SetViewportOrgEx`
`SetWindowExt`	Sets the window extents for a device context
`SetWindowExtEx`	Enhanced version of `SetWindowExt`
`SetWindowLong`	Modifies an integer attribute
`SetWindowOrg`	Sets the window origin for a device context
`SetWindowOrgEx`	Enhanced version of `SetWindowOrgEx`
`SetWindowPos`	Modifies a child or pop-up window's size, position, and ordering
`SetWindowsHook`	Specifies a system and/or application filter function
`SetWindowsHookEx`	Enhanced version of `SetWindowsHook`
`SetWindowText`	Defines the caption or text for a window
`SetWindowWord`	Modifies a word attribute
`ShellExecute`	Opens or prints the specified file
`ShowCaret`	Displays a new caret or redisplays a hidden caret
`ShowCursor`	Either increases or decreases the cursor display count
`ShowOwnedPopups`	Either shows or hides all pop-up windows
`ShowScrollBar`	Either hides or displays a scroll bar
`ShowWindow`	Either displays or removes the window
`SizeofResource`	Defines the size for a resource
`StackTraceCSIPFirst`	Gets information about a stack frame
`StackTraceFirst`	Gets information about the first stack frame
`StackTraceNext`	Gets information about the next stack frame
`StartDoc`	Starts a print job
`StartPage`	Prepares the printer driver to receive data
`StretchBlt`	Copies the bitmap to a destination device
`StretchDIBits`	Copies the device-independent bitmap to a destination device
`SwapMouseButton`	Switches the left and right mouse buttons
`SwapRecording`	Either starts or stops Swap analysis of the swapping behavior of the application
`SwitchStackBack`	Returns the stack of the current task to the task's data segment

Function	*Meaning*
`SwitchStackTo`	Changes the stack of the current task to the specified data segment
`SyncAllVoices`	Places a sync mark in each queue
`SystemHeapInfo`	Gets information about the User heap
`SystemParametersInfo`	Either queries or sets system-wide parameters
`TabbedTextOut`	Writes a string, using the specified font, with expanded tabs
`TaskFindHandle`	Gets information about a task
`TaskFirst`	Gets information about the first task in the task queue
`TaskGetCSIP`	Gets the next CS:IP value of a task
`TaskNext`	Gets information about the next task in the task queue
`TaskSetCSIP`	Sets the CS:IP value of a sleeping task
`TaskSwitch`	Switches to the specific address within a task
`TerminateApp`	Terminates an application
`TextOut`	Writes a character string using the current font
`Throw`	Restores the execution environment
`ToAscii`	Translates a virtual-key code to ANSI characters
`TrackPopupMenu`	Displays a pop-up menu at the specified position
`TranslateAccelerator`	Translates keyboard accelerators
`TranslateMDISysAccel`	Translates MDI child window command accelerators
`TranslateMessage`	Translates virtual key-stroke messages to character messages
`TransmitCommChar`	Puts a character at the top of the transmit queue
`UnAllocDiskSpace`	Deletes the file created by `AllocDiskSpace`
`UnAllocFileHandles`	Frees file handles allocated by `AllocFileHandles`
`UngetCommChar`	Specifies the next character to read
`UnhookWindowsHook`	Removes a filter function from the filter function chain
`UnhookWindowsHookEx`	Enhanced version of `UnhookWindowsHook`
`UnionRect`	Determines the union of two rectangles
`UnlockData`	Unlocks the current data segment
`UnlockResource`	Unlocks a resource
`UnlockSegment`	Unlocks the specified data segment
`UnrealizeObject`	Resets the origin of a brush
`UnregisterClass`	Removes a window class
`UpdateColors`	Translates each pixel's current color to the system palette

Function	*Meaning*
`UpdateWindow`	Tells the application that the window needs repainting
`ValidateCodeSegments`	Checks whether any code segments were modified by random memory overwrites
`ValidateFreeSpaces`	Checks free segments in memory for valid contents
`ValidateRect`	Validates the specified rectangle
`ValidateRgn`	Validates the specified region
`VerFindFile`	Indicates where to install a file
`VerInstallFile`	Installs a file
`VerLanguageName`	Converts a binary language ID into a string
`VerQueryValue`	Gets version information about a block
`VkKeyScan`	Converts the ANSI character to its corresponding virtual key code and shift state
`WaitMessage`	Yields control to other applications
`WindowFromPoint`	Finds the window that contains a specified point
`WinExec`	Executes a Windows or DOS application and specifies command parameters and the initial state of the application window
`WinHelp`	Executes the Windows Help application
`WNetAddConnection`	Adds a network connection
`WNetCancelConnection`	Removes a network connection
`WNetGetConnection`	Lists network connections
`WriteComm`	Writes from a buffer to a communication device
`WritePrivateProfileString`	Either writes a string to a private initialization file or deletes lines from a private initialization file
`WriteProfileString`	Either writes a string to WIN.INI or deletes lines from WIN.INI
`wsprintf`	Formats characters and values and places them in a buffer; format arguments are passed separately
`wvsprintf`	Formats characters and values and places them in a buffer; format arguments are passed in an array
`Yield`	Pauses the current task and begins a waiting task

B

Windows Functions by Category

This appendix lists the Windows functions by category. A general description of each function category and a list of its functions is provided.

Application Execution Functions

The Application Execution Functions are provided by Windows so that one application is able to execute another application. The following are categorized as application execution functions:

```
LoadModule
WinExec
WinHelp
```

Atom Functions

An *atom* is an integer value that uniquely identifies a character string. Atoms are stored in atom tables. Atom tables can either be local or global. A global atom table is accessible by all applications. A local atom table can be accessed by only one application. The following are categorized as atom management functions:

```
AddAtom                    GlobalDeleteAtom
DeleteAtom                 GlobalFindAtom
FindAtom                   GlobalGetAtomName
GetAtomHandle              InitAtomTable
GetAtomName                MAKEINTATOM
GlobalAddAtom
```

Bitmap Functions

Bitmaps are used extensively in Windows. A bitmap is a series of bits that define the appearance of a section of the display surface. The bits specify the color and pattern of the corresponding pixels on the display. Because bitmaps can be stored in memory, bitmaps can be quickly placed on the display and used for drawing, menus, charts, and so on. The following are categorized as bitmap functions:

```
BitBlt                     GetPixel
CreateBitmap               LoadBitmap
CreateBitmapIndirect       PatBlt
CreateCompatibleBitmap     SetBitmapBits
CreateDIBitmap             SetBitmapDimension
CreateDiscardableBitmap    SetBitmapDimensionEx
ExtFloodFill               SetDIBits
FloodFill                  SetDIBitsToDevice
GetBitmapBits              SetPixel
GetBitmapDimension         StretchBlt
GetBitmapDimensionEx       StretchDIBits
GetDIBits
```

Caret Functions

A *caret* is a blinking line, block, or bitmap that indicates a location inside the window's client area. The caret can be practically any pattern and any color. The caret is shown by inverting the pixels of the rectangular region that defines the caret. The rectangular region of the caret is defined in logical units. The inverted pixels are restored to their original values at specified intervals to give the caret a blinking effect. The interval between the inverting and blinking of the display is called the blink time.

Only one caret shape can be active at any one time. The active caret is shared between applications. A window, therefore, should manipulate the caret only when it has the input focus. The `CreateBitmap` function is used to create the bitmap for a caret. The `LoadBitmap` function is used to load an application resource for the caret. The following are categorized as caret functions:

```
CreateCaret
DestroyCaret
GetCaretBlinkTime
GetCaretPos
HideCaret
SetCaretBlinkTime
SetCaretPos
ShowCaret
```

Clipboard Functions

The *clipboard* is provided by Windows as temporary storage. The clipboard allows data to be exchanged between applications and provides cut-and-paste capabilities for those applications. The following are classified as clipboard functions:

```
ChangeClipboardChain
CloseClipboard
CountClipboardFormats
EmptyClipboard
EnumClipboardFormats
GetClipboardData
GetClipboardFormatName
GetClipboardOwner
GetClipboardViewer
GetPriorityClipboardFormat
IsClipboardFormatAvailable
OpenClipboard
RegisterClipboardFormat
SetClipboardData
SetClipboardViewer
```

Clipping Functions

A *clipping region* is a portion of a window's client area and restricts all graphics output. Any graphics output that extends beyond the boundaries of the clipping region is not displayed. The clipping functions create, monitor, and alter clipping regions. The following are categorized as clipping functions:

```
ExcludeClipRect
GetClipBox
IntersectClipRect
OffsetClipRgn
PtVisible
RectVisible
SelectClipRgn
```

Color Palette Functions

Color palettes are used to access the many colors that the system is able to generate. Most systems are able to generate thousands of colors but can display only up to 256 simultaneously. The color palette maintains a subset of the available system colors for use by an application.

Applications use logical palettes to maintain a list of colors. Each color in the palette has an appropriate palette index (the number of indexes available on the palette depends on the video mode and video hardware). By referencing the appropriate palette index, the corresponding color in the palette can be displayed. Color palette functions create and manipulate logical and system palettes. The following are categorized as color palette functions:

```
AnimatePalette              GetSystemPaletteUse
CreatePalette               RealizePalette
GetNearestColor             SelectPalette
GetNearestPaletteIndex      SetPaletteEntries
GetPaletteEntries           SetSystemPaletteUse
GetSystemPaletteEntries     UpdateColors
```

Common Dialog Functions

The common dialog functions are provided to manipulate the predefined common dialog boxes such as the Print dialog, the File Open dialog, and the Save File dialog. The following are common dialog functions:

```
CommDlgExtendedError
ChooseColor
ChooseFont
FindText
GetFileTitle
GetOpenFileName
GetSaveFileName
PrintDlg
ReplaceText
```

Communication Functions

The communication functions are provided by Windows for communications using the serial and parallel ports of the system. The following are categorized as communication functions:

```
BuildCommDCB
ClearCommBreak
CloseComm
EscapeCommFunction
FlushComm
GetCommError
GetCommEventMask
GetCommState
OpenComm
ReadComm
SetCommBreak
SetCommEventMask
SetCommState
TransmitCommChar
UngetCommChar
WriteComm
```

Coordinate Functions

Coordinate functions convert between the various coordinate systems and points. Client coordinates are converted to and from screen coordinates. Device points are converted to and from logical points. The following are categorized as coordinate functions:

```
ChildWindowFromPoint
ClientToScreen
DPtoLP
GetCurrentPosition
GetCurrentPositionEx
LPtoDP
MapWindowPoints
ScreenToClient
WindowFromPoint
```

Cursor Functions

The *cursor* is a bitmap that indicates the current position of the mouse. The cursor is automatically moved by Windows whenever input is received by the mouse. Cursor functions are used to manipulate the various aspects of the cursor. The following are categorized as cursor functions:

```
ClipCursor
CreateCursor
DestroyCursor
GetClipCursor
GetCursorPos
LoadCursor
SetCursor
SetCursorPos
ShowCursor
```

DDE Functions

The DDE functions provide the dynamic data exchange features for Windows. The following are dynamic data exchange (DDE) functions:

```
DdeAbandonTransaction      DdeFreeStringHandle
DdeAccessData              DdeGetData
DdeAddData                 DdeGetLastError
DdeClientTransaction       DdeInitialize
DdeCmpStringHandles        DdeKeepStringHandle
DdeConnect                 DdeNameService
DdeConnectList             DdePostAdvise
DdeCreateDataHandle        DdeQueryConvinfo
DdeCreateStringHandle      DdeQueryNextServer
DdeDisconnect              DdeQueryString
DdeDisconnectList          DdeSetUserHandle
DdeEnableCallback          DdeUnaccessData
DdeFreeDataHandle          DdeUninitialize
```

Debugging Functions

Debugging functions are provided by Windows to allow you to locate and isolate programming errors. The following are categorized as debugging functions:

```
DebugBreak
DirectedYield
FatalAppExit
FatalExit
GetSystemDebugState
OutputDebugString
QuerySendMessage
ValidateCodeSegments
ValidateFreeSpaces
```

Device Context Functions

A *device context* links Windows applications to device drivers and output devices. Through the device context link, a Windows application can pass device-independent information to the device driver. The device driver then creates the device-dependent operations required by the output device. The following are categorized as device context functions:

```
CreateCompatibleDC         GetDCOrg
CreateDC                   ReleaseDC
```

```
CreateIC                     ResetDC
DeleteDC                     RestoreDC
GetDC                        SaveDC
GetDCEx
```

Dialog Box Functions

Many applications use dialog boxes for user input. The dialog box is often advantageous because it can be customized for specialized input and is destroyed after it is used. There are three basic types of dialog boxes: the modeless dialog box, the modal dialog box, and the system modal dialog box.

The modeless dialog box accepts user input and allows the user to return to the previous task without removing the dialog box. The modal dialog box accepts user input but requires the user to respond to any requests in the dialog box before continuing. Only the parent window of the modal dialog box is disabled. The system modal dialog box is like a modal box except that all windows are disabled.

Windows provides a series of functions for the manipulation of dialog boxes and their corresponding controls. The following are categorized as dialog box functions:

```
CheckDlgButton               DlgDirSelectComboBox
CheckRadioButton             DlgDirSelectComboBoxEx
CreateDialog                 EndDialog
CreateDialogIndirect         GetDialogBaseUnits
CreateDialogIndirectParam    GetDlgItem
CreateDialogParam            GetDlgItemInt
DefDlgProc                   GetDlgItemText
DialogBox                    GetNextDlgGroupItem
DialogBoxIndirect            GetNextDlgTabItem
DialogBoxIndirectParam       IsDialogMessage
DialogBoxParam               IsDlgButtonChecked
DlgDirList                   MapDialogRect
DlgDirListComboBox           SendDlgItemMessage
DlgDirSelect                 SetDlgItemInt
DlgDirSelectEx               SetDlgItemText
```

Display and Movement Functions

Windows provides a set of functions that manipulate the number and position of the windows on the display. These functions are called display and movement functions and are as follows:

```
ArrangeIconicWindows
BeginDeferWindowPos
BringWindowToTop
CloseWindow
DeferWindowPos
EndDeferWindowPos
GetClientRect
GetWindowPlacement
GetWindowRect
GetWindowText
GetWindowTextLength
IsIconic
IsWindowVisible
IsZoomed
MoveWindow
OpenIcon
SetWindowPlacement
SetWindowPos
SetWindowText
ShowOwnedPopups
ShowWindow
```

Drag-Drop Functions

The drag-drop functions are used to implement the file drag and drop features for Windows 3.1. The following are drag-drop functions:

```
DragAcceptFiles
DragFinish
DragQueryFile
DragQueryPoint
```

Drawing Attribute Functions

Drawing attribute functions control the appearance of line, brush, text, and bitmap output. The following are categorized as drawing attribute functions:

```
GetBkColor
GetBkMode
GetPolyFillMode
GetROP2
GetStretchBltMode
GetTextColor
SetBkColor
SetBkMode
SetPolyFillMode
SetROP2
SetStretchBltMode
SetTextColor
```

Drawing Tool Functions

The Graphics Device Interface (GDI) uses drawing tools to create its output. The three drawing tools are the bitmap, brush, and pen. Drawing tool functions create, control, and delete the drawing tools. The following are categorized as drawing tool functions:

```
CreateBrushIndirect        EnumObjects
CreateDIBPatternBrush      GetBrushOrg
CreateHatchBrush           GetObject
CreatePatternBrush         GetStockObject
CreatePen                  IsGDIObject
CreatePenIndirect          SelectObject
CreateSolidBrush           SetBrushOrg
DeleteObject               UnrealizeObject
```

Ellipse and Polygon Functions

The ellipse and polygon functions provide fundamental drawing capabilities using the selected pen and brush. These functions can be included in applications to create graphics images such as bar charts, pie charts, or engineering drawings. The following are categorized as ellipse and polygon functions:

```
Chord
DrawFocusRect
Ellipse
Pie
Polygon
PolyPolygon
Rectangle
RoundRect
```

Environment Functions

Environment functions either modify or retrieve information on the environment associated with an output device. The following are categorized as environment functions:

```
GetDeviceCaps
GetEnvironment
SetEnvironment
```

Error Functions

Microsoft Windows provides functions for indicating errors such as invalid input. These functions flash the specified window, send a beep to the system speaker, and display a message box with the specified text and options. These functions are used

to tell the user that something is wrong. The following are categorized as error functions:

```
FlashWindow
MessageBeep
MessageBox
```

File I/O Functions

Windows provides the file I/O functions for creating, opening, reading, writing, and closing files from inside the Windows environment. The following are categorized as file I/O functions:

```
GetDriveType            _llseek
GetSystemDirectory      _lopen
GetTempDrive            _lread
GetTempFileName         _lwrite
GetWindowsDirectory     OpenFile
_lclose                 SetHandleCount
_lcreat
```

Font Functions

A font is a set of characters that have the same basic design and typeface. A font family is a set of typefaces with similar characteristics. The following are categorized as font functions:

```
AddFontResource                GetCharABCWidths
CreateFont                     GetCharWidth
CreateFontIndirect             GetFontData
CreateScalableFontResource     GetGlyphOutline
EnumFontFamilies               GetOutlineTextMetrics
EnumFonts                      GetRasterizerCaps
GetAspectRatioFilter           RemoveFontResource
GetAspectRatioFilterEx         SetMapperFlags
```

Hardware Functions

The following are classified as Windows hardware functions. These functions are used to monitor or alter the state of the keyboard and mouse input devices.

```
EnableHardwareInput     GetKeyNameText
GetAsyncKeyState        GetKeyState
```

```
GetInputState          MapVirtualKey
GetKBCodePage          OemKeyScan
GetKeyboardState       SetKeyboardState
GetKeyboardType        VkKeyScan
```

Hook Functions

System hooks are shared resources that install filter functions. Filter functions process events before they go to the application's message loop. The `SetWindowsHook` or the `SetWindowsHookEx` function specifies these filter functions. Messages generated by a specific type of event are sent to filter functions installed by the same type of hook. The following are categorized as hook functions:

```
CallMsgFilter
DefHookProc
SetWindowsHook
SetWindowHookEx
UnhookWindowsHook
UnhookWindowsHookEx
```

Icon Functions

Icons are used to represent minimized applications. The following are categorized as icon functions:

```
ArrangeIconicWindows
CopyIcon
CreateIcon
DestroyIcon
DrawIcon
IsIconic
LoadIcon
OpenIcon
```

Information Functions

Microsoft Windows information functions provide the capability to retrieve information pertaining to the number and position of the windows on the screen. The following are categorized as information functions:

```
AnyPopup                 GetParent
ChildWindowFromPoint     GetSysModalWindow
EnumChildWindows         GetTopWindow
```

```
EnumTaskWindows
EnumWindows
FindWindow
GetCurrentPosition
GetDesktopWindow
GetNextWindow
GetWindow
GetWindowTask
IsChild
IsWindow
SetParent
WindowFromPoint
```

Initialization File Functions

An *initialization file* contains run-time options for Windows applications. The Windows initialization file, WIN.INI contains information that affects the Windows environment and all applications. Private initialization files contain information for a particular application. Windows provides a set of functions for retrieving and setting information for initialization files. The following are categorized as initialization file functions:

```
GetPrivateProfileInt
GetPrivateProfileString
GetProfileInt
GetProfileString
WritePrivateProfileString
WriteProfileString
```

Input Functions

Windows input functions provide the interface to the system devices. The system devices are the mouse, the keyboard, and the timer. The functions allow you to control these system devices and specify how Windows will handle input from these devices. The following are categorized as input functions:

```
EnableWindow
GetActiveWindow
GetCapture
GetCurrentTime
GetDoubleClickTime
GetFocus
GetTickCount
IsWindowEnabled
KillTimer
ReleaseCapture
SetActiveWindow
SetCapture
SetDoubleClickTime
SetFocus
SetSysModalWindow
SetTimer
SwapMouseButton
```

Installable Driver Functions

Microsoft Windows provides the capability to create and manipulate installable device drivers. The following are categorized as installable driver functions:

```
CloseDriver
DefDriverProc
GetDriverModuleHandle
GetDriverInfo
GetNextDriver
OpenDriver
SendDriverMessage
```

Lempel-Ziv Expansion Functions

Lempel-Ziv expansion functions are used for data compression and decompression. The Lempel-Ziv expansion functions are contained in the dynamic link library LZEXPAND.DLL and include the following:

```
CopyLZFile
GetExpandedName
LZClose
LZCopy
LZDone
LZInit
LZOpenFile
LZRead
LZSeek
LZStart
```

Line Output Functions

The line output functions provide fundamental drawing capabilities using the selected pen. These functions can be used in applications to create graphics images such as bar charts, pie charts, or engineering drawings. The following are categorized as line output functions:

```
Arc
LineDDA
LineTo
MoveTo
MoveToEx
Polyline
```

Mapping Functions

The *mapping mode* specifies the relationship between units in logical space and the units for the device. The Graphics Device Interface operates with units in logical space. The use of logical space provides device independence. To create device-dependent coordinates, output to logical space is mapped to the device. Mapping functions control the Graphics Device Interface mapping modes. The following are categorized as mapping functions:

```
GetMapMode              ScaleViewportExt
GetViewportExt          ScaleViewportExtEx
GetViewportExtEx        ScaleWindowExt
GetViewportOrg          ScaleWindowExtEx
GetViewportOrgEx        SetMapMode
GetWindowExt            SetViewportExt
GetWindowExtEx          SetViewportExtEx
GetWindowOrg            SetViewportOrg
GetWindowOrgEx          SetViewportOrgEx
OffsetViewportOrg       SetWindowExt
OffsetViewportOrgEx     SetWindowExtEx
OffsetWindowOrg         SetWindowOrg
OffsetWindowOrgEx       SetWindowOrgEx
```

Memory Management Functions

Memory management functions are provided by Windows to manage both local and global memory. Global memory is system memory that has not been allocated by an application or reserved for the system. Local memory is the memory in the data segment of a Windows application. The following are categorized as memory management functions:

```
GetFreeSpace            LimitEMSPages
GetFreeSystemResources  LocalAlloc
GetSelectorBase         LocalCompact
GetSelectorLimit        LocalDiscard
GetWinFlags             LocalFlags
GlobalAlloc             LocalFree
GlobalCompact           LocalHandle
GlobalDiscard           LocalInit
GlobalDosAlloc          LocalLock
GlobalDosFree           LocalReAlloc
GlobalFlags             LocalShrink
```

GlobalFree
GlobalHandle
GlobalLock
GlobalLRUNewest
GlobalLRUOldest
GlobalNotify
GlobalReAlloc
GlobalSize
GlobalUnlock
GlobalUnwire
GlobalWire
LocalSize
LocalUnlock
LockData
LockSegment
SetSelectorBase
SetSelectorLimit
SetSwapAreaSize
SwitchStackBack
SwitchStackTo
UnlockData
UnLockSegment

Menu Functions

Menus in a Windows application are often used to present the user with a choice of selections, or items. These menu selections are then chosen through use of the mouse or keyboard. The selection from the menu indicates the action that the application should take. Menu selections can contain a single entry or provide a pop-up menu which provides additional menu selections. The following are categorized as menu functions:

AppendMenu
CheckMenuItem
CreateMenu
CreatePopupMenu
DeleteMenu
DestroyMenu
DrawMenuBar
EnableMenuItem
GetMenu
GetMenuCheckMarkDimensions
GetMenuItemCount
GetMenuItemID
GetMenuState
GetMenuString
GetSubMenu
GetSystemMenu
HiliteMenuItem
InsertMenu
IsMenu
LoadMenuIndirect
ModifyMenu
RemoveMenu
SetMenu
SetMenuItemBitmaps
TrackPopupMenu

Message Functions

A Windows message is generated each time an input event occurs. In general, the message is stored first in the system queue, then in the appropriate application queue. The application queue is a first-in-first-out queue. Some messages, however, are sent directly to the window function for the application. Windows sends messages in practically any sequence; the application, therefore, should not depend upon the order of the messages received.

Windows provides a set of functions for manipulating messages. The following are categorized as message functions:

```
CallWindowProc            PostQuitMessage
DispatchMessage           RegisterWindowMessage
GetMessage                ReplyMessage
GetMessageExtraInfo       SendMessage
GetMessagePos             SetMessageQueue
GetMessageTime            TranslateAccelerator
InSendMessage             TranslateMDISysAccel
PeekMessage               TranslateMessage
PostAppMessage            WaitMessage
PostMessage
```

Metafile Functions

A *metafile* is a series of Graphics Device Interface commands that create text or images. Because Graphics Device Interface commands are used to create the metafile, a metafile is device independent. Metafile functions create, delete, play, and manipulate metafiles. The following are categorized as metafile functions:

```
CloseMetaFile             GetMetaFileBits
CopyMetaFile              PlayMetaFile
CreateMetaFile            PlayMetaFileRecord
DeleteMetaFile            SetMetaFileBits
EnumMetaFile              SetMetaFileBitsBetter
GetMetaFile
```

Module Management Functions

Modules are executable units of code and data. Windows provides a set of functions for modifying and retrieving information for Windows modules. The following are categorized as module management functions:

```
FreeLibrary               GetModuleHandle
FreeModule                GetModuleUsage
FreeProcInstance          GetProcAddress
GetCodeHandle             GetVersion
GetInstanceData           LoadLibrary
GetModuleFileName         MakeProcInstance
```

Network Functions

Network functions are provided by Windows to support networked versions of Windows. The following functions are categorized as network functions:

WNetAddConnection
WNetCancelConnection
WNetGetConnection

OLE Functions

The OLE functions are used to implement the object linking and embedding features for creating compound documents. There are several subcategories for the OLE functions. The subcategories include:

OLE Client Functions

OleClose
OleExecute
OleLockServer
OleQueryOpen
OleQueryReleaseError
OleQueryReleaseMethod
OleQueryReleaseStatus
OleReconnect
OleRequestData
OleUnlockServer

OLE Document Functions

OleEnumObjects
OleRegisterClientDoc
OleRegisterServerDoc
OleRename
OleRenameClientDoc
OleRenameServerDoc
OleRevertClientDoc
OleRevertServerDoc
OleRevokeClientDoc
OleRevokeServerDoc
OleSavedClientDoc
OleSavedServerDoc

OLE Link Functions

OleGetLinkUpdateOptions
OleQueryLinkFromClip
OleQueryOutOfDate
OleSetLinkUpdateOptions
OleUpdate

OLE Object Creation Functions

OleClone
OleCopyFromLink
OleCreate
OleCreateFromClip
OleCreateFromFile
OleCreateFromTemplate
OleCreateInvisible
OleCreateLinkFromClip
OleCreateLinkFromFile
OleLoadFromStream
OleObjectConvert
OleQueryCreateFromClip

OLE Object Management Functions

```
OleActivate
OleCopyToClipboard
OleDelete
OleDraw
OleEnumFormats
OleEqual
OleGetData
OleIsDcMeta
OleQueryBounds
OleQueryClientVersion
OleQueryName
OleQueryProtocol
OleQuerySize
OleQueryType
OleRelease
OleSaveToStream
OleSetBounds
OleSetColorScheme
OldSetData
OleSetHostNames
OleSetTargetDevice
```

OLE Server Functions

```
OleBlockServer
OleQueryServerVersion
OleRegisterServer
OleRevokeObject
OleRevokeServer
OleUnblockServer
```

Operating System Interrupt Functions

The operating system interrupt functions are provided by Windows to permit assembly language applications to generate DOS and NETBIOS interrupts without coding the interrupt. The following are categorized as operating system interrupt functions:

```
DOS3Call
NetBIOSCall
```

Optimization Tool Functions

The optimization tool functions manipulate the Windows Profiler and Swap development tools. The following are categorized as optimization tool functions:

```
ProfClear
ProfFinish
ProfFlush
ProfInsChk
ProfSampleRate
```

```
ProfSetup
ProfStart
ProfStop
SwapRecording
```

Painting Functions

Windows provides functions that are used for simple graphics operations for the system display. The display system is shared by the applications running under Windows. Windows must carefully manage the display, therefore, to avoid conflicts among applications. The display context is used for managing the system display. The display context allows each window to be treated as a separate display surface. An application can control the display surface of a window by obtaining the display context. The four types of display contexts are *common*, *class*, *private*, and *window*.

The common display context allows drawing in the window's client area. This is the default context for all windows. The default selections for the pen, brush, font, clipping area, and other attributes are used. These selections can be modified.

The class display context is used when the window class has style `CS_CLASSDC`. The class display context is used by all windows in the class. The default selections for the pen, brush, font, clipping area, and other attributes are used. These selections can be modified.

The private display context is used when the window class has style `CS_OWNDC`. The private display context is used only by the specified window. The default selections for the pen, brush, font, clipping area, and other attributes are used. These selections can be modified.

The window display context does not limit drawing to the client area of the window. Drawing can occur anywhere inside the window. The default selections for the pen, brush, font, clipping area, and other attributes are used. These selections can be modified.

The following are categorized as painting functions:

```
BeginPaint
DrawFocusRect
DrawIcon
EndPaint
ExcludeUpdateRgn
FrameRect
GetDC
GetUpdateRect
GetUpdateRgn
GetWindowDC
GrayString
InvalidateRect
InvalidateRgn
InvertRect
InvertRgn
LockWindowUpdate
ReleaseDC
UpdateWindow
ValidateRect
ValidateRgn
```

Printer Control Functions

Printer control functions provide information on a printer and its device driver, and modify the initialization state of the printer. The following are categorized as printer control functions:

```
AbortDoc
DeviceCapabilities
DeviceMode
EndDoc
EndPage
Escape
ExtDeviceMode
SetAbortProc
StartDoc
```

Property Functions

A *property list* contains data handles associated with a window. Each window has a property list. This list is initially empty but can have entries added. Each entry consists of an ANSI string and a data handle. The data handle identifies any object or memory block associated with the window. By maintaining a property list, data associated with a window is easy to access and modify. The following are categorized as property functions:

```
EnumProps
GetProp
RemoveProp
SetProp
```

Rectangle Functions

Windows uses rectangles to specify certain areas of the display or window including the clipping area, client area, text area, and scroll area. Rectangles are also used for many other reasons. Rectangles, in Windows, are defined by the upper-left corner and lower-right corner. The dimensions of the rectangle are expressed in logical units. Rectangle functions are used to manipulate rectangles in a window's client area. The following are classified as rectangle functions:

```
CopyRect
EqualRect
FillRect
FrameRect
GetBoundsRect
InflateRect
IntersectRect
InvertRect
IsRectEmpty
OffsetRect
PtInRect
SetBoundsRect
SetRect
SetRectEmpty
UnionRect
```

Region Functions

A *region* is an area within a window used for output. Region functions create and modify regions. These functions can be used with the clipping functions to create clipping regions. The following are categorized as region functions:

```
CombineRgn                    FillRgn
CreateEllipticRgn             FrameRgn
CreateEllipticRgnIndirect     GetRgnBox
CreatePolygonRgn              InvertRgn
CreatePolyPolygonRgn          OffsetRgn
CreateRectRgn                 PaintRgn
CreateRectRgnIndirect         PtInRegion
CreateRoundRectRgn            RectInRegion
EqualRgn                      SetRectRgn
```

Registration Functions

The following are categorized as the Windows registration functions:

```
RegCloseKey
RegCreateKey
RegDeleteKey
RegEnumKey
RegOpenKey
RegQueryValue
RegSetValue
```

Resource Management Functions

Windows provides this set of functions for manipulating resources such as icons, bitmaps, cursors, fonts, and strings. The following are categorized as resource management functions:

```
AccessResource                LoadMenu
AllocResource                 LoadResource
FindResource                  LoadString
FreeResource                  LockResource
LoadAccelerators              SetResourceHandler
LoadBitmap                    SizeofResource
LoadCursor                    UnlockResource
LoadIcon
```

Scrolling Functions

Scrolling occurs when data is moved in and out of the client area. The scroll bar is the primary tool used to allow the user to scroll the contents of the client area. The scroll bar is a part of the nonclient area of the window and is created with the window. Both vertical and horizontal control bars can be created. The current display position of the contents, relative to the beginning and end of the contents being scrolled, is shown in the scroll bar thumb.

The scroll bar control is another tool to allow the user to scroll the contents of the client area. A scroll bar control is like a standard scroll bar but is not a part of the window. The scroll bar control can receive the input focus and permits the user to use the keyboard for scrolling.

Scrolling functions provide control over scroll bars and scroll bar controls. The following are categorized as scrolling functions:

```
EnableScrollBar
GetScrollPos
GetScrollRange
ScrollDC
ScrollWindow
ScrollWindowEx
SetScrollPos
SetScrollRange
ShowScrollBar
```

Segment Functions

Windows uses the segment functions to manipulate selectors and the memory blocks they reference and retrieve information on segments. The following are categorized as segment functions:

```
AllocDStoCSAlias        GlobalFix
AllocSelector           GlobalPageLock
ChangeSelector          GlobalPageUnlock
DefineHandleTable       GlobalUnfix
FreeSelector            LockSegment
GetCodeInfo             UnlockSegment
```

Shell Functions

The following are categorized as shell functions:

```
ExtractIcon
FindExecutable
ShellExecute
```

Stress Functions

The stress functions are included in the dynamic link library STRESS.DLL for application testing. The stress library consumes system resources for testing purposes. The following are categorized as stress functions:

```
AllocDiskSpace        FreeAllGDIMem
AllocFileHandles      FreeAllMem
AllocGDIMem           FreeAllUserMem
AllocMem              UnAllocDiskSpace
AllocUserMem          UnAllocFileHandles
```

String Manipulation Functions

Windows provides the string manipulation functions to manipulate and translate character strings. The following are categorized as string manipulation functions:

```
AnsiLower             IsCharUpper
AnsiLowerBuff         lstrcat
AnsiNext              lstrcmp
AnsiPrev              lstrcmpi
AnsiToOem             lstrcpy
AnsiToOemBuff         lstrlen
AnsiUpper             OemToAnsi
AnsiUpperBuff         OemToAnsiBuff
IsCharAlpha           ToAscii
IsCharAlphaNumeric    wsprintf
IsCharLower           wvsprintf
```

System Functions

Windows provides a set of functions used to retrieve information on system metrics, color, and time. These functions are the system functions. The following are categorized as system functions:

```
GetSysColor
GetSystemMetrics
```

```
GetTickCount
SetSysColors
SystemParametersInfo
```

Task Functions

A *task* is a Windows application call. Windows provides the task functions to manipulate tasks. The following are categorized as task functions:

```
Catch                   GetNumTasks
ExitWindows             IsTask
GetCurrentPDB           SetErrorMode
GetCurrentTask          Throw
GetDOSEnvironment       Yield
```

Text Functions

The Graphics Device Interface uses the text functions for text output and manipulation. The selected font is used by the Graphics Device Interface for text output. The following are categorized as text functions:

```
DrawText                GetTextFace
ExtTextOut              GetTextMetrics
GetTabbedTextExtent     SetTextAlign
GetTextAlign            SetTextCharacterExtra
GetTextCharacterExtra   SetTextJustification
GetTextExtent           TabbedTextOut
GetTextExtentEx         TextOut
GetTextExtentPoint
```

Toolhelp Functions

The following are categorized as Toolhelp functions:

```
ClassFirst              ModuleFindName
ClassNext               ModuleFirst
GlobalEntryHandle       ModuleNext
GlobalEntryModule       NotifyRegister
GlobalFirst             NotifyUnRegister
GlobalHandleToSel       StackTraceCSIPFirst
GlobalInfo              StackTraceFirst
GlobalNext              StrackTraceNext
InterruptRegister       SystemHeapInfo
```

```
InterruptUnRegister       TaskFindHandle
LocalFirst                TaskFirst
LocalInfo                 TaskGetCSIP
LocalNext                 TaskNext
LockInput                 TaskSetCSIP
MemManInfo                TaskSwitch
MemoryRead                TerminateApp
MemoryWrite               TimerCount
ModuleFindHandle
```

TrueType Functions

The TrueType functions are used to manipulate TrueType font resources. The following are categorized as TrueType functions:

```
CreateScalableFontResource
GetCharABCWidths
GetFontData
GetGlyphOutline
GetOutlineTextMetrics
GetRasterizerCaps
```

Version Functions

The File Version Stamping Library provides the functions to allow applications to install and analyze files. The following are version functions:

```
GetFileResource           GetWindowsDir
GetFileResourceSize       VerFindFile
GetFileVersionInfo        VerInstallFile
GetFileVersionInfoSize    VerLanguageName
GetSystemDir              VerQueryValue
```

Window Creation Functions

The first step in creating a window is to define a window class. The window class defines the appearance and behavior of the window. The three types of window classes are the *system global class*, the *application global class*, and the *application local class*.

System global classes are available from Windows. Windows creates these classes on startup. Applications can use these classes but cannot delete them.

Application global classes are created by the application by using the `CS_GLOBALCLASS` style for the particular class. The created class is then available to all the applications in the system. All application global classes created by an application are destroyed when the application ends.

Application global classes are created by the application and are available only to the application.

Once the class has been established, the class is registered. A window of that class type can then be created. Windows provides several functions for creating, destroying, modifying, and manipulating windows. These functions are called the window creation functions. The following are categorized as window creation functions.

```
AdjustWindowRect          GetClassName
AdjustWindowRectEx        GetClassWord
CreateWindow              GetLastActivePopup
CreateWindowEx            GetWindowLong
DefDlgProc                GetWindowWord
DefFrameProc              RegisterClass
DefMDIChildProc           SetClassLong
DefWindowProc             SetClassWord
DestroyWindow             SetWindowLong
GetClassInfo              SetWindowWord
GetClassLong              UnregisterClass
```

Windows Macros/Utility Functions

Windows provides a variety of macros and functions that perform utility-type operations to make programming in Windows a little easier. The following are categorized as Windows macros and utility functions:

```
COLORREF                  MAKEINTRESOURCE
HIBYTE                    MAKELONG
HIWORD                    MAKEPOINT
GetBValue                 max
GetGValue                 min
GetRValue                 MulDiv
LOBYTE                    PALETTEINDEX
LOWORD                    PALETTERGB
MAKEINTATOM               RGB
```

Windows Messages Quick Reference Guide

This appendix serves as a quick reference guide to the Windows messages. Table C.1 presents the categories into which Windows messages are divided, and provides a description of each category. To help you classify and group the messages, Table C.2 presents each Windows message with its appropriate category and a quick description of the message.

Table C.1. *The types of Windows messages.*

Category	*Meaning*
Button Control Messages	Sent by an application to a button control

continues

Table C.1. continued

Category	Meaning
Clipboard Messages	Sent to an application by the Windows system when another application attempts to use the window's clipboard
Combo Box Messages	Sent to a combo box from an application
Control Messages	Instruct controls to perform certain tasks; control messages are sent by the `SendMessage` function
Driver Messages	Sent to installable device drivers
Dynamic Data Exchange (DDE) Messages	Deal with client-server application relationships
Edit Control Messages	Sent to an edit control from an application. Control messages instruct controls to perform certain tasks and are sent by the `SendMessage` function.
Initialization Messages	Windows sends initialization messages whenever a menu or dialog box is created by an application
Input Messages	Windows sends input messages when an application receives input from the mouse, keyboard, scroll bars, or system timer
List Box Messages	Sent to a list box from an application
Multiple Document Interface (MDI) Messages	Used by applications to control child windows
Nonclient Area Messages	Windows sends nonclient area messages to create and maintain the nonclient area of an application window
Notification Codes	Sent to the parent window of a control as notification that certain actions have occurred. There are four basic types of notification codes: button, combo box, edit control, and list box
Button Notification Codes	Used with button controls
Combo Box Notification Codes	Used with combo boxes
Edit Control Notification	Used with edit controls
List Box Notification Codes	Used with list boxes
Owner-Draw Control Messages	Indicate to the owner of a control that the control needs to be drawn and needs to furnish drawing information

Category	*Meaning*
Scroll Bar Messages	Sent by the scroll bar control to the scroll bar owner when the scroll bar control is clicked
System Information Messages	Windows sends system information messages whenever an application makes a change that affects other applications
System Messages	Windows sends system messages whenever the window's System menu, scroll bars, or size box are accessed
Window Management Messages	Windows sends window management messages to an application when the window state changes

Table C.2. *Windows messages.*

Message	*Category*	*Meaning*
`BM_GETCHECK`	Button Control	Determines whether a radio button or check box is checked
`BM_GETSTATE`	Button Control	Determines the state of a button control
`BM_SETCHECK`	Button Control	Places or removes the checkmark for button controls
`BM_SETSTATE`	Button Control	Highlights a button control
`BM_SETSTYLE`	Button Control	Modifies the button style
`BN_CLICKED`	Button Notification	Indicates that a button has been clicked
`BN_DISABLE`	Button Notification	Indicates that a button has been disabled
`BN_DOUBLECLICKED`	Button Notification	Indicates that a button has been double-clicked
`CB_ADDSTRING`	Combo Box	Adds a string to the list box of a combo box
`CB_DELETESTRING`	Combo Box	Removes a string from the list box of a combo box

continues

Table C.2. continued

Message	Category	Meaning
CB_DIR	Combo Box	Gets a list of files from the current directory and places the list in the combo box
CB_FINDSTRING	Combo Box	Searches for the first string from the list box of a combo box that matches the specified prefix
CB_GETCOUNT	Combo Box	Determines the number of items in the list box of a combo box
CB_GETCURSEL	Combo Box	Gets the item index of the current selection
CB_GETDROPPEDCONTROLRECT	Combo Box	Retrieves the screen coordinates of the dropped-down list box of a combo box
CB_GETDROPPEDSTATE	Combo Box	Determines whether the list box of a combo box is dropped down and visible
CB_GETEDITSEL	Combo Box	Gets the starting and ending positions of the selected text in the edit control of a combo box
CB_GETEXTENDEDUI	Combo Box	Determines whether a combo box has the default or the extended user interface
CB_GETITEMDATA	Combo Box	Gets the 32-bit value associated with an item in an owner draw combo box
CB_GETITEMHEIGHT	Combo Box	Determines the height of a combo box component
CB_GETLBTEXT	Combo Box	Copies a string from a list box in a combo box to a buffer
CB_GETLBTEXTLEN	Combo Box	Determines the length of a string from a list box of a combo box
CB_INSERTSTRING	Combo Box	Inserts a string in a list box of a combo box
CB_LIMITTEXT	Combo Box	Specifies the maximum length of the text that can be entered in an edit control of a combo box
CB_RESETCONTENT	Combo Box	Deletes the strings from a combo box

Message	*Category*	*Meaning*
CB_SELECTSTRING	Combo Box	Selects the first string that has the specified prefix
CB_SETCURSEL	Combo Box	Selects a string and makes it visible in the list box of a combo box
CB_SETEDITSEL	Combo Box	Selects the text in the edit control within the specified starting and ending positions
CB_SETEXTENDEDUI	Combo Box	Specifies the user interface type, either extended or default, for a combo box
CB_SETITEMDATA	Combo Box	Sets the 32-bit value associated with an item in an owner-draw combo box
CB_SETITEMHEIGHT	Combo Box	Sets the height of the combo box component
CB_SHOWDROPDOWN	Combo Box	Either shows or hides a drop-down list box in a combo box
CBN_CLOSEUP	Combo Box Notification	Sent to the parent window of a combo box when the list box of the combo box is hidden
CBN_DBLCLK	Combo Box Notification	Sent when a string is double-clicked
CBN_DROPDOWN	Combo Box Notification	Sent to the owner of the combo box when a list box is to be dropped down
CBN_EDITCHANGE	Combo Box Notification	Sent when the text in the edit control is modified
CBN_EDITUPDATE	Combo Box Notification	Specifies that the edit control will display altered text
CBN_ERRSPACE	Combo Box Notification	Sent when there is no more system memory
CBN_KILLFOCUS	Combo Box Notification	Specifies that the combo box no longer has the input focus
CBN_SELCHANGE	Combo Box Notification	Specifies that the selection has been modified

continues

Table C.2. continued

Message	Category	Meaning
CBN_SELENDCANCEL	Combo Box Notification	Sent when an item is selected and the user closes the control by clicking another window or control
CBN_SELENDOK	Combo Box Notification	Sent when an item is selected and the user closes the control by pressing Enter or clicking the Down arrow
CBN_SETFOCUS	Combo Box Notification	Specifies that the combo box received the input focus
DM_GETDEFID	Button Control	Gets the default push button's ID for a dialog box
DM_SETDEFID	Button Control	Modifies the default push button control ID for a dialog box
DRV_CLOSE	Driver	Sent to an installable driver when the `CloseDriver` function is called
DRV_CONFIGURE	Driver	Tells a driver to display the private configuration dialog box
DRV_DISABLE	Driver	Sent to a driver when the driver is about to be removed from the system
DRV_ENABLE	Driver	Sent to a driver when the driver is loaded or reloaded
DRV_FREE	Driver	Tells the driver that it is about to be discarded
DRV_INSTALL	Driver	Sent to the driver during initialization
DRV_LOAD	Driver	Tells the driver that it has been loaded
DRV_OPEN	Driver	Sent to the driver each time the driver is opened
DRV_QUERYCONFIGURE	Driver	Determines whether the driver can be configured by the user
DRV_POWER	Driver	Informs the driver that the power supply to the associated device is about to be turned on or off

Message	*Category*	*Meaning*
DRV_REMOVE	Driver	Sent as the fourth message to a driver during driver configuration
EM_CANUNDO	Edit Control	Indicates whether an edit control can respond to an EM_UNDO message
EM_EMPTYUNDOBUFFER	Edit Control	Disables the undo capability of an edit control
EM_FMTLINES	Edit Control	Specifies whether the edit control should add or remove end-of-line characters from text that wraps around a line
EM_GETFIRSTVISIBLELINE	Edit Control	Determines the character index of the leftmost visible character in a single-line edit control and the index of the topmost visible line for multiline edit controls
EM_GETHANDLE	Edit Control	Gets the data handle of the buffer that stores the control window contents
EM_GETLINE	Edit Control	Gets a line from the edit control
EM_GETLINECOUNT	Edit Control	Gets the number of lines of text in the edit control
EM_GETMODIFY	Edit Control	Gets the setting of the modify flag for an edit control
EM_PASSWORDCHAR	Edit Control	Gets the edit control password character
EM_GETRECT	Edit Control	Gets the dimensions of the formatting rectangle of the edit control
EM_GETSEL	Edit Control	Gets the starting and ending positions of the current selection
EM_GETWORDBREAKPROC	Edit Control	Gets the edit control word break function
EM_LIMITTEXT	Edit Control	Specifies the maximum number of bytes that the user can enter

continues

Table C.2. continued

Message	*Category*	*Meaning*
EM_LINEFROMCHAR	Edit Control	Gets the line number of the line that contains the character at the specified position
EM_LINEINDEX	Edit Control	Gets the number of character positions that exist prior to the first character of a specified line
EM_LINELENGTH	Edit Control	Determines the length of a line from the text buffer for the edit control
EM_LINESCROLL	Edit Control	Scrolls the contents of the edit control a specified number of lines
EM_REPLACESEL	Edit Control	Replaces the current selection with the specified text
EM_SETHANDLE	Edit Control	Specifies the text buffer that holds the contents of the edit control window
EM_SETMODIFY	Edit Control	Sets the modify flag for the specified edit control
EM_SETPASSWORDCHAR	Edit Control	Defines the password character displayed in an edit control with style ES_PASSWORD
SETREADONLY	Edit Control	Specifies the read-only state of an edit control
EM_SETRECT	Edit Control	Sets the dimensions of the formatting rectangle for an edit control
EM_SETRECTNP	Edit Control	Sets the dimensions of the formatting rectangle for an edit control but does not repaint the control
EM_SETSEL	Edit Control	Selects the text within the specified starting and ending character positions
EM_SETTABSTOPS	Edit Control	Defines the tab stop settings for a multiline edit control

Message	*Category*	*Meaning*
EM_SETWORDBREAKPROC	Edit Control	Sent to a multiline edit control when the word-break function is replaced with a word-break function supplied by the application
EM_UNDO	Edit Control	Performs an "undo" of the last edit in an edit control
EN_CHANGE	Edit Control Notification	Indicates that an action has changed the content of the text
EN_ERRSPACE	Edit Control Notification	Specifies that an edit control is out of space
EN_HSCROLL	Edit Control Notification	Specifies that the horizontal scroll bar has been clicked and is active
EN_KILLFOCUS	Edit Control Notification	Specifies that the edit control has lost the input focus
EN_MAXTEXT	Edit Control Notification	Specifies that the inserted text exceeds the limits for the edit control
EN_SETFOCUS	Edit Control Notification	Specifies that the edit control has received the input focus
EN_UPDATE	Edit Control Notification	Specifies that the edit control will display altered text
EN_VSCROLL	Edit Control Notification	Specifies that the vertical scroll bar has been clicked and is active
LB_ADDSTRING	List Box	Adds a string to the list box
LB_DELETESTRING	List Box	Removes a string from the list box
LB_DIR	List Box	Gets a list of files from the current directory and places them in the list box
LB_FINDSTRING	List Box	Searches for a string in the list box that matches the prefix text
LB_GETCARETINDEX	List Box	Determines the index of the item from a multi-selection list box that has the focus rectangle
LB_GETCOUNT	List Box	Determines the number of items in a list box

continues

Table C.2. continued

Message	*Category*	*Meaning*
LB_GETCURSEL	List Box	Gets the item index for the currently selected item
LB_GETHORIZONTALEXTENT	List Box	Gets the horizontal scroll width of a list box
LB_GETITEMDATA	List Box	Gets the 32-bit value associated with an item in an owner draw list box
LB_GETITEMHEIGHT	List Box	Determines the height of the specified item from a list box
LB_GETITEMRECT	List Box	Gets the coordinates of the rectangle binding the list box item
LB_GETSEL	List Box	Gets the selection state of a list box item
LB_GETSELCOUNT	List Box	Determines the number of items selected from a list box
LB_GETSELITEMS	List Box	Gets the item indexes of the selected items from a list box
LB_GETTEXT	List Box	Copies a string from a list box into a buffer
LB_GETTEXTLEN	List Box	Determines the length of a string from the list box
LB_GETTOPINDEX	List Box	Gets the item index for the first visible item in a list box
LB_INSERTSTRING	List Box	Inserts a string into the list box
LB_RESETCONTENT	List Box	Deletes all the strings from a list box
LB_SELECTSTRING	List Box	Selects the first string that matches the specified prefix
LB_SELITEMRANGE	List Box	Selects one or more items from a list box
LB_SETCARETINDEX	List Box	Gives the focus rectangle to the specified item
LB_SETCOLUMNWIDTH	List Box	Defines the column width in pixels for a multi-column list box

Message	*Category*	*Meaning*
LB_SETCURSEL	List Box	Selects a string and puts it so that it can be seen in the list box
LB_SETHORIZONTALEXTENT	List Box	Defines the horizontal scroll width of a list box
LB_SETITEMDATA	List Box	Sets the 32-bit value associated with an item in an owner-draw list box
LB_SETITEMHEIGHT	List Box	Sets the height of the specified item in the list box
LB_SETSEL	List Box	Defines the selection state of a string
LB_SETTABSTOPS	List Box	Defines the tab stops in a list box
LB_SETTOPINDEX	List Box	Sets the first visible item in a list box to the specified item index
LBN_DBLCLK	List Box Notification	Specifies that a string has been double-clicked
LBN_ERRSPACE	List Box Notification	Specifies that there is no more system memory
LBN_KILLFOCUS	List Box Notification	Specifies that the list box has lost the input focus
LBN_SELCHANGE	List Box Notification	Specifies that the selection has been changed
LBN_SETFOCUS	List Box Notification	Specifies that the list box has received the input focus
STM_GETICON	Icon Control	Retrieves the handle of the icon that is associated with an icon control
STM_SETICON	Icon Control	Associates the specified icon with an icon control
WM_ACTIVATE	Window Management	Sent whenever a window becomes active or inactive
WM_ACTIVATEAPP	Window Management	Sent if the window being activated doesn't belong to the same application as the previously active window
WM_ASKCBFORMATNAME	Clipboard	Asks for the name of the CF_OWNERDISPLAY format
WM_CANCELMODE	Window Management	Sent when an application displays a message box and cancels the current system mode

continues

Table C.2. continued

Message	*Category*	*Meaning*
WM_CHANGECBCHAIN	Clipboard	Sent to the members of the viewing chain when the chain has been modified
WM_CHAR	Input	Sent when a WM_KEYUP and a WM_KEYDOWN message are translated
WM_CHARTOITEM	Input	Sent in response to the WM_CHAR message by a list box with style LBS_WANTKEYBOARDINPUT
WM_CHILDACTIVATE	Window Management	Sent to a child window's parent window when the SetWindowPos function is used to move a child window
WM_CHOOSEFONT_GETLOGFONT	Window Management	Sent to Font dialog box to get the current LOGFONT structure
WM_CLEAR	Edit Control	Deletes the current selection
WM_CLOSE	Window Management	Sent when a window is closed
WM_COMMAND	Input	Sent when a menu item is selected, a control passes a message to its parent window, or an accelerator key is translated
WM_COMMNOTIFY	Window Management	Sent when a COM port event occurs and indicates the status of the input and output queues of the window
WM_COMPACTING	System Information	Sent to top level windows when too much time is spent compacting memory, an indication that memory is low
WM_COMPAREITEM	Owner Draw Control	Compares two items to determine their relative position in a sorted owner draw list box or combo box
WM_COPY	Edit Control	Copies the current selection to the clipboard in CF_TEXT format

Message	*Category*	*Meaning*
WM_CREATE	Window Management	Sent whenever the CreateWindow function is called
WM_CTLCOLOR	Window Management	Sent to the parent window or a control or message box whenever the control or message box is to be drawn
WM_CUT	Edit Control	Copies the current selection to the clipboard in CF_TEXT format, then deletes the selection from the control window
WM_DDE_ACK	Dynamic Data Exchange	Tells the application that a WM_DDE_INITIATE, WM_DDE_EXECUTE, WM_DDE_DATA, WM_DDE_ADVISE, WM_DDE_UNADVISE, WM_DDE_POKE, or WM_DDE_REQUEST message has been received
WM_DDE_ADVISE	Dynamic Data Exchange	Posted by a client application to request a data item update from the server application
WM_DDE_DATA	Dynamic Data Exchange	Posted by the server application and sends a data item value to the client application
WM_DDE_EXECUTE	Dynamic Data Exchange	Posted by a client application and sends a command string to the server application
WM_DDE_INITIATE	Dynamic Data Exchange	Initiates conversations with applications that respond to the specified application and topic
WM_DDE_POKE	Dynamic Data Exchange	Sent by the client application to send unexpected data to a server application
WM_DDE_REQUEST	Dynamic Data Exchange	Posted by a client application and requests that the server application provide the value of a data item

continues

Table C.2. continued

Message	*Category*	*Meaning*
WM_DDE_TERMINATE	Dynamic Data Exchange	Terminates a conversation and can be posted by either a client or a server application
WM_DDE_UNADVISE	Dynamic Data Exchange	Sent by the client application to inform the server application that the specified item or clipboard format should not be updated
WM_DEADCHAR	Input	Sent when a WM_KEYUP and a WM_KEYDOWN message are translated
WM_DELETEITEM	Owner Draw Control	Sent to the owner of an owner draw list box or combo box when a list box item is removed
WM_DESTROY	Window Management	Sent when a window is destroyed with the DestroyWindow function
WM_DESTROYCLIPBOARD	Clipboard	Sent when the contents of the clipboard are being destroyed
WM_DEVMODECHANGE	System Information	Sent to top level windows when device mode settings are modified
WM_DRAWCLIPBOARD	Clipboard	Sent as notification to the next application that the clipboard has been modified
WM_DRAWITEM	Owner Draw Control	Indicates that an owner draw list or combo box needs redrawn
WM_DROPFILES	Window Management	Sent when the selected files are released over an application window that is registered to receive dropped files
WM_ENABLE	Window Management	Sent whenever a window is enabled or disabled
WM_ENDSESSION	Window Management	Indicates whether the session is ended

Message	*Category*	*Meaning*
WM_ENTERIDLE	Window Management	Sent to a window when a dialog box or menu is displayed and waiting for user response
WM_ERASEBKGND	Window Management	Sent whenever the window background needs erasing
WM_FONTCHANGE	System Information	Sent when font pool resources are modified
WM_GETDLGCODE	Window Management	Sent to an input procedure associated with a control
WM_GETFONT	Control	Gets the font used by a control
WM_GETHOTKEY	Window Management	Gets the hot key associated with a window
WM_GETMINMAXINFO	Window Management	Gets the maximized window size, the minimum or maximum tracking size, and the maximized window position
WM_GETTEXT	Window Management	Gets the text for a window
WM_GETTEXTLENGTH	Window Management	Gets the length of the window text
WM_HSCROLL	Input and Scroll Bar	Sent when the horizontal and scroll bar is activated
WM_HSCROLLCLIPBOARD	Clipboard	Sent to request horizontal scrolling for the CF_OWNERDISPLAY format
WM_ICONERASEBKGND	Window Management	Sent when the background of the icon needs to be erased
WM_INITDIALOG	Initialization	Sent before the dialog box is displayed
WM_INITMENU	Initialization	Sent to request the intialization of a menu
WM_INITMENUPOPUP	Initialization	Sent before a pop-up menu is displayed
WM_KEYDOWN	Input	Sent when a nonsystem key is pressed

continues

Table C.2. continued

Message	*Category*	*Meaning*
WM_KEYUP	Input	Sent when a nonsystem key is released
WM_KILLFOCUS	Window Management	Sent just before a window loses the input focus
WM_LBUTTONDBLCLK	Input	Sent when the left mouse button is double-clicked
WM_LBUTTONDOWN	Input	Sent when the left mouse button is pressed
WM_LBUTTONUP	Input	Sent when the left mouse button is released
WM_MBUTTONDBLCLK	Input	Sent when the middle mouse button is double-clicked
WM_MBUTTONDOWN	Input	Sent when the middle mouse button is pressed
WM_MBUTTONUP	Input	Sent when the middle mouse button is released
WM_MDIACTIVATE	MDI	Activates a child window
WM_MDICASCADE	MDI	Arranges child windows in a cascade fashion
WM_MDICREATE	MDI	Creates a child window
WM_MDIDESTROY	MDI	Closes a child window
WM_MDIGETACTIVE	MDI	Gets the active MDI child window
WM_MDIICONARRANGE	MDI	Arranges minimized child windows
WM_MDIMAXIMIZE	MDI	Maximizes an MDI child window
WM_MDINEXT	MDI	Makes the next child window active
WM_MDIRESTORE	MDI	Restores a child window
WM_MDISETMENU	MDI	Replaces the menu of the Window pop-up menu, an MDI frame window, or both
WM_MDITILE	MDI	Arranges child windows in a tiled format
WM_MEASUREITEM	Owner Draw Control	Determines the dimensions of an owner-draw combo box, list box, or menu item

Message	*Category*	*Meaning*
WM_MENUCHAR	Window Management	Sent to the window that owns the menu when the menu mnemonic character input by the user doesn't match any mnemonic characters in the menu
WM_MENUSELECT	Window Management	Sent when a menu item has been selected
WM_MOUSEACTIVATE	Input	Sent when a mouse button is pressed while the cursor is in an inactive window
WM_MOUSEMOVE	Input	Sent when the mouse is moved
WM_MOVE	Window Management	Sent when a window is moved
WM_NCACTIVATE	Nonclient Area	Sent to a window when the caption or icon needs to be updated to reflect an active or inactive state
WM_NCCALCSIZE	Nonclient Area	Sent when the client area's size needs to be determined
WM_NCCREATE	Nonclient Area	Sent before the WM_CREATE message is sent when a window is created
WM_NCDESTROY	Nonclient Area	Sent after the WM_DESTROY message when a nonclient area is destroyed
WM_NCHITTEST	Nonclient Area	Sent to the window containing the cursor whenever the mouse is moved
WM_NCLBUTTONDBLCLK	Nonclient Area	Sent when the left button is double-clicked with the cursor in a nonclient area
WM_NCLBUTTONDOWN	Nonclient Area	Sent when the left button is pressed with the cursor in a nonclient area
WM_NCLBUTTONUP	Nonclient Area	Sent when the left button is released with the cursor in a nonclient area

continues

Table C.2. continued

Message	*Category*	*Meaning*
WM_NCMBUTTONDBLCLK	Nonclient Area	Sent when the middle button is double-clicked with the cursor in a nonclient area
WM_NCMBUTTONDOWN	Nonclient Area	Sent when the middle button is pressed with the cursor in a nonclient area
WM_NCMBUTTONUP	Nonclient Area	Sent when the middle button is released with the cursor in a nonclient area
WM_NCMOUSEMOVE	Nonclient Area	Sent when the mouse moves the cursor in a nonclient area
WM_NCPAINT	Nonclient Area	Sent when the window border needs painting
WM_NCRBUTTONDBLCLK	Nonclient Area	Sent when the right button is double-clicked with the cursor in a nonclient area
WM_NCRBUTTONDOWN	Nonclient Area	Sent when the right button is pressed with the cursor in a nonclient area
WM_NCRBUTTONUP	Nonclient Area	Sent when the right button is pressed with the cursor in a nonclient area
WM_NEXTDLGCTL	Control	Sent to the window function of a dialog box to modify the control focus
WM_OTHERWINDOWCREATED	Window Management	Notifies all overlapped and pop-up windows that a top-level, unowned window has been created
WM_OTHERWINDOWDESTROYED	Window Management	Notifies all overlapped and pop-up windows that a top-level, unowned window has been destroyed
WM_PAINT	Window Management	Sent when a request to repaint a part of the application's window is made
WM_PAINTCLIPBOARD	Clipboard	Sent to request painting of the CF_OWNERDISPLAY format

Message	*Category*	*Meaning*
WM_PAINTICON	Window Management	Sent when a request to repaint a part of the application's minimized window is made
WM_PALETTECHANGED	System Information	Sent to all windows when the system color palette is modified
WM_PALETTEISCHANGING	Window Management	Tells windows that the palette is changing
WM_PARENTNOTIFY	Window Management	Sent to the parent of a child window when the child window is created or destroyed
WM_PASTE	Edit Control	Places the data from the control window at the position of the cursor
WM_POWER	Window Management	Indicates that the system is entering suspended mode
WM_QUERYDRAGICON	Window Management	Sent when a minimized window is about to be moved
WM_QUERYENDSESSION	Window Management	Sent when the End Session command is chosen
WM_QUERYNEWPALETTE	Window Management	Sent when a window is about to receive the input focus
WM_QUERYOPEN	Window Management	Sent when an icon is to be opened into a window
WM_QUEUESYNC	Window Management	Delimits CBT messages
WM_QUIT	Window Management	Sent upon request to terminate an application
WM_RBUTTONDBLCLK	Input	Sent when the right mouse button is double-clicked
WM_RBUTTONDOWN	Input	Sent when the right mouse button is pressed
WM_RBUTTONUP	Input	Sent when the right mouse button is released
WM_RENDERALLFORMATS	Clipboard	Sent to the clipboard owner telling it that data in the clipboard must be rendered in all formats

continues

Table C.2. continued

Message	Category	Meaning
WM_RENDERFORMAT	Clipboard	Sent to the clipboard owner telling it to format the last data sent to the clipboard
WM_SETCURSOR	Input	Sent when unable to capture the mouse input and the cursor has been moved
WM_SETFOCUS	Window Management	Sent after a window receives the input focus
WM_SETFONT	Control	Modifies the font used by a control
WM_SETHOTKEY	Window Management	Assigns a hot key to a window
WM_SETREDRAW	Window Management	Either sets or clears the redraw flag
WM_SETTEXT	Window Management	Sets the window text
WM_SHOWWINDOW	Window Management	Sent when a window is hidden or shown
WM_SIZE	Window Management	Sent when a window has been sized
WM_SIZECLIPBOARD	Clipboard	Sent to the clipboard owner when the clipboard application's window size is modified
WM_SPOOLERSTATUS	System Information	Sent from the Print Manager when a job is added to or removed from the print queue
WM_SYSCHAR	System	Sent when a WM_SYSKEYUP and a WM_SYSKEYDOWN message are translated
WM_SYSCOLORCHANGE	System Information	Sent to top-level windows when the system color changes
WM_SYSCOMMAND	System	Sent when a command is selected from the System menu
WM_SYSDEADCHAR	System	Sent when a WM_SYSKEYUP and a WM_SYSKEYDOWN message are translated

Message	*Category*	*Meaning*
WM_SYSKEYDOWN	System	Sent when an <ALT - key> sequence is pressed
WM_SYSKEYUP	System	Sent when an <ALT - key> sequence is released
WM_SYSTEMERROR	System	Indicates when a system error occurs
WM_TIMECHANGE	System Information	Sent when an application changes the system time
WM_TIMER	Input	Sent when the time limit for a timer has expired
WM_UNDO	Edit Control	Performs an "undo" for the last action
WM_VKEYTOITEM	Input	Sent by a list box with LBS_WANTKEYBOARDINPUT style to the owner of the list box in response to a WM_CHAR message
WM_VSCROLL	Input and Scroll Bar	Sent when the vertical and scroll bar is activated
WM_VSCROLLCLIPBOARD	Clipboard	Sent to request vertical scrolling for the CF_OWNDERDISPLAY format
WM_WINDOWPOSCHANGED	Window Management	Informs the window that its size or position has changed
WM_WINDOWPOSCHANGING	Window Management	Informs the windows that its size or position is about to change
WM_WININICHANGE	System Information	Sent when WIN.INI, the Windows initialization file, is modified

The Command-Line Compiler

This appendix serves as a reference to the command-line compiler. The command-line compiler provides direct control over the compilation process and is often called from a makefile to develop Windows applications. The command-line compiler provided by Borland automatically compiles and links the specified files while invoking the Turbo Assembler, TASM, if it is needed to compile .ASM source files. The command-line compiler can be operated in either real or protected mode.

The command-line compiler is very flexible and Borland offers a range of options to control the compilation process. The following formats are used to invoke the command-line compiler.

Real Mode:

```
bcc [option [option...]] filename [filename...]
```

in which

`option` represents compiler options (can be none or several)

`filename` represents the filename(s) to be compiled and linked

Protected Mode:

```
bccx [option [option...]] filename [filename...]
```

in which

`option` represents compiler options (can be none or several)

`filename` represents the filename(s) to be compiled and linked

For example, `bccx test.c` would compile the file `test.c` by using the command-line compiler in protected mode.

Table D.1 lists the command-line compiler options.

Table D.1. *Command-line compiler options.*

Option	*Meaning*
`@`*`filename`*	Use the response file name
`+`*`filename`*	Use the alternate configuration file specified in *`filename`*
`-1`	Generate 80186 instructions
`-1-`	Generate 8088/8086 instructions
`-2`	Generate 80286 protected-mode compatible instructions
`-A`	Use only ANSI keywords
`-A-` or `-AT`	Use Borland C++ keywords (the default)
`-AK`	Use only Kernighan and Ritchie keywords
`-AU`	Use only UNIX keywords
`-a`	Align word
`-a-`	Align byte (default)
`-B`	Compile and call the assembler to process inline assembly code
`-b`	Make enums word-sized (default)
`-b-`	Make enum signed or unsigned
`-C`	Turn on nested comments
`-C-`	Turn off nested comments
`-c`	Compile to .OBJ, do not link
`-D`*`name`*	Define the specified name to the string consisting of the null character

Option	*Meaning*
`-D`*name*`=`*string*	Define the specified name to the specified string
`-d`	Merge duplicate strings on
`-d-`	Merge duplicate strings off (default)
`-E`*filename*	Use the specified filename as the assembler
`-e`*filename*	Link and produce the specified filename
`-Fc`	Generate COMDEFs
`-Ff`	Create far variables automatically
`-Ff=size`	Create far variables automatically and set the threshold
`-Fm`	Enable `-Fc`, `-Ff`, and `-Fs` options
`-Fs`	Assume DS=SS in all memory models
`-f`	Emulate floating point (the default)
`-f-`	Don't do floating point
`-ff`	Do fast floating point (the default)
`-ff-`	Do ANSI floating point
`-f87`	Use 8087 instructions
`-f287`	Use 80287 instructions
`-G`	Optimize for speed
`-G-`	Optimize for size
`-g`*n*	Stop warnings after *n* messages
`-H`	Generate and use precompiled headers
`-H-`	Do not generate or use precompiled headers
`-Hu`	Use but do not generate precompiled headers
`-H=`*filename*	Set the name of the file for precompiled headers
`-h`	Use fast huge pointer arithmetic
`-I`*path*	Specify directories for include files
`-i`*n*	Set significant identifier length to *n*
`-j`*n*	Stop errors after *n* messages
`-K`	Make the default character type unsigned
`-K-`	Make the default character type signed (the default)
`-k`	Turn on the standard stack frame (the default)
`-L`*path*	Directories for libraries
`-l`*x*	Pass option in *x* to the linker
`-l-`*x*	Suppress the option in *x* for the linker
`-M`	Instruct the linker to create a map file

continues

Table D.1. continued

Option	*Meaning*
`-mc`	Compile using the compact memory model
`-mh`	Compile using the huge memory model
`-ml`	Compile using the large memory model
`-mm`	Compile using the medium memory model
`-mm!`	Compile using the medium memory model; assume DS != SS
`-ms`	Compile using the small memory model
`-ms!`	Compile using the small memory model; assume DS != SS
`-mt`	Compile using the tiny memory model
`-mt!`	Compile using the tiny memory model; assume DS != SS
`-N`	Check for stack overflow
`-n`*`path`*	Specify output directory
`-O`	Optimize jumps
`-O-`	Do not optimize (the default)
`-o`*`filename`*	Compile source file to *`filename`*.obj
`-P`	Perform a C++ compile
`-P`*`ext`*	Perform a C++ compile and set the default extension to the extension specified in *`ext`*
`-P-`	Perform a C++ or C compile depending on the source file extension (the default)
`-P-`*`ext`*	Perform a C++ or C compile depending on the source file extension; set the default extension to the extension specified in *`ext`*
`-p`	Use Pascal calling convention
`-p-`	Use C calling convention (the default)
`-Qe`	Use all available EMS memory
`-Qe-`	Use no EMS memory
`-Qx`	Use all available extended memory
`-Qx=`*`nnnn`*	Reserve the number of Kbytes in *`nnnn`* for other programs
`-Qx=`*`nnnn,yyyy`*	Reserve *`nnnn`* Kybtes of extended memory for other programs and *`yyyy`* for the compiler
`-Qx=`*`yyyy`*	Reserve *`yyyy`* Kbytes of extended memory for the compiler
`-Qx-`	Use no extended memory
`-r`	Use register variables
`-r-`	Do not use register variables

Option	Meaning
-rd	Keep only declared register variables in the registers
-S	Produce .ASM output
-T*string*	Pass the specified string as an option to TASM or the assembler specified with the -*E* option
-T-	Remove all assembler options
-U*name*	Undefine the specified name
-u	Generate underscores
-u-	Do not generate underscores
-V	Use smart C++ virtual tables
-Vf	Use far C++ virtual tables
-Vs	Use local C++ virtual tables
-V0,-V1	Use external and public C++ virtual tables
-v,-v-	Turn on source debugging
-vi,-vi-	Control the expansion of inline functions
-W	Create an .OBJ for Windows with all functions exportable
-WD	Create an .OBJ for Windows to be linked as a .DLL with all functions exportable
-WDE	Create an .OBJ for Windows to be linked as a .DLL with explicit export functions
-WE	Create an .OBJ for Windows with explicit export functions
-WS	Create an .OBJ for Windows that uses smart callbacks
-w	Display warnings
-w-	Do not display warnings
-w*xxx*	Allow the warning message in *xxx*
-w-*xxx*	Do not allow the warning message in *xxx*
-X	Disable compiler autodependency output
-Y	Enable overlay code generation
-Yo	Overlay the compiled files
-y	Turn on line numbers
-Z	Enable register usage optimization
-zA*name*	Specify code class
-zB*name*	Specify BSS class
-zC*name*	Specify code segment
-zD*name*	Specify BSS segment
-zE*name*	Specify far segment

continues

Table D.1. continued

Option	*Meaning*
`-zFname`	Specify far class
`-zGname`	Specify BSS group
`-zHname`	Specify far group
`-zPname`	Specify code group
`-zRname`	Specify data segment
`-zSname`	Specify data group
`-zTname`	Specify data class
`-zX*`	Use default name for X

Bibliography

Borland International. *Borland C++—Getting Started*. Scotts Valley, CA: Borland International, 1991.

———. *Borland C++—Library Reference*. Scotts Valley, CA: Borland International, 1991.

———. *Borland C++—Programmer's Guide*. Scotts Valley, CA: Borland International, 1991.

———. *Borland C++—User's Guide*. Scotts Valley, CA: Borland International, 1991.

———. *Borland C++—Whitewater Resource Toolkit*. Scotts Valley, CA: Borland International, 1991.

Microsoft Corporation. *Microsoft Windows Software Development Kit—Guide to Programming*. Redmond, WA: Microsoft Corporation, 1990.

———. *Microsoft Windows Software Development Kit—Reference Volume 1*. Redmond, WA: Microsoft Corporation, 1990.

———. *Microsoft Windows Software Development Kit—Reference Volume 2*. Redmond, WA: Microsoft Corporation, 1990.

Norton, Peter and Paul Yao. *Peter Norton's Windows 3.0 Power Programming Techniques*. New York: Bantam Computer Books, 1990.

Petzold, Charles. *Programming Windows: The Microsoft Guide to Writing Applications for Windows 3*. Redmond, WA: Microsoft Press, 1990.

P

Program Index

Listing 2.1. The module definition file for the fundamental window example, 27
Listing 2.2. C source code for the fundamental window example, 27-28
Listing 3.1. The definition file for the point drawing example, 36
Listing 3.2. The C source file for the point drawing example, 36-38
Listing 3.3. The definition file for the line drawing example, 40
Listing 3.4. The C source file for the line drawing example, 40-42
Listing 3.5. The definition file for the arc drawing example, 44
Listing 3.6. The C source file for the arc drawing example, 44-46
Listing 3.7. The definition file for the filled figure example, 50
Listing 3.8. The C source file for the filled figure example, 51-53
Listing 3.9. The definition file for the fill example, 54
Listing 3.10. The C source file for the fill example, 55-57
Listing 3.11. The definition file for the `TextOut` example, 59
Listing 3.12. The C source file for the `TextOut` example, 59-62
Listing 3.13. The definition file for the `TabbedTextOut` example, 63
Listing 3.14. The C source file for the `TabbedTextOut` example, 64-66
Listing 3.15. The definition file for the font example, 69

Listing 3.16. The C source file for the font example, 69-72
Listing 3.17. The definition file for the scrolling text example, 77
Listing 3.18. The C source file for the scrolling text example, 77-82
Listing 4.1. The definition file for the accelerator example, 87
Listing 4.2. The C source file for the accelerator example, 87-89
Listing 4.3. The resource file for the accelerator example, 89
Listing 4.4. The definition file for the bitmap example, 92-93
Listing 4.5. The C source file for the bitmap example, 93-95
Listing 4.6. The resource file for the bitmap example, 95
Listing 4.7. The definition file for the cursor example, 97
Listing 4.8. The C source file for the cursor example, 97-99
Listing 4.9. The resource file for the cursor example, 99
Listing 4.10. The definition file for the dialog box example, 101
Listing 4.11. The C source file for the dialog box example, 101-105
Listing 4.12. The resource file for the dialog box example, 105-106
Listing 4.13. The definition file for the icon example, 107
Listing 4.14. The C source file for the icon example, 107-109
Listing 4.15. The resource file for the icon example, 110
Listing 4.16. The definition file for the menu example, 112
Listing 4.17. The C source file for the menu example, 112-115
Listing 4.18. The resource file for the menu example, 115-116
Listing 4.19. The definition file for the string example, 118
Listing 4.20. The C source file for the string example, 118-121
Listing 4.21. The resource file for the string example, 121-122
Listing 5.1. The definition file for the keyboard example, 130-131
Listing 5.2. The C source file for the keyboard example, 131-136
Listing 6.1. The definition file for the mouse example, 143
Listing 6.2. The C source file for the mouse example, 143-146
Listing 7.1. The definition file for the child window example, 162
Listing 7.2. The C source file for the child window example, 162-164
Listing 9.1. The definition file for the MDI example, 180
Listing 9.2. The C source file for the MDI example, 180-186
Listing 9.3. The resource file for the MDI example, 186-187
Listing 10.1. The definition file for the DLL, 194
Listing 10.2. The C source file for the DLL, 194
Listing 10.3. The definition file for the DLL example, 195
Listing 10.4. The C source file for the DLL example, 196-198
Listing 12.1. The basic window example, 267-268
Listing 12.2. The module definition file for the fundamental window example, 269
Listing 12.3. C source code for the fundamental window example, 269-270
Listing 12.4. The line drawing example, 271-272

Listing 12.5. The arc drawing example, 273-275
Listing 12.6. The filled figures example, 276-277
Listing 12.7. The `TextOut` example, 278-280
Listing 12.8. The `TabbedTextOut` example, 281-282
Listing 12.9. The Scroller example, 284-285
Listing 12.10. The resource file for the accelerator example, 286-287
Listing 12.11. The C++ source file for the accelerator example, 287-289
Listing 12.12. The resource file for the bitmap example, 291
Listing 12.13. The C++ source file for the bitmap example, 291-292
Listing 12.14. The cursor example, 294
Listing 12.15. The resource file for the dialog example, 295-296
Listing 12.16. The C++ source file for the dialog example, 296-299
Listing 12.17. The resource file for the icon example, 301
Listing 12.18. The C++ source file for the icon example, 301-303
Listing 12.19. The resource file for the menu example, 304-305
Listing 12.20. The C++ source file for the menu example, 305-307
Listing 12.21. The resource file for the MDI example, 309
Listing 12.22. The C++ source file for the MDI example, 309-310

I

Index

Symbols

`\t` tab indicator, 63
386 enhanced mode, 166

A

abort functions, 889
  defining, 1196
`AbortDoc` function, 318, 1305
`ABORTDOC` printer escape, 1164
aborting jobs, 1164
Accelerator editor, 86, 1213-1214
accelerator
  keys, 85-89, 1210
    defining selection actions, 286-290
    translating into menu commands, 984-985
  table, loading, 712
accessing
  data, 425
  resource files, 319
  System menu, 631
  system palette, 635, 934
`AccessResource` function, 318-319, 1305
`ActivationResponse` member function, 1292, 1295
active windows, 124
`AddAtom` function, 319, 1305
`AddFontResource` function, 320-321, 1305
addresses
  base, locating, 624
  for functions, 612
  logical, 166
`AddString` member function, 1269

AdjustWindowRect function, 320, 1305
AdjustWindowRectEx function, 321, 1305
AfterDispatchHandler member function, 1295
Airbrush tool, 1222
aligning text, 75-76
  setting flags, 935
Alignment palette, Dialog editor, 1218-1219
allocated memory, freeing, 528
AllocDiskSpace function, 322-323, 1305
AllocDStoCSAlias function, 323, 1305
AllocFileHandles function, 324, 1306
AllocGDIMem function, 324, 1306
AllocMem function, 325, 1306
AllocResource function, 325, 1306
AllocSelector function, 326, 1306
AllocUserMem function, 326, 1306
alphabetical characters, 699
alphanumeric character, 699
AnimatePalette function, 327-328, 1306
ANSI
  character set, 129
  table, 582
AnsiLower function, 328, 1306
AnsiLowerBuff function, 329, 1306
AnsiNext function, 329, 1306
AnsiPrev function, 330, 1306
AnsiToOem function, 330-331, 1306
AnsiToOemBuff function, 331, 1306
AnsiUpper function, 331-332, 1306
AnsiUpperBuff function, 332, 1306
AnyPopup function, 332-333, 1306
AppendMenu function, 333-334, 1306
application-defined hook function, deleting, 990
applications
  behaviors, sharing with libraries, 1277-1279
  classes
    global, 1358
    local, 1358
  client, conversations, 428, 429
  creating, 22-24
  executing, 718-720, 1004-1005
  execution functions, 1333
  fundamental window, 26-29
  Help, 1006
  initializing in WinMain function, 19-20
  MDI, 173-175
    creating, 308-313
  ObjectWindows, 212
    code structure, 260-262
    defining structures and behaviors, 1233-1235
    developing with IDE, 264-265
    executing, 216
    initializing, 215-216
    main program, 214-215
    minimal, 266-270
    project files, 262-264
    terminating, 216-217
  receiving keyboard input, 124
  servers, conversations, 428-429
  suspending, 1003
  system palettes, accessing, 635
  terminating, 979
  using DLLs from, 195-198
  window components, 8-11
  see also utilities
Arc function, 39, 43, 334-335, 1306
arcs, drawing, 43-46, 273-275, 1198
  elliptical, 334-335
ArrangeIconicWindows function, 336, 1306
ArrangeIcons member function, 1273-1274
AssignMenu member function, 1292
asynchronous operations, errors, 809-810

atoms
- adding globally, 660
- integers, creating, 750
- locating
  - globally, 669
  - names, 674
- management functions, 1334
- reference count, decreasing, 662
- tables
  - adding strings, 319
  - hash, initializing, 690

auto-scrolling windows, 255-257, 283-285, 1284-1288

AutoScroll member function, 1286

B

background
- class brushes, 149-150
- color
  - setting device context, 892
  - text attribute, 68
- mode
  - setting device context, 893
  - text attribute, 68
- windows, light gray, 229, 1244

BANDINFO printer escape, 1164-1165

banding, 1164

base
- addresses, locating, 624
- classes, 204
  - for all ObjectWindows derived classes, 211-212, 1231-1232
- defining, selectors, 930
- units, dialog boxes, 564

BeforeDispatchHandler member function, 1296

BEGIN_PATH printer escape, 1165

BeginDeferWindowPos function, 336, 1306

BeginPaint function, 337, 1306

BeginView member function, 1286

behaviors
- defining for windows, dialog boxes, and controls, 1294-1303
- sharing between libraries and applications, 1277-1279

binary
- file formats supported by Resource Workshop, 1211
- raster operations (ROP2), 48

BitBlt function, 92, 338-339, 1306

bitmaps, 90-95, 1210
- bits
  - retrieving, 565-567
  - setting, 906
- BWCC push buttons, 1235-1236
- checkmark, default, 588
- copying to destination device, 338-339
- creating, 370-372, 375, 1220-1225
  - device-specific, 389-391
  - discardable, 392
- defining, 917
- device-independent, 909
  - stretching, 964-965
- dimensions, 891-892
- displaying splash images, 251-252
- editing, 1220-1225
- functions, 1334
- loading and displaying, 290-293, 713
- static text controls, 1241-1242
- stretching, 962
  - modes, device context, 626

bits
- retrieving for bitmaps, 565-567
- setting in bitmaps, 906

Black Rectangle tool, 1218

BM_GETCHECK message, 1018, 1361

BM_GETSTATE message, 1018, 1361

BM_SETCHECK message, 1019, 1361

BM_SETSTATE message, 1019, 1361

BM_SETSTYLE message, 1020, 1361

.BMP files, 1211
BMSetStyle member function, 1243
BN_CLICKED message, 1021, 1361
BN_DISABLE message, 1361
BN_DOUBLECLICKED message, 1021, 1361
BNClicked member function, 1245-1246, 1280
borders
  drawing for filled figures, 50-53
  windows, 9
bounding rectangles, 894
breaks, text, 1056
BringWindowToTop function, 339-340, 1306
brushes
  background class, 149-150
  creating, 53-57
  logical, creating, 372-373, 399-400
  origins, 895
    resetting, 993
  pattern, creating, 404
  solid, creating, 413
  stock, 53-54, 625-626
buffers
  allocating, 750
  freeing, 745
build member function, 1236-1244, 1246, 1248, 1252, 1255-1256, 1260, 1262-1263, 1266, 1268-1269, 1273, 1274-1275, 1280-1281, 1286, 1289, 1292, 1296
BuildCommDCB function, 340-343, 1306
bump divider controls, 251
BUTTON class controls, 159
  notification codes, 159-160
  styles, 154-155
buttons, 1242-1244
  BWCC controls, 243
    bitmap, 1235-1236
    radio, 242-243, 1239-1240
  clicking time span, 912
  control messages, 1359
  displaying in child windows, 161-164
  editing in dialog boxes, 347
  interpreting mouse, 967
  Maximize, 11
  Minimize, 11
  object types, 236
  radio, 1279-1280
    adding checkmarks, 349
    controls, 242
BWCC
  bitmap push buttons, 1235-1236
  button controls, 243
  check boxes, 1236-1237
    controls, 241
  group boxes, 1238-1239
  radio buttons, 1239-1240
    controls, 242-243
  static dividers, 1237-1238
    controls, 251
bypassing print-driver code, 1167, 1195
bytes
  allocating, 661
  high-order values, 686
  local memory block, specifying, 734
  low-order, 721
  resources, counting, 956

C

C source code files, 24-25
  accelerator example, 87-89
  arc drawing example, 44-46
  bitmap example, 93-95
  child window example, 162-164
  cursor example, 97-99
  dialog box example, 101-105
  DLL example, 196-198
  fill example, 55-57
  filled figure example, 51-53
  font example, 69-72

for DLLs, 191-194
fundamental window example, 27-28, 269-270
icon example, 107-109
keyboard example, 131-136
line drawing example, 40-42
MDI, 177
MDI example, 180-186
menu example, 112-115
mouse example, 143-146
point drawing example, 36-38
scrolling text example, 77-82
string example, 118-121
TabbedTextOut example, 64-66
TextOut example, 59-62
C++ source code files, 24-25
accelerator example, 287-289
arc drawing example, 273-275
bitmap example, 291-292
creating in ObjectWindows, 263
cursor example, 294
dialog example, 296-299
filled figures example, 276-277
icon example, 301-303
line drawing example, 271-272
MDI example, 309-310
menu example, 305-307
Scroller example, 284-285
TabbedTextOut example, 281-282
TextOut example, 278-280
callback functions
defining, 693
deleting, 693
installing, 926
notification, defining, 772
CallMsgFilter function, 343-344, 1306
CallNextHookEx function, 344, 1306
CallWindowProc function, 344-345, 1306
Cancel member function, 230, 1252
CanClear member function, 1264
CanClose member function, 217, 1234, 1262, 1264, 1296
CanUndo member function, 1256
Caption control, Dialog editor, 1216
captions, setting in windows, 949
carets, 129-136
blink rate, setting, 896
creating, 374
displaying, 952
functions, 1334-1335
positioning, 896
CascadeChildren member function, 1273, 1275
Catch function, 345, 1306
CB_ADDSTRING message, 1021, 1361
CB_DELETESTRING message, 1022, 1361
CB_DIR message, 1022, 1362
CB_FINDSTRING message, 1023, 1362
CB_GETCOUNT message, 1023, 1362
CB_GETCURSEL message, 1024, 1362
CB_GETDROPPEDCONTROLRECT message, 1024, 1362
CB_GETDROPPEDSTATE message, 1025, 1362
CB_GETEDITSEL message, 1025, 1362
CB_GETEXTENDEDUI message, 1026, 1362
CB_GETITEMDATA message, 1026, 1362
CB_GETITEMHEIGHT message, 1027, 1362
CB_GETLBTEXT message, 1027, 1362
CB_GETLBTEXTLEN message, 1027, 1362
CB_INSERTSTRING message, 1028, 1362
CB_LIMITTEXT message, 1028, 1362
CB_RESETCONTENT message, 1028, 1362
CB_SELECTSTRING message, 1029, 1363
CB_SETCURSEL message, 1029, 1363
CB_SETEDITSEL message, 1030, 1363
CB_SETEXTENDEDUI message, 1030, 1363
CB_SETITEMDATA message, 1031, 1363
CB_SETITEMHEIGHT message, 1031, 1363

CB_SHOWDROPDOWN message, 1031, 1363
CBN_CLOSEUP message, 1032, 1363
CBN_DBLCLK message, 1032, 1363
CBN_DROPDOWN message, 1032, 1363
CBN_EDITCHANGE message, 1033, 1363
CBN_EDITUPDATE message, 1033, 1363
CBN_ERRSPACE message, 1034, 1363
CBN_KILLFOCUS message, 1034, 1363
CBN_SELCHANGE message, 1034, 1363
CBN_SELENDCANCEL message, 1035, 1364
CBN_SELENDOK message, 1035, 1364
CBN_SETFOCUS message, 1035, 1364
ChangeClipboardChain function, 346, 1306
ChangeMenu function, 346-347, 1306
ChangeSelector function, 347, 1307
Character-to-glyph mapping, 578
characters
  alphabetical, 699
  alphanumeric, 699
  ANSI set, 129
  dead, 128
  double-byte, 702
  formatting, 1013-1014
  intercharacter spacing text attribute, 68
  lowercase, 700
    converting to, 328-329
  messages, 124-125, 128-129
  OEM set, 129
    converting to, 330-331
  placing
    in receive queues, 989
    in transmit queues, 987
  specifying with pointer, 329-330
  strings, displaying, 972, 980
  transmission
    restoring, 359
    suspending, 900
  uppercase, 700
    converting to, 332
  writing to communication device, 1010
Check Box tool, 1217
check boxes, 1245-1247
  BWCC, 1236-1237
    controls, 241
  checking, 1018
  controls, 240-241
Check member function, 1246
CheckDlgButton function, 347-348, 1307
checking
  check boxes, 1018
  radio buttons, 1018
checkmarks
  adding to radio buttons, 349
  bitmaps, default, 588
  deleting from menu items, 348-349
CheckMenuItem function, 348-349, 1307
CheckRadioButton function, 349, 1307
child windows, 124, 350, 701
  arranging, 336
  bringing to top, 339
  controls, 159-161
    displaying buttons with, 161-164
  handles, 646
  identification number (ID), 567
  maintaining lists of, 217-221
  MDI procedures, 177
  minimizing or maximizing, 178-180
  sizing, 770
ChildWindowFromPoint function, 349-350, 1307
ChildWithId member function, 1296
ChooseColor function, 350-352, 1307
ChooseFont function, 352-356, 1307
Chord function, 50-53, 356-357, 1307
chords, drawing, 356
class display context, 1351
class keyword, 203
classes
  application global, 1358
  application local, 1358

base, 204
names, registering with library, 815
object-oriented programming, 202-203
inheritance, 204-207
ObjectWindows, *see* ObjectWindows classes
streamable, 1290-1291
system global, 1357
window
BUTTON, 154-155
COMBOBOX, 155
creating, 225-226
defining, 148-150
EDIT, 156
LISTBOX, 156-157
SCROLLBAR, 157
STATIC, 158-164
types, 153
ClassFirst function, 357, 1307
ClassNext function, 358, 1307
classwords, setting, 898
Clear member function, 1248-1289
ClearCommBreak function, 359, 1307
ClearList member function, 1269
ClearModify member function, 1256
clicking mouse, 138
client
areas, 9
adding, 696-697
coordinate systems, 34-35
display context for specified windows, 558
mouse messages, 140-141
updating rectangles, 860
updating regions, 860
updating windows, 994
coordinates, converting to screen coordinates, 359-360
documents, registering with library, 815
windows, 173, 1272-1273
class, 254
ClientToScreen function, 359-360, 1307
CLIP_TO_PATH printer escape, 1166
clipboard
closing, 361
formats, 701
counting, 370
list priorities, 610
registering, 864
functions, 1335
messages, 1360
viewing, 900
ClipCursor function, 360-361, 1307
clipping
functions, 1335
regions, 1335
bounded, 1166
defining, 694
moving, 776
selecting, 885
CloseChildren member function, 1275
CloseClipboard function, 361, 1307
CloseComm function, 361, 1307
CloseDriver function, 362, 1307
CloseMetaFile function, 362, 1307
CloseWindow
function, 363, 1307
member function, 217, 1252, 1296
closing
clipboard, 361
communication devices, 361
device drivers, 362
documents, 821
files, 709, 744
keys, 862
metafile devices, 362
windows, 363
CMArrangeIcons member function, 1275
CMCascadeChildren member function, 1275
CMCloseChildren member function, 1275

CMCreateChild member function, 1275
CMEditClear member function, 1256
CMEditCopy member function, 1256
CMEditCut member function, 1256
CMEditDelete member function, 1256
CMEditFind member function, 1260
CMEditFindNext member function, 1260
CMEditPaste member function, 1256
CMEditReplace member function, 1260
CMEditUndo member function, 1256
CMExit member function, 1296
CMFileNew member function, 1264
CMFileOpen member function, 1264
CMFileSave member function, 1264
CMFileSaveAs member function, 1264
CMTileChildren member function, 1275
codes
  context, 126
  executing, data segment selectors, 323
  hit test, 139-140
  notification, 159-161
  OEM scan, 126
  segments
    defining tasks, 978
    selector, 323
    validating, 995
  selectors, converting to data selectors, 347
  virtual key, 126-128
    converting to ANSI, 982
colors
  background
    defining, 1199
    setting, 892
    text attribute, 68
  current, 627-628
  device contexts, updating, 994
  inverting, 699
  palette functions, 1336
  RGB, selecting, 875
  selecting, 350-352
  setting, 932-933
  specifying, 596
  text attribute, 68
  values, 619
    for pixels, 609
    green, 581
Colors palette, Paint editor, 1223
CombineRgn function, 363-364, 1307
Combo Box tool, 1217
combo boxes, 1247-1249
  control types, 238-241
  messages, 1360
COMBOBOX class controls, 159
  notification codes, 160-161
  styles, 155
command-line compiler options, 1381-1386
CommDlgExtendedError function, 364-366, 1307
common
  dialog functions, 1336
  display context, 1351
communication
  devices
    characters, writing, 1010
    closing, 361
    event masks, setting, 901
    states, setting, 902
  functions, 1336-1337
comparing strings, 428, 741-742
COMPRESS.EXE utility, 573
connections, cancelling, 1008
context code, 126
Control menu, 10
control messages, 1360
Control value table, 578
controls, 99
  behaviors, defining, 1294-1303
  button, 236

BWCC
button, 243
check box, 241
divider, 251
radio button, 242-243
Caption, 1216
check box, 240-241
child window, 159-161
combo box, 238-241
dialog box
defining actions, 295-300
locating, 597
retrieving, 568
edit, 246-248
functions
for creating, 1250-1251
member, 235
group box, 243-245
list box, 237-238
radio button, 242
scroll bar, 249-251
static, 245-246, 248-249
static bitmap, 251-252
conversations
initiating
with client applications, 428-429
with server applications, 428-430
terminating, 433
transactions
disabling, 434
enabling, 434
coordinates
client, converting to screen coordinates, 359-360
converting, 755
device, copying, 650
functions, 1337
logical, 555
rectangles, 617, 646-647
storing, 991
screen
converting to client coordinates, 880
messages, 592
systems, 34-35
viewports, 649
window origins, 653
`Copy` member function, 1256-1257
`CopyCursor` function, 366-367, 1307
`CopyIcon` function, 367, 1307
copying
bitmaps to destination devices, 338-339
cursors, 367
data, 436
device coordinates, 650
execution time for tasks, 981
files
source, to destination files, 368
titles, 575
version information, 575-576
icons, 367
metafiles, 368-369
rectangles, 369
strings, 611
key name, 614
text strings, 866
viewports, 649
Virtual Machine
executing, 981
execution time, 981
`CopyLZFile` function, 367-368, 1307
`CopyMetaFile` function, 368-369, 1307
`CopyRect` function, 369, 1307
`CountClipboardFormats` function, 370, 1307
`Create` member function, 225, 1252, 1292, 1296
`CreateBitmap` function, 370-371, 1307
`CreateBitmapIndirect` function, 371-372, 1307
`CreateBrushIndirect` function, 54-57, 372-373, 1307

CreateCaret function, 373-374, 1307
CreateChild member function, 1275-1276
CreateChildren member function, 1296
CreateCompatibleBitmap function, 374-375, 1308
CreateCompatibleDC function, 375, 1308
CreateCursor function, 375-376, 1308
CreateDC function, 376-381, 1308
CreateDialog function, 381-382, 1308
CreateDialogIndirect function, 382-384, 1308
CreateDialogIndirectParam function, 385-387, 1308
CreateDialogParam function, 387-389, 1308
CreateDIBitmap function, 389-391, 1308
CreateDIBPatternBrush function, 391-392, 1308
CreateDiscardableBitmap function, 392-393, 1308
CreateEllipticRgn function, 393, 1308
CreateEllipticRgnIndirect function, 394, 1308
CreateFont function, 69, 394-397, 1308
CreateFontIndirect function, 69-72, 397-399, 1308
CreateHatchBrush function, 54-57, 399-400, 1308
CreateIC function, 400, 1308
CreateIcon function, 401, 1308
CreateMenu function, 402, 1308
CreateMetaFile function, 402, 1308
CreatePalette function, 402-404, 1308
CreatePatternBrush function, 54-57, 404, 1308
CreatePen function, 47-48, 404-405, 1308
CreatePenIndirect function, 39, 47-48, 405-406, 1308
CreatePolygonRgn function, 406-407, 1308
CreatePolyPolygonRgn function, 407-408, 1308
CreatePopupMenu function, 409, 1308
CreateRectRgn function, 409-410, 1308
CreateRectRgnIndirect function, 410, 1308
CreateRoundRectRgn function, 411, 1309
CreateScalableFontResource function, 412, 1309
CreateSolidBrush function, 54-57, 413, 1309
CreateWindow function, 150-158, 413-421, 1309
CreateWindowEx function, 151-158, 422-423, 1309
creating
  applications, 22-24
  bitmaps, 370-372, 375
    discardable, 392
  brushes, 53-57
  carets, 374
  cursors, 376
  device context, 375-381
  device-specific bitmaps, 389-391
  dialog boxes, 229-232, 350-352, 381-383
    instance, 385-386
    system-defined, 601-604
  DLLs (dynamic link libraries), 191-194
  elliptical regions, 393-394
  filled figures, 49-50
  fonts, 394-399
    resources, 412

global memory objects, 432
handles
for metafiles, 593
string, 432
icons, 401
information context, 400-401
keys, 862
logical brushes
with device-independent bitmaps, 392
with hatch styles, 399-400
MDI documents, 177-187
metafiles, 402, 919
palettes, 402-404
paths, 1165
pattern brushes, 404
pens, 47-48, 405-406
polygonal regions, 406-408
popup-menus, 409-410
rectangles, 857, 924
rectangular regions, 410, 925
solid brushes, 413
system timer event, 937
timer event, 937
windows, 147-158, 222-226, 413-423
.CUR files, 1211
cursors, 96-99, 129, 138, 1210
copying, 367
creating and editing, 1220-1225
displaying, 953
functions, 1337
hiding, 953
loading, 713
movements
monitoring, 142-146
restricting, 360
positioning, 905
predefined, 138
redefining, 293-295
screen coordinates, retrieving, 557
shape, defining, 905
Custom Control tool, 1218
`Cut` member function, 1257

D

data
accessing, 425
adding, 425
bypassing the print-driver code, 1167
copying, 436
from instances, 582
handles
defining, 899
freeing, 435
locating from property list, 614
reading from files, 740
retrieving from server, 819
sending to printer, 1167
transactions, initiating, 426-427
writing, 743
data segments
current
locking, 735
unlocking, 992
selectors, executing codes, 323
stacks, returning, 968
data selectors, converting to code selectors, 347
data structures
`LOGFONT`, 69
`TEXTMETRIC`, 73-75
`TScrollBarData`, 1283
`TWindowAttr`, 222-223
`WNDCLASS`, 148-150
DDE (dynamic data exchange)
functions, 1338
messages, 1360
`DdeAbandonTransaction` function, 424, 1309
`DdeAccessData` function, 424-425, 1309

DdeAddData function, 425-426, 1309
DdeCallback function, 1309
DdeClientTransaction function, 426-427, 1309
DdeCmpStringHandles function, 427-428, 1309
DdeConnect function, 428-429, 1309
DdeConnectList function, 430, 1309
DdeCreateDataHandle function, 431-432, 1309
DdeCreateStringHandle function, 432, 1309
DdeDisconnect function, 433, 1309
DdeDisconnectList function, 433, 1309
DdeEnableCallback function, 434, 1309
DdeFreeDataHandle function, 434-435, 1309
DdeFreeStringHandle function, 435, 1309
DdeGetData function, 436, 1309
DdeGetLastError function, 436-439, 1309
DdeInitialize function, 439-441, 1309
DdeKeepStringHandle function, 441, 1309
DdeNameService function, 442, 1309
DdePostAdvise function, 443, 1309
DdeQueryConvInfo function, 443-446, 1309
DdeQueryNextServer function, 447, 1309
DdeQueryString function, 447-448, 1309
DdeReconnect function, 448, 1309
DdeSetUserHandle function, 449, 1309
DdeUnaccessData function, 449, 1309
DdeUninitialize function, 450, 1309
dead characters, 128
DebugBreak function, 450, 1309
debugging functions, 1338
DefChildProc member function, 1296
DefCommandProc member function, 1297
DefDlgProc function, 450-451, 1309
DefDriverProc function, 451, 1310
DeferWindowPos function, 452-453, 1310
DefFrameProc function, 177, 453-454, 1310
DefHookProc function, 454-455, 1310
DefineHandleTable function, 455
definition files, *see* module definition files
DefMDIChildProc function, 177, 455-456, 1310
DefNotificationProc member function, 1297
DefWindowProc function, 139-140, 456, 1310
DefWndProc member function, 1297
DeleteAtom function, 457, 1310
DeleteDC function, 457, 1310
DeleteLine member function, 1257
DeleteMenu function, 458, 1310
DeleteMetaFile function, 458-459, 1310
DeleteObject function, 459, 1310
DeleteSelection member function, 1257
DeleteString member function, 1269
DeleteSubText member function, 1257
deleting
  hook functions, 989
    application-defined, 990
  keys, 863
  strings, 1022
    list box, 1061
  update regions, rectangles, 996
  windows, 955
    class, 994
DeltaPos member function, 1281
desktop, Windows, 560
  handles, 560

Destroy member function, 1252-1253, 1297
DestroyCaret function, 459, 1310
DestroyCursor function, 460, 1310
DestroyIcon function, 460, 1310
DestroyMenu function, 461, 1310
DestroyWindow function, 461, 1310
device contexts, 32-33
  background
    color, setting, 892
    mode, setting, 893
  bitmap stretching mode, 626
  creating, 375-381
  drawing modes, 618
  functions, 1338-1339
  height, 652
  origin, 560
  releasing, 868
  restoring, 874
  retrieving, 651
  saving, 876
  text attributes, 67-68
  updating, 873
    colors, 994
  viewport extents, defining, 939
  viewport origin
    defining, 941
    setting, 940
  width, 652
  window extents, defining, 942
  window origin, defining, 944
device control block codes, 340-343
device coordinate systems, 34-35
device drivers
  closing, 362
  information, 570-571
  instances, enumerating, 598
  messages, 1360
    sending, 888
  module handles, 571
  mouse, 138
  printer, initializing, 961
device-dependent bitmaps, 90
device-independent bitmaps, 90, 909
device-specific bitmaps, creating, 389-391
DeviceCapabilities function, 462-467, 1310
DEVICEDATA printer escape, 1167
DeviceMode function, 467, 1310
devices
  communication, closing, 361
  metafile, closing, 362
  redirecting, 1007
    local, 1009
dialog box functions, 1339
dialog boxes, 99-106, 1210
  behaviors, defining, 1294-1303
  buttons, editing, 347
  controls, 1251-1255
    aligning, 1218-1219
    defining actions, 295-300
    locating, 597
    retrieving, 568
  creating, 229-232, 350-352, 381-383
    system-defined, 619
  file, 232-233, 1261-1263
  input, 233-234, 1267-1268
  search-and-replace, 234
  system-defined, creating, 601-604
  text, converting to integers, 568
  units
    base, 564
    converting to screen units, 753
dialog buttons, status, 703
Dialog editor, 99, 1215
  Alignment palette, 1218-1219
  Caption control, 1216
  Tools palette, 1216-1218
dialog procedure, 99
DialogBox function, 468-469, 1310
DialogBoxIndirect function, 469-471, 1310
DialogBoxIndirectParam function, 472-474, 1310

DialogBoxParam function, 474-476, 1310
dip divider controls, 251
DirectedYield function, 476, 1310
directory pathnames, 656
DisableAutoCreate member function, 1297
DisableTransfer member function, 1297
discardable moveable segments, 170-171
disk space, allocating, 322-323, 987
DispatchAMessage member function, 1297
DispatchMessage function, 476-477, 1310
DispatchScroll member function, 1297
display
  and movement functions, 1339-1340
  contexts, types, 1351
  devices, capability, 561-564
  elements, size, 631-633
dividers, static BWCC, 1237-1238
  controls, 251
DlgDirList function, 477-478, 1310
DlgDirListComboBox function, 479-480, 1310
DlgDirSelect function, 480-481, 1310
DlgDirSelectComboBox function, 481, 1310
DlgDirSelectComboBoxEx function, 1311
DlgDirSelectEx function, 1311
.DLL files, 1211
DLLs (dynamic link libraries)
  creating, 191-194
  import libraries, 190
  ObjectWindows, 264
  static versus dynamic linking, 189-190
  using from Windows applications, 195-198
DM_GETDEFID message, 1036, 1364
DM_SETDEFID message, 1036, 1364
documents
  closing, 821
  MDI, creating, 177-187
  registering
    client, 815
    with library, 816
  renaming, 818
  saving, 819
DOS
  attribute values, specifying, 1061
  Program Data Base (PDB), 554-555
  version numbers, 648
DOS3Call function, 481-482, 1311
DoSearch member function, 1260
double-byte characters, 702
double-clicking
  icons, 106
  length between clicks, 570
  mouse, 138
DPtoLP function, 482, 1311
draft modes, specifying, 1167
DRAFTMODE printer escape, 1167
DragAcceptFiles function, 483, 1311
DragFinish function, 483, 1311
dragging and dropping
  files, 6
  functions for, 1340
dragging mouse, 138
DragQueryFile function, 484, 1311
DragQueryPoint function, 484-485, 1311
DrawFocusRect function, 485-486, 1311
DrawIcon function, 486-487, 1311
drawing
  arcs, 273-275, 1198
    ellipitical, 43-46, 334-335
  attribute functions, 1340
  chords, 356
  filled figures, 275-278
    borders for, 50-53

in windows
disabling, 739
enabling, 739
lines, 39-49, 270-273, 711
modes, 48-49
device contexts, 618
locating, 618
setting, 927
points, 35-39
rectangles on printers, 1168
text, 58-67
grayed, 685-686
with Graphics Device Interface (GDI) output functions, 639
tool functions, 1340-1341
DrawItem member function, 1297
DrawMenuBar function, 487, 1311
DRAWPATTERNRECT printer escape, 1168-1169
DrawText function, 487-489, 1311
DriverProc function, 1311
drivers, *see* device drivers
drives
temporary, 636
types
fixed, 571-572
remote, 571-572
removable, 571-572
drop-down
combo boxes, 238
list combo boxes, 239
DRV_CLOSE message, 1036, 1364
DRV_CONFIGURE message, 1037, 1364
DRV_DISABLE message, 1038, 1364
DRV_ENABLE message, 1039, 1364
DRV_FREE message, 1039, 1364
DRV_INSTALL message, 1040, 1364
DRV_LOAD message, 1041, 1364
DRV_OPEN message, 1042, 1364
DRV_POWER message, 1043, 1364
DRV_QUERYCONFIGURE message, 1042, 1364
DRV_REMOVE message, 1044, 1365
DRV_USER message, 1045
dumps, MDI application, 311-313
Duplicate tool, 1216
dynamic binding, *see* polymorphism
dynamic link libraries, *see* DLLs
dynamic linking versus static linking, 189-190

E

EDIT class controls, 159
notification codes, 160
styles, 156
edit controls, 246-248, 1255-1259
input focus
losing, 1059
receiving, 1060
memory, allocating, 1058
messages, 1360
modify flags, values, 1053
operations, undoing, 1058
read-only states, 1054
scrolling, 1052
text
altering, 1058
limit, 1059
Edit Text Control tool, 1217
edit windows, creating, 226-227
editing
buttons in dialog boxes, 347
defining objects for, 1259-1261
files, 1263-1265
stacks in current tasks, 968
editors, single-line text, 130-136
elements, *see* interface elements
ellipse and polygon functions, 1341
Ellipse function, 50-53, 489-490, 1311
elliptical
arcs, drawing, 43-46, 334-335
regions, creating, 393-394
EM_CANUNDO message, 1045, 1365
EM_EMPTYUNDOBUFFER message, 1046, 1365

EM_FMTLINES message, 1046, 1365
EM_GETFIRSTVISIBLELINE message, 1046, 1365
EM_GETHANDLE message, 1047, 1365
EM_GETLINE message, 1047, 1365
EM_GETLINECOUNT message, 1047, 1365
EM_GETMODIFY message, 1048, 1365
EM_GETPASSWORDCHAR message, 1048
EM_GETRECT message, 1048, 1365
EM_GETSEL message, 1049, 1365
EM_GETWORDBREAKPROC message, 1050, 1365
EM_LIMITTEXT message, 1050, 1365
EM_LINEFROMCHAR message, 1050, 1366
EM_LINEINDEX message, 1051, 1366
EM_LINELENGTH message, 1051, 1366
EM_LINESCROLL message, 1052, 1366
EM_PASSWORDCHAR message, 1365
EM_REPLACESEL message, 1052, 1366
EM_SETHANDLE message, 1052, 1366
EM_SETMODIFY message, 1053, 1366
EM_SETPASSWORDCHAR message, 1053, 1366
EM_SETREADONLY message, 1053
EM_SETRECT message, 1054, 1366
EM_SETRECTNP message, 1055, 1366
EM_SETSEL message, 1055, 1366
EM_SETTABSTOPS message, 1056, 1366
EM_SETWORDBREAKPROC message, 1056, 1367
EM_UNDO message, 1057, 1367
embedding objects, 5
Empty Frames tools, 1222
EmptyClipboard function, 490, 1311
emToAnsi function, 774
EN_CHANGE message, 1058, 1367
EN_ERRSPACE message, 1058, 1367
EN_HSCROLL message, 1058, 1367
EN_KILLFOCUS message, 1059, 1367
EN_MAXTEXT message, 1059, 1367
EN_SETFOCUS message, 1060, 1367
EN_UPDATE message, 1060, 1367
EN_VSCROLL message, 1060, 1367
EnableAutoCreate member function, 1297-1298
EnableCommNotification function, 490-491, 1311
ENABLEDUPLEX printer escape, 1169
EnableHardwareInput function, 491-492, 1311
EnableKBHandler member function, 1298
EnableMenuItem function, 492-493, 1311
ENABLEPAIRKERNING printer escape, 1170
ENABLERELATIVEWIDTHS printer escape, 1170-1171
EnableScrollBar function, 493-494, 1311
EnableTransfer member function, 1298
EnableWindow function, 494, 1311
encapsulation, 202-203
END_PATH printer escape, 1171-1172
EndDeferWindowPos function, 494-495, 1311
EndDialog function, 495, 1311
EndDoc function, 496, 1311
ENDDOC printer escape, 1171
EndPage function, 496-497, 1311
EndPaint function, 497-498, 1311
EndView member function, 1286
ENErrSpace member function, 1257
EnumChildWindows function, 498, 1311
EnumClipboardFormats function, 499, 1311
EnumFontFamilies function, 499-500, 1311
EnumFonts function, 500-501, 1311
EnumMetaFile function, 501-502, 1311
EnumObjects function, 502-503, 1311
ENUMPAPERBINS printer escape, 1173
ENUMPAPERMETRICS printer escape, 1174
EnumProps function, 503-504, 1311

EnumTaskWindows function, 504-505, 1312
EnumWindows function, 505-506, 1312
environment
functions, 1341
strings, returning pointers, 570
EPSPRINTING printer escape, 1174
EqualRect function, 506-507, 1312
EqualRgn function, 507, 1312
Eraser tool, 1222
Error member function, 1277-1278
errors
asynchronous operations, 809-810
detecting, 364-366, 437-438
functions, 1341-1342
Escape function, 83, 508, 1163-1207, 1312
printer escapes, 1163-1207
EscapeCommFunction function, 508-509, 1312
event masks, communication devices, 901
event-driven versus procedure-driven programming, 16-18
ExcludeClipRect function, 509-510, 1312
ExcludeUpdateRgn function, 510-511, 1312
.EXE files, 1211
ExecDialog member function, 230, 1278
Execute member function, 1253
execution
environment, current, 345
time
copying, Virtual Machine, 981
tasks, current, 981
ExitWindows function, 511, 1312
EXT_DEVICE_CAPS printer escape, 1175-1176
ExtDeviceMode function, 512-513, 1312
extended tabs, 63-67
extents
viewports
editing, 878
scaling, 877
windows
defining, 942
editing, 880
ExtFloodFill function, 513-514, 1312
ExtractIcon function, 514-515, 1312
ExtTextOut function, 515-516, 1312
EXTTEXTOUT printer escape, 1176-1177

F

families, font, 72-73
FatalAppExit function, 516-517, 1312
FatalExit function, 517, 1312
file dialog boxes, 232-233, 1261-1263
file pointer, positioning, 749
files
closing, 709, 744
compressed, original name, 573
copying
multiple, 750
titles, 575
version information, 575-576
creating, 709, 747
deleting, 747
dragging and dropping, 6
editing, 1263-1265
creating windows for, 227-229
extension
GDI.EXE, 969
USER.EXE, 969
extensions for DLLs, 190
formats supported by Resource Workshop, 1211
handles
allocating, 324
defining, 914
freeing, 988
I/O functions, 1342
installing, 998, 1000

library, ObjectWindows, 264
module definition, *see* module definition files
naming, 619-622
opening, 737, 747
with file name, 601-604
OWL.DEF, 262-263
owl.h header, 266
pathnames, locating, 594
reading, 748
resource, *see* resource files
selecting from list boxes, 232-233
size of
resource, 574
version information buffer, 576
source code, 24-25
C, *see* C source code files
C++, *see* C++ source code files
copying, 368
temporary
names, 636-637
storage, 636
windows.h include, 14
filled figures
borders, drawing, 50-53
creating, 49-50
drawing, 275-278
filling, 53-57
Filled-in Frames tools, 1223
`FillRect` function, 517-518, 1312
`FillRgn` function, 518, 1312
`FindAtom` function, 519, 1312
`FindExactString` member function, 1269
`FindExecutable` function, 519-520, 1312
`FindResource` function, 520-521, 1312
`FindString` member function, 1269
`FindText` function, 521-523, 1312
`FindWindow` function, 523, 1312
`FirstThat` member function, 1298
`firstThat` member function, 1231
fixed
drives, 571-572
segments, 170
flags, text alignment, 75-76
setting, 935
`FlashWindow` function, 524, 1312
`FloodFill` function, 524-525, 1312
`FlushComm` function, 525, 1312
`FLUSHOUTPUT` printer escape, 1177
.FNT files, 1211
focus (input), for handles, 577
.FON files, 1211
Font header, 578
Font program, 578
fonts, 58, 68-73, 1210
character-to-glyph mapping, 578
control value table, 578
creating, 394-399, 1220-1225
current, in buffers, 642
CVT program, 578
editing, 1220-1225
families and typefaces, 72-73
functions, 1342
glyph data, 578
handles, 625-626
headers, 578
information, 577-578
kerning, 578
logical, mapping, 916
metrics, 578, 642-645
naming table, 578
outline curve data points, 580-581
postscript information, 578
reserved, 578
resources
adding, 320
deleting, 868
selecting, 352-356
text metrics, 73-75
TrueType, 6
installing, 616
metric data, 604-605
`ForEach` member function, 1298

forEach member function, 1231-1232
formats
  counting in Clipboard, 370
  file, supported by Resource Workshop, 1211
formatting characters, 1013-1014
frame windows, 173, 1274-1276
  class, 252-254
  procedures, 177
FrameRect function, 525-526, 1312
FrameRgn function, 526-527, 1312
free spaces, validating in memory, 995
FreeAllGDIMem function, 527, 1312
FreeAllMem function, 527-528, 1313
FreeAllUserMem function, 528, 1313
FreeLibrary function, 528-529, 1313
FreeModule function, 529, 1313
FreeProcInstance function, 529, 1313
FreeResource function, 530, 1313
FreeSelector function, 530, 1313
functions, 12
  abort, 889
  AbortDoc, 318, 1305
  AccessResource, 318-319, 1305
  AddAtom, 319, 1305
  AddFontResource, 320-321, 1305
  addresses, 612
  AdjustWindowRect, 320, 1305
  AdjustWindowRectEx, 321, 1305
  AllocDiskSpace, 322-323, 1305
  AllocDStoCSAlias, 323, 1305
  AllocFileHandles, 324, 1306
  AllocGDIMem, 324, 1306
  AllocMem, 325, 1306
  AllocResource, 325, 1306
  AllocSelector, 326, 1306
  AllocUserMem, 326, 1306
  AnimatePalette, 327-328, 1306
  AnsiLower, 328, 1306
  AnsiLowerBuff, 329, 1306
  AnsiNext, 329, 1306
  AnsiPrev, 330, 1306
  AnsiToOem, 330-331, 1306
  AnsiToOemBuff, 331, 1306
  AnsiUpper, 331-332, 1306
  AnsiUpperBuff, 332, 1306
  AnyPopup, 332-333, 1306
  AppendMenu, 333-334, 1306
  application execution, 1333
  Arc, 39, 43, 334-335, 1306
  ArrangeIconicWindows, 336, 1306
  atom management, 1334
  BeginDeferWindowPos, 336, 1306
  BeginPaint, 337, 1306
  BitBlt, 92, 338-339, 1306
  bitmap, 1334
  BringWindowToTop, 339-340, 1306
  BuildCommDCB, 340-343, 1306
  callback, 926
    defining, 693
    deleting, 693
  CallMsgFilter, 343-344, 1306
  CallNextHookEx, 344, 1306
  CallWindowProc, 344-345, 1306
  caret, 1334-1335
  Catch, 345, 1306
  ChangeClipboardChain, 346, 1306
  ChangeMenu, 346-347, 1306
  ChangeSelector, 347, 1307
  character-set conversion, 129
  CheckDlgButton, 347-348, 1307
  CheckMenuItem, 348-349, 1307
  CheckRadioButton, 349, 1307
  ChildWindowFromPoint, 349-350, 1307
  ChooseColor, 350-352, 1307
  ChooseFont, 352-356, 1307
  Chord, 50-53, 356-357, 1307
  ClassFirst, 357, 1307
  ClassNext, 358, 1307
  ClearCommBreak, 359, 1307
  ClientToScreen, 359-360, 1307
  clipboard, 1335
  ClipCursor, 360-361, 1307
  clipping, 1335

CloseClipboard, 361, 1307
CloseComm, 361, 1307
CloseDriver, 362, 1307
CloseMetaFile, 362, 1307
CloseWindow, 363, 1307
color palette, 1336
CombineRgn, 363-364, 1307
CommDlgExtendedError, 364-366, 1307
common dialog, 1336
communication, 1336-1337
coordinate, 1337
CopyCursor, 366-367, 1307
CopyIcon, 367, 1307
CopyLZFile, 367-368, 1307
CopyMetaFile, 368-369, 1307
CopyRect, 369, 1307
CountClipboardFormats, 370, 1307
CreateBitmap, 370-371, 1307
CreateBitmapIndirect, 371-372, 1307
CreateBrushIndirect, 54-57, 372-373, 1307
CreateCaret, 373-374, 1307
CreateCompatibleBitmap, 374-375, 1308
CreateCompatibleDC, 375, 1308
CreateCursor, 375-376, 1308
CreateDC, 376-381, 1308
CreateDialog, 381-382, 1308
CreateDialogIndirect, 382-384, 1308
CreateDialogIndirectParam, 385-387, 1308
CreateDialogParam, 387-389, 1308
CreateDIBitmap, 389-391, 1308
CreateDIBPatternBrush, 391-392, 1308
CreateDiscardableBitmap, 392-393, 1308
CreateEllipticRgn, 393, 1308
CreateEllipticRgnIndirect, 394, 1308
CreateFont, 69, 394-397, 1308
CreateFontIndirect, 69-72, 397-399, 1308
CreateHatchBrush, 54-57, 399-400, 1308
CreateIC, 400, 1308
CreateIcon, 401, 1308
CreateMenu, 402, 1308
CreateMetaFile, 402, 1308
CreatePalette, 402-404, 1308
CreatePatternBrush, 54-57, 404, 1308
CreatePen, 47-48, 404-405, 1308
CreatePenIndirect, 39, 47-48, 405-406, 1308
CreatePolygonRgn, 406-407, 1308
CreatePolyPolygonRgn, 407-408, 1308
CreatePopupMenu, 409, 1308
CreateRectRgn, 409-410, 1308
CreateRectRgnIndirect, 410, 1308
CreateRoundRectRgn, 411, 1309
CreateScalableFontResource, 412, 1309
CreateSolidBrush, 54-57, 413, 1309
CreateWindow, 150-158, 413-421, 1309
CreateWindowEx, 151-158, 422-423, 1309
cursor, 1337
DDE (dynamic data exchange), 1338
DdeAbandonTransaction, 424, 1309
DdeAccessData, 424-425, 1309
DdeAddData, 425-426, 1309
DdeCallback, 1309
DdeClientTransaction, 426-427, 1309
DdeCmpStringHandles, 427-428, 1309
DdeConnect, 428-429, 1309
DdeConnectList, 430, 1309

DdeCreateDataHandle, 431-432, 1309
DdeCreateStringHandle, 432, 1309
DdeDisconnect, 433, 1309
DdeDisconnectList, 433, 1309
DdeEnableCallback, 434, 1309
DdeFreeDataHandle, 434-435, 1309
DdeFreeStringHandle, 435, 1309
DdeGetData, 436, 1309
DdeGetLastError, 436-439, 1309
DdeInitialize, 439-441, 1309
DdeKeepStringHandle, 441, 1309
DdeNameService, 442, 1309
DdePostAdvise, 443, 1309
DdeQueryConvInfo, 443-446, 1309
DdeQueryNextServer, 447, 1309
DdeQueryString, 447-448, 1309
DdeReconnect, 448, 1309
DdeSetUserHandle, 449, 1309
DdeUnaccessData, 449, 1309
DdeUninitialize, 450, 1309
DebugBreak, 450, 1309
debugging, 1338
DefDlgProc, 450-451, 1309
DefDriverProc, 451, 1310
DeferWindowPos, 452-453, 1310
DefFrameProc, 177, 453-454, 1310
DefHookProc, 454-455, 1310
DefineHandleTable, 455
DefMDIChildProc, 177, 455-456, 1310
DefWindowProc, 139-140, 456, 1310
DeleteAtom, 457, 1310
DeleteDC, 457, 1310
DeleteMenu, 458, 1310
DeleteMetaFile, 458-459, 1310
DeleteObject, 459, 1310
DestroyCaret, 459, 1310
DestroyCursor, 460, 1310
DestroyIcon, 460, 1310
DestroyMenu, 461, 1310
DestroyWindow, 461, 1310
device context, 1338-1339
DeviceCapabilities, 462-467, 1310
DeviceMode, 467, 1310
dialog box, 1339
DialogBox, 468-469, 1310
DialogBoxIndirect, 469-471, 1310
DialogBoxIndirectParam, 472-474, 1310
DialogBoxParam, 474-476, 1310
DirectedYield, 476, 1310
DispatchMessage, 476-477, 1310
display and movement, 1339-1340
DlgDirList, 477-478, 1310
DlgDirListComboBox, 479-480, 1310
DlgDirSelect, 480-481, 1310
DlgDirSelectComboBox, 481, 1310
DlgDirSelectComboBoxEx, 1311
DlgDirSelectEx, 1311
DOS3Call, 481-482, 1311
DPtoLP, 482, 1311
drag-drop, 1340
DragAcceptFiles, 483, 1311
DragFinish, 483, 1311
DragQueryFile, 484, 1311
DragQueryPoint, 484-485, 1311
DrawFocusRect, 485-486, 1311
DrawIcon, 486-487, 1311
drawing attribute, 1340
drawing tool, 1340-1341
DrawMenuBar, 487, 1311
DrawText, 487-489, 1311
DriverProc, 1311
Ellipse, 50-53, 489-490, 1311
ellipse and polygon, 1341
EmptyClipboard, 490, 1311
emToAnsi, 774
EnableCommNotification, 490-491, 1311
EnableHardwareInput, 491-492, 1311
EnableMenuItem, 492-493, 1311
EnableScrollBar, 493-494, 1311
EnableWindow, 494, 1311
EndDeferWindowPos, 494-495, 1311

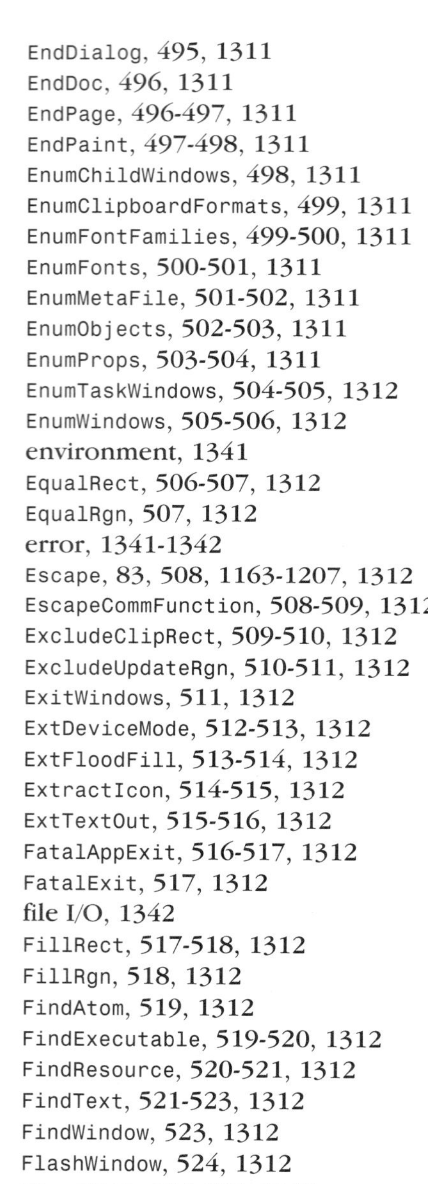

EndDialog, 495, 1311
EndDoc, 496, 1311
EndPage, 496-497, 1311
EndPaint, 497-498, 1311
EnumChildWindows, 498, 1311
EnumClipboardFormats, 499, 1311
EnumFontFamilies, 499-500, 1311
EnumFonts, 500-501, 1311
EnumMetaFile, 501-502, 1311
EnumObjects, 502-503, 1311
EnumProps, 503-504, 1311
EnumTaskWindows, 504-505, 1312
EnumWindows, 505-506, 1312
environment, 1341
EqualRect, 506-507, 1312
EqualRgn, 507, 1312
error, 1341-1342
Escape, 83, 508, 1163-1207, 1312
EscapeCommFunction, 508-509, 1312
ExcludeClipRect, 509-510, 1312
ExcludeUpdateRgn, 510-511, 1312
ExitWindows, 511, 1312
ExtDeviceMode, 512-513, 1312
ExtFloodFill, 513-514, 1312
ExtractIcon, 514-515, 1312
ExtTextOut, 515-516, 1312
FatalAppExit, 516-517, 1312
FatalExit, 517, 1312
file I/O, 1342
FillRect, 517-518, 1312
FillRgn, 518, 1312
FindAtom, 519, 1312
FindExecutable, 519-520, 1312
FindResource, 520-521, 1312
FindText, 521-523, 1312
FindWindow, 523, 1312
FlashWindow, 524, 1312
FloodFill, 524-525, 1312
FlushComm, 525, 1312
font, 1342
for creating controls and processing messages, 1250-1251
for drawing filled figures, 50
for drawing text, 58
FrameRect, 525-526, 1312
FrameRgn, 526-527, 1312
FreeAllGDIMem, 527, 1312
FreeAllMem, 527-528, 1313
FreeAllUserMem, 528, 1313
FreeLibrary, 528-529, 1313
FreeModule, 529, 1313
FreeProcInstance, 529, 1313
FreeResource, 530, 1313
FreeSelector, 530, 1313
GetActiveWindow, 530-531, 1313
GetAspectRatioFilter, 531, 1313
GetAspectRatioFilterEx, 531-532, 1313
GetAsyncKeyState, 532, 1313
GetAtomHandle, 532-533, 1313
GetAtomName, 533, 1313
GetBitmapBits, 533-534, 1313
GetBitmapDimension, 534, 1313
GetBitmapDimensionEx, 534-535, 1313
GetBkColor, 68, 535, 1313
GetBkMode, 68, 535, 1313
GetBoundsRect, 536, 1313
GetBrushOrg, 537, 1313
GetBValue, 537, 1313
GetCapture, 538, 1313
GetCaretBlinkTime, 538, 1313
GetCaretPos, 538-539, 1313
GetCharABCWidths, 539-540, 1313
GetCharWidth, 540, 1313
GetClassInfo, 541, 1313
GetClassLong, 541-542, 1313
GetClassName, 542, 1313
GetClassWord, 542-543, 1313
GetClientRect, 543-544, 1313
GetClipboardData, 544, 1313
GetClipboardFormatName, 545, 1313
GetClipboardOwner, 545, 1313
GetClipboardViewer, 546, 1314
GetClipBox, 546-547, 1314
GetClipCursor, 547-548, 1314

GetCodeHandle, 548, 1314
GetCodeInfo, 548-549, 1314
GetCommError, 549-550, 1314
GetCommEventMask, 551, 1314
GetCommState, 552-554, 1314
GetCurrentPDB, 554-555, 1314
GetCurrentPosition, 555, 1314
GetCurrentPositionEx, 555-556, 1314
GetCurrentTask, 556, 1314
GetCurrentTime, 556, 1314
GetCursor, 556-557, 1314
GetCursorPos, 557, 1314
GetDC, 558, 1314
GetDCEx, 558-559, 1314
GetDCOrg, 560, 1314
GetDesktopWindow, 560, 1314
GetDeviceCaps, 561-564, 1314
GetDialogBaseUnits, 564, 1314
GetDIBits, 565-567, 1314
GetDlgCtrlID, 567, 1314
GetDlgItem, 568, 1314
GetDlgItemInt, 568-569, 1314
GetDlgItemText, 569, 1314
GetDOSEnvironment, 570, 1314
GetDoubleClickTime, 570, 1314
GetDriverInfo, 570-571, 1314
GetDriverModuleHandle, 571, 1314
GetDriveType, 571-572, 1315
GetEnvironment, 572-573, 1315
GetExpandedName, 573, 1315
GetFileResource, 573-574, 1315
GetFileResourceSize, 574-575, 1315
GetFileTitle, 575, 1315
GetFileVersionInfo, 575-576, 1315
GetFileVersionInfoSize, 576-577, 1315
GetFocus, 577, 1315
GetFontData, 577-578, 1315
GetFreeFileHandles, 1315
GetFreeSpace, 578-579, 1315
GetFreeSystemResources, 579, 1315
GetGlyphOutline, 579-581, 1315
GetGValue, 581, 1315
GetInputState, 581-582, 1315
GetInstanceData, 582, 1315
GetKBCodePage, 582-583, 1315
GetKeyboardState, 583, 1315
GetKeyboardType, 584, 1315
GetKeyNameText, 585, 1315
GetKeyState, 585-586, 1315
GetLastActivePopup, 586, 1315
GetMapMode, 586-587, 1315
GetMenu, 587, 1315
GetMenuCheckMarkDimensions, 588, 1315
GetMenuItemCount, 588, 1315
GetMenuItemID, 588, 1315
GetMenuState, 589-590, 1315
GetMenuString, 590-591, 1315
GetMessage, 591-592, 1315
GetMessageExtraInfo, 592, 1316
GetMessagePos, 592-593, 1316
GetMessageTime, 593, 1316
GetMetaFile, 593-594, 1316
GetMetaFileBits, 594, 1316
GetModuleFileName, 594-595, 1316
GetModuleHandle, 595, 1316
GetModuleUsage, 595, 1316
GetNearestColor, 596, 1316
GetNearestPaletteIndex, 596, 1316
GetNextDlgGroupItem, 596-597, 1316
GetNextDlgTabItem, 597-598, 1316
GetNextDriver, 598, 1316
GetNextWindow, 599, 1316
GetNumTasks, 599, 1316
GetObject, 600, 1316
GetOpenClipboardWindow, 600, 1316
GetOpenFileName, 601-604, 1316
GetOutlineTextMetrics, 604-605, 1316
GetPaletteEntries, 607-608, 1316
GetParent, 608, 1316
GetPixel, 608-609, 1316

GetPolyFillMode, 609, 1316
GetPriorityClipboardFormat, 610, 1316
GetPrivateProfileInt, 610-611, 1316
GetPrivateProfileString, 611-612, 1316
GetProcAddress, 612, 1316
GetProfileInt, 612-613, 1316
GetProfileString, 613-614, 1316
GetProp, 614, 1316
GetQueueStatus, 615, 1317
GetRasterizerCaps, 616, 1317
GetRgnBox, 616-617, 1317
GetROP2, 49, 618-619, 1317
GetRValue, 619, 1317
GetSaveFileName, 619-622, 1317
GetScrollPos, 622-623, 1317
GetScrollRange, 623-624, 1317
GetSelectorBase, 624, 1317
GetSelectorLimit, 624-625, 1317
GetStockObject, 46-47, 53, 625-626, 1317
GetStretchBltMode, 626, 1317
GetSubMenu, 627, 1317
GetSysColor, 627-628, 1317
GetSysModalWindow, 628, 1317
GetSystemDebugState, 629, 1317
GetSystemDir, 629-630, 1317
GetSystemDirectory, 630, 1317
GetSystemMenu, 630, 1317
GetSystemMetrics, 631-633, 1317
GetSystemPaletteEntries, 633-634, 1317
GetSystemPaletteUse, 634, 1317
GetTabbedTextExtent, 635, 1317
GetTempDrive, 636, 1317
GetTempFileName, 636-637, 1317
GetTextAlign, 638, 1317
GetTextCharacterExtra, 68, 638, 1317
GetTextColor, 68, 639, 1317
GetTextExtent, 639-640, 1317
GetTextExtentEx, 640-641, 1317
GetTextExtentPoint, 641, 1317
GetTextFace, 642, 1318
GetTextMetrics, 642-645, 1318
GetThresholdEvent, 1318
GetThresholdStatus, 1318
GetTickCount, 645, 1318
GetTimerResolution, 1318
GetTopWindow, 1318
GetUpdateRect, 646-647, 1318
GetUpdateRgn, 647-648, 1318
GetVersion, 648, 1318
GetViewportExt, 648-649, 1318
GetViewportExtEx, 649, 1318
GetViewportOrg, 649, 1318
GetViewportOrgEx, 650, 1318
GetWindow, 650-651, 1318
GetWindowDC, 651, 1318
GetWindowExt, 652, 1318
GetWindowLong, 652-653, 1318
GetWindowOrg, 653, 1318
GetWindowOrgEx, 653, 1318
GetWindowPlacement, 654, 1318
GetWindowRect, 654-655, 1318
GetWindowsDir, 655-656, 1318
GetWindowsDirectory, 656, 1318
GetWindowTask, 656-657, 1318
GetWindowText, 657, 1318
GetWindowTextLength, 657-658, 1318
GetWindowWord, 658, 1318
GetWinFlags, 658-659, 1318
global memory management, 168
GlobalAddAtom, 659-660, 1318
GlobalAlloc, 660-661, 1319
GlobalCompact, 661, 1319
GlobalDeleteAtom, 662, 1319
GlobalDiscard, 662, 1319
GlobalDosAlloc, 662-663, 1319
GlobalDosFree, 663, 1319
GlobalEntryHandle, 664-666, 1319
GlobalEntryModule, 666-669, 1319
GlobalFindAtom, 669, 1319

GlobalFirst, 669-672, 1319
GlobalFix, 672-673, 1319
GlobalFlags, 673, 1319
GlobalFree, 673-674, 1319
GlobalGetAtomName, 674, 1319
GlobalHandle, 674-675, 1319
GlobalHandleToSel, 675, 1319
GlobalInfo, 675-676, 1319
GlobalLock, 676, 1319
GlobalLRUNewest, 677, 1319
GlobalLRUOldest, 677, 1319
GlobalNext, 678-680, 1319
GlobalNotify, 680-681, 1319
GlobalPageLock, 681-682, 1319
GlobalPageUnlock, 682, 1319
GlobalReAlloc, 682-683, 1319
GlobalSize, 683, 1319
GlobalUnfix, 684, 1319
GlobalUnlock, 684, 1319
GlobalUnWire, 1319
GlobalWire, 1320
GrayString, 685-686, 1320
hardware, 1342-1343
HIBYTE, 686, 1320
HideCaret, 686-687, 1320
HiliteMenuItem, 687-688, 1320
HIWORD, 688, 1320
hook, 1343
icon, 1343
IMPORTS, 195
InflateRect, 688-689, 1320
information, 1343-1344
InitAtomTable, 690, 1320
initialization file, 1344
input, 1344
InSendMessage, 690, 1320
InsertMenu, 691-692, 1320
installable driver, 1345
InterruptRegister, 693, 1320
InterruptUnRegister, 693-694, 1320
IntersectClipRect, 694, 1320
IntersectRect, 695, 1320
InvalidateRect, 696-697, 1320
InvalidateRgn, 697, 1320
InvertRect, 697-698, 1320
InvertRgn, 698-699, 1320
IsCharAlpha, 699, 1320
IsCharAlphaNumeric, 699-700, 1320
IsCharLower, 700, 1320
IsCharUpper, 700, 1320
IsChild, 701, 1320
IsClipboardFormatAvailable, 701, 1320
IsDBCSLeadByte, 702, 1320
IsDialogMessage, 702-703, 1320
IsDlgButtonChecked, 703-704, 1320
IsIconic, 704, 1320
IsMenu, 704, 1320
IsRectEmpty, 705, 1321
IsTask, 706, 1321
IsWindow, 706, 1321
IsWindowEnabled, 706-707, 1321
IsWindowVisible, 707, 1321
IsZoomed, 707, 1321
KillTimer, 708, 1321
_lclose, 708-709, 1321
_lcreat, 709, 1321
Lempel-Ziv expansion, 1345
line output, 1345
LineDDA, 710-711, 1321
LineTo, 39-40, 711, 1321
_llseek, 711-712, 1321
LoadAccelerators, 712, 1321
LoadBitmap, 92, 713, 1321
LoadCursor, 713-714, 1321
LoadIcon, 714-715, 1321
LoadLibrary, 715-716, 1321
LoadMenu, 716-717, 1321
LoadMenuIndirect, 717-718, 1321
LoadModule, 718-720, 1321
LoadResource, 720, 1321
LoadString, 118, 721, 1321
LOBYTE, 721-722, 1321
local memory management, 169-170

LocalAlloc, 722-723, 1321
LocalCompact, 723, 1321
LocalDiscard, 723, 1321
LocalFirst, 724-726, 1321
LocalFlags, 726-727, 1321
LocalFree, 1321
LocalHandle, 728, 1321
LocalInfo, 728-729, 1321
LocalInit, 729, 1321
LocalLock, 729-730, 1321
LocalNext, 730-732, 1321
LocalReAlloc, 733, 1322
LocalShrink, 733-734, 1322
LocalSize, 734, 1322
LocalUnlock, 734-735, 1322
LockData, 735, 1322
LockInput, 735-736
LockResource, 736, 1322
LockSegment, 736-737, 1322
LockWindowUpdate, 739
_lopen, 737-738, 1322
LOWORD, 738, 1322
LPtoDP, 739-740, 1322
_lread, 740, 1322
lstrcat, 740-741, 1322
lstrcmp, 741, 1322
lstrcmpi, 742, 1322
lstrcpy, 742-743, 1322
lstrlen, 743, 1322
_lwrite, 743-744, 1322
LZClose, 744, 1322
LZCopy, 744-745, 1322
LZDone, 745, 1322
LZInit, 746, 1322
LZOpenFile, 746-748, 1322
LZRead, 748-749, 1322
LZSeek, 749-750, 1322
LZStart, 750, 1322
macros and utility, 1358
MAKEINTATOM, 750, 1322
MAKEINTRESOURCE, 751, 1322
MAKELONG, 751, 1322
MAKEPOINT, 752, 1322
MakeProcInstance, 752, 1322
MapDialogRect, 753-754, 1322
mapping, 1346
MapVirtualKey, 754, 1322
MapWindowPoints, 755, 1323
max, 755, 1322
MemManInfo, 756-757, 1323
memory management, 1346-1347
MemoryRead, 757, 1323
MemoryWrite, 758, 1323
menu, 1347
message, 1347-1348
MessageBeep, 758, 1323
MessageBox, 118, 759-761, 1323
messages, processing, 690
metafile, 1348
min, 761, 1323
ModifyMenu, 761-763, 1323
module management, 1348
ModuleFindHandle, 764, 1323
ModuleFindName, 765-766, 1323
ModuleFirst, 766-767, 1323
ModuleNext, 767-768, 1323
movement, 1339-1340
MoveTo, 39, 768, 1323
MoveToEx, 769, 1323
MoveWindow, 769-770, 1323
MulDiv, 770, 1323
NetBIOSCall, 771, 1323
network, 1349
NotifyRegister, 771-773, 1323
NotifyUnRegister, 773, 1323
OemKeyScan, 773-774, 1323
OemToAnsi, 1323
OemToAnsiBuff, 775, 1323
OffsetClipRgn, 775-776, 1323
OffsetRect, 776-777, 1323
OffsetRgn, 777-778, 1323
OffsetViewportOrg, 778, 1323
OffsetViewportOrgEx, 779, 1323
OffsetWindowOrg, 779-780, 1323
OffsetWindowOrgEx, 780-781, 1323
OLE, 1349-1350

OleActivate, 781, 1323
OleBlockServer, 782, 1323
OleClone, 782-783, 1323
OleClose, 783, 1323
OleCopyFromLink, 783-784, 1324
OleCopyToClipboard, 784, 1324
OleCreate, 785-786, 1324
OleCreateFromClip, 786-787, 1324
OleCreateFromFile, 788-789, 1324
OleCreateFromTemplate, 789-790, 1324
OleCreateInvisible, 791-792, 1324
OleCreateLinkFromClip, 792-793, 1324
OleCreateLinkFromFile, 794-795, 1324
OleDelete, 796, 1324
OleDraw, 796-797, 1324
OleEnumFormats, 797, 1324
OleEnumObjects, 798, 1324
OleEqual, 798-799, 1324
OleExecute, 799, 1324
OleGetData, 799-800, 1324
OleGetLinkUpdateOptions, 800-801, 1324
OleIsDcMeta, 801
OleLoadFromStream, 802, 1324
OleLockServer, 803, 1324
OleObjectConvert, 803-804, 1324
OleQueryBounds, 804, 1324
OleQueryClientVersion, 805, 1324
OleQueryCreateFromClip, 805-806, 1324
OleQueryLinkFromClip, 806-807, 1324
OleQueryName, 808, 1324
OleQueryOpen, 808, 1324
OleQueryOutOfData, 809, 1324
OleQueryProtocol, 809, 1324
OleQueryReleaseError, 810, 1324
OleQueryReleaseMethod, 810-811, 1324
OleQueryReleaseStatus, 812, 1324
OleQueryServerVersion, 812, 1324
OleQuerySize, 813, 1324
OleQueryType, 813, 1324
OleReconnect, 814, 1324
OleRegisterClientDoc, 815, 1324
OleRegisterServer, 815, 1325
OleRegisterServerDoc, 816, 1325
OleRelease, 816-817, 1325
OleRename, 817, 1325
OleRenameClientDoc, 817-818, 1325
OleRenameServerDoc, 818, 1325
OleRequestData, 818-819, 1325
OleRevertClientDoc, 819, 1325
OleRevertServerDoc, 820, 1325
OleRevokeClientDoc, 820, 1325
OleRevokeObject, 821, 1325
OleRevokeServer, 821, 1325
OleRevokeServerDoc, 822, 1325
OleSavedClientDoc, 822, 1325
OleSavedServerDoc, 822-823, 1325
OleSaveToStream, 823, 1325
OleSetBounds, 824, 1325
OleSetColorScheme, 824, 1325
OleSetData, 825, 1325
OleSetHostNames, 825-826, 1325
OleSetLinkUpdateOptions, 827, 1325
OleSetTargetDevice, 827, 1325
OleUnblockServer, 827-828, 1325
OleUnlockServer, 828, 1325
OleUpdate, 829, 1325
OpenClipboard, 829, 1325
OpenComm, 830, 1325
OpenDriver, 831, 1325
OpenFile, 831-833, 1325
OpenIcon, 833, 1325
operating system interrupt, 1350
optimization tool, 1350-1351
OutputDebugString, 834, 1326
overloading, 207-209
painting, 1351
PaintRgn, 834, 1326
PALETTEINDEX, 835, 1326

PALETTERGB, 835, 1326
PatBlt, 836, 1326
PeekMessage, 837-838, 1326
Pie, 50-53, 838-840, 1326
PlayMetaFile, 840, 1326
PlayMetaFileRecord, 840, 1326
Polygon, 841, 1326
polygon, 1341
Polyline, 42, 842, 1326
PolyPolygon, 842-843, 1326
PostAppMessage, 844, 1326
PostMessage, 844, 1326
PostQuitMessage, 845, 1326
PrintDlg, 845-849, 1326
printer control, 1352
ProfClear, 849, 1326
ProfFinish, 849, 1326
ProfFlush, 850, 1326
ProfInsChk, 850, 1326
ProfSampRate, 850-851, 1326
ProfSetup, 851-852, 1326
ProfStart, 852, 1326
ProfStop, 852, 1326
property, 1352
PtInRect, 853, 1326
PtInRegion, 854, 1326
PtVisible, 854-855, 1326
QuerySendMessage, 855-856, 1326
ReadComm, 856, 1326
RealizePalette, 857, 1326
Rectangle, 50-53, 857, 1326
rectangle, 1352
RectInRegion, 858, 1326
RectVisible, 859, 1327
RedrawWindow, 860-861, 1327
RegCloseKey, 861-862, 1327
RegCreateKey, 862, 1327
RegDeleteKey, 862-863, 1327
RegEnumKey, 863, 1327
region, 1353
RegisterClass, 175-187, 864, 1327
RegisterClipboardFormat, 864, 1327
RegisterWindowMessage, 865, 1327
registration, 1353
RegOpenKey, 865-866, 1327
RegQueryValue, 866, 1327
RegSetValue, 867, 1327
ReleaseCapture, 867-868, 1327
ReleaseDC, 868, 1327
RemoveFontResource, 868-869, 1327
RemoveMenu, 869, 1327
RemoveProp, 870, 1327
ReplaceText, 870-872, 1327
ReplyMessage, 872-873, 1327
ResetDC, 873, 1327
ResizePalette, 874, 1327
resource management, 1353
RestoreDC, 874, 1327
RGB, 875, 1327
RoundRect, 50-53, 876, 1327
SaveDC, 876, 1327
ScaleViewportExt, 876-877, 1327
ScaleViewportExtEx, 877-878, 1327
ScaleWindowExt, 878-879, 1327
ScaleWindowExtEx, 879, 1327
ScreenToClient, 880, 1327
ScrollDC, 881-882, 1327
scrolling, 1354
ScrollWindow, 883, 1327
ScrollWindowEx, 883-885, 1327
segment, 171, 1354
SelectClipRgn, 885, 1327
SelectObject, 39, 92, 886, 1328
SelectPalette, 887, 1328
SendDlgItemMessage, 887, 1328
SendDriverMessage, 888, 1328
SendMessage, 889, 1328
SetAbortProc, 889, 1328
SetActiveWindow, 890, 1328
SetBitmapBits, 891, 1328
SetBitmapDimension, 891, 1328
SetBitmapDimensionEx, 892, 1328
SetBkColor, 68, 892, 1328
SetBkMode, 68, 893, 1328
SetBoundsRect, 894, 1328

SetBrushOrg, 895, 1328
SetCapture, 895, 1328
SetCaretBlinkTime, 896, 1328
SetCaretPos, 896, 1328
SetClassLong, 897, 1328
SetClassWord, 898, 1328
SetClipboardData, 899, 1328
SetClipboardViewer, 900, 1328
SetCommBreak, 900, 1328
SetCommEventMask, 900-901, 1328
SetCommState, 902-904, 1328
SetCursor, 905, 1328
SetCursorPos, 905, 1328
SetDIBits, 906-908, 1328
SetDIBitsToDevice, 909-910, 1328
SetDlgItemInt, 910-911, 1328
SetDlgItemText, 911, 1328
SetDoubleClickTime, 912, 1328
SetEnvironment, 912, 1328
SetErrorMode, 913, 1329
SetFocus, 914, 1329
SetHandleCount, 914, 1329
SetKeyboardState, 915, 1329
SetMapMode, 915, 1329
SetMapperFlags, 916, 1329
SetMenu, 917, 1329
SetMenuItemBitmaps, 917, 1329
SetMessageQueue, 918, 1329
SetMetaFileBits, 919, 1329
SetMetaFileBitsBetter, 919, 1329
SetPaletteEntries, 920, 1329
SetParent, 921, 1329
SetPixel, 35, 921-922, 1329
SetPolyFillMode, 922, 1329
SetProp, 923, 1329
SetRect, 923-924, 1329
SetRectEmpty, 924-925, 1329
SetRectRgn, 925, 1329
SetResourceHandler, 926, 1329
SetROP2, 49, 927, 1329
SetScrollPos, 928, 1329
SetScrollRange, 929, 1329
SetSelectorBase, 930, 1329
SetSelectorLimit, 930, 1329
SetStretchBltMode, 930-931, 1329
SetSwapAreaSize, 931, 1329
SetSysColors, 932, 1329
SetSysModalWindow, 933, 1329
SetSystemPaletteUse, 934, 1329
SetTextAlign, 75-76, 934-935, 1329
SetTextCharacterExtra, 68, 935, 1329
SetTextColor, 68, 936, 1329
SetTextJustification, 937, 1329
SetTimer, 937, 1330
SetViewportExt, 938, 1330
SetViewportExtEx, 939, 1330
SetViewportOrg, 940, 1330
SetViewportOrgEx, 940-941, 1330
SetWindowExt, 941, 1330
SetWindowExtEx, 942, 1330
SetWindowLong, 943, 1330
SetWindowOrg, 944, 1330
SetWindowOrgEx, 944, 1330
SetWindowPlacement, 945
SetWindowPos, 946, 1330
SetWindowsHook, 947, 1330
SetWindowsHookEx, 948, 1330
SetWindowText, 949, 1330
SetWindowWord, 949-950, 1330
shell, 1354-1355
ShellExecute, 950-951, 1330
ShowCaret, 952, 1330
ShowCursor, 953, 1330
ShowOwnedPopups, 953, 1330
ShowScrollBar, 954, 1330
ShowWindow, 955, 1330
SizeofResource, 956, 1330
SlashBox, 193
StackTraceCSIPFirst, 957, 1330
StackTraceFirst, 958, 1330
StackTraceNext, 959, 1330
StartDoc, 960, 1330
StartPage, 961, 1330
stress, 1355

StretchBlt, 962, 1330
StretchDIBits, 965-967, 1330
string manipulation, 1355
SwapMouseButton, 967, 1330
SwapRecording, 1330
SwitchStackBack, 968, 1330
SwitchStackTo, 968, 1331
SyncAllVoices, 1331
system, 1355-1356
SystemHeapInfo, 969, 1331
SystemParametersInfo, 969-971, 1331
TabbedTextOut, 63-67, 281-283, 972, 1331
task, 1356
TaskFindHandle, 973-974, 1331
TaskFirst, 974-975, 1331
TaskGetCSIP, 976, 1331
TaskNext, 976-977, 1331
TaskSetCSIP, 978, 1331
TaskSwitch, 978, 1331
TerminateApp, 979, 1331
text, 1356
TextOut, 58-62, 278-280, 979-980, 1331
Throw, 980, 1331
TimerCount, 981
ToAscii, 982, 1331
Toolhelp, 1356-1357
TrackPopupMenu, 982-983, 1331
TranslateAccelerator, 984, 1331
TranslateMDISysAccel, 175-176, 985, 1331
TranslateMessage, 125, 986, 1331
TransmitCommChar, 987, 1331
TrueType, 1357
UnAllocDiskSpace, 987, 1331
UnAllocFileHandles, 988, 1331
UngetCommChar, 988, 1331
UnhookWindowsHook, 989, 1331
UnhookWindowsHookEx, 990, 1331
UnionRect, 991, 1331
UnlockData, 991-992, 1331
UnlockResource, 992, 1331
UnlockSegment, 993, 1331
UnrealizeObject, 993, 1331
UnregisterClass, 994, 1331
UpdateColors, 994, 1331
UpdateWindow, 994, 1332
utility, 1358
ValidateCodeSegments, 995, 1332
ValidateFreeSpaces, 995, 1332
ValidateRect, 996, 1332
ValidateRgn, 996-997, 1332
VerFindFile, 998, 1332
VerInstallFile, 1000, 1332
VerLanguageName, 1001, 1332
VerQueryValue, 1002, 1332
version, 1357
VkKeyScan, 1002, 1332
WaitMessage, 1003, 1332
window creation, 1357-1358
WindowFromPoint, 1003, 1332
WinExec, 1004, 1332
WinHelp, 1006, 1332
WinMain, 18-20, 130, 260-261
WNetAddConnection, 1007, 1332
WNetCancelConnection, 1008, 1332
WNetGetConnection, 1009, 1332
WriteComm, 1010, 1332
WritePrivateProfileString, 1011, 1332
WriteProfileString, 1012, 1332
wsprintf, 1012-1013, 1332
wvsprintf, 1014, 1332
XBox, 193
Yield, 1015, 1332

fundamental window application, 26-29

G

GDI (Graphics Device Interface)
coordinate systems, 34-35
device context, 32-33
drawing modes, 48-49

filled figures, 49-57
fonts, 58, 68-73
text metrics, 73-75
lines, drawing, 39-46
mapping modes, 33-34
memory, allocating, 324
pens, 46-48
points, 35-39
printing, 83
text
aligning, 75-76
device context attributes, 67-68
drawing, 58-67, 639
justifying, 937
scrolling windows, 76-82
GDI.EXE extension file, 969
GetActiveWindow function, 530-531, 1313
GetApplication member function, 1298
GetAspectRatioFilter function, 531, 1313
GetAspectRatioFilterEx function, 531-532, 1313
GetAsyncKeyState function, 532, 1313
GetAtomHandle function, 532-533, 1313
GetAtomName function, 533, 1313
GetBitmapBits function, 533-534, 1313
GetBitmapDimension function, 534, 1313
GetBitmapDimensionEx function, 534-535, 1313
GetBkColor function, 68, 535, 1313
GetBkMode function, 68, 535, 1313
GetBoundsRect function, 536, 1313
GetBrushOrg function, 537, 1313
GetBValue function, 537, 1313
GetCapture function, 538, 1313
GetCaretBlinkTime function, 538, 1313
GetCaretPos function, 538-539, 1313
GetCharABCWidths function, 539-540, 1313
GetCharWidth function, 540, 1313
GetCheck member function, 1246
GetChildPtr member function, 1298-1299
GetChildren member function, 1299
GetClassInfo function, 541, 1313
GetClassLong function, 541-542, 1313
GetClassName function, 542, 1313
GetClassName member function, 226, 1236-1244, 1248, 1253, 1257, 1266, 1269, 1273, 1276, 1281, 1289, 1292, 1299
GetClassWord function, 542-543, 1313
GetClient member function, 1276, 1299
GetClientHandle member function, 1278
GetClientRect function, 543-544, 1313
GetClipboardData function, 544, 1313
GetClipboardFormatName function, 545, 1313
GetClipboardOwner function, 545, 1313
GetClipboardViewer function, 546, 1314
GetClipBox function, 546-547, 1314
GetClipCursor function, 547-548, 1314
GetCodeHandle function, 548, 1314
GetCodeInfo function, 548-549, 1314
GETCOLORTABLE printer escape, 1178
GetCommError function, 549-550, 1314
GetCommEventMask function, 551, 1314
GetCommState function, 552-554, 1314
GetCount member function, 1270
GetCurrentPDB function, 554-555, 1314
GetCurrentPosition function, 555, 1314
GetCurrentPositionEx function, 555-556, 1314

GetCurrentTask function, 556, 1314
GetCurrentTime function, 556, 1314
GetCursor function, 556-557, 1314
GetCursorPos function, 557, 1314
GetDC function, 558, 1314
GetDCEx function, 558-559, 1314
GetDCOrg function, 560, 1314
GetDesktopWindow function, 560, 1314
GetDeviceCaps function, 561-564, 1314
GetDialogBaseUnits function, 1314
GetDIBits function, 565-567, 1314
GetDlgCtrlID function, 567, 1314
GetDlgItem function, 568, 1314
GetDlgItemInt function, 568-569, 1314
GetDlgItemText function, 569, 1314
GetDOSEnvironment function, 570, 1314
GetDoubleClickTime function, 570, 1314
GetDriverInfo function, 570-571, 1314
GetDriverModuleHandle function, 571, 1314
GetDriveType function, 571-572, 1315
GetEditSel member function, 1248
GetEnvironment function, 572-573, 1315
GetExpandedName function, 573, 1315
GETEXTENDEDTEXTMETRICS printer escape, 1178-1180
GETEXTENTTABLE printer escape, 1181
GETFACENAME printer escape, 1182
GetFileResource function, 573-574, 1315
GetFileResourceSize function, 574-575, 1315
GetFileTitle function, 575, 1315
GetFileVersionInfo function, 575-576, 1315
GetFileVersionInfoSize function, 576-577, 1315
GetFirstChild member function, 1299
GetFocus function, 577, 1315
GetFontData function, 577-578, 1315
GetFreeFileHandles function, 1315
GetFreeSpace function, 578-579, 1315
GetFreeSystemResources function, 579, 1315
GetGlyphOutline function, 579-581, 1315
GetGValue function, 581, 1315
GetId member function, 1250, 1299
GetInputState function, 581-582, 1315
GetInstance member function, 1299
GetInstanceData function, 582, 1315
GetItemHandle member function, 1253
GetKBCodePage function, 582-583, 1315
GetKeyboardState function, 583, 1315
GetKeyboardType function, 584, 1315
GetKeyNameText function, 585, 1315
GetKeyState function, 585-586, 1315
GetLastActivePopup function, 586, 1315
GetLastChild member function, 1299
GetLine member function, 1257
GetLineFromPos member function, 1257
GetLineIndex member function, 1257
GetLineLength member function, 1257-1258
GetMapMode function, 586-587, 1315
GetMenu function, 587, 1315
GetMenuCheckMarkDimensions function, 588, 1315
GetMenuItemCount function, 588, 1315
GetMenuItemID function, 588, 1315
GetMenuState function, 589-590, 1315
GetMenuString function, 590-591, 1315
GetMessage function, 591-592, 1315

GetMessageExtraInfo function, 592, 1316
GetMessagePos function, 592-593, 1316
GetMessageTime function, 593, 1316
GetMetaFile function, 593-594, 1316
GetMetaFileBits function, 594, 1316
GetModule member function, 1299
GetModuleFileName function, 594-595, 1316
GetModuleHandle function, 595, 1316
GetModuleUsage function, 595, 1316
GetMsgID member function, 1248, 1270
GetNearestColor function, 596, 1316
GetNearestPaletteIndex function, 596, 1316
GetNextDlgGroupItem function, 596-597, 1316
GetNextDlgTabItem function, 597-598, 1316
GetNextDriver function, 598, 1316
GetNextWindow function, 599, 1316
GetNumLines member function, 1258
GetNumTasks function, 599, 1316
GetObject function, 600, 1316
GetOpenClipboardWindow function, 600, 1316
GetOpenFileName function, 601-604, 1316
GetOutlineTextMetrics function, 604-605, 1316
GETPAIRKERNTABLE printer escape, 1182
GetPaletteEntries function, 607-608, 1316
GetParent function, 608, 1316
GetParentObject member function, 1278
GETPHYSPAGESIZE printer escape, 1183
GetPixel function, 608-609, 1316
GetPolyFillMode function, 609, 1316
GetPosition member function, 1281-1282
GETPRINTINGOFFSET printer escape, 1184
GetPriorityClipboardFormat function, 610, 1316
GetPrivateProfileInt function, 610-611, 1316
GetPrivateProfileString function, 611-612, 1316
GetProcAddress function, 612, 1316
GetProfileInt function, 612-613, 1316
GetProfileString function, 613-614, 1316
GetProp function, 614, 1316
GetQueueStatus function, 615, 1317
GetRange member function, 1282
GetRasterizerCaps function, 616, 1317
GetRgnBox function, 616-617, 1317
GetROP2 function, 49, 618-619, 1317
GetRValue function, 619, 1317
GetSaveFileName function, 619-622, 1317
GETSCALINGFACTOR printer escape, 1184-1185
GetScrollPos function, 622-623, 1317
GetScrollRange function, 623-624, 1317
GetSelCount member function, 1270
GetSelection member function, 1258
GetSelectorBase function, 624, 1317
GetSelectorLimit function, 624-625, 1317
GetSelIndex member function, 1270
GetSelIndexes member function, 1270
GetSelString member function, 1270
GetSelStrings member function, 1270
GETSETPAPERBINS printer escape, 1185-1186

GETSETPAPERMETRICS printer escape, 1186
GETSETPAPERORIENT printer escape, 1187
GETSETSCREENPARAMS printer escape, 1188
GetSiblingPtr member function, 1299
GetStockObject function, 46-47, 53, 625-626, 1317
GetStretchBltMode function, 626, 1317
GetString member function, 1270
GetStringLen member function, 1271
GetSubMenu function, 627, 1317
GetSubText member function, 1258
GetSysColor function, 627-628, 1317
GetSysModalWindow function, 628, 1317
GetSystemDebugState function, 629, 1317
GetSystemDir function, 629-630, 1317
GetSystemDirectory function, 630, 1317
GetSystemMenu function, 630, 1317
GetSystemMetrics function, 631-633, 1317
GetSystemPaletteEntries function, 633-634, 1317
GetSystemPaletteUse function, 634, 1317
GetTabbedTextExtent function, 635, 1317
GETTECHNOLOGY printer escape, 1188
GetTempDrive function, 636, 1317
GetTempFileName function, 636-637, 1317
GetText member function, 1248, 1289
GetTextAlign function, 638, 1317
GetTextCharacterExtra function, 68, 638, 1317
GetTextColor function, 68, 639, 1317
GetTextExtent function, 639-640, 1317
GetTextExtentEx function, 640-641, 1317
GetTextExtentPoint function, 641, 1317
GetTextFace function, 642, 1318
GetTextLen member function, 1248
GetTextMetrics function, 642-645, 1318
GetThresholdEvent function, 1318
GetThresholdStatus function, 1318
GetTickCount function, 645, 1318
GetTimerResolution function, 1318
GetTopWindow function, 646, 1318
GETTRACKKERNTABLE printer escape, 1189-1190
GetUpdateRect function, 646-647, 1318
GetUpdateRgn function, 647-648, 1318
GETVECTORBRUSHSIZE printer escape, 1190-1191
GETVECTORPENSIZE printer escape, 1192
GetVersion function, 648, 1318
GetViewportExt function, 648-649, 1318
GetViewportExtEx function, 649, 1318
GetViewportOrg function, 649, 1318
GetViewportOrgEx function, 650, 1318
GetWindow function, 650-651, 1318
GetWindowClass member function, 226, 1244, 1253, 1276, 1293, 1299
  redefining, 295, 303
GetWindowDC function, 651, 1318
GetWindowExt function, 652, 1318
GetWindowLong function, 652-653, 1318
GetWindowOrg function, 653, 1318
GetWindowOrgEx function, 653, 1318
GetWindowPlacement function, 654, 1318

GetWindowRect function, 654-655, 1318
GetWindowsDir function, 655-656, 1318
GetWindowsDirectory function, 656, 1318
GetWindowTask function, 656-657, 1318
GetWindowText function, 657, 1318
GetWindowTextLength function, 657-658, 1318
GetWindowWord function, 658, 1318
GetWinFlags function, 658-659, 1318
global
  handles, specifying, 674
  heap, 166-168
    information, copying, 675-676
  memory, 663-666
    discarding, 662
  memory blocks
    bytes, specifying, 683
    freeing, 673
    lock counts, decrementing, 684
    locking into linear memory, 672
    reallocating, 683
    unlocking, 684
  memory objects, creating, 432
  modules, 666-669
GlobalAddAtom function, 659-660, 1318
GlobalAlloc function, 660-661, 1319
GlobalCompact function, 661, 1319
GlobalDeleteAtom function, 662, 1319
GlobalDiscard function, 662, 1319
GlobalDosAlloc function, 662-663, 1319
GlobalDosFree function, 663, 1319
GlobalEntryHandle function, 664-666, 1319
GlobalEntryModule function, 666-669, 1319
GlobalFindAtom function, 669, 1319
GlobalFirst function, 669-672, 1319
GlobalFix function, 672-673, 1319
GlobalFlags function, 673, 1319
GlobalFree function, 673-674, 1319
GlobalGetAtomName function, 674, 1319
GlobalHandle function, 674-675, 1319
GlobalHandleToSel function, 675, 1319
GlobalInfo function, 675-676, 1319
GlobalLock function, 676, 1319
GlobalLRUNewest function, 677, 1319
GlobalLRUOldest function, 677, 1319
GlobalNext function, 678-680, 1319
GlobalNotify function, 680-681, 1319
GlobalPageLock function, 681-682, 1319
GlobalPageUnlock function, 682, 1319
GlobalReAlloc function, 682-683, 1319
GlobalSize function, 683, 1319
GlobalUnfix function, 684, 1319
GlobalUnlock function, 684, 1319
GlobalUnWire function, 1319
GlobalWire function, 1320
glyph data, 578
graphics
  mode, 58
  static controls, 245-246
Graphics Device Interface, *see* GDI
gray-background windows, creating, 229, 1244
GrayString function, 685-686, 1320
Group Box tool, 1217
group boxes, 1266-1267
  BWCC, 1238-1239
  controls, 243-245

H

HandleDList member function, 1262
HandleFList member function, 1262

HandleFName member function, 1262
handles, 13-14, 595
  conversation, returning, 447
  creating for metafiles, 593
  current tasks, 556
  data
    defining, 899
    freeing, 435
  files
    allocating, 324
    defining, 914
    freeing, 988
  fonts, 625-626
  input focus, 577
  memory
    blocks, 594
    objects, local, 728
  menus, 704
    pop-up, 627
  module
    for device drivers, 571
    locating, 595
  returning, 600
    system modal windows, 628
  selectors, creating, 675
  specifying globally, 674
  stock pen, 625-626
  string
    creating, 432
    freeing, 435
    saving, 441
  validity, 706
  Windows desktop, 560
  windows, 650-651, 657
    child, 646
    locating, 599
    menus, 587
    parent, locating, 608
hardware functions, 1342-1343
hashValue member function, 1232, 1278, 1286, 1300
header files, owl.h, 266
heaps
  compacting, 723
  global, 166-168
    copying, 675-676
  local, 166, 168-170, 728
    initializing, 729
    shrinking, 734
Help applications, 1006
HIBYTE function, 686, 1320
HideCaret function, 686-687, 1320
HideList member function, 1248
hiding cursor, 953
high-order word, 688
highlights, removing from menus, 687
HiliteMenuItem function, 687-688, 1320
hit test
  codes, 139-140
  message, 139-140
HIWORD function, 688, 1320
hook
  codes, 344
  functions, 1343
    deleting, 989-990
Horizontal
  device metrics, 578
  header, 578
  metrics, 578
  Scroll Bar tool, 1217
horizontal scroll bars, 10, 1280-1283
HScroll member function, 1286
Hungarian notation, 12-13

I

.ICO files, 1211
Iconic Static Control tool, 1217
icons, 6-7, 106-110, 1210
  copying, 367
  creating, 401, 1220-1225
  displaying, 301-304
  editing, 1220-1225

functions, 1343
loading, 301-304, 715
IDE (Integrated Development Environment)
Project Manager, creating applications, 22-24
with ObjectWindows, 264-265
identification number (ID)
child windows, 567
menu items, 589
`IdleAction` member function, 1234
import libraries, 190
ObjectWindows, 264
`IMPORTS` function, 195
include files, windows.h, 14
`InflateRect` function, 688-689, 1320
information
context, creating, 400-401
functions, 1343-1344
inheritance, 204-207
`InitApplication` member function, 214-216, 1234
`InitAtomTable` function, 690, 1320
`InitChild` member function, 1276
`InitClientWindow` member function, 1276
initialization
file
functions, 1344
key values, 613
messages, 1360
initializing
ObjectWindows application objects, 215-216
printer drivers, 961
programs, `WinMain` function, 19-20
`InitInstance` member function, 214-216, 286, 290, 308, 1234
`InitMainWindow` member function, 214-215, 1234
redefining, 266-267
input
checking, 582
dialog boxes, 233-234, 1267-1268
focus, 1059
for handles, 577
functions, 1344
keyboards, 124
locking, 736
messages, 1360
mouse, 138
normal, restoring, 867
unlocking, 736
`InSendMessage` function, 690, 1320
`Insert` member function, 1258
`InsertMenu` function, 691-692, 1320
`InsertString` member function, 1271
installable driver functions, 1345
installing
callback functions, 926
files, 998-1000
instances
data, copying, 582
enumerating in device drivers, 598
registering with library, 815
instruction pointer, defining, 978
integers, 751
atoms, creating, 750
long, 751
intercharacter spacing, 639
text attribute, 68
interface
elements, 209-210
button, 243
check box, 241
group box, 244-245
radio button, 242-243
static bitmap, 251-252
static text, 248-249
window, 225
objects, 209, 217
defining shared behaviors, 217-221
dialog, 229-234
window, 221-229

InterruptRegister function, 693, 1320
interrupts, controlling, 693
InterruptUnRegister function, 693-694, 1320
IntersectClipRect function, 694, 1320
intersecting
  lines, 1203
  rectangles, 695
IntersectRect function, 695, 1320
InvalidateRect function, 696-697, 1320
InvalidateRgn function, 697, 1320
inverting
  colors, 699
  rectangles, 698
InvertRect function, 697-698, 1320
InvertRgn function, 698-699, 1320
isA member function, 1232, 1234, 1253, 1278, 1286, 1293, 1300
isAssociation member function, 1232
IsCharAlpha function, 699, 1320
IsCharAlphaNumeric function, 699-700, 1320
IsCharLower function, 700, 1320
IsCharUpper function, 700, 1320
IsChild function, 701, 1320
IsClipboardFormatAvailable function, 701, 1320
IsDBCSLeadByte function, 702, 1320
IsDialogMessage function, 702-703, 1320
IsDlgButtonChecked function, 703-704, 1320
isEqual member function, 1232, 1278, 1286-1287, 1300
IsFlagSet member function, 1300
IsIconic function, 704, 1320
IsMenu function, 704, 1320
IsModified member function, 1258
IsRectEmpty function, 705, 1321
isSortable member function, 1232
IsTask function, 706, 1321
IsVisibleRect member function, 1287
IsWindow function, 706, 1321
IsWindowEnabled function, 706-707, 1321
IsWindowVisible function, 707, 1321
IsZoomed function, 707, 1321

J-K

jobs, aborting, 1164
justifying text, 1197
  Graphics Device Interface (GDI), 937

kerning, 578
  track, defining, 1201
keyboards
  caret, 129-136
  enabling, 707
  input, 124
    sending to windows, 914
  messages, 130-136
    character, 128-129
    keystroke, 124-128
  state table, setting, 915
  types, 584
keys
  accelerator, 85-86
    translating, 984-985
  closing, 862
  creating, 862
  deleting, 863
  names, 585
    string, 614
  opening, 866
  status, 585
  strings, copying, 611
  values, specifying, 611

virtual
codes, 126-128
status, 583
Windows initialization file, 613
keystroke messages, 124-125
lParam variable, 125-126
wParam variable, 126-136
keywords
class, 203
struct, 203
union, 203
KillTimer function, 708, 1321

L

labels, menu items, 590
lastThat member function, 1232-1234
late binding, *see* polymorphism
LB_ADDSTRING message, 1061, 1367
LB_DELETESTRING message, 1061, 1367
LB_DIR message, 1061, 1367
LB_FINDSTRING message, 1062, 1367
LB_GETCARETINDEX message, 1063, 1367
LB_GETCOUNT message, 1063, 1367
LB_GETCURSEL message, 1063, 1368
LB_GETHORIZONTALEXTENT message, 1064, 1368
LB_GETITEMDATA message, 1064, 1368
LB_GETITEMHEIGHT message, 1064, 1368
LB_GETITEMRECT message, 1065, 1368
LB_GETSEL message, 1065, 1368
LB_GETSELCOUNT message, 1066, 1368
LB_GETSELITEMS message, 1066, 1368
LB_GETTEXT message, 1066, 1368
LB_GETTEXTLEN message, 1067, 1368
LB_GETTOPINDEX message, 1067, 1368
LB_INSERTSTRING message, 1067, 1368
LB_RESETCONTENT message, 1068, 1368
LB_SELECTSTRING message, 1068, 1368
LB_SELITEMRANGE message, 1069, 1368
LB_SETCARETINDEX message, 1069, 1368
LB_SETCOLUMNWIDTH message, 1069, 1368
LB_SETCURSEL message, 1070, 1369
LB_SETHORIZONTALEXTENT message, 1070, 1369
LB_SETITEMDATA message, 1070, 1369
LB_SETITEMHEIGHT message, 1071, 1369
LB_SETSEL message, 1071, 1369
LB_SETTABSTOPS message, 1072, 1369
LB_SETTOPINDEX message, 1072, 1369
LBN_DBLCLK message, 1072, 1369
LBN_ERRSPACE message, 1073, 1369
LBN_KILLFOCUS message, 1073, 1369
LBN_SELCHANGE message, 1073, 1369
LBN_SETFOCUS message, 1074, 1369
_lclose function, 708-709, 1321
_lcreat function, 709, 1321
least recently used (LRU) position, 677
Lempel-Ziv expansion functions, 1345
libraries
behaviors, sharing with applications, 1277-1279
import, 190
modules, loading, 715
ObjectWindows, 264
Line tool, 1222
LineDDA function, 710-711, 1321
lines
calculating points, 710-711
drawing, 39-46, 270-273, 711
modes, 48-49
end-cap, 1202
intersecting, 1203
length, 1051
output functions, 1345
pens, 46-48

LineTo function, 39-40, 711, 1321
linking
objects, 5
static versus dynamic, 189-190
List Box tool, 1217
list boxes, 1268-1272
controls, 237-238
displaying, 1025
items, 1063
heights, 1064
selecting, 1066
messages, 1360
rectangles, dimesions, 1065
width, scrollable, 1064
LISTBOX class controls, 159
notification codes, 160
styles, 156-157
_llseek function, 711-712, 1321
LoadAccelerators function, 712, 1321
LoadBitmap function, 92, 713, 1321
LoadCursor function, 713-714, 1321
LoadIcon function, 714-715, 1321
LoadLibrary function, 715-716, 1321
LoadMenu function, 716-717, 1321
LoadMenuIndirect function, 717-718, 1321
LoadModule function, 718-720, 1321
LoadResource function, 720, 1321
LoadString function, 118, 721, 1321
LOBYTE function, 721-722, 1321
local
devices, redirected, 1009
heaps, 166, 168-170, 728
shrinking, 734
memory blocks, 727
bytes, specifying, 734
locking, 730
reference count, decrementing, 735
size, modifying, 733
LocalAlloc function, 722-723, 1321
LocalCompact function, 723, 1321
LocalDiscard function, 723, 1321
LocalFirst function, 724-726, 1321
LocalFlags function, 726-727, 1321
LocalFree function, 1321
LocalHandle function, 728, 1321
LocalInfo function, 728-729, 1321
LocalInit function, 729, 1321
LocalLock function, 729-730, 1321
LocalNext function, 730-732, 1321
LocalReAlloc function, 733, 1322
LocalShrink function, 733-734, 1322
LocalSize function, 734, 1322
LocalUnlock function, 734-735, 1322
LockData function, 735, 1322
LockInput function, 735, 736
LockResource function, 736, 1322
LockSegment function, 736-737, 1322
LockWindowUpdate function, 739
LOGFONT data structure, 69
logical
addresses, 166
brushes, creating, 372-373
with device-independent bitmaps, 392
with hatch style, 399-400
coordinates, 35, 555
fonts, 68-69
mapping, 916
loops, message, 21-22
MDI, 175-176
WinMain function, 20
with ObjectWindows, 261
_lopen function, 737-738, 1322
low-order
bytes, 721
word, 738
lowercase characters, 700
LowMemory member function, 1278
LOWORD function, 738, 1322
lParam variable
character messages, 129
keystroke messages, 125-126
LPtoDP function, 739-740, 1322
_lread function, 740, 1322

LRU (least recently used position), 677
lstrcat function, 740-741, 1322
lstrcmp function, 741, 1322
lstrcmpi function, 742, 1322
lstrcpy function, 742-743, 1322
lstrlen function, 743, 1322
_lwrite function, 743-744, 1322
LZClose function, 744, 1322
LZCopy function, 744-745, 1322
LZDone function, 745, 1322
LZInit function, 746, 1322
LZOpenFile function, 746-748, 1322
LZRead function, 748-749, 1322
LZSeek function, 749-750, 1322
LZStart function, 750, 1322

M

macro functions, 1358
MAKEINTATOM function, 750, 1322
MAKEINTRESOURCE function, 751, 1322
MAKELONG function, 751, 1322
MAKEPOINT function, 752, 1322
MakeProcInstance function, 752, 1322
MakeWindow member function, 225, 230, 1278
MapDialogRect function, 753-754, 1322
mapping
  functions, 1346
  logical fonts, 916
  modes, 33-34
    current, 586-587
    defining, 915
    MM_ANISOTROPIC, 36
MapVirtualKey function, 754, 1322
MapWindowPoints function, 755, 1323
max function, 755, 1322
Maximize button, 11
maximizing child windows, 178-180
MDI (Multiple Document Interface)
  applications, 173-175
    creating, 308-313
  child window procedures, 177
  client windows, 1272-1273
    class, 254
  creating documents, 177-187
  frame windows, 1274-1276
    class, 252-254
    procedures, 177
  message loops, 175-176
  messages, 176, 1360
member functions, ObjectWindows
  ActivationResponse, 1292, 1295
  AddString, 1269
  AfterDispatchHandler, 1295
  ArrangeIcons, 1273-1274
  AssignMenu, 1292
  AutoScroll, 1286
  BeforeDispatchHandler, 1296
  BeginView, 1286
  BMSetStyle, 1243
  BNClicked, 1245-1246, 1280
  build, 1236-1244, 1246, 1248, 1252, 1255-1256, 1260, 1262-1263, 1266, 1268-1269, 1273-1275, 1280-1281, 1286, 1289, 1292, 1296
  Cancel, 230, 1252
  CanClear, 1264
  CanClose, 217, 1234, 1262, 1264, 1296
  CanUndo, 1256
  CascadeChildren, 1273, 1275
  Check, 1246
  ChildWithId, 1296
  Clear, 1248, 1289
  ClearList, 1269
  ClearModify, 1256
  CloseChildren, 1275
  CloseWindow, 217, 1252, 1296
  CMArrangeIcons, 1275
  CMCascadeChildren, 1275
  CMCloseChildren, 1275
  CMCreateChild, 1275
  CMEditClear, 1256

CMEditCopy, 1256
CMEditCut, 1256
CMEditDelete, 1256
CMEditFind, 1260
CMEditFindNext, 1260
CMEditPaste, 1256
CMEditReplace, 1260
CMEditUndo, 1256
CMExit, 1296
CMFileNew, 1264
CMFileOpen, 1264
CMFileSave, 1264
CMFileSaveAs, 1264
CMTileChildren, 1275
Copy, 1256-1257
Create, 225, 1252, 1292, 1296
CreateChild, 1275-1276
CreateChildren, 1296
Cut, 1257
DefChildProc, 1296
DefCommandProc, 1297
defining for controls, 235
DefNotificationProc, 1297
DefWndProc, 1297
DeleteLine, 1257
DeleteSelection, 1257
DeleteString, 1269
DeleteSubText, 1257
DeltaPos, 1281
Destroy, 1252-1253, 1297
DisableAutoCreate, 1297
DisableTransfer, 1297
DispatchAMessage, 1297
DispatchScroll, 1297
DoSearch, 1260
DrawItem, 1297
EnableAutoCreate, 1297-1298
EnableKBHandler, 1298
EnableTransfer, 1298
EndView, 1286
ENErrSpace, 1257
Error, 1277-1278
ExecDialog, 230, 1278
Execute, 1253
FindExactString, 1269
FindString, 1269
FirstThat, 1298
firstThat, 1231
ForEach, 1298
forEach, 1231-1232
GetApplication, 1298
GetCheck, 1246
GetChildPtr, 1298-1299
GetChildren, 1299
GetClassName, 226, 1236-1244, 1248, 1253, 1257, 1266, 1269, 1273, 1276, 1281, 1289, 1292, 1299
GetClient, 1276, 1299
GetClientHandle, 1278
GetCount, 1270
GetEditSel, 1248
GetFirstChild, 1299
GetId, 1250, 1299
GetInstance, 1299
GetItemHandle, 1253
GetLastChild, 1299
GetLine, 1257
GetLineFromPos, 1257
GetLineIndex, 1257
GetLineLength, 1257-1258
GetModule, 1299
GetMsgID, 1248, 1270
GetNumLines, 1258
GetParentObject, 1278
GetPosition, 1281-1282
GetRange, 1282
GetSelCount, 1270
GetSelection, 1258
GetSelIndex, 1270
GetSelIndexes, 1270
GetSelString, 1270
GetSelStrings, 1270
GetSiblingPtr, 1299
GetString, 1270
GetStringLen, 1271

GetSubText, 1258
GetText, 1248, 1289
GetTextLen, 1248
GetWindowClass, 226, 295, 303, 1244, 1253, 1276, 1293, 1299
HandleDList, 1262
HandleFList, 1262
HandleFName, 1262
hashValue, 1232, 1278, 1286, 1300
HideList, 1248
HScroll, 1286
IdleAction, 1234
InitApplication, 214-216, 1234
InitChild, 1276
InitClientWindow, 1276
InitInstance, 214-216, 286, 290, 308, 1234
InitMainWindow, 214-215, 266-267, 1234
Insert, 1258
InsertString, 1271
isA, 1232, 1234, 1253, 1278, 1286, 1293, 1300
isAssociation, 1232
isEqual, 1232, 1278, 1286-1287, 1300
IsFlagSet, 1300
IsModified, 1258
isSortable, 1232
IsVisibleRect, 1287
lastThat, 1232
LowMemory, 1278
MakeWindow, 225, 230, 1278
MessageLoop, 214, 216, 1234
nameOf, 1232, 1234, 1248, 1253, 1278-1279, 1287, 1289, 1293, 1300
new, 1232
NewFile, 1264
Next, 1300
ODADrawEntire, 1250
ODAFocus, 1250-1251
ODASelect, 1251
Ok, 230, 1253
Open, 1264
Paint, 272, 275, 277, 280, 283, 285, 293, 303, 1293
Paste, 1258
Previous, 1300
printOn, 1232, 1279, 1287, 1300
ProcessAccels, 216, 1234
ProcessAppMsg, 1234-1235
ProcessDlgMsg, 216, 1235
ProcessMDIAccels, 216, 1235
PutChildPtr, 1300
PutChildren, 1300
PutSiblingPtr, 1301
Read, 1264-1265
read, 1246, 1248-1249, 1253, 1260, 1265-1266, 1268, 1273, 1276, 1282, 1287, 1289-1291, 1293, 1301
Register, 1301
RemoveClient, 1301
ReplaceWith, 1265
RestoreMemory, 1279
Run, 214, 1235
Save, 1265
SaveAs, 1265
SBBottom, 1282
SBLineDown, 1282
SBLineUp, 1282
SBPageDown, 1282
SBPageUp, 1282
SBThumbPosition, 1282-1283
SBThumbTrack, 1283
SBTop, 1283
Scroll, 1258
ScrollBy, 1287
ScrollTo, 1287
Search, 1258
SelectFileName, 1262
SelectionChanged, 1266-1267
SendDlgItemMsg, 1254
SetCaption, 1254, 1301
SetCheck, 1246

SetEditSel, 1249
SetFileName, 1265
SetFlags, 1301
SetKBHandler, 1235
SetPageSize, 1287
SetParent, 1301
SetPosition, 1283
SetRange, 1283, 1287
SetSBarRange, 1287
SetSelection, 1259-1260
SetSelIndex, 1271
SetSelIndexes, 1271
SetSelString, 1271
SetSelStrings, 1271
SetText, 1249, 1290
SetTransferBuffer, 1301
SetUnits, 1288
SetupWindow, 1243, 1249, 1254, 1259, 1262, 1265, 1268, 1276, 1283, 1293, 1301
Show, 1301-1302
ShowList, 1249
ShutDownWindow, 1254, 1302
streamableName, 1291
TileChildren, 1273, 1276
Toggle, 1246
Transfer, 1246, 1249, 1271-1272, 1283, 1290, 1302
TransferData, 1268, 1302
Uncheck, 1246-1247
Undo, 1259
UpdateFileName, 1262
UpdateListBoxes, 1263
ValidWindow, 225, 1279
VScroll, 1288
WMActivate, 1276, 1302
WMClose, 1254, 1303
WMCommand, 1303
WMCreate, 1293
WMDestroy, 1303
WMDrawItem, 1251, 1303
WMGetDlgCode, 1243-1244
WMHScroll, 1293, 1303
WMInitDialog, 1254
WMLButtonDown, 1293
WMMDIActivate, 1273, 1293-1294
WMMove, 1294
WMNCDestroy, 1303
WMPaint, 1251, 1273, 1294
WMQueryEndSession, 1254, 1303
WMSetFocus, 1260-1261
WMSize, 1261, 1294
WMVScroll, 1294, 1303
Write, 1265
write, 1247, 1249, 1255, 1261, 1265, 1267-1268, 1273, 1276, 1283, 1288, 1290-1291, 1294, 1303
XRangeValue, 1288
XScrollValue, 1288
YRangeValue, 1288
YScrollValue, 1288

MemManInfo function, 756-757, 1323

memory
allocating, 325, 722, 746
for multiple windows, 336
from global heap, 660
in edit control, 1058
in Graphics Device Interface (GDI), 324
in User heap, 326
resources, 325
availability, 578, 931
configuring, 659
free spaces, validating, 995
freeing, 663
allocated, 528
global, 663-666
discarding, 662
freeing, 673
heap, 166-168, 675-676
locking into linear memory, 672
local heap, 166, 168-170
logical addresses, 166
management functions, 1346-1347
managers, 756

objects
global, moving, 677
handles, 728
operating modes, 165-166
page-lock count, 681-682
segments, 170-171
memory blocks
bytes, specifying, 683
discarding, 723
global
lock counts, 684
reallocating, 683
unlocking, 684
handles, 594
local, 727
bytes, 734
locking, 730
reference count, decrementing, 735
size, 733
locking globally, 676
MemoryRead function, 757, 1323
MemoryWrite function, 758, 1323
menu bar, 11
Menu editor, 110, 1219-1220
menus, 110-116, 1210
checkmark bitmap, default, 588
creating and testing, 1219-1220
functions, 1347
handles, 704
windows, 587
highlights, removing, 687
items
appending, 333-334
checkmarks, deleting, 348-349
defining actions, 286-290
defining responses, 304-308
deleting, 869
identification number (ID), 589
inserting, 691-692
labels, 590
modifying, 762
pop-up, 588
top-level, 588
loading, 717
resource, 716
pop-up
creating, 409-410
handles, 627
placing, 983
setting, 917
status, 589-590
System, accessing, 631
MessageBeep function, 758, 1323
MessageBox function, 118, 759-761, 1323
MessageLoop member function, 214-216, 1234
messages, 12
BM_GETCHECK, 1018, 1361
BM_GETSTATE, 1018, 1361
BM_SETCHECK, 1019, 1361
BM_SETSTATE, 1019, 1361
BM_SETSTYLE, 1020, 1361
BN_CLICKED, 1021, 1361
BN_DISABLE, 1361
BN_DOUBLECLICKED, 1021, 1361
CB_ADDSTRING, 1021, 1361
CB_DELETESTRING, 1022, 1361
CB_DIR, 1022, 1362
CB_FINDSTRING, 1023, 1362
CB_GETCOUNT, 1023, 1362
CB_GETCURSEL, 1024, 1362
CB_GETDROPPEDCONTROLRECT, 1024, 1362
CB_GETDROPPEDSTATE, 1025, 1362
CB_GETEDITSEL, 1025, 1362
CB_GETEXTENDEDDUI, 1362
CB_GETEXTENDEDUI, 1026
CB_GETITEMDATA, 1026, 1362
CB_GETITEMHEIGHT, 1027, 1362
CB_GETLBTEXT, 1027, 1362
CB_GETLBTEXTLEN, 1027, 1362
CB_INSERTSTRING, 1028, 1362
CB_LIMITTEXT, 1028, 1362
CB_RESETCONTENT, 1028, 1362
CB_SELECTSTRING, 1029, 1363

CB_SETCURSEL, 1029, 1363
CB_SETEDITSEL, 1030, 1363
CB_SETEXTENDEDDUI, 1363
CB_SETEXTENDEDUI, 1030
CB_SETITEMDATA, 1031, 1363
CB_SETITEMHEIGHT, 1031, 1363
CB_SHOWDROPDOWN, 1031, 1363
CBN_CLOSEUP, 1032, 1363
CBN_DBLCLK, 1032, 1363
CBN_DROPDOWN, 1032, 1363
CBN_EDITCHANGE, 1033, 1363
CBN_EDITUPDATE, 1033, 1363
CBN_ERRSPACE, 1034, 1363
CBN_KILLFOCUS, 1034, 1363
CBN_SELCHANGE, 1034, 1363
CBN_SELENDCANCEL, 1035, 1364
CBN_SELENDOK, 1035, 1364
CBN_SETFOCUS, 1035, 1364
character, 124-125, 128-129
coordinates, locating, 592
creating, 759
device drivers, sending to, 888
DM_GETDEFID, 1036, 1364
DM_SETDEFID, 1036, 1364
DRV_CLOSE, 1036, 1364
DRV_CONFIGURE, 1037, 1364
DRV_DISABLE, 1038, 1364
DRV_ENABLE, 1039, 1364
DRV_FREE, 1039, 1364
DRV_INSTALL, 1040, 1364
DRV_LOAD, 1041, 1364
DRV_OPEN, 1042, 1364
DRV_POWER, 1043, 1364
DRV_QUERYCONFIGURE, 1042, 1364
DRV_REMOVE, 1044, 1365
DRV_USER, 1045
EM_CANUNDO, 1045, 1365
EM_EMPTYUNDOBUFFER, 1046, 1365
EM_FMTLINES, 1046, 1365
EM_GETFIRSTVISIBLELINE, 1046, 1365
EM_GETHANDLE, 1047, 1365
EM_GETLINE, 1047, 1365
EM_GETLINECOUNT, 1047, 1365
EM_GETMODIFY, 1048, 1365
EM_GETPASSWORDCHAR, 1048
EM_GETRECT, 1048, 1365
EM_GETSEL, 1049, 1365
EM_GETWORDBREAKPROC, 1050, 1365
EM_LIMITTEXT, 1050, 1365
EM_LINEFROMCHAR, 1050, 1366
EM_LINEINDEX, 1051, 1366
EM_LINELENGTH, 1051, 1366
EM_LINESCROLL, 1052, 1366
EM_PASSWORDCHAR, 1365
EM_REPLACESEL, 1052, 1366
EM_SETHANDLE, 1052, 1366
EM_SETMODIFY, 1053, 1366
EM_SETPASSWORDCHAR, 1053, 1366
EM_SETREADONLY, 1053
EM_SETRECT, 1054, 1366
EM_SETRECTNP, 1055, 1366
EM_SETSEL, 1055, 1366
EM_SETTABSTOPS, 1056, 1366
EM_SETWORDBREAKPROC, 1056, 1367
EM_UNDO, 1057, 1367
EN_CHANGE, 1058, 1367
EN_ERRSPACE, 1058, 1367
EN_HSCROLL, 1058, 1367
EN_KILLFOCUS, 1059, 1367
EN_MAXTEXT, 1059, 1367
EN_SETFOCUS, 1060, 1367
EN_UPDATE, 1060, 1367
EN_VSCROLL, 1060, 1367
extra information, 592
functions, 1347-1348
  current filter, passing to, 343
  defining for processing, 1250-1251
  processing in, 690
keystroke, 124-128
LB_ADDSTRING, 1061, 1367
LB_DELETESTRING, 1061, 1367
LB_DIR, 1061, 1367
LB_FINDSTRING, 1062, 1367
LB_GETCARETINDEX, 1063, 1367

LB_GETCOUNT, 1063, 1367
LB_GETCURSEL, 1063, 1368
LB_GETHORIZONTALEXTENT, 1064, 1368
LB_GETITEMDATA, 1064, 1368
LB_GETITEMHEIGHT, 1064, 1368
LB_GETITEMRECT, 1065, 1368
LB_GETSEL, 1065, 1368
LB_GETSELCOUNT, 1066, 1368
LB_GETSELITEMS, 1066, 1368
LB_GETTEXT, 1066, 1368
LB_GETTEXTLEN, 1067, 1368
LB_GETTOPINDEX, 1067, 1368
LB_INSERTSTRING, 1067, 1368
LB_RESETCONTENT, 1068, 1368
LB_SELECTSTRING, 1068, 1368
LB_SELITEMRANGE, 1069, 1368
LB_SETCARETINDEX, 1069, 1368
LB_SETCOLUMNWIDTH, 1069, 1368
LB_SETCURSEL, 1070, 1369
LB_SETHORIZONTALEXTENT, 1070, 1369
LB_SETITEMDATA, 1070, 1369
LB_SETITEMHEIGHT, 1071, 1369
LB_SETSEL, 1071, 1369
LB_SETTABSTOPS, 1072, 1369
LB_SETTOPINDEX, 1072, 1369
LBN_DBLCLK, 1072, 1369
LBN_ERRSPACE, 1073, 1369
LBN_KILLFOCUS, 1073, 1369
LBN_SELCHANGE, 1073, 1369
LBN_SETFOCUS, 1074, 1369
length, 593
loops, 21-22
  MDI, 175-176
  of WinMain function, 20
  with ObjectWindows, 261
MDI, 176
modeless dialog boxes, 702-703
mouse
  client area, 140-141
  hit test, 139-140
  non-client area, 141-142
queues, 615
replying, 873
retrieving, 591-592
sending, 887-889
SETREADONLY, 1366
sound, 758
STM_GETICON, 1074, 1369
STM_SETICON, 1074, 1369
virtual key, translating, 986
Windows, 1017-1112
  types, 1359-1361
windows, defining, 865
WM_ACTIVATE, 1075, 1369
WM_ACTIVATEAPP, 1075, 1369
WM_ASKCBFORMATNAME, 1076, 1369
WM_CANCELMODE, 1076, 1369
WM_CHANGECBCHAIN, 1077, 1370
WM_CHAR, 130, 1077, 1370
WM_CHARTOITEM, 1078, 1370
WM_CHILDACTIVATE, 1079, 1370
WM_CHOOSEFONT_GETLOGFONT, 1079, 1370
WM_CLEAR, 1079, 1370
WM_CLOSE, 1080, 1370
WM_COMMAND, 111, 1080, 1370
WM_COMMNOTIFY, 1080, 1370
WM_COMPACTING, 1081, 1370
WM_COMPAREITEM, 1082, 1370
WM_COPY, 1083, 1370
WM_CREATE, 59, 76, 1083, 1371
WM_CTLCOLOR, 1084, 1371
WM_CUT, 1085, 1371
WM_DDE_ACK, 1085, 1371
WM_DDE_ADVISE, 1087, 1371
WM_DDE_DATA, 1088, 1371
WM_DDE_EXECUTE, 1089, 1371
WM_DDE_INITIATE, 1090, 1371
WM_DDE_POKE, 1091, 1371
WM_DDE_REQUEST, 1091, 1371
WM_DDE_TERMINATE, 1092, 1372
WM_DDE_UNADVISE, 1092, 1372
WM_DEADCHAR, 1093, 1372
WM_DELETEITEM, 1094, 1372

WM_DESTROY, 1094, 1372
WM_DESTROYCLIPBOARD, 1095, 1372
WM_DEVMODECHANGE, 1095, 1372
WM_DRAWCLIPBOARD, 1095, 1372
WM_DRAWITEM, 1096, 1372
WM_DROPFILES, 1097, 1372
WM_ENABLE, 1098, 1372
WM_ENDSESSION, 1098, 1372
WM_ENTERIDLE, 1098, 1373
WM_ERASEBKGND, 1099, 1373
WM_FONTCHANGE, 1099, 1373
WM_GETDLGCODE, 1100, 1373
WM_GETFONT, 1100, 1373
WM_GETHOTKEY, 1101, 1373
WM_GETMINMAXINFO, 1101, 1373
WM_GETTEXT, 1102, 1373
WM_GETTEXTLENGTH, 1102, 1373
WM_HSCROLL, 76, 1103, 1373
WM_HSCROLLCLIPBOARD, 1103, 1373
WM_ICONERASEBKGND, 1104, 1373
WM_INITDIALOG, 1105, 1373
WM_INITMENU, 1105, 1373
WM_INITMENUPOPUP, 1106, 1373
WM_KEYDOWN, 130, 1106, 1373
WM_KEYUP, 1107, 1374
WM_KILLFOCUS, 1108, 1374
WM_LBUTTONDBLCLK, 1108, 1374
WM_LBUTTONDOWN, 1108, 1374
WM_LBUTTONUP, 1109, 1374
WM_MBUTTONDBLCLK, 1110, 1374
WM_MBUTTONDOWN, 1110, 1374
WM_MBUTTONUP, 1111, 1374
WM_MDIACTIVATE, 1111, 1374
WM_MDICASCADE, 1112, 1374
WM_MDICREATE, 1374
WM_MDIDESTROY, 1114, 1374
WM_MDIGETACTIVE, 1114, 1374
WM_MDIICONARRANGE, 1115, 1374
WM_MDIMAXIMIZE, 1115, 1374
WM_MDINEXT, 1115, 1374
WM_MDIRESTORE, 1116, 1374
WM_MDISETMENU, 1116, 1374
WM_MDITILE, 1117, 1374
WM_MEASUREITEM, 1117, 1374
WM_MENUCHAR, 1118, 1375
WM_MENUSELECT, 1119, 1375
WM_MOUSEACTIVATE, 1119, 1375
WM_MOUSEMOVE, 142-143, 1121, 1375
WM_MOVE, 1121, 1375
WM_NCACTIVATE, 1122, 1375
WM_NCCALCSIZE, 1122, 1375
WM_NCCREATE, 1123, 1375
WM_NCDESTROY, 1124, 1375
WM_NCHITTEST, 1124, 1375
WM_NCLBUTTONDBLCLK, 1126, 1375
WM_NCLBUTTONDOWN, 1127, 1375
WM_NCLBUTTONUP, 1128, 1375
WM_NCMBUTTONDBLCLK, 1129, 1376
WM_NCMBUTTONDOWN, 1130, 1376
WM_NCMBUTTONUP, 1131, 1376
WM_NCMOUSEMOVE, 1133, 1376
WM_NCPAINT, 1134, 1376
WM_NCRBUTTONDBLCLK, 1134, 1376
WM_NCRBUTTONDOWN, 1135, 1376
WM_NCRBUTTONUP, 1136, 1376
WM_NEXTDLGCTL, 1138, 1376
WM_OTHERWINDOWCREATED, 1376
WM_OTHERWINDOWDESTROYED, 1376
WM_PAINT, 35-36, 76, 1138, 1376
WM_PAINTCLIPBOARD, 1138, 1376
WM_PAINTICON, 1377
WM_PALETTECHANGED, 1139, 1377
WM_PALETTEISCHANGING, 1377
WM_PARENTNOTIFY, 1140, 1377
WM_PASTE, 1141, 1377
WM_POWER, 1141, 1377
WM_QUERYDRAGICON, 1142, 1377
WM_QUERYENDSESSION, 1142, 1377
WM_QUERYNEWPALETTE, 1142, 1377
WM_QUERYOPEN, 1143, 1377
WM_QUEUESYNC, 1143, 1377
WM_QUIT, 1143, 1377
WM_RBUTTONDBLCLK, 1144, 1377
WM_RBUTTONDOWN, 1144, 1377

WM_RBUTTONUP, 1145, 1377
WM_RENDERALLFORMATS, 1145, 1377
WM_RENDERFORMAT, 1146, 1378
WM_SETCURSOR, 1147, 1378
WM_SETFOCUS, 1148, 1378
WM_SETFONT, 1148, 1378
WM_SETHOTKEY, 1148, 1378
WM_SETREDRAW, 1149, 1378
WM_SETTEXT, 1149, 1378
WM_SHOWWINDOW, 1150, 1378
WM_SIZE, 76, 1150, 1378
WM_SIZECLIPBOARD, 1151, 1378
WM_SPOOLERSTATUS, 1152, 1378
WM_SYSCHAR, 1152, 1378
WM_SYSCOLORCHANGE, 1153, 1378
WM_SYSCOMMAND, 1153, 1378
WM_SYSDEADCHAR, 1154, 1378
WM_SYSKEYDOWN, 1154, 1379
WM_SYSKEYUP, 1155, 1379
WM_SYSTEMERROR, 1156, 1379
WM_TIMECHANGE, 1156, 1379
WM_TIMER, 1157, 1379
WM_UNDO, 1157, 1379
WM_VKEYTOITEM, 1157, 1379
WM_VSCROLL, 76, 1158, 1379
WM_VSCROLLCLIPBOARD, 1159, 1379
WM_WINDOWPOSCHANGED, 1160, 1379
WM_WINDOWPOSCHANGING, 1160, 1379
WM_WININICHANGE, 1160, 1379
metafiles
copying, 368-369
creating, 402, 919
devices, closing, 362
functions, 1348
handles, creating, 593
pages, storing, 1164
MFCOMMENT printer escape, 1193
microprocessors, operating modes, 165-166
min function, 761, 1323
minimal ObjectWindows application, 266-270
Minimize button, 11
minimizing child windows, 178-179
mirror modes, setting, 1204
miter limits, defining, 1204
MM_ANISOTROPIC mapping mode, 36
modal dialog boxes, 99
creating, 229-232
modeless dialog boxes, 99
creating, 229-232
messages, 702-703
modes
386 enhanced, 166
background, 68
setting, 893
drawing, 48-49, 927
locating, 618
graphics, 58
mapping, 33-34
current, 586-587
defining, 915
mirror, 1204
poly, 1205
real, 165
standard, 166
stretching, 931
text, 58
modify flags, values, 1053
ModifyMenu function, 761-763, 1323
module definition files, 25-26
accelerator example, 87
arc drawing example, 44
bitmap example, 92-93
child window example, 162
creating in ObjectWindows, 262-263
cursor example, 97
dialog box example, 101
DLL example, 195
fill example, 54
filled figure example, 50
font example, 69
for DLLs, 193-194

fundamental window example, 27, 269
icon example, 107
keyboard example, 130-131
line drawing example, 40
MDI, 177
MDI example, 180
menu example, 112
mouse example, 143
point drawing example, 36
scrolling text example, 77
string example, 118
`TabbedTextOut` example, 63
`TextOut` example, 59
`ModuleFindHandle` function, 764, 1323
`ModuleFindName` function, 765-766, 1323
`ModuleFirst` function, 766-767, 1323
`ModuleNext` function, 767-768, 1323
modules
defining behaviors, 1277-1279
global, 666-669
handles
device drivers, 571
locating, 595
information, retrieving, 766
library, loading, 715
management functions, 1348
mouse
buttons, interpreting, 967
captures, releasing, 867
current position, 129
double-clicking, length of, 570
enabling, 707
input, 138, 895
messages
client area, 140-141
hit test, 139-140
non-client area, 141-142
monitoring movements, 142-146
moveable segments, 170-171
movement functions, 1339-1340
`MoveTo` function, 39, 768, 1323
`MoveToEx` function, 769, 1323
`MoveWindow` function, 769-770, 1323
`MulDiv` function, 770, 1323
multimedia, 6
Multiple Document Interface, *see* MDI
multitasking, 7

N

`nameOf` member function, 1232-1234, 1248, 1253, 1278-1279, 1287, 1289, 1293, 1300
naming
compressed files, original, 573
files, 619-622
renaming
documents, 818
objects, 817
table, fonts, 578
variables with Hungarian notation, 12-13
`NetBIOSCall` function, 771, 1323
network functions, 1349
`new` member function, 1232
`NewFile` member function, 1264
`NEWFRAME` printer escape, 1193
`Next` member function, 1300
`NEXTBAND` printer escape, 1194
non-client area messages, 1360
mouse messages, 141-142
non-system messages, 125
Notepad application window components, 8-9
notification
callback function, defining, 772
codes, 159-161, 1360
procedures for current tasks, 680-681
globally, 680-681
`NotifyRegister` function, 771-773, 1323
`NotifyUnRegister` function, 773, 1323

O

OBJ_ACC project, 286-290
OBJ_ARC project, 273-275
OBJ_BAS project, 266-268
OBJ_BIT project, 290-293
OBJ_CUR project, 293-295
OBJ_DLG project, 295-300
OBJ_FIG project, 276-278
OBJ_ICON project, 301-304
OBJ_LINE project, 270-273
OBJ_MDI project, 308-313
OBJ_MENU project, 304-308
OBJ_SCRL project, 283-285
OBJ_TTXT project, 281-283
OBJ_TXT project, 278-280
Object class, 211-212, 1231-1232
object linking and embedding (OLE), 5
  functions, 1349-1350
object-oriented programming, 202
  encapsulation, 202-203
  inheritance, 204-207
  polymorphism, 207-209
  with ObjectWindows, 209-210
objects, 202
  application, 212
    executing, 216
    initializing, 215-216
    main program, 214-215
    terminating, 216-217
  control
    button, 236
    BWCC button, 243
    BWCC check box, 241
    BWCC divider, 251
    BWCC radio button, 242-243
    check box, 240-241
    combo box, 238-240
    defining member functions for, 235
    edit, 246-248
    group box, 243-245
    list box, 237-238
    radio button, 242
    scroll bar, 249-251
    static, 245-246, 248-249
    static bitmap, 251-252
  defining for text editing, 1259-1261
  dialog
    creating, 229-232
    file, 232-233
    input, 233-234
    search-and-replace, 234
  global memory, creating, 432
  information, obtaining, 600
  interface, 209, 217
  MDI
    client windows, 254
    frame windows, 252-254
  names, copying, 808
  protocol, 809
  reconnecting, 814
  releasing, 817
  renaming, 817
  revoking, 821
  scroller, 255-257
  selecting, 886
  size, 813
  status, 808-809, 812
  types, 813
  window, 221
    creating, 222-226
    edit, 226-227
    file editing, 227-229
    gray background, 229
ObjectWindows
  application objects, 212
    executing, 216
    initializing, 215-216
    main program, 214-215
    terminating, 216-217
  classes
    hierarchy, 210-211
    Object, 211-212, 1231-1232

TApplication, 213-214, 1233-1235
TBButton, 243, 1235-1236
TBCheckBox, 241, 1236-1237
TBDivider, 251, 1237-1238
TBGroupBox, 1238-1239
TBRadioButton, 242-243, 1239-1240
TBStatic, 248-249, 1240-1241
TBStaticBmp, 251-252, 1241-1242
TButton, 236, 1242-1244
TBWindow, 229, 1244
TCheckBox, 240-241, 1245-1247
TComboBox, 238-240, 1247-1249
TControl, 235, 1250-1251
TDialog, 229-232, 1251-1255
TEdit, 246-248, 1255-1259
TEditWindow, 226-227, 1259-1261
TFileDialog, 232-233, 1261-1263
TFileWindow, 227-229, 1263-1265
TGroupBox, 243-245, 1265-1267
TInputDialog, 233-234, 1267-1268
TListBox, 237-238, 1268-1272
TMDIClient, 254, 1272-1273
TMDIFrame, 252-254, 1273-1276
TModule, 1277-1279
TRadioButton, 242, 1279-1280
TScrollBar, 249-251, 1280-1283
TScroller, 255-257, 283-285, 1284-1288
TSearchDialog, 234
TStatic, 245-246, 1288-1290
TStreamable, 1290-1291
TWindow, 223-225, 1291-1294
TWindowsObject, 217-221, 1294-1303
member functions, *see* member functions
object-oriented programming with, 209-210
ObjectWindows applications
code structure, developing, 260
message loop, 261
window procedures, 261-262
WinMain function, 260-261
defining structures and behaviors, 1233-1235
developing with IDE, 264-265
minimal, 266-270
projects
C++ source files, 263
libraries, 264
module definition files, 262-263
resource files, 263
ODADrawEntire member function, 1250
ODAFocus member function, 1250-1251
ODASelect member function, 1251
OEM
character set, 129
scan code, 126
table, 582
OemKeyScan function, 773-774, 1323
OemToAnsi function, 1323
OemToAnsiBuff function, 775, 1323
OffsetClipRgn function, 775-776, 1323
OffsetRect function, 776-777, 1323
OffsetRgn function, 777-778, 1323
offsets, 166
OffsetViewportOrg function, 778, 1323
OffsetViewportOrgEx function, 779, 1323
OffsetWindowOrg function, 779-780, 1323

OffsetWindowOrgEx function, 780-781, 1323
Ok member function, 230, 1253
OLE (object linking and embedding), 5
  functions, 1349-1350
OleActivate function, 781, 1323
OleBlockServer function, 782, 1323
OleClone function, 782-783, 1323
OleClose function, 783, 1323
OleCopyFromLink function, 783-784, 1324
OleCopyToClipboard function, 784, 1324
OleCreate function, 785-786, 1324
OleCreateFromClip function, 786-787, 1324
OleCreateFromFile function, 788-789, 1324
OleCreateFromTemplate function, 789-790, 1324
OleCreateInvisible function, 791-792, 1324
OleCreateLinkFromClip function, 792-793, 1324
OleCreateLinkFromFile function, 794-795, 1324
OleDelete function, 796, 1324
OleDraw function, 796-797, 1324
OleEnumFormats function, 797, 1324
OleEnumObjects function, 798, 1324
OleEqual function, 798-799, 1324
OleExecute function, 799, 1324
OleGetData function, 799-800, 1324
OleGetLinkUpdateOptions function, 800-801, 1324
OleIsDcMeta function, 801
OleLoadFromStream function, 802, 1324
OleLockServer function, 803, 1324
OleObjectConvert function, 803-804, 1324
OleQueryBounds function, 804, 1324
OleQueryClientVersion function, 805, 1324
OleQueryCreateFromClip function, 805-806, 1324
OleQueryLinkFromClip function, 806-807, 1324
OleQueryName function, 808, 1324
OleQueryOpen function, 808, 1324
OleQueryOutOfData function, 809, 1324
OleQueryProtocol function, 809, 1324
OleQueryReleaseError function, 810, 1324
OleQueryReleaseMethod function, 811, 1324
OleQueryReleaseStatus function, 812, 1324
OleQueryServerVersion function, 812, 1324
OleQuerySize function, 813, 1324
OleQueryType function, 813, 1324
OleReconnect function, 814, 1324
OleRegisterClientDoc function, 815, 1324
OleRegisterServer function, 815, 1325
OleRegisterServerDoc function, 816, 1325
OleRelease function, 817, 1325
OleRename function, 817, 1325
OleRenameClientDoc function, 818, 1325
OleRenameServerDoc function, 818, 1325
OleRequestData function, 819, 1325
OleRevertClientDoc function, 819, 1325
OleRevertServerDoc function, 820, 1325
OleRevokeClientDoc function, 820, 1325

OleRevokeObject function, 821, 1325
OleRevokeServer function, 821, 1325
OleRevokeServerDoc function, 822, 1325
OleSavedClientDoc function, 822, 1325
OleSavedServerDoc function, 823, 1325
OleSaveToStream function, 823, 1325
OleSetBounds function, 824, 1325
OleSetColorScheme function, 824, 1325
OleSetData function, 825, 1325
OleSetHostNames function, 826, 1325
OleSetLinkUpdateOptions function, 827, 1325
OleSetTargetDevice function, 827, 1325
OleUnblockServer function, 828, 1325
OleUnlockServer function, 828, 1325
OleUpdate function, 829, 1325
Open member function, 1264
OpenClipboard function, 829, 1325
OpenComm function, 830, 1325
OpenDriver function, 831, 1325
OpenFile function, 832-833, 1325
OpenIcon function, 833, 1325
operating system interrupt functions, 1350
operators, overloading, 207-209
optimization tool functions, 1350-1351
orientation, defining, 1187
OutputDebugString function, 834, 1326
overloading functions or operators, 207-209
OWL.DEF file, 262-263
owl.h header file, 266
owner draw control messages, 1360

P

pages in metafiles, storing, 1164
Paint Can tool, 1222
Paint editor, 90, 96, 106, 1220-1221
  Colors palette, 1223
  Tools palette, 1221-1223
  window pane, 1224-1225
Paint member function, 1293
  redefining, 272, 275, 277, 280, 283, 285, 293, 303
Paintbrush tool, 1222
painting
  functions, 1351
  windows, 337
PaintRgn function, 834, 1326
PALETTEINDEX function, 835, 1326
PALETTERGB function, 835, 1326
palettes
  Alignment, Dialog editor, 1218-1219
  Colors, Paint editor, 1223
  creating, 402-404
  entries
    index, locating, 596
    locating, 607-608
    replacing, 327-328
  selecting, 887
  size, editing, 874
  system, setting, 934
  Tools
    Dialog editor, 1216-1218
    Paint editor, 1221-1223
paper orientation, defining, 1187
parameters
  CreateWindow function, 151
  system-wide
    querying, 969
    setting, 969
parent windows
  handles, locating, 608
  setting, 921

PASSTHROUGH printer escape, 1195
passwords, setting, 1053
Paste member function, 1258
PatBlt function, 836, 1326
pathnames
  subdirectories, 630
  Windows directory, 656
paths
  copying to Windows directory, 655
  creating, 1165
  subdirectory, locating, 630
pattern brushes, creating, 404
PDB (Program Data Base), 554-555
PeekMessage function, 837-838, 1326
Pen tool, 1222
pens
  creating, 47-48, 405-406
  stock, 46-47
physical fonts, 68-69
Pick Rectangle tool, 1216, 1221
Pie function, 50-53, 839-840, 1326
pixels
  color values, 609
  defining, 1206
  painting, 922
PlayMetaFile function, 840, 1326
PlayMetaFileRecord function, 840, 1326
POINT data structure, 752
pointers
  instruction, defining, 978
  positioning, 749
  repositioning, 712
  returning to environment string, 570
points, 35-39, 752
  calculating in lines, 710-711
  in Windows, 1003
poly modes, defining, 1205
Polygon function, 841, 1326
polygonal regions, creating, 406-408
polygons
  filling, 609
  functions, 1341
  setting, 922
Polyline function, 42, 842, 1326
polymorphism, 207-209
PolyPolygon function, 843, 1326
pop-up
  menus
    creating, 409-410
    placing, 983
    handles, 627
  windows
    bringing to top, 339
    displaying, 953
    hiding, 953
    locating, 333
    retrieving, 586
    sizing, 770
PostAppMessage function, 844, 1326
PostMessage function, 844, 1326
PostQuitMessage function, 845, 1326
predefined
  cursor types, 96
  cursors, 138
  ObjectWindows definition file OWL.DEF, 262-263
  window classes, 159
previous key state, 126
Previous member function, 1300
print jobs
  current, ending, 318
  exiting, 318
  starting, 960, 1206
print-driver code, bypassing, 1167, 1195
PrintDlg function, 845-849, 1326
printer escapes
  ABORTDOC, 1164
  BANDINFO, 1164-1165
  BEGIN_PATH, 1165
  CLIP_TO_PATH, 1166

DEVICEDATA, 1167
DRAFTMODE, 1167
DRAWPATTERNRECT, 1168-1169
ENABLEDUPLEX, 1169
ENABLEPAIRKERNING, 1170
ENABLERELATIVEWIDTHS, 1170-1171
END_PATH, 1171-1172
ENDDOC, 1171
ENUMPAPERBINS, 1173
ENUMPAPERMETRICS, 1174
EPSPRINTING, 1174
EXT_DEVICE_CAPS, 1175-1176
EXTTEXTOUT, 1176-1177
FLUSHOUTPUT, 1177
GETCOLORTABLE, 1178
GETEXTENDEDTEXTMETRICS, 1178-1180
GETEXTENTTABLE, 1181
GETFACENAME, 1182
GETPAIRKERNTABLE, 1182
GETPHYSPAGESIZE, 1183
GETPRINTINGOFFSET, 1184
GETSCALINGFACTOR, 1184-1185
GETSETPAPERBINS, 1185-1186
GETSETPAPERMETRICS, 1186
GETSETPAPERORIENT, 1187
GETSETSCREENPARAMS, 1188
GETTECHNOLOGY, 1188
GETTRACKKERNTABLE, 1189-1190
GETVECTORBRUSHSIZE, 1190-1191
GETVECTORPENSIZE, 1192
MFCOMMENT, 1193
NEWFRAME, 1193
NEXTBAND, 1194
PASSTHROUGH, 1195
QUERYESCSUPPORT, 1195
RESTORE_CTM, 1196
SAVE_CTM, 1196
SET_ARC_DIRECTION, 1198
SET_BACKGROUND_COLOR, 1199
SET_BOUNDS, 1199
SET_MIRROR_MODE, 1203
SET_POLY_MODE, 1204
SET_SCREEN_ANGLE, 1205
SET_SPREAD, 1206
SETABORTPROC, 1196
SETALLJUSTVALUES, 1197
SETCOLORTABLE, 1200
SETCOPYCOUNT, 1201
SETKERNTRACK, 1201
SETLINECAP, 1202
SETLINEJOIN, 1203
SETMITERLIMIT, 1204
STARTDOC, 1206
TRANSFORM_CTM, 1207

printers
control functions, 1352
drivers, initializing, 961
rectangles, drawing, 1168
printing in GDI (Graphics Device Interface), 83
printOn member function, 1232, 1279, 1287, 1300
private display context, 1351
procedure-driven versus event-driven programming, 16-18
procedures, 22
child windows, 177
dialog, 99
frame windows, 177
with ObjectWindows, 261-262
WndProc, 28-29
ProcessAccels member function, 216, 1234
ProcessAppMsg member function, 1234-1235
ProcessDlgMsg member function, 216, 1235
ProcessMDIAccels member function, 216, 1235
ProfClear function, 849, 1326
ProfFinish function, 849, 1326
ProfFlush function, 850, 1326
profile strings, 614
assigning, 1012
ProfInsChk function, 850, 1326

ProfSampRate function, 851, 1326
ProfSetup function, 852, 1326
ProfStart function, 852, 1326
ProfStop function, 852, 1326
Program Data Base (PDB), 554-555
Program Segment Prefix (PSP), 554-555
programmers, Windows advantages for, 7-8
programming
  event-driven versus procedure-driven, 16-18
  object-oriented, 202-210
programs, *see* applications, utilities
Project window, Resource Workshop, 1212
projects
  creating applications, 22-24
  in Resource Workshop, 1212-1213
  OBJ_ACC, 286-290
  OBJ_ARC, 273-275
  OBJ_BAS, 266-268
  OBJ_BIT, 290-293
  OBJ_CUR, 293-295
  OBJ_DLG, 295-300
  OBJ_FIG, 276-278
  OBJ_ICON, 301-304
  OBJ_LINE, 270-273
  OBJ_MDI, 308-313
  OBJ_MENU, 304-308
  OBJ_SCRL, 283-285
  OBJ_TTXT, 281-283
  OBJ_TXT, 278-280
  ObjectWindows applications
    C++ source files, 263
    libraries, 264
    module definition files, 262-263
    resource files, 263
  WIN_ARC, 44-46
  WIN_BIT, 92-95
  WIN_CHLD, 162-164
  WIN_CUR, 96-99
  WIN_DLG, 100-106
  WIN_DLL, 193-194
  WIN_DLLE, 195-198
  WIN_FIGS, 50-53
  WIN_FILL, 54-57
  WIN_FONT, 69-72
  WIN_ICO, 107-110
  WIN_KEY, 130-136
  WIN_LINE, 40-42
  WIN_MDI, 180-187
  WIN_MENU, 112-116
  WIN_MOUS, 143-146
  WIN_ONE, 26-28, 268-270
  WIN_PT, 36-39
  WIN_SCR, 77-82
  WIN_STR, 118-122
  WIN_TTXT, 63-67
  WIN_TXT, 59-62
property
  functions, 1352
  lists, 1352
    data handles, 614
    entries, removing, 870
PSP (Program Segment Prefix), 554-555
PtInRect function, 853, 1326
PtInRegion function, 854, 1326
PtVisible function, 855, 1326
Push Button tool, 1217
push buttons, *see* buttons
PutChildPtr member function, 1300
PutChildren member function, 1300
PutSiblingPtr member function, 1301

Q

QUERYESCSUPPORT printer escape, 1195
QuerySendMessage function, 855-856, 1326
queues
  messages, 615
  receive, 989
  transmit, 987

R

Radio Button tool, 1217
radio buttons, 1279-1280
  adding checkmarks, 349
  BWCC, 1239-1240
    controls, 242-243
  checking, 1018
  controls, 242
ranges for scroll bars
  defining, 929
  maximum, 624
  minimum, 624
raster operations (ROP2), binary, 48
.RC files, 1211
rcdata resources, 1211
`Read` member function, 1264-1265
`read` member function, 1246-1249, 1253, 1260, 1265-1266, 1268, 1273, 1276, 1282, 1287, 1289-1291, 1293, 1301
read-only states, edit control, 1054
`ReadComm` function, 856, 1326
real mode, 165
`RealizePalette` function, 857, 1326
receive queues, placing characters, 989
`Rectangle` function, 50-53, 857, 1326
rectangles
  bounding, setting, 894
  client areas
    adding, 696
    updating, 860
  clipping regions
    defining, 694
    position within, 859
  coordinates, 617, 646
    storing, 991
  copying, 369
  creating, 857, 924
  deleting update regions, 996
  dimesions, list boxes, 1065
  drawing on printers, 1168
  functions, 1352
  intersections, 695
  inverting, 698
  resizing, 688-689
  rounding, 876
  scrolling, 881
  status, 705
rectangular regions, creating, 410, 925
`RectInRegion` function, 858, 1326
`RectVisible` function, 859, 1327
redirected local device, 1009
redirecting device, 1007
`RedrawWindow` function, 860-861, 1327
reference counts
  decreasing in atoms, 662
  decrementing in local memory block, 735
`RegCloseKey` function, 862, 1327
`RegCreateKey` function, 862, 1327
`RegDeleteKey` function, 863, 1327
`RegEnumKey` function, 863, 1327
regions
  client areas, updating, 860
  combining, 363-364
  elliptical, creating, 393-394
  functions, 1353
  polygonal, creating, 406-408
  rectangular, creating, 410
  removing, 997
`Register` member function, 1301
`RegisterClass` function, 175-187, 864, 1327
`RegisterClipboardFormat` function, 864, 1327
registering window class, 864
`RegisterWindowMessage` function, 865, 1327
registration functions, 1353
`RegOpenKey` function, 866, 1327
`RegQueryValue` function, 866, 1327
`RegSetValue` function, 867, 1327
`ReleaseCapture` function, 868, 1327

ReleaseDC function, 868, 1327
releasing
  device contexts, 868
  mouse captures, 867
remote drives, 571-572
removable drives, 571-572
RemoveClient member function, 1301
RemoveFontResource function, 869, 1327
RemoveMenu function, 869, 1327
RemoveProp function, 870, 1327
repeat count, keystroke messages, 126
ReplaceText function, 870-872, 1327
ReplaceWith member function, 1265
replacing, *see* searching and replacing
replying to messages, 873
ReplyMessage function, 873, 1327
.RES files, 1211
reserved fonts, 578
ResetDC function, 873, 1327
ResizePalette function, 874, 1327
resource files, 26
  accelerator example, 89, 286-287
  accessing, 319
  bitmap example, 95, 291
  creating in ObjectWindows, 263
  cursor example, 99
  dialog box example, 105-106
  dialog example, 295-296
  icon example, 110, 301
  MDI example, 186-187, 309
  menu example, 115-116, 304-305
  string example, 121-122
Resource Workshop
  Accelerator editor, 86, 1213-1214
  Dialog editor, 99, 1215-1219
  file formats supported by, 1211
  Menu editor, 110, 1219-1220
  Paint editor, 90, 96, 106, 1220-1225
  projects, 1212-1213
  resource types, 1209-1211
  String editor, 116, 1226-1227
resources
  accelerator, 85-89
  bitmap, 90-95
  byte count, 956
  cursor, 96-99
  dialog box, 99-106
  file, size of, 574
  font
    adding, 320
    creating, 412
    deleting, 868
  icon, 106-110
  loading, 720
  locking, 736
  management functions, 1353
  memory, allocating, 325
  menu, 110-116
  script files, MDI, 177
  string, 116-122
    copying, 721
  system, 579
  types, 1209-1211
  unlocking, 992
  values, 751
    converting, 751
RESTORE_CTM printer escape, 1196
RestoreDC function, 874, 1327
RestoreMemory member function, 1279
restoring
  device contexts, 874
  normal input, 867
  transformation matrix to previous state, 1196
retrieving
  bits, bitmaps, 565-567
  messages, 591-592
  text, 569
  version information, 1002
RGB (Royal, Green, Blue)
  color, selecting, 875
  values, defining, 1200

RGB function, 875, 1327
ROP2 (binary raster operations), 48
rounding rectangles, 876
RoundRect function, 50-53, 876, 1327
Run member function, 214, 1235

S

Save member function, 1265
SAVE_CTM printer escape, 1196
SaveAs member function, 1265
SaveDC function, 876, 1327
saving
    device contexts, 876
    string handles, 441
    transformation matrix, 1196
SBBottom member function, 1282
SBLineDown member function, 1282
SBLineUp member function, 1282
SBPageDown member function, 1282
SBPageUp member function, 1282
SBThumbPosition member function, 1282-1283
SBThumbTrack member function, 1283
SBTop member function, 1283
ScaleViewportExt function, 877, 1327
ScaleViewportExtEx function, 878, 1327
ScaleWindowExt function, 879, 1327
ScaleWindowExtEx function, 880, 1327
Scissors tool, 1221
screen
    angles, defining, 1205
    coordinate systems, 34
    coordinates
        converting to client coordinates, 880
        messages, locating, 592
        retrieving, 557
        windows, 654-655
    dumps, MDI application, 311-313
ScreenToClient function, 880, 1327
scroll bars, 1280-1283
    auto-scrolling windows, 255-257
    controls, 249-251
    displaying, 954
    hiding, 954
    horizontal, 10
    messages, 1361
    ranges
        defining, 929
        maximum, 624
        minimum, 624
    thumb position, 623
        setting, 928
    vertical, 11
Scroll member function, 1258
SCROLLBAR class controls, 159-161
    styles, 157
ScrollBy member function, 1287
ScrollDC function, 881-882, 1327
scrolling
    auto-scrolling, 1284-1288
    edit controls, 1052
    functions, 1354
    list boxes, 1064
    rectangles, 881
    windows, 76-82, 883-885
ScrollTo member function, 1287
ScrollWindow function, 883, 1327
ScrollWindowEx function, 883-885, 1327
Search member function, 1258
search-and-replace dialog boxes, 234
searching for
    and replacing text, 870, 1052
    palette entry index, 596
    strings, 1023
segments, 170-171
    code, defining, 978
    data, unlocking, 992
    descriptors, 166
    functions, 1354
    identifiers, 166

locking, 737
selectors, 166
unlocking, 993
SelectClipRgn function, 885, 1327
SelectFileName member function, 1262
SelectionChanged member function, 1266-1267
SelectObject function, 39, 92, 886, 1328
selectors
allocating, 326
base
addresses, locating, 624
defining, 930
code, 347
creating, 675
data, 347
limits, 625
defining, 930
SelectPalette function, 887, 1328
SendDlgItemMessage function, 887, 1328
SendDlgItemMsg member function, 1254
SendDriverMessage function, 888, 1328
SendMessage function, 889, 1328
servers
registering with library, 815
version, 812
service names
registering, 442
unregistering, 442
Set Groups tool, 1216
Set Order tool, 1216
SET_ARC_DIRECTION printer escape, 1198
SET_BACKGROUND_COLOR printer escape, 1199
SET_BOUNDS printer escape, 1199
SET_MIRROR_MODE printer escape, 1203
SET_POLY_MODE printer escape, 1204
SET_SCREEN_ANGLE printer escape, 1205
SET_SPREAD printer escape, 1206
SetAbortProc function, 889, 1328
SETABORTPROC printer escape, 1196
SetActiveWindow function, 890, 1328
SETALLJUSTVALUES printer escape, 1197
SetBitmapBits function, 891, 1328
SetBitmapDimension function, 891, 1328
SetBitmapDimensionEx function, 892, 1328
SetBkColor function, 68, 892, 1328
SetBkMode function, 68, 893, 1328
SetBoundsRect function, 894, 1328
SetBrushOrg function, 895, 1328
SetCaption member function, 1254, 1301
SetCapture function, 895, 1328
SetCaretBlinkTime function, 896, 1328
SetCaretPos function, 896, 1328
SetCheck member function, 1246
SetClassLong function, 897, 1328
SetClassWord function, 898, 1328
SetClipboardData function, 899, 1328
SetClipboardViewer function, 900, 1328
SETCOLORTABLE printer escape, 1200
SetCommBreak function, 900, 1328
SetCommEventMask function, 901, 1328
SetCommState function, 902-904, 1328
SETCOPYCOUNT printer escape, 1201
SetCursor function, 905, 1328
SetCursorPos function, 905, 1328
SetDIBits function, 906-908, 1328
SetDIBitsToDevice function, 909-910, 1328
SetDlgItemInt function, 911, 1328
SetDlgItemText function, 911, 1328
SetDoubleClickTime function, 912, 1328

SetEditSel member function, 1249
SetEnvironment function, 912, 1328
SetErrorMode function, 913, 1329
SetFileName member function, 1265
SetFlags member function, 1301
SetFocus function, 914, 1329
SetHandleCount function, 914, 1329
SetKBHandler member function, 1235
SETKERNTRACK printer escape, 1201
SetKeyboardState function, 915, 1329
SETLINECAP printer escape, 1202
SETLINEJOIN printer escape, 1203
SetMapMode function, 915, 1329
SetMapperFlags function, 916, 1329
SetMenu function, 917, 1329
SetMenuItemBitmaps function, 917, 1329
SetMessageQueue function, 918, 1329
SetMetaFileBits function, 919, 1329
SetMetaFileBitsBetter function, 919, 1329
SETMITERLIMIT printer escape, 1204
SetPageSize member function, 1287
SetPaletteEntries function, 920, 1329
SetParent
  function, 921, 1329
  member function, 1301
SetPixel function, 35, 922, 1329
SetPolyFillMode function, 922, 1329
SetPosition member function, 1283
SetProp function, 923, 1329
SetRange member function, 1283, 1287
SETREADONLY message, 1366
SetRect function, 924, 1329
SetRectEmpty function, 925, 1329
SetRectRgn function, 925, 1329
SetResourceHandler function, 926, 1329
SetROP2 function, 49, 927, 1329
SetSBarRange member function, 1287
SetScrollPos function, 928, 1329
SetScrollRange function, 929, 1329
SetSelection member function, 1259-1260
SetSelectorBase function, 930, 1329
SetSelectorLimit function, 930, 1329
SetSelIndex member function, 1271
SetSelIndexes member function, 1271
SetSelString member function, 1271
SetSelStrings member function, 1271
SetStretchBltMode function, 931, 1329
SetSwapAreaSize function, 931, 1329
SetSysColors function, 932, 1329
SetSysModalWindow function, 933, 1329
SetSystemPaletteUse function, 934, 1329
SetText member function, 1249, 1290
SetTextAlign function, 75-76, 935, 1329
SetTextCharacterExtra function, 68, 935, 1329
SetTextColor function, 68, 936, 1329
SetTextJustification function, 937, 1329
SetTimer function, 937, 1330
SetTransferBuffer member function, 1301
SetUnits member function, 1288
SetupWindow member function, 1243, 1249, 1254, 1259, 1262, 1265, 1268, 1276, 1283, 1293, 1301
SetViewportExt function, 938, 1330
SetViewportExtEx function, 939, 1330
SetViewportOrg function, 940, 1330
SetViewportOrgEx function, 941, 1330
SetWindowExt function, 941, 1330
SetWindowExtEx function, 942, 1330
SetWindowLong function, 943, 1330
SetWindowOrg function, 944, 1330
SetWindowOrgEx function, 944, 1330

SetWindowPlacement function, 945
SetWindowPos function, 946, 1330
SetWindowsHook function, 947, 1330
SetWindowsHookEx function, 948, 1330
SetWindowText function, 949, 1330
SetWindowWord function, 950, 1330
shell functions, 1354-1355
ShellExecute function, 950-951, 1330
shift states, returning, 1002
Show member function, 1301-1302
ShowCaret function, 952, 1330
ShowCursor function, 953, 1330
ShowList member function, 1249
ShowOwnedPopups function, 953, 1330
ShowScrollBar function, 954, 1330
ShowWindow function, 955, 1330
ShutDownWindow member function, 1254, 1302
simple combo boxes, 238
SizeofResource function, 956, 1330
SlashBox function, 193
software, installing, 655
solid brushes, creating, 413
sound messages, 758
source code files, 24-25
  C, *see* C source code files
  C++, *see* C++ source code files
source files, copying to destination files, 368
spacing, intercharacter, 639
  text attribute, 68
stacks
  editing in current tasks, 968
  returning to data segment in tasks, 968
StackTraceCSIPFirst function, 957, 1330
StackTraceFirst function, 958, 1330
StackTraceNext function, 959, 1330
standard mode, 166
StartDoc function, 960, 1330
STARTDOC printer escape, 1206
starting print jobs, 1206
StartPage function, 961, 1330
state table, keyboards, 915
static
  BWCC dividers, 1237-1238
  linking versus dynamic linking, 189-190
  text, 245-246, 248-249, 1288-1290
  text controls, 1240-1241
    bitmap, 251-252, 1241-1242
STATIC class controls, 159-161
  styles, 158-164
STM_GETICON message, 1074, 1369
STM_SETICON message, 1074, 1369
stock
  brushes, 53-54, 625-626
  pens, 46-47
    handles, 625-626
storing
  metafile pages, 1164
  rectangle coordinates, 991
streamable classes, 1290-1291
streamableName member function, 1291
stress functions, 1355
StretchBlt function, 962, 1330
StretchDIBits function, 965-967, 1330
stretching
  device-independent bitmaps, 964-965
  mode, setting, 931
String editor, 116, 1226-1227
strings, 116-122
  adding, 1022, 1061
    to atom table, 319
  appending, 741
  character, displaying, 972, 980
  comparing, 428, 741-742
  copying, 611, 742
  deleting, 1022
  environment, 570
  extents, 640-641

handles
creating, 432
freeing, 435
saving, 441
height, 640
indexes, specifying, 1061
list box, deleting, 1061
locating, 1023
manipulation functions, 1355
profile, 614
assigning, 1012
resources, copying, 721
tables, 1210, 1226-1227
text, height and width, 636
width, 640
`struct` keyword, 203
structures, *see* data structures
Style Selections tools, 1223
styles
`BUTTON` class control, 154-155
`COMBOBOX` class control, 155
`CreateWindowEx` function bits, 152
`EDIT` class control, 156
`LISTBOX` class control, 156-157
`SCROLLBAR` class control, 157
`STATIC` class control, 158-164
window, 153-154
window class, 148-149
subdirectories, pathnames, 630
suspending applications, 1003
`SwapMouseButton` function, 967, 1330
`SwapRecording` function, 1330
switching to tasks, 978
`SwitchStackBack` function, 968, 1330
`SwitchStackTo` function, 968, 1331
`SyncAllVoices` function, 1331
system
functions, 1355-1356
global classes, 1357
hooks, 1343
information messages, 1361
interrupts, controlling, 693
messages, 125, 1361
modal windows, handles, 628
palettes
accessing, 635
setting, 934
resource space, 579
state information, 629
timer event, 937
System menu, accessing, 631
`SystemHeapInfo` function, 969, 1331
`SystemParametersInfo` function, 969-971, 1331

T

Tab Set tool, 1216
tabbed text, 281-283
`TabbedTextOut` function, 63-67, 281-283, 972, 1331
tables
ANSI, 582
atom, 319
OEM, 582
string, 1210, 1226-1227
tabs
\t indicator, 63
extended, 63-67
stops, setting, 1056
`TApplication` class, 213-214, 1233-1235
`TaskFindHandle` function, 973-974, 1331
`TaskFirst` function, 974-975, 1331
`TaskGetCSIP` function, 976, 1331
`TaskNext` function, 976-977, 1331
tasks
code segments, defining, 978
current
execution time, 981
handles, 556
stacks, 968
stopping, 1015

executing, amount, 599
functions, 1356
instruction pointer, defining, 978
starting, 1015
switching to, 978
TaskSetCSIP function, 978, 1331
TaskSwitch function, 978, 1331
TBButton class, 243, 1235-1236
TBCheckBox class, 241, 1236-1237
TBDivider class, 251, 1237-1238
TBGroupBox class, 1238-1239
TBRadioButton class, 242-243, 1239-1240
TBStatic class, 248-249, 1240-1241
TBStaticBmp class, 251-252, 1241-1242
TButton class, 236, 1242-1244
TBWindow class, 229, 1244
TCheckBox class, 240-241, 1245-1247
TComboBox class, 238-241, 1247-1249
TControl class, 235, 1250-1251
TDialog class, 229-232, 1251-1255
TEdit class, 246-248, 1255-1259
TEditWindow class, 226-227, 1259-1261
TerminateApp function, 979, 1331
terminating
applications, 979
ObjectWindows application objects, 216-217
transactions, 424
Test Dialog tool, 1216
testing menus, 1219-1220
text
aligning, 75-76
alignment flags
setting, 935
status, 638
breaks, 1056
buffers, setting, 1052
color, 68, 639
converting to integers, dialog boxes, 568
current position, 129
device context attributes, 67-68
displaying in client area, 278-280
drawing, 58-67, 639
edit controls, 246-248, 1058-1059
editing, 1259-1261
editors
edit controls, 1255-1259
single-line, 130-136
extended tabs, 63-67
file formats supported by Resource Workshop, 1211
fonts, 68-73
functions, 1356
grayed, 685-686
intercharacter spacing, 639
justifying, 937, 1197
length, 658
metrics of fonts, 73-75
mode, 58
retrieving, 569
scrolling windows, 76-82
searching for and replacing, 870, 1052
setting, 911
static, 1288-1290
static controls, 245-246, 248-249, 1240-1241
bitmap, 1241-1242
strings, 116-122, 1226-1227
copying, 866
extents, calculating, 641
height, 636
values, 867
width, 636
tabbed, 281-283
values, setting, 911
windows, 657
Text Static Control tool, 1217
Text tool, 1222
TEXTMETRIC data structure, 73-75
TextOut function, 58-62, 278-280, 980, 1331

`TFileDialog` class, 232-233, 1261-1263
`TFileWindow` class, 227-229, 1263-1265
`TGroupBox` class, 243-245, 1265-1267
three-state boxes, 1245
`Throw` function, 980, 1331
thumb positions, scroll bars, 623, 928
`TileChildren` member function, 1273, 1276
timer events
  creating, 937
  terminating, 708
`TimerCount` function, 981
`TInputDialog` class, 233-234, 1267-1268
title bar, 11
`TListBox` class, 237-238, 1268-1272
`TMDIClient` class, 254, 1272-1273
`TMDIFrame` class, 252-254, 1273-1276
`TModule` class, 1277-1279
`ToAscii` function, 982, 1331
`Toggle` member function, 1246
Toolhelp functions, 1356-1357
tools
  Alignment palette, Dialog editor, 1218-1219
  Colors palette, Paint editor, 1223
  Tools palette
    Dialog editor, 1216-1218
    Paint editor, 1221-1223
Tools palette
  Dialog editor, 1216-1218
  Paint editor, 1221-1223
top-level window, designating, 890
`TrackPopupMenu` function, 982-983, 1331
`TRadioButton` class, 242, 1279-1280
transactions, terminating, 424
`Transfer` member function, 1246, 1249, 1271-1272, 1283, 1290, 1302
`TransferData` member function, 1268, 1302
`TRANSFORM_CTM` printer escape, 1207
transformation matrix
  defining, 1207
  restoring to previous state, 1196
  saving, 1196
transition state, keystroke messages, 126
`TranslateAccelerator` function, 984, 1331
`TranslateMDISysAccel` function, 175-176, 985, 1331
`TranslateMessage` function, 125, 986, 1331
transmit queues, placing characters, 987
`TransmitCommChar` function, 987, 1331
TrueType
  fonts, 6
    installing, 616
    metric data, 604-605
  functions, 1357
`TScrollBar` class, 249-251, 1280-1283
`TScrollBarData` structure, 1283
`TScroller` class, 255-257, 283-285, 1284-1288
`TSearchDialog` class, 234
`TStatic` class, 245-246, 1288-1290
`TStreamable` class, 1290-1291
`TWindow` class, 223-225, 1291-1294
`TWindowAttr` data structure, 222-223
`TWindowsObject` class, 217-221, 1294-1303
two-state boxes, 1245
typefaces, 72-73

U

`UnAllocDiskSpace` function, 987, 1331
`UnAllocFileHandles` function, 988, 1331
`Uncheck` member function, 1246-1247
`Undo` member function, 1259
Undo tool, 1216

UngetCommChar function, 988, 1331
UnhookWindowsHook function, 989, 1331
UnhookWindowsHookEx function, 990, 1331
union keyword, 203
UnionRect function, 991, 1331
units of measure, 33-34
UnlockData function, 992, 1331
unlocking
  data segments, current, 992
  resources, 992
  segments, 993
UnlockResource function, 992, 1331
UnlockSegment function, 993, 1331
UnrealizeObject function, 993, 1331
UnregisterClass function, 994, 1331
update regions (rectangles), deleting, 996
UpdateColors function, 994, 1331
UpdateFileName member function, 1262
UpdateListBoxes member function, 1263
UpdateWindow function, 994, 1332
updating
  client area, 994
    rectangles, 860
    regions, 860
  device contexts, 873
    colors, 994
uppercase characters, 700
user-defined resources, 1211
USER.EXE extension file, copying, 969
users, Windows advantages, 6-7
utilities
  COMPRESS.EXE, 573
  functions, 1358

V

ValidateCodeSegments function, 995, 1332
ValidateFreeSpaces function, 995, 1332
ValidateRect function, 996, 1332
ValidateRgn function, 997, 1332
validating
  code segments, 995
  memory free spaces, 995
ValidWindow member function, 225, 1279
values, 755
  color, 619
  converting resources, 751
  high-order
    byte, 686
    words, 688
  justification, for text, 1197
  modify flags, 1053
  setting, 897-898
    in text, 911
variables
  Hungarian notation, 12-13
  lParam, 125-126, 129
  wParam, 126-129
VerFindFile function, 998, 1332
VerInstallFile function, 1000, 1332
VerLanguageName function, 1001, 1332
VerQueryValue function, 1002, 1332
versions
  functions, 1357
  information, retrieving, 1002
Vertical Scroll Bar tool, 1217
vertical scroll bars, 11, 1280-1283
viewports
  coordinates, 649
  copying, 649
  extents
    defining, 939
    editing, 878
    scaling, 877

height, 648, 938
origin
defining for device context, 941
setting, 940
width, 648, 938
virtual keys
codes, 126-128, 754
converting to ANSI, 982
returning, 1002
messages, 986
status, 583
Virtual Machine, copying execution time, 981
VkKeyScan function, 1002, 1332
VScroll member function, 1288

W

WaitMessage function, 1003, 1332
White Frame Static Control tool, 1218
whole-window coordinate systems, 34-35
WIN_ARC project, 44-46
WIN_BIT project, 92-95
WIN_CHLD project, 162-164
WIN_CUR project, 96-99
WIN_DLG project, 100-106
WIN_DLL project, 193-194
WIN_DLLE project, 195-198
WIN_FIGS project, 50-53
WIN_FILL project, 54-57
WIN_FONT project, 69-72
WIN_ICO project, 107-110
WIN_KEY project, 130-136
WIN_LINE project, 40-42
WIN_MDI project, 180-187
WIN_MENU project, 112-116
WIN_MOUS project, 143-146
WIN_ONE project, 26-28, 268-270
WIN_PT project, 36-39
WIN_SCR project, 77-82
WIN_STR project, 118-122
WIN_TTXT project, 63-67
WIN_TXT project, 59-62
window pane, Paint editor, 1224-1225
WindowFromPoint function, 1003, 1332
Windows
advantages
to programmers, 7-8
to users, 6-7
applications, *see* applications
class list, 357-358
desktop, 560
directory paths, 655
history, 4-5
initialization file keys, 613
messages, 1017-1112
points, 1003
version 3.1 new features, 5-6
version numbers, 648
windows
active, 124
auto-scrolling, 255-257, 283-285, 1284-1288
basic, 1291-1294
behaviors, defining, 1294-1303
captions, setting, 949
child, 124, 350, 701
arranging, 336
bringing to top, 339
controls, 159-161
identification number (ID), 567
MDI, 177
sizing, 770
class
creating, 225-226
defining, 148-150
deleting, 994
registering, 864
types, 153
client, 173, 1272-1273
area, updating, 994
class, 254
closing, 363
components, 8-11
creating, 225

creating, 147-158, 222-226, 413-423
creation functions, 1357-1358
deleting, 955
from clipboard chain of viewers, 346
device contexts, 1351
height, 652
retrieving, 651
width, 652
displaying, 707, 955
drawing, enabling/disabling, 739
edit, creating, 226-227
extents
defining in device contexts, 942
editing, 880
file editing, creating, 227-229
frame, 173, 177, 1274-1276
class, 252-254
fundamental application, 26-29
gray background, 229, 1244
handles, 650-651, 657
input focus, 577
locating, 599
returning, 600
height, 941
keyboard input, sending, 914
length, 658
management messages, 1361
maximizing, 708
menus, handles, 587
messages, defining, 865
minimizing, 704
multiple, 336
objects, 221
creating, 222-226
edit, 226-227
file editing, 227-229
gray background, 229
origins, 780
coordinates, 653
in device contexts, 944
painting, 337
parent, 921
handles, 608
placement information, 945
pop-up
bringing to top, 339
displaying, 953
hiding, 953
locating, 333
retrieving, 586
sizing, 770
positioning, 654, 946
procedures, 261-262
Project, Resource Workshop, 1212
regions, deleting, 997
scaling, 879
screen coordinate, 654-655
scrolling, 76-82, 883-885
show state, 654
sizing, 320-322, 946
subclassing, 344-345
system modal, handles, 628
text, 657
top-level, designating, 890
update regions, copying, 647, 648
validity, 706
width, 941
windows.h include file, 14
WinExec function, 1004, 1332
WinHelp function, 1006, 1332
WinMain function, 18-20, 130
with ObjectWindows, 260-261
WM_ACTIVATE message, 1075, 1369
WM_ACTIVATEAPP message, 1075, 1369
WM_ASKCBFORMATNAME message, 1076, 1369
WM_CANCELMODE message, 1076, 1369
WM_CHANGECBCHAIN message, 1077, 1370
WM_CHAR message, 130, 1077, 1370
WM_CHARTOITEM message, 1078, 1370
WM_CHILDACTIVATE message, 1079, 1370
WM_CHOOSEFONT_GETLOGFONT message, 1079, 1370

WM_CLEAR message, 1079, 1370
WM_CLOSE message, 1080, 1370
WM_COMMAND message, 111, 1080, 1370
WM_COMMNOTIFY message, 1080, 1370
WM_COMPACTING message, 1081, 1370
WM_COMPAREITEM message, 1082, 1370
WM_COPY message, 1083, 1370
WM_CREATE message, 59, 76, 1083, 1371
WM_CTLCOLOR message, 1084, 1371
WM_CUT message, 1085, 1371
WM_DDE_ACK message, 1085, 1371
WM_DDE_ADVISE message, 1087, 1371
WM_DDE_DATA message, 1088, 1371
WM_DDE_EXECUTE message, 1089, 1371
WM_DDE_INITIATE message, 1090, 1371
WM_DDE_POKE message, 1091, 1371
WM_DDE_REQUEST message, 1091, 1371
WM_DDE_TERMINATE message, 1092, 1372
WM_DDE_UNADVISE message, 1092, 1372
WM_DEADCHAR message, 1093, 1372
WM_DELETEITEM message, 1094, 1372
WM_DESTROY message, 1094, 1372
WM_DESTROYCLIPBOARD message, 1095, 1372
WM_DEVMODECHANGE message, 1095, 1372
WM_DRAWCLIPBOARD message, 1095, 1372
WM_DRAWITEM message, 1096, 1372
WM_DROPFILES message, 1097, 1372
WM_ENABLE message, 1098, 1372
WM_ENDSESSION message, 1098, 1372
WM_ENTERIDLE message, 1098, 1373
WM_ERASEBKGND message, 1099, 1373
WM_FONTCHANGE message, 1099, 1373
WM_GETDLGCODE message, 1100, 1373
WM_GETFONT message, 1100, 1373
WM_GETHOTKEY message, 1101, 1373
WM_GETMINMAXINFO message, 1101, 1373
WM_GETTEXT message, 1102, 1373
WM_GETTEXTLENGTH message, 1102, 1373
WM_HSCROLL message, 76, 1103, 1373
WM_HSCROLLCLIPBOARD message, 1103, 1373
WM_ICONERASEBKGND message, 1104, 1373
WM_INITDIALOG message, 1105, 1373
WM_INITMENU message, 1105, 1373
WM_INITMENUPOPUP message, 1106, 1373
WM_KEYDOWN message, 130, 1106, 1373
WM_KEYUP message, 1107, 1374
WM_KILLFOCUS message, 1108, 1374
WM_LBUTTONDBLCLK message, 1108, 1374
WM_LBUTTONDOWN message, 1108, 1374
WM_LBUTTONUP message, 1109, 1374
WM_MBUTTONDBLCLK message, 1110, 1374
WM_MBUTTONDOWN message, 1110, 1374
WM_MBUTTONUP message, 1111, 1374
WM_MDIACTIVATE message, 1111, 1374
WM_MDICASCADE message, 1112, 1374
WM_MDICREATE message, 1374
WM_MDIDESTROY message, 1114, 1374
WM_MDIGETACTIVE message, 1114, 1374
WM_MDIICONARRANGE message, 1115, 1374
WM_MDIMAXIMIZE message, 1115, 1374
WM_MDINEXT message, 1115, 1374
WM_MDIRESTORE message, 1116, 1374
WM_MDISETMENU message, 1116, 1374
WM_MDITILE message, 1117, 1374
WM_MEASUREITEM message, 1117, 1374
WM_MENUCHAR message, 1118, 1375
WM_MENUSELECT message, 1119, 1375
WM_MOUSEACTIVATE message, 1119, 1375
WM_MOUSEMOVE message, 142-143, 1121, 1375
WM_MOVE message, 1121, 1375
WM_NCACTIVATE message, 1122, 1375

WM_NCCALCSIZE message, 1122, 1375
WM_NCCREATE message, 1123, 1375
WM_NCDESTROY message, 1124, 1375
WM_NCHITTEST message, 139-140, 1124, 1375
WM_NCLBUTTONDBLCLK message, 1126, 1375
WM_NCLBUTTONDOWN message, 1127, 1375
WM_NCLBUTTONUP message, 1128, 1375
WM_NCMBUTTONDBLCLK message, 1129, 1376
WM_NCMBUTTONDOWN message, 1130, 1376
WM_NCMBUTTONUP message, 1131, 1376
WM_NCMOUSEMOVE message, 1133, 1376
WM_NCPAINT message, 1134, 1376
WM_NCRBUTTONDBLCLK message, 1134, 1376
WM_NCRBUTTONDOWN message, 1135, 1376
WM_NCRBUTTONUP message, 1136, 1376
WM_NEXTDLGCTL message, 1138, 1376
WM_OTHERWINDOWCREATED message, 1376
WM_OTHERWINDOWDESTROYED message, 1376
WM_PAINT message, 35-36, 76, 1138, 1376
WM_PAINTCLIPBOARD message, 1138, 1376
WM_PAINTICON message, 1377
WM_PALETTECHANGED message, 1139, 1377
WM_PALETTEISCHANGING message, 1377
WM_PARENTNOTIFY message, 1140, 1377
WM_PASTE message, 1141, 1377
WM_POWER message, 1141, 1377
WM_QUERYDRAGICON message, 1142, 1377
WM_QUERYENDSESSION message, 1142, 1377
WM_QUERYNEWPALETTE message, 1142, 1377
WM_QUERYOPEN message, 1143, 1377
WM_QUEUESYNC message, 1143, 1377
WM_QUIT message, 1143, 1377
WM_RBUTTONDBLCLK message, 1144, 1377
WM_RBUTTONDOWN message, 1144, 1377
WM_RBUTTONUP message, 1145, 1377
WM_RENDERALLFORMATS message, 1145, 1377
WM_RENDERFORMAT message, 1146, 1378
WM_SETCURSOR message, 1147, 1378
WM_SETFOCUS message, 1148, 1378
WM_SETFONT message, 1148, 1378
WM_SETHOTKEY message, 1148, 1378
WM_SETREDRAW message, 1149, 1378
WM_SETTEXT message, 1149, 1378
WM_SHOWWINDOW message, 1150, 1378
WM_SIZE message, 76, 1150, 1378
WM_SIZECLIPBOARD message, 1151, 1378
WM_SPOOLERSTATUS message, 1152, 1378
WM_SYSCHAR message, 1152, 1378
WM_SYSCOLORCHANGE message, 1153, 1378
WM_SYSCOMMAND message, 1153, 1378
WM_SYSDEADCHAR message, 1154, 1378
WM_SYSKEYDOWN message, 1154, 1379
WM_SYSKEYUP message, 1155, 1379
WM_SYSTEMERROR message, 1156, 1379
WM_TIMECHANGE message, 1156, 1379
WM_TIMER message, 1157, 1379
WM_UNDO message, 1157, 1379
WM_VKEYTOITEM message, 1157, 1379
WM_VSCROLL message, 76, 1158, 1379
WM_VSCROLLCLIPBOARD message, 1159, 1379
WM_WINDOWPOSCHANGED message, 1160, 1379
WM_WINDOWPOSCHANGING message, 1160, 1379

`WM_WININICHANGE` message, 1160, 1379
`WMActivate` member function, 1276, 1302
`WMClose` member function, 1254, 1303
`WMCommand` member function, 1303
`WMCreate` member function, 1293
`WMDestroy` member function, 1303
`WMDrawItem` member function, 1251, 1303
`WMGetDlgCode` member function, 1243-1244
`WMHScroll` member function, 1293, 1303
`WMInitDialog` member function, 1254
`WMLButtonDown` member function, 1293
`WMMDIActivate` member function, 1273, 1293-1294
`WMMove` member function, 1294
`WMNCDestroy` member function, 1303
`WMPaint` member function, 1251, 1273, 1294
`WMQueryEndSession` member function, 1254, 1303
`WMSetFocus` member function, 1260-1261
`WMSize` member function, 1261, 1294
`WMVScroll` member function, 1294, 1303
`WNDCLASS` data structure, 148-150
`WndProc` procedure, 28-29
`WNetAddConnection` function, 1007, 1332
`WNetCancelConnection` function, 1008, 1332
`WNetGetConnection` function, 1009, 1332
`wParam` variable
  character messages, 129
  keystroke messages, 126-136
`write` member function, 1247, 1249, 1255, 1261, 1265, 1267-1268, 1273, 1276, 1283, 1288, 1290-1291, 1294, 1303
`WriteComm` function, 1010, 1332
`WritePrivateProfileString` function, 1011, 1332
`WriteProfileString` function, 1012, 1332
`wsprintf` function, 1013, 1332
`wvsprintf` function, 1014, 1332
WYSIWYG (what-you-see-is-what-you-get), 4, 7, 58

X-Z

`XBox` function, 193
`XRangeValue` member function, 1288
`XScrollValue` member function, 1288

`Yield` function, 1015, 1332
`YRangeValue` member function, 1288
`YScrollValue` member function, 1288

Zoom tool, 1221

Companion Disk Offer!

Get the companion disk for this book on your choice of 5.25-inch or 3.5-inch disk. This offer provides you with all the files that you need to build the examples in this book using your Borland C++ compiler. The C and C++ source files, module definition files, project files, and resource files used for the examples in this book are included on the companion disk. To order your companion disk, send your name, address (complete with ZIP code), disk preference (specify either 5.25-inch or 3.5-inch disk), and a check or money order for $12.50 ($15 for foreign orders) to:

Borland Disk Offer
Code 3
MC Software
P.O. Box 115
Woodland, AL 36280-0115

If you prefer, you can simply copy this page, fill in the blanks, and send with the check or money order to the preceding address.

Cost Including Shipping and Handling:

$12.50 U.S. orders
$15.00 Foreign orders

Disk Preference:

5.25-inch high-density (1.2M) _______
3.5-inch high-density (1.44M) _______

Payment Method:

Check _______
Money order_______

Name: ______________________________

Street Address: ______________________________

City: ______________________________

State: ______________________________ **Zip:** _______________

Check or money orders should be made to:

MC Software

Allow two weeks for delivery.

(This offer is made by MC Software.)